INTERACTIVE CASEBOOK SERIES[SM]

BUSINESS ORGANIZATIONS

A Contemporary Approach

FOURTH EDITION

Frank Partnoy

ADRIAN A. KRAGEN PROFESSOR OF LAW
UC BERKELEY SCHOOL OF LAW

Elizabeth Pollman

PROFESSOR OF LAW
UNIVERSITY OF PENNSYLVANIA CAREY LAW SCHOOL

WEST
ACADEMIC
PUBLISHING

Interactive Casebook Series is a servicemark registered in the U.S. Patent and Trademark Office.

© 2010 Thomson Reuters
© 2014, 2019 LEG, Inc. d/b/a West Academic
© 2023 LEG, Inc. d/b/a West Academic
    860 Blue Gentian Road, Suite 350
    Eagan, MN 55121
    1-877-888-1330

Printed in the United States of America

ISBN: 978-1-63659-537-5

Editors' Note

We have written this book to be a teaching resource, not a research tool. Toward this end, we have edited the cases heavily, generally without adding ellipses or brackets to signal our edits. This means we have omitted citations and footnotes, even whole paragraphs and sections, without any identifying notations. Likewise, to aid readability, we have sometimes removed words, phrases, and sections from statutes, official comments, and regulations, again without signaling these edits.

In short, as with many secondary references, you should use caution when quoting primary materials from this book. The full text of the cases and other primary materials are readily available by using the online version of the book, which has hyperlinks to the original sources.

In addition, the book does not have a suggested printed statutory supplement. Instead, we expect that students will rely on the statutory excerpts in the text, as well as the online statutory materials (including the Delaware General Corporation Law and the Model Business Corporation Act, both of which are linked here).

Acknowledgments

We are grateful to our students for their comments and enthusiasm. We also thank Alan Palmiter for his enormous contributions to earlier editions and Amy Westbrook for her extensive related materials to those editions. We have also benefited greatly from the help of many research assistants at Berkeley Law and Penn Carey Law, and express our gratitude to them and our institutions for their support. Further, we profoundly appreciate the many wonderful conversations with professor friends and colleagues who share our love for business law and teaching.

Table of Contents

Table of Cases

The principal cases are in bold type. Cases cited or discussed in the text are in roman type. Cases cited in principal cases and within other quoted materials are not included.

BUSINESS ORGANIZATIONS

A Contemporary Approach

FOURTH EDITION

CHAPTER 1

Introduction

This is a dramatic casebook about business organizations.

We say "dramatic" because the study and practice of business law is infused with human drama. There is dramatic tension everywhere: between people who own businesses and people who control them, between people who profit from businesses and people who are harmed by them, between people who care about making as much money as they possibly can and people who care more about the environment, social issues, and the welfare of employees and their communities.

As with theater and film, you might not see every element of the drama at first. But as you learn the vocabulary and concepts in this book, you likely will begin to notice tensions beneath the surfaces of the statutes, cases, and examples we discuss. And we predict that you also will notice, in real time, how the material you explore here echoes some of the real-world dramas in the business world as they play out during this semester.

Every time we teach this course, we find that dramatic events in the news pop up to illustrate, and help students understand, the concepts in this book. An activist shareholder knocks at the door of a public company. A wealthy individual is accused of committing widespread fraud. A law firm controversy erupts among its partners. A business is investigated for failing to oversee some significant harm. Or the founders of a startup become unimaginably rich as they develop a new drug or innovative technology. You might even notice that some concepts in this book relate to the activities of your family or friends. Your personal real-world dramas probably won't rival the disputes in television shows that involve the business world, but you should expect that there will be tension lurking, even in the most happily run businesses and business relationships.

As with the academic study of drama, we will provide you with the tools you need to understand the various elements of this course, including concepts related to plot, character, and language. Even aspects of accounting and finance have the potential to engage your imagination, especially as you master the details. The issues we cover in this book will range from the highly practical (as in how to incorporate a business or run a board meeting) to the realm of theory and policy (as in the role of the public corporation in society and politics).

As you will discover, this book has many traditional elements: it lays out the rules and principles of business law and uses statutes and court decisions to identify key issues. But we hope you will notice and appreciate that this book has a modern feel: it uses interactive elements, such as examples, hypos, real-life documents, and sidebar boxes. It covers novel and complex areas of law and legal practice with more narrative description than you would find in a traditional casebook. It streamlines judicial decisions and cuts out extraneous material, including citations. The "Points for Discussion" and questions are brief and straightforward, to help you think through concepts rather than quiz you for a particular "right" answer. And the online version of this book allows you to search for particular terms, highlight and add notes, and easily access hyperlinked material.

> Check out the inside front cover for instructions on how to access the on-line version of this Interactive Casebook.

Who is this book for? We designed it for anyone taking a course on Business Associations, Business Organizations, or Corporations. Whether you are taking the course because you know the topic will be on the bar exam, because you want to understand how corporations impact the world, or because you have dreamed of being a business lawyer, we have tried to make this book relevant to you. You will find lots of useful new vocabulary and black-letter rules, a good dose of novel concepts and policy analysis, and the tools to help you become a top-notch business lawyer.

For those of you who are not interested in business law, and are taking this course because you feel obligated to do so, we will try to pique your interest as well. At minimum, we promise you will see, explore, and understand some new forms of drama.

Before you dig in, we want to give you an overview of how we have organized the vast subject of business law.

Organization of this Book: 6 Modules, 20 Chapters

The law of business organizations is a sprawling topic. The business firm, especially the corporation, reaches into every aspect of our social, economic, and political lives. To help you keep things organized, we have broken up the book into six modules: (1) un-corporations, (2) corporations, (3) directors and officers, (4) stakeholders, (5) shareholders, and (6) markets. Under each module below are several questions, each of which represents a chapter in the book. We also give you a brief answer to each question, which includes a description of the topics we will cover in each chapter.

Don't worry right now if some of the words in this outline are unfamiliar. We just want you to have a sense of what we will be covering. You might want to return to this outline periodically to remind yourself where you are in the "big picture" of this course.

(1) Un-Corporations

Our first module introduces business organizations other than the corporation, which some label "un-corporations," and covers the basic building blocks of agency and partnership, as well as the relatively new and flexible limited liability company, or LLC.

- ### *What rules govern principal-agent relationships?*

Chapter 2 addresses agency relationships, our first and most fundamental drama. We use the Restatement (Third) of Agency and a few cases to show how agency relationships are formed between principals and agents, and to illustrate how the law addresses the tensions between these parties. Agents owe fiduciary duties to principals, in significant part because they have conflicting incentives. We cover the important concepts of actual and apparent authority, and when principals are liable to third parties.

- ### *What are the basic principles of partnership law?*

Chapter 3 examines partnerships, which are important not only for lawyers. Partnerships can be formed by operation of law, even when people don't think they are forming a partnership. We cover partnership duties, including notions of equality and other rules that apply whenever two or more people associate to carry on as co-owners a business for profit. One message of the uniform rules that govern partnerships is to be wary of the default form of partnership and the potential for unlimited personal liability.

- ### *What are the key attributes of limited liability companies?*

Chapter 4 covers LLC basics, including some details about LLC "members" and "managers." We show how LLCs can be conceptualized as a contractual form of doing business, and we cover the uniform rules that apply to LLCs, including many of the concepts that arise later in the course, such as how businesses are formed, and what risks and tensions the parties should anticipate in advance. The LLC is a common choice for people who are setting up a new business.

(2) Corporations

Our second module introduces the key vocabulary and legal principles relating to corporations, starting with how they are formed and the importance of limited liability, and then covering the basics of accounting, valuation, and capital structure.

- ***What are the basic features of corporations?***

Chapter 5 introduces the fundamental aspects of corporations, including corporate vocabulary and descriptions of key corporate characteristics, such as centralized management and limited liability. We introduce the main actors in the corporate drama: directors and officers, stakeholders, and shareholders (each of whom gets their own module after this one), and describe the tension in corporations that arises from the separation of ownership and control. We also cover "nuts and bolts" topics, such as how corporations are formed, and we introduce two important judicial concepts, equitable review and the internal affairs doctrine, where courts apply the law of the state of incorporation, most commonly, Delaware.

- ***When do people who incorporate lose the "gift" of limited liability?***

Chapter 6 covers "piercing the corporate veil," one of the most litigated and contentious issues in business law. We describe the factors that most commonly lead courts to "pierce" through the corporate veil of limited liability to hold shareholders liable for tort and contract violations. The fact patterns in veil piercing cases are colorful and often involve scheming of various kinds. We also discuss "reverse veil piercing," a particularly controversial doctrine that can take away limited liability from corporations.

- ***What do lawyers really need to know about accounting and valuation?***

Chapter 7 might look like a bunch of numbers but hidden in those numbers are interesting stories about how businesses describe themselves. We go through three key financial statements: the balance sheet, income statement, and cash flow statement. We use the example of a simple company to show how accounting principles reflect art as well as science. We also describe how to figure out what a business is worth based on two methods: discounted cash flow and comparables analysis.

- ***What is "capital structure" and how does it matter to corporations?***

Chapter 8 zooms in on the right side of the balance sheet to explore the tensions between equity and debt, as well as hybrid securities such as preferred stock and options. We describe the impact of taxes and bankruptcy on capital structure, as well as the concepts of "legal capital" and "par value," which are important when companies distribute cash to shareholders through dividends or share repurchases. We also discuss policy questions related to capital structure and distributions.

(3) Directors and Officers

Our third module covers the fiduciary duties of care and loyalty that directors and officers owe to the corporation and its shareholders, as well as the evolution of a new modern version of the duty of loyalty, focused on good faith and oversight.

- ### *What is the duty of care?*

Chapter 9 covers the fiduciary duty of care owed by directors and officers and the related "business judgment rule," the judicial presumption that directors act on an informed basis, in good faith, and in the honest belief that actions were taken in the best interests of the corporation. We discuss a few important cases illustrating these issues, along with the concept of "exculpation," which permits corporations to include in their charters a provision that insulates directors (and, recently, officers) from personal liability in many circumstances concerning breaches of the duty of care.

- ### *What is the "classic" duty of loyalty?*

Chapter 10 covers the traditional duty of loyalty, which requires that directors and officers act in a manner they reasonably believe to be in the best interests of the corporation. We focus on conflicts of interest, beginning with some confusing statutes about interested transactions, and we discuss some common law approaches that provide some clarity with respect to statutory provisions about fairness and the effect of approval by disinterested directors or shareholders for fiduciary breach claims. We also address the "corporate opportunity doctrine," a subset of duty of loyalty cases that prohibit directors and officers from taking business opportunities that belong to the corporation without disclosure and consent.

- ### *What is the modern "good faith and oversight" version of the duty of loyalty?*

Chapter 11 traces the evolution of a second version of the duty of loyalty. We cover the development of each of two key concepts, good faith and oversight, focusing on Delaware law, and we then turn to the recent judicial assessment of shareholder claims of oversight failures, many of which have resulted in the loss of human lives. We analyze a line of recent cases involving what are known as "*Caremark* claims," after a 1990s Delaware case, and describe the increasing judicial focus on the oversight of "essential and mission critical" risks.

(4) Stakeholders

Our fourth module considers a range of "big picture" and policy issues related to the role of corporations in society, and is particularly focused on questions about which, if any, stakeholder constituencies corporations should serve.

- ### *What kind of a "person" is the corporation and what is its purpose?*

Chapter 12 covers the debate over corporate purpose and the corporation's role in society. We examine various theories that scholars have used to conceptualize the corporation over time, including the polar views of those who see the corporation as essentially private property versus those who see the corporation as a social institution. We consider two important topics related to these theories: corporate rights related to political activity and the potential for corporations to be charged as criminals.

- ### *What are the legal and policy issues raised by corporate social responsibility and ESG?*

Chapter 13 covers the topic many people regard as the most controversial in business law: environmental, social, and governance concerns, or ESG. We discuss the history of corporate social responsibility and the law related to corporations and charitable giving. We examine forms of business organization that are explicitly tasked with providing a social benefit, rather than only making profits. We also cover the ongoing debate about ESG, including questions about what role the corporation should play in society.

(5) Shareholders

Our fifth module covers the roles, rights, and duties of shareholders, the owners of corporations. We use a poem to help remember the basic shareholder rights: vote, sue, sell, yell.

- ### *How is litigation used to enforce shareholder rights?*

Chapter 14 is an overview of shareholder litigation. We discuss the central distinction between derivative and direct forms of litigation, and we describe the "demand requirement" that plaintiffs in derivative lawsuits must either demand that directors file suit on behalf of the corporation or show that the demand is excused because it would be futile. We examine "special litigation committees" that assess potential litigation, and we assess some civil procedure aspects of shareholder litigation, such as adequacy and standing. We also consider how directors and officers are often protected from personal liability in shareholder litigation through indemnification and insurance.

- ***What are the details and scope of shareholder voting rights?***

Chapter 15 examines shareholder voting, a fundamental right of shareholders. We describe the basics of shareholder voting at annual and special meetings, including voting procedures. We cover some battles for board seats between shareholders and directors, and we describe the limited shareholder power to initiate action, some restrictions on directors' responses to shareholder initiatives, as well as the "poison pill" defense. We also examine several issues related to shareholder activism, which often is aimed at shareholder votes, either to replace directors or on shareholder proposals about various concerns.

- ***What information can shareholders obtain from a company?***

Chapter 16 focuses on an important right that is related to all four words in the poem, the right of shareholders to obtain information. We examine Delaware's statute, Section 220, that gives shareholders the right to inspect books and records but requires a "proper purpose." We distinguish between requests for a list of shareholders versus requests for other information, such as board minutes, financial information, or other internal corporate documents, including correspondence. We also discuss the information required for shareholder voting, including federal law related to proxy statements.

- ***What duties do controlling shareholders owe?***

Chapter 17 switches from shareholder rights to shareholder duties and describes doctrines related to shareholders who have large ownership stakes or otherwise can exercise control over a corporation. We begin by considering what constitutes shareholder control, including not only control of a majority of voting shares, but also circumstances where a minority shareholder nevertheless exercises control. Then we consider four distinct doctrinal areas where controlling shareholders can owe duties: "intra-group" transactions, "cash-out" transactions, "oppression" in closely held corporations, and the sale of control for a premium.

(6) Markets

Our final module examines important ways that corporations interface with the markets, including the purchase and sale of corporations, litigation about misstatements that are alleged to have inflated the price of stock, and trading by people with inside information.

- ***What are the basic aspects of mergers and acquisitions law?***

Chapter 18 is an introduction to mergers and acquisitions. We describe basic M&A deal structures, including different rules for shareholder voting and appraisal rights. We explore the fiduciary duties of directors in the M&A context, distinguishing between the *Unocal* standard of intermediate review of board actions to preserve the corporation versus the *Revlon* standard that, at some point, imposes on directors an obligation to achieve the highest value that is reasonably available for shareholders. We also consider a range of anti-takeover devices and defensive tactics and describe some recent extensions and developments in M&A case law.

• *What are the key elements of securities class action litigation?*

Chapter 19 examines securities class action litigation. We begin with an overview of securities markets and notions of market efficiency, which underpin some of the key concepts in the case law. We focus on Rule 10b-5, promulgated under Section 10(b) of the Securities Exchange Act of 1934, and the cases that have interpreted this rule. Specifically, we cover three important elements of a securities class action: the materiality of alleged misrepresentations, the scienter (or state of mind) of any defendants, and the reliance of shareholders in public markets on alleged misrepresentations.

• *What is "insider trading"?*

Chapter 20 covers insider trading, including both policy and law. We begin with state law on insider trading and some history, but our primary focus is on three Supreme Court cases that define the contours of insider trading law. We distinguish between the "classical theory" of insider trading, where a violation arises from the relationship between a corporate insider who trades and the corporation's shareholders versus the more expansive "misappropriation theory," where a violation arises from the relationship between a person who trades and the source of information. We also discuss "tippee" liability as well as liability for disgorgement of "short-swing" profits.

This is a lot of material, and you probably have some questions. We hope to answer your questions as we move through these modules and chapters. But we want to emphasize here that the questions and answers should be clearer if you keep in mind how they fit into the bigger picture.

That's it for our introduction. Now you are ready to begin your study of business organizations.

———

MODULE I – UN-CORPORATIONS

CHAPTER 2

Agency Basics

In Chapter 1, we introduced you to some business law basics and hopefully piqued your interest in this course. Now we turn to questions about the legal rules that govern participants in a business, beginning with how the law addresses principal-agent relationships, and then partnerships, LLCs, and corporations. We start here with the law of agency.

The law has long had rules concerning when an agency relationship is formed, the duties and obligations between a principal and agent, and legal consequences with third parties that flow from the agency relationship. These are the basic principles of agency law that we will study in this chapter.

At the outset, you might take a moment to notice that agency relationships are ubiquitous. You interact with agents in your everyday life, from a store clerk who assists you with a purchase to the professor who acts on behalf of the university in teaching a course. An agency relationship exists between employer and employee, corporation and officer, client and lawyer, and partnership and general partner. People often retain agents to perform specific services such as in real estate transactions and in the sports and entertainment industry where, for example, authors, performers, and athletes often retain agents to represent their interests in dealing with third parties. In short, agency is a building block concept that has relevance for many types of business relationships and organizations, including sole proprietorships, partnerships, corporations, and limited liability companies (LLCs). That's why we start with it.

Each state has its own agency law that has been enacted as a statute by the state legislature or judicially created over time through case law. In addition, the general principles of agency law are captured in the Restatement (Third) of the Law of Agency. The Restatement is an influential secondary source of law drafted by the American Law Institute. Originally published in 1933 (First), the Restatement was updated in 1958 (Second), and again in 2006 (Third). Thus, if you were to deal with a real-world agency law issue in practice you would consider what is the relevant jurisdiction and then research the state agency law applicable to your matter at hand. Here, the focus is on understanding general principles, and we refer to the Restatement (Third) of Agency.

A.　Formation of the Agency Relationship

The Restatement (Third) of Agency § 1.01 provides the definition of the agency relationship:

> Agency is the fiduciary relationship that arises when one person (a "principal") manifests assent to another person (an "agent") that the agent shall act on the principal's behalf and subject to the principal's control, and the agent manifests assent or otherwise consents so to act.

Thus, the agency relationship is created between two parties—an agent and a principal—and includes three basic elements: (1) mutual assent, (2) control, and (3) acting on behalf of a principal.

The facts are important for each of these three elements. First, the parties must assent that the agent will act on behalf, and subject to the control, of the principal. However, it is not required that the parties intend to enter into something called an agency relationship or that they are aware of the legal consequences. Generally, no writing is required. In addition, how the parties characterize the relationship or popular usage is not dispositive in determining whether an agency relationship exists. This means, for example, that a contract provision disclaiming an agency relationship could be relevant, but not dispositive, in determining whether an agency relationship exists.

To determine whether the agent and principal have assented to their relationship with each other, courts look to the parties' outward manifestations from the viewpoint of a reasonable person rather than to their inner, subjective thoughts. Each party must have objectively manifested assent to the agency relationship, whether by words or conduct. Notably, the consensual aspect of agency does not mean that agency is limited to commercial settings or that an enforceable contract with consideration necessarily underlies the relationship. Many agents act or promise to act gratuitously, without compensation or bargained-for exchange, and this assent still suffices for purposes of creating an agency relationship. You might be surprised to learn that just agreeing to do a requested favor for a friend could create an agency relationship.

[handwritten margin note: objective assent]

Second, control is evidenced in agency by a consensual relationship in which the principal has the power and right to direct the agent as to the goal of the relationship. We might colloquially refer to this as whether the principal is "in charge" or able to instruct the agent.

Finally, in an agency relationship, the agent is acting on behalf of the principal. From the principal's perspective, this is indeed the point of creating the agency relationship—the principal wants someone else to take some action on their behalf. For example, a sole proprietor who wants to grow her business might hire an agent so that someone else can act on her behalf in carrying out business matters. This element gets at the idea that the agent is acting in a representative capacity or to further the interests of the principal.

The following case examines the elements that constitute the formation of an agency relationship. The plaintiffs, a group of farmers, brought action against Cargill, Inc. (Cargill), and Warren Grain & Seed Co. (Warren), after Warren defaulted on contracts with the plaintiffs for the sale of grain. The case turned on whether an agency relationship had been formed between Cargill and Warren such that Cargill could be held responsible as a principal for the liabilities of Warren to the plaintiff farmers.

Warren operated a grain elevator. As an intermediary in the agricultural business of the region, it bought and stored grain and seed from local farmers. In 1964, Warren applied for financing from Cargill. Cargill officials from the regional office investigated Warren's operations. Subsequently, Cargill entered into a security agreement which provided that Cargill would loan money for working capital to Warren up to a stated limit, originally set at $175,000. Under this contract, Warren would receive funds and pay its expenses drawn on Cargill's bank account by issuing bank drafts imprinted with both Warren and Cargill's names. In return for the financing, Warren appointed Cargill as its grain agent for a certain transaction with a third party and Cargill was also given a right of first refusal to buy grain sold by Warren to the terminal market.

From 1964 to 1970, Warren and Cargill executed multiple new contracts extending the available credit. The contracts incorporated provisions of the original contract and added some new ones: Cargill got a right of first refusal to purchase grain sold by Warren; Warren promised to provide Cargill annual financial statements and access to their books for inspections; and Warren promised not to make repairs or improvements of more than $5,000, declare dividends, or buy and sell stock without Cargill's approval. Cargill also visited Warren to review its financial records and informed Warren that Cargill would periodically recommend improvements. However, Warren apparently never implemented some of Cargill's recommendations. A memo to the Cargill official in charge of the Warren account stated: "This organization (Warren) needs very strong paternal guidance."

In 1970, Cargill contracted with Warren to act as its agent for a new type of wheat as well as in the sunflower seed business. Warren contracted with farmers on Cargill's behalf, and Warren cleaned and packaged the seeds in Cargill bags while farmers were paid directly by Cargill. Cargill continued to review Warren's financial statements and recommend that certain actions should be taken. Warren purchased from Cargill various business forms printed by Cargill and used sample forms from Cargill. Warren was at that time shipping Cargill 90% of its cash grain. When Cargill's facilities were full, Warren shipped grain to other companies. About 25% of Warren's total sales was seed grain, which it sold directly to its customers.

As Warren became indebted in excess of its credit line, Cargill began to contact Warren daily regarding financial affairs and, in 1973, Cargill headquarters informed Warren that a regional manager would be working with them on a day-to-day basis.

By 1977, it became clear that Warren had serious financial problems. Several farmers, who had heard that Warren's checks were not being paid, inquired at Cargill and were initially told that there would be no problem with payment. When Cargill discovered that Warren had deliberately falsified financial statements, Cargill refused to provide additional financing. As Warren was winding down operations, Cargill sent an official to supervise the grain elevator and the disbursement of funds. At the time Warren ceased operations, it was $3.6 million in debt to Cargill. Warren was also indebted to plaintiff farmers in the amount of $2 million, and they brought action against Cargill seeking to recover that sum.

A. *Gay Jenson Farms Co. v. Cargill, Inc.*

309 N.W.2d 285 (Minn. 1981)

PETERSON, JUSTICE.

Plaintiffs, 86 individual, partnership or corporate farmers, brought this action against defendant Cargill, Inc. (Cargill) and defendant Warren Grain & Seed Co. (Warren) to recover losses sustained when Warren defaulted on the contracts made with plaintiffs for the sale of grain. After a trial by jury, judgment was entered in favor of plaintiffs, and Cargill brought this appeal. We affirm.

The major issue in this case is whether Cargill, by its course of dealing with Warren, became liable as a principal on contracts made by Warren with plaintiffs.[6] Cargill contends that no agency relationship was established with Warren, notwithstanding its financing of Warren's operation and its purchase of the majority of Warren's grain. However, we conclude that Cargill, by its control and influence over Warren, became a principal with liability for the transactions entered into by its agent Warren.

Agency is the fiduciary relationship that results from the manifestation of consent by one person to another that the other shall act on his behalf and subject to his control, and consent by the other so to act. *Jurek v. Thompson*, 308 Minn. 191 (1976); *Lee v. Peoples Cooperative Sales Agency*, 201 Minn. 266 (1937); Restatement (Second) of Agency § 1 (1958). In order to create an agency there must be an agreement, but not necessarily a contract between the parties. Restatement (Second) of Agency § 1, comment b (1958). An agreement may result in the creation of an agency relationship although the parties did not call it an agency and did not intend the legal consequences of the relation to follow. *Id*. The existence of the agency may be proved by circumstantial evidence which shows a course of dealing between the two parties. *Rausch v. Aronson*, 211 Minn. 272 (1941). When an agency relationship is to be proven

---

[6]   At trial, plaintiffs sought to establish actual agency by Cargill's course of dealing between 1973 and 1977 rather than "apparent" agency or agency by estoppel, so that the only issue in this case is one of actual agency.

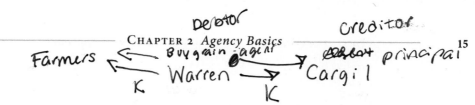

by circumstantial evidence, the principal must be shown to have consented to the agency since one cannot be the agent of another except by consent of the latter. *Larkin v. McCabe*, 211 Minn. 11 (1941).

Cargill contends that the prerequisites of an agency relationship did not exist because Cargill never consented to the agency, Warren did not act on behalf of Cargill, and Cargill did not exercise control over Warren. We hold that all three elements of agency could be found in the particular circumstances of this case. By directing Warren to implement its recommendations, Cargill manifested its consent that Warren would be its agent. Warren acted on Cargill's behalf in procuring grain for Cargill as the part of its normal operations which were totally financed by Cargill.[7] Further, an agency relationship was established by Cargill's interference with the internal affairs of Warren, which constituted de facto control of the elevator.

A creditor who assumes control of his debtor's business may become liable as principal for the acts of the debtor in connection with the business. Restatement (Second) of Agency § 140 (1958). It is noted in comment a to section 140 that:

> A security holder who merely exercises a veto power over the business acts of his debtor by preventing purchases or sales above specified amounts does not thereby become a principal. However, if he takes over the management of the debtor's business either in person or through an agent, and directs what contracts may or may not be made, he becomes a principal, liable as a principal for the obligations incurred thereafter in the normal course of business by the debtor who has now become his general agent. The point at which the creditor becomes a principal is that at which he assumes de facto control over the conduct of his debtor, whatever the terms of the formal contract with his debtor may be.

A number of factors indicate Cargill's control over Warren, including the following:

(1) Cargill's constant recommendations to Warren by telephone;

(2) Cargill's right of first refusal on grain;

(3) Warren's inability to enter into mortgages, to purchase stock or to pay dividends without Cargill's approval;

(4) Cargill's right of entry onto Warren's premises to carry on periodic checks and audits;

---

[7] Although the contracts with the farmers were executed by Warren, Warren paid for the grain with drafts drawn on Cargill. While this is not in itself significant, *see Lee v. Peoples Cooperative Sales Agency*, 201 Minn. 266 (1937), it is one factor to be taken into account in analyzing the relationship between Warren and Cargill.

(5) Cargill's correspondence and criticism regarding Warren's finances, officers salaries and inventory;

(6) Cargill's determination that Warren needed "strong paternal guidance";

(7) Provision of drafts and forms to Warren upon which Cargill's name was imprinted;

(8) Financing of all Warren's purchases of grain and operating expenses; and

(9) Cargill's power to discontinue the financing of Warren's operations.

We recognize that some of these elements, as Cargill contends, are found in an ordinary debtor-creditor relationship. However, these factors cannot be considered in isolation, but, rather, they must be viewed in light of all the circumstances surrounding Cargill's aggressive financing of Warren.

It is also Cargill's position that the relationship between Cargill and Warren was that of buyer-supplier rather than principal-agent. Restatement (Second) of Agency § 14K (1958) compares an agent with a supplier as follows: "One who contracts to acquire property from a third person and convey it to another is the agent of the other only if it is agreed that he is to act primarily for the benefit of the other and not for himself."

Factors indicating that one is a supplier, rather than an agent, are: "(1) That he is to receive a fixed price for the property irrespective of price paid by him. This is the most important. (2) That he acts in his own name and receives the title to the property which he thereafter is to transfer. (3) That he has an independent business in buying and selling similar property." Restatement (Second) of Agency § 14K, Comment a (1958).

Under the Restatement approach, it must be shown that the supplier has an independent business before it can be concluded that he is not an agent. The record establishes that all portions of Warren's operation were financed by Cargill and that Warren sold almost all of its market grain to Cargill. Thus, the relationship which existed between the parties was not merely that of buyer and supplier.

A case analogous to the present one is *Butler v. Bunge Corporation*, 329 F. Supp. 47 (N.D. Miss. 1971). In *Butler*, the plaintiff brought an action to recover the price of a soybean crop sold to an elevator that was operated by Bayles, a purported agent of the defendant Bunge Corporation. Bayles had agreed to operate a former Bunge elevator pursuant to an agreement in which Bayles was designated as manager. Although Bunge contended that Bayles was an independent contractor, the court determined that the elevator was an agent of Bunge.

In this case, as in *Butler*, Cargill furnished substantially all funds received by the elevator. Cargill did have a right of entry on Warren's premises, and it, like Bunge, required maintenance of insurance against hazards of operation. Warren's activities, like Bayles' operations, formed a substantial part of Cargill's business that was developed in that area. In addition, Cargill did not think of Warren as an operator who was free to become Cargill's competitor, but rather conceded that it believed that Warren owed a duty of loyalty to Cargill. The decisions made by Warren were not independent of Cargill's interest or its control.

Further, we are not persuaded by the fact that Warren was not one of the "line" elevators that Cargill operated in its own name. The Warren operation, like the line elevator, was financially dependent on Cargill's continual infusion of capital. The arrangement with Warren presented a convenient alternative to the establishment of a line elevator. Cargill became, in essence, the owner of the operation without the accompanying legal indicia.

The amici curiae assert that, if the jury verdict is upheld, firms and banks which have provided business loans to county elevators will decline to make further loans. The decision in this case should give no cause for such concern. We deal here with a business enterprise markedly different from an ordinary bank financing, since Cargill was an active participant in Warren's operations rather than simply a financier. Cargill's course of dealing with Warren was, by its own admission, a paternalistic relationship in which Cargill made the key economic decisions and kept Warren in existence.

Although considerable interest was paid by Warren on the loan, the reason for Cargill's financing of Warren was not to make money as a lender but, rather, to establish a source of market grain for its business. As one Cargill manager noted, "We were staying in there because we wanted the grain." For this reason, Cargill was willing to extend the credit line far beyond the amount originally allocated to Warren. It is noteworthy that Cargill was receiving significant amounts of grain and that, notwithstanding the risk that was recognized by Cargill, the operation was considered profitable.

On the whole, there was a unique fabric in the relationship between Cargill and Warren which varies from that found in normal debtor-creditor situations. We conclude that, on the facts of this case, there was sufficient evidence from which the jury could find that Cargill was the principal of Warren within the definitions of agency set forth in Restatement (Second) of Agency §§ 1 and 140.

Affirmed.

Points for Discussion

1. Cargill's defense?

The plaintiffs argued that Cargill was the principal in an agency relationship with Warren. Cargill disputed this characterization of its relationship with Warren. How did Cargill characterize the relationship? *Buyer – Supplier*

2. Fact-specific inquiries.

What facts supported a conclusion that Cargill controlled Warren? What facts supported a conclusion that Warren was acting on behalf of Cargill? And what facts supported assent by each party? On the whole, do you think these facts were sufficient for a ruling that an agency relationship was formed between Cargill and Warren?

3. Lender liability?

Creditors and lenders are often concerned about whether or not they will get paid back, and so they often take steps to protect their interests. It is customary for commercial loan documents to specify certain protections such as events of default and remedies the lender may exercise upon a default. Typical events of default include, for example: failure to make timely payments, material adverse changes in the borrower's financial condition or the adequacy of the collateral, and breach of any covenants made by the borrower. Typical remedies include suspension or termination of further advances from the lender, acceleration of unpaid principal and interest, and possession of collateral or the posting of additional security by the borrower.

———

Lenders have to act carefully when deciding what to do when a borrower shows signs of distress. If the lender does nothing, the borrower might fail and not pay back the lender. But if the lender declares an event of default, and requires a remedy such as requiring the loan to be paid back in full or possessing the collateral, it could have a devastating impact on the borrower that could also endanger the borrower's ability to pay back the loan.

Another concern is illustrated by the *Cargill* case—lender liability. Lender liability claims have been asserted (1) by borrowers using various theories to attempt to prevent or recover damages from the lender's exercise of contractual rights, and (2) by third parties attempting to hold the lender liable for the debts of the borrower using an agency theory based on control, as in *Cargill*.

A small handful of lender liability cases like *Cargill* exist, but not a huge number—the *Cargill* case could thus be understood as a cautionary tale, representing an unlikely but possible risk for creditors or lenders that exercise significantly more than the typical amount of control or become unusually involved in the borrower's business. The comments to the Restatement (Third) of Agency § 1.01 provide the following: "Control, however defined, is by itself insufficient to establish agency. In the debtor-creditor context, most courts are reluctant to find relationships of agency on the basis of provisions in agreements that protect the creditor's interests . . . An unusual example to the contrary is *A. Gay Jenson Farms Co. v. Cargill, Inc.,* 309 N.W.2d 285 (Minn. 1981) . . ."

B.   Rights and Duties Between Principal and Agent

Why does it matter that an agency relationship exists? One reason is because once this relationship is created, the principal and agent owe each other certain obligations and duties under the law.

1.   Principal's Obligations to Agent

The obligations owed by the principal to the agent are relatively straightforward. Restatement (Third) of Agency § 8.14 provides that the principal has a duty to reimburse or indemnify the agent for any promised payments, any payments the agent makes within the scope of actual authority, and when the agent "suffers a loss that fairly should be borne by the principal in light of their relationship." In addition, under § 8.15, a principal has an obligation to deal with the agent fairly and in good faith. The principal should also generally cooperate with the agent and not unreasonably interfere with the agent's performance of his or her duties.

2.   Agent's Fiduciary Duties to Principal

More notably, the duties that are owed by the agent to the principal are not just obligations, but they are *fiduciary duties.* This is an important topic that we will see throughout the course, as fiduciary duties arise or can arise in agency, partnership, LLCs, and corporations.

A fiduciary is someone, such as an agent, a partner, or a corporate director, who stands in a special relation of trust, confidence, or responsibility in certain obligations to others. A fiduciary relationship requires one party to put the other party's interests ahead of her own. In a broad sense, fiduciary duties seek to protect those who delegate authority against the negligence, disloyalty, or worse of those who exercise this author-

To many economists and legal scholars, "agency costs" are a key concept or theory used to explain the relationships between business principals and their agents. Imagine one party (the principal) delegates work to another party (the agent). The agent's interests might diverge from those of the principal. For example, the agent might want to steal or shirk (not put in their best efforts). The divergence of interests between the principal and agent gives rise to what are known as "agency costs." These costs can be minimized, such as by the principal monitoring the agent, but in theory, given the costs of doing so, there will always be some residual agency costs that exist when there is a separation of ownership from managerial control. The topic of agency costs can be relevant in all forms of business organizations that we study, including partnerships, LLCs, and corporations.

ity on their behalf. Without the protection of fiduciary duties, people might be less inclined to hire someone to work for them, join a partnership, or invest money in a business enterprise.

Fiduciary duties are well established and deeply ingrained in the law, and rationales for these duties have been stated in various ways, ranging from moralistic terms to efficiency rationales, such as reducing transaction and monitoring costs. Drawing on influences from economists, some describe the separation or divergence of interests between principals and agents as "agency costs," recognizing that agents might shirk or act opportunistically out of self-interest rather than doing what is best for the principal. Agency costs might be reduced through various legal rules and business practices but cannot be entirely eliminated. Fiduciary duties might be thought of as "gap fillers" that help to reduce agency costs or build trust between parties as it would be nearly impossible, and prohibitively costly, to negotiate for and draft a "complete" contract given the difficulty of foreseeing every possible scenario of conflict between the parties. Instead, the law steps in with its own (often vague and flexible) rules that state broadly that the fiduciary must exercise care, diligence, honesty, and loyalty with respect to the principal or the firm and its participants. When litigation arises, courts apply fiduciary principles to the particular facts at hand in a case.

An agent is a fiduciary with respect to matters within the scope of the agency relationship. The Restatement (Third) of Agency §§ 8.01–8.11 explains that the agent owes the principal the duties of care and loyalty, and certain duties related to information and confidentiality. The duty of care refers to the level of care, competence, and diligence that an agent exercises. If an agent claims to have special skills or knowledge, then the agent has a duty to act with the care normally exercised by agents with such skills or knowledge. Otherwise, the standard is simply the ordinary care that an agent would use in similar circumstances, if the agent is paid, or gross negligence for unpaid agents.

The duty of loyalty refers to the idea that the agent must not put their own interests ahead of those of the principal when the agent is acting within the agency relationship. The agent should act for the benefit of the principal in all matters connected with the agency. For example, the agent must not compete with the principal, act adversely to the principal, take a business opportunity that belongs to the principal, or abuse the agent position to earn unauthorized side profits, bribes, or tips.

Finally, the agent has duties related to information. An agent has a duty to provide information to the principal that the agent knows or has reason to know that the principal would wish to have, as well as to provide the facts that are material to the agent's duties to the principal. Further, the duty of confidentiality means that the agent must not disclose or misuse confidential information. Unlike the other duties, the duty of confidentiality notably remains in force even after the agency relationship has terminated.

If an agent breaches any of these duties without the consent of the fully informed principal, the agent could be liable to the principal for any resulting damages. The agent could also be liable to disgorge to the principal any profit made by the agent in breach of a duty.

The following case involves a lawsuit brought by a small machine shop business, General Automotive Manufacturing Company ("Automotive"), against John Singer, a former employee. Singer was a well-regarded expert at machine work, known for being able to use special techniques and qualified in estimating the costs and competitive prices of machine-shop products.

Automotive hired Singer as the general manager of its business pursuant to a written contract which set out his compensation as a fixed monthly salary and a commission of 3% of the gross sales. In exchange, the contract provided that Singer promised "to devote his entire time, skill, labor and attention to said employment, during the term of this employment, and not to engage in any other business or vocation of a permanent nature during the term of this employment." He was not to disclose any information concerning the business or affairs that he acquired in the course of his employment for his own benefit or to the detriment of his employer. It also provided that, as a manager, Singer was a fiduciary agent with respect to solicitation of business and was bound to exercise the utmost good faith and loyalty to his employer.

A dispute later arose when it came to Automotive's attention that Singer was secretly profiting while in its employ. The trial court found in favor of Automotive. Singer appealed.

General Automotive Mfg. v. Singer

120 N.W.2d 659 (Wis. 1963)

BROWN, CHIEF JUSTICE.

Study of the record discloses that Singer was engaged as general manager of Automotive's operations. Among his duties was solicitation and procurement of machine shop work for Automotive. Because of Singer's high reputation in the trade he was highly successful in attracting orders.

Automotive is a small concern and has a low credit rating. Singer was invaluable in bolstering Automotive's credit. For instance, when collections were slow for work done by Automotive, Singer paid the customer's bill to Automotive and waited for his own reimbursement until the customer remitted. Also, when work was slack, Singer set Automotive's shop to make parts for which there were no present orders and himself financed the cost of materials for such parts, waiting for recoupment until such stock-piled parts could be sold. Some parts were never sold and Singer personally absorbed the loss upon them.

As time went on a large volume of business attracted by Singer was offered to Automotive but which Singer decided could not be done by Automotive at all, for lack of suitable equipment, or which Automotive could not do at a competitive price. When Singer determined that such orders were unsuitable for Automotive he neither informed Automotive of these facts nor sent the orders back to the customer. Instead, he made the customer a price, then dealt with another machine shop to do the work at a less price, and retained the difference between the price quoted to the customer and the price for which the work was done. Singer was actually behaving as a broker for his own profit in a field where by contract he had engaged to work only for Automotive. We concur in the decision of the trial court that this was inconsistent with the obligations of a faithful agent or employee.

Singer finally set up a business of his own, calling himself a manufacturer's agent and consultant, in which he brokered orders for products of the sort manufactured by automotive—this while he was still Automotive's employee and without informing Automotive of it. Singer had broad powers of management and conducted the business activities of Automotive. In this capacity he was Automotive's agent and owed a fiduciary duty to it. Under his fiduciary duty to Automotive Singer was bound to the exercise of the utmost good faith and loyalty so that he did not act adversely to the interests of Automotive by serving or acquiring any private interest of his own. He was also bound to act for the furtherance and advancement of the interest of Automotive.

Singer did things to benefit himself, not his principal

If Singer violated his duty to Automotive by engaging in certain business activities in which he received a secret profit he must account to Automotive for the amounts he illegally received.

The present controversy centers around the question whether the operation of Singer's side line business was a violation of his fiduciary duty to Automotive. The trial court found this business was conducted in secret and without the knowledge of Automotive. There is conflicting evidence regarding this finding but it is not against the great weight and clear preponderance of the evidence and, therefore, cannot be disturbed.

The trial court found that Singer's side line business, the profits of which were $64,088.08, was in direct competition with Automotive. However, Singer argues that in this business he was a manufacturer's agent or consultant, whereas Automotive was a small manufacturer of automotive parts. The title of an activity does not determine the question whether it was competitive but an examination of the nature of the business must be made. In the present case the conflict of interest between Singer's business and his position with Automotive arises from the fact that Singer received orders, principally from a third-party called Husco, for the manufacture of parts. As a manufacturer's consultant he had to see that these orders were filled as inexpensively as possible, but as Automotive's general manager he could not act adversely to the corporation and serve his own interests. On this issue Singer argues that when Automotive had the shop capacity to fill an order he would award Automotive the job, but he contends that it was in the exercise of his duty as general manager of Automotive to refuse orders which in his opinion Automotive could not or should not fill and in that case he was free to treat the order as his own property. However, this argument ignores, as the trial court said, "defendant's agency with plaintiff and the fiduciary duties of good faith and loyalty arising therefrom."

Rather than to resolve the conflict of interest between his side line business and Automotive's business in favor of serving and advancing his own personal interests, Singer had the duty to exercise good faith by disclosing to Automotive all the facts regarding this matter. Upon disclosure to Automotive it was in the latter's discretion to refuse to accept the orders from Husco or to fill them if possible or to sub-job them to other concerns with the consent of Husco if necessary, and the profit, if any, would belong to Automotive. Automotive would then be able also to decide whether to expand its operations, install suitable equipment, or to make further arrangements with Singer or Husco. By failing to disclose all the facts relating to the orders from Husco and by receiving secret profits from these orders, Singer violated his fiduciary duty to act solely for the benefit of Automotive. Therefore he is liable for the amount of the profits he earned in his side line business.

maybe its not the act but the lack of Disclosure

We conclude that Singer's independent activities were in competition with Automotive and were in violation of his obligation of fidelity to that corporation, as stated in Finding of Fact No. 10 and Singer must account for his profits so obtained. Judgment affirmed.

Points for Discussion

1. Judge-made law.

The case applies common law principles established through judge-made precedent. The opinion does not cite to any statutes. What is the purpose of extensive statutes if some of the most important aspects of business organization law are decided by judges without reference to those statutes? As we will see, business law is a mix of statutes and case law—a dialogue between legislatures and courts.

Old law Some things or so settled

2. Gap-filling function.

Imagine a hypothetical bargain that might have taken place between the parties in advance of the dispute. Would the parties have negotiated to allow Singer to maintain a side business if he was not taking business away from the company and did not interfere with work that Automotive was capable of handling? Consider the importance of Singer to Automotive's business. Since Automotive was incapable of doing the work Singer rerouted, should Singer be allowed to operate a side business or otherwise send work to other shops? How would we know what Automotive would have been willing to allow Singer to do if it was not even informed of the customer inquiries and given an opportunity to use this information to make changes to its business operations or pricing?

3. Interaction of contract and fiduciary duties.

Did it matter that the parties had a contract that specified that Singer was an agent who owed the fiduciary duty of loyalty? Or would the court have applied agency and fiduciary law principles anyway based on the facts? What remedy does Automotive get from Singer? How is this different from what the remedy would have been had the court's ruling been based on breach of contract?

4. Avoiding liability.

How could Singer have avoided liability in these circumstances? Would it have been enough to avoid liability if Singer had told General Automotive what he was doing?

———

We have so far examined the inward-looking consequences of the agency relationship—the rights and duties between the principal and agent. The next section examines the outward-looking consequences of the agency relationship—the contract and tort liability that the principal can incur based on the agent's actions and related topics.

C.　Contract Liability: Principals

When can a third party hold a principal liable in contract for the actions of the agent? There are five bases by which a principal (or purported principal) can incur contract liability: actual authority, apparent authority, undisclosed principal liability, ratification, and estoppel.

It is possible for more than one of these bases to be present in a particular factual circumstance, but any one of these would be sufficient for holding a principal (or purported principal) liable. We will give special attention to the first two—actual authority and apparent authority—which are the most common.

1.　Actual Authority

Actual authority is authority that the agent reasonably believes she has based on the principal's manifestations, expressed through words or other conduct. Restatement (Third) of Agency § 2.01 tells us:

An agent acts with actual authority when, at the time of taking action that has legal consequences for the principal, the agent reasonably believes, in accordance with the principal's manifestations to the agent, that the principal wishes the agent so to act.

For example, a principal tells an agent: "Do X." Upon hearing this, the agent reasonably believes that the principal wants her to do X, and she has actual authority to do so. If the agent carries out the instruction by entering into a contract on behalf of the principal, the principal is bound to the contract.

How do you know if the agent's understanding of the principal's manifestations is reasonable? An agent's belief is reasonable if it reflects any meaning that the agent knows from the principal is to be ascribed or if it accords with the inferences that a reasonable person in the agent's position would draw in light of the context.

Actual authority may be express or implied. That is, actual authority encompasses both the authority to do what the principal explicitly instructs (i.e. express) as well as what a reasonable person in the agent's position would understand to be reasonably included (i.e. implied) in those instructions in order to accomplish the objective. Implied authority can be inferred from the words the principal used, from custom, or from the relations between the parties. It includes the notion that the agent can do incidental acts that are related to a transaction that is authorized.

Mill St. Church of Christ v. Hogan

785 S.W.2d 263 (Ky. Ct. App. 1990)

HOWARD, JUDGE.

Samuel Hogan filed a claim for workers' compensation benefits for an injury he received while painting the interior of the Mill Street Church of Christ on December 15, 1986. In 1986, the Elders of the Mill Street Church of Christ decided to hire church member, Bill Hogan, to paint the church building. The Elders decided that another church member, Gary Petty, would be hired to assist if any assistance was needed. In the past, the church had hired Bill Hogan for similar jobs, and he had been allowed to hire his brother, Sam Hogan, the respondent, as a helper. Sam Hogan had earlier been a member of the church but was no longer a member.

Dr. David Waggoner, an Elder of the church, soon contacted Bill Hogan, and he accepted the job and began work. Apparently Waggoner made no mention to Bill Hogan of hiring a helper at that time. Bill Hogan painted the church by himself until he reached the baptistry portion of the church. This was a very high, difficult portion of the church to paint, and he decided that he needed help. After Bill Hogan had reached this point in his work, he discussed the matter of a helper with Dr.

Waggoner at his office. According to both Dr. Waggoner and Hogan, they discussed the possibility of hiring Gary Petty to help Hogan. None of the evidence indicates that Hogan was told that he had to hire Petty. In fact, Dr. Waggoner apparently told Hogan that Petty was difficult to reach. That was basically all the discussion that these two individuals had concerning hiring a helper. None of the other Elders discussed the matter with Bill Hogan.

On December 14, 1986, Bill Hogan approached his brother, Sam, about helping him complete the job. Bill Hogan told Sam the details of the job, including the pay, and Sam accepted the job. On December 15, 1986, Sam began working. A half hour after he began, he climbed the ladder to paint a ceiling corner, and a leg of the ladder broke. Sam fell to the floor and broke his left arm. The church Elders did not know that Bill Hogan had approached Sam Hogan to work as a helper until after the accident occurred.

After the accident, Bill Hogan reported the accident and resulting injury to Charles Payne, a church Elder and treasurer. Payne stated in a deposition that he told Bill Hogan that the church had insurance. At this time, Bill Hogan told Payne the total number of hours worked which included a half hour that Sam Hogan had worked prior to the accident. Payne issued Bill Hogan a check for all of these hours.

It is undisputed in this case that Mill Street Church of Christ is an insured employer under the Workers' Compensation Act. Sam Hogan filed a claim under the Workers' Compensation Act. As part of their argument, petitioners argue the Workers' Compensation Board erred in finding that Bill Hogan possessed implied authority as an agent to hire Sam Hogan. Petitioners contend there was neither implied nor apparent authority in the case at bar.

It is important to distinguish implied and apparent authority before proceeding further. Implied authority is actual authority circumstantially proven which the principal actually intended the agent to possess and includes such powers as are practically necessary to carry out the duties actually delegated. Apparent authority on the other hand is not actual authority but is the authority the agent is held out by the principal as possessing. It is a matter of appearances on which third parties come to rely.

Petitioners attack the Workers' Compensation Board's findings concerning implied authority. In examining whether implied authority exists, it is important to focus upon the agent's understanding of his authority. It must be determined whether the agent reasonably believes because of present or past conduct of the principal that the principal wishes him to act in a certain way or to have certain authority. The nature of the task or job may be another factor to consider. Implied authority may be necessary in order to implement the express authority. The existence of prior similar practices is one of the most important factors. Specific conduct by the principal in the past permitting the agent to exercise similar powers is crucial.

The person alleging agency and resulting authority has the burden of proving that it exists. Agency cannot be proven by a mere statement, but it can be established by circumstantial evidence including the acts and conduct of the parties such as the continuous course of conduct of the parties covering a number of successive transactions. Specifically one must look at what had gone on before to determine if the agent had certain authority. If considering past similar acts done in a similar manner, it is found that the present action was taken within the scope of the agent's authority, the act is binding upon the principal.

In considering the above factors in the case at bar, Bill Hogan had implied authority to hire Sam Hogan as his helper. First, in the past the church had allowed Bill Hogan to hire his brother or other persons whenever he needed assistance on a project. Even though the Board of Elders discussed a different arrangement this time, no mention of this discussion was ever made to Bill or Sam Hogan. In fact, the discussion between Bill Hogan and Church Elder Dr. Waggoner, indicated that Gary Petty would be difficult to reach and Bill Hogan could hire whomever he pleased. Further, Bill Hogan needed to hire an assistant to complete the job for which he had been hired. The interior of the church simply could not be painted by one person. Maintaining a safe and attractive place of worship clearly is part of the church's function, and one for which it would designate an agent to ensure that the building is properly painted and maintained.

Finally, in this case, Sam Hogan believed that Bill Hogan had the authority to hire him as had been the practice in the past. To now claim that Bill Hogan could not hire Sam Hogan as an assistant, especially when Bill Hogan had never been told this fact, would be very unfair to Sam Hogan. Sam Hogan relied on Bill Hogan's representation. The church treasurer in this case even paid Bill Hogan for the half hour of work that Sam Hogan had completed prior to the accident. Considering the above facts, we find that Sam Hogan was within the employment of the Mill Street Church of Christ at the time he was injured. The decision of the Workers' Compensation Board is affirmed. All concur.

---

2. Apparent Authority

Apparent authority arises, according to Restatement (Third) of Agency § 2.03, "when a third party reasonably believes the actor has authority to act on behalf of the principal and that belief is traceable to the principal's manifestations." Claims of apparent authority commonly arise when a third party seeks to bind a principal who created the impression that an agent had authority for a particular action when in fact he or she did not. It is a doctrine that protects the reasonable beliefs of third parties.

Apparent authority may be the basis for contract liability where an agent acts beyond the scope of their actual authority or even where there is not a true agency

The comments to the Restatement (Third) of Agency provide explanations for each provision along with hypothetical illustrations. For example, Comment a to § 2.03 provides: "The definition [of apparent authority] in this section does not presuppose the present or prior existence of an agency relationship . . . The definition thus applies to actors who appear to be agents but are not, as well as to agents who act beyond the scope of their actual authority."

relationship. This is because the focus of apparent authority is on what a third party reasonably believes one person has authorized another to do. When we think about apparent authority, there might not be an "actual" principal arising from the principal-agent relationship; instead, there might only be an "apparent" principal, from the third party's perspective.

Thus, whereas *actual authority* depends on the *agent's* reasonable beliefs, *apparent authority* depends on the *third party's* reasonable beliefs. For apparent authority, it is critical to determine whether a principal or purported principal has made a manifestation that led a third party to reasonably believe that the agent or actor had authority to act on behalf of the principal or purported principal. A manifestation could be words or conduct, and for apparent authority it must be traceable to the principal, for example, through an intermediary or by the principal giving an agent a certain title or position.

Comment c to § 2.03 explains:

[Manifestations] include explicit statements that a principal makes directly to a third party, as well as statements made by others concerning an actor's authority that reach the third party and are traceable to the principal. For example, a principal may make a manifestation about an agent's authority by directing that the agent's name and affiliation with the principal be included in a listing of representatives that is provided to a third party. The principal may make a manifestation by directing an agent to make statements to third parties or directing or designating an agent to perform acts or conduct negotiations, placing an agent in a position within an organization, or placing the agent in charge of a transaction or situation.

The following case illustrates how apparent authority can bind a principal to contract liability. The case involved OSL, an ophthalmology medical practice, owned by Dr. William J. Andreoni, that entered into a contract with Paychex for payroll processing services. Paychex's office handled payroll services for about 7,000 clients based on the information provided by the clients. Paychex would ask each new client for a designated payroll contact who would provide Paychex with the relevant employee information including names, addresses, social security numbers, and salary information so that it could process the client's payroll. Paychex provides reports on a regular basis to clients, including information about checks before they are paid to employees, and invoices indicating how many paychecks were issued per pay period because Paychex charges its clients per check processed.

For over ten years, OSL's office manager Carleen Connor was the designated payroll contact. For several of those years, Connor told Paychex to direct deposit into her bank account more money than she was supposed to receive—indeed, she was paid $233,159 more than her authorized salary during that time. Paychex sent to OSL reports confirming all payments made. These reports were sent to Connor's attention, and OSL's owner, Dr. Andreoni, said that he saw none of these reports because they were not sent directly to his attention. When another employee took over Connor's duties, OSL discovered the unauthorized payments. OSL then tried to get out of the responsibility for the extra money that had been paid to Connor by filing a breach of contract action against Paychex. The district court issued summary judgment in favor of Paychex. OSL appealed.

Ophthalmic Surgeons, Ltd. v. Paychex, Inc.

632 F.3d 31 (1st Cir. 2011)

TORRUELLA, CIRCUIT JUDGE.

Although we have found that the contract creates no obligation for Paychex to verify the information that the payroll contact provides, we must now examine whether agency law creates such an obligation. OSL argues that the district court erred by ignoring a disputed issue of material fact regarding Connor's lack of apparent authority to "specify" the withdrawal of payments adding up to more than her authorized weekly salary. We find that OSL's argument is without merit.

A corporation must, by necessity, act through its agents. It is undisputed that Connor was in fact authorized to handle payroll and was the designated payroll contact assigned to communicate with Paychex. Connor's actual authority, however, did not extend to embezzling funds by authorizing the issuance of paychecks in amounts in excess of her salary as this is not what OSL, the principal, instructed her to do. The question remains, however, as to whether Connor was cloaked with apparent authority such that Paychex could have reasonably relied upon her authority to issue additional paychecks in her name. Restatement (Third) of Agency § 2.03 cmt. a ("Apparent authority may survive the termination of actual authority or of an agency relationship."). OSL argues that Connor had no apparent authority where OSL, as principal, did not act in a way that gave the appearance that Connor had the authority to order the paychecks at issue here and that Paychex is therefore liable for making the unauthorized payments.

We recognize that "[t]he mere creation of an agency for some purpose does not automatically invest the agent with 'apparent authority' to bind the principal without limitation." Under New York law, apparent authority can only be created through "words *or conduct of the principal*, communicated to a third party" such that a third party can reasonably rely on the "appearance and belief that the agent possesses authority to enter into a transaction."

We find that Paychex's reliance was reasonable and that Connor had apparent authority because OSL put Connor in a position where it appeared that she had the power to authorize additional paychecks. *Telenor Mobile Commc'ns AS v. Storm LLC*, 584 F.3d 396, 411 (2d Cir. 2009) ("Under New York law, an agent has apparent authority if 'a principal places [the] agent in a position where it appears that the agent has certain powers which he may or may not possess.' "). In her position as the designated payroll contact, Connor often called in more than one week's worth of payroll at a time without objection from OSL. Further, Dr. Andreoni admits that, after 1989, he had no further contact with Paychex. Even if we assume that, in 1989, the purported conversation between Dr. Andreoni, as agent of OSL, and a representative of Paychex occurred and that during that conversation, Dr. Andreoni informed Paychex that he wanted OSL employees to be paid weekly for fifty-two weeks each year, OSL's argument fails. This conversation does not expressly convey a limitation on Connor's authority, especially where the conversation did not occur in connection with the formation of the 1994 Agreement. Further, it was reasonable for Paychex to assume its clients' needs might change and that the payroll contact would be authorized to convey such a change.

Paychex's reliance was also reasonable because of OSL's failure to object to the transactions that Connor authorized.

> A principal's inaction creates apparent authority when it provides a basis for a third party reasonably to believe the principal intentionally acquiesces in the agent's representations or actions. . . . If the third party has observed prior interactions between the agent and the principal, the third party may reasonably believe that a subsequent act or representation by the agent is authorized because it conforms to the prior pattern observed by the third party. The belief is thus traceable to the principal's participation in the pattern and failure to inform the third party that no inferences about the agent's authority should be based upon it.

Restatement (Third) of Agency § 3.03 cmt. b (internal citation omitted). In *Minskoff v. American Express Travel Related Services. Co., Inc.*, 98 F.3d 703 (2d Cir. 1996), the Second Circuit found such inaction or omission sufficient to create apparent authority in an agent who was fraudulently using her employer's credit card.

We find the Second Circuit's reasoning in *Minskoff* persuasive. *Minskoff* involved an office assistant, Susan Schrader Blumenfeld, who was explicitly responsible for the personal and business affairs of a company's president and CEO. Her duties included screening her employer's mail, reviewing credit card statements, and forwarding these statements to the company's bookkeepers for payment. Less than a year after she began working for the company, Blumenfeld fraudulently requested that American Express issue an additional credit card in her name for the company's corporate account. After discovering the fraud over one year later, the company filed a suit to recover the money the company had paid in connection with the unauthorized charges and sought a declaration that it was not liable for the outstanding balances. The court held that, pursuant to the Truth in Lending Act, Blumenfeld acted without actual, implied, or apparent authority when she forged the credit card applications. However, the court held that there was apparent authority for Blumenfeld's subsequent use of the fraudulently obtained credit card where the company failed to examine credit card and bank statements documenting the fraudulent charges. *Id.* at 709–10 ("A cardholder's failure to examine credit card statements that would reveal fraudulent use of the card constitutes a negligent omission that creates apparent authority for charges that would otherwise be considered unauthorized under the [Truth in Lending Act].").

We find *Minskoff* directly applicable to these circumstances. Like the company in *Minskoff*, OSL failed to examine the payroll reports that Paychex sent. That these reports were sent to Connor's attention is not dispositive where OSL, as principal, did not convey any instructions to Paychex that it should do otherwise. Further, OSL's failure to object to the "extraordinary" transactions would reasonably convey to a third party that it acquiesced in its agent's acts. *Cf. id.* at 710 (noting that the company's omissions created a continuing impression that nothing was wrong with the accounts); *Bus. Integration Servs., Inc. v. AT&T Corp.*, 251 F.R.D. 121, 128 (S.D.N.Y. 2008) ("Applying the general principles of agency, we find that [the principal's] failure to respond in any way to the allegedly unauthorized disclosure [of its agent], . . . of which it obviously has been aware for a long time, justifies the 'reasonable assumption' [of assent]. . . . Silence may constitute a manifestation when . . . a reasonable person would express dissent to the inference that other persons will draw from silence.").

We find that by placing Connor in a position where it appeared that she had authority to order additional checks and by acquiescing to Connor's acts through its failure to examine the payroll reports, OSL created apparent authority in Connor such that Paychex reasonably relied on her authority to issue the additional paychecks.

Points for Discussion

1. Doctrinal motivations.

Was OSL or Paychex in a better position to avoid paying Connor an extra $233,159? Does the apparent authority rule put the burden on the party better able to avoid the loss?

OSL

2. Inward and outward-facing aspects of agency law.

Paychex illustrates how a principal can be held liable on a contract with a third party on the basis of apparent authority even when the agent acted beyond the scope of actual authority. In a situation like this, what were the principal's options? Who did it have a claim against?

---

3.   Undisclosed Principal Liability

Most of the time when a third party is dealing with an agent, the third party knows the identity of the principal on whose behalf the agent is acting. But sometimes situations arise in which a third party does not have notice that the person they are dealing with is an agent acting on behalf of someone else—we refer to the principal in this situation as "undisclosed." If the agent was acting within the scope of authority when dealing with the third party, the undisclosed principal can be held liable on the basis of actual authority. But even if the agent was not acting within the scope of actual authority, the undisclosed principal could still be held liable.

The Restatement acknowledges that there are only a "small universe of cases" applying the undisclosed principal doctrine, and it previously used a vague broader category called "inherent authority" for these cases.

Restatement (Third) of Agency § 2.06

Liability of Undisclosed Principal

(1) An undisclosed principal is subject to liability to a third party who is justifiably induced to make a detrimental change in position by an agent acting on the principal's behalf and without actual authority if the principal, having notice of the agent's conduct and that it might induce others to change their positions, did not take reasonable steps to notify them of the facts.

(2) An undisclosed principal may not rely on instructions given an agent that qualify or reduce the agent's authority to less than the authority a third party would reasonably believe the agent to have under the same circumstances if the principal had been disclosed.

Among the few undisclosed principal cases, the best known remains an old English case, *Watteau v. Fenwick*, 1 Q.B. 346 (Queen's Bench 1893), which involved a beerhouse named the Victoria Hotel. The business was originally owned by Humble, who sold it to the defendants, Fenwick et al. After the sale of the business, Humble stayed on as manager, the license remained in his name, and his name was still painted over the door. Fenwick told Humble that he had no authority to buy any goods for the business except bottled ales and minerals; all other goods would be supplied by Fenwick. Despite this limitation of authority, Humble had bought for the business other items such as cigars and bovril (a popular wintertime drink) from a third-party supplier, Watteau.

At the time of entering into these transactions, Watteau did not know that Humble was an agent. Thus, Watteau could not invoke the doctrine of apparent authority since he did not even know of the existence of the principal. But when Watteau later learned of Fenwick, the court allowed Watteau to hold Fenwick to the contract, noting, "otherwise, in every case of undisclosed principal, or at least in every case where the fact of there being a principal was undisclosed, the secret limitation of authority would prevail and defeat the action of the person dealing with the agent and then discovering that he was an agent and had a principal." The court reasoned that if it did not uphold liability in these circumstances, "very mischievous consequences would often result."

Restatement (Third) of Agency § 2.06 includes two subsections, which can be read disjunctively to capture two ways in which an undisclosed principal could be subject to liability. The famous Watteau case is reflected in subsection (2). As comment c to § 2.06 to explains, "[u]nder subsection (1), a principal is subject to liability to a third party who is justifiably induced to make a detrimental change in position by the conduct of an agent acting without actual authority when the principal has notice of the agent's conduct and its likely impact on third parties and fails to take reasonable steps to inform them of the facts." It provides the following illustration:

> P, who owns Blackacre, coinhabits it with A, who manages Blackacre on P's behalf. T, who wishes to purchase Blackacre, mistakenly believes that A has authority to sell it on the basis of A's representation that A has such authority. P is aware of T's error and could easily inform T of the facts. P is subject to liability to T if T justifiably makes a detrimental change in position as a consequence of A's conduct.

As to rationales for undisclosed principal liability, comment c to § 2.06 provides a variety of explanations. First, similar to the doctrine of apparent authority, this rule "protects third parties by backstopping actual authority when circumstances might otherwise permit the principal opportunistically to speculate at the expense of third parties." Further, "[t]he doctrine allocates to the principal the risk that the agent will deviate from the principal's instructions while doing acts that are consistent with the apparent position the agent occupies, which are acts that third parties would anticipate an agent in such a position would have authority to do and may well be acts that are foreseeable to the principal." A reasonable third party is unlikely to make inquiries into the status of the agent in the circumstances in which the undisclosed principal doctrine applies, and "making the inquiry may be difficult or its costs may seem excessive relative to the magnitude of the particular transaction." In addition, on a separate note, when an undisclosed principal has notice of an agent's unauthorized actions and that a third party might be induced to make a detrimental change in position, the rule of liability in these circumstances operates similarly to estoppel under equitable principles.

4.   Ratification

Ratification is a doctrine that allows a person to retroactively bind herself to a contract entered into purportedly on her behalf, even though the agent or purported agent was not acting with authority at the time he entered into the contract. In the words of § 4.01 of the Restatement (Third) of Agency, it is "the affirmance of a prior act done by another, whereby the act is given effect as if done by an agent acting with actual authority." The effect of ratification is to validate the contract as if the principal or purported principal had originally authorized it. Upon ratification, the agent or purported agent is relieved of liability for breach of her duty to her principal. Both parties to the contract are bound following a valid ratification.

Ratification can be express or implied. Express ratification refers to when a person objectively manifests acceptance of the transaction, such as through oral or written statements. Implied ratification occurs when the person engages in conduct that justifies a reasonable assumption that the person consents to the transaction. For example, implied ratification commonly occurs when a principal accepts the benefits of an unauthorized transaction entered into purportedly on her behalf, such as by accepting payment. In either case, whether express or implied, there must be a manifestation of assent or other conduct indicative of consent by the principal.

There are a number of additional rules about ratification, captured in the Restatement (Third) of Agency §§ 4.02–4.07, including that valid ratification requires that the principal or purported principal is fully aware of all material facts involved in the transaction. Further, ratification is all or nothing—there is no partial ratification or cherry picking parts of an act or contract that a principal wants to ratify. Ratification operates through equitable principles so the ratification is ineffective if it would be inequitable to the third party as a result of a material change in circumstances or if a third party has already manifested an intention to withdraw from the transaction.

> According to comment b of § 4.01: "In most jurisdictions, ratification may create a relationship of agency when none existed between the actor and the ratifier at the time of the act. It is necessary that the actor have acted or purported to act on behalf of the ratifier. This limits the range of ratifiable acts to those done by an actor who is an agent or who is not an agent but pretends to be."

5.   Estoppel

Estoppel is an equitable doctrine. In the context of agency, the idea is that the principal or purported principal is "estopped" from disclaiming contractual liability. Estoppel does not create a binding contract between the parties, it is simply a doctrine that can prevent a principal or purported principal from avoiding an obligation by arguing that no authority existed at the time the agent or actor entered into a contract.

The estoppel doctrine can apply regardly of whether an agency relationship actually existed—it is typically raised where a purported agent did not have actual or apparent authority, but the plaintiff asks the court to hold the defendant liable due to some fault.

Notice that estoppel is similar to apparent authority in that both apply where a principal or purported principal leads a third party to believe that an agent or actor is authorized to act on the principal's behalf, even though no actual authority exists. However, there are two ways in which estoppel is different from apparent authority. First, estoppel does not require showing that the principal made manifestations of authority to the third party, but it does require showing that the third party detrimentally changed position in reliance on the principal or purported principal. Second, estoppel is a one-way street: it allows the third party to hold the principal liable but does not give the principal any rights against the third party (unless the principal were to ratify the transaction). The remedy is generally for damages rather than making the defendant a party to the contract.

> **Restatement (Third) of Agency § 2.05**
>
> **Estoppel to Deny Existence of Agency Relationship**
>
> A person who has not made a manifestation that an actor has authority as an agent and who is not otherwise liable as a party to a transaction purportedly done by the actor on that person's account is subject to liability to a third party who justifiably is induced to make a detrimental change in position because the transaction is believed to be on the person's account, if
>
> (1) the person intentionally or carelessly caused such belief, or
>
> (2) having notice of such belief and that it might induce others to change their positions, the person did not take reasonable steps to notify them of the facts.

Consider two illustrations from comment d to Restatement (Third) of Agency § 2.05:

1. P has two coagents, A and B. P has notice that B, acting without actual or apparent authority, has represented to T that A has authority to enter into a transaction that is contrary to P's instructions. T does not know that P's instructions forbid A from engaging in the transaction. T cannot establish conduct by P on the basis of which T could reasonably believe that A has the requisite authority. T can, however, establish that P had notice of B's representation and that it would have been easy for P to inform T of the limits on A's authority. T detrimentally changes position in reliance on B's representation by making a substantial down payment. If it is found that T's action was justifiable, P is estopped to deny B's authority to make the representation.

2. P owns a large retail furniture store, known as "P's Furniture Emporium." P, who is often absent from the premises, does not otherwise maintain surveillance over the store's sales force. T, a prospective customer, enters the store and is approached by A, whose demeanor and attire lend A the appearance of a salesperson. After examining

floor samples, T purchases several items of furniture for cash, giving the cash to A. A gives T a receipt written on a standard-looking form, with "P's Furniture Emporium" printed at the top. A explains to T that the items purchased are not presently in inventory but will be delivered to T's home within two weeks. A is an imposter who is not an employee or other agent of P. A does not remit any of the cash paid by T to P. No furniture is delivered to T. T's change of position is justified by T's belief that A is what A purports to be, a salesperson with authority to sell from P's inventory. Whether P may deny A's authority is a question for the trier of fact.

D. Contract Liability: Agents

We started by studying the five different bases by which a principal (or purported principal) may be bound to contract liability. But what about *the agent's* liability?

The answer depends on whether the agent has entered into the contractual obligation with the third party on behalf of a disclosed, unidentified, or undisclosed principal. *See* Restatement (Third) of Agency §§ 6.01–6.03.

When an agent acting with actual or apparent authority makes a contract on behalf of a **disclosed principal**, it is only the principal and the third party who are parties to the contract. The agent is not a party to the contract unless the agent and third party agree otherwise. This rule conforms to common sense—the third party knows that the agent is acting on behalf of a principal and the third party knows who that principal is, and so the third party's expectation is that she is contracting with that principal and not the agent. When you go to a store and make a purchase, you understand your transaction is between you and the store owner and not the clerk who might have assisted you.

Keep in mind that the foregoing statement concerns the outward-facing aspects of contract liability with respect to the third party. As between the principal and the agent, we have seen that the agent owes fiduciary duties to the principal. Accordingly, if the principal were to be bound by an agreement under a third party's apparent authority claim, the principal might in turn have a claim against the agent for actions that were taken without actual authority. *See* Restatement (Third) of Agency § 8.09 (Duty to Act Only Within the Scope of Actual Authority and to Comply with Principal's Lawful Instructions).

When an agent acting with actual or apparent authority makes a contract on behalf of an **unidentified principal**, all three—the principal, agent, and third party—are parties to the contract unless the agent and the third party agree otherwise regarding the agent's liability. A principal is "unidentified" if, when an agent and a third party interact, the third party has notice that the agent is acting for a principal but does not have notice of the principal's identity.

Similarly, when an agent acting with actual authority makes a contract on behalf of an **undisclosed principal**, the agent and third party are parties to the contract; and unless excluded, the principal is also a party to the contract. The lesson for the agent is clear: if the agent does not want to be liable on the contract, then she must disclose that she is acting on behalf of a principal and provide the identity of that principal.

Finally, there is another way an agent might have liability to a third party: a claim known as breach of the implied warranty of authority. This claim, if successful, does not bind the agent to the contract, or make them a party to it, but it can hold the agent responsible for representing authority to bind the principal if it turns out to be false. That is, a person (or agent) who enters into an agreement with a third party, purporting to bind another person (or principal), yet actually lacking the authority to do so, may be sued by the third party if the implied representation is false.

> When both the agent and the principal can be bound, if the third party sues for breach of the contract, in many states, she must elect to sue either the agent or the principal. In other states, the third party may sue both the agent and the principal but may recover damages only once. The terms of the contract may also bear on the effect given to a judgment obtained against a principal or agent. For example, a contract may explicitly make the principal and agent joint and several obligors.

When both 3rd

As the comments to § 6.10 of the Restatement explain: "The person who makes the implied representation bears the risk of its falsity because that person is better able than is the third party to ascertain the truth at the time of making the representation." In this way, "[a]n agent's implied warranty of authority is a solution to a problem otherwise confronted by third parties who deal with persons whom they believe to act as agents with power to bind a principal." Indeed, "[u]nless an agent risks some liability when a third party believes the agent acts with authority to bind the principal, agents may be tempted to act beyond the bounds imposed by the principal's manifestation of assent to the agent, in the hopes that, if the transaction turns out to be advantageous for the principal, the principal will ratify what the agent has done." Further, if a person (or agent) knowingly makes a false representation, or does so negligently, there is the possibility of liability for fraud or negligent misrepresentation.

Restatement (Third) of Agency § 6.10
Agent's Implied Warranty of Authority

A person who purports to make a contract, representation, or conveyance to or with a third party on behalf of another person, lacking power to bind that person, gives an implied warranty of authority to the third party and is subject to liability to the third party for damages for loss caused by breach of that warranty, including loss of the benefit expected from performance by the principal, unless

(1)   the principal or purported principal ratifies the act as stated in § 4.01; or

(2)   the person who purports to make the contract, representation, or conveyance gives notice to the third party that no warranty of authority is given; or

(3)   the third party knows that the person who purports to make the contract, representation, or conveyance acts without actual authority.

E.   Tort Liability

As you probably learned in your Torts class, a person is liable for a tort that he or she commits. When can a *principal* also be held liable in tort? That is what agency law adds to the equation.

There are a few instances in which a third party can hold a principal directly liable. *See* Restatement (Third) of Agency §§ 7.04–7.06. Most notably, a principal can be held directly liable when an agent acts with actual authority to commit a tort or when the principal ratifies the agent's conduct. A principal can also be subject to liability if harm to a third party was caused by the principal's negligence in selecting or supervising the agent. In addition, the law has established circumstances for direct or strict liability such as if the activity engaged in by the agent is "inherently" or "abnormally" dangerous—activity involving demolition, blasting, a wild animal, or any activity which is likely to cause harm or damage unless precautions are taken. This principle is more generally referred to as one of "nondelegable" duty because delegating duty does not in itself discharge the principal's duties in special circumstances in which the law imposes duties to use reasonable care.

If the third party succeeds in holding the principal vicariously liable for the agent's tort, the principal is usually separately entitled to indemnification from the agent. As a practical matter, however, the principal may have deeper pockets than the agent and may not be able to actually obtain the indemnification.

More commonly, third parties attempt to hold a principal liable for the tort of an agent through the doctrine of vicarious liability. The Restatement (Third) of Agency provides for two forms or means of holding a principal vicariously liable:

- When an agent is an employee who commits a tort while acting within the scope of employment. § 7.07.

- When an agent commits a tort when acting with apparent authority in dealing with a third party on or purportedly on behalf of the principal. § 7.08.

We will begin our study with the first, which is sometimes referred to as the doctrine of "respondeat superior," under which a third party can hold a principal liable for the agent's tort if the agent was an "employee" who committed a tort while acting "within the scope of employment."

1. Vicarious Liability for an Employee's Tort Occurring Within the Scope of Employment

a. Employee Status

Agency law distinguishes between types of agents—some are "employees" and some are "independent contractors" (also referred to as "non-employee agents"). The Restatement (Third) of Agency § 7.07(3) provides that an agent is an "employee" for purposes of vicarious liability if the principal controls or has the right to control the manner and means by which the agent performs his or her duties. Both the right to exercise control and the actual exercise of control are typically evaluated.

There are at least a couple of main policy justifications for distinguishing between the two types of agents and holding the principal vicariously liable for the torts of agents over which it holds a higher level of control. One is that where a principal gets the benefits of control of an agent, the principal should also have the corresponding obligation of liability for the agent's actions. This rationale is rooted in a fairness principle that holds accountable the person or enterprise that stands to benefit from the risk-creating activities rather than the innocent injured plaintiff.

The other main policy rationale is economic—the concept often referred to as placing the loss on the "lowest cost avoider." The party with control over the agent is in the best position to prevent the agent from engaging in careless or improper conduct and has the greatest incentive to take cost-effective precautions or get insurance. Creating a legal rule that holds the principal liable encourages efficient precautions to be taken and spreads the risk. The employer can anticipate the risks inherent in the enterprise, spread the risk through insurance, take into account the cost of insurance in setting the price for its goods and services, and spread the risk among those who benefit from the goods and services. By definition, the principal does not supervise the details of the independent contractor's work and therefore is not in as good a position to monitor the work and prevent negligent performance.

b.   Scope of Employment

A principal's vicarious liability only results if the employee's tort occurred within the scope of employment. The same rationales of fairness and economic policy apply to this second element.

What counts as "within the scope of employment"? This is a question that many courts have addressed, but not always consistently.

Courts have used two main approaches to determining whether a tort occurred within the scope of employment. The first is referred to as the "motive" or "purpose" test, and it is reflected in the Restatement (Third) of Agency § 7.07(2), which provides:

> An employee acts within the scope of employment when performing work assigned by the employer or engaging in a course of conduct subject to the employer's control. An employee's act is not within the scope of employment when it occurs within an independent course of conduct not intended by the employee to serve any purpose of the employer.

An example would be when a bouncer in a bar is aggressive and commits a tort such as assault or battery while doing his or her job. Notice that "within the scope of employment" is not strictly limited to the employee's proper or authorized conduct. There is some wiggle room around the concept such that an employee might be taking an action incidental to that instructed by the employer and still be held to have acted within the scope of employment. This line is sometimes described as the difference between "frolic and detour." A "frolic" is when an employee substantially deviates from or abandons the scope of employment. By contrast, if an employee is still engaged in the scope of employment but strays slightly from the assignment, this is a mere "detour."

> Can an employee's intentional tort be within the scope of employment? Yes. Although most vicarious liability cases involve torts of negligence, the intentional nature of the tort does not preclude vicarious liability. As a practical matter, it is just less likely that an intentional tort would be held to have occurred within the scope of employment.

Some courts have criticized the purpose test and have instead used a "foreseeability" test, asking whether the employee's conduct should fairly have been foreseen from the nature of the employment or whether the risk of such conduct was typical or incidental to the employer's enterprise.

A famous case using this approach is *Ira S. Bushey & Sons, Inc. v. United States*, 398 F.2d 167 (2d Cir. 1968), a Second Circuit opinion written by Judge Henry Friendly. The case involved a sailor who, after a night of drinking, came back to the ship where he was supposed to sleep and damaged the dock. The court held the employer, the United States government, liable for the damage to the dock owner. Although the court acknowledged that the sailor was not motivated by the purpose of serving his employer, the court held the conduct was nonetheless within the scope of employment because it was foreseeable activity: "[T]he proclivity of seamen to find solace for solitude by copious resort to the bottle while ashore has been noted in opinions too numerous to warrant citation." The court explained the underlying rationale, "that a business enterprise cannot justly disclaim responsibility for accidents which may fairly be said to be characteristic of its activities."

In contrast, the following case gives a colorful example of vicarious liability that uses an approach like that summarized by the Restatement (Third) of Agency. The plaintiff, Margaret Clover, sued the Snowbird Ski Resort for injuries she sustained from a ski accident in which one of the resort's employees collided with her. The employee, Chris Zulliger, worked as a chef at the Plaza Restaurant, which was located at the base of the resort. Zulliger was also instructed by his supervisor to make periodic trips to monitor the operations at the Mid-Gad, a restaurant halfway to the top of the mountain. Snowbird gave employees ski passes as part of their compensation and preferred that their employees know how to ski because it made it easier for them to get to and from work.

On the day of the accident, Zulliger was asked to inspect the operation of the Mid-Gad before starting work at the Plaza Restaurant at 3 p.m. Zulliger went skiing with another employee-friend and they stopped at the Mid-Gad in the middle of their first run. Zulliger and his employee-friend then skied four runs before heading down the mountain to begin work. On their final run, they took a route that was often taken by Snowbird employees to travel from the top of the mountain to the Plaza. About mid-way down the mountain, at a point above the Mid-Gad, Zulliger decided to take a jump off a crest. There was a sign instructing skiers to ski slowly at this point in the run. The ski patrol often instructed people at this location not to become airborne because of the steep drop off, which also impaired visibility of skiers below. Zulliger, however, ignored the sign and skied over the crest at a significant speed. When Zulliger went over the jump, he collided with Clover, who was injured.

Clover brought claims against Zulliger and Snowbird. Zulliger settled separately with Clover. On a motion for summary judgment, the trial judge dismissed Clover's claims against Snowbird on the basis that Zulliger was not acting within the scope of his employment at the time of the collision. Clover appealed.

Clover v. Snowbird Ski Resort

808 P.2d 1037 (Utah 1991)

HALL, CHIEF JUSTICE.

Under the doctrine of respondeat superior, employers are held vicariously liable for the torts their employees commit when the employees are acting within the scope of their employment. Clover's respondeat superior claim was dismissed on the ground that as a matter of law, Zulliger's actions at the time of the accident were not within the scope of his employment. In a recent case, *Birkner v. Salt Lake County*, this court addressed the issue of what types of acts fall within the scope of employment. In *Birkner*, we stated that acts within the scope of employment are " 'those acts which are so closely connected with what the servant is employed to do, and so fairly and reasonably incidental to it, that they may be regarded as methods, even though quite improper ones, of carrying out the objectives of the employment.' " The question of whether an employee is acting within the scope of employment is a question of fact that must be submitted to a jury "whenever reasonable minds may differ as to whether the [employee] was at a certain time involved wholly or partly in the performance of his [employer's] business or within the scope of employment."

In *Birkner*, we observed that the Utah cases that have addressed the issue of whether an employee's actions, as a matter of law, are within or without the scope of employment have focused on three criteria. "First, an employee's conduct must be of the general kind the employee is employed to perform. . . . In other words, the employee must be about the employer's business and the duties assigned by the employer, as opposed to being wholly involved in a personal endeavor." Second, the employee's conduct must occur substantially within the hours and ordinary spatial boundaries of the employment. "Third, the employee's conduct must be motivated at least in part, by the purpose of serving the employer's interest."

In applying the *Birkner* criteria to the facts in the instant case, it is important to note that if Zulliger had returned to the Plaza Restaurant immediately after he inspected the operations at the Mid-Gad Restaurant, there would be ample evidence to support the conclusion that on his return trip Zulliger's actions were within the scope of his employment. There is evidence that it was part of Zulliger's job to monitor the operations at the Mid-Gad and that he was directed to monitor the operations on the day of the accident. There is also evidence that Snowbird intended Zulliger to use the ski lifts and the ski runs on his trips to the Mid-Gad. It is clear, therefore, that Zulliger's actions could be considered to "be of the general kind that the employee is employed to perform." It is also clear that there would be evidence that Zulliger's actions occurred within the hours and normal spatial boundaries of his employment. Zulliger was expected to monitor the operations at the Mid-Gad during the time the lifts were operating and when he was not working as a chef at the Plaza. Furthermore, throughout the trip he would have been on his employer's premises. Finally, it is clear that Zulliger's actions in monitoring the operations at the Mid-Gad, per his employer's instructions, could be considered "motivated, at least in part, by the purpose of serving the employer's interest."

The difficulty, of course, arises from the fact that Zulliger did not return to the Plaza after he finished inspecting the facilities at the Mid-Gad. Rather, he skied four more runs and rode the lift to the top of the mountain before he began his return to the base. Snowbird claims that this fact shows that Zulliger's primary purpose for skiing on the day of the accident was for his own pleasure and that therefore, as a matter of law, he was not acting within the scope of his employment.

There is ample evidence that there was a predominant business purpose for Zulliger's trip to the Mid-Gad. Therefore, this case is better analyzed under our decisions dealing with situations where an employee has taken a personal detour in the process of carrying out his duties.

Under the circumstances of the instant case, it is entirely possible for a jury to reasonably believe that at the time of the accident, Zulliger had resumed his employment and that Zulliger's deviation was not substantial enough to constitute a total abandonment of employment. First, a jury could reasonably believe that by beginning his return to the base of the mountain to begin his duties as a chef and to report concerning his observations at the Mid-Gad, Zulliger had resumed his employment. In past cases, in holding that the actions of an employee were within the scope of employment, we have relied on the fact that the employee had resumed the duties of employment prior to the time of the accident. This is an important factor because if the employee has resumed the duties of employment, the employee is then "about the employer's business" and the employee's actions will be "motivated, at least in part, by the purpose of serving the employer's interest." The fact that due to Zulliger's deviation, the accident occurred at a spot above the Mid-Gad does not disturb this analysis. In situations where accidents have occurred substantially within the normal spatial boundaries of employment, we have held that employees may be within the scope of employment if, after a personal detour, they return to their duties and an accident occurs.

Second, a jury could reasonably believe that Zulliger's actions in taking four ski runs and returning to the top of the mountain do not constitute a complete abandonment of employment. It is important to note that by taking these ski runs, Zulliger was not disregarding his employer's directions. In *Cannon v. Goodyear Tire & Rubber Co.*, wherein we held that the employee's actions were a substantial departure from the course of employment, we focused on the fact that the employee's actions were in direct conflict with the employer's directions and policy. In the instant case, far from directing its employees not to ski at the resort, Snowbird issued its employees season ski passes as part of their compensation.

These two factors, along with other circumstances—such as, throughout the day Zulliger was on Snowbird's property, there was no specific time set for inspecting the restaurant, and the act of skiing was the method used by Snowbird employees to travel among the different locations of the resort—constitute sufficient evidence for a jury to conclude that Zulliger, at the time of the accident, was acting within the scope of his employment. In light of the genuine issues of material fact in regard to each of Clover's claims, summary judgment was inappropriate. Reversed and remanded for further proceedings.

whether operating within scope of employment is a MOF not MOL

Points for Discussion

1. Within the scope of employment?

Why did the *Clover* court conclude that it would be possible for a jury to reasonably believe that at the time of the accident, Zulliger had resumed his employment and that Zulliger's deviation was not substantial enough to constitute a total abandonment of employment?

2. Foreseeability vs. purpose.

Is the foreseeability or purpose test a better test for determining activity "within the scope of employment"? Why?

---

2.   Franchisor Tort Liability

A common situation in which vicarious liability claims arise is franchise arrangements. A franchise arrangement involves a company or individual (the "franchisee") operating a business pursuant to a license to do so (the "franchising agreement") from another company or individual (the "franchisor"). The key question is typically whether a franchisor has exercised sufficient control over the franchisee to create an agency relationship through which the franchisor can be held liable for the franchisee's tortious conduct (or for the franchisee's employees as a "joint employer"). Courts typically look at the franchising agreement to determine the extent of the franchisor's right of control and the facts demonstrating the franchisor's level of involvement in the day-to-day operations of the franchisee's business.

The following case is an illustrative example from California. A company named Sui Juris, LLC ("Sui Juris", "franchisee") owned by Daniel Poff had contracted with Domino's Pizza Franchising, LLC ("Domino's", "franchisor") to operate a Domino's franchise location. The plaintiff (Patterson) alleged that she was sexually harassed by her supervisor (Miranda) during the course of her work at the franchisee's pizza store. Patterson sued both Sui Juris (franchisee) and Domino's (franchisor), arguing that Domino's should be liable as a joint employer under agency principles. Domino's filed for summary judgment claiming that it lacked the requisite day-to-day control to be considered a joint employer of the franchisee's employees.

The trial court granted summary judgment for Domino's on all counts. The Court of Appeals conversely concluded that a reasonable inference could be drawn that Sui Juris lacked managerial independence and that there was a triable issue of fact on Domino's role as a principal and joint employer. The California Supreme court granted review.

Patterson v. Domino's Pizza, LLC

333 P.3d 723 (Cal. 2014)

BAXTER, J.

We granted review to address the novel question dividing the lower courts in this case: Does a franchisor stand in an employment or agency relationship with the franchisee and its employees for purposes of holding it vicariously liable for workplace injuries allegedly inflicted by one employee of a franchisee while supervising another employee of the franchisee? The answer lies in the inherent nature of the franchise relationship itself.

Over the past 50 years, the Courts of Appeal, using traditional "agency" terminology, have reached various results on whether a franchisor should be held liable for torts committed by a franchisee or its employees in the course of the franchisee's business. In analyzing these questions, the appellate courts have focused on the degree to which a particular franchisor exercised general "control" over the "means and manner" of the franchisee's operations.

Meanwhile, franchising has seen massive growth. A franchisor, which can have thousands of stores located far apart, imposes comprehensive and meticulous standards for marketing its trademarked brand and operating its franchises in a uniform way. To this extent, the franchisor controls the enterprise. However, the franchisee retains autonomy as a manager and employer. It is the franchisee who implements the operational standards on a day-to-day basis, hires and fires store employees, and regulates workplace behavior.

Analysis of the franchise relationship for vicarious liability purposes must accommodate these contemporary realities. The imposition and enforcement of a uniform marketing and operational plan cannot automatically saddle the franchisor with responsibility for employees of the franchisee who injure each other on the job. The contract-based operational division that otherwise exists between the franchisor and the franchisee would be violated by holding the franchisor accountable for misdeeds committed by employees who are under the direct supervision of the franchisee, and over whom the franchisor has no contractual or operational control. It follows that potential liability on the theories pled here requires that the franchisor exhibit the traditionally understood characteristics of an "employer" or "principal;" i.e., it has retained or assumed a general right of control over factors such as hiring, direction, supervision, discipline, discharge, and relevant day-to-day aspects of the workplace behavior of the franchisee's employees.

Here, the franchisor prescribed standards and procedures involving pizza-making and delivery, general store operations, and brand image. These standards were vigorously enforced through representatives of the franchisor who inspected franchised stores. However, there was considerable, essentially uncontradicted evidence that the franchisee made day-to-day decisions involving the hiring, supervision, and disciplining of his employees. Plaintiff herself testified that after the franchisee hired her, she followed his policy, and reported the alleged sexual harassment to him. The franchisee suspended the offender. Nothing contractually required or allowed the franchisor to intrude on this process.

Plaintiff highlights the franchisee's testimony that a representative of the franchisor said the harasser should be fired. But, any inference that this statement represented franchisor "control" over discipline for sexual harassment complaints cannot reasonably be drawn from the evidence. The uncontradicted evidence showed that the franchisee imposed discipline consistent with his own personnel policies, declined to follow the ad hoc advice of the franchisor's representative, and neither expected nor sustained any sanction for doing so. [W]e reverse the Court of Appeal's decision overturning the grant of summary judgment in the franchisor's favor.

II. DISCUSSION

A. Special Features of the Franchise Relationship

Companies can market goods and services in more than one way. In an integrated method of distribution, the company uses its own employees and other assets to operate chain or branch stores. In doing so, it reaps the full benefits (e.g., maximizing profits) and bears the full burdens (e.g., investing capital and risking liability) of running a business.

Franchising is different. It is a distribution method that has existed in this country in one form or another for over 150 years. However, it was not until the 1950's that a form of franchising called the "business format" model began to emerge. This model is used heavily, but not exclusively, in the fast food industry. The rise of business format franchising has been attributed to the post-World War II growth in population, personal income, retail spending, and automobile use. Today, the economic effects of franchising are profound. Annually, this sector of the economy, including the fast food industry, employs millions of people, carries payrolls in the billions of dollars, and generates trillions of dollars in total sales.

Under the business format model, the franchisee pays royalties and fees for the right to sell products or services under the franchisor's name and trademark. In the process, the franchisee also acquires a business plan, which the franchisor has crafted for all of its stores. This business plan requires the franchisee to follow a system of standards and procedures. A long list of marketing, production, operational, and administrative areas is typically involved. The franchisor's system can take the form of printed manuals, training programs, advertising services, and managerial support, among other things.

The business format arrangement allows the franchisor to raise capital and grow its business, while shifting the burden of running local stores to the franchisee. The systemwide standards and controls provide a means of protecting the trademarked brand at great distances. The goal—which benefits both parties to the contract—is to build and keep customer trust by ensuring consistency and uniformity in the quality of goods and services, the dress of franchise employees, and the design of the stores themselves.

The franchisee is often an entrepreneurial individual who is willing to invest his time and money, and to assume the risk of loss, in order to own and profit from his own business. In the typical arrangement, the franchisee decides who will work as his employees, and controls day-to-day operations in his store. The franchise arrangement puts the franchisee in a better position than other small businesses. It gives him access to resources he otherwise would not have, including the uniform operating system itself.

B. Analysis of the Arguments and the Law

[T]he venerable respondeat superior rule provides that "an employer may be held vicariously liable for torts committed by an employee within the scope of employment." Under certain circumstances, the employer may be subject to this form of vicarious liability even for an employee's willful, malicious, and criminal conduct. Three policy justifications for the respondeat superior doctrine have been cited—prevention, compensation, and risk allocation. They do not always apply. We know of no decision by a California court addressing a franchisor's statutory or common law liability under the California Fair Employment and Housing Act (FEHA) for sexual harassment claims made by one employee of a franchisee against another employee (or supervisor) of the franchisee. Nor has this court decided whether a franchisor may be considered an "employer" who is vicariously liable for torts committed by someone working for the franchisee.

C. Application of the Law to the Present Case

We start with the contract itself. The contract said there was no principal-agent relationship between Domino's and Sui Juris. Notwithstanding any training, support, or oversight on Domino's part, Sui Juris agreed to act as an "independent contractor." Likewise, the contract stated that persons who worked in the Sui Juris store were the employees of Sui Juris, and that no employment or agency relationship existed between them and Domino's. Domino's disclaimed any rights or responsibilities as to Sui Juris's employees. Nor did Domino's have the right to direct Sui Juris's employees in store operations. Domino's disclaimed liability under the contract for any damages arising out of the operation of the store. Consistent with the exclusive control vested in Sui Juris over its own employees, neither the contract nor the Managers Reference Guide (the MRG) empowered Domino's to establish a sexual harassment policy or training program for Sui Juris's employees. Nor was there any procedure by which Sui Juris's employees could report such complaints to Domino's. In fact, the topic did not appear in the franchise documents at all. Thus, under the foregoing terms, Domino's lacked contractual authority to manage the behavior of Sui Juris's employees while performing their jobs, including any acts that might involve sexual harassment.

Of course, the parties' characterization of their relationship in the franchise contract is not dispositive. We must also consider those evidentiary facts set forth in the summary judgment materials as to which objections were not made and sustained. According to the testimonial evidence, Poff exercised sole control over selecting the individuals who worked in his store. He did not include Domino's in the application, interview, or hiring process. Nor did anyone attempt to intervene on Domino's behalf. It was Poff's decision to hire Patterson as a new employee and to otherwise retain the existing staff when he bought the franchise.

Evidence about the training of Sui Juris's employees is more nuanced, but did not indicate control over relevant day-to-day aspects of employment and employee conduct. It appears the parties did not follow the literal language of the contract placing sole responsibility on Sui Juris for handling all training programs for its employees. Domino's provided new employees with orientation materials in both electronic and handbook form. Such programs supplemented the training that Poff was required to conduct. However, with respect to training employees on how to treat each other at work, and how to avoid sexual harassment, it appears that Sui Juris, not Domino's, was in control. No Domino's representative, including Lee, trained Sui Juris employees on sexual harassment. [Lee was an "area leader" for Domino's who monitored 101 Domino's franchises for compliance with operational and marketing standards.] Nothing in the record indicates that any Domino's representative reviewed Poff's sexual harassment policy, discussed its substance with Poff or his employees, or observed any training sessions at the store.

Of particular relevance is that Poff's sexual harassment policy and training program came with the authority to impose discipline for any violations. The record shows that Poff, not Domino's, wielded such significant control.

First, Poff encouraged the reporting of sexual harassment complaints directly to him. The apparent purpose of Poff's admonitions was to give him the chance to respond by taking appropriate disciplinary action against the offending employee. Second, Domino's had no procedure for monitoring or reporting sexual harassment complaints between the employees of franchisees. Third, Poff acted on Patterson's complaint by taking unilateral disciplinary action. There is no evidence that Poff solicited Domino's advice or consent on any of these decisions, or that he was required to do so.

Like the dissenting opinion, Patterson emphasizes evidence that Lee said Poff should "get rid" of Miranda. It is not clear when this statement was made. For several reasons, however, no reasonable inference can be drawn that it was intended or interpreted to mean that Poff had no choice in the matter, that Domino's was in charge, or that consequences would ensue if Poff did not follow Lee's advice. As noted above, Poff acted with the obvious understanding that the decision whether and how to discipline Miranda was his alone to make. He chose to proceed in a prudent and methodical way by investigating the complaint before a final decision was made.

In addition, Poff acknowledged that Lee's statement was not accompanied by a specific threat, express or implied. She never stated that Poff would risk any sanction if he did not terminate Miranda's employment. Indeed, her statement left Poff with no negative memory about possible repercussions at all. When Lee arrived at the Sui Juris store a short time later, Miranda's disciplinary fate was not discussed. The only concern was whether and how to retrain the Sui Juris staff. By Poff's own account, Lee made helpful training suggestions, not demands.

No reasonable inference can be drawn that Domino's, through Lee, retained or assumed the traditional right of general control an "employer" or "principal" has over hiring, direction, supervision, discipline, discharge, and relevant day-to-day aspects of the workplace behavior of the franchisee's employees. Hence, there is no basis on which to find a triable issue of fact that an employment or agency relationship existed between Domino's and Sui Juris and its employees in order to support Patterson's claims against Domino's on vicarious liability grounds.

III. CONCLUSION

Nothing we say herein is intended to minimize the seriousness of sexual harassment in the workplace, particularly by a supervisor. Nor do we mean to imply that franchisors, including those of immense size, can never be held accountable for sexual harassment at a franchised location. A franchisor will be liable if it has retained or assumed the right of general control over the relevant day-to-day operations at its franchised locations that we have described, and cannot escape liability in such a case merely because it failed or declined to establish a policy with regard to that particular conduct. Our holding is limited to determining the circumstances under which an employment or agency relationship exists as a prerequisite to pursuing statutory and tort theories like those alleged against the franchisor here.

Dissenting Opinion by WERDEGAR, J.

I write separately to express my disagreement with the majority's application of the law to the facts of this case. The California Fair Employment and Housing Act (FEHA) makes employers liable for sexual harassment. Thus, as the majority recognizes, plaintiff Patterson may recover from defendant Domino's Pizza, LLC (Domino's), on her statutory claim of sexual harassment if Domino's did something to become a joint employer with its franchisee Daniel Poff (doing business as Sui Juris, LLC), of Poff's employees. Because the FEHA's statutory definition of "employer" is essentially tautological, a court properly looks to the common law for guidance, bearing in mind "the spirit and letter of the law that it [is] interpreting."

The common law offers various definitions of employment. The prevailing view is to consider the totality of the circumstances, reflecting upon the nature of the work relationship between the parties, and placing emphasis on the control exercised by the employer over the employee's performance of employment duties. The outcome depends on the factual inquiry. For example, a franchisor, pursuing its legitimate interest in ensuring that customers enjoy a similar experience in each franchised location, may implement the franchise agreement in various ways, including ways short of day-to-day oversight, to exercise control over employee selection, training, personal appearance, interaction with customers, and compliance with in-store procedures. This retention of control by the franchisor, enforced by regular inspections and the threat that a noncompliant franchisee will be placed in default, presents occasions for the franchisor to act as an employer by forcing the termination of problematic employees. The majority finds that Domino's successfully walked this tightrope between enforcing contractual standards and becoming an employer by leaving to Poff all decisions about the discharge of his employees, even when cause for discharge existed. Because the case has not been tried, we will never know whether Domino's succeeded or not. Unlike the majority, I would hold that plaintiff has raised a triable issue of fact.

Asked whether Domino's area leader Lee had "ever t[old] you that you needed to fire any employees," Poff answered "Yes." Those employees were Knight, a manager who had delivered non-Domino's food to schools, and Miranda, plaintiff's alleged harasser. Asked whether Poff rather than Lee had "ultimately ma[d]e the decision to terminate" Knight, Poff answered that he "had to pull the trigger on the termination, but it was very strongly hinted that there would be problems if I did not do so." Asked "[h]ow was it strongly hinted," Poff explained that "[t]he area leaders would pull you into your office at the store, for example, and tell you what they wanted. If they did not get what they wanted, they would say you would be in trouble." In fact, Lee indicated to Poff that not firing Knight might cause Poff to lose his franchise. Lee candidly testified she told Poff that, " '[i]f you have anyone that works for you that is damaging the brand or going to cause you to lose your franchise agreement, that person is not the person you want working for you.' And I told him, 'Right now, [Knight] is hurting your franchise.' " Poff fired Knight a few weeks later.

This interaction between Poff and Lee provides essential context for their later interaction concerning Miranda. Upon learning of plaintiff's allegations of harassment against Miranda, Lee told Poff, "You've got to get rid of this guy." Asked how he had answered, Poff testified that his "response always to the area leader was 'yes' or 'I'll get it done' or, you know, 'Give me a little time.' I never said 'no' intentionally to [Lee]." Poff could not "recall specifically" whether Lee "allude[d] to anything that would happen to [Poff] if [he] didn't fire Miranda," but it was hardly necessary for

Lee to repeat the warning she had recently given Poff that the failure to follow her wishes concerning the termination of a problematic employee could lead to the loss of his franchise. Consistently with his statement that he "never said 'no' " to Lee, Poff confirmed that he "never t[old] her over the phone or to her face that [he] did not intend to fire Miranda." A franchisee who did not follow Lee's suggestions, Poff testified, was "out of business very quickly." Ultimately, Miranda's failure to return to work made it unnecessary for Poff to risk the loss of his franchise by refusing Lee's demand.

Under the common law, " '[p]erhaps no single circumstance is more conclusive to show the relationship of an employee than the right of the employer to end the service whenever he sees fit to do so.' " While no one factor is determinative, the power to discharge an employee offers " 'strong evidence' " both of the fact of control and of the ultimate existence of an employment relationship. This is because the employer's power to terminate the employee's services gives the employer the means of controlling the employee's activities and because, as a matter of logic, a person's reservation of the power to terminate another's employee "is incompatible with the full control of the work by another." For these purposes "[i]t is not essential that the right of control be exercised or that there be actual supervision of the work of the [employee]." "What matters is whether the hirer 'retains all necessary control' over its operations."

In summary, if Domino's relationship with Poff gave it the power to force him to fire his employees, then those employees were subject not just to Poff's control but also to Domino's and thus were the employees of both. Viewing the evidence in the light most favorable to plaintiff, as we must when reviewing an order granting a defense motion for summary judgment, the record would clearly permit the trier of fact to conclude that Domino's retained and exercised that power.

As mentioned, my disagreement with the majority is not so much with its statement of the applicable law as with its application of the law to the facts. In concluding Domino's did not have the power to force Poff to discharge his employees, the majority places too much emphasis on the terms of the franchise agreement and not enough on the parties' real world interaction. The language of the governing contract is only "one factor to be considered in determining the nature of the employment relationship" and "is not controlling." This is because our principal responsibility in FEHA cases is not to give effect to private contracts intended to shift or avoid liability, nor is it to promote the use of franchising as a business model or to avoid "disrupt[ing] the franchise relationship." Instead, our duty is to vindicate the Legislature's "fundamental public interest in a workplace free from the pernicious influence of sexism." When this task requires us to construe FEHA's definition of employer, we are bound by the Legislature's command that "[t]he provisions of [FEHA] shall be construed liberally for the accomplishment of [its] purposes. . . ." To emphasize contractual language intended to shield a franchisor from employment-related claims over evidence the franchisor in practice retained and exercised the power to terminate the franchisee's employees tends to undermine FEHA's goals by permitting the franchisor, in effect, to opt out of the statutory duties of a California employer.

For these reasons, I dissent.

We Concur: LIU, J., and CHANEY, J.

Points for Discussion

1. *Majority or dissent?*

Do you find the majority or dissent more persuasive? On what basis do they diverge? What values are at stake? What incentives does the majority's ruling create for franchisors? How do public law issues such as the enforcement of state anti-discrimination and anti-harassment laws connect with business law?

2. *Evaluating policy justifications in franchise relationships.*

The court cited three policy justifications for the respondeat superior doctrine—prevention, compensation, and risk allocation. How well do these policy justifications fit the franchise business model? In what direction do these policies push when applied to franchisor-franchisee relationships?

---

3.   Tort Liability and Apparent Agency

We started this section on agency issues involving torts by noting that the Restatement sets out two situations in which vicarious liability for the principal can arise:

- When an agent is an employee who commits a tort while acting within the scope of employment. § 7.07.

- When an agent commits a tort when acting with apparent authority in dealing with a third party on or purportedly on behalf of the principal. § 7.08.

We have focused in detail on the first situation of respondeat superior as it is the typical basis on which a principal's vicarious tort liability is established. We now briefly turn to the second basis—apparent agency (sometimes also called "ostensible agency"). Our coverage of this topic will be much briefer because the doctrine of apparent agency is not as frequently used by litigants and does not have as long a history as respondeat superior.

The doctrine emerged as some courts agreed to extend the concept of apparent authority from the contract context to the tort context. The Restatement (Third) of

Agency § 7.08 provides: "A principal is subject to vicarious liability for a tort committed by an agent in dealing or communicating with a third party on or purportedly on behalf of the principal when actions taken by the agent with apparent authority constitute the tort or enable the agent to conceal its commission." The comment to § 7.08 explains that apparent agency applies in situations in which an agent appears to deal or communicate on behalf of a principal and the agent's appearance of authority enables the agent to commit a tort or conceal its commission. Examples of such torts include defamation and fraudulent or negligent misrepresentations.

Looking to case law, we can see that claims of apparent agency generally arise in: (1) circumstances which led an injured third party to reasonably believe that an agency or employment relationship existed between the principal or alleged principal and the alleged agent tortfeasor; and (2) those circumstances existed because of some action or inaction on the part of the principal in creating or failing to dispel that belief. Many, but not all, courts also require (3) a showing that the third party's injury arose out of the third party's justifiable reliance that an agency or employee relationship existed.

A relatively small number of cases examine claims of apparent agency. Beyond the torts of defamation and misrepresentation, the case law mainly concerns two common scenarios in which everyday people do not realize they are dealing with an independent contractor or party. The first involve medical malpractice claims against a hospital for the actions of an independent contractor physician. The second involve claims against a franchisor for injuries that a plaintiff suffered at a franchisee's business operation.

For example, in *Miller v. McDonald's Corporation*, 945 P.2d 1107 (Or. Ct. App. 1997), the plaintiff sued McDonald's Corporation for injuries she sustained when she bit into a heart-shaped sapphire stone inside a Big Mac hamburger that she bought at a McDonald's franchise. The crucial issues were whether the putative principal had held out the franchisee as an agent and whether the plaintiff had relied in that holding out. The first issue was not seriously disputed as McDonald's pursues a common image, appearance, and operation for all of its restaurants even those independently run, such that it could create a reasonable belief that McDonald's was the principal. As to the second issue, the plaintiff testified that she relied on the reputation of McDonald's in patronizing that restaurant and in her expectation of the quality of food and service she would receive. The court ruled that a jury could find that her reliance was objectively reasonable.

Notice that in many instances in which torts occur, the concept of apparent agency will simply not apply because the tort victim's injury does not arise out of a reasonable belief that a party is an agent for a principal.

F.　Termination of the Agency Relationship

We have now studied formation of the agency relationship, the duties and obligations of the agent and principal to each other, and the liability in contract and tort of the principal and agent to third parties. What is left is to learn about how the agency relationship comes to an end.

Recall that agency is a relationship that requires mutual assent to exist. Consequently, either the principal or the agent can terminate the agency relationship at any time and for any reason by communicating to the other that the relationship is at an end. The terminology is "renunciation" by the agent and "revocation" by the principal. A renunciation or revocation is effective when the other party has notice of it. If the parties have a contractual relationship as well as agency, it is possible that one of the parties could be in breach, but that does not impinge upon each party's unilateral power to terminate the agency relationship.

The Restatement (Third) of Agency §§ 3.06–3.10 also provides several other ways that an agency relationship can end, including by:

- Death of the agent or principal (when the agent or third party has notice)

- Loss of capacity of the principal (when the agent or third party has notice)

- The expiration of a specified term, if there was one, for the agency relationship

- The occurrence of circumstances on the basis of which the agent should reasonably conclude that the principal no longer would assent to the agent's taking action on the principal's behalf (i.e., accomplishment of a specified purpose of the agency relationship, facts constituting a supervening frustration in the agent's ability to accomplish the principal's objectives)

If the original manifestations of agency set no specific time or purpose, the agency continues until a reasonable time has passed. Determining whether the agency is at end would then require a reasonable, objective appraisal of the parties' conduct, which would be highly fact-specific.

What are the consequences of terminating the agency relationship? Under traditional common law principles, the agent's actual authority to bind the principal ends when the agency ends. The agent may compete with her former principal after the agency relationship is terminated, but some duties continue such as the duty to not disclose confidential or proprietary information learned during the agency relationship.

As apparent authority arises because of the reasonable beliefs of a third party, the termination of actual authority does not by itself end any apparent authority held by an agent. Section 3.11 provides: "Apparent authority ends when it is no longer reasonable for the third party with whom an agent deals to believe that the agent continues to act with actual authority." Thus to avoid lingering apparent authority, the principal may need to give notice of the termination to third parties and take away items or references that might give rise to a third party's belief that the former agent still has authority such as uniforms, business cards, webpage listings, and the like.

CHAPTER 3

Partnership Basics

The partnership is one the oldest forms of business organization. Let's start with the definition: a partnership is "an association of two or more persons to carry on as co-owners of a business for profit." RUPA § 202(a). As with agency, the formation of a general partnership requires no written agreement or governmental action. The association must be voluntary, but the partners do not need to know or intend to form a partnership. Thus, the partnership is a "residual form" of business organization: it exists even if some other form such as a corporation or LLC does not.

We note four key features of general partnerships at the outset. First, and perhaps most important, general partnerships do not have limited liability. Instead, each partner is jointly and severally liable for the debts of the partnership—they have unlimited personal liability. Second, unless otherwise agreed, each partner has the ability to participate in the control and management of the partnership. Third, unless otherwise agreed, partners share profits equally (and allocate losses in the same proportion). Fourth, partnerships have "pass-through" taxation, meaning that partnership income is not taxed and instead the profits or losses of the partnership flow through to the partners to include on their personal tax returns.

Partnerships are mostly governed by state law. A majority of states have adopted a uniform partnership statute that is known as "RUPA"—the Revised Uniform Partnership Act of 1997 (last amended 2013). Unless otherwise noted, all references to RUPA in this book are to the 2013 harmonized and renumbered version of the Uniform Partnership Act of 1997, which you can find on the Uniform Law Commission's website (uniformlaws.org). Several states continue to operate under the predecessor, Uniform Partnership Act (1914), also known as "UPA." The codified versions of RUPA or UPA (together with state case law) are the "default rules" of partnership law: they are the rules that typically apply if the partners have not agreed otherwise.

RUPA § 105 sets forth the relatively few rights and duties that are nonwaivable, meaning partners cannot contract around them. For example, a partnership agreement may not unreasonably restrict a partner's right of access to partnership books and records, eliminate the duty of care or loyalty, or restrict the rights of third parties. With few mandatory rules, partnership is a highly flexible form of business organization. We will study the basic rules for general partnerships and then the variety of limited liability forms of partnership that have developed in the law.

A. Partnership Formation

Because certain legal consequences follow from the partnership relationship, such as fiduciary duties owed between the partners and the personal liability of partners for the partnership debts to third parties, many cases have involved a determination of whether a particular relationship constitutes a partnership or something else (e.g., borrower-lender, employer-employee). The starting point of analysis is RUPA Section 202 below, and then courts have reasoned based on whether the relationship has characteristics of a typical partnership, such as profit sharing, participation in management, and risk of loss.

The statute provides the definition of a partnership and establishes a presumption of partnership if there is profit sharing unless it is of a listed type that does not connote co-ownership of a business.

§ 202. Formation of Partnership

(a) Except as otherwise provided in subsection (b), the association of two or more persons to carry on as co-owners a business for profit forms a partnership, whether or not the persons intend to form a partnership.

(b) An association formed under a statute other than this [act], a predecessor statute, or a comparable statute of another jurisdiction is not a partnership under this [act].

(c) In determining whether a partnership is formed, the following rules apply:

(1) Joint tenancy, tenancy in common, tenancy by the entireties, joint property, common property, or part ownership does not by itself establish a partnership, even if the co-owners share profits made by the use of the property.

(2) The sharing of gross returns does not by itself establish a partnership, even if the persons sharing them have a joint or common right or interest in property from which the returns are derived.

(3) A person who receives a share of the profits of a business is presumed to be a partner in the business, unless the profits were received in payment:

(A) of a debt by installments or otherwise;

(B) for services as an independent contractor or of wages or other compensation to an employee;

(C)   of rent;

(D)   of an annuity or other retirement or health benefit to a deceased or retired partner or a beneficiary, representative, or designee of a deceased or retired partner;

(E)   of interest or other charge on a loan, even if the amount of payment varies with the profits of the business, including a direct or indirect present or future ownership of the collateral, or rights to income, proceeds, or increase in value derived from the collateral; or

(F)   for the sale of the goodwill of a business or other property by installments or otherwise.

Now we turn to a classic case on the issue of partnership formation. It involved a story of friendship and financial disaster that put at risk the fortunes of the wealthy defendants who had helped out a friend by investing in his partnership. It all started in the spring of 1921 when the partnership of Knauth, Nachod, & Kuhne (K. N. & K.) found itself in serious financial difficulties after having engaged in unwise speculations. The partnership had securities, but of a quality too risky to be able to use as collateral to get a bank loan. One of the partners, John Hall, had friends who were willing to help him—the defendants, William Peyton, George W. Perkins, Jr., and Edward W. Freeman.

Peyton, Perkins, and Freeman entered into an agreement in which they would loan to K. N. & K. $2.5 million worth of securities, which were to be returned to them on or before April 1923. During the loan period, the partnership could use these securities as collateral to secure business loans for the partnership up to $2 million. In order to protect the defendants against loss, K. N. & K. would meanwhile turn over to them a large number of speculative securities to hold. In compensation for this loan, the defendants were to receive 40% of the partnership profits until the return was made, but in any event not less than $100,000 and not more than $500,000. The defendants were also given an option to join the partnership if any of them expressed a desire to do so before June 1923.

Other creditors to K. N. & K. later sued Peyton, Perkins, and Freeman, claiming they were partners of K. N. & K. who could be held personally responsible for the debts of the firm. As the old saying goes, no good deed goes unpunished!

Martin v. Peyton

158 N.E. 77 (N.Y. 1927) → pretty much great depression

ANDREWS, JUDGE.

Partnership results from contract, express or implied. If denied it may be proved by the production of some written instrument; by testimony as to some conversation; by circumstantial evidence. If nothing else appears, the receipt by the defendant of a share of the profits of the business is enough.

Assuming some written contract between the parties, the question may arise whether it creates a partnership. If it be complete, if it expresses in good faith the full understanding and obligation of the parties, then it is for the court to say whether a partnership exists. It may, however, be a mere sham intended to hide the real relationship. Then other results follow. In passing upon it, effect is to be given to each provision. Mere words will not blind us to realities. Statements that no partnership is intended are not conclusive. If as a whole a contract contemplates an association of two or more persons to carry on as co-owners a business for profit, a partnership there is. On the other hand, if it be less than this, no partnership exists. Passing on the contract as a whole, an arrangement for sharing profits is to be considered. It is to be given its due weight. But it is to be weighed in connection with all the rest. It is not decisive. It may be merely the method adopted to pay a debt or wages, as interest on a loan or for other reasons.

In the case before us the claim that the defendants became partners in the firm of Knauth, Nachod & Kuhne, doing business as bankers and brokers, depends upon the interpretation of certain instruments. We refer to circumstances surrounding their execution only so far as is necessary to make them intelligible. And we are to remember that although the intention of the parties to avoid liability as partners is clear, although in language precise and definite they deny any design to then join the firm of K. N. & K.; although they say their interests in profits should be construed merely as a measure of compensation for loans, not an interest in profits as such; although they provide that they shall not be liable for any losses or treated as partners, the question still remains whether in fact they agree to so associate themselves with the firm as to "carry on as co-owners a business for profit."

The answer depends upon an analysis of various provisions. As representing the lenders, Mr. Peyton and Mr. Freeman are called "trustees." The loaned securities when used as collateral are not to be mingled with other securities of K. N. & K., and the trustees at all times are to be kept informed of all transactions affecting them. To them shall be paid all dividends and income accruing therefrom. They may also substitute for any of the securities loaned securities of equal value. With their consent the firm may sell any of its securities held by the respondents, the proceeds to go, however, to the trustees. In other similar ways the trustees may deal with these same securities, but the securities loaned shall always be sufficient in value to permit of their hypothecation for $2,000,000. If they rise in price the excess may be withdrawn by the defendants. If they fall, they shall make good the deficiency.

So far, there is no hint that the transaction is not a loan of securities with a provision for compensation. Later a somewhat closer connection with the firm appears. Until the securities are returned, the directing management of the firm is to be in the hands of John R. Hall, and his life is to be insured for $1,000,000, and the policies are to be assigned as further collateral security to the trustees. These requirements are not unnatural. Hall was the one known and trusted by the defendants. Their acquaintance with the other members of the firm was of the slightest. These others had brought an old and established business to the verge of bankruptcy. As the respondents knew, they also had engaged in unsafe speculation. The respondents were about to loan $2,500,000 of good securities. As collateral they were to receive others of problematical value. What they required seems but ordinary caution. Nor does it imply an association in the business.

The trustees are to be kept advised as to the conduct of the business and consulted as to important matters. They may inspect the firm books and are entitled to any information they think important. Finally, they may veto any business they think highly speculative or injurious. Again we hold this but a proper precaution to safeguard the loan. The trustees may not initiate any transaction as a partner may do. They may not bind the firm by any action of their own. Under the circumstances the safety of the loan depended upon the business success of K. N. & K. This success was likely to be compromised by the inclination of its members to engage in speculation. No longer, if the respondents were to be protected, should it be allowed. The trustees, therefore, might prohibit it, and that their prohibition might be effective, information was to be furnished them. Not dissimilar agreements have been held proper to guard the interests of the lender.

As further security each member of K. N. & K. is to assign to the trustees their interest in the firm. No loan by the firm to any member is permitted and the amount each may draw is fixed. No other distribution of profits is to be made. So that realized profits may be calculated the existing capital is stated to be $700,000, and profits are to be realized as promptly as good business practice will permit. In case the trustees think this is not done, the question is left to them and to Mr. Hall, and if they differ then to an arbitrator. There is no obligation that the firm shall continue the business. It may dissolve at any time. Again we conclude there is nothing here not properly adapted to secure the interest of the respondents as lenders. If their compensation is dependent on a percentage of the profits still provision must be made to define what these profits shall be.

The "indenture" is substantially a mortgage of the collateral delivered by K. N. & K. to the trustees to secure the performance of the "agreement." It certainly does not strengthen the claim that the respondents were partners.

Finally we have the "option." It permits the respondents, or any of them, or their assignees or nominees to enter the firm at a later date if they desire to do so by buying 50 per cent or less of the interests therein of all or any of the members at a stated price. Or a corporation may, if the respondents and the members agree, be formed in place of the firm. Meanwhile, apparently with the design of protecting the firm business against improper or ill-judged action which might render the option valueless, each member of the firm is to place his resignation in the hands of Mr. Hall. If at any time he and the trustees agree that such resignation should be accepted, that member shall then retire, receiving the value of his interest calculated as of the date of such retirement.

This last provision is somewhat unusual, yet it is not enough in itself to show that on June 4, 1921, a present partnership was created nor taking these various papers as a whole do we reach such a result. It is quite true that even if one or two or three like provisions contained in such a contract do not require this conclusion, yet it is also true that when taken together a point may come where stipulations immaterial separately cover so wide a field that we should hold a partnership exists. As in other branches of the law, a question of degree is often the determining factor. Here that point has not been reached. The judgment appealed from should be affirmed, with costs.

Partnership by Estoppel

So far, we have focused on the notion of true general partnerships, in which the issue is whether there is an "association of two or more persons to carry on as co-owners a business for profit." A doctrine also exists to protect creditors in situations where there is reliance on a purported partner. A claim of "partnership by estoppel" does not allege a real partnership existed, but instead that a person becomes subject to partnership liability if that person purported to be a partner or consented to being represented as such, and a third party relied on that representation in entering into the transaction. RUPA § 308.

B.   Partnership Management

One of the distinctive characteristics of a general partnership is its default structure of decentralized management: each partner is an agent of the partnership for conducting the partnership's business. This means that unless the partnership agreement says otherwise, each partner has actual authority to bind the partnership in the ordinary course of business. RUPA § 301 provides this rule and also the rule that a partner has apparent authority that can bind the partnership to a contract in the ordinary course of the partnership business or business of the kind carried on by the partnership, unless the third party knew or had notice that the partner lacked actual authority. RUPA § 305 provides that a partnership is liable for a partner's tort when the partner was acting in the ordinary course of partnership business when the tort occurred or with authority of the partnership.

§ 301. Partner Agent of Partnership

Subject to the effect of a statement of partnership authority under Section 303, the following rules apply:

(1) Each partner is an agent of the partnership for the purpose of its business. An act of a partner, including the signing of an instrument in the partnership name, for apparently carrying on in the ordinary course the partnership business or business of the kind carried on by the partnership binds the partnership, unless the partner did not have authority to act for the partnership in the particular matter and the person with which the partner was dealing knew or had notice that the partner lacked authority.

(2) An act of a partner which is not apparently for carrying on in the ordinary course the partnership's business or business of the kind carried on by the partnership binds the partnership only if the act was actually authorized by all the other partners.

§ 305. Partnership Liable for Partner's Actionable Conduct

(a) A partnership is liable for loss or injury caused to a person, or for a penalty incurred, as a result of a wrongful act or omission, or other actionable conduct, of a partner acting in the ordinary course of business of the partnership or with the actual or apparent authority of the partnership.

(b) If, in the course of the partnership's business or while acting with actual or apparent authority of the partnership, a partner receives or causes the partnership to receive money or property of a person not a partner, and the money or property is misapplied by a partner, the partnership is liable for the loss.

In addition to making each partner a managerial agent by default, partnership rules also provide each partner with equal voting rights in management. For example, imagine a three-person partnership of A, B, and C. A contributes 70% of the partnership capital, B contributes 20%, and C contributes 10%. By default, the amounts of capital contribution make no difference to their voting power in management—A, B, and C each have one equal vote.

What happens when the partners disagree about how to manage the partnership? RUPA § 401 provides: "A difference arising as to a matter in the ordinary course of business may be decided by a majority of the partners. An act outside the ordinary course of business of a partnership and an amendment to the partnership agreement may be undertaken only with the affirmative vote or consent of all of the partners." This is a default rule that can be altered by agreement, such as often happens in large law firms where it may be unworkable for decisions to be made by majority rule or unanimity. Large partnerships will often have executive committees with delegated authority because of the high costs of communication and negotiation between all partners, collective action problems, and the risk of hold-outs.

Notably, the default rules of management can lead to potential deadlock problems in partnerships with an even number of partners, especially those with just two partners. The following case applies the basic partnership management rules to a deadlock.

National Biscuit Company, Inc. v. Stroud

106 S.E.2d 692 (N.C. 1959)

PARKER, JUSTICE.

partnership to sell groceries

C. N. Stroud and Earl Freeman entered into a general partnership to sell groceries under the firm name of Stroud's Food Center. There is nothing in the agreed statement of facts to indicate or suggest that Freeman's power and authority as a general partner were in any way restricted or limited by the articles of partnership in respect to the ordinary and legitimate business of the partnership. Certainly, the purchase and sale of bread were ordinary and legitimate business of Stroud's Food Center during its continuance as a going concern.

Several months prior to February 1956 Stroud advised plaintiff that he personally would not be responsible for any additional bread sold by plaintiff to Stroud's Food Center. After such notice to plaintiff, it from 6 February 1956 to 25 February 1956, at the request of Freeman, sold and delivered bread in the amount of $171.04 to Stroud's Food Center.

The General Assembly of North Carolina in 1941 enacted a Uniform Partnership Act, which became effective 15 March 1941.

G.S. § 59–39 is entitled "Partner Agent of Partnership as to Partnership Business," and subsection (1) reads: "Every partner is an agent of the partnership for the purpose of its business, and the act of every partner, including the execution in the partnership name of any instrument, for apparently carrying on in the usual way the business of the partnership of which he is a member binds the partnership, unless the partner so acting has in fact no authority to act for the partnership in the particular matter, and the person with whom he is dealing has knowledge of the fact that he has no such authority." G.S. § 59–39(4) states: "No act of a partner in contravention of a restriction on authority shall bind the partnership to persons having knowledge of the restriction."

[handwritten: neither partner can prevent the other from binding the partnership in the ordinary course of business.]

G.S. § 59–45 provides that "all partners are jointly and severally liable for the acts and obligations of the partnership."

G.S. § 59–48 is captioned "Rules Determining Rights and Duties of Partners." Subsection (e) thereof reads: "All partners have equal rights in the management and conduct of the partnership business." Subsection (h) hereof is as follows: "Any difference arising as to ordinary matters connected with the partnership business may be decided by a majority of the partners; but no act in contravention of any agreement between the partners may be done rightfully without the consent of all the partners."

Freeman as a general partner with Stroud, with no restrictions on his authority to act within the scope of the partnership business so far as the agreed statement of facts shows, had under the Uniform Partnership Act "equal rights in the management and conduct of the partnership business." Under G.S. § 59–48(h) Stroud, his co-partner, could not restrict the power and authority of Freeman to buy bread for the partnership as a going concern, for such a purchase was an "ordinary matter connected with the partnership business," for the purpose of its business and within its scope, because in the very nature of things Stroud was not, and could not be, a majority of the partners. Therefore, Freeman's purchases of bread from plaintiff for Stroud's Food Center as a going concern bound the partnership and his co-partner Stroud.

In *Crane on Partnership*, 2d Ed., p. 277, it is said: "In cases of an even division of the partners as to whether or not an act within the scope of the business should be done, of which disagreement a third person has knowledge, it seems that logically no restriction can be placed upon the power to act. The partnership being a going concern, activities within the scope of the business should not be limited, save by the expressed will of the majority deciding a disputed question; half of the members are not a majority." *Sladen, Fakes & Co. v. Lance*, 151 N.C. 492, 66 S.E. 449, is distinguishable. That was a case where the terms of the partnership imposed special restrictions on the power of the partner who made the contract.

At the close of business on 25 February 1956 Stroud and Freeman by agreement dissolved the partnership. By their dissolution agreement all of the partnership assets, including cash on hand, bank deposits and all accounts receivable, with a few exceptions, were assigned to Stroud, who bound himself by such written dissolution agreement to liquidate the firm's assets and discharge its liabilities. It would seem a fair inference from the agreed statement of facts that the partnership got the benefit of the bread sold and delivered by plaintiff to Stroud's Food Center, at Freeman's request, from 6 February 1956 to 25 February 1956. *See Blackstone Guano Co. v. Ball*, 201 N.C. 534, 160 S.E. 769. But whether it did or not, Freeman's acts, as stated above, bound the partnership and Stroud.

The judgment of the court below is affirmed.

Points for Discussion

1. Understanding the case.

Explain the court's basis for deciding in favor of National Biscuit. Why wasn't Stroud's notification to National Biscuit enough for him to restrict Freeman's ability to bind the partnership?

2. Deadlock in partnerships.

What kinds of problems might arise in partnerships that have two partners with equal management rights? How might you have drafted the partnership agreement to avert or mitigate the problem that gave rise to the litigation in this case? In a "deadlock" situation where there is one partner "for" a proposed action and one partner "against," how do you know which partner wins?

C. Partnership Fiduciary Duties and Information Rights

Each partner owes fiduciary duties to the other partners and to the partnership itself. Next is the most famous case involving partnership fiduciary duties: *Meinhard v. Salmon*. It arose from a dispute between two "coadventurers" in a commercial real estate project.

Meinhard v. Salmon

164 N.E. 545 (N.Y. 1928)

CARDOZO, C. J.

On April 10, 1902, Louisa M. Gerry leased to the defendant Walter J. Salmon the premises known as the Hotel Bristol at the northwest corner of Forty-Second street and Fifth avenue in the city of New York. The lease was for a term of 20 years, commencing May 1, 1902, and ending April 30, 1922. The lessee undertook to change the hotel building for use as shops and offices at a cost of $200,000. Alterations and additions were to be accretions to the land.

Salmon, while in course of treaty with the lessor as to the execution of the lease, was in course of treaty with Meinhard, the plaintiff, for the necessary funds. The result was a joint venture with terms embodied in a writing. Meinhard was to pay to Salmon half of the moneys requisite to reconstruct, alter, manage, and operate the property. Salmon was to pay to Meinhard 40 per cent. of the net profits for the first five years of the lease and 50 per cent. for the years thereafter. If there were losses, each party was to bear them equally. Salmon, however, was to have sole power to "manage, lease, underlet and operate" the building. There were to be certain pre-emptive rights for each in the contingency of death.

The two were coadventurers, subject to fiduciary duties akin to those of partners. As to this we are all agreed. The heavier weight of duty rested, however, upon Salmon. He was a coadventurer with Meinhard, but he was manager as well. During the early years of the enterprise, the building, reconstructed, was operated at a loss. If the relation had then ended, Meinhard as well as Salmon would have carried a heavy burden. Later the profits became large with the result that for each of the investors there came a rich return. For each the venture had its phases of fair weather and of foul. The two were in it jointly, for better or for worse.

When the lease was near its end, Elbridge T. Gerry had become the owner of the reversion. He owned much other property in the neighborhood, one lot adjoining the Bristol building on Fifth avenue and four lots on Forty-Second street. He had a plan to lease the entire tract for a long term to some one who would destroy the buildings then existing and put up another in their place. In the latter part of 1921, he submitted such a project to several capitalists and dealers. He was unable to carry it through with any of them. Then, in January, 1922, with less than four months of the lease to run, he approached the defendant Salmon. The result was a new lease to the Midpoint Realty Company, which is owned and controlled by Salmon, a lease covering the whole tract, and involving a huge outlay. The term is to be 20 years, but successive covenants for renewal will extend it to a maximum of 80 years at the will of either party. The existing buildings may remain unchanged for seven years. They are then to be torn down, and a new building to cost $3,000,000 is to be placed upon the site. The rental, which under the Bristol lease was only $55,000, is to be from $350,000 to $475,000 for the properties so combined. Salmon personally guaranteed the performance by the lessee of the covenants of the new lease until such time as the new building had been completed and fully paid for.

The lease between Gerry and the Midpoint Realty Company was signed and delivered on January 25, 1922. Salmon had not told Meinhard anything about it. Whatever his motive may have been, he had kept the negotiations to himself. Meinhard was not informed even of the bare existence of a project. The first that he knew of it was in February, when the lease was an accomplished fact. He then made demand on the defendants that the lease be held in trust as an asset of the venture, making offer upon the trial to share the personal obligations incidental

The building project undertaken by Salmon, one of the most important in New York City in the 1920s, resulted in the "Salmon Tower." The 60-story building at 42nd Street and Fifth Avenue, across from the New York City Public Library, was for a time the second tallest building in the city. Designed by the architectural firm Shreve Lamb & Harmon (the same firm that designed the Empire State Building), it remains a landmark of the New York skyline.

to the guaranty. The demand was followed by refusal, and later by this suit. A referee gave judgment for the plaintiff, limiting the plaintiff's interest in the lease, however, to 25 per cent. The limitation was on the theory that the plaintiff's equity was to be restricted to one-half of so much of the value of the lease as was contributed or represented by the occupation of the Bristol site. Upon cross-appeals to the Appellate Division, the judgment was modified so as to enlarge the equitable interest to one-half of the whole lease. With this enlargement of plaintiff's interest, there went, of course, a corresponding enlargement of his attendant obligations. The case is now here on an appeal by the defendants.

Joint adventurers, like copartners, owe to one another, while the enterprise continues, the duty of the finest loyalty. Many forms of conduct permissible in a workaday world for those acting at arm's length, are forbidden to those bound by fiduciary ties. A trustee is held to something stricter than the morals of the market place. Not honesty alone, but the punctilio of an honor the most sensitive, is then the standard of behavior. As to this there has developed a tradition that is unbending and inveterate. Uncompromising rigidity has been the attitude of courts of equity when petitioned to undermine the rule of undivided loyalty by the "disintegrating erosion" of particular exceptions. Only thus has the level of conduct for fiduciaries been kept at a level higher than that trodden by the crowd. It will not consciously be lowered by any judgment of this court.

The owner of the reversion, Mr. Gerry, had vainly striven to find a tenant who would favor his ambitious scheme of demolition and construction. Baffled in the search, he turned to the defendant Salmon in possession of the Bristol, the keystone of the project. He figured to himself beyond a doubt that the man in possession would prove a likely customer. To the eye of an observer, Salmon held the lease as owner in his own right, for himself and no one else. In fact he held it as a fiduciary, for himself and another, sharers in a common venture. If this fact had been proclaimed, if the lease by its terms had run in favor of a partnership, Mr. Gerry, we may fairly assume, would have laid before the partners, and not merely before one of them, his plan of reconstruction. The pre-emptive privilege, or, better, the pre-emptive opportunity, that was thus an incident of the enterprise, Salmon appropriate to himself in secrecy and silence. He might have warned Meinhard that the plan had been submitted, and that either would be free to compete for the award. If he had done this, we do not need to say whether he would have been under a duty, if successful in the competition, to hold the lease so acquired for the benefit of a venture than about to end, and thus prolong by indirection its responsibilities and duties. The trouble about his conduct is that he excluded his coadventurer from any chance to compete, from any chance to enjoy the opportunity for benefit that had come to him alone by virtue of his agency. This chance, if nothing more, he was under a duty to concede. The price of its denial is an extension of the trust at the option and for the benefit of the one whom he excluded.

No answer is it to say that the chance would have been of little value even if seasonably offered. Such a calculus of probabilities is beyond the science of the chancery. Salmon, the real estate operator, might have been preferred to Meinhard, the woolen merchant. On the other hand, Meinhard might have offered better terms, or reinforced his offer by alliance with the wealth of others. Perhaps he might even have persuaded the lessor to renew the Bristol lease alone, postponing for a time, in return for higher rentals, the improvement of adjoining lots. We know that even under the lease as made the time for the enlargement of the building was delayed for seven years. All these opportunities were cut away from him through another's intervention. He knew that Salmon was the manager. As the time drew near for the expiration of the lease, he would naturally assume from silence, if from nothing else, that the lessor was willing to extend it for a term of years, or at least to let it stand as a lease from year to year. Not impossibly the lessor would have done so, whatever his protestations of unwillingness, if Salmon had not given assent to a project more attractive. At all events, notice of termination, even if not necessary, might seem, not unreasonably, to be something to be looked for, if the business was over the another tenant was to enter. In the absence of such notice, the matter of an extension was one that would naturally be attended to by the manager of the enterprise, and not neglected altogether. At least, there was nothing in the situation to give warning to any one that while the lease was still in being, there had come to the manager an offer of extension which he had locked within his breast to be utilized by himself alone. The very fact that Salmon was in control with exclusive powers of direction charged him the more obviously with the duty of disclosure, since only through disclosure could opportunity be equalized. If he might cut off renewal by a purchase for his own benefit when four months were to pass before the lease would have an end, he might do so with equal right while there remained as many years. He might steal a march on his comrade under cover of the darkness, and then hold the captured ground. Loyalty and comradeship are not so easily abjured.

Little profit will come from a dissection of the precedents. Authority is, of course, abundant that one partner may not appropriate to his own use a renewal of a lease, though its term is to begin at the expiration of the partnership. The lease at hand with its many changes is not strictly a renewal. Even so, the standard of loyalty for those in trust relations is without the fixed divisions of a graduated scale. To say that a partner is free without restriction to buy in the reversion of the property where the business is conducted is to say in effect that he may strip the good will of its chief element of value, since good will is largely dependent upon continuity of possession. Equity refuses to confine within the bounds of classified transactions its precept of a loyalty that is undivided and unselfish. Certain at least it is that a "man obtaining his locus standi, and his opportunity for making such arrangements, by the position he occupies as a partner, is bound by his obligation to his copartners in such dealings not to separate his interest from theirs, but, if he acquires any benefit, to communicate it to them." Certain it is also that there may be no abuse of special opportunities growing out of a special trust as manager or agent. A constructive trust is, then, the remedial device through which preference of self is made subordinate to loyalty to others.

> Notice that the rule (or duty) applied by Judge Cardozo is contextual. If Salmon had received information about a real estate opportunity far removed geographically or involving a non-real estate investment opportunity, Judge Cardozo suggests the result would have been different. Does it make sense for the application of fiduciary duties to vary depending on the parties' specific relationship?

We have no thought to hold that Salmon was guilty of a conscious purpose to defraud. Very likely he assumed in all good faith that with the approaching end of the venture he might ignore his coadventurer and take the extension for himself. He had given to the enterprise time and labor as well as money. He had made it a success. Meinhard, who had given money, but neither time nor labor, had already been richly paid. There might seem to be something grasping in his insistence upon more. Such recriminations are not unusual when coadventurers fall out. They are not without their force if conduct is to be judged by the common standards of competitors. That is not to say that they have pertinency here. Salmon had put himself in a position in which thought of self was to be renounced, however hard the abnegation. He was much more than a coadventurer. He was a managing coadventurer. For him and for those like him the rule of undivided loyalty is relentless and supreme. A different question would be here if there were lacking any nexus of relation between the business conducted by the manager and the opportunity brought to him as an incident of management. For this problem, as for most, there are distinctions of degree. If Salmon had received from Gerry a proposition to lease a building at a location far removed, he might have held for himself the privilege thus acquired, or so we shall assume. Here the subject-matter of the new lease was an extension and enlargement of the subject-matter of the old one.

A question remains as to the form and extent of the equitable interest to be allotted to the plaintiff. The trust as declared has been held to attach to the lease which was in the name of the defendant corporation. We think it ought to attach at the option of the defendant Salmon to the shares of stock which were owned by him or were under his control. The difference may be important if the lessee shall wish to execute an assignment of the lease, as it ought to be free to do with the consent of the lessor. On the other hand, an equal division of the shares might lead to other hardships. It might take away from Salmon the power of control and management which under the plan of the joint venture he was to have from first to last. The number of shares to be allotted to the plaintiff should, therefore, be reduced to such an extent as may be necessary to preserve to the defendant Salmon the expected measure of dominion. To that end an extra share should be added to his half.

Andrews, J. (dissenting)

. . . . I am of the opinion that the issue here is simple. Was the transaction, in view of all the circumstances surrounding it, unfair and inequitable? I reach this conclusion for two reasons. There was no general partnership, merely a joint venture for a limited object, to end at a fixed time. The new lease, covering additional property, containing many new and unusual terms and conditions, with a possible duration of 80 years, was more nearly the purchase of the reversion than the ordinary renewal with which the authorities are concerned.

Were this a general partnership between Mr. Salmon and Mr. Meinhard, I should have little doubt as to the correctness of this result, assuming the new lease to be an offshoot of the old. Such a situation involves questions of trust and confidence to a high degree; it involves questions of good will; many other considerations. As has been said, rarely if ever may one partner without the knowledge of the other acquire for himself the renewal of a lease held by the firm, even if the new lease is to begin after the firm is dissolved. Warning of such an intent, if he is managing partner, may not be sufficient to prevent the application of this rule.

We have here a different situation governed by less drastic principles. I assume that where parties engage in a joint enterprise each owes to the other the duty of the utmost good faith in all that relates to their common venture. Within its scope they stand in a fiduciary relationship.

What then was the scope of the adventure into which the two men entered? It is to be remembered that before their contract was signed Mr. Salmon had obtained the lease of the Bristol property. Very likely the matter had been earlier discussed between them. The $5,000 advance by Mr. Meinhard indicates that fact. But it has been held that the written contract defines their rights and duties. Having the lease, Mr. Salmon assigns no interest in it to Mr. Meinhard. He is to manage the property. It is for him to decide what alterations shall be made and to fix the rents. But for 20 years from May 1, 1902, Salmon is to make all advances from his own funds and Meinhard is to pay him personally on demand one-half of all expenses incurred and all losses sustained "during the full term of said lease," and during the same period Salmon is to pay him a part of the net profits. There was no joint capital provided.

It seems to me that the venture so inaugurated had in view a limited object and was to end at a limited time. There was no intent to expand it into a far greater undertaking lasting for many years. The design was to exploit a particular lease. Doubtless in it Mr. Meinhard had an equitable interest, but in it alone. This interest terminated when the joint adventure terminated. There was no intent that for the benefit of both any advantage should be taken of the chance of renewal—that the adventure should be continued beyond that date. Mr. Salmon has done all he promised to do in return for Mr. Meinhard's undertaking when he distributed profits up to May 1, 1922.

Points for Discussion

1. What roles?

What roles do you think Meinhard and Salmon expected that each would play? How might their expectations have affected the judges' views of their business relationship? Should their expectations matter?

2. What risks?

How did Meinhard and Salmon divide the risks of their business relationship? How would you have advised them to do so? Could they have allocated the risks in advance, so that they could have avoided this dispute?

————————

RUPA § 409 sets two main standards of conduct, providing that a partner owes to the partnership and the other partners duties of care and loyalty.

The duty of care of a partner "is to refrain from engaging in grossly negligent or reckless conduct, willful or intentional misconduct, or a knowing violation of law."

The fiduciary duty of loyalty includes the duties: to account to the partnership for any property, profit, or benefit derived by the partner from using or appropriating partnership property; to refrain from dealing with the partnership on behalf of a person having an interest adverse to the partnership; and to refrain from competing with the partnership in the conduct of the partnership's business. All partners may authorize or ratify, after full disclosure of all material facts, a specific act or transaction by a partner that otherwise would violate the duty of loyalty. Thus, applying RUPA to the set of facts in *Meinhard v. Salmon*, if Salmon had told his partner Meinhard all of the material facts about the lease opportunity and Meinhard had consented to Salmon taking it, then Salmon would not have breached his fiduciary duty of loyalty by taking the opportunity for himself.

§ 409. Standards of Conduct for Partners

(a) A partner owes to the partnership and the other partners the duties of loyalty and care stated in subsections (b) and (c).

(b) The fiduciary duty of loyalty of a partner includes the duties:

    (1) to account to the partnership and hold as trustee for it any property, profit, or benefit derived by the partner:

        (A) in the conduct or winding up of the partnership's business;

        (B) from a use by the partner of the partnership's property; or

   (C) from the appropriation of a partnership opportunity;

 (2) to refrain from dealing with the partnership in the conduct or winding up of

the partnership business as or on behalf of a person having an interest adverse to the partnership; and

 (3) to refrain from competing with the partnership in the conduct of the partnership's business before the dissolution of the partnership.

(c) The duty of care of a partner in the conduct or winding up of the partnership business is to refrain from engaging in grossly negligent or reckless conduct, willful or intentional misconduct, or a knowing violation of law.

(d) A partner shall discharge the duties and obligations under this [act] or under the partnership agreement and exercise any rights consistently with the contractual obligation of good faith and fair dealing.

(e) partner does not violate a duty or obligation under this [act] or under the partnership agreement solely because the partner's conduct furthers the partner's own interest.

(f) All the partners may authorize or ratify, after full disclosure of all material facts, a specific act or transaction by a partner that otherwise would violate the duty of loyalty.

(g) It is a defense to a claim under subsection (b)(2) and any comparable claim in equity or at common law that the transaction was fair to the partnership.

(h) If, as permitted by subsection (f) or the partnership agreement, a partner enters into a transaction with the partnership which otherwise would be prohibited by subsection (b)(2), the partner's rights and obligations arising from the transaction are the same as those of a person that is not a partner.

Because partners owe fiduciary duties, generally participate in management, and are exposed to liability for partnership debts, it is important that they have access to information about the partnership. RUPA § 408 sets out the relevant rules. It requires a partnership to keep its books and records at its principal office. Further, it provides that the partnership shall furnish to each partner any information concerning the partnership's business and other circumstances which the partnership knows and is material to the proper exercise of the partner's rights and duties. Upon a partner's request, the partnership must also provide any other information except to the extent the request is unreasonable or otherwise improper under the circumstances.

D. Partnership Property, Liability, and Finances

Now that we have examined how a partnership is formed, the basic rules of management, and the fiduciary duties of partners, let's turn to the financial aspects of this form of business organization.

1. Property

Partnerships are businesses and businesses typically need money or other property in order to carry out their operations, and if things go well, then they are making profits. "Partnership property" refers to everything the partnership owns, including both capital and property that is subsequently acquired in partnership transactions and operations. Partnership "capital," by the way, is the property or money contributed by each partner for the partnership's business.

A partner has a certain financial interest as a co-owner of the business, but she does not directly own or control the property of the partnership. Under default rules, a partner may use or possess partnership property only on behalf of the partnership, not for her personal purposes.

Does a partner have any interest in the partnership that she can transfer? The answer is yes, but it is a limited economic right or asset. The partner's "transferable interest" is treated as "personal property" that can be transferred without dissociating the partner or dissolving the partnership and it is attachable by personal creditors of the partner. Transfer of the partner's transferable interest gives the transferee no rights of management of the partnership or access to partnership records. It merely entitles the transferee to receive distributions to which the transferring partner would otherwise be entitled (and a right to an accounting in a dissolution of the partnership). This is because, under RUPA §§ 402(b) and 503, a partner may not transfer her status as partner or unilaterally make someone else a partner without the unanimous consent of the other partners.

Regarding the point that the partner's transferable interest is attachable by creditors as it is personal property, RUPA § 504 provides that a judgment creditor of a partner or transferee may apply to a court for a "charging order" against the transferable interest for the unsatisfied amount of the judgment. A charging order is a lien on a judgment debtor's transferable interest. It requires the partnership to pay over to the person with the charging order any distribution that would otherwise be paid to the judgment debtor.

2. Liability

Under general partnership law, all partners are jointly and severally liable to outside creditors for the partnership's obligations. Creditors must first seek to recover from partnership assets before proceeding against an individual partner's assets, but the rule of joint and several liability ultimately means that partners have personal, unlimited liability for the entire amount of partnership liabilities. This is one of the major consequences of operating as a general partnership and one of the key reasons for choosing to operate instead as a limited liability entity such as an LLP, LLC, or corporation.

Although each partner is subject to joint and several liability from outside creditors, as between the partners, each partner is only responsible for his share of the partnership obligation. A partner is not personally liable for a partnership debt or other liability of the partnership incurred before the person became a partner. If one partner pays off a partnership obligation, he is entitled to indemnification from the partnership. If the partnership lacks the funds to indemnify the partner, the partners are required to contribute according to their share of the loss. *See* RUPA §§ 306–307, 401, 806.

3. Finances

How do the finances—that is, the accounting and profit-sharing—in a partnership work? Under RUPA (1997), each partner has an account that is credited (increased) with the amount equal to the value of the partner's contribution (the "capital" the partner puts in), plus her share of the profits. The account is debited (decreased) when there are distributions to the partner, as well as for her share of any losses and partnership liabilities. The account is a book-keeping tally that tracks each partner's financial position in the partnership.

Capital contributions are not required from partners. If a partner does make a contribution, it becomes partnership property, and she gets credit for the value of it in the partnership accounting. But, unless otherwise agreed, a partner generally has no right to be compensated for services rendered to the partnership.

By default, profit sharing is done on an equal basis and losses are allocated in the same proportion as profits. *See* RUPA § 401(a). This default rule applies regardless of how much capital a partner has contributed or how much a partner has worked for the partnership. So, for example, if the partners did not make an agreement on this topic, then their sharing would be equal as to both profits and losses (i.e., if there were two partners, then 50/50 profits and losses). This default rule also means that if a partnership agreement established a profit-sharing percentage but neglected to specify an allocation for loss-sharing, the loss-sharing percentage would mirror the profit-sharing percentage. For example, if the partners agreed to share profits 60/40 but did not specify the loss allocation, then losses would also be shared 60/40.

Note that loss-sharing agreements among partners do not affect the personal liability of each partner to third party creditors for the debts of the partnership. That is, partners in a general partnership remain jointly and severally liable for all of the partnership debts. But they can agree how to allocate losses among themselves.

When do partners get to take profits out of the partnership for their own personal use? RUPA is silent on when such distributions occur. A well-drafted partnership agreement will address this. If not, a comment to § 401 of the 1997 version of RUPA provides the following guidance: "Absent an agreement to the contrary . . . the interim distribution of profits [is] a matter arising in the ordinary course of business to be decided by majority vote of the partners."

The following case considers application of the loss-sharing rules in a "service" partnership, in which one partner contributed capital and the other labor, at the time of dissolution—the topic to which we will subsequently turn.

Kovacik v. Reed

315 P.2d 314 (Cal. 1957)

Schauer, Justice.

In this suit for dissolution of a joint venture and for an accounting, defendant appeals from a judgment that plaintiff recover from defendant one half the losses of the venture. We have concluded that inasmuch as the parties agreed that plaintiff was to supply the money and defendant the labor to carry on the venture, defendant is correct in his contention that the trial court erred in holding him liable for one half the monetary losses, and that the judgment should therefore be reversed.

It appears that plaintiff, a licensed building contractor in San Francisco, operated his contracting business as a sole proprietorship under the fictitious name of "Asbestos Siding Company." Defendant had for a number of years worked for various building contractors in that city as a job superintendent and estimator.

Early in November, 1952, Kovacik (plaintiff) told Reed (defendant) that Kovacik had an opportunity to do kitchen remodeling work for Sears Roebuck Company in San Francisco and asked Reed to become his job superintendent and estimator in this venture. Kovacik said that he had about $10,000.00 to invest in the venture and that, if Reed would superintend and estimate the jobs, Kovacik would share the profits with Reed on a 50-50 basis. Kovacik did not ask Reed to agree to share any loss that might result and Reed did not offer to share any such loss. The subject of a possible loss was not discussed in the inception of this venture. Reed accepted Kovacik's proposal and commenced work for the venture shortly after November 1, 1952. Reed's only contribution was his own labor. Kovacik provided all of the venture's financing through the credit of Asbestos Siding Company, although at times Reed purchased materials for the jobs in his own name or on his account for which he was reimbursed.

The venture bid on and was awarded a number of remodeling jobs in San Francisco. Reed worked on all of the jobs as job superintendent. During August,

1953, Kovacik, who at that time had all of the financial records of the venture in his possession, informed Reed that the venture had been unprofitable and demanded contribution from Reed as to amounts which Kovacik claimed to have advanced in excess of the income received from the venture. Reed at no time promised, represented or agreed that he was liable for any of the venture's losses, and he consistently and without exception refused to contribute to or pay any of the loss resulting from the venture. The venture was terminated on August 31, 1953.

Kovacik thereafter instituted this proceeding, seeking an accounting of the affairs of the venture and to recover from Reed one half of the losses. Despite the evidence above set forth from the statement of the oral proceedings, showing that at no time had defendant agreed to be liable for any of the losses, the trial court "found"—more accurately, we think, concluded as a matter of law—that "plaintiff and defendant were to share equally all their joint venture profits and losses between them," and that defendant "agreed to share equally in the profits and losses of said joint venture." Following an accounting taken by a referee appointed by the court, judgment was rendered awarding plaintiff recovery against defendant of some $4,340, as one half the monetary losses found by the referee to have been sustained by the joint venture.

It is the general rule that in the absence of an agreement to the contrary the law presumes that partners and joint adventurers intended to participate equally in the profits and losses of the common enterprise, irrespective of any inequality in the amounts each contributed to the capital employed in the venture, with the losses being shared by them in the same proportions as they share the profits.

However, it appears that in the cases in which the above stated general rule has been applied, each of the parties had contributed capital consisting of either money or land or other tangible property, or else was to receive compensation for services rendered to the common undertaking which was to be paid before computation of the profits or losses. Where, however, as in the present case, one partner or joint adventurer contributes the money capital as against the other's skill and labor, all the cases cited, and which our research has discovered, hold that neither party is liable to the other for contribution for any loss sustained. Thus, upon loss of the money the party who contributed it is not entitled to recover any part of it from the party who contributed only services. The rationale of this rule, as expressed in *Heran v. Hall* and *Meadows v. Mocquot*, both *supra*, is that where one party contributes money and the other contributes services, then in the event of a loss each would lose his own capital—the one his money and the other his labor. Another view would be that in such a situation the parties have, by their agreement to share equally in profits, agreed that the values of their contributions—the money on the one hand and the labor on the other—were likewise equal; it would follow that upon the loss, as here, of both money and labor, the parties have shared equally in the losses. Actually, of course, plaintiff here lost only some $8,680—or somewhat less than the $10,000 which he originally proposed and agreed to invest.

Plaintiff contended on oral argument before this court that it must be assumed that there was evidence outside the record which would support the trial court's 'finding' (conclusion) of an agreement between the parties to share monetary losses as well as profits. But, this appeal is taken upon a settled statement. Rule 52, Rules on Appeal, provides that "If a record on appeal does not contain all of the papers, records and oral proceedings, . . . it shall be presumed . . . that it includes all matters material to a determination of the points on appeal . . ." Thus, the evidence to support the essential findings and conclusions here must be found in the settled statement or the judgment must fall. Plaintiff's contention is therefore without merit.

It follows that the conclusion of law upon which the judgment in favor of plaintiff for recovery from defendant of one half the monetary losses depends is untenable, and that the judgment should be reversed. Consequently, it is unnecessary to dispose of defendant's further contention that plaintiff could not in any event recover, because the joint venture did not hold or apply for a general contractor's license or any other license, and was thus tainted with illegality.

The judgment is reversed.

———

· **Points for Discussion**

1. RUPA strikes back?

Kovacik v. Reed came after the UPA (1914), but before RUPA (1997). A comment to RUPA § 401 addresses *Kovacik*, noting:

> Subject to contrary agreement and the effect of Section 806(e), this subsection's loss sharing rules apply, even where one or more of the partners contribute no capital. The rule was the same under UPA (1914) § 18(a), although there is some case law to the contrary. *See, e.g., Kovacik v. Reed*, 315 P.2d 314 (Cal. 1957); *Becker v. Killarney*, 523 N.E.2d 467 (Ill. App. Ct. 1988). It may seem unfair that the contributor of services, who contributes little or no capital, should be obligated to contribute toward the capital loss of the large contributor who contributed no services. In entering a partnership with such a capital structure, the partners should foresee that application of the default rule might bring about unusual results and take advantage of their power to vary by agreement the allocation of capital losses.

A small number of cases applying California law have continued to cite *Kovacik v. Reed* for the proposition that in a partnership in which one partner contributed capital and the other services, each party "bears its own losses" and neither party is liable to the other. *See, e.g., David Lee Bradley Productions, Inc. v. Henderson*, 2001 WL 1636834 (Cal. App. 4. Dist. 2001); *Farhang v. Indian Institute of Tech.*, 2020 WL 2228936 (N.D. Cal. 2010).

Can *Kovacik* be reconciled with the RUPA default rule by understanding that courts are implying an agreement between the parties to deem the capital and labor as equal losses? Or is *Kovacik* better thought of as a minority rule or approach, diverging from RUPA, and applying in some states in the context of a "service" partnership like the one in the case?

2. *Which is better?*

In the context of a "service" partnership like the one in this case, what are the advantages of the approach in *Kovacik* compared to a strict application of RUPA's default? What are the disadvantages?

E. Partnership Tax Treatment

As we mentioned at the outset of this chapter, the "pass-through" tax treatment of partnerships is a notable feature of the organizational form. It is worth studying this topic in more detail as it can be an important factor in choice-of-entity decisions.

The key point to observe is that the Internal Revenue Code classifies every business organization as either a partnership or a corporation—with very different tax treatment for each. A partnership is treated as an aggregate of individuals rather than a separate entity. The partnership is not a taxpayer, though partnerships must file an information return so the partners (and the IRS) know how much business income or loss to include on the partners' personal income tax returns. Partnership income and expenses "pass through" (or "flow through") to the partners in proportion to their ownership interests. This applies to partners who participate materially in the partnership's business. An individual partner who does not participate materially in the business can only use partnership losses to offset ordinary income from other sources *after* the partner disposes of his entire interest in the partnership. A corporation, by contrast, is treated as a taxpaying entity separate from its shareholders. The corporation itself pays taxes on business income and the shareholders are also taxed on any dividends they receive—what is known as "double taxation."

So, what counts as a corporation or a partnership for tax purposes? The answer might surprise you. Under so-called "check the box" regulations adopted by the IRS in 1997, every unincorporated entity can choose to be taxed as a partnership. *See* Treas. Reg. § 301.7701. This means that every GP, LLP, LP, LLLP, and LLC is taxed as a partnership, unless its owners elect for the entity to be taxed as a corporation by checking a box. *See* I.R.S. Form 8832.

Corporations are generally subject to business-level tax under IRC Subchapter C (and are commonly referred to as "C Corporations"). There is an exception for certain corporations that elect to be taxed on a pass-through basis under IRC Subchapter S (so-called "S corporations," which we are subject to extensive restrictions such as having no more than 100 shareholders who must be individuals, estates, qualified trusts, or tax-exempt entities).

Why do business planners seek to avoid being taxed as a corporation? The answer: corporations are subject to "double taxation." The corporation pays tax on income it earns. When the corporation distributes a portion of that income to its shareholders as dividends, the shareholders pay income tax on the dividends, with no deduction or other allowance for the tax the corporation has paid. In contrast, a partnership pays no tax. The income from the business is taxed only once—to the partners—whether or not the income is actually distributed. (Note that business planners should pay attention to this potential for tax liability when planning the timing and amount of distributions.)

Consider an example. Suppose Anita and Brandon come to own a partnership (or other unincorporated entity, like an LLC). At the end of each year, the partnership will compute its net income and file an information return. The partnership pays "salaries" to Anita and Brandon and distributes to them some or all of the business net income. The partnership pays no tax on its net income. Anita and Brandon pay taxes, at their respective individual tax rates, on the "salaries" they received plus the net business income, whether or not distributed to them. To determine how much of the business income profit is attributed to each partner, reference is made initially to the partnership agreement. If there is no agreement on this point, the tax rules assume equal partners. And if the partnership operates at a loss, each partner can use his proportionate share of that loss to offset income received from other sources.

Now suppose that Anita and Brandon own the business as a corporation that pays them the same salaries and retains the same amount of net business income. Unlike a partnership, the corporation pays taxes on its net income, after deducting the owners' salaries as a business expense. The owners pay taxes on their salaries but, unlike partners in a partnership, they will not pay taxes on any business income, unless the corporation distributes profits as dividends. Nor can they claim a personal income deduction if the corporation operates at a loss.

Two examples illustrate the costs of corporate "double taxation" compared to a "pass-through" partnership, whether the business is profitable or operates at a loss (both examples use recent tax rates for individuals and corporations). The examples include lots of numbers, but, as we promised in the Introduction, there is drama here as well.

Example A
(business is profitable)

Assume a business with *net income* of $80,000, after Owners pay themselves salaries totaling $70,000. If the business is taxed as a pass-through partnership (no business level tax), Owners must include distributions from the business in their personal income taxes and thus are taxed on $150,000 in total income. If the business is taxed as a corporation, the corporation will incur income tax. If the corporation distributes its profits as dividends, Owners are taxed on their combined salaries and dividends.

	Partnership (000)	Corporation (000)
Business		
Income (loss)	$80	$80
Business tax	$0	$16.8
Distribution to Owners	$80	$62.2
Personal		
Salaries	$70	$70
Distributions from business	$80	$62.2
Taxable income	$150	$132.2
Personal tax*	$11.4	$9.2
TOTAL TAX	**$11.4**	**$26.0**

* assumes Owners received equal salaries and are married, filing jointly.

Thus, owners can reduce their overall tax bill by about $14,600 by using the pass-through partnership as opposed to the double-taxed corporation.

Example B
(business operates at a loss)

Assume a business with *net losses* of $20,000, after Owners pay themselves salaries totaling $70,000. If the business is taxed as a pass-through partnership (no business level tax), Owners deduct the business losses in their individual tax returns and are taxed on $50,000 in income. If the business is taxed as a corporation, the corporation will not incur income tax, but can carry forward its tax losses to offset income in future years (if there is any), but Owners cannot reduce their individual taxable income using the corporate business losses.

	Partnership (000)	Corporation (000)
Business		
Income (loss)	($20)	($20)
Business tax	$0	$0
Personal		
Salaries	$70	$70
Distributions	($20)	$0
Taxable income	$50	$70
Personal tax*	$0.1	$2.1
TOTAL TAX	**$0.1**	**$2.1**

* assumes Owners received equal salaries and are married, filing jointly.

Thus, owners can reduce overall taxes by about $2,000 by using the pass-through partnership. The corporation's carry-forward losses may (or may not) be usable in future years and are unlikely to have a present value of more than $2,000.

F.   Partnership Dissociation and Dissolution

Our last topic on the general partnership form is a challenging one. Articles 6, 7, and 8 of RUPA provide rules concerning two different concepts:

- *Partner dissociation* refers to a change in the relationship of the partners caused by any partner ceasing to be associated in the carrying on of the business. In other words, this happens when a partner leaves the partnership.

- *Partnership dissolution* is the first of three phases (dissolution, winding up, termination) by which a partnership can come to an end.

The UPA used to provide only for the concept of "dissolution," and thus when a partner left a partnership it was automatically deemed a dissolution. This made the general partnership form unstable since it would be dissolved anytime a partner died or left the partnership. RUPA establishes the new concept of "dissociation" to refer to when a partner leaves (voluntarily or involuntarily), and RUPA sets out default rules providing that a dissociation leads to dissolution in some but not all circumstances.

We will study both scenarios—dissociation with and without dissolution. These two scenarios lead to very different outcomes. When dissolution is triggered, unless it is rescinded, the partnership needs to begin winding up its affairs, pay off its debts, and settle the partners' accounts in accordance with RUPA § 806. After this process is completed, the partnership ends. By contrast, when there is a dissociation without triggering dissolution, then a partner leaves the partnership and the partnership continues to operate so long as there are still two or more partners. The dissociated partner is entitled to a buyout of his or her interest.

One more bit of vocabulary is in order before we proceed. There are two types of partnerships regarding their duration: "term" and "at will." A "term" partnership refers to a situation in which the partners have agreed to carry on the partnership for a particular term of time or for the accomplishment of a particular undertaking. If the partners have not so agreed, the partnership is "at will." Whether a partnership is "term" or "at will" can have implications for the consequences of a partner's dissociation under the default rules provided by RUPA.

1.   Dissociation Triggering Dissolution

If any of these circumstances listed in RUPA § 801 occur, then dissolution is triggered:

- In an at-will partnership, any partner who gives notice of his express will to withdraw;

- In a term partnership, if all agree to dissolve or if the term expires;

- In a term partnership if one partner dissociates wrongfully, dissolution occurs if, within 90 days after the dissociation, one-half of the remaining partners agree to wind up the partnership;

- Upon an event agreed to in the partnership agreement resulting in the dissolution and winding up of the partnership business;

- Upon an event that makes it unlawful for all or substantially all of the business of the partnership to be continued;

- Upon application by a partner to a court for an order of judicial dissolution on the grounds that the economic purpose of the partnership is likely to be unreasonably frustrated, another partner has engaged in conduct that makes it not reasonably practicable to carry on business with that partner, or it is otherwise not reasonably practicable to carry on the partnership business in conformity with the partnership agreement;

- Upon the passage of 90 consecutive days during which the partnership does not have at least two partners.

Remember these are default rules and it is possible for partners to agree otherwise. It is indeed common for partnership agreements to provide for buyout and continuation agreements to avoid dissolution in the circumstances listed above. RUPA also includes a provision that enables a partnership to rescind its dissolution. If a partnership rescinds its dissolution, the partnership resumes carrying on its business as if dissolution had never occurred.

One question puzzling legal observers concerns a potential ambiguity in the 2013 amendments to RUPA about rescinding dissolution. Recall that in an at-will partnership any partner may dissociate and thereby trigger dissolution by simply giving notice to the partnership of his will to withdraw. Under § 802(b) of RUPA (1997), rescinding dissolution requires "all of the partners, including any dissociating partner other than a wrongfully dissociating partner." Therefore, under RUPA (1997), if a partner expressed his will to withdraw in an at-will partnership, pursuant to § 801(1), that triggered dissolution and if the partner did not agree to rescind then the dissolution would lead to winding up the business. By contrast, the harmonized language from the 2013 amendment, RUPA § 803, provides that a partnership may "rescind its dissolution" if it receives "the affirmative vote or consent of each partner," and § 102(10) defines the term "partner" as someone who "has not dissociated as a partner under Section 601." Following this line of analysis, does the harmonized version still require the consent of all partners, including the dissociating partner, for rescinding dissolution? Or does it simply require the consent of the remaining partners to rescind dissolution? If it has been changed, does that mean that a dissociating partner in an at-will partnership can no longer express his will to withdraw and force dissolution leading to winding up of the partnership business?

As we have seen with the *Kovacik v. Reed* case above, if a dissociation triggers a dissolution and it is not rescinded, then the partnership must wind up the partnership business. This generally involves the partnership concluding its business, selling its assets, and settling accounts in accordance with RUPA § 806, an excerpt of which is below.

§ 806. Disposition of Assets in Winding Up; When Contributions Required.

(a) In winding up its business, a partnership shall apply its assets, including the contributions required by this section, to discharge the partnership's obligations to creditors, including partners that are creditors.

(b) After a partnership complies with subsection (a), any surplus must be distributed in the following order, subject to any charging order in effect under Section 504:

    (1) to each person owning a transferable interest that reflects contributions made and not previously returned, an amount equal to the value of the unreturned contributions; and

    (2) among persons owning transferable interests in proportion to their respective rights to share in distributions immediately before the dissolution of the partnership.

(c) If a partnership's assets are insufficient to satisfy all its obligations under subsection (a), . . . the following rules apply:

(1) Each person that was a partner when the obligation was incurred and that has not been released from the obligation under Section 703(c) and (d) shall contribute to the partnership for the purpose of enabling the partnership to satisfy the obligation. The contribution due from each of those persons is in proportion to the right to receive distributions in the capacity of a partner in effect for each of those persons when the obligation was incurred.

(2) If a person does not contribute the full amount required under paragraph (1) with respect to an unsatisfied obligation of the partnership, the other persons required to contribute . . . shall contribute the additional amount necessary to discharge the obligation. The additional contribution due from each of those other persons is in proportion to the right to receive distributions in the capacity of a partner in effect for each of those other persons when the obligation was incurred.

(3) If a person does not make the additional contribution required by paragraph (2), further additional contributions are determined and due in the same manner as provided in that paragraph.

(d) A person that makes an additional contribution under subsection (c)(2) or (3) may recover from any person whose failure to contribute under subsection (c)(1) or (2) necessitated the additional contribution. . .

(e) If a partnership does not have sufficient surplus to comply with subsection (b)(1), any surplus must be distributed among the owners of transferable interests in proportion to the value of the respective unreturned contributions.

Once winding up is complete, the partnership terminates. No magic words or filings are required for a general partnership. The partnership may file with the Secretary of State a statement of dissolution stating the name of the partnership and that it is dissolved, or the same regarding termination. Additional details on winding up, the power to bind the partnership after dissolution, and liability after dissolution are in §§ 802–805 of RUPA.

In a term partnership, when a partner withdraws before the end of the term, that partner "wrongfully dissociates." The partner is still entitled to a buyout, but it is minus any damages from the wrongful dissociation and the partner does not have to be paid the buyout amount until the end of the term, unless she goes to court and proves it would not be an undue hardship for the partnership to pay it out earlier.

2.   Dissociation Without Dissolution

Not all circumstances in which a partner withdraws from a partnership leads to dissolution. If the event of dissociation is not listed in RUPA § 801, then the partner leaves the partnership and the partnership continues as the same entity. Some examples include when a partner dies, leaves a term partnership before the end of the term, or is expelled pursuant to a partnership agreement, judicial determination, or a unanimous vote of the other partners in certain circumstances.

The "buyout price" to which the dissociated partner is entitled is defined in § 701(b) as the amount distributable to the partner if, on the date of dissociation, the assets of the partnership were sold using the greater of either the "going concern" value or the "liquidation value" of the partnership. "Going concern" value refers to the value of the business as an operating entity. "Liquidation value" refers to the price one could get by selling all of the assets of the business. The value is therefore determined by imagining hypothetically that the partnership is being sold or liquidated—it is not actually, this is simply a default way of determining a valuation for the partner's buyout price. Interest accrues on the buyout price from the date of dissociation to the date of payment. If no agreement for the buyout has been reached by 120 days after a written demand for the payment, then the partnership must pay the default buyout amount.

If it was a "wrongful dissociation," however, then the damages for that action get taken out of that buyout amount and the payment may be deferred. A wrongful dissociation occurs when a partner leaves a term partnership in breach of a provision of the partnership agreement or before the end of the term or completion of the undertaking that was agreed upon.

What are the other consequences of dissociation? When a partner dissociates, they are no longer a partner in the partnership. Dissociation terminates the departing partner's right to participate in the management of the business and limits their remaining duties and liabilities. A person's dissociation does not by itself discharge the person from an obligation or liability to the partnership or other partners which the person incurred *while* a partner, but, with limited exception, the dissociating partner is no longer personally liable for a partnership obligation or liability that arises *after* their dissociation. An exception exists concerning a dissociating partner's lingering apparent authority and liability. RUPA §§ 702, 703. Also note that a partner's obligation to safeguard confidential or proprietary information continues post-dissociation. Although the dissociated partner remains personally liable for pre-dissociation debts, the dissociated partner has the right to seek indemnification from the partnership, and ultimately from the partners, for any claims made against the dissociated partner after the buyout. Additional details on the consequences of dissociation are in §§ 603 and 701–704 of RUPA.

Finally, you may have noticed that most events of dissociation and dissolution do not require courts for resolution, but RUPA does contain provisions that allow partners to seek a judicial determination to dissolve the partnership or expel a partner. What kind of conduct might constitute grounds for such an action? The following case provides an example.

Giles v. Giles Land Co.

279 P.3d 139 (Kan. Ct. App. 2012)

GREEN, J.

Kelly Giles (Kelly), a general partner in a family farming partnership, filed suit against the partnership and his partners, arguing that he had not been provided access to partnership books and records. The remaining members of the partnership then filed a counterclaim requesting that Kelly be dissociated from the partnership. The trial court held that Kelly was not denied access to the partnership books and records. Kelly does not appeal from this decision. Moreover, the trial court held that Kelly should be dissociated from the partnership. Kelly, however, contends that the trial court's ruling regarding his dissociation from the partnership was improper. We disagree. Accordingly, we affirm.

The dispute in this case centers on a family owned and operated limited partnership, Giles Land Company, L.P. (partnership). On one side is the plaintiff, Kelly, the second youngest of seven children in the Giles family. On the other side are the defendants: the partnership; Norman Lee Giles and Dolores Giles, the mother and father of the seven children involved; and Kelly's six siblings: Norman Roger Giles (Roger), Lorie Giles Horacek, Trudy Giles Giard, Audry Giles Gates, Jody Giles Peintner, and Julie Giles Cox. Kelly appeals from the trial court's judgment granting the counterclaim filed by the defendants, which included Norman and Dolores Giles along with their six other children, seeking the dissociation of Kelly from the partnership, under K.S.A. 56a–601.

The record reveals the following facts. The partnership was formed in the mid-1990's. One-half of the assets in the partnership came from a trust held for the benefit of the children of Norman and Dolores, and the other half of the assets came from Norman. Over the years, Norman and Dolores transferred interests in the partnership to their children. The ownership in the partnership is as follows:

	General Partnership Interest	Limited Partnership Interest
Norman Lee Giles	4.634500	03.3357145
Dolores N. Giles	4.634500	03.3357145
Trudy Giles Giard		12.857143
Norman Roger Giles	.243667	12.857143
Audry Giles Gates		12.857143
Jody Giles Peintner		12.857143
Lorie Giles Horacek	.243666	12.857143
Kelly K. Giles	.243667	06.185714
Julie Giles Cox		12.857143
Totals:	10.00%	90.00%

The partnership owns both ranchland and farmland. This partnership is not the only Giles family business; there is also Giles Ranch Company and H.G. Land and Cattle Company. In 1999, Kelly was a partner in the Giles Ranch Company, but he became so overwhelmed with the debt he had incurred in the operations of the ranch company that he insisted that he be bought out of the ranch company and relieved of all debt. The other partners managed to buy out Kelly's interest in the ranch company. At the time of the lawsuit, Kelly only had an ownership interest in the partnership at issue, i.e., Giles Land Company.

On March 26, 2007, the partnership held a meeting to discuss converting the partnership into a limited liability company. Kelly was unable to attend the meeting, but he later received a letter explaining the family's interest in converting the partnership to a limited liability company. Kelly did not sign the articles of organization for the proposed conversion and instead had his attorney request production of all of the partnership's books and records for his review. Kelly was not satisfied with the records that the partnership had provided, so he filed suit asking the court to force the partnership to turn over all of the documents he was requesting. In response, the defendants filed an answer and a counterclaim seeking to dissociate Kelly from the partnership.

After a 2-day trial, the trial court determined that the partnership had properly complied with the document requests. The trial court also held that Kelly should be dissociated from the partnership under K.S.A. 56a–601(e)(3) or, in the alternative, K.S.A. 56a–601(e)(1). The trial court found that due to Kelly's threats and the total distrust between Kelly and his family, it was not practicable to carry on the business of the partnership so long as Kelly was a partner.

Did the Trial Court Err in Finding that Kelly Should Be Dissociated from the Partnership?

On appeal, Kelly argues that the trial court erred in finding that he should be dissociated from the partnership under K.S.A. 56a–601(e)(3) or, alternatively, K.S.A. 56a–601(e)(1). K.S.A. 56a–601 states the following: "A partner is dissociated from a partnership upon the occurrence of any of the following events:. . . .(e) on application by the partnership or another partner, the partner's expulsion by judicial determination because: (1) The partner engaged in wrongful conduct that adversely and materially affected the partnership business; . . . . (3) the partner engaged in conduct relating to the partnership business which makes it not reasonably practicable to carry on the business in partnership with the partner."

The trial court relied primarily on K.S.A. 56a–601(e)(3) to dissociate Kelly; therefore, the record must demonstrate that (1) Kelly engaged in conduct relating to the partnership business and (2) such conduct makes it not reasonably practicable to carry on the business in partnership with Kelly.

Kansas' partnership statutes were dramatically changed on the enactment of the Kansas Revised Uniform Partnership Act in 1998, K.S.A. 56a–101 et seq. These changes brought about the concept of dissociation, which previously did not formally exist in our law. Thus, it is not surprising that our research has revealed no Kansas cases and very few cases from other jurisdictions that have discussed and applied the dissociation provisions of the Uniform Partnership Act 1997 (UPA). The statutory dissociation language in K.S.A. 56a–601(e) is very similar to the dissolution provisions set out in K.S.A. 56a–801(e). The comment to § 601 of the UPA, which is the source of K.S.A. 56a–601(e), confirms that the dissociation provisions were based on the preexisting grounds for dissolution under the UPA. Consequently, caselaw addressing the analogous UPA dissolution provisions is probative in analyzing the defendants' dissociation claim.

First, the trial court found that Kelly did not trust the other general partners and that he did not trust some of his sisters who are limited partners in the partnership. The trial court also found that the general partners as well as all of the other partners did not trust Kelly.

The trial court further found that the relationship between Kelly and the other family members was irreparably broken. In reaching that conclusion, the trial court focused on a meeting between the partners in 2006. Kelly turned to each of the general partners and said that they would each die, in turn, and that he would be the last man standing and that he would then get to control the partnership. Although Kelly testified that this was not a threat and that he was simply trying to explain the right of survivorship, the trial court believed the testimony of the rest of the family that it was taken as a threat. The trial court also relied on evidence that Kelly had said that "paybacks are hell" and that he intended to get even with his partners. The trial court also found this to be a threat. Another fact that the trial court relied on in finding that the family relationship was irreparably broken was that it was impossible for any of the family members to communicate with Kelly regarding the partnership. Each family member testified that he or she believed that it was in the best interest of the partnership to not have Kelly remain a partner.

Additionally, to support its argument that the trial court correctly applied K.S.A. 56a–601(e)(3), the defendants direct this court to consider *Brennan v. Brennan Associates*, 293 Conn. 60, 977 A.2d 107 (2009). The *Brennan* court applied a totality of the circumstances approach in finding that the alleged misconduct was related to the partnership. The court explained that a 17-year-old conviction involving an unrelated enterprise likely would not meet the broad definition of related to, but when that evidence is combined with the other issues between the partners, the court found that dissociation was proper. The *Brennan* court held that "an irreparable deterioration of a relationship between partners is a valid basis to order dissolution, and, therefore, is a valid basis for the alternative remedy of dissociation."

Here, like in *Brennan*, Kelly argues that the evidence that the trial court relied on was not related to the partnership business. Reviewing the record as a whole, it is clear that the trial court found the evidence to be related to the partnership business because this was a family partnership and all of the alleged disputes were between family members in that partnership. It is also telling that both of the parents and all of the other siblings joined in this lawsuit seeking Kelly's dissociation. Clearly, the relationship between Kelly and his family was broken, and although Kelly attempted to argue that their personal issues were not interfering with the partnership, the trial court did not find his testimony to be credible.

In light of the animosity that Kelly harbors toward his partners and his distrust of them (which distrust is mutual), it is clear that Kelly can no longer do business with his partners and vice-versa. Indeed, the partnership has reached an impasse regarding important business because of a lack of communication between Kelly and his partners. The evidence indicated that most communications with Kelly had to be conducted through his attorney. Moreover, Kelly's statement predicting the deaths of his general partners, his statement that "paybacks are hell," and his statement that he would get even showed a naked ambition on his part to control the partnership, contrary to the interests of the other partners.

Alternative Theory for Dissociation

The trial court also found that there was enough evidence to dissociate Kelly under K.S.A. 56a–601(e)(1). In applying the alternative theory of dissociation, the trial court held the following: "In addition, Kelly Giles' conduct toward the General Partners who own the largest General Partnership interests by far, his parents, would also constitute wrongful conduct that materially affected the partnership business under 56a–601(e)(1), and the Court so finds."

As stated earlier, the *Brennan* court held that "an irreparable deterioration of a relationship between partners is a valid basis to order dissolution, and, therefore, is a valid basis for the alternative remedy of dissociation." To support this conclusion, the Brennan court noted that one of the grounds for dissolution was identical to one of the grounds for dissociation, namely, that another partner has engaged in conduct relating to the partnership which makes it not reasonably practicable to carry on the business in partnership with that partner. The court further held that the grounds for dissociation do not need to be construed more strictly than the grounds for dissolution.

Like in the previously cited case of *Ferrick v. Barry*, 320 Mass. 217, 68 N.E.2d 690 (1946), Kelly had created a situation where the partnership could no longer carry on its business to the mutual advantage of the other partners. For example, Lorie testified that Kelly would berate and belittle Norman in an attempt to make Norman do what Kelly wanted. There was also testimony given by John Horacek, Lorie's husband, that in a phone conversation between Kelly and Norman, Kelly yelled and cursed at his father and his father was in tears by the end of the conversation. Norman further testified that it would be better for everyone if Kelly were no longer in the partnership because it was clear that Kelly did not agree with what the other partners were wanting to do with the future of the partnership. Norman testified: " 'Cause I think the route we're on now, Judge, if we continue on this, and we don't—we're just at a standstill on what we plan to do." There was also evidence that Kelly had frustrated the partnership's opportunities to purchase more land. Kelly is clearly not cooperating with the other partners and the distrust between Kelly and his partners runs both ways. Thus, even though there is no evidence that Kelly has been dishonest, and even though the partnership has continued to be successful, this does not mean that the other partners should be forced to remain in partnership with an uncooperative and distrustful partner.

Because this is a family partnership, the evidence of Kelly making threats or berating his parents to get them to give him what he wants qualifies as wrongful conduct. None of the partners were able to interact or communicate with Kelly. Additionally, Norman clearly testified that the partnership was at a standstill because of the disputes between Kelly and the rest of the partners. This is evidence that Kelly was materially or adversely affecting the partnership. Moreover, this evidence is clearly enough to support dissolution based on the caselaw listed earlier; therefore, it is also sufficient for dissociation. Based on this evidence, we determine that the trial court properly held that Kelly could also be dissociated under K.S.A. 56a–601(e)(1).

Affirmed.

Points for Discussion

1. Dissociation or dissolution?

The members of the partnership besides Kelly Giles had sought a judicial determination that Kelly be dissociated from the partnership. The court noted that there was sufficient evidence to support dissociation or dissolution. What had Kelly done to materially affect the partnership business or make it not reasonably practicable to carry on business in partnership with him? Why might expulsion of Kelly by dissociation be preferable to dissolution?

2. Planning; power vs. right.

As we conclude our discussion of general partnerships, you might recall that RUPA is mostly a set of default rules that will apply where the partners have not agreed otherwise. What sorts of provisions might a partnership want to customize with regard to exit rights of dissociation? Why might a partnership choose a term? In addition, there are certain provisions in RUPA pertaining to dissociation, expulsion, and dissolution that cannot be varied. Why do you think this is so? Why does a partner always have the "power" but not necessarily the "right" to dissociate?

———

G. Other Partnership Forms (LPs, LLPs, LLLPs)

A key characteristic of the general partnership is that the partners are subject to personal liability for the debts and obligations of the partnership. Other partnership forms have developed to provide a form of limited liability for some or all of the partners. Each of these partnership forms requires filing a certificate with the secretary of state in the jurisdiction chosen by the parties in order to accomplish formation (and if this is not done or not done correctly, the parties may have inadvertently formed a general partnership). To understand these other partnership forms, it is helpful to know about their history and typical uses, as well as their defining characteristics.

1. Limited Partnerships (LPs)

A limited partnership is a partnership composed of one or more general partners and one or more limited partners. You can think of the limited partners as silent partners who do not participate in the management of the business—they invest money in return for transferable interests in the partnership. Because the limited partners do not control how the business is run, the law provides that their liability is limited to the amount of their investment. As noted above, forming a limited partnership requires filing a certificate of limited partnership with the secretary of state in the jurisdiction chosen by the parties.

The defining characteristics are:

- Separation of ownership and management functions. Under statutory default norms, the limited partners are passive investors with essentially no day-to-day management power and no authority to act as agents for the business. General partners are the active managers, empowered to carry out the limited partnership's business. Because of their management role, only the general partners owe fiduciary duties of care and loyalty to the partnership.

- Limited liability. The limited partners are not personally liable for the obligations of the limited partnership. General partners are jointly and severally liable for the limited partnership's obligations.

The LP form of business organization developed in part as a matter of historical circumstance. Before the mid-nineteenth century, states required a special act of the legislature in order to get a charter for a corporation (and in turn, at least a measure of limited liability for shareholders). As a result, before the mid-nineteenth century, corporate charters were often difficult or expensive to obtain. In 1822, New York became the first state to enact a limited partnership act, which served some of the same purposes as incorporation—allowing for a form of passive investment to be done in the business organization and to provide limited liability for that role. Put differently, the LP form was desirable because it helped solve the economic problem of how to finance a business that required significant capital from a large number of individuals. Giving management rights to a large number of partners could be unwieldy for running the business and investors worried about putting all of their personal assets at risk, as they would have to do as a general partner in a partnership. The LP solved the problem by allowing for one or a small group of general partners to manage the enterprise and for a large number of limited partners to invest without risking more than the amount invested.

The LP form spread across states and the Uniform Limited Partnership Act (ULPA) was first adopted in 1916. The Revised Uniform Limited Partnership Act (RULPA) was updated in 2001.

RULPA differs in some ways from RUPA, the uniform partnership act. For example, RULPA §§ 503 and 504 provide that absent a partnership agreement otherwise, profits and losses in a limited partnership are allocated and distributed in proportion to "the value . . . of contributions made by each partner and to the extent they have been received by the partnership and have not been returned."

A frequently litigated question regarding LPs, at least historically, was whether a limited partner had exercised control in the business, thereby subjecting herself to liability as a general partner (i.e., unlimited personal liability for partnership debts). Amendments to ULPA have liberalized the "control" rule, broadening the ability of limited partners to engage in voting oversight and some management of the business, thus narrowing the instances in which limited partners can be held personally liable.

Another development regarding LP law has been to allow the general partner to be a corporation. This allows the "general partner" to enjoy limited liability.

At this point, you might wonder why anyone would use the LP form anymore, since other forms like the corporation and LLC have become readily available. Indeed, the LP is used in somewhat limited settings in current times.

First, it is used in certain sophisticated business settings in which the parties want a customizable form for limited investments. A key example is in the venture capital setting in which a firm seeks to raise a large amount of money to invest in start-up companies, and the investment capital typically comes as investment opportunities arise. The LP form allows for making the investors' ownership interests "assessable," so that they can be made to forfeit their ownership interest if they do not contribute on demand to cover the need for additional investment capital.

Second, the LP form is sometimes used as an estate planning device. For example, parents might form a LP with the family business and serve as general partners. Over time, they might give portions of their limited partnership interests to their children. Because of the restrictions on transfer and management power that might come with those limited partnership interests, the value is often discounted, and the parents can transfer family wealth to future generations while maintaining control of the business and reducing tax costs.

In both of these settings, the general partner of the limited partnership can be a corporation or an LLC. The general partner is jointly and severally liable for the limited partnership's obligations but using a limited liability entity as the general partner can reduce the exposure to liability for that party.

2. Limited Liability Partnerships (LLPs) and Limited Liability Limited Partnerships (LLLPs)

LLPs are general partnerships that have made an election to be treated as limited liability partnerships (LLPs) and file a form with the secretary of state. The effect is to shield the partners from personal liability for all partnership debts. Partners remain liable for their own actions as partners, but when they are part of an LLP, they are shielded from being held personally liable for their partners' actions. For example, a partner in a law firm structured as an LLP remains liable for her own malpractice, and the partnership itself can be held liable for such malpractice, but the other partners cannot be held personally liable for any shortfall. The same liability shield is provided to general partners in an LP that elects to become a limited liability limited partnership (LLLP).

The partnership forms developed in the law before the limited liability company (LLC), which we will study in Chapter 4. LLPs are somewhat less commonly used now that the LLC form has become available, but some states have limitations on certain professional business firms (such as law firms and accounting firms) using the LLC form and so if they still want limited liability, they turn to the LLP form.

CHAPTER 4

LLC Basics

Now that we've covered the basics of agency and partnership, we are ready to start discussing the forms of business organization that are most common today. One of those is the limited liability company, or LLC. When people are starting a business, they often choose to set up an LLC. Note that the "LL" part of LLC stands for limited liability, just as it did for LLPs in the previous chapter. Limited liability is a key motivation for choosing the LLC. The basic idea is that the personal assets of the people who invest money in the LLC are protected. With limited exceptions, they cannot be liable beyond their investment.

There are some advantages to discussing LLCs before we get to corporations. The class you are taking is, in many ways, a vocabulary class, and LLCs introduce many of the most important vocabulary terms. We have found that students often benefit from seeing these terms several times, in different contexts. LLCs are a good opportunity for us to start using our new vocabulary, in the same way you might have experienced during the early weeks of a language class. If this material is new to you, don't worry: we will revisit these concepts several times in later chapters.

The first thing to know about LLCs is that they are created under state statutes that combine certain aspects of corporation and partnership law. That is why they are sometimes labeled a "hybrid," even though an LLC is its own form of business entity and is not a species of corporation. The "C" in "LLC" stands for company not corporation. To form an LLC, you prepare and file a short document (often one page) called the "articles of organization" with the relevant state agency (often called the "Secretary of State").

In addition, the LLC is required to have an "operating agreement," which sets forth details about how the LLC will be operated. These details include the purpose of the LLC, the rights and duties of managers, the rights and obligations of members, provisions for meetings of members, and contributions of "capital" (meaning investment).

In contrast, the vocabulary for corporations is different. Corporations are required to file a document with the relevant state agency, but it is called a "certificate of incorporation" or "articles of incorporation." Although this document often is relatively simple, at least when a corporation is first formed, it can include more complex terms. Instead of the LLC's "operating agreement," corporations have "bylaws," which specify the details about how the corporation will be operated. The table below includes the basic vocabulary for the partnership, corporation, and LLC.

Basic Vocabulary

	Partnership	**Corporation**	**LLC**
Required document for formation	None	Certificate of incorporation (aka articles of incorporation or charter)	Articles of organization (aka certificate of organization or formation)
Other key organizational documents	Partnership agreement	Bylaws	Operating agreement (aka LLC agreement)
Participants holding a financial interest	Partners	Shareholders (aka stockholders)	Members

Each of the above forms of business organization has a different approach to the agency issues we covered in Chapter 2, including fiduciary duties and other rights, duties, and obligations. In general, you can think about the rights of investors in any business entity as falling into four categories: vote, sue, sell, and "yell." What voting rights do investors have? When and whom can they sue? When and how can they transfer their investments? And do they have any other rights to express their views about the business? These questions become important as the number investors increases.

Although the LLC is a legal entity, it needs human beings (at least one person) to engage in business. For LLCs, agency questions can arise because of the distinction between "managers" (the people who manage the business of the LLC) and "members" (the people who invest in the LLC). For a one-member LLC, the answers to agency questions are usually straightforward, because that member can also be the sole manager. But the answers become more complicated as more people become involved in the business. Some LLCs are "member-managed"; others are "manager-managed." The LLC operating agreement is designed to anticipate and answer questions that might arise as the LLC conducts its business.

One of the most distinctive aspects of the LLC form is that it allows for pass-through taxation like a partnership and limited liability like a corporation. As we discussed in Chapter 3, pass-through taxation is often desirable because it allows business losses to "pass-through" and serve as deductions on personal tax returns and it avoids the "double taxation" that occurs in the corporate context where the business entity itself is taxed and the shareholders are also taxed on any dividends they receive. And limited liability is desirable for investors to shield themselves from personal liability for the obligations of the business.

Another defining characteristic of LLC law is its strong focus on contractual freedom to structure the company's internal governance by agreement. Depending on the state, LLC law can be highly flexible, allowing for customization of LLCs even beyond that allowed for partnerships and corporations. For example, one particularly controversial topic has been whether LLCs should be allowed under state law to eliminate fiduciary duties owed by LLC managers by including a waiver provision in the operating agreement. More generally, the qualities of freedom and flexibility in the LLC form are evidenced by the choice that LLC law gives to planners to choose either a partnership or corporation-like allocation of management functions.

In short, the LLC is a distinctive, highly contractual form of business organization that has some characteristics similar to partnerships, some similar to corporations, and some that are unique to LLCs. In this chapter, we will examine the key characteristics of LLCs and the developing law on this form of business enterprise.

A. History

To understand LLC law, it helps to know a bit about history. The LLC form of business organization originated in Wyoming in the late 1970s. Oil and gas companies, important to the state economy, pushed for a form of business that would allow for pass-through taxation like a partnership, and also for limited liability, to shield the investors from business risk. Before LLCs were developed, the only options that would accomplish these basic goals were limited partnerships, which required at least one general partner to be subject to liability for the partnership obligations, and corporations qualifying for subchapter S status under IRS rules that are subject to certain constraints that limit their flexibility and utility.

The Wyoming legislature aimed to attract investors in its state oil and gas production and to make it easier to organize investment entities for this purpose. It designed its LLC Act around IRS rulings at the time, referred to as the "Kintner rules," which provided that an entity would be taxed as a corporation if it possessed a certain number of corporate-like characteristics (perpetual life, transferable ownership interests, limited liability, centralized management). The Wyoming LLC Act provided for limited liability, but in many other ways provided for characteristics resembling partnerships, with the aim of receiving partnership status for pass-through taxation purposes.

A decade after Wyoming passed its LLC Act, the IRS issued a ruling confirming that a Wyoming LLC would be taxed as a partnership despite the entity's corporate-like limited liability. Subsequently, states around the country started to pass their own LLC acts. Many of the early statutes were similarly based on the IRS ruling and thus were designed to have many partnership-like characteristics in order to receive pass-through taxation.

In 1997, the IRS implemented new rules, the so-called "check-the-box" regulations, which allow unincorporated business entities to choose whether they want to be taxed as a corporation or a partnership. Without the previous constraint of the more rigid Kintner rules, many states thereafter began to revise their LLC acts to allow for greater organizational flexibility.

B.   Sources of Law

All U.S. states and the District of Columbia have adopted LLC statutes, but there is significant variation among the states on their LLC laws. One reason for this variation is because states developed their LLC statutes in response to changing IRS tax rulings over time, and because many states had already passed an LLC act before a uniform act was drafted.

The first Uniform Limited Liability Company Act was promulgated in 1996, revised in 2006, and again in 2011 and 2013, through amendments enacted as part of the Harmonization of Business Entity Acts project carried out by the National Conference of Commissioners on Uniform State Laws. This uniform LLC statute, as amended, is referred to as the Revised Uniform Limited Liability Company Act ("Re-ULLCA" or "RULLCA"). More than twenty states have adopted RULLCA.

Another influential LLC statute is the Delaware Limited Liability Company Act ("DLLCA"). Most businesses that choose to organize as an LLC select either their home state where the business is primarily operated or Delaware. The internal affairs doctrine applies and thus choosing the state of formation is a choice of law.

Because the LLC is of relatively recent vintage, the body of LLC case law is developing but not nearly as extensive as older business forms such as partnerships and corporations. Further, because of the emphasis on the contractual nature of the LLC, the operating agreement often predominates analysis, to the extent it does not conflict with mandatory statutory provisions.

This chapter focuses on general principles—to the extent widely varying LLC statutes can be summarized—as well as on the influential uniform act and the Delaware statute.

C.   Formation

As noted above, an LLC is formed by filing articles of organization with the designated state office, usually the Secretary of State. Most LLC statutes require a relatively minimal amount of information to be included in the articles of organization—typically the name of the LLC (which must include an indication that it is an LLC), the address of its principal place of business or its registered office, and the name and address of its agent for service of process. Many LLC statutes require the articles to additionally state information such as the name of a member or manager, the purpose of the LLC (which can be broadly stated as any lawful act or activity for an LLC), and whether it is to be manager-managed or member-managed. Most LLC statutes allow the use of the LLC entity form for for-profit businesses as well as for charitable non-profit activities. For example, RULLCA 104(b) provides that an LLC "may have any lawful purpose regardless of whether for profit."

In most LLCs, the articles of organization are typically a bare bones document that is simply a requirement for formation and instead the critical document setting out the internal governance is the operating agreement. The LLC form of business organization is highly flexible and "private ordering" is expected—those choices are usually put in the operating agreement.

The principle of contractual freedom and the centrality of the operating agreement is captured in LLC statutes. For example, DLLCA § 18–1101(b) provides: "It is the policy of this chapter to give the maximum effect to the principle of freedom of contract and to the enforceability of limited liability company agreements." Likewise, the prefatory note to RULLCA states: "Like the partnership agreement in a general or limited partnership, an LLC's operating agreement serves as the foundational contract among the entity's owners."

LLC statutes allow for operating agreements to select the company's governance rules, except as to a few matters that are provided as mandatory. For example, RULLCA § 105(c) provides a list of mandatory provisions of LLC law. Under this section, the operating agreement may not:

- vary the choice of law that applies under the internal affairs doctrine;

- vary the LLC's capacity to sue and be sued;

- vary any statutory provision pertaining to registered agents or records authorized or required to be filed with the Secretary of State;

- alter or eliminate the duty of loyalty or the duty of care, except as provided (and discussed below in the section on fiduciary duties);

- eliminate the contractual obligation of good faith and fair dealing, but the operating agreement may prescribe the standards, if not manifestly unreasonable, by which the performance of the obligation is to be measured;

- relieve or exonerate a person from liability for conduct involving bad faith, willful or intentional misconduct, or knowing violation of law;

- unreasonably restrict the rights to information of members and managers provided for under the statute, but the operating agreement may impose reasonable restrictions and may define appropriate remedies, including liquidated damages, for a breach of any reasonable restriction on use;

- vary certain statutory provisions concerning dissolution and winding up of the company;

- unreasonably restrict the statutory rights of a member to maintain a direct or derivative action;

- vary the statutory provisions concerning a special litigation committee, but the operating agreement may provide that the company may not have a special litigation committee;

- vary certain rights and requirements pertaining to mergers;

- restrict the rights of a person other than a member or manager.

Some of the vocabulary in the above statutory language might be unfamiliar. We will see many of these terms throughout this course, including in the next module. The "internal affairs doctrine" provides that "internal affairs" of a business are governed by the state where the LLC articles of organization are filed. The "duty of loyalty" and "duty of care" are two of the fiduciary duties that LLC managers can owe to members. A "derivative action" is an equitable lawsuit by a member on behalf of the LLC, essentially seeking to hold fiduciaries accountable or persuade the managers of the LLC to sue third parties. Derivative actions can be counterintuitive and challenging, and we will encounter them in several contexts in future chapters.

The other provisions of RULLCA are not mandatory. They are instead statutory default rules that may be contracted around in the operating agreement. Other LLC statutes follow a similar structure of listing certain mandatory provisions and otherwise allowing operating agreements significant contractual freedom and flexibility.

Statutes vary regarding whether the operating agreement must be in writing. RULLCA, for example, provides that it can be "oral, implied, in a record, or in any combination thereof." § 102(13). Similarly, Delaware's act provides that the operating agreement (whether referred to by such term or the "LLC agreement" or otherwise) means any agreement "written, oral or implied, of the member or members as to the affairs of a limited liability company and the conduct of its business." DLLCA § 18–101(9).

Most statutes, including RULLCA and the Delaware act, provide a default rule requiring unanimous member approval for amendments to operating agreements. This means, for example, that after formation of the LLC, it requires the unanimous consent of the members to admit another member to the company.

The following excerpt comes from a well-known decision of the Supreme Court of Delaware that demonstrates the central importance of the operating agreement in defining the rights and obligations of the participants in the LLC.

Elf Atochem North America, Inc. v. Jaffari

<u>727 A.2d 286 (Del. 1999)</u>

VEASEY, CHIEF JUSTICE.

This is a case of first impression before this Court involving the Delaware Limited Liability Company Act (the "Act"). The wording and architecture of the Act is somewhat complicated, but it is designed to achieve what is seemingly a simple concept—to permit persons or entities ("members") to join together in an environment of private ordering to form and operate the enterprise under an LLC agreement with tax benefits akin to a partnership and limited liability akin to the corporate form.

This is a purported derivative suit brought on behalf of a Delaware LLC calling into question whether: (1) the LLC, which did not itself execute the LLC agreement in this case ("the Agreement") defining its governance and operation, is nevertheless bound by the Agreement; and (2) contractual provisions directing that all disputes be resolved exclusively by arbitration or court proceedings in California are valid under the Act. Resolution of these issues requires us to examine the applicability and scope of certain provisions of the Act in light of the Agreement.

We hold that: (1) the Agreement is binding on the LLC as well as the members; and (2) since the Act does not prohibit the members of an LLC from vesting exclusive subject matter jurisdiction in arbitration proceedings (or court enforcement of arbitration) in California to resolve disputes, the contractual forum selection provisions must govern.

Facts

Plaintiff below-appellant Elf Atochem North America, Inc., a Pennsylvania Corporation ("Elf"), manufactures and distributes solvent-based maskants to the aerospace and aviation industries throughout the world. Defendant below-appellee Cyrus A. Jaffari is the president of Malek, Inc., a California Corporation. Jaffari had developed an innovative, environmentally-friendly alternative to the solvent-based maskants that presently dominate the market.

In the mid-nineties, Elf approached Jaffari and proposed investing in his product and assisting in its marketing. Jaffari found the proposal attractive since his company, Malek, Inc., possessed limited resources and little international sales expertise. Elf and Jaffari agreed to undertake a joint venture that was to be carried out using a limited liability company as the vehicle.

On October 29, 1996, Malek, Inc. caused to be filed a Certificate of Formation with the Delaware Secretary of State, thus forming Malek LLC, a Delaware limited liability company under the Act. The certificate of formation is a relatively brief and formal document that is the first statutory step in creating the LLC as a separate legal entity. The certificate does not contain a comprehensive agreement among the parties, and the statute contemplates that the certificate of formation is to be complemented by the terms of the Agreement.

Next, Elf, Jaffari and Malek, Inc. entered into a series of agreements providing for the governance and operation of the joint venture. Of particular importance to this litigation, Elf, Malek, Inc., and Jaffari entered into the Agreement, a comprehensive and integrated document of 38 single-spaced pages setting forth detailed provisions for the governance of Malek LLC, which is not itself a signatory to the Agreement. Elf and Malek LLC entered into an Exclusive Distributorship Agreement in which Elf would be the exclusive, worldwide distributor for Malek LLC. The Agreement provides that Jaffari will be the manager of Malek LLC. Jaffari and Malek LLC entered into an employment agreement providing for Jaffari's employment as chief executive officer of Malek LLC.

The Agreement is the operative document for purposes of this Opinion, however. Under the Agreement, Elf contributed $1 million in exchange for a 30 percent interest in Malek LLC. Malek, Inc. contributed its rights to the water-based maskant in exchange for a 70 percent interest in Malek LLC.

The Agreement contains an arbitration clause covering all disputes. The clause, Section 13.8, provides that "any controversy or dispute arising out of this Agreement, the interpretation of any of the provisions hereof, or the action or inaction of any Member or Manager hereunder shall be submitted to arbitration in San Francisco, California. . . ." Section 13.8 further provides: "No action . . . based upon any claim arising out of or related to this Agreement shall be instituted in any court by any Member except (a) an action to compel arbitration . . . or (b) an action to enforce an award obtained in an arbitration proceeding. . . ." The Agreement also contains a forum selection clause, Section 13.7, providing that all members consent to: "exclusive jurisdiction of the state and federal courts sitting in California in any action on a claim arising out of, under or in connection with this Agreement or the transactions contemplated by this Agreement, provided such claim is not required to be arbitrated pursuant to Section 13.8"; and personal jurisdiction in California.

Elf's Suit in the Court of Chancery

On April 27, 1998, Elf sued Jaffari and Malek LLC, individually and derivatively on behalf of Malek LLC, in the Delaware Court of Chancery, seeking equitable remedies. Among other claims, Elf alleged that Jaffari breached his fiduciary duty to Malek LLC, pushed Malek LLC to the brink of insolvency by withdrawing funds for personal use, interfered with business opportunities, failed to make disclosures to Elf, and threatened to make poor quality maskant and to violate environmental regulations.

The Court of Chancery granted defendants' motion to dismiss based on lack of subject matter jurisdiction. The court held that Elf's claims arose under the

Agreement, or the transactions contemplated by the agreement, and were directly related to Jaffari's actions as manager of Malek LLC. Therefore, the court found that the Agreement governed the question of jurisdiction and that only a court of law or arbitrator in California is empowered to decide these claims. Elf now appeals the order of the Court of Chancery dismissing the complaint.

General Summary of Background of the Act

The Delaware Act was adopted in October 1992. The Act is codified in Chapter 18 of Title 6 of the Delaware Code. To date, the Act has been amended six times with a view to modernization. The LLC is an attractive form of business entity because it combines corporate-type limited liability with partnership-type flexibility and tax advantages. The Act can be characterized as a "flexible statute" because it generally permits members to engage in private ordering with substantial freedom of contract to govern their relationship, provided they do not contravene any mandatory provisions of the Act. Indeed, the LLC has been characterized as the "best of both worlds."

Policy of the Delaware Act

The basic approach of the Delaware Act is to provide members with broad discretion in drafting the Agreement and to furnish default provisions when the members' agreement is silent. The Act is replete with fundamental provisions made subject to modification in the Agreement (e.g. "unless otherwise provided in a limited liability company agreement. . . .").

Although business planners may find comfort in working with the Act in structuring transactions and relationships, it is a somewhat awkward document for this Court to construe and apply in this case. To understand the overall structure and thrust of the Act, one must wade through provisions that are prolix, sometimes oddly organized, and do not always flow evenly. Be that as it may as a problem in mastering the Act as a whole, one returns to the narrow and discrete issues presented in this case.

Freedom of Contract

Section 18–1101(b) of the Act, like the essentially identical Section 17–1101(c) of the LP Act, provides that "[i]t is the policy of [the Act] to give the maximum effect to the principle of freedom of contract and to the enforceability of limited liability company agreements." Accordingly, the following observation relating to limited partnerships applies as well to limited liability companies:

> The Act's basic approach is to permit partners to have the broadest possible discretion in drafting their partnership agreements and to furnish answers only in situations where the partners have not expressly made provisions in their partnership agreement. Truly, the partnership agreement is the cornerstone of a Delaware limited partnership, and effectively constitutes the entire agreement among the partners with respect to the admission of partners to, and the creation, operation and termination of, the limited

partnership. Once partners exercise their contractual freedom in their partnership agreement, the partners have a great deal of certainty that their partnership agreement will be enforced in accordance with its terms.

In general, the commentators observe that only where the agreement is inconsistent with mandatory statutory provisions will the members' agreement be invalidated. Such statutory provisions are likely to be those intended to protect third parties, not necessarily the contracting members. As a framework for decision, we apply that principle to the issues before us, without expressing any views more broadly.

The Arbitration and Forum Selection Clauses in the Agreement are a Bar to Jurisdiction in the Court of Chancery

In vesting the Court of Chancery with jurisdiction, the Act accomplished at least three purposes: (1) it assured that the Court of Chancery has jurisdiction it might not otherwise have because it is a court of limited jurisdiction that requires traditional equitable relief or specific legislation to act; (2) it established the Court of Chancery as the default forum in the event the members did not provide another choice of forum or dispute resolution mechanism; and (3) it tends to center interpretive litigation in Delaware courts with the expectation of uniformity. Nevertheless, the arbitration provision of the Agreement in this case fosters the Delaware policy favoring alternate dispute resolution mechanisms, including arbitration. Such mechanisms are an important goal of Delaware legislation, court rules, and jurisprudence.

Malek LLC's Failure to Sign the Agreement Does Not Affect the Members' Agreement Governing Dispute Resolution

Elf argues that because Malek LLC, on whose behalf Elf allegedly brings these claims, is not a party to the Agreement, the derivative claims it brought on behalf of Malek LLC are not governed by the arbitration and forum selection clauses of the Agreement.

Elf argues that Malek LLC came into existence on October 29, 1996, when the parties filed its Certificate of Formation with the Delaware Secretary of State. The parties did not sign the Agreement until November 4, 1996. Elf contends that Malek LLC existed as an LLC as of October 29, 1996, but never agreed to the Agreement because it did not sign it. Because Malek LLC never expressly assented to the arbitration and forum selection clauses within the Agreement, Elf argues it can sue derivatively on behalf of Malek LLC pursuant to 6 Del. C. § 18–1001.

We are not persuaded by this argument. Section 18–101(7) defines the limited liability company agreement as "any agreement, written or oral, of the member or members as to the affairs of a limited liability company and the conduct of its business." Here, Malek, Inc. and Elf, the members of Malek LLC, executed the Agreement to carry out the affairs and business of Malek LLC and to provide for arbitration and forum selection.

Notwithstanding Malek LLC's failure to sign the Agreement, Elf's claims are subject to the arbitration and forum selection clauses of the Agreement. The Act is a statute designed to permit members maximum flexibility in entering into an agreement to govern their relationship. It is the members who are the real parties in interest. The LLC is simply their joint business vehicle. This is the contemplation of the statute in prescribing the outlines of a limited liability company agreement.

Classification by Elf of its Claims as Derivative is Irrelevant

Elf argues that the Court of Chancery erred in failing to classify its claims against Malek LLC as derivative. Elf contends that, had the court properly characterized its claims as derivative instead of direct, the arbitration and forum selection clauses would not have applied to bar adjudication in Delaware.

Although Elf correctly points out that Delaware law allows for derivative suits against management of an LLC, Elf contracted away its right to bring such an action in Delaware and agreed instead to dispute resolution in California. That is, Section 13.8 of the Agreement specifically provides that the parties (*i.e.*, Elf) agree to institute "[n]o action at law or in equity based upon any claim arising out of or related to this Agreement" except an action to compel arbitration or to enforce an arbitration award. Furthermore, under Section 13.7 of the Agreement, each member (*i.e.*, Elf) "consent[ed] to the exclusive jurisdiction of the state and federal courts sitting in California in any action on a claim arising out of, under or in connection with this Agreement or the transactions contemplated by this Agreement."

Sections 13.7 and 13.8 of the Agreement do not distinguish between direct and derivative claims. They simply state that the members may not initiate any claims outside of California. Elf initiated this action in the Court of Chancery in contravention of its own contractual agreement. As a result, the Court of Chancery correctly held that all claims, whether derivative or direct, arose under, out of or in connection with the Agreement, and thus are covered by the arbitration and forum selection clauses.

The Court of Chancery was correct in holding that Elf's claims bear directly on Jaffari's duties and obligations under the Agreement. Thus, we decline to disturb its holding.

The Argument that Chancery Has "Special" Jurisdiction for Derivative Claims Must Fail

Elf claims that 6 Del. C. §§ 18–110(a), 18–111 and 18–1001 vest the Court of Chancery with subject matter jurisdiction over this dispute. According to Elf, the Act grants the Court of Chancery subject matter jurisdiction over its claims for breach of fiduciary duty and removal of Jaffari, even though the parties contracted to arbitrate all such claims in California. In effect, Elf argues that the Act affords the Court of Chancery "special" jurisdiction to adjudicate its claims, notwithstanding a clear contractual agreement to the contrary.

Again, we are not persuaded by Elf's argument. Elf is correct that 6 Del. C. §§ 18–110(a) and 18–111 vest jurisdiction with the Court of Chancery in actions involving removal of managers and interpreting, applying or enforcing LLC agreements respectively. Nevertheless, for the purpose of designating a more convenient forum, we find no reason why the members cannot alter the default jurisdictional provisions of the statute and contract away their right to file suit in Delaware.

———————

Points for Discussion

1. *"Creatures of contract"?*

LLCs are sometimes said to be "creatures of contract." How does *Elf Atochem* demonstrate a contractarian view of the LLC form? How does it also reveal limitations to the idea that LLCs are contractual in nature?

Professor Mohsen Manesh, a leading scholar of LLCs, has highlighted several non-contractual dimensions, including the state filing requirement to form an LLC, the binding of nonparties to an LLC agreement, judicially implied fiduciary duties, and entity attributes such as separate legal existence and limited liability. *See* Mohsen Manesh, *Creatures of Contract: A Half-Truth About LLCs*, 42 Del. J. Corp. L. 391 (2018). Considering these features, would it be more accurate to say that LLCs are creatures of contract, statutes, and equity?

2. *Delaware's role.*

Delaware's LLC Act, § 18–109(d), provides: "Except by agreeing to arbitrate any arbitrable matter in a specified jurisdiction or in the State of Delaware, a member who is not a manager may not waive its right to maintain a legal action or proceeding in the courts of the State of Delaware with respect to matters relating to the organization or internal affairs of a limited liability company." Why do you think Delaware allows an LLC to include a term in its operating agreement compelling arbitration in a "specified jurisdiction" outside of Delaware? Why do you think this is the only exception to otherwise mandating a right for non-manager members to bring suit in Delaware courts with respect to internal affairs of the LLC?

———————

D.   Limited Liability and Veil Piercing

As a general matter, members and managers are not personally liable for the LLC's obligations—it is a limited liability form of business entity. RULLCA § 304(a) explains: "A debt, obligation or other liability of a limited liability company is solely the debt, obligation, or other liability of the company. A member or manager is not personally liable, directly or indirectly, by way of contribution or otherwise, . . . solely by reason of being or acting as a member or manager."

Although the general rule is limited liability, some courts have employed "veil piercing" concepts. Veil piercing refers to a situation in which a court disregards the limited liability of the entity and allows a plaintiff to seek recompense for a debt owed by the business entity from a shareholder or member of the entity. Imagine, for example, that a creditor to the business is owed a debt, but there are not sufficient assets in the business to satisfy the debt. If the general rule of limited liability applies, the creditor is out of luck and will bear the loss. By contrast, if the creditor is allowed to pierce the veil, they may seek satisfaction of the debt from the shareholders or members of the business.

We will cover veil piercing in depth in our study of corporations. Indeed, many professors might prefer to first cover the topic in the corporate law context because corporate veil piercing has a longer history and a more extensively developed doctrine. For our purposes here, it suffices to say that courts have used a variety of elements and factors to decide when to allow a plaintiff to pierce the veil to reach the personal assets of LLC members. For example, in *Utzler v. Braca*, 972 A.2d 743 (Conn. App. 2009), the court held that veil piercing was appropriate under an "alter-ego" theory when the owner deposited LLC funds into a commingled bank account from which he also made withdrawals for personal unrelated needs and projects. We will read cases based on similar theories in Chapter 6.

One commonly used factor for veil piercing in the corporate context is if there was a failure to observe corporate formalities such as adopting and keeping corporate records including bylaws and minutes of board and shareholder meetings. Whether or not to use this as a factor in the LLC context has been the subject of some debate. Some authorities, including RULLCA, provide that failure to observe company formalities of governance should not be a ground for piercing the LLC veil. The comments to RULLCA § 304(b) explain: "In the corporate realm 'disregard of corporate formalities' is a key factor in the piercing analysis. In the realm of LLCs, that factor is inappropriate because informality of organization and operation is both common and desired."

E. Management

The management structure of LLCs is highly flexible. It is not constrained by the limitations often imposed by corporate law. For example, under many statutes, managers do not have to be natural persons.

As noted above, LLCs can either be member-managed or manager-managed. In a member-managed LLC, the management and conduct of the company are vested in the members—that is, the investors or equity holders. Thus, member-managed companies are similar to general partnerships in terms of having decentralized governance. The members themselves are both investors and managers in the company.

What are the default voting rules in member-managed companies? LLC statutes vary regarding whether they set the default rule at per capita voting (one vote per member) or pro rata voting (by percentage of financial interest or sometimes the term "units" is used). RULLCA provides for the per capita approach by default in § 407(b)—the management and conduct of the company are vested in the members and each member has equal rights in the company's management. You might notice that this is the same default rule as under RUPA for general partnerships. By contrast, the Delaware act, in § 18–402, provides for pro rata voting by default. The management of a Delaware LLC is vested in its members and in proportion to the percentage or other interest of members in the profits of the company. Under either approach, by default, decisions in the ordinary course of business operations typically require a majority vote, and those outside the ordinary course require unanimity. These rules may be customized in the operating agreement.

LLCs also have an entirely different option for their management: they can choose to be manager-managed. Pursuant to this option, LLCs can structure their management in a wide variety of ways—for example, by hiring a CEO or arranging for a corporate-like board of managers, or having each member designate a manager for representative management. Members can decide to hire outsiders to serve in manager roles or some members may dually serve in a managerial role. RULLCA provides a default rule that in a manager-managed LLC: "any matter relating to the activities and affairs of the company is decided exclusively by the manager, or, if there is more than one manager, by a majority of the managers" and "[e]ach manager has equal rights in the management and conduct of the company's activities and affairs." § 407(c).

In a manager-managed LLC, managers run the ordinary operations of the company, but by default still need the consent of members for decisions outside the ordinary course such as a sale or lease of substantially all of the company assets, merging with another company, or amending the operating agreement. And, unless otherwise provided in the LLC operating agreement, a member or manager has broad authority to delegate to other persons any of their powers and duties to manage and control the business and affairs of the LLC. DLLCA § 18–407.

How do you know which type of management an LLC has in place? The answer is that it is often difficult to know for sure without having access to review the company's operating agreement. Most LLC statutes, including RULLCA and the Delaware act, set the default as member-managed. If the members intend their LLC to be manager-managed, most statutes require a written statement of that intention in the LLC's operating agreement—and some statutes also require a statement of manager-management in the articles of organization.

We have now reviewed the basics of management and voting. But what about the authority of the members and managers to act as agents of the company and bind it to liability? This has been an area of some difficulty and confusion given that LLCs may be member-managed or manager-managed, and issues of both actual and apparent authority can arise.

Under many statutory formulations, in a member-managed LLC, each member, as a member, has apparent authority in the ordinary course of the LLC's business to bind the LLC, but in a manager-managed LLC, only managers have apparent authority to bind the LLC. Most statutes require LLCs to elect in the articles of organization to be member-managed or manager-managed, and LLC acts often link the choice of internal management structure to the agency authority, both actual and apparent.

RULLCA provides a contrary default rule: "A member is not an agent of a limited liability company solely by reason of being a member." § 301(a). Furthermore, RULLCA rejects "statutory apparent authority" that would create through LLC law a default or automatic binding of the LLC for acts of members in a member-managed LLC and managers in a manager-managed LLC. A prefatory note to the uniform statute explains: "The concept does not make sense for modern LLC law, because: (i) an LLC's status as member-managed or manager-managed is not apparent from the LLC's name (creating traps for unwary third parties); and (ii) although most LLC statutes provide templates for member management and manager-management, variability of management structure is a key strength of the LLC as a form of business organization." Other law, such as agency law, will handle power-to-bind questions that may arise regarding LLCs governed by RULLCA. Likewise, the Delaware statute does not differentiate as to statutory apparent authority between member-managed and manager-managed LLCs and does not require a designation of the LLC as member-managed or manager-managed in the certificate of formation. DLLCA § 18–402. Under the approaches taken by RULLCA and Delaware, the operating agreement has an important role to play in establishing agency authority, and common law agency principles resolve issues of apparent authority.

F. Finance

1. Contributions

LLC statutes do not require any minimum amount of capital to be contributed to an LLC, nor do all members need to make capital contributions. Members are free to decide among themselves how much cash, property, or services, if any, each member will contribute.

2. Allocation of Profits and Losses

The operating agreement of the LLC typically provides for how the profits and losses of the company will be allocated among the members. As you can imagine, this is often a topic of great interest for members who are investing in the company!

Many LLCs choose to allocate profits and losses among the members on a pro rata basis that is proportionate to their investment. But this is not necessarily the case.

Further, profits and losses may be allocated differently—for example, an LLC might choose to allocate to one member more of the profits and less of the losses than other members in recognition of that member also serving in a managerial role.

If the operating agreement does not so provide, many LLC statutes provide a default rule, typically that profits and losses shall be allocated on a pro rata basis according to the members' contributions. This is the approach that the Delaware act takes in § 18–503. The RULLCA does not provide a default rule for allocating profits; it provides a default rule only for rights to share in distributions, as explained below.

3. Distributions

A distribution refers to the transfer of LLC property (e.g., cash) to members. Members typically have no statutory right to compel a distribution, but rather will receive a distribution as agreed in the operating agreement. Most LLC statutes such as Delaware's provide by default that, unless otherwise agreed, any distribution made to members is on a pro rata basis according to the members' contributions. *See, e.g.,* DLLCA § 18–504.

Some LLC statutes (including the RULLCA) instead provide for per capita distributions by default. *See, e.g.,* RULLCA § 404. The comments to RULLCA § 404 explain the drafters' perspective in focusing on distributions: "Capital accounts are maintained for one purpose, to determine how distributions will be made to members. The rules for maintenance of capital accounts can be very complex. Generally, however, profits increase capital account balances (and increase the amounts that will be distributed to the members), and losses reduce capital account balances (and reduce the amounts that will be distributed to the members). If the statute has a simple default rule for how distributions are to be made to the members, providing an additional set of default profit and loss allocation provisions and capital account rules will be, at best, duplicative and, at worse, inconsistent with the distribution rules."

Finally, most LLC statutes prohibit distributions that would render the company unable to pay its bills as they come due or that would render the company insolvent.

4. Transferability of Members' Interests

A member has a financial "interest" in the LLC. Generally, a member may freely transfer her financial interest in the LLC (the RULLCA refers to this as a "transferable interest"; the Delaware act refers to this simply as a "limited liability company interest"). Such a transfer only confers the member's right to receive distributions and not governance rights or rights to participate in management. In this respect, the default LLC rules resemble the rules for a general partnership.

For example, the Delaware statute provides in § 18–702: "The assignee of a member's limited liability company interest shall have no right to participate in the management of the business and affairs of a limited liability company except as provided in a limited liability company agreement or, unless otherwise provided in the limited liability company agreement, upon the vote or consent of all of the members of the limited liability company." And regarding the rights of the assignee of the interest: "An assignment of a limited liability company interest entitles the assignee to share in such profits and losses, to receive such distribution or distributions, and to receive such allocation of income, gain, loss, deduction, or credit or similar item to which the assignor was entitled, to the extent assigned."

Does RULLCA provide a default rule for transferring governance rights?
Comment to RULLCA § 501.

As to whether a member may transfer governance rights to a fellow member, the question is moot absent a provision in the operating agreement changing the default rule, see Section 407(b)(2) (allocating governance rights per capita). In the default mode, a member's transfer of governance rights to another member: (i) does not increase the transferee's governance rights; (ii) eliminates the transferor's governance rights; and (iii) thereby changes the denominator but not the numerator in calculating governance rights.

EXAMPLE:

LCN Company, LLC is a member-managed limited liability company with three members, Laura, Charles, and Nora. The operating agreement does not displace this act's default rule on the allocation of governance rights among members. Thus, each member has 1/3 of those rights. Laura transfers her entire ownership interest to Charles. The transfer does not increase Charles's governance rights but does eliminate Laura's. After the transfer, Laura has no governance rights . . . As a result, Charles and Nora each have 1/2 of the governance rights.

The economic structure of LLCs can be complex given the rules for capital accounts, allocations, and default rules on transferable interests that do not include management rights. Equity compensation in particular can be complex. Nevertheless, LLCs offer enormous flexibility for private ordering that can be attractive to sophisticated businesspeople or those who do not anticipate large numbers of members or frequent transfers.

G. Information Rights

LLC statutes, such as RULLCA, generally provide members with a default right to access the LLC's books and records, upon demand describing the particular information sought and a proper purpose related to the member's interest. The Delaware act authorizes the private ordering of member inspection rights. For example, § 18–305 provides that the operating agreement or the manager can set forth "reasonable standards" to obtain information from the LLC "reasonably related to the member's interest as a member." In a manager-managed LLC, the managers also have rights to information to exercise their duties.

H.   Fiduciary Duties

Fiduciary duties in LLCs, and the extent to which they can be contracted around or eliminated, have been a subject of considerable controversy. What is the purpose and role of fiduciary duties? Are they essential to every form of business organization? Or is an LLC sufficiently contractual in nature that it should be possible to completely disclaim all fiduciary duties with a provision in the operating agreement?

States have taken a variety of approaches to the thorny question of fiduciary duties. The RULLCA approach to fiduciary duties in LLCs is similar to RUPA's approach to fiduciary duties in partnerships. Specifically, RULLCA provides for fiduciary duties owed by members (in a member-managed LLC) and managers (in a manager-managed LLC) and sets limitations on modifications to such duties. Section 409 provides that members in a member-managed LLC, and managers in a manager-managed LLC, owe the fiduciary duties of loyalty and care, including the duties:

(1) to account to the company and hold as trustee for it any property, profit, or benefit derived:

(A) in the conduct or winding up of the company's activities and affairs;

(B) from a use of the company's property; or

(C) from the appropriation of a company opportunity;

(2) to refrain from dealing with the company in the conduct or winding up of the company's activities and affairs as or on behalf of a person having an interest adverse to the company; and

(3) to refrain from competing with the company in the conduct of the company's activities and affairs before the dissolution of the company.

The duty of care requires the members in a member-managed LLC, and managers in a manager-managed LLC, to refrain from engaging in grossly negligent or reckless conduct, willful or intentional misconduct, or knowing violation of law. Furthermore, members (and managers in a manager-managed LLC) shall discharge their duties and obligations under the statute or under their operating agreement consistently with the contractual obligation of good faith and fair dealing.

RULLCA allows an LLC to alter but not eliminate these fiduciary duties in its operating agreement. Specifically, the statute provides that, if not manifestly unreasonable, the operating agreement may: (A) alter or eliminate aspects of the duty of loyalty; (B) identify specific types or categories of activities that do not violate the duty of loyalty; and (C) alter the duty of care, but it may not authorize conduct involving bad faith, willful or intentional misconduct, or knowing violation of law. In addition, the contractual obligation of good faith and fair dealing cannot be eliminated, but the operating agreement may prescribe the standards, if not manifestly unreasonable, by which the performance of the obligation is to be measured.

Delaware allows even broader flexibility for the private ordering of fiduciary duties in LLCs. Delaware's statute provides that the rules of law and equity, including the rules of law and equity relating to fiduciary duties" govern "[i]n any case not provided for in this chapter"—and it allows fiduciary duties to be "expanded or restricted or eliminated" in the operating agreement. DLLCA §§ 18–1104, 18–1101(c). Only the contractual covenant of good faith and fair dealing cannot be eliminated.

Under Delaware corporate law, some aspects of fiduciary duties are mandatory—they cannot be entirely eliminated. By contrast, under Delaware LLC law, fiduciary duties are default duties that can be eliminated in the operating agreement. This difference reflects the emphasis in LLC law on flexibility and the freedom of contract. As a practical matter for the business lawyer, this underscores the importance of clear drafting and diligent research into the relevant jurisdiction's approach and recent case law.

What are the benefits of this broad flexibility and freedom of contract philosophy? What are the pitfalls?

Consider the following case which discusses the application of fiduciary duties in the absence of a provision unambiguously eliminating them in a Delaware LLC. The factual background involved the manager of an LLC who, together with his family, acquired majority voting control over the company's equity during the course of its operations and thereby held a veto over any strategic option. The court found that the manager used his control over the LLC to deliver the LLC to himself and his family on unfair terms.

Auriga Capital Corp. v. Gatz Properties

40 A.3d 839 (Del. Ch. 2012)

STRINE, CHANCELLOR.

A group of minority investors have sued for damages, arguing the manager breached his contractual and fiduciary duties through this course of conduct. The manager, after originally disclaiming that he owed a fiduciary duty of loyalty to the minority, now rests his defense on two primary grounds. The first is that the manager and his family were able to veto any option for the LLC as their right as members. As a result, they could properly use a chokehold over the LLC to pursue their own interests and the minority would have to live with the consequences of their freedom of action. The second defense is that by the time of the auction, the LLC was valueless.

In this post-trial decision, I find for the plaintiffs. For reasons discussed in the opinion, I explain that the LLC agreement here does not displace the traditional duties of loyalty and care that are owed by managers of Delaware LLCs to their investors in the absence of a contractual provision waiving or modifying those duties. The Delaware Limited Liability Company Act (the "LLC Act") explicitly applies equity as a default and our Supreme Court, and this court, have consistently held that default fiduciary duties apply to those managers of alternative entities who would qualify as fiduciaries under traditional equitable principles, including managers of LLCs. Here, the LLC agreement makes clear that the manager could only enter into a self-dealing transaction, such as its purchase of the LLC, if it proves that the terms were fair. In other words, the LLC agreement essentially incorporates a core element of the traditional fiduciary duty of loyalty. Not only that, the LLC agreement's exculpatory provision makes clear that the manager is not exculpated for bad faith action, willful misconduct, or even grossly negligent action, i.e., a breach of the duty of care. The manager's course of conduct here breaches both his contractual and fiduciary duties.

Default Fiduciary Duties Do Exist In The LLC Context

The Delaware LLC Act does not plainly state that the traditional fiduciary duties of loyalty and care apply by default as to managers or members of a limited liability company. In that respect, of course, the LLC Act is not different than the DGCL, which does not do that either. In fact, the absence of explicitness in the DGCL inspired the case of *Schnell v. Chris–Craft*. Arguing that the then newly-revised DGCL was a domain unto itself, and that compliance with its terms was sufficient to discharge any obligation owed by the directors to the stockholders, the defendant corporation in that case won on that theory at the Court of Chancery level. But our Supreme Court reversed and made emphatic that the new DGCL was to be read in concert with equitable fiduciary duties just as had always been the case, stating famously that "inequitable action does not become legally permissible simply because it is legally possible."

The LLC Act is more explicit than the DGCL in making the equitable overlay mandatory. Specifically, § 18–1104 of the LLC Act provides that "[i]n any case not provided for in this chapter, the rules of law and equity . . . shall govern." In this way, the LLC Act provides for a construct similar to that which is used in the corporate context. But unlike in the corporate context, the rules of equity apply in the LLC context by statutory mandate, creating an even stronger justification for application of fiduciary duties grounded in equity to managers of LLCs to the extent that such duties have not been altered or eliminated under the relevant LLC agreement.

It seems obvious that, under traditional principles of equity, a manager of an LLC would qualify as a fiduciary of that LLC and its members. Under Delaware law, "[a] fiduciary relationship is a situation where one person reposes special trust in and reliance on the judgment of another or where a special duty exists on the part of one person to protect the interests of another." Corporate directors, general partners and trustees are analogous examples of those who Delaware law has determined owe a "special duty." Equity distinguishes fiduciary relationships from straightforward commercial arrangements where there is no expectation that one party will act in the interests of the other.

The manager of an LLC—which is in plain words a limited liability "company" having many of the features of a corporation—easily fits the definition of a fiduciary. The manager of an LLC has more than an arms-length, contractual relationship with the members of the LLC. Rather, the manager is vested with discretionary power to manage the business of the LLC.

Thus, because the LLC Act provides for principles of equity to apply, because LLC managers are clearly fiduciaries, and because fiduciaries owe the fiduciary duties of loyalty and care, the LLC Act starts with the default that managers of LLCs owe enforceable fiduciary duties.

This reading of the LLC Act is confirmed by the Act's own history. Before 2004, § 18–1101(c) of the LLC Act provided that fiduciary duties, to the extent they existed, could only be "expanded or restricted" by the LLC agreement. Following our Supreme Court's holding in Gotham Partners, *L.P. v. Hallwood Realty Partners, L.P.*, 817 A.2d 160 (Del. 2002), which questioned whether default fiduciary duties could be fully eliminated in the limited partnership context when faced with similar statutory language and also affirmed our law's commitment to protecting investors who have not explicitly agreed to waive their fiduciaries' duties and therefore expect their fiduciaries to act in accordance with their interests, the General Assembly amended not only the Delaware Revised Limited Uniform Partnership Act ("DRULPA"), but also the LLC Act to permit the "eliminat[ion]" of default fiduciary duties in an LLC agreement. At the same time, the General Assembly added a provision to the LLC Act (the current § 18–1101(e)) that permits full contractual exculpation for breaches of fiduciary and contractual duties, except for the implied contractual covenant of good faith and fair dealing.

If the equity backdrop I just discussed did not apply to LLCs, then the 2004 "Elimination Amendment" would have been logically done differently. Why is this so? Because the Amendment would have instead said something like: "The managers, members, and other persons of the LLC shall owe no duties of any kind to the LLC and its members except as set forth in this statute and the LLC agreement." Instead, the Amendment only made clear that an LLC agreement could, if the parties so chose, "eliminat[e]" default duties altogether, thus according full weight to the statutory policy in favor of giving maximum effect to the principle of freedom of contract and to the enforceability of [LLC] agreements. The General Assembly left in place the explicit equitable default in § 18–1104 of the Act. Moreover, why would the General Assembly amend the LLC Act to provide for the elimination of (and the exculpation for) "something" if there were no "something" to eliminate (or exculpate) in the first place? The fact that the legislature enacted these liability-limiting measures against the backdrop of case law holding that default fiduciary duties did apply in the LLC context, and seemed to have accepted the central thrust of those decisions to be correct, provides further weight to the position that default fiduciary duties do apply in the LLC context to the extent they are not contractually altered.

Thus, our cases have to date come to the following place based on the statute. The statute incorporates equitable principles. Those principles view the manager of an LLC as a fiduciary and subject the manager as a default principle to the core fiduciary duties of loyalty and care. But, the statute allows the parties to an LLC agreement to entirely supplant those default principles or to modify them in part. Where the parties have clearly supplanted default principles in full, we give effect to the parties' contract choice. Where the parties have clearly supplanted default principles in part, we give effect to their contract choice. But, where the core default fiduciary duties have not been supplanted by contract, they exist as the LLC statute itself contemplates.

There are two issues that would arise if the equitable background explicitly contained in the statute were to be judicially excised now. The first is that those who crafted LLC agreements in reliance on equitable defaults that supply a predictable structure for assessing whether a business fiduciary has met his obligations to the entity and its investors will have their expectations disrupted. The equitable context in which the contract's specific terms were to be read will be eradicated, rendering the resulting terms shapeless and more uncertain. The fact that the implied covenant of good faith and fair dealing would remain extant would do little to cure this loss.

The common law fiduciary duties that were developed to address those who manage business entities were, as the implied covenant, an equitable gap-filler. If, rather than well thought out fiduciary duty principles, the implied covenant is to be used as the sole default principle of equity, then the risk is that the certainty of contract law itself will be undermined. The implied covenant has rightly been narrowly interpreted by our Supreme Court to apply only "when the express terms of the contract indicate that the parties would have agreed to the obligation had they negotiated the issue." The implied covenant is to be used "cautious[ly]" and does not apply to situations that could be anticipated, which is a real problem in the business context, because fiduciary duty review typically addresses actions that are anticipated and permissible under the express terms of the contract, but where there is a potential for managerial abuse. For these reasons, the implied covenant is not a tool that is designed to provide a framework to govern the discretionary actions of business managers acting under a broad enabling framework like a barebones LLC agreement. In fact, if the implied covenant were used in that manner, the room for subjective judicial oversight could be expanded in an inefficient way. The default principles that apply in the fiduciary duty context of business entities are carefully tailored to avoid judicial second-guessing. A generalized "fairness" inquiry under the guise of an "implied covenant" review is an invitation to, at best, reinvent what already exists in another less candid guise, or worse, to inject unpredictability into both entity and contract law, by untethering judicial review from the well-understood frameworks that traditionally apply in those domains.

The second problem is a related one, which is that a judicial eradication of the explicit equity overlay in the LLC Act could tend to erode our state's credibility with investors in Delaware entities. To have told the investing public that the law of equity would apply if the LLC statute did not speak to the question at issue, and to have managers of LLCs easily qualify as fiduciaries under traditional and settled principles of equity law in Delaware, and then to say that LLC agreements could "expan[d] or restric[t] or eliminat [e]" these fiduciary duties, would lead any reasonable investor to conclude the following: the managers of the Delaware LLC in which I am investing owe me the fiduciary duties of loyalty and care except to the extent the agreement "expand [s]," "restrict[s]," or "eliminate[s]" these duties. That expectation has been reinforced by our Supreme Court in decisions like *William Penn Partnership v. Saliba,* where it stated that "[t]he parties here agree that managers of a Delaware [LLC] owe traditional fiduciary duties of loyalty and care to the members of the LLC, unless the parties expressly modify or eliminate those duties in an operating agreement;" in a consistent line of decisions by this court affirming similar principles; in the reasoning of Gotham Partners in the analogous limited partnership context; and culminating with legislative reinforcement in the 2004 Elimination Amendment inspired by Gotham Partners that allowed LLC agreements to eliminate fiduciary duties altogether. Reasonable investors in Delaware LLCs would, one senses, understand even more clearly after the Elimination Amendment that they were protected by fiduciary duty review unless the LLC agreement provided to the contrary, because they would of course think that there would have been no need for our General Assembly to pass a statute authorizing the elimination of something that did not exist at all.

Reasonable minds can debate whether it would be wise for the General Assembly to create a business entity in which the managers owe the investors no duties at all except as set forth in the statute and the governing agreement. Perhaps it would be, perhaps it would not. That is a policy judgment for the General Assembly. What seems certain is that the General Assembly, and the organs of the Bar who propose alteration of the statutes to them, know how to draft a clear statute to that effect and have yet to do so. The current LLC Act is quite different and promises investors that equity will provide the important default protections it always has, absent a contractual choice to tailor or eliminate that protection. Changing that promise is a job for the General Assembly, not this court.

With that statement of the law in mind, let us turn to the relevant terms of Peconic Bay's LLC Agreement.

[The court concluded that the LLC Agreement did not by its language clearly displace the traditional fiduciary duties of loyalty and care, and that the manager breached such fiduciary duties and had not proven that the breaches were exculpated.]

Points for Discussion

1. How far does this go?

On appeal, in affirming the decision on the merits, the Delaware Supreme Court commented that the case could be decided solely by reference to the LLC Agreement and so the Court of Chancery's discussion of default fiduciary duties was "dictum." *Gatz Properties, LLC v. Auriga Capital Corp.*, 59 A.3d 1206, 1218 (Del. 2012). In 2013, the Delaware legislature amended the LLC statute to confirm that fiduciary duties apply as a default matter. *See* DLLCA § 18–1104.

A difficult question arises regarding whether to apply this principle one step further such as to reach the human controllers of an "entity fiduciary." When a manager in an LLC is not a natural person but a limited liability entity, should courts hold the individual controllers liable for the duty of loyalty?

2. Are fiduciary duties essential?

Should there be a non-waivable fiduciary duty of loyalty in LLCs or in certain LLCs such as those that are publicly-traded? What dangers might exist in allowing parties to completely eliminate fiduciary duties in LLCs?

I.   Direct and Derivative Litigation

A member who has been injured personally may maintain a direct action against another member, a manager, or the LLC to enforce and protect their rights and interests. To maintain a direct action, the member must "plead and prove an actual threatened injury that is not solely the result of an injury suffered or threatened to be suffered by the limited liability company." RULLCA § 801(b). As we will see in corporate law, LLC law draws a distinction between what is known as direct and derivative claims.

Members also have rights to bring derivative claims on behalf of the company, such as to pursue a breach of fiduciary duty. As noted above, derivative claims can be complex. Many LLC statutes provide for a "demand requirement" for derivative claims. For example, Delaware's statute, § 18–1001, provides:

"A member or an assignee of a limited liability company interest may bring an action in the Court of Chancery in the right of a limited liability company to recover a judgment in its favor if managers or members with authority to do so have refused to bring the action or if an effort to cause those managers or members to bring the action is not likely to succeed."

The complaint must set forth "with particularity the effort, if any, of the plaintiff to secure initiation of the action by a manager or member or the reasons for not making the effort." § 18–1003.

Similarly, RULLCA provides that a member may maintain a derivative action to enforce a right of an LLC if: (1) the member first makes a demand on the other members in a member-managed LLC, or the managers of a manager-managed LLC, requesting that they cause the company to bring an action to enforce the right, and the managers or other members do not bring the action within a reasonable time; or (2) a demand would be futile. § 802.

In addition, RULLCA contains a provision allowing an LLC to appoint a special litigation committee, or "SLC," to investigate claims asserted in a proceeding and to determine whether pursuing the action is in the best interests of the company. § 805. The comments to RULLCA § 805 describe the standard for judicial review of the SLC determination: "If a court determines that the members of the committee were disinterested and independent and whether the committee conducted its investigation and made its recommendation in good faith, independently, and with reasonable care, with the committee

Direct vs. Derivative Claims

Comment to RULLCA § 801

Although in ordinary contractual situations it is axiomatic that each party to a contract has standing to sue for breach of that contract, within a limited liability company different circumstances typically exist. A member does not have a direct claim against a manager or another member merely because the manager or other member has breached the operating agreement. Likewise a member's violation of this act does not automatically create a direct claim for every other member. To have standing in his, her, or its own right, a member plaintiff must be able to show a harm that occurs independently of the harm caused or threatened to be caused to the limited liability company.

EXAMPLE:

Through grossly negligent conduct, in violation of Section 409(c), the manager of a manager-managed LLC reduces the net assets of an LLC by fifty percent, which in turns decreases the value of Member A's investment by $3,000,000. Member A has no standing to bring a direct claim; the damage is merely derivative of the damage first suffered by the LLC. Member A may, however, bring a derivative claim.

EXAMPLE:

Same facts, except in addition to violating Section 409(c), the manager's conduct breaches an express provision of the operating agreement to which Member A is a signatory. The analysis and the result are the same.

EXAMPLE:

An operating agreement defines "distributable cash" and requires the LLC to periodically distribute that cash among all members. The LLC's manager fails to distribute the cash. Each member has a direct claim against the manager and the LLC.

having the burden of proof, it makes no sense to substitute the court's legal judgment for the business judgment of the SLC." (internal quotation marks omitted). We will study SLCs in the corporate context as well, where courts follow differing approaches.

Some courts have recognized that members of an LLC may bring a derivative suit on the LLC's behalf, even where there are no provisions governing such suits in the relevant LLC statute. *See Tzolis v. Wolff*, 10 N.Y. 3d 100 (Ct. App. N.Y. 2008).

J. Dissociation and Dissolution

Most LLC statutes provide that one becomes a member of the LLC by unanimous consent of the existing members or by the terms of the operating agreement. States have widely differing default approaches, however, to the question of how a member may leave an LLC. We will focus on the default approaches of the RULLCA and the Delaware statute.

1. RULLCA

Under RULLCA, dissociation can occur by the withdrawal or expulsion of a member. The uniform statute provides that "a person has the power to dissociate as a member at any time, rightfully or wrongfully, by withdrawing as a member by express will." § 601(a). Wrongful dissociation occurs in a list of enumerated situations such as where the departing member is in breach of an express provision of the operating agreement. Importantly, RULLCA does not provide for buyout rights for members, but they may contract for such rights in the operating agreement.

In addition, the uniform statute provides for means of expelling a member, thus forcing dissociation, for example where there has been a transfer of all of a member's transferable interest and upon unanimous consent of all other members; or pursuant to a judicial order because a member has engaged in wrongful conduct that has adversely and materially affected the company, willfully committed a material breach of the operating agreement, or has engaged in conduct that makes it not reasonably practicable to carry on the company business with the person as a member.

The uniform statute explains that the effect of dissociation is to terminate the member's right to participate in the management and conduct of the company, as well as their fiduciary duties. Any transferable interest owned by the person in their capacity as a member becomes owned by the person solely as a transferee. A person's dissociation as a member does not of itself discharge the person from any debt, obligation, or other liability to the LLC or the other members that the person incurred while a member. The LLC continues after the member's withdrawal from the company.

Similar to general partnership law, the uniform LLC statute includes separate provisions concerning the dissolution of the company. An LLC will be dissolved when any of the following occurs: (1) an event or circumstance that the operating agreement states causes dissolution; (2) the consent of all the members to dissolve the company; (3) the passage of 90 consecutive days during which the LLC had no members; (4) on application by a member, the entry by a court of an order for judicial dissolution; or (5) administrative dissolution by the state (such as for failure to pay required fees or timely make required filings).

A court may grant an application for judicial dissolution of the LLC if:

- The conduct of all or substantially all of the LLC's activities is unlawful;

- It is not reasonably practicable to carry on the company's activities in conformity with the articles of organization and the operating agreement; or

- The managers or members in control of the company have acted, are acting, or will act in a manner that is illegal or fraudulent; or in a manner that is oppressive and was, is, or will be directly harmful to the applicant for dissolution.

Absent a rescission of the LLC dissolution, the company continues after dissolution only for the purpose of winding up. After its debts to creditors are paid, the surplus is distributed "(1) to each person owning a transferable interest that reflects contributions made and not previously returned, an amount equal to the value of the unreturned contributions; and (2) among persons owning transferable interests in proportion to their respective rights to share in distributions immediately before the dissolution of the company." § 707(b).

2. Delaware

The Delaware LLC statute takes a different approach, providing simple default rules for dissolution, but not mentioning dissociation. And, in fact, § 18–603 states that unless otherwise provided in the operating agreement, a member cannot unilaterally resign or withdraw until the LLC has been dissolved and wound up. Members of a Delaware LLC should therefore carefully consider whether to include a term in the operating agreement providing for an exit mechanism besides dissolution. Otherwise, a member that wants to exit the LLC will have very limited options: she could try to negotiate with the other members for a buyout or to dissolve the LLC, or petition the Court of Chancery for judicial dissolution (which is generally used sparingly in the court's discretion concerning circumstances where it is not reasonably practicable to continue carrying on the business, such as where the purpose for which the LLC was created has been frustrated or a deadlock exists).

Under § 18–801, an LLC is dissolved and its affairs shall be wound up upon any of the following events:

- At the time, or upon the happening of events, specified in the operating agreement;

- Unless otherwise provided in the operating agreement, upon the vote or consent of members who own more than 2/3 of the then-current percentage interests in the LLC;

- Within 90 days of an event that terminated the membership of the last remaining member (with limited exceptions); or

- Upon the entry of a decree of judicial dissolution.

Points for Discussion

1. Withdrawal and dissolution rights.

As we have seen, LLC statutes vary widely across states. Many take restrictive approaches to creating default rules for dissociation or buyouts that would facilitate liquidating an equity position. Do they help to promote "locking in" capital to facilitate business development? Do they help family-owned LLCs minimize the tax value of an equity interest in a closely held business? Are they fail-safes intended to encourage legal planners to contract for customized provisions? What do you make of these default rules?

2. Why not just use LLCs?

We started this chapter by noting the LLC is a common choice of entity, especially for new businesses. Do you think LLCs are always superior to partnerships? When would you choose a partnership instead of an LLC? Are there aspects to LLCs that you find problematic? Although LLCs are common, many new businesses instead choose the corporate entity, instead of the LLC. Moreover, almost all large public corporations are corporate entities, not LLCs. We address corporations in the next module.

Test Your Knowledge

To assess your understanding of the Chapter 1, 2, 3, and 4 material in this module, <u>click here</u> to take a quiz.

MODULE II – CORPORATIONS

CHAPTER 5

Corporation Basics

Corporations are the dominant structure through which joint business enterprise is conducted in the United States and throughout the world. Corporate law is central to economics and business. Most of you deal with numerous corporations every day, when you buy your morning coffee, fill your car with gas or electricity, withdraw money from the bank, or watch a show or movie. For better or worse, you cannot avoid corporations. Corporations range from multinational, publicly owned firms, such as ExxonMobil and Amazon, to local family-owned businesses.

Corporations also have a dramatic effect on society. They are important in economic and financial terms: they hire employees and provide investments for people to save for retirement. But they also are important in social and political terms: they affect the environment, contribute to charities, and influence government.

This chapter gives you an overview of several basic concepts that provide a useful starting point for our study of corporations and corporate law. We start with some history. Then we turn to the fundamental aspects of corporations, and the basic vocabulary you will need for this course, as well as the "nuts and bolts" of the incorporation process. After that, we examine two categories of judicial doctrines that are important in corporate law: "internal affairs," a doctrine that courts discuss in determining which state's law applies to a corporation, and "equitable" principles, which judges often reference in disputes involving corporations. We close with several policy issues.

> There are millions of business firms in the U.S. states. Of these, most are closely held by private owners, and their shares do not trade on public stock markets. Only a few thousand operating corporations have their shares traded on public stock markets like the New York Stock Exchange and NASDAQ.

A. A Brief History of Corporate Law

The concept of a corporation is not new. In ancient Rome, the government created business entities that had mixed private-state ownership. In the Middle Ages, governments in Continental Europe (particularly Italy) created corporations to undertake state functions, such as the monopoly to trade in a particular commodity.

In sixteenth-century England, ecclesiastical, municipal, and charitable corporations emerged as devices to hold property and to ensure continuity. In addition, borrowing from their Italian counterparts, English business corporations (known as joint stock companies) obtained concessions from the state and typically were granted monopoly rights in trade.

Joint stock companies, such as the East India Company, took on many of the characteristics of modern corporations. They were separate legal entities that took stock subscriptions from many investors, who then could transfer their interests in the enterprise to others. A joint stock company's trading business was ongoing and perpetual, and the investors' liability was often limited to the cost of their stock.

Some English joint stock companies were not created by state concession, but instead obtained their corporate attributes through complex deeds of settlement that provided for transferability of shares, continuity of life, and central management. The incorporated and unincorporated joint stock companies were the forerunners of the U.S. business corporation.

During the early 1700s, England experienced a speculative boom in joint stock companies, stimulated by the scheme of the South Sea Company to acquire almost the entire English national debt by buying out existing debt holders, often with South Sea Company shares. In response, Parliament in 1720 enacted the "Bubble Act" (not very subtly subtitled "An Act to Restrain the Extravagant and Unwarranted Practice of Raising Money by Voluntary Subscriptions for Carrying on Projects Dangerous to the Trade and Subjects of this Kingdom"). But by prohibiting unincorporated companies with transferable shares, the Bubble Act actually protected the incorporated South Sea Company's access to investors' capital.

In the American colonies, duly chartered corporations were permitted and existed, and the Bubble Act prohibited the formation of unincorporated joint stock companies. After independence, however, corporate chartering became more common. The earliest U.S. corporations were primarily non-business entities such as charities, churches, and municipalities. Soon after, state legislatures granted charters by special acts to banks, insurance, and infrastructure companies building turnpikes and canals—businesses with large capital needs and often special monopoly privileges.

By 1800 there were about 335 incorporated businesses in the United States. Corporate law and policy during this period was shaped by legislative practice. A corporate charter was considered a valuable privilege, and the legislative monopoly conferring this privilege created obvious temptations, to which many legislators and entrepreneurs inevitably yielded—to their mutual profit.

The resulting corruption and perception of corruption led the business community to argue that incorporation should be a right, not a privilege. For many businesses, incorporation had become a matter of economic necessity. As industrial and manufacturing concerns grew, individuals and partnerships no longer had enough capital to finance such enterprises. In response, states enacted general corporation laws that allowed any group of persons to organize a corporation by complying with prescribed statutory conditions. New York was an early pioneer. In 1811, it permitted self-incorporation to the organizers of certain manufacturing companies, limiting their capital to $100,000 and their existence to 20 years.

From the beginning, a corporation was considered a "person" for many purposes. Although not a natural person, it had many legal attributes of a natural person that flowed from state law. A corporation could own property, enter into contracts, sue and be sued in its own name, and be held liable for its debts.

In the early nineteenth century, the Supreme Court began to address questions concerning the treatment of corporations under the U.S. Constitution. One of the most notable early decisions is *Trustees of Dartmouth College v. Woodward*, 17 U.S. 518 (1819). In 1769, the British Crown had granted articles of incorporation to the trustees of Dartmouth College. After the American Revolution, New Hampshire, as successor to the Crown, enacted laws amending Dartmouth's charter so as to give state officials a major role in the governance of the college. Dartmouth sued, claiming the amendments violated the Contract Clause of the Constitution.

The Court invalidated New Hampshire's action on the ground the charter constituted a contract between the state and the college that was "within the letter of the Constitution and within its spirit also." Although the Court held that a state could not unilaterally amend the provisions of the state-granted charter, Justice Story (in a concurring opinion) suggested states could avoid this restriction by granting future charters subject to a reserved right to amend them. States seized upon this suggestion and began to include in all corporate charters a clause reserving the state's power to amend or repeal any authority granted to the corporation. When general corporation laws came into vogue, states added similar reserved powers clauses to their constitutions, their general corporation laws, or both. Currently, all states reserve the power to amend the statutes that govern corporations. *See* MBCA § 1.02; DGCL § 394.

The liberalization of the U.S. corporation continued into the second half of the 1800s. Unfettered from the constraints of special charters and shaped by the burgeoning railroad industry, corporations continued to flourish. Railway companies, which required a larger central organization and significant capital inputs, used a variety of financial instruments, for which the corporate form proved convenient. In addition, railway companies generally became more dependent on the availability of an open market for their securities to raise necessary capital.

This rapid growth of corporations in size and number did not occur without opposition. Throughout U.S. history, some have feared the aggregations of capital and the power in American society that corporations represent. But this opposition did little to stem the tide of corporate growth; other states soon followed New York's lead from the early 1800s and enacted general corporation laws. Many of the restrictions on size and duration were lifted.

The growth of corporate power and unchecked abuses concerned many Americans. Pressure grew to reform internal corporate governance and to impose limits on corporations' power. By the 1860s, the device of the shareholder "derivative" suit (in which individual shareholders can sue on behalf of the corporation to enforce corporate duties) had been developed to deal with managers' corruption and fraud, and other doctrines were emerging aimed at imposing greater control over corporate management. (Remember the shareholder derivative suit: it will play an important role in various chapters.)

Railway regulation was a leading public issue in the 1870s, and in the 1880s the Interstate Commerce Commission was created, primarily for the purpose of controlling the railroads. In 1890 the Sherman Act was passed to combat "trusts" that dominated major industries. Thus, while businesses were free to adapt the corporate instrument to their will, regulatory efforts also were initiated to circumscribe some of the power and impact of large corporations and their managers.

New Jersey was the first state to depart from the philosophy of strict limitations on corporations, beginning with its 1888 incorporation statute, which it revised in 1896. Delaware, a small state, passed a statute in 1899 modeled on New Jersey's statute with a view to attracting incorporations and thereby generating franchise tax revenues. When New Jersey amended its corporation law in 1913 to reimpose a number of restrictive provisions, Delaware kept the "enabling" nature of its statute, and emerged as the venue of choice, at least for publicly traded corporations.

In early U.S. corporations, one of the most important features of the statutory charter was a statement of corporate purposes. Under the common law doctrine of *ultra vires* ("beyond the power"), a corporation could not engage in activities outside the scope of its defined purposes. The doctrine reflected both the public suspicion of concentrations of private economic power and the desire of corporate investors to limit their financial exposure to specified business risks and constrain the corporations they invested in to do business in specified spheres such as providing services in their local community.

In the nineteenth century, a central focus of the law of corporations was the resolution of disputes arising under the ultra vires doctrine. Once states began in the mid-1800s to enact general incorporation statutes, however, corporate lawyers began circumventing the limitations of the ultra vires doctrine simply by drafting the articles of incorporation in broad terms. "Purpose clauses" sometimes went on for pages, listing every conceivable activity in which a corporation might engage, even if the promoters intended only to undertake limited activities.

Today, such drafting is unnecessary. Modern statutes typically allow for broad purpose provisions such as the one in Section 3.01(a) of the MBCA stating: "Every corporation incorporated under this Act has the purpose of engaging in any lawful business unless a more limited purpose is set forth in the articles of incorporation." A similar breadth is found with respect to corporate powers. As a result, the *ultra vires* doctrine is relevant today in only limited circumstances. *See* MBCA § 3.04; DGCL § 124. Statements of corporate purpose include a limit of *lawful* activity. Further, the purpose and powers language in the articles can limit the scope of a corporation's business and management discretion. Similarly, "benefit corporations" specify in their articles particular social or environmental purposes that could limit the scope of their corporate activities. Otherwise, the doctrine of *ultra vires* is not relevant as a defense to an otherwise valid obligation.

> As we will see in Chapter 13, entrepreneurs increasingly are forming corporations with a stated social purpose or purposes, and states have adopted various statutory provisions that govern these new categories of entities. For example, "benefit corporations" often include a specified social purpose in their articles or a "general social benefit" statement (for example, "a material positive impact on society and the environment, taken as a whole"). States take varying approaches to benefit corporations, and the types of descriptions of corporate powers and purposes in benefit corporations' articles is evolving: some descriptions are specific and narrow, while others are general and broad.

B. Fundamental Aspects of the Corporation

The corporation can be defined in many ways. It is a legal entity that can own property, enter into contracts, sue and be sued. It is a team of people, including suppliers of money and labor, who work together to earn a return on their investments. It is a web of contracts among investors, employees, customers, and community. It is an investment vehicle that can be used for good or for ill. In many ways, the corporation is a drama: over time, the corporate actors—shareholders, directors, officers, and other employees—work through the conflicts that arise from their different investments, incentives, and goals.

Public and private ordering. Corporations can be seen as an amalgam of statutory, judicial, and private rules. To create a corporation, one must file the articles or certificate of incorporation with a designated state office and pay required fees. The governing documents for corporations (the articles or certificate of incorporation and the bylaws) allocate rights and responsibilities among the shareholders and directors. Shareholders elect directors to a corporate board with authority to manage the business and affairs of the corporation, including by delegating responsibilities to the corporation's officers and employees.

Fundamental shareholder rights. The corporation's board of directors, not shareholders, makes or delegates most business decisions. This a basic principle of corporate law. Corporate law limits the role of shareholders to a handful of fundamental rights, which we label generally as the rights (1) to voice views on various issues, primarily by voting, (2) to litigate claims against the corporation and its directors, officers, and controlling shareholders, (3) to exit the corporation, by selling shares. In shorthand, so they are easy for you to remember, we refer to these rights as the rights to vote, sue, and sell.

All of these rights can be limited in various ways, as we will see throughout this book. For example, some shareholders receive only limited voting rights. Corporations can specify the forum in which shareholders may sue the corporation and its directors and officers. And some shareholders face restrictions on their ability to sell shares without approval of the board of directors.

One central question of corporate law is how shareholders can maintain an appropriate amount of power, while ceding responsibility for most corporate decisions to directors and officers, sometimes referred to collectively as managers. Put another way, how can shareholders ensure that corporate managers will be accountable? Imagine that you own shares in a corporation, but you don't like how the managers are running the business. You might believe the directors have paid the officers too much money. Or perhaps you believe it is socially irresponsible for the corporation to be engaged in a particular activity. What can you do?

One strategy is simply to sell your shares. By selling, you exit the corporation, effectively severing your connection. Another strategy is to try to influence directors and officers by speaking out, submitting shareholder proposals to change their approach, attending the annual shareholders meeting, or even mounting a voting contest to replace the directors.

Which would you choose? Exit through selling is typically the cheaper option, particularly for investors who own a relatively small number of shares that are tradeable on public markets. For many shareholders, the cost of trying to influence directors and officers is greater than the potential benefit. In theory, shareholders can exert pressure or influence directors and officers by threatening to sell their shares, or by actually selling. However, if selling is the favored option, the most quality-conscious participants in the corporation are likely to exit first, leaving shareholders who are less able to help the corporation overcome its problems. Further, the stock price at which a shareholder sells will typically reflect the mismanagement or other problems that may be creating the shareholder's dissatisfaction.

Some shareholders and directors have recognized the limits of exit, and recent structural changes in markets have promoted the role of voice. Technological advances have made voice less costly. Increasingly, institutional investors such as mutual funds and pension funds hold shares in large blocks, and therefore would capture a larger portion of any gains to the corporation from the exercise of voice. Moreover, because many such institutional investors must maintain a diversified portfolio of investments in different companies, exit has become a less viable option and exercising voice is a more important avenue.

Finally, there is the possibility of shareholders bringing what is known as a derivative suit on behalf of the corporation against its directors in situations where the directors have harmed the corporation, such as by breaching their fiduciary duties of care or loyalty. As we will learn, the law has established obstacles to bringing these suits and a judicial presumption that directors exercise their business judgment properly. The law has also created ways for directors to be exculpated, indemnified, or insured for settlements and damages, such that directors rarely pay out of pocket. Accountability through litigation can be elusive except in egregious circumstances.

These concepts illustrate some of the central themes in this book. At their core, corporate law and policy are about the dramatic tensions among the participants in the corporation. The overarching legal question we will address is: how do law, markets, and contract enable each of these participants to protect themselves? And the overarching policy question we will address is: for whose benefit should the corporation be run?

You can also see the essential structure of the corporation by looking at a corporate statute (which you can find online). Browsing the table of contents will tell you a lot. For example, here are the main topics of the Delaware General Corporation Law (DGCL), the country's leading state for incorporation of public corporations:

- (§§ 101–111) the incorporation process
- (§§ 121–124) the powers of the corporation
- (§§ 131–136) the corporation's registered agent and office for service of process
- (§§ 141–146) the powers of the corporation's board of directors and officers
- (§§ 151–169) the corporation's issuance of shares
- (§§ 170–174) the corporation's payment of profits to shareholders
- (§§ 201–203) the transfers of shares
- (§§ 211–233) the voting of shares at shareholder meetings
- (§§ 251–264) the merger or other combination of corporations
- (§§ 271–285) the sale of corporate assets and dissolution of the corporation
- (§§ 291–296) the treatment of insolvent corporations
- (§§ 341–356) the special rules that govern close corporations

Notice that the statute describes key events for corporations—how they are created, what they can do, how they make decisions, how they conduct their affairs, how they can merge, and how they are dissolved.

C. Basic Corporate Vocabulary, Characteristics, and Actors

1. The Corporation

A corporation is a legal entity. Like human beings, corporations can enter into contracts, commit torts, sue and be sued. They are creatures of state law, which permits the formation of corporations as separate legal entities. When lawyers think about or deal with a corporation, they often start by drawing a diagram. When you read cases that involve many corporations, you might find it useful to draw boxes, with each representing a corporation, particularly if there are complex relationships among them.

> Suppose that "ABC, Inc." (one box) and "XYZ Corp." (another box) enter into a contract. You can show this relationship as a line connecting the two boxes. The diagram provides a visual way to see the two corporate entities and their legal relationship.
>
> **ABC, Inc.**
>
> ↑
> **contract**
> ↓
>
> **XYZ Corp.**

Corporate categories. There are numerous categories of corporations, and several important distinctions among types of corporations:

"For-profit" vs. "nonprofit." Although the typical corporations we discuss in this book are "for-profit" corporations (also known as business corporations), many corporations are not-for-profit or "nonprofit" corporations. In general, a "for-profit" corporation aims to generate financial wealth which it can distribute to shareholders, whereas a "nonprofit" corporation may be established for a range of purposes and does not have shareholders. Charities, and most hospitals and private universities, are examples of nonprofit corporations. Unless we note otherwise in this book, when we refer to corporations we mean for-profit business corporations.

Other statutory corporate forms. Most state statutes permit the formation of other types of corporations. For example, some states permit certain professionals to form "professional corporations," which have many of the attributes of normal for-profit corporations, though with ownership limits and sometimes special liability rules. In addition, entrepreneurs who seek to blend profits and social good can form a "benefit corporation," which requires that managers consider the impact of their decisions not only on shareholders, but also society and the environment or for a public benefit. We will discuss benefit corporations in more detail in Chapter 13, Corporate Social Responsibility, Benefit Corporations, and ESG.

"Public" vs. "private." Corporations whose shares are publicly traded on stock exchanges are known as "public" corporations, whereas corporations without publicly

traded stock are called "close," "closely held," or "private" corporations. ExxonMobil is a public corporation, but many individual Exxon gas stations are franchisees, often organized as private corporations.

In a private corporation, there is no ready market for the corporation's securities and there is usually a substantial overlap among some or all of the participants in how they govern the corporation's business. For example, directors and officers of private corporations often have substantial ownership stakes, and shareholders are often involved in management. In contrast, the shares of public corporations are freely traded: shareholders of public corporations typically can sell their shares easily on stock markets, and people without any relationship to the corporation can become shareholders by buying shares in the market. Shareholders of public corporations typically do not play a management role; although directors and officers of public corporations often own shares of their corporations, their ownership percentage typically is much smaller than the ownership stakes of private company shareholders.

Tax status. Although corporations are creatures of state law, federal income tax treatment is also an important consideration.

The Internal Revenue Code classifies every business organization as either a corporation or a partnership—with very different tax treatment for each. A corporation is treated as a taxpaying entity separate from its shareholders. The corporation itself pays taxes on business income and the shareholders are also taxed on any dividends or gains they receive—what is known as "double taxation." Specifically, corporations are generally subject to business-level tax under IRC Subchapter C (and are commonly referred to as "C Corporations").

There is an exception for certain corporations that elect to be taxed on a flow-through basis under IRC Subchapter S. To qualify as an "S corporation,"

> There is a curious ambiguity in corporate nomenclature. The terms "private" and "public" corporation mean different things in different contexts. Sometimes people refer to close corporations as "private" corporations since their shares are not traded on a public stock exchange. But sometimes people refer to "private" corporations as those that are not owned by the government. In this sense Bank of America is a "private" corporation since its shares (as of this writing) are not owned by the government, but instead by shareholders who acquired their shares on stock markets open to the public. In this sense, the Federal Deposit Insurance Corporation (a corporation owned by the government) is a "public" corporation since it is not "private." Got it?
>
> In this book, when we refer to "public" corporations we are talking about non-governmental, for-profit corporations whose shares are traded on public stock markets. And when we refer to "private" corporations, we are referring to "close" or "closely held" corporations that are non-governmental, for-profit corporations whose shares are not traded on public stock markets.

the corporation must be a domestic corporation (or LLC) with no more than 100 shareholders. The shareholders themselves must be individuals, estates or qualified trusts, or tax-exempt entities (such as employee stock ownership plans, pension plans, and charities). No shareholder can be a nonresident alien. The corporation can have only one class of stock, although shares with different voting rights are treated as part of the same class if they are otherwise alike. All the shareholders must consent to election of Subchapter S treatment. Once an election is made, corporate income, losses, and credits are attributed to shareholders according to the number of shares they hold. (But shareholders of an S Corporation can only write off losses up to the amount of capital they invested, with losses above capital investment carried forward and recognized in future years.)

Thus, public corporations are generally "C Corporations," and many (but certainly not all) private corporations are instead formed as "S Corporations."

Corporate characteristics. We will discuss various conceptions of the corporation in this book, but it is worth noting upfront that there are certain key characteristics of the basic business corporation. These characteristics illustrate not only the advantages of the corporate form, but also some of the reasons why tensions arise among the main actors in the corporate drama.

Separate entity. Every corporation is a legal entity that is separate from the investors who provide it with money and the people who manage its business. Investors who buy ownership interests in a corporation are known as shareholders or stockholders. The people who manage the corporation's business are known as directors and officers. The corporation is a separate legal entity from all of these people.

Perpetual existence. As a general rule, corporations have an unlimited existence. The individual corporate actors inevitably will change over time. Shareholders sell their shares. Corporate directors come and go. Employees retire, quit, are fired, or die. But the corporation remains intact and can exist forever. Notably, the parties may agree in advance that the corporation has a specific term or they may seek voluntary dissolution of the corporation (that is, liquidation of its assets, payment of creditors, and distribution of the net proceeds to shareholders) pursuant to the relevant statutory provision. But absent specification otherwise or dissolution, a corporation has perpetual existence and shareholders have no right to withdraw and demand payment for their shares from the corporation.

Limited liability. A corporation's shareholders cannot lose more money than they invested. In other words, a shareholder's liability is limited to the amount of money she paid for her shares. It is the corporation, not the shareholders, that owns the assets of the business and is liable for business debts.

Centralized management. Shareholders elect a corporation's directors, who have the power to manage and oversee the corporation's business. Shareholders agree to play only a limited governance role, in part because the directors have fiduciary duties to act in the best interests of the corporation. The directors typically delegate responsibility for daily decisions to corporate officers. The separation between shareholder ownership and managerial control is one of the distinctive features of modern public corporations.

Transferability of ownership interests. Shareholders can transfer to others their ownership interests in a corporation. In publicly owned corporations, this is accomplished on stock exchanges and similar stock trading markets.

These are the basic characteristics of corporations, but there are many exceptions. Indeed, corporate law essentially is a set of enabling "default rules" setting forth the relationship among corporate actors unless they agree otherwise. Particularly for small firms, the law governing the participants in a corporation is largely contractual, and the parties can and do alter or amend many of the basic corporate terms. Large firms, in contrast, are increasingly governed by government regulation, which they often cannot avoid by contract.

2.   Sources of Corporate Law and Private Ordering

Although there are federal statutes that govern a good deal of corporate activity, there is no federal corporation law (although some legislators have proposed that). The legal rules governing the corporation's actors are an amalgam of state statutes, judicial decisions, and privately created governance. State corporation statutes are not all-encompassing, and court decisions fill many of the gaps. In fact, a central aspect of corporate law—corporate fiduciary duties—is largely judge-made. Although each state's corporate case law is based on that state's corporate statute, many court decisions refer to corporate law principles that are generally accepted throughout the country.

> Unlike other areas of law where Restatements collect and synthesize judge-made rules, there is no restatement for U.S. corporate law. Instead, in 1994, the American Law Institute produced a set of statements and suggested rules on corporate law, the "ALI Principles of Corporate Governance: Analysis and Recommendations." These "ALI Principles" have been controversial and only somewhat influential. We will refer to them at various points, but bear in mind that they often differ from prevailing corporate law practices.

No two state statutes are identical, yet there has been a trend toward uniformity in many areas. Many states rely on the "model" corporate law rules in the Model Business Corporation Act (MBCA), which was drafted and continues to be revised by the Corporate Laws Committee of the Business Law Section of the American Bar Association. However, many state statutes—importantly, California and New York—differ from the MBCA in certain areas, either because the legislators have adopted different policies or because the MBCA has changed and states have not yet updated their statutes to reflect these revisions. We will point out many of these differences in various chapters.

We frequently will cite to the law of one state: Delaware. Delaware is the leading corporate law state. A majority of publicly traded corporations, and many private corporations, are incorporated there. Delaware's corporate law statute, the Delaware General Corporation Law (DGCL), is unique and differs in many areas from the MBCA. Delaware's courts have provided significant guidance in interpreting the DGCL and in understanding corporate law more generally. Courts of other states often refer to court decisions from Delaware, whose case law is the most comprehensive and highly regarded among the states. This book contains many Delaware court decisions.

> Our citations to the Delaware corporate statute are linked to the state's online statutory code. *See* Delaware Code, Title 8, Chapter 1 (General Corporation Law). Our citations to the MBCA are linked to the version available from the American Bar Association.

In your study of corporate law, you will find it invaluable to understand the text and meaning of these and other state corporate statutes. We will refer to various statutory provisions in this book and will quote from some of them. Links to these statutes are available in the online version of this book. The statutes are also available from numerous sources online (including through Westlaw).

And, although corporate law is primarily within the purview of states, we will also see a number of situations in which federal law has created an overlay of rules concerning corporate governance, typically for public corporations (which are also subject to extensive disclosure obligations under federal securities laws).

Furthermore, as noted, the governance of a corporation is also a matter of "private ordering." The articles of incorporation and bylaws are sometimes referred to as the "organic documents" or "constitutive documents" of the corporation. They set out the essential information about the corporation and its internal governance.

Articles of incorporation. Just about anyone can create a corporation by filing "articles of incorporation" with the relevant state officials and paying the required (often modest) fees. Remember that corporations are creatures of state law. The people who form a corporation will file the articles in one particular state. The basic structure and most rules for the corporation will be set forth in that state's corporation statute and judicial interpretation.

The "articles of incorporation" are like the "constitution" of the corporation. Although the term "articles" is plural, the "articles" of incorporation are really just one legal document, with a number of provisions or articles. The document typically is brief, sometimes just one page, though in public corporations they can be much longer. The articles establish the corporation and contain basic provisions required by the state, such as the precise name of the corporation, its agent and address for service of process, and the number of authorized shares. The articles must be filed and accepted for filing by the relevant state officials, typically the Secretary of State, Corporations Division. The articles are sometimes called the "certificate of incorporation," depending on the state, or colloquially referred to as the "corporate charter."

> Besides browsing corporate statutes, you will find it useful to browse some typical articles and bylaws.
>
> For corporations subject to disclosure requirements under the federal securities laws, these organic documents can often be found as attachments to disclosure documents filed with the Securities and Exchange Commission at https://www.sec.gov/edgar/search-edgar/companysearch.html.
>
> In addition, most public corporations provide links to these documents on their websites—usually under "investor relations."

Bylaws. In addition to the articles of incorporation, a corporation's founders also will draft and adopt "bylaws." The bylaws, which are not filed with the state, set out the governing details of the corporation. Bylaws typically are lengthier than the articles of incorporation. Bylaws vary widely, but frequently include items such as: the powers of directors and officers, procedures for electing directors and filling director vacancies, required notice periods and details for calling and holding meetings of shareholders and directors, and similar internal governance issues.

In this course, we will see numerous planning challenges and conflicts among the various corporate participants. In theory, the organic documents are supposed to work together to assist these participants in achieving their objectives. In practice, shareholders, directors, and officers can disagree about how these documents can or should be changed during the life of a corporation. In general, corporate law creates a simple and powerful legal hierarchy: the corporation's articles cannot conflict with the statute under which the corporation is organized, and the corporation's bylaws cannot conflict with the statute or the articles.

3. Corporate Securities

Corporations raise money by issuing shares or other securities to their investors. Securities used to be issued as hard copy certificates that the corporation gave to investors in exchange for cash. Today, there are no pieces of paper for most securities. Instead, ownership of securities is documented through computer records.

There are three basic categories of securities: common shares, preferred shares, and debt. These categories vary in terms of risk and expected return.

Debt securities. Debt is the least risky security and has the lowest expected return. A holder of debt typically expects to receive only fixed payments of interest over time.

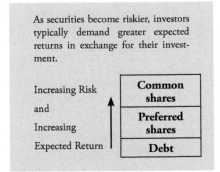

As securities become riskier, investors typically demand greater expected returns in exchange for their investment.

Increasing Risk
and
Increasing
Expected Return

| Common shares |
| Preferred shares |
| Debt |

Even if the corporation does well, debt securities will receive only fixed payments—debtholders are creditors. If the corporation becomes insolvent, and its assets must be sold for cash (liquidated), debt securities will have priority.

Equity securities. Common shares take on greater risk and also have greater expected return. Common shares have a claim to the residual financial rights to the corporation's income and assets. Once the corporation has paid everyone it owes, the common shares are entitled (at the discretion of the board of directors) to whatever is left. Common shares can receive payment through "dividends," which are cash payments the corporation can make, upon approval by the board. If the corporation becomes insolvent and cannot pay its debts, common shares—as the residual claim—are the last to receive any proceeds. This last-in-line position (sometimes referred to as being the "residual claimant") is often said to be the rationale for giving the common shareholders the right to vote in the corporation.

Preferred shares are "equity," like common shares, but preferred shares have certain priorities over the common stock. For example, preferred shares often carry the right to receive dividends before common shares receive a dividend. Likewise, preferred shares typically have priority over common shares if the corporation becomes insolvent. Thus, preferred shares typically have less risk than common shares, but more risk than debt. The exact "preferences" that the preferred stock is entitled to is a matter of contract.

Authorized, issued, and outstanding shares. There are three terms to describe the three stages that shares can occupy. First is "authorized." The corporation's articles of incorporation specify how many shares of common and preferred stock the corporation is "authorized" to issue. Additional shares can be issued only if the articles are amended to increase the number of authorized shares.

The term "stock" is often used interchangeably with the term "shares" to refer to ownership units of "equity" securities. Likewise, the terms "bonds," "debentures," and "notes" often are used to describe different classes of "debt" securities. Ultimately, the claims of securities are generally governed by their terms, not their labels.

Second is "issued." Of the corporation's authorized shares, the corporation might issue all, or just a portion, of those shares to its shareholders. Frequently, a corporation will not issue all of its authorized shares. One reason for this practice is that a corporation's board of directors generally is free to sell authorized but unissued shares on whatever terms it decides are reasonable—without shareholder approval. In contrast, if the board wants to raise capital by issuing more shares than the number of authorized shares, the corporation will need to amend its articles of incorporation, which requires shareholder approval.

Third is "outstanding." The portion of the authorized stock that has been sold and remains in the hands of stockholders is the stock "outstanding." Because the corporation can repurchase issued shares (which are called "treasury shares" and are held by the corporation, and this practice is referred to as "stock buybacks"), some of the issued shares might not be outstanding.

Example

The articles of XYZ, Inc. authorize 100 common shares. The board approves the issuance of 80 shares, which are sold to investors. At that point 80 shares are outstanding. The board can issue 20 more shares, but if it wants to issue more than that, the articles would have to be amended.

The corporation then repurchases 10 of the 80 shares that are issued and outstanding. This means that of the 100 shares authorized, there are now 70 shares outstanding. There are also 10 treasury shares (repurchased and not outstanding) and 20 authorized, but unissued shares.

---

4. Corporate Actors

The corporation can be thought of as a drama, with several actors. Within the governance of the corporation, there are three categories of actors: shareholders, directors, and officers. There also are numerous categories of corporate stakeholders. Each of these actors can play an important role in corporate decision making. Moreover, some individuals can play more than one of these roles simultaneously. For example, a person might be a shareholder, a director, and an officer. Corporate actors can wear more than one hat.

Shareholders. "Shareholders"—sometimes called "stockholders"—are often described as the "owners" of the corporation, but more precisely they are owners of stock. In the simplest case, shareholders contribute capital to the corporation in exchange for "common shares" of the corporation. These common shares represent a divided economic stake in the equity of the corporation. Although corporate law often seems to envision this simplest case, and some corporations raise capital exclusively through common shares, many corporations also use other forms to raise capital, including other corporate "securities," which are described below.

Like participants in a representative democracy, shareholders do not control the corporation directly. Instead, shareholders generally play a mostly passive role, and their voting rights are limited. Shareholders elect directors and must approve (after board initiation) certain fundamental transactions, such as amendments to the articles or a merger with another corporation. Shareholders also can amend the bylaws, although the extent to which shareholders can do so unilaterally, when the directors oppose the amendment, is controversial.

The relationships of corporate actors are also the subject of other courses in a typical law school curriculum. Here are a few:

Corporate Finance covers the corporation's capital structure, the valuation of corporate securities, and the issuance of corporate debt.

Debtor-Creditor Law and Bankruptcy cover the rights of creditors when a debtor, including a corporate debtor, is unwilling or unable to pay its debts.

Labor and Employment Law covers the rights of employees under the many laws (federal and state) that regulate the employment relationship.

Securities Regulation covers the federal registration and public disclosure regime and exemptions for private placements of securities.

Directors. "Directors" are individuals who are elected by the shareholders to be responsible for managing or supervising the corporation's business. The directors (also referred to as "board members") act on behalf of the corporation only collectively as the "board" or "board of directors." Directors owe duties to act on behalf of the corporation, and directors are supposed to represent the interests of the corporation. Given the potentially competing interests among the various corporate actors, it can be difficult for directors to determine when a particular decision will be in the corporation's interests, as opposed to the narrow interest of one of the corporate actors. They must inform themselves and use their good faith business judgment.

Directors are not considered employees or agents of the corporation, although corporate employees can serve as directors. An "outside" director is a person who generally does not have any affiliation with the corporation, other than his or her role as a director. An "inside" director is a person who is both a director and a corporate employee—such as when the company's CEO (an employee) also serves as a director on the board. The question of whether a director is "disinterested" (not financially interested in a particular corporate decision) or "independent" (not beholden to an interested party) will recur throughout this course.

Officers. "Officers" are corporate employees. Corporate statutes and bylaws give broad discretion to directors to delegate responsibility to officers and describe the duties of officers in only general terms. Typically, the board delegates the responsibility for running the corporation's day-to-day business to the Chief Executive Officer (CEO) and other officers such as the Chief Financial Officer (CFO) and Chief Operating Officer (COO). The board selects the most senior officers, and one of the important responsibilities of the board is the hiring, and potential firing, of the CEO.

In practice, the roles of these categories of corporate actors can be complex and overlapping, particularly in private corporations. When you consider a problem, or read a case, first consider whether the corporation at issue is public or private. In a public corporation, the roles of the parties often are cleanly divided, with shareholders playing a limited role in the business. In contrast, the shareholders of a private corporation typically are more active, and often wear several hats. The directors and officers of a private corporation frequently will be substantial shareholders. In a private corporation, personal and family relationships can matter more than title or position.

Stakeholders. Other corporate actors are known as "stakeholders." They include creditors, employees, customers, and the community, people and institutions who are involved with and depend on the corporation but do not fit the legal categories of shareholders, directors, or officers. Creditors are people and entities that lend money to a corporation in exchange for the corporation's promise to make periodic interest payments and to return the principal of the loan after a specified time or maturity. Although corporate directors and officers generally owe fiduciary duties to the corporation and its shareholders, they typically do not owe such duties to creditors. Instead, creditors typically protect themselves by contract, including covenants in bond or loan documents that restrict certain corporate actions. Bankruptcy law also protects creditors. They are entitled to payment first, before shareholders.

Employees obviously have a stake in the corporation, too. However, their protections derive primarily from sources other than corporate law. Employees can be protected by employment contracts, common law, and regulatory statutes, which govern workplace safety, discrimination, and various labor issues. Likewise, suppliers and customers enter into contractual relationships with the corporation or are covered by common and statutory law.

Finally, the community can be an important corporate stakeholder because it depends on the corporation to employ its citizens, pay taxes, and contribute to various cultural and community affairs. When a major corporation leaves a community, its departure can be a serious blow to the community's health or even survival.

Who does the corporation serve? One question that will resurface throughout this course, and in corporate law, is this: for whose benefit should the corporation be run?

The following schematic represents one way to diagram the relationships in the corporation:

Influenced by the law and economics movement, some scholars argue that shareholders occupy the role of "owners" or "principals." The board of directors acts as "agent" for the shareholders, with delegated power to manage and supervise the business and affairs of the corporation. The board selects the officers, who along with employees, carry out the day-to-day business of the corporation. The stakeholders reside "outside" the corporation and have contractual, tort, regulatory, and social claims on the corporation. There are other ways of thinking about the corporation, which we explore in Chapter 12 on Corporate Purpose and Personhood.

There are no easy answers to this question. Probably, each of you already has some notion of the kinds of roles you ideally would want the for-profit corporation to play in society. Should it be managed for the exclusive benefit of shareholders? Should it be managed for the benefit of society overall? Or is it possible to describe how the corporate objective might occupy some middle ground between these seemingly polar goals? We will return to this question at several points, especially in Chapter 12, Corporate Purpose and Personhood.

5. Authority and Actions Binding the Corporation

Who acts for the corporation? We've introduced you to the standard governance model of the corporation in which shareholders elect the corporation's directors, the board of directors is charged with managing the corporation's business, and officers and employees carry on day-to-day operations under power delegated by the board of directors. The corporation, a legal construct, can act only through the agency of human beings. What is the authority of corporate directors and officers?

Corporate law vests authority in the board of directors as a collective body. Individual directors are not agents by virtue of their role as directors. They have authority to act as a board of directors through the means specified by corporate law: board meetings and written consents.

- Unless the articles or bylaws provide otherwise, the vote of a majority of the directors present at a board meeting at which there is a quorum is necessary to pass a resolution. DGCL § 141(b); MBCA § 8.24. Let's break this rule for action at board meetings down into more detail. Quorum refers to the minimum number of directors that must be present at a meeting to make the proceedings of that meeting valid. The purpose of the quorum requirement is to preclude action by a minority of the directors. The statutory norm for a quorum is a majority of the total number of directors, although the articles of incorporation or bylaws may increase the quorum requirement or reduce it to no less than one-third of the board. The MBCA requires at least two days' notice for special meetings of the board of directors, but directors can waive any required notice. MBCA §§ 8.22, 8.23. Thus, putting it all together, the default quorum is a majority of the total number of directors, and once there is a quorum present, and any required notice has been

Boards often find it difficult to discharge all of their responsibilities acting through the full board. Many boards delegate responsibility for many board functions to committees empowered to exercise, in defined areas, the authority of the board. Corporate statutes authorize this practice. Public corporations are required under federal law and stock exchange rules to have certain standing committees, with independent directors, such as for audit, compensation, as well as nominations and governance. In addition, boards often create specialized committees to deal with specific problems. For example, in Chapter 14 we discuss the use of special litigation committees in connection with derivative suits.

properly given, the board can take action by the vote of a majority of the directors present. For example, assuming the default rules, a board with a total of ten directors would need six directors for a quorum, and if that number were present, it would require the vote of at least four directors to pass a resolution.

- State corporate law rules vary regarding the ability of a board of directors to take action by written consent without a board meeting. Delaware's statute, like the MBCA, authorizes a board to act without a meeting by means of unanimous written consent. DGCL § 141(f); MBCA § 8.21. Written consents generally set out by resolution the specific action or actions being taken by the board followed by the signatures of the approving directors.

As for officers, agency principles apply. In some cases, courts find that officers have authority by being appointed to their office by the board of directors. The key corporate officers, along with their functions and general authority, are usually specified in the corporation's bylaws. It is also possible that the board of directors, acting at a board meeting or through a written consent, could create actual authority for officers to act on behalf of the corporation. In other cases, where actual authority is not established, courts may find that the officer was acting with apparent authority because a person dealing with the corporation reasonably believes the officer has authority. Or, sometimes courts find ratification has occurred because a board has taken action at a board meeting or through a written consent to expressly affirm an agent's action, or ratification is implied based on prior dealings between the officer and a third party that the board never challenged.

6.   Corporate Fiduciary Duties

Duties of care and loyalty. We have seen fiduciary duties in agency and partnership law, in Chapters 2 and 3, and we will also study the specific law on fiduciary duties in the corporate context in several chapters of this book. The relationships among the various corporate actors are governed in part by express legal rules and in part by fiduciary principles created mostly by the courts. The basic fiduciary duties that directors and officers owe to the corporation are the duty of care and the duty of loyalty.

The duty of care requires managers to be attentive and prudent in making decisions. The duty of loyalty requires managers to put the corporation's interests ahead of their own. The duties of care and loyalty are embodied in numerous statutes and cases, and arise in a wide range of contexts. For now, we simply want to highlight the general nature of these twin duties.

Business judgment rule. Notwithstanding these duties, a central thesis of corporate law is that courts defer to the board of directors, who have significant discretion in making corporate decisions, even when their well-meaning decisions result in failure. Courts have developed a rule of abstention or standard of review—known as the "business judgment rule" (BJR)—under which courts defer to the judgment of the board of directors absent a conflict of interest, bad faith, or gross inattention.

In general, the BJR presumes that director decisions (1) are informed, (2) made in good faith, and (3) in the honest belief that the action taken is in the best interests of the corporation. As a procedural matter, this judicial presumption is important. In order for a plaintiff to shift the burden to the directors (which typically means that the directors must establish that a decision was fair to the corporation), the plaintiff must show that a decision: (1) was grossly uninformed (2) did not have a rational business purpose (i.e., constituted waste), (3) was made by directors with a personal or financial interest in the decision, or (4) was made by directors who were not independent (i.e., were beholden to someone who had an interest in the decision).

We will cover the details of the BJR later in the course. For now, it is enough to recognize that the BJR plays a central role in the American system of corporate law. The BJR creates a presumption that, absent evidence of self-dealing, illegality, or the directors not being reasonably informed, all board decisions are intended to advance the interests of the corporation and its shareholders. Consequently, courts will not entertain shareholder suits that challenge the wisdom of such decisions. Structurally, the BJR implements the basic corporate attribute of centralized management by insulating the board's decision-making prerogatives from shareholder, and judicial, second guessing.

Liability to corporation and shareholders. Corporate managers who breach their fiduciary duties can be held liable for any losses they cause the corporation. Fashioning procedures to enforce managers' fiduciary duties raises difficult issues about who can enforce corporate interests. More often than not, the managers whose conduct is at issue control the corporate decision-making apparatus and are not likely to sue themselves. Moreover, shareholders are not authorized to act directly for the corporation, and thus cannot enforce a corporate claim against the managers.

The "derivative suit" was developed to solve this problem. The derivative suit is an action in equity brought by a shareholder on behalf of the corporation. The action is brought against the corporation as a nominal defendant, and the plaintiff-shareholder (and his lawyer) controls prosecution of the suit against other defendants such as directors and officers. Any recovery belongs to the corporation for whose benefit the suit has been brought.

In addition, shareholder plaintiffs (and their lawyers) also file federal, and less frequently state, class action lawsuits against corporations and their managers alleging various violations of law, in particular federal securities fraud. At any point in time, hundreds of public corporations face the threat of civil liability in both derivative and class action lawsuits brought by shareholders. However, most of these corporations have agreed to indemnify or insure their managers against liability in many instances, and nearly all the suits (even when meritorious) are settled without going to trial. As a result, it is rare for a non-interested director personally to pay money damages in a lawsuit brought by shareholders.

Duties of shareholders. Although directors owe fiduciary duties, shareholders generally do not. Of course, a person might be a shareholder and a director, and therefore owe duties because of her director role. But simply being a shareholder generally will not subject a shareholder to any fiduciary duties. There is, however, one major exception. If shareholders exercise control through their share ownership (as opposed to any other role they might play within the corporation), courts often will hold that such controlling shareholders owe fiduciary duties to other shareholders.

D. Process of Incorporation and Related Topics

Now, that we know the basic vocabulary of corporations, we turn to the process of incorporation. The filing requirements and procedures for forming a corporation are simple and quick. But there are pitfalls. Obtaining limited liability is important, and it's important to do it right. We next examine the logistics of how to form a corporation and what can happen if a promoter engages in activity for a corporation before it is formed or if the corporation is defectively formed.

1. The Basics of Forming a Corporation

Although the procedures vary slightly from state to state, the MBCA is typical. Incorporation is formally accomplished by an "incorporator"—a capacity that has no further significance once the corporation is organized. The incorporator signs and files the articles of incorporation (a public document) with the Secretary of State or another designated official. There is a filing fee, which is usually a flat rate or in some states, notably Delaware, calculated on the basis of the number of authorized shares. Under most statutes, formal corporate existence commences with the filing of the articles of incorporation.

MBCA § 2.01
Incorporators

One or more persons may act as the incorporator or incorporators of a corporation by delivering articles of incorporation to the secretary of state for filing.

What goes into the articles? Very little is required, though much can be included. Under most statutes the articles must include only (1) the name of the corporation, (2) the number of shares it is authorized to issue, (3) the name and address of each incorporator, and (4) the name and address of the corporation's registered office and registered agent (the person and place to receive service of process or other official notices). There is no need to identify the directors, the officers, or the shareholders—the internal functioning and ownership of the corporation is mostly a private matter, at least under state law. Nor is there a need to disclose the corporation's specific purposes, powers, and responsibilities—as we have seen, these are typically described only in general terms as engaging in any lawful business.

Under the MBCA (and most state statutes), the articles can include provisions that insulate directors from liability, or "exculpate" them. An exculpation clause limits the personal liability of directors to the corporation or its shareholders in certain circumstances. Some states such as Delaware also allow for officer exculpation, subject to important exclusions. Indemnification provisions also can obligate the corporation to reimburse directors and officers for personal liability, again with exceptions.

MBCA § 2.02
Articles of Incorporation

(a)   The articles of incorporation must set forth:

(1)   a corporate name for the corporation that satisfies the requirements of section 4.01;

(2)   the number of shares the corporation is authorized to issue;

(3)   the street and mailing addresses of the corporation's initial registered office and the name of its initial registered agent at that office; and

(4)   the name and address of each incorporator.

(b) The articles of incorporation may set forth:

(1)   the names and addresses of the individuals who are to serve as the initial directors;

(2)   provisions not inconsistent with law regarding: (i) the purpose or purposes for which the corporation is organized; (ii) managing the business and regulating the affairs of the corporation; (iii) defining, limiting, and regulating the powers of the corporation, its board of directors, and shareholders; (iv) a par value for authorized shares or classes of shares; or (v) the imposition of interest holder liability on shareholders;

(3)   any provision that under this Act is required or permitted to be set forth in the bylaws;

(4)   a provision eliminating or limiting the liability of a director to the corporation or its shareholders for money damages for any action taken, or any failure to take any action, as a director, except liability for (i) the amount of a financial benefit received by a director to which the director is not entitled; (ii) an intentional infliction of harm on the corporation or the shareholders; (iii) a violation of section 8.32; or (iv) an intentional violation of criminal law;

(5)   a provision permitting or making obligatory indemnification of a director for liability as defined in section 8.50 to any person for any action taken, or any failure to take any action, as a director, except liability for (i) receipt of a financial benefit to which the director is not entitled, (ii) an intentional infliction of harm on the corporation or the shareholders, (iii) a violation of section 8.32, or (iv) an intentional violation of criminal law; and

(6)   a provision limiting or eliminating any duty of a director or any other person to offer the corporation the right to have or participate in any, or one or more classes or categories of, business opportunities, before the pursuit or taking of the opportunity by the director or other person; provided that any application of such a provision to an officer or a related person of that officer (i) also requires approval of that application by the board of directors, subsequent to the effective date of the provision, by action of qualified directors taken in compliance with the same procedures as are set forth in section 8.62, and (ii) may be limited by the authorizing action of the board.

(c) The articles of incorporation need not set forth any of the corporate powers enumerated in this Act.

(d) Provisions of the articles of incorporation may be made dependent upon facts objectively ascertainable outside the articles of incorporation in accordance with section 1.20(k).

(e) As used in this section, "related person" has the meaning specified in section 8.60.

After the corporation comes into legal existence, an organizational meeting must be held. This is done either by the incorporator or by the initial board. At this first meeting (or when the incorporator simply signs a consent form), a number of standard tasks happen: (1) the election of directors (or of additional directors if directors were named in the articles); (2) the adoption of bylaws; (3) the appointment of officers; (4) the designation of a bank as depository for corporate funds; and (5) approval of the sale of stock to the initial shareholders.

MBCA § 2.05
Organization of Corporation

(a) After incorporation:

(1) if initial directors are named in the articles of incorporation, the initial directors shall hold an organizational meeting, at the call of a majority of the directors, to complete the organization of the corporation by appointing officers, adopting bylaws, and carrying on any other business brought before the meeting; or

(2) if initial directors are not named in the articles, the incorporator or incorporators shall hold an organizational meeting at the call of a majority of the incorporators:

(i) to elect directors and complete the organization of the corporation; or

(ii) to elect a board of directors who shall complete the organization of the corporation.

(b) Action required or permitted by this Act to be taken by incorporators at an organizational meeting may be taken without a meeting if the action taken is evidenced by one or more written consents describing the action taken and signed by each incorporator.

(c) An organizational meeting may be held in or out of this state.

It is not necessary to have a lawyer to incorporate a business. In fact, many people incorporate without a lawyer, either on their own or by using a corporation service company or online provider. Service companies can provide standard articles of incorporation, bylaws, and forms of stock certificate. They also file the necessary documents with the state, act as registered agent for the corporation, qualify the corporation to do business in other jurisdictions, and assist in the filing of annual and other reports required by the state of incorporation and other states where the corporation is registered as a foreign corporation. In many cases, the service companies charge less than lawyers for comparable work. Lawyers offer planning counsel regarding governance and other considerations that can provide value beyond the task of incorporation.

2. Promoter Liability and Defective Formation

When does the corporation come to life? The question is important for those who want the advantage of corporate limited liability, so business liabilities do not create personal liability. Modern corporate statutes (the MBCA is typical) identify a precise moment when the corporation comes into existence: the filing of the articles.

> Most states have websites with information about corporations and other business entities. The websites include business-entity statutes, descriptions of the different business-entity types, information on fees, instructions on forming a corporation or unincorporated entity, and forms for downloading and filing. Some states are moving towards on-line "paperless" filing systems.

MBCA § 2.03
Incorporation

(a) Unless a delayed effective date is specified, the corporate existence begins when the articles of incorporation are filed.

(b) The secretary of state's filing of the articles of incorporation is conclusive proof that the incorporators satisfied all conditions precedent to incorporation except in a proceeding by the state to cancel or revoke the incorporation or involuntarily dissolve the corporation.

What happens if a "corporation" enters into a business transaction—but before the corporation exists? This problem used to be common, when the incorporation process took longer than a simple filing and required approval by a state official and formalities such as multiple signatures, notarization, and local county filings done in person or by mail. Given these difficulties, third parties sometimes would do deals with a "corporation to be formed." Other times, parties thought the corporation existed, unaware of some incorporation delay or defect.

The heavily litigated question that arose was whether third parties could sue *personally* those individuals who purported to act for the corporation. When both parties knew that the corporation had not yet been formed, the question was whether the "promoter" was liable. When one or both of the parties was unaware that there was a defect in incorporation, the question was whether the court should infer limited liability on equity grounds. Today, with incorporation so simple, these cases do not arise as often, but it is still helpful to know the basics.

a. Promoter Liability

Suppose two parties enter into a contract, and one acts on behalf of a corporation to be formed. If both parties know that there has been no incorporation, traditional principles of contract and agency law present some conceptual questions: Can the corporation, once formed, become bound by the contract and, if so, under what theory? Is the "promoter" who executes the contract liable on the contract if the corporation never comes into existence? If the corporation comes into existence and adopts the contract as its own, is the promoter off the hook? And can the corporation now sue on the contract?

> The term "promoter" refers to an individual who organizes or makes financing or other arrangements for a corporation before it is formed. As an agent for the proposed corporation, promoters have fiduciary duties to the corporation they promote and to those who will eventually buy stock in the corporation.

Here's the general rule: when a promoter contracts for the benefit of a corporation that is contemplated but not yet organized, the promoter is personally liable on the contract in the absence of an agreement otherwise. Furthermore, the promoter is not discharged from liability simply because the corporation is later organized and receives the benefits of the contract, even where the corporation adopts the contract. The parties may agree to discharge the promoter's liability—but to do so they must agree there will be a novation once the corporation is formed and formally accepts the contract.

The question becomes one of intent. When the parties' contract does not directly address the issue, courts have discerned the parties' intent from their contract and their dealings. Factors include:

> A "novation" is a three-party arrangement in which a new party replaces an existing party to a contract. In a pre-incorporation contract, the newly formed corporation assumes all of the rights and liabilities of the promoter under the contract, thus discharging the promoter.

- the form of signature—did the promoter sign as an agent of the corporation?

- actions of the third party—did the third party plan to look only to the corporation for performance?

- partial performance—did the promoter's partial performance of the contract indicate an intent to be held personally liable?

- novation—did later actions taken by the parties discharge the promoter's liability?

Consider the following signature line: "D.J. Geary, for a bridge company to be organized and incorporated." What did the parties intend? Perhaps Geary would use his best efforts to bring a corporation into existence and to have it adopt the contract as its own; thus, Geary would not be bound personally. Perhaps Geary would be liable on the contract until such time as he has successfully incorporated the corporation and it has adopted the contract. Perhaps Geary would be bound on the contract and would remain bound even if the corporation came into existence and adopted the contract.

Which of these interpretations is most logical? The Restatement (Second) of Agency § 326 (1958) provides: "Unless otherwise agreed, a person who, in dealing with another, purports to act as agent for a principal whom both know to be non-existent or wholly incompetent, becomes a party to such contract." Under this default rule, Geary would be bound on the contract and would remain bound even if the corporation were ultimately to adopt it. A novation or release of Geary would be needed to discharge him from the contract.

b. *De Facto* Corporation Doctrine and Corporation by Estoppel

Two doctrines have developed that deal with circumstances in which a business organization has failed to become a *de jure* corporation (a corporation by law) but will nonetheless be treated as a corporation.

Under the doctrine of *de facto* corporation, courts infer limited liability if (1) the promoters in the would-be corporation had made a good faith effort to incorporate; (2) the promoters were unaware that the incorporation had not happened; and (3) the promoters used the corporate form in a transaction with a third party.

Under the doctrine of *corporation by estoppel*, courts prevent a contracting party from asserting the promoter's personal liability when the contracting party assumed the only recourse would be against the business assets.

MBCA § 2.04
Liability for Preincorporation Transactions

All persons purporting to act as or on behalf of a corporation, knowing there was no incorporation under this Act, are jointly and severally liable for all liabilities created while so acting.

OFFICIAL COMMENT

Ordinarily, only the filing of articles of incorporation should create the privilege of limited liability. Situations may arise, however, in which the protection of limited liability arguably should be recognized even though the simple incorporation process established by the Act has not been completed.

As a result, the Act imposes liability only on persons who act as or on behalf of corporations "knowing" that no corporation exists. In addition, section 2.04 does not foreclose the possibility that persons who urge defendants to execute contracts in the corporate name knowing that no steps to incorporate have been taken may be estopped to impose personal liability on individual defendants. This estoppel may be based on the inequity perceived when persons, unwilling or reluctant to enter into a commitment under their own name, are persuaded to use the name of a nonexistent corporation, and then are sought to be held personally liable under section 2.04 by the party advocating execution in the name of the corporation. While no special provision is made in section 2.04, the section does not foreclose the possibility that persons who urge defendants to execute contracts in the corporate name knowing that no steps to incorporate have been taken may be estopped to impose personal liability on individual defendants. This estoppel may be based on the inequity perceived when persons, unwilling or reluctant to enter into a commitment under their own name, are persuaded to use the name of a nonexistent corporation, and then are sought to be held personally liable under section 2.04 by the party advocating that form of execution.

Academic studies have sought to find consistency in the disarray of judicial doctrines. One early study, looking at cases through 1952, concluded that courts rarely provided "either real reasons or good reasons" when deciding defective formation cases. Subsequent studies have found that courts generally uphold the understandings and expectations of the parties, and infer limited liability if there is a good faith attempt to incorporate and both parties believe the transaction was with a corporation. Other research shows that courts continue to apply the *de facto* and *estoppel* doctrines, and that the doctrines are largely indistinguishable and depend on whether the person acting on behalf of the defectively incorporated entity was found to have acted in good faith. In sum, courts have continued to infer limited liability when parties assume in good faith that a corporation exists.

CHAPTER 5 *Corporation Basics*

Finally, you might note that contracting with a non-existent corporation can also happen when a corporation, though properly formed, has been dissolved by administrative order for failure to pay franchise taxes, to report a change in registered agent, or to file annual reports. Many state statutes address these situations by allowing the corporation to pay the back taxes or make the required filings, and then apply for reinstatement. For example, MBCA § 14.22 provides for reinstatement within two years of administrative dissolution. The effect of reinstatement is the retroactive recognition of the corporation, along with all corporate attributes including limited liability.

E.   Equitable Review by the Courts

As we have seen, a state's corporate law is not limited to its statute, but also includes judge-made case law. A fundamental issue that arises throughout corporate case law is the tension between the text of corporate statutes and principles of equity. The issue often arises when one or more corporate law statutory provisions are in conflict, or when directors have interpreted a statutory provision in a way that share-holders believe is unfair. In some cases, the plaintiff shareholders have challenged the actions of directors by arguing that they were improperly motivated. The following case is a classic example of how the Delaware courts have dealt with these kinds of conflicts and may subject a director's action to being "twice tested"—first for legal authorization, and second for equity. Directors must exercise their authority consistently with equitable principles of fiduciary duty.

Schnell v. Chris-Craft Industries, Inc.

285 A.2d 437 (Del. 1971)

[Plaintiffs, a group of Chris-Craft shareholders, were dissatisfied with the company's economic performance. They resolved to seek control by electing a new board of directors at Chris-Craft's next annual shareholders' meeting. On October 16, 1971, as required by federal law, they filed documents announcing their intentions with the Securities and Exchange Commission.

On October 18, Chris-Craft's board met and amended the corporation's bylaws, which had previously fixed January 11, 1972, as the date of the annual meeting. The new bylaws read as follows:

1. Annual Meeting. The annual meeting of stockholders of Chris-Craft Industries, Inc. shall be held for the election of the directors in the two month period commencing December 1 and ending on January 31 and at such time as shall be designated by the Board.

At this same October 18 meeting, the directors fixed December 8, 1971, at 9:30 a.m. as the date and time for the annual meeting, and named the Holiday Inn at Cortland, New York, where Chris-Craft operated a plant, as the place.

Cortland is a small town far from any transportation hubs. The board said it changed the meeting date because weather conditions made it difficult to get to Cortland in January and because holding the meeting well before Christmas would reduce problems with the mail. A notice with this information was mailed to shareholders on November 8, 1971, more than 60 days before January 11, 1972.

The trial court found that the defendants' actions, including the change in the date of the annual meeting, were designed to obstruct the plaintiffs' efforts to gain control. But the court declined to reschedule the meeting on its original date, holding that the plaintiffs had delayed too long in seeking judicial relief. On appeal, the Supreme Court reversed.]

HERRMANN, JUSTICE for the majority of the Court: It will be seen that the Chancery Court considered all of the reasons stated by management as business reasons for changing the date of the meeting; but that those reasons were rejected by the Court below in making the following findings:

The case involves a "proxy contest" in which a group of shareholders dissatisfied with current management sought to replace the incumbent directors with their own slate of directors. The new board, they hoped, would steer the corporation in a new and more profitable direction. The insurgent group sought voting authority—or "proxies"—from other shareholders to vote their shares for the new board slate.

Proxy contests are relatively rare. As we will see in Chapter 15, Voting, the insurgent must bear the expenses of the contest (such as hiring lawyers, obtaining a shareholders' list to solicit proxies, and mailing disclosure documents to all shareholders) and can hope for reimbursement from the corporation for its election expenses only if successful.

More frequently, shareholders or other outsiders who think the corporation will be more profitable under new management will seek to buy sufficient shares to have a controlling interest—a takeover! We will see takeover fights throughout this book, including in the next case and particularly in Chapter 18, M&A.

"I am satisfied, however, in a situation in which present management has disingenuously resisted the production of a list of its stockholders to plaintiffs or their confederates and has otherwise turned a deaf ear to plaintiffs' demands about a change in management designed to lift defendant from its present business doldrums, management has seized on Delaware Corporation Law for the purpose of cutting down on the amount of time which would otherwise have been available to plaintiffs and others for the waging of a proxy battle. Management thus enlarged the scope of its scheduled October 18 directors' meeting to include the bylaw amendment in controversy after the stockholders committee had filed with the S.E.C. its intention to wage a proxy fight on October 16.

"Thus plaintiffs reasonably contend that because of the tactics employed by management (which involve the hiring of two established proxy solicitors as well as a refusal to produce a list of its stockholders, coupled with its use of Delaware Corporation Law to limit the time for contest), they are given little chance, because of the exigencies of time, including that required to clear material at the S.E.C., to wage a successful proxy fight between now and December 8."

In our view, those conclusions amount to a finding that management has attempted to utilize the corporate machinery and the Delaware Law for the purpose of perpetuating itself in office; and, to that end, for the purpose of obstructing the legitimate efforts of dissident stockholders in the exercise of their rights to undertake a proxy contest against management. These are inequitable purposes, contrary to established principles of corporate democracy. The advancement by directors of the bylaw date of a stockholders' meeting, for such purposes, may not be permitted to stand.

When the bylaws of a corporation designate the date of the annual meeting of stockholders, it is to be expected that those who intend to contest the reelection of incumbent management will gear their campaign to the bylaw date. It is not to be expected that management will attempt to advance that date in order to obtain an inequitable advantage in the contest.

Management contends that it has complied strictly with the provisions of the new Delaware Corporation Law in changing the bylaw date. The answer to that contention, of course, is that inequitable action does not become permissible simply because it is legally possible.

Accordingly, the judgment below must be reversed and the cause remanded, with instructions to nullify the December 8 date as a meeting date for stockholders; to reinstate January 11, 1972 as the sole date of the next annual meeting of the stockholders of the corporation; and to take such other proceedings and action as may be consistent herewith regarding the stock record closing date and any other related matters.

Points for Discussion

1. Source of law.

There is no doubt that the bylaw change in *Schnell* was authorized by the applicable statute. Indeed, although the trial court's opinion, quoted by the Supreme

Court, stated that "management has seized on a relatively new section of the Delaware Corporation Law," the change would also have complied with the old provision. What, then, is the law that the Supreme Court found defendants to have violated?

2. Fact-specific inquiries.

In *Stahl v. Apple Bancorp, Inc.*, 579 A.2d 1115 (Del. Ch. 1990), the court was presented with another dispute related to setting the date of an annual meeting. In both *Schnell* and *Stahl*, plaintiffs argued that the board's decision to change the meeting date, though it complied with the statute, should be enjoined because the transaction was improperly motivated. In *Schnell* the court sided with the insurgent shareholders; in *Stahl* the court sided with the incumbent board of directors. The *Stahl* court explained:

> "It is an elementary proposition of corporation law that, where they exist, fiduciary duties constitute a network of responsibilities that overlay the exercise of even undoubted legal power. Thus it is well established, for example, that where corporate directors exercise their legal powers for an inequitable purpose their action may be rescinded or nullified by a court at the instance of an aggrieved shareholder. The leading Delaware case of *Schnell v. Chris-Craft Industries, Inc.* announced this principle and applied it in a setting in which directors advanced the date of an annual meeting in order to impede an announced proxy contest.

> I place my opinion [in this case] on the narrow ground that the action of deferring this company's annual meeting where no meeting date has yet been set and no proxies even solicited does not impair or impede the effective exercise of the franchise to any extent. To speak of the effective exercise of the franchise is to imply certain assumptions concerning the structure and mechanism that define the vote and govern its exercise. Shares are voted at meetings; meetings are generally called as fixed in bylaws. While the refusal to call a shareholder meeting when the board is not obligated to do so might under some imaginable circumstance breach a fiduciary duty, such a decision does not itself constitute an impairment of the exercise of the franchise that sparked the close judicial scrutiny of *Schnell*."

———————

F.   The Internal Affairs Doctrine

The internal affairs doctrine is a widely accepted choice of law rule. It provides that the law of the state of incorporation should govern any disputes regarding that corporation's "internal affairs." Thus, a business with shareholders in Florida, headquartered in California, doing business throughout the South, and incorporated in Delaware would be subject to the corporate law rules of—Delaware! And this would be the result wherever litigation involving the corporation's shareholders and managers might arise.

A strong argument for the internal affairs doctrine is that any other choice of law rule would be extremely difficult to administer when the corporation conducts a multi-state business. For example, how could one decide which shareholders were entitled to vote at an annual meeting if it were necessary to follow each potentially conflicting law of every state in which the corporation did business? Obviously, a choice must be made, and the internal affairs doctrine tells courts to make this choice by deciding questions of internal corporate affairs according to the law of the state of incorporation.

What are internal affairs? Courts have said they are the matters peculiar to the relationships among the corporation and its officers, directors, and shareholders. For example, internal affairs typically include the right of shareholders to vote, to receive distributions of corporate property (including dividends), to receive information from the management about corporate affairs, to limit the powers of the corporation to specified activities, and to bring suit on behalf of the corporation when the managers refuse to do so. Internal affairs include the duties that managers owe to shareholders, as well as certain actions by the board of directors, such as decisions to indemnify officers, issue stock, or merge with other corporations.

In contrast, a corporation's external affairs are generally governed by the law where the activities occur and by federal and state regulatory statutes—not by the state of incorporation. For example, a state's employment laws govern conditions of employment of all business operations within the state, wherever the business might be incorporated. State tax laws generally apply to activities of any corporation within the state, especially taxes on corporate real estate and income. When corporations enter into contracts, commit torts, and deal in property, the internal affairs doctrine does not apply.

Sometimes corporate activities can be governed by both internal and external rules. For example, state corporation law controls the right to merge and the procedure to be followed, but mergers are also independently subject to federal antitrust laws and securities laws (federal securities laws specify the disclosure that shareholders must receive when they vote on a merger).

What happens when a court in one state is asked to resolve a corporate dispute involving a corporation incorporated in a state whose corporate law is at odds with that state's corporate law? The following is a leading case from Delaware that addresses this situation. You will notice that the corporate law of Panama, where the corporation at issue was incorporated, conflicted with the corporate law of Delaware and, in fact, that of all U.S. states. The result in the case may surprise you.

McDermott Inc. v. Lewis

531 A.2d 206 (Del. 1987)

MOORE, JUSTICE

We confront an important issue of first impression whether a Delaware subsidiary of a Panamanian corporation may vote the shares it holds in its parent company under circumstances which are prohibited by Delaware law, but not the law of Panama. Necessarily, this involves questions of foreign law, and applicability of the internal affairs doctrine under Delaware law.

[Plaintiffs sued in the Court of Chancery to enjoin the 1982 Reorganization under which McDermott Incorporated, a Delaware corporation ("McDermott Delaware"), became a 92%-owned subsidiary of McDermott International, Inc., a Panamanian corporation ("International"). Plaintiffs are stockholders of McDermott Delaware, which emerged from the Reorganization owning approximately 10% of International's common stock. Plaintiffs challenged this aspect of the Reorganization, and the Court of Chancery granted partial summary judgment in their favor, holding that McDermott Delaware could not vote its stock in International.]

> A "subsidiary" is a corporation that is controlled by another corporation, often referred to as the "parent." The subsidiary can be "wholly owned" when the parent holds 100% of the subsidiary's voting shares, or "partially owned" when the parent holds less than all of the subsidiary's shares, but effectively controls the subsidiary's board of directors.

We conclude that the trial court erred in refusing to apply the law of Panama to the internal affairs of International. Accordingly, we reverse. In so doing, we reaffirm the principle that the internal affairs doctrine is a major tenet of Delaware corporation law having important federal constitutional underpinnings.

I.

International was incorporated in Panama on August 11, 1959, and is principally engaged in providing worldwide marine construction services to the oil and gas industry. Its executive offices are in New Orleans, Louisiana, and there are no operations in Delaware.

McDermott Delaware and its subsidiaries operate throughout the United States in three principal industry segments: marine construction services,

> A "prospectus" is a disclosure document that a company provides investors to inform them about the securities being offered. The document includes material information about the company, its risks, its financial condition, its management, and the securities being offered. Federal securities laws specify the contents of the prospectus and how it is distributed to investors.

power generation systems and equipment, and engineered materials. McDermott Delaware's principal offices are in New Orleans.

Following the 1982 Reorganization, McDermott Delaware became a 92%-owned subsidiary of International. The public stockholders of International hold approximately 90% of the voting power of International, while McDermott Delaware holds about 10%.

At the time of the reorganization, International's prospectus admitted the 10% voting interest given to McDermott Delaware would be voted by International, "and such voting power could be used to oppose an attempt by a third party to acquire control of International if the management of International believes such use of the voting power would be in the best interests of the stockholders of International."

The applicable Panamanian law is set forth in the record by affidavits and opinion letters of Ricardo A. Durling, Esquire [a practicing Panamanian lawyer who wrote the first treatise on Panama corporate law], and the deans of two Panamanian law schools, to support the claim that McDermott Delaware's retention of a 10% interest in International, and its right to vote those shares, is permitted by the laws of Panama. Significantly, the plaintiffs have not offered any contrary evidence.

II.

We note at the outset that if International were incorporated either in Delaware or Louisiana, its stock could not be voted by a majority-owned subsidiary. 8 Del.C. § 160(c); La. Rev. Stat. Ann. § 12:75(G). No United States jurisdiction of which we are aware permits that practice.

The trial court concluded that since both Delaware and Louisiana law prohibit a majority-owned subsidiary from voting its parent's stock, the device was improper. We consider this an erroneous application of both Delaware and Panamanian law.

It is apparent that under limited circumstances the laws of Panama permit a subsidiary to vote the shares of its parent. All three legal experts agreed that McDermott Delaware could vote the shares it held in International. Further, Dean Fernandez specifically stated that it "is a principle of law that in matters of public law one can only do what is expressly allowed by the law; while in private law all acts not prohibited by law can be performed." This fully accords with basic principles of Delaware corporate law.

Given the uncontroverted evidence of Panamanian law, establishing that a Panamanian corporation may place voting shares in a majority-owned subsidiary of a publicly traded corporation registered with the National Securities Commission of Panama, we turn to the fundamental issues presented by application of the internal affairs doctrine.

III.

Internal corporate affairs involve those matters which are peculiar to the relationships among or between the corporation and its current officers, directors, and shareholders. The internal affairs doctrine requires that the law of the state of incorporation should determine issues relating to internal corporate affairs. Under Delaware conflict of laws principles and the United States Constitution, there are appropriate circumstances which mandate application of this doctrine.

Delaware's well established conflict of laws principles require that the laws of the jurisdiction of incorporation—here the Republic of Panama—govern this dispute involving McDermott International's voting rights.

The traditional conflicts rule developed by courts has been that internal corporate relationships are governed by the laws of the forum of incorporation. As early as 1933, the Supreme Court of the United States noted:

> It has long been settled doctrine that a court, state or federal, sitting in one state will, as a general rule, decline to interfere with, or control by injunction or otherwise, the management of the internal affairs of a corporation organized under the laws of another state but will leave controversies as to such matters to the courts of the state of the domicile.

Rogers v. Guaranty Trust Co. of New York, 288 U.S. 123, 130 (1933) (citations omitted).

A review of cases over the last twenty-six years finds that in all but a few, the law of the state of incorporation was applied without any discussion.

A "foreign corporation" is one incorporated in a jurisdiction other than the one where it is doing business or involved in litigation. To "do business" in a state where it is not incorporated, the foreign corporation must register. ("Doing business" involves a minimum contacts analysis, similar to that for personal jurisdiction under the Fourteenth Amendment.) All state corporate statutes permit foreign corporations to register, which typically involves a simple informational filing and small filing fee. MBCA § 15.03; DGCL § 371. A foreign corporation that does business in a state, but fails to register, will not be recognized in that state as a corporation. This prevents the corporation from suing in the state and exposes its participants to individual liability for any corporate contracts or torts.

The policy underlying the internal affairs doctrine is an important one, and we decline to erode the principle:

> Under the prevailing conflicts practice, neither courts nor legislatures have maximized the imposition of local corporate policy on foreign corporations but have consistently applied the law of the state of incorporation to the entire gamut of internal corporate affairs. In many cases, this is a wise, practical, and equitable choice. It serves the vital need for a single, constant and equal law to avoid the fragmentation of

continuing, interdependent internal relationships. The lex incorporationis validates the autonomy of the parties in a subject where the underlying policy of the law is enabling. It facilitates planning and enhances predictability. In fields like torts, where the typical dispute involves two persons and a single or simple one-shot issue and where the common substantive policy is to spread the loss through compensation and insurance, the preference for forum law and the emphasis on the state interest in forum residents which are the common denominators of the new conflicts methodologies do not necessarily lead to unacceptable choices. By contrast, applying local internal affairs law to a foreign corporation just because it is amenable to process in the forum or because it has some local shareholders or some other local contact is apt to produce inequalities, intolerable confusion, and uncertainty, and intrude into the domain of other states that have a superior claim to regulate the same subject matter.

Kozyris, *Corporate Wars and Choice of Law,* 1985 Duke L.J. 1, 98.

Given the significance of these considerations, application of the internal affairs doctrine is not merely a principle of conflicts law. It is also one of serious constitutional proportions—under due process, the commerce clause and the full faith and credit clause—so that the law of one state governs the relationships of a corporation to its stockholders, directors and officers in matters of internal corporate governance. The alternatives present almost intolerable consequences to the corporate enterprise and its managers. With the existence of multistate and multinational organizations, directors and officers have a significant right, under the fourteenth amendment's due process clause, to know what law will be applied to their actions. Stockholders also have a right to know by what standards of accountability they may hold those managing the corporation's business and affairs. That is particularly so here, given the significant fact that in the McDermott Group reorganization, and after full disclosure, 89.59% of the total outstanding common shares of McDermott Delaware were tendered in the exchange offer.

Addressing the facts originally presented to the trial court and to us, we must conclude that due process and the commerce clause, in addition to principles of Delaware conflicts law, mandate reversal. Due process requires that directors, officers and shareholders be given adequate notice of the jurisdiction whose laws will ultimately govern the corporation's internal affairs. Under such circumstances, application of 8 Del. C. § 160(c) to International would unfairly and, in our opinion, unconstitutionally, subject those intimately involved with the management of the corporation to the laws of Delaware.

Moreover, application of Section 160(c) to International would violate the commerce clause. Delaware and Panama law clearly differ in their treatment of a subsidiary's voting rights under the facts originally presented here. For Delaware now to interfere in the internal affairs of a foreign corporation having no relationship whatever to this State clearly implies that International can be subjected to the differing laws of all fifty states on various matters respecting its internal affairs. Such a prohibitive burden has obvious commerce clause implications, and could not pass constitutional muster.

————————

Points for Discussion

1. *Corporation voting its own shares.*

One of plaintiffs' complaints was that, after the recapitalization, the board of McDermott International would be able to control the voting of some of its own shares, because those shares would be held by its subsidiary, McDermott Delaware. This is a puzzling issue: what specifically is wrong with a subsidiary holding shares of its parent's stock and then voting those shares?

To see the concern, suppose that a parent company controls its subsidiary, because it owns the majority of the subsidiary's shares. If you are a minority shareholder of the subsidiary, the parent will outvote you, all of the time, on every decision. If the subsidiary holds shares of the parent, one of those decisions will be how to vote those parent shares. You might disagree with the directors of the parent and the subsidiary about how to vote those shares, but that will not matter: you will not be able to influence how the subsidiary votes the parent shares it owns.

The policy concern is that directors of the parent could use the votes of parent shares that are held by subsidiaries to entrench themselves. One way to avoid this danger is by not counting the subsidiary's votes of parent shares at all, and that is the approach followed in every state in the U.S. (though not in Panama). In theory, the votes of parent company shares that are held by subsidiaries could be counted proportionately, based on how the shareholders of the subsidiary voted, but in practice the approach in the U.S. has been simply not to count the votes at all.

2. *Importance of internal affairs doctrine to Delaware.*

Notice the effort that the Delaware court made to justify the application of Panamanian law. At one level, it would seem the court should have wanted to uphold the corporate rule in Delaware (and every other U.S. jurisdiction) that parent companies cannot place their voting shares in a controlled subsidiary. Yet the court went out of its way to apply "rogue" Panamanian law. Why?

Perhaps the answer is that Delaware is the home to roughly half of all public corporations. As such, it has an interest in the uniform and unswerving application of the internal affairs doctrine. Under this choice of law rule, any business that chooses to incorporate in Delaware will be assured—wherever corporate litigation might arise—that Delaware corporate law will apply to the internal disputes between shareholders and managers, and among shareholders.

3. *State regulation of pseudo-foreign corporations.*

Despite the internal affairs doctrine, a few states have chosen by statute to impose their own corporate rules on the internal affairs of "pseudo-foreign corporations"—that is, corporations that are incorporated outside the state, but conduct most of their business and have most of their shareholders in the state.

Cal. Corp. Code
§ 2115

(a)   A foreign corporation is subject to the requirements of subdivision (b) if:

    (1)   the average of the property factor, the payroll factor, and the sales factor with respect to it is more than 50 percent during its latest full income year and

    (2)   more than one-half of its outstanding voting securities are held of record by persons having addresses in this state appearing on the books of the corporation.

(c)   This section does not apply to any corporation (1) with outstanding securities listed on the New York Stock Exchange, the NYSE Amex, the NASDAQ Global Market, or the NASDAQ Capital Market, or (2) if all of its voting shares (other than directors' qualifying shares) are owned directly or indirectly by a corporation or corporations not subject to this section.

The California "pseudo-foreign corporation" statute is both broad and narrow. On one hand, § 2115(b) covers a wide range of corporate "internal affairs," such as the annual election of directors, removal of directors, filling of director vacancies, directors' standard of care, indemnification of directors and officers, limitations on corporate distributions of cash or property, annual shareholders' meeting, shareholder's right to cumulative voting, limitations on sale of assets or mergers, dissenters' rights, and rights of inspection. On the other hand, § 2115 does not apply to public corporations whose shares are traded on a national exchange.

Two cases illustrate the different approaches taken by courts faced with "pseudo-foreign corporations" operating in California but incorporated in another state (in one case Utah and the other case Delaware). Both cases raised the question of which law applied to shareholder voting rights. The first case—decided by a California appellate court—chose California law. The second case—decided by the Delaware Supreme Court—chose Delaware law. Why the inconsistency?

California approach. The California court framed the issue as being whether California could "constitutionally impose its law requiring cumulative voting by shareholders upon a corporation which is domiciled elsewhere, but whose contacts with California are greater than those with any other jurisdiction." *Wilson v. Louisiana-Pacific Resources, Inc.,* 187 Cal. Rptr. 852 (Cal. Ct. App. 1982).

Since Congress had not exercised its Commerce Clause powers to regulate the corporate internal affairs at issue, the decision turned on "the negative implications of dormant congressional authority." The court pointed out that California's corporate law was even-handed and applied cumulative voting equally to foreign corporations and domestic corporations. The corporation argued that the California statute might lead some foreign corporations "already operating in California to reduce their property, payroll, and sales in this state below the statutory 50 percent level, and could deter foreign corporations contemplating the transaction of business in this state from increasing their business activities above that level." But the court was not persuaded that cumulative voting interfered with interstate commerce, since the corporation's president said "he knew of no adverse effect on the corporation's business which would be caused by cumulative voting."

> Finally, the California court pointed out:

> The potential for conflict and resulting uncertainty from California's statute is substantially minimized by the nature of the criteria specified in section 2115. A corporation can do a majority of its business in only one state at a time; and it can have a majority of its shareholders resident in only one state at a time. If a corporation meets those requirements in this state, no other state is in a position to regulate the method of voting by shareholders on the basis of the same or similar criteria. It might also be said that no other state could claim as great an interest in doing so. In any event, it does not appear that any other state has attempted to do so. If California's statute were replicated in all states, no conflict would result. We conclude that the potential for conflict is, on this record, speculative and without substance.

Delaware approach. In a similar case, but in Delaware, the Delaware Supreme Court addressed the applicability of Delaware law (the state of incorporation) or California law (the state where the business had most of its operations and shareholders) as both a matter of choice of law and constitutional law. *VantagePoint Venture Partners 1996 v. Examen, Inc.,* 871 A.2d 1108 (Del. 2005).

The Delaware court showed little concern that the complaining shareholder, which controlled a majority of the corporation's preferred shares, could have vetoed the merger if California law applied. Nor was the court impressed with the argument that California had significant interests in regulating corporations doing the bulk of their business in the state.

The Delaware court stated it is "an accepted part of the business landscape in this country for States to create corporations, to prescribe their powers, and to define the rights that are acquired by purchasing their shares. A State has an interest in promoting stable relationships among parties involved in the corporations it charters, as well as in ensuring that investors in such corporations have an effective voice in corporate affairs." The Delaware court explained that the internal affairs doctrine reflects "a long-standing choice of law principle" that only one state—the state of incorporation—should regulate a corporation's internal affairs.

Finally, the Delaware court then turned to the U.S. Constitution:

> The internal affairs doctrine is not, however, only a conflicts of law principle. Pursuant to the Fourteenth Amendment Due Process Clause, directors and officers of corporations "have a significant right to know what law will be applied to their actions" and "stockholders have a right to know by what standards of accountability they may hold those managing the corporation's business and affairs." Under the Commerce Clause, a state "has no interest in regulating the internal affairs of foreign corporations." Therefore, this Court has held that an "application of the internal affairs doctrine is mandated by constitutional principles, except in the 'rarest situations,'" e.g., when "the law of the state of incorporation is inconsistent with a national policy on foreign or interstate commerce."

> Accordingly, we hold Delaware's well-established choice of law rules and the federal constitution mandated that the corporation's internal affairs, and in particular, the complaining shareholder's voting rights, be adjudicated exclusively in accordance with the law of its state of incorporation, in this case, the law of Delaware.

G. Some Initial Policy Questions About Corporations

U.S. corporate law is essentially a matter of incorporation-based private choice. The choice of the parties to incorporate (or reincorporate) the business in a particular state is respected both at the state level under the internal affairs doctrine and at the federal level under the assumption that states operate as adaptive laboratories and efficient producers of corporate law. As a result, U.S. corporate law can be seen as a product that states offer to persons interested in joining together in business firms.

This leads to a couple questions. First, how is state corporate law actually produced—particularly in Delaware, the leading producer of corporate law for public corporations? Second, has the state competition to produce corporate law led to efficient results? Or is corporate law the result of a "race to bottom" as states seek to attract self-serving managers? Or perhaps is corporate law the result of a "race to the top" as states seek to balance the interests of managers and shareholders?

1. Production of Corporate Law

State corporate law is a combination of statutory law and judge-made law. Most of statutory corporate law, as we have seen, is a set of default rules. The statutes establish the basic rules on corporate formation, financial rights and duties, governance structure, procedures for structural changes, transfer of corporate interests, and access to judicial protection.

Judges are critical in interpreting the corporate law statutes and filling in the gaps, particularly by defining and shaping corporate fiduciary duties. As you will see in this book, most of the important corporate law cases are resolved not by turning to statutory rules, but by deciding on the existence and reach of corporate fiduciary duties. And corporate innovations often arise when corporate lawyers dream up new financing and other corporate mechanisms, later approved by judges.

We focus on the production of corporate law in Delaware—both by its legislature and its judiciary—since the state is the dominant producer of U.S. corporate law, particularly for public corporations. Other states produce statutory corporate law in much the same way as Delaware—through bar association drafting committees. But Delaware is unique among the states in the way it produces judge-made law—through its expert, independent judges.

Delaware's corporate statute. Delaware's corporate statute is the most far-reaching and innovative of any U.S. corporate statute—even though its dense wording is also sometimes the hardest to decipher. Its legislature is usually the first mover on corporate law reforms, such as simplified merger procedures, teleconferencing at board meetings, hybrid financing techniques, and electronic shareholder voting. Once Delaware acts, other states tend to mimic the leader.

Delaware's corporate statute, however, is not really the product of the state's legislature. Instead, virtually all reforms to the corporate statute are drafted by a special committee of the Delaware bar association—the Council of the Corporate Law Section—and then passed by the state legislature. The Council is composed mostly of private corporate lawyers who represent corporate management, but also includes shareholder plaintiffs' lawyers and representatives of the Delaware's secretary of state's office.

To ensure that corporate law reforms come only from the Council and not special-interest groups, the Delaware constitution requires that all amendments to the state's corporate statute be passed by two-thirds of each legislative chamber. And to seal the deal, the Delaware constitution cannot be amended through the legislative process. Thus, no single corporation or corporate interest group can wield control over Delaware's corporate statute.

Although some have asserted that the Delaware statute balances the interests of the modern corporation's multiple constituencies (managers, shareholders, creditors, employees, suppliers, consumers, communities), the reality is that the statutory drafters focus almost exclusively on management prerogatives and shareholder rights. That is, the production of Delaware corporate law has favored ever more enabling state corporate statutes.

Other states, most of which have adopted some variant of the MBCA, produce corporate statutory law in similar ways. The MBCA—drafted by a special ABA subcommittee composed of by-invitation-only corporate lawyers, law professors, and in-house counsel—generally mirrors the Delaware corporate statute with some notable differences. Although most states have revised and adapted the MBCA provisions to meet their state's special needs, the redrafting has typically been done not by legislative committee, but instead by each state's bar association and its corporate law committee. This is also true for states, such as California and New York, that have not followed the MBCA but have their own special corporate statute.

Nonetheless, the corporate statutes in states other than Delaware may reflect input by powerful corporations in the state—particularly with respect to anti-takeover laws. But otherwise there is no corporate or other special-interest lobby behind corporate statutory revisions. As in Delaware, corporate law is generally the product of a private group of corporate law practitioners, law professors, and state bureaucrats. State legislatures are usually happy that somebody else has done the specialized work of creating and updating the state's corporate statute.

> When the sale of corporate shares changes the control of a corporation—and thus affects the people and communities where the corporation operations—states have sought to regulate the changes in control in what is known as "anti-takeover laws." Starting in the 1960s and 1970s, states started to adopt laws designed to protect corporations conducting business in the state from takeover bids opposed by the corporation's management. Corporate managers argued that hostile bidders would restructure the business, lay off employees, and abandon communities where the corporation operated. Anti-takeover laws vary in their design and are subject to federal Commerce Clause limitations regarding commercial transactions occurring outside the state.

Delaware's corporate judiciary. In Delaware, all cases involving corporate law issues go to the Delaware Court of Chancery, whose judges are appointed on the basis of their corporate law expertise. The chancery court sits in equity without a jury and has a docket with large numbers of corporate law cases. This means that chancery court judges both ascertain the facts and decide how the law applies to them, thus resolving corporate law cases with remarkable speed. Delaware judges are the rock stars of corporate law. Their opinions, speeches, and law review articles are widely followed and discussed by corporate lawyers and academics.

Delaware seeks to ensure that its judges are independent of the political process in a number of ways. Delaware judges are nominated by a bipartisan nominating committee charged with selecting the best-qualified candidates. Delaware judges are then appointed by the governor to 12-year terms, among the longest in the country. Delaware law requires that judicial appointments maintain an equal balance between the two political parties.

Delaware's judiciary is especially known for its large, well-developed body of case law on corporate law. On many corporate law topics, Delaware decisions outnumber those of all other U.S. courts combined. Delaware's large body of case law is seen as providing predictability on a wide range of corporate law issues. Furthermore, with a large number of cases involving Delaware corporations and knowledgeable and sophisticated jurists and practitioners, the law continually evolves in response to a changing business environment.

A number of states have sought to replicate Delaware's judicial advantage in corporate law by creating special business courts. These state courts have special jurisdiction to hear business cases, especially those arising under the state's corporate statutes. But these special courts suffer from a number of disadvantages in competing for incorporation business. In many, the facts are determined by juries, not judges; the judges are appointed through a political process and serve relatively short terms; and decisions by trial judges do not have precedential value. In addition, no state has a body of case law that compares with Delaware's.

Private ordering. Delaware envisions that the participants in a corporation should be able to engage in "private ordering," changing the terms of their arrangement by amending the certificate of incorporation and bylaws. *See* DGCL §§ 109, 242. However, there are limits. For example, some companies have added provisions to their certificates of incorporation or bylaws (known as "forum selection" clauses) that purport to establish the forum or fora for specified types of shareholder litigation. Forum selection clauses can help avoid the costs and dangers of inconsistent rulings from multijurisdictional litigation, but they can also restrict shareholder litigation rights to sue on certain claims in particular jurisdictions.

Litigation concerning the validity of forum selection clauses, and other issues related to private ordering, has stirred controversy. While the law is still evolving, recent years have witnessed a number of important developments. For example, in a 2013 case, *Boilermakers Local 154 Retirement Fund v. Chevron Corp.,* the Delaware Court of Chancery ruled that a forum selection bylaw may validly restrict the forum in which shareholders can bring state corporate law claims. In 2015, the Delaware legislature added a new Section 115 to the DGCL authorizing Delaware corporations to select Delaware courts, both state and federal, as the exclusive forum for "internal corporate claims," and invalidating any provision prohibiting plaintiffs from bringing internal corporate claims in Delaware courts. It also added a new Section 102(f) providing that a certificate of incorporation may not contain any provision imposing liability on a stockholder for the attorneys' fees or expenses of the corporation or any other party in connection with an "internal corporate claim" as defined in new Section 115. Building on these various developments, in 2020, the Delaware Supreme Court in *Salzberg v. Sciabacucchi* upheld a corporate charter provision restricting the forum in which shareholders may bring certain federal securities law claims.

2.   Race to the Bottom or to the Top?

The crucial policy question that arises from Delaware's dominance in the market for corporate chartering of public corporations is the quality of the Delaware product. Although there is no doubt that Delaware has been a leader in U.S. corporate law—the question is whether Delaware has sold out to corporate managers, at the expense of corporate shareholders and other constituencies.

The early debate. Beginning in the 1960s many academics concluded that Delaware was in the for-profit business of selling its corporation law in exchange for filing fees. The prevailing assumption was that corporate managers, who controlled the decision of where to incorporate or reincorporate the business, pressed for incorporation in Delaware to increase their power (and compensation) as managers.

William Cary (a law school professor and former SEC chair) was the main spokesperson for the thesis that Delaware was engaged in a "race to the bottom." He contended that Delaware systematically had eliminated or reduced shareholder protections. As evidence, he pointed to statutory provisions that had reduced the shareholder vote to approve mergers from two-thirds to a majority, as well as numerous court decisions that he interpreted as liberally applying the business judgment rule and permitting corporate managers to resist hostile tender offers.

> Reincorporation usually happens by means of a merger where the corporation seeking a new corporate home forms a shell corporation in the "destination state." The corporation then merges into this shell and, in the process, disappears. The result is a new corporation with all the business, assets and liabilities of the original corporation, but now with a new state of incorporation. The merger requires the approval of the corporation's board of directors and its shareholders.

Central to Cary's argument was that horizontal corporate federalism allowed managers to choose among fifty states. If one state imposed policies that managers didn't like, they could simply reincorporate the business in a different, more management-friendly state. Cary proposed minimum federal standards to prevent this managerial opportunism.

In response to Cary's argument, Ralph Winter (a federal appeals court judge and former law school professor) argued that market forces resulted in a "race to the top" that Delaware was winning. Winter argued that it did not make sense that Delaware was engaged in a race to the bottom, since doing so would disadvantage Delaware corporations in attracting capital. In particular, Winter explained that if Delaware actually permitted managers to profit at the expense of its shareholders, shareholders would discover this and not invest in Delaware corporations. This would cause share prices to decline and create incentives for hostile bidders to buy the cheap shares and reincorporate in a more shareholder-friendly state.

Winter noted that although Cary's argument enjoyed almost universal academic support, it was implausible on its face. Why would shareholders voluntarily invest in corporations permitted to steal from them? Winter argued that competition for corporate charters led states to create corporate law that provided the greatest benefit to shareholders. He opposed interference in this market, particularly at the federal level. According to Winter, the greater danger was not that states would compete for charters but that they would not.

Research developments. Since Cary and Winter, many academics have contributed to this debate. There have been numerous *event studies* of whether reincorporation in Delaware affects share prices. Some studies find moving to Delaware increases share prices, though it is unclear whether this is due to Delaware law or an increased chance the corporation will be sold.

An "event study" is a statistical assessment of how an event (such as a merger or the passage of a new law) affects the share prices of a firm. The fluctuation in the firm's shares prices around the event date are compared to fluctuations in share prices of comparable firms or even the market as a whole. The idea is to find abnormal returns (positive or negative) that would indicate the event created or destroyed firm value.

Other studies have tried to measure whether Delaware corporations are more financially successful. Results are mixed: one study found a "Delaware effect" during the 1990s, when by one measure Delaware firms were more valuable, but more recent studies have questioned those results and show that the effect disappeared in later years. The debate continues.

Whether or not Delaware offers a superior product, its corporate law is likely to remain on top. Corporate managers are lured to Delaware by flexible laws regarding executive compensation, self-dealing, and indemnification. Corporate counsel often prefer the Delaware brand. Investment bankers (who help companies sell shares to the public) prefer Delaware's certainty (and its case law encouraging the use of investment bankers).

A good portion of Delaware's state budget is funded by corporate franchise taxes and incorporation fees, not to mention revenues from litigation. The state bar, legislature, administrative agencies, and judiciary understand the importance of maintaining Delaware's dominance and don't want to jeopardize the goose that lays the golden eggs—an attitude that reassures the U.S. business community, which regularly chooses Delaware as one of the most business-friendly states in the nation.

Given Delaware's dominance, you might wonder whether there really is vigorous competition among the states for corporate charters. After all, the vast majority of companies that incorporate out of their home state do so in Delaware—no other state is even close. Maybe the "race to the top or bottom" debate is misconceived, and Delaware's primary competition comes not from other states but from the federal government. Delaware authorities are always aware that if they misstep, the federal authorities may step in—as has happened after financial scandals and crises.

_____

Points for Discussion

1. *Corporate law as product.*

Is it appropriate to describe state corporate law (statutes, court system, lawyers) as a "product"? If so, is corporate law unique, or do states sell other law products?

2. *Delaware's partial dominance.*

Although Delaware is the legal home of about half of public corporations in the United States, it is far less dominant with respect to private corporations. If Delaware corporate law offers so many advantages to public corporations, why don't private corporations also flock to Delaware? (Delaware also offers special statutory provisions, DGCL §§ 341–356, just for close corporations.)

3. *Assessing Delaware's corporate law.*

The Cary-Winter debate, which still persists, is ultimately based on two testable views of Delaware corporate law. Cary sought to prove that Delaware law was deficient since it had abandoned two-thirds voting for mergers and adopted a majority-voting requirement in its place. Winter pointed to the willingness of investors to invest in Delaware companies as proof that Delaware's corporate law is no worse, and perhaps better, than any other. How would you assess whether Delaware corporate law is, indeed, a superior product?

_____

CHAPTER 6

Limited Liability and Piercing the Corporate Veil

Recall that the corporate capital structure is split between shareholders and creditors. This split creates tension, but it also illuminates one major attraction of the corporate form for shareholders: limited liability. In general, a shareholder's liability is limited to the amount she invests in the business. After that money is gone, creditors bear any additional losses. With limited liability, the corporation is like a sealed box, a no-recourse structure in which creditors can look only to corporate assets for payment of their claims (unless shareholders personally guarantee the corporate obligation).

But sometimes courts disregard the corporate entity and allow creditors to recover directly from shareholders—that is, they "pierce the corporate veil" (or PCV). Many states have established the PCV doctrine through case law, rather than statute. Piercing the corporate veil can be thought of as an exception to the general rule of limited liability and it arises when the corporation lacks sufficient assets to satisfy a plaintiff's claim, and the plaintiff seeks to hold shareholders personally liable. Plaintiffs could be tort victims or contract claimants against the corporation. And the concept of piercing can apply within corporate groups, such as when a plaintiff seeks to hold a parent corporation liable for the debt of a subsidiary. PCV is the most litigated issue in corporate law, and the one most often confronted by attorneys who specialize in areas outside corporate law.

In this chapter, we discuss the general rule of limited liability and the exception of piercing the corporate veil, as well as several related doctrines. Let us note in advance: veil piercing case law is notoriously murky. Courts use metaphors, templates, and multi-pronged tests that can disguise doctrinal uncertainty. The case law is sprinkled with colorful terms such as "alias," "alter ego," "corporate double," "dummy," and "instrumentality."

We will try to help you understand piercing, first by providing a "scorecard" of the key factors that courts often discuss in deciding whether to pierce the corporate veil, and second by examining the policy issues related to limited liability. But this assistance will be brief and fleeting and will last just a few pages. It is no substitute for carefully reading cases in the area, to get a better sense of relevant arguments and issues. Accordingly, the bulk of this chapter is an assortment of cases. The devil will be in the details, and lawyers who confront piercing—either in advising corporate clients about how to avoid it, or in advising litigants after the fact—spend most of their time dealing with the unique facts of particular cases.

A. Considerations for Piercing the Corporate Veil

Piercing the corporate veil is an equitable doctrine created by the courts to "prevent fraud and achieve justice." There is no one PCV test or rule that governs all cases. States generally have adopted some version of a test that looks at whether (1) there is a "unity of interest and ownership" between the corporation and the shareholder being sued (sometimes phrased as an "alter ego relationship" or one of "domination and control"), and (2) whether there was deceit or wrongdoing, or some element of unfairness or wrong that goes beyond the mere fact of the creditor's inability to collect. But courts have stated the legal test in many different ways and the cases often seem to turn on whether the court sees the defendants as "good" or "bad." The fact-dependent question is often: did the defendants abuse the "privilege" of corporate limited liability?

Although piercing cases vary depending on the facts, as a general matter courts are more likely to pierce in the following situations—a sort of scorecard, or checklist, for assessing the likelihood of piercing in a particular case.

Corporation is closely held. Nearly all conventional piercing cases involve closely held corporations. Shareholder-managers of closely held corporations typically have more to gain personally by taking risks that shift losses to creditors than do the managers of public companies. An individual is more likely to be able to dominate and control a closely held corporation than a public corporation.

The defendant actively participated in the business. Courts are more likely to disregard limited liability when a shareholder actively participated in the business. The reason is simple: passive shareholders are less likely to have acted to disadvantage creditors. As with other factors such as deception, much of piercing doctrine is about fairness.

Insiders failed to observe corporate formalities. Judges perceive a sense of injustice in permitting someone who has not respected the corporate form (such as by failing to hold regular corporate meetings, obtain board authorizations, or keep proper minutes) to seek insulation through the corporate form. The lack of corporate formalities also may indicate that the insiders were indifferent about the corporation's obligations to outsiders.

Insiders commingled business and personal assets. Commingling is another sign that insiders did not respect the corporate form and that creditors might have been confused. Judges want insiders to respect the separateness of the corporation and to make sure the corporation takes its obligations seriously.

Insiders did not adequately capitalize the business. Courts are reluctant to permit insiders to "externalize" the risks of the business and place them on outsiders, particularly in tort cases. (Externalization happens when business losses are borne by outsiders, such as contract creditors or tort victims, rather than insiders protected by limited liability.) Courts will look to whether the business was adequately capitalized when formed and whether it then continued to maintain adequate capital or carried insurance to cover the risks of its activities.

Insiders deceived creditors. Deception is an important consideration in piercing cases, in part because courts perceive inequities in protecting individuals who engage in deceptive conduct from personal liability, but also because—at least in contract cases—deception prevents injured parties from protecting themselves in advance.

* * *

The above checklist is not foolproof, and it does not always capture the important facts in particular cases. But it is a good starting point in your analysis of why and when a court might pierce the corporate veil.

To give you a sense of history, in a landmark study on PCV, Professor Robert Thompson looked at all the reported piercing cases on Westlaw through 1985. *Piercing the Corporate Veil: An Empirical Study*, 76 Cornell L. Rev. 1036 (1991). The study found that piercing rarely happens in public companies (in fact, it was attempted in only 9 of the some 1600 cases in the study).

The Thompson study also found that the most predictive factor in PCV was misrepresentation by corporate insiders. When a court found such misrepresentation, piercing happened 91.6% of the time.

Other PCV factors were also predictive of when courts pierce. When courts found the commingling of personal and business assets, piercing happened 85.3% of the time. For a finding of inadequate capitalization, the piercing rate was 73.3%. And for a finding of failure to observe corporate formalities, the piercing rate was 66.9%.

In addition, piercing happened more frequently in one-person corporations (49.6%) than in those with more than three shareholders (35.0%). And piercing also happened more often against individual shareholders (43.1%) than against corporate shareholders (37.2%).

B. Piercing Policy

To understand piercing cases, it helps to understand a bit about the policy implications of piercing. Limited liability can result in creditors, rather than shareholders, bearing much of the costs of business failure. Piercing shifts those costs back to shareholders. So a preliminary question is this: why do states allow shareholders to limit their liability? Why give shareholders this "gift"?

1. Rationales for Limited Liability

The concept of limited liability spread in the nineteenth century to encourage capital formation from many small investors. Early incorporation statutes authorized manufacturing firms to incorporate without the risks of operating in the partnership form—thus permitting the firm to be centrally managed and relieving investors of any responsibility beyond their initial subscription or a specified limit. This policy allowed people to feel comfortable investing in companies without putting their personal assets at risk and it enabled companies to pool large amounts of investment for large-scale ventures. For example, New York's legislative policy in the nineteenth century to promote incorporation through limited liability fostered the growth of an urban society whose members could participate broadly in business firms organized as corporations.

> Limited liability is a default rule. Parties can (and frequently do) contract around the rule and create personal liability for corporate insiders. For example, banks' lending to small closely held corporations will often demand personal guarantees from the owners of the business.

Limited liability continues to promote these social and democratic goals. In recent years state legislatures have authorized new forms of limited liability business organizations, such as LLCs and LLPs—forms widely used by small-scale entrepreneurs who often invest much of their personal wealth in their businesses.

Limited liability also promotes the organization of large, publicly held corporations. It helps reduce costs that shareholders might otherwise feel obligated to bear, such as closely monitoring managers or even other shareholders. Further, limited liability allows shareholders to diversify their investments without exposing their personal assets to additional liability with each investment. In turn, diversified shareholders are willing to let managers take on valuable, but risky projects they might otherwise avoid. And, to the extent limited liability makes shares fungible, it creates the potential for additional monitoring by shareholders who can buy large blocks of shares and pressure directors and officers.

Many of the economic arguments in favor of limited liability do not apply to closely held corporations, where ownership and management are often not separated. Monitoring costs doesn't matter if the owners and managers are the same people. The effects on share trading doesn't matter if shares don't trade. These are some reasons why piercing typically occurs in the closely held corporation context.

A separate set of issues arises when dealing with corporate groups (companies that operate through subsidiary corporations), our third category of cases in the next section. The central question here is whether disregarding separate incorporation should be easier in a holding company structure. That is, should corporate (compared to individual) shareholders have more responsibility for the debts of their subsidiaries?

As originally conceived, the corporation was an "enterprise" to carry on the operations of a given business. Early corporate statutes prohibited one corporation from holding the stock of another. But these prohibitions disappeared, and many corporations began to operate through subsidiaries that were more or less indistinguishable parts of a larger enterprise. At first, courts responded by employing "enterprise liability" theories to hold parent corporations responsible for the liabilities of their subsidiaries. But over time, the courts accepted the separate legal personality, so long as the subsidiary was funded with assets sufficient to give it a reasonable chance of business success.

More recently, courts have tended to apply the same rule of limited liability to individual and corporate shareholders. Does it make sense that corporate investment should be encouraged as much as individual investment? Although it might seem unjust to hold individual public shareholders liable for the actions of corporate managers, this argument seems less persuasive when applied to a parent corporation that controls a subsidiary. Do any of the advantages of limited liability—such as encouraging investment—apply when one corporation capitalizes another corporation? Some argue that reinvigorating the doctrine of enterprise liability for corporate groups would make it difficult for corporations to externalize risk by using thinly capitalized subsidiaries.

On the other hand, a rule of enterprise liability would discourage some worthwhile investments. Why penalize a corporation that has integrated some of its economic functions into a corporate group? If Widget, Inc. purchased Raw Materials, Inc. and held it as a subsidiary, should a court be more likely to pierce in a suit against the integrated corporate group than when the two companies remained separate? One key issue in such cases is whether a person dealing with separate companies is led to believe the companies are operating as a group. In other words, deceit can be an especially important factor in corporate group cases.

2.   Alternative Exceptions to Limited Liability

You should keep in mind that there are alternative exceptions to limited liability outside of the piercing context. Examples include the doctrines of fraudulent conveyance and equitable subordination.

Under the doctrines of fraudulent conveyance and equitable subordination, courts can set aside transactions that defraud creditors. The Uniform Fraudulent Conveyance Act (UFCA), codified in the U.S. Bankruptcy Code and many state statutes, protects creditors from two types of transfers: (1) transfers with the intent to defraud creditors, and (2) transfers that constructively defraud creditors. Showing intentional fraud requires that the court find an actual intent by the debtor to "hinder, delay or defraud." But constructive fraud can be shown if the debtor makes a transfer while insolvent or near insolvency—if the transfer lacks fair consideration.

In the bankruptcy context, the UFCA is used instead of veil piercing to set aside transfers by the corporation to its shareholders when the transfer undermines creditor claims. The courts set aside the transfer and apply it against the corporation's debts to its creditors. For example, the UFCA has been used to set aside "excess" salary payments from a corporation to its sole shareholder that far exceeded the value of the shareholder's services to the corporation.

The UFCA helps explain why courts consider corporate formalities and the intermingling of corporate and personal assets in veil piercing cases. The disregard of corporate formalities often provides indirect evidence of fraudulent conveyances; and the intermingling of corporate and personal assets often provides direct evidence of fraudulent conveyances.

But the UFCA has limitations—compared to veil piercing. First, the UFCA requires a specific finding of a fraudulent transaction, which may be difficult to establish, particularly when there is a lack of corporate formalities. Second, unlike veil piercing, which imposes unlimited liability on shareholders, the UFCA only allows a court to set aside specific fraudulent conveyances, which may not satisfy a creditor's entire claim.

In addition, the doctrine of equitable subordination is another method to protect creditors' interests. This doctrine, applicable only in federal bankruptcy proceedings, subordinates—or pushes to the back of the line—some creditors' claims (typically those of corporate insiders) to reach an equitable result. Subordination thus allows outside creditors to receive payment before insiders. The result is significant since priority in bankruptcy often determines which creditors will get paid.

Before courts invoke the equitable subordination doctrine, there must be a showing of fraudulent conduct, mismanagement, or inadequate capitalization. As a baseline, courts generally look to whether a claimant engaged in some form of "inequitable conduct" and whether the misconduct resulted in injury to the debtor's creditor or conferred an unfair advantage on the claimant.

Equitable subordination also has limitations—compared to veil piercing and fraudulent conveyance principles. Equitable subordination does not increase the overall size of the pie available to creditors. Nor does it hold shareholders personally liable for corporate obligations. It only alters the normal priority of insider claims against the available corporate resources.

However, these alternatives should give you a sense that piercing is not the only exception to limited liability. Still, piercing is an important part of corporate law, and given that it is litigated so frequently, it is worth studying it with some care. As you read through the following six cases, think about the PCV scorecard and policy arguments. Which factors were key to the decision to pierce, and which were not? And why?

C. Piercing in Tort Cases

Now we turn to an assortment of cases. First are tort cases, in which a plaintiff seeks to pierce the veil of the corporate tortfeasor and get to a shareholder who has sufficient assets. Second are contract cases, in which a plaintiff seeks to pierce the veil of the corporate counterparty and recover from a shareholder who is not a party to the agreement. Third are corporate group cases in which a plaintiff seeks to disregard the corporate veil of a wrongdoing subsidiary to recover from its parent, or to recover from some other entity or entities related to the wrongdoer. Courts sometimes apply the same test in all of these contexts and do not draw distinctions, but commentators have long debated whether they raise different policy concerns. And, finally, at the end we will turn to a controversial variation on the PCV doctrine known as reverse veil piercing.

———————

Tort creditors are involuntary. That means they have limited opportunities to protect themselves from a corporation that causes them a loss. A pedestrian does not have an opportunity to bargain with the corporation that owns a delivery van before the van hits them.

As a result, one might expect that courts would be much more willing to pierce the corporate veil in the tort context than in the contract context. Yet some studies suggest that the opposite is true: that courts are equally likely or even less likely to pierce in tort actions. Can you think of any reasons why courts might be reluctant to pierce in tort actions? Which factors are likely to be most important to piercing cases brought by tort victims? The following two cases are examples of numerous similar cases. Which factors were dispositive in these cases?

Walkovszky v. Carlton

223 N.E.2d 6 (N.Y. 1966)

FULD, JUDGE.

This case involves what appears to be a rather common practice in the taxicab industry of vesting the ownership of a taxi fleet in many corporations, each owning only one or two cabs.

The complaint alleges that the plaintiff was severely injured four years ago in New York City when he was run down by a taxicab owned by the defendant Seon Cab Corporation and negligently operated at the time by the defendant Marchese. The individual defendant, Carlton, is claimed to be a stockholder of 10 corporations, including Seon, each of which has but two cabs registered in its name, and it is implied that only the minimum automobile liability insurance required by law (in the amount of $10,000) is carried on any one cab. Although seemingly independent of one another, these corporations (and the corporate owner of the garage) are alleged to be "operated as a single entity, unit and enterprise" with regard to financing, supplies, repairs, employees and garaging, and all are named as defendants. The plaintiff asserts that he is also entitled to hold their stockholders personally liable for the damages sought because the multiple corporate structure constitutes an unlawful attempt "to defraud members of the general public" who might be injured by the cabs.

The defendant Carlton has moved to dismiss the complaint on the ground that as to him it "fails to state a cause of action." The Appellate Division, by a divided vote, held that a valid cause of action was sufficiently stated.

The law permits the incorporation of a business for the very purpose of enabling its proprietors to escape personal liability but, manifestly, the privilege is not without its limits. Broadly speaking, the courts will disregard the corporate form, or, to use accepted terminology, "pierce the corporate veil," whenever necessary "to prevent fraud or to achieve equity." Such liability, moreover, extends not only to the corporation's commercial dealings but to its negligent acts as well.

In the case before us, the plaintiff has explicitly alleged that none of the corporations "had a separate existence of their own." However, it is one thing to assert that a corporation is a fragment of a larger corporate combine which actually conducts the business. It is quite another to claim that the corporation is a "dummy" for its individual stockholders who are in reality carrying on the business in their personal capacities for purely personal rather than corporate ends. Either circumstance would justify treating the corporation as an agent and piercing the corporate veil to reach the principal but a different result would follow in each case. In the first, only a larger corporate entity would be held financially responsible while, in the other, the stockholder would be personally liable.

The individual defendant is charged with having "organized, managed, dominated and controlled" a fragmented corporate entity but there are no allegations that he was conducting business in his individual capacity. The fact that the fleet ownership has been deliberately split up among many corporations does not ease the plaintiff's burden in that respect. The corporate form may not be disregarded merely because the assets of the corporation, together with the mandatory insurance coverage of the vehicle which struck the plaintiff, are insufficient to assure him the recovery sought. If Carlton were to be held individually liable on those facts alone, the decision would apply equally to the thousands of cabs which are owned by their individual drivers who conduct their businesses through corporations organized pursuant to the Business Corporation Law, and carry the minimum insurance required by the Vehicle and Traffic Law. These taxi owner-operators are entitled to form such corporations, and we agree with the court at Special Term that, if the insurance coverage required by statute "is inadequate for the protection of the public, the remedy lies not with the courts but with the Legislature." The responsibility for imposing conditions on the privilege of incorporation has been committed by the Constitution to the Legislature and it may not be fairly implied, from any statute, that the Legislature intended, without the slightest discussion or debate, to require of taxi corporations that they carry automobile liability insurance over and above that mandated by the Vehicle and Traffic Law.

This is not to say that it is impossible for the plaintiff to state a valid cause of action against the defendant Carlton. However, the simple fact is that the plaintiff has just not done so here. While the complaint alleges that the separate corporations were undercapitalized and that their assets have been intermingled, it is barren of any "sufficiently particular(ized) statements" that the defendant Carlton and his associates are actually doing business in their individual capacities, shuttling their personal funds in and out of the corporations "without regard to formality and to suit their immediate convenience." Such a "perversion of the privilege to do business in a corporate form" would justify imposing personal liability on the individual stockholders. Nothing of the sort has in fact been charged, and it cannot reasonably or logically be inferred from the happenstance that the business of Seon Cab Corporation may actually be carried on by a larger corporate entity composed of many corporations which, under general principles of agency, would be liable to each other's creditors in contract and in tort.[3]

In sum, then, the complaint falls short of adequately stating a cause of action against the defendant Carlton in his individual capacity.

The order of the Appellate Division should be reversed, with leave to serve an amended complaint.

KEATING, JUDGE dissenting:

The defendant Carlton, the shareholder here sought to be held for the negligence of the driver of a taxicab, was a principal shareholder and organizer of the defendant corporation which owned the taxicab. The sole assets of these taxicab corporations are the vehicles themselves and they are apparently subject to mortgages.

> The medallions were considered judgment proof when the case was decided. Since the case, NYC taxicab medallions are no longer considered judgment proof. In fact, when a medallion is sold, the new owner must set up an escrow account to ensure compensation of tort victims by the previous owner. In many locations around the world, ride-hailing companies have disrupted the taxi industry and the value of medallions.

---

[3]   In his affidavit in opposition to the motion to dismiss, the plaintiff's counsel claimed that corporate assets had been "milked out" of, and "siphoned off" from the enterprise. Quite apart from the fact that these allegations are far too vague and conclusory, the charge is premature. If the plaintiff succeeds in his action and becomes a judgment creditor of the corporation, he may then sue and attempt to hold the individual defendants accountable for any dividends and property that were wrongfully distributed.

From their inception these corporations were intentionally undercapitalized for the purpose of avoiding responsibility for acts which were bound to arise as a result of the operation of a large taxi fleet having cars out on the street 24 hours a day and engaged in public transportation. And during the course of the corporations' existence all income was continually drained out of the corporations for the same purpose.

The issue presented by this action is whether the policy of this State, which affords those desiring to engage in a business enterprise the privilege of limited liability through the use of the corporate device, is so strong that it will permit that privilege to continue no matter how much it is abused, no matter how irresponsibly the corporation is operated, no matter what the cost to the public. I do not believe that it is.

Under the circumstances of this case the shareholders should all be held individually liable to this plaintiff for the injuries he suffered. At least, the matter should not be disposed of on the pleadings by a dismissal of the complaint. "If a corporation is organized and carries on business without substantial capital in such a way that the corporation is likely to have no sufficient assets available to meet its debts, it is inequitable that shareholders should set up such a flimsy organization to escape personal liability. The attempt to do corporate business without providing any sufficient basis of financial responsibility to creditors is an abuse of the separate entity and will be ineffectual to exempt the shareholders from corporate debts." (Ballantine, Corporations (rev. ed., 1946), § 129, pp. 302–303.)

The defendant Carlton claims that, because the minimum amount of insurance required by the statute was obtained, the corporate veil cannot and should not be pierced despite the fact that the assets of the corporation which owned the cab were "trifling compared with the business to be done and the risks of loss" which were certain to be encountered. I do not agree.

The Legislature in requiring minimum liability insurance of $10,000, no doubt, intended to provide at least some small fund for recovery against those individuals and corporations who just did not have and were not able to raise or accumulate assets sufficient to satisfy the claims of those who were injured as a result of their negligence. It certainly could not have intended to shield those individuals who organized corporations, with the specific intent of avoiding responsibility to the public, where the operation of the corporate enterprise yielded profits sufficient to purchase additional insurance. Moreover, it is reasonable to assume that the Legislature believed that those individuals and corporations having substantial assets would take out insurance far in excess of the minimum in order to protect those assets from depletion. Given the costs of hospital care and treatment and the nature of injuries sustained in auto collisions, it would be unreasonable to assume that the Legislature believed that the minimum provided in the statute would in and of itself be sufficient to recompense "innocent victims of motor vehicle accidents for the injury and financial loss inflicted upon them."

The defendant contends that the court will be encroaching upon the legislative domain by ignoring the corporate veil and holding the individual shareholder [liable]. This argument was answered by Mr. Justice Douglas: "In the field in which we are presently concerned, judicial power hardly oversteps the bounds when it refuses to lend its aid to a promotional project which would circumvent or undermine a legislative policy. To deny it that function would be to make it impotent in situations where historically it has made some of its most notable contributions. If the judicial power is helpless to protect a legislative program from schemes for easy avoidance, then indeed it has become a handy implement of high finance."

The defendant contends that a decision holding him personally liable would discourage people from engaging in corporate enterprise. What I would merely hold is that a participating shareholder of a corporation vested with a public interest, organized with capital insufficient to meet liabilities which are certain to arise in the ordinary course of the corporation's business, may be held personally responsible for such liabilities. Where corporate income is not sufficient to cover the cost of insurance premiums above the statutory minimum or where initially adequate finances dwindle under the pressure of competition, bad times or extraordinary and unexpected liability, obviously the shareholder will not be held liable. The only types of corporate enterprises that will be discouraged as a result of a decision allowing the individual shareholder to be sued will be those such as the one in question, designed solely to abuse the corporate privilege at the expense of the public interest.

For these reasons I would vote to affirm the order of the Appellate Division.

———————

Radaszewski v. Telecom Corp.

981 F.2d 305 (8th Cir. 1992)

RICHARD S. ARNOLD, CHIEF JUDGE.

This is an action for personal injuries filed on behalf of Konrad Radaszewski, who was seriously injured in an automobile accident on August 21, 1984. Radaszewski, who was on a motorcycle, was struck by a truck driven by an employee of Contrux, Inc. The question presented on this appeal is whether the District Court had jurisdiction over the person of Telecom Corporation, which is the corporate parent of Contrux. This question depends, in turn, on whether, under Missouri law, Radaszewski can "pierce the corporate veil," and hold Telecom liable for the conduct of its subsidiary, Contrux, and Contrux's driver.

I.

In general, someone injured by the conduct of a corporation or one of its employees can look only to the assets of the employee or of the employer corporation for recovery. The shareholders of the corporation, including, if there is one, its parent corporation, are not responsible. To the general rule, though, there are exceptions. There are instances in which an injured person may "pierce the corporate veil," that is, reach the assets of one or more of the shareholders of the corporation whose conduct has created liability.

Under Missouri law, a plaintiff in this position needs to show three things.

(1) Control, not mere majority or complete stock control, but complete domination, not only of finances, but of policy and business practice in respect to the transaction attacked so that the corporate entity as to this transaction had at the time no separate mind, will or existence of its own; and

(2) Such control must have been used by the defendant to commit fraud or wrong, to perpetrate the violation of a statutory or other positive legal duty, or dishonest and unjust act in contravention of plaintiff's legal rights; and

(3) The aforesaid control and breach of duty must proximately cause the injury or unjust loss complained of.

Collet v. American National Stores, Inc., 708 S.W.2d 273, 284 (Mo. App. 1986).

Because Telecom, as such, has had no contact with Missouri, whether Missouri courts have jurisdiction over Telecom depends on whether the corporate veil of Contrux can be pierced. The parties have argued the case as one of jurisdiction, and so will we, but in fact the underlying issue is whether Telecom can be held liable for what Contrux did.

II.

To satisfy the second element of the *Collet* formulation, plaintiff cites no direct evidence of improper motivation or violation of law on Telecom's part. He argues, instead, that Contrux was undercapitalized.

Undercapitalizing a subsidiary, which we take to mean creating it and putting it in business without a reasonably sufficient supply of money, has become a sort of proxy under Missouri law for the second *Collet* element. The reason, we think, is not because undercapitalization, in and of itself, is unlawful (though it may be for some purposes), but rather because the creation of an undercapitalized subsidiary justifies an inference that the parent is either deliberately or recklessly creating a business that will not be able to pay its bills or satisfy judgments against it.

Here, the District Court held, and we assume, that Contrux was undercapitalized in the accounting sense. Most of the money contributed to its operation by Telecom was in the form of loans, not equity, and, when Contrux first went into business, Telecom did not pay for all of the stock that was issued to it. Telecom says, however, that this doesn't matter, because Contrux had $11,000,000 worth of liability insurance available to pay judgments like the one that Radaszewski hopes to obtain. No one can say, therefore, the argument runs, that Telecom was improperly motivated in setting up Contrux, in the sense of either knowingly or recklessly establishing it without the ability to pay tort judgments.

In fact, Contrux did have $1,000,000 in basic liability coverage, plus $10,000,000 in excess coverage. This coverage was bound on March 1, 1984, about five and one-half months before the accident involving Radaszewski. Unhappily, Contrux's insurance carrier became insolvent two years after the accident and is now in receivership. But this insurance, Telecom points out, was sufficient to satisfy federal financial-responsibility requirements applicable to interstate carriers such as Contrux.

The District Court rejected this argument. Undercapitalization is undercapitalization, it reasoned, regardless of insurance. The Court said:

> The federal regulation does not speak to what constitutes a properly
> capitalized motor carrier company. Rather, the regulation speaks to what
> constitutes an appropriate level of *financial responsibility*.

This distinction escapes us. The whole purpose of asking whether a subsidiary is "properly capitalized," is precisely to determine its "financial responsibility." If the subsidiary is financially responsible, whether by means of insurance or otherwise, the policy behind the second part of the *Collet* test is met. Insurance meets this policy just as well, perhaps even better, than a healthy balance sheet.

At the oral argument, counsel for Radaszewski described the insurance company in question as "fly-by-night." He pointed out, and this is in the record, that the insurance agency that placed the coverage, Dixie Insurance Agency, Inc., was, like Contrux, a wholly owned subsidiary of Telecom. (Apparently the $1,000,000 primary policy is still in force. It is only the $10,000,000 excess policy that is inoperative on account of the insolvency of the excess carrier, Integrity Insurance Co.) Plaintiff argues that if the case went to trial he could show that the excess carrier "was an insurance company with wobbly knees for years before its receivership." He also says that the excess carrier was not strong enough even to receive a minimum rating in the Best Insurance Guide. Finally, plaintiff suggests that Contrux bought "its insurance from a financially unsound company which most certainly charged a significantly lower premium."

Here, it is beyond dispute that Contrux had insurance, and that it was considered financially responsible under the applicable federal regulations. We see nothing sinister in the fact that the insurance was purchased through an agency wholly owned by Telecom. This is a common business practice. The assertion that a reduced premium was paid is wholly without support in the record. It is based on speculation only. There is no evidence that Telecom or Contrux knew that the insurance company was going to become insolvent, and no reason, indeed, that we can think of why anyone would want to buy insurance from a company that he thought would become insolvent.

The doctrine of limited liability is intended precisely to protect a parent corporation whose subsidiary goes broke. That is the whole purpose of the doctrine, and those who have the right to decide such questions, that is, legislatures, believe that the doctrine, on the whole, is socially reasonable and useful. We think that the doctrine would largely be destroyed if a parent corporation could be held liable simply on the basis of errors in business judgment. Something more than that should be shown, and *Collet* requires something more than that. In our view, this record is devoid of facts to show that "something more."

Heaney, Senior Circuit Judge, dissenting:

I respectfully dissent. In every respect on the basis of the record now before us, Contrux was nothing but a shell corporation established by Telecom to permit it to operate as a nonunion carrier without regard to the consequences that might occur to those who did business with Contrux or those who might be affected by its actions.

The majority asks why anyone would want to buy insurance from an insolvent company. An answer readily comes to mind. The purchase was a cheap way of complying with federal regulations and furthered the illusion to all concerned that Contrux was a viable company able to meet its responsibilities.

As the matter now stands, the innocent victim may have to bear most of the costs of his disabling injuries without having the opportunity to prove that Contrux was intentionally undercapitalized. I believe this is wrong and inconsistent with Missouri law. I would thus remand for trial.

————

Points for Discussion

1. *Enterprise liability.*

The plaintiff in *Walkovszky* sought liability from two sources: (1) the ten taxicab corporations and corporate garage under common ownership, and (2) Carlton individually. The case was appealed only on the issue of whether the plaintiff sufficiently stated a valid cause of action against Carlton. The possibility of "enterprise liability" against corporations that are operated as a single economic unit expands the assets available to corporate creditors, without imposing liability on individual shareholders. In some instances, this may be enough to satisfy liabilities to creditors. But in *Walkovszky* the assets of the other corporations were heavily mortgaged or otherwise judgment-proof. (*Radaszewski* involved a parent-subsidiary corporate relationship and a tort claimant. We include it here as a tort case, but you can also think about it as an example of a corporate group case, which we'll study in more detail later in this chapter.)

2. Advising.

Following the decision in *Walkovszky*, the plaintiff amended his complaint to allege with more specificity that Carlton had conducted business in his individual capacity. Carlton again moved to dismiss but this time the trial court denied his motion, which was affirmed on appeal. The case then settled. Given this outcome, how would you advise an owner of a taxi fleet in New York City to organize and run their business?

3. Compare Walkovszky and Radaszewski.

Both cases involved involuntary tort claimants; both cases involved operating companies that had carried the minimum insurance required by law; and both cases (over a strong dissent) concluded that piercing was not appropriate. Do you think both courts got it right? Are the cases different in any way that should matter?

4. Formalities in the tort setting.

Many cases mention "disregard of corporate formalities" as a factor in PCV. But why should the internal operations of a corporation (regular meetings, minutes, resolutions, and so on) be relevant to liability for torts? More specifically, why would formalities matter to tort victims who never interacted with the corporation before the unfortunate event? Some argue that if corporate formalities are flouted, corporate owners should not be allowed to rely on limited liability. What is the justification for such a quid pro quo?

5. Undercapitalization.

Some courts also mention undercapitalization (the failure to maintain an adequate financial cushion) as a piercing factor, particularly if the business engages in potentially hazardous activities. Courts are more likely to pierce, especially in tort cases, when the decisions mention undercapitalization. Why? And, by the way, what is undercapitalization? Should it be measured when the business was organized or at the time of the corporate wrong? If a business begins operating with sufficient capital to cover its anticipated business losses, but then loses money over time, must shareholders invest additional capital on pain of losing their limited liability? What if the business enters a new, riskier line of business? Should buying the minimum-required insurance be enough to preserve the limited liability shield? What if the business operates in an industry without minimum insurance requirements?

D. Piercing in Contract Cases

Contract creditors are in a different position than tort creditors. Most important, they are voluntary. They know or can ascertain that they are dealing with a no-recourse corporation and have the opportunity to bargain for a risk premium, shareholder guarantees, or restrictions on distributions.

Yet the fact that a plaintiff had a contractual relationship with a corporation—and therefore had the opportunity to negotiate in advance—does not necessarily prevent the plaintiff from piercing the corporate veil. Indeed, many contract cases involve misrepresentations that undermine the expectation of a non-recourse relationship. That is one reason why courts pierce so frequently in contract cases. As with the tort cases, these two contract cases are representative. The relationships among the various parties are complex. What are the key factors in these cases?

Freeman v. Complex Computing Co.

119 F.3d 1044 (2d Cir. 1997)

MINER, CIRCUIT JUDGE.

While pursuing graduate studies under a fellowship at Columbia University in the early 1990s, defendant Jason Glazier co-developed computer software with potential commercial value and negotiated with Columbia to obtain a license for the software. Columbia apparently was unwilling to license software to a corporation of which Glazier was an officer, director, or shareholder. Nonetheless, Columbia was willing to license the software to a corporation that retained Glazier as an independent contractor.

Accordingly, in September of 1992, Complex Computing Co., Inc. ("C3") was incorporated, with an acquaintance of Glazier's as the sole shareholder and initial director, and Seth Akabas (a partner of Glazier's counsel in this action) as the president, treasurer and assistant secretary. In November of 1992, another corporation, Glazier, Inc., of which Glazier was the sole shareholder, entered into an agreement with C3 (the "consulting agreement").[1] Under the consulting agreement, Glazier, Inc. was retained as an independent contractor (titled as C3's "Scientific Advisor") to develop and market Glazier's software, which was licensed from Columbia, and to provide support services to C3's clients. Glazier was designated the sole signatory on C3's bank account, and was given a written option to purchase all of C3's stock for $2,000.

---

[1] Although the consulting agreement was between C3 and Glazier, Inc., numerous provisions in the agreement made express reference to Glazier personally. For example, the consulting agreement provided that it was terminable if Glazier himself was unable to perform or supervise performance of Glazier, Inc.'s obligations.

In September of 1993, C3 entered into an agreement with plaintiff Daniel Freeman (the "C3–Freeman Agreement"), under which Freeman agreed to sell and license C3's computer software products for a five-year term. In exchange, C3 agreed to pay Freeman commissions on the revenue received by C3 over a ten-year period from the client-base developed by Freeman, including the revenue received from sales and licensing, maintenance and support services. The C3–Freeman Agreement included provisions relating to Freeman's compensation if C3 terminated the agreement prior to its expiration, or if C3 made a sale that did not result in revenues because of a future merger, consolidation, or stock acquisition. The agreement included an arbitration clause.

Schedule 1 of the C3–Freeman Agreement listed the customers from whom Freeman would receive commissions. Although C3's president signed the C3–Freeman Agreement, Glazier personally signed the periodic amendments to Schedule 1. On March 24, 1994, Glazier signed an amended Schedule 1 that listed as customers, among numerous others, Thomson Financial, Banker's Trust and Chemical Bank. The amendment provided that "to date, Dan Freeman has performed—and will continue to perform—material marketing services" as regards these customers.

On August 22, 1994, C3 and Thomson Investment Software (Thomson) entered into a licensing agreement that granted Thomson exclusive worldwide sales and marketing rights of C3's products. Freeman contends that the licensing agreement resulted from efforts made by him over approximately nine months to bring the transaction to fruition.

In October of 1994, C3 gave Freeman the requisite 60-days notice of the termination of its agreement with him. The letter of termination, signed by Glazier, explained that C3's exercise of its option to terminate Freeman's employment was "an action to combat the overly generous termination clause we committed to, and to force a renegotiation of your sales contract."

Glazier was hired in January of 1995 as Thomson's Vice President and Director of Research and Development at a starting salary of $150,000 plus additional payments of "incentive compensation" based in part upon the revenues received by Thomson in connection with the sale or license of products developed by Glazier. On the same day, Thomson and C3 entered into an assets purchase agreement. As part of the transaction, Thomson assumed C3's intellectual products, trademarks and tradenames. The Thomson Agreement set forth a list of C3 agreements assumed by Thomson, but expressly excluded the C3–Freeman Agreement. Thomson paid a total of $750,000, from which Glazier was paid $450,000 as a "signing bonus" in connection with his new employment contract.

In May of 1995, Freeman commenced the action giving rise to this appeal. He estimated that he was due more than $100,000, and that the moneys due him in the future under the agreement would be in excess of $5 million.

The district court found that both C3 and Glazier should be compelled to arbitrate their disputes with Freeman in accordance with the C3–Freeman Agreement. The district court found that Glazier was subject to the arbitration clause of the C3–Freeman Agreement because he "did not merely dominate and control C3—to all intents and purposes, he was C3" and because he held the "sole economic interest of any significance" in the corporation.

II. Piercing the Corporate Veil

Neither party disputes that New York law applies to these issues. We review de novo the district court's legal conclusions.

A. Glazier's Equitable Ownership of C3

Glazier contends that he should not be held personally liable under a veil-piercing theory because he is not a shareholder, officer, director, or employee of C3. We reject this argument.

New York courts have recognized for veil-piercing purposes the doctrine of equitable ownership, under which an individual who exercises sufficient control over the corporation may be deemed an "equitable owner," notwithstanding the fact that the individual is not a shareholder of the corporation.

Because Glazier "exercised considerable authority over the corporation to the point of completely disregarding the corporate form and acting as though its assets were his alone to manage and distribute," he is appropriately viewed as C3's equitable owner for veil-piercing purposes. If there were board meetings, no minutes were kept from August 1994 through May 1995. Glazier agreed to personally indemnify C3's sole shareholder and director against any liability arising from the performance of his duties as C3's director. The president of C3 never attended a meeting of the Board of Directors. No shareholder received dividends or other distributions, despite the corporate income of $563,257 in 1994 and $200,000 from the assets sale to Thomson.

Glazier used C3 to sell his intellectual product and powers, including the software that he had co-developed at Columbia and which Columbia licensed to C3. Through payments from C3 to Glazier, Inc., he received the vast majority of the resulting revenues.[5] Both Glazier, Inc. and C3 were located at Glazier's apartment, and Glazier was the sole signatory on C3's bank account. Glazier, Inc.'s consulting agreement with C3 expressly provided that it was terminable if Glazier himself was unable to perform or supervise the performance of Glazier, Inc.'s obligations to C3, which were described as "marketing C3's software products, developing new software

---

[5]   The consulting agreement provided that C3 would not pay anyone compensation unless Glazier, Inc. had first received its share in full. The consulting agreement obligated C3 to pay Glazier, Inc. annual compensation of $150,000, with "cost-of-living" adjustments. In addition, it was to pay Glazier, Inc. a bonus for each calendar year equal to 60% of the first $200,000 in revenues received by C3, 70% of the next $200,000, 80% of the third $200,000, and 85% of all revenues received thereafter.

products, enhancing C3's existing software products, and providing support services to C3's clients." These obligations essentially described C3's entire business.

Glazier himself gave Thomson a resume stating that from 1992 to the present, Glazier was the principal, owner and manager of C3, and that Glazier, Inc. was the predecessor to C3. C3 paid over $8000 to the law firm that represented Glazier personally in his negotiations with Thomson. These negotiations resulted in Thomson employing Glazier and paying him a $450,000 signing bonus. C3 then paid Glazier, through Glazier, Inc., an additional $210,000 out of the proceeds of the assets and other funds that were in the C3 bank account following the assets purchase. After payment of taxes and other expenses, this left only $10,000 in C3's account. Freeman contends that this balance renders C3 unable to fulfill its alleged obligations to him. Additionally, Glazier had an option to purchase all the shares of C3 from its sole shareholder for $2000. Thus, at his discretion, he could have become the sole shareholder for a small payment.

The district court found that "to regard Glazier as anything but the sole stockholder and controlling person of C3 would be to exalt form over substance." Under the unique facts of the instant case, viewed in their totality, we agree that it is appropriate to treat Glazier as an "equitable owner" for veil-piercing purposes.

B. Piercing the C3 Veil

Glazier next argues that the district court's determination that he controlled C3 does not justify piercing the corporate veil in the absence of a factual finding that he used his control over C3 to wrong Freeman. We agree that the district court erred in piercing the corporate veil before finding that Glazier used his domination of C3 to wrong Freeman.

The presumption of corporate independence and limited shareholder liability serves to encourage business development. Nevertheless, that presumption will be set aside, and courts will pierce the corporate veil under certain limited circumstances. To pierce the corporate veil under New York law, a plaintiff must prove that "(1) the owner has exercised such control that the corporation has become a mere instrumentality of the owner, which is the real actor; (2) such control has been used to commit a fraud or other wrong; and (3) the fraud or wrong results in an unjust loss or injury to plaintiff."

The element of domination and control never was considered to be sufficient of itself to justify the piercing of a corporate veil. Even if a plaintiff showed that the dominator of a corporation had complete control over the corporation so that the corporation "had no separate mind, will, or existence of its own," New York law will not allow the corporate veil to be pierced in the absence of a showing that this control "was used to commit wrong, fraud, or the breach of a legal duty, or a dishonest and unjust act in contravention of plaintiff's legal rights, and that the control and breach of duty proximately caused the injury complained of."

As discussed in the context of equitable ownership, the record is replete with examples of Glazier's control over C3. Therefore, the district court's finding of control was not erroneous. However, the district court erred in the decision to pierce C3's corporate veil solely on the basis of a finding of domination and control. Thus, while we accept the district court's factual finding that Glazier controlled C3, we remand to the district court the issue of whether Glazier used his control over C3 to commit a fraud or other wrong that resulted in unjust loss or injury to Freeman. Though there is substantial evidence of such wrongdoing, a finding on this issue must be made in the first instance by the district court before veil-piercing occurs.

GODBOLD, SENIOR CIRCUIT JUDGE, concurring in part, dissenting in part:

I concur in affirming the district court's holding that Glazier was in total control of C3. I see no need, however, to remand the case to the district court for it to determine whether "Glazier used his control over C3 to commit a fraud or other wrong that resulted in an unjust loss or injury to Freeman." The record before us discloses fraud or other wrong by Glazier, through C3, resulting in an unjust loss or injury to Freeman. Consequently C3's corporate veil is to be pierced, and, without more, arbitration should proceed against Glazier as well as C3.

C3 is Glazier's creature, subject to his "complete control" ("he was C3"). C3 agreed with Freeman for him to sell and license C3's software products for five years and to receive commissions for ten years on revenue received from Freeman's clients. Plus, if C3 merged or consolidated, Freeman was to receive an additional payment of 10 percent of the total consideration conveyed. The agreement contained a termination clause. C3 could terminate on sixty days notice, but Freeman was entitled to receive all compensation for services previously rendered as well as the commissions that accrued over a ten year period (presumably to include 10 percent of the consideration for a buy out or merger).

Approximately a year after the C3–Freeman agreement was made C3 entered into an agreement with Thomson Trading Services, Inc., an account developed by Freeman, to make Thomson its exclusive worldwide marketer. Thomson took over existing C3 agreements, but not C3's agreement with Freeman. That agreement remained C3's responsibility. But C3 has paid Freeman nothing.

It remained for C3 to get rid of Freeman. It did so by a purported termination of the C3–Freeman agreement. C3 recited that it was exercising its option to terminate as "an action to combat the overly generous termination clause we committed to, and to force a renegotiation of your sales contract." In short, Freeman was not to receive the benefits guaranteed him by the termination clause; the termination was to force him to give up the "overly generous" termination benefits he was entitled to receive. The asserted termination was not to implement the provision for termination but in derogation of it.

By this Tinker-to-Evers-to-Chance play:

- C3's business has gone to Thomson.

- Thomson has handsomely rewarded Glazier.

- Thomson, in acquiring C3, has not assumed responsibility for the Freeman agreement.

- Glazier is enjoying the generous fruits of the C3–Thomson deal while C3 has been reduced to a shell.

- Freeman has been stripped of his benefits, paid nothing, and hung out to dry, on the asserted ground that benefits (past and future) agreed to be paid to him by C3 were too generous.

This is fraud by Glazier—a fully revealed rip off. But if one shrinks from the word "fraud" it is at least a "wrongful injury."

The next case, *Theberge v. Darbro, Inc.*, also raises the issue of piercing in a contract case. The business is commercial real estate, with the selling and buying of real estate among various business groups—with first, second, and third mortgages, sometimes with personal guarantees and sometimes without. The case involves seller financing for which there were no written personal guarantees.

The story begins with Michael and Thomas Theberge, who owned seven rental properties, which in August 1986 they sold for $900,000 to the Worden Group for cash and a $180,000 promissory note secured by a second mortgage (the "Theberge mortgage"). Later that year, the Worden Group agreed to sell the seven properties for $970,000 to Darbro, Inc., which was owned by Albert and Mitchell Small. Prior to the closing, the Smalls informed the Worden Group and the Theberges that the purchaser would not be Darbro, but instead Horton Street Associates, Inc., a newly formed corporation owned by the Smalls.

To finance the purchase of the seven buildings, Horton Street borrowed a total of $840,000 from Casco Northern Bank and executed promissory notes secured by first and third mortgages on the premises. Horton Street also assumed the existing $180,000 Theberge mortgage note owed by the Worden Group to the Theberges. Finally, Horton Street executed a $20,000 note payable to the Worden Group.

The lenders to Horton Street received various guarantees and other financial protections. Darbro guaranteed $450,000—and Albert Small personally guaranteed $330,000—of the Casco Northern first mortgage. Albert co-signed the promissory note given to Casco Northern on the third mortgage, as well as the $20,000 note payable to the Worden Group.

Soon after the purchase, Horton Street began to lose money. There was a downturn in the real estate market, an increase in vacancy rates, a flood that damaged one of the buildings, and unexpected repairs that were required on the properties. To compensate for these losses, Albert loaned money to Darbro, which in turn loaned money to Horton Street.

In the spring of 1989, Horton Street sold two of the seven buildings. As a result of these sales, and pursuant to the terms of the Theberge mortgage, Horton Street paid the Theberges to partially discharge the second mortgage, retired the third mortgage to Casco Northern, and reduced the balance on the Casco Northern first mortgage.

By May 1989, Darbro had loaned to Horton Street approximately $225,000 and had received only "a couple small payments." Albert then decided that Darbro would not loan additional monies to Horton Street, and advised the Theberges that he could not make any further payments and that he wished to negotiate "a solution."

When these negotiations failed, the Theberges and the Worden Group brought an action against Horton Street to recover the outstanding balance on the $180,000 promissory note. The court issued a default judgment against Horton Street.

The Theberges and the Worden Group then instituted a second action against Darbro, Albert Small, and Mitchell Small, seeking a judgment on the unpaid balance of the note. The plaintiffs alleged (1) Horton Street was the alter ego of Darbro, Albert, and Mitchell; (2) the sale to Horton Street was based on representations that Albert would "stand behind" the Theberge mortgage.

The trial court made factual findings, some of which favored the Smalls. The court specifically found that the defendants had not acted illegally or fraudulently and that they had not guaranteed the payment of the Theberge promissory note. The court further found that the Theberges were sophisticated real estate investors and understood the formalities, and the effect, of a personal guarantee in a real estate transaction.

But the court also found that Horton Street had no separate offices, utilities, or employees; maintained no corporate records or books; commingled its business with that of the other defendants; and failed to conduct formal corporate meetings. According to the court, both Horton Street and Darbro were, in essence, Albert—as evidenced by the fact that, when in a financial crisis, Albert "unilaterally assumed full control of Horton Street on his own initiative" and acted to the defendants' own benefit and to the detriment of the plaintiffs.

The trial court concluded that "notions of equitable estoppel ought to preclude" the defendants from asserting Horton Street's corporate status and that the defendants were liable to the plaintiffs for the outstanding balance on the Theberge mortgage.

Theberge v. Darbro, Inc.

684 A.2d 1298 (Me. 1996)

GLASSMAN, JUSTICE.

On appeal, the defendants contend that the trial court erred by determining that their conduct justified piercing the corporate veil of Horton Street. We agree. It is well established that "corporations are separate legal entities with limited liability." Although the corporate entity may be pierced if it is merely the alter ego of an individual or other corporation, we will "disregard the legal entity of a corporation with caution and only when necessary in the interest of Justice." When the plaintiff attempts, in the context of a contractual dispute, to pierce the corporate veil, courts generally apply "more stringent standards because the party seeking relief in a contract case is presumed to have voluntarily and knowingly entered into an agreement with a corporate entity, and is expected to suffer the consequences of the limited liability associated with the corporate business form."

The plaintiffs contend, and the trial court determined, that the oral representations that Albert was a person of financial substance who would stand behind the obligations of Horton Street, and the financial arrangement between Albert and Casco Northern, effectively extinguishing the Theberge mortgage, justifies piercing the corporate veil. We disagree. The court found, and the record supports, that the defendants did not act illegally or fraudulently, but, rather conducted themselves "shrewdly" and employed "sharp business practices." The court determined that the defendants did not formally, personally guarantee the transaction and that the plaintiffs were sophisticated real estate professionals who understood the significance of a personal guarantee. Indeed, the success of the Worden Group in securing Albert's personal liability on the $20,000 note to them belies the contention of a reasonable expectation that Albert would "stand behind" the Theberge mortgage in the absence of a formal guarantee.

When the Theberges permitted the assumption by Horton Street of their mortgage, they protected themselves by refusing to release the Worden Group from liability. Casco Northern also protected its interest in the loans to Horton Street by obtaining guarantees from Darbro and Albert in amounts sufficient to cover the loan amounts. The plaintiffs, by contrast, failed to obtain any such guarantee from any of the defendants and instead opted to proceed with the transaction. We decline to reconstruct the agreement negotiated between the parties to effect a result beyond the plain meaning of that bargain.

Considering all the evidence in the instant case, we determine that it is insufficient to justify piercing the corporate veil of Horton Street.

———————

Points for Discussion

The Thompson study, which looked at all PCV cases through 1985, found that piercing is more frequent in contract cases (42.0% of the time) compared to tort cases (31.0% of the time). This is contrary to the assumption that courts in piercing cases are more sympathetic to tort victims, who cannot protect themselves by contract. In fact, some commentators have argued that contract creditors should not be able to pierce the corporate veil at all, on the theory they can always obtain personal guarantees. For some contract creditors, PCV is arguably a financial windfall.

In a follow-up study of piercing cases through 2006, Professor Peter Oh found a similar rate of piercing in contract cases (46.2% of the time) as in tort cases (47.8% of the time), after excluding cases involving fraud claims. *Veil-Piercing*, 89 Tex. L. Rev. 81 (2010). Although less dramatic than the Thompson study, the Oh study raises the question why piercing happens as often in contract cases as tort cases. Perhaps contract PCV cases are brought by commercial litigators, who recognize that sometimes businesses fail and don't bring borderline claims, while tort PCV are brought by personal-injury lawyers, who are always looking for a deep pocket, even when the odds are against them?

1. *Advising.*

On remand, the district court in *Freeman* found that Glazier's actions constituted fraudulent or other wrongful behavior because they left Freeman as "a general creditor of an essentially defunct corporation with virtually no assets." The court entered an order compelling Glazier to arbitrate plaintiff's claim. How does this resolution affect how you might advise parties contemplating negotiations after *Freeman*?

2. *Formalities.*

Compare the observance of corporate formalities in *Freeman* and *Theberge.* Who seemed to have followed corporate formalities more rigorously—Jason Glazier or the Smalls? The court pierces in *Freeman*, not in *Theberge.* Isn't this the opposite of what you would expect?

3. *Deceit.*

Compare the level of deceit in the two cases. Was Freeman led to believe that C3 was well-capitalized or falsely told that Glazier would stand behind the corporation? And why didn't the court in *Theberge* find it relevant that Albert Small had said he would stand behind the corporation's obligations or that the Smalls had engaged in "sharp business practices"?

E.   Piercing in Corporate Groups

Which entity or entities should be liable when there is a group of corporations? For example, what if one corporation owns the stock of another, but only the subsidiary damaged the plaintiff? The plaintiff might seek damages against the parent corporation as well the subsidiary. Or what if the parent corporation owns the stock of many subsidiaries, which are affiliates of each other? The plaintiff might seek damages against all of the corporations, on a theory of "enterprise liability." There are legitimate reasons to divide a business into multiple corporations, including convenience and profit maximization. Sometimes courts will respect the limited liability of each corporation, but other times they will disregard one or more of the veils in a corporate group. Here are two examples.

Gardemal v. Westin Hotel Co.

186 F.3d 588 (5th Cir. 1999)

DeMoss, Circuit Judge.

Lisa Cerza Gardemal sued Westin Hotel Company (Westin) and Westin Mexico, S.A. de C.V. (Westin Mexico), under Texas law, alleging that the defendants were liable for the drowning death of her husband in Cabo San Lucas, Mexico. The district court granted Westin's motion for summary judgment, and Westin Mexico's motion to dismiss for lack of personal jurisdiction. We affirm the district court's rulings.

In June 1995, Gardemal and her husband John W. Gardemal, a physician, traveled to Cabo San Lucas, Baja California Sur, Mexico, to attend a medical seminar held at the Westin Regina Resort Los Cabos (Westin Regina). The Westin Regina is owned by Desarollos Turisticos Integrales Cabo San Lucas, S.A. de C.V. (DTI), and managed by Westin Mexico. Westin Mexico is a subsidiary of Westin, and is incorporated in Mexico. During their stay at the hotel, the Gardemals decided to go snorkeling with a group of guests. According to Gardemal, the concierge at the Westin Regina directed the group to "Lovers Beach" which, unbeknownst to the group, was notorious for its rough surf and strong undercurrents. While climbing the beach's rocky shore, five men in the group were swept into the Pacific Ocean by a rogue wave and thrown against the rocks. Two of the men, including John Gardemal, drowned.

Gardemal, as administrator of her husband's estate, brought wrongful death and survival actions under Texas law against Westin and Westin Mexico, alleging that her husband drowned because Westin Regina's concierge negligently directed the group to Lovers Beach and failed to warn her husband of its dangerous condition. Westin then moved for summary judgment, alleging that although it is the parent company of Westin Mexico, it is a separate corporate entity and thus could not be held liable for acts committed by its subsidiary. [The magistrate judge recommended that Westin be dismissed from the action, accepting Westin's separate corporate identity. The magistrate also recommended granting Westin Mexico's motion to dismiss on the ground that it had insufficient minimum contacts to bring it within the personal jurisdiction of the court.] The district court then accepted the magistrate judge's recommendations and dismissed Gardemal's suit. We affirm.

In this action Gardemal seeks to hold Westin liable for the acts of Westin Mexico by invoking two separate, but related, state-law doctrines. Gardemal first argues that liability may be imputed to Westin because Westin Mexico functioned as the alter ego of Westin. Gardemal next contends that Westin may be held liable on the theory that Westin Mexico operated a single business enterprise.

Under Texas law the alter ego doctrine allows the imposition of liability on a corporation for the acts of another corporation when the subject corporation is organized or operated as a mere tool or business conduit. Alter ego is demonstrated "by evidence showing a blending of identities, or a blurring of lines of distinction, both formal and substantive, between two corporations." An important consideration is whether a corporation is underfunded or undercapitalized, which is an indication that the company is a mere conduit or business tool.

On appeal Gardemal points to several factors which, in her opinion, show that Westin is operating as the alter ego of Westin Mexico. She claims, for example, that Westin owns most of Westin Mexico's stock; that the two companies share common corporate officers; that Westin maintains quality control at Westin Mexico by requiring Westin Mexico to use certain operations manuals; that Westin oversees advertising and marketing operations at Westin Mexico through two separate contracts; and that Westin Mexico is grossly undercapitalized. We are not convinced.

The record, even when viewed in a light most favorable to Gardemal, reveals nothing more than a typical corporate relationship between a parent and subsidiary. It is true, as Gardemal points out, that Westin and Westin Mexico are closely tied through stock ownership, shared officers, financing arrangements, and the like. But this alone does not establish an alter-ego relationship.

In this case, there is insufficient record evidence that Westin dominates Westin Mexico to the extent that Westin Mexico has, for practical purposes, surrendered its corporate identity. In fact, the evidence suggests just the opposite, that Westin Mexico functions as an autonomous business entity. There is evidence, for example, that Westin Mexico banks in Mexico and deposits all of the revenue from its six hotels into that account. The facts also show that while Westin is incorporated in Delaware, Westin Mexico is incorporated in Mexico and faithfully adheres to the required corporate formalities. Finally, Westin Mexico has its own staff, its own assets, and even maintains its own insurance policies.

Gardemal is correct in pointing out that undercapitalization is a critical factor in our alter-ego analysis, especially in a tort case like the present one. But as noted by the district court, there is scant evidence that Westin Mexico is in fact undercapitalized and unable to pay a judgment, if necessary. This fact weighs heavily against Gardemal because the alter ego doctrine is an equitable remedy which prevents a company from avoiding liability by abusing the corporate form. In this case, there is insufficient evidence that Westin Mexico is undercapitalized or uninsured. Moreover, there is no indication that Gardemal could not recover by suing Westin Mexico directly.

Likewise, we reject Gardemal's attempt to impute liability to Westin based on the single business enterprise doctrine. Under that doctrine, when corporations are not operated as separate entities, but integrate their resources to achieve a common business purpose, each constituent corporation may be held liable for the debts incurred in pursuit of that business purpose. Like the alter-ego doctrine, the single business enterprise doctrine is an equitable remedy which applies when the corporate form is "used as part of an unfair device to achieve an inequitable result."

On appeal, Gardemal attempts to prove a single business enterprise by calling our attention to the fact that Westin Mexico uses the trademark "Westin Hotels and Resorts." She also emphasizes that Westin Regina uses Westin's operations manuals. Gardemal also observes that Westin allows Westin Mexico to use its reservation system. Again, these facts merely demonstrate what we would describe as a typical, working relationship between a parent and subsidiary. Gardemal has pointed to no evidence in the record demonstrating that the operations of the two corporations were so integrated as to result in a blending of the two corporate identities. Moreover, Gardemal has come forward with no evidence that she has suffered some harm, or injustice, because Westin and Westin Mexico maintain separate corporate identities.

Reviewing the record in the light most favorable to Gardemal, we conclude that there is insufficient evidence that Westin Mexico was Westin's alter ego. Similarly, there is insufficient evidence that the resources of Westin and Westin Mexico are so integrated as to constitute a single business enterprise.

[The court also affirmed the district court's decision granting Westin Mexico's motion to dismiss for lack of personal jurisdiction.]

OTR Associates v. IBC Services, Inc.

801 A.2d 407 (N.J. Super. Ct. App. Div. 2002)

PRESSLER, P.J.A.D.

The single dispositive issue raised by this appeal is whether the trial court, based on its findings of fact following a bench trial, was justified, as a matter of law, in piercing the corporate veil and thus holding a parent corporation liable for the debt incurred by its wholly owned subsidiary. We are satisfied that the facts, both undisputed and as found, present a textbook illustration of circumstances mandating corporate-veil piercing.

Plaintiff OTR Associates, a limited partnership, owns a shopping mall in Edison, New Jersey, in which it leased space in 1985 for use by a Blimpie franchisee, Samyrna, Inc., a corporation owned by Sam Iskander and his wife. The franchise agreement, styled as a licensing agreement, had been entered into in 1984 between

Samyrna and the parent company, International Blimpie Corporation (Blimpie). Blimpie was the sole owner of a subsidiary named IBC Services, Inc. (IBC), created for the single purpose of holding the lease on premises occupied by a Blimpie franchisee. Accordingly, it was IBC that entered into the lease with OTR in July 1985 and, on the same day and apparently with OTR's consent, subleased the space to the franchisee. The history of the tenancy was marked by regular and increasingly substantial rent arrearages, and it was terminated by a dispossess judgment and warrant for removal in 1996. In 1998 OTR commenced this action for unpaid rent, then in the amount of close to $150,000, against Blimpie. The action was tried in December 2000, and judgment was entered in favor of OTR against Blimpie in the full amount of the rent arrearages plus interest thereon, then some $208,000. Blimpie appeals, and we affirm.

We consider the facts in the context of the well-settled principles respecting corporate-veil piercing. Nearly three-quarters of a century ago, the Court of Errors and Appeals made clear that while "ownership alone of capital stock in one corporation by another, does not create any relationship that by reason of which the stockholding company would be liable for torts of the other," nevertheless "where a corporation holds stock of another, not for the purpose of participating in the affairs of the other corporation, in the normal and usual manner, but for the purpose of control, so that the subsidiary company may be used as a mere agency or instrumentality for the stockholding company, such company will be liable for injuries due to the negligence of the subsidiary." The conceptual basis of the rule, which is equally applicable to contractual obligations, is simply that "it is where the corporate form is used as a shield behind which injustice is sought to be done by those who have control of it that equity penetrates the corporate veil."

Thus, the basic finding that must be made to enable the court to pierce the corporate veil is "that the parent so dominated the subsidiary that it had no separate existence but was merely a conduit for the parent." But beyond domination, the court must also find that the "parent has abused the privilege of incorporation by using the subsidiary to perpetrate a fraud or injustice, or otherwise to circumvent the law." And the hallmarks of that abuse are typically the engagement of the subsidiary in no independent business of its own but exclusively the performance of a service for the parent and, even more importantly, the undercapitalization of the subsidiary rendering it judgment-proof.

Blimpie concedes that it formed IBC for the sole purpose of holding the lease on the premises of a Blimpie franchisee. It is also clear that IBC had virtually no assets other than the lease itself, which, in the circumstances, was not an asset at all but only a liability since IBC had no independent right to alienate its interest therein but was subject to Blimpie's exclusive control. It had no business premises of its own, sharing the New York address of Blimpie. It had no income other than the rent payments by the franchisee, which appear to have been made directly to OTR. It does not appear that it had its own employees or office staff. We further note that

Blimpie not only retained the right to approve the premises to be occupied by the franchisee and leased by IBC, but itself, in its Georgia headquarters, managed all the leases held by its subsidiaries on franchisee premises. As explained by Charles G. Leaness, presently Executive Vice President of Blimpie and formerly corporate counsel as well as vice-president and secretary of IBC, in 1996, the year of IBC's eviction for non-payment of rent, he was Blimpie's Corporate Counsel Compliance Officer. Blimpie, he testified, is exclusively a franchising corporation with "hundreds and hundreds" of leases held by its wholly-owned leasehold companies, which are, however, overseen by Blimpie's administrative assistants, that is "people in our organization that do this communicate with landlords as their everyday job. Because we have—you know—there are various leases, various assignments." Leaness also made clear that the leasing companies, whose function he explained as assisting franchisees in negotiating leases, "don't make a profit. There's no profit made in a leasehold."

Domination and control by Blimpie of IBC is patent and was not, nor could have been, reasonably disputed. The question then is whether Blimpie abused the privilege of incorporation by using IBC to commit a fraud or injustice or other improper purpose. We agree with the trial judge that the evidence overwhelmingly requires an affirmative answer. The leit motif of the testimony of plaintiff's partners who were involved in the dealings with IBC was that they believed that they were dealing with Blimpie, the national and financially responsible franchising company, and never discovered the fact of separate corporate entities until after the eviction. While it is true that IBC never apparently expressly claimed to be Blimpie, it not only failed to explain its relationship to Blimpie as a purported independent company but it affirmatively, intentionally, and calculatedly led OTR to believe it was Blimpie. Illustratively, when OTR was pre-leasing space in the mall, the first approach to it was the appearance at its on-site office of two men in Blimpie uniforms who announced that they wanted to open a Blimpie sandwich shop. One of the men was the franchisee, Iskander. The other was never identified but presumably was someone with a connection to Blimpie. It is also true that the named tenant in the lease was IBC Services, Inc., but the tenant was actually identified in the first paragraph of the lease as "IBC Services, Inc. having an address at c/o International Blimpie Corporation, 1414 Avenue of the Americas, New York, New York." It hardly required a cryptographer to draw the entirely reasonable inference that IBC stood for International Blimpie Corporation. The suggestion, unmistakably, was that IBC was either the corporate name or a trading-as name and that International Blimpie Corporation was the other of these two possibilities.

Beyond the circumstances surrounding the commencement of the tenancy relationship, the correspondence through the years between plaintiff and the entity it believed to be its tenant confirmed plaintiff's belief that Blimpie was its tenant. Blimpie's letters to OTR were on stationary headed only by the Blimpie logo. There is nothing in any of that correspondence that would have suggested the existence of an independent company standing between the franchisor and the franchisee, and, indeed, the correspondence received by OTR from its lessee typically referred to the sub-tenant, Samyrna, as "our franchisee."

As we understand Blimpie's defense and its argument on this appeal, it asserts that it is entitled to the benefit of the separate corporate identities merely because IBC observed all the corporate proprieties—it had its own officers and directors albeit interlocking with Blimpie's, it filed annual reports, kept minutes, held meetings, and had a bank account. But that argument begs the question. The separate corporate shell created by Blimpie to avoid liability may have been mechanistically impeccable, but in every functional and operational sense, the subsidiary had no separate identity. It was moreover not intended to shield the parent from responsibility for its subsidiary's obligations but rather to shield the parent from its own obligations. And that is an evasion and an improper purpose, fraudulently conceived and executed. The corporate veil was properly pierced.

Points for Discussion

1. *Do the rules matter?*

Both Westin and Blimpie observed corporate formalities. Why in *Gardemal* is it a "typical corporate relationship between a parent and subsidiary" and in *OTR Associates* "a textbook illustration of circumstances mandating corporate-veil piercing"? Do the results in the cases vary because of the different PCV rules used by the courts?

2. *Distinguish the cases.*

The *Gardemal* case involved a tort claimant, but the court did not pierce. The *OTR Associates* case involved a contract claimant, and the court did pierce. Does this make sense? Arguably, the Gardemals justifiably assumed that the Westin logo on the hotel in Mexico assured quality and responsibility. And, arguably, the mall lessor (of all people) should have known to ask what entity was signing the lease and to demand a guarantee from the parent corporation.

3. *Contract vs. tort.*

Would the results have been the same if Westin Mexico had been sued in contract, and Blimpie had been sued in tort?

F. Reverse Veil Piercing

In traditional veil piercing, a creditor of the corporation seeks to pierce the veil of limited liability to access a shareholder's assets. In contrast, "reverse veil piercing" aims in the opposite direction, at the assets of the corporation. It is controversial and can take one of two forms.

In "insider" reverse veil piercing, a corporate insider such as a shareholder seeks to have the corporate entity disregarded to claim the corporation's assets as their own, seek a right or benefit under the law, or avail the shareholder of corporate claims against third parties. Courts and commentators have not been very sympathetic to insider reverse veil piercing cases, although some have argued that insider reverse veil piercing should permit shareholders to assert constitutional rights on behalf of corporations whose shares they own. Insider reverse veil piercing can arise in corporate bankruptcy, when a shareholder targets corporate assets that would otherwise be used to satisfy the debts of senior creditors. It has also been used to treat a parent and subsidiary entities as a singular employer so that both receive workers' compensation immunity.

By contrast, "outsider" reverse veil piercing is sought by a third-party outsider—a creditor of a shareholder typically seeks to access an entity's assets in satisfaction of the creditor's claim against the shareholder. For example, a creditor of a parent corporation might seek to hold a subsidiary liable for conduct by the corporate parent.

The Delaware courts recently recognized "outsider" reverse veil piercing, in the case excerpted below. The facts are complicated, but they provide an opportunity to study, not only a novel judicial ruling, but also how a defendant might try to avoid paying a judgment, and how plaintiffs can try to stop them.

The action was brought by Manichaean Capital, LLC, a Delaware LLC, along with individual plaintiffs, who owned common stock in a company called SourceHOV Holdings, Inc. ("SourceHOV Holdings"). The defendant was Exela, a Delaware corporation, which acquired SourceHOV Holdings in a merger. Exela sat atop a network of subsidiaries, including more than one entity with "SourceHOV" in its name. Plaintiffs voted against the merger and sought a statutory appraisal. The court ruled that the fair value of their shares was significantly higher than what they would have received in the merger—they received an appraisal judgment for $57 million. So far, so good.

However, Source HOV Holdings had no direct operating assets, meaning that it could not pay the appraisal judgment. But plaintiffs didn't give up. Instead, they dug one level lower in the Exela network, and moved for a "charging order" (a court-ordered lien) against the membership interest that SourceHOV Holdings held in its wholly owned subsidiary named SourceHOV, LLC. The court granted this motion and required that any distributions made by this subsidiary and payable to SourceHOV Holdings must be paid to plaintiffs first, before reaching Exela.

The dispute arose from a clever move by Exela: before the charging order was issued, certain of Exela's subsidiaries entered into an accounts receivable securitization facility (the "A/R Facility"), which transferred their accounts receivable to a newly formed subsidiary. (Accounts receivable are payments owed to a company.) The A/R facility thus diverted money around SourceHOV Holdings, so that plaintiffs had no avenue to collect.

To enforce the spirit of the charging order, the plaintiffs sought to "reverse pierce" up to parent Exela, and then down to the other subsidiaries. This was a question of first impression in Delaware.

Manichaean Capital, LLC v. Exela Techs., Inc.

251 A.3d 694 (Del. Ch. 2021)

SLIGHTS, VICE CHANCELLOR.

Traditional Veil-Piercing

Delaware courts consider a number of factors in determining whether to disregard the corporate form and pierce the corporate veil, including: "(1) whether the company was adequately capitalized for the undertaking; (2) whether the company was solvent; (3) whether corporate formalities were observed; (4) whether the dominant shareholder siphoned company funds; and (5) whether, in general, the company simply functioned as a facade for the dominant shareholder." While these factors are useful, any single one of them is not determinative. An ultimate decision regarding veil-piercing is largely based on some combination of these factors, in addition to "an overall element of injustice or unfairness."

Plaintiffs make a compelling case in their Complaint that Exela and SourceHOV Holdings "operate[ ] as a single economic entity such that it would be inequitable for this Court to uphold a legal distinction between them." First, it is reasonably conceivable that SourceHOV Holdings is insolvent and that its insolvency, at least in part, is the result of Exela's undercapitalization of SourceHOV Holdings. SourceHOV Holdings is a holding company with no direct operating assets. In fact, its only asset is its membership interest in SourceHOV, LLC, which in turn holds interests in its solvent subsidiaries. SourceHOV Holdings has no bank account, money market account or brokerage account. The Complaint alleges funds that once flowed up from the SourceHOV Subsidiaries to SourceHOV Holdings as a matter of course, are now bypassing SourceHOV Holdings and flowing directly to Exela. Now that SourceHOV Holdings has no funds, and no prospect of securing funds, it is unable to meet its obligations as they become due, and it is at least reasonably conceivable that it will never be able to do so.

Plaintiffs further allege that Exela: (1) is headquartered at the same address as SourceHOV Holdings, (2) has failed to maintain proper business registrations for SourceHOV Holdings, (3) has significantly overlapping personnel with SourceHOV Holdings, (4) has referred to Exela and its subsidiaries as one combined enterprise in

SEC filings and (5) requires SourceHOV Holdings to obtain Exela's consent before SourceHOV Holdings may pay its own creditors. Plaintiffs compellingly allege that fraud and injustice has resulted and will result from the diversion of funds from SourceHOV Holdings to Exela in an explicit attempt to avoid payment of the Appraisal Judgment.

Taking Plaintiffs' well-pled characterization as fact, it is reasonably conceivable the A/R Facility was created in order deliberately to prevent funds from flowing through SourceHOV Holdings and to enable SourceHOV Holdings to avoid its obligations to creditors, including Plaintiffs. Assuming the pled facts are true, it is reasonably conceivable that it is necessary to pierce the SourceHOV Holdings corporate veil to avoid fraud and injustice.

Reverse Veil-Piercing

The question of whether and to what extent courts of Delaware should allow so-called reverse veil-piercing is one of first impression. . . . For reasons explained below, I am satisfied that Delaware law allows for reverse veil-piercing in limited circumstances and in circumscribed execution.

1. The Mechanics of Reverse Veil-Piercing and its Proper Application

At its most basic level, reverse veil-piercing involves the imposition of liability on a business organization for the liabilities of its owners. Outsider reverse veil-piercing is implicated where "an outside third party, frequently a creditor, urges a court to render a company liable on a judgment against its member." Given Plaintiffs are creditors of SourceHOV Holdings, the single member and 100% owner of SourceHOV LLC, which in turn is the single member and owner of the SourceHOV Subsidiaries, and Plaintiffs seek to hold the subsidiaries liable for a judgment held against the member, this case concerns outsider veil-piercing.

Courts declining to allow reverse veil-piercing have relied primarily on a desire to protect innocent parties. Reverse veil-piercing has the potential to bypass normal judgement collection procedures by permitting the judgment creditor of a parent to jump in front of the subsidiary's creditors. For obvious reasons, this dynamic would "unsettle the expectations of corporate creditors who understand their loans to be secured . . . by corporate assets" and could lead to corporate creditors "insist[ing] on being compensated for the increased risk of default posed by outside reverse-piercing claims." As (if not more) important, "to the extent that the corporation has other non-culpable shareholders, they obviously will be prejudiced if the corporation's assets can be attached directly." Courts rejecting reverse veil-piercing have emphasized that the risk of harm to innocent stakeholders is often avoidable because judgment creditors can invoke other claims and remedies to achieve the same outcome.

The risks that reverse veil-piercing may be used as a blunt instrument to harm innocent parties, and to disrupt the expectations of arms-length bargaining, while real, do not, in my view, justify the rejection of reverse veil-piercing outright. Rather, the recognition of the risks creates an opportunity to manage them, and to do so in a manner that serves the interests of equity.

The natural starting place when reviewing a claim for reverse veil-piercing are the traditional factors Delaware courts consider when reviewing a traditional veil-piercing claim—the so-called "alter ego" factors that include insolvency, undercapitalization, commingling of corporate and personal funds, the absence of corporate formalities, and whether the subsidiary is simply a facade for the owner. The court should then ask whether the owner is utilizing the corporate form to perpetuate fraud or an injustice. This inquiry should focus on additional factors, including: "(1) the degree to which allowing a reverse pierce would impair the legitimate expectations of any adversely affected shareholders who are not responsible for the conduct of the insider that gave rise to the reverse pierce claim, and the degree to which allowing a reverse pierce would establish a precedent troubling to shareholders generally; (2) the degree to which the corporate entity whose disregard is sought has exercised dominion and control over the insider who is subject to the claim by the party seeking a reverse pierce; (3) the degree to which the injury alleged by the person seeking a reverse pierce is related to the corporate entity's dominion and control of the insider, or to that person's reasonable reliance upon a lack of separate entity status between the insider and the corporate entity; (4) the degree to which the public convenience, as articulated by [the DGCL and Delaware's common law], would be served by allowing a reverse pierce; (5) the extent and severity of the wrongful conduct, if any, engaged in by the corporate entity whose disregard is sought by the insider; (6) the possibility that the person seeking the reverse pierce is himself guilty of wrongful conduct sufficient to bar him from obtaining equitable relief"; (7) the extent to which the reverse pierce will harm innocent third-party creditors of the entity the plaintiff seeks to reach; and (8) the extent to which other claims or remedies are practically available to the creditor at law or in equity to recover the debt. Fundamentally, reverse veil-piercing, like traditional veil-piercing, is rooted in equity, and the court must consider all relevant factors, including those just noted, to reach an equitable result.[124]

2. Plaintiffs' Reverse Veil-Piercing Claim Is Well-Pled

After carefully reviewing the Complaint, I am satisfied this is one of those "exceptional circumstances" where a plaintiff has well pled a basis for reverse veil-piercing. It is at least reasonably conceivable that the SourceHOV Subsidiaries are alter egos of SourceHOV Holdings and that the subsidiaries have actively participated in a scheme to defraud or work an injustice against SourceHOV Holdings creditors, like Plaintiffs, by diverting funds that would normally flow to SourceHOV Holdings away from that entity to Exela. At this stage, from the well pled allegations in the

---

[124] I recognize that, as a practical matter, the consideration of whether the reverse pierce will cause harm to innocent third parties will substantially limit the doctrine's application. Borrowing from our "bad faith" jurisprudence in the fiduciary duty context, the case meeting this rigid framework for reverse veil-piercing can safely be classified as a "rare bird."

Complaint, I see no innocent shareholders or creditors of the SourceHOV Subsidiaries that would be harmed by reverse veil-piercing, nor any potential alternative claims at law or in equity, as against the SourceHOV Subsidiaries or SourceHOV Holdings itself, that would for certain remedy the harm. [The court provided additional analysis of the "alter ego" factors, the fraud or injustice inquiry, and the additional elements to sustain a reverse veil-piercing claim.]

Points for Discussion

1. Rare bird?

Manichaean Capital involved plaintiffs that had faced "the highly unusual circumstance where an appraisal judgment debtor cannot or will not pay" and the judgment debtor had only a membership interest in an LLC, against which the plaintiffs got a charging order. 251 A.3d at 699-700. Delaware LLC law provides that a charging order is the "exclusive remedy" by which a creditor may satisfy judgment out of the LLC interest, and thus equitable claims and remedies, such as unjust enrichment, are not available as separate means to reach LLC assets. Thus, it seemed the plaintiffs' only hope was reverse veil piercing to expand the entities against whom the charging order could be enforced. In light of these particular facts, and the eight factors for outsider reverse veil piercing that the court set out, just how rare do you think successful reverse veil piercing cases are likely to be?

2. Reverse veil piercing policy.

Courts have split on whether they recognize a claim of reverse veil piercing. Courts that have declined to adopt reverse veil piercing have cited a variety of policy-related concerns, including that these types of claims can adversely affect nonculpable shareholders and creditors, can be dealt with through other remedies, and have negative implications for the stability of the corporate form. Other courts have observed that traditional veil piercing and outsider reverse veil piercing share similar policy goals of achieving an equitable result to prevent fraud or injustice. Which policy arguments do you find most compelling? If you were to craft a test for outsider reverse veil piercing, what factors do you think would be most important?

CHAPTER 7

Accounting and Valuation

This chapter covers accounting and valuation basics. We start with two pages filled with a bunch of numbers. You might think of skipping these, but please don't. Hidden in these numbers are interesting "stories" about a fictional business called Widget, Inc. One of our goals in this chapter is to explore these kinds of stories. We think an intuitive understanding of accounting and valuation will help you greatly, not only if you work in the business world, but with personal financial decisions as well.

Like many businesses, Widget, Inc. has three financial statements, labeled a Balance Sheet, a Statement of Income, and a Statement of Cash Flows. (Such labels are often capitalized in the financial statements, but you also will see these terms discussed without capitalization.) The Balance Sheet depicts a "snapshot" of Widget, Inc.'s assets and liabilities at the end of each of the previous two years. Take a look at the Balance Sheet now. The first line shows that cash declined from $275,000 to $100,000 during this time. Why might Widget, Inc.'s cash have declined so much? What do you think is the story behind that?

The Statement of Income depicts a "moving picture" of Widget, Inc.'s income and expenses for each of the previous three years. Look at Widget, Inc.'s "bottom line," its annual Net Income. That number has been increasing each year, from $226,000 to $254,000 and then to a whopping $390,000 during the most recent year. Why might that have happened? What is that story?

Finally, and in contrast, the Statement of Cash Flows adjusts these net income numbers to show how Widget, Inc.'s cash flows changed each year. Look at the bottom line there: ($175,000). That number confirms that cash declined by $175,000 last year, just as the Balance Sheet also showed (the parentheses in the financial statements indicate that the number is negative, just like a minus sign would). Again, there's a story there. What do you think it is?

In short, what is going on at this company? What might a potential investor, such as a venture capital firm, ask about Widget, Inc.? What might you ask, as a potential employee or general counsel? Perhaps most importantly, what do you think Widget, Inc. is worth?

Accounting and financial valuation are fundamentally different tools. Accounting looks back in time to understand past numbers. It describes the details and facts about a company historically. In contrast, financial valuation looks forward in time. It describes potential visions of how a company might do in the future, and then uses those projections to assess how much the company is worth today.

The two key valuation methods we will explore are known as the "comparables" method ("comps," for short) and the "discounted cash flow" method ("DCF," for short). Both comps and DCF can vary depending on whether a company has publicly traded shares. We will discuss accounting and valuation of both private and public firms.

In this chapter, we give you some tools to help you answer these questions, not only for Widget, Inc. but for any company, large or small, based on its financial statements. First, we introduce some basic accounting concepts and work through a simple example. Then we go through each of the three financial statements, step by step. Finally, we discuss some common ways to value a business.

That last question is one that threads through this chapter, and often arises when people think about any business. You might begin your thinking about accounting and valuation by taking a look at the next two pages with one simple question in mind: how much would you pay to buy Widget, Inc.?

WIDGET, INC. BALANCE SHEET
(As of December 31)

Assets	Year 2	Year 1
Current Assets		
Cash	100,000	275,000
Accounts receivable	1,380,000	1,145,000
Inventories	1,310,000	1,105,000
Prepaid expenses	40,000	35,000
Total Current Assets	2,830,000	2,560,000
Property, Plant, and Equipment		
Land*	775,000	775,000
Buildings**	2,000,000	2,000,000
Machinery**	1,000,000	935,000
Office Equipment**	225,000	205,000
Total PP&E	4,000,000	3,915,000
Accumulated Depreciation***	(1,620,000)	(1,370,000)
Intangible Assets****	50,000	0
Total Long-term Assets	2,430,000	2,545,000
Total Assets	5,260,000	5,105,000
Liabilities and Equity		
Current Liabilities		
Accounts payable	900,000	825,000
Notes payable, 11% due next July 1	0	355,000
Accrued expenses payable	250,000	235,000
Other liabilities	600,000	570,000
Total Current Liabilities	1,750,000	1,985,000
Long-term Notes payable, 12.5% due in ten years	2,000,000	2,000,000
Total Liabilities	3,750,000	3,985,000
Stockholders' Equity		
Common stock (1,000 shares authorized and outstanding)		
Paid-in capital	200,000	200,000
Retained earnings	1,310,000	920,000
Total Equity	1,510,000	1,120,000
Total Liabilities and Equity	5,260,000	5,105,000

* The land was purchased 15 years ago for $775,000, the price shown on the balance sheet. A comparable property nearby recently sold for $975,000.

** The machinery and equipment are in good repair. The fair market value of the building and equipment are about $200,000 more than historical cost.

*** Depreciation is on a level (straight line) basis over the estimated useful life.

*** Depreciation is on a level (straight line) basis over the estimated useful life.

**** Intangible assets include patent acquired for $50,000 during Year 2.

STATEMENT OF INCOME (Year Ended December 31)			
	Year 2	Year 1	Year 0
Net sales	7,500,000	7,000,000	6,800,000
Cost of goods sold	4,980,000	4,650,000	4,607,000
Gross Profit	2,520,000	2,350,000	2,193,000
Operating Expenses			
Depreciation	250,000	240,000	200,000
Selling and admin expense*	1,300,000	1,220,000	1,150,000
R&D	50,000	125,000	120,000
Operating Income	920,000	765,000	723,000
Interest expense	320,000	375,000	375,000
Income before taxes	600,000	390,000	348,000
Income taxes	210,000	136,000	122,000
Net Income	**390,000**	**254,000**	**226,000**

* Includes $130,000 salaries paid to the owners in Year 2; $100,000 in Year 1; and $100,000 in Year 0, and bonuses totaling $120,000 in Year 2; $100,000 in Year 1; and $80,000 in Year 0.

STATEMENT OF CASH FLOWS (Year Ended December 31)			
	Year 2	Year 1	Year 0
From Operating Activities			
Net Income	390,000	254,000	226,000
Decrease (Increase) in accts receivable	(235,000)	(34,000)	(32,000)
Decrease (Increase) in inventories	(205,000)	(28,000)	(33,000)
Decrease (Increase) in prepaid expenses	(5,000)	(3,000)	(3,000)
Increase (Decrease) in accounts payable	75,000	25,000	20,000
Increase (Decrease) in accr exp payable	15,000	7,000	5,000
Depreciation	250,000	240,000	200,000
Total from Operating Activities	285,000	461,000	383,000
From Investing Activities			
Sales (Purchases) of machinery	(65,000)	(378,000)	(263,000)
Sales (Purchases) of office equipment	(20,000)	(27,000)	(25,000)
Sales (Purchases) of patents	(50,000)	0	0
Total from Investing Activities	(135,000)	(405,000)	(288,000)
From Financing Activities			
Increase (Decrease) in short-term debt	30,000	(40,000)	(35,000)
Increase (Decrease) in long-term debt	(355,000)	0	0
Total from Financing Activities	(325,000)	(40,000)	(35,000)
Increase (Decrease) in Cash Position	**(175,000)**	**16,000**	**60,000**

A. Financial Accounting for Lawyers

We include this chapter, and believe it is important, because the reality is that you cannot escape accounting and numbers, even in law school, and especially in law practice. Whether you practice corporate law or litigation, whether you work in the private sector or in government, you inevitably will confront financial accounting. You will find basic accounting and financial numeracy to be useful, whatever you decide to do with your life. So if you don't have a basic understanding of these concepts yet, you might as well learn them now, in the relative comfort of a law school course. It will be easier than picking it up on the job. And for those of you who have taken accounting courses or already have experience with financial statements, our advice is to approach this chapter with an open mind. We are going to cover accounting from a different perspective than you may have encountered before—that of law and policy.

Example

You represent an investor group interested in buying Widget, Inc. Looking at the financial statements, which aspects of the business appear to be attractive? Which are worrisome? Which accounting entries raise questions for you and the group?

How might you value the business of Widget, Inc.? What should you focus on—the accounting value of the business assets? The extent that assets exceed liabilities? The annual revenues of the business? Net income? Cash flow? And should you focus on these items just for the past year, or over time?

Purposes for accounting. This chapter is designed to introduce basic accounting and valuation concepts to law students who have *no* training in accounting or finance. It also introduces an approach to accounting that students with training in accounting or finance might find unfamiliar. Most accounting and finance courses are oriented to the perspective of idealized business owners and managers, who use financial information to keep track of, and exercise control over, the businesses they own or operate. From the perspective of such idealized owner/managers, the most useful financial statements are those that come as close as possible to presenting the objective truth about the firm's financial status and the results of its operations.

In contrast, lawyers frequently must deal with financial statements in adversarial or quasi-adversarial settings. When a financial statement has been prepared by or on behalf of an opposing party, the lawyer must appreciate the possibility that this statement—even if it has been prepared by a Certified Public Accountant (CPA) who has opined that it presents financial information "fairly" and "in accordance with generally accepted accounting principles" (GAAP, pronounced "gap")—will in fact represent a subjective and self-serving picture of the opposing party's financial situation. Lawyers know that the idealized business person does not exist. The numbers might be close to accurate. But they also might be lies.

Lawyers also deal with financial statements when advising parties in a non-adversarial manner. For example, the seller and buyer of a business ideally will agree to a deal that is a "win-win" for both of them. Transactional lawyers often act as dealmakers or advisers in situations different from the adversarial role assumed in the litigation-focused world of many law school courses. For lawyers to play such a role effectively, so that they add value to their clients' transactions, they must understand the business, including accounting and valuation issues.

State law typically requires corporations to furnish their shareholders with annual balance sheets and income statements, but allows corporations to decide which accounting principles to use when preparing those statements. Most firms, and all public corporations, use GAAP, but recognize that the rules do not embody immutable scientific or mathematical truths. Instead, GAAP represents the often-controversial judgments and policy preferences of a group of accounting professionals from the Financial Accounting Standards Board (FASB). As the perceptions, judgments, and preferences of FASB change over time, so does GAAP.

There are many assumptions under GAAP. A business is assumed to be separate from its owners and managers, even if it does not have a separate legal existence. A business is assumed to be a "going concern," meaning it will continue in operation for the foreseeable future. Businesses are also supposed to apply the same accounting concepts, standards, and procedures from one period to the next, and to disclose all material information. Another assumption is that businesses will follow a *Conservatism Principle, meaning they will record only actual, not anticipated, profits and will recognize* probable losses as soon as possible.

Accounting is subjective. Although financial statements appear precise, the numbers often reflect highly subjective judgments. Many transactions can be conceptualized in different ways, all of them consistent with GAAP. People have incentives to use the flexibility inherent in GAAP to present financial information in a way that best serves their interests. A manager might want the business to appear as profitable as possible. A divorcing spouse might try to minimize a business's asset values. A person selling a business might attempt to make the business appear free of risks. An accountant might want to keep clients happy by painting the picture of their business that they want to see. We are all human.

It is important to note that the choices people make regarding GAAP might be entirely legitimate without being manipulative. Simply put, there are different ways to account for different items. If your company buys a building, you should list that building as an asset. But how should you record its worth? The amount you paid? What if you got a really good deal and bought it for half of its market value—should you then record this amount rather than its cost? Should you record changes in the value of the building over time? And how much? These are difficult questions, and there are different legitimate answers.

There is an old joke about a client conducting interviews in search of a new CPA. The client asks each candidate several detailed accounting questions. One candidate answers all of the questions correctly. Then, the client asks one final "killer" question, the answer to which clinches the job:

> Client: OK, and finally, how much is two plus two? (Previous candidates had answered "four.")
>
> CPA: How much do you want it to be?

The joke illustrates not only the willingness of some accountants and managers to stretch the rules, but also the fact that GAAP is a flexible framework that can be shaped favorably. Of course, many managers and accountants are honest and do their best to follow the rules. But it is important to note that the two fundamental aspects of accounting we have mentioned—the lack of objective truth and the incentives for people to present favorable information—can be a dangerous combination, or at least a reason to apply a critical eye.

Although GAAP can appear scientific at times, and some accounting rules have an air of precision, you should keep in mind two fundamental aspects of accounting that matter crucially to law and policy. If you are formally trained in accounting, you might view these two propositions as heresy.

- There is no such thing as objective truth in accounting.

- People naturally will present financial information that suits their interests.

For example, some business people are tempted to manipulate accounting to make a company look better than it is. Corporate officers, and their accountants, are frequently accused of "managing earnings" by manipulating the corporation's financial statements to make it appear that the corporation is earning consistent and increasing profits. The extent of earnings management can vary, from merely smoothing quarterly or annual income over time to outright fraud.

Lawyers in both the deal-making and litigation settings frequently bring a healthy skepticism to their assessment of financial statements.

Stages of accounting. Financial statements are produced through a three-stage process. First is the "recording and controls" stage, in which a company records in its books information concerning every transaction in which it is involved. Second is the "audit" stage, in which the company, perhaps with the assistance of independent accountants, verifies the accuracy of the information it has recorded. Third is the "accounting" stage, in which the company classifies and analyzes the audited information and presents it in a set of financial statements. At each stage, there are opportunities for managers and accountants to be truthful and forthcoming, or not.

Although public companies always go through these three stages, private companies often do not. The audit and accounting process is expensive, and many small companies are not in a position to pay to have their financial statements audited by an outside, independent accounting firm. Managers of private companies often have business priorities other than accounting, and lower expectations about the benefits of a robust accounting process. Accordingly, someone considering buying a private business might be skeptical about the details in financial statements and would want to know who prepared the financial statements, how they were prepared, and whether any third party reviewed them. In our example, the buyers of Widget, Inc. certainly would want answers to these questions, particularly because the company's financial statements are not audited. (If they had been audited, a signed audit opinion would have accompanied the financial statements—there is no such opinion here.)

Decades of accounting scandals and related litigation have sharpened the focus of lawyers on financial accounting issues. You might have heard of some of the firms involved in such scandals: Enron and WorldCom during the early 2000s, or numerous financial institutions during the global financial crisis of 2007–08. One major accounting firm, Arthur Andersen, collapsed under the pressure of the Enron scandal, and other accounting firms, and some law firms, have been sued because of accounting improprieties. Lawyers involved in planning and disclosing the affairs of corporations frequently deal with complex accounting issues.

Accounting as art, not science. Inevitably, preparing and reading financial statements is an art, not a science. Even though numbers are involved, this is not mathematics. It is more like a forensic investigation, an attempt to construct a plausible story about what has happened in a business, to evaluate its risks and value. The goal of financial statements is to convey information, but financial statements alone rarely tell the entire story. As you read the materials that follow, ask yourself what additional information a prospective buyer would want to understand the real story of Widget, Inc. With these inquiries, you will begin to perform one of a lawyer's most important functions in a business transaction: helping clients ask the right questions.

The materials that follow will help you understand the basics of financial accounting. We just cover the basics, though. Public companies' financial statements can stretch to dozens, or even hundreds, of pages, with detailed footnotes describing contingent liabilities and complex financial instruments. Our focus is on the three financial statements set forth above: the balance sheet, the income statement, and the cash flow statement. We will give you several examples based on Widget, Inc. so that you can discern a more detailed story of that company. We then will spend some time on valuation, again using the story of Widget, Inc. to give you a sense of how business people value a corporation. In other chapters, we offer "Points for Discussion" after various sections of materials; here, there are so many points for discussion that we raise them as questions throughout the materials.

B.   The Fundamental Equation

We begin with the balance sheet. As noted above, the balance sheet is a "snap-shot"—it is a picture of the business at a particular moment. In the case of Widget, Inc. you have a picture as of two moments. The first column is a snapshot of its assets and liabilities as of December 31 of Year 2, and the second column is a snapshot as of December 31 of Year 1.

Note that the balance sheet is in "balance"—total assets are equal to total liabilities plus total equity. For Year 2, Total Assets are $5,260,000, and Total Liabilities and Equity are also $5,260,000. This also holds true for Year 1. This equating of assets to liabilities plus equity is known as the "fundamental equation" of financial accounting:

ASSETS = LIABILITIES + EQUITY

"Assets" refers to the property, both tangible and intangible, owned by the firm. "Liabilities" refers to the amount that the firm owes to others, whether pursuant to written evidence of indebtedness or otherwise. "Equity" represents the accounting value of the interest of the firm's owners. Equity initially includes the value of the property (including money) the owners contribute when they organize the firm.

Assets are sometimes referred to as the "left side" of the balance sheet, and liabilities and equity the "right side." (Imagine that the balance sheet was presented with assets on the left, and liabilities and equity on the right, rather than assets on top, and liabilities and equity on the bottom). In simple terms, the right side of the balance sheet shows where the firm's money came from, and the left side of the balance sheet shows where it went. How did Widget, Inc. obtain money? It issued common stock to its owners, and it also borrowed money from outside parties. It then used this money to buy assets.

Cookie jar accounting. Before we go through the balance sheet in detail, we want to work through an example to show how the fundamental equation works. Imagine that our corporation is an empty jar. It has no assets, no liabilities, and no equity. At the start, the fundamental equation looks like this:

Step One: Suppose the owner of the firm invests $12. You might imagine that the owner actually puts $12 in the jar. Now, the firm's balance sheet is:

Note that the balance sheet is in balance. The $12 of assets recorded on the left balances the $12 of equity recorded to the right.

Step Two: Next assume the firm borrows an additional $10. You might imagine that a lender puts $10 in the jar and records an "IOU" for $10. Now, the balance sheet is:

The balance sheet is still in balance, but this time the increased assets were matched with an increase in liabilities. The same will be true every time the firm obtains money from the outside, whether in the form of equity or debt. Every such transaction will increase assets and increase either liabilities or equity, depending on the source of the money. Each transaction will affect both the left and right side of the balance sheet, which will always remain in balance.

Step Three: Next the firm buys two felt-tip pens for $2 each. You might imagine that the firm takes $4 of cash out of the jar and puts $4 of pens into the jar. Because one asset is exchanged for another, the balance sheet remains unchanged.

Note that in recording the value of the pens as an asset, we follow the Cost Principle, which holds that historical cost provides the best basis for recording a transaction, because it can be determined objectively and is verifiable. If you wanted to be more precise, you could break the assets into two groups: $18 of cash and $4 of pens. Either way, the total assets are $22.

<u>Step Four</u>: Then the firm buys scissors on credit for $5. It puts scissors worth $5 in the jar and incurs a liability of $5, which can be envisioned as a bill for $5 also placed in the jar.

<u>Step Five</u>: Then the firm sells one of the felt-tip pens for $3. It exchanges a pen that cost $2 for $3 in cash. The $1 profit results in an increase in assets of $1.

Note that the cookie jar is now weighted more heavily on the left side than on the right, because the assets are greater than the sum of liabilities plus equity. We have a problem now, because we know that the balance sheet must balance. How can we get it to balance? Recall that the right side of the balance sheet represents where the firm's money came from. We know that the value of the equity entry on the balance sheet increased when the owner put money into the firm. In addition, the equity entry will change to reflect the firm's profits and losses. When the firm makes money, equity will increase; when it loses money, equity will decline.

Because the firm has made $1, the equity entry also should increase by $1. The actual increase appears in "Retained Earnings," which is a component of equity. Once we reflect the increased value of equity, the fundamental equation again holds.

See if you can provide the explanation for how the firm would account for the following three transactions:

<u>Step Six</u>: The firm pays the bill for the scissors.

<u>Step Seven</u>: The firm pays $2 in rent for the use of the jar.

<u>Step Eight</u>: Finally, the owner takes $5 out of the jar so she can get herself a treat.

C. Balance Sheet

Now that we understand the basics of the balance sheet, we will work through each of the most important balance sheet accounts. As you read this section, you should look at each individual number on Widget, Inc.'s balance sheet to be sure you understand what the number means and why it might have changed over time.

1. Balance Sheet Assets

Assets are listed in the balance sheet in the order of their liquidity, beginning with cash, followed by assets that the firm expects to convert to cash in the reasonably near future, and continuing to other assets, such as plant and equipment, that the firm uses in its business over the longer term.

Current assets. We will begin with the four items of current assets on Widget, Inc.'s balance sheet. Current assets include cash and other assets that in the normal course of business will be converted into cash in the reasonably near future, generally within one year of the date of the balance sheet. Note that Widget, Inc.'s cash declined from Year 1 to Year 2, while its other current assets increased.

Current Assets	Year 2	Year 1
Cash	100,000	275,000
Accounts receivable	1,380,000	1,145,000
Inventories	1,310,000	1,105,000
Prepaid expenses	40,000	35,000
Total Current Assets	2,830,000	2,560,000

Cash. Cash, the first current asset, represents not just physical bills and coins, but also money deposited in the bank. Widget, Inc. had $275,000 of cash at the end of Year 1, but only $100,000 of cash at the end of Year 2. Why such a significant decline? Is Widget, Inc. financially weaker now, with less cash? Or is it stronger, because it found more attractive business opportunities, and spent more cash on them?

You might think that accounting for cash is straightforward, and for many businesses it is. But many firms use extra cash to buy liquid securities, such as commercial paper and treasury bills, with a view to generating interest income. Some firms also purchase publicly traded debt and equity securities.

Commercial paper is short-term highly rated debt issued by public corporations, typically with a maturity of less than 270 days. Treasury bills are obligations of the U.S. government with a maturity of less than one year. You should be wary of descriptions of short-term investments. What some companies describe as "cash" or "marketable securities" might actually consist of riskier investments. For example, during the Financial Crisis of 2008, investors learned that many corporations, most notably American International Group (AIG), had exposure to the risks of subprime mortgages through their short-term, highly rated investments.

Larger public corporations separately record "cash and cash equivalents" and "short term investments." Some of the investments in these categories are not really equivalent to "cash."

Some investments are recorded on the balance sheet at their cost, especially if their value cannot readily be determined. But other investments are "marked to market," meaning that the recorded number on the balance sheet reflects changes in the fair market value of the investment since the previous period. These changes are then recorded as income or loss on the reporting firm's income statement.

In recent years, it has become common for firms to buy and sell large amounts of a variety of financial instruments, either to hedge against fluctuations in interest rates, exchange rates, commodity prices, or other values or to seek trading gains. In general, such instruments also must be "marked to market" as of the date of the balance sheet, and the difference between their cost and market value must be recorded as a gain or loss. If Widget, Inc. had held cryptocurrency instead of U.S. dollar bank deposits, its current assets might have fluctuated much more. If market prices cannot readily be determined, management is required to make a good faith estimate of market value.

As you might imagine, this is an area where managers and accountants might try to be aggressive. For example, Enron and several financial institutions in the early 2000s were accused of assigning unrealistic values to some of the financial instruments they held. During the Financial Crisis of 2008, there was extensive debate about whether financial assets with exposure to subprime mortgages should be "marked to market" or recorded at a higher value given the belief that market prices were artificially depressed due to mistaken market pessimism. Over time, many banks have recorded financial assets—including assets backed by home mortgages or corporate loans—at values that were greater than the prices they would have fetched in the market. Likewise, many firms involved in trading cryptoassets recorded those assets at artificially high prices.

Accounts receivable. The second current asset is accounts receivable, sometimes just called "receivables" or "A/R." These are amounts not yet collected from customers who received goods or services. Widget, Inc. had $1,145,000 of receivables at the end of Year 1, and $1,380,000 of receivables at the end of Year 2. What might have caused this increase?

Accounts receivable might have increased for two reasons. First, sales might have increased. That's a good story: a higher number might indicate that more customers purchased goods or services. Second, receivables might have increased because customers were paying more slowly, or not at all. That's not such a good story. A higher number might be that lower amounts are being collected. Thus, a significant change in accounts receivable might be a positive sign or a negative sign.

When a firm sells to customers on credit and the customers don't pay their bills on time, GAAP requires a reduction in accounts receivable by deducting an allowance (or "reserve") for bad debts. Firms usually calculate bad debt allowances based on past customer behavior. However, when a firm's customer base or business conditions change, those calculations might not prove accurate. Likewise, some firms sell goods subject to a right of return. They record sales based on assumptions about returns, but those assumptions also might change.

How much of Widget, Inc.'s accounts receivable reflect a reduction for "doubtful accounts"? Who do you think determined that amount, and how did they arrive at the number?

Corporations often record other kinds of receivables on their balance sheets. For example, notes or loans receivable represent money owed to the corporation. Widget, Inc. did not record these receivables, but they can be significant for firms engaged in businesses that involve customer financing. For these firms, the allowance for bad debts can have a major impact on results. Financial institutions frequently are forced to "write off" payments they expect to receive from customers and counterparties.

Inventory. Inventory, the third current asset, represents goods held for use in production or for sale to customers. Widget, Inc.'s inventory—a recorded value of the widgets it holds and hopes to sell—increased from $1,105,000 at the end of Year 1 to $1,310,000 at the end of Year 2. Is this increase good or bad?

As with receivables, the increase might be positive if it reflects increasing sales. But the increase might instead reflect declining customer purchases. Which is it? At this point, you probably are beginning to see that, although the numbers in the financial statements appear to be objective, behind those numbers there are more complex, real-life stories about what has happened inside the corporation.

Firms that want to play games to maximize the value of their reported assets might "cherry pick" their inventories by assuming that only the least expensive items are the ones sold. If costs were increasing, they might assume that the first (and cheapest) items on the shelf were sold. In contrast, if costs were declining, they might assume that the most recent (and cheapest) items on the shelf were sold. If the inventories are fungible—as with widgets—firms might manipulate their decisions about which items were sold.

GAAP establishes a uniform set of rules for inventory reporting, in part to prevent such gaming. Firms can opt to use one of three methods to value their closing inventory: (1) average cost; (2) first in, first out (FIFO); and (3) last in, first out (LIFO). Each of these methods is an assumption about which items in inventory actually are sold to customers. Many firms find it more practical to use an assumption than to keep track of the cost of each item.

Here are some ways to visualize each of the three assumptions about how firms sell inventory:

- Average cost: inventory is sold at random from a bin

- FIFO: inventory is pushed through a pipeline

- LIFO: inventory is added and sold from the top of a stack

Example
LIFO/FIFO

Imagine that Widget, Inc. produced three widgets over time, at costs that increased from $10 to $20 to $30. The total value of its inventory, as listed in its balance sheet, would be $60. Next, imagine that Widget, Inc. sold two of the three widgets in its inventory. The inventory that Widget, Inc. would assume was sold would depend on its assumptions, as follows:

- Average cost: each widget sold cost $20

- FIFO: the first widget sold cost $10; the second widget sold cost $20

- LIFO: the first widget sold cost $30; the second widget sold cost $20

The value of Widget, Inc.'s remaining inventory then depends on the valuation method it chose. The balance sheet value of the one remaining widget in inventory under each method would be:

- Average cost: $20 ($60 minus the assumed cost of the two sold widgets of $40)

- FIFO: $30 ($60 minus the assumed cost of the two sold widgets of $30)

- LIFO: $10 ($60 minus the assumed cost of the two sold widgets of $50)

As you might have noticed, the inventory valuation method will affect income, and therefore income taxes. If the cost of inventory is increasing, a firm using LIFO will record a lower inventory value, lower income, and lower taxes—this is because it will assume that it was selling from the more expensive "last in" inventory. In contrast, a firm using FIFO will record a higher inventory value, higher income, and higher taxes. Higher costs reduce income and therefore reduce taxes, whereas lower costs have the opposite effect. The opposite conclusions will hold if the cost of inventory is decreasing. The average cost method will generate values in between FIFO and LIFO.

Which method is most realistic? The answer depends on how the costs of inventory actually change over time. In some lines of business, inventory values decline sharply: technologies improve; clothing goes out of style. If the value of items in inventory drops below their cost, GAAP requires that the balance sheet "book" value of the inventory be reduced. (This decline also is recorded on the income statement, as a charge against earnings of an equivalent amount—we will get to the income statement soon.)

A corporation's managers usually are in the best position to decide on an appropriate inventory method, or to determine when an inventory charge is necessary. On the other hand, managers might make such decisions to maximize reported income and to avoid charges. These determinations inevitably involve value judgments.

Prepaid expenses. Balance sheets often contain other current assets. We have included one, prepaid expenses, which are payments the corporation has made in advance for services it will receive in the coming year. Widget, Inc. had relatively small prepaid expenses, which increased only slightly during Year 2.

Remember that this category is part of current assets, meaning prepaid expenses during the upcoming year. For example, prepaid expenses might include the value of ten months' worth of payments on a one-year insurance policy that was paid in full two months before the beginning of the current year.

Prepaid expenses are an example of a "deferred charge," an asset that reflects payments made in one period for goods or services that will generate income in subsequent periods. Advertising a new product is another example. Firms sometimes play games with deferred charges to inflate profits in one period vs. another. You might be wary of a large and growing deferred charge account. Fortunately, Widget, Inc. has not recorded such an asset.

Fixed assets. Next are Widget, Inc.'s fixed assets, longer-term assets that, unlike current assets, are not expected to be converted into cash within a year. Notice that the fixed assets are accompanied by footnotes, which sometimes tell more of a story than the numbers themselves.

Property, Plant, and Equipment	Year 2	Year 1
Land*	775,000	775,000
Buildings**	2,000,000	2,000,000
Machinery**	1,000,000	935,000
Office Equipment**	225,000	205,000
Total PP&E	4,000,000	3,915,000
Accumulated Depreciation***	(1,620,000)	(1,370,000)
Intangible Assets****	50,000	0
Total Long-term Assets	2,480,000	2,545,000

* The land was purchased 15 years ago for $775,000, the price shown on the balance sheet. A comparable property nearby recently sold for $975,000.

** The machinery and equipment are in good repair. The fair market value of the building and equipment are about $200,000 more than historical cost.

*** Depreciation is on a level (straight line) basis over the estimated useful life.

**** Intangible assets include patent acquired for $50,000 during Year 2.

PP&E and depreciation. Fixed assets are often grouped under the label "Property, Plant, and Equipment," or PP&E. PP&E represent assets the firm uses to conduct its operations, as opposed to assets it holds for sale. Under GAAP, when a firm acquires a fixed asset, it records the asset on its balance sheet at cost. This approach reflects a compromise between the goals of presenting accurate and reliable information and the fact that it is easier to record the cost of an asset than to investigate and assess its market value.

Note that Widget, Inc. has recorded several types of fixed assets—land, buildings, machinery, and office equipment—all at cost. As a result, the balance sheet value of these fixed assets will remain constant over time, set at historical cost. They will not be "marked to market." What, then, accounts for the increase in the amount of the entries for machinery and office equipment during Year 2?

The footnotes to the balance sheet contain additional information about the fixed assets. How much do you think Widget, Inc. land is worth? The reported value in the balance sheet is just the cost of $775,000. But if a comparable nearby property recently sold for $975,000, Widget, Inc.'s land might be worth a lot more. As you might imagine, assessing the value of land is less straightforward than assessing the value of marketable securities, which is why land is typically recorded at cost.

For some fixed assets that are used to generate revenue, such as machinery and equipment (but not land), GAAP attempts to track the likely decline in the value of the assets by using an accounting concept called "depreciation." When we get to the income statement, we will see that for some of its fixed assets Widget, Inc. records a depreciation expense each year as an estimate of the decline in those assets' value during that year. Depreciation is an accounting fiction that reduces a corporation's reported income even though it does not reflect any current cash expense; the cash was spent when the asset was acquired.

There are various GAAP formulas used to calculate depreciation. The simplest "straight line" method is to divide the total cost of a fixed asset by an estimate of its useful life, and then record that amount each year as a "depreciation expense." The accumulated decline in the value of such an asset is then reflected in the balance sheet as "accumulated depreciation." For some assets, the GAAP rules state that accumulated depreciation should increase in a straight line; for others, the assumptions are more complicated.

For example, suppose a computer costs $1,000 and has an estimated useful life of five years. The annual depreciation expense for the computer would be $200, and that amount would be part of the annual depreciation expense on the income statement. The balance sheet would keep track of the value of the computer by recording both (1) the $1,000 cost, and (2) the accumulated depreciation each year ($200 for the first year, then $400, and so on).

Under GAAP, all depreciation expenses accrued with respect to a firm's fixed assets are added up and recorded, on the asset side of the balance sheet, in an account called "allowance for depreciation" or "accumulated depreciation," which is then subtracted from the cost of the firm's fixed assets. Widget, Inc. has included entries for accumulated depreciation. These entries are adjustments to the historical cost of assets, to account for the assumption that the value of these assets has declined as the company continues to use them to generate revenue. In its footnotes, Widget, Inc. has indicated that its depreciation is on a "straight line" basis. In other words, if Widget, Inc. purchased a machine for $10,000, and estimated the useful life of the machine as 10 years, it would record depreciation of $1,000 per year, the same "straight line" amount per year.

Once an asset has been fully depreciated, it will have a balance sheet value of zero, even if it is still a valuable asset. This somewhat odd result occurs because the accounting concept of the useful life of an asset does not necessarily correspond to the asset's actual useful life.

The balance sheet "book" value of a firm's fixed assets—cost less the allowance for depreciation—often does not reflect either the current market value of those assets or what the firm would have to pay to replace them. In times of inflation, the book value of fixed assets often is much lower than either their current value or their replacement value. The book value of fixed assets also can exceed those assets' market value if the assets have become obsolete. If that happens, as with inventory, the balance sheet entry for those assets must be reduced, or "written down," and earnings must be reduced by an equivalent amount.

Intangible assets. Intangible assets, the other main category of fixed assets, have no physical existence, but often have substantial value. Common examples are patents and trademarks, or licenses for a franchise. Under GAAP, firms must record intangible assets they purchase at cost, less an allowance for "amortization" (the equivalent of depreciation, applied to intangibles). However, firms typically do not record as an asset the value of intangible assets they developed or promote, rather than purchase. Consequently, the values of many well-known and valuable intangible assets, such as the brand names "Coke" or "iPhone," are not reflected on the balance sheets of the firms that own them.

How might you assess the value of Widget, Inc.'s intangible assets? The only intangible asset on the balance sheet is a patent acquired during Year 2 for $50,000. Why should this intangible asset be listed, while others are not? How might you tell whether the cost of this patent is a reliable measure of its value?

Money spent on research and development (R&D) is treated differently. R&D expenses appears on the income statement, but not on the balance sheet. You might ask why, given that R&D, like intangible assets, is a potentially valuable asset that could lead to new discoveries or products that will generate substantial revenue in future years. The not-very-satisfying answer is that accounting has a conservative bias with respect to R&D, meaning that balance sheets often understate the value of assets. There is some evidence that this bias leads managers who are preoccupied with short term earnings to underinvest in R&D.

Financial statements sometimes include an intangible asset called "goodwill." The accounting concept of "goodwill" can be confusing, since it differs from the way we normally think of that word. The idea is that when an acquiring firm buys a target firm's stock for more than the amount of the equity recorded on the target firm's balance sheet, the acquirer will need to record the difference between the purchase price and the recorded equity amount as an asset. Under GAAP, this asset is called "goodwill." Companies that buy a lot of other companies often have large "goodwill" entries on their balance sheets. It is important to distinguish between this accounting notion of "goodwill" and "goodwill" in the way people normally use the term, as in a favorable business reputation. A business might be particularly valuable if it has a good location or enjoys a positive reputation with its clients, employees, and other stakeholders, but that kind of economic goodwill will not appear on the balance sheet.

2. Balance Sheet Liabilities

Liabilities usually are divided into current liabilities and long-term liabilities. Reproduced below is the liability section of Widget, Inc.'s balance sheet. Traditionally, assets appeared on the left-hand side of the balance sheet, while liabilities appeared on the right. Today, it is common for corporations to record their assets first, and then their liabilities below the assets.

Current Liabilities	Year 2	Year 1
Accounts payable	900,000	825,000
Notes payable, 11% due next July 1	0	355,000
Accrued expenses payable	250,000	235,000
Other liabilities	600,000	570,000
Total Current Liabilities	1,750,000	1,985,000
Long-term Notes payable, 12.5% due in ten years	2,000,000	2,000,000

Current liabilities. Current liabilities are the debts a firm owes that must be paid within one year of the balance sheet date. Current liabilities often are evaluated in relation to current assets, which in a sense are the source from which current liabilities must be paid. Hopefully, at this point, you are getting a better sense of how accounting conventions work, so we won't belabor each entry with a lengthy description.

Widget, Inc.'s current liabilities include accounts payable, which represents short-term obligations of Widget, Inc. to suppliers. Some of Widget, Inc.'s notes are due within one year as well. Widget, Inc. also has accrued expenses payable, which represents short-term debts it has incurred but not yet paid, as well as a category of "other liabilities." How do Widget, Inc.'s total current liabilities of $1,750,000 affect your assessment of the firm?

Long-term liabilities. Long-term liabilities, the other main category of liabilities, are debts due more than one year from the balance sheet date. Balance sheets usually list fixed liabilities, such as mortgages and bonds, by their maturities and the interest rates they bear. Some long-term liabilities, like insurance, are harder to predict and must be estimated.

Widget, Inc. lists just one long-term liability, $2,000,000 of "Notes payable, 12.5% due in ten years." If these Notes required an annual payment, Widget, Inc. would be obligated to pay $250,000 of interest every year for ten years and then at the end of the ten-year period to repay the principal amount of $2,000,000.

Off balance sheet liabilities. In recent years, business firms have developed a variety of techniques for engaging in "off balance sheet financing"—transactions that involve long-term financial obligations, but which, because of their form, are not recorded as liabilities on the balance sheet. Firms typically discuss off balance sheet liabilities in footnotes to their financial statements. These footnotes can be extraordinarily complex. Likewise, footnote disclosures can include descriptions of "contingent liabilities" such as loan guarantees, warranty obligations, and potential litigation claims. These items might not appear as liabilities on the balance sheet, even though they matter to someone assessing the business.

3. Balance Sheet Equity

Equity represents the owners' interest in a firm. A firm's equity—also often referred to as its "net worth"—equals the difference between the book values of the firm's assets and liabilities. Recall the fundamental equation:

$$\text{ASSETS} = \text{LIABILITIES} + \text{EQUITY}$$

The balance sheet value of equity typically does not represent the actual market value of a firm's equity. For many firms, the "book" value of equity, from the balance sheet, will be well below the market value of equity. (For some firms, the opposite will be true.) It is possible for balance sheet equity to be a negative number, if the firm has recorded liabilities that exceed its assets, and yet the market value of the equity (ownership interest) of the firm still might be positive. This is because the balance sheet does not include many of a corporation's assets, such as intangibles, and because it does not record every entry at market value.

Corporations' balance sheets often include two or three lines in the equity section. State laws once required, and now permit, corporations to issue stock with "par value" or "stated value." As explained in more detail in the next chapter, par or stated value can be established arbitrarily, but once established, it has legal and accounting significance. When a corporation issues stock with a "par value" or "stated value," its balance sheet must include a "stated capital" or "legal capital" account for each class of such stock. The amount in each of those accounts is calculated by multiplying the par value of that class of stock by the number of shares issued and outstanding.

In economic terms, a corporation's equity has two components. The first, often recorded as "paid-in capital," reflects the total amount the corporation has received from those who have purchased its stock. (A corporation with par value stock often will divide paid-in capital between two accounts entitled "stated capital" and "capital surplus." Terminology varies though, and other account titles sometimes are used.) The second, called "retained earnings" or "earned surplus," reflects the cumulative results of the corporation's operations since it was formed. Each year, this account increases or decreases in an amount equal to the corporation's net income or net loss. This account also is reduced by an amount equal to any distributions the corporation has made to its shareholders in the form of "dividends" or any amounts the corporation has paid to repurchase its shares.

Now consider Widget, Inc.'s equity. The details are reproduced below.

Stockholders' Equity	**Year 2**	**Year 1**
Common stock (1,000 shares authorized		
and outstanding)		
Paid-in capital	200,000	200,000
Retained earnings	1,310,000	920,000
Total Equity	1,510,000	1,120,000

Widget, Inc.'s paid-in capital did not change, because the corporation did not issue any new shares. If it had issued new shares, its paid-in capital would have increased. However, Widget, Inc.'s total equity did increase, by $390,000. Why did the book value of the equity increase by this amount? The answer to this question comes from the income statement, which we will discuss in a moment. You will notice that this change is equal to the net income Widget, Inc. generated during Year 2.

4.   Balance Sheet Analysis

The balance sheet provides useful information about the ability of a company to meet its obligations. For example, do you think Widget, Inc. has sufficient "liquidity" from cash, or assets it is likely to convert into cash, to meet its financial obligations as they come due? One commonly used indicator of a firm's liquidity is its *current ratio*, which is computed by dividing current assets by current liabilities.

Some analysts prefer a current ratio of at least 2:1—current assets at least twice as large as current liabilities. But this is a generalization. Many firms can operate safely with a lower current ratio, while other firms, such as firms with a large amount of inventory (which can be converted into cash only by first selling the goods in inventory and then collecting the resulting accounts receivable) might need a higher current ratio.

A gradual increase in a firm's current ratio, based on a comparison of successive balance sheets, could be a sign of financial strength. But too large a current ratio might signal that the firm is not managing current assets efficiently.

Creditors also are interested in the right-hand side of the balance sheet because it gives them information about whether a firm will be able to pay its debts on time. They often look at a firm's *debt-equity ratio*: long-term debt divided by the book value of equity. A debt-equity ratio of significantly more than 1:1 might pose some danger to debtholders, because if the firm's business falters, it might be unable to generate sufficient revenues to pay the interest due on its debt.

Likewise, creditors sometimes look at a firm's *interest coverage ratio*: annual earnings divided by annual interest payments due on long-term debt. Some analysts consider debt a safe investment if a firm's interest coverage ratio is at least 3:1. What do you think of Widget, Inc.'s ability to meet its obligations, based on the right side of its balance sheet?

D. Income Statement

Managers, investors, and creditors are interested in more than just a snapshot of the firm's assets and liabilities. They also want to know about the firm's operations over time. The balance sheet provides only limited information about how much money the firm made during a particular period of time. By examining the change in retained earnings on the balance sheet over time, we can get some sense of how much money the firm made or lost during a particular period. For example, we can tell that Widget, Inc. had retained earnings of $920,000 at the end of Year 1 and $1,310,000 at the end of Year 2. We have a sense that this increase in retained earnings occurred because the firm made money during Year 2, just as the jar made money by selling the pen.

In other words, the balance sheet shows that assets and retained earnings increased, but it doesn't show details about the firm's accounting income. The income statement (sometimes called the "statement of earnings" or "profit and loss statement") provides this information. The income statement is also the "bridge" between successive balance sheets: the profit or loss in one period appears at the bottom of the income statement, and this same number is reflected on the firm's balance sheet as an increase or decrease in "retained earnings" in the equity part of the balance sheet. For example, Widget, Inc.'s Net Income during Year 2 was $390,000, and the increase in the balance sheet value of Widget, Inc.'s equity from the end of Year 1 to the end of Year 2 also was $390,000 ($390,000 equals $1,510,000 minus $1,120,000).

Whereas the balance sheet was a "snapshot," the income statement is a "motion picture." The income statement shows how the firm has performed during a period of time. Widget, Inc.'s balance sheet is just one frame of the motion picture—it shows the value of Widget, Inc.'s assets, liabilities, and equity as of December 31. In contrast, Widget, Inc.'s income statement includes every frame, from the beginning to the end of the year—it shows how much accounting income Widget, Inc. had during the year ended December 31.

Investors and creditors are often more interested in a firm's income statement than its balance sheet. The idea is that if you are trying to predict a firm's ability to generate profits in the future it is more helpful to look at the results of past operations than the book value of assets. Moreover, investors seem to place a very high value on firms whose profits rise steadily. Most people are risk averse and pay more attention to potential losses than potential gains. Thus, the more volatile a firm's income, the less they will be prepared to pay for any given level of anticipated earnings. This gives managers an economic incentive to "manage" the earnings their firm reports to eliminate volatility.

Not surprisingly, managers pay attention to the fact that investors prefer steady profits or, better yet, steadily rising profits. In the discussion of financial statement terms and concepts in this and the following section, we note several areas in which GAAP provides opportunities for managers to "massage" financial statement numbers to improve their appearance. As you read these sections, consider whether there is anything in Widget, Inc.'s financial statements that suggests the owners were "massaging" the company's income.

The GAAP requirement that most firms use accrual accounting to prepare their financial statements is central here. Under the Realization Principle, a firm must recognize revenue in the period that services are rendered or goods are shipped, even if payment is not received in that period (and cannot recognize revenue until services are rendered or goods are shipped). Under the *Matching Principle*, a firm must allocate the expenses it incurred to generate certain revenues to the period in which those revenues are recognized. Consider how these requirements would affect a lawyer who provided $1,000 in services in Year 1, who paid $250 of expenses in that year, and whose bill for $1,000 was not paid until Year 2. If the lawyer used *cash accounting*, she would report the $1,000 as earned in Year 2, when payment was received, but deduct the expense in Year 1, when it was paid. Using accrual accounting, which focuses not on cash movements but on the performance of services and on matching income to expenses, the lawyer would recognize the $1,000 in income in Year 1 and would also record the $250 expense in Year 1.

Taken together, the Realization and Matching Principles go a long way toward ensuring that an income statement prepared using accrual accounting presents a conceptually sound picture of the economic results of a firm's operations for a given period. Those principles also limit substantially a firm's ability to manipulate its payment and receipt of cash so as to "manage" the earnings it reports. But because recognition of revenues and recording of expenses are tied to events more difficult to measure than the movement of cash, the Realization and Matching Principles also increase substantially the subjectivity of the information included in accrual basis financial statements. How, for example, should a lawyer record the cost, paid in Year 1, of a party to publicize the opening of her office? Is it all an expense incurred in Year 1, since the lawyer paid it all in Year 1, or should only a portion of the publicity expense be allocated to Year 1 and the remainder be deducted in future years so long as the lawyer believes that the publicity will continue to produce benefits for several years?

1. Income Statement Items

Next, we will go through the details of the income statement, in the same way we did with the balance sheet. For each entry, you should look at Widget, Inc.'s numbers, and the changes from year to year. What "story" can you tell about how these numbers changed over time?

	Year 2	Year 1	Year 0
Net sales	7,500,000	7,000,000	6,800,000
Operating Expenses			
Cost of goods sold	4,980,000	4,650,000	4,607,000
Depreciation	250,000	240,000	200,000
Selling and admin expense*	1,300,000	1,220,000	1,150,000
R&D	50,000	125,000	120,000
Operating Income	920,000	765,000	723,000
Interest expense	320,000	375,000	375,000
Income before taxes	600,000	390,000	348,000
Income taxes	210,000	136,000	122,000
Net Income	390,000	254,000	226,000

* Includes $130,000 salaries paid to the owners in Year 2; $100,000 in Year 1; and $100,000 in Year 0, and bonuses totaling $120,000 in Year 2; $100,000 in Year 1; and $80,000 in Year 0.

Net sales. The statement of income begins with Net Sales, sometimes listed as "Revenue" and referred to colloquially as "Top Line" revenue (because it is on the top line). This number represents the total value of Widget, Inc.'s revenue during the relevant year. Notice that Widget, Inc.'s net sales increased steadily during the three years.

Once we know the total revenues, we can deduct expenses. We start with Cost of Goods Sold, or COGS. COGS generally represents the cost of items sold from inventory. You'll notice that for Widget, Inc., as for many corporations, the COGS entry represents the largest expense, and that this expense increases along with the increase in net sales. We subtract COGS from Net Sales and record the difference as "Gross Profit." Gross Profit, sometimes called gross margin, represents the profit a firm makes after deducting the direct expenses of manufacturing and selling its goods and services. We distinguish between these direct expenses and the more indirect expenses associated with operating the business.

Operating expenses. We begin by deducting *depreciation*, which also was discussed above when we covered balance sheet details. Depreciation is a non-cash expense that represents the decline in the value of fixed assets that we "match," following GAAP, with each particular year. Widget, Inc.'s depreciation expense increased somewhat over time, because the total amount of the fixed assets it was depreciating increased over time.

As you might imagine, the assessment of the value of COGS could be quite subjective. GAAP generally requires inventory to be valued at the lower of cost or market value. The value a firm reports for its inventory will affect both the firm's balance sheet and its income statement. Firms that hold a relatively small number of identifiable items in inventory often use the "specific identification method." They value each inventory item at cost, unless its market value is lower than cost, and compute COGS by adding up the actual cost of all inventory items sold during the relevant period.

In addition, GAAP requires that firms apply uniform assumptions about which items are sold to customers. To compute COGS, these firms add their *purchases* during a reporting period to the value of their inventory at the start of the period (called *opening inventory*) and then subtract the value of their *closing inventory*. By conducting a physical count at the end of an accounting period, a firm can determine the number of items in its closing inventory. Thus, GAAP attempts to require a process that will produce relatively uniform assessments of COGS.

Remember that depreciation is fiction, not fact. Depreciation is not an actual cash expense. Therefore, although depreciation expenses will reduce accounting income, they will not reduce the amount of operating cash a corporation generates. Indeed, many managers prefer to maximize depreciation expenses—even though these expenses reduce net income—for one simple reason: depreciation is a tax-deductible expense. A depreciation expense might not matter directly to how much money the corporation actually is making, but it matters indirectly because depreciation reduces tax payments, which are based on income.

Selling and administrative expense is the general catch-all category for expenses, sometimes referred to as "overhead."

These expenses have different names. You might see them referred to as selling, general, and administrative expenses. Widget, Inc. included salaries in this category. Other firms will include a separate line in the statement of income for salary or compensation expenses.

Research and development also is an expense, often called "R&D." How should we interpret Widget, Inc.'s declining R&D expenses? On one hand, the decline in expenses increased Widget, Inc.'s income. On the other hand, if Widget, Inc. is not spending enough money on R&D, its future income might suffer. Whether a firm is balancing these effects properly, such as by buying third-party patents, is a difficult question: too little spending on R&D might be a bad sign, but so might too much R&D spending.

All of the above expenses are *operating expenses*, because they are costs associated with the operation of a business. To obtain *operating income*, we subtract all of these expenses from net sales. Operating income is sometimes referred to as *EBIT*, for Earnings Before Interest and Taxes.

EBITDA. In assessing firms, many investors like to examine EBITDA, initials that stand for a firm's Earnings Before Interest, Taxes, Depreciation, and Amortization. In other words, EBITDA represents net sales minus all operating expenses except depreciation. To calculate EBITDA, you simply add depreciation to EBIT. For example, in Year 2 Widget, Inc. had operating income, or EBIT, of $920,000. It had depreciation expenses during that period of $250,000. Accordingly, its EBITDA would be the sum of these two numbers, or $1,170,000.

The rationale for examining EBITDA is that it gives an investor a clearer sense of how much money the firm generated from its "core" business, just taking into account operations, and not accounting for non-cash items such as depreciation and amortization or non-core items such as taxes and interest. Although the "ITDA" part affects the company's net income, some investors believe that they can get a better sense of how a firm is performing by looking at earnings before the "ITDA" factors are taken into account.

Interest expense and taxes. Finally, the statement of income also accounts for interest payments and taxes. *Interest expense* represents the amount of interest the firm paid on its debt during the year. Note that Widget, Inc.'s interest expense declined during Year 2. Why?

Income before taxes is obtained by subtracting interest expense from operating income. Income before taxes is sometimes called "taxable income." This is the number the Internal Revenue Service cares about. Note that Widget, Inc.'s *income taxes* track its income before taxes. This is because Widget, Inc.'s tax rate is roughly the same over time. Income taxes are not necessarily constant and can vary based on changes in tax regulations and legislation, or changes in a firm's approach to its

You'll notice that the Widget, Inc. financials reflect a corporate tax rate of approximately 35%. Tax rates have fluctuated over time, and often vary by company, depending on numerous factors. Later in the chapter when we look at how the Widget, Inc. financials might be used to value the company, it's conceivable that the company's valuation might increase if future earnings and cash flows were expected to rise—on the assumption of a smaller tax bill.

taxes during a particular year. Again, depreciation is important, in part, because it reduces a corporation's taxable income.

Net income. We have reached net income, an important number in the financial statements. It is often referred to as the "bottom line," because it typically is just that: the bottom line of the income statement. Many investors look simply at net income, or net income per share, in assessing investments. Moreover, net income is the link to both the balance sheet and the cash flow statements. Whatever is left from net income, after a firm pays dividends, goes to Retained Earnings in the firm's balance sheet. If net income after dividends is positive, retained earnings increases by the same amount. Can you see that link for Widget, Inc.?

Note that Widget, Inc.'s net sales increased by about 3% from Year 0 to Year 1 and by about 7% from Year 1 to Year 2, while net income increased by more than 12% in Year 1 and by more than 53% in Year 2. What might explain these disproportionate increases in Widget, Inc.'s profitability?

Two possibilities are that Widget, Inc. was able to increase its *profit margin* on the products it produced and sold or that it was able to generate increased sales without increasing, or even reducing, its fixed costs and overhead. It also is possible, though less likely, that profits increased because Widget, Inc. was able to reduce significantly either its interest expense or the percentage of income it was paying as taxes. To determine which of these factors explains the increases in Widget, Inc.'s profitability, an analyst would calculate the ratio of the expense items in Widget, Inc.'s income statement to its net sales.

Which of Widget, Inc.'s expenses increased as a percentage of its net sales in each of the three years for which information is provided? Which decreased? Would doing these calculations provide you with a better idea now of how the managers were able to increase Widget, Inc.'s profits so dramatically? Was it due to an increase in efficiency or a reduction in discretionary expenses? What do you think of the change in R&D expenses? Does it seem likely that any new owners or managers of Widget, Inc. would be able to sustain similar profits?

One could obtain added insight into the potential value of Widget, Inc.'s business by comparing its profit margin to those of other firms in the same line of business. If Widget, Inc.'s profit margin is comparatively low, the potential may exist to improve profits by improving management. If Widget, Inc.'s profit margin is comparatively high, the potential for such improvement is less likely to exist. If profit margins of all firms in Widget, Inc.'s line of business are relatively low, then competition probably is intense and increasing its profit margin is likely to be difficult.

2. Comparison of Income Statement to Balance Sheet Items

Inferences also can be drawn by comparing certain balance sheet data to income statement data. For example, one might expect a firm's accounts receivable and inventory to change at about the same rate as its sales. If sales increased by 15%, accounts receivable and inventory both could be expected to increase by roughly 15% to reflect a higher level of sales on credit and the higher level of inventory needed to support a higher level of sales. Changes in these accounts that are not proportionate are not necessarily a sign of problems—an unanticipated increase in sales might lead to a short-term decline in a firm's inventory—but they often are a signal that further inquiry is required. Look at the relative changes in these accounts at Widget, Inc. and consider what additional questions, if any, you would ask about these changes.

One commonly referenced number based on the income statement and balance sheet is *return on equity*, which is the net income reported for the current year divided by the balance sheet entry for equity at the end of the previous year. That percentage return then can be compared to the returns available on alternative investments. For example, if return on a firm's equity is less than the return available on a risk-free investment such as U.S. Treasury notes (and if reported income accurately reflects the results of the firm's operations), an analyst is likely to conclude that the firm is worth considerably less than its net book value. After all, why bear the risk of buying a business for its book value if one could earn a larger return on a risk-free investment of the same amount?

Similarly, if a firm's return on equity greatly exceeds the returns available from risk-free investments, an analyst might conclude (again, assuming the numbers are accurate) that the firm is worth considerably more than its book value. In essence, the analyst would infer that a significant portion of the firm's earning power is attributable to the existence of intangible assets, the value of which, due to GAAP, is not reflected on the firm's balance sheet.

Net income is not only important for analyzing accounting income or calculating return on equity. It also is the starting point for the statement of cash flows, the third financial statement we have provided.

E. Statement of Cash Flows

The use of GAAP addresses some of the problems of subjectivity in accounting by requiring firms to prepare a *statement of cash flows*. Cash is important—some even say it is king. A firm must use cash, not income, to pay its bills, repay its debts, and make distributions to its owners. Over a period of many years, a firm's total income and cash flow usually will approximate each other. But over a shorter period of time, income and cash flow may differ substantially. As one accounting adage goes, "income is a fiction, but cash is a fact."

The statement of cash flows, as its name suggests, reports on the movement of cash into and out of a firm. The statement reflects all transactions that involve the receipt or disbursement of cash, whether they relate to operations or involve only balance sheet accounts such as purchases of plant and equipment, new borrowings, repayment of loans, equity investments, or distributions to equity holders. The statement of cash flows is split into three parts, based on whether the cash flow is from *operating activities, investing activities, or financing activities.*

Many investors focus on cash flow from operating activities as being of primary importance, because operating cash flow is the best indicator of how much cash the firm is generating from its core operations. In contrast, cash flow from investing activities merely reflects how much cash was invested in the firm, and cash flow from financing activities merely reflects how much cash the firm borrowed. Of course, investing and borrowing matter to a firm's bottom line—cash is cash, after all—but operating cash flows provide a better gauge of how much cash the firm's true operations are generating, and hopefully will generate in the future.

Structurally, the statement of cash flows starts with net income and then "corrects" for each of the non-cash changes reflected in the balance sheet and income statement. For example, if the firm reported an increase in non-cash assets, such as accounts receivable, inventories, or prepaid expenses, it would need to correct for that increase by reducing its net income. In other words, the firm, in calculating net income, assumed that it got the benefit of income from the increase in these non-cash items. However, that increase was an accounting increase only—it wasn't cash. In order to get back to cash, the statement of cash flows reduces net income for the increase in non-cash assets. Conversely, it increases net income for any decrease in non-cash assets.

The cash flow statement follows the opposite approach for liabilities. For example, if the firm reported an increase in non-cash liabilities, such as accounts payable or accrued expenses payable, it would need to correct for that increase by increasing its net income. Remember that any increase in liabilities was an accounting increase only—it wasn't cash. In order to get back to cash, the statement of cash flows increases net income for the increase in non-cash liabilities. Conversely, it reduces net income for any decrease in non-cash items.

Boy, that sounds confusing! To clarify, we will go through an example from Widget, Inc.'s statement of cash flows. Remember that parentheses indicate that a number is negative, just like putting a minus sign in front.

	Year 2	Year 1	Year 0
From Operating Activities			
Net Income	390,000	254,000	226,000
Decrease (Increase) in accts receivable	(235,000)	(34,000)	(32,000)
Decrease (Increase) in inventories	(205,000)	(28,000)	(33,000)
Decrease (Increase) in prepaid expenses	(5,000)	(3,000)	(3,000)
Increase (Decrease) in accounts payable	75,000	25,000	20,000
Increase (Decrease) in accr exp payable	15,000	7,000	5,000
Depreciation	250,000	240,000	200,000
Total from Operating Activities	285,000	461,000	383,000
From Investing Activities			
Sales (Purchases) of machinery	(65,000)	(378,000)	(263,000)
Sales (Purchases) of office equipment	(20,000)	(27,000)	(25,000)
Sales (Purchases) of patents	(50,000)	0	0
Total from Investing Activities	(135,000)	(405,000)	(288,000)
From Financing Activities			
Increase (Decrease) in short-term debt	30,000	(40,000)	(35,000)
Increase (Decrease) in long-term debt	(355,000)	0	0
Total from Financing Activities	(325,000)	(40,000)	(35,000)
Increase (Decrease) in Cash Position	**(175,000)**	**16,000**	**60,000**

Note that Widget, Inc.'s net income for Year 2 was $390,000. This is our starting point for analyzing cash flows. Recall that in calculating Widget, Inc.'s net income, the income statement included numerous non-cash items. These items have to be corrected in the cash flow statement. The first such item is accounts receivable, an asset. According to the balance sheet, Widget, Inc.'s accounts receivable increased in Year 2 from $1,145,000 to $1,380,000, an increase of $235,000. That means that, as a result of Widget, Inc.'s sales during the year, it was owed an additional $235,000. This amount is an asset, but it is a non-cash asset. It is a valuable asset for Widget, Inc. to be owed an extra $235,000—it hopes it will collect that full amount in cash someday. But it hasn't done that yet, and so if we assumed that $235,000 was received in cash, we made a mistake.

Where did we make this mistake? In the statement of income, Widget, Inc.'s net sales included both sales for cash and sales on credit. However, the sales on credit increased during Year 2. By how much? $235,000. If we had been focused on the "fact" of cash, rather than the accounting "fiction" of income, when we prepared the statement of income, we wouldn't have included that $235,000.

We correct this mistake in the statement of cash flows. Specifically, we reduce Widget, Inc.'s net income by $235,000 to account for the fact that net income reflected increased sales on credit, for which the company has not yet collected cash. The second line of the statement of cash flows contains this correction for Year 2.

The same analysis applies to the other entries on the cash flow statement. If net income assumed Widget, Inc. received cash, but it did not, we subtract. If net income assumed Widget, Inc. paid cash, but it did not, we add. For example, the amount Widget, Inc. charges as a depreciation expense each year shows up as a positive entry in the statement of cash flows, while Widget, Inc.'s purchases of machinery reduces cash flows.

Many students find it difficult to "translate" income into cash flows by making these corrections. We suggest that you try picking a few of the numbers in the statement of cash flows and tell the story of what these numbers mean. Why are they positive or negative? What correction are they making to the income statement? If you can tell these stories, you can be reasonably confident that you understand financial statement analysis.

What does Widget, Inc.'s statement of cash flows tell you about the firm that its balance sheet and statement of income did not? Are you worried about the $175,000 overall decrease in Widget, Inc.'s cash position during Year 2? Why or why not? What about the difference between Widget, Inc.'s statement of cash flow for Year 2, which shows a decrease in cash position, and its statement of income for the same year, which shows an increase in net income?

As should be clear by now, income is a concept, and computation of a firm's income generally depends on numerous subjective judgments and is heavily influenced by the assumptions underlying GAAP. Cash, on the other hand, is tangible; one can touch, smell, and even taste it. More importantly, a company needs cash to pay its bills, repay its debts, and make distributions to its owners.

Firms frequently report significantly different amounts of income and cash flow for any given year. The disparity most often is attributable, at least in part, to GAAP requirements relating to accounting for fixed assets. Recall that when a firm acquires a fixed asset, it records that asset at cost on its balance sheet and then, over the useful life of that asset, records a portion of its cost as a charge against income—a depreciation expense—on its income statement. That "expense" does not reflect a current disbursement of cash; the cash was spent when the asset was acquired. As a result, cash flow will be lower than reported income in years in which large amounts of fixed assets are purchased and will be higher than reported income in years in which (non-cash) depreciation expenses are greater than the amounts spent to purchase fixed assets.

Comparison of a firm's income and cash flow statements often will provide insights into the direction of its business or suggest further inquiries that one might make. Consider, for example, the implications when cash flow from operations lags income. Is the shortfall due to rapid growth in the firm's business? If so, is substantial additional financing necessary to sustain that growth? Do increases in inventory and accounts receivable reflect long-term growth in the firm's business, or a short-term effort to pump up reported earnings? If accounts receivable and inventory decreased, does that suggest the firm is managing its current assets more efficiently or that its business is declining? By asking these and similar questions, one can obtain a better understanding of a firm's business than would be the case if one analyzed that firm's balance sheet and income statement alone. Note again that while the financial statements provide a good deal of useful data, it is the user's task to recognize and ask the additional questions that arise from that data.

F.   The Basics of Business Valuation

Now that we've covered the basics of financial statements, we can use them to value the business of Widget, Inc. Valuing a business can be tough and inevitably involves judgment calls. The simplest method is to calculate the value of the business's assets and subtract its liabilities. If the values on the balance sheet are accurate, perhaps with some minor adjustments, this "asset" approach can work reasonably well.

But often the value of a business is not simply assets minus liabilities. For example, one widely used valuation approach is to estimate how much cash the business is likely to produce each year for its owners, and then determine how much that cash should be worth in today's dollars. This method is known as "discounted cash flow" analysis, or DCF, and is regarded by many as the most reliable method of valuation.

A third approach is to look at comparable businesses, particularly ones that have been valued recently or traded in the market. For example, you might find some companies you believe are comparable to Widget, Inc. and base your valuation of Widget, Inc. on information about these companies. This method takes various forms and is often called the "comparables" approach.

These three valuation methods can be important to lawyers in various contexts, not just in the sale of a business. The concepts of "fairness" and "fair value" can arise in disputes about distributions, appraisals, voting contests, and other settings. Many business people think about valuation on an almost daily basis. Valuation can be complicated, even when it might seem simple.

For many companies, including startups, the above valuation methods have limitations: the value of the business is not merely based on assets, future cash flows are uncertain, and there are few or no comparable peers. In these cases, valuation can involve a lot of guesswork. Sometimes valuation is mostly a bet on the founders or key employees, or on new technology. Imagine, for example, that Widget, Inc.'s founders have just developed a new drug or social media platform, or created a new cryptocurrency. Valuing such companies can feel more like art than science. Still, there are some basic principles to keep in mind when talking about valuation. We describe them next.

1. The "Asset" Approach

One method of valuing a business is simply to look at its assets and liabilities. For example, the book value of Widget Inc.'s assets minus liabilities was $1,510,000 in the most recent year. If you look back at the Balance Sheet now, you'll see that this number equals Assets of $5,260,000 minus Liabilities of $3,750,000—or Total Equity. This value represents what Widget, Inc. would be worth if its balance sheet *actually* reflected all of its assets and liabilities.

But as we pointed out in discussing financial statements, these assumptions are often false. That is, book value often does not reflect actual value. Many assets are recorded at historical cost, not market value. Accounting depreciation and other markdowns might not reflect market realities. Book value often excludes intangible assets, such as intellectual property and economic goodwill, which are important to the value of many businesses. The asset approach also does not take into account the potential for a business to generate more cash flow or income in the future.

Sometimes a business would be worth more being liquidated (its assets sold for cash) than continuing as a going concern. To make this determination, the market value of the assets and liabilities, including those not on the balance sheet, can be determined, by making appropriate adjustments to the balance sheet. For example, it is possible—given some of Widget, Inc.'s apparent trouble in moving inventory and collecting from customers—that a liquidation of the company might be a viable option and thus a useful way to value the business.

Consider what the "adjusted book value" of Widget, Inc. might be if we adjusted the value of certain of its assets. Here is an example. Many of the numbers in the "Adjusted" column differ from the actual balance sheet numbers for Year 2. Note which ones are different, and think about why we might make such changes.

Assets	Year 2	Adjusted
Current Assets		
Cash	100,000	100,000
Accounts Receivable *	1,380,000	690,000
Inventories * *	1,310,000	655,000
Prepaid expenses	40,000	40,000
Total Current Assets	2,830,000	1,485,000
Property, Plant, and Equipment		
Land* * *	775,000	1,200,000
Buildings* * * *	2,000,000	2,000,000
Machinery* * * *	1,000,000	1,000,000
Office Equipment* * * *	225,000	225,000
Total PP&E	4,000,000	4,425,000
Accumulated Depreciation* * * *	(1,620,000)	(620,000)
Intangible Assets		
Patent	50,000	50,000
Trademarks* * * * *		400,000
Total Intangible Assets	50,000	450,000
Total Long-term Assets	2,430,000	4,255,000
Total Assets	5,260,000	5,740,000

* Assuming only half of accounts receivable will be paid

* * Assuming only half of inventory will be sold

* * * Assuming FMV of land is $1,200,000

* * * * Assuming Accumulated Depreciation is $1,000,000 more than actual loss in FMV of Buildings, Machinery and Office Equipment

* * * * * Assuming Trademarks (brand and customer loyalty) is $400,000

Based on these assumptions, we can recalculate Widget, Inc.'s adjusted book value to be $1,990,000 (Total Assets of $5,740,000 minus Total Liabilities of $3,750,000). We assume in our example that total liabilities stay the same, because these are the values of actual amounts owed, but the market value of those liabilities also might change, and we could adjust those as well. Do you think the new balance sheet asset values are reasonable? You can imagine a lively debate about valuation based on disputes about what assets really are worth, even when the assets are simple. Are inventories really worth so little? Are the trademarks really worth so much?

The asset approach might be used for simple assets, such as office equipment. Widget, Inc.'s entry above is $225,000, based on the cost of its office equipment. Depending on the amount of accumulated depreciation for this office equipment, it might appear on the balance sheet to be worthless. But is it really worth zero? Even for simple assets, the valuation can become complicated. Suppose the office equipment still has salvage value, meaning that it could be sold to another firm or for the value of its recycled parts. The footnote suggests that accumulated depreciation is more than the actual loss in the FMV, or fair market value. You can imagine that people might disagree about these valuations, even for simple assets.

Although the asset approach has limitations, many company valuations nevertheless are based on assets. For example, stock analysis often refers to the book value of assets of financial institutions, such as banks and insurance companies, in determining and assessing their valuations. Regulators also use calculations based on asset values in examining such institutions. For many small businesses, owners and prospective purchasers base their valuations on the book value of assets on the balance sheet, and then make common sense adjustments based on how accurate they think those numbers really are. For example, you might start a negotiation by saying Widget, Inc.'s office equipment is worth just $25,000, even though you understand there are good reasons it should be worth more.

2.   The "DCF" Approach

But how much more? Or less? The "gold standard" for figuring this out is the discounted cash flow method, or DCF. The DCF method is routinely accepted by courts and regulators as a reliable method for experts to use in valuing a business, and it is widely used in practice. Following the DCF method, you calculate the value of a business in two steps. First, estimate the future cash flows. Second, "discount" those cash flows to calculate their "present value." Both of these steps involve some art, but also some science. They also involve some important vocabulary that might be new.

For the first step, a DCF typically starts with the income statement or the cash flow statement and then normalizes or adjusts the numbers up or down based on estimates of likely future changes. If you look back at Widget Inc.'s financial statements, you will see that it reported $390,000 of net income last year, and $285,000 of operating cash flow. How much annual cash flow should we expect from Widget, Inc. in the future?

The answer to this question, like so many answers in this chapter, involves art as well as science. For example, recall that Widget, Inc. reported in a footnote that it paid $120,000 of bonuses to the owners. These payments were not part of net income or operating cash flow, meaning that, if Widget, Inc. hadn't paid bonuses, its net income and operating cash flow would have been much higher. Shouldn't you take these bonuses into account in valuing the company? If you bought Widget, Inc., you wouldn't have to pay the former owners that $120,000. Instead, you could pay it to yourself (as salary or dividends), or reinvest it in the business.

In addition, there are numerous other judgments to be paid about Widget, Inc.'s future prospects. Will next year be better? What about the year after that? Will there be some bad years? How bad? When will the old equipment need to be replaced? What other costs might the company incur? Some of these estimates inevitably will involve educated guesses.

Valuation experts have a range of techniques that they use to make these adjustments. Suppose that after doing all of this, we end up with the following expected future cash flows for Widget, Inc.:

Year 1	$440,000 (an increase from the most recent year)
Year 2	$410,000 (a tough year)
Year 3	$520,000 (a good year)
Year 4	$480,000 (old equipment must be replaced)
Year 5	$550,000 (new equipment pays off)
Year 6 and beyond	$560,000 (a guess into the indefinite future)

Now we are ready for the second step of our DCF valuation: discount each of these future cash flows to determine their present value. If you haven't seen the concepts of present value and future value before, please take a moment think through the following example. These concepts are important, not just for your career but for your personal financial decisions.

The basic idea is called the "time value of money," and it is one of the most important concepts in business and finance. To illustrate this "time value," suppose you have $100 today. You could just keep that money in cash or a checking account that doesn't pay interest, and then you'd still have $100 in the future. Alternatively, you could put the money in a bank account that pays a return or some other invest-ment. If you could earn 10% annually on that $100, you would have about $200 after 7 years. If you could only earn 7% on that $100, it would take you longer—about 10 years—until you doubled your money. (As a rough approximation, the "Rule of 72" is that the number 72 divided by your % return is how long it will take for your money to double. 72 divided by 10 is about 7, so it will take 7 years for $100 to become $200 at a rate of 10%; 72 divided by 7 is about 10, so it will take 10 years for $100 to become $200 at a rate of 7%. It will take longer for your money to double if the rate is lower, shorter if the rate is higher.)

In a corporate finance course or in business school, we would do more math so we could calculate precisely how much time it would take our money to double, or to grow at other rates. But in this course we want to emphasize the intuition behind the time value of money. Most important, we want you to see that $100 today is not worth the same as $100 tomorrow. Instead, a *present value* of $100 today can grow to be worth a *future value* of $200. The higher the assumed percentage rate, the higher the future value relative to the present value. The main lesson is that we should not compare $100 today to $100 tomorrow. We should not add or subtract present vs. future values; they are like apples and oranges. Instead, we should try to convert future values into present values by using a technique known as "discounting."

There is some basic math behind discounting, but again we want to emphasize the intuition. Essentially, each future value cash flow is discounted to present value by using a "discount factor" based on a "discount rate," a rate of interest that corresponds to the cash flow. The higher the discount rate, the more the future cash flow is discounted in order to calculate its present value. For example, suppose we estimate that we will receive a cash flow in 7 years with a future value of $200, and we want to figure out its present value. If we use a discount rate of 7%, then we will calculate the present value as being about $100 (remember the rule of 72). But if we instead assume a discount rate of 25%, the present value of that future cash flow would be a lot less than $100. The lingo is that the future cash flow is "discounted" more, so that its present value is less.

How should we figure out what discount rate to use when valuing a business? That is a complicated question, based on numerous factors, including the risk associated with the future cash flows. Again, these concepts are covered in detail in other courses.

We'll start with an example, just to show you a few dozen examples of the differences between the future value of a cash flow and its present value. Below is a table with a projection (in the second column) of annual cash flows for the next fifteen years. You can think of these cash flows as arising from the net profits or operating cash flow from a business, or from something as simple as the sale of apples produced by an apple tree. We assume that the cash flows will be $50 for each of the next five years, then $40 for the next ten years, and then a final cash flow of $50 representing the salvage value. Each of these cash flows is an estimate of a future value. We can then discount each of those cash flows to obtain a present value. The third and fourth columns in the chart below illustrate such an approach at two discount rates, 5% and 15%.

		Present Value of Cash Flows	
		Discount rate	
Year	Cash flow	5%	15%
1	$50.00	$47.62	$43.48
2	$50.00	$45.35	$37.81
3	$50.00	$43.19	$32.88
4	$50.00	$41.14	$28.59
5	$50.00	$39.18	$24.86
6	$40.00	$29.85	$17.29
7	$40.00	$28.43	$15.04
8	$40.00	$27.07	$13.08
9	$40.00	$25.78	$11.37
10	$40.00	$24.56	$9.89
11	$40.00	$23.39	$8.60
12	$40.00	$22.27	$7.48
13	$40.00	$21.21	$6.50
14	$40.00	$20.20	$5.65
15	$40.00	$19.24	$4.92
Salvage	$50.00	$24.05	$6.14
	Total	$482.58	$273.71

Note that the total present value of the cash flows is $482.58 if we use a 5% discount rate (the total of all of the numbers in the third column), and $273.71 if we use a 15% discount rate (the fourth column total). Why is that? Which discount rate do you think is more accurate? Also note that we did not simply add up the 16 cash flows under the "Cash flow" column. Doing so would have ignored the time value of money and overestimated the present value.

Valuing Widget, Inc. is conceptually no more difficult than this example. We already have estimated the cash flows, so we just need to come up with a discount rate. Below, we have assumed a 25% discount rate, just to show you an example of the conversion from the future value of the estimated cash flows for Widget, Inc. (FV in the chart below) to present value (PV in the chart below). Here it is:

Year	FV	PV
1	$440,000	$352,000
2	$410,000	$262,400
3	$520,000	$266,240
4	$480,000	$196,608
5	$550,000	$180,224
Terminal value	$2,240,000	$734,003
	Total PV	$1,991,475

The final row above is called "terminal value." A DCF analysis often involves this kind of estimate of the value of all of the future cash flows as of some final date, so we don't have to keep calculating these numbers for every year, forever. Here, we assumed that the value of the annual cash flows in Year 6 and beyond would be worth $2,240,000, so we called that the terminal value. That kind of calculation is common in DCF analysis and involves a lot of assumptions. You might be skeptical of its accuracy; attorneys and experts often are skeptical of terminal value calculations. Still, they are common in practice, so we want you to see one.

However one values a business, the company's financial statements will be a source of important information. But the financial statements should not be accepted at face value. Prospective purchasers will want to perform their "due diligence" and look behind the financial statement numbers. For example, a purchaser should inquire what is behind the cost of goods sold, investigate overhead charges, understand the selling and marketing expenses, determine whether receivables really are collectible, and ascertain whether inventory is obsolete. In addition, an important part of "due diligence" is to inquire into contingent liabilities, such as possibly costly environmental claims or potential liability to customers.

Each of the FV cash flows in the middle column are then discounted to obtain the PV numbers in the far-right column. (For example, the FV of $550,000 we estimate as a cash flow in year 5 is discounted to a PV of $180,224 today.) All the years' present values—discounted cash flows—are then summed in the number in the bottom right. The value of Widget, Inc. under these assumptions is about $1,990,000.

That was a lot of math! We hope that you followed it (if not the first time through, perhaps the second time) and that you noticed how our calculations made assumptions about market valuations and transactions, prevailing discount rates, and assessments of future business conditions. That is, each of the methods that we used in valuing Widget, Inc. was really a style of art.

3.   The "Comparables" Approach

A third commonly used valuation method looks at "comparables," or "comps." This approach uses comparable assets or businesses as a guide. For example, if you are thinking of buying a house, and you trying to figure out what a house should be worth, you might find some comparable houses that have sold recently, and then assume that this house's value is similar. If houses in a neighborhood have been selling for around $500 per square foot, you might assume that a 2,000-square-foot house you are looking at is worth $1 million.

The comps approach also involves some art. For example, the seller of a house and their broker might assert that there have been just a few recent sales of houses that they claim are most like their house, and then claim that true comps have been selling for $600 per square foot. That is why they have listed this house at a price of $1.2 million. You might respond by arguing that these houses are nicer than their house, or in a better location, so that they are not accurate comps. Instead, you might find recent house sales at closer to $400 per square foot, and claim that the house is worth much less.

Buyers and sellers often negotiate about which comps are truly comparable, and which are not. Some buyers might have overpaid, or gotten a bargain. The market might have changed recently. Good comps should be comparable. It's a little like using somebody else's course outline for a business law final exam, it is important to make sure their outline was based on the same questions and assumptions you are making.

To value Widget, Inc. using the comparables method, we'll have to make some assumptions about how similar businesses have been valued. A frequent valuation method is to use a price-earnings ratio (or P/E ratio). Suppose that a basket of companies similar to Widget, Inc. have recently been purchased on average at 6 times "trailing earnings." That is, the P/E ratio in these transactions has been 6—meaning that the purchase price paid for these companies has been 6.3 times recent annual net earnings as stated in the companies' financial statements. (This information, as you might guess, is collected and carefully guarded by business valuators.)

If Widget, Inc. were to be valued on this basis, a prospective purchaser might be willing to pay $2,340,000 based on the company's most recent earnings of $390,000 (where 6 times $390,000 is equal to $2,340,000). Or, the purchaser might look at an average of Widget Inc.'s earnings over the past several years and apply the P/E ratio to this average. Given that Widget Inc.'s net earnings averaged $290,000 for the three most recent years, the purchaser might be willing to pay instead only $1,740,000 (where $290,000 times 6 equals $1,740,000).

The comparables method of valuation ultimately depends on prices paid for the companies in market transactions and the assumption that these other companies were valued accurately. That might or might not be true. For example, "comps" of publicly held companies with multiple lines of business may not be accurate when valuing a closely held company that operates only in one line of business. And valuations of publicly traded companies fluctuate with values in financial markets, which have a propensity to cycle through periods of mania, panic, and crash. If you value a company based on "comps," the valuation will gyrate along with the markets.

Another indication of value using comparables might be the price at which shares of comparable companies have been trading. For publicly traded companies, this is one of the most frequent methods for company valuation. We could pick some companies we think resemble Widget, and then calculate Widget, Inc.'s value based on their publicly available financial information, perhaps also using a P/E ratio or similar information.

We know that buyers are typically willing to purchase control of publicly traded companies for more than the total market price of their issued shares (their "market capitalization," or "market cap"). This "control premium" is often in the range of 30–35%. We would need to adjust our valuation based on publicly traded comps to include this control premium. As the sole shareholder of Widget, Inc., we obviously would have control.

Using these various approaches, we could come up with a range of valuations based on comps. As with the valuation of a house, we would need to justify our choice of comps, and all of that would become part of our negotiations. Suppose that we come up with a range and claim that the average is $1,875,000. We might even include a detailed spreadsheet, with calculations that appear to be very scientific.

4. A Final Thought on Valuing Businesses

So how much should Widget, Inc. sell for? Notice that our three valuation methods—based on assets, DCF, and comps—came to similar results, ranging between $1.8 million and $2.0 million. You might conclude that the value must be in that range. But you might also be suspicious. Our tight range of valuations reflected—as you might have noticed—some convenient assumptions that we made about asset market values, earnings, market comparables, and discount rates.

It can be even more difficult to value startup companies, or companies that depend a lot on unpredictable events or technologies. Assets can be difficult to value. Future cash flows can be difficult to predict. And some companies are unique, and don't really have comparables. Ultimately, valuation is similar to financial analysis and accounting more generally. We are studying art, not science.

CHAPTER 8

Capital Structure

In the previous chapter, we focused on the details of financial statements, including the assets on the left-hand side of the balance sheet. Now we take a more detailed look at the right-hand side of the balance sheet. These entries—including debt and equity—are a window into the key attributes and tensions of many corporations. They show how the corporation raised its funds and who have claims on the corporation's income. They also reveal the potential for dramatic conflict.

When we say "capital structure," we refer to the "structure" of the right-hand side of the balance sheet. How did the corporation raise its capital? Did it simply issue shares of stock? Or did it also borrow money? What are the relative portions of equity and debt? Did the corporation raise money by issuing more complex financial instruments? Did it grant stock options to employees? These are questions of capital structure, which essentially ask how the corporation has been financed and whether money has been (and can be) paid to those who hold the corporation's debt and equity.

In theory, capital structure should not matter much to corporate decision making. Instead, at least theoretically, the value of the corporation should depend on the return of the assets represented by the left-hand side of the balance sheet. Two financial economists, Franco Modigliani and Merton Miller, won Nobel Prizes in Economics partly for their suggestion that in an efficient market with perfect information (and no taxes or bankruptcy costs) the value of a corporation would not be affected by how it was financed. The simple metaphor for their theorem is a pizza: the value of the pizza depends on the ingredients, not on how it is sliced. Likewise, the value of a corporation depends on its income-producing assets, not whether it obtained financing by issuing equity or debt, or some portion of each.

In reality, the Modigliani-Miller assumptions rarely hold, and capital structure matters greatly to corporations. Managers of a corporation with no debt obviously worry less about bankruptcy than managers of a corporation with massive obligations. Corporations can deduct interest payments on debt for tax purposes (recall that taxes were calculated based on income after interest payments). However, dividend payments on equity are not tax deductible.

Companies often go through a kind of life cycle of capital structure, starting with something simple, such as one class of common stock and no debt, and then evolving to add new slices to that structure. You can imagine that Widget, Inc. might have begun, like many startups, by simply dividing its common stock among a few founders and early employees. Many startups also have "friends and family" investors, who buy stock at an early stage. By the time we discovered Widget, Inc., in the previous chapter, its capital structure was still relatively simple, with one class of common stock and one major liability, some 10-year notes.

For many startups, the next stage in their life would be to raise money from outside investors, often by issuing a "seed" round and then successive rounds of preferred stock (Series A, Series B, and so on). Later, the company might sell itself to a larger company, or issue shares to the public in an initial public offering. As a company adds to its capital structure, the relative stakes of each investor can change, and lawyers and investors keep track of these changes using a "cap table" that lists all of the securities the company has issued, including stock, convertible notes, warrants, and stock option grants. Investors negotiate terms at each stage, including their relative ownership and voting control, as well as many other terms that we will discuss in this chapter. The founders often resist giving up control, even in an IPO, and many public companies now have "dual-class" capital structures, where one class of common shares (still held by the founders) has more votes per share than a second class of common shares (issued to the public). Some companies, especially financial institutions, have even more complex capital structures.

As this chapter illustrates, corporations with different capital structures—that is, different ratios of debt and equity—face different challenges. Remember the central question of this course: for whose benefit should the corporation be run? Should corporate managers run the corporation for the exclusive benefit of equity? Or for some combination or equity and debt? And, if so, how should managers take debt into account in making decisions?

These are just a few questions we will pose about capital structure in this chapter. We begin by describing different possible capital structures depending on the mix of debt, equity, preferred, and options. Then we turn to how inevitable conflicts arise when there are different claimants to the corporation's assets and cash flow, as reflected on the right-hand side of the balance sheet. Finally, we analyze two legal and policy issues that arise from the capital structure: the treatment of so-called "legal capital" and the corporation's payment of dividends to equity.

A. Slicing up the Corporation: Some Details on Capital Structure

Recall that corporations can raise money by issuing securities to investors. The investors are willing to give money to the corporation, in exchange for securities, because they expect a return on their investment. Corporations have considerable flexibility in tailoring the terms of their securities to allocate control, profit, and risk among the various investors.

Corporate securities can be divided into two broad categories: equity and debt. In general, equity securities represent permanent commitments of capital to a corporation, while debt securities represent capital invested for a limited period of time. Returns on equity securities generally depend on the corporation earning a profit. Although equity securities might share in the corporation's assets in the event of liquidation, the rights of equity securities are subordinated to the claims of creditors, including those who hold the corporation's debt securities. On the other hand, holders of equity securities typically elect the corporation's board of directors and thus exert more control over the conduct of the corporation's business and the risks it incurs.

In contrast, debt securities typically represent temporary contributions of capital (for example, until the maturity date of a loan). Debt securities are more likely to have priority in terms of payment if the firm becomes insolvent or liquidates voluntarily. Because debt securities are less risky, they typically are entitled only to a fixed return. Holders of debt securities can secure their rights by placing liens on some or all of a corporation's assets or by negotiating contractual covenants restricting the corporation's operations. Apart from such covenants, however, debtholders ordinarily play no role in the management of the firm.

Although the distinction between equity and debt is not always sharp or well defined, it is a standard distinction, and most people use it. In the remainder of this section, we will describe more details about the differences between equity and debt. But before we do so, let's start with an example, so you can see that the tensions inherent in the capital structure are not merely abstractions, but actually arise in real life and are often part of real human drama. Some of the terms in the example might not be entirely clear—we will go through everything in detail in a moment. Later, once we have covered the detailed capital structure descriptions, we will return to this example, to be sure you have a sense of how capital structure matters.

1.   The Drama of Widget, Inc.

Three of our former students—Justin, Kathy, and Lorenzo—have read through the financial statements of Widget, Inc. from the previous chapter. After much debate, they agree that an appropriate valuation of Widget, Inc. is in the range of $2 million. They form JKL Corporation and offer to pay $2 million to acquire all of Widget's assets, tangible and intangible, and to assume all of the liabilities listed on Widget's balance sheet. In addition to financing the purchase of Widget's business, Justin, Kathy, and Lorenzo want to provide JKL Corporation with an additional $150,000 to finance an expansion of the business. Thus, they need to raise a total of $2,150,000.

Justin and Kathy each are prepared to commit $200,000 to JKL Corporation. Kathy can provide that amount in cash, but Justin cannot provide more than $100,000, though he is prepared to sign a note obligating him to pay JKL Corporation the additional $100,000 in the future. In exchange for their investments, Justin and Kathy each expect to receive 40% of JKL's common shares.

Lorenzo is prepared to invest $600,000 of cash in JKL. In exchange for $100,000 of his investment, he will receive 20% of JKL's common shares. Lorenzo is willing to invest the remaining $500,000 either by purchasing preferred shares or making a long-term loan to JKL. Whatever the form of that investment, Lorenzo wants to be assured that he will receive at least $50,000 in income from JKL every year before any payments (other than salary) are made to Justin and Kathy. In addition, if JKL is liquidated, the $500,000 will be repaid to him before any payments are made with respect to JKL's common shares.

In addition to the $900,000 of cash that Justin, Kathy, and Lorenzo are prepared to invest, JKL has arranged to borrow $500,000 from First National Bank ("Bank"). JKL has agreed to repay that principal amount in five annual installments of $100,000 each, the first of which will be due in five years, and to pay interest at 10% per annum on the unpaid principal. The bank will not have any right to participate in the management of JKL or any right to receive payments other than those just described. However, the bank has required JKL and Lorenzo to agree that, whatever form Lorenzo's $500,000 investment takes, Lorenzo's funds will remain committed to JKL until the bank's loan has been repaid in full and, in the event JKL is liquidated, Lorenzo's claims will be subordinated to those of the bank.

Even with the $500,000 loan from Bank, Justin, Kathy, and Lorenzo would be $750,000 short of the total they need. However, the Widget brothers, who founded Widget, Inc. and are eager to retire, have agreed to offer "seller financing" to cover this shortfall and take a note for $750,000 of the $2 million purchase price. The note will require JKL to make annual interest payments of $75,000 (equal to 10% of the face value of the note) and to repay the principal of $750,000 to the Widget brothers in 10 years. If JKL fails to make any interest payment when due, the $750,000 in principal will become due immediately. The Widget brothers will not have any right to participate in the management of JKL or any right to receive payments, except as just described.

The capital structure that will result from these different sources of financing is fairly typical for a corporation such as JKL. Justin, Kathy, and Lorenzo will own 40%, 40% and 20% of JKL's common shares, respectively. Lorenzo also will own preferred shares or a debt security. First National Bank and the Widget brothers will hold debt securities that provide no right to participate in the general management of JKL.

2.   Equity Securities

We use the terms *common shares* and *preferred shares* to describe the two basic kinds of equity securities. Corporate statutes require that at least one class of equity security have voting rights and the right to receive the net assets of the corporation in dissolution or liquidation. These rights usually are assigned to common shares, although they also can be assigned to preferred shares. We begin by describing some basic terms that apply to all equity securities and then some differences between common and preferred shares.

Basic terms of equity securities. When a corporation is formed, its articles of incorporation create authorized shares. Until shares are first sold to shareholders, they are authorized but unissued. When sold, they are authorized and issued or authorized and outstanding. If repurchased by the corporation, they become authorized and issued, but not outstanding—commonly referred to as treasury shares.

Corporation statutes do not dictate how many or what kind of shares must be authorized. But the statutes do require that the articles specify the number of shares that a corporation is authorized to issue and, unless they are common shares, describe the characteristics of those shares. If a corporation has issued all the shares authorized in its articles, it cannot issue more shares unless the articles are amended to authorize additional shares. For this to happen, the board of directors must recommend the amendment, which must then be approved by holders of at least a majority of its outstanding voting shares. However, if a corporation has not issued all the shares authorized in its articles, then the board can decide on what terms to issue these authorized but unissued shares. Consequently, if a corporation's shareholders authorize more shares than the corporation currently plans to issue, they also delegate authority to the board to decide if, when, and on what terms additional shares should be issued.

You might be wondering: should the organizers of a corporation authorize more shares than they initially plan to issue? They might want to issue additional shares at a later date to raise new money, to use for employee benefit plans, or to acquire other companies. As a practical matter, it may seem tempting to authorize a large number of shares at first so the corporation has the flexibility to issue additional shares in the future without the bother of amending the articles.

However, convenience might not be the only issue, especially in a close corporation. Shareholders might wish to keep control over the issuance of new shares by authorizing only the number of shares the company will issue immediately. For example, the articles might authorize 100 shares. For the company to issue more shares in the future, there would have to be another shareholder vote to amend the articles (to increase the number of authorized shares above 100). The need for an additional vote can protect minority shareholders and preserve existing control relationships. However, such a limitation might enable one or more shareholders to prevent the company from raising additional capital by blocking the vote to authorize additional shares.

In large corporations, shareholders usually exert relatively little influence over day-to-day management, and allowing the board to issue additional common shares may not constitute the surrender of much real power. Convenience usually decides the question in favor of an initial (and subsequent) authorization of many more shares than the corporation has current plans to issue. Under the MBCA, shareholders nonetheless retain some power over the issuance of additional shares of authorized stock, in that shareholder approval is required if the corporation issues, for consideration other than cash or a cash equivalent, shares with voting power equal to more than 20% of the voting power outstanding immediately before the issuance.

The precise number of shares that a shareholder owns in a corporation at a particular time determines her position relative to other shareholders. What is important, however, is not the absolute *number* of shares owned, but the *percentage* of the corporation's outstanding stock those shares represent (or more specifically, the voting power). Assume that two corporations are identical except that Corp. A has two shares of common shares outstanding and Corp. B has 1,000 shares outstanding. One share of Corp. A, representing 50% of its outstanding shares, clearly would have more value and greater proportionate voting power than 100 shares of Corp. B, representing 10% of its outstanding shares.

When additional shares are sold to other investors, the voting power of existing shareholders is diminished in relative terms—or "diluted." This is a problem for shareholders who want to maintain their proportionate voting interest to exercise a degree of control.

The common law doctrine of "preemptive rights" addressed concerns about dilution. Courts held a shareholder had an inherent right to maintain her proportionate interest in a corporation by purchasing a proportionate number of any new shares issued for cash. For example, a shareholder who owned 100 shares in a corporation with 1,000 shares issued and outstanding would be entitled to purchase 10% of any new issue. Although the preemption rights worked in closely held corporations with simple capital structures, it became problematic in corporations with several classes of shares or those that issued shares in exchange for property to be used in the business. Preemptive rights also were of questionable value in publicly held corporations: a typical public shareholder, owning far less than 1% of the outstanding shares, presumably would care little about being diluted, so long as the overall value of her shares were not affected. Moreover, if she believed the firm was selling new shares at too low a price, she could protect herself simply by purchasing additional shares on the open market.

Over time, courts and legislatures addressed the problems posed by preemptive rights. First, courts developed several exceptions to the rule that shareholders always had preemptive rights. Later legislatures modified state corporate laws to allow corporations to avoid preemptive rights and almost all public corporations exercised this option.

Today, many states have adopted an "opt-in" approach to preemptive rights. MBCA § 6.30(a) provides that "The shareholders of a corporation do not have a preemptive right to acquire the corporation's unissued shares except to the extent the articles of incorporation so provide." To provide shareholders with such rights, the articles must include an appropriate provision. A simple declaration, such as "The corporation elects to have preemptive rights," will do. Absent such a declaration in the articles, no preemptive rights exist.

Delaware's corporate statute no longer explicitly addresses preemptive rights. Nonetheless, DGCL § 157 authorizes a corporation to issue rights to purchase its shares, which can include preemptive rights. In addition, a Delaware corporation can include a provision in its articles creating preemptive rights.

Common shares. Common shares are the most basic of all corporate securities. All corporations have common shares, and many small corporations issue no other kind of equity security. Holders of common shares usually have the exclusive power to elect a corporation's board of directors, although in some corporations one or more classes of common shares are non-voting and, in many corporations, preferred shares have limited voting rights.

Common shares represent a "residual claim" on both the current income and the assets of a corporation. All income that remains after a corporation has satisfied the claims of creditors and holders of its more senior securities—preferred shares and debt—"belongs" in a conceptual sense to the holders of common shares. If no income remains, shareholders receive nothing. If some income remains, the board of directors can distribute it to shareholders in the form of a "dividend" or can choose to have it reinvested in the business. At least in theory, the board should choose to reinvest income only if it believes that the future returns from that investment will be greater than those that shareholders could generate by investing that income on their own elsewhere.

If the corporation is liquidated, common shares also represent a residual claim on the corporation's assets. This means that in liquidation the corporation must first pay the claims of creditors and holders of preferred shares. Common shareholders receive whatever "residual" remains. As a consequence, common shareholders are the first to lose their investment if the corporation experiences economic difficulties and have the greatest potential for gain if the corporation is successful.

Common shares generally represent a permanent commitment of capital to a corporation. Holders of common shares, if they wish to get out of their investment, generally do so by "exit"—selling their shares to other investors, who buy at a price that reflects the firm's current value. Generally, common shares are not redeemable, and the corporation has no obligation to repurchase them from shareholders. If a corporation is paying large current dividends or is reinvesting its income successfully, shareholders often will be able to realize substantial gains by selling their common shares to other investors. However, as we've noted earlier, shareholders of close corporations might not be able to find a ready market for their shares.

Although common shareholders are last in line when it comes to distributions of income and in liquidation, they generally are first in line with respect to control. They often have the exclusive right to elect the board of directors and to vote on other matters that require shareholders' approval. This combination of voting rights and a residual claim on profits and assets gives shareholders a strong incentive to ensure that the corporation is operated efficiently. If shareholders elect competent directors and monitor their performance effectively, they will realize the benefits of those directors' sound business decisions. If shareholders elect incompetent directors or fail to monitor their performance effectively, they will bear the loss if the directors mismanage the corporation's business or misappropriate its assets.

Common shareholders also are seen as the primary beneficiaries of the fiduciary duties that corporate law imposes on the board of directors. As we have seen, courts defer to a considerable degree to directors' business judgments, but they do so on the assumption that directors have exercised reasonable diligence and acted in the corporation's and thus the shareholders' best interests. These obligations extend to decisions concerning whether a corporation should reinvest its profits or distribute them as dividends. In addition, directors have a duty to refrain from engaging in transactions that will provide them with unfair profits at the corporation's expense. In short, directors have broad discretion to manage, but must bear in mind that they are managing other people's money and that they have obligations to do so with care, loyalty, and good faith.

Preferred shares. Preferred shares have economic rights senior to those customarily assigned to common shares. Preferred shares vary widely, depending on the attributes assigned to them in the articles of incorporation. If no attribute is assigned to a class of shares with respect to its voting rights, right to dividends, or rights to redemption or in liquidation, courts generally will presume that "stock is stock"—that stock with certain preferences otherwise have the same rights as does common stock. Thus, although the rights attached to preferred shares are set forth in or pursuant to the articles authorizing such shares, the rights of preferred shares are viewed as part of a contract between the preferred shareholders and the corporation.

Preferred shares almost always have dividend rights senior to those of common shares. This means that payment of dividends on common shares cannot happen until dividends due on preferred shares have been paid. A preferred share's dividend preference usually will be stated as a fixed amount that must be paid annually or quarterly. The preference may expire if a dividend due for a given period is not paid, or it may be "cumulative"—meaning that if a dividend is not paid when due, the right to receive that dividend accumulates and all accrued dividend arrearages must be paid before any dividends can be paid on common shares.

Preferred shares also may be "participating." This means preferred shares will receive dividends whenever they are paid on common shares, either in the same amount as or as a multiple of the amount paid on common shares.

In addition to a dividend preference, preferred shares often have a preference in liquidation, generally stated as a right to receive a specified amount before any amounts are distributed with respect to common shares. The amount of this preference most often is the amount that the corporation received when it sold the preferred shares plus, in the case of cumulative preferred, any accumulated unpaid dividends. In some instances, there may also be a specified "liquidation premium" that must be paid. However, as with common shares, the liquidation rights of preferred shares are subordinate to the claims of creditors. Consequently, when a corporation does not have assets sufficient to pay its debts, the preferred shareholders receive nothing in the event of liquidation.

Preferred shares sometimes represent a permanent commitment of capital to a corporation and sometimes do not. In the latter event, the shares are "redeemable" for some specified amount—that is, the corporation will repurchase the shares from the preferred shareholders. The right to require redemption may be held by the shareholder, by the corporation, or by both. The amount for which shares are to be redeemed generally is equal to the preference to which they are entitled in the event of liquidation, although it is not unusual to provide that, when shares are redeemable by the corporation, some premium above that amount must be paid by the corporation.

Preferred shares can have voting rights and will be deemed to have voting rights equal to those of common shares, unless the articles of incorporation provide otherwise. Sometimes the preferred have voting rights on an "as-converted" basis with the common shares, but often the voting rights of preferred shares are limited to specified issues and circumstances. Preferred shares usually have a statutory right to vote on changes in the corporate structure that affect adversely their rights and preferences. In addition, preferred shares are often given the right to elect some or all of a corporation's directors if dividends due on the preferred shares are not paid for some designated period. Such provisions reflect the nature of the contract between holders of preferred shares and the corporation. In short, the preferred shareholders may relinquish their right to participate in control in exchange for a priority claim to periodic dividends, but if the corporation fails to pay those dividends, preferred shareholders then become entitled to exert control.

The standard features of preferred shares may be supplemented by a variety of other features, including the right to convert preferred shares into common shares at some specified ratio, the right to vote on certain transactions, or the right to require the corporation to redeem preferred shares if and when specified events should occur. As noted, these rights are essentially contractual in nature and must be spelled out in the articles. Moreover, most courts have taken the position that the preferred shareholders are owed fiduciary duties only when they rely on a right shared equally with the common stock and not when they invoke their special contractual rights.

Preferred shares are a favorite way for "venture capital" (VC) firms to finance "start-up" or "early-stage" businesses, particularly in areas of new technology. After such companies have raised their initial capital and need more money to expand or survive, they often will raise money from VC firms, which manage investment pools comprised of wealthy individuals and large institutional investors, like pension plans and university endowments.

Why do VC firms prefer convertible preferred stock? A number of explanations exist, ranging from tax motivations to governance. For example, convertible preferred stock has long been attractive to VCs because of its hybrid nature, which gives VC firms some protection on the downside and the ability to convert their equity to common stock on the upside. VC firms can negotiate specific protections in their preferred, including a liquidation preference, the right to elect a certain number of directors to the board, and the ability to convert their preferred shares into common shares if the company goes public.

Corporations often raise money by selling preferred shares in lieu of taking on debt. The two have obvious similarities. The price at which a company can sell preferred shares is influenced by factors similar to those that determine the price at which it can borrow—the dividend rate, the redemption features, whether the preferred can be converted into common shares and, if so, at what price. Consequently, the requirement that the terms of preferred shares be spelled out in the articles can pose real timing problems, especially in the case of a publicly held company. It usually takes a minimum of 30 days to obtain shareholder approval of an amendment to the articles of incorporation authorizing new preferred shares. By the end of that period, market conditions are likely to have changed enough so that whatever terms were specified at the beginning of the period must again be modified.

Most corporation statutes address this timing problem by permitting the articles to authorize "blank check preferred shares," the essential characteristics of which—rights to dividends, liquidation preferences, redemption rights, voting rights, and conversion rights—can be set by the board of directors at the time the shares are sold. Such an authorization may facilitate the sale of preferred shares, but it also enhances substantially the power of a corporation's board of directors by allowing it to issue preferred shares with rights that may materially impinge on those of common shares without first obtaining explicit shareholder approval. For example, many corporate boards use blank check preferred shares as part of "poison pill" rights plans, because the issuance does not require shareholder approval.

3.   Debt Securities

Debt securities represent a corporation's liabilities to lenders. They can be labeled *notes*, *debentures*, or *bonds*—and sometimes these terms are used interchangeably. Typically, notes and debentures have shorter maturities than bonds, and debentures are usually not secured by corporate assets. Some short-term debt securities resemble accounts payable or the debts of trade creditors. But typically, debt securities are part of a company's long-term capital structure and reflect long-term interests in a corporation's financial fortunes.

A "poison pill" is an anti-takeover device that dilutes the financial position of an acquiror that buys an interest exceeding a specified threshold in a corporation without first obtaining the permission of the corporation's board of directors. The device thus compels would-be acquirors to negotiate with the board. We will see poison pills again a few times in this book, when we talk about shareholder voting rights, shareholder activism, and M&A.

The terms of a bond typically are fixed by a complex contract known as an *indenture* that specifies the rights and obligations of the bondholders and the corporation. Whether or not an indenture is used, certain fundamental terms are set forth in every debt contract. For example, the corporate borrower is obliged to repay a fixed amount of *princi-*

pal on a particular date. Typically, *interest* must be paid at periodic intervals, whether the interest is a floating rate that varies over time or is fixed throughout the term of the contract. Importantly, the interest obligation does not depend on whether the corporation earns a profit. If the corporation fails to pay interest on a bond when interest is due, it will be deemed in default. Typically, an event of default will cause the entire principal amount of the bond to become due immediately, and this "acceleration" entitles the bondholders to pursue all legal remedies for which they have bargained, including the right to initiate bankruptcy proceedings.

The indenture can require that the corporation repay the entire principal amount all at once at maturity, or it can specify that the corporation make periodic principal payments, so that the principal amount is "amortized" over time. Some indentures require that borrowers make payments into a "sinking fund" that will be used to repay part of the principal prior to the bond's maturity date.

If a bond is secured, the debt contract also must specify the terms of the security arrangement and the collateral that secures the bond. The debt contract also may include provisions, known as *covenants* or *negative covenants*, requiring the borrower to refrain from taking certain actions that might jeopardize the position of the bondholders. A corporation may agree, for example, not to pay any dividends or repurchase any of its own shares unless it meets certain financial conditions.

Bonds may be made redeemable or "callable" at a fixed price at the option of the corporation. This right can be valuable to a corporation; if interest rates decline, it can redeem outstanding high-interest bonds by issuing lower-interest bonds or otherwise borrowing at a lower interest rate. To compensate bondholders for their loss of income, a bond's redemption price usually is set at something above the principal that the bondholders would be entitled to receive when the bonds mature.

Because the terms and conditions of debt securities are fixed entirely by contract and often are the result of extensive negotiations, many other provisions may be included in a debt contract. For example, the corporation might give the bondholder the right to convert bonds into common shares. So-called convertible debentures are hybrid securities that closely resemble convertible preferred shares—indeed, two such instruments might have all of the same substantive terms so that the only real difference is the label.

Unless the articles of incorporation provide to the contrary, a corporation's board of directors has the authority to issue debt securities without shareholder

> Bonds usually do not carry the right to vote, although many corporate statutes, authorize voting debt. Moreover, a borrower corporation's directors owe bondholders only such obligations as are spelled out in the debt contract, or are otherwise part of contract law. Directors generally are not fiduciaries for bondholders. Consequently, bondholders' interests generally are protected only to the extent that they have negotiated appropriate covenants as part of their debt contracts.

approval. The board decides whether the corporation should incur new debt, in what amount, and on what terms and conditions. The board must involve shareholders only if it decides to issue bonds that will be convertible into shares and the corporation does not have enough authorized shares to satisfy the bonds' conversion rights. In such a case, the board must seek shareholder approval of an amendment to the articles increasing the number of authorized shares. However, shareholders need not approve the issuance of the convertible debt securities.

The use of long-term debt as part of a corporation's capital structure creates a tension between debt and equity investors. Both have stakes in the long-term health of the corporation, and both benefit if the corporation accumulates funds in excess of the amount it needs for current operations. But holders of debt and equity have agreed to different trade-offs between risk and reward, and each thus has a different perspective on how much risk that a corporation should assume.

Unless she has bargained for a right to convert her debt into equity, a bondholder has accepted rights to fixed payments of interest and repayment of her capital in lieu of the possibly higher, but uncertain, returns available to holders of equity securities, especially common shares. Common shareholders have assumed more risk, but also can exercise more control over the conduct of the corporation's business. A debtholder is viewed as an outsider entitled only to the protection specified in her contract. In contrast, common shareholders are protected by directors' fiduciary duties, including the duty to advance the interests of the common shareholders even if at the expense of the interests of non-shareholders.

4. Options

In addition to debt and equity, companies often issue *options*, which are the right to buy securities, typically common shares, at a specified time and price. Stock options are important pieces of the financial accounting and valuation puzzle. Corporate lawyers frequently deal with options, in part because most publicly traded companies and many private companies award stock options to managers and employees.

The definition of an option is simple: it is the right to buy or sell something in the future. Options are everywhere. A tenant with the right to renew a lease at a particular monthly rate owns an option. A car rental company that permits a client to purchase the car's tank of gasoline in advance is selling an option. Any corporation that gives its employees the right to buy its shares at a set time and price also has issued an option.

Options generally are known as *contingent claims*, because they are assets whose value and future payoff depend on the outcome of some uncertain contingent event, such as fluctuations in rental markets, gasoline use on a trip, or changes in the corporation's stock price. Remember: a party who owns an option has a contractual *right* (to buy or sell), but not a contractual *obligation* to do so. A tenant with a right to renew the lease need not renew; a car renter who pre-purchases a tank of gas need not use all of it; and an employee with stock options is not obligated to buy corporate stock. Simply stated, option holders have rights, not obligations.

The most familiar type of option is the stock option. Corporations frequently grant stock options to their employees, particularly senior managers, as compensation. Again, the option holder has the right—but not the obligation—to buy shares of the company.

Options have a special terminology:

In 1995 The Walt Disney Company hired Michael Ovitz, a Hollywood talent broker. Besides agreeing to pay Ovitz a base salary of $1 million and a discretionary bonus, Disney issued stock options that entitled Ovitz to purchase five million shares of Disney stock. When Disney's stock price went up, the right to buy five million shares of Disney stock proved to be highly valuable. Fourteen months after being hired, Disney terminated Ovitz, who exercised his stock options and made $130 million. Disney shareholders claimed this was excessive—particularly for someone who had done a poor job. We discuss these options in greater detail when we take up the Delaware judicial response to this famous shareholder suit in the *Disney* litigation.

- The right to buy shares is known as a *call option*, whereas the right to sell is known as a *put option*.

- The price specified in an option contract is known as the *strike price* or *exercise price*.

- The date specified in an option contract is known as the *maturity date* or *expiration date*.

Corporations typically issue only call options. When issued to the public, call options are sometimes known as *warrants*. Stock options awarded to managers typically are call options with a ten-year maturity date and an exercise price equal to the market price when the options were awarded. As incentive compensation, the options may be subject to a vesting period over which time the rights become exercisable.

Points for Discussion

1. *Allocating risk and return.*

Return to the capital structure of our JKL Corporation. What are the rights of each of the parties with regard to (1) participating in the management of JKL, (2) receiving current income with respect to their investments, and (3) recovering the capital they are committing to JKL? How are the parties' attitudes toward risk likely to differ? How does JKL's capital structure allocate risk—assume, for example, that the corporation becomes insolvent or that it becomes a huge financial success? How does the way they have elected to slice JKL's capital structure affect the expected returns of each party?

2. Debt vs. equity.

How can the Widget brothers protect their interests as creditors of JKL? How does their approach differ from the approach Justin, Kathy or Lorenzo might use to protect their interests as shareholders?

3. Debt vs. preferred.

Would it be better for Lorenzo to receive preferred shares or a debt security for the $500,000 he proposes to invest beyond what will be allocated to common shares? What business and legal risks does the choice entail for JKL and the three shareholders? What risks and benefits does the choice entail for Lorenzo? If Lorenzo elects to purchase preferred shares, how should the terms be structured to protect Lorenzo's interest in receiving income of $50,000 a year with respect to this portion of his investment?

4. Options?

How might you advise the parties to use options, if at all? For example, would you advise the Widget brothers to ask for options in lieu of other protections? How should JKL respond if the Widget brothers request that the corporation issue stock options to them?

B.   Capital Structure in the Real World: Taxes, Bankruptcy, and Conflicts

As noted above, the term "capital structure" describes how a company has raised funds using corporate securities. Some corporations have an all-equity capital structure consisting only of common shares. Other corporations have small amounts of equity and large amounts of debt. Some corporations have complicated capital structures, with numerous slices, each with different claims on the corporation.

Investing is a voluntary act. People with funds to invest will buy a security only if they perceive it to be more attractive than other available investments. Consequently, those who organize a corporation cannot simply select a capital structure and impose it on potential investors. They must design a capital structure for the firm in general, and specify the terms of the securities it will issue in particular, so that investors find the rights embodied in those securities—relating to participation in management, claims on the firm's income, rights in the event of liquidation and potential financial rewards—sufficiently attractive to justify investing in one or more of them.

Within the limits imposed by market forces, however, persons organizing a corporation generally have the ability to select among different capital structures that reflect differing allocations of control, risk, and claims on the corporation's income and assets. As is the case when choosing an organizational form, federal income tax considerations often will influence the organizers' choice. Likewise, the costs of bankruptcy will constrain a corporation's ability to issue increasing amounts of debt. Finally, capital structure choices inevitably create conflict among parties with potentially competing claims to a corporation's income, and frequently different agendas and risk preferences. We next address each of these issues: taxes, bankruptcy, and conflicts.

1. Taxes

The Internal Revenue Code gives corporations a powerful incentive to favor debt in their capital structure. Specifically, it allows corporations to deduct from their taxable income all interest paid on bonds they have issued. The code does not allow corporations to deduct dividends paid on preferred or common shares. Repayment of the principal of a bond also typically is treated as a tax-free return of capital.

Recall the capital structure of Widget, Inc., from the financial statements at the beginning of the previous chapter. The Balance Sheet showed that Widget, Inc. had issued $2 million of Notes payable, 12.5%. The annual interest payment on that debt was $250,000 ($2 million times 12.5%). Widget, Inc. was entitled to deduct this amount from its income to calculate its "Income before taxes."

What if Widget, Inc. had decided that instead of issuing debt it would raise the $2 million by issuing preferred shares with a 12.5% dividend? If Widget, Inc. paid a dividend of $250,000 in its most recent year, it would *not* have been entitled to deduct that payment, because it was a "dividend" not "interest." Accordingly, the company's "Income before taxes" for the most recent year would have been $850,000, not $600,000, and it would have paid tax on this higher amount.

Given the tax advantages of characterizing corporate payments as payments on debt and not on equity, the IRS will not simply accept the label used by the corporation. Instead, the IRS and the courts consider numerous factors in assessing whether debt really is debt. The court in *Slappey Drive Industrial Park v. United States*, 561 F.2d 572 (5th Cir. 1977), provided a useful list, although not exhaustive:

(1) the names given to the certificates evidencing the indebtedness;

(2) the presence or absence of a fixed maturity date;

(3) the source of payments;

(4) the right to enforce payment of principal and interest;

(5) participation in management flowing as a result;

(6) the status of the contribution in relation to regular corporate creditors;

(7) the intent of the parties;

(8) "thin" or adequate capitalization;

(9) identity of interest between creditor and stockholder;

(10) source of interest payments;

(11) the ability of the corporation to obtain loans from outside lenders;

(12) the extent to which the advance was used to acquire capital assets;

(13) the failure of the debtor to repay or seek to postpone on the due date.

So why don't corporations always issue bonds rather than preferred shares? And why don't corporations raise as much of their capital as possible by selling debt to persons who might otherwise purchase common shares? One answer is that preferred stock has other advantages. For example, preferred stock is more flexible than debt. The corporation must make interest payments to debtholders but can choose to forego dividend payments on preferred stock when the corporation has a bad year. Because debtholders have the ability to accelerate debt and force bankruptcy proceedings if the company fails to make payments, many equity investors prefer that companies not have too much debt. For most companies, there is some optimal mix of capital structure that includes both debt and equity, notwithstanding the tax advantages of debt.

Thus, because of taxes, capital structure matters. For tax purposes, corporations have an incentive to issue debt instead of equity. On the other hand, corporations that issue too much debt might lose the tax advantage if challenged. On balance, taxes are a "thumb" on the capital structure scale that favors debt over equity.

2. Bankruptcy and Leverage

In contrast to taxes, the specter of bankruptcy is a disincentive for corporations to issue debt. At the extreme, an equity-only corporation will never have to worry about bankruptcy. If business goes poorly, the equity investors lose their money; but if there are no debts to repay, there are no potential bankruptcy costs.

Financing a corporation with debt has advantages. A corporation will find it profitable to finance business activities with borrowed money whenever it can earn more income from those activities than it will pay in interest on the borrowed money. This concept is known as *leverage*. Whatever the corporation earns in excess of its interest costs will increase the corporation's income and benefit its shareholders. In effect, the corporation is using the borrowed money as a lever to increase its shareholders' income.

But leverage also increases shareholders' risk. If a corporation earns less from the activities being financed than the interest on the borrowed money, the corporation's income will decline because the corporation must pay interest on the borrowed funds whether or not the investment financed proves to be profitable. Consequently, if a corporation is not confident that leverage will work to its advantage, it often will choose to issue new equity rather than rely on borrowed money to finance its activities.

For example, suppose that you have $1 million and want to start a corporation. You have determined that your corporation needs $2 million of initial capital. Therefore, you must raise an additional $1 million by issuing corporate securities. Assuming debt is available at an interest rate of 10%, so that annual interest payments are $100,000, should the corporation issue equity or debt to raise the additional $1 million?

The answer depends on how much money you expect the corporation to make. (For this analysis, we are isolating the effects of leverage, and therefore we will ignore the effect of taxes, which as we know would make debt relatively more attractive.) If the corporation earns $200,000 of income before interest, you will earn $100,000 in both scenarios. If you borrow, you will pay $100,000 of interest, leaving $100,000 of income for the equity, all of which you own. If you issue equity, you will not owe any interest, so you will split 50-50 the corporation earnings of $200,000 with the other equity holder, leaving you with $100,000 of income. The results of this break-even scenario are depicted below.

Break-Even Scenario

	Issue debt	Issue equity
Income Before Interest	$200,000	$200,000
(Interest)	($100,000)	$0
Net Income	$100,000	$200,000
Return on equity	10%	10%

If the corporation earns less than $200,000, the negative effects will be magnified if you borrow. For example, if the corporation earned just $50,000, you would lose $50,000 if you borrowed, whereas you would earn $25,000 if you sold shares. This Negative Scenario is depicted below.

Negative Scenario

	Issue debt	Issue equity
Income Before Interest	$50,000	$50,000
(Interest)	($100,000)	$0
Net Income	($50,000)	$50,000
Return on equity	(5%)	2.5%

If the corporation earns more than $200,000, the positive effects will be magnified if you borrow. For example, if the corporation earned $500,000, you would earn $400,000 if you borrowed, but just $250,000 if you sold shares.

Positive Scenario

	Issue debt	Issue equity
Income Before Interest	$500,000	$500,000
(Interest)	($100,000)	$0
Net Income	$400,000	$500,000
Return on equity	40%	25%

Thus, leverage increases risk—both on the upside and downside. Shareholders who are risk seekers might prefer debt, while shareholders that are risk averse might prefer more equity. There is no "rule of thumb" describing the optimal share of equity and debt.

What about debt taken by insiders? If a corporation has too much inside debt—that is, debt taken by shareholders of the corporation—a bankruptcy court might re-characterize this debt as equity, pushing it further down in the capital structure, and making it less likely that the inside debtholders will receive anything in the bankruptcy process. Under the "Deep Rock Doctrine," named for a bankrupt company involved in the leading case of *Taylor v. Standard Gas & Electric Co.*, 306 U.S. 307 (1939), bankruptcy courts have exercised their equity jurisdiction to subordinate the claims of inside creditors to those of outside creditors when they conclude the insiders have not invested adequate equity capital in a corporation. When this "equitable subordination" doctrine is invoked, inside creditors usually receive no repayment with respect to the "debt" they hold.

3. Tension in the Capital Structure

Capital structure also matters to corporations because slicing the capital structure creates tensions among the parties who contribute money to the corporation. Consider the inevitable tensions between managers and shareholders of a corporation. Capital structure can minimize these agency costs. For example, a corporation might use debt as a disciplining device to constrain managers, who might be less likely to slack if they must be sure the corporation repays its debts.

Some of these tensions arise because of "optionality" in the capital structure. Remember that an option is a right. For example, the holder of a call option has the right to buy some asset at a specified price—such as if Widget, Inc. were to issue options to employees giving them the right to buy 100 shares for $100 per share anytime during the next four years.

There is a separate, different way to think about options in the context of capital structure. Some people find this concept difficult, but it illustrates the inevitable tensions among different parts of the capital structure. Here is the basic idea: equity is an option. Can you see how?

Imagine a company with $100 of debt. You can think of equity as having the right to buy the company's assets for $100 from the debt holder. If the equity doesn't pay the $100 debt, the corporation goes into bankruptcy and the equity receives little or nothing of the remaining assets. But if the equity repays the $100 debt, then equity keeps all of the upside from the assets. This is why equity is sometimes called the "residual" claim. Equity gets to keep what is left after repaying the debt—that potential for upside is option-like.

Thus, options are more than merely types of corporate securities. They also are conceptual tools that help illuminate the roles of various participants in a corporation. For example, in the JKL problem at the beginning of this chapter, the relative positions of Justin, Kathy, and Lorenzo, on one hand, and First National Bank, on the other hand, can be described using options.

One way of thinking about the shareholder-bank relationship is that the shareholders have bought a call option from the Bank. The shareholders have the right to receive the residual profits of the corporation after it repays the Bank's loan. The exercise price of this option is the amount of the loan, and the expiration dates are the dates that payments are due under the loan. Like any call option, the shareholders' position increases in value as the underlying assets increase in value. And like any call option, the shareholders' position has a limited downside. Shareholders have the right, but not the obligation, to the upside associated with JKL's assets. If those assets are worth less than the loan amount, the shareholders simply decline to exercise their call option, which becomes worthless (along with their initial investment). The Bank, which takes on the risk associated with JKL's assets as they decline in value, suffers the losses.

Thinking about the shareholders and Bank from the perspective of options theory helps illuminate the principle of leverage. A person who owns assets and buys a put option is limiting her downside, just as a person who borrows money to invest in a business is limiting her downside. Likewise, a person who buys a call option is magnifying her exposure to the underlying assets: she has the potential to increase the profit associated with an investment, with limited downside risk.

Leverage and the limited liability of shareholders are also related in an important way. As a company's leverage increases, so does the chance that the shareholders lose all of their initial investment. Because limited liability means that shareholders cannot lose more than their initial investment, higher leverage increases the risks of other corporate creditors, including holders of debt and preferred stock.

Another way of thinking about the relationship between the shareholders and the bank is that the shareholders own the assets of JKL and have purchased a "put option" from the bank. This put option gives the shareholders the right to "sell" the corporate assets to the bank in the event of bankruptcy. In other words, the put option is an insurance policy that protects the shareholders from losing more than their initial investment—the bank bears any additional declines in value. This insurance protection is another way of thinking about limited liability, one of the central concepts of corporate law. Typically, the most shareholders can lose is the amount of their investment.

As you read the next case, which highlights the tension that arises from the capital structure, consider how corporate law allocates rights to the various participants in the corporation. The case highlights the tension between common shareholders and preferred shareholders in a startup corporation, where the preferred shareholders (venture capital firms) wanted to cut their losses and have the corporation dissolve and liquidate its assets, repaying them at least some of their investment. Meanwhile, the common shareholders didn't anticipate they would get much of anything in liquidation and instead wanted to take on new financing (here, debt financing) and hope that the corporation could recover and become profitable. The case presents a quite common scenario in VC-financed startups.

Equity-Linked Investors, L.P. v. Adams

705 A.2d 1040 (Del. Ch. 1997)

Allen, Chancellor.

This case involves a conflict between the financial interests of the holders of a convertible preferred stock with a liquidation preference, and the interests of the common stock. The conflict arises because the company, Genta Incorporated, is on the lip of insolvency and in liquidation it would probably be worth substantially less than the $30 million liquidation preference of the preferred stock. Thus, if the liquidation preference of the preferred were treated as a liability of Genta, the firm would certainly be insolvent now.

Yet Genta, a bio-pharmaceutical company that has never made a profit, does have several promising technologies in research and there is some ground to think that the value of products that might be developed from those technologies could be very great. Were that to occur, naturally, a large part of the "upside" gain would accrue to the benefit of the common stock, in equity the residual owners of the firm's net cash flows. (Of course, whatever the source of funds that would enable a nearly insolvent company to achieve that result would also negotiate for a share of those future gains—which is what this case is about). But since the current net worth of the company would be put at risk in such an effort—or more accurately would continue at risk—if Genta continues to try to develop these opportunities, any loss that may eventuate will in effect fall, not on the common stock, but on the preferred stock.

The Genta board sought actively to find a means to continue the firm in operation so that some chance to develop commercial products from its promising technologies could be achieved. It publicly announced its interest in finding new sources of capital. Contemporaneously, the holders of the preferred stock, relatively few institutional investors, were seeking a means to cut their losses, which meant, in effect, liquidating Genta and distributing most or all of its assets to the preferred. The contractual rights of the preferred stock did not, however, give the holders the necessary legal power to force this course of action on the corporation. Negotiations held between Genta's management and representatives of the preferred stock with respect to the rights of the preferred came to an unproductive and somewhat unpleasant end in January 1997.

Shortly thereafter, Genta announced that a third-party source of additional capital had been located and that an agreement had been reached that would enable the corporation to pursue its business plan for a further period. The evidence indicates that at the time set for the closing of that transaction, Genta had available sufficient cash to cover its operations for only one additional week. A Petition in Bankruptcy had been prepared by counsel.

This suit by a lead holder of the preferred stock followed the announcement of the loan transaction. Plaintiff is Equity-Linked Investors, one of the institutional investors that holds Genta's Series A preferred stock. The suit challenges the transaction in which Genta borrowed on a secured basis some $3,000,000 from Paramount Capital Asset Management, Inc. in exchange for a note, warrants exercisable into half of Genta's outstanding stock, and other consideration.

From a realistic or finance perspective, the heart of the matter is the conflict between the interests of the preferred stock and the economic interests of the common stock.

While the facts indisputably entail the imposition by the board of (or continuation of) economic risks upon the preferred stock which the holders of the preferred did not want, and while this board action was taken for the benefit largely of the common stock, those facts do not constitute a breach of duty. While the board in these circumstances could have made a different business judgment, in my opinion, it violated no duty owed to the preferred in not doing so. The special protections offered to the preferred are contractual in nature. The corporation is, of course, required to respect those legal rights. But, aside from the insolvency point, generally it will be the duty of the board, where discretionary judgment is to be exercised, to prefer the interests of common stock—as the good faith judgment of the board sees them to be—to the interests created by the special rights, preferences, etc., of preferred stock, where there is a conflict. The facts of this case do not involve any violation by the board of any special right or privilege of the Series A preferred stock.

I conclude that the directors of Genta were independent with respect to the loan transaction, acted in good faith in arranging and committing the company to that transaction, and, in the circumstances faced by them and the company were well informed of the available alternatives to try to bring about the long-term business plan of the company. In my opinion, they breached no duty owed to the company or any of the holders of its equity securities. While certainly some corporations at some points ought to be liquidated, when that point occurs is a question of business judgment ordinarily and in this instance.

Points for Discussion

1. Resolving tensions.

Where are the tensions? If you could have anticipated the problems at Genta Incorporated, could you have set up a different structure to avoid the conflict that arose in the case? For example, what do you think would have happened if the preferred shareholders had sought to obtain greater governance rights to influence corporate action? Would the parties likely have agreed to different terms?

2. Fiduciary duties in startups.

Startup companies that take venture capital financing typically have a capital structure with common and preferred stock as we saw in *Equity-Linked Investors*. The composition of the board of directors is usually negotiated and includes designated seats for venture capital investors who hold preferred stock. Designated members of the board are known as "constituency directors."

In carrying out their fiduciary duties, can such constituency directors favor the interests of the preferred shareholders over those of the common shareholders? Delaware courts have answered no. In a notable decision, the Court of Chancery explained: "[T]he standard of conduct for directors requires that they strive in good faith and on an informed basis to maximize the value of the corporation for the benefit of its residual claimants, the ultimate beneficiaries of the firm's value, not for the benefit of its contractual claimants." *In re Trados, Inc. Sh. Litig.*, 73 A.3d 17, 40-41 (Del. Ch. 2013). The court criticized the directors who "did not understand their job was to maximize the value of the corporation for the benefit of the common shareholders." *Id.* at 62. How are constituency directors to navigate dual obligations they have to the company on whose board they sit and to the investment funds which they represent?

3. Do labels matter?

Options offer new ways of thinking about the economic positions of equity and debt. But they also present challenging questions. What if JKL had issued $1,500,000 of call options to Justin, Kathy, and Lorenzo, and issued $500,000 of equity to the Bank? JKL still would have raised the same amount of equity and capital, and the parties still would have the same priority in JKL's capital structure. But now the labels have changed. Should those labels matter? Should you think about the corporation any differently if its capital structure is composed of "options" instead of "equity" and "equity" instead of "debt"? Does *Equity-Linked Investors* depend on labels?

4. Corporate insolvency.

Note that Chancellor Allen intimates that "at the point of insolvency" the duties of the board may shift from maximizing the interests of the common stock to protecting the interests of the corporation's creditors. But what if the corporation has not yet reached the point of insolvency? Delaware courts have rejected an approach that would shift fiduciary duties when the corporation is merely in the "zone of insolvency." *See N. Am. Catholic Educ. Programming Found. v. Gheewalla*, 930 A.2d 92 (Del. 2007). Furthermore, insolvency is now best understood as giving the board a choice in discharging its fiduciary duty. The board can decide whether to maximize the interests of creditors or shareholders within the purview of its business judgment. *See Quadrant Structured Products Co. v. Vertin*, 102 A.3d 155 (Del. Ch. 2014).

C. Capital Structure Law and Policy

Next we turn to three legal and policy issues related to capital structure. First, we describe the legal capital regime, which is antiquated and often makes little sense, yet still affects the behavior of corporations and their lawyers. Second, we cover some related—and sometimes counterintuitive—rules governing distributions to shareholders. Finally, we address some law and policy questions surrounding two judicial decisions on the payment of dividends, which highlight the challenges boards face related to capital structure.

1. Legal Capital

Historically, state corporation laws purported to protect debtholders by regulating "legal capital," sometimes called "stated capital." You can think of legal capital as a "cushion" of capital designed to ensure there is enough money to protect the interests of debtholders. The law generally provided that the corporation could not "eat into" this cushion of legal capital by paying out too much money to shareholders.

a. The Basic Concept

If you imagine the right-hand side of the balance sheet, legal capital represents a portion of the equity that is off limits to shareholders. The idea is that this should give the debtholders some confidence that this cushion amount will be available to repay the money they are owed.

Legal capital is a counterintuitive concept. It is easy to calculate the amount of legal capital, but hard—if not impossible—to understand how and why legal capital might actually protect debtholders. Let's get the easy part out of the way first. The formula for calculating legal capital is simple. It is the product of the number of shares outstanding and the "par value" of those shares. For now, just think of par value as an arbitrary number set by the corporation. All you have to do to compute legal capital is multiply those two numbers.

Legal capital = outstanding shares x par value

The number of outstanding shares is straightforward: you simply add up the number of issued shares held by the corporation's shareholders. Although we will discuss par value in greater detail in a moment, for now all you need to know is that par value is set forth in the articles of incorporation. If the corporation has set a par value of $1 per share, and there are 100 shares outstanding, that corporation's legal capital is $100. That's it.

b. Some Context and History

The more difficult part is to understand how and why legal capital and par value came to be an important part of corporate law. This story begins with a vivid metaphor: stock watering. Imagine a rancher from the nineteenth century filling his livestock with water before selling them. This process of "aquatizing" the herd made them appear larger and heavier than they really were, which—the rancher hoped—would yield a higher price for them at market.

As the story goes, Daniel Drew, a cattle-driver-turned-financier, brought this practice to Wall Street—but with shares instead of cows. Corporations would issue shares for more than the corporation's assets were worth. These overvalued shares became known as "watered stock," after their livestock counterparts, referring to the fact that the value of the stock was artificially inflated.

As sharp promoters prowled the countryside, selling shares of dubious corporations for progressively higher prices, the concept of "par value" developed. Equity investors began to expect, or at least hope, that every subscriber would pay the same amount and receive the same value. Ideally, the stock they bought would have some benchmark value reflecting that equal amounts of cash had been contributed for each share and that none of the shares would have been watered. This benchmark amount came to be known "par value," or just "par" for short. Investors imagined that it reflected both the amount paid for the stock and its value.

Concepts of legal capital arose from the concept of par value. Judges and legislators were concerned about the potential inequities of watered stock. For example, suppose a promoter had contributed land worth $20,000 to a corporation, and drafted articles of incorporation that authorized 1,000 shares of common stock at $100 par value. Then, the promoter (after taking 500 shares for contributing the land, which he over-valued at $50,000) would try to sell the remaining shares for $100 each, even though their value had been watered. Such abuses led some to believe that strong legal capital rules would protect outside shareholders and creditors. Such rules would ensure that all investors (both insiders and outsiders) paid the same amount for their shares and would assure lenders and other creditors that the amounts invested in the business by shareholders actually existed.

Over time, the received wisdom became that legal capital, based on par value, was a proxy for the value of a corporation's assets. Judges and legislators began to accept the notion that creditors were willing to lend on the basis of "par value," because that amount represented the contributions of shareholders, and was a rough approximation of the value of the firm's assets. That value, the story went, gave lenders confidence that they would be repaid.

In fact, this received wisdom was a ruse far from reality. Several scholars, led by Bayless Manning, demonstrated that the idealized world of legal capital was a fiction. Manning argued that par value was an arbitrary number that persisted only because corporate statutes required that it be used and stated in the corporate charter. Creditors didn't actually rely on par value for protection, and par value usually didn't reflect economic value. By the 1970s, few people believed that par value reflected actual value or that legal capital actually protected anyone.

Nevertheless, corporate statutes continued to require that corporations state a par value for their shares, and corporations were prohibited from distributing more than their legal capital to shareholders. Over time, rules were liberalized, and states permitted corporations to issue low-par or no-par stock. In the modern context, par value, when used, is understood as the minimum price at which the stock can be issued, and it can be set at a tiny number such as a fraction of a cent. In 1984, the MBCA did away with the concept of par value. But other states, including Delaware, maintain traditional legal capital rules. Thus, legal capital statutes govern a majority of public corporations today and remain as potential traps for the unwary lawyer.

> From an investor's perspective, holding debt is typically less risky than holding equity. Why is this? One reason is that the claims of debtholders (often called creditors) have priority over the claims of equity holders in bankruptcy. When a corporation goes under, debt is paid first, before equity. Another reason debt is less risky is that debtholders typically bargain for contractual protections in their agreements with the corporation. Thus, debtholders are protected by covenants, written provisions that limit the corporation's ability to put them at risk. In addition, some debts are secured by the corporation's assets. In practice, these factors matter more than legal capital in reducing the risk of debt.

Lawyers need to understand legal capital rules, old or new, for at least three reasons. First, one condition of many financing transactions is that the corporation's lawyer opine that all of the corporation's stock is "validly issued, fully paid and nonassessable." To render such an opinion, a lawyer must review all transactions in which the corporation has issued stock to see whether they were effectuated in compliance with the governing statutory provisions, including legal capital provisions.

Second, although many states once limited the consideration the corporation could accept for the issuance of shares—for example, not permitting future services or unsecured promissory notes as consideration—those limits have been supplanted. Today, the only requirement (in Delaware and the MBCA) is that the board determine the consideration is adequate, and this determination is conclusive. Thus, the corporate lawyer must also ensure that the board has properly determined that the consideration for the issued shares is adequate.

Third, most corporate statutes explicitly provide that directors can be held personally liable if they approve the issuance of shares or other distributions to shareholders in violation of applicable statutory provisions. Understandably, directors often seek the advice of counsel before making what might otherwise seem to be no more than a garden variety business judgment.

c.   Delaware Example

To help you see legal capital in action, we set forth below some relevant portions of Delaware's corporate statute. These provisions contain the legal capital rules that should help you advise Justin, Kathy, and Lorenzo about being sure their new corporation complies with Delaware's legal capital regime.

DGCL § 151
Classes and Series of Stock

(a)   Every corporation may issue 1 or more classes of stock or 1 or more series of stock within any class thereof, any or all of which classes may be of stock with par value or stock without par value.

DGCL § 152
Issuance of Stock

The consideration [for] the capital stock to be issued by a corporation shall be paid in such form and in such manner as the board of directors shall determine. The board of directors may authorize capital stock to be issued for consideration consisting of cash, any tangible or intangible property or any benefit to the corporation, or any combination thereof. In the absence of actual fraud in the transaction, the judgment of the directors as to the value of such consideration shall be conclusive.

> ### DGCL § 153
> ### Consideration for Stock
>
> (a) Shares of stock with par value may be issued for such consideration, having a value not less than the par value thereof, as determined from time to time by the board of directors, or by the stockholders if the certificate of incorporation so provides.
>
> (b) Shares of stock without par value may be issued for such consideration as is determined from time to time by the board of directors, or by the stockholders if the certificate of incorporation so provides.

Recall from our example that Justin, Kathy, and Lorenzo have agreed to pay a total of $500,000 for the common shares of JKL. Suppose that they also have agreed that JKL initially will issue 5,000 shares of common shares. Kathy will pay $200,000 in cash for 2,000 shares ($100 per share). Justin will pay $100,000 in cash and give JKL a note for $100,000 in exchange for another 2,000 shares. Lorenzo will pay $100,000 in cash for the remaining 1,000 shares. Lorenzo also will invest an additional $500,000 in 20-year subordinated notes.

Assume that JKL is incorporated in Delaware. Justin, Kathy, and Lorenzo have asked the following questions:

- Will the corporation need to set a par value for its common shares?

- What would be the consequence of setting the par value of JKL's shares at $100 per share—the price for which the shares will be sold—or at some lower value, such as $1 per share?

- Does the Delaware legal capital regime limit JKL's choice in setting par value?

- How would JKL reflect the transaction on its balance sheet if it sets the par value at $100 per share? At $1 per share?

- If JKL decides to issue no-par stock, is its board of directors required to take any further action? Would any such action be desirable?

- Can JKL accept Justin's personal note as partial payment for the 2,000 shares he will receive?

d. Reality of Legal Capital Rules

Although you might imagine some interesting interpretative questions under these statutory provisions, in practice they virtually never arise. Corporate lawyers avoid problems by setting par value far below the price at which the corporation plans to sell its shares. One choice is whether to use low-par or no-par stock. The choice usually depends on the manner in which the relevant jurisdiction calculates the tax or "franchise fee" payable on incorporation. That fee frequently is calculated on the basis of the aggregate authorized capital of the corporation, with no-par stock "deemed" to have some arbitrary par value for this purpose.

States that follow the MBCA have jettisoned the traditional approach to legal capital. They abandon the concept of par value as a rule (although they permit corporations to use par value in their articles). Instead, corporations may issue shares for whatever consideration the board authorizes, based on a variety of factors. The crucial determination for the board is based on business conditions, not the artificial notion of par value. According to the Official Comment to MBCA § 6.21, "there is no minimum price at which specific shares must be issued and therefore there can be no 'watered stock' liability for issuing shares below an arbitrarily fixed price." This reflects the drafters' belief that the old system of legal capital did not protect creditors' interests.

2. Distributions to Shareholders

A second capital structure issue—when a corporation may pay money to shareholders—is related to the concept of legal capital. The conflict between equity and debt is particularly acute when it comes to such distributions. If a corporation pays a dividend to shareholders or uses cash to repurchase shares, that money is no longer available to repay holders of debt.

The traditional approach to regulating distributions to shareholders looked back to the concept of legal capital. Recall that legal capital was a kind of "cushion" that corporations were required to maintain for the protection of creditors. The law provided that corporations could not make distributions that eroded this cushion.

However, corporations could make distributions out of "surplus" that left the cushion intact. Let's return to the right-hand side of the balance sheet. Recall that the equity portion of the balance sheet consists of both legal capital or stated capital (sometimes referred to as paid-in capital) as well as additional equity (sometimes referred to as retained earnings or earned surplus). Traditional statutes provided that corporations could make distributions out of this surplus as long as it did not impair their legal capital.

Today, states vary in their approach to distributions, but generally prohibit corporations from making distributions that will render them unable to pay debts or make them essentially insolvent. Some states, such as California, go further and also require that the corporation's balance sheet assets equal a specified percentage of its balance sheet liabilities. Any distribution that reduces assets below this level is not permitted. For example, Section 170 of the Delaware Corporations Code provides that the directors may declare and pay dividends (1) out of "surplus" or (2) if there is no surplus, out of "net profits."

The legal capital rules are complex, but essentially boil down to the board first calculating the company's "net assets" by subtracting total assets from liabilities, and

CHAPTER 8 *Capital Structure* 279

second subtracting "legal capital" from "net assets." For example, if a company has $100 of assets and $70 of liabilities, the first step is to calculate that the company has $30 of net assets ($100 minus $70). Then, if the company's "legal capital" is $10 (based on the board's earlier determination of par value), there is "surplus" of $20 ($30 minus $10). The board could then distribute up to $20 of this surplus through dividends or share repurchases. The basic idea is that the board should not make a distribution if it would impair legal capital.

The consequences of violating a state's unlawful distribution rules can be serious. When an unlawful distribution leads to creditor losses, the directors who authorized the distribution can be held personally liable. For example, in Delaware, directors remain liable for unlawful distributions even if they acted in good faith. (Later in this book, we will see that Delaware and other states permit corporations to "exculpate" directors from liability for breaches of the duty of care if they satisfied a good faith requirement; however, exculpation is not permitted for directors' liability for unlawful distributions.)

In reality, the strict rules and harsh penalties for unlawful distributions are rarely a serious concern, and restrictions on distributions based on the concept of legal capital are largely ineffective. For example, corporations can avoid the applicable statutes by amending their articles of incorporation to reduce the par value of its outstanding stock, thus expanding the available "surplus" and minimizing the "cushion" designed to protect creditors.

Courts also have permitted directors to justify distributions by "revaluing" their assets. In basic terms, the "revaluation" of the corporation's assets (on the left-hand side of the balance sheet) increases the available "surplus" for distributions (on the right-hand side of the balance sheet). For example, if a corporation held property carried at a cost of $1 million, but the board determined the fair market value of that property was $2 million, the board could justify a larger distribution to shareholders, without putting creditors at risk.

Not all dividends involve the distribution of cash to stockholders. Corporations occasionally declare "stock dividends" and distribute additional shares of stock to their shareholders. In economic terms, such dividends result in no meaningful change in the financial status of the corporation or its shareholders. They merely divide shareholders' ownership interests in the corporation into a greater number of pieces while leaving each shareholder's proportionate interest unchanged. Indeed, such "dividends" may be declared to produce the appearance that shareholders are receiving something of value with respect to their stock when the corporation is not in a position to pay a dividend in cash.

Since stock dividends do not result in the distribution of any real assets, there is no need to limit them for the protection of creditors. Indeed, because the par value (if any) of the shares distributed must be added to stated capital, a stock dividend can actually benefit creditors. The MBCA recognizes that a stock dividend involves the issuance of shares "without consideration" and thus stock dividends are excluded from the definition of "distribution."

The following case relies on similar reasoning to allow a Delaware corporation to repurchase a substantial portion of its outstanding stock—an action that has the same impact on creditors as the payment of a dividend. Under the DGCL and other corporate statutes, a repurchase of shares by the corporation is treated as a "distribution" subject to essentially the same restrictions applicable to payment of a dividend.

Klang v. Smith's Food & Drug Centers, Inc.

702 A.2d 150 (Del.1997)

Veasey, Chief Justice.

> During the 1990s and 2000s, many of the most important decisions on corporate law were authored by E. Norman Veasey, who served as Chief Justice of the Delaware Supreme Court from 1992 to 2004. Besides solidifying Delaware's reputation for "fair, reasonable and efficient" litigation (according to the U.S. Chamber of Commerce), Veasey also was a national leader on professionalism reform. He chaired a special ABA committee that proposed ethics rules for lawyers that, among other things, permitted lawyers to violate attorney-client confidences to prevent financial crimes.

Smith's Food & Drug Centers, Inc. ("SFD") is a Delaware corporation that owns and operates a chain of supermarkets in the Southwestern United States. Slightly more than three years ago, Jeffrey P. Smith, SFD's Chief Executive Officer, began to entertain suitors with an interest in acquiring SFD.

On January 29, 1996, SFD entered into an agreement with The Yucaipa Companies ("Yucaipa"), a California partnership also active in the supermarket industry. Under the agreement, the following would take place:

(1) Smitty's Supermarkets, Inc. ("Smitty's"), a wholly-owned subsidiary of Yucaipa that operated a supermarket chain in Arizona, was to merge into Cactus Acquisition, Inc. ("Cactus"), a subsidiary of SFD, in exchange for which SFD would deliver to Yucaipa slightly over 3 million newly-issued shares of SFD common stock; and

(2) SFD was to undertake a recapitalization, in the course of which SFD would assume a sizable amount of new debt, retire old debt, and offer to repurchase up to fifty percent of its outstanding shares (other than those issued to Yucaipa) for $36 per share.

SFD hired the investment firm of Houlihan Lokey Howard & Zukin ("Houlihan") to examine the transactions and render a solvency opinion. Houlihan eventually issued a report to the SFD Board replete with assurances that the transactions would not endanger SFD's solvency, and would not impair SFD's capital in violation of 8 Del.C. § 160. On May 17, 1996, in reliance on the Houlihan opinion, SFD's

Board determined that there existed sufficient surplus to consummate the transactions, and enacted a resolution proclaiming as much. On May 23, 1996, SFD's stockholders voted to approve the transactions, which closed on that day. The self-tender offer was over-subscribed, so SFD repurchased fully fifty percent of its shares at the offering price of $36 per share.

A corporation may not repurchase its shares if, in so doing, it would cause an impairment of capital under 8 Del.C. § 160. A repurchase impairs capital if the funds used in the repurchase exceed the amount of the corporation's "surplus," defined by 8 Del.C. § 154 to mean the excess of net assets over the par value of the corporation's issued stock.

Plaintiff asked the Court of Chancery to rescind the transactions in question as violative of Section 160.

Plaintiff relies on an April 25, 1996 proxy statement in which the SFD Board released a pro forma balance sheet showing that the merger and self-tender offer would result in a deficit to surplus on SFD's books of more than $100 million. Plaintiff asks us to adopt an interpretation of 8 Del.C. § 160 whereby balance-sheet net worth is controlling for purposes of determining compliance with the statute. In response, defendants do not dispute that SFD's books showed a negative net worth in the wake of its transactions with Yucaipa, but argue that corporations should have the presumptive right to revalue assets and liabilities to comply with Section 160.

> "Pro forma" is from Latin meaning "as a matter of form." Pro forma financial statements are produced only as a matter of form, or—more precisely—in a way that does not conform to GAAP. Typically, a pro forma financial statement will look better than a financial statement that conforms to GAAP. Regulators have been concerned about companies using pro forma figures to mislead investors and require that they be clearly disclosed. The rationale for preparing a pro forma balance sheet is that there are unusual or nonrecurring transactions that distort the GAAP picture of a company's financial position. But notice that even the pro forma balance sheet for SFD, which reflected the effects of the merger and self-tender offer, showed that SFD had a negative net worth. Do you think anyone believed that this result was accurate?

Plaintiff advances an erroneous interpretation of Section 160. We understand that the books of a corporation do not necessarily reflect the current values of its assets and liabilities. Among other factors, unrealized appreciation or depreciation can render book numbers inaccurate. It is unrealistic to hold that a corporation is bound by its balance sheets for purposes of determining compliance with Section 160. Accordingly, we adhere to the principles of *Morris v. Standard Gas & Electric Co.*, 63 A.2d 577 (Del. Ch. 1949), allowing a corporation to revalue properly its assets and liabilities to show a surplus and thus conform to the statute.

Plaintiff further contends that SFD's repurchase of shares violated Section 160 even without regard to the corporation's balance sheets. Plaintiff claims that the SFD Board was not entitled to rely on the solvency opinion of Houlihan, which showed that the transactions would not impair SFD's capital given a revaluation of corporate assets.

On May 17, 1996, Houlihan released its solvency opinion to the SFD Board, expressing its judgment that the merger and self-tender offer would not impair SFD's capital. Houlihan reached this conclusion by comparing SFD's "Total Invested Capital" of $1.8 billion—a figure Houlihan arrived at by valuing SFD's assets under the "market multiple" approach—with SFD's long-term debt of $1.46 billion. This comparison yielded an approximation of SFD's "concluded equity value" equal to $346 million, a figure clearly in excess of the outstanding par value of SFD's stock. Thus, Houlihan concluded, the transactions would not violate 8 Del.C. § 160.

Plaintiff contends that Houlihan's analysis relied on inappropriate methods to mask a violation of Section 160. Noting that 8 Del.C. § 154 defines "net assets" as "the amount by which total assets exceeds total liabilities," plaintiff argues that Houlihan's analysis is erroneous as a matter of law because of its failure to calculate "total assets" and "total liabilities" as separate variables.

We believe that plaintiff reads too much into Section 154. The statute simply defines "net assets" in the course of defining "surplus." It does not mandate a "facts and figures balancing of assets and liabilities" to determine by what amount, if any, total assets exceeds total liabilities. The statute is merely definitional. It does not require any particular method of calculating surplus, but simply prescribes factors that any such calculation must include. Although courts may not determine compliance with Section 160 except by methods that fully take into account the assets and liabilities of the corporation, Houlihan's methods were not erroneous as a matter of law simply because they used Total Invested Capital and long-term debt as analytical categories rather than "total assets" and "total liabilities."

We are satisfied that the Houlihan opinion adequately took into account all of SFD's assets and liabilities. In cases alleging impairment of capital under Section 160, the trial court may defer to the board's measurement of surplus unless a plaintiff can show that the directors failed to fulfill their duty to evaluate the assets on the basis of acceptable data and by standards which they are entitled to believe reasonably reflect present values. In the absence of bad faith or fraud on the part of the board, courts will not substitute our concepts of wisdom for that of the directors. Therefore, we defer to the board's determination of surplus, and hold that SFD's self-tender offer did not violate 8 Del.C. § 160.

Points for Discussion

1. *The balance sheet?*

If the Court's description of the balance sheet is correct, what good is the balance sheet? Why did SFD's pro forma books show a negative net worth?

2. *Valuation.*

Looking back to the previous chapter, what valuation method does it appear that Houlihan used in rendering its solvency opinion? What is the "market multiple" approach that Houlihan used to calculate the value of SFD's assets? Do you agree that Houlihan had adequately taken into account SFD's assets and liabilities, even though the investment firm did not calculate "net assets" and "total liabilities"?

---

3. Corporate Law on Dividend Policy

Decisions as to whether distributions lawfully can be made arise mostly when corporations are in financial difficulty. In solvent corporations, decisions relating to whether and in what amounts to make distributions involve a basic financial policy issue: should cash not needed for current operations be reinvested in the business or distributed to shareholders? Statutory constraints are a legal formality, not an impediment, in these circumstances and the decision usually turns on business strategy.

Decisions about payment of dividends generally are governed by the business judgment rule. Thus, generally, only if it can be shown that the decision was tainted by fraud, illegality, or a conflict of interest can the presumption be overcome that the directors acted on an informed basis, with good faith and in the best interests of the corporation. Of all business decisions, the decision whether to distribute profits to shareholders or to re-invest them in the business is one of the most important, and courts are loathe to intervene.

We include as an example below a New York case that involved a dividend decision by the board of a public corporation that ended up favoring "accounting fiction" over "tax reality." In 1972, American Express purchased almost two million shares of stock in Donaldson, Lufkin & Jenrette, Inc. (DLJ), for $29.9 million. By 1975, the stock had declined in value to approximately $4 million. American Express announced that it would distribute the DLJ stock as a dividend. Two shareholders sued to enjoin the distribution. They argued that American Express would be better off selling the DLJ stock.

The shareholders pointed out that a distribution of the DLJ stock would not have any impact on American Express's liability for income taxes. On the other hand, if American Express sold the DLJ stock, it could reduce otherwise taxable capital gains by an amount equal to its roughly $26 million loss on the DLJ stock and thus save approximately $8 million in taxes. In effect, the shareholders' argument was that rather than distribute $4 million in DLJ stock as a dividend, American Express could sell the stock, save $8 million in taxes, and then (if it wished) distribute $12 million (the sale price plus the tax savings) as a dividend. This was the "tax reality."

The American Express board of directors considered the shareholders' argument at a meeting on October 17, 1975 and decided to proceed with the dividend. The board had previously been advised by its accountants that if the DLJ stock was distributed as a dividend, rather than sold, American Express would not have to reduce its reported income for 1975 to reflect its loss on its investment. Rather, it could bypass its income statement and simply reduce retained earnings by $29.9 million—the book value of the stock it would be distributing. This was the "accounting fiction."

Kamin v. American Express Co.

383 N.Y.S.2d 807 (Sup. Ct. 1976)

GREENFIELD, JUSTICE.

Examination of the complaint reveals that there is no claim of fraud or self-dealing, and no contention that there was any bad faith or oppressive conduct. The law is quite clear as to what is necessary to ground a claim for actionable wrongdoing.

More specifically, the question of whether or not a dividend is to be declared or a distribution of some kind should be made is exclusively a matter of business judgment for the Board of Directors.

> Courts will not interfere with such discretion unless it be first made to appear that the directors have acted or are about to act in bad faith and for a dishonest purpose. It is for the directors to say, acting in good faith of course, when and to what extent dividends shall be declared.

Thus, a complaint must be dismissed if all that is presented is a decision to pay dividends rather than pursuing some other course of conduct. The directors' room rather than the courtroom is the appropriate forum for thrashing out purely business questions which will have an impact on profits, market prices, competitive situations, or tax advantages.

The affidavits of the defendants and the exhibits annexed thereto demonstrate that the objections raised by the plaintiffs to the proposed dividend action were carefully considered and unanimously rejected by the Board at a special meeting called precisely for that purpose at the plaintiffs' request. The minutes of the special meeting indicate that the defendants were fully aware that a sale rather than a distribution of the DLJ shares might result in the realization of a substantial income tax saving. Nevertheless, they concluded that there were countervailing considerations primarily with respect to the adverse effect such a sale, realizing a loss of $25 million, would have on the net income figures in the American Express financial statement. Such a reduction of net income would have a serious effect on the market value of the publicly traded American Express stock. This was not a situation in which the defendant directors totally overlooked facts called to their attention. They gave them consideration, and attempted to view the total picture in arriving at their decision.

The business judgment rule (BJR) is a presumption protecting board decision making. The BJR is analogous to rational basis review for legislative actions: the courts give deference with the understanding they lack the expertise to sustain a more intense level of review or should not engage in judicial second-guessing. In applying the BJR to challenges to ordinary business decisions for breach of the duty of care, courts typically focus on whether the decision was rational from a business perspective or whether the board engaged in a satisfactory process.

In *Kamin*, the court determined that the board's decision had a business justification and was the product of a satisfactory process. It applied the business judgment rule and dismissed the complaint. Does that mean that the court is condoning the board's decision to avoid showing a loss on the DLJ stock in its financial statements?

The only hint of self-interest which is raised, not in the complaint but in the papers on the motion, is that four of the twenty directors were officers and employees of American Express and members of its Executive Incentive Compensation Plan. Hence, it is suggested, by virtue of the action taken earnings may have been overstated and their compensation affected thereby. Such a claim is highly speculative and standing alone can hardly be regarded as sufficient to support an inference of self-dealing. There is no claim or showing that the four company directors dominated and controlled the sixteen outside members of the Board.

Points for Discussion

1. *Accounting vs. markets.*

Do you think the American Express board was correct in its belief that stock market investors are more interested in the accounting treatment of a dividend payment, here American Express's divestiture of its interest in DLJ, than in that transaction's actual financial impact on American Express? Even if the board's assessment was correct, should the court have allowed the board to seek to increase the market price of American Express stock by rejecting a transaction (selling the DLJ stock and recording the loss) that would have produced a real economic benefit worth $8 million to the company? Would it matter if the compensation of the inside directors was based on accounting performance rather than the corporation's share price?

2. *Public vs. private corporations and dividend policy.*

Judges are reluctant to interfere with dividend policies in public corporations. By contrast, as we will see in Chapter 17 when we cover oppression in closely held corporations, courts in some states are willing to rigorously review these decisions in closely held corporations.

Why is this? Basically, in the public corporation a poorly conceived dividend policy will be subject to market discipline, including even a takeover. But in the closely held corporation there is generally no market for corporate shares and the discipline for misguided dividend policies has sometimes come from the courts. Under the "oppression" doctrine, courts in some states have protected the reasonable expectations of minority shareholders, including to be paid dividends or to have their shares bought out by the majority.

For example, in *Bonavita v. Corbo*, 692 A.2d 119 (N.J. Ch. Div. 1996), a longtime family business came to be held 50-50 by the sister of one of the co-founders and her nephew, who ran the business. The court found that the sister had "reasonable expectations" of having money for retirement from the business, and ordered the corporation to repurchase her shares—in effect, a lump-sum payment of her dividend rights.

Test Your Knowledge

To assess your understanding of the Chapter 5, 6, 7, and 8 material in this module, click here to take a quiz.

MODULE III — DIRECTORS AND OFFICERS

CHAPTER 9

Duty of Care

Corporate fiduciary duties have a long and complex history. Traditionally, it has been common to regard fiduciary duties as being split between the duty of care and the duty of loyalty. We will study each duty in various contexts, some overlapping. We start with the duty of care.

In general, the duty of care has been described as a duty to act with the care that an ordinarily prudent person would reasonably be expected to exercise in a like position and under similar circumstances. However, this standard of *conduct* is not always the same as the standard of *liability*. In other words, there is often a difference between how lawyers advise directors and officers about what is appropriate conduct, and how courts decide when to impose liability.

Many students are surprised by how rarely corporate directors are found personally liable for breaching their fiduciary duties. There are two key concepts at work here. One is the "business judgment rule," a judicial presumption in favor of directors. The other is "exculpation," the ability of corporations to include in their charters a provision that insulates directors (and, recently, officers) from personal liability for monetary damages in many circumstances concerning breach of the duty of care.

We begin this chapter with some detail on the business judgment rule, and a colorful case about the Chicago Cubs' decision to shun nighttime baseball. We then turn to a famous Delaware case that generated an equally famous statutory provision. The case, *Smith v. Van Gorkom*, held directors personally liable for breaching their duty of care in deciding to sell the company and is one of the most widely criticized—and cited—corporate law cases. The case led the Delaware legislature to adopt DGCL § 102(b)(7), which allows corporations to adopt exculpation provisions. We conclude the chapter with the classic case of *Francis v. United Jersey Bank*, which raises the issue of the duty of care in a situation of director "nonfeasance" rather than a business decision.

A. The Business Judgment Rule (BJR)

The BJR protects directors from liability for business decisions, even those that were unwise and resulted in losses to the corporation. The BJR has been part of the common law for at least one hundred fifty years. Traditionally, it has shielded directors from personal liability and their decisions from review. If the BJR applies, courts do not interfere with or second-guess directors' actions and board decisions—in essence, it's a doctrine of judicial abstention. If the BJR does not apply, courts may scrutinize the decision as to its fairness to the corporation and its shareholders.

As a procedural matter, the BJR creates a rebuttable presumption that the directors acted on an informed basis, in good faith, and in the honest belief that the action taken was in the best interests of the corporation. Therefore, a plaintiff challenging a board's decision bears the burden of rebutting this presumption, by showing that the directors engaged in self-dealing or acted in bad faith, or that the decision was not a proper exercise of business judgment. A plaintiff might, for example, rebut the BJR by showing that the directors were grossly negligent in failing to inform themselves in making a business decision.

As a policy matter, the BJR reflects the view that directors are better than courts at making business judgments or that boards need wide discretion for making decisions and should not be subject to judicial second-guessing in hindsight. Although the basic idea behind the BJR seems simple, it is hard to express the boundaries of the rule and courts refer to application of the BJR in a variety of ways. Many corporate statutes, including Delaware's, do not even try to codify the common law doctrine; instead, they leave it to courts to define the scope of the BJR and determine whether and how to apply BJR in particular cases.

In light of the BJR, and the potential for exculpation discussed later in this chapter, the MBCA sets out separate provisions for "standards of conduct for directors" and "standards of liability for directors." Consider the excerpt below.

MBCA § 8.30
Standards of Conduct for Directors

(a)   Each member of the board of directors, when discharging the duties of a director, shall act: (i) in good faith, and (ii) in a manner the director reasonably believes to be in the best interests of the corporation.

(b)   The members of the board of directors or a board committee, when becoming informed in connection with their decision-making function or devoting attention to their oversight function, shall discharge their duties with the care that a person in a like position would reasonably believe appropriate under similar circumstances.

(c)   In discharging board or board committee duties, a director shall disclose, or cause to be disclosed, to the other board or committee members information not already known by them but known by the director to be material to the discharge of their decision-making or oversight functions,

> except that disclosure is not required to the extent that the director reasonably believes that doing so would violate a duty imposed under law, a legally enforceable obligation of confidentiality, or a professional ethics rule.

Notice that the MBCA's language related to business judgment is not sharply defined. For example, consider the meaning of one phrase, which appears in § 8.30, stating that a director has the latitude to take action that he or she "reasonably believes to be in the best interests of the corporation."

First, the Official Comment to MBCA § 8.30 states it "sets standards of conduct for directors that focus on the manner in which directors make their decisions, not the correctness of the decisions made." It further explains that "the phrase 'reasonably believes' is both subjective and objective in character. Its first level of analysis is geared to what the particular director, acting in good faith, actually believes. . . The second level of analysis is focused specifically on 'reasonably.' Although a director has wide discretion in gathering information and reaching conclusions, whether a director's belief is reasonable (*i.e.*, could—not would—a reasonable person in a like position and acting in similar circumstances, taking into account that director's knowledge and experience, have arrived at that belief) ultimately involves an overview that is objective in character."

> Any discussion of the "best interests of the corporation" raises the recurring question whether the corporation is a device for the maximization of share-holder profits or whether the corporation is a social institution with responsibilities to its many constituents. Consider the two key parts of this phrase. What is the "corporation"? Whose interests does it include, and how much focus should there be on shareholders? And what are the corporation's "best interests"? How should directors decide what is "best"?

Second, the Comment states that the phrase "best interests of the corporation" is "key to an understanding of a director's duties": "The term 'corporation' is a surrogate for the business enterprise as well as a frame of reference encompassing the shareholder body. In determining the corporation's 'best interests,' the director has wide discretion in deciding how to weigh near-term opportunities versus long-term benefits as well as in making judgments where the interests of various groups of shareholders or other corporate constituencies may differ."

The bottom line is that the BJR gives directors broad latitude in making decisions. If the decision is within the realm of reason, it generally will be protected—a sort of "rational basis" test. This is captured in the Official Comment to MBCA § 8.31, "Standards of Liability for Directors," which provides:

Boards of directors and corporate managers make numerous decisions that involve the balancing of risks and benefits for the enterprise. Although some decisions turn out to have been unwise or the result of a mistake of judgment, it is not reasonable to impose liability for an informed decision made in good faith which with the benefit of hindsight turns out to be wrong or unwise. Therefore, as a general rule, a director is not exposed to personal liability for injury or damage caused by an unwise decision and conduct conforming with the standards of section 8.30 will almost always be protected regardless of the end result. Moreover, the fact that a director's performance fails to meet the standards of section 8.30 does not in itself establish personal liability for damages that the corporation or its shareholders may have suffered as a consequence. Nevertheless, a director can be held liable for misfeasance or nonfeasance in performing his or her duties. Section 8.31 sets forth the standards of liability of directors as distinct from the standards of conduct set forth in section 8.30.

How is the BJR relevant to the court's decision in the case that follows?

Shlensky v. Wrigley

237 N.E.2d 776 (Ill. Ct. App. 1968)

SULLIVAN, JUSTICE.

Deny Suit

This is an appeal from a dismissal of plaintiff's amended complaint on motion of the defendants. The action was a stockholders' derivative suit against the directors for negligence and mismanagement. The corporation was also made a defendant. Plaintiff sought damages and an order that defendants cause the installation of lights in Wrigley Field and the scheduling of night baseball games.

Plaintiff is a minority stockholder of defendant corporation, Chicago National League Ball Club (Inc.), a Delaware corporation with its principal place of business in Chicago, Illinois. Defendant corporation owns and operates the major league professional baseball team known as the Chicago Cubs. The corporation also engages in the operation of Wrigley Field, the Cubs' home park, the concessionaire sales during Cubs' home games, television and radio broadcasts of Cubs' home games, the leasing of the field for football games and other events and receives its share, as visiting team, of admission moneys from games played in other National League stadia. The individual defendants are directors of the Cubs and have served for varying periods of years. Defendant Philip K. Wrigley is also president of the corporation and owner of approximately 80% of the stock therein.

Plaintiff alleges that since night baseball was first played in 1935 nineteen of the twenty major league teams have scheduled night games. In 1966, out of a total of

1620 games in the major leagues, 932 were played at night. Plaintiff alleges that every member of the major leagues, other than the Cubs, scheduled substantially all of its home games in 1966 at night, exclusive of opening days, Saturdays, Sundays, holidays and days prohibited by league rules. Allegedly this has been done for the specific purpose of maximizing attendance and thereby maximizing revenue and income.

The Cubs, in the years 1961–65, sustained operating losses from its direct baseball operations. Plaintiff attributes those losses to inadequate attendance at Cubs' home games. He concludes that if the directors continue to refuse to install lights at Wrigley Field and schedule night baseball games, the Cubs will continue to sustain comparable losses and its financial condition will continue to deteriorate.

Plaintiff alleges that, except for the year 1963, attendance at Cubs' home games has been substantially below that at their road games, many of which were played at night. Plaintiff compares attendance at Cubs' games with that of the Chicago White Sox, an American League club, whose weekday games were generally played at night. The weekend attendance figures for the two teams was similar; however, the White Sox week-night games drew many more patrons than did the Cubs' weekday games.

Plaintiff alleges that the funds for the installation of lights can be readily obtained through financing and the cost of installation would be far more than offset and recaptured by increased revenues and incomes resulting from the increased attendance.

Plaintiff further alleges that defendant Wrigley has refused to install lights, not because of interest in the welfare of the corporation but because of his personal opinions "that baseball is a 'daytime sport' and that the installation of lights and night baseball games will have a deteriorating effect upon the surrounding neighborhood." It is alleged that he has admitted that he is not interested in whether the Cubs would benefit financially from such action because of his concern for the neighborhood, and that he would be willing for the team to play night games if a new stadium were built in Chicago.

Plaintiff alleges that the other defendant directors, with full knowledge of the foregoing matters, have acquiesced in the policy laid down by Wrigley and have permitted him to dominate the board of directors in matters involving the installation of lights and scheduling of night games, even though they knew he was not motivated by a good faith concern as to the best interests of defendant corporation, but solely by his personal views set forth above. It is charged that the directors are acting for a reason or reasons contrary and wholly unrelated to the business interests of the corporation; that such arbitrary and capricious acts constitute mismanagement and waste of corporate assets, and that the directors have been negligent in failing to exercise reasonable care and prudence in the management of the corporate affairs.

The question on appeal is whether plaintiff's amended complaint states a cause of action. It is plaintiff's position that fraud, illegality and conflict of interest are not the only bases for a stockholder's derivative action against the directors. Contrariwise, defendants argue that the courts will not step in and interfere with honest business judgment of the directors unless there is a showing of fraud, illegality or conflict of interest.

The cases in this area are numerous and each differs from the others on a factual basis. However, the courts have pronounced certain ground rules which appear in all cases and which are then applied to the given factual situation. The court in *Wheeler v. Pullman Iron and Steel Co.*, 143 Ill. 197, 207, 32 N.E. 420, 423 (1892), said:

> It is, however, fundamental in the law of corporations, that the majority of its stockholders shall control the policy of the corporation, and regulate and govern the lawful exercise of its franchise and business. Every one purchasing or subscribing for stock in a corporation impliedly agrees that he will be bound by the acts and proceedings done or sanctioned by a majority of the shareholders, or by the agents of the corporation duly chosen by such majority, within the scope of the powers conferred by the charter, and courts of equity will not undertake to control the policy or business methods of a corporation, although it may be seen that a wiser policy might be adopted and the business more successful if other methods were pursued. The majority of shares of its stock, or the agents by the holders thereof lawfully chosen, must be permitted to control the business of the corporation in their discretion, when not in violation of its charter or some public law, or corruptly and fraudulently subversive of the rights and interests of the corporation or of a shareholder.

Plaintiff in the instant case argues that the directors are acting for reasons unrelated to the financial interest and welfare of the Cubs. However, we are not satisfied that the motives assigned to Philip K. Wrigley, and through him to the other directors, are contrary to the best interests of the corporation and the stockholders. For example, it appears to us that the effect on the surrounding neighborhood might well be considered by a director who was considering the patrons who would or would not attend the games if the park were in a poor neighborhood. Furthermore, the long run interest of the corporation in its property value at Wrigley Field might demand all efforts to keep the neighborhood from deteriorating. By these thoughts we do not mean to say that we have decided that the decision of the directors was a correct one. That is beyond our jurisdiction and ability. We are merely saying that the decision is one properly before directors and the motives alleged in the amended complaint showed no fraud, illegality or conflict of interest in their making of that decision.

Finally, we do not agree with plaintiff's contention that failure to follow the example of the other major league clubs in scheduling night games constituted negligence. Plaintiff made no allegation that these teams' night schedules were profitable or that the purpose for which night baseball had been undertaken was fulfilled. Furthermore, it cannot be said that directors, even those of corporations that are losing money, must follow the lead of the other corporations in the field. Directors are elected for their business capabilities and judgment and the courts cannot require them to forego their judgment because of the decisions of directors of other companies. Courts may not decide these questions in the absence of a clear showing of dereliction of duty on the part of the specific directors and mere failure to "follow the crowd" is not such a dereliction.

For the foregoing reasons the order of dismissal entered by the trial court is affirmed.

Points for Discussion

1. Negligence?

Should directors be subject to liability under a negligence standard when making business decisions? Consider three factors: voluntariness, judicial expertise, and risk. Does it matter that shareholders have voluntarily invested in the corporation, and therefore have taken the risk of bad board decisions? What are the pros and cons of after-the-fact litigation as a tool to evaluate board decisions? Finally, do shareholders—particularly diversified shareholders—worry about directors taking too much risk, or not enough risk? Given your answers to these questions, does it make sense that courts have not adopted a negligence standard when evaluating claims challenging directors' ordinary business decisions for breach of the duty of care? Is the duty of care an "aspirational" standard of conduct?

2. Policy rationales.

How might directors act if they did not receive the protection of BJR for their

Under the waste standard and through the operation of the BJR, good-faith board decisions are protected from judicial second-guessing. As we have seen in *Shlensky v. Wrigley* and *Kamin v. American Express Co.* (Chapter 8, Capital Structure), courts are prepared to uphold business decisions without looking into their merits.

In only a handful of cases have courts found good-faith board action so imprudent as to fall outside the BJR, such as when there are suspicions of conflicts of interest or other malfeasance, though the evidence is lacking. For example, in one famous case involving high-risk bank transactions during the height of the Great Depression, the court imposed liability on bank directors for approving the transactions during the precarious period after the 1929 stock market crash. *Litwin v. Allen*, 25 N.Y.S.2d 667 (N.Y. Sup. Ct. 1940). The court faulted the bank directors for approving a transaction "so improvident, so risky, so unusual and unnecessary to be contrary to fundamental conceptions of prudent banking practice."

Although some commentators have explained *Litwin* as imposing higher duties on bank directors, who were often viewed as appropriate deep pockets before federal bank deposit insurance, the case had overtones of self-dealing. The company benefited by the financing transactions was the holding company for a business group in which the bank's parent, J.P. Morgan & Company, was deeply committed. Although the court concluded the plaintiffs had failed to show a conflict of interest, the heightened court scrutiny of the transaction suggested doubts about the good faith of the bank directors.

business decisions? Who might be willing to serve on corporate boards of directors if there were no BJR protection? How much litigation might fill court dockets if plaintiffs did not bear the burden of rebutting the BJR when challenging a board decision for breach of the duty of care?

3. Corporate waste.

One "residual" or "leftover" claim plaintiffs challenging a board decision can make is called "waste." Essentially, the claim is that a decision or transaction was a waste or spoliation of corporate assets. Waste claims rarely succeed because they face an extraordinarily high bar. As the Delaware Supreme Court has stated, there is waste only if "what the corporation has received is so inadequate in value that no person of ordinary, sound business judgment would deem it worth that which the corporation has paid." *Grobow v. Perot*, 539 A.2d 180, 189 (Del. 1988). Thus, the waste standard shields directors from liability and board decisions from review, even when the decision seems clearly unwise or imprudent.

Only if a corporate transaction results in no benefit to the corporation—such as issuing stock without consideration or using corporate funds to discharge personal obligations—have courts found corporate waste. As one court observed, "rarest of all—and indeed, like Nessie, possibly non-existent—would be the case of disinterested business people making non-fraudulent deals (non-negligently) that meet the legal standard of waste!" *Steiner v. Meyerson*, 1995 WL 441999 at *5 (Del. Ch. 1995). Why wasn't the board's refusal in *Wrigley* to adopt nighttime baseball an instance of corporate waste?

—————

B. *Smith v. Van Gorkom*

Given this backdrop, one would expect judges to hold directors liable for poor decisions rarely, if at all. We now turn to one such rare case. We begin with a summary of the facts and then provide an extended excerpt of this landmark case. Delaware judicial opinions tend to be long and fact intensive, especially in important corporate law cases. Finally, we discuss the reaction to the court's decision and some of the policy issues it raised.

1. Background of the Case

The Trans Union Corporation was a publicly traded company in the rail leasing business. Its chairman and chief executive officer was Jerome W. Van Gorkom, who was nearing retirement age when the events in the case occurred. Its board of directors consisted of five company officers and five outside directors. Four of the latter were CEOs of large public corporations; the fifth was the former dean of the University of Chicago Business School.

Trans Union had been facing a major business problem relating to investment tax credits (ITCs). Its competitors generated sufficient taxable income to allow them to make use of all ITCs they generated and took these tax benefits into account in setting the terms of their railcar leases. Trans Union, however, did not have sufficient income to take advantage of all of its ITCs, but nevertheless had to match its competitors' prices. In July 1980, Trans Union management submitted its annual revision of the company's five-year forecast to the board. That report discussed alternative solutions to the ITC problem and concluded that the company had sufficient time to develop its course of action. The report did not mention the possible sale of the company.

On August 27, Van Gorkom met with senior management to consider the ITC problem. Among the ideas mentioned were selling Trans Union to a company with a large amount of taxable income and engaging in a leveraged buyout. This latter alternative was discussed again at a management meeting on September 5. At that meeting, the chief financial officer, Donald Romans, presented preliminary calculations for a leveraged buyout based on a price between $50 and $60 per share, but did not state that these calculations established a fair price for the company. They merely "ran the numbers" at $50 and $60 per share for a "rough" estimate of the cash flow needed for a leveraged buyout. While Van Gorkom rejected the leveraged buyout idea at the time, he stated that he would be willing to sell his own shares at $55 per share.

> The named plaintiff in *Van Gorkom*, B. Alden Smith, was also motivated by tax concerns, but of a different kind. Smith's main beef with the deal was not the price, but the fact that it would trigger his obligation to pay capital gains taxes. Smith wanted the deal to be done as a tax-free reorganization in which he would receive stock instead of cash, but the board had decided differently. It would have been fruitless for Smith to challenge the board's decision about how to structure the deal—that would fall under the BJR—so he decided to institute a class action and challenge the way the board had decided on and disclosed the negotiations of the price instead.

Then, without consulting the board of directors or any officers, Van Gorkom decided to meet with Jay A. Pritzker, a corporate takeover specialist he knew socially. Prior to that meeting, Van Gorkom instructed Trans Union's controller, Carl Peterson, to prepare a confidential calculation of the feasibility of a leveraged buyout at $55 per share. On September 13, Van Gorkom proposed a sale of Trans Union to Pritzker at $55 per share. Two days later, Pritzker advised Van Gorkom that he was interested in a purchase at that price. By September 18, after two more meetings that included two Trans Union officers and an outside consultant, Van Gorkom knew that Pritzker was ready to propose a cash-out merger at $55 per share if Pritzker could also have the option to buy one million shares of Trans Union treasury stock at $38 per share (a price which was 75 cents above the current market price). Pritzker also insisted that the Trans Union board act on his proposal within three days, *i.e.,* by Sunday, September 21, and instructed his attorney to draft the merger documents.

On September 19, without consulting Trans Union's legal department, Van Gorkom engaged outside counsel as merger specialists. He called for meetings of senior management and the board of directors for the next day, but only those officers who had met with Pritzker knew the subject of the meetings.

Senior management's reaction to Pritzker's proposal was completely negative. Romans objected both to the price and to the sale of treasury shares (shares that Trans Union previously had repurchased in the market) to Pritzker as a "lock-up." Immediately after this meeting, Van Gorkom met with the board. He made a twenty-minute oral presentation outlining the Pritzker offer but did not furnish copies of the proposed merger agreement. Nor did he tell the board that he was the one who had approached Pritzker and mentioned the $55 price. Van Gorkom stated that: Pritzker would purchase all outstanding Trans Union shares for $55 each and Trans Union would be merged into a wholly owned entity Pritzker formed for this purpose; for 90 days Trans Union would be free to receive, but not to solicit competing offers; other bidders could be furnished only published, rather than proprietary, information; the Trans Union board had to act by Sunday evening, September 21; the offer was subject to Pritzker obtaining financing by October 10, 1980; and if Pritzker met or waived the financing contingency, Trans Union was obliged to sell him one million newly issued shares at $38 per share. According to Van Gorkom, the issue for the board was whether $55 was a fair price rather than the best price. He said that putting Trans Union "up for auction" through a 90-day "market test" would allow the free market an opportunity to judge whether $55 was fair. Outside counsel advised the board that they might be sued if they did not accept the offer, and that a fairness opinion from an investment banker was not legally required.

At the board meeting, Romans stated that his prior studies in connection with a possible leveraged buyout did not indicate a fair price for the stock or a valuation of the company. However, it was his opinion that $55 was "at the beginning of the range" of a fair price.

The board meeting lasted two hours, at the end of which the board approved the merger, with two conditions: (1) Trans Union reserved the right to accept any better offer during the 90-day market test period; and (2) Trans Union could share its proprietary information with other potential bidders. At that time, however, the board did not reserve the right to actively solicit other bids.

That evening Van Gorkom signed the as-yet-unamended merger agreement, still unread either by himself or the other board members, "in the midst of a formal party which he hosted for the opening of the Chicago Lyric Opera."

On September 22, Trans Union issued a press release announcing a "definitive" merger agreement with Marmon Group, Inc., an affiliate of a Pritzker holding company. Within ten days, rebellious key officers threatened to resign. Van Gorkom met with Pritzker, who agreed to modify the agreement to include the conditions imposed by the board, provided that the "dissident" officers agreed to stay with Trans Union for at least six months following the merger.

The board reconvened on October 8 and, without reading the text, approved the proposed amendments regarding the 90-day market test and solicitation of other bids. The board also authorized the company to employ its investment banker to solicit other offers.

Although the amendments had not yet been prepared, Trans Union issued a press release on the following day stating that it could actively seek other offers and had retained an investment banker for that purpose. The release also said that Pritzker had obtained the necessary financing commitments and had acquired one million shares of Trans Union at $38 per share and that if Trans Union had not received a more favorable offer by February 1, 1981, its shareholders would meet to vote on the Pritzker bid. Van Gorkom executed the amendments to the merger agreement on October 10, without consulting the board and apparently without fully understanding that the amendments significantly constrained Trans Union's ability to negotiate a better deal.

Trans Union received only two serious offers during the market test period. One, from General Electric Credit Corporation, fell through when Trans Union would not rescind its agreement with Pritzker to give GE Credit extra time. The other offer, a leveraged buyout by management (except Van Gorkom) arranged through Kohlberg, Kravis, Roberts & Co. (KKR) was made in early December at $60 per share. It was contingent upon completing equity and bank financing, which KKR said was 80% complete, with terms and conditions substantially the same as the Pritzker deal. Van Gorkom, however, did not view the KKR deal as "firm" because of the financing contingency (even though the Pritzker offer had been similarly conditioned), and he refused to issue a press release about it. KKR planned to present its offer to the Trans Union board, but withdrew shortly before the scheduled meeting, noting that a senior Trans Union officer had withdrawn from the KKR purchasing group after Van Gorkom spoke to him. Van Gorkom denied influencing the officer's decision, and he made no mention of it to the board at the meeting later that day.

The shareholder lawsuit was brought on December 19, 1980. Management's proxy statement was mailed on January 21 for a meeting scheduled for February 10, 1981. The Trans Union board met on January 26 and gave final approval to the Pritzker merger, as well as a supplement to its proxy statement that was mailed the next day. On February 10, 1981, the shareholders approved the Pritzker merger by a large majority.

Smith v. Van Gorkom

488 A.2d 858 (Del. 1985)

Horsey, Justice (for the majority).

We turn to the issue of the application of the business judgment rule to the September 20 meeting of the Board.

The Court of Chancery concluded from the evidence that the Board of Directors' approval of the Pritzker merger proposal fell within the protection of the business judgment rule. The Court found that the Board had given sufficient time and attention to the transaction, since the directors had considered the Pritzker proposal on three different occasions, on September 20, and on October 8, 1980 and finally on January 26, 1981. On that basis, the Court reasoned that the Board had acquired, over the four-month period, sufficient information to reach an informed business judgment on the cash-out merger proposal. The Court ruled:

> that given the market value of Trans Union's stock, the business acumen of the members of the board of Trans Union, the substantial premium over market offered by the Pritzkers and the ultimate effect on the merger price provided by the prospect of other bids for the stock in question, that the board of directors of Trans Union did not act recklessly or improvidently in determining on a course of action which they believed to be in the best interest of the stockholders of Trans Union.

The Court of Chancery made but one finding; *i.e.*, that the Board's conduct over the entire period from September 20 through January 26, 1981 was not reckless or improvident, but informed. This ultimate conclusion was premised upon three subordinate findings, one explicit and two implied. The Court's explicit finding was that Trans Union's Board was "free to turn down the Pritzker proposal" not only on September 20 but also on October 8, 1980 and on January 26, 1981. The Court's implied, subordinate findings were: (1) that no legally binding agreement was reached by the parties until January 26; and (2) that if a higher offer were to be forthcoming, the market test would have produced it, and Trans Union would have been contractually free to accept such higher offer. However, the Court offered no factual basis or legal support for any of these findings; and the record compels contrary conclusions.

Under Delaware law, the business judgment rule is the offspring of the fundamental principle, codified in 8 Del. C. § 141(a), that the business and affairs of a Delaware corporation are managed by or under its board of directors. In carrying out their managerial roles, directors are charged with an unyielding fiduciary duty to the corporation and its shareholders. The business judgment rule exists to protect and promote the full and free exercise of the managerial power granted to Delaware directors. The rule itself "is a presumption that in making a business decision, the directors of a corporation acted on an informed basis, in good faith and in the honest belief that the action taken was in the best interests of the company." *Aronson v. Lewis,* 473 A.2d 805, 812 (Del. 1984). Thus, the party attacking a board decision as uninformed must rebut the presumption that its business judgment was an informed one.

The determination of whether a business judgment is an informed one turns on whether the directors have informed themselves "prior to making a business decision, of all material information reasonably available to them." *Id.*

Under the business judgment rule there is no protection for directors who have made "an unintelligent or unadvised judgment." *Mitchell v. Highland-Western Glass,* 167 A. 831, 833 (Del. Ch. 1933). A director's duty to inform himself in preparation for a decision derives from the fiduciary capacity in which he serves the corporation and its stockholders. Since a director is vested with the responsibility for the management of the affairs of the corporation, he must execute that duty with the recognition that he acts on behalf of others. Such obligation does not tolerate faithlessness or self-dealing. But fulfillment of the fiduciary function requires more than the mere absence of bad faith or fraud. Representation of the financial interests of others imposes on a director an affirmative duty to protect those interests and to proceed with a critical eye in assessing information of the type and under the circumstances present here.

Thus, a director's duty to exercise an informed business judgment is in the nature of a duty of care, as distinguished from a duty of loyalty. Here, there were no allegations of fraud, bad faith, or self-dealing, or proof thereof. Hence, it is presumed that the directors reached their business judgment in good faith, and considerations of motive are irrelevant to the issue before us.

The standard of care applicable to a director's duty of care has also been recently restated by this Court. In *Aronson,* we stated:

> While the Delaware cases use a variety of terms to describe the applicable standard of care, our analysis satisfies us that under the business judgment rule director liability is predicated upon concepts of gross negligence. (footnote omitted).

We again confirm that view. We think the concept of gross negligence is also the proper standard for determining whether a business judgment reached by a board of directors was an informed one.

In the specific context of a proposed merger of domestic corporations, a director has a duty under 8 Del. C. § 251(b), along with his fellow directors, to act in an informed and deliberate manner in determining whether to approve an agreement of merger before submitting the proposal to the stockholders. Certainly in the merger context, a director may not abdicate that duty by leaving to the shareholders alone the decision to approve or disapprove the agreement. Only an agreement of merger satisfying the requirements of 8 Del. C. § 251(b) may be submitted to the shareholders under § 251(c).

It is against those standards that the conduct of the directors of Trans Union must be tested, as a matter of law and as a matter of fact, regarding their exercise of an informed business judgment in voting to approve the Pritzker merger proposal.

III.

The issue of whether the directors reached an informed decision to "sell" the Company on September 20, 1980 must be determined only upon the basis of the information then reasonably available to the directors and relevant to their decision to accept the Pritzker merger proposal. This is not to say that the directors were precluded from altering their original plan of action, had they done so in an informed manner. What we do say is that the question of whether the directors reached an informed business judgment in agreeing to sell the Company, pursuant to the terms of the September 20 Agreement presents, in reality, two questions: (A) whether the directors reached an informed business judgment on September 20, 1980; and (B) if they did not, whether the directors' actions taken subsequent to September 20 were adequate to cure any infirmity in their action taken on September 20. We first consider the directors' September 20 action in terms of their reaching an informed business judgment.

–A–

On the record before us, we must conclude that the Board of Directors did not reach an informed business judgment on September 20, 1980 in voting to "sell" the Company for $55 per share pursuant to the Pritzker cash-out merger proposal. Our reasons, in summary, are as follows:

The directors (1) did not adequately inform themselves as to Van Gorkom's role in forcing the "sale" of the Company and in establishing the per share purchase price; (2) were uninformed as to the intrinsic value of the Company; and (3) given these circumstances, at a minimum, were grossly negligent in approving the "sale" of the Company upon two hours' consideration, without prior notice, and without the exigency of a crisis or emergency.

As has been noted, the Board based its September 20 decision to approve the cash-out merger primarily on Van Gorkom's representations. None of the directors, other than Van Gorkom and Chelberg, had any prior knowledge that the purpose of the meeting was to propose a cash-out merger of Trans Union. No members of Senior Management were present, other than Chelberg, Romans and Peterson; and the latter two had only learned of the proposed sale an hour earlier. Both general counsel Moore and former general counsel Browder attended the meeting, but were equally uninformed as to the purpose of the meeting and the documents to be acted upon.

Without any documents before them concerning the proposed transaction, the members of the Board were required to rely entirely upon Van Gorkom's 20-minute oral presentation of the proposal. No written summary of the terms of the merger was presented; the directors were given no documentation to support the adequacy of $55 price per share for sale of the Company; and the Board had before it nothing more than Van Gorkom's statement of his understanding of the substance of an agreement which he admittedly had never read, nor which any member of the Board had ever seen.

Under 8 Del. C. § 141(e) "directors are fully protected in relying in good faith on reports made by officers." The term "report" has been liberally construed to include reports of informal personal investigations by corporate officers. However, there is no evidence that any "report," as defined under § 141(e), concerning the Pritzker proposal, was presented to the Board on September 20. Van Gorkom's oral presentation of his understanding of the terms of the proposed Merger Agreement, which he had not seen, and Romans' brief oral statement of his preliminary study regarding the feasibility of a leveraged buy-out of Trans Union do not qualify as § 141(e) "reports" for these reasons: The former lacked substance because Van Gorkom was basically uninformed as to the essential provisions of the very document about which he was talking. Romans' statement was irrelevant to the issues before the Board since it did not purport to be a valuation study. At a minimum for a report to enjoy the status conferred by § 141(e), it must be pertinent to the subject matter upon which a board is called to act, and otherwise be entitled to good faith, not blind, reliance. Considering all of the surrounding circumstances—hastily calling the meeting without prior notice of its subject matter, the proposed sale of the Company without any prior consideration of the issue or necessity therefore, the urgent time constraints imposed by Pritzker, and the total absence of any documentation whatsoever—the directors were duty bound to make reasonable inquiry of Van Gorkom and Romans, and if they had done so, the inadequacy of that upon which they now claim to have relied would have been apparent.

The defendants rely on the following factors to sustain the Trial Court's finding that the Board's decision was an informed one: (1) the magnitude of the premium or spread between the $55 Pritzker offering price and Trans Union's current market price of $38 per share; (2) the amendment of the Agreement as submitted on September 20 to permit the Board to accept any better offer during the "market test" period; (3) the collective experience and expertise of the Board's "inside" and "outside" directors; and (4) their reliance on Brennan's legal advice that the directors might be sued if they rejected the Pritzker proposal. We discuss each of these grounds *seriatim:*

(1)

A substantial premium may provide one reason to recommend a merger, but in the absence of other sound valuation information, the fact of a premium alone does not provide an adequate basis upon which to assess the fairness of an offering price. Here, the judgment reached as to the adequacy of the premium was based on a comparison between the historically depressed Trans Union market price and the amount of the Pritzker offer. Using market price as a basis for concluding that the premium adequately reflected the true value of the Company was a clearly faulty, indeed fallacious, premise, as the defendants' own evidence demonstrates.

The record is clear that before September 20, Van Gorkom and other members of Trans Union's Board knew that the market had consistently undervalued the worth of Trans Union's stock, despite steady increases in the Company's operating income in the seven years preceding the merger. The Board related this occurrence in large part to Trans Union's inability to use its ITCs as previously noted. Van Gorkom testified that he did not believe the market price accurately reflected Trans Union's true worth; and several of the directors testified that, as a general rule, most chief executives think that the market undervalues their companies' stock. Yet, on September 20, Trans Union's Board apparently believed that the market stock price accurately reflected the value of the Company for the purpose of determining the adequacy of the premium for its sale.

The parties do not dispute that a publicly-traded stock price is solely a measure of the value of a minority position and, thus, market price represents only the value of a single share. Nevertheless, on September 20, the Board assessed the adequacy of the premium over market, offered by Pritzker, solely by comparing it with Trans Union's current and historical stock price.

Indeed, as of September 20, the Board had no other information on which to base a determination of the intrinsic value of Trans Union as a going concern. As of September 20, the Board had made no evaluation of the Company designed to value the entire enterprise, nor had the Board ever previously considered selling the Company or consenting to a buy-out merger. Thus, the adequacy of a premium is indeterminate unless it is assessed in terms of other competent and sound valuation information that reflects the value of the particular business.

Despite the foregoing facts and circumstances, there was no call by the Board, either on September 20 or thereafter, for any valuation study or documentation of the $55 price per share as a measure of the fair value of the Company in a cash-out context. It is undisputed that the major asset of Trans Union was its cash flow. Yet, at no time did the Board call for a valuation study taking into account that highly significant element of the Company's assets.

We do not imply that an outside valuation study is essential to support an informed business judgment; nor do we state that fairness opinions by independent investment bankers are required as a matter of law. Often insiders familiar with the business of a going concern are in a better position than are outsiders to gather relevant information; and under appropriate circumstances, such directors may be fully protected in relying in good faith upon the valuation reports of their management.

Here, the record establishes that the Board did not request its Chief Financial Officer, Romans, to make any valuation study or review of the proposal to determine the adequacy of $55 per share for sale of the Company. The Board rested on Romans' elicited response that the $55 figure was within a "fair price range" within the context of a leveraged buy-out. No director sought any further information from Romans. No director asked him why he put $55 at the bottom of his range. No director asked Romans for any details as to his study, the reason why it had been undertaken or its depth. No director asked to see the study; and no director asked Romans whether Trans Union's finance department could do a fairness study within the remaining 36-hour period available under the Pritzker offer.

Had the Board, or any member, made an inquiry of Romans, he presumably would have responded as he testified: that his calculations were rough and preliminary; and, that the study was not designed to determine the fair value of the Company, but rather to assess the feasibility of a leveraged buy-out financed by the Company's projected cash flow, making certain assumptions as to the purchaser's borrowing needs. Romans would have presumably also informed the Board of his view, and the widespread view of Senior Management, that the timing of the offer was wrong and the offer inadequate.

The record also establishes that the Board accepted without scrutiny Van Gorkom's representation as to the fairness of the $55 price per share for sale of the Company—a subject that the Board had never previously considered. The Board thereby failed to discover that Van Gorkom had suggested the $55 price to Pritzker and, most crucially, that Van Gorkom had arrived at the $55 figure based on calculations designed solely to determine the feasibility of a leveraged buy-out.[19] No questions were raised either as to the tax implications of a cash-out merger or how the price for the one million share option granted Pritzker was calculated.

We do not say that the Board of Directors was not entitled to give some credence to Van Gorkom's representation that $55 was an adequate or fair price. Under § 141(e), the directors were entitled to rely upon their chairman's opinion of value and adequacy, provided that such opinion was reached on a sound basis. Here, the issue is whether the directors informed themselves as to all information that was reasonably available to them. Had they done so, they would have learned of the source and derivation of the $55 price and could not reasonably have relied thereupon in good faith.

subject to $55

---

[19]   As of September 20 the directors did not know: that Van Gorkom had arrived at the $55 figure alone, and subjectively, as the figure to be used by Controller Peterson in creating a feasible structure for a leveraged buy-out by a prospective purchaser; that Van Gorkom had not sought advice, information or assistance from either inside or outside Trans Union directors as to the value of the Company as an entity or the fair price per share for 100% of its stock; that Van Gorkom had not consulted with the Company's investment bankers or other financial analysts; that Van Gorkom had not consulted with or confided in any officer or director of the Company except Chelberg; and that Van Gorkom had deliberately chosen to ignore the advice and opinion of the members of his Senior Management group regarding the adequacy of the $55 price.

None of the directors, Management or outside, were investment bankers or financial analysts. Yet the Board did not consider recessing the meeting until a later hour that day (or requesting an extension of Pritzker's Sunday evening deadline) to give it time to elicit more information as to the sufficiency of the offer, either from inside Management (in particular Romans) or from Trans Union's own investment banker, Salomon Brothers, whose Chicago specialist in merger and acquisitions was known to the Board and familiar with Trans Union's affairs.

Thus, the record compels the conclusion that on September 20 the Board lacked valuation information adequate to reach an informed business judgment as to the fairness of $55 per share for sale of the Company.

(2)

This brings us to the post-September 20 "market test" upon which the defendants ultimately rely to confirm the reasonableness of their September 20 decision to accept the Pritzker proposal. In this connection, the directors present a two-part argument: (a) that by making a "market test" of Pritzker's $55 per share offer a condition of their September 20 decision to accept his offer, they cannot be found to have acted impulsively or in an uninformed manner on September 20; and (b) that the adequacy of the $17 premium for sale of the Company was conclusively established over the following 90 to 120 days by the most reliable evidence available—the marketplace. Thus, the defendants impliedly contend that the "market test" eliminated the need for the Board to perform any other form of fairness test either on September 20, or thereafter.

Again, the facts of record do not support the defendants' argument. There is no evidence: (a) that the Merger Agreement was effectively amended to give the Board freedom to put Trans Union up for auction sale to the highest bidder; or (b) that a public auction was in fact permitted to occur.

(3)

The directors' unfounded reliance on both the premium and the market test as the basis for accepting the Pritzker proposal undermines the defendants' remaining contention that the Board's collective experience and sophistication was a sufficient basis for finding that it reached its September 20 decision with informed, reasonable deliberation.[21] Compare *Gimbel v. Signal Companies, Inc.*, 316 A.2d 599 (Del. Ch.

---

[21] Trans Union's five "inside" directors had backgrounds in law and accounting, 116 years of collective employment by the Company and 68 years of combined experience on its Board. Trans Union's five "outside" directors included four chief executives of major corporations and an economist who was a former dean of a major school of business and chancellor of a university. The "outside" directors had 78 years of combined experience as chief executive officers of major corporations and 50 years of cumulative experience as directors of Trans Union. Thus, defendants argue that the Board was eminently qualified to reach an informed judgment on the proposed "sale" of Trans Union notwithstanding their lack of any advance notice of the proposal, the shortness of their deliberation, and their determination

1974), aff'd per curiam, 316 A.2d 619 (Del. 1974). There, the Court of Chancery preliminarily enjoined a board's sale of stock of its wholly-owned subsidiary for an alleged grossly inadequate price. It did so based on a finding that the business judgment rule had been pierced for failure of management to give its board "the opportunity to make a reasonable and reasoned decision." The Court there reached this result notwithstanding the board's sophistication and experience; the company's need of immediate cash; and the board's need to act promptly due to the impact of an energy crisis on the value of the underlying assets being sold—all of its subsidiary's oil and gas interests. The Court found those factors denoting competence to be outweighed by evidence of gross negligence; that management in effect sprang the deal on the board by negotiating the asset sale without informing the board; that the buyer intended to "force a quick decision" by the board; that the board meeting was called on only one-and-a-half days' notice; that its outside directors were not notified of the meeting's purpose; that during a meeting spanning "a couple of hours" a sale of assets worth $480 million was approved; and that the Board failed to obtain a current appraisal of its oil and gas interests. The analogy of Signal to the case at bar is significant.

(4)

Part of the defense is based on a claim that the directors relied on legal advice rendered at the September 20 meeting by James Brennan, Esquire, who was present at Van Gorkom's request. Unfortunately, Brennan did not appear and testify at trial even though his firm participated in the defense of this action.

Several defendants testified that Brennan advised them that Delaware law did not require a fairness opinion or an outside valuation of the Company before the Board could act on the Pritzker proposal. If given, the advice was correct. However, that did not end the matter. Unless the directors had before them adequate information regarding the intrinsic value of the Company, upon which a proper exercise of business judgment could be made, mere advice of this type is meaningless; and, given this record of the defendants' failures, it constitutes no defense here.[22]

A second claim is that counsel advised the Board it would be subject to lawsuits if it rejected the $55 per share offer. It is, of course, a fact of corporate life that today when faced with difficult or sensitive issues, directors often are subject to suit, irrespective of the decisions they make. However, counsel's mere acknowledgement of this circumstance cannot be rationally translated into a justification for a board permitting itself to be stampeded into a patently unadvised act. While suit might

---

not to consult with their investment banker or to obtain a fairness opinion.

[22] Nonetheless, we are satisfied that in an appropriate factual context a proper exercise of business judgment may include, as one of its aspects, reasonable reliance upon the advice of counsel. This is wholly outside the statutory protections of 8 Del. C. § 141(e) involving reliance upon reports of officers, certain experts and books and records of the company.

result from the rejection of a merger or tender offer, Delaware law makes clear that a board acting within the ambit of the business judgment rule faces no ultimate liability. Thus, we cannot conclude that the mere threat of litigation, acknowledged by counsel, constitutes either legal advice or any valid basis upon which to pursue an uninformed course.

–B–

[The court examined the board's post-September 20 conduct and determined this conduct did not cure the deficiencies in its September 20 actions.]

IV.

As to questions which were not originally addressed by the parties in their briefing of this case the parties' response, including reargument, has led the majority of the Court to conclude: (1) that since all of the defendant directors, outside as well as inside, take a unified position, we are required to treat all of the directors as one as to whether they are entitled to the protection of the business judgment rule; and (2) that considerations of good faith, including the presumption that the directors acted in good faith, are irrelevant in determining the threshold issue of whether the directors as a Board exercised an informed business judgment. For the same reason, we must reject defense counsel's *ad hominem* argument for affirmance: that reversal may result in a multi-million dollar class award against the defendants for having made an allegedly uninformed business judgment in a transaction not involving any personal gain, self-dealing or claim of bad faith.

Plaintiffs have not claimed, nor did the Trial Court decide, that $55 was a grossly inadequate price per share for sale of the Company. That being so, the presumption that a board's judgment as to adequacy of price represents an honest exercise of business judgment (absent proof that the sale price was grossly inadequate) is irrelevant to the threshold question of whether an informed judgment was reached.

V.

The defendants ultimately rely on the stockholder vote of February 10 for exoneration. The defendants contend that the stockholders' "overwhelming" vote approving the Pritzker Merger Agreement had the legal effect of curing any failure of the Board to reach an informed business judgment in its approval of the merger.

The parties tacitly agree that a discovered failure of the Board to reach an informed business judgment in approving the merger constitutes a voidable, rather than a void, act. Hence, the merger can be sustained, notwithstanding the infirmity of the Board's action, if its approval by majority vote of the shareholders is found to have been based on an informed electorate. *Cf. Michelson v. Duncan*, 407 A.2d 211 (Del. 1979), *aff'g in part and rev'g in part*, 386 A.2d 1144 (Del. Ch. 1978). The disagreement between the parties arises over: (1) the Board's burden of disclosing to the shareholders all relevant and material information; and (2) the sufficiency of the evidence as to whether the Board satisfied that burden.

In *Lynch v. Vickers Energy Corp.,* this Court held that corporate directors owe to their stockholders a fiduciary duty to disclose all facts germane to the transaction at issue in an atmosphere of complete candor. Applying this standard to the record before us, we find that Trans Union's stockholders were not fully informed of all facts material to their vote on the Pritzker Merger and that the Trial Court's ruling to the contrary is clearly erroneous. We list the material deficiencies in the proxy materials: (1) The fact that the Board had no reasonably adequate information indicative of the intrinsic value of the Company, other than a concededly depressed market price, was without question material to the shareholders voting on the merger. (2) We find false and misleading the Board's characterization of the Romans report in the Supplemental Proxy Statement. Nowhere does the Board disclose that Romans stated to the Board that his calculations were made in a "search for ways to justify a price in connection with" a leveraged buy-out transaction, "rather than to say what the shares are worth." (3) We find misleading the Board's references to the "substantial" premium offered. The Board gave as their primary reason in support of the merger the "substantial premium" shareholders would receive. But the Board did not disclose its failure to assess the premium offered in terms of other relevant valuation techniques, thereby rendering questionable its determination as to the substantiality of the premium over an admittedly depressed stock market price.

The burden must fall on defendants who claim ratification based on shareholder vote to establish that the shareholder approval resulted from a fully informed electorate. On the record before us, it is clear that the Board failed to meet that burden.

VI.

To summarize: we hold that the directors of Trans Union breached their fiduciary duty to their stockholders (1) by their failure to inform themselves of all information reasonably available to them and relevant to their decision to recommend the Pritzker merger; and (2) by their failure to disclose all material information such as a reasonable stockholder would consider important in deciding whether to approve the Pritzker offer.

We hold, therefore, that the Trial Court committed reversible error in applying the business judgment rule in favor of the director defendants in this case.

On remand, the Court of Chancery shall conduct an evidentiary hearing to determine the fair value of the shares represented by the plaintiffs' class, based on the intrinsic value of Trans Union on September 20, 1980. Thereafter, an award of damages may be entered to the extent that the fair value of Trans Union exceeds $55 per share.

Reversed and Remanded for proceedings consistent herewith.

McNEILLY, JUSTICE, dissenting:

The majority opinion reads like an advocate's closing address to a hostile jury. And I say that not lightly. Throughout the opinion great emphasis is directed only to the negative, with nothing more than lip service granted the positive aspects of this case. In my opinion Chancellor Marvel (retired) should have been affirmed. The Chancellor's opinion was the product of well reasoned conclusions, based upon a sound deductive process, clearly supported by the evidence and entitled to deference in this appeal. Because of my diametrical opposition to all evidentiary conclusions of the majority, I respectfully dissent.

It would serve no useful purpose, particularly at this late date, for me to dissent at great length. I restrain myself from doing so, but feel compelled to at least point out what I consider to be the most glaring deficiencies in the majority opinion. The majority has spoken and has effectively said that Trans Union's Directors have been the victims of a "fast shuffle" by Van Gorkom and Pritzker. That is the beginning of the majority's comedy of errors. The first and most important error made is the majority's assessment of the directors' knowledge of the affairs of Trans Union and their combined ability to act in this situation under the protection of the business judgment rule.

Trans Union's Board of Directors consisted of ten men, five of whom were "inside" directors and five of whom were "outside" directors. The "inside" directors were Van Gorkom, Chelberg, Bonser, William B. Browder, Senior Vice–President–Law, and Thomas P. O'Boyle, Senior Vice–President–Administration. At the time the merger was proposed the inside five directors had collectively been employed by the Company for 116 years and had 68 years of combined experience as directors. The "outside" directors were A.W. Wallis, William B. Johnson, Joseph B. Lanterman, Graham J. Morgan and Robert W. Reneker. With the exception of Wallis, these were all chief executive officers of Chicago based corporations that were at least as large as Trans Union. The five "outside" directors had 78 years of combined experience as chief executive officers, and 53 years cumulative service as Trans Union directors.

The inside directors wear their badge of expertise in the corporate affairs of Trans Union on their sleeves. But what about the outsiders? Dr. Wallis is or was an economist and math statistician, a professor of economics at Yale University, dean of the graduate school of business at the University of Chicago, and Chancellor of the University of Rochester. Dr. Wallis had been on the Board of Trans Union since 1962. He also was on the Board of Bausch & Lomb, Kodak, Metropolitan Life Insurance Company, Standard Oil and others.

William B. Johnson is a University of Pennsylvania law graduate, President of Railway Express until 1966, Chairman and Chief Executive of I.C. Industries Holding Company, and member of Trans Union's Board since 1968.

Joseph Lanterman, a Certified Public Accountant, is or was President and Chief Executive of American Steel, on the Board of International Harvester, Peoples Energy, Illinois Bell Telephone, Harris Bank and Trust Company, Kemper Insurance Company and a director of Trans Union for four years.

Graham Morgan is a chemist, was Chairman and Chief Executive Officer of U.S. Gypsum, and in the 17 and 18 years prior to the Trans Union transaction had been involved in 31 or 32 corporate takeovers.

Robert Reneker attended University of Chicago and Harvard Business Schools. He was President and Chief Executive of Swift and Company, director of Trans Union since 1971, and member of the Boards of seven other corporations including U.S. Gypsum and the Chicago Tribune.

Directors of this caliber are not ordinarily taken in by a "fast shuffle." I submit they were not taken into this multi-million dollar corporate transaction without being fully informed and aware of the state of the art as it pertained to the entire corporate panorama of Trans Union. True, even directors such as these, with their business acumen, interest and expertise, can go astray. I do not believe that to be the case here. These men knew Trans Union like the back of their hands and were more than well qualified to make on the spot informed business judgments concerning the affairs of Trans Union including a 100% sale of the corporation. Lest we forget, the corporate world of then and now operates on what is so aptly referred to as "the fast track." These men were at the time an integral part of that world, all professional business men, not intellectual figureheads.

The majority of this Court holds that the Board's decision, reached on September 20, 1980, to approve the merger was not the product of an *informed* business judgment, that the Board's subsequent efforts to amend the Merger Agreement and take other curative action were *legally and factually* ineffectual, and that the Board did *not deal with complete candor* with the stockholders by failing to disclose all material facts, which they knew or should have known, before securing the stockholders' approval of the merger. I disagree.

At the time of the September 20, 1980 meeting the Board was acutely aware of Trans Union and its prospects. The problems created by accumulated investment tax credits and accelerated depreciation were discussed repeatedly at Board meetings, and all of the directors understood the problem thoroughly. Moreover, at the July 1980 Board meeting the directors had reviewed Trans Union's newly prepared five-year forecast, and at the August 1980 meeting Van Gorkom presented the results of a comprehensive study of Trans Union made by The Boston Consulting Group. This study was prepared over an 18 month period and consisted of a detailed analysis of all Trans Union subsidiaries, including competitiveness, profitability, cash throw-off, cash consumption, technical competence and future prospects for contribution to Trans Union's combined net income.

At the September 20 meeting Van Gorkom reviewed all aspects of the proposed transaction and repeated the explanation of the Pritzker offer he had earlier given to senior management. Having heard Van Gorkom's explanation of the Pritzker's offer, and Brennan's explanation of the merger documents the directors discussed the matter. Out of this discussion arose an insistence on the part of the directors that two modifications to the offer be made. First, they required that any potential competing bidder be given access to the same information concerning Trans Union that had been provided to the Pritzkers. Second, the merger documents were to be modified to reflect the fact that the directors could accept a better offer and would not be required to recommend the Pritzker offer if a better offer was made.

I have no quarrel with the majority's analysis of the business judgment rule. It is the application of that rule to these facts which is wrong. An overview of the entire record, rather than the limited view of bits and pieces which the majority has exploded like popcorn, convinces me that the directors made an informed business judgment which was buttressed by their test of the market.

---

2.   Aftermath of the Case

The defendant directors of Trans Union settled the case by agreeing to pay $23.5 million to the plaintiff class. The payments were made to approximately 12,000 former shareholders of Trans Union who held stock between September 19, 1980 and February 10, 1981. Of that amount, the directors' liability insurance carrier paid about $10 million. The $13.5 million balance was paid by the Pritzker group on behalf of the Trans Union directors, even though the Pritzker group was not a defendant. The Pritzker group made the payment on the condition the individual directors would each contribute 10% of their uninsured liability to a charity of Pritzker's choice, although Van Gorkom actually ended up making charitable contributions on behalf of some of the directors.

Van Gorkom created a firestorm in much of the corporate community and among academics, judges, and commentators. Few had believed that the Delaware Supreme Court would hold experienced directors personally liable in a case in which the shareholders received a 50% premium over the existing market price for their stock. Some praised the case for its focus on corporate governance and fiduciary duty. Others criticized *Van Gorkom* as a fundamentally misguided decision, one of the worst in corporate law. As you can see from the roundtable discussion below, the embers of the firestorm still glowed fifteen years after the decision:

> *Ira Millstein*: This case sent shock waves through the boardrooms of the United States because I guarantee you 99% of boards didn't think that anything wrong had happened. Most everybody wrote about the decision as "the Delaware courts are going nuts." Most academics thought it was crazy. Most directors were horrified.

Boris Yavitz: What Ira is describing as a typical board is pretty much what I saw in the very early years of my service, which goes back to about 1975. Most boards were not much more than rubber stamps. The CEO said "Jump" and directors were allowed just one question: How high? It wasn't a matter of not arguing with the boss—you typically didn't even question him.

Steven Friedman: Everybody seems to imply that the process was wrong but the end result was right. You see in the published accounts that KKR was willing to pay $60, and also that GE Capital was willing to pay more. Both of them were turned off by the fact that there was a signed merger agreement and a clear message of "Don't mess with my deal." So I think that we should criticize this board not just for the process but for their decision.

Boris Yavitz: What happened is that all directors got the message: It is *procedure, procedure, procedure* that counts. Everything else doesn't mean very much. We were clearly panicked about what could happen if we didn't do what the lawyers said. We went through a tightly scripted process, which we hoped would end up with us not being sued but, even more hopefully, end up with the right decision. It was of great concern to me that we directors seemed to abandon much of our judgment to the security guards.

Ira Millstein: On behalf of the legal community, I will say that this was happening for a good reason, which was that you *hadn't* been doing your job. What happened with *Smith v. Van Gorkom* is it gave the lawyers an opportunity to act like lawyers for change. Most lawyers knew generally what was required—that the board had to make a good faith judgment. But if you went into a boardroom before *Smith v. Van Gorkom* and tried to talk about legal obligations, they'd say, "We have more important things to do than listen to you tell us about what we ought to be doing." When *Smith* came down, you were able to walk into a boardroom for the first time in my experience and really be heard. That was a good thing to have happen. Up until then it was more missionary work—talking about good and evil and how you really "ought" to do your jobs.

Roundtable: The Legacy of "Smith v. Van Gorkom," 24 Directors and Boards 28, 32–37 (Spring 2000).

Points for Discussion

1. *Becoming informed.*

Van Gorkom focused attention on the board decision-making process. Spurred in part by the case, a certain board meeting decorum has come to be understood as standard. The Official Comment to MBCA § 8.30(b) describes the standard of conduct for how directors should become informed:

The phrase "becoming informed," in the context of the decision-making function, refers to the process of gaining sufficient familiarity with the background facts and circumstances in order to make an informed judgment. Unless the circumstances would permit a reasonable director to conclude that he or she is already sufficiently informed, the standard of care requires every director to take steps to become informed about the background facts and circumstances before taking action on the matter at hand. The process typically involves review of written materials provided before or at the meeting and attention to/participation in the deliberations leading up to a vote. In addition to considering information and data on which a director is expressly entitled to rely under section 8.30(e), "becoming informed" can also involve consideration of information and data generated by other persons, for example, review of industry studies or research articles prepared by third parties. It can also involve direct communications, outside of the boardroom, with members of management or other directors. There is no one way for "becoming informed," and both the method and measure—"how to" and "how much"—are matters of reasonable judgment for the director to exercise.

Does this description suggest that board decision making must adhere to standards of boardroom "due process," as some commentators reading the case have suggested?

2. *Individual vs. collective decision making.*

Is every director individually required to perform duties in good faith and in a manner they believe is in the best interests of the corporation? Or is the standard of conduct applied to the board as a whole? Boards generally are collegial bodies that make collective decisions. So what should the court do if a particular director plays a more prominent role? Conversely, what if one director is a slacker? Can deficient performance of one director be overcome? Or does every director need to be sufficiently informed? Suppose that the Trans Union defendants had accepted the court's invitation to invoke individual defenses. What legal theory would the court have used to exonerate individual directors, even though the court found the directors collectively to have been grossly negligent in not being fully informed about the fair value of Trans Union? Are there varying degrees of gross negligence for different directors? These questions remain difficult, and open.

3. *Reliance.*

Directors frequently rely on opinions provided by attorneys, accountants, engineers, financial specialists, and other expert professional advisors. In general, such reliance is justified and protects directors who rely on such advice in good faith, even if the advice turns out to be poor.

In *Van Gorkom*, the court rejected the directors' argument that they were protected from liability because they relied on the information that Van Gorkom presented to them. Was that decision sound policy? Or should the directors have been entitled to rely on the information? Reliance might not be justified if a report contains on its face sufficient warning of its own inadequacy to put a reasonable director on notice that better information should be demanded. And reports prepared by or under the supervision of corporate employees who have a personal interest in the outcome of the decision on which they bear may require closer scrutiny than usual. How much homework do you think a director should do before relying on others? Consider DGCL § 141(e) and MBCA § 8.30(e), (f).

DGCL 141

(e)   A member of the board of directors, or a member of any committee designated by the board of directors, shall, in the performance of such member's duties, be fully protected in relying in good faith upon the records of the corporation and upon such information, opinions, reports or statements presented to the corporation by any of the corporation's officers or employees, or committees of the board of directors, or by any other person as to matters the member reasonably believes are within such other person's professional or expert competence and who has been selected with reasonable care by or on behalf of the corporation.

MBCA § 8.30
Standards of Conduct for Directors

(e)   In discharging board or board committee duties, a director who does not have knowledge that makes reliance unwarranted is entitled to rely on information, opinions, reports, or statements, including financial statements and other financial data, prepared or presented by any of the persons specified in subsection (f).

(f)   director is entitled to rely, in accordance with subsection (d) or (e), on: (1) one or more officers or employees of the corporation whom the director reasonably believes to be reliable and competent in the functions performed or the information, opinions, reports or statements provided; (2) legal counsel, public accountants, or other persons retained by the corporation as to matters involving skills or expertise the director reasonably believes are matters (i) within the particular person's professional or expert competence, or (ii) as to which the particular person merits confidence; or (3) a board committee of which the director is not a member if the director reasonably believes the committee merits confidence.

4. Causation.

In decision-making cases, the plaintiffs charge that if directors had been sufficiently informed, they would not have approved the deal that caused losses to the corporation or its shareholders. In other words, plaintiffs allege that the defendant directors' breach of duty, and not other factors, caused the loss. For example, in *Van Gorkom* the plaintiffs established that Trans Union's directors had been grossly negligent in agreeing to sell the company for $55 per share. However, that did not necessarily mean the directors were liable, because their gross negligence might not have caused any damages. Indeed, the Delaware Supreme Court remanded the case with instructions that the Court of Chancery "conduct an evidentiary hearing to determine the fair value of Trans Union's stock as of the date of the board's decision. Thereafter, an award of damages may be entered to the extent that the fair value of Trans Union exceeds $55 per share." The implication of the Supreme Court's use of "may" appeared to be that if the Court of Chancery determined Trans Union had not been worth more than $55 per share, no damages would be awarded.

Should the court in *Van Gorkom* have addressed causation earlier in its decision, before conducting a detailed inquiry into the board's conduct?

5. Fairness opinions.

One significant issue in *Van Gorkom* was whether the board was required to seek a "fairness opinion" from an investment bank. Although the court did not hold that such an opinion is really required, many commentators and lawyers have assumed that a fairness opinion is a necessity in every corporate acquisition. In fact, the Trans Union board may actually have been presented with a valuation study of the company before the first September meeting. According to Robert Pritzker (brother of Jay Pritzker and later CEO of the Marmon Group), the Boston Consulting Group had prepared an 18-month study of Trans Union, which apparently concluded the company had a value of $55/share. The Delaware Supreme Court was aware of the Boston Consulting Group study, and Justice McNeilly's dissent refers to it as "a comprehensive study" supporting his conclusion that the board was "acutely aware of Trans Union and its prospects." The majority opinion in a footnote, however, states "no one even referred to [the Boston Consulting Group study] at the September 20 meeting; and it is conceded that these materials do not represent valuation studies." What role should a fairness opinion have played in the merger decision, and in the case? What are the pros and cons of fairness opinions?

The value of Pritzker's option to buy Trans Union shares can be calculated with some precision using the Black-Scholes option pricing model. Only a handful of data points is required, and it is not necessary to understand the intricacies of the model in order to intuit and use its results. Versions of the model are available online for free—just search for "Black-Scholes option pricing model."

Some of the data required are given in the case; the other data are available elsewhere. The six required variables are: (1) the stock price at the time the option was granted, (2) the exercise price of the option, (3) the time remaining before expiration, (4) the risk-free interest rate, (5) the stock's dividend yield, and (6) the stock's volatility.

We can look at data from the case and other sources: (1) the stock price at the relevant time is given in the opinion as $37.25; (2) the exercise price of the option also is given, $38; (3) the time remaining before expiration is 134 days, the number of days from September 20, 1980, until February 1, 1981; (4) the risk-free interest rate in effect until the date of maturity of the option, based on available data for the yields on comparable maturity United States treasury bills, was 10.17%; (5) given that Trans Union paid an annual dividend of $2.36 per share during 1980, its dividend yield was approximately 6.3%.

The remaining variable, volatility, is more difficult to estimate. The most accurate method of estimating volatility would be to calculate the volatility implied by the prices of Trans Union options being traded in September 1980; however, there were no such options traded at the time. The next most accurate method is to calculate volatility using historical prices of Trans Union stock. This method suggests a volatility measure of approximately 25.4%. Given these data, the Black-Scholes estimate of the value of Pritzker's option on September 20 is approximately $2.48 million. The table below summarizes these results.

Stock Price	$37.25
Exercise Price	$38.00
Days to Expiration	134
Risk-free Rate	10.17%
Dividend Yield	6.30%
Volatility	29.30%
Option Value	$2.48 per share

The bottom line is that the grant of one million options to Pritzker on September 20, 1980, was extremely valuable ($2.48 million). Suppose that instead of granting Pritzker an option, the board had given him a suitcase filled with that much cash. Would that have changed the board's approach? Or the court's? Likewise, Van Gorkom's negotiation of the option down to one million from 1.75 million shares saved Trans Union a considerable sum of money—about $1.8 million.

Today, one would expect both the prospective purchaser of a company and its board to attempt to evaluate such an option using the above methodology. In such instances, lawyers advising participants in mergers need to understand the basics of option valuation. Trans Union's directors, and its counsel, might have fared better if they had.

C. Director and Officer Exculpation

In large part as a reaction to *Van Gorkom*, many states enacted legislation during the 1980s to reduce the risk of directors' personal liability. While there is some variation between state approaches to exculpation, as a general matter, these statutes permitted corporations to include in their charters "exculpation" provisions, which eliminated or reduced the personal liability of directors for monetary damages for breach of the duty of care.

Our discussion of exculpation begins with DGCL § 102(b)(7), the first iteration of which was adopted by the Delaware legislature in response to *Van Gorkom* and allowed a corporation to include a director exculpation provision in its certificate of incorporation. Exculpation provisions (often referred to by the Delaware statutory section as "102(b)(7) provisions") are ubiquitous, particularly in the charters of public corporations. The effect of these provisions on shareholder litigation is significant. For example, Delaware courts have held that if a complaint alleges only a duty of care claim against directors for monetary damages, it can be dismissed for failure to state a claim on which relief may be granted if the corporation has an exculpation provision in its certificate of incorporation. *See Malpiede v. Townson*, 780 A.2d 1075 (Del. 2001).

Historically, the protections of § 102(b)(7) extended only to directors and did not include officers. In 2022, however, § 102(b)(7) was amended to further allow a corporation to include an officer exculpation provision in its certificate of incorporation. Still, directors and officers are not treated uniformly under the amended provision. Consider the differences, which are discussed in greater detail below, as you read the excerpt of § 102(b)(7) that follows.

DGCL § 102
Contents of Certificate of Incorporation

(b)   the certificate of incorporation may also contain any or all of the following matters:

(7)   A provision eliminating or limiting the personal liability of a director or officer to the corporation or its stockholders for monetary damages for breach of fiduciary duty as a director or officers, provided that such provision shall not eliminate or limit the liability of a director:

(i)   A director or officer for any breach of the director's or officer's duty of loyalty to the corporation or its stockholders;

(ii)   A director or officer for acts or omissions not in good faith or which involve intentional misconduct or a knowing violation of law;

(iii)   A director under § 174 of this title [which covers unlawful payment of dividends]; or

(iv)   A director or officer for any transaction from which the director or officer derived an improper personal benefit; or

(v)   An officer in any action by or in the right of the corporation.

Following the 2022 amendment, § 102(b)(7) remains an enabling provision that allows, but does not require, the corporation to include an exculpation provision in its certificate of incorporation. If not in the initial certificate of incorporation, the board must therefore propose the adoption of such a provision and obtain shareholder approval to amend the certificate of incorporation. Such will be the case for any existing Delaware corporation that wishes to adopt an officer exculpation provision in line with the 2022 amendment.

1.   Exculpation Exclusions

Section 102(b)(7) does not permit corporations to limit directors' and officers' personal liability for all breaches of duty. Instead, there are five important exceptions.

Looking first at subsections (i) through (iv), you'll notice they cover situations involving violations of the duty of loyalty, acts or omissions not in good faith, intentional misconduct or a knowing violation of law, unlawful payment of dividends and the like under § 174, and transactions from which the director or officer derived an improper personal benefit. The statute does not expressly state that duty of care claims can be exculpated; instead, the reader can deduce or negatively infer this conclusion given that violations of the duty of care are not excluded.

The result is that plaintiffs' attorneys will often try to characterize conduct in such a way so that it is not exculpated by a § 102(b)(7) provision in the corporation's certificate of incorporation. Indeed, some cases can be reframed as involving a failure of oversight or self interest that cannot be exculpated rather than exculpable gross negligence. For example, instead of pleading a breach of the duty of care in *Van Gorkom* the plaintiff might have argued that Van Gorkom acted out of a desire to maximize his personal gain before his impending retirement and the other directors acceded to his "fast shuffle."

The contours of the duty of loyalty, referenced in subsection (i) of § 102(b)(7), and implicated by (iv) regarding improper personal benefit, are covered in greater detail in Chapter 10.

Subsection (ii) has three parts, which we can label "not in good faith," "intentional misconduct," and "knowing violations." The second two parts are relatively straightforward. If a director or officer engages in intentional or knowing wrongdoing, the director or officer remains potentially liable. That is, we can think of directors as having a duty of obedience to corporate norms and non-corporate law that cannot be exculpated.

The key remaining phrase—"not in good faith"—has been an important focus of the courts in recent decades. Whether a director's actions are "not in good faith"—which the Delaware courts have understood to mean the director "consciously disregarded" his or her duties—often will be the determining factor in deciding if he or she can be personally liable. In the past, plaintiffs' attorneys commonly alleged oversight failures as breach of the duty of care, but now more typically frame the conduct as non-exculpable claims for breach of the duty of good faith. We will explore this issue in depth in Chapter 11.

As for subsection (iii) of § 102(b)(7), recall from the discussion of capital structure in Chapter 8 that directors can be personally liable for declaring dividends or approving other distributions that violate the legal capital requirements. Whatever you might think of the wisdom of legal capital restrictions on corporate distributions, corporations cannot exculpate directors from liability for violating those restrictions. In other words, even after § 102(b)(7), directors are always potentially on the hook for declaring an improper dividend. Note that directors, not officers, are authorized to declare and cause the corporation to pay dividends. For that reason, the scope of subsection (iii) remains unchanged following the 2022 amendment.

It was noted at the beginning of this section that although the 2022 amendment lessened the disparity of treatment between directors and officers, it did not eliminate it. Subsection (v) of § 102(b)(7) illustrates why. In excluding derivative claims from exculpation, subsection (v) refers only to officers. Accordingly, exculpation is not available to an officer in any derivative action, including those which allege an officer's violation of the duty of care. Directors, on the other hand, remain eligible for exculpation for both direct and derivative claims alike, provided the exclusions set forth in subsections (i)–(iv) are not triggered. (The distinction between direct and derivative claims is discussed in greater detail in Chapter 14 on Shareholder Litigation.)

Further, note that § 102(b)(7) allows an exculpation clause to apply to directors and only certain officers, namely a person who (during the course of conduct alleged to be wrongful) (1) is or was president, CEO, COO, CFO, CLO, controller, treasurer, or chief accounting officer; (2) is or was identified in the corporation's public filings with the U.S. Securities and Exchange Commission because such person is or was one of the most highly compensated executive officers of the corporation; or (3) has, by written agreement with the corporation, consented to be identified as an officer for purposes of accepting service of process. (You can pull up the full text of § 102(b)(7) and see if you can find how it defines "officer" to provide for this limitation.)

Two additional points should be kept in mind. First, § 102(b)(7) expressly refers to "eliminating or limiting the personal liability of a director or officer to the corporation or its stockholders for monetary damages. . . ." Therefore, exculpation provisions will not block or forestall suits seeking other types of relief such as the equitable remedy of an injunction. Second, prior to the 2022 amendment, § 102(b)(7) explicitly referred to "directors," not "officers." Consequently, Delaware courts interpreted the statute to allow exculpation of directors for conduct or actions taken in their capacity as directors. Plaintiffs' attorneys often targeted officers as defendants with the hopes of surviving motions to dismiss. And, individuals who served as both an officer and a director (such as a CEO who also sat on the corporation's board) faced exposure to liability for breach of the duty of care for actions taken when wearing their "hat" as an officer for the corporation. The 2022 amendment lessens the disparity of treatment between exculpation for directors and officers, but does not treat them the same—thus raising the question of whether and how the strategies of plaintiffs' attorneys might change, if at all.

2. Compare Delaware and MBCA

Other state statutes resemble Delaware's in some ways, but differ in others. For example, MBCA § 2.02(b)(4) permits corporations to adopt a provision in the articles of incorporation to eliminate or limit directors' personal liability for certain fiduciary duty breaches. The MBCA excludes from its coverage liability for improperly received financial benefits, intentional infliction of harm on the corporation or the shareholders, intentional violations of criminal law, and unlawful distributions, including dividends. Thus, the MBCA avoids the Delaware terms of "duty of loyalty" and "not in good faith," but introduces questions about what is an "improper financial benefit" or "intentional infliction of harm."

> Does the MBCA allow for exculpation of officers? Take a look at MBCA § 2.02(b)(4).

One thing you should notice is that both the Delaware and MBCA exculpation provisions apply only to liability for monetary damages; they do not permit corporations to exculpate directors from equitable relief for breaching their fiduciary duties. In addition, both provisions require that the exculpation provision be placed in the charter, thus requiring initial adoption or shareholder approval.

3.   Policy Questions

Exculpating directors and officers raises serious public policy questions. Why shouldn't directors and officers be liable for grossly negligent actions? Why would shareholders agree to an exculpation provision? On the other hand, if corporations can exculpate directors and officers from liability for gross negligence, why not permit them to go further? If shareholders want to exculpate their directors from violations of the duty of loyalty, why shouldn't they be permitted to do so? And should claims against directors and officers for breaching their fiduciary duties hinge on how plaintiffs' lawyers frame the claims and how judges interpret them? Consider the 2022 amendment. Why do you think exculpation was historically limited to directors' liability? Do you agree with the 2022 amendment allowing for officer exculpation? How significant is the subsection (v) exclusion of § 102(b)(7)?

D.   The Duty of Care and Nonfeasance

In this final section, we turn to *Francis v. United Jersey Bank*, a "classic" case in the area of directors' obligations of care and oversight. It is an unusual case in some ways: the corporation was a family business, and the family was not very well functioning. Moreover, the corporation was in the reinsurance industry, which has some peculiar features not common to other businesses. Nevertheless, the case remains a well-known application of the duty of care to a suit alleging harm from a director's nonfeasance. Although most corporations these days have director exculpation provisions in their charters that would obviate a claim for breach of the duty of care even in the face of director nonfeasance, it is worth considering the possibility of such a suit for corporations that do not protect their directors in this way.

The corporation at issue, Pritchard & Baird, Intermediaries Corp., was a reinsurance broker, a firm that arranged contracts between insurance companies by means of which companies that wrote large policies sold participations in those policies to other companies in order to share the risks. According to the custom in the industry, the selling company paid the applicable portion of the premium to the broker, which deducted its commission and forwarded the balance to the reinsuring company. Thus, the broker handled large amounts of money as a fiduciary for its clients.

As of 1964, all the stock of Pritchard & Baird was owned by Charles Pritchard, Sr., one of the firm's founders, his wife, and his two sons, Charles, Jr. and William. They were also the four directors. Charles, Sr. dominated the corporation until 1971, when he became ill, and the two sons took over management of the business. Charles, Sr. died in 1973, leaving Mrs. Pritchard and the sons as the only remaining directors.

Contrary to the industry practice, Pritchard & Baird did not segregate its operating funds from those of its clients; instead, it deposited all funds in the same account. From this account Charles, Sr. had drawn "loans" that correlated with corporate profits and were repaid at the end of each year. After his death, Charles, Jr. and William began to draw ever larger amounts that greatly exceeded profits (they continued to characterize these payments as "loans"). The sons drew these payments from something known as the "float," the extra money available to them after Pritchard & Baird had received an insurance premium and before it had to forward the premium to the reinsurer.

By 1975 the corporation was bankrupt. This action was brought by the trustees in bankruptcy against Mrs. Pritchard and the bank as administrator of her husband's estate. Mrs. Pritchard died during the pendency of the proceedings, and her executrix was substituted as defendant. As to Mrs. Pritchard, the principal claim was that she had been negligent in the conduct of her duties as a director of the corporation.

Francis v. United Jersey Bank

432 A.2d 814 (N.J. 1981)

POLLOCK, J.

The "loans" were reflected on financial statements that were prepared annually as of January 31, the end of the corporate fiscal year. Although an outside certified public accountant prepared the 1970 financial statement, the corporation prepared only internal financial statements from 1971–1975. In all instances, the statements were simple documents, consisting of three or four 8 x11 inch sheets.

The statements of financial condition from 1970 forward demonstrated:

	Working Capital Deficit	Shareholders' Loans	Net Brokerage Income
1970	$389,022	$509,941	$807,229
1971	Not available	Not available	Not available
1972	$1,684,289	$1,825,911	$1,546,263
1973	$3,506,460	$3,700,542	$1,736,349
1974	$6,939,007	$7,080,629	$876,182
1975	$10,176,419	$10,298,039	$551,598

Mrs. Pritchard was not active in the business of Pritchard & Baird and knew virtually nothing of its corporate affairs. She briefly visited the corporate offices in

Morristown on only one occasion, and she never read or obtained the annual financial statements. She was unfamiliar with the rudiments of reinsurance and made no effort to assure that the policies and practices of the corporation, particularly pertaining to the withdrawal of funds, complied with industry custom or relevant law. Although her husband had warned her that Charles, Jr. would "take the shirt off my back," Mrs. Pritchard did not pay any attention to her duties as a director or to the affairs of the corporation.

After her husband died in December 1973, Mrs. Pritchard became incapacitated and was bedridden for a six-month period. She became listless at this time and started to drink rather heavily. Her physical condition deteriorated, and in 1978 she died. The trial court rejected testimony seeking to exonerate her because she "was old, was grief-stricken at the loss of her husband, sometimes consumed too much alcohol and was psychologically overborne by her sons." That court found that she was competent to act and that the reason Mrs. Pritchard never knew what her sons "were doing was because she never made the slightest effort to discharge any of her responsibilities as a director of Pritchard & Baird."

Individual liability of a corporate director for acts of the corporation is a prickly problem. Generally directors are accorded broad immunity and are not insurers of corporate activities. The problem is particularly nettlesome when a third party asserts that a director, because of nonfeasance, is liable for losses caused by acts of insiders, who in this case were officers, directors and shareholders. Determination of the liability of Mrs. Pritchard requires findings that she had a duty to the clients of Pritchard & Baird, that she breached that duty and that her breach was a proximate cause of their losses.

As a general rule, a director should acquire at least a rudimentary understanding of the business of the corporation. Accordingly, a director should become familiar with the fundamentals of the business in which the corporation is engaged. Because directors are bound to exercise ordinary care, they cannot set up as a defense lack of the knowledge needed to exercise the requisite degree of care. If one feels that he has not had sufficient business experience to qualify him to perform the duties of a director, he should either acquire the knowledge by inquiry, or refuse to act.

Directors are under a continuing obligation to keep informed about the activities of the corporation. Otherwise, they may not be able to participate in the overall management of corporate affairs. Directors may not shut their eyes to corporate misconduct and then claim that because they did not see the misconduct, they did not have a duty to look. The sentinel asleep at his post contributes nothing to the enterprise he is charged to protect.

Directorial management does not require a detailed inspection of day-to-day activities, but rather a general monitoring of corporate affairs and policies. Accordingly, a director is well advised to attend board meetings regularly. Regular attendance does not mean that directors must attend every meeting, but that directors should attend meetings as a matter of practice. A director of a publicly held corporation might be expected to attend regular monthly meetings, but a director of a small, family corporation might be asked to attend only an annual meeting. The point is that one of the responsibilities of a director is to attend meetings of the board of which he or she is a member.

While directors are not required to audit corporate books, they should maintain familiarity with the financial status of the corporation by a regular review of financial statements. In some circumstances, directors may be charged with assuring that bookkeeping methods conform to industry custom and usage. The extent of review, as well as the nature and frequency of financial statements, depends not only on the customs of the industry, but also on the nature of the corporation and the business in which it is engaged. Financial statements of some small corporations may be prepared internally and only on an annual basis; in a large publicly held corporation, the statements may be produced monthly or at some other regular interval. Adequate financial review normally would be more informal in a private corporation than in a publicly held corporation.

The review of financial statements, however, may give rise to a duty to inquire further into matters revealed by those statements. Upon discovery of an illegal course of action, a director has a duty to object and, if the corporation does not correct the conduct, to resign.

In certain circumstances, the fulfillment of the duty of a director may call for more than mere objection and resignation. Sometimes a director may be required to seek the advice of counsel concerning the propriety of his or her own conduct, the conduct of other officers and directors or the conduct of the corporation. Sometimes the duty of a director may require more than consulting with outside counsel. A director may have a duty to take reasonable means to prevent illegal conduct by co-directors; in any appropriate case, this may include threat of suit.

A director is not an ornament, but an essential component of corporate governance. Consequently, a director cannot protect himself behind a paper shield bearing the motto, "dummy director." The New Jersey Business Corporation Act, in imposing a standard of ordinary care on all directors, confirms that dummy, figurehead and accommodation directors are anachronisms with no place in New Jersey law.

The factors that impel expanded responsibility in the large, publicly held corporation may not be present in a small, close corporation. Nonetheless, a close corporation may, because of the nature of its business, be affected with a public interest. For example, the stock of a bank may be closely held, but because of the nature of banking the directors would be subject to greater liability than those of another close corporation. Even in a small corporation, a director is held to the standard of that degree of care that an ordinarily prudent director would use under the circumstances.

A director's duty of care does not exist in the abstract, but must be considered in relation to specific obligees. In general, the relationship of a corporate director to the corporation and its stockholders is that of a fiduciary. Shareholders have a right to expect that directors will exercise reasonable supervision and control over the policies and practices of a corporation. The institutional integrity of a corporation depends upon the proper discharge by directors of those duties.

While directors may owe a fiduciary duty to creditors also, that obligation generally has not been recognized in the absence of insolvency. With certain corporations, however, directors are deemed to owe a duty to creditors and other third parties even when the corporation is solvent. Although depositors of a bank are considered in some respects to be creditors, courts have recognized that directors may owe them a fiduciary duty. Directors of nonbanking corporations may owe a similar duty when the corporation holds funds of others in trust.

As a reinsurance broker, Pritchard & Baird received annually as a fiduciary millions of dollars of clients' money which it was under a duty to segregate. To this extent, it resembled a bank rather than a small family business. Accordingly, Mrs. Pritchard's relationship to the clientele of Pritchard & Baird was akin to that of a director of a bank to its depositors.

As a director of a substantial reinsurance brokerage corporation, she should have known that it received annually millions of dollars of loss and premium funds which it held in trust for ceding and reinsurance companies. Mrs. Pritchard should have obtained and read the annual statements of financial condition of Pritchard & Baird. Although she had a right to rely upon financial statements prepared in accordance with [New Jersey law], such reliance would not excuse her conduct.

From those statements, she should have realized that, as of January 31, 1970, her sons were withdrawing substantial trust funds under the guise of "Shareholders' Loans." The financial statements for each fiscal year commencing with that of January 31, 1970, disclosed that the working capital deficits and the "loans" were escalating in tandem. Detecting a misappropriation of funds would not have required special expertise or extraordinary diligence; a cursory reading of the financial statements would have revealed the pillage. Thus, if Mrs. Pritchard had read the financial statements, she would have known that her sons were converting trust funds. When financial statements demonstrate that insiders are bleeding a corporation to death, a director should notice and try to stanch the flow of blood.

In summary, Mrs. Pritchard was charged with the obligation of basic knowledge and supervision of the business of Pritchard & Baird. Under the circumstances, this obligation included reading and understanding financial statements, and making reasonable attempts at detection and prevention of the illegal conduct of other officers and directors. She had a duty to protect the clients of Pritchard & Baird against the policies and practices that would result in the misappropriation of money they had entrusted to the corporation. She breached that duty.

The judgment of the Appellate Division is affirmed.

Points for Discussion

1. *When does the BJR apply?*

The court stated, "a director is held to the standard of that degree of care that an ordinarily prudent director would use under the circumstances." Did the court give Mrs. Pritchard business judgment rule protection? Why or why not?

2. *How much more?*

Clearly, directors must do more than Mrs. Pritchard did to fulfill their oversight duties. But how much more? Consider the guidance to directors offered in the Official Comment to MBCA § 8.30.

3. *A "simple housewife"?*

The trial court's opinion in *Francis v. United Jersey Bank*, 392 A.2d 1233 (Law Div. 1978), contains the following passage:

> It has been urged in this case that Mrs. Pritchard should not be held responsible for what happened while she was a director of Pritchard & Baird because she was a simple housewife who served as a director as an accommodation to her husband and sons. Let me start by saying that I reject the sexism which is unintended but which is implicit in such an argument. There is no reason why the average housewife could not adequately discharge the functions of a director of a corporation such as Pritchard & Baird, despite a lack of business career experience, if she gave some reasonable attention to what she was supposed to be doing. The problem is not that Mrs. Pritchard was a simple housewife. The problem is that she was a person who took a job which necessarily entailed certain responsibilities and she then failed to make any effort whatever to discharge those responsibilities. The ultimate insult to the fundamental dignity and equality of women would be to treat a grown woman as though she were a child not responsible for her acts and omissions.

Should courts take into account the background of directors in determining whether they satisfied their oversight responsibilities? If so, what factors are most appropriate and relevant? Some statutes refer to "the care a person in a like position" would reasonably believe appropriate; others refer to the care "an ordinarily prudent person in a like position would exercise." Do these statutes mean there is a single, unitary standard of care, or are the director's expertise and experience relevant in determining the appropriate standard of care?

For example, would a director with an accounting background have greater responsibilities to uncover management fraud? Would a labor union representative elected to the board under a collective bargaining agreement be more responsible for overseeing employee relations? Are lawyers serving on a board supposed to be sensitive to legal compliance? What are the responsibilities of an investment banker whose only contribution at board meetings is in connection with proposed financings?

4. Bad faith?

A failure of oversight could be framed as a breach of the duty of care, as the plaintiffs in *Francis* alleged. Could such a failure instead be alleged as a non-exculpable breach of the duty of good faith? What standard must be met to successfully win a claim against directors for breach of the duty of good faith? What is the appropriate remedy for failure of oversight when the directors did not personally gain? We will consider these questions more fully in Chapter 11.

CHAPTER 10

Duty of Loyalty

This chapter addresses the "traditional" duty of loyalty, which requires that directors and officers act in a manner they reasonably believe to be in the best interests of the corporation. The duty of loyalty arises in numerous contexts, some of which we will consider in later chapters, including transactions involving controlling shareholders (Chapter 17), various kinds of corporate deals (Chapter 18), and insider trading (Chapter 20). The nature of judicial review may differ with each context, but the basic question remains the same: how should a court evaluate business transactions when a corporate fiduciary has a personal interest in the transaction that conflicts with corporate interests?

In this chapter, we examine two commonplace contexts in which the duty of loyalty arises: interested transactions and corporate opportunities. Such transactions raise the possibility that the officer or director's personal interests may be contrary to those of the corporation. The duty of loyalty requires an officer or director to place the corporation's best interests above their own, and opens the door for a reviewing court to be sure this is true.

Keep in mind that director "conflicts" are not necessarily bad. Indeed, for many corporations conflicted transactions may be a fact of life. Suppose a corporate director proposes to sell land to their corporation. Obviously, there is a conflict, because a high price will benefit the director personally, while a low price will benefit the corporation whose interest the director is supposed to serve. This is a classic "interested" transaction (sometimes referred to as "conflicted" or "self dealing"). A director or officer is

> The Introductory Comment to the 1989 version of MBCA Subchapter F took great care not to disparage director conflicts.
>
> "It is important to keep firmly in mind that it is a contingent risk we are dealing with—that an interest conflict is not in itself a crime or a tort or necessarily injurious to others. Contrary to much popular usage, having a 'conflict of interest' is not something one is 'guilty of'; it is simply a state of affairs. Indeed, in many situations, the corporation and the shareholders may secure major benefits from a transaction despite the presence of a director's conflicting interest. Further, while history is replete with selfish acts, it is also oddly counterpointed by numberless acts taken contrary to self interest."

"interested" in connection with a transaction when they stand to gain monetarily while other shareholders do not. But an interested transaction is not necessarily unfair to the corporation. Indeed, it might be beneficial, or even crucial, to the corporation. Directors are often uniquely positioned to help their corporations, even if they personally benefit from the dealings as well.

This chapter begins with an overview of the issues presented in interested transactions and the historical evolution of the duty of loyalty. First, we consider the statutory approaches to director and officer conflicts, including the concept of *per se* voidability and the importance of process, particularly approval by directors or shareholders. Next, we explore more deeply these statutory concepts by considering the common law analysis of breach of fiduciary duty for interested transactions, including elements that courts examine in determining the fairness of a transaction—namely, fair price and fair process. Finally, we discuss the ability of corporate directors and executives to take business opportunities that properly belong to the corporation, a problem that has generated a separate doctrine known as the "corporate opportunity doctrine."

A.   *Per Se* Voidability and Statutory Approaches

We begin by describing the common law background of modern duty of loyalty statutes. You will notice a steady relaxation of the standards that courts use, starting with a flat prohibition on such transactions and ending with statutory safe harbors that rescue certain interested transactions from per se voidability under common law.

1.   Historical Phases of Doctrinal Evolution

The law applicable to conflicts evolved significantly during the nineteenth and twentieth centuries. Legal scholars and commentators have pointed to a variety of possible explanations for this evolution, including a general common law shift from rules to standards, different fact patterns emerging over time from the nineteenth-century railroad robber barons, experience with interested transactions casting them in a more favorable light for corporations, and the potential that state courts and legislatures had been politically captured by corporate managers.

The evolution of the common law has been periodized as follows. First, as of the late nineteenth century, the general common law rule was that a corporation or its shareholders could void a conflicted transaction between a director and the corporation. At the time, judges doubted that the conflicted director or the remaining directors could put the corporation's interests ahead of the conflicted director's personal interests. It didn't matter if conflicted directors removed themselves from the decision-making process on the transaction. A director, like a trustee, simply wasn't supposed to engage in self-dealing. Period.

Second, by the early twentieth century, courts recognized the need for some flexibility in approaching conflicted transactions, and the general rule changed to focus on a two-pronged approach that permitted certain forms of interested transactions. A conflicted deal was valid if it was both (1) approved by a disinterested board majority and (2) found fair by a reviewing court. This meant that even if the process of approval was fair, the transaction was voidable if its substance was unfair to the corporation. Further, in this second phase, a transaction approved by an interested board majority remained subject to avoidance at the corporation's option. Importing trust law principles to corporate law, courts reasoned that approval by a majority-interested board was similar to a trustee transacting with herself, and thus disfavored.

Third, by the mid-twentieth century, courts adopted a more permissive approach. By 1960, some courts had held that interested transactions were no longer automatically voidable. Instead, the courts reviewed such transactions to assess whether the transaction was substantively fair, taking into account

Director conflicts are not necessarily limited to board members who benefit directly from a transaction. Even directors who do not have a direct financial interest in a transaction may have corporate or other positions that are linked to the transacting director.

For example, an outside director may be a member of a law firm that depends on receiving work from an inside director (such as the company's general counsel) who assigns legal work for the corporation. Can such an outside director exercise truly independent judgment on a transaction involving the general counsel, even if the director will not directly benefit financially from the transaction? And even if there were no financial interest, there may be personal dimensions if the interested director is a family member or lifelong friend.

Today, corporate statutes dealing with director conflicts of interest are generally narrow in scope. They define conflicts that trigger heightened judicial review as those in which a director has a "financial" interest, although sometimes commentary to the statutes and judicial interpretations take into account the structural bias among directors to accommodate fellow directors. What are the advantages and disadvantages of such an approach?

the transaction's terms and price. Under the common law of many states, however, *per se* invalidity was still a possibility absent disinterested majority approval.

Fourth, state legislatures began to adopt statutory provisions concerning interested transactions. Contemporary statutes, such as DGCL § 144 and former MBCA § 8.31, codify the common law development that conflicted transactions are not automatically invalid. Although they mention both disinterested approval (by shareholders or the board) and a judicial finding of fairness, these statutes do not specify when a transaction is valid. Over time, courts have had to resolve whether approval by directors or shareholders should be dispositive, or whether the court should engage in its own review of director self-dealing.

A key question has concerned the common law's interaction with the statutory provisions. Does the statute save a transaction from challenge on the basis of *per se* invalidity? Further, does the statute only come to bear when a corporation (or a representative plaintiff suing on the corporation's behalf) seeks to void the contract? Or do interested transaction statutes have broader applicability to suits for breach of fiduciary duty in addition to suits to void the agreement?

One extensive study of the issue has explained that the answers to these questions "vary from state to state and from statute to statute, for the statutes' linguistic formulations differ, along with judicial attitudes." *See* William W. Bratton, *Reconsidering the Evolutionary Erosion Account of Corporate Fiduciary Law*, 76 Bus. Law. 1157 (2021).

2.   Delaware's Interested Transaction Statute

Delaware has a typical interested transaction statute, which provides that an interested-director or officer transaction will not automatically be void or voidable if *either* there has been informed, disinterested board approval *or* informed shareholder approval *or* the transaction is fair to the corporation.

DGCL § 144
Interested Directors; Quorum

(a)   No contract or transaction between a corporation and 1 or more of its directors or officers, or between a corporation and any other corporation, partnership, association, or other organization in which 1 or more of its directors or officers, are directors or officers, or have a financial interest, shall be void or voidable solely for this reason, or solely because the director or officer is present at or participates in the meeting of the board or committee which authorizes the contract or transaction, or solely because any such director's or officer's votes are counted for such purpose, if:

   (1)   The material facts as to the director's or officer's relationship or interest and as to the contract or transaction are disclosed or are known to the board of directors or the committee, and the board or committee in good faith authorizes the contract or transaction by the affirmative votes of a majority of the disinterested directors, even though the disinterested directors be less than a quorum; or

   (2)   The material facts as to the director's or officer's relationship or interest and as to the contract or transaction are disclosed or are known to the shareholders entitled to vote thereon, and the con-

> tract or transaction is specifically approved in good faith by vote of the shareholders; or
>
> (3) The contract or transaction is fair as to the corporation as of the time it is authorized, approved or ratified, by the board of directors, a committee or the shareholders.
>
> (b) Common or interested directors may be counted in determining the presence of a quorum at a meeting of the board of directors or of a committee which authorizes the contract or transaction.

a. Meaning of DGCL § 144

Under this statute, what role does a court have in reviewing the transaction's fairness to the corporation? Because the statute is written in the disjunctive, one possible answer is that there should be judicial review for fairness only if there had been no prior approval by an informed, disinterested decision maker. If this interpretation were correct, it would reduce judicial scrutiny (and, hence, potentially be less protective for minority shareholders), particularly when compared to the early days of the common law. This approach, however, could be viewed as efficient because it would give prospective certainty to a transaction in which the decisional process is fair, presumably on the theory that good process identifies substantive fairness in most instances.

Alternatively, the statute might be read as simply removing the absolute prohibition against interested-director transactions without specifying when such transactions are valid. Support for this reading comes from the statutory language that a transaction that satisfies one or more of the tests is not void or voidable solely because of the director's interest. Under this construction, the statute can be seen as relating primarily to the burden of proof in litigation challenging a conflict of interest transaction rather than establishing standards for the validity of the transaction itself. Thus, under this interpretation, the burden of establishing validity initially would be on the interested director, but would shift to the shareholder challenging the transaction if there had been full disclosure and approval by disinterested decision makers. This interpretation leaves to the court the question of the transaction's fairness, with approval by informed, disinterested decision makers only shifting the burden on the question of fairness.

b. Evolving Court Interpretations of DGCL § 144

Delaware court decisions illustrate the difficulties in interpreting DGCL § 144. Some earlier decisions stated that the court retains a role in determining fairness, even if the self-dealing transaction is approved by informed, disinterested decision makers. Other decisions suggest that the review by appropriate corporate decision makers displaces judicial review.

In *Fliegler v. Lawrence*, 361 A.2d 218 (Del. 1976), a shareholder brought a derivative suit on behalf of Agau Mines against its officers and directors (including the named defendant Lawrence) and another corporation, United States Antimony Corp. (USAC), which was owned primarily by Lawrence and the other defendants. Lawrence had acquired, in his individual capacity, certain mining properties which he transferred to USAC. Agau later acquired USAC in exchange for 800,000 shares of Agau stock. Fliegler, a minority shareholder of Agau, challenged Agau's acquisition of USAC, claiming it was unfair. The defendants contended that they had been relieved of the burden of proving fairness because Agau's shareholders had ratified the transaction pursuant to § 144(a)(2).

The court held that the purported ratification did not affect the burden of proof because the majority of shares voted in favor of the acquisition were cast by the defendants in their capacity as Agau stockholders. Only one-third of the disinterested shareholders cast votes. Thus, the *Fliegler* court determined that despite the absence of any provision in § 144(a)(2) requiring *disinterested* shareholder approval of an interested-director transaction, it would impose such a requirement before shifting the burden of proof from the interested director to the challenging shareholder.

The court then addressed the proper interpretation of the disjunctive language of § 144. The court rejected the argument that compliance with § 144(a)(2) automatically validated the transaction and concluded that the statute "merely removes an 'interested director' cloud when its terms are met and provides against invalidation of an agreement 'solely' because such a director or officer is involved. Nothing in the statute sanctions unfairness to Agau or removes the transaction from judicial scrutiny."

In *Marciano v. Nakash*, 535 A.2d 400 (Del. 1987), the court found to be fair a director self-dealing transaction that, because of a deadlock at both the shareholder and director level, had not been approved by either disinterested shareholders or directors. The court characterized *Fliegler* as having "refused to view § 144 as either completely preemptive of the common law duty of director fidelity or as constituting a grant of broad immunity" and cited with approval *Fliegler's* "merely removes an 'interested director' cloud" language. In a footnote, however, the court observed:

> Although in this case none of the curative steps afforded under section 144(a) were available because of the director-shareholder deadlock, a non-disclosing director seeking to remove the cloud of interestedness would appear to have the same burden under section 144(a)(3), as under prior case law, of proving the intrinsic fairness of a questioned transaction which had been approved or ratified by the directors or shareholders. On the other hand, approval by fully-informed disinterested directors under section 144(a)(1), or disinterested stockholders under section 144(a)(2),

permits invocation of the business judgment rule and limits judicial review to issues of gift or waste with the burden of proof upon the party attacking the transaction.

Without explicitly addressing the tension between *Fliegler* and *Marciano*, the following decision by the Delaware Supreme Court embraces the view that § 144 creates a safe harbor for interested director transactions from *per se* invalidity.

Benihana of Tokyo, Inc. v. Benihana, Inc.

906 A.2d 114 (Del. 2006)

BERGER, JUSTICE.

In this appeal, we consider whether Benihana, Inc. was authorized to issue $20 million in preferred stock and whether Benihana's board of directors acted properly in approving the transaction. We conclude that the Court of Chancery's factual findings are supported by the record and that it correctly applied settled law in holding that the stock issuance was lawful and that the directors did not breach their fiduciary duties. Accordingly, we affirm.

Factual and Procedural Background

Rocky Aoki founded Benihana of Tokyo, Inc. (BOT), and its subsidiary, Benihana, which own and operate Benihana restaurants in the United States and other countries. Aoki owned 100% of BOT until 1998, when he pled guilty to insider trading charges. In order to avoid licensing problems created by his status as a convicted felon, Aoki transferred his stock to the Benihana Protective Trust. The trustees of the Trust were Aoki's three children and the family's attorney.

Benihana, a Delaware corporation, has two classes of common stock. There are approximately 6 million shares of Class A common stock outstanding. Each share has 1/10 vote and the holders of Class A common are entitled to elect 25% of the directors. There are approximately 3 million shares of Common stock outstanding. Each share of Common has one vote and the holders of Common stock are entitled to elect the remaining 75% of Benihana's directors. Before the transaction at issue, BOT owned 50.9% of the Common stock and 2% of the Class A stock. The nine member board of directors is classified and the directors serve three-year terms.

In 2003, conflicts arose between Aoki and his children. In August, the children were upset to learn that Aoki had changed his will to give his new wife Keiko control over BOT.

The Aoki family's turmoil came at a time when Benihana also was facing challenges. Many of its restaurants were old and outmoded. Benihana hired WD

Partners to evaluate its facilities and to plan and design appropriate renovations. The resulting Construction and Renovation Plan anticipated that the project would take at least five years and cost $56 million or more. Wachovia offered to provide Benihana a $60 million line of credit for the Construction and Renovation Plan, but the restrictions Wachovia imposed made it unlikely that Benihana would be able to borrow the full amount. Because the Wachovia line of credit did not assure that Benihana would have the capital it needed, the company retained Morgan Joseph & Co. to develop other financing options.

On January 9, 2004, after evaluating Benihana's financial situation and needs, Fred Joseph, of Morgan Joseph, met with Joel Schwartz (Benihana's CEO), Darwin Dornbush (Benihana's general counsel) and John E. Abdo (a member of the board's executive committee). Joseph expressed concern that Benihana would not have sufficient available capital to complete the Construction and Renovation Plan and pursue appropriate acquisitions. Benihana was conservatively leveraged, and Joseph discussed various financing alternatives, including bank debt, high yield debt, convertible debt or preferred stock, equity and sale/leaseback options.

The full board met with Joseph on January 29, 2004. He reviewed all the financing alternatives that he had discussed with the executive committee, and recommended that Benihana issue convertible preferred stock. Joseph explained that the preferred stock would provide the funds needed for the Construction and Renovation Plan and also put the company in a better negotiating position if it sought additional financing from its bank.

Joseph gave the directors a board book, marked "Confidential," containing an analysis of the proposed stock issuance (the Transaction). The book included, among others, the following anticipated terms: (i) issuance of $20,000,000 of preferred stock, convertible into Common stock; (ii) dividend of 6% +/- 0.5%; (iii) conversion premium of 20% +/- 2.5%; (iv) buyer's approval required for material corporate transactions; and (v) one to two board seats to the buyer. At trial, Joseph testified that the terms had been chosen by looking at comparable stock issuances and analyzing the Morgan Joseph proposal under a theoretical model.

The board met again on February 17, 2004, to review the terms of the Transaction. The directors discussed Benihana's preferences and Joseph predicted what a buyer likely would expect or require. For example, Schwartz asked Joseph to try to negotiate a minimum on the dollar value for transactions that would be deemed "material corporation transactions" and subject to the buyer's approval. Schwartz wanted to give the buyer only one board seat, but Joseph said that Benihana might have to give up two. Joseph told the board that he was not sure that a buyer would agree to an issuance in two tranches, and that it would be difficult to make the second tranche non-mandatory. As the Court of Chancery found, the board understood that the preferred terms were akin to a "wish list."

Shortly after the February meeting, Abdo contacted Joseph and told him that BFC Financial Corporation was interested in buying the new convertible stock. In April 2004, Joseph sent BFC a private placement memorandum. Abdo negotiated with Joseph for several weeks.[5] They agreed to the Transaction on the following basic terms: (i) $20 million issuance in two tranches of $10 million each, with the second tranche to be issued one to three years after the first; (ii) BFC obtained one seat on the board, and one additional seat if Benihana failed to pay dividends for two consecutive quarters; (iii) BFC obtained preemptive rights on any new voting securities; (iv) 5% dividend; (v) 15% conversion premium; (vi) BFC had the right to force Benihana to redeem the preferred stock in full after ten years; and (vii) the stock would have immediate "as if converted" voting rights. Joseph testified that he was satisfied with the negotiations, as he had obtained what he wanted with respect to the most important points.

On April 22, 2004, Abdo sent a memorandum to Dornbush, Schwartz and Joseph, listing the agreed terms of the Transaction. He did not send the memorandum to any other members of the Benihana board. Schwartz did tell four directors that BFC was the potential buyer. At its next meeting, held on May 6, 2004, the entire board was officially informed of BFC's involvement in the Transaction. Abdo made a presentation on behalf of BFC and then left the meeting. Joseph distributed an updated board book, which explained that Abdo had approached Morgan Joseph on behalf of BFC, and included the negotiated terms. The trial court found that the board was not informed that Abdo had negotiated the deal on behalf of BFC. But the board did know that Abdo was a principal of BFC. After discussion, the board reviewed and approved the Transaction, subject to the receipt of a fairness opinion.

On May 18, 2004, after he learned that Morgan Joseph was providing a fairness opinion, Schwartz publicly announced the stock issuance. Two days later, Aoki's counsel sent a letter asking the board to abandon the Transaction and pursue other, more favorable, financing alternatives. The letter expressed concern about the directors' conflicts, the dilutive effect of the stock issuance, and its "questionable legality." Schwartz gave copies of the letter to the directors at the May 20 board meeting, and Dornbush advised that he did not believe that Aoki's concerns had merit. Joseph and another Morgan Joseph representative then joined the meeting by telephone and opined that the Transaction was fair from a financial point of view. The board then approved the Transaction.

During the following two weeks, Benihana received three alternative financing proposals. Schwartz asked three outside directors to act as an independent committee and review the first offer. The committee decided that the offer was inferior and not

---

[5]   BFC, a publicly traded Florida corporation, is a holding company for several investments. Abdo is a director and vice chairman. He owns 30% of BFC's stock.

worth pursuing. Morgan Joseph agreed with that assessment. Schwartz referred the next two proposals to Morgan Joseph, with the same result.

On June 8, 2004, Benihana and BFC executed the Stock Purchase Agreement. On June 11, 2004, the board met and approved resolutions ratifying the execution of the Stock Purchase Agreement and authorizing the stock issuance. Schwartz then reported on the three alternative proposals that had been rejected by the ad hoc committee and Morgan Joseph. On July 2, 2004, BOT filed this action against all of Benihana's directors, except Kevin Aoki, alleging breaches of fiduciary duties; and against BFC, alleging that it aided and abetted the fiduciary violations.

The Court of Chancery held that Benihana was authorized to issue the preferred stock with preemptive rights, and that the board's approval of the Transaction was a valid exercise of business judgment. This appeal followed.

Discussion

[The court first decided that Benihana's certificate of incorporation authorized the board to issue preferred stock with preemptive rights.]

A. Section 144(a)(1) Approval

Section 144 of the Delaware General Corporation Law provides a safe harbor for interested transactions, like this one, if "the material facts as to the director's relationship or interest and as to the contract or transaction are disclosed or are known to the board of directors . . . and the board . . . in good faith authorizes the contract or transaction by the affirmative votes of a majority of the disinterested directors."

After approval by disinterested directors, courts review the interested transaction under the business judgment rule, which "is a presumption that in making a business decision, the directors of a corporation acted on an informed basis, in good faith and in the honest belief that the action taken was in the best interest of the company."

BOT argues that § 144(a)(1) is inapplicable because, when they approved the Transaction, the disinterested directors did not know that Abdo had negotiated the terms for BFC.[14] Abdo's role as negotiator is material, according to BOT, because Abdo had been given the confidential term sheet prepared by Joseph and knew which of those terms Benihana was prepared to give up during negotiations. We agree that the board needed to know about Abdo's involvement in order to make an informed decision. The record clearly establishes, however, that the board possessed that material information when it approved the Transaction on May 6, 2004 and May 20, 2004.

Shortly before the May 6 meeting, Schwartz told three of the outside directors that BFC was the proposed buyer. Then, at the meeting, Abdo made the presentation on behalf of BFC. Joseph's board book also explained that Abdo had made the initial

---

[14]   BOT argued to the trial court that the directors who voted on the Transaction were not disinterested or independent. BOT is not pressing that claim on appeal.

contact that precipitated the negotiations. The board members knew that Abdo is a director, vice-chairman, and one of two people who control BFC. Thus, although no one ever said, "Abdo negotiated this deal for BFC," the directors understood that he was BFC's representative in the Transaction. As one of the outside directors testified, "whoever actually did the negotiating, [Abdo] as a principal would have to agree to it. So whether he sat in the room and negotiated it or he sat somewhere else and was brought the results of someone else's negotiation, he was the ultimate decision-maker." Accordingly, we conclude that the disinterested directors possessed all the material information on Abdo's interest in the Transaction, and their approval at the May 6 and May 20 board meetings satisfies § 144(a)(1).

B. Abdo's alleged fiduciary violation

BOT next argues that the Court of Chancery should have reviewed the Transaction under an entire fairness standard because Abdo breached his duty of loyalty when he used Benihana's confidential information to negotiate on behalf of BFC. This argument starts with a flawed premise. The record does not support BOT's contention that Abdo used any confidential information against Benihana. Even without Joseph's comments at the February 17 board meeting, Abdo knew the terms a buyer could expect to obtain in a deal like this. Moreover, as the trial court found, "the negotiations involved give and take on a number of points" and Benihana "ended up where it wanted to be" for the most important terms. Abdo did not set the terms of the deal; he did not deceive the board; and he did not dominate or control the other directors' approval of the Transaction. In short, the record does not support the claim that Abdo breached his duty of loyalty.

C. Dilution of BOT's voting power

Finally, BOT argues that the board's primary purpose in approving the Transaction was to dilute BOT's voting control. BOT points out that Schwartz was concerned about BOT's control in 2003 and even discussed with Dornbush the possibility of issuing a huge number of Class A shares. Then, despite the availability of other financing options, the board decided on a stock issuance, and agreed to give BFC "as if converted" voting rights. According to BOT, the trial court overlooked this powerful evidence of the board's improper purpose.

Here, however, the trial court found that "the primary purpose of the . . . Transaction was to provide what the directors subjectively believed to be the best financing vehicle available for securing the necessary funds to pursue the agreed upon Construction and Renovation Plan for the Benihana restaurants." That factual determination has ample record support, especially in light of the trial court's credibility determinations. Accordingly, we defer to the Court of Chancery's conclusion that the board's approval of the Transaction was a valid exercise of its business judgment, for a proper corporate purpose.

Points for Discussion

1. Process.

Notice how the Delaware Supreme Court in *Benihana* details the board deliberations in the case. Does this suggest that the focus on board process, which began in *Smith v. Van Gorkom*, has now reached its zenith in Delaware? That is, even when director loyalty is questioned, will Delaware courts refuse to inquire into the substance of the transaction if it was approved by informed, disinterested, independent directors?

2. Burden shifting.

Generally, as we have seen, the challenger of an interested director transaction bears the initial burden to show that a director had a conflicting interest in a corporate transaction, and then the burden shifts to the director (and those who seek to uphold the transaction). How does the court in *Benihana* deal with the question of burden shifting in director self-dealing transactions?

───────────────

3.   MBCA Procedural Safe Harbor

Subchapter F of the MBCA, adopted in 1989 and revised in 2005, sought to overcome the interpretive problems that statutes like DGCL § 144 can pose. Subchapter F follows a safe harbor approach. By providing bright-line definitions of who is an "interested" director, what constitutes a "conflicting interest transaction," and who are "qualified directors," Subchapter F attempts to provide greater prospective certainty and reduce judicial intervention.

Specifically, it defines a "director's conflicting interest transaction" (or "DCIT") and states that a DCIT is immune from attack if it is authorized by "qualified" directors, disinterested shareholders, or a court under a fairness standard. Any of these three forms of authorization insulates the transaction from judicial review on the basis of the director conflict. The MBCA thus takes a broad approach by providing a safe harbor from the *per se* invalidity issue as well as suits for breach of fiduciary duty of loyalty.

Subchapter F thus raises two key questions: what is a DCIT? who is a "qualified" director? MBCA § 8.60 defines a DCIT as a transaction by the corporation in which the director (1) is a party, (2) has a "material financial interest," or (3) knows that a "related person" is a party or had a material financial interest. Each of the terms in quotes is further defined. A "material financial interest" is one that would reasonably be expected to impair the director's judgment when authorizing the transaction. A "related person" is someone on a precisely enumerated family tree (from spouse to half sibling), someone who lives in the director's house, an entity controlled by the director or someone on the family tree, an entity in which the director serves as director, partner or trustee, or an entity controlled by the director's employer.

Who is a qualified director? MBCA § 1.43 defines a "qualified director" as someone who does not have a conflicting interest in the transaction or one who has no "material relationship" with a conflicted director (that is, there is no "actual or potential benefit or detriment that would reasonably be expected to impair the director's judgment" when considering the DCIT). The MBCA clarifies that directors do not become unqualified just because he was nominated or elected to the board by a conflicted director, or serve with the conflicted director on the board of another corporation.

In order for a DCIT to be insulated from judicial review, a majority of "qualified directors" (at least two) must authorize it. They must deliberate and vote on their own, without the presence or participation of the conflicted director. Normal quorum requirements are relaxed, and a quorum exists if a majority of the board's qualified directors (again, at least two) is present.

As you can see, the MBCA seeks to provide clear yes-or-no answers to directors and lawyers who shepherd interested director transactions through the corporate board. For example, a conflicted director who fails to disclose to the board his interest in a transaction (where the other directors do not know) or fails to reveal material information (such as that the land he is selling is sinking into an abandoned coal mine) cannot claim the MBCA safe harbor for board approval. On the other hand, if the DCIT is approved by informed directors who have neither a conflicting interest in the transaction nor financial ties to the conflicted director, the transaction falls within the safe harbor even if the directors are all close personal friends.

Points for Discussion

1. How bright?

What are the advantages and disadvantages of Subchapter F and its bright-line definition of a "director's conflicting interest transaction"? For example, what if the corporation enters into a transaction with a director's young cousin, who was orphaned and raised by the director? Are you satisfied by the explanation that the narrowly circumscribed definition of "related person" under Subchapter F was intended to leave some questionable situations immune from judicial scrutiny on the ground (as explained in the Official Comment) that "the legislative draft[er] who chooses to suppress marginal anomalies by resorting to generalized statements of principle will pay a cost in terms of predictability"?

2. *Can a court dodge Subchapter F?*

What is the standard of review if the requisite number of qualified directors approve a DCIT, following the procedures laid out in Subchapter F? What are the alternatives for a court convinced that the terms of the DCIT are manifestly unfair to the corporation?

B. Common Law Approaches

Given the complex and evolving history as well as different approaches across states, there remains a great deal of confusion regarding the relationship between common law voidability, fairness review, business judgment review, and the interplay between common law and statutes. In this section, we explore more deeply the statutory concepts we introduced above by analyzing several common law approaches and various doctrines on fiduciary duties in interested transactions.

As we have seen, both narrow and broad interpretations of interested transaction statutes exist. The narrow interpretation views the statute as concerning only the issue of voidability, and would subject claims of breach of fiduciary duty to separate common law analysis. In this view, the sole purpose of the statutory provision is to save the transaction from a common law claim of *per se* voidability. For example, the statute enables a board to avoid the voidability problem by having a majority of the voting and disinterested directors approve the transaction. By contrast, under a broad interpretation, the statute applies for breach of fiduciary duty in addition to suits to void the agreement.

The MBCA's safe harbor has evolved from a statute that could be read narrowly to a statute that explicitly incorporates the broad reading and makes clear that disinterested director approval triggers a business judgment standard of review.

Delaware's statute is not so clear and the case law has straddled both narrow and broad readings. Which reading do you think is a better fit for Delaware? Consider that DGCL § 144(a) covers only completed transactions between the corporation and its directors or officers, and transactions between companies with interlocked boards. Further consider the language of section 144(a) that no contract or transaction "shall be void or voidable solely for this reason." The realm of actionable fiduciary misconduct under the duty of loyalty is broader than the covered transactions, and section 144 cannot possibly preempt the common law entirely. By its plain language, it seems to make clear that if a transaction complies with a section 144 safe harbor, it will not be invalidated solely on the grounds of the offending interest, but it does not address fiduciary duty claims. For these reasons, a number of legal scholars and practitioners have argued that the narrow interpretation is the best understanding of DGCL § 144.

Although the statutory tests vary for determining the validity of a director self-dealing transaction, they tend to focus on three factors: board approval, shareholder approval, and fairness. The statutory safe harbors parallel the common law analysis for fiduciary claims, but are not exactly the same in all instances. Therefore, we now consider these factors in greater detail and from the additional perspective of common law analysis of a claim for breach of the fiduciary duty of loyalty.

1. Court-Determined Fairness

As we've seen, judicial review of director self-dealing transactions has changed over time. Statutes take the view that approval by informed, disinterested, independent directors or shareholders will rescue certain transactions from *per se* voidability under common law. But absent such approval, courts are still called on to review the "fairness" of director self-dealing transactions. Further, in states such as Delaware that have a statute susceptible to a narrow interpretation, it is possible that there was insufficient process for cleansing a transaction at common law for purposes of a breach of fiduciary duty of loyalty claim, and thus the defendants would bear the burden of showing fairness. So we begin with the question: what is "fairness"?

The judicial inquiry into fairness looks at both procedure and substance. The procedural inquiry typically focuses on the internal corporate process followed in obtaining approval by directors or shareholders. The courts focus on how the transaction was negotiated and approved, the disclosure given to decision makers, the ability of directors to be objective, and the effect of shareholder ratification.

Substantive fairness focuses on a comparison of the fair market value of the transaction to the price the corporation actually paid or was paid, as well as the corporation's need for and ability to consummate the transaction. The test has often been articulated as "whether the proposition submitted would have commended itself

> Consider the following description of the factors relevant to a fairness inquiry. Do you agree with this list? Are there any factors you think are missing?
>
> "While the concept of 'fairness' is incapable of precise definition, courts have stressed such factors as whether the corporation received in the transaction full value in all the commodities purchased; the corporation's need for the property; its ability to finance the purchase; whether the transaction was at the market price, or below, or constituted a better bargain than the corporation could have otherwise obtained in dealings with others; whether there was a detriment to the corporation as a result of the transaction; whether there was a possibility of corporate gain siphoned off by the directors directly or through corporations they controlled; and whether there was full disclosure—although neither disclosure nor shareholder assent can convert a dishonest transaction into a fair one."
>
> *Shlensky v. South Parkway Building Corp.*, 166 N.E.2d 793, 801–02 (Ill. 1960).

to an independent corporation." To the extent that this formulation contemplates independent arm's-length negotiation as providing the basis for fair market value, a range of prices can satisfy the test of substantive fairness. Consider the Official Comment to Subchapter F, MBCA § 8.60: "If the issue in a transaction is the 'fairness' of a price, 'fair' is not to be taken to imply that there is one single 'fair' price, all others being 'unfair.' Generally a 'fair' price is any price within a range that an unrelated party might have been willing to pay or willing to accept, as the case may be, for the relevant property, asset, service or commitment, following a normal arm's-length business negotiation. The same approach applies not only to gauging the fairness of price, but also to the fairness evaluation of any other key term of the deal."

The following classic case illustrates a court's application of the entire fairness standard in the context of a claim for breach of fiduciary duty of loyalty regarding an interested transaction.

Bayer v. Beran

49 N.Y.S. 2d 2 (Sup. Ct. 1944)

Shientag, Justice.

Three derivative stockholders' suits present for review two transactions upon which plaintiffs seek to charge the individual defendants, who are directors, with liability in favor of the corporate defendant, the Celanese Corporation of America. There are two causes of action alleging breach of fiduciary duty by the directors, one in connection with a program of radio advertising embarked upon by the corporation towards the end of 1941, and the other relating to certain payments of $30,000 a year made to Henri Dreyfus, one of its vice-presidents and a director, pursuant to a contract of employment entered into with him by the corporation.

Directors are fiduciaries. The fiduciary has two paramount obligations: responsibility and loyalty. The concept of loyalty, of constant, unqualified fidelity, has a definite and precise meaning. The fiduciary must subordinate his individual and private interests to his duty to the corporation whenever the two conflict.

The director of a business corporation is given a wide latitude of action. The law does not seek to deprive him of initiative and daring and vision. Business has its adventures, its bold adventures; and those who in good faith, and in the interests of the corporation they serve, embark upon them, are not to be penalized if failure, rather than success, results from their efforts. The law will not permit a course of conduct by directors, which would be applauded if it succeeded, to be condemned with a riot of adjectives simply because it failed. Directors of a commercial corporation may take chances, the same kind of chances that a man would take in his own business. Because they are given this wide latitude, the law will not hold directors liable for honest errors, for mistakes of judgment. To encourage freedom of action on the part of directors, or to put it another way, to discourage interference with the exercise of their free and independent judgment, there has grown up what is known as the "business judgment rule."

The "business judgment rule," however, yields to the rule of undivided loyalty. This great rule of law is designed "to avoid the possibility of fraud and to avoid the temptation of self-interest." The dealings of a director with the corporation for which he is the fiduciary are therefore viewed "with jealousy by the courts." *Globe Woolen Co. v. Utica Gas & Electric Co.*, 224 N.Y. 483, 121 N.E. 378, 380. Such personal transactions of directors with their corporations, such transactions as may tend to produce a conflict between self-interest and fiduciary obligation, are, when challenged, examined with the most scrupulous care, and if there is any evidence of improvidence or oppression, any indication of unfairness or undue advantage, the transactions will be voided . . . . "Their dealings with the corporation are subjected to rigorous scrutiny and where any of their contracts or engagements with the corporation are challenged the burden is on the director not only to prove the good faith of the transaction but also to show its inherent fairness from the viewpoint of the corporation and those interested therein." *Pepper v. Litton,* 308 U.S. 295, 306, 60 S. Ct. 238, 245, 84 L.Ed. 281.

The first, or 'advertising', cause of action charges the directors with negligence, waste and improvidence in embarking the corporation upon a radio advertising program beginning in 1942 and costing about $1,000,000 a year. It is further charged that they were negligent in selecting the type of program and in renewing the radio contract for 1943. More serious than these allegations is the charge that the directors were motivated by a noncorporate purpose in causing the radio program to be undertaken and in expending large sums of money therefor. It is claimed that this radio advertising was for the benefit of Miss Jean Tennyson, one of the singers on the program, who in private life is Mrs. Camille Dreyfus, the wife of the president of the company and one of its directors; that it was undertaken to 'further, foster and subsidize her career'; to 'furnish a vehicle' for her talents.

Eliminating for the moment the part played by Miss Tennyson in the radio advertising campaign, it is clear that the character of the advertising, the amount to be expended therefor, and the manner in which it should be used, are all matters of business judgment and rest peculiarly within the discretion of the board of directors. Under the authorities previously cited, it is not, generally speaking, the function of a court of equity to review these matters or even to consider them. Had the wife of the president of the company not been involved, the advertising cause of action could have been disposed of summarily. Her connection with the program, however, makes it necessary to go into the facts in some detail.

Before 1942 the company had not resorted to radio advertising. While it had never maintained a fixed advertising budget, the company had, through its advertising department, spent substantial sums of money for advertising purposes. In 1941, for example, the advertising expense was $683,000, as against net sales for that year of $62,277,000 and net profits (before taxes) of $13,972,000. The advertising was at all times directed towards the creation of a consumer preference which would compel or induce the various trade elements linking the corporation to the consumer to label the corporation's products so that the consumer would know he was buying the material he wanted. The company had always claimed that its products, which it had called or labeled 'Celanese', were different from rayon, chemically and physically; that its products had qualities, special and unique, which made them superior to rayon. The company had never called or designated its products as rayon.

As far back as ten years ago, a radio program was considered, but it did not seem attractive. In 1937, the Federal Trade Commission promulgated a rule, the effect of which was to require all celanese products to be designated and labeled rayon. The name 'Celanese' could no longer be used alone. The products had to be called or labeled 'rayon' or 'celanese rayon.' This gave the directors much concern. As one of them expressed it, 'When we were compelled to put our product under the same umbrella with rayon rather than being left outside as a separate product, a thermo-plastic such as nylon is, we believed we were being treated in an unfair manner and that it was up to us, however, to do the best we could to circumvent the situation in which we found ourselves . . . All manner of things were considered but there seemed only one thing we could do. We could either multiply our current advertising and our method of advertising in the same mediums we had been using, or we could go into radio.'

The directors decided towards the end of 1941 to resort to the radio and to have the company go on the air with a dignified program of fine music, the kind of program which they felt would be in keeping with what they believed to be the beauty and superior quality of their products. The radio program was not adopted on the spur of the moment or at the whim of the directors. They acted after studies reported to them, made by the advertising department, beginning in 1939. A radio consultant was employed to advise as to time and station. An advertising agency of national repute was engaged to take charge of the formulation and production of the program. It was decided to expend about $1,000,000 a year, but the commitments were to be subject to cancellation every thirteen weeks, so that the maximum obligation of the company would be not more than $250,000.

So far, there is nothing on which to base any claim of breach of fiduciary duty. Some care, diligence and prudence were exercised by these directors before they committed the company to the radio program. It was for the directors to determine whether they would resort to radio advertising; it was for them to conclude how much to spend; it was for them to decide the kind of program they would use.

Now we have to take up an unfortunate incident, one which cannot be viewed with the complacency displayed by some of the directors of the company. The Doctors

Dreyfus and their families own about 135,000 shares of common stock, the other directors about 10,000 shares out of a total outstanding issue of 1,376,500 shares. Some of these other directors were originally employed by Dr. Camille Dreyfus, the president of the company. His wife, to whom he has been married for about twelve years, is known professionally as Miss Jean Tennyson and is a singer of wide experience.

Dr. Dreyfus, as was natural, consulted his wife about the proposed radio program; he also asked the advertising agency, that had been retained, to confer with her about it. She suggested the names of the artists, all stars of the Metropolitan Opera Company, and the name of the conductor, prominent in his field. She also offered her own services as a paid artist. All of her suggestions as to personnel were adopted by the advertising agency. While the record shows Miss Tennyson to be a competent singer, there is nothing to indicate that she was indispensable or essential to the success of the program. She received $500 an evening. It would be far-fetched to suggest that the directors caused the company to incur large expenditures for radio advertising to enable the president's wife to make $24,000 in 1942 and $20,500 in 1943.

Of course it is not improper to appoint relatives of officers or directors to responsible positions in a company. But where a close relative of the chief executive officer of a corporation, and one of its dominant directors, takes a position closely associated with a new and expensive field of activity, the motives of the directors are likely to be questioned. The board would be placed in a position where selfish, personal interests might be in conflict with the duty it owed to the corporation. That being so, the entire transaction, if challenged in the courts, must be subjected to the most rigorous scrutiny to determine whether the action of the directors was intended or calculated "to subserve some outside purpose, regardless of the consequences to the company, and in a manner inconsistent with its interests."

After such careful scrutiny I have concluded that, up to the present, there has been no breach of fiduciary duty on the part of the directors. The president undoubtedly knew that his wife might be one of the paid artists on the program. The other directors did not know this until they had approved the campaign of radio advertising and the general type of radio program. The evidence fails to show that the program was designed to foster or subsidize 'the career of Miss Tennyson as an artist' or to 'furnish a vehicle for her talents.' That her participation in the program may have enhanced her prestige as a singer is no ground for subjecting the directors to liability, as long as the advertising served a legitimate and a useful corporate purpose and the company received the full benefit thereof.

The musical quality of 'Celanese Hour' has not been challenged, nor does the record contain anything reflecting on Miss Tennyson's competence as an artist. There is nothing in the testimony to show that some other soprano would have enhanced the artistic quality of the program or its advertising appeal. There is no suggestion that the present program is inefficient or that its cost is disproportionate to what a program of that character reasonably entails. Miss Tennyson's contract with the advertising agency retained by the directors was on a standard form, negotiated through her professional agent. Her compensation, as well as that of the other artists, was in conformity with that paid for comparable work. She received less than any of the other artists on the program. Although she appeared with a greater regularity than any other singer, she received no undue prominence, no special build-up. Indeed, all of the artists were subordinated to the advertisement of the company and of its products. The company was featured. It appears also that the popularity of the program has increased since it was inaugurated.

It is clear, therefore, that the directors have not been guilty of any breach of fiduciary duty, in embarking upon the program of radio advertising and in renewing it. The complaint is accordingly dismissed on the merits.

---

2. Approval by Informed, Disinterested, Independent Directors

As modern courts (and corporate statutes) have come to accept that disinterested and independent directors can have a cleansing effect on transactions involving director conflicts, one of the most litigated questions has been whether the directors who approved the deal were informed, disinterested, and independent.

There is also the possibility that a court will take a narrow interpretation of the statutory safe harbor. Notice that DGCL § 144 refers to "a majority of the disinterested directors, even though the disinterested directors be less than a quorum," whereas common law for fiduciary breach has generally required approval by a disinterested majority of the entire board in order to achieve cleansing effect. To see the difference, consider a nine-member board with a single informed, disinterested director. Under the section 144(a) statutory analysis, so long as she approves the transaction in good faith, it would not be presumptively voidable due to the offending interest. But under common law, there would not have been approval by a disinterested majority board, and thus the transaction could be subjected to the entire fairness standard instead of the business judgment rule with respect to a fiduciary breach claim. *See, e.g., Cumming v. Edens*, 2018 WL 992877 (Del. Ch. Feb. 20, 2018). Further, common law analysis of fiduciary duty has gener-

> Judicial deference to process, whether the self-dealing transaction was approved by directors or shareholders, depends on all material facts as to the transaction and the director's interest being properly disclosed. A useful illustration is the *Benihana* case. Remember that the court's conclusion that the business judgment rule applied turned on the court's finding that the directors who approved the financing package at issue in the case were sufficiently informed, including about the conflicted director's role in negotiating the terms of the package.

ally required that a majority of the board not only be disinterested but also independent in order to have cleansing effect.

To help you understand the limits to board approval, we consider the distinction between "interest" and "independence." Chancellor Chandler explained this distinction, which frequently arises when the plaintiff alleges demand futility in a derivative suit:

> Although interest and independence are two separate and distinct issues, these two attributes are sometimes confused by parties.
>
> A disabling "interest," as defined by Delaware common law, exists in two instances. The first is when (1) a director personally receives a benefit (or suffers a detriment), (2) as a result of, or from, the challenged transaction, (3) which is not generally shared with (or suffered by) the other shareholders of his corporation, and (4) that benefit (or detriment) is of such subjective material significance to that particular director that it is reasonable to question whether that director objectively considered the advisability of the challenged transaction to the corporation and its shareholders. The second instance is when a director stands on both sides of the challenged transaction. This latter situation frequently involves the first three elements listed above. As for the fourth element, whenever a director stands on both sides of the challenged transaction he is deemed interested and allegations of materiality have not been required.
>
> "Independence" does not involve a question of whether the challenged director derives a benefit *from the transaction* that is not generally shared with the other shareholders. Rather, it involves an inquiry into whether the director's decision resulted from that director being *controlled* by another. A director can be controlled by another if in fact he is *dominated* by that other party, whether through close personal or familial relationship or through force of will. A director can also be controlled by another if the challenged director is *beholden* to the allegedly controlling entity. A director may be considered beholden to (and thus controlled by) another when the allegedly controlling entity has the unilateral power (whether direct or indirect through control over other decision makers), to decide whether the challenged director continues to receive a benefit, financial or otherwise, upon which the challenged director is so dependent or is of such subjective material importance to him that the threatened loss of that benefit might create a reason to question whether the controlled director is able to consider the corporate merits of the challenged transaction objectively.
>
> Confusion over whether specific facts raise a question of interest or independence arises from the reality that similar factual circumstances may implicate *both* interest and independence, one but not the other, or neither.

By way of example, consider the following: Director *A* is both a director and officer of company *X*. Company *X* is to be merged into company *Z*. Director *A*'s vote in favor of recommending shareholder approval of the merger is challenged by a plaintiff shareholder.

Scenario One. Assume that one of the terms of the merger agreement is that director *A* was to be an officer in surviving company *Z, and* that maintaining his position as a corporate officer in the surviving company was material to director *A*. That fact might, when considered in light of all of the facts alleged, lead the Court to conclude that director A had a disabling interest.

Scenario Two. Assume that director *C* is both a director and the majority shareholder of company X. Director *C* had the power plausibly to threaten director *A*'s position as officer of corporation *X* should director *A* vote against the merger. Assume further that director *A*'s position as a corporate officer is material to director *A*. Those circumstances, when considered in light of *all* of the facts alleged, might lead the Court to question director *A*'s independence from director *C*, because it could reasonably be assumed that director *A* was controlled by director *C*, since director *A* was beholden to director *C* for his position as officer of the corporation. Confusion over whether to label this disability as a disqualifying "interest" or as a "lack of independence" may stem from the fact that, colloquially, director *A* was "interested" in keeping his job as a corporate officer. Scenario Two, however, raises only a question as to director *A*'s independence since there is nothing that suggests that director *A* would receive something *from the transaction* that might implicate a disabling interest.

If a plaintiff's allegations combined all facts described in both Scenario One *and* Scenario Two, it might be reasonable to question *both* director *A*'s interest and independence. Conversely, if all the facts in both scenarios were alleged *except* for the materiality of director *A*'s position as a corporate officer (perhaps because director *A* is a billionaire and his officer's position pays $20,000 per year and is not even of prestige value to him) then *neither* director *A*'s interest nor his independence would be reasonably questioned. The key issue is not simply whether a particular director receives a benefit from a challenged transaction not shared with the other shareholders, or solely whether another person or entity has the ability to take some benefit away from a particular director, but whether the possibility of gaining some benefit or the fear of losing a benefit is likely to be of such importance to that director that it is reasonable for the Court to question whether valid business judgment or selfish considerations animated that director's vote on the challenged transaction.

Orman v. Cullman, 794 A.2d 5, 25–26 n.50 (Del. Ch. 2002).

Finally, corporate statutes make clear that directors with a direct or indirect financial interest are deemed "interested." But the statutes usually do not address what kind of *non-financial relationship* with an interested director will call into question the approval by a director who otherwise would be considered disinterested.

As we have seen, federal law, including stock exchange rules, requires a certain degree of director independence. But state law goes further with respect to the approval of conflicted transactions. For example, Official Comment 5 to former MBCA § 8.31 suggests such a director with such a non-financial interest would be considered "interested" (though perhaps the statute should have used the term "non-independent") if the director had "a relationship with the other parties to the transaction such that the relationship might reasonably be expected to affect his judgment in the particular matter in a manner adverse to the corporation."

3. Disinterested Shareholder Approval

An interested transaction can be insulated from judicial review if it is approved or subsequently ratified by shareholders, provided that the material facts as to the transaction and the director's interest were disclosed to the shareholders. At common law, informed shareholder ratification created a presumption that the transaction was fair. Thus, many courts indicated that shareholder ratification shifts the burden of proof to the party challenging the transaction to show that the terms were so unequal as to amount to waste. However, when interested directors owned a majority of the shares, shareholder ratification generally did not shift the burden.

The shareholder-approval provisions of the interested-director statutes seem to codify the common law. Thus, an interested-director transaction is not void or voidable if the director's interest is disclosed to the shareholders and the shareholders approve the transaction. Technical compliance with the statutory procedures, however, will not immunize a transaction from scrutiny for fairness where the interested directors hold a majority of the shares voted in favor of the transaction. At common law for breach of fiduciary duty claims, shareholder ratification must be informed and disinterested to have cleansing effect.

To avoid the uncertainty of whether shareholder approval is valid if the interested directors vote their shares, it is now common to obtain "majority of the minority" shareholder approval as a condition of the transaction. In fact, some statutes do not permit the voting of shares owned by interested directors when shareholders are asked to approve a director self-dealing transaction. *See* Cal. Corp. Code § 310(a)(1).

Approval by shareholders, compared to that by directors, has the disadvantage that shareholders are not in a position to negotiate the terms of the transaction. Their approval or ratification is "take it or leave it." Should approval by a majority of disinterested shareholders be given conclusive weight? Or is there still a role for the court to ensure fairness? And what is the role of a "waste" claim, an allegation that shareholder approval should not—or cannot—insulate the transaction from review because it was a waste of corporate assets?

The following cases discuss these questions. The first involves a director stock option plan that was ratified by shareholders of a public company. The second involves an acquisition of a public company by another company in which directors of the acquired company had a substantial financial interest.

Lewis v. Vogelstein

699 A.2d 327 (Del. Ch. 1997)

Allen, Chancellor.

This shareholders' suit challenges a stock option compensation plan for the directors of Mattel, Inc., which was approved or ratified by the shareholders of the company at its 1996 Annual Meeting of Shareholders ["1996 Plan" or "Plan"].

I.

The facts as they appear in the pleading are as follows. The Plan was adopted in 1996 and ratified by the company's shareholders at the 1996 annual meeting. It contemplates two forms of stock option grants to the company's directors: a one-time grant of options on a block of stock and subsequent, smaller annual grants of further options.

With respect to the one-time grant, the Plan provides that each outside director will qualify for a grant of options on 15,000 shares of Mattel common stock at the market price on the day such options are granted (the "one-time options"). The one-time options are alleged to be exercisable immediately upon being granted although they will achieve economic value, if ever, only with the passage of time. It is alleged that if not exercised, they remain valid for ten years.

With respect to the second type of option grant, the Plan qualifies each director for a grant of options upon his or her re-election to the board each year (the "Annual Options"). The maximum number of options grantable to a director pursuant to the annual options provision depends on the number of years the director has served on the Mattel board. Those outside directors with five or fewer years of service will qualify to receive options on no more than 5,000 shares, while those with more than five years service will qualify for options to purchase up to 10,000 shares. Once granted, these options vest over a four year period, at a rate of 25% per year. When exercisable, they entitle the holder to buy stock at the market price on the day of the grant. According to the complaint, options granted pursuant to the annual options provision also expire ten years from their grant date, whether or not the holder has remained on the board.

When the shareholders were asked to ratify the adoption of the Plan, as is typically true, no estimated present value of options that were authorized to be granted under the Plan was stated in the proxy solicitation materials.

II.

As the presence of valid shareholder ratification of executive or director compensation plans importantly affects the form of judicial review of such grants, it is logical to begin an analysis of the legal sufficiency of the complaint by analyzing the sufficiency of the attack on the disclosures made in connection with the ratification vote.

A. Disclosure Obligation:

[The court rejected plaintiff's claim that defendants had a duty to disclose the estimated present value of the stock option grants to which directors might become entitled under the 1996 Plan.]

III.

I turn to the motion to dismiss the complaint's allegation to the effect that the Plan, or grants under it, constitute a breach of the directors' fiduciary duty of loyalty. As the Plan contemplates grants to the directors that approved the Plan and who recommended it to the shareholders, we start by observing that it constitutes self-dealing that would ordinarily require that the directors prove that the grants involved were, in the circumstances, entirely fair to the corporation. However, it is the case that the shareholders have ratified the directors' action. That ratification is attacked only on the ground just treated. Thus, for these purposes I assume that the ratification was effective. The question then becomes what is the effect of informed shareholder ratification on a transaction of this type (i.e., officer or director pay).

A. Shareholder Ratification Under Delaware Law:

What is the effect under Delaware corporation law of shareholder ratification of an interested transaction? The answer to this apparently simple question appears less clear than one would hope or indeed expect. Four possible effects of shareholder ratification appear logically available: First, one might conclude that an effective shareholder ratification acts as a complete defense to any charge of breach of duty. Second, one might conclude that the effect of such ratification is to shift the substantive test on judicial review of the act from one of fairness that would otherwise be obtained (because the transaction is an interested one) to one of waste. Third, one might conclude that the ratification shifts the burden of proof of unfairness to plaintiff, but leaves that shareholder-protective test in place. Fourth, one might conclude (perhaps because of great respect for the collective action disabilities that attend shareholder action in public corporations) that shareholder ratification offers no assurance of assent of a character that deserves judicial recognition. Thus, under this approach, ratification on full information would be afforded no effect. Excepting the fourth of these effects, there are cases in this jurisdiction that reflect each of these approaches to the effect of shareholder voting to approve a transaction.

In order to state my own understanding I first note that by shareholder ratification I do not refer to every instance in which shareholders vote affirmatively with respect to a question placed before them. I exclude from the question those instances in which shareholder votes are a necessary step in authorizing a transaction. Thus the law of ratification as here discussed has no direct bearing on shareholder action to amend a certificate of incorporation or bylaws. Nor does that law bear on shareholder votes necessary to authorize a merger, a sale of substantially all the corporation's assets, or to dissolve the enterprise. For analytical purposes one can set such cases aside.

1. *Ratification generally*: I start with principles broader than those of corporation law. Ratification is a concept deriving from the law of agency which contemplates the ex post conferring upon or confirming of the legal authority of an agent in circumstances in which the agent had no authority or arguably had no authority. To be effective, of course, the agent must fully disclose all relevant circumstances with respect to the transaction to the principal prior to the ratification. Beyond that, since the relationship between a principal and agent is fiduciary in character, the agent in seeking ratification must act not only with candor, but with loyalty. Thus an attempt to coerce the principal's consent improperly will invalidate the effectiveness of the ratification.

Assuming that a ratification by an agent is validly obtained, what is its effect? One way of conceptualizing that effect is that it provides, after the fact, the grant of authority that may have been wanting at the time of the agent's act. Another might be to view the ratification as consent or as an estoppel by the principal to deny a lack of authority. In either event the effect of informed ratification is to validate or affirm the act of the agent as the act of the principal.

Application of these general ratification principles to shareholder ratification is complicated by three other factors. First, most generally, in the case of shareholder ratification there is of course no single individual acting as principal, but rather a class or group of divergent individuals—the class of shareholders. This aggregate quality of the principal means that decisions to affirm or ratify an act will be subject to collective action disabilities; that some portion of the body doing the ratifying may in fact have conflicting interests in the transaction; and some dissenting members of the class may be able to assert more or less convincingly that the "will" of the principal is wrong, or even corrupt and ought not to be binding on the class. In the case of individual ratification these issues won't arise, assuming that the principal does not suffer from multiple personality disorder. Thus the collective nature of shareholder ratification makes it more likely that following a claimed shareholder ratification, nevertheless, there is a litigated claim on behalf of the principal that the agent lacked authority or breached its duty. The second, mildly complicating factor present in shareholder ratification is the fact that in corporation law the "ratification" that shareholders provide will often not be directed to lack of legal authority of an agent but will relate to the consistency of some authorized director action with the equitable duty of loyalty. Thus shareholder ratification sometimes acts not to confer legal authority—but as in this case—to affirm that action taken is consistent with shareholder interests. Third, when what is "ratified" is a director conflict transaction, the statutory law—in Delaware Section 144 of the Delaware General Corporation Law—may bear on the effect.

2. *Shareholder ratification*: These differences between shareholder ratification of director action and classic ratification by a single principal, do lead to a difference in the effect of a valid ratification in the shareholder context. The principal novelty added to ratification law generally by the shareholder context, is the idea—no doubt analogously present in other contexts in which common interests are held—that, in addition to a claim that ratification was defective because of incomplete information or coercion, shareholder ratification is subject to a claim by a member of the class that the ratification is ineffectual (1) because a majority of those affirming the transaction had a conflicting interest with respect to it or (2) because the transaction that is ratified constituted a corporate waste. As to the second of these, it has long been held that shareholders may not ratify a waste except by a unanimous vote. The idea behind this rule is apparently that a transaction that satisfies the high standard of waste constitutes a gift of corporate property and no one should be forced against their will to make a gift of their property. In all events, informed, uncoerced, disinterested shareholder ratification of a transaction in which corporate directors have a material conflict of interest has the effect of protecting the transaction from judicial review except on the basis of waste.

B. The Waste Standard:

The judicial standard for determination of corporate waste is well developed. Roughly, a waste entails an exchange of corporate assets for consideration so disproportionately small as to lie beyond the range at which any reasonable person might be willing to trade. Most often the claim is associated with a transfer of corporate assets that serves no corporate purpose; or for which no consideration at all is received. Such a transfer is in effect a gift. If, however, there is *any substantial* consideration received by the corporation, and if there is a *good faith judgment* that in the circumstances the transaction is worthwhile, there should be no finding of waste, even if the fact finder would conclude *ex post* that the transaction was unreasonably risky. Any other rule would deter corporate boards from the optimal rational acceptance of risk. Courts are ill-fitted to attempt to weigh the "adequacy" of consideration under the waste standard or, ex post, to judge appropriate degrees of business risk.

[The court concluded that plaintiff's complaint should not be dismissed because the one time option grants to the directors were sufficiently unusual as to require further inquiry into whether they constituted waste.]

Harbor Finance Partners v. Huizenga

751 A.2d 879 (Del. Ch. 1999)

Strine, Vice Chancellor.

This matter involves a challenge to the acquisition of AutoNation, Incorporated by Republic Industries, Inc. A shareholder plaintiff contends that this acquisition (the "Merger") was a self-interested transaction effected for the benefit of Republic directors who owned a substantial block of AutoNation shares, that the terms of the transaction were unfair to Republic and its public stockholders, and that stockholder approval of the transaction was procured through a materially misleading proxy statement (the "Proxy Statement").

The Rule 12(b)(6) motion: The complaint fails to state a claim that the disclosures in connection with the Merger were misleading or incomplete. The affirmative stockholder vote on the Merger was informed and uncoerced, and disinterested shares constituted the overwhelming proportion of the Republic electorate. As a result, the business judgment rule standard of review is invoked and the Merger may only be attacked as wasteful. As a matter of logic and sound policy, one might think that a fair vote of disinterested stockholders in support of the transaction would dispose of the case altogether because a waste claim must be supported by facts demonstrating that "no person of ordinary sound business judgment" could consider the merger fair to Republic and because many disinterested and presumably rational Republic stockholders voted for the Merger. But under an unbroken line of authority dating from early in this century, a non-unanimous, although overwhelming, free and fair vote of disinterested stockholders does not extinguish a claim for waste. The waste vestige does not aid the plaintiff here, however, because the complaint at best alleges that the Merger was unfair and does not plead facts demonstrating that no reasonable person of ordinary business judgment could believe the transaction advisable for Republic. Thus I grant the defendants' motion to dismiss under Chancery Court Rule 12(b)(6).

II. Legal Analysis

4. Why Doesn't A Fully Informed, Uncoerced Vote Of Disinterested Stockholders Foreclose A Waste Claim?

Although I recognize that our law has long afforded plaintiffs the vestigial right to prove that a transaction that a majority of fully informed, uncoerced independent stockholders approved by a non-unanimous vote was wasteful, I question the continued utility of this "equitable safety valve."

The origin of this rule is rooted in the distinction between voidable and void acts, a distinction that appears to have grown out of the now largely abolished *ultra vires* doctrine. Voidable acts are traditionally held to be ratifiable because the corporation can lawfully accomplish them if it does so in the appropriate manner. Thus if directors who could not lawfully effect a transaction without stockholder approval did so anyway, and the requisite approval of the stockholders was later attained, the transaction is deemed fully ratified because the subsequent approval of the stockholders cured the defect.

In contrast, void acts are said to be non-ratifiable because the corporation cannot, in any case, lawfully accomplish them. Such void acts are often described in conclusory terms such as "ultra vires" or "fraudulent" or as "gifts or waste of corporate assets." Because at first blush it seems it would be a shocking, if not theoretically impossible, thing for stockholders to be able to sanction the directors in committing illegal acts or acts beyond the authority of the corporation, it is unsurprising that it has been held that stockholders cannot validate such action by the directors, even on an informed basis.

One of the many practical problems with this seemingly sensible doctrine is that its actual application has no apparent modern day utility insofar as the doctrine covers claims of waste or gift, except as an opportunity for Delaware courts to second-guess stockholders. There are several reasons I believe this to be so.

First, the types of "void" acts susceptible to being styled as waste claims have little of the flavor of patent illegality about them, nor are they categorically *ultra vires*. Put another way, the oft-stated proposition that "waste cannot be ratified" is a tautology that, upon close examination, has little substantive meaning. I mean, what rational person would ratify "waste"? Stating the question that way, the answer is, of course, no one. But in the real world stockholders are not asked to ratify obviously wasteful transactions. Rather than lacking any plausible business rationale or being clearly prohibited by statutory or common law, the transactions attacked as waste in Delaware courts are ones that are quite ordinary in the modern business world. Thus a review of the Delaware cases reveals that our courts have reexamined the merits of stockholder votes approving such transactions as: stock option plans; the fee agreement between a mutual fund and its investment advisor; corporate mergers; the purchase of a business in the same industry as the acquiring corporation; and the repurchase of a corporate insider's shares in the company. These are all garden variety transactions that may be validly accomplished by a Delaware corporation if supported by sufficient consideration, and what is sufficient consideration is a question that fully informed stockholders seem as well positioned as courts to answer. That is, these transactions are neither per se *ultra vires* or illegal; they only become "void" upon a determination that the corporation received no fair consideration for entering upon them.

Second, the waste vestige is not necessary to protect stockholders and it has no other apparent purpose. While I would hesitate to permit stockholders to ratify a blatantly illegal act—such as a board's decision to indemnify itself against personal liability for intentionally violating applicable environmental laws or bribing government officials to benefit the corporation—the vestigial exception for waste has little to do with corporate integrity in the sense of the corporation's responsibility to society as a whole. Rather, if there is any benefit in the waste vestige, it must consist in protecting stockholders. And where disinterested stockholders are given the information necessary to decide whether a transaction is beneficial to the corporation or wasteful to it, I see little reason to leave the door open for a judicial reconsideration of the matter.

The fact that a plaintiff can challenge the adequacy of the disclosure is in itself a substantial safeguard against stockholder approval of waste. If the corporate board failed to provide the voters with material information undermining the integrity or financial fairness of the transaction subject to the vote, no ratification effect will be accorded to the vote and the plaintiffs may press all of their claims. As a result, it is difficult to imagine how elimination of the waste vestige will permit the accomplishment of unconscionable corporate transactions, unless one presumes that stockholders are, as a class, irrational and that they will rubber stamp outrageous transactions contrary to their own economic interests.

In this regard, it is noteworthy that Delaware law does not make it easy for a board of directors to obtain "ratification effect" from a stockholder vote. The burden to prove that the vote was fair, uncoerced, and fully informed falls squarely on the board. Given the fact that Delaware law imposes no heightened pleading standards on plaintiffs alleging material nondisclosures or voting coercion and given the pro-plaintiff bias inherent in Rule 12(b)(6), it is difficult for a board to prove ratification at the pleading stage. If the board cannot prevail on a motion to dismiss, the defendant directors will be required to submit to discovery and possibly to a trial.

Nor is the waste vestige necessary to protect minority stockholders from oppression by majority or controlling stockholders. Chancellor Allen recently noted that the justification for the waste vestige is "apparently that a transaction that satisfies the high standard of waste constitutes a gift of corporate property and no one should be forced against their will to make a gift of their property." This justification is inadequate to support continued application of the exception. As an initial matter, I note that property of the corporation is not typically thought of as personal property of the stockholders, and that it is common for corporations to undertake important value-affecting transactions over the objection of some of the voters or without a vote at all.

In any event, my larger point is that this solicitude for dissenters' property rights is already adequately accounted for elsewhere in our corporation law. Delaware fiduciary law ensures that a majority or controlling stockholder cannot use a stockholder vote to insulate a transaction benefiting that stockholder from judicial examination. Only votes controlled by stockholders who are not "interested" in the transaction at issue are eligible for ratification effect in the sense of invoking the business judgment rule rather than the entire fairness form of review. That is, only the votes of those stockholders with no economic incentive to approve a wasteful transaction count.

Third, I find it logically difficult to conceptualize how a plaintiff can ultimately prove a waste or gift claim in the face of a decision by fully informed, uncoerced, independent stockholders to ratify the transaction. The test for waste is whether any person of ordinary sound business judgment could view the transaction as fair.

If fully informed, uncoerced, independent stockholders have approved the transaction, they have, it seems to me, made the decision that the transaction is "a fair exchange." As such, it is difficult to see the utility of allowing litigation to proceed in which the plaintiffs are permitted discovery and a possible trial, at great expense to the corporate defendants, in order to prove to the court that the transaction was so devoid of merit that each and every one of the voters comprising the majority must be disregarded as too hopelessly misguided to be considered a "person of ordinary sound business judgment." In this day and age in which investors also have access to an abundance of information about corporate transactions from sources other than boards of directors, it seems presumptuous and paternalistic to assume that the court knows better in a particular instance than a fully informed corporate electorate with real money riding on the corporation's performance.

Finally, it is unclear why it is in the best interests of disinterested stockholders to subject their corporation to the substantial costs of litigation in a situation where they have approved the transaction under attack. Enabling a dissident who failed to get her way at the ballot box in a fair election to divert the corporation's resources to defending her claim on the battlefield of litigation seems, if anything, contrary to the economic well-being of the disinterested stockholders as a class. Why should the law give the dissenters the right to command the corporate treasury over the contrary will of a majority of the disinterested stockholders? The costs to corporations of litigating waste claims are not trifling.

For all these reasons, a reexamination of the waste vestige would seem to be in order. Although there may be valid reasons for its continuation, those reasons should be articulated and weighed against the costs the vestige imposes on stockholders and the judicial system.

Points for Discussion

1. A place for "waste" review?

Note that Chancellor Allen and Vice Chancellor Strine expressed different views on whether a court should review a corporate transaction ratified by a majority of disinterested shareholders. Allen concluded that under Delaware law the transaction is still subject to judicial review under a "waste" standard. Strine applied this approach, but called for a reexamination of the "waste vestige" and noted in dicta that it is unnecessary, paternalistic, and costly. Who is more persuasive? And, by the way, what is the law in Delaware when judges on the Court of Chancery take different stances on the same question?

2. *Review under "waste" standard and the business judgment rule.*

As you may have also noticed, judicial review of corporate transactions for "waste" inquires into whether corporate decision makers approved a transaction in which no rational businessperson could conclude the corporation received fair value in the transaction. Is review under the "waste" standard consistent with the premises of the business judgment rule? How can it be said that directors are presumed to be informed, to act in good faith, and to not have conflicting interests when a court can determine that they approved an irrational business deal? Or is it that sometimes lack of information, bad faith, and conflicts of interest may not be provable—but something smells wrong—and the "waste" standard provides judges a safety valve?

———————

C.   Corporate Opportunity Doctrine

The corporate opportunity doctrine is a subset of director conflicts and the duty of loyalty. It forbids a director, officer, or managerial employee from diverting to himself any business opportunity that "belongs" to the corporation. In a 1939 decision laying out the doctrine, the Delaware Supreme Court held that a corporate fiduciary cannot take a business opportunity if (1) it is one that the corporation can financially undertake, (2) it is within the line of the corporation's business and advantageous to the corporation, and (3) it is one in which the corporation has an interest or a reasonable expectancy. *Guth v. Loft*, 5 A.2d 503 (Del. 1939). *Guth v. Loft* significantly expanded the corporate opportunity doctrine and represents the transformative case in this area.

As with many loyalty concepts, the corporate opportunity doctrine is simple to state but difficult to apply. Which "opportunities" should be turned over to the corporation and which can properly be exploited by the individual? When a business opportunity is presented to a corporate insider (usually a director or officer), can he accept it for himself or must he first offer it to the corporation? And are there opportunities that belong to the corporation so that the insider cannot take them even if the corporation, for some reason, is unable to do so?

To answer these questions, one must balance competing interests. On one hand, corporate managers are expected to further the corporation's expansion potential, and should not be allowed to advance their own economic interests at the expense of their corporation. On the other hand, corporate managers have their own entrepreneurial interests, and society benefits when persons are permitted to develop and exploit new business opportunitites.

Guth v. Loft involved a dispute between Charles G. Guth and a company he once ran, known as Loft, Inc. But it really is a story about Pepsi-Cola, the soft drink. Pepsi-Cola was invented in the late nineteenth century, and quickly became a popular drink. However, the Pepsi-Cola company rode a roller coaster of spiraling costs and declining profits and by 1931 it was declared bankrupt for a second time.

Guth, a colorful businessman who had made a fortune in candy and bottling businesses, took over Pepsi-Cola when Coca-Cola Company, a supplier to his businesses, rejected his demands for a volume discount. Guth vowed he would "show them" by purchasing Pepsi-Cola. Guth tweaked Pepsi-Cola's formula and reduced prices, and within a few years the company was thriving. Guth owned 91% of Pepsi-Cola's shares.

Meanwhile, Guth's other company, Loft, Inc., was crumbling, and Guth agreed to sell back his Loft shares. The remaining shareholders of Loft were furious about how Guth had treated them, pointing out that Loft had paid Pepsi-Cola's startup expenses and that it was Loft's soda fountains, capital, and employees that had made Pepsi-Cola a success. The shareholders brought a suit on behalf of Loft against Guth, alleging that Guth's investment in Pepsi-Cola had been the taking of a corporate opportunity of Loft. The complaint alleged Guth could not have undertaken the Pepsi-Cola venture on his own: he lacked the funds; and it was his position at Loft that made the deal possible. Guth responded that the Pepsi-Cola opportunity was not an opportunity meant for Loft, which was primarily in the retail candy business.

After a 46-day trial, Loft won and the Delaware Supreme Court affirmed, expanding the corporate opportunity doctrine to include a broader "line of business" test in addition to a narrower "interest or expectancy" test (both are described below).

Notice that the corporate opportunity doctrine, compared to other types of fiduciary duties, focuses on *potential* harm to the corporation, not actual harm. The unlawful usurpation of a corporate opportunity happens when the corporate manager takes the opportunity, without presenting it to the corporation. The corporation might have rejected the opportunity, and even if the corporation had accepted it, the opportunity might not have been profitable. For this reason, the usual remedy for the unlawful taking of a corporate opportunity is for the corporation to receive the profits the manager derived from the opportunity, if any—that is, the corporate manager must hold the opportunity in "constructive trust" for the corporation.

We cover the corporate opportunity doctrine by presenting a well-known Delaware case and then examining several categories of tests. Our goal is to give you a sense of where the lines are drawn between those opportunities that belong to the corporation and those that do not.

1. Delaware's Approach to Corporate Opportunities

Broz v. Cellular Information Systems, Inc.

673 A.2d 148 (Del. 1996)

VEASEY, CHIEF JUSTICE.

Robert F. Broz ("Broz") is the President and sole stockholder of RFB Cellular, Inc. ("RFBC"), a Delaware corporation engaged in the business of providing cellular telephone service in the Midwestern United States. At the time of the conduct at issue in this appeal, Broz was also a member of the board of directors of plaintiff below-appellee, Cellular Information Systems, Inc. ("CIS"). CIS is a publicly held Delaware corporation and a competitor of RFBC.

Broz has been the President and sole stockholder of RFBC since 1992. RFBC owns and operates an FCC license area, known as the Michigan-4 Rural Service Area Cellular License ("Michigan-4"). The license entitles RFBC to provide cellular telephone service to a portion of rural Michigan. Although Broz' efforts have been devoted primarily to the business operations of RFBC, he also served as an outside director of CIS at the time of the events at issue in this case. CIS was at all times fully aware of Broz' relationship with RFBC and the obligations incumbent upon him by virtue of that relationship.

In April of 1994, Mackinac Cellular Corp. ("Mackinac") sought to divest itself of Michigan-2, the license area immediately adjacent to Michigan-4. To this end, Mackinac contacted Daniels & Associates ("Daniels") and arranged for the brokerage firm to seek potential purchasers for Michigan-2. In compiling a list of prospects, Daniels included RFBC as a likely candidate. In May of 1994, David Rhodes, a representative of Daniels, contacted Broz and broached the subject of RFBC's possible acquisition of Michigan-2. Broz later signed a confidentiality agreement at the request of Mackinac, and received the offering materials pertaining to Michigan-2.

Michigan-2 was not, however, offered to CIS. Apparently, Daniels did not consider CIS to be a viable purchaser for Michigan-2 in light of CIS' recent financial difficulties. The record shows that, at the time Michigan-2 was offered to Broz, CIS had recently emerged from lengthy and contentious Chapter 11 proceedings. Pursuant to the Chapter 11 Plan of Reorganization, CIS entered into a loan agreement that substantially impaired the company's ability to undertake new acquisitions or to incur new debt. In fact, CIS would have been unable to purchase Michigan-2 without the approval of its creditors.

During the period from early 1992 until the time of CIS' emergence from bankruptcy in 1994, CIS divested itself of some fifteen separate cellular license systems. CIS contracted to sell four additional license areas on May 27, 1994, leaving CIS with only five remaining license areas, all of which were outside of the Midwest.

On June 13, 1994, following a meeting of the CIS board, Broz spoke with CIS' Chief Executive Officer, Richard Treibick ("Treibick"), concerning his interest in acquiring Michigan-2. Treibick communicated to Broz that CIS was not interested in Michigan-2. Treibick further stated that he had been made aware of the Michigan-2 opportunity prior to the conversation with Broz, and that any offer to acquire Michigan-2 was rejected. After the commencement of the PriCellular tender offer, in August of 1994, Broz contacted another CIS director, Peter Schiff ("Schiff"), to discuss the possible acquisition of Michigan-2 by RFBC. Schiff, like Treibick, indicated that CIS had neither the wherewithal nor the inclination to purchase Michigan-2. In late September of 1994, Broz also contacted Stanley Bloch ("Bloch"), a director and counsel for CIS, to request that Bloch represent RFBC in its dealings with Mackinac. Bloch agreed to represent RFBC, and, like Schiff and Treibick, expressed his belief that CIS was not at all interested in the transaction. Ultimately, all the CIS directors testified at trial that, had Broz inquired at that time, they each would have expressed the opinion that CIS was not interested in Michigan-2.

On June 28, 1994, following various overtures from PriCellular concerning an acquisition of CIS, six CIS directors entered into agreements with PriCellular to sell their shares in CIS at a price of $2.00 per share. These agreements were contingent upon, *inter alia*, the consummation of a PriCellular tender offer for all CIS shares at the same price. Financing difficulties ultimately caused PriCellular to delay the closing date of the tender offer from September 16, 1994 until October 14, 1994 and then again until November 9, 1994.

On August 6, September 6 and September 21, 1994, Broz submitted written offers to Mackinac for the purchase of Michigan-2. During this time period, PriCellular also began negotiations with Mackinac to arrange an option for the purchase of Michigan-2. PriCellular's interest in Michigan-2 was fully disclosed to CIS' chief executive, Treibick, who did not express any interest in Michigan-2, and was actually incredulous that PriCellular would want to acquire the license. Nevertheless, CIS was fully aware that PriCellular and Broz were bidding for Michigan-2 and did not interpose CIS in this bidding war.

In late September of 1994, PriCellular reached agreement with Mackinac on an option to purchase Michigan-2. The exercise price of the option agreement was set at $6.7 million, with the option remaining in force until December 15, 1994. Pursuant to the agreement, the right to exercise the option was not transferrable to any party other than a subsidiary of PriCellular. Therefore, it could not have been transferred to CIS. The agreement further provided that Mackinac was free to sell Michigan-2 to any party who was willing to exceed the exercise price of the Mackinac-PriCellular option contract by at least $500,000. On November 14, 1994, Broz agreed to pay Mackinac $7.2 million for the Michigan-2 license, thereby meeting the terms of the option agreement. An asset purchase agreement was thereafter executed by Mackinac and RFBC.

Nine days later, on November 23, 1994, PriCellular completed its financing and closed its tender offer for CIS. Prior to that point, PriCellular owned no equity interest in CIS.

APPLICATION OF THE CORPORATE OPPORTUNITY DOCTRINE

The doctrine of corporate opportunity represents but one species of the broad fiduciary duties assumed by a corporate director or officer. A corporate fiduciary agrees to place the interests of the corporation before his or her own in appropriate circumstances. The classic statement of the doctrine is derived from the venerable case of *Guth v. Loft, Inc.*

The corporate opportunity doctrine, as delineated by *Guth* and its progeny, holds that a corporate officer or director may not take a business opportunity for his own if: (1) the corporation is financially able to exploit the opportunity; (2) the opportunity is within the corporation's line of business; (3) the corporation has an interest or expectancy in the opportunity; and (4) by taking the opportunity for his own, the corporate fiduciary will thereby be placed in a position inimicable to his duties to the corporation. The Court in *Guth* also derived a corollary which states that a director or officer *may* take a corporate opportunity if: (1) the opportunity is presented to the director or officer in his individual and not his corporate capacity; (2) the opportunity is not essential to the corporation; (3) the corporation holds no interest or expectancy in the opportunity; and (4) the director or officer has not wrongfully employed the resources of the corporation in pursuing or exploiting the opportunity. *Guth*, 5 A.2d at 509.

Thus, the contours of this doctrine are well established. It is important to note, however, that the tests enunciated in *Guth* and subsequent cases provide guidelines to be considered by a reviewing court in balancing the equities of an individual case. No one factor is dispositive and all factors must be taken into account insofar as they are applicable. Cases involving a claim of usurpation of a corporate opportunity range over a multitude of factual settings. Hard and fast rules are not easily crafted to deal with such an array of complex situations. In the instant case, we find that the facts do not support the conclusion that Broz misappropriated a corporate opportunity.

We note at the outset that Broz became aware of the Michigan-2 opportunity in his individual and not his corporate capacity. As the Court of Chancery found, "Broz did not misuse proprietary information that came to him in a corporate capacity nor did he otherwise use any power he might have over the governance of the corporation to advance his own interests." 663 A.2d at 1185. In fact, it is clear from the record that Mackinac did not consider CIS a viable candidate for the acquisition of Michigan-2. Accordingly, Mackinac did not offer the property to CIS. In this factual posture, many of the fundamental concerns undergirding the law of corporate opportunity are not present (*e.g.*, misappropriation of the corporation's proprietary information). The burden imposed upon Broz to show adherence to his fiduciary duties to CIS is thus lessened to some extent. Nevertheless, this fact is not dispositive.

We turn now to an analysis of the factors relied on by the trial court. First, we find that CIS was not financially capable of exploiting the Michigan-2 opportunity. The record shows that CIS was in a precarious financial position at the time Mackinac presented the Michigan-2 opportunity to Broz. Having recently emerged from lengthy and contentious bankruptcy proceedings, CIS was not in a position to commit capital to the acquisition of new assets. Further, the loan agreement entered into by CIS and its creditors severely limited the discretion of CIS as to the acquisition of new assets and substantially restricted the ability of CIS to incur new debt.

Second, while it may be said with some certainty that the Michigan-2 opportunity was within CIS' line of business, it is not equally clear that CIS had a cognizable interest or expectancy in the license. Under the third factor laid down by this Court in *Guth*, for an opportunity to be deemed to belong to the fiduciary's corporation, the corporation must have an interest or expectancy in that opportunity. As this Court stated in *Johnston*, 121 A.2d at 924, "[f]or the corporation to have an actual or expectant interest in any specific property, there must be some tie between that property and the nature of the corporate business." Despite the fact that the nature of the Michigan-2 opportunity was historically close to the core operations of CIS, changes were in process. At the time the opportunity was presented, CIS was actively engaged in the process of divesting its cellular license holdings. CIS' articulated business plan did not involve any new acquisitions. Further, as indicated by the testimony of the entire CIS board, the Michigan-2 license would not have been of interest to CIS even absent CIS' financial difficulties and CIS' then current desire to liquidate its cellular license holdings. Thus, CIS had no interest or expectancy in the Michigan-2 opportunity.

Finally, the corporate opportunity doctrine is implicated only in cases where the fiduciary's seizure of an opportunity results in a conflict between the fiduciary's duties to the corporation and the self-interest of the director as actualized by the exploitation of the opportunity. In the instant case, Broz' interest in acquiring and profiting from Michigan-2 created no duties that were inimicable to his obligations to CIS. Broz, at all times relevant to the instant appeal, was the sole party in interest in RFBC, a competitor of CIS. CIS was fully aware of Broz' potentially conflicting duties. Broz, however, comported himself in a manner that was wholly in accord with his obligations to CIS. Broz took care not to usurp any opportunity which CIS was willing and able to pursue. Broz sought only to compete with an outside entity, PriCellular, for acquisition of an opportunity which both sought to possess. Broz was not obligated to refrain from competition with PriCellular. Therefore, the totality of the circumstances indicates that Broz did not usurp an opportunity that properly belonged to CIS.

In concluding that Broz had usurped a corporate opportunity, the Court of Chancery placed great emphasis on the fact that Broz had not formally presented the matter to the CIS board. In so holding, the trial court erroneously grafted a new requirement onto the law of corporate opportunity, *viz.*, the requirement of formal presentation under circumstances where the corporation does not have an interest, expectancy or financial ability.

The teaching of *Guth* and its progeny is that the director or officer must analyze the situation *ex ante* to determine whether the opportunity is one rightfully belonging to the corporation. If the director or officer believes, based on one of the factors articulated above, that the corporation is not entitled to the opportunity, then he may take it for himself. Of course, presenting the opportunity to the board creates a kind of "safe harbor" for the director, which removes the specter of a *post hoc* judicial determination that the director or officer has improperly usurped a corporate opportunity. Thus, presentation avoids the possibility that an error in the fiduciary's assessment of the situation will create future liability for breach of fiduciary duty. It is not the law of Delaware that presentation to the board is a necessary prerequisite to a finding that a corporate opportunity has not been usurped.

In concluding that Broz usurped an opportunity properly belonging to CIS, the Court of Chancery held that "[f]or practical business reasons CIS' interests with respect to the Mackinac transaction came to merge with those of PriCellular, even before the closing of its tender offer for CIS stock." Based on this fact, the trial court concluded that Broz was required to consider PriCellular's prospective, post-acquisition plans for CIS in determining whether to forego the opportunity or seize it for himself. Had Broz done this, the Court of Chancery determined that he would have concluded that CIS was entitled to the opportunity by virtue of the alignment of its interests with those of PriCellular.

We disagree. Broz was under no duty to consider the interests of PriCellular when he chose to purchase Michigan-2. At the time Broz purchased Michigan-2, PriCellular had not yet acquired CIS. Any plans to do so would still have been wholly speculative. Accordingly, Broz was not required to consider the contingent and uncertain plans of PriCellular in reaching his determination of how to proceed.

In reaching our conclusion on this point, we note that certainty and predictability are values to be promoted in our corporation law. Broz, as an active participant in the cellular telephone industry, was entitled to proceed in his own economic interest in the absence of any countervailing duty. The right of a director or officer to engage in business affairs outside of his or her fiduciary capacity would be illusory if these individuals were required to consider every potential, future occurrence in determining whether a particular business strategy would implicate fiduciary duty concerns.

We hold that Broz did not breach his fiduciary duties to CIS.

2. Corporate Opportunity Tests

We now consider several categories of corporate opportunity tests applied by the courts. It is important to note up front that these tests are often characterized as default rules, which corporate participants can waive. Indeed, Delaware has a statutory provision, DGCL § 122(17), which explicitly permits corporations to waive the protections of the corporate opportunity doctrine.

DGCL § 122
Specific Powers

Every corporation created under this chapter shall have power to—

(17) Renounce, in its certificate of incorporation or by action of its board of directors, any interest or expectancy of the corporation in, or in being offered an opportunity to participate in, specified business opportunities or specified classes or categories of business opportunities that are presented to the corporation or one or more of its officers, directors or stockholders.

A corporation or board of directors can choose to identify "classes or categories of business opportunities" by line or type of business, identity of originator, identity of the party or parties to or having an interest in the business opportunity, identity of the recipient of the business opportunity, periods of time, or geographical location. Many investors find waiver attractive, particularly for close or early-stage corporations. For example, venture capitalists often invest in numerous companies and are presented with numerous corporate opportunities. They might not invest in a corporation if they thought the investment would restrict their other opportunities.

However, the application of DGCL § 122(17) is not as clear as many would like. The comment to the subsection says it "does not change the level of judicial scrutiny that will apply to the renunciation of an interest or expectancy of the corporation in a business opportunity, which will be determined by the common law of fiduciary duty, including the duty of loyalty." Does that mean DGCL § 122(17) really is not much of a default rule, and the courts will analyze corporate opportunity disputes even when corporations have opted out of the doctrine? What should be the standard of review if the board renounces a business opportunity (business judgment rule or fairness)? Does it matter how the corporation renounces (in its articles or by board resolution)? Does the absence of a renunciation suggest that the corporation has an interest or expectancy in an opportunity?

Given these uncertainties, even corporations that opt out of the corporate opportunity doctrine may be subject to one or more of the categories of judicial tests. Below are a few of these categories. There are no clear lines here, and cases depend greatly on the facts, so we have included a few excerpts from some of the classic cases in the area.

Interest or expectancy. The interest or expectancy analysis is the earliest judicial test, and it is difficult to apply. The key point is that corporate opportunities are not limited to actual ownership. They include "interests" or "expectancies" that are less than an enforceable legal right. In *Litwin v. Allen*, 25 N.Y.S.2d 667, 686 (Sup. Ct. 1940), the court suggested how to discern whether the corporation has an interest or expectancy:

> This corporate right or expectancy, this mandate upon directors to act for the corporation, may arise from various circumstances, such as, for example, the fact that directors had undertaken to negotiate in the field on behalf of the corporation, or that the corporation was in need of the particular business opportunity to the knowledge of the directors, or that the business opportunity was seized and developed at the expense, and with the facilities of the corporation. It is noteworthy that in cases which have imposed this type of liability upon fiduciaries, the thing determined by the court to be the subject of the trust was a thing of special and unique value to the beneficiary; for example, real estate, a proprietary formula valuable to the corporation's business, patents indispensable or valuable to its business, a competing enterprise or one required for the growth and expansion of the corporation's business or the like.

Line of business. Under the line of business test, a corporation has a prior claim to a business opportunity presented to an officer or director that falls within the firm's particular line of business. The test is closely related to the "interest or expectancy" standard, but includes a practicality assessment of the corporation's ability to take on the business opportunity. In *Guth v. Loft*, 5 A.2d 503, 514 (Del. 1939), the court explained the concept as follows:

> The phrase is not within the field of precise definition, nor is it one that can be bounded by a set formula. It has a flexible meaning, which is to be applied reasonably and sensibly to the facts and circumstances of the particular case. Where a corporation is engaged in a certain business, and an opportunity is presented to it embracing an activity as to which it has fundamental knowledge, practical experience and ability to pursue, which, logically and naturally is adaptable to its business having regard for its financial position, and is one that is consonant with its reasonable needs and aspirations for expansion, it may be properly said that the opportunity is in the line of the corporation's business.

Thus, if a business proposition would require a corporation to modify its operating infrastructure beyond a certain threshold, the business opportunity would be found to be outside the corporation's line of business. Courts will typically apply the test to extend beyond a corporation's existing operations. The rationale for such an application is simple. Courts recognize that corporations are dynamic entities. Furthermore, shareholders reasonably expect that a corporation will go beyond the status quo and take advantage of highly profitable, but safe, opportunities.

The line of business test becomes even more difficult to apply when a director or officer wears more than one hat. In *Johnston v. Greene*, 121 A.2d 919 (Del. 1956), Odlum, a financier, who was an officer and director of numerous corporations, was offered in his individual capacity the chance to acquire all the stock of Nutt-Shel, as well as some related patents. Although the business of Nutt-Shel had no close relation to the business of Airfleets, Inc., of which Odlum was president, Odlum turned over to Airfleets the opportunity to buy the stock of Nutt-Shel. But he purchased the patents for his friends and associates and, to a limited extent, for himself. Airfleets, which had a large amount of cash, had the financial capability to buy the patents. The board of Airfleets, dominated by Odlum, voted to buy only the stock. In a shareholders' derivative action against Odlum and the directors, the Delaware Supreme Court found that Odlum had not breached his duty in the purchase of the patents. In discussing the problem of multiple conflicting loyalties, the court stated:

> At the time when the Nutt-Shel business was offered to Odlum, his position was this: He was the part-time president of Airfleets. He was also president of Atlas—an investment company. He was a director of other corporations and a trustee of foundations interested in making investments. If it was his fiduciary duty, upon being offered any investment opportunity, to submit it to a corporation of which he was a director, the question arises, Which corporation? Why Airfleets instead of Atlas? Why Airfleets instead of one of the foundations? So far as appears, there was no specific tie between the Nutt-Shel business and any of these corporations or foundations. Odlum testified that many of his companies had money to invest, and this appears entirely reasonable. How, then, can it be said that Odlum was under any obligation to offer the opportunity to one particular corporation? And if he was not under such an obligation, why could he not keep it for himself?

> Plaintiff suggests that if Odlum elects to assume fiduciary relationships to competing corporations he must assume the obligations that are entailed by such relationships. So he must, but what are the obligations? The mere fact of having funds to invest does not ordinarily put the corporations "in competition" with each other, as that phrase is used in the law of corporate opportunity. There is nothing inherently wrong in a man of large business and financial interests serving as a director of two or more investment companies, and both Airfleets and Atlas (to mention only two companies) must reasonably have expected that Odlum would be free either to offer to any of his companies any business opportunity that came to him personally, or to retain it for himself—provided always that

there was no tie between any of such companies and the new venture or any specific duty resting upon him with respect to it.

In short, which corporation does a director serve when on multiple boards?

Economic capacity. Another important factor in deciding whether there has been a usurpation of a corporate opportunity is whether the corporation has the economic capacity to take the opportunity. The importance of the corporation's ability to pay for the opportunity varies case by case. Some courts treat incapacity as an indication the opportunity was not of interest to the corporation, others that the corporation would have rejected it. Further, some courts focus on whether the corporation had liquid assets available, while others look to the corporation's financial solvency more generally and ask whether it could raise enough money to pay for the opportunity.

Corporate rejection. Courts broadly accept the notion that a manager can take a corporate opportunity if the corporation has rejected it. The important question is whether the opportunity was presented to, and rejected after full disclosure by, disinterested, independent corporate decision makers. By accepting the opportunity, the corporation precludes the manager from developing it individually. Proper rejection, however, precludes the corporation from later claiming the corporate opportunity.

Remedies. In general, the remedy for a breach of fiduciary duty is the award of damages in the amount of the harm the corporation suffered from the breach. When dealing with the taking of a corporate opportunity, however, the problem of the appropriate remedy is more complex. Recall that the harm when a corporate manager takes a corporate opportunity occurs before it is known how the corporation might have developed it and whether it will be profitable. The harm to the corporation is not actual, but instead the deprivation of the right to take the opportunity for itself.

One possible remedy for usurpation of a corporate opportunity is to assess damages according to the potential profits lost by the corporation, based on a calculation of the estimated value of the opportunity at the time of the taking given its likely returns and their risk. Another possible remedy is to assess the actual profits realized by the usurping manager on the theory of unjust enrichment. Such profits would be easy to measure if the manager had already sold the opportunity, although valuation problems may arise.

Courts have chosen the latter approach. The traditional remedy is the imposition of a constructive trust on the manager's new business. This approach eliminates messy valuation problems and assumes that the manager's actual profits approximate the corporation's potential lost profits. However, the offending manager is entitled to expenditures made in pursuing and developing the opportunity, including reasonable compensation.

————————

Points for Discussion

1. *Corporate expansion vs. entrepreneurship.*

Notice that the corporate-opportunity cases seem to go in two directions. Sometimes the courts focus on the corporation's expectancies and line of business—that is, the corporation's expansion potential. Sometimes the courts focus on the insider's interests in developing an outside business—that is, individual entrepreneurial motivations. Why not consider business opportunities only from the perspective of the corporation?

2. *Waiver of fiduciary duties.*

Delaware's statutory provision that allows the corporation to renounce an interest in specified business opportunities effectively means that the corporation is permitted to waive fiduciary duties. Notice that this provision applies only to the waiver of the corporate opportunity doctrine, but not to the waiver of director duties related to other aspects of the duty of loyalty. Why should the corporation be able to waive its interests in business opportunities, but not director loyalty in interested transactions? And does the statutory provision allow directors on the board to approve such a renunciation when they have an interest in the outside business opportunity?

CHAPTER 11

Good Faith and Oversight

The previous chapter covered the "classic" duty of loyalty, based on conflicts of interest. But a second version of the duty of loyalty has emerged in recent years, involving the concepts of "good faith" and "oversight." In this chapter, we focus on the evolution of this new version of the duty of loyalty, and the developing meaning of these two concepts. You can think of this new version as a "good faith and oversight" duty of loyalty.

We'll warn you at the outset that this new version of the duty of loyalty can seem confusing, particularly because it stems from the duty of care. The basic idea is that directors must make a good faith effort to exercise their duty of care in overseeing the corporation's business. If they fail to make this effort, and such failure is sufficiently serious, then they have breached their duties, and courts have determined that it should not be exculpable, and therefore is deemed a violation of the duty of loyalty.

We begin with the evolution of "good faith" focusing on the landmark Delaware case of *Disney*, which addressed questions about the board's responsibilities in awarding executive compensation. We consider the Delaware Supreme Court's insights into the categories of conduct that would violate the obligation of good faith.

Then we discuss the evolution of "oversight." The Delaware case law on the oversight duties of directors has evolved since early cases arose under the duty of care. Claims for failure of oversight have become known as *Caremark* claims after a Court of Chancery case from the 1990s.

Finally, armed with our understanding of these two terms, we then analyze the modern "good faith and oversight" version of the duty of loyalty, based on three important Delaware cases. *Stone v. Ritter*, the first case to articulate this modern duty, provides an opportunity to consider the oversight of financial risk. *Marchand v. Barnhill* clarifies aspects of *Caremark* claims, including oversight of "essential and mission critical" risks. And *Boeing* applies the modern approach to two horrific accidents, raising questions about the oversight responsibilities of directors when there is risk to human life.

In sum, the Delaware Supreme Court has categorized good faith as "a subsidiary element," or part of the duty of loyalty, and has set out standards for plaintiffs bringing claims for bad faith or failure of oversight. This area of law has been a hot area of litigation in recent years and is worth detailed study.

A. Evolution of "Good Faith"

Before we dive into *Disney*, it is worth noting that the payment of corporate executives presents unique challenges. Executive compensation is a double-edged sword. On one hand, it presents a classic (some say outrageous) conflict of interest. CEOs are paid hundreds of times more than average workers, and there has been much public debate and outrage about how much corporate executives receive. On the other hand, these lavish pay packages are publicly disclosed and shareholders frequently vote to approve them, in part because they help align the incentives of executives and shareholders, and potentially reduce the agency costs that arise from the separation of ownership and control.

Federal law regulates various aspects of public company executive pay, including requirements that companies discuss and analyze executive compensation in proxy statements, hold an annual "say on pay" shareholder advisory vote, and have compensation committees made up of independent directors. But state law has been central to disputes over both the process and substance of board decisions about executive compensation.

Under state corporate law, directors must act with care and in good faith in informing themselves and making decisions about executive compensation, but courts generally defer to their business judgment in the absence of conflicts of interest. Judicial review usually focuses on the decision-making process rather than the amount or structure of compensation. So long as the board or compensation committee consulted with pay experts, considered the pay scales at comparable companies, and deliberated in good faith, courts have accepted board process over judicial second-guessing. The waste standard represents the outer limit of this deference—it inquires into whether the directors irrationally squandered corporate assets.

By contrast, when interested or dominated directors set their own or others' compensation, the duty of loyalty is implicated as we have seen with our study of interested transactions. Although the standards for the duty of care and the duty of loyalty were relatively well developed, before the *Disney* case it was not very clear what standard would apply to a claim for lack of good faith.

The *Disney* dispute was notable for the size of the challenged award: The Walt Disney Company paid a $130 million severance package of cash and stock options to Michael Ovitz, a Hollywood talent agent who had been hired as the number-two executive at Disney and was terminated after just 14 months. The litigation also was notable for its twists and turns. In 1998, the Delaware Court of Chancery dismissed the shareholder-plaintiffs' derivative suit, stating that a large severance package alone was not enough to show a lack of due care or to constitute waste. On appeal, the

Delaware Supreme Court (*Brehm v. Eisner*) concluded the complaint was weak, but suggested the plaintiffs seek an inspection of Disney's "books and records" and granted leave to amend the complaint. In 2002, after obtaining documents and e-mails from Disney, the plaintiffs filed an amended complaint that painted a picture of board indifference and abdication of responsibility. In 2003, the Chancery Court accepted the amended complaint, concluding that it adequately alleged the Disney directors breached their "duty of good faith."

After extensive discovery, the Chancery Court conducted a 37-day trial with 24 witnesses and 1,033 trial exhibits that filled more than 22 binders. In its 2005 decision, the court found for the defendants on all counts, concluding that the directors' conduct was less than ideal, but not in bad faith or grossly negligent. The plaintiffs appealed again to the Delaware Supreme Court.

The facts were as follows. In 1994, Disney President and Chief Operating Officer, Frank Wells, died in a tragic helicopter crash. Only three months later, Michael Eisner, Disney's Chairman and Chief Executive Officer, had quadruple bypass heart surgery. The two events crystallized that successor planning had to become a priority at the company.

For nearly 25 years, Eisner had a social and professional relationship with Hollywood power-player Michael Ovitz, the leading partner and co-founder of Creative Artists Agency ("CAA"), a premier talent agency. At that time, CAA had 550 employees and a roster of about 1,400 of Hollywood's top actors, directors, writers, and musicians, generating about $150 million in annual revenues and an annual income of over $20 million for Ovitz. In 1995, when Ovitz began negotiations to leave CAA and join Music Corporation of America ("MCA"), Eisner became interested in recruiting Ovitz to join Disney.

Eisner and Irwin Russell, who was a Disney director and chairman of the compensation committee, first approached Ovitz about joining Disney. Both Russell and Eisner negotiated with Ovitz. Eisner had talks with Ovitz about the skills and experience needed at Disney. At some point in these talks, Ovitz came to believe that he and Eisner would run Disney together as co-CEOs. Russell led negotiations on the financial terms of the Ovitz employment contract. From the beginning Ovitz made it clear he was making $20 to $25 million a year at CAA, and he would not give up his 55% interest in the firm without "downside protection." During the summer of 1995, the parties agreed to a draft version of Ovitz's employment agreement (the "OEA") modeled after Eisner's and the late Mr. Wells' employment contracts.

Under the draft OEA, Ovitz would receive a five-year contract with two tranches of options—first, a tranche with three million options vesting in equal parts in the third, fourth, and fifth years of employment, and if the value of those options at the end of the five years had not appreciated to $50 million, Disney would make up the difference; second, a tranche of two million options that would vest immediately if

Disney and Ovitz opted to renew the contract. The proposed OEA also provided that absent defined causes, neither party could terminate the agreement without penalty. If Ovitz walked away for any reason other than those permitted under the OEA, he would forfeit any benefits remaining under the OEA and could be enjoined from working for a competitor. If Disney fired Ovitz for any reason other than gross negligence or malfeasance, Ovitz would be entitled to a non-fault payment (Non-Fault Termination or "NFT"), which consisted of his remaining salary, $7.5 million a year for unaccrued bonuses, the immediate vesting of his first tranche of options, and a $10 million cash out payment for the second tranche of options.

Russell prepared and gave Ovitz and Eisner a "case study" to explain the terms of the draft OEA. Russell expressed concern that the negotiated terms represented an extraordinary level of executive compensation, but he acknowledged that Ovitz was an "exceptional corporate executive" and "highly successful and unique entrepreneur" who merited "downside protection and upside opportunity." Coming from being a leading partner in a private firm, Ovitz would have to adjust to a smaller amount of cash compensation, but Russell noted that the negotiated salary for Ovitz would still be very large for Disney as it was higher than any other corporate officer's salary, even the CEO's. Moreover, the stock options granted under the OEA would exceed the standards applied within Disney and would "raise very strong criticism." Russell recommended additional study of this issue.

To assist in evaluating the financial terms of the OEA, Russell recruited Graef Crystal, an executive compensation consultant, and Raymond Watson, a member of Disney's compensation committee and a past Disney board chairman who had helped structure Wells' and Eisner's compensation packages. On August 10, Russell, Watson, and Crystal met and discussed a set of values using different and various inputs and assumptions, accounting for different numbers of options, vesting periods, and potential proceeds of option exercises at various times and prices.

Two days later, Crystal faxed to Russell a memo concluding that the OEA would provide Ovitz with approximately $23.6 million per year for the first five years, or $23.9 million a year over seven years if Ovitz exercised the two-year renewal option. Crystal opined those amounts would approximate Ovitz's current annual compensation at CAA. Additional discussion, however, led to Crystal's concern that the draft OEA gave Ovitz a situation of low risk and high return: Ovitz could hold the first tranche of options, wait out the five-year term, collect the $50 million guarantee, and then exercise the in-the-money options and receive an additional windfall. Russell responded that the guarantee wouldn't function as Crystal believed. Crystal then revised his original memo, adjusting the value of the OEA to $24.1 million per year. Up to that point, only three Disney directors—Eisner, Russell, and Watson—had been involved in the negotiations and knew the status of the draft OEA.

While Russell, Watson, and Crystal were finalizing their analysis of the OEA, Eisner told Ovitz about the options being structured in the two tranches rather than a single grant, and that Ovitz would join Disney only as President, not as a co-CEO with Eisner. After deliberating, Ovitz said he would accept those terms, and that evening Ovitz, Eisner, and their families celebrated together.

On August 14, Eisner and Ovitz signed a letter agreement, which outlined the basic terms of Ovitz's employment, and stated that the agreement (which would ultimately be drafted as a formal contract) was subject to approval by Disney's compensation committee and board of directors. Russell, Watson, and Eisner contacted each of the board members and informed them of the impending new hire. At that time, Disney also issued a public press release announcing the hiring of Ovitz and the reaction was extremely positive: Disney's stock price rose 4.4% in a single day, thereby increasing Disney's market capitalization by over $1 billion.

On September 26, 1995, the compensation committee (Russell, Watson, Poitier, and Lozano) met for one hour to consider the proposed terms of the OEA, among other agenda items. A term sheet was distributed at the meeting, although a draft of the OEA was not. The committee discussed historical comparables, such as Eisner's and Wells' option grants, and the factors that Russell, Watson, and Crystal had considered in setting the size of the option grants and the termination provisions of the contract. Watson shared the spreadsheet analysis that he had performed in August and discussed his findings with the committee. Crystal did not attend the meeting, although he was available by telephone to respond to questions if needed, but no one from the committee called. After Russell's and Watson's presentations, the General Counsel Sandy Litvack also responded to substantive questions. The committee voted unanimously to approve the OEA terms, subject to "reasonable further negotiations within the framework of the terms and conditions" described in the OEA.

Immediately after, the Disney board met in executive session. Eisner led the discussion relating to Ovitz, and Watson then explained his analysis, and both Watson and Russell responded to questions from the board. After further deliberation, the board voted unanimously to elect Ovitz as President.

Ovitz's tenure as President began on October 1, 1995, the date that the OEA was executed. When Ovitz took office, the initial reaction was optimistic. By the fall of 1996, however, it had become clear that Ovitz was "a poor fit with his fellow executives." By then the Disney directors were discussing that the disconnect with Ovitz was likely irreparable and that he would have to be terminated. Multiple theories arose as to why Ovitz did not succeed: he failed to follow Eisner's directives and generally did very little; Eisner's micromanaging prevented Ovitz from having the authority necessary to make the changes that Ovitz thought were appropriate; Ovitz was not given enough time for his efforts to bear fruit; Ovitz simply did not adapt to the Disney culture or fit in with other executives. General Counsel Litvack, with Eisner's approval, told Ovitz that he was not working out at Disney and that he should start looking for a graceful exit from Disney and a new job. Eisner also met several times with Ovitz and tried to persuade him to leave Disney. On September

30, 1996, the Disney board met. During an executive session of that meeting, and in small group discussions where Ovitz was not present, Eisner told the other board members of the continuing problems with Ovitz's performance.

During this period, Eisner was also working with Litvack to explore whether Disney could terminate Ovitz for cause so that it would not owe Ovitz the NFT payment. Litvack reviewed the OEA, refreshed himself on the meaning of "gross negligence" and "malfeasance," reviewed all the facts concerning Ovitz's performance, and consulted the co-head of Disney's litigation department and another in-house attorney. Litvack advised Eisner that he did not believe there was cause to terminate Ovitz under the OEA, and that it would be inappropriate, unethical, and a bad idea to attempt to coerce Ovitz (by threatening a for-cause termination) into negotiating for a smaller NFT package than the OEA provided. If pressed by Ovitz's attorneys, Disney would have to admit that in fact there was no cause, which could subject Disney to a wrongful termination lawsuit. Litvack also believed that attempting to avoid legitimate contractual obligations would harm Disney's reputation as an honest business partner and would affect its future business dealings.

In December 1996, Disney terminated Ovitz. Although the board did not meet to vote on the termination, most, if not all, of the Disney directors trusted Eisner's and Litvack's conclusion that there was no cause to terminate Ovitz, and that Ovitz should be terminated without cause even though that involved making the costly NFT payment.

In re The Walt Disney Company Derivative Litigation

906 A.2d 27 (Del. 2006)

Jacobs, Justice.

II. SUMMARY OF APPELLANTS' CLAIMS OF ERROR

The appellants claim that the Disney defendants breached their fiduciary duties to act with due care and in good faith by (1) approving the OEA, and specifically, its NFT provisions; and (2) approving the NFT severance payment to Ovitz upon his termination—a payment that is also claimed to constitute corporate waste. [The appellants also asserted claims against Ovitz, which the Court rejected in Part III.]

IV. THE CLAIMS AGAINST THE DISNEY DEFENDANTS

1. The Due Care Determinations

Our law presumes that "in making a business decision the directors of a corporation acted on an informed basis, in good faith, and in the honest belief that the action taken was in the best interests of the company." Those presumptions can be rebutted if the plaintiff shows that the directors breached their fiduciary duty of care or of loyalty or acted in bad faith. If that is shown, the burden then shifts to the director defendants to demonstrate that the challenged act or transaction was entirely fair to the corporation and its shareholders.

Because no duty of loyalty claim was asserted against the Disney defendants, the only way to rebut the business judgment rule presumptions would be to show that the Disney defendants had either breached their duty of care or had not acted in good faith. At trial, the plaintiff-appellants attempted to establish both grounds, but the Chancellor determined that the plaintiffs had failed to prove either.

The appellants challenge the Court of Chancery's determination that the full Disney board was not required to consider and approve the OEA, because the Company's governing instruments allocated that decision to the compensation committee. This challenge also cannot survive scrutiny.

As the Chancellor found, under the Company's governing documents the board of directors was responsible for selecting the corporation's officers, but under the compensation committee charter, the committee was responsible for establishing and approving the salaries, together with benefits and stock options, of the Company's CEO and President. The compensation committee also had the charter-imposed duty to "approve employment contracts, or contracts at will" for "all corporate officers who are members of the Board of Directors regardless of salary." That is exactly what occurred here. The full board ultimately selected Ovitz as President, and the compensation committee considered and ultimately approved the OEA, which embodied the terms of Ovitz's employment, including his compensation.

The Delaware General Corporation Law (DGCL) expressly empowers a board of directors to appoint committees and to delegate to them a broad range of responsibilities, which may include setting executive compensation. Nothing in the DGCL mandates that the entire board must make those decisions. At Disney, the responsibility to consider and approve executive compensation was allocated to the compensation committee, as distinguished from the full board. The Chancellor's ruling—that executive compensation was to be fixed by the compensation committee—is legally correct.

The appellants next challenge the Chancellor's determination that although the compensation committee's decision-making process fell far short of corporate governance "best practices," the committee members breached no duty of care in considering and approving the NFT terms of the OEA. That conclusion is reversible error, the appellants claim, because the record establishes that the compensation committee members did not properly inform themselves of the material facts and, hence, were grossly negligent in approving the NFT provisions of the OEA.

In our view, a helpful approach is to compare what actually happened here to what would have occurred had the committee followed a "best practices" (or "best case") scenario, from a process standpoint. In a "best case" scenario, all committee members would have received, before or at the committee's first meeting on September 26, 1995, a spreadsheet or similar document prepared by (or with the assistance of) a compensation expert (in this case, Graef Crystal). Making different, alternative assumptions, the spreadsheet would disclose the amounts that Ovitz could receive under the OEA in each circumstance that might foreseeably arise. One variable in that matrix of possibilities would be the cost to Disney of a non-fault termination for each of the five years of the initial term of the OEA. The contents of the spreadsheet would be explained to the committee members, either by the expert who prepared it or by a fellow committee member similarly knowledgeable about the subject. That spreadsheet, which ultimately would become an exhibit to the minutes of the compensation committee meeting, would form the basis of the committee's deliberations and decision.

Had that scenario been followed, there would be no dispute (and no basis for litigation) over what information was furnished to the committee members or when it was furnished. Regrettably, the committee's informational and decisionmaking process used here was not so tidy. That is one reason why the Chancellor found that although the committee's process did not fall below the level required for a proper exercise of due care, it did fall short of what best practices would have counseled.

The Disney compensation committee met twice: on September 26 and October 16, 1995. The minutes of the September 26 meeting reflect that the committee approved the terms of the OEA (at that time embodied in the form of a letter agreement), except for the option grants, which were not approved until October 16—after the Disney stock incentive plan had been amended to provide for those options. At the September 26 meeting, the compensation committee considered a "term sheet" which, in summarizing the material terms of the OEA, relevantly disclosed that in the event of a non-fault termination, Ovitz would receive: (i) the present value of his salary ($1 million per year) for the balance of the contract term, (ii) the present value of his annual bonus payments (computed at $7.5 million) for the balance of the contract term, (iii) a $10 million termination fee, and (iv) the acceleration of his options for 3 million shares, which would become immediately exercisable at market price.

Thus, the compensation committee knew that in the event of an NFT, Ovitz's severance payment alone could be in the range of $40 million cash, plus the value of the accelerated options. Because the actual payout to Ovitz was approximately $130 million, of which roughly $38.5 million was cash, the value of the options at the time of the NFT payout would have been about $91.5 million. Thus, the issue may be framed as whether the compensation committee members knew, at the time they approved the OEA, that the value of the option component of the severance package could reach the $92 million order of magnitude if they terminated Ovitz without cause after one year. The evidentiary record shows that the committee members were so informed.

On this question the documentation is far less than what best practices would have dictated. There is no exhibit to the minutes that discloses, in a single document, the estimated value of the accelerated options in the event of an NFT termination after one year. The information imparted to the committee members on that subject is, however, supported by other evidence, most notably the trial testimony of various witnesses about spreadsheets that were prepared for the compensation committee meetings.

The compensation committee members derived their information about the potential magnitude of an NFT payout from two sources. The first was the value of the "benchmark" options previously granted to Eisner and Wells and the valuations by Watson of the proposed Ovitz options. The committee's second source of information was the amount of "downside protection" that Ovitz was demanding. The committee members knew that by leaving CAA and coming to Disney, Ovitz would be sacrificing "booked" CAA commissions of $150 to $200 million—an amount that Ovitz demanded as protection against the risk that his employment relationship with Disney might not work out. Ovitz wanted at least $50 million of that compensation to take the form of an "up-front" signing bonus. Had the $50 million bonus been paid, the size of the option grant would have been lower. Because it was contrary to Disney policy, the compensation committee rejected the up-front signing bonus demand, and elected instead to compensate Ovitz at the "back end," by awarding him options that would be phased in over the five-year term of the OEA.

Despite its imperfections, the evidentiary record was sufficient to support the conclusion that the compensation committee had adequately informed itself of the potential magnitude of the entire severance package, including the options, that Ovitz would receive in the event of an early NFT.

The appellants' final claim in this category is that the Court of Chancery erroneously held that the remaining members of the old Disney board had not breached their duty of care in electing Ovitz as President of Disney. The only properly reviewable action of the entire board was its decision to elect Ovitz as Disney's President. The Chancellor determined that in electing Ovitz, the directors were informed of all information reasonably available and, thus, were not grossly negligent. We agree.

Well in advance of the September 26, 1995 board meeting the directors were fully aware that the Company needed—especially in light of Wells' death and Eisner's medical problems—to hire a "number two" executive and potential successor to Eisner. There had been many discussions about that need and about potential candidates who could fill that role even before Eisner decided to try to recruit Ovitz. Before the September 26 board meeting Eisner had individually discussed with each director the possibility of hiring Ovitz, and Ovitz's background and qualifications. The directors thus knew of Ovitz's skills, reputation and experience, all of which they believed would be highly valuable to the Company. The directors also knew that to accept a position at Disney, Ovitz would have to walk away from a very successful business—a reality that would lead a reasonable person to believe that Ovitz would likely succeed in similar pursuits elsewhere in the industry. The directors also knew of the public's highly positive reaction to the Ovitz announcement, and that Eisner and senior management had supported the Ovitz hiring. Indeed, Eisner, who had long desired to bring Ovitz within the Disney fold, consistently vouched for Ovitz's qualifications and told the directors that he could work well with Ovitz.

The board was also informed of the key terms of the OEA (including Ovitz's salary, bonus and options). Russell reported this information to them at the September 26, 1995 executive session, which was attended by Eisner and all non-executive directors. Russell also reported on the compensation committee meeting that had immediately preceded the executive session. And, both Russell and Watson responded to questions from the board. Relying upon the compensation committee's approval of the OEA and the other information furnished to them, the Disney directors, after further deliberating, unanimously elected Ovitz as President.

Based upon this record, we uphold the Chancellor's conclusion that, when electing Ovitz to the Disney presidency the remaining Disney directors were fully informed of all material facts, and that the appellants failed to establish any lack of due care on the directors' part.

2. The Good Faith Determinations

The Court of Chancery held that the business judgment rule presumptions protected the decisions of the compensation committee and the remaining Disney directors, not only because they had acted with due care but also because they had not acted in bad faith. In its Opinion the Court of Chancery defined bad faith as follows:

> Upon long and careful consideration, I am of the opinion that the concept of intentional dereliction of duty, a conscious disregard for one's responsibilities, is an appropriate (although not the only) standard for determining whether fiduciaries have acted in good faith. Deliberate indifference and inaction in the face of a duty to act is, in my mind, conduct that is clearly disloyal to the corporation. It is the epitome of faithless conduct.

Because of the increased recognition of the importance of good faith, some conceptual guidance to the corporate community may be helpful. The precise question is whether the Chancellor's articulated standard for bad faith corporate fiduciary conduct—intentional dereliction of duty, a conscious disregard for one's responsibilities—is legally correct. In approaching that question, we note that the Chancellor characterized that definition as "an appropriate (although not the only) standard for determining whether fiduciaries have acted in good faith." That observation is accurate and helpful, because as a matter of simple logic, at least three different categories of fiduciary behavior are candidates for the "bad faith" pejorative label.

The first category involves so-called "subjective bad faith," that is, fiduciary conduct motivated by an actual intent to do harm. That such conduct constitutes classic, quintessential bad faith is a proposition so well accepted in the liturgy of fiduciary law that it borders on axiomatic. We need not dwell further on this category, because no such conduct is claimed to have occurred, or did occur, in this case.

The second category of conduct, which is at the opposite end of the spectrum, involves lack of due care—that is, fiduciary action taken solely by reason of gross negligence and without any malevolent intent. In this case, appellants assert claims of gross negligence to establish breaches not only of director due care but also of the directors' duty to act in good faith. Although the Chancellor found, and we agree, that the appellants failed to establish gross negligence, to afford guidance we address the issue of whether gross negligence (including a failure to inform one's self of available material facts), without more, can also constitute bad faith. The answer is clearly no.

Both our legislative history and our common law jurisprudence distinguish sharply between the duties to exercise due care and to act in good faith, and highly significant consequences flow from that distinction. The Delaware General Assembly has addressed the distinction between bad faith and a failure to exercise due care (i.e., gross negligence) in two separate contexts [director exculpation and indemnification pursuant to sections 102(b)(7) and 145 of the DGCL].

That leaves the third category of fiduciary conduct, which falls in between the first two categories of (1) conduct motivated by subjective bad intent and (2) conduct resulting from gross negligence. This third category is what the Chancellor's definition of bad faith—intentional dereliction of duty, a conscious disregard for one's responsibilities—is intended to capture. The question is whether such misconduct is properly treated as a non-exculpable, nonindemnifiable violation of the fiduciary duty to act in good faith. In our view it must be, for at least two reasons.

First, the universe of fiduciary misconduct is not limited to either disloyalty in the classic sense (i.e., preferring the adverse self-interest of the fiduciary or of a related person to the interest of the corporation) or gross negligence. Cases have arisen where corporate directors have no conflicting self-interest in a decision, yet engage in misconduct that is more culpable than simple inattention or failure to be informed of all facts material to the decision. To protect the interests of the corporation and its shareholders, fiduciary conduct of this kind, which does not involve disloyalty (as traditionally defined) but is qualitatively more culpable than gross negligence, should be proscribed. A vehicle is needed to address such violations doctrinally, and that doctrinal vehicle is the duty to act in good faith. The Chancellor implicitly so recognized in his Opinion, where he identified different examples of bad faith as follows:

> A failure to act in good faith may be shown, for instance, where the fidu-
> ciary intentionally acts with a purpose other than that of advancing the

best interests of the corporation, where the fiduciary acts with the intent to violate applicable positive law, or where the fiduciary intentionally fails to act in the face of a known duty to act, demonstrating a conscious disregard for his duties. There may be other examples of bad faith yet to be proven or alleged, but these three are the most salient.

Those articulated examples of bad faith are not new to our jurisprudence. Indeed, they echo pronouncements our courts have made throughout the decades.

Second, the legislature has also recognized this intermediate category of fiduciary misconduct, which ranks between conduct involving subjective bad faith and gross negligence. Section 102(b)(7)(ii) of the DGCL expressly denies money damage exculpation for "acts or omissions not in good faith or which involve intentional misconduct or a knowing violation of law." By its very terms that provision distinguishes between "intentional misconduct" and a "knowing violation of law" (both examples of subjective bad faith) on the one hand, and "acts . . . not in good faith," on the other. Because the statute exculpates directors only for conduct amounting to gross negligence, the statutory denial of exculpation for "acts . . . not in good faith" must encompass the intermediate category of misconduct captured by the Chancellor's definition of bad faith.

For these reasons, we uphold the Court of Chancery's definition as a legally appropriate, although not the exclusive, definition of fiduciary bad faith. We need go no further. [The Court then concluded that payment of the severance payout to Ovitz was in good faith on the facts presented.]

V. THE WASTE CLAIM

The appellants' final claim is that even if the approval of the OEA was protected by the business judgment rule presumptions, the payment of the severance amount to Ovitz constituted waste. This claim is rooted in the doctrine that a plaintiff who fails to rebut the business judgment rule presumptions is not entitled to any remedy unless the transaction constitutes waste. The Court of Chancery rejected the appellants' waste claim, and the appellants claim that in so doing the Court committed error.

To recover on a claim of corporate waste, the plaintiffs must shoulder the burden of proving that the exchange was "so one sided that no business person of ordinary, sound judgment could conclude that the corporation has received adequate consideration." A claim of waste will arise only in the rare, "unconscionable case where directors irrationally squander or give away corporate assets." This onerous standard for waste is a corollary of the proposition that where business judgment presumptions are applicable, the board's decision will be upheld unless it cannot be "attributed to any rational business purpose."

The claim that the payment of the NFT amount to Ovitz, without more, constituted waste is meritless on its face, because at the time the NFT amounts were paid, Disney was contractually obligated to pay them. The payment of a contractually obligated amount cannot constitute waste, unless the contractual obligation is itself wasteful. Accordingly, the proper focus of a waste analysis must be whether the amounts required to be paid in the event of an NFT were wasteful ex ante.

[The appellants'] claim does not come close to satisfying the high hurdle required to establish waste. The approval of the NFT provisions in the OEA had a rational business purpose: to induce Ovitz to leave CAA, at what would otherwise be a considerable cost to him, in order to join Disney.

VI. CONCLUSION

For the reasons stated above, the judgment of the Court of Chancery is affirmed.

Points for Discussion

1. Disney *vs.* Van Gorkom.

In *Van Gorkom*, thirteen directors of Trans Union were held personally liable for approving a merger in a two-hour meeting without receiving documents summarizing the deal or relevant valuation information. By contrast, in *Disney*, the directors were exonerated after approving Ovitz's pay package in a one-hour meeting of the compensation committee without discussing or receiving documentation on the financial impact of a "no-fault termination." What explains the different conclusions in these two major cases? Do you think the members of the Disney compensation committee really understood that if Ovitz were terminated after one year without cause he would be entitled to receive $130 million—basically for not having worked out?

2. *Advise.*

What advice can you give directors about how to meet their burden of showing their actions were in good faith to claim protection under a § 102(b)(7) exculpation clause? When, according to the Supreme Court, might the members of a compensation committee have acted without good faith? For example, after the *Disney* decision, would the committee members lack good faith if they failed to obtain a pay consultant's report on the financial implications of a pay package under various assumptions? That is, are *pro forma* reports by pay consultants (showing different "what if" scenarios) now required by Delaware law? Should the directors be required to obtain a valuation of option grants?

3. *Who cares?*

Ovitz's $130 million would seem like a lot of money, but it was nothing to Disney, a fraction of one percent of the value of the corporation's shares. Why the fuss?

4. Director compensation.

Historically, executive compensation has attracted far greater attention than the compensation that directors receive for their board service. However, director compensation can also present issues of excessive pay and give rise to claims of breach of fiduciary duties and waste.

Directors have the responsibility to determine their own compensation. Although boards and committees often seek the advice of an independent compensation consultant, they cannot eliminate the inherent conflict of interest by having management or a consultant make the determination. In setting their own pay, directors unavoidably enter into an interested transaction, which may be subject to entire fairness review if challenged. Shareholder approval of specific awards or a self-executing compensation plan, which does not give the board any further discretion to determine award levels, may provide a defense to a shareholder challenge and result in the application of the business judgment rule.

Some see director compensation as an opportunity to align directors' interests with those of shareholders. Many corporations use restricted stock grants or stock options as a component of director compensation. Some corporations even have stock ownership guidelines that require directors to hold a minimum amount of the corporation's stock while serving as a director.

If you were advising directors about setting their compensation, what practices would you recommend? What should directors be mindful about in this context?

5. Categories of conduct constituting bad faith.

The *Disney* Court gives several examples of bad faith. What are they? How are these different from traditional duty of loyalty violations such as involving interested transactions or corporate opportunities?

———

B. Evolution of "Oversight"

We next turn to the evolution of the concept of "oversight." Recall that the power to manage and direct the corporation's affairs is vested in the board of directors. The board then delegates some of that power to the corporation's officers and employees. Directors are not expected to directly oversee every aspect of a corporation's business. Therefore, one of the difficult questions with respect to oversight is: how do directors fulfill their oversight responsibilities? How much should they do? How much must they do? Are the duties of care and loyalty both implicated? How does good faith fit in?

Historically, the debate about monitoring compliance centered on whether directors *should* institute legal compliance programs (an aspirational standard) or whether directors face *liability* for failure to do so (a legal duty). Questions also arose about whether a monitoring duty arose only after a "triggering event" that put directors on notice that the corporation was not in compliance or whether such programs were part of a legal duty of care.

1. *Graham v. Allis-Chalmers*: Respond to Red Flags

One much-cited statement of a director's duty to create legal compliance programs comes from *Graham v. Allis-Chalmers Manufacturing Co.*, 188 A.2d 125 (Del. 1963). The case involved a derivative action against the directors of Allis-Chalmers, a multi-division manufacturing firm with over 31,000 employees. Suit was brought after the company and four non-director employees were indicted for price-fixing violations of the federal antitrust laws.

The derivative action alleged that the director defendants had either actual knowledge of the illegal price-fixing or knowledge of facts that should have put them on notice. In discovery, however, there was no evidence that any director actually knew of the price-fixing or of facts suggesting that lower-level employees were violating the antitrust laws. So the plaintiffs shifted their theory to claim the directors were liable for failing to institute a monitoring system that would have allowed directors to learn of and prevent the antitrust violations.

The Delaware Supreme Court pointed out that the company's operating policy was to delegate price-setting authority "to the lowest possible management level capable of fulfilling the delegated responsibility." The board, although it annually reviewed departmental profit goals, did not participate in decisions setting specific product prices. The Court stated, "By reason of the extent and complexity of the company's operations, it is not practicable for the Board to consider in detail specific problems of the various divisions."

The plaintiffs pointed to two 1937 FTC decrees against Allis-Chalmers that had enjoined the company from fixing prices on certain electrical equipment. The plaintiffs argued that the decrees, which should have alerted the directors to past antitrust activity, put them on notice to identify and prevent such activity in the future. The Court was not impressed:

> The difficulty the argument has is that only three of the present directors knew of the decrees, and all three of them satisfied themselves that Allis-Chalmers had not engaged in the practice enjoined and had consented to the decrees merely to avoid expense and the necessity of defending the company's position. Under the circumstances, we think knowledge by three of the directors that in 1937 the company had consented to the entry of decrees enjoining it from doing something they had satisfied themselves it had never done, did not put the Board on notice of the possibility of future illegal price fixing.

Plaintiffs have wholly failed to establish either actual notice or imputed notice to the Board of Directors of facts which should have put them on guard, and have caused them to take steps to prevent the future possibility of illegal price fixing and bid rigging. Plaintiffs say that as a minimum in this respect the Board should have taken the steps it took in 1960 when knowledge of the facts first actually came to their attention as a result of the Grand Jury investigation. Whatever duty, however, there was upon the Board to take such steps, the fact of the 1937 decrees has no bearing upon the question, for under the circumstances they were [put on] notice of nothing.

Plaintiffs are thus forced to rely solely upon the legal proposition advanced by them that directors of a corporation, as a matter of law, are liable for losses suffered by their corporations by reason of their gross inattention to the common law duty of actively supervising and managing the corporate affairs.

The precise charge made against these director defendants is that, even though they had no knowledge of any suspicion of wrongdoing on the part of the company's employees, they still should have put into effect a system of watchfulness which would have brought such misconduct to their attention in ample time to have brought it to an end. On the contrary, it appears that directors are entitled to rely on the honesty and integrity of their subordinates until something occurs to put them on suspicion that something is wrong. If such occurs and goes unheeded, then liability of the directors might well follow, but absent cause for suspicion there is no duty upon the directors to install and operate a corporate system of espionage to ferret out wrongdoing which they have no reason to suspect exists.

In the last analysis, the question of whether a corporate director has become liable for losses to the corporation through neglect of duty is determined by the circumstances. If he has recklessly reposed confidence in an obviously untrustworthy employee, has refused or neglected cavalierly to perform his duty as a director, or has ignored either willfully or through inattention obvious danger signs of employee wrongdoing, the law will cast the burden of liability upon him. This is not the case at bar, however, for as soon as it became evident that there were grounds for suspicion, the Board acted promptly to end it and prevent its recurrence.

Graham grew out of the heavy electrical equipment price-fixing conspiracy, one of the first instances in which executives of major corporations received jail terms for antitrust violations. Despite evidence in the criminal cases and similar evidence in *Graham* that subordinate employees had concealed their illegal behavior from their supervisors, there was skepticism in the press and Congress that senior executives were, in fact, unaware of what was going on.

Instead, under Allis-Chalmers' decentralized structure, there were indications that the heads of the various organizational units faced significant pressure to show steadily increasing profits for their segments. Profits were expected regardless of the conditions in the particular markets in which the organizational units operated. If true, was the court too quick to say that when a board creates such a mode of management it need not establish "a corporate system of espionage"?

2. *Caremark*: Institute Monitoring Systems

Three decades after *Graham v. Allis-Chalmers*, the Delaware Court of Chancery set a new direction for the board's oversight duties by stating (in dicta) that a board's oversight duties required more than simply responding to red flags. *In re Caremark International Inc.*, 698 A.2d 959 (Del. Ch. 1996). The company involved, Caremark, had been the subject of an extensive four-year investigation by the United States Department of Health and Human Services and the Department of Justice regarding its compliance with health care provider regulations. In 1994, Caremark pleaded guilty to mail fraud and agreed to pay civil and criminal fines to various private and public parties, totaling approximately $250 million.

A shareholder derivative suit followed, alleging the Caremark directors breached their duty of care. As the court explained:

> The claim is that the directors allowed a situation to develop and continue which exposed the corporation to enormous legal liability and that in so doing they violated a duty to be active monitors of corporate performance. The complaint thus does not charge either director self-dealing or the more difficult loyalty-type problems arising from cases of suspect director motivation, such as entrenchment or sale of control contexts. The theory here advanced is possibly the most difficult theory in corporation law upon which a plaintiff might hope to win a judgment.

The Court of Chancery's opinion ruled on a proposed settlement as to which there were no objectors. Although appeal was unlikely, the court took the opportunity to explain its view of the law in this area, more than thirty years after the Delaware Supreme Court's opinion in *Graham v. Allis-Chalmers*:

> Director liability for a breach of the duty to exercise appropriate attention may, in theory, arise in two distinct contexts. First, such liability may be said to follow from a board decision that results in a loss because that decision was ill advised or "negligent." [This] class of cases will typically be subject to review under the director-protective business judgment rule, assuming the decision made was the product of a process that was either deliberately considered in good faith or was otherwise rational.
>
> The second class of cases in which director liability for inattention is theoretically possible entail circumstances in which a loss eventuates

not from a decision but, from unconsidered inaction. Most of the decisions that a corporation, acting through its human agents, makes are, of course, not the subject of director attention. Legally, the board itself will be required only to authorize the most significant corporate acts or transactions: mergers, changes in capital structure, fundamental changes in business, appointment and compensation of the CEO, etc. As the facts of this case graphically demonstrate, ordinary business decisions that are made by officers and employees deeper in the interior of the organization can, however, vitally affect the welfare of the corporation and its ability to achieve its various strategic and financial goals. In the face of financial and organizational disasters, what is the board's responsibility with respect to the organization and monitoring of the enterprise to assure that the corporation functions within the law to achieve its purposes?

In 1963, the Delaware Supreme Court in *Graham v. Allis-Chalmers Mfg. Co.* addressed the question of potential liability of board members for losses experienced by the corporation as a result of the corporation having violated the antitrust laws of the United States. The claim asserted was that the directors ought to have known of it and if they had known they would have been under a duty to bring the corporation into compliance with the law and thus save the corporation from the loss. The Delaware Supreme Court concluded that, under the facts as they appeared, there was no basis to find that the directors had breached a duty to be informed of the ongoing operations of the firm. In notably colorful terms, the court stated that "absent cause for suspicion there is no duty upon the directors to install and operate a corporate system of espionage to ferret out wrongdoing which they have no reason to suspect exists." The Court found that there were no grounds for suspicion in that case and, thus, concluded that the directors were blamelessly unaware of the conduct leading to the corporate liability.

How does one generalize this holding today? Can it be said today that, absent some ground giving rise to suspicion of violation of law, that corporate directors have no duty to assure that a corporate information gathering and reporting systems exists which represents a good faith attempt to provide senior management and the Board with information respecting material acts, events or conditions within the corporation, including compliance with applicable statutes and regulations? I certainly do not believe so.

A broad interpretation of *Graham v. Allis-Chalmers*—that it means that a corporate board has no responsibility to assure that appropriate information and reporting systems are established by management—would not, in any event, be accepted by the Delaware Supreme Court in 1996, in my opinion. In stating the basis for this view, I start with the recognition that in recent years the Delaware Supreme Court has made it clear—especially in its jurisprudence concerning takeovers, from *Smith v. Van Gorkom* through *QVC v. Paramount Communications*—the seriousness with which the corporation law views the role of the corporate board. Secondly, I note the elementary fact that relevant and timely information is an essential predicate for satisfaction of the board's supervisory and monitoring role under Section 141 of the Delaware General Corporation Law. Thirdly, I note the potential impact of the federal organizational sentencing guidelines on any business organization. Any rational person attempting in good faith to meet an organizational governance responsibility would be bound to take into account this development and the enhanced penalties and the opportunities for reduced sanctions that it offers.

In light of these developments, it would, in my opinion, be a mistake to conclude that our Supreme Court's statement in *Graham* concerning "espionage" means that corporate boards may satisfy their obligation to be reasonably informed concerning the corporation, without assuring themselves that information and reporting systems exist in the organization that are reasonably designed to provide to senior management and to the board itself timely, accurate information sufficient to allow management and the board, each within its scope, to reach informed judgments concerning both the corporation's compliance with law and its business performance.

Obviously the level of detail that is appropriate for such an information system is a question of business judgment. And obviously too, no rationally designed information and reporting system will remove the possibility that the corporation will violate laws or regulations, or that senior officers or directors may nevertheless sometimes be misled or otherwise fail reasonably to detect acts material to the corporation's compliance with the law. But it is important that the board exercise a good faith judgment that the corporation's information and reporting system is in concept and design adequate to assure the board that appropriate information will come to its attention in a timely manner as a matter of ordinary operations, so that it may satisfy its responsibility.

Thus, I am of the view that a director's obligation includes a duty to attempt in good faith to assure that a corporate information and reporting system, which the board concludes is adequate, exists, and that failure to do so under some circumstances may, in theory at least, render a director liable for losses caused by non-compliance with applicable legal standards.

Generally where a claim of directorial liability for corporate loss is predicated upon ignorance of liability creating activities within the corporation, as in *Graham* or in this case, in my opinion only a sustained or systematic failure of the board to exercise oversight—such as an utter failure to attempt to assure a reasonable information and reporting system exits—will establish the lack of good faith that is a necessary condition to liability. Such a test of liability—lack of good faith as evidenced by sustained or systematic failure of a director to exercise reasonable oversight—is quite high.

The court concluded, based on the facts in the case at hand, that the directors had not breached a duty:

> I conclude, in light of the discovery record, that there is a very low probability that it would be determined that the directors of Caremark breached any duty to appropriately monitor and supervise the enterprise. Indeed the record tends to show an active consideration by Caremark management and its Board of the Caremark structures and programs that ultimately led to the company's indictment and to the large financial losses incurred in the settlement of those claims. It does not tend to show knowing or intentional violation of law. Neither the fact that the Board, although advised by lawyers and accountants, did not accurately predict the severe consequences to the company that would ultimately follow from the deployment by the company of the strategies and practices that ultimately led to this liability, nor the scale of the liability, gives rise to an inference of breach of any duty imposed by corporation law upon the directors of Caremark.

Although state law has traditionally been the source of oversight responsibility, increasingly federal law plays a role. After the corporate and accounting scandals that came to light in the early 2000s, Congress federalized a number of areas of corporate governance, including internal controls over financial accounting and disclosure systems in public companies. The Public Company Accounting Reform and Investor Protection Act of 2002 (known as the Sarbanes-Oxley Act), besides creating a new self-regulatory body called the Public Company Accounting Oversight Board to regulate the accounting profession, mandates oversight by corporate boards, senior management, and even company lawyers of company financial reporting. One of the most onerous provisions of Sarbanes-Oxley is Section 404, which requires that managers of public corporations establish and maintain an adequate internal control structure and procedures for financial reporting, and include an assessment of these controls in the corporation's annual report.

Although Chancellor Allen's description of the updated oversight duty of directors was only dicta (there was no need for him to reject the *Graham* "red flags" test in approving the *Caremark* settlement), the claim laid out by Allen became known as a "*Caremark* claim." After the case, plaintiff-shareholders began to sue directors for breaching their fiduciary duty by failing to assure that an adequate corporate information and reporting system existed to help prevent corporate malfeasance (e.g., employee misconduct or violations of law) and was monitored with proper oversight. As we will see below, a decade after *Caremark*, the Delaware Supreme Court clarified the board of directors' oversight duty and the role of good faith.

C. Modern Approach to Good Faith and Oversight

In 2006, about forty years after *Graham v. Allis-Chalmers*, the issue of oversight responsibility squarely came before the Delaware Supreme Court again. By this time, a decade had also passed since the Court of Chancery's opinion in *Caremark*, and the Delaware Supreme Court had begun giving more attention to "good faith."

The concept of "good faith" arises in several aspects of director fiduciary duties. Recall that the BJR presumes that directors act in good faith. When directors rely on experts, courts ask whether the reliance was made in good faith. When judges analyze the independence of directors, they often inquire into whether decisions by the directors were made in good faith.

In addition, Delaware's § 102(b)(7) specifically permits companies to limit the personal liability of directors (and officers) for monetary damages for breaches of fiduciary duties, with an important exception for actions "not in good faith." In other words, even if a company adopts an exculpation clause to the full extent permitted by § 102(b)(7), directors still can be personally liable if they do not act in "good faith." This is important because it means that when a corporation has a § 102(b)(7) provision in its certificate of incorporation, plaintiffs are deterred from bringing breach of the duty of care claims against directors, but could potentially still go forward with a suit if they instead characterized the conduct as "not in good faith."

For many years, it was unclear whether directors owed an independent duty of good faith, in addition to the duties of care and loyalty. Some courts and commentators referred to a "triad" of duties, including good faith. Others assumed that there was no free-standing duty of good faith; instead, good faith was a component of the of the duty of care or the duty of loyalty. The Delaware courts used the term "good faith" in analyzing the board's action, although ultimately the Delaware Supreme Court stopped short of establishing an independent duty of good faith.

In *Disney*, the Delaware Supreme Court stated that a failure to act in good faith amounted to something more than a violation of the duty of care. It did not delineate the precise differences between good faith and care, but it gave some examples. When the concept of "good faith" arose in a monitoring or oversight case, the claims generally were characterized as *Caremark* claims that fell under the duty of care. Then, in *Stone v. Ritter*, the Delaware Supreme Court finally clarified some of the questions surrounding the application of good faith and applied a new good faith approach under the duty of loyalty in the context of a *Caremark* claim. That case is next, along with a more recent excerpt from a Delaware Supreme Court decision applying some of the good faith, and *Caremark* concepts.

Stone v. Ritter

911 A.2d 362 (Del. 2006)

HOLLAND, JUSTICE.

This is an appeal from a final judgment of the Court of Chancery dismissing a derivative complaint against fifteen present and former directors of AmSouth Bancorporation ("AmSouth"), a Delaware corporation. The plaintiffs-appellants, William and Sandra Stone, are AmSouth shareholders and filed their derivative complaint without making a pre-suit demand on AmSouth's board of directors (the "Board"). The Court of Chancery held that the plaintiffs had failed to adequately plead that such a demand would have been futile.

The Court of Chancery characterized the allegations in the derivative complaint as a "classic *Caremark* claim," and recognized that: "generally where a claim of directorial liability for corporate loss is predicated upon ignorance of liability creating activities within the corporation . . . only a sustained or systematic failure of the board to exercise oversight—such as an utter failure to attempt to assure a reasonable information and reporting system exists-will establish the lack of good faith that is a necessary condition to liability."

In this appeal, the plaintiffs acknowledge that the directors neither "knew nor should have known that violations of law were occurring," i.e., that there were no "red flags" before the directors. Nevertheless, the plaintiffs argue that the Court of Chancery erred by dismissing the derivative complaint which alleged that "the defendants had utterly failed to implement any sort of statutorily required monitoring, reporting or information controls that would have enabled them to learn of problems requiring their attention." The defendants argue that the plaintiffs' assertions are contradicted by the derivative complaint itself and by the documents incorporated therein by reference.

During the relevant period, AmSouth's wholly-owned subsidiary, AmSouth Bank, operated about 600 commercial banking branches in six states throughout the southeastern United States and employed more than 11,600 people. In 2004, AmSouth and AmSouth Bank paid $40 million in fines and $10 million in civil penalties to resolve government and regulatory investigations pertaining principally to the failure by bank employees to file "Suspicious Activity Reports" ("SARs"), as required by the federal Bank Secrecy Act ("BSA") and various anti-money-laundering ("AML") regulations. No fines or penalties were imposed on AmSouth's directors, and no other regulatory action was taken against them.

The government investigations arose originally from an unlawful "Ponzi" scheme operated by Louis D. Hamric, II and Victor G. Nance. In August 2000, Hamric, then a licensed attorney, and Nance, then a registered investment advisor with Mutual of New York, contacted an AmSouth branch bank in Tennessee to arrange for custodial trust accounts to be created for "investors" in a "business venture." That venture (Hamric and Nance represented) involved the construction of medical clinics overseas. In reality, Nance had convinced more than forty of his clients to invest in promissory notes bearing high rates of return, by misrepresenting the nature and the risk of that investment. Relying on similar misrepresentations by Hamric and Nance, the AmSouth branch employees in Tennessee agreed to provide custodial accounts for the investors and to distribute monthly interest payments to each account upon receipt of a check from Hamric and instructions from Nance.

The Hamric-Nance scheme was discovered in March 2002, when the investors did not receive their monthly interest payments. Thereafter, Hamric and Nance became the subject of several civil actions brought by the defrauded investors in Tennessee and Mississippi (and in which AmSouth also was named as a defendant), and also the subject of a federal grand jury investigation in the Southern District of Mississippi. Hamric and Nance were indicted on federal money-laundering charges, and both pled guilty.

The government authorities found that since April 24, 2002, AmSouth has been in violation of the anti-money-laundering program requirements of the Bank Secrecy Act, that "AmSouth's compliance program lacked adequate board and management oversight," and that "reporting to management for the purposes of monitoring and oversight of compliance activities was materially deficient."

It is a fundamental principle of the Delaware General Corporation Law that "the business and affairs of every corporation organized under this chapter shall be managed by or under the direction of a board of directors." Thus, "by its very nature a derivative action impinges on the managerial freedom of directors." Court of Chancery Rule 23.1, accordingly, requires that the complaint in a derivative action "allege with particularity the efforts, if any, made by the plaintiff to obtain the action the plaintiff desires from the directors or the reasons for the plaintiff's failure to obtain the action or for not making the effort."

To excuse demand "a court must determine whether or not the particularized factual allegations of a derivative stockholder complaint create a reasonable doubt that, as of the time the complaint is filed, the board of directors could have properly exercised its independent and disinterested business judgment in responding to a demand." The plaintiffs assert that the incumbent defendant directors "face a substantial likelihood of liability" that renders them "personally interested in the outcome of the decision on whether to pursue the claims asserted in the complaint," and are therefore not disinterested or independent.[12]

---

[12] The fifteen defendants include eight current and seven former directors. The complaint concedes that seven of the eight current directors are outside directors who have never been employed by AmSouth. One board member, C. Dowd Ritter, the Chairman, is an officer or employee of AmSouth.

Critical to this demand excused argument is the fact that the directors' potential personal liability depends upon whether or not their conduct can be exculpated by the section 102(b)(7) provision contained in the AmSouth certificate of incorporation. Such a provision can exculpate directors from monetary liability for a breach of the duty of care, but not for conduct that is not in good faith or a breach of the duty of loyalty. The standard for assessing a director's potential personal liability for failing to act in good faith in discharging his or her oversight responsibilities has evolved beginning with our decision in *Graham v. Allis-Chalmers Manufacturing Company*, through the Court of Chancery's *Caremark* decision to our most recent decision in *Disney*.

[The Court then summarized the *Graham* and *Caremark* decisions, quoting extensively from each decision.]

The *Caremark* Court recognized that "the duty to act in good faith to be informed cannot be thought to require directors to possess detailed information about all aspects of the operation of the enterprise." The Court of Chancery formulated the following standard for assessing the liability of directors where the directors are unaware of employee misconduct that results in the corporation being held liable:

> Generally where a claim of directorial liability for corporate loss is predicated upon ignorance of liability creating activities within the corporation, as in *Graham* or in this case, only a sustained or systematic failure of the board to exercise oversight—such as an utter failure to attempt to assure a reasonable information and reporting system exists—will establish the lack of good faith that is a necessary condition to liability.

As evidenced by the language quoted above, the *Caremark* standard for so-called "oversight" liability draws heavily upon the concept of director failure to act in good faith. That is consistent with the definition(s) of bad faith recently approved by this Court in its recent *Disney* decision, where we held that a failure to act in good faith requires conduct that is qualitatively different from, and more culpable than, the conduct giving rise to a violation of the fiduciary duty of care (i.e., gross negligence). In *Disney*, we identified the following examples of conduct that would establish a failure to act in good faith:

> A failure to act in good faith may be shown, for instance, where the fiduciary intentionally acts with a purpose other than that of advancing the best interests of the corporation, where the fiduciary acts with the intent to violate applicable positive law, or where the fiduciary intentionally fails to act in the face of a known duty to act, demonstrating a conscious disregard for his duties. There may be other examples of bad faith yet to be proven or alleged, but these three are the most salient.

The third of these examples describes, and is fully consistent with, the lack of good faith conduct that the *Caremark* court held was a "necessary condition" for director oversight liability, i.e., "a sustained or systematic failure of the board to exercise oversight—such as an utter failure to attempt to assure a reasonable information and reporting system exists." Indeed, our opinion in *Disney* cited *Caremark* with approval for that proposition. Accordingly, the Court of Chancery applied the correct standard in assessing whether demand was excused in this case where failure to exercise oversight was the basis or theory of the plaintiffs' claim for relief.

It is important, in this context, to clarify a doctrinal issue that is critical to understanding fiduciary liability under *Caremark* as we construe that case. The phraseology used in *Caremark* and that we employ here—describing the lack of good faith as a "necessary condition to liability"—is deliberate. The purpose of that formulation is to communicate that a failure to act in good faith is not conduct that results, ipso facto, in the direct imposition of fiduciary liability. The failure to act in good faith may result in liability because the requirement to act in good faith "is a subsidiary element," i.e., a condition, "of the fundamental duty of loyalty." It follows that because a showing of bad faith conduct, in the sense described in *Disney* and *Caremark*, is essential to establish director oversight liability, the fiduciary duty violated by that conduct is the duty of loyalty.

This view of a failure to act in good faith results in two additional doctrinal consequences. First, although good faith may be described colloquially as part of a "triad" of fiduciary duties that includes the duties of care and loyalty, the obligation to act in good faith does not establish an independent fiduciary duty that stands on the same footing as the duties of care and loyalty. Only the latter two duties, where violated, may directly result in liability, whereas a failure to act in good faith may do so, but indirectly. The second doctrinal consequence is that the fiduciary duty of loyalty is not limited to cases involving a financial or other cognizable fiduciary conflict of interest. It also encompasses cases where the fiduciary fails to act in good faith. As the Court of Chancery aptly put it in *Guttman*, "a director cannot act loyally towards the corporation unless she acts in the good faith belief that her actions are in the corporation's best interest."

We hold that *Caremark* articulates the necessary conditions predicate for director oversight liability: (a) the directors utterly failed to implement any reporting or information system or controls; or (b) having implemented such a system or controls, consciously failed to monitor or oversee its operations thus disabling themselves from being informed of risks or problems requiring their attention. In either case, imposition of liability requires a showing that the directors knew that they were not discharging their fiduciary obligations. Where directors fail to act in the face of a known duty to act, thereby demonstrating a conscious disregard for their responsibilities, they breach their duty of loyalty by failing to discharge that fiduciary obligation in good faith.

The plaintiffs contend that demand is excused under Rule 23.1 because AmSouth's directors breached their oversight duty and, as a result, face a "substantial likelihood of liability" as a result of their "utter failure" to act in good faith to put into place policies and procedures to ensure compliance with BSA and AML obligations. The Court of Chancery found that the plaintiffs did not plead the existence of "red flags"—"facts showing that the board ever was aware that AmSouth's internal controls were inadequate, that these inadequacies would result in illegal activity, and that the board chose to do nothing about problems it allegedly knew existed." In dismissing the derivative complaint in this action, the Court of Chancery concluded:

> This case is not about a board's failure to carefully consider a material corporate decision that was presented to the board. This is a case where information was not reaching the board because of ineffective internal controls. . . . With the benefit of hindsight, it is beyond question that AmSouth's internal controls with respect to the Bank Secrecy Act and anti-money laundering regulations compliance were inadequate. Neither party disputes that the lack of internal controls resulted in a huge fine—$50 million, alleged to be the largest ever of its kind. The fact of those losses, however, is not alone enough for a court to conclude that a majority of the corporation's board of directors is disqualified from considering demand that AmSouth bring suit against those responsible.

The KPMG Report evaluated the various components of AmSouth's longstanding BSA/AML compliance program. The KPMG Report reflects that AmSouth's Board dedicated considerable resources to the BSA/AML compliance program and put into place numerous procedures and systems to attempt to ensure compliance. According to KPMG, the program's various components exhibited between a low and high degree of compliance with applicable laws and regulations.

The KPMG Report describes the numerous AmSouth employees, departments and committees established by the Board to oversee AmSouth's compliance with the BSA and to report violations to management and the Board:

> **BSA Officer.** Since 1998, AmSouth has had a "BSA Officer" "responsible for all BSA/AML-related matters including employee training, general communications, CTR reporting and SAR reporting," and "presenting AML policy and program changes to the Board of Directors, the managers at the various lines of business, and participants in the annual training of security and audit personnel;"
>
> **BSA/AML Compliance Department.** AmSouth has had for years a BSA/AML Compliance Department, headed by the BSA Officer and comprised of nineteen professionals, including a BSA/AML Compliance Manager and a Compliance Reporting Manager;
>
> **Corporate Security Department.** AmSouth's Corporate Security Department has been at all relevant times responsible for the detection and reporting of suspicious activity as it relates to fraudulent activity, and

William Burch, the head of Corporate Security, has been with AmSouth since 1998 and served in the U.S. Secret Service from 1969 to 1998; and

Suspicious Activity Oversight Committee. Since 2001, the "Suspicious Activity Oversight Committee" and its predecessor, the "AML Committee," have actively overseen AmSouth's BSA/AML compliance program. The Suspicious Activity Oversight Committee's mission has for years been to "oversee the policy, procedure, and process issues affecting the Corporate Security and BSA/AML Compliance Programs, to ensure that an effective program exists at AmSouth to deter, detect, and report money laundering, suspicious activity and other fraudulent activity."

The KPMG Report reflects that the directors not only discharged their oversight responsibility to establish an information and reporting system, but also proved that the system was designed to permit the directors to periodically monitor AmSouth's compliance with BSA and AML regulations. For example, as KPMG noted in 2004, AmSouth's designated BSA Officer "has made annual high-level presentations to the Board of Directors in each of the last five years." Further, the Board's Audit and Community Responsibility Committee (the "Audit Committee") oversaw AmSouth's BSA/AML compliance program on a quarterly basis. The KPMG Report states that "the BSA Officer presents BSA/AML training to the Board of Directors annually," and the "Corporate Security training is also presented to the Board of Directors."

The KPMG Report shows that AmSouth's Board at various times enacted written policies and procedures designed to ensure compliance with the BSA and AML regulations. For example, the Board adopted an amended bank-wide "BSA/AML Policy" on July 17, 2003—four months before AmSouth became aware that it was the target of a government investigation. That policy was produced to plaintiffs in response to their demand to inspect AmSouth's books and records pursuant to section 220 and is included in plaintiffs' appendix. Among other things, the July 17, 2003, BSA/AML Policy directs all AmSouth employees to immediately report suspicious transactions or activity to the BSA/AML Compliance Department or Corporate Security.

In this case, the adequacy of the plaintiffs' assertion that demand is excused depends on whether the complaint alleges facts sufficient to show that the defendant directors are potentially personally liable for the failure of non-director bank employees to file SARs. Delaware courts have recognized that "most of the decisions that a corporation, acting through its human agents, makes are, of course, not the subject of director attention." Consequently, a claim that directors are subject to personal liability for employee failures is "possibly the most difficult theory in corporation law upon which a plaintiff might hope to win a judgment."

For the plaintiffs' derivative complaint to withstand a motion to dismiss, "only a sustained or systematic failure of the board to exercise oversight—such as an utter failure to attempt to assure a reasonable information and reporting system exists—will establish the lack of good faith that is a necessary condition to liability." As the *Caremark* decision noted:

> Such a test of liability—lack of good faith as evidenced by sustained or systematic failure of a director to exercise reasonable oversight—is quite high. But, a demanding test of liability in the oversight context is probably beneficial to corporate shareholders as a class, as it is in the board decision context, since it makes board service by qualified persons more likely, while continuing to act as a stimulus to good faith performance of duty by such directors.

> The KPMG Report—which the plaintiffs explicitly incorporated by reference into their derivative complaint—refutes the assertion that the directors "never took the necessary steps to ensure that a reasonable BSA compliance and reporting system existed." KPMG's findings reflect that the Board received and approved relevant policies and procedures, delegated to certain employees and departments the responsibility for filing SARs and monitoring compliance, and exercised oversight by relying on periodic reports from them. Although there ultimately may have been failures by employees to report deficiencies to the Board, there is no basis for an oversight claim seeking to hold the directors personally liable for such failures by the employees.

> With the benefit of hindsight, the plaintiffs' complaint seeks to equate a bad outcome with bad faith. The lacuna in the plaintiffs' argument is a failure to recognize that the directors' good faith exercise of oversight responsibility may not invariably prevent employees from violating criminal laws, or from causing the corporation to incur significant financial liability, or both, as occurred in *Graham*, *Caremark* and this very case. In the absence of red flags, good faith in the context of oversight must be measured by the directors' actions "to assure a reasonable information and reporting system exists" and not by second-guessing after the occurrence of employee conduct that results in an unintended adverse outcome. Accordingly, we hold that the Court of Chancery properly applied *Caremark* and dismissed the plaintiffs' derivative complaint for failure to excuse demand by alleging particularized facts that created reason to doubt whether the directors had acted in good faith in exercising their oversight responsibilities.

> The judgment of the Court of Chancery is affirmed.

————————

Points for Discussion

1. Decisions vs. oversight.

Should the Delaware courts treat claims involving decision making (as in the *Van Gorkom* and *Disney* cases) similarly to those involving oversight (as in *Caremark* and *Stone v. Ritter*)? Why might the courts distinguish between these two categories of cases?

2. Good faith and monitoring.

What must a plaintiff allege to establish that a defendant director violated their obligation to act in good faith? After *Stone v. Ritter*, how would you advise directors regarding their monitoring duties?

3. Duties of loyalty and care.

After *Stone v. Ritter*, is a *Caremark* claim categorized as a breach of the duty of care or the duty of loyalty? If it is a duty of loyalty claim, what is left for the duty of care?

4. Red flags.

Graham v. Allis-Chalmers imposed a duty of inquiry only when there were "obvious signs" of employee wrongdoing. In contrast, *Caremark* required some sort of monitoring system even absent a red flag. How would you advise a board implementing a system of monitoring legal compliance? Is it enough just to set up a monitoring system? Or do the directors also bear some independent responsibility for detecting or responding to red flags? In other words, what should be the board's approach to red flags?

5. Duty of obedience.

By the way, are the duties of care and loyalty enough to describe the corporate legal landscape? Consider a board decision to have the corporation engage in conduct that violates the law. If after careful deliberations and a well-informed cost-benefit analysis, a board composed entirely of directors without any personal financial stake in the decision arrived at the conclusion it would be in the best (financial) interests of the corporation to violate a particular legal norm, what duty is violated?

First, there would seem to be no duty of care breach: the directors were informed and deliberative. Second, there would seem to be no duty of loyalty breach: none had a conflicting personal financial interest, and they were all genuinely seeking only to promote the best interests of the corporation. Yet, from *Allis-Chalmers* to *Caremark* to *Stone v. Ritter*, there is a clear judicial consensus that decisions to knowingly violate the law are beyond the pale.

It would seem there is another duty at work: a duty of obedience. Do directors have a duty to respect legal norms, both internal and external? And should failure to respect such norms trigger personal liability? How can such a duty of obedience be rationalized as part of the duty of loyalty?

6. *Oversight of risk management.*

Stone v. Ritter involved director oversight of risk management, an increasingly important topic at companies, especially financial institutions. The judicial approach to this particular category of oversight has been mixed. Historically, some courts held directors to heightened duties in their role overseeing financial risks. *See Brane v. Roth,* 590 N.E.2d 587 (Ind. Ct. App. 1992); *Hoye v. Meek,* 795 F.2d 893 (10th Cir. 1986). One issue in such cases has been the complexity of financial risks, and the potential for complex financial risks to lead to hidden exposure and serious losses.

But Delaware courts have been more skeptical of some allegations that directors failed to manage financial risk. For example, in *In re Citigroup Inc. S'holder Deriv. Litig.,* 964 A.2d 106 (Del. Ch. 2009), a prominent case arising out of the 2008 global financial crisis, the court confronted a complaint that did not include details about red flags or other oversight failures and concluded:

> "Business decision-makers must operate in the real world, with imperfect information, limited resources, and an uncertain future. To impose liability on directors for making a 'wrong' business decision would cripple their ability to earn returns for investors by taking business risks. Indeed, this kind of judicial second guessing is what the business judgment rule was designed to prevent, and even if a complaint is framed under a *Caremark* theory, this Court will not abandon such bedrock principles of Delaware fiduciary duty law."

The 2008 crisis brought numerous corporations—and the markets themselves—to the brink of collapse. It also led many directors to reevaluate their approach to risk management, particularly with respect to complex financial risks. Oversight of risk management, especially financial risks, has been increasingly important, at an increasing number of companies.

It is unclear which path the courts will follow in cases that allege risk management failures. Arguably, financial risks are categorically different from other business risks: they can pose an existential threat to a company, they can be very difficult to understand, and they are likely to impose externalized costs on others (including taxpayers, who are asked to fund bailouts, as they did after the 2008 crisis). Moreover, judges, especially in Delaware, have specialized financial expertise from cases that involve complex financial issues and independent valuation assessments, and they are arguably better positioned to assess financial risks than other business risks.

The question remains: should "financial risks" be treated differently than more routine "business risks"? And are there certain categories of business risks that warrant closer scrutiny? The case addressed this question, in the context of a threat to human health.

Marchand v. Barnhill

212 A.3d 805 (Del. 2019)

STRINE, CHIEF JUSTICE.

Blue Bell Creameries USA, Inc., one of the country's largest ice cream manufacturers, suffered a *listeria* outbreak in early 2015, causing the company to recall all of its products, shut down production at all of its plants, and lay off over a third of its workforce. Blue Bell's failure to contain *listeria*'s spread in its manufacturing plants caused listeria to be present in its products and had sad consequences. Three people died as a result of the *listeria* outbreak. Less consequentially, but nonetheless important for this litigation, stockholders also suffered losses because, after the operational shutdown, Blue Bell suffered a liquidity crisis that forced it to accept a dilutive private equity investment.

Based on these unfortunate events, a stockholder brought a derivative suit against two key executives and against Blue Bell's directors claiming breaches of the defendants' fiduciary duties. The complaint alleges that the executives—Paul Kruse, the President and CEO, and Greg Bridges, the Vice President of Operations—breached their duties of care and loyalty by knowingly disregarding contamination risks and failing to oversee the safety of Blue Bell's food-making operations, and that the directors breached their duty of loyalty under *Caremark*.

As to the *Caremark* claim, the Court of Chancery held that the plaintiff did not plead any facts to support "his contention that the [Blue Bell] Board 'utterly' failed to adopt or implement any reporting and compliance systems." Although the plaintiff argued that Blue Bell's board had no supervisory structure in place to oversee "health, safety and sanitation controls and compliance," the Court of Chancery reasoned that "[w]hat Plaintiff really attempts to challenge is not the existence of monitoring and reporting controls, but the effectiveness of monitoring and reporting controls in particular instances," and "[t]his is not a valid theory under . . . *Caremark*." In this opinion, we reverse as to both holdings.

We hold that the complaint alleges particularized facts that support a reasonable inference that the Blue Bell board failed to implement any system to monitor Blue Bell's food safety performance or compliance. Under *Caremark* and this Court's opinion in *Stone v. Ritter*, directors have a duty "to exercise oversight" and to monitor the corporation's operational viability, legal compliance, and financial performance. A board's "utter failure to attempt to assure a reasonable information and reporting system exists" is an act of bad faith in breach of the duty of loyalty.

As a monoline company that makes a single product—ice cream—Blue Bell can only thrive if its consumers enjoyed its products and were confident that its products were safe to eat. That is, one of Blue Bell's central compliance issues is food safety. Despite this fact, the complaint alleges that Blue Bell's board had no committee overseeing food safety, no full board-level process to address food safety issues, and no protocol by which the board was expected to be advised of food safety reports and developments. Consistent with this dearth of any board-level effort at monitoring, the complaint pleads particular facts supporting an inference that during a crucial period when yellow and red flags about food safety were presented to management, there was no equivalent reporting to the board and the board was not presented with any material information about food safety. Thus, the complaint alleges specific facts that create a reasonable inference that the directors consciously failed "to attempt to assure a reasonable information and reporting system exist[ed]."

I. Background

[Although Blue Bell was subject to various state and federal regulations, the plaintiff's complaint alleged that the Company's health and safety issues emerged as early as 2009 and remained ongoing until the *listeria* outbreak in 2015. From 2009 to 2014, several regulators found compliance failures at Blue Bell's facilities such as condensation drips, standing water, open containers of ingredients, and generally unsanitary and insufficient conditions. In 2013, the Company had five positive *listeria* tests. By 2014, it had ten. Management was informed about this growing *listeria* threat, but the board never received reports about *listeria* or about the Company's broader food safety issues. On February 13, 2015, Blue Bell was notified that the Texas Department of State Health Services had also found *listeria* in its samples. The board was not told of this alarming update and its February 19, 2015 meeting contained no discussion of *listeria*.

Four days later, Blue Bell initiated a limited recall. Two days after the limited recall was announced, the board met for the first time to discuss the *listeria* issue, despite two years of mounting evidence that *listeria* was a growing problem for the Company. Instead of holding more frequent meetings going forward so as to remain updated on the presence of *listeria* in its products, Blue Bell's board delegated the Company's response to management. By April 20, 2015, Blue Bell had recalled all of its products and the Center for Diseases Control and Prevention ("CDC") had begun its own investigation. Ultimately, eight people were sickened and three of those people died. The FDA subsequently inspected each of the Company's plants in Texas, Oklahoma, and Alabama and found major deficiencies in all three. Various news outlets also interviewed former Blue Bell employees, who claimed that management had ignored their complaints about factory conditions.]

II. Analysis

B. The Caremark Claim

The plaintiff also challenges the Court of Chancery's dismissal of his *Caremark* claim. Although *Caremark* claims are difficult to plead and ultimately to prove out, we nonetheless disagree with the Court of Chancery's decision to dismiss the plaintiff's claim against the Blue Bell board.

Under *Caremark* and *Stone v. Ritter*, a director must make a good faith effort to oversee the company's operations. Failing to make that good faith effort breaches the duty of loyalty and can expose a director to liability. In other words, for a plaintiff to prevail on a *Caremark* claim, the plaintiff must show that a fiduciary acted in bad faith—"the state of mind traditionally used to define the mindset of a disloyal director."

Bad faith is established, under *Caremark*, when "the directors [completely] fail[ ] to implement any reporting or information system or controls[,] or . . . having implemented such a system or controls, consciously fail[ ] to monitor or oversee its operations thus disabling themselves from being informed of risks or problems requiring their attention." In short, to satisfy their duty of loyalty, directors must make a good faith effort to implement an oversight system and then monitor it.

As with any other disinterested business judgment, directors have great discretion to design context- and industry-specific approaches tailored to their companies' businesses and resources. But *Caremark* does have a bottom-line requirement that is important: the board must make a good faith effort—*i.e.*, try—to put in place a reasonable board-level system of monitoring and reporting. Thus, our case law gives deference to boards and has dismissed *Caremark* cases even when illegal or harmful company activities escaped detection, when the plaintiffs have been unable to plead that the board failed to make the required good faith effort to put a reasonable compliance and reporting system in place.

For that reason, our focus here is on the key issue of whether the plaintiff has pled facts from which we can infer that Blue Bell's board made no effort to put in place a board-level compliance system. That is, we are not examining the effectiveness of a board-level compliance and reporting system after the fact. Rather, we are focusing on whether the complaint pleads facts supporting a reasonable inference that the board did not undertake good faith efforts to put a board-level system of monitoring and reporting in place.

Under *Caremark*, a director may be held liable if she acts in bad faith in the sense that she made no good faith effort to ensure that the company had in place any "system of controls." Here, the plaintiff did as our law encourages and sought out books and records about the extent of board-level compliance efforts at Blue Bell regarding what has to be one of the most central issues at the company: whether it is ensuring that the only product it makes—ice cream—is safe to eat. Using these books and records, the complaint fairly alleges that before the *listeria* outbreak engulfed the company:

- no board committee that addressed food safety existed;

- no regular process or protocols that required management to keep the board apprised of food safety compliance practices, risks, or reports existed;

- no schedule for the board to consider on a regular basis, such as quarterly or biannually, any key food safety risks existed;

- during a key period leading up to the deaths of three customers, management received reports that contained what could be considered red, or at least yellow, flags, and the board minutes of the relevant period revealed no evidence that these were disclosed to the board;

- the board was given certain favorable information about food safety by management, but was not given important reports that presented a much different picture; and

- the board meetings are devoid of any suggestion that there was any regular discussion of food safety issues.

And the complaint goes on to allege that after the *listeria* outbreak, the FDA discovered a number of systematic deficiencies in all of Blue Bell's plants—such as plants being constructed "in such a manner as to [not] prevent drip and condensate from contaminating food, food-contact surfaces, and food-packing material"—that might have been rectified had any reasonable reporting system that required management to relay food safety information to the board on an ongoing basis been in place.

In sum, the complaint supports an inference that no system of board-level compliance monitoring and reporting existed at Blue Bell. Although *Caremark* is a tough standard for plaintiffs to meet, the plaintiff has met it here. When a plaintiff can plead an inference that a board has undertaken no efforts to make sure it is informed of a compliance issue intrinsically critical to the company's business operation, then that supports an inference that the board has not made the good faith effort that *Caremark* requires.

In defending this case, the directors largely point out that by law Blue Bell had to meet FDA and state regulatory requirements for food safety, and that the company had in place certain manuals for employees regarding safety practices and commissioned audits from time to time. In the same vein, the directors emphasize that the government regularly inspected Blue Bell's facilities, and Blue Bell management got the results.

But the fact that Blue Bell nominally complied with FDA regulations does not imply that the *board* implemented a system to monitor food safety *at the board level*. Indeed, these types of routine regulatory requirements, although important, are not typically directed at the board. At best, Blue Bell's compliance with these requirements shows only that management was following, in a nominal way, certain standard requirements of state and federal law. It does not rationally suggest that the board implemented a reporting system to monitor food safety or Blue Bell's operational performance. The mundane reality that Blue Bell is in a highly regulated industry and complied with some of the applicable regulations does not foreclose any pleading-stage inference that the directors' lack of attentiveness rose to the level of bad faith indifference required to state a *Caremark* claim.

In answering the plaintiff's argument, the Blue Bell directors also stress that management regularly reported to them on "operational issues." This response is telling. In decisions dismissing *Caremark* claims, the plaintiffs usually lose because they must concede the existence of board-level systems of monitoring and oversight such as a relevant committee, a regular protocol requiring board-level reports about the relevant risks, or the board's use of third-party monitors, auditors, or consultants. For example, in *Stone v. Ritter,* although the company paid $50 million in fines related "to the failure by bank employees" to comply with "the federal Bank Secrecy Act," the "[b]oard dedicated considerable resources to the [Bank Secrecy Act] compliance program and put into place numerous procedures and systems to attempt to ensure compliance." Accordingly, this Court affirmed the Court of Chancery's dismissal of a *Caremark* claim. Here, the Blue Bell directors just argue that because Blue Bell management, in its discretion, discussed general operations with the board, a *Caremark* claim is not stated.

But if that were the case, then *Caremark* would be a chimera. At every board meeting of any company, it is likely that management will touch on some operational issue. Although *Caremark* may not require as much as some commentators wish, it does require that a board make a good faith effort to put in place a reasonable system of monitoring and reporting about the corporation's central compliance risks. In Blue Bell's case, food safety was essential and mission critical. The complaint pled facts supporting a fair inference that no board-level system of monitoring or reporting on food safety existed.

If *Caremark* means anything, it is that a corporate board must make a good faith effort to exercise its duty of care. A failure to make that effort constitutes a breach of the duty of loyalty. Where, as here, a plaintiff has followed our admonishment to seek out relevant books and records and then uses those books and records to plead facts supporting a fair inference that no reasonable compliance system and protocols were established as to the obviously most central consumer safety and legal compliance issue facing the company, that the board's lack of efforts resulted in it not receiving official notices of food safety deficiencies for several years, and that, as a failure to take remedial action, the company exposed consumers to *listeria*-infected ice cream, resulting in the death and injury of company customers, the plaintiff has met his onerous pleading burden and is entitled to discovery to prove out his claim.

III. Conclusion

We therefore reverse the Court of Chancery's decision and remand for proceedings consistent with this opinion.

————

Points for Discussion

1. Prong one vs. prong two.

What are the two different "prongs" of *Caremark*? What is a plaintiff required to show under each? Must a plaintiff show only one or both prongs? How likely do you think it is for a plaintiff to succeed on a motion to dismiss on a prong one vs. prong two claim?

2. Mission critical risk in a monoline business.

In rejecting defendants' motion to dismiss, how much weight did the Court place on the notion that food safety was "essential and mission critical" to Blue Bell? What was the relevance to *Caremark* analysis that the company was a "monoline" business?

How much of the analysis in *Marchand* depended on the fact that the oversight failures posed a threat to human life? The next case even more directly confronted this question.

————

In re The Boeing Company Derivative Litigation

2021 WL 4059934 (Del. Ch. Sept. 7, 2021)

ZURN, VICE CHANCELLOR.

A 737 MAX airplane manufactured by The Boeing Company ("Boeing" or the "Company") crashed in October 2018, killing everyone onboard; a second one crashed in March 2019, to the same result. Those tragedies have led to numerous investigations and proceedings in multiple regulatory and judicial arenas to find out what went wrong and who is responsible. Those investigations have revealed that the 737 MAX tended to pitch up due to its engine placement; that a new software program designed to adjust the plane downward depended on a single faulty sensor and therefore activated too readily; and that the software program was insufficiently explained to pilots and regulators. In both crashes, the software directed the plane down.

The primary victims of the crashes are, of course, the deceased, their families, and their loved ones. While it may seem callous in the face of their losses, corporate law recognizes another set of victims: Boeing as an enterprise, and its stockholders. The crashes caused the Company and its investors to lose billions of dollars in value. Stockholders have come to this Court claiming Boeing's directors and officers failed them in overseeing mission-critical airplane safety to protect enterprise and stockholder value.

Because the crashes' second wave of harm affected Boeing as a company, the claim against its leadership belongs to the Company. In order for the stockholders to pursue the claim, they must plead with particularity that the board cannot be entrusted with the claim because a majority of the directors may be liable for oversight failures. This is extremely difficult to do. The defendants have moved to dismiss this action, arguing the stockholders have failed to clear this high hurdle.

The narrow question before this Court today is whether Boeing's stockholders have alleged that a majority of the Company's directors face a substantial likelihood of liability for Boeing's losses. This may be based on the directors' complete failure to establish a reporting system for airplane safety, or on their turning a blind eye to a red flag representing airplane safety problems. I conclude the stockholders have pled both sources of board liability. The stockholders may pursue the Company's oversight claim against the board.

I.   Background

[In the years leading up to the 2018 crash (the "Lion Air Crash") and the 2019 crash (the "Ethiopian Airlines Crash"), Boeing had consistently prioritized production and sales over the implementation of meaningful systems to monitor airplane safety.] In 2010, Boeing's primary competitor, Airbus, announced its fuel-efficient A320neo, which sold well and quickly gained ground on Boeing's 737, which had not been updated since the late 1990s. As Boeing clients began considering Airbus's fuel-efficient jets, Boeing felt production and sales pressure.

At an August 2011 Board meeting, the Board approved development of the 737 MAX, which would be a reconfigured version of the 737 NG that incorporated new engine technology and other modifications and upgrades. The August 2011 Board minutes [state that] the "strategy and objectives associated with the 737 MAX include increasing customer value, maintaining market share and competitive advantage over the Airbus A320neo, reducing risk, and enabling wide body product investment." No Board member inquired about the safety implications of reconfiguring the 737 NG with larger engines.

In developing and marketing the 737 MAX, Boeing prioritized (1) expediting regulatory approval and (2) limiting expensive pilot training required to fly the new model. [The] "frenetic" pace [set for] the 737 MAX program result[ed] in hastily delivered technical drawings and sloppy, deficient blueprints. In particular, the 737 MAX's larger engine needed to be situated differently on the airplane's wings, shifting its center of gravity. Because of that engine placement, the 737 MAX tended to tilt too far upwards, or "pitch up," in flight. Boeing addressed the issue with a new software: the Maneuvering Characteristics Augmentation System, or "MCAS." MCAS moved the leading edge of the plane's entire horizontal tail, known as the "horizontal stabilizer," to push the airplane's tail up and its nose down.

[MCAS was designed to activate if the plane pitched up at a high angle of attack (or "AOA").] [But] [t]he external sensor for AOA was highly vulnerable to false readings or failure for numerous reasons, such as general weather, lightning, freezing temperatures, software malfunctions, or birds. The AOA's sensor's vulnerability was well-known: between 2004 and 2019, failed AOA sensors were flagged to the FAA in more than 216 incident reports, including instances that required emergency landings. MCAS had only one AOA sensor, creating a "single point of failure" that violated the fundamental engineering principle requiring redundancy "so that one single error in a complex system does not cause total system failure." If the single AOA sensor was triggered, even for a flawed reason unrelated to the plane's pitch, MCAS would "correct" the aircraft by pushing its nose down.

On October 29, 2018, a new 737 MAX flying as Lion Air Flight 610 crashed into the Java Sea minutes after taking off from Jakarta, Indonesia, killing all 189 passengers and crew. Satellite data show the plane rising and falling repeatedly, as MCAS continually activated to force the airplane's nose downwards. [Subsequently, on March 10, 2019, another 737 MAX crashed.] Ethiopian Airlines Flight ET 302 went down shortly after taking off, killing all 157 passengers and crew. The pilots followed Boeing's recommended emergency procedures, but could not regain control of the plane because MCAS repeatedly activated.

II.   Analysis

1.   Plaintiffs Have Pled Particularized Facts Demonstrating A Majority Of The Director Defendants Face A Substantial Likelihood Of *Caremark* Liability.

Plaintiffs' *Caremark* theory breaks the Company's 737 MAX trauma into three periods of time: before the first crash, between the two crashes, and after the second crash. As crystallized at argument, Plaintiffs' theory before the Lion Air Crash maps onto *Caremark*'s first prong, asserting the Board utterly failed to implement any reporting or information systems or controls. Plaintiffs further assert the first Lion Air Crash was a red flag the Board ignored under prong two, while continuing to fall short under prong one. Plaintiffs contend the Board's prong two deficiencies culminated in the Ethiopian Airlines Crash. Plaintiffs have sufficiently alleged the Director Defendants face a substantial likelihood of liability under their *Caremark* theories.

a. Plaintiffs Have Stated A Claim Under *Caremark* Prong One.

Directors may use their business judgment to "design context- and industry- specific approaches tailored to their companies' businesses and resources. But *Caremark* does have a bottom-line requirement that is important: the board must make a good faith effort—*i.e.*, try—to put in place a reasonable board-level system of monitoring and reporting." This oversight obligation is "designed to ensure reasonable reporting and information systems exist that would allow directors to know about and prevent wrongdoing that could cause losses for the Company." "[O]nly a sustained or systematic failure of the board to exercise oversight—such as an utter failure to attempt to assure a reasonable information and reporting system exists—will establish the lack of good faith that is a necessary condition to liability."

Our Supreme Court's recent decision in *Marchand* addressed the contours of a *Caremark* prong one claim when the company is operating in the shadow of "essential and mission critical" regulatory compliance risk. *Marchand* addressed the regulatory compliance risk of food safety and the failure to manage it at the board level, which allegedly allowed the company to distribute mass quantities of ice cream tainted by listeria. Food safety was the "most central safety and legal compliance issue facing the company."

Marchand held that the board had not made a "good faith effort to put in place a reasonable system of monitoring and reporting" when it left compliance with food safety mandates to management's discretion, rather than implementing and then overseeing a more structured compliance system.

Like food safety in *Marchand*, airplane safety "was essential and mission critical" to Boeing's business, and externally regulated. Considering *Marchand*'s mandate that the board rigorously exercise its oversight function with respect to mission critical aspects of the company's business, such as the safety of its products that are widely distributed and used by consumers, as well as the failings *Marchand* identified as giving rise to the reasonable inference that the board faced a substantial likelihood of liability under prong one, I conclude that Plaintiffs have not carried their burden under Rule 23.1 for their prong one claim. To be clear, I do not track the deficiencies *Marchand* identified because they are any sort of prescriptive list . . . I echo *Marchand* because it is dispositive in view of Plaintiffs' remarkably similar factual allegations.

i. *The Board had no committee charged with direct responsibility to monitor airplane safety.*

The Amended Complaint alleges the Board had no committee charged with direct responsibility to monitor airplane safety. While the Audit Committee was charged with "risk oversight," safety does not appear in its charter. Rather, its oversight function was primarily geared toward monitoring Boeing's financial risks.

Perhaps because the Audit Committee was not asked to do so, the pleading stage record indicates the Audit Committee did not regularly or meaningfully address or discuss airplane safety. The yearly report the Audit Committee received on Boeing's compliance risk management process did not include oversight of airplane safety. Specifically as to the 737 MAX, the Audit Committee never assessed its safety risks, including those regarding MCAS and the AOA sensor, during its development before the Lion Air Crash or after; nor did the Audit Committee ask for presentations or information on the topic. Similarly, the ERV process and the Corporate Audit group did not address airplane safety.

Defendants press that the Audit Committee addressed "risk" broadly, pointing to one-off instances like when it responded to FAA questions about [an unrelated safety] incident, or when it referred to "quality" or "safety" in passing. But those occasional occurrences fail to dislodge Plaintiffs' allegations that the Board did not specifically charge the Audit Committee with monitoring airplane safety.

The lack of Board-level safety monitoring was compounded by Boeing's lack of an internal reporting system by which whistleblowers and employees could bring their safety concerns to the Board's attention.

ii. *The Board did not monitor, discuss, or address airplane safety on a regular basis.*

Zooming out from the committee level, Plaintiffs have alleged specific facts supporting the conclusion that the Board writ large did not formally address or monitor safety. The Board did not regularly allocate meeting time or devote discussion to airplane safety and quality control until after the second crash. Nor did the Board establish a schedule under which it would regularly assess airplane safety to determine whether legitimate safety risks existed.

The period after the Lion Air Crash is emblematic of these deficiencies. The Board's first call on November 23 was explicitly optional. The crash did not appear on the Board's formal agenda until the Board's regularly scheduled December meeting; those board materials reflect discussion of restoration of profitability and efficiency, but not product safety, MCAS, or the AOA sensor. The Audit Committee devoted slices of five-minute blocks to the crash, through the lens of supply chain, factory disruption, and legal issues—not safety.

The next board meeting, in February 2019, addressed factory production recovery and a rate increase, but not product safety or MCAS. At that meeting, the Board affirmatively decided to delay its investigation into the 737 MAX, notwithstanding publicly reported concerns about the airplane's safety. Weeks later, after the Ethiopian Airlines Crash, the Board still did not consider the 737 MAX's safety. It was not until

April 2019—after the FAA grounded the 737 MAX fleet—that the Board built in time to address airplane safety.

Defendants argue the Board "regularly discussed" safety as part of its strategic initiatives, pointing to slide decks that nod to "safety" as an "enduring value" and as part of a "production system" that was simultaneously focused on "[a]ccelerating productivity." They also point out that the Board was updated on the 737 MAX's development, production, and certification, and that the Board inspected the plants where the 737 MAX was assembled. Defendants stress that the Board "oversaw the quality and safety of the 737 MAX program through monitoring the progress of the FAA's extensive certification review of the 737 MAX."

[But] under *Marchand*, minimal regulatory compliance and oversight do not equate to a per se indicator of a reasonable reporting system. "[T]he fact that [Boeing] nominally complied with F[A]A regulations does not imply that the board implemented a system to monitor [airplane] safety at the board level. As *Marchand* made plain, [that] the company's product facially satisfies regulatory requirements does not mean that the board has fulfilled its oversight obligations to prevent corporate trauma.

iii. *The Board had no regular process or protocols requiring management to apprise the Board of airplane safety; instead, the Board only received* ad hoc *management reports that conveyed only favorable or strategic information.*

As alleged, the Board did not simply fail to assess safety itself; it also failed to expect or demand that management would deliver safety reports or summaries to the Board on a consistent and mandatory basis. The Amended Complaint's allegations and exhibits incorporated by reference show that the Board received intermittent, management-initiated communications that mentioned safety in name, but were not safety-centric and instead focused on the Company's production and revenue strategy. And when safety was mentioned to the Board, it did not press for further information, but rather passively accepted management's assurances and opinions.

For mission-critical safety, discretionary management reports that mention safety as part of the Company's overall operations are insufficient to support the inference that the Board expected and received regular reports on product safety. Boeing's Board cannot leave "compliance with [airplane] safety mandates to management's discretion rather than implementing and then overseeing a more structured compliance system."

Here, the reports the Board received throughout the 737 MAX's development and FAA certification were high-level reports focused on the Company's operations and business strategy; the Board did not expect any safety content. After the Lion Air Crash, management's communications to the Board demonstrate the lack of a Board process or protocol governing such communications. None of Muilenburg's [Boeing's CEO and Chairman of the Board] communications in the weeks following the Lion Air Crash were initiated by a Board request, either as a one-off or as part of a standing protocol. Muilenburg sent them at his discretion. In the absence of a safety mandate,

Muilenburg's self-directed communications to the Board focused on discrediting media reports faulting MCAS, and on blaming Lion Air repair shops and crew.

Muilenburg did not send any communication to the Board about the Lion Air Crash until November 5, 2018, roughly one week after it happened. In that email, he disclosed that an airspeed indicator was damaged, but treated the Lion Air crash as a public relations problem and maintained to the Board that the "737 MAX fleet is safe." Muilenburg contacted the Board again after the WSJ Article was printed: he gave lip service to the idea that "[t]he safety of our planes is our top priority," but claimed that references to withholding information "are categorically false," and existing flight crew procedures were adequate, and that the 737 MAX was safe.

The Board's reliance on management-directed intermittent safety reporting continued after the Ethiopian Airline Crash. The Board passively accepted Muilenburg's assurances that Boeing's "teams are centered on our priorities, including safety, quality and stability," and as an "outgoing" component of its "production operations"; and that public and regulatory backlash was driven solely by "public/political pressure, not by any new facts" about the 737 MAX's safety. The Board did not press for more information.

It was not until April 2019, the month following the Ethiopian Airline Crash, that Boeing's Vice President of BCA Engineering and BCA's Vice President of Safety, Security, & Compliance presented to the Board. This was the first time that the Board or any of its committees heard a presentation from either member of management, "despite their roles leading engineering and safety, respectively, for Boeing's largest segment."

Management's ad hoc reports were also one-sided at best and false at worst, conveying only favorable and optimistic safety updates and assurances that the quality of Boeing's aircraft would drive production and revenue. Management reported its unsupported conclusion that MCAS and the AOA sensor did not cause the crashes and that the 737 MAX remained airworthy and able to meet production goals.

The fact that management only communicated with the Board regarding safety on an ad hoc basis as necessary to further business strategy, and the fact that management only gave the board "certain favorable information" but not "important reports that presented a much different picture," indicate that the Board failed to implement a reasonable reporting system to monitor the safety of Boeing's airplanes.

iv.   *Management saw red, or at least yellow, flags, but that information never reached the Board.*

In *Marchand*, the Supreme Court agreed with the plaintiff that management's knowledge about growing safety issues in the company and failure to report those issues to the board was "further evidence that the board had no food safety reporting system in place." Where management received reports that contained what could be considered red, or at least yellow, flags, and the board minutes of the relevant period revealed no evidence that these were disclosed to the board, it is reasonable to infer the absence of a reporting system. Here, as in *Marchand*, Boeing management knew that the 737 MAX had numerous safety defects, but did not report those facts to the Board.

In the critical period leading up to the Lion Air Crash, Boeing management received formal complaints from employees who questioned the safety of the 737 MAX. Further, Boeing's Internal Safety Analysis found that if a pilot took more than ten seconds to identify and respond to the MCAS activation, the result would be catastrophic. [Chief Technical Pilot] Forkner made MCAS's vulnerability issues known within the Company. But before the Lion Air Crash, there was no evidence that management apprised the Board of the AOA disagree sensor's malfunctions or the probability of catastrophic failure.

After the Lion Air Crash, Boeing started revising MCAS and, like the FAA, performed a risk assessment that concluded an unacceptably high risk of catastrophic failure. Boeing also pushed out the Manual Bulletin, and the FAA issued the Emergency Directive. But management told the Board the 737 MAX was safe, and did not brief the Board on the risks of MCAS.

Thus, safety concerns known to management filed to make their way to the Board, supporting the conclusion that the Board failed to establish a reporting system.

b. Plaintiffs Have Stated A Post-Lion Air Claim Under *Caremark* Prong Two.

Plaintiffs also contend that Director Defendants face a substantial likelihood of liability under *Caremark* prong two because they ignored the Lion Air Crash and other red flags about the 737 MAX's safety before the Ethiopian Airlines Crash. "To state a prong two *Caremark* claim, Plaintiff must plead particularized facts that the board knew of evidence of corporate misconduct—the proverbial red flag—yet acted in bad faith by consciously disregarding its duty to address that misconduct." Plaintiffs have done so here.

A classic prong two claim acknowledges the board had a reporting system, but alleges that system brought information to the board that the board then ignored. In this case, Plaintiffs' prong two claim overlaps and coexists with their prong one claim; Plaintiffs assert the Board ignored red flags at the same time they utterly failed to establish a reporting system.

I can appreciate the breadth of Plaintiffs' theory in view of the Board's pervasive failures under prong one and the scale of the tragedy that followed. Boeing's safety issues manifested in the Lion Air Crash—an accident the Board could not help but learn about, despite the lack of a Board-level monitoring system. Unlike many harms in the *Caremark* context, which include financial misconduct that the board can likely discover only through an internal system, the Board did not require an internal system to learn about the Lion Air Crash and the attendant MCAS failures.

The Lion Air Crash and its causes were widely reported in the media; those reports reached the Board; and the Board ignored them.

But I need not decide today whether Plaintiffs' prong two theory is cognizable in view of my conclusion that the Board utterly failed under prong one. Defendants press that "the Board had extensive reporting systems and controls," including its Audit Committee, ERV, ethics and compliance reporting portals, internal audits group, and regular management and legal updates. Assuming Defendants are correct, the Board nonetheless ignored the Lion Air Crash and the consequent revelations about the unsafe 737 MAX.

The Lion Air Crash was a red flag about MCAS that the Board should have heeded but instead ignored. The Board did not request any information about it from management, and did not receive any until November 5, 2018, over one week after it happened. In that communication, Muilenburg advanced management's position that the 737 MAX was safe, and the Board passively accepted that position. The November 12 WSJ Article circulated the theory that MCAS had serious engineering defects that were concealed from regulators and pilots, which required immediate investigation and remediation. The Board was aware of that article, but did not question management's contrary position. The Section 220 record does not reveal evidence of any director seeking or receiving additional written information about MCAS or the AOA sensor, Boeing's dealings with the FAA, how it had obtained FAA certification, the required amount of pilot training for the 737 MAX, or about airplane safety generally.

When the Board finally convened to address the Lion Air Crash, the call was optional. The full Board did not anchor the tragedy as an agenda item until it met for its regularly scheduled Board meeting in December 2018, and its focus at that meeting was on the continued production of the 737 MAX, rather than MCAS, potential remedial steps, or safety generally. And when the Board eventually considered whether it should investigate the causes of the Lion Air Crash, at the February 2019 Board meeting, the Board formally resolved to "delay any investigation until the conclusion of the regulatory investigations or until such time as the Board determines that an internal investigation would be appropriate."

Electing to follow management's steady misrepresentations that the 737 MAX fleet was safe and airworthy, the Board treated the crash as an "anomaly," a public relations problem, and a litigation risk, rather than investigating the safety of the aircraft and the adequacy of the certification process. The Board's declination to test the modicum of information it received and seek the truth of the 737 MAX's safety, despite reported information calling it into question, do not indicate a mere "failed attempt" to address a red flag. As alleged and supported by the Section 220 record, the Board was aware or should have been aware that its response to the Lion Air Crash fell short.

———

Points for Discussion

1. Posing a threat to human life.

How should risk to human life be included in the jurisprudence of oversight? Should corporate law cases apply a heightened standard of scrutiny in cases when boards have traded off corporate profits today for human lives lost tomorrow? It appears from *Marchand* and *Boeing* that the risk to human life was an important part of the court's determinations regarding the board's oversight responsibilities.

However, the courts have not yet created a separate category for oversight cases that involve a threat to human life, or otherwise recognized that such cases differ from cases that involve mission critical oversight failures that pose only financial risks. Should the courts be explicit about what appears to be implicit in these decisions, and treat cases involving risk to human life as requiring a heightened oversight standard?

2. Quantifying safety risks.

How should boards assess safety risks? Should they explicitly quantify safety risks, or is it sufficient for directors to discuss and consider safety, without using numbers? For example, suppose that the Blue Bell directors had been informed that, given the safety risks, there would be on average one outbreak of *listeria* every ten years, and that such an outbreak would on average result in eight people being sickened and three deaths. How should a court assess oversight by directors who explicitly consider numerical estimates of average safety risks?

Likewise, what if the Boeing directors had established extensive safety protocols but nevertheless believed that, even with these protocols in place, there was still a small risk of a 737-MAX crash in a given year? Would these actions satisfy the directors' oversight responsibilities if their estimate of the probability of a crash was 1%? Or 0.0001%?

Research on the value of a statistical human life has estimated, based on both surveys about risk and studies of risky behavior, that the value of a statistical human life is approximately $10 million. In fact, government agencies use this value in assessing the costs and benefits of public projects, such as building a bridge. Should boards similarly quantify safety risks based on these numbers?

Test Your Knowledge

To assess your understanding of the Chapter 9, 10, and 11 material in this module, click here to take a quiz.

MODULE IV – STAKEHOLDERS

CHAPTER 12

Corporate Purpose and Personhood

This chapter introduces you to the debate over corporate purpose and the corporation's place in society. What is the corporation? Is it essentially the private property of the shareholders, or is it a social institution that should serve public ends? Is it contractual in nature or is it a creature of the state that created it and to which it is responsible? To whom are the corporation and its directors and officers accountable? What interests must or may the board consider? Under what circumstances may the directors favor interests other than those of shareholders? What rights may a corporation assert? Can the corporation be held criminally liable?

We begin by examining various ways that thinkers have conceptualized the corporation over time, with particular focus on the allocation of power within the corporation. Next, we lay out the corporate purpose debate, which basically pits those who see the corporation as a set of contractual/property rights against those who see the corporation as a social institution with responsibilities to its many constituents or stakeholders. Finally, we consider two important topics related to corporate personhood—the rights and liability of corporations. Specifically, we focus on corporate rights related to political activity and the issue of corporate criminality.

A. Theories of the Corporation

How should we conceptualize corporations? Who should stand at the center of corporate governance? What should the relationship be between shareholders and the board of directors? In this section, we introduce you to some of the key academic literature on theories of the corporation that have developed over the past century. Although a number of changes in law, markets, and culture have occurred during this time, the different theories of corporations and their governance that have developed remain relevant to policy debates and doctrinal questions, as well as the deeper question of corporate purpose.

1. Berle-Means Corporation

An important moment in the modern debate about corporations dates to the 1932 publication of *The Modern Corporation and Private Property* by Adolf Berle and Gardiner Means. The book, which studied the characteristics of the 200 largest corporations listed on the New York Stock Exchange, identified a separation between stock ownership and managerial control. According to Berle and Means, the large body of shareholders in public corporations had no real control over the enterprise. Instead, control resided with the board of directors and the corporation's top executives—that is, with corporate management.

Berle and Means found that public shareholders had little say in the composition of the board:

> In the election of the board the stockholder ordinarily has three alternatives. He can refrain from voting, he can attend the annual meeting and personally vote his stock, or he can sign a proxy transferring his voting power to certain individuals selected by the management of the corporation, the proxy committee. As his personal vote will count for little or nothing at the meeting unless he has a very large block of stock, the stockholder is practically reduced to the alternative of not voting at all or else of *handing over his vote to individuals over whom he has no control and in whose selection he did not participate.* In neither case will he be able to exercise any measure of control. Rather, control will tend to be in the hands of those who select the proxy committee by whom, in turn, the election of directors for the ensuing period may be made. Since the proxy committee is appointed by the existing management, the latter can virtually dictate their own successors. Where ownership is sufficiently sub-divided, the management can thus become a self-perpetuating body even though its share in the ownership is negligible. This form of control can properly be called "management control."

For Berle and Means, the separation of ownership from control raised important questions about the legitimacy of actions taken by managers and the problem of corporate power. The abuses exposed by the stock market crash of 1929 cast doubt on market forces as adequate protection against management overreaching. The prescription to mitigate the separation of ownership from control was added legal protection for shareholders to protect them from unfettered management self-interest. This also would serve, they thought, to control the power of corporations in society. One solution was greater information to shareholders in the voting process; another was heightened fiduciary duties so that the powers of corporate managers would be exercised for the benefit of the shareholders. Although a number of thinkers, such as Professor Henry Manne, later invigorated the notion that market forces, such as "the market for corporate control," serve an important role in the functioning of the corporate system, Berle and Means' focus on the separation of ownership and control as a key problem of corporations has had long-lasting influence.

2. "Nexus of Contracts" Corporation

In the late 1970s, a number of economists and law professors advanced a theory of the corporation as a "nexus of contracts" among the corporate participants. Under this theory, investment is voluntary and the relationships between shareholders and managers are essentially contractual. Freedom of contract dictates that the parties be permitted to structure their relations as they choose, and the role of the state is limited to identifying and enforcing their voluntary consensual arrangements. Because corporations must compete for investors' capital, they will design governance structures to reduce the risks of management overreaching—to attract investment.

The "nexus of contracts" corporation stands in stark contrast with the corporation as an "entity" or "creature of law," which supports state intervention through direct regulation and shareholder litigation. The contractual theory views the corporation as a private contract, where the state's role is limited to enforcing the parties' understandings. The corporation, rather than a ward of the state, is the result of contracts among the owners and managers. In short, the role of shareholders is whatever they have voluntarily chosen.

The contractarians recognized, however, that market forces did not always protect against opportunistic managers. For example, in "final period" transactions (such as a merger) where there is no market after the transaction, managers may rationally seek to benefit themselves at the expense of shareholders. For the contractarians, the answer to such opportunism lay in corporate fiduciary duties that they viewed as filling the gaps in the corporation's contractual structure.

The contractarian theory—the first systematic effort to respond to Berle and Means—has influenced the intellectual development of corporate law. Drawing on economic rather than legal literature, it suggested a new way to view the corporate structure. Its leading proponents, Frank Easterbrook and Daniel Fischel, argued that corporate law rules, such as limited liability and board prerogatives, could be explained as a reflection of the bargains that corporate constituents would have agreed to on their own. Shareholders have (limited) rights under corporate law as residual claimants because this outcome would be the efficient result of hypothetical bargaining.

Although some writers continue to advocate a strict contractarian view that public shareholders have the rights that they have voluntarily accepted, many have come to recognize that the linchpin of the contractarian theory (the market for corporate control) has not operated as predicted. First, the stock market—upon which the market in corporate control depends—has not been as efficient as contractarians supposed. Second, takeovers are expensive, and not every badly managed company is subject to their discipline. Third, management has installed anti-takeover devices (sometimes with shareholder consent) even though contractarian theory predicts that the managers should have faced market discipline for installing such devices and shareholders should have rejected them as contrary to their best interests. Finally, state anti-takeover statutes passed at the behest of corporate managers, generally without shareholder participation, have undermined the effectiveness of the market for corporate control.

3. "Political Product" Corporation

If the contractarian model does not explain the Berle and Means separation of ownership and control in the modern U.S. public corporation, what does? Some scholars, most notably Mark Roe, have suggested the role of the public shareholder is the product of a combination of political and economic forces.

The prevailing paradigm is that the modern corporation survived because it was the fittest means of dealing with large-scale organization. But if politics cut off lines of development, then whether it is the inevitable form for large-scale firms becomes doubtful. Politics and the organization of financial intermediaries cannot be left out of the equation.

Professor Roe has asserted that corporate structures with strong managers and weak owners developed in the United States partly due to path dependence—that is, because of the unique history of circumstances and choices in the United States, as contrasted with those in other countries. The path taken by U.S. corporate law does not necessarily reflect the approach that would be chosen today or the best arrangement for economic efficiency. But, having invested in the original path, and given the subsequent set of institutions and practices that developed in tandem, it is easier staying on this path than charting a new one.

Historically, the American public abhorred private concentrations of economic power. As large-scale industry arose at the end of the nineteenth century, it faced two financing problems created by the absence of nationwide financial institutions: big industry needed to gather lots of capital nationally, and certain organizational forms that worked well with strong financial institutions were unavailable given the longstanding disdain for concentrated economic power. We developed very good substitutes. We developed, for example, high-quality securities markets, which allowed firms to raise capital in a national market, to remedy the absence of truly national financial institutions. We developed antitrust rules that promoted competition and, because competition pushes even firms with substandard internal governance toward efficiency, the costs of internal governance problems were reduced.

In time, we adopted new legal and economic institutions. Corporate boards now have well defined legal duties that partly constrain managers, and we have an active bar that pursues lawsuits, some of which are legitimate and functional. We have developed professional norms and incentive structures that motivate some managers.

We have had hostile takeovers, which constrained managers. And so continues the development of the path taken, subject to the political as well as economic forces in society.

4. "Team Production" Corporation

Notice that these theories of the corporation do not resolve whether the corporation should be run for the benefit of shareholders. Most contractarians assert that the corporation should be run for shareholders—a "shareholder primacy" norm. Contractarians justify this view by pointing out that shareholders are residual claimants in the corporation, entitled to whatever remains after payment is made to others such as employees, managers, and creditors. This last-in-line position makes shareholders most sensitive to corporate performance, and thus most like "owners."

But as we have seen, shareholders do not "own" the corporation in the same way a proprietor owns her own business. The shareholders cannot determine what products the corporation will sell, who will run the day-to-day operations, whether profits will be paid to the owners, when the business will take on new debt, or even whether the business should be sold.

The shareholder primacy norm has therefore been the subject of significant debate. Must directors make every business decision solely on the basis of maximizing the financial wealth of current shareholders? Some commentators have argued that corporate law does not require this. Instead, corporate fiduciary duties are generally understood as running to the "corporation" itself or the "corporation and its shareholders" and are framed from a long-term perspective. And the business judgment rule gives directors broad latitude to make decisions that do not necessarily maximize shareholder value.

Furthermore, contemporary corporate statutes that authorize charitable contributions and, in some states, permit directors to consider nonshareholder constituencies seem inconsistent with shareholder wealth maximization. In fact, corporate directors often say they operate by considering the impact of their business decisions on all the corporation's constituencies, not just shareholders.

Seeking to bridge theory and reality, Professors Margaret Blair and Lynn Stout offered an alternative model that they described as "team production." Drawing on work by financial economists, they argue that a business corporation "requires inputs from a large number of individuals, including shareholders, creditors, managers, and rank-and-file employees"—all of whom constitute a "team." Corporate law calls on team members to cede control of the enterprise to the board of directors. In so doing, "the team members have created a new and separate entity that takes on a life of its own and could, potentially, act against their interests, leading them to lose what they have invested in the enterprise."

Why would team members give up control to the board in this way? For Blair and Stout, the answer is that team members believe there will be more efficient team production and their share will reflect this if they and other corporate participants defer to the board. In this model, the board becomes the focal point for resolving the claims of all the team members—a "mediating hierarchy." They explain:

> Our argument suggests that it is misleading to view a public corporation as merely a bundle of assets under common ownership. Rather, a public corporation is a team of people who enter into a complex agreement to work together for their mutual gain. Participants—including shareholders, employees, and perhaps other stakeholders such as creditors or the local community—enter into a "pactum subjectionis" under which they yield control over outputs and key inputs (time, intellectual skills, or financial capital) to the hierarchy. They enter into this mutual agreement in an effort to reduce wasteful shirking and rent-seeking by relegating to the internal hierarchy the right to determine the division of duties and resources in the joint enterprise. They thus agree not to specific terms or outcomes (as in a traditional "contract"), but to participation in a process of internal goal setting and dispute resolution. . . .

> The mediating hierarchy model of the public corporation necessarily implies that authority for making some allocative decisions—those that take place "within" the firm—ultimately rests with the board of directors, whose decisions cannot be overturned by appealing to some outside authority, like a court. This claim should not be read too broadly. When members of the hierarchy behave in ways that threaten the hierarchy itself (as when corporate directors violate their duty of loyalty to the firm through self-dealing), courts will intervene. . . .

> We realize that this approach may seem odd—even counterintuitive—to corporate theorists accustomed to thinking of corporations in terms of a grand-design principal-agent model where shareholders are the principals and directors are their agents. Nevertheless, our claim that directors should be viewed as disinterested trustees charged with faithfully representing the interests not just of shareholders, but of all team members, is consistent with the way that many directors have historically described their own roles. Our claim also resonates with the views of legal scholars who argue that directors should view their jobs in these terms. Most importantly, our model of corporations is consistent with the law itself.

5. "Board-Centric" Corporation

Notice that the various theories of the corporation (with particular focus on the public corporation) assume that legal (if not actual) control of the corporation resides with the board of directors. Some see this as a potential problem and favor increased regulation to move control back to shareholders. Others see board centrality as the result of implicit bargaining and would seek to ensure that markets, particularly the market in corporate control, remain functional. Yet others see the powerful role of the board as the outcome of politics (the political realists) or the current state of the law (the team production theorists)—without coming to a view on the efficiency of the status quo.

Some corporate scholars, most notably Professor Stephen Bainbridge, have resolved these questions by asserting that the Berle-Means separation of ownership and control, and centralized management in particular, serves to allow the system to operate more efficiently. By placing control in the board of directors, the modern corporation, particularly in the United States, has succeeded in organizing social resources (labor, capital, goods) to produce enormous social wealth. Further empowering of shareholders, beyond minor modifications to existing rules, would be a mistake—for shareholders. Professor <u>Bainbridge</u> argues:

> Any model of corporate governance must answer two basic sets of questions: (1) Who decides? In other words, which corporate constituency possesses ultimate decision-making power? (2) When the ultimate decisionmaker, whoever it may be, is presented with a zero sum game in which it must prefer the interests of one corporate constituency over those of all others, whose interests prevail?

> On the means question, prior scholarship typically favored either shareholder primacy or managerialism. In contrast, . . . the power and right to exercise decision-making fiat is vested neither in the shareholders nor the managers, but in the board of directors. According to this director primacy model, the board of directors is not a mere agent of the shareholders, but rather is a sort of Platonic guardian serving as the nexus of the various contracts making up the corporation. As a positive theory of corporate governance, the director primacy model strongly emphasizes the role of fiat—i.e., the centralized decision-making authority possessed by the board of directors. As a normative theory of corporate governance, director primacy claims that resolving the resulting tension between authority and accountability is the central problem of corporate law.

> The substantial virtues of fiat can be realized only by preserving the board's decision-making authority from being trumped by either shareholders or courts. . . . At some point, greater accountability necessarily makes the decision-making process less efficient, while highly efficient decision-making structures necessarily reduce accountability. In general, that tension is resolved in favor of authority. Because only shareholders are entitled to elect directors, boards of public corporations are insulated from pressure by nonshareholder corporate constituencies, such as employees or creditors. At the same time, the diffuse nature of U.S.

stock ownership and regulatory impediments to investor activism insulate directors from shareholder pressure. Accordingly, the board has virtually unconstrained freedom to exercise business judgment. . . . Ultimately, fiat is both the defining characteristic of corporate governance and its overarching value. . . .

As an account of the ends of corporate governance, prior scholarship has tended to favor either shareholder primacy or various forms of stakeholderism. Again, the director primacy model developed herein rejects both approaches. [D]irector decisionmaking primacy can be reconciled with a contractual obligation on the board's part to maximize the value of the shareholders' residual claim.

Points for Discussion

1. Which theory?

Which theory best matches your views of corporations and what should be the role of shareholders and the board of directors in corporate governance?

2. Role of law?

What might the role of law be under each of these theories? Which theories anticipate that the law should seek to "reform" the role of shareholders in the corporation? Which theories seek to maintain corporate law as it is—or as the theorists perceive it to be?

B. The Corporate Purpose Debate

We have now examined a variety of theories about corporations and the allocation of power in their governance. Underlying these theories is a deeper question regarding the purpose of the corporation. For whose benefit should the corporation be run—for the primary benefit of its shareholders or to benefit society overall, or some combination of both? The answer to this question can lead to different conclusions about whether particular corporate decisions are proper.

The debate over the purpose of the corporation has dominated corporate law since the aftermath of the "Great Crash" of 1929 and the economic depression that followed. During the early 1930s, Congress held a series of hearings about the role of the modern corporation. Testimony focused on the major scandals of that era and leading scholars debated the appropriate role of corporate law, policy, and power. Historically, the debate was framed by two polar views, generally referred to now as "shareholder primacy" and "stakeholderism" (the latter sometimes framed as "corporate social responsibility").

1.   Corporation as Private Property

Adolf Berle, a Wall Street lawyer and law professor, developed an early version of the shareholder primacy view during the early 1930s (around the time that he published *The Modern Corporation* with Gardiner Means, discussed above). Berle argued in an influential law review article that corporate powers were held in trust "at all times exercisable only for the ratable benefit of all the shareholders." During the following three decades, Berle modified his views to become more sympathetic to stakeholders and the social obligations of corporations, and a prominent economist from the University of Chicago, Milton Friedman, emerged in the 1960s and 1970s as the leading proponent of what became known as shareholder primacy.

Friedman argued that the only social responsibility of a corporation is to maximize profits for its shareholders within the confines of the law. According to Friedman, for-profit corporations had developed a proven ability to maximize shareholder wealth, and he argued that they should pursue this goal. In his view, "there is one and only one social responsibility of business: to use its resources and engage in activities designed to increase its profits so long as it stays within the rules of the game, which is to say, engages in open and free competition, without deception or fraud."

Friedman was not opposed to social responsibility in general. But he argued that social responsibility was for individuals and government, not corporations. If individual shareholders wanted to be socially responsible by contributing their own money to social causes, that was fine. And Friedman favored government intervention to correct market failures, to provide important public services, and to protect and enforce contract and property rights. But those responsibilities were not the job of business corporations in his view.

Over time, many "law and economics" academics and financial leaders have come to share Friedman's view that the corporation exists primarily to generate shareholder value or wealth. They have explained that other corporate constituencies, such as employees and creditors, are protected by contracts with the corporation and other areas of law. They have seen other constituencies' interests as incidental and subordinate to the goal of maximizing shareholder value. Delaware Chancellor William Allen labeled this view the "property" model, because it envisions the corporation as a form of privately held property.

Notice that the property model explicitly assumes the corporation is run for the benefit of shareholders rather than other stakeholders. In fact, U.S. corporate law focuses on contributors of capital (shareholders) instead of contributors of other inputs (employees, suppliers, creditors, communities). Why should corporate law favor capital over these other inputs, which often may be as or more important to the success of the corporation? The answer by those who advocate for shareholder primacy has been that these other inputs are protected by free markets, contractual negotiations, and government regulation—not corporate law.

2.   Corporation as Social Institution

The leading 1930s proponent of the contrary view was law professor E. Merrick Dodd. A year after Berle published his influential pro-shareholder article, Dodd countered that the business corporation was more properly seen "as an economic institution which has a social service as well as a profit making function."

Dodd's view spread widely. It appealed to people who found the notion of corporate citizenship and responsibility attractive. Many corporate executives complained that shareholders were too short-sighted, with no real stake in the long-term health of the corporation. They asserted that shareholders wrongly viewed the corporation as their private property, when the superior view was that directors should focus on the corporation's long-term interests, including attention to non-shareholder constituencies. In this view, the directors owed duties to the corporation itself as an entity, not merely to the corporation's shareholders. Chancellor Allen labeled this competing view the "entity" model.

Many students find the 2003 documentary "The Corporation" entertaining and thought provoking. The film portrays the modern corporation as often dysfunctional, even sociopathic. Featuring clips of several prominent commentators, including Milton Friedman and Bob Monks, it describes the shareholder primacy and CSR arguments. "The Corporation" is available on YouTube, and a sequel, "The New Corporation," came out in 2022. *See* http:// www.thecorporation.com.

More recently, consumers and other corporate stakeholders have pressed corporations to consider issues of business ethics and sustainability. Social awareness initiatives and socially responsible investing have led to increased pressure on corporations to behave responsibly. Some prominent corporate leaders, including Warren Buffett, have asserted that corporations must focus on "people, communities, and the environment"—the keys to profitability and thus shareholder value. And some leading academics have argued that corporate law actually gives directors broad discretion to consider non-shareholder constituents, corporate boards are not bound to allocate residual profits only to shareholders, and long-term corporate returns are not necessarily linked to shareholder empowerment. Instead, these academics point out that the most successful corporations often focus on maximizing "firm value," which includes the value to all corporate constituents, not just shareholders. (In the next chapter, we will examine in more detail the concepts of corporate social responsibility and "environmental, social, and governance" or "ESG.")

Points for Discussion

1. *Different corporate purposes?*

The above discussion highlights the corporate purpose debate through the legal lens of fiduciary duties as pitting those who believe that directors should manage the corporation to maximize shareholders' economic interests against those who believe that directors ought to consider other social aims. Is this the best way to think about corporate purpose? Perhaps it is better thought of as a business issue concerning the corporation's business objective? Or as a moral issue concerning business ethics? Does it make sense to think of corporations as having more than one corporate purpose?

2. *The corporate purpose clause.*

Historically, under the system of special chartering, corporate charters were granted one by one, and each charter of a for-profit business corporation typically listed a specific activity or corporate purpose related to the type of business being operated. Through the nineteenth century, as states adopted general incorporation statutes, the requirement of stating a corporate purpose in the charter remained, but over time such statutes allowed for broad statements of pursuing "any lawful activity." Although some corporations choose to state a customized corporate purpose in their charters, most corporations state their purpose broadly, as allowed by modern statutes. How does the corporate purpose clause relate to the corporate purpose debate?

C. Corporate Purpose in Context

The tension between the corporation as profit maximizer and social institution, though it arises regularly in business practice, does not come up that often in court cases. In this section, we look at some notable examples as well as other perspectives on corporate purpose in practice.

First, we look at *Dodge v. Ford Motor Co.* involving the dispute between the Dodge brothers and Henry Ford—a famous, one hundred-year-old case in corporate law from the Michigan Supreme Court. The case is often discussed in debates about the purpose of the modern for-profit corporation, with differing views about whether its statement about corporate purpose is a classic and important articulation or mere dicta that was unnecessary to its holding resolving a dispute involving oppression between majority and minority shareholders in a closely held corporation. Second, we look at a more modern case from Delaware's Court of Chancery, *eBay Domestic Holdings, Inc. v. Newmark*, which has also attracted significant attention (and debate) due to its language concerning corporate purpose. Finally, this section turns to a prominent voice in legal debates that has championed a stakeholder perspective and "new paradigm" for understanding corporate purpose.

1.   The "Classic" Case

Dodge v. Ford Motor is one of the most famous corporate law decisions, and best remembered for its discussion of corporate purpose, given Henry Ford's insistence on stating his motives for business decisions in terms of social rather than economic values.

Ford Motor Company was organized in 1903 with an initial capitalization of $150,000. The Dodge brothers were originally suppliers of auto parts to the company and minority shareholders. The articles of incorporation stated the following purpose of the corporation: "To purchase, manufacture and plac[e] on the market for sale automobiles or the purchase, manufacture and placing on the market for sale of motors and of devices and appliances incident to their construction and operation." By 1913, Ford had set up his famous assembly line for automobile manufacturing, and the Dodge brothers were no longer supplying most of Ford Motor Company's parts. Ford was moving toward vertically integrating the business, and was positioning the company to build an inexpensive car of good quality that would be widely accessible to middle-class Americans. The Dodge brothers had started their own automotive company and were building and selling upscale cars.

Originally, Ford cars had sold for more than $900. But over time, the selling price was lowered and the car itself was improved. In 1916, the car's sales price was reduced from $440 to $360. As the company lowered the price of its cars, sales soared. The following chart shows the company's remarkable success:

Fiscal Year	Cars sold	Profits	Special dividends
1910	18,664	$4,521,509	
1911	34,466	$6,275,031	
1912	68,544	$13,057,312	$3,000,000
1913	168,304	$25,046,767	$12,000,000
1914	248,307	$30,338,454	$11,000,000
1915 (10 mos.)	264,351	$24,641,423	$14,000,000
1916	472,350	$59,994,918	$5,000,000

Besides the regular quarterly dividends amounting to $1,200,000 per year, the company also paid special dividends totaling $45 million from 1911 through 1916. Then, in 1916, Ford "declared it to be the settled policy of the company not to pay in the future any special dividends, but to put back into the business for the future all of the earnings of the company other than the regular dividend." Ford had also announced that it would be extending its operations by investing in iron ore mines and building manufacturing plants on the River Rouge, increasing the number of employees "to spread the benefits of this industrial system to the greatest possible number."

A lawsuit was brought by the Dodge brothers, two minority shareholders, against the Ford Motor Company, Henry Ford, and other members of the board of directors. At the time the suit was brought, the company's paid-in capital was $2,000,000, with the Dodge brothers owning 10% of the outstanding shares, and Ford owning 58% and dominating the company's board of directors and serving as president. The plaintiffs sought (1) to compel the payment of a special dividend, and (2) to enjoin Ford's expansion plan regarding the River Rouge property. The lower court granted all relief requested by plaintiffs.

The defendants appealed from the lower court order directing the corporation to pay a special dividend of $19 million, enjoining it from building the smelter and steel manufacturing facilities at the River Rouge property, and restraining it from "increasing the fixed capital assets" or "holding liquid assets in excess of such as may be reasonably required in the proper conduct and carrying on of the business and operations" of the corporation.

Dodge v. Ford Motor Co.

170 N.W. 668 (Mich. 1919)

OSTRANDER, C.J.

When plaintiffs made their complaint and demand for further dividends, the Ford Motor Company had concluded its most prosperous year of business. The demand for its cars at the price of the preceding year continued. It could make and could market in the year beginning August 1, 1916, more than 500,000 cars. The cost of materials was likely to advance, and perhaps the price of labor; but it reasonably might have expected a profit for the year of upwards of $60,000,000. In justification of their dividend policy and business plan, the defendants proved the following facts: It had been the policy of the corporation for a considerable time to annually reduce the selling price of cars, while keeping up, or improving, their quality. As early as in June, 1915, a general plan for the expansion of the productive capacity of the concern by a practical duplication of its plant had been talked over by the executive officers and directors and agreed upon. It is hoped, by Mr. Ford, that eventually 1,000,000 cars will be annually produced. The contemplated changes will permit the increased output.

The plan, as affecting the profits of the business for the year beginning August 1, 1916, and thereafter, calls for a reduction in the selling price of the cars. It is true that this price might be at any time increased, but the plan called for the reduction in price of $80 a car. The capacity of the plant, without the additions thereto voted to be made, would produce more than 600,000 cars annually. This number, and more, could have been sold for $440 instead of $360, a difference in the return for capital, labor, and materials employed of at least $48,000,000. In short, the plan does not call for and is not intended to produce immediately a more profitable business, but a less profitable one; not only less profitable than formerly, but less profitable than it is admitted it might be made. The apparent immediate effect will be to diminish the value of shares and the returns to shareholders.

It is the contention of plaintiffs that the apparent effect of the plan is intended to be the continued and continuing effect of it, and that it is deliberately proposed to continue the corporation henceforth as a semi-eleemosynary institution and not as a business institution. In support of this contention, they point to the attitude and to the expressions of Mr. Henry Ford.

Mr. Henry Ford is the dominant force in the business of the Ford Motor Company. No plan of operations could be adopted unless he consented, and no board of directors can be elected whom he does not favor. A business, one of the largest in the world, and one of the most profitable, has been built up. It employs many men, at good pay.

"My ambition," said Mr. Ford, "is to employ still more men, to spread the benefits of this industrial system to the greatest possible number, to help them build up their lives and their homes. To do this we are putting the greatest share of our profits back in the business."

"With regard to dividends, the company paid sixty per cent on its capitalization of two million dollars, or $1,200,000, leaving $58,000,000 to reinvest for the growth of the company. This is Mr. Ford's policy at present, and it is understood that the other stockholders cheerfully accede to this plan."

He had made up his mind in the summer of 1916 that no dividends other than the regular dividends should be paid, "for the present."

"Q. For how long? Had you fixed in your mind any time in the future, when you were going to pay? A. No.

"Q. That was indefinite in the future? A. That was indefinite; yes, sir."

The record, and especially the testimony of Mr. Ford, convinces that he has to some extent the attitude towards shareholders of one who has dispensed and distributed to them large gains and that they should be content to take what he chooses to give. His testimony creates the impression, also, that he thinks the Ford Motor Company has made too much money, has had too large profits, and that, although large profits might be still earned, a sharing of them with the public, by reducing the price of the output of the company, ought to be undertaken. We have no doubt that certain sentiments, philanthropic and altruistic, creditable to Mr. Ford, had large influence in determining the policy to be pursued by the Ford Motor Company—the policy which has been herein referred to.

It is said by his counsel that—

Although a manufacturing corporation cannot engage in humanitarian works as its principal business, the fact that it is organized for profit does not prevent the existence of implied powers to carry on with humanitarian motives such charitable works as are incidental to the main business of the corporation.

The cases referred to by counsel, like all others in which the subject is treated, turn finally upon the question whether it appears that the directors were not acting for the best interests of the corporation. The case presented here is not like any of them. The difference between an incidental humanitarian expenditure of corporate funds for the benefit of the employees, like the building of a hospital for their use and the employment of agencies for the betterment of their condition, and a general purpose and plan to benefit mankind at the expense of others, is obvious. There should be no confusion (of which there is evidence) of the duties which Mr. Ford conceives that he and the stockholders owe to the general public and the duties which in law he and his codirectors owe to protesting, minority stockholders. A business corporation is organized and carried on primarily for the profit of the stockholders. The powers of the directors are to be employed for that end. The discretion of directors is to be exercised in the choice of means to attain that end, and does not extend to a change in the end itself, to the reduction of profits, or to the nondistribution of profits among stockholders in order to devote them to other purposes.

There is committed to the discretion of directors, a discretion to be exercised in good faith, the infinite details of business, including the wages which shall be paid to employees, the number of hours they shall work, the conditions under which labor shall be carried on, and the price for which products shall be offered to the public.

It is said by appellants that the motives of the board members are not material and will not be inquired into by the court so long as their acts are within their lawful powers. As we have pointed out, and the proposition does not require argument to sustain it, it is not within the lawful powers of a board of directors to shape and conduct the affairs of a corporation for the merely incidental benefit of shareholders and for the primary purpose of benefiting others, and no one will contend that, if the avowed purpose of the defendant directors was to sacrifice the interests of shareholders, it would not be the duty of the courts to interfere.

We are not, however, persuaded that we should interfere with the proposed expansion of the business of the Ford Motor Company. In view of the fact that the selling price of products may be increased at any time, the ultimate results of the larger business cannot be certainly estimated. The judges are not business experts. It is recognized that plans must often be made for a long future, for expected competition, for a continuing as well as an immediately profitable venture. The experience of the Ford Motor Company is evidence of capable management of its affairs. It may be noticed, incidentally, that it took from the public the money required for the execution of its plan, and that the very considerable salaries paid to Mr. Ford and to certain executive officers and employees were not diminished. We are not satisfied that the alleged motives of the directors, in so far as they are reflected in the conduct of the business, menace the interests of shareholders. It is enough to say, perhaps, that the court of equity is at all times open to complaining shareholders having a just grievance.

The decree of the court below fixing and determining the specific amount to be distributed to stockholders is affirmed. In other respect, the said decree is reversed.

———

Points for Discussion

1. *Shareholder wealth maximization.*

Dodge v. Ford Motor is often cited by legal scholars as support for the shareholder primacy view. "A business corporation is organized and carried on primarily for the profit of the stockholders." Does it support that view? Notice the court used the word "primarily," not "exclusively," suggesting that "an incidental humanitarian expenditure for the benefit of the employees" would be permissible. In addition, it is worth noting that the court refused to question the business judgment of management and enjoin the proposed vertical expansion of the company even though that expansion would reduce short-term profits. Thus, the decision seems to allow for discretion in business strategy and to leave room for activities that are not profit maximizing if they are "incidental" to the "primary" purpose of the corporation.

What is the precedential value of the decision regarding corporate purpose? Is it just an old Michigan case about minority shareholder oppression in a closely held corporation? Or is it a classic articulation of corporate purpose with contemporary relevance?

2. *What really happened?*

Ford had asserted on numerous occasions that he wanted to benefit customers and employees, and to gain for himself only a small or reasonable profit from his venture:

> I hold this view because it enables a large number of people to buy and enjoy the use of a car and because it gives a larger number of men employment at good wages. Those are the two aims I have in life. But I would not be counted a success if I could not accomplish that and at the same time make a fair amount of profit for myself and the men associated with me in the business.
>
> And let me say right here, that I do not believe that we should make such an awful profit on our cars. A reasonable profit is right, but not too much. So it has been my policy to force the price of the car down as fast

as production would permit, and give the benefits to users and laborers, with resulting surprisingly enormous benefits to ourselves.

Does Ford's refusal to "make such an awful profit" actually make good business sense and contain the seeds of substantial future profits (and dividends) for the shareholders? In assessing this question, keep in mind the underlying business situation.

At the time of the case, Ford Motor Company had monopoly power. It was capturing ninety-six percent of the popular car market and half of the total unit production of cars in the United States, making the company extremely profitable. But the company was seeking to vertically integrate and expand with its huge River Rouge complex, and it had a labor problem—many workers would not regularly show up for work and unionizing pressures were building. Offering workers a $5/day wage helped to ensure a steady workforce for the assembly line. The River Rouge expansion and labor-friendly strategy, however, left little available cash for dividends. Further, Ford might have been concerned that if he stated his business strategy explicitly, it might undermine his business relations with labor, the consuming public, and attract the attention of newly active antitrust forces. Instead of saying that high wages and the River Rouge expansion were means to pursue profitability and maintain the company's monopoly, Ford said he wanted to do good for all.

Was this public-regarding litigation stance ultimately a good strategy for Ford? Why do you think the Dodge brothers brought the lawsuit? In ruling (in part) for the Dodges, what do you think concerned the Michigan Supreme Court? Was it oppression of minority shareholders, the economic and political implications of a one-company industry, or something else?

---

2. A Modern Case

Next we have a more recent case from the Delaware Court of Chancery. It involved craigslist, Inc., an online classifieds site started by Craig Newmark and James Buckmaster, who together owned a majority of the company's shares and dominated its board. The company had a third shareholder—the company eBay, which bought its stake in craigslist from an outgoing craigslist CEO who had pressured craigslist to seek increased profits by monetizing more of its website, and said that if Jim and Craig didn't follow this advice he would sell his minority interest to a competitor. As Jim and Craig resisted this pressure, three-way negotiations ensued and the former CEO sold his stock to eBay. After eBay's purchase, Craig owned 42.6% of craigslist, Jim owned 29% of craigslist, and eBay owned 28.4% of craigslist.

The parties had a shareholders' agreement that expressly permitted eBay to compete with craigslist in the online classifieds arena. Under the agreement, when eBay chose to compete by launching its own classifieds site, its stock became freely transferable but it lost certain contractual consent rights that gave eBay the right to approve or disapprove of a variety of corporate actions at craigslist. Although eBay had an express right to compete, Jim and Craig were nonetheless not very happy when eBay did so and the relationship had "soured quickly" after eBay's purchase when it became clear they had different views on capitalizing on the "tremendous untapped monetization potential" of craigslist. Jim and Craig asked eBay to sell its shares back to the company or a third party that would be compatible with Jim, Craig, and "craigslist's unique corporate culture." When eBay refused to sell, Jim and Craig, acting in their capacity as directors, responded by: (1) adopting a rights plan (also known as a poison pill) that restricted eBay from buying more craigslist shares and hampered eBay's ability to sell its craigslist shares; (2) implementing a staggered board that made it impossible for eBay to unilaterally elect a director to the craigslist board; and (3) seeking a right of first refusal over eBay's shares or subjecting it to a dilutive stock issuance.

eBay filed a lawsuit challenging all three measures, asserting that Jim and Craig, as directors and controlling shareholders, had breached fiduciary duties they owed to eBay as a minority shareholder. The following excerpt comes from the court's analysis of the first challenged action—the adoption of a rights plan (poison pill). The court used an intermediate standard of review for enhanced scrutiny, known as the *Unocal* test, which requires the directors to "(1) identify the proper corporate objectives served by their actions; and (2) justify their actions as reasonable in relationship to those objectives." We will study *Unocal* in more detail in the chapter on M&A. For now, consider the following question: What does the court's analysis tell us about its view of corporate purpose under Delaware corporate law?

eBay Domestic Holdings, Inc. v. Newmark

16 A.3d 1 (Del. Ch. 2010)

CHANDLER, CHANCELLOR.

Facts

Oil and Water

In 1995, two individuals in northern California began to develop modest ideas that would take hold in cyberspace and grow to become household names. Craig Newmark, founder of craigslist, started an email list for San Francisco events that in time has morphed into the most-used classifieds site in the United States. Pierre Omidyar, founder of eBay, Inc., started an online auction system that has grown to become one of the largest auction and shopping websites in the United States. As they grew, both companies expanded overseas and established a presence in international markets.

Now, even though both companies enjoy household-name status, craigslist and eBay are, to put it mildly, different animals. Indeed, the two companies are a study in contrasts, with different business strategies, different cultures, and different perspectives on what it means to run a successful business. It is curious these two companies ever formed a business relationship. Each, however, felt it had something to offer to and gain from the other. Thus, despite all differences, eBay and craigslist formed a relationship.

The dissimilarities between these two companies drive this dispute, so I will spend a moment discussing them. I will begin with craigslist. Though a for-profit concern, craigslist largely operates its business as a community service. Nearly all classified advertisements are placed on craigslist free of charge. Moreover, craigslist does not sell advertising space on its website to third parties. Nor does craigslist advertise or otherwise market its services, craigslist's revenue stream consists solely of fees for online job postings in certain cities and apartment listings in New York City.

Despite ubiquitous name recognition, craigslist operates as a small business. It is headquartered in an old Victorian house in a residential San Francisco neighborhood. It employs approximately thirty-four employees. It is privately held and has never been owned by more than three stockholders at a time. It is not subject to the reporting requirements of federal securities laws, and its financial statements are not in the public domain. It keeps its internal business data, such as detailed site metrics, confidential.

Almost since its inception, the craigslist website has maintained the same consistent look and simple functionality. Classified categories the site offers are broad (for example, antiques, personal ads, music gigs, and legal services), but craigslist has largely kept its focus on the classifieds business. It has not forayed into ventures beyond its core competency in classifieds, craigslist's management team—consisting principally of defendants Jim, CEO and President of craigslist, and Craig, Chairman and Secretary of the craigslist board—is committed to this community-service approach to doing business. They believe this approach is the heart of craigslist's business. For most of its history, craigslist has not focused on "monetizing" its site. The relatively small amount of monetization craigslist has pursued (for select job postings and apartment listings) does not approach what many craigslist competitors would consider an optimal or even minimally acceptable level. Nevertheless, craigslist's unique business strategy continues to be successful, even if it does run counter to the strategies used by the titans of online commerce. Thus far, no competing site has been able to dislodge craigslist from its perch atop the pile of most-used online classifieds sites in the United States, craigslist's lead position is made more enigmatic by the fact that it maintains its dominant market position with small-scale physical and human capital. Perhaps the most mysterious thing about craigslist's continued success is the fact that craigslist does not expend any great effort seeking to maximize its profits or to monitor its competition or its market share.

Now to eBay. Initially a venture with humble beginnings, eBay has grown to be a global enterprise. eBay is a for-profit concern that operates its business with an eye to maximizing revenues, profits, and market share. Sellers who use eBay's site pay eBay a commission on each sale. These commissions formed the initial revenue stream for eBay, and they continue to be an important source of revenue today. Over the years eBay has tapped other revenue sources, expanding its product and service offerings both internally and through acquisitions of online companies such as PayPal, Skype, Half.com, and Rent.com. eBay advertises its services and actively seeks to drive web traffic to its sites. It has a large management team and a formal management structure. It employs over 16,000 people at multiple locations around the world. It actively monitors its competitive market position. Its shares trade on the NASDAQ. It maintains a constant focus on monetization, turning online products and services into revenue streams. In terms of business objectives, eBay is vastly different from craigslist; eBay focuses on generating income from each of the products and services it offers rather than from only a small subset of services. It might be said that "eBay" is a moniker for monetization, and that "craigslist" is anything but.

Analysis

Rights Plan

The two main issues I confront are: First, did Jim and Craig properly and reasonably perceive a threat to craigslist's corporate policy and effectiveness? Second, if they did, is the Rights Plan a proportional response to that threat?

I conclude, based on all of the evidence, that Jim and Craig in fact did not adopt the Rights Plan in response to a reasonably perceived threat or for a proper corporate purpose.

Jim and Craig contend that they identified a threat to craigslist and its corporate policies that will materialize after they both die and their craigslist shares are distributed to their heirs. At that point, they say, "eBay's acquisition of control [via the anticipated acquisition of Jim or Craig's shares from some combination of their heirs] would fundamentally alter craigslist's values, culture and business model, including departing from [craigslist's] public-service mission in favor of increased monetization of craigslist." To prevent this unwanted potential future reality, Jim and Craig have adopted the Rights Plan now so that their vision of craigslist's culture can bind future fiduciaries and stockholders from beyond the grave.

It is true that on the unique facts of a particular case—*Paramount Communications, Inc. v. Time Inc.*—this Court and the Delaware Supreme Court accepted defensive action by the directors of a Delaware corporation as a good faith effort to protect a specific corporate culture. It was a muted embrace. Chancellor Allen wrote only that he was "not persuaded that there may not be instances in which the law might recognize as valid a perceived threat to a 'corporate culture' that is shown to be palpable (for lack of a better word), distinctive and advantageous." This conditional, limited, and double-negative-laden comment was offered in a case that involved the journalistic independence of an iconic American institution. Even in that fact-specific context, the acceptance of the amorphous purpose of "cultural protection" as a justification for defensive action did not escape criticism.

More importantly, Time did not hold that corporate culture, standing alone, is worthy of protection as an end in itself. Promoting, protecting, or pursuing non-stockholder considerations must lead at some point to value for stockholders.[105] When director decisions are reviewed under the business judgment rule, this Court will not question rational judgments about how promoting non-stockholder interests—be it through making a charitable contribution, paying employees higher salaries and benefits, or more general norms like promoting a particular corporate culture—ultimately promote stockholder value. Under the *Unocal* standard, however, the directors must act within the range of reasonableness.

Ultimately, defendants failed to prove that craigslist possesses a palpable, distinctive, and advantageous culture that sufficiently promotes stockholder value to support the indefinite implementation of a poison pill. Jim and Craig did not make any serious attempt to prove that the craigslist culture, which rejects any attempt to further monetize its services, translates into increased profitability for stockholders. I am sure that part of the reason craigslist is so popular is because it offers a free service that is also extremely useful. It may be that offering free classifieds is an essential component of a successful online classifieds venture. After all, by offering free classifieds, craigslist is able to attract such a large community of users that real estate brokers in New York City gladly pay fees to list apartment rentals in order to access the vast community of craigslist users. Likewise, employers in select cities happily pay fees to advertise job openings to craigslist users. Neither of these fee-generating activities would have been possible if craigslist did not provide brokers and employers access to a sufficiently large market of consumers, and brokers and employers may not have reached that market without craigslist's free classifieds.

Giving away services to attract business is a sales tactic, however, not a corporate culture. Jim, Craig, and the defense witnesses advisedly described craigslist's business using the language of "culture" because that was what carried the day in *Time*. To the extent business measures like loss-leading products, money-back coupons, or putting

---

[105]   *E.g.*, Revlon Inc. v. MacAndrews & Forbes Holdings, Inc., 506 A.2d 173, 183 (Del.1986) ("Although such considerations [of non-stockholder corporate constituencies and interests] may be permissible, there are fundamental limitations upon that prerogative. A board may have regard for various constituencies in discharging its responsibilities, provided there are rationally related benefits accruing to the stockholders."). *See also* Robert C. Clark, Corporate Law § 16.2 (1986) (discussing views about the corporation's proper role); Jonathan Macey, *A Close Read of an Excellent Commentary on Dodge v. Ford*, 3 Va. L. & Bus. Rev. 177, 179 (2008) (suggesting that boards can take action that may not seem to directly maximize profits, so long as there is some plausible connection to a rational business purpose that ultimately benefits stockholders in some way; the benefit to other constituencies cannot be at the stockholders' expense).

products on sale are cultural artifacts, they reflect the American capitalist culture, not something unique to craigslist. Having heard the evidence and judged witness credibility at trial, I find that there is nothing about craigslist's corporate culture that *Time* or *Unocal* protects. The existence of a distinctive craigslist "culture" was not proven at trial. It is a fiction, invoked almost talismanically for purposes of this trial in order to find deference under *Time's* dicta.

The defendants also failed to prove at trial that when adopting the Rights Plan, they concluded in good faith that there was a sufficient connection between the craigslist "culture" (however amorphous and intangible it might be) and the promotion of stockholder value. No evidence at trial suggested that Jim or Craig conducted any informed evaluation of alternative business strategies or tactics when adopting the Rights Plan. Jim and Craig simply disliked the possibility that the Grim Reaper someday will catch up with them and that a company like eBay might, in the future, purchase a controlling interest in craigslist. They considered this possible future state unpalatable, not because of how it affects the value of the entity for its stockholders, but rather because of their own personal preferences. Jim and Craig therefore failed to prove at trial that they acted in the good faith pursuit of a proper corporate purpose when they deployed the Rights Plan. Based on all of the evidence, I find instead that Jim and Craig resented eBay's decision to compete with craigslist and adopted the Rights Plan as a punitive response. They then cloaked this decision in the language of culture and post mortem corporate benefit. Although Jim and Craig (and the psychological culture they embrace) were the only known beneficiaries of the Rights Plan, such a motive is no substitute for their fiduciary duty to craigslist stockholders.

Jim and Craig did prove that they personally believe craigslist should not be about the business of stockholder wealth maximization, now or in the future. As an abstract matter, there is nothing inappropriate about an organization seeking to aid local, national, and global communities by providing a website for online classifieds that is largely devoid of monetized elements. Indeed, I personally appreciate and admire Jim's and Craig's desire to be of service to communities. The corporate form in which craigslist operates, however, is not an appropriate vehicle for purely philanthropic ends, at least not when there are other stockholders interested in realizing a return on their investment. Jim and Craig opted to form craigslist, Inc. as a for-profit Delaware corporation and voluntarily accepted millions of dollars from eBay as part of a transaction whereby eBay became a stockholder. Having chosen a for-profit corporate form, the craigslist directors are bound by the fiduciary duties and standards that accompany that form. Those standards include acting to promote the value of the corporation for the benefit of its stockholders. The "Inc." after the company name has to mean at least that. Thus, I cannot accept as valid for the purposes of implementing the Rights Plan a corporate policy that specifically, clearly, and admittedly seeks not to maximize the economic value of a for-profit Delaware corporation for the benefit of its stockholders—no matter whether those stockholders are individuals of modest means or a corporate titan of online commerce. If Jim and

Craig were the only stockholders affected by their decisions, then there would be no one to object. eBay, however, holds a significant stake in craigslist, and Jim and Craig's actions affect others besides themselves.

Jim and Craig's defense of the Rights Plan thus fails the first prong of *Unocal* both factually and legally. I find that defendants failed to prove, as a factual matter, the existence of a distinctly protectable craigslist culture and further failed to prove, both factually and legally, that they actually decided to deploy the Rights Plan because of a craigslist culture. I find, instead, that Jim and Craig acted to punish eBay for competing with craigslist. Directors of a for-profit Delaware corporation cannot deploy a rights plan to defend a business strategy that openly eschews stockholder wealth maximization—at least not consistently with the directors' fiduciary duties under Delaware law.

Up to this point, I have evaluated the Rights Plan primarily through the lens of the first prong of *Unocal*. To the extent I assume for purposes of analysis that a craigslist culture was something that Jim and Craig reasonably could seek to protect, the Rights Plan nonetheless does not fall within the range of reasonable responses. In evaluating the range of reasonableness, it is important to note that Jim and Craig actually do not seek to protect the craigslist "culture" today. They are perfectly able to ensure the continuation of craigslist's "culture" so long as they remain majority stockholders. What they instead want is to preserve craigslist's "culture" over some indefinite period that starts at the (happily) unknowable moment when their natural lives come to a close. The attenuated nature of that goal further undercuts the degree to which "culture" can provide a basis for heavy-handed defensive action.

In their fight against the imperatives of time, Jim and Craig deployed a rights plan that singles out eBay and effectively precludes eBay from selling the entirety of its shares as one complete block. Because the Rights Plan is not fully preclusive—in that eBay can sell its shares in chunks no larger than 14.99%—the plan is more appropriately evaluated against the range of reasonableness.

The avowed purpose of the Rights Plan is to protect the craigslist "culture" at some point in the future unrelated to when eBay sells some or all of its shares. As long as Jim and Craig have control, however, they can maintain the craigslist "culture" regardless of whether eBay sells some or all of its shares. The Rights Plan neither affects when eBay can sell its shares nor affects when the craigslist culture can change. It therefore does not have a reasonable connection to Jim and Craig's professed goal. Assuming Jim and Craig sought to establish a corporate Académie Française to protect the cultural integrity of craigslist's business model, the Rights Plan simply does not serve that goal. It therefore falls outside the range of reasonableness. On the factual record presented at trial, therefore, the defendants also failed to meet their burden of proof under the second prong of *Unocal*.

Because defendants failed to prove that they acted to protect or defend a legitimate corporate interest and because they failed to prove that the rights plan was a reasonable response to a perceived threat to corporate policy or effectiveness, I rescind the Rights Plan in its entirety.

────────────

3.   Stakeholder Perspectives

A number of legal scholars and practitioners have championed concepts of corporate purpose that include stakeholder interests. Here is an excerpt of one vision of corporate purpose by prominent corporate lawyer Marty Lipton (who created the poison pill in the 1980s, an important legal innovation that we will study in the chapter on M&A).

IT'S TIME TO ADOPT THE NEW PARADIGM
Martin Lipton, Wachtell, Lipton, Rosen & Katz
Harvard Law School Forum on Corporate Governance (Feb. 11, 2019)

Capitalism is at an inflection point. For the past 50 years, corporate law and policy has been misguided by Nobel Laureate Milton Friedman's ex-cathedra doctrinal announcement that the sole purpose of business is to maximize profits for shareholders. Corporations have also been faced with technological disruption, globalization and the rise of China, capital markets dominated by short-term trading and focused on quarterly profits, and unrelenting attacks and threats by activist hedge funds. In response to these pressures, corporations focused primarily on increasing shareholder wealth in the short-term, at the expense of employees, customers, suppliers, long-term value and the local and national communities in which they operate. The prioritization of the wealth of shareholders at the expense of employee wages and retirement benefits, with a concomitant loss of the Horatio Alger dream, gave rise to the deepening inequality and populism that today threaten capitalism from both the left and the right.

Action by corporations, asset managers, and investors is imperative. We have developed *The New Paradigm*—a roadmap for an implicit corporate governance and stewardship partnership—based on the idea that corporations and shareholders can forge a meaningful and successful private-sector solution to attacks by short-term financial activists and the short-termism that significantly impedes long-term economic prosperity. *The New Paradigm* is structured to obtain its benefits without the ill-fitting encumbrance of legislation and regulation. It is flexible and self-executing by corporations notifying their investors that they have adopted it and by investors notifying the corporations in which they have invested that they have adopted it. It is not a contract and can be unilaterally modified. . . .

The New Paradigm

The New Paradigm is a roadmap for an implicit corporate governance and stewardship partnership between corporations and investors and asset managers to achieve sustainable long-term investment and growth rejects shareholder primacy and is instead premised on the idea that stakeholder governance and ESG are in the best interests of shareholders. While it recognizes a pivotal role for boards of directors in harmonizing the interests of shareholders and other stakeholders, it also assumes that shareholders and other stakeholders have more shared objectives than differences—namely, they have the same basic interest in facilitating sustainable, long-term value creation. In this framework, the board of directors can exercise business judgment to implement the company's objectives, and the company and its shareholders engage on a regular basis to achieve mutual understanding and agreement as to corporate purpose, societal purpose and performance. Ultimately, the shareholders' power to elect the directors determines how any conflicts are resolved, if they are not resolved by engagement. However, since the company and its shareholders have the same fundamental objectives, there should be little room for activism and short-termism.

The New Paradigm is premised on the idea that companies and shareholders can forge a meaningful and successful private-sector solution to attacks by short-term financial activists and the short-termism that significantly impedes long-term economic prosperity. It is not a contract and can be unilaterally modified. The framework of *The New Paradigm* is divided into three buckets:

First, *governance* is about the relationship between a company and its shareholders (asset managers and investors) and between company management and the board of directors. Companies will embrace core principles of good governance and, in cultivating genuine and candid relationships with shareholders, will be in a position to demonstrate that they have engaged, thoughtful boards overseeing reasonable, long-term business strategies.

Second, *engagement* is the exchange of information and requests between a company and its shareholders. Engagement is dialogue, not dictates from either side. Engagement connotes expectations around a two-way commitment between companies and shareholders to proactively engage with each other on issues and concerns that affect the company's long-term value, and provide each other with the access necessary to cultivate long-term relationships. Companies commit to being responsive to the issues and concerns of shareholders, while shareholders will proactively communicate their preferences and expectations.

Third, *stewardship* is the relationship between shareholders (asset managers and investors) and a company. Stewardship reflects a commitment on the part of asset managers and investors to be accountable to the beneficial owners whose money they invest, and to use their power as shareholders to foster sustainable, long-term value creation. In embracing stewardship principles, asset managers and investors will develop an understanding of a company's governance and long-term business strategy, and commit to constructive dialogue as the primary means for addressing subpar strategies or operations.

In this framework, if a company, its board of directors and its CEO and management team are diligently pursuing well-conceived strategies that were developed with the participation of independent, competent and engaged directors, and its operations are in the hands of competent executives, asset managers and investors will support the company and refuse to support short-term financial activists seeking to force short-term value enhancements without regard to long-term value implications.

———————

Points for Discussion

1. *Compare* Dodge v. Ford *and* eBay v. Newmark.

In what ways are the cases similar? Does the Delaware Court of Chancery in *eBay* propound a similar view of corporate purpose as the Michigan Supreme Court did in *Ford* nearly a century earlier? What are the limits of these decisions?

2. *Constituency statutes.*

A central tenet of modern U.S. corporate law is that the board of directors supervises and manages the business and affairs of the corporation. Does the board have the discretion to decide that the corporation pursue an agenda other than exclusively maximizing shareholder value? Many modern corporate statutes, though interestingly not Delaware's, specifically recognize the discretion of the board to make decisions that take into account stakeholder interests. Such statutes are generally known as "constituency statutes." An example is below. What do you think is the practical impact of constituency statutes? Does it matter that constituency statutes are phrased to give directors the discretion, but not an obligation, to consider non-shareholder stakeholders? What does the lack of a constituency statute in Delaware law suggest about corporate purpose under Delaware corporate law?

Ohio Revised Code § 1701.59
Authority of Directors

(A) Except where the law, the articles, or the regulations require action to be authorized or taken by shareholders, all of the authority of a corporation shall be exercised by or under the direction of its directors.

(F) For purposes of this section, a director, in determining what the director reasonably believes to be in the best interests of the corporation, shall consider the interests of the corporation's shareholders and any beneficial purposes and related provisions set forth in the corporation's articles. The director shall consider any priority among purposes provided in the corporation's articles and shall consider any other method for balancing the purposes of the corporation that is set forth in the corporation's articles. In addition, the director may, in the director's discretion, consider any of the following:

(1) The interests of the corporation's employees, suppliers, creditors, and customers;

(2) The economy of the state and nation;

(3) Community and societal considerations;

(4) The long-term as well as short-term interests of the corporation and its shareholders, including the possibility that these interests may be best served by the continued independence of the corporation.

3. *The Business Roundtable statement.*

In August 2019, the Business Roundtable, an association of CEOs of some of the largest U.S. corporations, announced a "Statement on the Purpose of a Corporation," signed by nearly 200 CEOs. The statement provided: "While each of our individual companies serves its own corporate purpose, we share a fundamental commitment to all of our stakeholders." It further stated that the signatories "commit to deliver value" to all stakeholders, and specifically identified those as customers, employees, suppliers, communities, and shareholders. On the topic of shareholders, it committed to "[g]enerating long-term value for shareholders." The statement reflected an "update" to the Business Roundtable's 1997 "Statement on Corporate Governance," in which it said that "the paramount duty of management and of boards of directors is to the corporation's stockholders." In Q&A discussing the 2019 update, the Business Roundtable explained that "in recent years, an increasing number of members began to tell us that the 1997 language did not mirror their view of how a well-run company operates." Further: "The Statement is not a repudiation of shareholder interests in favor of political and social goals. Rather, the Statement reflects the fact that for corporations to be successful, durable and return value to shareholders, they must consider the interests and meet the fair expectations of a wide range of stakeholders in addition to shareholders."

Why do you think the Business Roundtable issued the updated statement? Do you think it might affect the behavior of corporations or would you expect business as usual?

4. *Corporate purpose in global context.*

The discretion and responsibilities of the board are particularly tested in corporations that operate globally. Multinational corporations must account for the different legal, regulatory, and business risks they face in the many countries where they operate. Simply complying with national laws and regulations often might not be enough. In many countries, particularly in continental Europe, non-shareholder stakeholders wield greater power, and various conceptions of stakeholderism are more widely accepted. Multinational corporations must decide whether to treat workers better than local workplace rules may require, or whether to implement environmentally friendlier policies than otherwise would apply. These decisions depend not only on the legal rules of the countries where the corporation operates, but also on the perceptions and preferences of the corporation's shareholders and stakeholders throughout the world. Does *The New Paradigm* better reflect contemporary expectations of a multinational corporation's shareholders such as large asset managers? Can it be reconciled with existing law on the fiduciary duties of the board of directors?

———————————

So far this chapter has explored the topic of corporate purpose. In the remaining sections of the chapter, we turn to other topics related to corporations' role in society, and specifically how corporations can bear rights and liabilities. How do these legal features in turn impact corporate law and shape our understanding of corporate purpose?

D. Corporate Personhood and Rights

A corporation is a "person" for many, but not all, purposes. It can own property, enter into contracts, and sue and be sued. Furthermore, under the Supreme Court's interpretations of the U.S. Constitution, a corporation is entitled to equal protection and due process under the law, can seek fair compensation when the government takes its property, and even has speech rights. But a corporation cannot vote, claim the privilege against self-incrimination, or expect the same privacy interests as individuals. That is, although corporations have some rights similar to those of individuals, their rights are not entirely the same.

We begin this section with a thumbnail sketch of corporations under the Constitution. We then turn to corporations as political actors and examine an important

Supreme Court decision, *Citizens United v. Federal Election Commission*, which found unconstitutional a legislative ban on corporate spending in federal elections. The various opinions of the justices reflect a long-standing dialogue on the Court about corporations in society and politics. Is the corporation an artificial being as to which the state can "giveth and taketh"? Is the corporation a real entity, greater than the sum of its parts, with its own separate existence and interests? Is the corporation a voluntary association with rights similar to those of the individuals who constitute it? The decision has already had an impact in both U.S. electoral democracy and modern corporate governance.

1.   Corporations Under the Constitution

At the founding of the United States in 1787, most corporations were municipal, religious, or charitable institutions, and very few business corporations existed. The Constitution does not expressly refer to corporations. In 1819, when the Supreme Court decided one of the earliest cases on corporate rights, the corporation at issue was Dartmouth College and it claimed protection under the Contracts Clause of the Constitution. Chief Justice Marshall's opinion described the corporation as an "artificial being" and explained that it "possesses only those properties which the charter of its creation confers upon it either expressly or as incidental to its very existence." But, the Court also recognized that a corporate charter is a contract between the state and the private individuals forming the corporation, and once granted it cannot be impaired by the state absent a reservation of authority giving the state the power to do so.

Early decisions such as <u>*Dartmouth College*</u> granting contracts clause protection were narrow in scope and the Court also established limitations to corporate rights. For example, in a pre-Civil War decision, the Court held that out-of-state corporations were not "citizens" under the Privileges and Immunities Clause of Article IV of the Constitution. As a result, states could regulate, or even keep out, corporations that were chartered in other states.

In the late 1800s, as the size and number of business corporations increased in the United States, the Supreme Court expanded the rights of corporations. In a series of headnotes and dicta, the Court stated that a corporation is included in the designation of "person" under the Fourteenth Amendment and has the right to equal protection and due process. By the turn of the century, there was little doubt that corporations could claim constitutional protections related to contract and property interests.

The Court, however, did not extend the same constitutional protections to corporations' non-commercial activities. In the early twentieth century, the Court stated that the liberty protected by the Fourteenth Amendment is "the liberty of natural, not artificial persons." Further, in <u>*Hale v. Henkel*</u>, the Court held that a corporation is not a "person" for the purpose of the privilege against self-incrimination because that right "is purely a personal privilege of the witness." But a corporation could claim Fourth Amendment protections against unreasonable searches and seizures because it "is, after all, but an association of individuals under an assumed name and with a distinct legal entity." And, as the twentieth century continued, the Court displayed a willingness to grant expressive and associational protections to media corporations and nonprofits.

2.　Regulation of Corporations as "Political Actors" and First Amendment Rights

The early case law left open the question of how corporations could be regulated as political actors. Before the "progressive era," corporate political contributions, and even bribes, were at the center of allegations of political corruption. Congress responded to these scandals by prohibiting corporations from contributing to or supporting the campaign of any candidate or party in connection with any federal election. President Theodore Roosevelt heralded this legislation as necessary to instill the confidence of "the plain people of small means" in the electoral process and eradicate perceived political corruption. The legislation also prevented corporate managers from using "other people's money" to advance their own political agendas.

> Regulation of the financing of federal elections arises under the Federal Election Campaign Act (FECA), passed by Congress in 1971. In 1976, Congress amended FECA to establish the Federal Election Commission (FEC) to ensure compliance with federal election law and to further regulate federal campaign finance.
>
> In 2002, Congress amended FECA in the McCain-Feingold Bipartisan Campaign Reform Act (BCRA) to regulate certain types of "electioneering" activities on the eve of a federal election.

Specifically, the Tillman Act of 1907 prohibited corporations from spending "treasury funds" (general corporate assets) on campaign contributions or independent expenditures "advocating the election or defeat of a clearly identified candidate." 2 U.S.C. § 441.

Despite these limits, corporations found other ways to be politically involved. In 1971, Congress passed the Federal Elections Campaign Act (FECA), which allowed corporations and unions to establish "separate segregated funds," popularly called political action committees (PACs). PACs receive voluntary contributions from people with ties to the corporation, not from the corporation's treasury funds. In other words, PAC money comes directly from shareholders, executives, and employees with their consent, instead of coming from the corporation's general funds as determined by the managers who control the corporation.

In addition to using PACs, corporations can pay for communications to their employees and shareholders that expressly support or oppose candidates and pay for "issue ads." Corporations can also donate to charitable and educational organizations, including "think tanks" that advocate political views.

Corporations also can, and do, lobby. Corporate lobbyists must register and disclose any payments they receive if they engage in "direct communications with members of Congress on pending or proposed federal legislation." But many activities that might pass as lobbying—such as congressional testimony, letter-writing campaigns, and comments on government regulations—are not subject to lobbyist disclosure rules.

Further, in several key cases starting in the 1970s, the Supreme Court recognized commercial speech protection, and addressed whether corporations have First Amendment rights to engage in political spending. One of the most important recent decisions involving corporate rights was *Citizens United*, involving a political advocacy nonprofit corporation that released "Hillary," a video documentary that was critical of then-Senator Hillary Clinton, a leading candidate at the time. Citizens United planned to run TV ads announcing that "Hillary" would be available before the primary elections on cable television through video-on-demand. Citizens United was mostly funded by donations from individuals, but also accepted a small portion of funds from for-profit corporations. Concerned about possible civil and criminal penalties for violating a provision of federal campaign finance law, § 441b of the Bipartisan Campaign Reform Act, it sued the Federal Election Commission (FEC) seeking declaratory and injunctive relief. Citizens United argued that § 441b and BCRA's disclaimer, disclosure, and reporting requirements were unconstitutional as applied to "Hillary" and its proposed TV ads. The District Court granted summary judgment to the FEC.

The Court's various opinions in *Citizens United* span more than 100 pages. Justice Kennedy wrote the majority opinion, which concluded that the federal statute banning corporations from using their general treasury funds to make independent expenditures that expressly advocate for or against a candidate in connection with federal elections, 2 U.S.C. § 441b, could not be read narrowly to avoid constitutional infirmity and held that *Austin*, a key campaign finance precedent, had to be overruled. Nonetheless, the majority opinion upheld certain disclosure and disclaimer requirements of FECA.

As you read the excerpts below, ask yourself how the justices seem to view the modern corporation.

(1) **Creature of state law:** The corporation is an artificial entity created by the state, which can broadly regulate its creations or concessions.

(2) **Real entity:** The corporation itself is a speaker. The corporate person has autonomy and appropriately speaks through management, subject to oversight by shareholders who can replace misguided managers.

(3) Private voluntary association: The corporation is an aggregate of its participants who understand that management will speak and act on behalf of their collective interests. Shareholders who don't like this can invest elsewhere or use their corporate governance tools to change corporate decision making.

Citizens United v. Federal Election Commission

558 U.S. 310 (2010)

Justice Kennedy delivered the opinion of the Court.

Federal law prohibits corporations and unions from using general treasury funds to make independent expenditures for speech expressly advocating the election or defeat of a candidate. *Austin v. Michigan Chamber of Commerce* had held that political speech may be banned based on the speaker's corporate identity.

In this case, we are asked to reconsider *Austin*. We hold that *stare decisis* does not compel the continued acceptance of *Austin*. The Government may regulate corporate political speech through disclaimer and disclosure requirements, but it may not suppress that speech altogether. We decline to adopt an interpretation that requires intricate (and chilling) case-by-case determinations to verify whether political speech is banned, especially if we are convinced that this corporation has a constitutional right to speak on this subject.

III

The law before us is an outright ban, backed by criminal sanctions. Section 441b makes it a felony for all corporations—including nonprofit advocacy corporations—either to expressly advocate the election or defeat of candidates. These prohibitions are classic examples of censorship.

We find no basis for the proposition that, in the context of political speech, the Government may impose restrictions on certain disfavored speakers. Both history and logic lead us to this conclusion.

The Court has recognized that First Amendment protection extends to corporations. This protection has been extended by explicit holdings to the context of political speech. Under the rationale of these precedents, political speech does not lose First Amendment protection "simply because its source is a corporation." *Bellotti* at 784; *Pacific Gas & Elec. Co. v. Public Util. Comm'n of Cal.*, 475 U.S. 1, 8 (1986) (plurality opinion) ("The identity of the speaker is not decisive in determining whether speech is protected. Corporations and other associations, like individuals, contribute to the 'discussion, debate, and the dissemination of information and ideas' that the First Amendment seeks to foster").

Bellotti struck down a state-law prohibition on corporate independent expenditures related to referenda issues. Thus the law stood until *Austin*, which "upheld a direct restriction on the independent expenditure of funds for political speech for the first time in [this Court's] history." There, the Michigan Chamber of Commerce sought to use general treasury funds to run a newspaper ad supporting a specific candidate. Michigan law, however, prohibited corporate independent expenditures that supported or opposed any candidate for state office. A violation of the law was punishable as a felony. The Court sustained the speech prohibition.

To bypass *Bellotti*, the *Austin* Court identified a new governmental interest in limiting political speech: an antidistortion interest. *Austin* found a compelling governmental interest in preventing "the corrosive and distorting effects of immense aggregations of wealth that are accumulated with the help of the corporate form and that have little or no correlation to the public's support for the corporation's political ideas.

The Court is thus confronted with conflicting lines of precedent: a pre-*Austin* line that forbids restrictions on political speech based on the speaker's corporate identity and a post-*Austin* line that permits them.

In its defense of the corporate-speech restrictions in § 441b, the Government notes the antidistortion rationale on which *Austin* and its progeny rest in part, yet it all but abandons reliance upon it. It argues instead that two other compelling interests support *Austin*'s holding that corporate expenditure restrictions are constitutional: an anticorruption interest, and a shareholder protection interest.

1

If the First Amendment has any force, it prohibits Congress from fining or jailing citizens, or associations of citizens, for simply engaging in political speech. If the antidistortion rationale were to be accepted, however, it would permit Government to ban political speech simply because the speaker is an association that has taken on the corporation form. The Government contends that *Austin* permits it to ban corporate expenditures for almost all forms of communication stemming from a corporation.

Political speech is "indispensable to decision making in a democracy, and this is no less true because the speech comes from a corporation rather than an individual." *Bellotti* (the worth of speech "does not depend upon the identity of its source, whether corporation, association, union, or individual"). This protection of speech is inconsistent with *Austin*'s anti-distortion rationale. *Austin* sought to defend the antidistortion rationale as a means to prevent corporations from obtaining 'an unfair advantage in the market place' by using 'resources amassed in the economic marketplace.' But *Buckley* rejected the premise that the Government has an interest "in equalizing the relative ability of individuals and groups to influence the outcome of elections." *Buckley* was specific in stating that "the skyrocketing cost of political campaigns could not sustain the governmental prohibition. The First Amendment's protections do not depend on the speaker's financial ability to engage in public discussion."

The *Austin* majority undertook to distinguish wealthy individuals from corporations on the ground that "state law grants corporations special advantages such as limited liability, perpetual life, and favorable treatment of the accumulation and distribution of assets." This does not suffice, however, to allow laws prohibiting speech. "It is rudimentary that the State cannot exact as the price of those special advantages the forfeiture of First Amendment rights."

All speakers, including individuals and the media, use money amassed from the economic marketplace to fund their speech. The First Amendment protects the resulting speech, even if it was enabled by economic transactions with persons or entities who disagree with the speaker's ideas. "Many persons can trace their funds to corporations, if not in the form of donations, then in the form of dividends, interest, or salary."

Austin's antidistortion rationale would produce the dangerous, and unacceptable, consequence that Congress could ban political speech of media corporations. Media corporations are now exempt from § 441b's ban on corporate expenditures. Yet media corporations accumulate wealth with the help of the corporate form, the largest media corporations have "immense aggregations of wealth," and the views expressed by media corporations often "have little or no correlation to the public's support" for those vies. Thus, under the Government's reasoning, wealthy media corporations could have their voices diminished to put them on part with other media entities. There is no precedent for permitting this under the First Amendment.

Austin interferes with the "open marketplace" of ideas protected by the First Amendment. It permits the Government to ban the political speech of millions of associations of citizens. Most of these are small corporations without large amounts of wealth.

2

The Government falls back on the argument that corporate political speech can be banned in order to prevent corruption or its appearance.

The absence of prearrangement and coordination of an expenditure with the candidate or his agent not only undermines the value of the expenditure to the candidate, but also alleviates the danger that expenditures will be given as a *quid pro quo* for improper commitments from the candidate. Limits on independent expenditures, such as § 441b, have a chilling effect extending well beyond the Government's interest in preventing *quid pro quo* corruption. The anticorruption interest is not sufficient to displace the speech here in question.

Independent expenditures do not lead to, or create the appearance of *quid pro quo* corruption. In fact, there is only scant evidence that independent expenditures even ingratiate. Ingratiation and access, in any event, are not corruption.

3

The Government contends further that corporate independent expenditures can be limited because of its interest in protecting dissenting shareholders from being compelled to fund corporate political speech. This asserted interest, like *Austin's* antidistortion rationale, would allow the Government to ban the political speech even of media corporations. Assume, for example that a shareholder of a corporation that owns a newspaper disagrees with the political views the newspaper expresses. Under the Government's view, that potential disagreement could give the Government the authority to restrict the media corporation's political speech. The First Amendment does not allow that power. There is, furthermore, little evidence of abuse that cannot be corrected by shareholders "through the procedures of corporate democracy."

Our Nation's speech dynamic is changing, and informative voices should not have to circumvent onerous restrictions to exercise their First Amendment rights. Speakers have become adept at presenting citizens with sound bites, talking points, and scripted messages that dominate the 24-hour news cycle. Corporations, like individuals, do not have monolithic views. On certain topics corporations may possess valuable expertise, leaving them the best equipped to point out errors or fallacies in speech of all sorts, including the speech of candidates and elected officials.

Rapid changes in technology—and the creative dynamic inherent in the concept of free expression—counsel against upholding a law that restricts political speech in certain media or by certain speakers. Today, 30-second television ads may be the most effective way to convey a political message. Soon, however, it may be that Internet sources such as blogs and social networking Web sites, will provide citizens with significant information about political candidates and issues. Yet, § 441b would seem to ban a blog post expressly advocating the election or defeat of a candidate if that blog were created with corporate funds. The First Amendment does not permit Congress to make these categorical distinctions based on the corporate identity of the speaker and the content of the political speech.

Due consideration leads to this conclusion: *Austin* should be and now is overruled. We return to the principle established in *Buckley* and *Bellotti* that the Government may not suppress political speech on the basis of the speaker's corporate identity. No sufficient governmental interest justifies limits on the political speech of nonprofit or for-profit corporations.

IV.

Citizens United next challenges BCRA's disclaimer and disclosure provisions as applied to *Hillary* and the three advertisements for the movie. Under BCRA § 311, televised electioneering communications funded by anyone other than a candidate must include a disclaimer that " _____ is responsible for the content of this advertising." Under BCRA § 201, any person who spends more than $10,000 on electioneering communications within a calendar year must file a disclosure statement with the FEC. That statement must identify the person making the expenditure, the amount of the expenditure, the election to which the communication was directed, and the names of certain contributors.

Disclaimer and disclosure requirements may burden the ability to speak, but they impose no ceiling on "campaign-related activities," and "do not prevent anyone from speaking." In *Buckley*, the Court explained that disclosure could be justified based on a governmental interest in "providing the electorate with information" about the sources of election-related spending that would help citizens "make informed choices in the political marketplace."

Shareholder objections raised through the procedures of corporate democracy can be more effective today because modern technology makes disclosures rapid and informative. With the advent of the Internet, prompt disclosure of expenditures can provide shareholders and citizens with the information needed to hold corporations and elected officials accountable for their positions and supporters. Shareholders can determine whether their corporation's political speech advances the corporation's interest in making profits, and citizens can see whether elected officials are " 'in the pocket' of so-called moneyed interests." The First Amendment protects political speech; and disclosure permits citizens and shareholders to react to the speech of corporate entities in a proper way. This transparency enables the electorate to make informed decisions and give proper weight to different speakers and messages.

The judgment of the District Court is reversed with respect to the constitutionality of 2 U.S.C. § 441b's restrictions on corporate independent expenditures. The judgment is affirmed with respect to BCRA's disclaimer and disclosure requirements. The case is remanded for further proceedings consistent with this opinion.

JUSTICE SCALIA, concurring.

I write separately to address Justice STEVENS' discussion of the original understanding of the First Amendment. The dissent embarks on a detailed exploration of the Framers' views about the "role of corporations in society." The Framers didn't like corporations, the dissent concludes, and therefore it follows (as night the day) that corporations had no rights of free speech.

To the contrary, colleges, towns, and cities, religious institutions, and guilds had long been organized as corporations at common law and under the King's charter, and the practice of incorporation only expanded in the United States. Both corporations and voluntary associations actively petitioned the Government and expressed their views in newspapers and pamphlets. For example: An antislavery Quaker corporation petitioned the First Congress, distributed pamphlets, and communicated through the press in 1790. The New York Sons of Liberty sent a circular to colonies farther south in 1766. And the Society for the Relief and Instruction of Poor Germans circulated a biweekly paper from 1755 to 1757. The dissent offers no evidence—none whatever—that the First Amendment's unqualified text was originally understood to exclude such associational speech from its protection.

The dissent says that "speech" refers to oral communications of human beings, and since corporations are not human beings they cannot speak. This is sophistry. The authorized spokesman of a corporation is a human being, who speaks on behalf of the human beings who have formed that association—just as the spokesman of an unincorporated association speaks on behalf of its members.

The Amendment is written in terms of "speech," not speakers. Its text offers no foothold for excluding any category of speaker, from single individuals to partnerships of individuals, to unincorporated associations of individuals, to incorporated associations of individuals—and the dissent offers no evidence about the original meaning of the text to support any such exclusion. A documentary film critical of a potential Presidential candidate is core political speech, and its nature as such does not change simply because it was funded by a corporation. Nor does the character of that funding produce any reduction whatever in the "inherent worth of the speech" and "its capacity for informing the public." Indeed, to exclude or impede corporate speech is to muzzle the principal agents of the modern free economy. We should celebrate rather than condemn the addition of this speech to the public debate.

JUSTICE STEVENS, with whom JUSTICE GINSBURG, JUSTICE BREYER, and JUSTICE SOTOMAYOR join, concurring in part and dissenting in part.

The real issue in this case concerns how, not if, the appellant may finance its electioneering. Citizens United is a wealthy nonprofit corporation that runs a political action committee (PAC) with millions of dollars in assets. Under the Bipartisan Campaign Reform Act of 2002 (BCRA), it could have used those assets to televise and promote *Hillary: The Movie* wherever and whenever it wanted to. Neither Citizens United's nor any other corporation's speech has been "banned." All that the parties dispute is whether Citizens United had a right to use the funds in its general treasury to pay for broadcasts. The notion that the First Amendment dictates an affirmative answer to that question is, in my judgment, profoundly misguided. Even more misguided is the notion that the Court must rewrite the law relating to campaign expenditures by *for-profit* corporations and unions to decide this case.

In the context of elections to public office, the distinction between corporate and human speakers is significant. Although they make enormous contributions to our society, corporations are not actually members of it. They cannot vote or run for office. Because they may be managed and controlled by nonresidents, their interests may conflict in fundamental respects with the interests of eligible voters. The financial resources, legal structure, and instrumental orientation of corporations raise legitimate concerns about their role in the electoral process. Our lawmakers have a compelling constitutional basis, if not also a democratic duty, to take measures designed to guard against the potentially deleterious effects of corporate spending in local and national races.

Thomas Jefferson famously fretted that corporations would subvert the Republic. General incorporation statutes, and widespread acceptance of business corporations as socially useful actors, did not emerge until the 1800's.

The Framers thus took it as a given that corporations could be comprehensively regulated in the service of the public welfare. Unlike our colleagues, they had little trouble distinguishing corporations from human beings, and when they constitutionalized the right to free speech in the First Amendment, it was the free speech of individual Americans that they had in mind. While individuals might join together to exercise their speech rights, business corporations, at least, were plainly not seen as facilitating such associational or expressive ends. Even "the notion that business corporations could invoke the First Amendment would probably have been quite a novelty," given that "at the time, the legitimacy of every corporate activity was thought to rest entirely in a concession of the sovereign." In light of these background practices and understandings, it seems to me implausible that the Framers believed "the freedom of speech" would extend equally to all corporate speakers, much less than it would preclude legislatures from taking limited measures to guard against corporate capture of elections.

It is an interesting question "who" is even speaking when a business corporation places an advertisement that endorses or attacks a particular candidate. Presumably it is not the customers or employees, who typically have no say in such matters. It cannot realistically be said to be the shareholders, who tend to be far removed from the day-to-day decisions of the firm and whose political preferences may be opaque to management. Perhaps the officers or directors of the corporation have the best claim to be the ones speaking, except their fiduciary duties generally prohibit them from using corporate funds for personal ends. Some individuals associated with the corporation must make the decision to place the ad, but the idea that these individuals are thereby fostering their self-expression or cultivating their critical faculties is fanciful. It is entirely possible that the corporation's electoral message will conflict with their personal convictions. Take away the ability to use general treasury funds for some of those ads, and no one's autonomy, dignity, or political equality has been impinged upon in the least.

The majority's unwillingness to distinguish between corporations and humans similarly blinds it to the possibility that corporations' "war chests" and their special "advantages" in the legal realm may translate into special advantages in the market for legislation. Corporations, that is, are uniquely equipped to seek laws that favor their owners, not simply because they have a lot of money but because of their legal and organizational structure. Remove all restrictions on their electioneering, and the door may be opened to a type of rent seeking that is "far more destructive" than what noncorporations are capable of.

Points for Discussion

1. *What kind of person is the corporation?*

The Supreme Court (and different justices) have variously viewed the corporation (1) as a creature of state law (a "concession" theory), (2) as a distinct legal entity separate from the incorporating state and its shareholders (a "real entity" theory), and (3) as a voluntary association of participants (an "aggregate" theory).

The "concession" theory is reflected in the *Dartmouth College* case, in which the Supreme Court disallowed states from unilaterally changing the corporate charter, viewing the corporation as an "artificial being" created by the law and a binding contract between two parties—the state and the private individuals who formed the corporation. The "real entity" theory has also appeared in Court decisions, such as when the Court denied "citizen" status to corporations under the Privileges and Immunities Clause, and when it has referred to corporations as having dignity or autonomy interests. In *Citizens United* and other cases granting protections to corporations, the Court has often used the language of the "aggregate" theory, characterizing the corporation as a group of individuals from whom rights can be derived.

Which view best describes the corporation? Does it make sense to determine corporate rights based on these theories of the corporation?

2. *Do shareholders have a voice in corporate political activities?*

Justice Kennedy pointed out that dissenting shareholders can protect themselves "through the procedures of corporate democracy." How might this happen? The Court did not explain. In the earlier *Bellotti* opinion, the Court referenced state corporate law:

> Acting through their power to elect the board of directors or to insist upon protective provisions in the corporation's charter, shareholders normally are presumed competent to protect their own interests. In addition to intracorporate remedies, minority shareholders generally have access to the judicial remedy of a derivative suit to challenge corporate disbursements alleged to have been made for improper corporate purposes or merely to further the personal interests of management.

Further, the *Bellotti* opinion noted that "the shareholder invests in a corporation of his own volition and is free to withdraw his investment at any time and for any reason."

However, in pointing to the "procedures of corporate democracy" in *Bellotti* and *Citizens United*, the Court did not acknowledge that shareholders often have incomplete information about a corporation's political spending. In addition, many Americans invest indirectly through pension funds and mutual funds and lack a ready means of exit. And, in any case, selling stock provides a solution only prospectively and does nothing to address the political spending that has already occurred.

As a matter of state corporate law, while shareholders elect the board of directors, they generally do not have proxy access to nominate directors. Waging a proxy fight is expensive and it's unclear whether shareholders would vote to oust directors for approving political spending the directors believed was in the corporation's best interests. Shareholders can also sue the directors for violating their fiduciary duties, but absent fraud or self-dealing, the business judgment rule protects political spending decisions if the board had plausible reasons for its decision.

Shareholders have another avenue for voice—they can propose and vote on shareholder proposals. But many proposals get settled before going to a shareholder vote and even if the proposal receives majority support, the board is not required to follow the shareholders' recommendations. Nonetheless, since *Citizens United*, shareholder proposals concerning corporate political spending have dramatically increased and resulted in some corporations making voluntary reports about their spending.

Are the "procedures of corporate democracy" sufficient to protect shareholders? Should political expenditures be considered ordinary business decisions subject to business judgment rule protection? Should the Securities and Exchange Commission mandate disclosure of corporate political spending? Are corporate directors best equipped to make political decisions for the corporation?

————————

In the last section of this chapter, we turn from the topic of corporate rights to corporate criminal liability. When a corporate agent commits a crime in her corporate capacity, who is criminally liable—the agent alone, the agent's supervisor, the corporate managers who could have prevented the crime, the corporation, or no one? What does this tell us about corporations' role in society and the ability to hold them accountable for their actions?

E.   Corporate Criminality

For over a century, the Supreme Court has recognized not only corporate rights, but also corporate criminal liability. Further, among the panoply of corporate rights are certain protections related to trials, searches, and seizures. This section considers corporate criminality and how criminal law has been used as a tool to internalize corporate social harms. We look at the prosecution of the corporation for the bad acts of its agents. This raises questions about why the corporation (not just its human agents or their supervisors) should be punished, how the corporation can have criminal intent, and why the corporation and ultimately its shareholders should be subject to fines and other monetary punishment for the actions of rogue agents.

As you consider the question of corporate criminality, you will notice the animating question is whether corporate criminality is a useful way to induce the corporation to consider and respond to its natural tendency to externalize costs and risks. Perhaps making the corporation civilly liable for failures to protect consumers, provide a safe workplace, or comply with environmental regulation is enough. And, perhaps, the piercing doctrine compels shareholders to ensure that their corporation complies with external legal norms. In the end, you will want to ask whether criminal liability (where fines imposed on the corporation are the usual sanction) accomplishes the purposes of criminal law: retribution, deterrence, incapacitation, rehabilitation, and restoration.

Although the corporation by its nature is a "person" for purposes of owning property, contracting, and being a party to civil litigation, the early common law treated criminal conduct by corporate agents as *ultra vires* and thus beyond corporate capacity. Since the twentieth century, criminal statutes, and cases interpreting them, have come to define the corporation as a person for purposes of criminal liability.

Corporate criminality is a messy concept. What is accomplished by holding the corporation criminally responsible for the bad acts (almost always unauthorized) of corporate agents? Why isn't individual criminality enough? How can the corporation, itself a legal fiction, harbor criminal intent? Since the corporation cannot be flogged or imprisoned, what punishment is appropriate? Why should shareholders (and sometimes other corporate constituents) pay for the misdeeds of corporate agents? What does criminal liability accomplish that civil liability doesn't?

The following case addresses many of these questions.

State v. Christy Pontiac-GMC, Inc.

354 N.W.2d 17 (Minn. 1984)

Simonett, Justice.

We hold that a corporation may be convicted of theft and forgery, which are crimes requiring specific intent, and that the evidence sustains defendant corporation's guilt.

In a bench trial, defendant-appellant Christy Pontiac-GMC, Inc., was found guilty of two counts of theft by swindle and two counts of aggravated forgery, and was sentenced to a $1,000 fine on each of the two forgery convictions. Defendant argues that as a corporation it cannot, under our state statutes, be prosecuted or

Pontiac was one of the divisions of General Motors Corporation, before the company went bankrupt in 2009. The Pontiac brand, which began in 1928 and came to be known for its sporty "muscle" cars, was discontinued as part of the company's restructuring.

convicted for theft or forgery and that, in any event, the evidence fails to establish that the acts complained of were the acts of the defendant corporation.

Christy Pontiac is a Minnesota corporation, doing business as a car dealership. It is owned by James Christy, a sole stockholder, who serves also as president and as director. In the spring of 1981, General Motors offered a cash rebate program for its dealers. A customer who purchased a new car delivered during the rebate period was entitled to a cash rebate, part paid by GM and part paid by the dealership. GM would pay the entire rebate initially and later charge back, against the dealer, the dealer's portion of the rebate. Apparently it was not uncommon for the dealer to give the customer the dealer's portion of the rebate in the form of a discount on the purchase price.

At this time Phil Hesli was employed by Christy Pontiac as a salesman and fleet manager. On March 27, 1981, James Linden took delivery of a new Grand Prix. Although the rebate period on this car had expired on March 19, the salesman told Linden that he would still try to get the $700 rebate for Linden. Later, Linden was told by a Christy Pontiac employee that GM had denied the rebate. Subsequently, it was discovered that Hesli had forged Linden's signature twice on the rebate application form submitted by Christy Pontiac to GM, and that the transaction date had been altered and backdated to March 19 on the buyer's order form. Hesli signed the order form as "Sales Manager or Officer of the Company."

On April 6, 1981, Ronald Gores purchased a new Le Mans, taking delivery the next day. The rebate period for this model car had expired on April 4, and apparently Gores was told he would not be eligible for a rebate. Subsequently, it was discovered that Christy Pontiac had submitted a $500 cash rebate application to GM and that Gores' signature had been forged twice by Hesli on the application. It was also discovered that the purchase order form had been backdated to April 3. This order form was signed by Gary Swandy, an officer of Christy Pontiac.

Both purchasers learned of the forged rebate applications when they received a copy of the application in the mail from Christy Pontiac. Both purchasers complained to James Christy, and in both instances the conversations ended in angry mutual recriminations. Christy did tell Gores that the rebate on his car was "a mistake" and offered half the rebate to "call it even." After the Attorney General's office made an inquiry, Christy Pontiac contacted GM and arranged for cancellation of the Gores rebate that had been allowed to Christy Pontiac. Subsequent investigation disclosed that of 50 rebate transactions, only the Linden and Gores sales involved irregularities.

In a separate trial, Phil Hesli was acquitted of three felony charges but found guilty on the count of theft for the Gores transaction and was given a misdemeanor disposition. An indictment against James Christy for theft by swindle was dismissed, as was a subsequent complaint for the same charge, for lack of probable cause. Christy Pontiac, the corporation, was also indicted, and the appeal here is from the four convictions on those indictments. Before trial, Mr. Christy was granted immunity and was then called as a prosecution witness. Phil Hesli did not testify at the corporation's trial.

Christy Pontiac argues on several grounds that a corporation cannot be held criminally liable for a specific intent crime. Minn.Stat. § 609.52, subd. 2 (1982), says "whoever" swindles by artifice, trick or other means commits theft. Minn.Stat. § 609.625, subd. 1 (1982), says "whoever" falsely makes or alters a writing with intent to defraud, commits aggravated forgery. Christy Pontiac agrees that the

> Specific intent is "the intent to accomplish the precise criminal act that one is later charged with."

term "whoever" refers to persons, and it agrees that the term "persons" may include corporations, but it argues that when the word "persons" is used here, it should be construed to mean only natural persons. This should be so, argues defendant, because the legislature has defined a crime as "conduct which is prohibited by statute and for which the actor may be sentenced to imprisonment, with or without a fine," Minn. Stat. § 609.02, subd. 1 (1982), and a corporation cannot be imprisoned. Neither, argues defendant, can an artificial person entertain a mental state, let alone have the specific intent required for theft or forgery.

We are not persuaded by these arguments. The Criminal Code is to "be construed according to the fair import of its terms, to promote justice, and to effect its purposes." The legislature has not expressly excluded corporations from criminal liability and, therefore, we take its intent to be that corporations are to be considered persons within the meaning of the Code in the absence of any clear indication to the contrary. We do not think the statutory definition of a crime was meant to exclude corporate criminal liability; rather, we construe that definition to mean conduct which is prohibited and, if committed, *may* result in imprisonment. Interestingly, the specific statutes under which the defendant corporation was convicted, sections 609.52 (theft) and 609.625 (aggravated forgery), expressly state that the sentence may be either imprisonment or a fine.

Nor are we troubled by any anthropomorphic implications in assigning specific intent to a corporation for theft or forgery. There was a time when the law, in its logic, declared that a legal fiction could not be a person for purposes of criminal liability, at least with respect to offenses involving specific intent, but that time is gone. If a corporation can be liable in civil tort for both actual and punitive damages for libel, assault and battery, or fraud, it would seem it may also be criminally liable for conduct requiring specific intent. Most courts today recognize that corporations may be guilty of specific intent crimes. Particularly apt candidates for corporate criminality are types of crime, like theft by swindle and forgery, which often occur in a business setting.

We hold, therefore, that a corporation may be prosecuted and convicted for the crimes of theft and forgery.

There remains, however, the evidentiary basis on which criminal responsibility of a corporation is to be determined. Criminal liability, especially for more serious crimes, is thought of as a matter of personal, not vicarious, guilt. One should not be convicted for something one does not do. In what sense, then, does a corporation "do" something for which it can be convicted of a crime? The case law, as illustrated by the authorities above cited, takes differing approaches. If a corporation is to be criminally liable, it is clear that the crime must not be a personal aberration of an employee acting on his own; the criminal activity must, in some sense, reflect corporate policy so that it is fair to say that the activity was the activity of the corporation. There must be, as Judge Learned Hand put it, a "kinship of the act to the powers of the officials, who commit it." *United States v. Nearing*, 252 F. 223, 231 (S.D.N.Y. 1918).

We believe, first of all, the jury should be told that it must be satisfied beyond a reasonable doubt that the acts of the individual agent constitute the acts of the corporation. Secondly, as to the kind of proof required, we hold that a corporation may be guilty of a specific intent crime committed by its agent if: (1) the agent was acting within the course and scope of his or her employment, having the authority to act for the corporation with respect to the particular corporate business which was conducted criminally; (2) the agent was acting, at least in part, in furtherance of the corporation's business interests; and (3) the criminal acts were authorized, tolerated, or ratified by corporate management.

This test is not quite the same as the test for corporate vicarious liability for a civil tort of an agent. The burden of proof is different, and, unlike civil liability, criminal guilt requires that the agent be acting at least in part in furtherance of the corporation's business interests. Moreover, it must be shown that corporate management authorized, tolerated, or ratified the criminal activity. Ordinarily, this will be shown by circumstantial evidence, for it is not to be expected that management authorization of illegality would be expressly or openly stated. Indeed, there may be instances where the corporation is criminally liable even though the criminal activity has been expressly forbidden. What must be shown is that from all the facts and circumstances, those in positions of managerial authority or responsibility acted or failed to act in such a manner that the criminal activity reflects corporate policy, and it can be said, therefore, that the criminal act was authorized or tolerated or ratified by the corporation.

This brings us, then, to the third issue, namely, whether under the proof requirements mentioned above, the evidence is sufficient to sustain the convictions. We hold that it is.

The evidence shows that Hesli, the forger, had authority and responsibility to handle new car sales and to process and sign cash rebate applications. Christy Pontiac, not Hesli, got the GM rebate money, so that Hesli was acting in furtherance of the corporation's business interests. Moreover, there was sufficient evidence of management authorization, toleration, and ratification. Hesli himself, though not an officer, had middle management responsibilities for cash rebate applications. When the customer Gores asked Mr. Benedict, a salesman, about the then discontinued rebate, Benedict referred Gores to Phil Hesli. Gary Swandy, a corporate officer, signed the backdated retail buyer's order form for the Linden sale. James Christy, the president, attempted to negotiate a settlement with Gores after Gores complained. Not until after the Attorney General's inquiry did Christy contact divisional GM headquarters. As the trial judge noted, the rebate money "was so obtained and accepted by Christy Pontiac and kept by Christy Pontiac until somebody blew the whistle. We conclude the evidence establishes that the theft by swindle and the forgeries constituted the acts of the corporation.

We wish to comment further on two aspects of the proof. First, it seems that the state attempted to prosecute both Christy Pontiac and James Christy, but its prosecution of Mr. Christy failed for lack of evidence. We can imagine a different situation where the corporation is the alter ego of its owner and it is the owner who alone commits the crime, where a double prosecution might be deemed fundamentally unfair. Secondly, it may seem incongruous that Hesli, the forger, was acquitted of three of the four criminal counts for which the corporation was convicted. Still, this is not the first time different trials have had different results. We are reviewing this record, and it sustains the convictions.

Points for Discussion

1. *Vicarious specific intent.*

As *Christy Pontiac* makes clear, a corporation can harbor criminal intent vicariously. But not every individual in the corporation—or his state of mind—can bind the corporation in a criminal case. Instead, the question is whether the individual was in some sense acting on behalf of the corporation. Courts have taken different approaches to discerning a corporation's intent.

Some courts, including the federal courts, accept the same *respondeat superior* standard that applies for civil liability—namely that the agents' acts fall "within the scope of their employment." Thus, criminal liability extends to actions taken within the employee's general line of work where outsiders would assume the employee had the authority to act.

Many state courts (including *Christy Pontiac*), however, require more to prove vicarious corporate liability. The jury must find beyond a reasonable doubt (1) the agent was acting within the course and scope of employment; (2) the agent was furthering the corporation's business interests; and (3) corporate management authorized, tolerated, or ratified the conduct.

A few courts go further and apply the higher standard of the Model Penal Code, which requires that criminal conduct be "authorized, requested, commanded, performed or recklessly tolerated by the board of directors or by a high managerial agent acting in behalf of the corporation within the scope of his office or employment." Model Penal Code § 2.07(1)(c) (Proposed Official Draft 1962).

What if an employee engages in illegal conduct contrary to specific instructions or stated corporate policies—thus belying any actual corporate authority? At one level, prosecuting the corporation would seem to miss the mark. But without the threat of corporate criminality, there would be fewer incentives for corporate shareholders and boards of directors to institute safeguards against illegal conduct by corporate employees. As the Supreme Court explained in upholding corporate criminal liability for the first time, adhering to "the old and exploded doctrine that a corporation cannot commit a crime would virtually take away the only means of effectually controlling the subject-matter and correcting the abuses aimed at." *New York Cent. & Hudson River R.R. Co. v. United States*, 212 U.S. 481 (1909). And allowing the corporation to disown the crimes of its employees carried out in the corporate name would raise serious questions about the corporation as a legitimate member of society.

2. Organizational crime.

Corporate criminality also recognizes that prosecuting individuals for the crimes of the organization is sometimes difficult. When there is illegal conduct that benefits a company, such as in *Christy Pontiac* where the car dealership stood to gain from customers receiving the GM rebates, the individual agents might understandably assert, "I was just doing what the boss expected me to do." Exposing the corporation to the threat of conviction may spur corporate decision makers to prevent violations by employees.

Limiting prosecutions to responsible individuals might also leave many commercial crimes unpunished. Juries and judges may be sympathetic with corporate agents who are just doing their job (as may have happened in *Christy Pontiac*, where Hesli was mostly exonerated). Further, it may be hard to identify responsible individuals in complex and decentralized business structures. Given that many corporate crimes are profitable for the business, corporate criminality serves to induce corporate decision makers to have the corporation internalize the costs of illegal conduct within the organization.

An interesting question that arises when the corporation is charged with a crime is how to determine whether the entity had the requisite criminal intent. Federal courts have looked at the corporation's "collective" knowledge and action, even when no one individual committed the offense. Thus, the state of mind and conduct of multiple employees are aggregated and imputed to the corporation. For example, in *U.S. v. Bank of New England*, 821 F.2d 844 (1st Cir. 1987), the court deemed a corporation to have full knowledge if "one part of the corporation has half the information making up the item, and another part of the entity has the other half." This aggregation can lead to corporate criminal liability even when no individual in the corporation had the necessary *mens rea*.

3. Punishing shareholders?

Does punishment of the corporation serve the general criminal justice goals of retribution, deterrence, incapacitation, rehabilitation, and restoration? Although it is easy to make the case for locking up white-collar criminals, it is harder to justify corporate criminality. The corporation cannot be jailed or physically punished, so incapacitation has to happen through other means. Instead, the corporation can be fined—with the financial burden falling on investors who often had nothing to do with the crime. And a fine, particularly if corporate management simply sees it as a cost of doing business, does not necessarily keep the corporation from committing the same crimes again.

Do fines and other forms of monetary punishment imposed against the corporation actually lead to changes in corporate behavior? Or are fines paid by the corporation simply a way for corporate executives to shift the blame and the liability on someone else? When the corporation is punished, shareholders inevitably bear the brunt of the monetary punishment. Should shareholders be punished for the bad acts of corporate employees and managers?

4. Corporate executives and directors as criminals.

Corporate statutes specify that the board of directors manages and supervises the corporation's business and affairs. Given their oversight role, can directors be subject to individual criminal liability for failing to adequately supervise subordinates' activities? What about executives who manage the day-to-day business? If the animating purpose of corporate criminality is deterrence, wouldn't criminal liability for corporate directors and high-level executives be a better (and more certain) way to ensure legal compliance by the corporation?

The answer is that the law is ambivalent. Although corporate managers can be held liable for failing to prevent criminal conduct in the corporation, judges have shown some reluctance to punish individuals for organizational misdeeds. Nonetheless, the legislative trend has been toward greater accountability, and corporate managers live under a real threat of individual prosecution if the corporation spirals into criminality.

Making corporate executives criminally liable reflects a sense of social condemnation of corporate executives who in the name of increasing corporate profits disregard how corporate activities affect others. But if the goal is primarily deterrence and rehabilitation, isn't corporate-level punishment more effective and thus preferable for inducing attitudes of corporate responsibility?

————————

CHAPTER 13

Corporate Social Responsibility, Benefit Corporations, and ESG

As we explored in the previous chapter, there are myriad ways to understand corporate purpose. Many view corporations as having an obligation to be socially responsible. Some believe that because corporations wield power, they should have corresponding responsibilities to various stakeholders such as customers, employees, community members, and others. To some observers, this view stems from the idea that because states charter corporations and bestow on them certain privileges such as limited liability, corporations should in turn be good corporate citizens. Many argue that corporate social responsibility ("CSR") is simply good business—engaging in corporate philanthropy and treating stakeholders well often aligns with long-term value maximization as it can enhance corporate reputation, help manage risk, and constrain corporate fraud or illegal conduct. On the other end of the spectrum are shareholder primacy advocates who argue that corporations can of course pursue an activity that benefits stakeholders to the extent that it also serves the bottom line of corporate profits, but corporations exist to maximize shareholder value and should not make trade-offs with that goal.

In the twenty-first century, two new concepts have emerged. More than thirty states have adopted legislation for a new form of corporation—the benefit corporation—that allows entrepreneurs to incorporate in a form that requires the pursuit of dual purposes. Benefit corporations are for-profit corporations that seek profit while also pursuing a public benefit, and their boards must consider the interests of stakeholders as well as shareholders. Further, the concept of "ESG"—an acronym that refers to environmental, social and governance—has spread around the world. Considering ESG issues in investment decisions has become mainstream since the term was coined in the early 2000s. ESG investing has soared into trillions of dollars and represents one third of private capital under management globally. Debate has intensified about whether ESG investing or corporate activity aligns with long-term risk-adjusted shareholder value and whether it is a force for social good.

This chapter examines each of these three topics in turn—CSR, benefit corporations, and ESG. As you are digging in, consider how they relate to the central question of corporate purpose and fit into or adapt corporate law principles.

A. Corporate Social Responsibility

1. The Roots of CSR

Evidence of the business community's concern for society can be traced back centuries. More specifically, the concept of CSR as we know it today might be said to have roots in corporate charitable giving that began in the mid-to-late 1800s.

In *The Gospel of Wealth*, Andrew Carnegie, the steel industry magnate, called upon wealthy individuals to support social causes through philanthropy. Although questionable or even unscrupulous practices led a number of famous business leaders during this era to be dubbed "robber barons," industrialists such as John D. Rockefeller and Cornelius Vanderbilt also gave large sums in charity and were patrons of the arts, endowers of educational institutions, and supporters of various community projects. Many of these philanthropic efforts were effectuated in their individual capacities. Before the twentieth century, corporate charitable giving was perceived by many in a negative light as giving away shareholders' assets without their approval. Corporate contributions were legally restricted to causes that benefited the company. The connection of famous industrialists and philanthropy to their business empires, however, raised one of the major issues of the day: could limited charter powers and a conception of managers as trustees of shareholders' property create a legal basis for *corporate* charitable giving?

The classification of the "nonprofit" sector also appeared in the late nineteenth century. Nonprofit corporations could make profits and use donations in pursuit of their stated goals, but had no shareholders or equity holders to whom gains would be distributed. Several noted business leaders created nonprofit corporations through which they pursued various philanthropic and social endeavors. For example, the Rockefeller Foundation's 1913 charter stated its purpose as promoting "the well-being of mankind throughout the world."

Notably, during this time, criticisms of the factory system as the source of various social problems also led reformers to push for improved conditions as part of a broader industrial welfare movement. Many businesses became more concerned with employees and how to make them more productive. Some provided hospital clinics, lunch rooms, profit sharing, recreational facilities, and engaged in other practices to improve the workers' conditions, although this was not at the time called "social responsibility" and some have characterized it as paternalism. These practices may have reflected both a business motive as well as a social decision to take some care for the plight of workers.

By the 1930s, corporations began to be seen as institutions that had social obligations to fulfill. The rise of large corporations with dispersed shareholders contributed to views of managers as trustees for the different set of external relations with the company. In the decades that followed, awareness of the role of business in community affairs grew. Researchers pinpoint Howard Bowen's publication of his landmark book *Social Responsibilities of the Businessman* (1953) as the beginning of the modern period of literature on the subject. He asked: "What responsibilities to society may businessmen reasonably be expected to assume?" And he defined "social responsibilities" as "the obligations of business[people] to pursue those policies, to make those decisions, or to follow those lines of action which are desirable in terms of the objectives and values of our society." Thus, by the 1950s, CSR had begun to take shape, although it still largely took the form of corporate philanthropy.

2. Corporate Charitable Giving and Beyond

In the early twentieth century, many courts held that corporate charitable contributions were *ultra vires*, or beyond the powers granted by the articles of incorporation with respect to the corporation's business. In response to these decisions, nearly all states amended their corporate statutes to authorize corporate charitable giving. These statutes, like the statute in the case that follows, gave corporations the power to make charitable gifts, but did not specify whether such gifts had to be aimed at advancing the corporation's business interests.

The following case raises the question whether corporate charitable giving is appropriate and how courts should evaluate a shareholder's challenge to such giving. The case arose out of the ill will from a family divorce in which the wife (and her daughter) challenged the husband's decision to have the corporation he dominated donate company stock to fund a camp for "underprivileged boys."

Girard Henderson had dominated the affairs of Alexander Dawson, Inc. for many years, through his controlling interest in that corporation. In 1955, as part of a separation agreement, he transferred 11,000 shares of common stock to his wife, Theodora Henderson, who also owned in her own name 37,000 shares of Alexander Dawson preferred stock. In 1967, Mrs. Henderson formed the Theodora Holding Corp. (plaintiff in the case) and transferred to the holding company her 11,000 shares of Alexander Dawson common stock, which at the time had a market value of $15,675,000. During the year of the disputed corporate charitable donation, the corporation paid dividends on the preferred and common stock held by Mrs. Henderson and her holding company totaling $286,240.

From 1960 to 1966, Girard Henderson had caused Alexander Dawson to make annual corporate contributions ranging from $60,000 to more than $70,000 to the Alexander Dawson Foundation (the Foundation), which Henderson had formed in 1957. All contributions were unanimously approved by the shareholders. In 1966, Alexander Dawson donated to the Foundation a large tract of land valued at $467,750 for the purpose of establishing a camp for under-privileged boys. In April 1967, Mr. Henderson proposed that the board approve a $528,000 gift of company stock to the Foundation to finance the camp. One director, Theodora Ives (the daughter of Mrs. Henderson), objected and suggested that the gift be made instead to a charitable corporation supported by her mother and herself. Girard Henderson responded by causing a reduction in the Alexander Dawson board of directors from eight members to three. The newly composed board, which did not include Theodora Ives, thereafter approved the gift of stock to the Foundation.

Theodora Holding Corp. then brought suit against certain individuals, including Girard Henderson, challenging the stock gift and seeking an accounting and the appointment of a liquidating receiver for Alexander Dawson.

Theodora Holding Corp. v. Henderson

257 A.2d 398 (Del. Ch. 1969)

MARVEL, VICE CHANCELLOR.

Title 8 Del.C. § 122 provides as follows:

Every corporation created under this chapter shall have power to—

(9) Make donations for the public welfare or for charitable, scientific or educational purposes, and in time of war or other national emergency in aid thereof.

There is no doubt but that the Alexander Dawson Foundation is recognized as a legitimate charitable trust by the Department of Internal Revenue. It is also clear that it is authorized to operate exclusively in the fields of "religious, charitable, scientific, literary, or educational purposes, or for the prevention of cruelty to children or animals." Furthermore, contemporary courts recognize that unless corporations carry an increasing share of the burden of supporting charitable and educational causes that the business advantages now reposed in corporations by law may well prove to be unacceptable to the representatives of an aroused public. The recognized obligation of corporations towards philanthropic, educational and artistic causes is reflected in the statutory law of all of the states, other than the states of Arizona and Idaho.

In *A.P. Smith Mfg. Co. v. Barlow*, 13 N.J. 145, 98 A.2d 581 (1953), a case in which the corporate donor had been

> The study of corporate law frequently requires knowledge of the tax code and regulations. For example, corporate directors and officers typically are more likely to approve, and shareholders are less likely to contest, charitable contributions if they are tax deductible by the corporation, so that the charitable contribution reduces the amount of corporate income subject to tax. Internal Revenue Code § 170(a) generally allows tax deductions for charitable contributions. Today, § 170(b)(2)(A) provides that, with certain limited exceptions: "The total deductions under subsection (a) for any taxable year . . . shall not exceed 10 percent of the taxpayer's taxable income." When Henderson was decided, the limitation on charitable deductions was only 5 percent.

organized long before the adoption of a statute authorizing corporate gifts to charitable or educational institutions, the Supreme Court of New Jersey upheld a gift of $1500 by the plaintiff corporation to Princeton University, being of the opinion that the trend towards the transfer of wealth from private industrial entrepreneurs to corporate institutions, the increase of taxes on individual income, coupled with steadily increasing philanthropic needs, necessitate corporate giving for educational needs even were there no statute permitting such gifts. The court also noted that the gift tended to bolster the free enterprise system and the general social climate in which plaintiff was nurtured. And while the court pointed out that there was no showing that the gift in question was made indiscriminately or to a pet charity in furtherance of personal rather than corporate ends, the actual holding of the opinion appears to be that a corporate charitable or educational gift to be valid must merely be within reasonable limits both as to amount and purpose.

I conclude that the test to be applied in passing on the validity of a gift such as the one here in issue is that of reasonableness, a test in which the provisions of the Internal Revenue Code pertaining to charitable gifts by corporations furnish a helpful guide. The gift here under attack was made from gross income and had a value as of the time of giving of $528,000 in a year in which Alexander Dawson's total income was $19,144,229.06, or well within the federal tax deduction limitation of 5% of such income.

The contribution under attack can be said to have "cost" all of the stockholders of Alexander Dawson including plaintiff, less than $80,000, or some fifteen cents per dollar of contribution, taking into consideration the federal tax provisions applicable to holding companies as well as the provisions for compulsory distribution of dividends received by such a corporation. It is accordingly obvious, in my opinion, that the relatively small loss of immediate income otherwise payable to plaintiff and the corporate defendant's other stockholders had it not been for the gift in question, is far out-weighed by the overall benefits flowing from the placing of such gift in channels where it serves to benefit those in need of philanthropic or educational support, thus providing justification for large private holdings, thereby benefiting plaintiff in the long run. Finally, the fact that the interests of the Alexander Dawson Foundation appear to be increasingly directed towards the rehabilitation and education of deprived but deserving young people is peculiarly appropriate in an age when a large segment of youth is alienated even from parents who are not entirely satisfied with our present social and economic system.

On notice, an order in conformity with the holdings of this opinion may be presented.

Points for Discussion

1. Relevance of statute.

Notice that the court, while initially reciting the Delaware statute that authorizes corporate charitable giving, does not mention it again. Instead, the court adopted a rule of "reasonableness" for reviewing corporate giving, even though the statute states no such limitation. Where does the "reasonableness" standard come from?

2. Corporate gifts as profit maximizers.

How much do corporations give to charities? In its annual report for 2022, the Giving USA Foundation found that total corporate charitable giving (including by corporate foundations) amounted to over $20 billion. This represented only 4.3% of all charitable giving in the country. By comparison, charitable giving by non-corporate foundations totaled over $90 billion, or 18.7% of all charitable giving. And giving by individuals, mostly to churches, amounted to nearly $327 billion, representing 67.4% of all charitable contributions.

Corporations frequently cite their own economic interests in justifying corporate gifts. The New Jersey Supreme Court, in *A.P. Smith Manufacturing Co. v. Barlow*, cited by the *Henderson* court, upheld the corporate gift to Princeton University, citing the company's argument that the gift arguably advanced its long-run business interests. Would you advise a corporation to make only those gifts that managers believe further the corporation's long-run business interests? Must the managers quantify how much the charitable contributions will enhance the corporation's business interests or its reputation for social responsibility? Should corporations be permitted to make contributions that do not generate demonstrable benefits for the corporation? Put another way, must the corporation limit its activities solely to maximizing profits?

3. Corporate gifts as social function.

As Professor Berle observed, *Barlow* recognized that "modern directors are not limited to running business enterprise for maximum profit, but are in fact and recognized in law as administrators of a community system." Is *Henderson* also consistent with this view? Does the corporation owe something to society in exchange for the privileges that society bestows on corporations, including limited liability for shareholders? Can corporate philanthropy be seen a kind of repayment? If so, should it be required?

4. Corporate gifts as self dealing.

Does the calculus change when corporate charity is tinged with conflicts of interest? For example, suppose a major oil company agrees to donate $50 million to help build an art museum that will house the art collection of the company's founder and CEO. Is the fairness of the gift subject to searching judicial review? That is, given the apparent conflict of interest, should a court scrutinize whether the corporation will actually realize $50 million worth of advertising and reputational benefits? Or will it be enough that the gift was considered by a group of independent directors (not financially beholden to the CEO) who concluded the donation was reasonable in light of the company's revenues and earnings? For Delaware's answer, see *Kahn v. Sullivan*, 594 A.2d 48 (Del. 1991) (upholding chancery court's conclusion that charitable donations approved by independent directors are subject to review under business judgment rule).

5. *Should shareholders decide?*

Shareholders generally cannot challenge corporate gifts, given the discretion afforded corporate directors under the business judgment rule, and shareholders have no formal voice in how and in what amounts corporations engage in charitable giving. Some commentators have argued that, after directors decide how much money a corporation will give to charities, shareholders should then be able to select the beneficiaries. Does this seem like a useful solution to the problem of directors giving away "other people's money"?

6. *Disclosure of corporate gifts?*

Managers also have broad discretion over charitable contributions because corporations generally are not required to disclose such contributions to shareholders. Securities regulators are reluctant to require such disclosure. As former SEC Chairman, Richard Breeden, once said, "If I were still in government, I would not want to touch the issue of 'regulating' corporate philanthropy with a 500 foot pole." If disclosure rules are unlikely, should corporate law play a more prominent role in making corporate charitable contributions more transparent?

7. *Expanded notions of CSR in contemporary business.*

Since the mid-twentieth century era of *Henderson*, CSR in many firms has moved towards a more complete integration with strategic management and corporate governance. As a reflection of this evolution, many firms have developed management and organizational mechanisms for internal controls and reporting on business's socially conscious policies and practices. Business ethics, stakeholder management, and the "triple bottom line" of people, planet, and profit became part of the business vocabulary. The range of stakeholders and issues defining CSR has also notably broadened, especially in the past several decades. What examples come to mind for you of corporate CSR initiatives? How do you hear of such practices and when do you support them?

B.   Benefit Corporations

Recall from the previous chapter the Delaware Court of Chancery's statement in *eBay Domestic Holdings, Inc. v. Newark,* that "Directors of a for-profit Delaware corporation cannot defend a business strategy that openly eschews stockholder wealth maximization." Further: "Having chosen a for-profit corporate form, the directors are bound by the fiduciary duties and standards that accompany that form. Those standards include acting to promote the value of the corporation for the benefit of its stockholders. The 'Inc.' after the company name has to mean at least that."

> Take care not to confuse benefit corporations (or public benefit corporations known as "PBCs") with Certified B Corporations—or "B Corps," as they're commonly called. A benefit corporation is a legal business entity, whereas B Corp certification is a standards-based designation similar to "Fairtrade."

If one were to take seriously this language, but wish to do differently in their business venture, what options are available? Since 2010, a new corporate form known as the benefit corporation has emerged.

The benefit corporation was the invention of B Lab, a nonprofit organization, formed by entrepreneurs who sought to establish paths for business to operate as a "force for good." B Lab's first initiative was to create a third-party certification standard for companies meeting standards that B Lab assesses across five categories: governance, workers, community, the environment, and customers. Regardless of their legal structure or state of incorporation, companies can apply to B Lab to be recognized as a "Certified B Corporation." Such accreditation is similar in many ways to other third-party certification schemes such as "Fairtrade" for coffee or chocolate and a "UL"-rated seal on a lightbulb that has been tested for consumer safety, but with its certification B Lab aims to signal that an entire business has achieved a minimum threshold score on its impact assessment. B Lab's second initiative was to design a new form of corporation—the legal structure itself—under state corporate law that would allow for the pursuit of dual purposes: profit and public benefit.

1.   The Model Benefit Corporation Legislation

B Lab, together with the help of corporate lawyers, drafted a model version of benefit corporation legislation that could be adopted by state legislatures. The following excerpt, from a symposium exploring the benefit corporation movement, explains the B Lab co-founders' motivations in catalyzing the development and spread of Model Benefit Corporation Legislation ("MBCL").

BENEFIT CORPORATIONS AND THE FIRM COMMITMENT UNIVERSE

Bart Houlahan, Andrew Kassoy & Jay Coen Gilbert, B Lab Co-founders

40 Seattle U. L. Rev. 299 (2017)

B Lab was created . . . to address the challenges created by a financial system focused only on shareholder value. We seek to create an infrastructure that will enable business to be a force for good, but believe that shareholder primacy leads to the misapplication of resources and limits the ability of corporations to raise money in mainstream capital markets while operating in a responsible and sustainable manner. For this reason, we asked Bill Clark (whose contribution to this Symposium discusses the basis for society to demand stakeholder governance) to draft legislation addressing this concern. His model was the one adopted in Maryland in 2010 and in most other jurisdictions that have authorized benefit corporations. Two other contributors to the issue (Larry Hamermesh and Rick Alexander) were involved in the drafting of another model, which has been adopted in Delaware. But all jurisdictions adopting benefit corporation legislation, whatever model they use, allow corporations to reject shareholder primacy, and to place the interests of stakeholders (including employees, the community, and the environment) on par with the interests of shareholders.

We promoted this legislation because want all stakeholders to be able to distinguish good companies from good marketing. We have developed a certification for corporations that demonstrate a positive impact on all of their stakeholders (Certified B Corps), but we do not want those certified entities to experience mission drift due to legal pressure to produce short term profits for shareholders. The benefit corporation is a way to resist this pressure. Indeed, where the form is available, we now require that corporations become benefit corporations.

By rejecting shareholder primacy, the benefit corporation endeavors to create a solid foundation for long-term mission alignment and value creation. It protects mission through capital raises and leadership changes, creates more flexibility when evaluating potential sale and liquidity options, and prepares closely held businesses to lead a mission-driven life post-IPO. Most importantly, this legal form changes the purpose of business from one focused on the creation of shareholder value to one that creates shared value.

Benefit corporation statutes differ from current corporate law by (1) providing for a broad corporate purpose to create a material positive impact on society and the environment; (2) creating accountability that gives shareholders the ability to hold directors responsible for pursuing the public purpose; and (3) requiring transparent reporting of overall social and environmental performance in order to allow both shareholders and other stakeholders to know what the company is doing to achieve its purpose. This model creates better governance, mitigates risk, and allows business to create value for society and shareholders.

Benefit corporation law is a critical tool to allow private capital to be invested in a manner that creates shared and durable value for everyone. But a tool is only as good as the person who uses it. As highlighted in Rick Alexander's essay, shareholders must understand the value of firm commitment, and, more importantly, the ultimate source of wealth for universal investors, which is thriving financial markets and a healthy, peaceful, and prosperous planet. These goals can only be attained and maintained for the long term if private capital is allocated and invested in a manner that creates value for everyone. So investors must learn to use benefit corporation law as a tool to require the companies they own to create value in a responsible and sustainable manner.

* * * *

The need for this new corporate form has never been more urgent. There is a populist movement against the establishment. Brexit, recent U.S. elections, and political developments across Europe and beyond suggest a populace that believes the system is rigged against them. Global events, including financial crises, increasing inequality, and climate and food injustices, indicate that the fundamental dissatisfaction with the status quo stems from economic circumstance. Led by Colin Mayer's work on corporate betrayal of the stakeholders corporations should be serving, the conference addressed how this "rigging" may be as much a result of the structure of our financial system as of our political institutions. The work reflected in this symposium issue will contribute to this important discussion, and highlight the leadership opportunities and responsibilities of the business and financial communities. Their leadership can help to create a more inclusive economy that works for everyone.

We believe business needs a new operating system, a set of normative and institutional changes that allow capitalism to equal its promise. The evolution of capitalism requires an evolution in corporate law, one that allows company directors to serve all stakeholders and creates mechanisms so that investors can hold them accountable. Business, as one of the most powerful forces in society, has an historic opportunity and obligation to drive a positive culture shift to use business as a force for good. If business has had a role in leading us to our current point, then it must have a role in forging the path forward.

———————

Turning now to the basics of benefit corporations, the heart of the MBCL is section 301(a), which establishes a standard of conduct for directors that places all stakeholders at the center of the corporation's governance.

Model Benefit Corporation Legislation § 301

(a) Consideration of interests.—In discharging the duties of their respective positions and in considering the best interests of the benefit corporation, the board of directors, committees of the board, and individual directors of a benefit corporation:

(1) Shall consider the effects of any action or inaction upon:

  i.   the shareholders of the benefit corporation;

  ii.   the employees and work force of the benefit corporation, its subsidiaries, and its suppliers;

  iii. the interests of customers as beneficiaries of the general public benefit or a specific public benefit purpose of the benefit corporation;

  iv.   community and societal factors, including those of each community in which offices or facilities of the benefit corporation, its subsidiaries, or its suppliers are located;

  v.   the local and global environment;

  vi.   the short-term and long-term interests of the benefit corporation, including benefits that may accrue to the benefit corporation from its long-term plans and the possibility that these interests may be best served by the continued independence of the benefit corporation; and

  vii. the ability of the benefit corporation to accomplish its general public benefit purpose and any specific public benefit purpose.

Two points are particularly notable. First, unlike the constituency statutes enacted into some state corporate laws, which allow for board consideration of stakeholder interests, the MBCL *requires* it. Second, the MBCL specifies a list of stakeholders. Under Section 301(a), directors of a benefit corporation must consider the corporation's effect on shareholders, employees, customers, the community where the corporation operates, the local and global environment, and its ability to accomplish its general public

> States that have adopted the MBCL as their state benefit corporation law have in many instances adapted various provisions. Remember to check a particular jurisdiction's benefit corporation law in practice.

benefit purpose and any specific purpose. No particular stakeholder interest has primacy. Further, paragraph 2 of Section 301 provides that the board may consider "other factors or interests" the board deems "appropriate." And paragraph 3 establishes that the board is not required to prioritize among those interests unless the corporation's articles of incorporation so provide. The mandate of Section 301 is thus procedural in nature—it mandates that the board consider a wide range of constituencies, but it does not mandate any particular outcome.

Section 201 of the MBCL provides that "a benefit corporation shall have a purpose of creating a general public benefit." The model legislation defines "general public benefit" as a "material positive impact on society and the environment, taken as a whole, from the business and operations of a benefit corporation assessed taking into account the impacts of the benefit corporation as reported against a third-party standard." The board may select the third-party standard, but it must address all of the interests that the directors must consider under Section 301 and meet requirements of independence, credibility, and transparency. The model legislation notes that it must be a "recognized standard for defining, reporting, and assessing corporate social and environmental performance."

In addition, a benefit corporation may add a "specific benefit purpose" in its articles of incorporation. This term is given broad meaning and can include any of the following: "[p]roviding low-income or underserved individuals or communities with beneficial products or services; [p]romoting economic opportunity for individuals or communities beyond the creation of jobs in the normal course of business; [p]rotecting or restoring the environment; [i]mproving human health; [p]romoting the arts, sciences, or advancement of knowledge; [i]ncreasing the flow of capital to entities with a purpose to benefit society or the environment; and [c]onferring any other particular benefit on society or the environment." Including a specific benefit is optional, and may help ensure that a particular interest is salient so that it does not get lost in the mix.

Another innovation of the MBCL is the creation of a remedy known as the "benefit enforcement proceeding," in which the benefit corporation, or its shareholders on a derivative basis, may bring suit to allege: "(1) failure of a benefit corporation to pursue or create general public benefit or a specific public benefit set forth in its articles; or (2) violation of any obligation duty or standard of conduct under this [chapter]." MBCL § 305. Although the MBCL preserves the business judgment rule for fiduciary claims, the benefit enforcement proceeding provision can be seen as a departure from traditional corporate law as it invokes a substantive inquiry into whether the corporation has failed to achieve or pursue its benefit purpose. Corporate shareholders must own at least two percent of a class or series of stock in order to bring a claim (or five percent for parent shareholders). Other stakeholders cannot bring a benefit enforcement proceeding.

Finally, the MBCL requires benefit corporations to prepare and make available an "annual benefit report." The report must include a narrative section, an assessment, and a compliance statement. It must also include the name of the benefit officer and director, where applicable, and the director's compensation. The report must be sent to allshareholders, posted on the website of the corporation (or, if the corporation doesn't have a website, made available without charge to any person who requests it), and filed with the state corporate filing office. States have varied in whether they have adopted this draft legislation language in its entirety and

> How can a corporation opt in or out of benefit corporation law? The MBCL requires a two-thirds vote of shareholders, by class, to authorize becoming a benefit corporation. The same vote is required for a transaction in which the benefit corporation ceases to be a benefit corporation or sells substantially all of its assets.

several states have added express penalties for failure to file the report. To further aid in accountability, the MBCL permits the board of directors to include a "benefit director," who satisfies certain independence requirements and provides an annual compliance statement for inclusion in the annual benefit report.

In 2010, Maryland was the first state to adopt the MBCL. Since that time, over thirty states have adopted benefit corporation statutes, either based on the MBCL or a variation reflected in Delaware's approach—the topic we turn to next.

2. The Delaware Public Benefit Corporation Statute

A second model of benefit corporation law, first adopted in Delaware in 2013, has now been followed (with adaptation) in several states. This version is known as the "public benefit corporation" or "PBC." It is important because Delaware is the jurisdiction most often chosen by companies that raise significant venture capital or private equity, and it is the jurisdiction chosen most often by companies that go public.

To add the PBC as an option on its menu of forms of business organization, Delaware added new Subchapter XV to its DGCL, of which Section 361 provides: "If a corporation elects to become a public benefit corporation under this subchapter in the manner prescribed in this subchapter, it shall be subject in all respects to the provisions of this chapter, except to the extent this subchapter imposes additional or different requirements, in which case such requirements shall apply."

PBC law is similar to the MBCL but has several important differences that were crafted with an eye toward designing benefit corporation governance in a manner that could appeal to investors and public companies. First, PBC law mandates that in addition to considering all stakeholders, a PBC must choose a specific public benefit to promote. Further, Delaware's Section 362 sets up a three-part balancing act that invokes a materiality test, balancing "the stockholders' pecuniary interests, the best interests of those materially affected by the corporation's conduct, and the public benefit or public benefits identified in its certificate of incorporation."

DGCL § 362. Public benefit corporation defined; contents of certificate of incorporation.

(a)   A "public benefit corporation" is a for-profit corporation organized under and subject to the requirements of this chapter that is intended to produce a public benefit or public benefits and to operate in a responsible and sustainable manner. To that end, a public benefit corporation shall be managed in a manner that balances the stockholders' pecuniary interests, the best interests of those materially affected by the corporation's conduct, and the public benefit or public benefits identified in its certificate of incorporation. In the certificate of incorporation, a public benefit corporation shall:

(1)   Identify within its statement of business or purpose pursuant to § 102(a)(3) of this title one or more specific public benefits to be promoted by the corporation; and

(2)   State within its heading that it is a public benefit corporation.

(b)   "Public benefit" means a positive effect (or reduction of negative effects) on 1 or more categories of persons, entities, communities or interests (other than stockholders in their capacities as stockholders) including, but not limited to, effects of an artistic, charitable, cultural, economic, educational, environmental, literary, medical, religious, scientific or technological nature. "Public benefit provisions" means the provisions of a certificate of incorporation contemplated by this subchapter.

Second, PBC law does not mandate the use of a third-party standard and instead leaves the mechanism of implementing stakeholder values to the board's discretion. In this regard, the PBC model is less stringent. Similarly in this vein, PBC dictates reporting to shareholders only once every two years, and there is no public disclosure requirement.

Third, PBC statutes do not include a provision for "benefit enforcement proceedings," and so any legal challenge regarding whether a PBC is properly implementing the governance mandate must consist of a fiduciary claim. That is, in contrast to the MBCL, PBC law does not contemplate a separate substantive legal claim that a corporation has failed to pursue or create public benefit. The balancing decisions of PBC boards will not be disturbed by courts if the board was independent, informed, and acting in good faith.

Initially, Delaware's PBC statute provided some protection against shareholder activism in the form of a supermajority vote requirement for conversion into or out of the PBC form. But in 2020, the Delaware legislature changed to a simple majority vote, making it easier to both opt into or out of PBC status. *See* DGCL §§ 242(b), 251.

Points for Discussion

1. Different approaches to benefit corporations: MBCL vs. PBC.

What are the strengths of each of the approaches to benefit corporation statutes? Why did Delaware go in a different direction from the model created by B Lab?

2. Shareholder or stakeholder governance?

One of the distinctive features of the benefit corporation model is its requirement that directors consider stakeholder interests and pursue a public benefit. For this reason, some refer to benefit corporations as a form of stakeholder governance. In what ways, however, might benefit corporations still be understood as a variation of shareholder governance? Can boards of directors consider shareholder and stakeholder interests in balance without giving any constituency primacy? Does the existence of the benefit corporation form impact our understanding of whether traditional corporations should consider the interests of stakeholders or pursue CSR?

3. Going public as a PBC.

Since the spread of benefit corporation and PBC statutes across the country, several thousand businesses have been incorporated in this form. A relatively small number have gone public as PBCs, including Lemonade, Vital Farms, Coursera, and AllBirds. What challenges might exist for publicly traded PBCs and how might they navigate those to preserve their social mission? Would it be advisable for PBCs to go public with other governance features such as dual-class stock in order to lock in the commitment to public benefit?

C. ESG

We started this chapter by examining the history and evolution of CSR, and the law related to corporations and charitable giving. We have also explored benefit corporations, a form of business organization that explicitly requires the pursuit of a public benefit in addition to profits. In this final section, we examine the rise of a more recent term than CSR that has spread widely in investment practices and corporate activity: ESG. The acronym stands for "environmental, social, governance," and it has become a mainstream concept in investing and business management as well as a focal point for regulatory developments around the globe. With its meteoric rise, debate about the term's meaning and the merits of investors and corporations focusing on ESG issues has also gained increasing attention.

1. The Rise of ESG

In 2000, the United Nations (UN) launched the Global Compact, a multi-stakeholder initiative that aims to align business operations and strategies with ten principles in the areas of human rights, labor, the environment, and anti-corruption, and to catalyze actions in support of broader UN goals. The Global Compact is a non-binding framework to which individual companies can make a voluntary pledge of commitment. With 7,000 corporate signatories around the world, it is the largest voluntary corporate sustainability initiative.

Following on the heels of the Global Compact, in 2004 the UN launched another initiative, titled "Who Cares Wins," that brought together major players in the financial industry for a collaboration to pursue a wide variety of stated goals including sustainable development, resilient financial markets, and building awareness and mutual understanding of stakeholders. Out of this initiative, and related efforts at the UN, came the term ESG.

ESG has no singular definition besides referring to "environmental, social, and governance." As originally used, the aim was to "integrate environmental, social and governance issues in analysis, asset management and securities brokerage." Explaining this goal, the *Who Cares Wins* report from 2004 noted: "We are convinced that it is in the interest of investors, asset managers and securities brokerage houses alike to improve the integration of ESG factors in financial analysis. This will contribute to better investment markets as well as to the sustainable development of the planet."

Further underlying this view was the belief that "[c]ompanies with better ESG performance can increase shareholder value by better managing risks related to emerging ESG issues, by anticipating regulatory changes or consumer trends, and by accessing new markets or reducing costs" and "hav[ing] a strong impact on reputation and brands." Accordingly, companies should not focus on single issues, but instead the "entire range of ESG issues relevant to their business." Examples of ESG issues include climate change, human rights, workplace health and safety, human capital management, board diversity, and management of corruption and bribery issues. The ESG issues that are relevant to investment decisions can differ across regions, industries, and companies.

WHO CARES WINS: CONNECTING FINANCIAL MARKETS TO A CHANGING WORLD

The United Nations Global Compact

Recommendations by the financial industry to better integrate environmental, social and governance issues in analysis, asset management and securities brokerage (2004)

Executive Summary

This report is the result of a joint initiative of financial institutions which were invited by United Nations Secretary-General Kofi Annan to develop guidelines and recommendations on how to better integrate environmental, social and corporate governance issues in asset management, securities brokerage services and associated research functions. Eighteen financial institutions from 9 countries with total assets under management of over 6 trillion USD have participated in developing this report. The initiative is supported by the chief executive officers of the endorsing institutions. The U.N. Global Compact oversaw the collaborative effort that led to this report and the Swiss Government provided the necessary funding.

The institutions endorsing this report are convinced that in a more globalised, interconnected and competitive world the way that environmental, social and corporate governance issues are managed is part of companies' overall management quality needed to compete successfully. Companies that perform better with regard to these issues can increase shareholder value by, for example, properly managing risks, anticipating regulatory action or accessing new markets, while at the same time contributing to the sustainable development of the societies in which they operate. Moreover, these issues can have a strong impact on reputation and brands, an increasingly important part of company value.

The report aims at increasing the awareness of all involved financial market actors, at triggering a broader discussion, and supporting creativity and thoughtfulness in approach, rather than being prescriptive. It also aims to enhance clarity concerning the respective roles of different market actors, including companies, regulators, stock exchanges, investors, asset managers, brokers, analysts, accountants, financial advisers and consultants. It therefore includes recommendations for different actors, striving to support improved mutual understanding, collaboration and constructive dialogue on these issues.

The endorsing institutions are committed to start a process to further deepen, specify and implement the recommendations outlined in this report by means of a series of individual and collaborative efforts at different levels. They are also keen to start a dialogue with other stakeholders on ways to implement the recommendations because they are convinced that only if all actors contribute to the integration of environmental, social and governance issues in investment decisions, can significant improvements in this field be achieved. As an important next step, endorsing institutions plan to approach the relevant accounting standard-setting, professional and self-regulatory organizations, and investor relations associations in order to ensure that their intentions are fully understood and supported. They invite the Global Compact or one of its implementing bodies to review the state of the implementation of this report's recommendations in a year's time with the goal of assessing how market actors have responded to the call for action by this report.

Endorsing institutions are convinced that a better consideration of environmental, social and governance factors will ultimately contribute to stronger and more resilient investment markets, as well as contribute to the sustainable development of societies. The report's recommendations can be summarized as follows:

- Analysts are asked to better incorporate environmental, social and governance (ESG) factors in their research where appropriate and to further develop the necessary investment know-how, models and tools in a creative and thoughtful way. Based on the existing know-how in especially exposed industries, the scope should be expanded to include other sectors and asset classes. Because of their importance for sustainable development, emerging markets should receive particular consideration and environmental, social and governance criteria should be adapted to the specific situation in these markets. Academic institutions, business schools and other research organisations are invited to support the efforts of financial analysts by contributing high-level research and thinking.

- Financial institutions should commit to integrating environmental, social and governance factors in a more systematic way in research and investment processes. This must be supported by a strong commitment at the Board and senior management level. The formulation of long-term goals, the introduction of organisational learning and change processes, appropriate training and incentive systems for analysts are crucial in achieving the goal of a better integration of these issues.

- Companies are asked to take a leadership role by implementing environmental, social and corporate governance principles and polices and to provide information and reports on related performance in a more consistent and standardised format. They should identify and communicate key challenges and value drivers and prioritise environmental, social and governance issues accordingly. We believe that this information is best conveyed to financial markets through normal investor relation communication channels and encourage, when relevant, an explicit mention in the annual report of companies. Concerning the outcomes of financial research in this field, companies should accept positive as well as critical results.

- Investors are urged to explicitly request and reward research that includes environmental, social and governance aspects and to reward well-managed companies. Asset managers are asked to integrate research on such aspects in investment decisions and to encourage brokers and companies to provide better research and information. Both investors and asset managers should develop and communicate proxy voting strategies on ESG issues as this will support analysts and fund managers in producing relevant research and services.

- Pension fund trustees and their selection consultants are encouraged to consider environmental, social and governance issues in the formulation of investment mandates and the selection of investment managers, taking into account their fiduciary obligations to participants and beneficiaries. Governments and multilateral agencies are asked to proactively consider the investment of their pension funds according to the principles of sustainable development, taking into account their fiduciary obligations to participants and beneficiaries.

- Consultants and financial advisers should help create a greater and more stable demand for research in this area by combining research on environmental, social and governance aspects with industry level research and sharing their experience with financial market actors and companies in order to improve their reporting on these issues.

- Regulators are invited to shape legal frameworks in a predictable and transparent way as this will support integration in financial analysis. Regulatory frameworks should require a minimum degree of disclosure and accountability on environmental, social and governance issues from companies, as this will support financial analysis. The formulation of specific standards should, on the other hand, rely on market-driven voluntary initiatives. We encourage financial analysts to participate more actively in ongoing voluntary initiatives, such as the Global Reporting Initiative, and help shape a reporting framework that responds to their needs.

- Stock exchanges are invited to include environmental, social and governance criteria in listing particulars for companies as this will ensure a minimum degree of disclosure across all listed companies. As a first step, stock exchanges could communicate to listed companies the growing importance of environmental, social and governance issues. Similarly, other self-regulatory organizations (e.g. NASD, FSA), professional credential-granting organizations (e.g. AIMR, EFFAS), accounting standard-setting bodies (e.g. FASB, IASB), public accounting entities, and rating agencies and index providers should all establish consistent standards and frameworks in relation to environmental, social and governance factors.

- Non-Governmental Organisations (NGOs) can also contribute to better transparency by providing objective information on companies to the public and the financial community.

———

A wide variety of actors helped to spread the concept of integrating ESG issues into investment analysis. For example, early in the history of ESG, a group of United Nations Environment Programme Finance Initiative (UNEP FI) asset managers commissioned the international law firm Freshfields Bruckhaus Deringer to produce a study analyzing whether integration of ESG issues into investment policy is consistent with the fiduciary duties of asset managers. The Freshfields report concluded that "integrating ESG considerations into an investment analysis so as to more reliably predict financial performance is clearly permissible and is arguably required in all jurisdictions." Debate about the fiduciary duties of asset managers concerning ESG integration into investment decisions and stewardship did not end, but the Freshfields report was widely influential.

Further, the UNEP FI and UN Global Compact launched the Principles for Responsible Investment (PRI). Under the PRI, institutional investors can voluntarily commit to supporting and implementing six core principles that promote the disclosure of ESG issues by portfolio companies and the integration of ESG issues in investment analysis, ownership policies, and within the investment industry itself. PRI has grown significantly and now counts thousands of signatories. Many asset managers offer ESG-labeled funds. Efforts at standard setting for "impact" or "sustainability" reporting such as the Global Reporting Initiative (GRI) and the Sustainability Accounting Standards Board (SASB) have also developed as well as scores or ESG ratings created by commercial and nonprofit organizations. A number of additional actors and developments have catapulted ESG to a global phenomenon.

———

Points for Discussion

1. CSR, benefit corporations, and ESG.

What do these three concepts have in common regarding their approaches to incorporating stakeholder interests? In what ways do they differ? How do they each relate to existing corporate law principles?

2. The meaning of ESG.

To many observers and market participants, ESG refers to environmental, social, and governance factors for investment analysis. Over time, the term has taken on additional usages. For example, some view ESG as a tool for risk management. For many companies, ESG provides a framework for identifying and managing social risks to their business. And, relatedly, for many investors, the key justification for incorporating ESG factors into investment analysis relates to their potential impact on portfolio-level risk-adjusted returns or the relationship between ESG factors and risk management at the company level. Thus you may hear references to "ESG risks" or discussions of integrating ESG into board oversight practices. By contrast, some view ESG as a synonym for CSR or sustainability, or as an expression of ideological preference.

3. E, S, and G at the firm level and portfolio level.

ESG encompasses wide-ranging issues. Some issues that fall within the ESG umbrella might be in tension with each other at times. For example, a business that is divesting or decommissioning brown assets or transforming to new technology with less environmental impact may have workers that are losing relevant skills or getting laid off. To take another example, institutional investors that hold a broadly diversified portfolio across the market may have incentives to reduce systematic risk and internalize intra-portfolio negative externalities. Considering ESG factors or risk management for one company may point in a different direction than for an overall portfolio.

---

2. Emerging Issues and the ESG Debate

With trillions of dollars in investment funds under ESG-labels or using ESG factors for investment analysis, and lawmakers and agencies around the world implementing ESG regulations, debate about ESG has also grown heated. A number of rulemaking initiatives and policies are in flux. To conclude this chapter, we explore some of the important topics of debate.

One enduring question has been whether the relationship between ESG and economic performance can be empirically proven. Do ESG-related practices create long-term risk-adjusted value for companies and investors? Significant evidence exists of such a link, but the empirical evidence has been mixed overall. Studies often bundle ESG issues together or rely on ESG performance ratings that do so, which can leave open questions of which, if any, corporate policies or activities are actually related to financial performance and whether the relationship is causal. Thus both advocates and critics of ESG can find empirical evidence to point to, or questions to raise, as they are making their case. ESG ratings are likewise a thorny topic as they vary widely by provider and are not subject to standardized approaches or accountability mechanisms that ensure reliability.

Further, both empirical studies and ESG ratings rely on available data and disclosure rules vary around the world on different aspects of E, S, and G. Many investors, including under the auspices of the PRI, have pushed for increased disclosure of

ESG-related information on a voluntary and mandatory basis. The disclosure rules on issues ranging from board diversity to climate risks have provoked contentious debate in the United States such as regarding the authority of the Securities and Exchange Commission (SEC), and whether the concept of investor materiality or the First Amendment impose limits on mandatory disclosure.

Concerns about ESG as a marketing gimmick and "greenwashing" also abound. Asset managers could, for instance, market a fund under an ESG or green label and charge higher fees without changing their investment activities to back up their claims. Regulators have cracked down on some large financial institutions for greenwashing and have created new taxonomies and systems for labeling funds.

Another area of debate concerns the role of asset managers with regard to ESG. With changing administrations, the Department of Labor has changed its guidelines over time concerning how, and whether, ERISA fund managers can consider ESG issues in investment decisions. Further, investment trends in the past several decades, including the rise of index funds, have resulted in just a small handful of asset managers holding a large amount of all U.S. public equities. The "Big Three" index fund managers, BlackRock, State Street, and Vanguard, often hold significant stakes in large public corporations and can wield power as shareholders. Should they use this power to push companies to engage in ESG practices or reduce externalities that impact stakeholders? Should they support pro-ESG shareholder proposals and the campaigns of ESG activists? Is this consistent with their fiduciary duties? How can leaders of large institutional investors maintain legitimacy when they manage other peoples' money? Consider the following excerpt of an open letter that Larry Fink, the chairperson and CEO of BlackRock, the world's largest asset manager, addressed to the CEOs of its portfolio companies.

Larry Fink's *2021* Letter to CEOs

Larry Fink, Chairperson and Chief Executive Officer

BlackRock (2021)

Dear CEO,

BlackRock is a fiduciary to our clients, helping them invest for long-term goals. Most of the money we manage is for retirement—for individuals and pension beneficiaries like teachers, firefighters, doctors, businesspeople, and many others. It is their money we manage, not our own. The trust our clients place in us, and our role as the link between our clients and the companies they invest in, gives us a great responsibility to advocate on their behalf.

This is why I write to you each year, seeking to highlight issues that are pivotal to creating durable value—issues such as capital management, long-term strategy, purpose, and climate change. We have long believed that our clients, as shareholders in your company, will benefit if you can create enduring, sustainable value for *all* of your stakeholders. . . .

A Tectonic Shift Accelerates

We know that climate risk is investment risk. But we also believe the climate transition presents a historic investment opportunity.

Essential to this transition has been the growing availability and affordability of sustainable investment options. Not long ago, building a climate-aware portfolio was a painstaking process, available only to the largest investors. But the creation of sustainable index investments has enabled a massive acceleration of capital towards companies better prepared to address climate risk.

Today we are on the cusp of another transformation. Better technology and data are enabling asset managers to offer customized index portfolios to a much broader group of people—another capability once reserved for the largest investors. As more and more investors choose to tilt their investments towards sustainability-focused companies, the tectonic shift we are seeing will accelerate further. And because this will have such a dramatic impact on how capital is allocated, every management team and board will need to consider how this will impact their company's stock. . . .

Sustainability and Deeper Connections to Stakeholders Drives Better Returns

In 2018, I wrote urging every company to articulate its purpose and how it benefits all stakeholders, including shareholders, employees, customers, and the communities in which they operate. Over the course of 2020, we have seen how purposeful companies, with better environmental, social, and governance (ESG) profiles, have outperformed their peers. During 2020, 81% of a globally-representative selection of sustainable indexes outperformed their parent benchmarks. This outperformance was even more pronounced during the first quarter downturn, another instance of sustainable funds' resilience that we have seen in prior downturns. And the broader array of sustainable investment options will continue to drive investor interest in these funds, as we have seen in 2020.

But the story goes deeper. It's not just that broad-market ESG indexes are outperforming counterparts. It's that within industries—from automobiles to banks to oil and gas companies—we are seeing another divergence: companies with better ESG profiles are performing better than their peers, enjoying a "sustainability premium."

It is clear that being connected to stakeholders—establishing trust with them and acting with purpose—enables a company to understand and respond to the changes happening in the world. Companies ignore stakeholders at their peril—companies that do not earn this trust will find it harder and harder to attract customers and talent, especially as young people increasingly expect companies to reflect their values. The more your company can show its purpose in delivering value to its customers, its employees, and its communities, the better able you will be to compete and deliver long-term, durable profits for shareholders.

I cannot recall a time where it has been more important for companies to respond to the needs of their stakeholders. We are at a moment of tremendous economic pain. We are also at a historic crossroads on the path to racial justice—one that cannot be solved without leadership from companies. A company that does not seek to benefit from the full spectrum of human talent is weaker for it—less likely to hire the best talent, less likely to reflect the needs of its customers and the communities where it operates, and less likely to outperform.

While issues of race and ethnicity vary greatly across the world, we expect companies in all countries to have a talent strategy that allows them to draw on the fullest set of talent possible. As you issue sustainability reports, we ask that your disclosures on talent strategy fully reflect your long-term plans to improve diversity, equity, and inclusion, as appropriate by region. We hold ourselves to this same standard.

Questions of racial justice, economic inequality, or community engagement are often classed as an "S" issue in ESG conversations. But it is misguided to draw such stark lines between these categories. For example, climate change is already having a disproportionate impact on low-income communities around the world—is that an E or an S issue? What matters is less the category we place these questions in, but the information we have to understand them and how they interact with each other. Improved data and disclosures will help us better understand the deep interdependence between environmental and social issues.

I am an optimist. I have seen how many companies are taking these challenges seriously—how they are embracing the demands of greater transparency, greater accountability to stakeholders, and better preparation for climate change. I am encouraged by what I have seen from businesses. And now, business leaders and boards will need to show great courage and commitment to their stakeholders. We need to move even faster—to create more jobs, more prosperity, and more inclusivity.

————————

The pro-ESG approach of many asset managers has been controversial and generated an "anti-woke" backlash. Some investors, including individuals, state pension funds, and investment funds, have criticized BlackRock's approach and adopted an anti-ESG agenda, favoring investments in companies that are alleged to be causing social or environmental harm.

For example, consider the following statement from Strive Asset Management:

We created Strive to offer everyday Americans a way to invest in the stock market without mixing business with politics.

Many Americans invest in the market by selecting large asset managers to oversee their retirement and investment accounts. These asset managers charge low fees, but there is a hidden cost: these firms tell America's public companies to adopt divisive social and political agendas that most

Americans disagree with. Even worse, they cause America's companies to perform more poorly by mixing politics with business, which harms the investment accounts of everyday Americans.

At Strive, we are solving that problem by creating index funds that deliver our message to American public companies.

Why Strive?, *Strive Asset Management*, https://strive.com/why-strive/ (2023).

Further, Strive Asset Management explains its philosophy with the following description:

We cater to everyday Americans who don't want their investments and retirement accounts to be used to push political agendas onto American companies. Our goal is to offer very similar investment options to existing large asset managers, at similar or identical fees. The key distinction is our approach to shareholder voting and engagement.

We take our fiduciary duty to our clients seriously. Our voting and advocacy decisions are made with the sole interest of maximizing the value of our clients' investment accounts—with no "mixed motivation" to also advance a social objective.

Our investment products do not exclude "bad-acting" companies. Why? Because we believe in engagement over divestment.

Instead, we use our voice and vote as a shareholder to drive positive behavior by advancing Excellence Capitalism in the boardroom—a new movement that leads companies to focus exclusively on delivering excellent products and services to their customers over all other agendas.

We aim to maximize the value of our clients' investments by depoliticizing corporate America. Strive hopes that this will also create a more unified private sector that brings together individuals of all backgrounds and beliefs to work together to improve the lives of their customers and shareholders.

Id.

Points for Discussion

1. ESG in an era of politicization.

Some politicians have criticized asset managers for pushing "progressive" or "woke" policies in companies through ESG. Asset managers such as Larry Fink have rejected this backlash and noted that ESG is aligned with the pursuit of shareholder value in a capitalist system. What incentives might motivate large asset managers in charting their paths with respect to ESG? What incentives might motivate new or smaller asset managers, such as Strive Asset Management?

2. *ESG-related regulation.*

The SEC has engaged in rulemaking that mandates disclosure of a number of ESG-related areas ranging from human capital management to climate risk. Other regulators around the world have similarly been active in this area. Are such disclosures for investors, stakeholders, or both? What is the role of government in facilitating ESG investing?

3. *The future of ESG?*

What might be the future of ESG? Will it fade or rise in popularity? What are the pros and cons of the ESG acronym? Should ESG be expanded with additional letters or shrunk by taking one out? Would investors, or society more generally, be better off with a different term and concept? What accounts for the renaissance in debate about corporate purpose, CSR, and developments such as the benefit corporation and ESG?

———————

MODULE V – SHAREHOLDERS

CHAPTER 14

Litigation

Shareholders can vote, sue, and sell. In the previous chapter, we focused on the right of shareholders to vote and use their voice to influence corporate behavior. In this chapter we turn to the right of shareholders to bring derivative suits under state corporate law to enforce the duties of corporate fiduciaries. We also discuss issues related to shareholders' rights to sue based on federal securities laws.

Shareholder litigation is an important topic, and in this chapter we can only brush the surface. We won't get into the details of shareholder litigation that are covered in a securities course or an upper-level course in corporate governance or M&A. Our primary ambition here is to give you a basic overview of how shareholder litigation matters to corporations and to cover some of the key distinctions in the area.

Hundreds of securities class action lawsuits are filed every year, along with many more derivative lawsuits. In the 2000s, there was an increase in the number of "mega" settlements of shareholder litigation, with several multi-billion dollar settlements, including those based on scandals at Enron, WorldCom, AOL Time Warner, and other large public companies. The Financial Crisis of 2008 also generated a surge in shareholder lawsuits, such as those arising from the collapse of Lehman Brothers, the role of Citibank in the subprime mortgage market, and Bank of America's acquisition of Merrill Lynch. For many years, merger litigation focused on Delaware, but recent cases dismissing shareholder litigation have led many suits to migrate to federal court, where they are framed in terms of the violation of federal disclosure rules instead of the breach of state fiduciary duties.

Opinion about these lawsuits is sharply divided. Some argue that shareholder litigation benefits all shareholders because the threat of litigation polices the conduct of managers and private lawsuits fill gaps left by lapses in regulation and the weaknesses of market forces. Others argue that shareholder litigation is parasitic and imposes great costs on corporations with little benefit. Whatever one's view, it is clear that litigation plays an important role in the relationship between shareholders and directors.

Keep in mind that the central actor in shareholder litigation typically is not the shareholder. Instead, it is the plaintiffs' lawyer. The law provides plaintiffs' lawyers with strong financial incentives to monitor corporate behavior and to litigate when information about fiduciary misconduct comes to light or an alleged fraud is revealed and has a negative impact on the value of a corporation's securities. Whenever a plaintiffs' law firm detects apparent wrongdoing, litigates, and then settles a lawsuit that a court deems to be successful, the court will award the firm attorneys' fees that, in most cases, will compensate it relatively generously for the time devoted to bringing the action and the risk incurred by undertaking to represent shareholders' interests on a contingent fee basis. Of course, not every case settles or is successful.

In this chapter, we tackle several of the questions posed by shareholder litigation. First, we examine a choice many plaintiffs' attorneys—and therefore courts—must make in individual cases: is the case appropriately a derivative action or a direct action? Often, the distinction is not clear, and some cases may fit both categories. Second, we focus on one particularly important aspect of derivative actions, known as the demand requirement. In simple terms, courts (especially in Delaware) have developed tests to decide whether plaintiffs must first "demand" that a corporation's board take action before they are permitted to sustain their own lawsuit. In practice, the fate of a lawsuit depends on whether demand is required. Third, we ask who is an appropriate plaintiff, with a focus on the adequacy and standing of particular types of plaintiffs. Fourth, we consider indemnification and insurance. Finally, we consider some of the policy implications of shareholder litigation.

A.   Derivative vs. Direct

Many plaintiffs' securities firms view federal class actions and state derivative actions as alternatives: they might file one, or the other, depending on the relative costs and benefits. We begin by analyzing one crucial distinction between these two types of litigation: whether the nature of the injury to shareholders is direct or derivative.

> The derivative action is a strange animal. Historically, it arose in the United States during the nineteenth century, as courts recognized the importance of permitting minority shareholders to sue when corporate directors breached their duties. Judges saw derivative actions as an equitable remedy designed to give shareholders the ability to enforce corporate rights against directors or other wrongdoers when the people who controlled the corporation refused to do so. You already have read several cases involving derivative actions. Take a few minutes to flip back through the earlier cases in this book. Which ones involve derivative actions? Why were they brought as derivative actions? Keep the derivative vs. direct distinction in mind as you read cases in future chapters.

1.   Derivative

Recall that a derivative action is a special type of lawsuit. It typically is brought by a shareholder *on behalf of the corporation* in which they hold stock. The shareholder asserts rights belonging to the corporation because the board of directors has failed to do so. The corporation is named as a nominal defendant. Any amounts recovered belong to the corporation, not the shareholder-plaintiff. The incentive for bringing a derivative suit often lies in the rule that a successful plaintiff can recover attorneys' fees from the corporation.

In theory, a shareholder can bring a derivative action against any party who has harmed the corporation, whether an insider or outsider. In practice, nearly all derivative actions are brought against directors, officers, or controlling shareholders who have breached duties to the corporation. Suing an outside party—for example, claiming breach of a contract with the corporation—is more often seen as a business judgment reserved for the board of directors.

The shareholder-plaintiff who brings a derivative action represents the corporation to vindicate the interests of all shareholders. For example, Federal Rule of Civil Procedure 23.1 requires that the derivative suit "fairly and adequately represent the interests of the shareholders similarly situated in enforcing the rights of the corporation." The shareholder-plaintiff "is a self-chosen representative and a volunteer champion"—and thus assumes fiduciary responsibilities. For example, a plaintiff cannot later abandon a derivative action for personal gain.

2. Direct

Shareholders can also sue directly *on their own behalf* to vindicate individual rights, rather than corporate rights. In public corporations, direct actions are often brought as class actions, in which a shareholder-representative brings the action on behalf of similarly situated shareholders. Direct actions, though they have their own procedural rules, are attractive because they avoid the procedural hurdles that apply to derivative actions—principally, the requirement of pre-suit demand on the board and the board's power to seek dismissal of the derivative suit before trial. (We will discuss this demand requirement in detail in the next section.) On the other hand, direct actions are subject to other limitations and restrictions, many arising under federal securities law. So the question of whether a direct action is superior to a derivative action can be a difficult one.

> Two important kinds of "direct" shareholder actions are covered elsewhere in the book. Claims by shareholders that the corporation (or others) has deceived them in connection with the voting of their shares can be brought in federal and state court as direct actions. *See* Chapter 16, Information. And, claims by investors involving deception in connection with the buying and selling of securities can be brought in federal court as direct class actions. *See* Chapter 19, Securities Fraud.

3. Direct vs. Derivative Distinction

As you can imagine, corporate actions often affect shareholders both directly and derivatively. When is an action direct and when is it derivative? The answers—to the extent there are any—are in a handful of judicial opinions, primarily in Delaware. As we learned during our discussion of the internal affairs doctrine, derivative actions typically are based on the law of the state of incorporation. Derivative actions are often filed in Delaware, where roughly half of all publicly traded corporations are incorporated. Accordingly, the Delaware courts are the most frequent arbiter of whether an injury is direct or derivative.

Although the case law is not a model of clarity, the following actions are generally treated as direct, thus not subject to derivative action procedures:

- **Protection of financial rights**—compel dividends or protect accrued dividend arrearages, compel dissolution, appoint a receiver, or obtain similar equitable relief

- **Protection of voting rights**—enforce the right to vote, prevent the improper dilution of voting rights, protect preemptive rights, or enjoin the improper voting of shares

- **Protection of governance rights**—enjoin an ultra vires or unauthorized act, challenge the use of corporate machinery or the issuance of stock for a wrongful purpose (such as to perpetuate management in control), require notice or holding of a shareholders' meeting

- **Protection of minority rights**—challenge the improper expulsion of shareholders through mergers, redemptions, or other means, prevent oppression of, or fraud against, minority shareholders, or hold controlling shareholders liable for their acts that depress minority share value

- **Protection of informational rights**—inspect corporate books and records

Historically, some courts sought to distinguish direct actions from derivative actions by looking at whether the shareholder-plaintiff suffered a special injury (direct) or whether all shareholders were affected equally (derivative). This "special injury" approach created confusion. In response, the Delaware Supreme Court tried to simplify the task of distinguishing the two actions. Here is that attempt.

Tooley v. Donaldson, Lufkin, & Jenrette, Inc.

845 A.2d 1031 (Del. 2004)

Veasey, Chief Justice.

Plaintiff-stockholders brought a purported class action in the Court of Chancery, alleging that the members of the board of directors of their corporation breached their fiduciary duties by agreeing to a 22-day delay in closing a proposed merger. Plaintiffs contend that the delay harmed them due to the lost time-value of the cash paid for their shares. The Court of Chancery granted the defendants' motion to dismiss on the sole ground that the claims were, "at most," claims of the corporation being asserted derivatively. They were, thus, held not to be direct claims of the stockholders, individually. Thereupon, the Court held that the plaintiffs lost their standing to bring this action when they tendered their shares in connection with the merger.

Although the trial court's legal analysis of whether the complaint alleges a direct or derivative claim reflects some concepts in our prior jurisprudence, we believe those concepts are not helpful and should be regarded as erroneous. We set forth in this Opinion the law to be applied henceforth in determining whether a stockholder's claim is derivative or direct. That issue must turn *solely* on the following questions: (1) who suffered the alleged harm (the corporation or the suing stockholders, individually); and (2) who would receive the benefit of any recovery or other remedy (the corporation or the stockholders, individually)?

Plaintiffs are former minority stockholders of Donaldson, Lufkin & Jenrette, Inc. (DLJ). DLJ was acquired by Credit Suisse Group (Credit Suisse) in the Fall of 2000. Before that acquisition, AXA Financial, Inc. (AXA), which owned 71% of DLJ stock, controlled DLJ. Pursuant to a stockholder agreement between AXA and Credit Suisse, AXA agreed to exchange with Credit Suisse its DLJ stockholdings for a mix of stock and cash.

The tender offer price was set at $90 per share in cash. The tender offer was to expire 20 days after its commencement. The merger agreement, however, authorized two types of extensions. First, Credit Suisse could unilaterally extend the tender offer if certain conditions were not met. Alternatively, DLJ and Credit Suisse could agree to postpone acceptance by Credit Suisse of DLJ stock tendered by the minority stockholders.

Credit Suisse availed itself of both types of extensions to postpone the closing of the tender offer. Plaintiffs challenge the second extension that resulted in a 22-day delay. They contend that this delay was not properly authorized and harmed minority stockholders while improperly benefiting AXA. They claim damages representing the time-value of money lost through the delay.

The order of the Court of Chancery dismissing the complaint is based on the plaintiffs' lack of standing to bring the claims asserted therein. Thus, when plaintiffs tendered their shares they lost standing under the contemporaneous holding rule. The ruling before us on appeal is that the plaintiffs' claim is derivative, purportedly brought on behalf of DLJ. The Court of Chancery, relying upon our confusing jurisprudence on the direct/derivative dichotomy, based its dismissal on the following ground: "Because this delay affected all DLJ shareholders equally, plaintiffs' injury was not a special injury, and this action is, thus, a derivative action, at most."

In our view, the concept of "special injury" that appears in some Supreme Court and Court of Chancery cases is not helpful to a proper analytical distinction between direct and derivative actions. We now disapprove the use of the concept of "special injury" as a tool in that analysis.

The analysis must be based solely on the following questions: Who suffered the alleged harm—the corporation or the suing stockholder individually—and who would receive the benefit of the recovery or other remedy? This simple analysis is well imbedded in our jurisprudence, but some cases have complicated it by injection of the amorphous and confusing concept of "special injury."

The Chancellor, in *Agostino v. Hicks*, 845 A.2d 1110 (Del. Ch. 2004), correctly points this out and strongly suggests that we should disavow the concept of "special injury." In a scholarly analysis of this area of the law, he also suggests that the inquiry should be whether the stockholder has demonstrated that he or she has suffered an injury that is not dependent on an injury to the corporation. In the context of a claim for breach of fiduciary duty, the Chancellor articulated the inquiry as follows: "Looking at the body of the complaint and considering the nature of the wrong alleged and the relief requested, has the plaintiff demonstrated that he or she can prevail without showing an injury to the corporation?"[9] We believe that this approach is helpful in analyzing the first prong of the analysis: what person or entity has suffered the alleged harm? The second prong of the analysis should logically follow.

Determining whether an action is derivative or direct is sometimes difficult and has many legal consequences, some of which may have an expensive impact on the parties to the action. For example, if an action is derivative, the plaintiffs are then required to comply with the requirements of Court of Chancery Rule 23.1, that the stockholder: (a) retain ownership of the shares throughout the litigation; (b) make presuit demand on the board; and (c) obtain court approval of any settlement. Further, the recovery, if any, flows only to the corporation. The decision whether a suit is direct or derivative may be outcome-determinative. Therefore, it is necessary that a standard to distinguish such actions be clear, simple and consistently articulated and applied by our courts.

A court should look to the nature of the wrong and to whom the relief should go. The stockholder's claimed direct injury must be independent of any alleged injury to the corporation. The stockholder must demonstrate that the duty breached was owed to the stockholder and that he or she can prevail without showing an injury to the corporation.

In this case it cannot be concluded that the complaint alleges a derivative claim. There is no derivative claim asserting injury to the corporate entity. There is no relief that would go the corporation. Accordingly, there is no basis to hold that the complaint states a derivative claim.

But, it does not necessarily follow that the complaint states a direct, individual claim. While the complaint purports to set forth a direct claim, in reality, it states

---

[9]   The Chancellor further explains that the focus should be on the person or entity to whom the relevant duty is owed. As noted in *Agostino*, this test is similar to that articulated by the American Law Institute (ALI), a test that we cited with approval in *Grimes v. Donald*, 673 A.2d 1207 (Del. 1996).

no claim at all. The trial court analyzed the complaint and correctly concluded that it does not claim that the plaintiffs have any rights that have been injured. Their rights have not yet ripened. The contractual claim is nonexistent until it is ripe, and that claim will not be ripe until the terms of the merger are fulfilled, including the extensions of the closing at issue here. Therefore, there is no direct claim stated in the complaint before us.

Due to the reliance on the concept of "special injury" by the Court of Chancery, the ground set forth for the dismissal is erroneous, there being no derivative claim. That error is harmless, however, because, in our view, there is no direct claim either.

Points for Discussion

1. *ALI Principles.*

The ALI Principles of Corporate Governance attempt to distinguish between direct and derivative actions. The following Comment to ALI Principles § 7.01 sets forth four policy considerations that the ALI Principles say "deserve to be given close attention by the court." Are these criteria helpful? Or are they merely conclusory results of the characterization?

> ## <u>ALI Principles § 7.01</u>
> ## <u>Direct and Derivative Actions Distinguished</u>
>
> First, a derivative action distributes the recovery more broadly and evenly than a direct action. Because the recovery in a derivative action goes to the corporation, creditors and others having a stake in the corporation benefit financially from a derivative action and not from a direct one. Similarly, although all shareholders share equally, if indirectly, in the corporate recovery that follows a successful derivative action, the injured shareholders other than the plaintiff will share in the recovery from a direct action only if the action is a class action brought on behalf of all these shareholders.
>
> Second, once finally concluded, a derivative action will have a preclusive effect that spares the corporation and the defendants from being exposed to a multiplicity of actions.
>
> Third, a successful plaintiff is entitled to an award of attorneys' fees in a derivative action directly from the corporation, but in a direct action the plaintiff must generally look to the fund, if any, created by the action.

Finally, characterizing the action as derivative may entitle the board to take over the action or to seek dismissal of the action. Thus, in some circumstances the characterization of the action will determine the available defenses.

2. Applying the tests.

Are the *Tooley* and ALI approaches the same? Would they lead courts to reach different conclusions? For example, how would each test suggest a court should assess a shareholder claiming denial of preemptive rights, which ensure proportional voting and financial rights? Is such a claim direct or derivative? What about a suit challenging the board's decision to give a CEO guaranteed lifetime employment?

3. What about closely held corporations?

The policy reasons for requiring a shareholder to sue derivatively when her claim is based on an alleged injury to the corporation may not be present when the suit involves a close corporation in which there is a close identity between shareholders and managers. In addition, litigation-related agency costs are much less likely to arise in a suit involving a close corporation because the plaintiff generally will have substantial financial interests in the action and is more likely to monitor the attorneys. Nevertheless, there may be other reasons for requiring that such an action be maintained as a derivative suit; for example, having damages awarded to the corporation, rather than to an individual shareholder, may be necessary to protect creditors' interests. Should courts consider different factors in derivative suits involving closely held corporations?

4. The difficulty of distinguishing direct vs. derivative.

In *Brookfield Asset Management, Inc. v. Rosson*, 261 A.3d 1251 (Del. 2021), the Delaware Supreme Court reexamined principles of direct and derivative standing in what is known as a "corporate overpayment/dilution claim," based on a transaction that transfers economic value and voting power from minority stockholders to a controlling stockholder. One way of viewing such a transaction is as an overpayment, or over-issuance of stock, that harms the corporation because of the reduction in the value of the corporate entity. Another way of viewing the transaction focuses instead on the harm to the minority shareholders whose stakes in the corporation are diluted when a controlling shareholder causes the corporation to issue "excessive" shares for inadequate consideration, such as for assets of the controlling shareholder that have a lesser value.

The Court weighed these various perspectives and clarified that corporation overpayment/dilution claims are "exclusively derivative." The harm to shareholders in this context "was not *independent* of the harm to the Company, but rather flowed indirectly to them in proportion to, and via their shares." In so holding, it overruled an earlier decision, *Gentile v. Rossette*, 906 A.2d 91 (Del. 2006), that had treated such claims as "dual-natured" and had been characterized as an exception to the *Tooley* test. The Delaware courts have thus gone back and forth on this particular type of claim. So if you find the distinction between direct and derivative claims sometimes hard to determine, you are in good company! Whenever in doubt in practice, it is a good idea to research how recent case law has handled a claim similar to the one you are handling.

B.   Demand Requirement

Rule 23.1 of the Federal Rules of Civil Procedure provides that the complaint in a derivative suit shall "allege with particularity the efforts, if any, made by the plaintiff to obtain the action plaintiff desires from the directors and the reasons for the plaintiff's failure to obtain the action or for not making the effort." Delaware Chancery Court Rule 23.1 contains a similar provision. Although the demand requirement is framed as a pleading rule, courts treat it as a matter of substantive law governing the allocation of power within the corporation.

> As a practical matter, it is rare for a shareholder to make a demand. The reason for this is that if a shareholder makes a demand, and the board refuses the demand, a court will apply the business judgment rule to the board's decision. The shareholder would only have a potential claim for wrongful refusal of demand—which would be an exceedingly difficult claim to win. Accordingly, the plaintiff typically just files a derivative action and includes in the complaint a claim that demand should be excused as futile.

The demand requirement is a way for judges to filter those derivative suits that appear to have merit from those that do not. By deciding whether "demand" on the board is required, courts essentially decide whether the shareholder can proceed with a lawsuit on behalf of the corporation. If demand is required, the derivative suit ends—and the shareholder is left to intra-corporate remedies. If demand is excused, the suit proceeds. The demand requirement applies only to derivative actions, not to direct actions.

The premise of the demand requirement arises from the general rule that the board, not shareholders, manages the corporation. Accordingly, the board normally would have the power to decide whether the corporation should bring a lawsuit. Derivative actions are an exception to the general rule, because they permit shareholders—rather than the board—to act on behalf of the corporation in bringing, maintaining, and settling litigation. Thus, the demand requirement is a way for judges to balance the board's managerial prerogatives and the desirability, in certain circumstances, of allowing shareholders to litigate on behalf of the corporation.

1. Demand Futility

Early cases made it easy for shareholders to meet the demand requirement by making boilerplate allegations that demand would be futile because the corporation's directors either had benefitted improperly from the transaction at issue or were dominated or controlled by the people who had benefitted. Alternatively, courts allowed shareholder-plaintiffs to name all directors as defendants and then assert that the board could not be expected to sue because the directors were potentially liable for having approved the transaction at issue or for failing to seek to hold liable whoever was responsible for approving it. Courts soon realized, however, that permitting plaintiffs to make conclusory allegations begged the key question posed by the statutory demand requirement: when would demand be excused as futile?

The following case—the leading case on "demand futility"—represents the Delaware Supreme Court's attempt to clarify this question. The Court adopted a "refined" three-part test that synthesized two of its longstanding demand futility precedents: *Aronson v. Lewis*, 473 A.2d 805 (Del. 1984) and *Rales v. Blasband*, 634 A.2d 927 (Del. 1993).

The case arose out of a proposed stock reclassification of Facebook, Inc. (now Meta) that would allow Mark Zuckerberg (controlling shareholder, chairperson, and CEO) to dispose of a substantial amount of his company stock while retaining voting control. Numerous shareholder challenges in the Court of Chancery ensued, and were ultimately consolidated into a class action. Before the trial began, however, Facebook withdrew the reclassification proposal and settled the case. At that point, it had spent over $20 million defending the class action and $68 million in plaintiffs' attorneys' fees.

Subsequently, another Facebook shareholder—United Food and Commercial Workers Union and Participating Food Industry Employers Tri-State Pension Fund ("Tri-State")—sued Facebook's current and former directors to recover costs that the company had incurred in connection with the class action. Tri-State pleaded that demand was futile for two reasons: (1) that the board's negotiation and approval of the reclassification was not a valid exercise of its business judgment, and (2) that the majority of Facebook's directors were beholden to Zuckerberg. The Court of Chancery dismissed Tri-State's complaint and Tri-State appealed.

United Food and Commercial Workers Union and Participating Food Industry Employers Tri-State Pension Fund v. Zuckerberg

262 A.3d 1034 (Del. 2021)

MONTGOMERY-REEVES, JUSTICE.

"A cardinal precept" of Delaware law is "that directors, rather than shareholders, manage the business and affairs of the corporation." This precept is reflected in Section 141(a) of the Delaware General Corporation Law ("DGCL"), which provides that "[t]he business and affairs of every corporation organized under this chapter *shall be managed by or under the direction of a board of directors* except as may be otherwise provided in this chapter or in [a corporation's] certificate of incorporation." The board's authority to govern corporate affairs extends to decisions about what remedial actions a corporation should take after being harmed, including whether the corporation should file a lawsuit against its directors, its officers, its controller, or an outsider.

"In a derivative suit, a stockholder seeks to displace the board's [decision-making] authority over a litigation asset and assert the corporation's claim." Thus, "[b]y its very nature[,] the derivative action" encroaches "on the managerial freedom of directors" by seeking to deprive the board of control over a corporation's litigation asset. "In order for a stockholder to divest the directors of their authority to control the litigation asset and bring a derivative action on behalf of the corporation, the stockholder must" (1) make a demand on the company's board of directors or (2) show that demand would be futile. The demand requirement is a substantive requirement that " '[e]nsure[s] that a stockholder exhausts his intracorporate remedies,' 'provide[s] a safeguard against strike suits,' and 'assure[s] that the stockholder affords the corporation the opportunity to address an alleged wrong without litigation and to control any litigation which does occur.' "

Court of Chancery Rule 23.1 implements the substantive demand requirement at the pleading stage by mandating that derivative complaints "allege with particularity the efforts, if any, made by the plaintiff to obtain the action the plaintiff desires from the directors or comparable authority and the reasons for the plaintiff's failure to obtain the action or for not making the effort." To comply with Rule 23.1, the plaintiff must meet "stringent requirements of factual particularity that differ substantially from . . . permissive notice pleadings." When considering a motion to dismiss a complaint for failing to comply with Rule 23.1, the Court does not weigh the evidence, must accept as true all of the complaint's particularized and well-pleaded allegations, and must draw all reasonable inferences in the plaintiff's favor.

The plaintiff in this action did not make a pre-suit demand. Thus, the question before the Court is whether demand is excused as futile. This Court has articulated two tests to determine whether the demand requirement should be excused as futile: the *Aronson* test and the *Rales* test. The *Aronson* test applies where the complaint challenges a decision made by the same board that would consider a litigation demand. Under *Aronson*, demand is excused as futile if the complaint alleges particularized facts that raise a reasonable doubt that "(1) the directors are disinterested and independent[,] [or] (2) the challenged transaction was otherwise the product of a valid business judgment." This reflects the "rule . . . that where officers and directors are under an influence which sterilizes their discretion, they cannot be considered proper persons to conduct litigation on behalf of the corporation. Thus, demand would be futile."

The *Rales* test applies in all other circumstances. Under *Rales*, demand is excused as futile if the complaint alleges particularized facts creating a "reasonable doubt that, as of the time the complaint is filed," a majority of the demand board "could have properly exercised its independent and disinterested business judgment in responding to a demand." "Fundamentally, *Aronson* and *Rales* both 'address the same question of whether the board can exercise its business judgment on the corporat[ion]'s behalf' in considering demand." For this reason, the Court of Chancery has recognized that the broader reasoning of *Rales* encompasses *Aronson*, and therefore the *Aronson* test is best understood as a special application of the *Rales* test.

While Delaware law recognizes that there are circumstances where making a demand would be futile because a majority of the directors "are under an influence which sterilizes their discretion" and "cannot be considered proper persons to conduct litigation on behalf of the corporation," the demand requirement is not excused lightly because derivative litigation upsets the balance of power that the DGCL establishes between a corporation's directors and its stockholders. Thus, the demand-futility analysis provides an important doctrinal check that ensures the board is not improperly deprived of its decision-making authority, while at the same time leaving a path for stockholders to file a derivative action where there is reason to doubt that the board could bring its impartial business judgment to bear on a litigation demand.

In this case, Tri-State alleged that demand was excused as futile for several reasons, including that the board's negotiation and approval of the Reclassification would not be "protected by the business judgment rule" because "[t]heir approval was not fully informed" or "duly considered," and that a majority of the directors on the Demand Board lacked independence from Zuckerberg. The Court of Chancery held that Tri-State failed to plead with particularity facts establishing that demand was futile and dismissed the complaint because it did not comply with Court of Chancery Rule 23.1.

On appeal, Tri-State raises two issues with the Court of Chancery's demand-futility analysis. First, Tri-State argues that the Court of Chancery erred by holding that exculpated care violations do not satisfy the second prong of the *Aronson* test. Second, Tri-State argues that its complaint contained particularized allegations establishing that a majority of the directors on the Demand Board were beholden to Zuckerberg.

For the reasons provided below, this Court affirms the Court of Chancery's judgment.

A. Exculpated Care Violations Do Not Satisfy *Aronson*'s Second Prong

Tri-State alleges that the Director Defendants breached their duty of care in negotiating and approving the Reclassification.

Facebook's charter contains a Section 102(b)(7) clause; as such, the Director Defendants face no risk of personal liability from the allegations asserted in this action. Thus, Tri-State's demand-futility allegations raise the question whether a derivative plaintiff can rely on exculpated care violations to establish that demand is futile under the second prong of the *Aronson* test. The Court of Chancery held that exculpated care claims do not excuse demand because the second prong of the *Aronson* test focuses on whether a director faces a substantial likelihood of liability. Tri-State argues that this analysis was wrong because *Aronson*'s second prong focuses on whether the challenged transaction "satisfies the applicable standard of review," not on whether directors face a substantial likelihood of liability.

The following discussion is divided into three parts. The first part affirms the Court of Chancery's holding that, in light of subsequent developments, exculpated care claims do not excuse demand under *Aronson*'s second prong. The second part explains why Tri-State's counterarguments do not change our analysis [*omitted in this excerpt*]. The third part adopts the Court of Chancery's three-part test as the universal test for demand futility

The second prong of *Aronson* focuses on whether the directors face a substantial likelihood of liability

The main question on appeal is whether allegations of exculpated care violations can establish that demand is excused under *Aronson*'s second prong. According to Tri-State, the second prong excuses demand whenever the complaint raises a reasonable doubt that the challenged transaction was a valid exercise of business judgment, regardless of whether the directors face a substantial likelihood of liability for approving the challenged transaction. Thus, exculpated care violations can establish that demand is futile.

Tri-State's argument hinges on the plain language of *Aronson*'s second prong, which focuses on whether "the challenged transaction was . . . the product of a valid business judgment". . . Later opinions issued by this Court contain similar language that can be read to suggest that *Aronson*'s second prong focuses on the propriety of the challenged transaction. These passages do not address, however, why *Aronson* used the standard of review as a proxy for whether the board could impartially consider a litigation demand. The likely answer is that, before the General Assembly adopted Section 102(b)(7) in 1995, rebutting the business judgment rule through allegations of care violations exposed directors to a substantial likelihood of liability.

Thus, even if the demand board was independent and disinterested with respect to the challenged transaction, the litigation presented a threat that would "sterilize [the board's] discretion" with respect to a demand.

Aronson supports this conclusion. For example, in *Aronson* the Court noted that, although naming directors as defendants is not enough to establish that demand would be futile, "in rare cases a transaction may be so egregious on its face that board approval cannot meet the test of business judgment, and a substantial likelihood of liability therefore exists. . . . [I]n that context demand is excused." This passage helps to illuminate the connection that the Court drew between rebutting the business judgment rule and the board's ability to consider a litigation demand. At that time, if the business judgment rule did not apply, allowing the derivative litigation to go forward would expose the directors to a substantial likelihood of liability for breach-of-care claims supported by well-pleaded factual allegations. It is reasonable to doubt that a director would be willing to take that personal risk. Thus, demand is excused.

On the other hand, if the business judgment rule would apply, allowing the derivative litigation to go forward would expose the directors to a minimal threat of liability. A remote threat of liability is not a good enough reason to deprive the board of control over the corporation's litigation assets. Thus, demand is required.

Accordingly, this Court affirms the Court of Chancery's holding that exculpated care claims do not satisfy *Aronson*'s second prong. This Court's decisions construing *Aronson* have consistently focused on whether the demand board has a connection to the challenged transaction that would render it incapable of impartially considering a litigation demand. When *Aronson* was decided, raising a reasonable doubt that directors breached their duty of care exposed them to a substantial likelihood of liability and protracted litigation, raising doubt as to their ability to impartially consider demand. The ground has since shifted, and exculpated breach of care claims no longer pose a threat that neutralizes director discretion. These developments must be factored into demand-futility analysis, and Tri-State has failed to provide a reasoned explanation of why rebutting the business judgment rule should automatically render directors incapable of impartially considering a litigation demand given the current landscape. For these reasons, the Court of Chancery's judgment is affirmed

This Court adopts the Court of Chancery's three-part test for demand futility

This issue raises one more question—whether the three-part test for demand futility the Court of Chancery applied below is consistent with *Aronson*, *Rales*, and their progeny. The Court of Chancery noted that turnover on Facebook's board, along with a director's decision to abstain from voting on the Reclassification, made it difficult to apply the *Aronson* test to the facts of this case.

To address these concerns, the Court of Chancery applied [a] three-part test on a director-by-director basis to determine whether demand should be excused as futile. . . This approach treated "*Rales* as the general demand futility test," while "draw[ing] upon *Aronson*-like principles when evaluating whether particular directors face a substantial likelihood of liability as a result of having participated in the decision to approve the Reclassification."

This Court adopts the Court of Chancery's three-part test as the universal test for assessing whether demand should be excused as futile. When the Court decided *Aronson*, it made sense to use the standard of review to assess whether directors were subject to an influence that would sterilize their discretion with respect to a litigation demand. Subsequent changes in the law have eroded the ground upon which that framework rested. Those changes cannot be ignored, and it is both appropriate and necessary that the common law evolve in an orderly fashion to incorporate those developments. The Court of Chancery's three-part test achieves that important goal. Blending the *Aronson* test with the *Rales* test is appropriate because "both 'address the same question of whether the board can exercise its business judgment on the corporat[ion]'s behalf' in considering demand"; and the refined test does not change the result of demand-futility analysis.

Further, the refined test "refocuses the inquiry on the decision regarding the litigation demand, rather than the decision being challenged." Notwithstanding text focusing on the propriety of the challenged transaction, this approach is consistent with the overarching concern that *Aronson* identified: whether the directors on the demand board "cannot be considered proper persons to conduct litigation on behalf of the corporation" because they "are under an influence which sterilizes their discretion." The purpose of the demand-futility analysis is to assess whether the board should be deprived of its decision-making authority because there is reason to doubt that the directors would be able to bring their impartial business judgment to bear on a litigation demand. That is a different consideration than whether the derivative claim is strong or weak because the challenged transaction is likely to pass or fail the applicable standard of review. It is helpful to keep those inquiries separate. And the Court of Chancery's three-part test is particularly helpful where, like here, board turnover and director abstention make it difficult to apply the *Aronson* test as written.

Finally, because the three-part test is consistent with and enhances *Aronson*, *Rales*, and their progeny, the Court need not overrule *Aronson* to adopt this refined test, and cases properly construing *Aronson*, *Rales*, and their progeny remain good law.

Accordingly, from this point forward, courts should ask the following three questions on a director-by-director basis when evaluating allegations of demand futility:

(i) whether the director received a material personal benefit from the alleged misconduct that is the subject of the litigation demand;

(ii) whether the director faces a substantial likelihood of liability on any of the claims that would be the subject of the litigation demand; and

(iii) whether the director lacks independence from someone who received a material personal benefit from the alleged misconduct that would be the subject of the litigation demand or who would face a substantial likelihood of liability on any of the claims that are the subject of the litigation demand.

If the answer to any of the questions is "yes" for at least half of the members of the demand board, then demand is excused as futile. It is no longer necessary to determine whether the *Aronson* test or the *Rales* test governs a complaint's demand-futility allegations.

B. The Complaint Does Not Plead with Particularity Facts Establishing that Demand Would Be Futile

The second issue on appeal is whether Tri-State's complaint pleaded with particularity facts establishing that a litigation demand on Facebook's board would be futile. The Court resolves this issue by applying the three-part test adopted above on a director-by-director basis.

The Demand Board was composed of nine directors. Tri-State concedes on appeal that two of those directors, Chenault and Zients, could have impartially considered a litigation demand. And Facebook does not argue on appeal that Zuckerberg, Sandberg, or Andreessen could have impartially considered a litigation demand. Thus, in order to show that demand is futile, Tri-State must sufficiently allege that two of the following directors could not impartially consider demand: Thiel, Hastings, Bowles, and Desmond-Hellmann.

Tri-State concedes on appeal that neither Thiel, Hastings, Bowles, nor Desmond-Hellmann had a personal interest in the Reclassification. This eliminates the possibility that demand could be excused under the first prong of the demand-futility test, as none of the remaining four directors obtained a material personal benefit from the alleged misconduct that is the subject of the litigation demand.

Similarly, there is no dispute that Facebook has a broad Section 102(b)(7) provision; and Tri-State concedes on appeal that the complaint does not plead with particularity that Thiel, Hastings, Bowles, or Desmond-Hellmann committed a *non-exculpated* breach of their fiduciary duties with respect to the Reclassification. This eliminates the possibility that demand could be excused under the second prong of the demand-futility test, as none of the remaining four directors would face a substantial likelihood of liability on any of the claims that would be the subject of the litigation demand.

This leaves one unanswered question: whether the complaint pleaded with particularity facts establishing that two of the four remaining directors lacked independence from Zuckerberg.

"The primary basis upon which a director's independence must be measured is whether the director's decision is based on the corporate merits of the subject before

the board, rather than extraneous considerations or influences." Whether a
director is independent "is a fact-specific
determination" that depends upon "the
context of a particular case." To show a
lack of independence, a derivative complaint must plead with particularity facts
creating "a reasonable doubt that a director is . . . so 'beholden' to an interested
director . . . that his or her 'discretion
would be sterilized.' "

> Independence analysis under Del-
> aware law is distinct from stock
> exchange rules, which take a more
> bright-line approach. While Delaware
> courts have noted that independence
> under stock exchange rules is a factor
> they consider, the analysis under Del-
> aware law is highly fact specific, nu-
> anced, and holistic.

"A plaintiff seeking to show that a director was not independent must satisfy a
materiality standard." The plaintiff must allege that "the director in question had ties
to the person whose proposal or actions he or she is evaluating that are sufficiently
substantial that he or she could not objectively discharge his or her fiduciary duties."
In other words, the question is "whether, applying a subjective standard, those ties
were *material*, in the sense that the alleged ties could have affected the impartiality
of the individual director." "Our law requires that all the pled facts regarding a
director's relationship to the interested party be considered in full context in making
the, admittedly imprecise, pleading stage determination of independence." And while
"the plaintiff is bound to plead particularized facts in . . . a derivative complaint, so
too is the court bound to draw all inferences from those particularized facts in favor
of the plaintiff, not the defendant, when dismissal of a derivative complaint is sought."

"A variety of motivations, including friendship, may influence the demand futility inquiry. But, to render a director unable to consider demand, a relationship must be
of a bias-producing nature." Alleging that a director had a "personal friendship" with
someone else, or that a director had an "outside business relationship," are "insufficient
to raise a reasonable doubt" that the director lacked independence. "Consistent with
[the] predicate materiality requirement, the existence of some financial ties between
the interested party and the director, without more, is not disqualifying."

Like the Court of Chancery below, we hold that Tri-State failed to raise a
reasonable doubt that either Thiel, Hastings, or Bowles was beholden to Zuckerberg.

1. Hastings

The complaint does not raise a reasonable doubt that Hastings lacked independence from Zuckerberg. According to the complaint, Hastings was not independent
because:

- "Netflix purchased advertisements from Facebook at relevant times,"
  and maintains "ongoing and potential future business relationships
  with" Facebook.

- According to an article published by *The New York Times*, Facebook gave to Netflix and several other technology companies "more intrusive access to users' personal data than it ha[d] disclosed, effectively exempting those partners from privacy rules."

- "Hastings (as a Netflix founder) is biased in favor of founders maintaining control of their companies."

- "Hastings has . . . publicly supported large philanthropic donations by founders during their lifetimes. Indeed, both Hastings and Zuckerberg have been significant contributors . . . [to] a well-known foundation known for soliciting and obtaining large contributions from company founders and which manages donor funds for both Hastings . . . and Zuckerberg . . . ."

These allegations do not raise a reasonable doubt that Hastings was beholden to Zuckerberg. Even if Netflix purchased advertisements from Facebook, the complaint does not allege that those purchases were material to Netflix or that Netflix received anything other than arm's length terms under those agreements. Similarly, the complaint does not make any particularized allegations explaining how obtaining special access to Facebook user data was material to Netflix's business interests, or that Netflix used its special access to user data to obtain any concrete benefits in its own business.

Further, having a bias in favor of founder-control does not mean that Hastings lacks independence from Zuckerberg. Hastings might have a good-faith belief that founder control maximizes a corporation's value over the long-haul. If so, that good-faith belief would play a valid role in Hasting's exercise of his impartial business judgment.

Finally, alleging that Hastings and Zuckerberg have a track record of donating to similar causes falls short of showing that Hastings is beholden to Zuckerberg. As the Court of Chancery noted below, "[t]here is no logical reason to think that a shared interest in philanthropy would undercut Hastings' independence. Nor is it apparent how donating to the same charitable fund would result in Hastings feeling obligated to serve Zuckerberg's interests." Accordingly, the Court affirms the Court of Chancery's holding that the complaint does not raise a reasonable doubt about Hastings's independence.

2. Thiel

The complaint does not raise a reasonable doubt that Thiel lacked independence from Zuckerberg. According to the complaint, Thiel was not independent because:

- "Thiel was one of the early investors in Facebook," is "its longest-tenured board member besides Zuckerberg," and "has . . . been instrumental to Facebook's business strategy and direction over the years."

- "Thiel has a personal bias in favor of keeping founders in control of the companies they created . . . ."

- The venture capital firm at which Thiel is a partner, Founders Fund, "gets 'good deal flow' " from its "high-profile association with Facebook."

- "According to Facebook's 2018 Proxy Statement, the Facebook shares owned by the Founders Fund (*i.e.*, by Thiel and Andreessen) will be released from escrow in connection with" an acquisition.

- "Thiel is Zuckerberg's close friend and mentor."

- In October 2016, Thiel made a $1 million donation to an "organization that paid [a substantial sum to] Cambridge Analytica" and "cofounded the Cambridge Analytica-linked data firm Palantir." Even though "[t]he Cambridge Analytica scandal has exposed Facebook to regulatory investigations" and litigation, Zuckerberg did not try to remove Thiel from the board.

- Similarly, Thiel's "acknowledge[ment] that he secretly funded various lawsuits aimed at bankrupting [the] news website Gawker Media" lead to "widespread calls for Zuckerberg to remove Thiel from Facebook's Board given Thiel's apparent antagonism toward a free press." Zuckerberg ignored those calls and did not seek to remove Thiel from Facebook's board.

These allegations do not raise a reasonable doubt that Thiel is beholden to Zuckerberg. The complaint does not explain why Thiel's status as a long-serving board member, early investor, or his contributions to Facebook's business strategy make him beholden to Zuckerberg. And for the same reasons provided above, a director's good faith belief that founder controller maximizes value does not raise a reasonable doubt that the director lacks independence from a corporation's founder.

While the complaint alleges that Founders Fund "gets 'good deal flow' " from Thiel's "high-profile association with Facebook," the complaint does not identify a single deal that flowed to—or is expected to flow to—Founders Fund through this association, let alone any deals that would be material to Thiel's interests. The complaint also fails to draw any connection between Thiel's continued status as a director and the vesting of Facebook stock related to the acquisition. And alleging that Thiel is a personal friend of Zuckerberg is insufficient to establish a lack of independence.

The final pair of allegations suggest that because "Zuckerberg stood by Thiel" in the face of public scandals, "Thiel feels a sense of obligation to Zuckerberg." These allegations can only raise a reasonable doubt about Thiel's independence if remaining a Facebook director was financially or personally material to Thiel. As the Court of Chancery noted below, given Thiel's wealth and stature, "[t]he complaint does not support an inference that Thiel's service on the Board is financially material to him. Nor does the complaint sufficiently allege that serving as a Facebook director confers such cachet that Thiel's independence is compromised." Accordingly, this Court affirms the Court of Chancery's holding that the complaint does not raise a reasonable doubt about Thiel's independence.

3. Bowles

The complaint does not raise a reasonable doubt that Bowles lacked independence from Zuckerberg. According to the complaint, Thiel was not independent because:

- "Bowles is beholden to the entire board" because it granted "a waiver of the mandatory retirement age for directors set forth in Facebook's Corporate Governance Guidelines," allowing "Bowles to stand for reelection despite having reached 70 years old before" the May 2018 annual meeting.

- "Morgan Stanley—a company for which [Bowles] . . . served as a longstanding board member at the time (2005–2017)—directly benefited by receiving over $2 million in fees for its work . . . in connection with the Reclassification . . . ."

- Bowles "ensured that Evercore and his close friend Altman financially benefitted from the Special Committee's engagement" without properly vetting Evercore's competency or considering alternatives.

These allegations do not raise a reasonable doubt that Bowles is beholden to Zuckerberg or the other members of the Demand Board. The complaint does not make any particularized allegation explaining why the board's decision to grant Bowles a waiver from the mandatory retirement age would compromise his ability to impartially consider a litigation demand or engender a sense of debt to the other directors. For example, the complaint does not allege that Bowles was expected to do anything in exchange for the waiver, or that remaining a director was financially or personally material to Bowles.

The complaint's allegations regarding Bowles's links to financial advisors are similarly ill-supported. None of these allegations suggest that Bowles received a personal benefit from the Reclassification, or that Bowles's ties to these advisors made him beholden to Zuckerberg as a condition of sending business to Morgan Stanley, Evercore, or his "close friend Altman." Accordingly, this Court affirms the Court of Chancery's holding that the complaint does not raise a reasonable doubt about Bowles's independence.

IV. CONCLUSION

For the reasons provided above, the Court of Chancery's judgment is affirmed.

Points for Discussion

1. How high is the bar?

As we have seen, a plaintiff must demonstrate demand futility by setting forth "particularized facts," rather than "conclusory allegations." Does this requirement put plaintiffs in a Catch-22? Without discovery, a plaintiff may not be able to learn the facts necessary to establish demand futility. Yet without those facts, a plaintiff will not be entitled to engage in discovery. How difficult do you think it would be for a plaintiff to satisfy the demand futility test?

2. Why a special test for demand futility?

The Court in *Zuckerberg* explained that the demand requirement reflects the "cardinal precept" of DGCL § 141(a) that the board of directors shall manage or oversee the management of the corporation. Yet the court does not automatically apply the business judgment rule to derivative suits. Why not? How do directors' decisions about litigation differ from other decisions? Is it just the threat of personal liability? Are courts more qualified to evaluate directors' ability to make decisions about potential corporate litigation than about other commercial or financial issues?

3. Director's wealth and stature?

As in *Zuckerberg*, Delaware courts usually go "director by director" in examining independence, and it is a highly fact-specific determination about each individual director. Should a director's personal wealth or professional stature be relevant to this analysis? What did you think of the Court's consideration of Thiel's "wealth and stature" regarding claims about becoming beholden to Zuckerberg by being a long-serving Facebook board member or having access to deal flow from such "high-profile association with Facebook"? Are there public policy concerns at play when wealth is used as a factor in analyzing independence?

4. The MBCA approach: universal demand.

The MBCA does away with the demand excused/required distinction. To avoid two separate litigation phases (first to determine whether demand was required and then to decide the substance of the plaintiff's claim), the MBCA requires demand on the board in all derivative suits. After making the demand, the claimant-shareholder must then wait 90 days for the board to take corrective action, unless the board rejects the demand earlier or the corporation would suffer irreparable injury by waiting. MBCA § 7.42. Once the 90 days have expired, the shareholder may then bring a derivative claim in court. If the board has rejected the demand, the shareholder must plead with particularity that the board's rejection was flawed because it was either not informed, not disinterested, or not in good faith.

Even if the demand is not rejected, the board under the MBCA continues to have a voice after the derivative suit is filed. For example, the board can move for dismissal of the suit based on a showing that a majority of independent directors determined in good faith and after a "reasonable inquiry" that maintaining the suit is not in the corporation's best interests. MBCA § 7.44. As we'll see next, director "independence" under the MBCA has been interpreted much the same way as in Delaware. *See Einhorn v. Culea* below.

---

2. Special Litigation Committees

In response to a derivative action, a corporation often will form a "Special Litigation Committee," or SLC. The central premise of an SLC is that it will be independent: its members typically are independent directors, who are not defendants in the derivative action, and the SLC typically hires independent lawyers and advisors. The SLC investigates the claims in the complaint, and then acts for the corporation to recommend to the court whether to allow the litigation to proceed. SLCs frequently recommend against the litigation proceeding and move to dismiss.

Early cases held that the business judgment rule precluded judicial review of the substance of a recommendation by an SLC that a derivative suit be dismissed. More recent cases have scrutinized SLC recommendations more closely. One of the primary concerns about SLCs is the degree to which their members might be influenced by other non-SLC directors, including the defendants in the derivative action. The judicial focus on SLCs is often on the independence or interest of individual directors. Many cases address "structural bias," the notion that even members of independent committees can be subject to the influence of other directors.

Ultimately, two different approaches emerged, reflected in two leading SLC cases that we summarize here. *Auerbach* applies a business judgment rule-style analysis to SLCs and defers to their judgment. *Zapata* scrutinizes the SLC more carefully.

BJR deference. *Auerbach v. Bennett*, 393 N.E.2d 994 (N.Y. 1979), a leading early SLC decision, involved a derivative suit filed by shareholders of General Telephone and Electronics Corporation (GTE) to recover from the responsible GTE officials more than $11 million in bribes and kickbacks that GTE, in an SEC filing, acknowledged it had paid. An SLC, comprised of three directors who had joined the GTE board after the incidents in question, was appointed to consider the shareholders' claim. The SLC conducted an investigation and concluded that none of the defendants had breached his duty of care or profited personally from the challenged payments and that it was not in GTE's best interest for the suit to proceed. (Had the suit proceeded to trial, GTE no doubt would have been forced to disclose publicly the identities of those to whom it had paid bribes and kickbacks—information that it had not disclosed in its

SEC filing.) Based on the findings of the SLC, the corporation then filed, and the trial court granted, a motion for summary judgment dismissing the shareholders' claim.

On appeal, the court held that the business judgment rule would not foreclose inquiry into either the disinterestedness and independence of the members of the SLC or the adequacy and appropriateness of the SLC's investigative procedures and methodologies. However, plaintiffs had not called either of these matters into question. As to plaintiffs' request that the court review the merits of the SLC's "ultimate substantive decision" that it was not in GTE's interests to pursue the claims advanced, the New York Court of Appeals took the position that such an inquiry would be inappropriate:

> [The committee's substantive decision] falls squarely within the embrace of the business judgment doctrine, involving as it did the weighing and balancing of legal, ethical, commercial, promotional, public relations, fiscal and other factors familiar to the resolution of many if not most corporate problems. To this extent the conclusion reached by the special litigation committee is outside the scope of our review. Thus, the courts cannot inquire as to which factors were considered by that committee or the relative weight accorded them in reaching that substantive decision. Inquiry into such matters would go to the very core of the business judgment made by the committee. To permit judicial probing of such issues would be to emasculate the business judgment doctrine as applied to actions and determinations of the special litigation committee.

Two-tiered judicial scrutiny. In contrast, *Zapata Corp. v. Maldonado*, 430 A.2d 779 (Del. 1981), rejected *Auerbach*'s deferential approach. The court concluded that empathy can make directors appointed to an SLC reluctant to support the continuance of claims against their fellow board members. In *Zapata*, the plaintiff alleged that certain actions constituted a breach of fiduciary duty and that demand was excused because a majority of the directors had benefited from the challenged decision. The corporation did not contest plaintiff's claim of demand futility. Instead, it created an "Independent Investigation Committee of Zapata Corporation," composed of two new directors. This Committee retained counsel, filed a report recommending that the suit be dismissed, and caused Zapata to move to have the suit dismissed. The Delaware Chancery Court denied Zapata's motion. The Delaware Supreme Court agreed, and proposed a two-part test for assessing an SLC's decision to dismiss a derivative suit:

> After an objective and thorough investigation of a derivative suit, an independent committee may cause its corporation to file a pretrial motion to dismiss in the Court of Chancery. The basis of the motion is the best interests of the corporation, as determined by the committee. The Court should apply a two-step test to the motion.

First, the Court should inquire into the independence and good faith of the committee and the bases supporting its conclusions. Limited discovery may be ordered to facilitate such inquiries. The corporation should have the burden of proving independence, good faith and a reasonable investigation, rather than presuming independence, good faith and reasonableness. If the Court determines either that the committee is not independent or has not shown reasonable bases for its conclusions, or, if the Court is not satisfied for other reasons relating to the process, including but not limited to the good faith of the committee, the Court shall deny the corporation's motion. If, however, the Court is satisfied that the committee was independent and showed reasonable bases for good faith findings and recommendations, the Court may proceed, in its discretion, to the next step.

The second step provides, we believe, the essential key in striking the balance between legitimate corporate claims as expressed in a derivative stockholder suit and a corporation's best interests as expressed by an independent investigating committee. The Court should determine, applying its own independent business judgment, whether the motion should be granted.[18] This means, of course, that instances could arise where a committee can establish its independence and sound bases for its good faith decisions and still have the corporation's motion denied. The second step is intended to thwart instances where corporate actions meet the criteria of step one, but the result does not appear to satisfy its spirit, or where corporate actions would simply prematurely terminate a stockholder grievance deserving of further consideration in the corporation's interest. The Court of Chancery of course must carefully consider and weigh how compelling the corporate interest in dismissal is when faced with a non-frivolous lawsuit. The Court of Chancery should, when appropriate, give special consideration to matters of law and public policy in addition to the corporation's best interests.

Other courts have expressed concerns similar to those expressed in *Zapata*, primarily because of "structural bias" concerns that SLC members might be influenced by other directors, including defendants in the relevant derivative action.

The following cases illustrate the way courts approach the question whether SLC members are "independent."

---

[18] This step shares some of the same spirit and philosophy of the statement by the Vice Chancellor: "Under our system of law, courts and not litigants should decide the merits of litigation."

Einhorn v. Culea

<u>612 N.W.2d 78 (Wis. 2000)</u>

ABRAHAMSON, CHIEF JUSTICE.

Under Wis. Stat. § 180.0744, the corporation may create a special litigation committee consisting of two or more independent directors appointed by a majority vote of independent directors present at a meeting of the board of directors. The independent special litigation committee determines whether the derivative action is in the best interests of the corporation. If the independent special litigation committee acts in good faith, conducts a reasonable inquiry upon which it bases its conclusions and concludes that the maintenance of the derivative action is not in the best interests of the corporation, the circuit court shall dismiss the derivative action. The statute thus requires the circuit court to defer to the business judgment of a properly composed and properly operating special litigation committee.

Given the finality of the ultimate decision of the committee to dismiss the action, judicial oversight is necessary to ensure that the special litigation committee is independent so that it acts in the corporation's best interest. At issue is whether the special litigation committee created in the present case under Wis. Stat. § 180.0744 was composed of independent directors as required by statute.

Although the plain language of Wis. Stat. § 180.0744 requires the directors who are members of the special litigation committee to be independent, the statute does not define the word "independent." Rather, § 180.0744(3) merely instructs that whether a director on the committee is independent should not be determined solely on the basis of any of the following three factors set forth in the statute: (1) whether the director is nominated to the special litigation committee or elected by persons who are defendants in the derivative action, (2) whether the director is a defendant in the action, or (3) whether the act being challenged in the derivative action was approved by the director if the act resulted in no personal benefit to the director.

The legislature allows the circuit court to give weight to these factors; but the presence of one or more of these factors is not solely determinative of the issue of whether a director is independent. The legislature recognized, for example, that a shareholder could prevent the entire board of directors from serving on the special litigation committee merely by naming all the directors as defendants in the derivative action.

We now discuss the appropriate test to be applied to determine whether directors who are members of a special litigation committee are independent under Wis. Stat. § 180.0744. This question is one of first impression in Wisconsin. Nothing in the statute expressly states the factors to be examined to determine whether directors who are members of a committee are independent.

The Model Business Corporation Act (upon which Wis. Stat. § 180.0744 is based) builds on the law relating to special litigation committees developed by a number of states. We are therefore informed by the case law of other states, and we derive from this case law the following test to determine whether a member of a special litigation committee is independent.

Whether members are independent is tested on an objective basis as of the time they are appointed to the special litigation committee. Considering the totality of the circumstances, a court shall determine whether a reasonable person in the position of a member of a special litigation committee can base his or her decision on the merits of the issue rather than on extraneous considerations or influences. In other words, the test is whether a member of a committee has a relationship with an individual defendant or the corporation that would reasonably be expected to affect the member's judgment with respect to the litigation in issue. The factors a court should examine to determine whether a committee member is independent include, but are not limited to, the following:

(1) A committee member's status as a defendant and potential liability. Optimally members of a special litigation committee should not be defendants in the derivative action and should not be exposed to personal liability as a result of the action.

(2) *A committee member's participation in or approval of the alleged wrong-doing or financial benefits from the challenged transaction.* Optimally members of a special litigation committee should not have been members of the board of directors when the transaction in question occurred or was approved. Nor should they have participated in the transaction or events underlying the derivative action. Innocent or pro forma involvement does not necessarily render a member not independent, but substantial participation or approval or personal financial benefit should.

(3) *A committee member's past or present business or economic dealings with an individual defendant.* Evidence of a committee member's employment and financial relations with an individual defendant should be considered in determining whether the member is independent.

(4) *A committee member's past or present personal, family, or social relations with individual defendants.* Evidence of a committee member's non-financial relations with an individual defendant should be considered in determining whether the member is independent. A determination of whether a member is independent is affected by the extent to which a member is directly or indirectly dominated by, controlled by or beholden to an individual defendant.

(5) *A committee member's past or present business or economic relations with the corporation.* For example, if a member of the special litigation com-

mittee was outside counsel or a consultant to the corporation, this factor should be considered in determining whether the member is independent.

(6) *The number of members on a special litigation committee.* The more members on a special litigation committee, the less weight a circuit court may assign to a particular disabling interest affecting a single member of the committee.

(7) *The roles of corporate counsel and independent counsel.* Courts should be more likely to find a special litigation committee independent if the committee retains counsel who has not represented individual defendants or the corporation in the past.

Some courts and commentators have suggested that a "structural bias" exists in special litigation committees that taints their decisions. They argue that members of a committee, appointed by the directors of the corporation, are instinctively sympathetic and empathetic towards their colleagues on the board of directors and can be expected to vote for dismissal of any but the most egregious charges. They assert that the committees are inherently biased and untrustworthy. Wisconsin Stat. § 180.0744 and the Model Business Corporation Act are designed to combat this possibility.

A court should not presuppose that a special litigation committee is inherently biased. Although members of a special litigation committee may have experiences similar to those of the defendant directors and serve with them on the board of directors, the legislature has declared that independent members of a special litigation committee are capable of rendering an independent decision. The test we set forth today is designed, as is the statute, to overcome the effects of any "structural bias."

A circuit court is to look at the totality of the circumstances. A finding that a member of the special litigation committee is independent does not require the complete absence of any facts that might point to non-objectivity. A director may be independent even if he or she has had some personal or business relation with an individual director accused of wrongdoing.

It is vital for a circuit court to review whether each member of a special litigation committee is independent. The special litigation committee is, after all, the "only instance in American Jurisprudence where a defendant can free itself from a suit by merely appointing a committee to review the allegations of the complaint." We agree with the Delaware Court of Chancery that the trial court must be "certain that the SLC is truly independent." While ill suited to assessing business judgments, courts are well suited by experience to evaluate whether members of a special litigation committee are independent.

Delaware courts assess the independence of SLC members by ascertaining whether those directors are, "*for any substantial reason, incapable of making* [decisions] *with only the best interests of the corporation in mind.*" The following case, *In re Oracle Corp. Derivative Litigation*, illustrates the application of the *Zapata* test in the context of a board whose directors were embedded in overlapping professional and academic circles. There, plaintiff-shareholders filed a derivative action alleging that four of Oracle's directors had engaged in insider trading. Oracle's board assembled an SLC that included two new directors who had assumed their positions after the alleged insider trading occurred. When the SLC ultimately recommended dismissal of the action, plaintiffs argued that the committee's two board members were not sufficiently independent.

In re Oracle Corp. Derivative Litigation

824 A.2d 917 (Del. Ch. 2003)

STRINE, VICE CHANCELLOR.

In this opinion, I address the motion of the special litigation committee ("SLC") of Oracle Corporation to terminate this action, "the Delaware Derivative Action," and other such actions pending in the name of Oracle against certain Oracle directors and officers. These actions allege that these Oracle directors engaged in insider trading while in possession of material, non-public information showing that Oracle would not meet the earnings guidance it gave to the market for the third quarter of Oracle's fiscal year 2001. The SLC bears the burden of persuasion on this motion and must convince me that there is no material issue of fact calling into doubt its independence. This requirement is set forth in *Zapata Corp. v. Maldonado* and its progeny.

The question of independence "turns on whether a director is, *for any substantial reason,* incapable of making a decision with only the best interests of the corporation in mind." That is, the independence test ultimately "focus[es] on impartiality and objectivity." In this case, the SLC has failed to demonstrate that no material factual question exists regarding its independence.

During discovery, it emerged that the two SLC members—both of whom are professors at Stanford University—are being asked to investigate fellow Oracle directors who have important ties to Stanford, too. Among the directors who are accused by the derivative plaintiffs of insider trading are: (1) another Stanford professor, who taught one of the SLC members when the SLC member was a Ph.D. candidate and who serves as a senior fellow and a steering committee member alongside that SLC member at the Stanford Institute for Economic Policy Research or "SIEPR"; (2) a Stanford alumnus who has directed millions of dollars of contributions to Stanford during recent years, serves as Chair of SIEPR's Advisory Board and has a conference center named for him at SIEPR's facility, and has contributed nearly $600,000 to SIEPR and the Stanford Law School, both parts of Stanford with which one of the

SLC members is closely affiliated; and (3) Oracle's CEO, who has made millions of dollars in donations to Stanford through a personal foundation and large donations indirectly through Oracle, and who was considering making donations of his $100 million house and $170 million for a scholarship program as late as August 2001, at around the same time period the SLC members were added to the Oracle board. Taken together, these and other facts cause me to harbor a reasonable doubt about the impartiality of the SLC.

It is no easy task to decide whether to accuse a fellow director of insider trading. For Oracle to compound that difficulty by requiring SLC members to consider accusing a fellow professor and two large benefactors of their university of conduct that is rightly considered a violation of criminal law was unnecessary and inconsistent with the concept of independence recognized by our law. The possibility that these extraneous considerations biased the inquiry of the SLC is too substantial for this court to ignore. I therefore deny the SLC's motion to terminate.

Factual Background

The Delaware Derivative Complaint centers on alleged insider trading by four members of Oracle's board of directors-Lawrence Ellison, Jeffrey Henley, Donald Lucas, and Michael Boskin (collectively, the "Trading Defendants"). Each of the Trading Defendants had a very different role at Oracle.

Ellison is Oracle's Chairman, Chief Executive Officer, and its largest stockholder, owning nearly twenty-five percent of Oracle's voting shares. By virtue of his ownership position, Ellison is one of the wealthiest men in America. By virtue of his managerial position, Ellison has regular access to a great deal of information about how Oracle is performing on a week-to-week basis.

Henley is Oracle's Chief Financial Officer, Executive Vice President, and a director of the corporation. Like Ellison, Henley has his finger on the pulse of Oracle's performance constantly.

Lucas is a director who chairs Oracle's Executive Committee and its Finance and Audit Committee. Although the plaintiffs allege that Lucas's positions gave him access to material, non-public information about the company, they do so cursorily. On the present record, it appears that Lucas did not receive copies of week-to-week projections or reports of actual results for the quarter to date. Rather, his committees primarily received historical financial data.

Boskin is a director, Chairman of the Compensation Committee, and a member of the Finance and Audit Committee. As with Lucas, Boskin's access to information was limited mostly to historical financials and did not include the week-to-week internal projections and revenue results that Ellison and Henley received.

On February 1, 2002, Oracle formed the SLC in order to investigate the Delaware Derivative Action and to determine whether Oracle should press the claims raised by the plaintiffs, settle the case, or terminate it.

Two Oracle board members were named to the SLC. Both of them joined the Oracle board on October 15, 2001, more than a half a year after Oracle's 3Q FY 2001 closed. The SLC members also share something else: both are tenured professors at Stanford University. . . . Professor Hector Garcia-Molina is Chairman of the Computer Science Department at Stanford . . . The other SLC member, Professor Joseph Grundfest, is the W.A. Franke Professor of Law and Business at Stanford University. . . .

The SLC's investigation was, by any objective measure, extensive. The SLC reviewed an enormous amount of paper and electronic records. SLC counsel interviewed seventy witnesses, some of them twice. SLC members participated in several key interviews, including the interviews of the Trading Defendants. . .

During the course of the investigation, the SLC met with its counsel thirty-five times for a total of eighty hours. In addition to that, the SLC members, particularly Professor Grundfest, devoted many more hours to the investigation.

In the end, the SLC produced an extremely lengthy Report totaling 1,110 pages (excluding appendices and exhibits) that concluded that Oracle should not pursue the plaintiffs' claims against the Trading Defendants or any of the other Oracle directors serving during the 3Q FY 2001. . . [T]he SLC concluded that even a hypothetical Oracle executive who possessed all information regarding the company's performance in December and January of 3Q FY 2001 would not have possessed material, non-public information that the company would fail to meet the earnings and revenue guidance it provided the market in December. Although there were hints of potential weakness in Oracle's revenue growth, especially starting in mid-January 2001, there was no reliable information indicating that the company would fall short of the mark, and certainly not to the extent that it eventually did. . . [T]aking into account all the relevant information sources, the SLC concluded that even Ellison and Henley—who were obviously the two Trading Defendants with the most access to inside information—did not possess material, non-public information. As to Lucas and Boskin, the SLC noted that they did not receive the weekly updates (of various kinds) that allegedly showed a weakening in Oracle's performance during 3Q FY 2001. As a result, there was even less of a basis to infer wrongdoing on their part. . .

Consistent with its Report, the SLC moved to terminate this litigation. The plaintiffs were granted discovery focusing on three primary topics: the independence of the SLC, the good faith of its investigative efforts, and the reasonableness of the bases for its conclusion that the lawsuit should be terminated. Additionally, the plaintiffs received a large volume of documents comprising the materials that the SLC relied upon in preparing its Report.

The Applicable Procedural Standard

In order to prevail on its motion to terminate the Delaware Derivative Action, the SLC must persuade me that: (1) its members were independent; (2) that they acted in good faith; and (3) that they had reasonable bases for their recommendations. If the SLC meets that burden, I am free to grant its motion or may, in my discretion, undertake my own examination of whether Oracle should terminate and permit the suit to proceed if I, in my oxymoronic judicial "business judgment," conclude that procession is in the best interests of the company. This two-step analysis comes, of course, from *Zapata*.

Is the SLC Independent? The Facts Disclosed in the Report

In its Report, the SLC took the position that its members were independent. In support of that position, the Report noted several factors including:

- the fact that neither Grundfest nor Garcia-Molina received compensation from Oracle other than as directors;

- the fact that neither Grundfest nor Garcia-Molina were on the Oracle board at the time of the alleged wrongdoing;

- the fact that both Grundfest and Garcia-Molina were willing to return their compensation as SLC members if necessary to preserve their status as independent;

- the absence of any other material ties between Oracle, the Trading Defendants, and any of the other defendants, on the one hand, and Grundfest and Garcia-Molina, on the other; and

- the absence of any material ties between Oracle, the Trading Defendants, and any of the other defendants, on the one hand, and the SLC's advisors, on the other.

Noticeably absent from the SLC Report was any disclosure of several significant ties between Oracle or the Trading Defendants and Stanford University, the university that employs both members of the SLC. In the Report, it was only disclosed that:

- defendant Boskin was a Stanford professor;

- the SLC members were aware that Lucas had made certain donations to Stanford; and

- among the contributions was a donation of $50,000 worth of stock that Lucas donated to Stanford Law School after Grundfest delivered a speech to a venture capital fund meeting in response to Lucas's request. It happens that Lucas's son is a partner in the fund and that approximately half the donation was allocated for use by Grundfest in his personal research.

The "Stanford" Facts that Emerged During Discovery

In view of the modesty of these disclosed ties, it was with some shock that a series of other ties among Stanford, Oracle, and the Trading Defendants emerged during discovery. Although the plaintiffs have embellished these ties considerably beyond what is reasonable, the plain facts are a striking departure from the picture presented in the Report. . . . [T]he question is whether the ties I am about to identify would be of a material concern to two distinguished, tenured faculty members whose current jobs would not be threatened by whatever good faith decision they made as SLC members.

Boskin

Defendant Michael J. Boskin is the T.M. Friedman Professor of Economics at Stanford University. . . . During the 1970s, Boskin taught Grundfest when Grundfest was a Ph.D. candidate. Although Boskin was not Grundfest's advisor and although they do not socialize, the two have remained in contact over the years, speaking occasionally about matters of public policy.

Furthermore, both Boskin and Grundfest are senior fellows and steering committee members at the Stanford Institute for Economic Policy Research, which was previously defined as "SIEPR." . . . . [B]oth Boskin and Grundfest publish working papers under the SIEPR rubric and that SIEPR helps to publicize their respective works.

Lucas

. . . Lucas's ties with Stanford are far, far richer than the SLC Report lets on. To begin, Lucas is a Stanford alumnus, having obtained both his undergraduate and graduate degrees there. By any measure, he has been a very loyal alumnus. [The court explained that Lucas donated $4.1 million to Stanford and served as chairman of a family foundation established by his brother who died of cancer and which donated $11.7 million to Stanford.] Lucas is not only a major contributor to SIEPR, he is the Chair of its Advisory Board. At SIEPR's facility at Stanford, the conference center is named the Donald L. Lucas Conference Center.

From these undisputed facts, it is inarguable that Lucas is a very important alumnus of Stanford and a generous contributor to not one, but two, parts of Stanford important to Grundfest: the Law School and SIEPR.

Ellison

There can be little doubt that Ellison is a major figure in the community in which Stanford is located. The so-called Silicon Valley has generated many success stories, among the greatest of which is that of Oracle and its leader, Ellison. One of the wealthiest men in America, Ellison is a major figure in the nation's increasingly important information technology industry. Given his wealth, Ellison is also in a position to make-and, in fact, he has made-major charitable contributions. . .

[including through the Ellison Medical Foundation, which pledged $10 million to Stanford, and through Oracle, which made over $300,000 in donations to Stanford. Oracle also established and endowed an educational foundation to help provide technology education to disadvantaged populations and gave Stanford the right to name four of the foundation's seven directors.]

Beginning in the year 2000 and continuing well into 2001—the same year that Ellison made the trades the plaintiffs contend were suspicious and the same year the SLC members were asked to join the Oracle board-Ellison and Stanford discussed a much more lucrative donation. The idea Stanford proposed for discussion was the creation of an Ellison Scholars Program modeled on the Rhodes Scholarship at Oxford. The proposed budget for Stanford's answer to Oxford: $170 million. The Ellison Scholars were to be drawn from around the world and were to come to Stanford to take a two-year interdisciplinary graduate program in economics, political science, and computer technology. During the summer between the two academic years, participants would work in internships at, among other companies, Oracle.

The omnipresent SIEPR was at the center of this proposal, which was put together by John Shoven, the Director of SIEPR. Ellison had serious discussions and contact with SIEPR around the time Shoven's proposal first surfaced. Indeed, in February 2001, Ellison delivered a speech at SIEPR-at which he was introduced by defendant Lucas. In a CD-ROM that contains images from the speech, Shoven's voice-over touts SIEPR's connections with "some of the most powerful and prominent business leaders."

As part of his proposal for the Ellison Scholars Program, Shoven suggested that three of the four Trading Defendants-Ellison, Lucas, and Boskin-be on the Program board. In the hypothetical curriculum that Shoven presented to Ellison, he included a course entitled "Legal Institutions and the Modern Economy" to be taught by Grundfest. Importantly, the Shoven proposal included a disclaimer indicating that listed faculty members may not have been consulted, and Grundfest denies that he was. The circumstances as a whole make that denial credible, although there is one confounding factor.

Lucas, who was active in encouraging Ellison to form a program of this kind at Stanford, testified at his deposition that he had spoken to Grundfest about the proposed Ellison Scholars Program "a number of years ago," Lucas seems to recall having asked Grundfest if he would be involved with the yet-to-be created Program, but his memory was, at best, hazy. At his own deposition, Grundfest was confronted more generically with whether he had heard of the Program and had agreed to teach in it if it was created, but not with whether he had discussed the topic with Lucas.

Candidly, this sort of discrepancy is not easy to reconcile on a paper record. My conclusion, however, is that Grundfest is being truthful in stating that he had not participated in shaping the Shoven proposal, had not agreed to teach in the Program, and could not recall participating in any discussions about the Program.

That said, I am not confident that Grundfest was entirely unaware, in 2001 and/or 2002 of the possibility of such a program or that he did not have a brief conversation with Lucas about it before joining the Oracle board. Nor am I convinced that the discussions about the Ellison Scholars Program were not of a very serious nature, indeed, the record evidence persuades me that they were serious. To find otherwise would be to conclude that Ellison is a man of more than ordinary whimsy, who says noteworthy things without caring whether they are true. . .

In order to buttress the argument that Stanford did not feel beholden to him, Ellison shared with the court the (otherwise private) fact that one of his children had applied to Stanford in October 2000 and was not admitted. If Stanford felt comfortable rejecting Ellison's child, the SLC contends, why should the SLC members hesitate before recommending that Oracle press insider trading-based fiduciary duty claims against Ellison?

But the fact remains that Ellison was still talking very publicly and seriously about the possibility of endowing a graduate interdisciplinary studies program at Stanford during the summer *after* his child was rejected from Stanford's undergraduate program.

The SLC's Argument

The SLC contends that even together, these facts regarding the ties among Oracle, the Trading Defendants, Stanford, and the SLC members do not impair the SLC's independence. In so arguing, the SLC places great weight on the fact that none of the Trading Defendants have the practical ability to deprive either Grundfest or Garcia-Molina of their current positions at Stanford. Nor, given their tenure, does Stanford itself have any practical ability to punish them for taking action adverse to Boskin, Lucas, or Ellison-each of whom, as we have seen, has contributed (in one way or another) great value to Stanford as an institution. As important, neither Garcia-Molina nor Grundfest are part of the official fundraising apparatus at Stanford; thus, it is not their on-the-job duty to be solicitous of contributors, and fundraising success does not factor into their treatment as professors.

In so arguing, the SLC focuses on the language of previous opinions of this court and the Delaware Supreme Court that indicates that a director is not independent only if he is dominated and controlled by an interested party, such as a Trading Defendant. The SLC also . . . Put another way, much of our law focuses the bias inquiry on whether there are economically material ties between the interested party and the director whose impartiality is questioned, treating the possible effect on one's personal wealth as the key to the independence inquiry. Putting a point on this, the SLC cites certain decisions of Delaware courts concluding that directors who are personal friends of an interested party were not, by virtue of those personal ties, to be labeled non-independent. . .

The Court's Analysis of the SLC's Independence

I begin with an important reminder: the SLC bears the burden of proving its independence. It must convince me.

But of what? According to the SLC, its members are independent unless they are essentially subservient to the Trading Defendants-*i.e.,* they are under the "domination and control" of the interested parties. If the SLC is correct and this is the central inquiry in the independence determination, they would win. Nothing in the record suggests to me that either Garcia-Molina or Grundfest are dominated and controlled by any of the Trading Defendants, by Oracle, or even by Stanford.

But, in my view, an emphasis on "domination and control" would serve only to fetishize much-parroted language, at the cost of denuding the independence inquiry of its intellectual integrity. Take an easy example. Imagine if two brothers were on a corporate board, each successful in different businesses and not dependent in any way on the other's beneficence in order to be wealthy. The brothers are brothers, they stay in touch and consider each other family, but each is opinionated and strong-willed. A derivative action is filed targeting a transaction involving one of the brothers. The other brother is put on a special litigation committee to investigate the case. If the test is domination and control, then one brother could investigate the other. Does any sensible person think that is our law? I do not think it is.

And it should not be our law. Delaware law should not be based on a reductionist view of human nature that simplifies human motivations on the lines of the least sophisticated notions of the law and economics movement. *Homo sapiens* is not merely *homo economicus.* We may be thankful that an array of other motivations exist that influence human behavior; not all are any better than greed or avarice, think of envy, to name just one. But also think of motives like love, friendship, and collegiality, think of those among us who direct their behavior as best they can on a guiding creed or set of moral values.

Nor should our law ignore the social nature of humans. To be direct, corporate directors are generally the sort of people deeply enmeshed in social institutions. Such institutions have norms, expectations that, explicitly and implicitly, influence and channel the behavior of those who participate in their operation. Some things are "just not done," or only at a cost, which might not be so severe as a loss of position, but may involve a loss of standing in the institution. In being appropriately sensitive to this factor, our law also cannot assume-absent some proof of the point-that corporate directors are, as a general matter, persons of unusual social bravery, who operate heedless to the inhibitions that social norms generate for ordinary folk.

For all these reasons, this court has previously held that the Delaware Supreme Court's teachings on independence can be summarized thusly:

> At bottom, the question of independence turns on whether a director is, *for any substantial reason,* incapable of making a decision with only the best interests of the corporation in mind. That is, the Supreme Court cases ultimately focus on impartiality and objectivity. (citation omitted) . . .

The SLC Has Not Met Its Burden to Demonstrate the Absence of a Material Dispute of Fact About Its Independence

Using the contextual approach I have described, I conclude that the SLC has not met its burden to show the absence of a material factual question about its independence. I find this to be the case because the ties among the SLC, the Trading Defendants, and Stanford are so substantial that they cause reasonable doubt about the SLC's ability to impartially consider whether the Trading Defendants should face suit. The concern that arises from these ties can be stated fairly simply, focusing on defendants Boskin, Lucas, and Ellison in that order, and then collectively.

As SLC members, Grundfest and Garcia-Molina were already being asked to consider whether the company should level extremely serious accusations of wrongdoing against fellow board members. As to Boskin, both SLC members faced another layer of complexity: the determination of whether to have Oracle press insider trading claims against a fellow professor at their university. Even though Boskin was in a different academic department from either SLC member, it is reasonable to assume that the fact that Boskin was also on faculty would-to persons possessing typical sensibilities and institutional loyalty-be a matter of more than trivial concern. Universities are obviously places of at-times intense debate, but they also see themselves as communities. In fact, Stanford refers to itself as a "community of scholars." To accuse a fellow professor-whom one might see at the faculty club or at inter-disciplinary presentations of academic papers-of insider trading cannot be a small thing-even for the most callous of academics.

As to Boskin, Grundfest faced an even more complex challenge than Garcia-Molina. Boskin was a professor who had taught him and with whom he had maintained contact over the years. Their areas of academic interest intersected, putting Grundfest in contact if not directly with Boskin, then regularly with Boskin's colleagues. Moreover, although I am told by the SLC that the title of senior fellow at SIEPR is an honorary one, the fact remains that Grundfest willingly accepted it and was one of a select number of faculty who attained that status. And, they both just happened to also be steering committee members. Having these ties, Grundfest (I infer) would have more difficulty objectively determining whether Boskin engaged in improper insider trading than would a person who was not a fellow professor, had not been a student of Boskin, had not kept in touch with Boskin over the years, and who was not a senior fellow and steering committee member at SIEPR.

In so concluding, I necessarily draw on a general sense of human nature. It may be that Grundfest is a very special person who is capable of putting these kinds of things totally aside. But the SLC has not provided evidence that that is the case. In this respect, it is critical to note that I do not infer that Grundfest would be less likely to recommend suit against Boskin than someone without these ties. Human nature being what it is, it is entirely possible that Grundfest would in fact be tougher on Boskin than he would on someone with whom he did not have such connections. The inference I draw is subtly, but importantly, different. What I infer is that a person in Grundfest's position would find it difficult to assess Boskin's conduct without pondering his own association with Boskin and their mutual affiliations. Although these connections might produce bias in either a tougher or laxer direction, the key inference is that these connections would be on the mind of a person in Grundfest's position, putting him in the position of either causing serious legal action to be brought against a person with whom he shares several connections (an awkward thing) or not doing so (and risking being seen as having engaged in favoritism toward his old professor and SIEPR colleague).

The same concerns also exist as to Lucas. For Grundfest to vote to accuse Lucas of insider trading would require him to accuse SIEPR's Advisory Board Chair and major benefactor of serious wrongdoing-of conduct that violates federal securities laws. Such action would also require Grundfest to make charges against a man who recently donated $50,000 to Stanford Law School after Grundfest made a speech at his request

And, for both Grundfest and Garcia-Molina, service on the SLC demanded that they consider whether an extremely generous and influential Stanford alumnus should be sued by Oracle for insider trading. Although they were not responsible for fundraising, as sophisticated professors they undoubtedly are aware of how important large contributors are to Stanford, and they share in the benefits that come from serving at a university with a rich endowment. A reasonable professor giving any thought to the matter would obviously consider the effect his decision might have on the University's relationship with Lucas, it being (one hopes) sensible to infer that a professor of reasonable collegiality and loyalty cares about the well-being of the institution he serves. . . .

The SLC's motion to terminate is DENIED. . .

Points for Discussion

1. Love and friendship in corporate law?

The *Oracle* court discussed motives for behavior including "love, friendship, and collegiality" that might impinge upon a director's independence. Does it surprise you to see these concepts in corporate law? How do you know if a friendship or personal relationship is close or significant enough to call into question a director's independence? Are courts well situated to make these determinations? Do the independence determinations in *Zuckerberg* seem consistent with those in *Oracle*? Should independence inquiries be limited to material financial or familial interests?

2. Independence in different contexts.

Director independence plays an important role in a number of situations including demand futility analysis for shareholder derivative litigation and when a board is asked to consider an interested director transaction. Is the independence inquiry the same across these different contexts? Do courts apply the standard evenly across these standards?

C. Who Qualifies as Plaintiff?

As noted above, shareholder litigation typically is driven by plaintiffs' law firms. But obviously, to file lawsuits those firms must have clients. Who are those clients? In federal securities class actions, the nature of the clients has changed dramatically since 1995, when the Private Securities Litigation Reform Act instructed federal courts to select as a lead plaintiff the one "most capable of adequately representing the interests of class members." In response, plaintiffs' law firms increasingly have courted clients who could satisfy this "most capable" requirement.

In general, courts have found that the "most capable" plaintiff is the one with the greatest financial stake in the outcome of the case, so long as the plaintiff satisfied the requirements of Rule 23 of the Federal Rules of Civil Procedure, which governs class actions. Indeed, the 1995 Act established a rebuttal presumption that the plaintiff with the greatest financial stake will be the lead plaintiff.

Derivative actions are not governed by the 1995 Act, but still are subject to the general requirement that a named plaintiff must be capable of adequately and fairly representing the interests of shareholders on whose behalf the suit has been brought. (These requirements are set forth in F.R.C.P. 23.1 and in various state statutes.)

We discuss two procedural issues that arise in the context of determining who qualifies as a plaintiff. First is the "adequacy" requirement, which is relatively easy to satisfy. Second is "standing," which can be more complicated. This is not a civil procedure class, so we will not delve into the nuances of the rules. But these two requirements are at the heart of shareholder litigation, particularly derivative actions, so they deserve some attention.

1. Adequacy

As noted above, F.R.C.P. 23 (which governs class actions) and F.R.C.P. 23.1 (which governs derivative suits) both require that a named plaintiff be capable of adequately and fairly representing the interests of the shareholders (in a class action) and the corporation (in a derivative suit) on whose behalf the suit has been brought. Most states have similar requirements. In the vast majority of decisions by federal and state courts, so long as a plaintiff is represented by a qualified attorney and does not have interests antagonistic to the class or the corporation, they satisfy the adequacy requirement.

Example

Surowitz v. Hilton Hotels Corp., 383 U.S. 363 (1966), involved a derivative claim filed by a Polish immigrant who had a very limited grasp of English and who, when deposed by defendants, had demonstrated almost no understanding of the charges in the complaint. The record, however, also contained evidence that Mrs. Surowitz, the named plaintiff, had filed suit only after her attorney in the case and her son-in-law—a prominent attorney and investment advisor—had investigated certain transactions involving the defendant corporation and found evidence that strongly suggested manipulation of the price of its stock and egregious self dealing.

Reversing a lower court decision dismissing the suit, the Court noted that although one purpose of Rule 23.1 was to "discourage 'strike suits' by people who might be interested in getting quick dollars by making charges without regard to their truth so as to coerce corporate managers to settle worthless claims in order to get rid of them," it also was true that "derivative suits have played a rather important role in protecting shareholders of corporations from the designing schemes and wiles of insiders who are willing to betray their company's interests in order to enrich themselves." Noting that "it is not easy to conceive of anyone more in need of protection against such schemes than little investors like Mrs. Surowitz," the Court held that it was error to dismiss this apparently meritorious claim simply because Mrs. Surowitz had advanced it on the advice of others.

Courts analyzing the adequacy requirement often look to the role the plaintiffs' lawyer plays in the litigation. The following case is representative.

In re Fuqua Industries, Inc. Shareholder Litigation

752 A.2d 126 (Del. Ch. 1999)

Chandler, Chancellor.

The question I must answer is whether I should disqualify a derivative plaintiff who is unfamiliar with the basic facts of his or her lawsuit and who exercises little, if any, control over the conduct of such suit?

The first derivative plaintiff Mrs. Abrams has held Fuqua shares for over thirty years. The quantity of her holdings has ranged from as much as 12,008 Fuqua shares to the current level of 8000 shares. The decision to purchase Fuqua shares, as most all of Abrams' investment decisions including the decision to file this suit, was made jointly with her husband, Burton Abrams, a retired trial attorney.

During the long pendency of this litigation Mrs. Abrams fell ill. As she concedes, her memory and faculties have suffered as a result. In a 1998 deposition, it was evident that Mrs. Abrams lacked a meaningful grasp of the facts and allegations of the case prosecuted in her name. While at times she appeared able to provide a general understanding of her claim, she was unable to articulate the understanding with any particularity and she was obviously confused about basic facts regarding her lawsuit.

Alan Freberg, the second derivative plaintiff in this action, purchased twenty-five Fuqua shares in 1989. In 1991, presumably upon concluding that Fuqua directors and Triton had engaged in self-dealing transactions, Freberg retained counsel and filed his first complaint.

Freberg's deposition testimony evidences that his knowledge of the case is at best elliptical. Defendants argue that before his "cram" session immediately before the deposition, Freberg knew absolutely nothing about this matter and had not even been privy to the third amended complaint. Defendants also point out (with much scorn) Freberg's general ignorance of the six or seven other lawsuits in which he was, or still is, the named representative plaintiff. The subtext of defendants' motion is that Freberg has no knowledge of this case because he has no real economic interest at stake. In defendants' view, Freberg is a puppet for his fee-hungry lawyers.

Court of Chancery decisions hold that a representative plaintiff will not be barred from the courthouse for lack of proficiency in matters of law and finance and poor health so long as he or she has competent support from advisors and attorneys and is free from disabling conflicts. This conclusion is both just and sensible.

Defendants' attack on Abrams' and Freberg's adequacy raises serious concerns. The allegation that attorneys bring actions through puppet plaintiffs while the real parties in interest are the attorneys themselves in search of fees is an oft-heard complaint from defendants in derivative suits. Sometimes, no doubt, the allegation rings true.

By the same token, however, the mere fact that lawyers pursue their own economic interest in bringing derivative litigation cannot be held as grounds to disqualify a derivative plaintiff. To do so is to impeach a cornerstone of sound corporate governance. Our legal system has privatized in part the enforcement mechanism for policing fiduciaries by allowing private attorneys to bring suits on behalf of nominal shareholder plaintiffs. In so doing, corporations are safeguarded from fiduciary breaches and shareholders thereby benefit. Through the use of cost and fee shifting mechanisms, private attorneys are economically incentivized to perform this service on behalf of shareholders.

To be sure, a real possibility exists that the economic motives of attorneys may influence the remedy sought or the conduct of the litigation. This influence, however, is inherent in private enforcement mechanisms and does not necessarily vitiate the substantial beneficial impact upon the conduct of fiduciaries.

Nonetheless, in some instances, the attorney in pursuit of his own economic interests may usurp the role of the plaintiff and exploit the judicial system entirely for his own private gain. Such extreme facts call for the court to exercise its discretion and to curb the agency costs inherent in private regulatory and enforcement mechanisms. These agency costs should not be borne by society, defendant corporations, directors or the courts.

I cannot say that either Abrams or Freberg is an inadequate plaintiff in this case. Contrary to defendants' assertions, Freberg does in fact understand the basic nature of the derivative claims brought in his name, even if barely so.

As defendants have adduced no evidence that Freberg has interests antagonistic to the interests he purports to represent, or that class counsel is incompetent or inexperienced, I conclude that Freberg meets Rule 23.1's minimum adequacy requirements. Interestingly, much of defendants' brief is devoted to demonstrating Freberg's surprising level of ignorance with respect to *other* lawsuits in which he is a representative plaintiff. For better or worse, however, no limit exists on the number of lawsuits one individual can bring in a lifetime. Thus, this fact alone is insufficient to disqualify Freberg.

Like Mrs. Surowitz with the aid of her son-in-law, Mrs. Abrams discovered her injury and filed this lawsuit with the aid of her husband. Even though the defendant in *Surowitz* demonstrated that Mrs. Surowitz did not "understand" her complaint and did not make any decisions with respect to the prosecution of the litigation, a unanimous Supreme Court did not dismiss her case; nor did it disqualify her as an inadequate plaintiff. I am reluctant to do differently here.

Abrams has been a substantial holder of Fuqua stock for thirty years. When she and her husband grew dissatisfied with Fuqua management, Mr. Abrams wrote letters to Fuqua's board demanding that certain measures be taken to improve the company's share price. His letters were disregarded. Determining that she had suffered legally cognizable harm, Mr. and Mrs. Abrams retained counsel in an effort to redress their grievances. They placed their trust and confidence in their lawyers as clients have always done.

Our legal system has long recognized that lawyers take a dominant role in prosecuting litigation on behalf of clients. A conscientious lawyer should indeed take a leadership role and thrust herself to the fore of a lawsuit. This maxim is particularly relevant in cases involving fairly abstruse issues of corporate governance and fiduciary duties.

I deny defendants' motions to disqualify Virginia Abrams and Alan Freberg as representative plaintiffs in this action.

---

2. Standing

Because a derivative suit seeks to enforce a right in the name of the corporation, standing generally has been limited to those with an equity interest in the corporation. But what does it mean to have an equity interest in the corporation? The question presents three issues: the nature of the plaintiff's holding, timing, and the plaintiff's countervailing interests.

Nature of the holding. First, consider the nature of the plaintiff's holding. In most jurisdictions, a derivative suit may be brought by either a shareholder of record or a beneficial owner of stock. A "shareholder" includes both a person whose shares are held in a voting trust as well as the more traditional "street name" owner of shares.

"Street name" refers to shares that are held electronically in the account of a stock broker. Historically, shareholders received physical share certificates, pieces of paper representing their ownership interest. The shareholder could either keep those pieces of paper at home, or "deposit" them—in the same way one might deposit money at a bank—with a Wall Street stock broker. Over time, corporations shifted to electronic ownership, with the actual shareholder holding a "beneficial ownership" interest. Today, shares typically are held in the name of the broker, or in "street" name.

What about other participants in the corporation's capital structure, such as creditors? Remember the right-hand side of the balance sheet—can holders of debt also bring derivative actions?

In general, the answer is no. A creditor typically is not allowed to maintain a derivative suit, although, when a corporation becomes bankrupt, its receiver may assert its rights in a suit that primarily will benefit its creditors. One reason for this rule is that the interests of creditors often are adverse to those of shareholders; risky investments that have the potential to enrich shareholders often jeopardize creditors' interests. A second is that creditors can negotiate contractual provisions restricting managers' discretion and therefore do not need the added protection of the derivative suit.

Some commentators have argued for a more relaxed rule. Although large creditors might be able to protect themselves contractually against an increased risk of default arising after the loan has been made, smaller creditors often do not have the economic leverage to negotiate such protection. Some have argued that directors should owe fiduciary duties to creditors and that creditors should have standing to bring a derivative suit where stockholder action is unlikely to occur or it is necessary to provide adequate protection to creditors. Whatever the theoretical force of these arguments, courts have almost universally rejected them.

However, in some "mega" settlements, the recovery has gone primarily to holders of securities other than shares. In some cases, the company becomes insolvent after the alleged fraud is revealed, and holders of securities with claims more senior than shares assume priority. This was true in both the *Cendant* litigation, where the primary recovery was to holders of hybrid preferred securities, and the *WorldCom* litigation, where the primary recovery was to certain bondholders. In the *Enron* litigation, the plaintiffs included not only shareholders, but also holders of numerous other securities, including preferred stock and options. These three cases involved some of the largest settlements in history, yet the focus was on non-shareholder claimants.

Another question about the nature of the holding arises when the plaintiff is not and never was a shareholder of the corporation injured by the transaction of which she complains, but instead owns stock in a direct or indirect parent of that corporation. The action would then be a "double" derivative action (or possibly a "triple"). In other words, the plaintiff would bring a derivative action to force the parent to force the subsidiary to bring a suit. The rationale for such claims, which sometimes are allowed, is that the same wrongdoers controlled both the parent and the subsidiary.

Timing. In many jurisdictions, the plaintiff must have been a shareholder at the time of the wrongdoing and at the time suit is filed and must remain a shareholder throughout the litigation. The idea is that the plaintiff not only must have been injured by the wrongdoing, but also must fairly and adequately represent the interest of other shareholders. Put simply, the question is whether someone who is no longer a shareholder can enforce the rights of the corporation.

The issue often arises when shareholders assert a claim on behalf of a corporation that has been merged out of existence or on behalf of the surviving corporation in a merger. The general rule is that a shareholder of a corporation that did not survive a merger lacks standing to sue derivatively for misconduct that occurred before the merger because the claim now is an asset of the surviving corporation. Courts generally do not apply this rule where the merger itself is the subject of a claim or when the merger involved a reorganization that did not eliminate the plaintiff's economic interest in the enterprise. In addition, shareholders who claim they were defrauded in connection with a merger often will have standing to maintain a direct suit on their own behalf or a class action on behalf of all similarly situated former shareholders of the merged corporation.

Such contemporaneous ownership requirements often are justified on the grounds that they serve to assure that the corporation's rights will be prosecuted by a plaintiff who has incurred actual harm and who will benefit from a successful outcome. This justification assumes that the principal purpose of the derivative suit is compensation. Absent the contemporaneous ownership requirement, a person could purchase stock in a company at a price that reflected the harm already done, bring a derivative suit and, if the suit succeeded, realize a windfall equal to a pro rata share of whatever amount the company recovered.

Example

In *Bangor Punta Operations, Inc. v. Bangor & Aroostook Railroad Co.*, 417 U.S. 703 (1974), the Court dismissed a suit brought by a railroad corporation against its former owner for damages caused by its alleged breaches of fiduciary duty. The Court reasoned that because the shareholder currently in control of the railroad had acquired more than 99% of its stock from the former owner after the alleged wrongs occurred, equitable principles relating to unjust enrichment required it to dismiss the suit, even though it had been filed by the railroad itself, rather than derivatively by its new controlling shareholder. The Court acknowledged that, if the purpose of derivative suits was deterrence, a different result would follow. Then, "any plaintiff willing to file a complaint would suffice. No injury or violation of a legal duty to the particular plaintiff would have to be alleged."

When a derivative suit is filed on behalf of a typical public corporation, however, the rationale supporting the contemporaneous ownership requirement is less compelling. Some shareholders will have sold their stock at prices that reflect the harm the wrongdoers caused and will not share in any subsequent recovery, while other shareholders will have purchased their stock after the wrong occurred and will realize a windfall if the suit succeeds. This suggests that the main purpose of the contemporaneous ownership requirement, at least in public companies, may not be to prevent a windfall but to make it more difficult for a plaintiffs' attorney to "buy into a lawsuit." *Fuqua* makes clear that courts will allow a plaintiffs'

For over a century, legal commentators have criticized contemporaneous ownership requirements as illogical and inconsistent with policy rationales for derivative litigation.

See J. Travis Laster, *Goodbye to the Contemporaneous Ownership Requirement*, 33 Del. J. Corp. L. 673 (2008); *Bamford v. Penfold, L.P.*, 2020 WL 967942, at *24 (Del. Ch. Feb. 28, 2020).

attorney to file a derivative suit in the name of a "figurehead plaintiff," but the contemporary ownership requirement imposes on a plaintiffs' attorney the burden of locating a plaintiff who owned the subject corporation's stock at the time the alleged wrongdoing occurred.

Some jurisdictions, such as California, have relaxed the contemporaneous ownership requirement. California permits a suit if there is a strong *prima facie* case in favor of the claim asserted on behalf of the corporation and the plaintiff acquired the shares before there was disclosure to the public or to the plaintiff of the wrongdoing. A plaintiff who qualifies under this standard will not realize a windfall because, if the wrongdoing has not been disclosed, the price at which they purchased will not reflect that wrongdoing. But the requirement that the wrongdoing not yet be disclosed also largely eliminates the possibility that the plaintiff acquired stock so as to qualify to bring a derivative suit.

In a class action, the typicality requirement serves much the same function as does the contemporaneous ownership requirement in a derivative suit. If a plaintiff did not hold stock at the time of the alleged wrongful conduct, their injuries, if any, will differ from those of shareholders who did hold stock and their claims then will not be typical of those asserted on behalf of the purported class.

Countervailing interests. Plaintiff shareholders also can face standing or other challenges based on their other interests. For example, suppose a shareholder who owns just one share of a corporation files a derivative action, and the court learns that the shareholder also holds a large "short" position. That shareholder's net position will benefit if the corporation loses money. Is that the kind of shareholder who should be permitted to bring a derivative action on behalf of the corporation?

> A "short seller" borrows shares they do not own and then sells the shares in the market. They remain obligated to deliver shares to the lender in the future. If the shares decline in value, they make money by repurchasing lower priced shares to return to the lender. If the shares increase in value, they lose money. Conceptually, selling short is the opposite of buying stock: short sellers make money when the share price declines and lose money when it rises.

Increasingly, shareholders hold such countervailing positions, and therefore are "economically encumbered." They are burdened by their other positions, and therefore face very different incentives, suffer different losses, and reap different gains than other shareholders. A person who owns shares of a company and who also has sold short shares is not injured by a corporate action that causes the value of shares to decline. Should such a person be permitted to double dip, by making money on their short position from the corporation's wrongdoing, and then suing to recover the losses on the shares they own based on the same wrongdoing?

Another problem associated with security ownership arises from share lending. Shares of public companies are held by brokers who can and do lend them to other shareholders. Brokerage agreements frequently provide that shareholders agree to such lending. Short sellers borrow shares from brokers, who obtain those shares from shareholders' accounts (in particular, from *margin accounts*, accounts in which shareholders are entitled to borrow money to buy shares "on margin").

When Mylan Pharmaceuticals made a bid for King Pharmaceuticals, Carl Icahn—a major shareholder of Mylan—was not pleased. He thought the offering price for King was too high, and he wanted to block the deal and persuade other shareholders to vote against it. In contrast, shareholders of King Pharmaceuticals, including Perry Corporation, wanted Mylan to approve the deal. To help ensure that Mylan shareholders would vote yes, Perry Corporation bought 9.99% of the outstanding shares of Mylan—in addition to its stake in King. It then entered into a "swap" transaction with a bank, in which it offloaded the economic risk of its stake in Mylan. In other words, the sum of Perry's two positions—the 9.99% ownership in Mylan minus the swap—was zero. It had no financial stake in Mylan. However, Perry nevertheless owned the Mylan shares, and it voted those shares in favor of the deal. Icahn sued and the deal fell apart. But it raised an issue that continues to perplex courts and regulators: how should they treat someone like Perry, who owns shares but also has an offsetting financial interest? For example, what if Perry wanted to file a derivative suit to force Mylan's board to go through with the deal?

Whereas the shorting party can, and does, undertake to pay any dividend declared by the corporation, the shorting party cannot similarly undertake to transfer standing or other plaintiff's rights. Consequently, because there are only a finite number of shares, when a shareholder permits a share to be borrowed for shorting, they essentially create a new shareholder. Share lending thereby creates the illusion that there are more shares owned beneficially than are actually registered. The last buyer of shares in the chain of lending and shorting is the final shareholder of record. Should only that person have standing as a plaintiff?

In a shareholder class action, distributions (either in a settlement or judgment) are made to any shareholder who can demonstrate ownership of the stock during the class period. The settlement and judgment amount is based upon the number of record shares outstanding during the class period; however, due to lending and shorting, the actual number of shares is greater than this number. Moreover, economically encumbered shareholders are entitled to recover, even if they were not damaged (or even if, as a result of their net short position, they profited). Because encumbered shares are entitled to recover pro rata, unencumbered shares receive less than the compensation necessary to make them whole, and encumbered shares receive a windfall. Overall, countervailing interests can make shareholder litigation complex, and puzzling.

D. Indemnification and D&O Insurance

In Chapter 9 on the Duty of Care, we have seen that exculpation, otherwise known as a "102(b)(7) provision," provides one way to avoid personal liability. Such provisions in the corporate charter allow for exculpation of directors and officers for personal liability for monetary damages for breach of the duty of care (note, however, that exculpation of officers is limited to certain officers and they are not exculpated from derivative claims).

How else can directors and officers avoid liability from shareholder litigation? First, corporate statutes permit corporations to "indemnify" directors and officers, not only for liability, but for the expenses of defending against lawsuits. The details of indemnification statutes can be complicated, but they generally permit corporations to protect directors and officers in even broader contexts than those covered by exculpation. Second, corporations may "insure" directors and officers against liability, sometimes in ways that go beyond indemnification. Such director and officer, or D&O, insurance is common, and serves as yet another protection.

1. Indemnification

Corporations can directly pay for, or reimburse, the damages and costs of directors and officers, as well as other corporate officials. Corporate statutes provide for both permissive and mandatory indemnification. In analyzing indemnification issues, you can think of three categories. First are the payments that corporations may indemnify (permissive). Second are the payments that corporations must indemnify (mandatory). Third are the payments that corporations may not indemnify (prohibited). The statutes attempt to draw the lines among these three categories.

Historically, courts addressed indemnification issues case by case, with unclear and often unsatisfactory results. In 1941, New York enacted the first indemnification statute. Today, every state has adopted such a statute, and many are comprehensive.

a. Permissive Indemnification

We now consider Delaware's approach to indemnification in greater detail. The provisions are contained in DGCL § 145. Sections 145(a) and (b) provide for permissive indemnification. Section 145(a) covers lawsuits brought by third parties, including class actions. Section 145(b) applies to derivative actions brought on behalf of the corporation. Thus, you'll notice the direct-derivative distinction that we discussed in the previous chapter also matters to indemnification.

The Delaware statutory provisions are a bit of a slog, but worth the effort. As you read them, notice (1) who is covered, (2) what is indemnified, (3) the standards of conduct required for indemnification, and (4) the effect of an action being concluded against the covered person.

DGCL § 145
Indemnification of Officers, Directors, Employees and Agents

(a) A corporation shall have power to indemnify any person who was or is a party or is threatened to be made a party to any threatened, pending or completed action, suit or proceeding, whether civil, criminal, administrative or investigative (other than an action by or in the right of the corporation) by reason of the fact that the person is or was a director, officer, employee or agent of the corporation, or is or was serving at the request of the corporation as a director, officer, employee or agent of another corporation, partnership, joint venture, trust or other enterprise, against expenses (including attorneys' fees), judgments, fines and amounts paid in settlement actually and reasonably incurred by the person in connection with such action, suit or proceeding if the person acted in good faith and in a manner the person reasonably believed to be in or not opposed to the best interests of the corporation, and, with respect to any criminal action or proceeding, had no reasonable cause to believe the person's conduct was unlawful. The termination of any action, suit or proceeding by judgment, order, settlement, conviction, or upon a plea of nolo contendere or its equivalent, shall not, of itself, create a presumption that the person did not act in good faith and in a manner which the person reasonably believed to be in or not opposed to the best interests of the corporation, and, with respect to any criminal action or proceeding, had reasonable cause to believe that the person's conduct was unlawful.

(b) A corporation shall have power to indemnify any person who was or is a party or is threatened to be made a party to any threatened, pending or completed action or suit by or in the right of the corporation to procure a judgment in its favor by reason of the fact that the person is or was a director, officer, employee or agent of the corporation, or is or was serving at the request of the corporation as a director, officer, employee or agent of another corporation, partnership, joint venture, trust or other enterprise against expenses (including attorneys' fees) actually and reasonably incurred by the person in connection with the defense or settlement of such action or suit if the person acted in good faith and in a manner the person reasonably believed to be in or not opposed to the best interests of the corporation and except that no indemnification shall be made in respect of any claim, issue or matter as to which such person shall have been adjudged to be liable to the corporation unless and only to the extent that the Court of Chancery or the court in which such action or suit was brought shall determine upon application that, despite the adjudication of liability but in view of all the circumstances

> of the case, such person is fairly and reasonably entitled to indemnity for such expenses which the Court of Chancery or such other court shall deem proper.

Notice that both Section 145(a) and 145(b) cover a broad range of corporate actors—directors, officers, employees, and agents (even when from another entity serving at the request of the corporation). Notice also the standard of conduct required for indemnification, which requires "good faith" and a specified "reasonable belief."

The primary difference between Section 145(a) and 145(b) is coverage. Section 145(a) permits broad indemnification of both expenses and amounts paid in damages or settlement of non-corporate claims. Section 145(b) permits narrower indemnification only of expenses in a corporate (derivative) suit, and only if the person to be indemnified was not adjudged liable to the corporation. In other words, Section 145(b)—on its own—does not provide indemnification for judgments or amounts paid in settlement of derivative suits. The rationale for this distinction is that because the ultimate plaintiff in a derivative suit is the corporation, the corporation should keep any judgment or settlement amount. If the corporation reimbursed a director for that amount, the corporation would essentially be paying from one pocket what it had just received in another pocket—a circularity problem.

Before you conclude that Section 145(b) prohibits indemnification of amounts paid in derivative suits, consider Section 145(f).

DGCL § 145
Indemnification of Officers, Directors, Employees and Agents

(f)   The indemnification and advancement of expenses provided by, or granted pursuant to, the other subsections of this section shall not be deemed exclusive of any other rights to which those seeking indemnification or advancement of expenses may be entitled under any bylaw, agreement, vote of stockholders or disinterested directors or otherwise, both as to action in such person's official capacity and as to action in another capacity while holding such office.

Does Section 145(f) permit a corporation to indemnify a director for settlement or judgment amounts in derivative actions?

Finally, read Sections 145(a) and 145(b) again, carefully. What is the function of the "good faith" language in both sections? How does this language fit with the "not in good faith" language in Section 102(b)(7), which was adopted at the same time? What kind of director conduct is in the "prohibited" category, and may not be subject to indemnification?

b.   Mandatory Indemnification

The Delaware indemnification provisions then change gears. Section 145(c) provides for *mandatory indemnification* when the director or officer has prevailed. Even if there has been a falling out with a particular corporate actor, indemnification is as of right when the covered person has successfully defended an action or proceeding arising from his or her corporate role. Notice, though, that this mandatory indemnification covers only expenses.

> ## DGCL § 145
> ## Indemnification of Officers, Directors, Employees and Agents
>
> (c)   To the extent that a present or former director or officer of a corporation has been successful on the merits or otherwise in defense of any action, suit or proceeding referred to in subsections (a) and (b) of this section, or in defense of any claim, issue or matter therein, such person shall be indemnified against expenses (including attorneys' fees) actually and reasonably incurred by such person in connection therewith.

What constitutes "success on the merits or otherwise"? The phrase "on the merits" is clear enough. If a director actually prevails, even on a technical defense, the corporation must indemnify him or her for expenses. The meaning of "or otherwise" is less clear. For example, indemnification of expenses would be required for a settlement in which a director pays no money and assumes no liability, and the case is dismissed with prejudice. But if a suit is dismissed without prejudice, indemnification may not be required.

c.   Advancement of Expenses

Notice that thus far the focus has been after-the-fact indemnification—that is, payment by the corporation to the covered person after the litigation or proceeding has concluded. For many corporate actors, this may present a serious financial burden if they must undertake their own defense and pay the ongoing costs of litigation, hoping for corporate indemnification (mandatory or permissive) later on. Can the corporation advance payments for litigation expenses? Should a director or officer who later will be indemnified have to pay for the ongoing costs of litigation, or can the corporation make advance payments for litigation expenses? Section 145(e) permits such advances, but it also raises difficult policy issues.

> ### DGCL § 145
> ### Indemnification of Officers, Directors, Employees and Agents
>
> (e) Expenses (including attorneys' fees) incurred by an officer or director in defending any civil, criminal, administrative or investigative action, suit or proceeding may be paid by the corporation in advance of the final disposition of such action, suit or proceeding upon receipt of an undertaking by or on behalf of such director or officer to repay such amount if it shall ultimately be determined that such person is not entitled to be indemnified by the corporation as authorized in this section. Such expenses (including attorneys' fees) incurred by former directors and officers or other employees and agents may be so paid upon such terms and conditions, if any, as the corporation deems appropriate.

Requiring directors to fund their own litigation expenses or post a bond up front would create a divide between rich and poorer directors. Moreover, as a practical matter, shareholder litigation can be expensive, and directors and officers without sufficient resources to pay for ongoing litigation expenses might be forced to settle on terms unfavorable to the corporation. The advancement-of-expenses provision essentially allows corporations to "lend" money to their directors or officers for these expenses. Advancement of expenses remains controversial. Agreements for the advancement of expenses are frequently litigated, especially when there are reasons to doubt that the director or officer had been acting in the corporation's best interests.

d. Policy Questions

In general, corporate indemnification of corporate officials raise difficult policy questions. Will responsible people be willing to serve as directors if they are forced to bear the upfront cost of defending their conduct whenever it is challenged? On the other hand, why help directors or officers who intentionally harm their corporations? Civil and criminal laws exist to deter wrongful conduct—doesn't indemnification frustrate the purpose of those laws? Indemnification policy requires a balancing act between encouraging good director behavior and deterring bad.

2. D&O Insurance

Finally, corporations are permitted to purchase insurance policies that cover their directors and officers. Unlike the statutory provisions for exculpation and indemnification, the statutes authorizing the purchase of D&O insurance are typically straightforward. DGCL § 145(g) is representative.

> ## DGCL § 145
> ## Indemnification of Officers, Directors,
> ## Employees and Agents: Insurance
>
> (g) A corporation shall have power to purchase and maintain insurance on behalf of any person who is or was a director, officer, employee or agent of the corporation, or is or was serving at the request of the corporation as a director, officer, employee or agent of another corporation, partnership, joint venture, trust or other enterprise against any liability asserted against such person and incurred by such person in any such capacity, or arising out of such person's status as such, whether or not the corporation would have the power to indemnify such person against such liability under this section.

Insurance companies began to offer D&O insurance policies during the 1960s, when an increasing number of lawsuits began to generate fears of personal liability for corporate officials. During the corporate litigation explosion of the 1980s, which coincided with a rise in merger and acquisition activity, some insurance companies cut back on their D&O coverage and significantly increased premiums. In the 1990s, coverage returned and premiums stabilized. Following the spate of corporate scandals that came to light in the early 2000s, D&O premiums and deductibles rose, fewer items were covered, and the number of insurance companies offering D&O coverage dwindled to a handful. During the 2010s, the market for D&O insurance remained concentrated, and premiums diverged based on industry and size. Most corporate directors will insist on significant D&O insurance coverage.

a.   Two Parts of D&O Policies

D&O policies consist of two separate but integral parts. The first part reimburses the corporation for its lawful expenses in connection with indemnifying its directors and officers, thus encouraging indemnification by the corporation. The second part of the D&O policy covers claims against individual directors or officers acting in their corporate capacity, thus reducing their exposure when the corporation is unable or unwilling to indemnify. This coverage often extends to claims (including judgments, settlements, and attorneys' fees) arising in court litigation, as well as administrative, regulatory, and investigative proceedings.

D&O insurance protects beyond corporate indemnification. First, the standard D&O policy may cover amounts paid in judgment or settlement in a derivative suit. Second, D&O insurance may cover conduct that does not satisfy the statutory standards for indemnification. For example, in *Van Gorkom*, because the directors were adjudged to have been grossly negligent in not informing themselves sufficiently prior to approving the merger, statutory indemnification might not have been available. Nonetheless, since the directors had not been "dishonest or fraudulent," the corporation's insurance carrier paid $10 million—the full policy limit—as part of the $23.5 million settlement of the case. Finally, D&O coverage is available even if the corporation becomes insolvent or refuses to pay indemnification, assuming the policy requirements are satisfied.

b.   D&O Exclusions and Coverage Denial

The D&O insurance exclusion of "dishonest, fraudulent or criminal conduct" has potentially important ramifications for executives in corporations that have experienced "accounting irregularities" and have had to restate their financial statements. Some policy exclusions only apply if there is a *judgment* finding such conduct, creating incentives for executives to settle the charges without admitting liability. When a corporation restates its financials, coverage may also turn on whether the financial misstatements were dishonest or intentional, or merely the result of an honest error in accounting or business judgment. To ensure access to D&O coverage, plaintiffs in securities fraud class actions will often couch their claims in terms of both fraud and negligence. Nonetheless, under some policies, mere *allegations* of dishonest or intentional conduct are enough to exclude coverage.

> D&O coverage is subject to significant limitations. Many policies have a deductible amount for each director and officer and for the corporation. Sometimes there are co-pays, which means the insured bears a certain percentage (such as 5%) of the loss above the deductible amount. In addition, D&O exclusions are many and significant, and they vary from policy to policy:
>
> - Dishonest, fraudulent, or criminal acts. Sometimes these exclusions are triggered merely if there are *allegations* of such conduct, while others require an actual *adjudication*.
>
> - Claims alleging conduct by directors or officers detrimental to the corporation for their own personal gain or profit. A common example is insider trading.
>
> - Claims involving libel and slander, bodily harm or property damages, and pollution.
>
> - Claims against a director or officer brought directly by the corporation, though not necessarily derivative suits (most insurers seek to stay clear of internal disputes).

D&O policies, like other insurance policies, can allow the insurance company to deny coverage and rescind the policies if there were "material misrepresentations" in the policy application. As you would expect, D&O policy applications include extensive descriptions of the corporation and its finances, including the latest annual report, and financial statements. In addition, the insured must disclose knowledge of "any act, error or omission that might give rise to a claim under the policy."

Rescission gained much importance after recent financial scandals in the 2000s. For example, several insurance companies that underwrote D&O policies for Enron sought to rescind coverage on the ground that Enron misled insurers when it renewed its D&O policies based on earnings that were subsequently significantly restated. One issue was whether the misrepresentations must have been knowing or intentional, or whether merely showing a material misrepresentation could be grounds for rescission. Some states permit rescission if the misrepresentation is material *or* fraudulent. If materiality is at issue, the insurance company will have to show that the financial statements were important in writing the policy or evaluating the risk.

c.   Policy Questions

To some, it is troubling that corporate law permits a corporation to insure its executives for conduct sufficiently egregious to be outside the scope of indemnification. Moreover, these critics point out, D&O insurance can be expensive and is paid for almost entirely by the corporation.

Defenders of D&O insurance respond with a simple argument: the scope of insurance coverage is a question of insurance law rather than corporate law. The statute only authorizes the purchase of insurance and leaves the determination of coverage limits to insurance companies and state insurance commissioners. In addition, if corporations did not purchase D&O insurance for their executives, one would expect that the executives would demand additional compensation to purchase it for themselves.

Who should bear the risks of executive malfeasance? Supporters of the present system argue that insurance companies, and their regulators, should decide this through exclusions and pricing decisions. They say the markets will police any problems, because if D&O insurance is harmful to a corporation, shareholders can choose to invest in corporations that do not insure. However, this argument assumes that shareholders have information about the D&O coverage and payments, that they act on this information, and that their actions influence executive behavior. Are any of these assumptions true?

The bottom line policy question is simple: law or markets? The phenomenon of D&O insurance presents this question in stark form. How much should society entrust to insurance markets the setting of limits on corporate governance? But the question is not limited to D&O insurance. Indeed, it is a question fundamental to director decision making, which—as we have seen—is limited somewhat by law, but is more generally an area where society entrusts to directors—subject to market pressures—the oversight of corporate behavior, for better or for worse.

E.   Some Policy Implications of Shareholder Litigation

We close this chapter by touching on several policy issues. Shareholder litigation is enormously controversial, and many of these thorny questions will not be resolved anytime soon.

Agency costs of litigation. Most shareholder lawsuits are brought in a representative capacity, as class actions or derivative suits. Collective action problems limit the ability of shareholders to police managers through litigation. A shareholder who chooses to devote resources to monitoring managers' performance must bear the costs of such efforts, as well as the risk that no wrongdoing will be found. Moreover, even if the shareholder succeeds in identifying a breach of fiduciary duty and remedying it through a class or derivative action, the only benefit will be a pro rata portion of whatever is recovered in a class action or whatever increase in the value of that shareholder's shares results from a successful derivative suit. Instead, it is the shareholder-plaintiffs' lawyer who stands to earn attorneys' fees and thus has a much greater incentive to bring litigation based on managerial misconduct.

Just as agency costs arise from the different incentives of principal and agent, or metaphorically shareholder and manager, so do agency costs arise from the different incentives of shareholder and lawyer. The plaintiffs' attorney typically will have a much greater financial stake in shareholder litigation than an individual shareholder. Moreover, plaintiffs' attorneys can sometimes benefit from shortchanging or even injuring the interests of the shareholders whose interests they supposedly represent. For example, a plaintiffs' law firm might agree to a settlement that shareholders collectively would reject, rather than take a case to trial, so as to assure the firm will receive a fee for the work it has done. Alternatively, a firm might file a suit that has little merit from the standpoint of most shareholders, but substantial nuisance value, in the hope that a defendant corporation will agree to a settlement that includes substantial attorneys' fees.

Plaintiffs' attorneys are constantly on the watch for cases. They typically look for evidence of two factors in deciding whether to file a lawsuit on behalf of shareholders. First, is there sufficient evidence of liability so that they can survive the pleading stage? For this question, evidence can come from publicly filed restatements of a corporation's financial condition, whistleblowers who have evidence of wrongdoing, government investigations, or even the plaintiffs' lawyers' own investigation.

If there is evidence of liability, the second question is whether there is sufficient evidence of damages so that the plaintiffs' lawyers can obtain an attractive settlement. The primary source of evidence regarding damages is public information. Was news about the allegations revealed on a particular date or dates? If so, how much did the company's share price decline when news about the allegations was announced? If the news filtered out in stages, how much did each stage impact the share price? How many shares were outstanding and how actively traded were those shares? Are the plaintiffs' lawyers confident they can establish that the price declines were caused by the revelation of information about the allegations?

As discussed above, even if there is sufficient evidence of these factors, one important question remains: who will be the plaintiff? Before the enactment of the Private Securities Litigation Reform Act of 1995 (PSLRA), plaintiffs' lawyers would file cases immediately after a company's share price declined on behalf of one or more individual investors with relatively small shareholdings. Some "professional" plaintiffs held a few shares of many companies in anticipation of a lawsuit, and courts selected the "lead plaintiff" and his law firm based in part on who had been the first to file a complaint.

In 2006, one of the most prominent plaintiffs' law firms, Milberg Weiss Bershad & Schulman, and two of its name partners, were criminally indicted for allegedly participating in a scheme in which several individuals were paid millions of dollars in secret kickbacks in exchange for serving as named plaintiffs in more than 150 class-action and shareholder derivative-action lawsuits. The indictment alleged that the firm received more than $200 million in attorneys' fees from these lawsuits.

The PSLRA changed the landscape of federal securities litigation by shifting from a first-to-file presumption to a size-of-loss presumption. Congress mandated that in appointing a lead plaintiff, "the court shall adopt a presumption that the most adequate plaintiff . . . is the person or group of persons that . . . has the largest financial interest in the relief sought by the class." Securities Exchange Act § 27(a)(3)(B)(iii)(I). The PSLRA's Conference Report explained that "class members with large amounts at stake will represent the interests of the plaintiff class more effectively than class members with small amounts at stake." H.R. Conf. Rep. 104–369, at 34 (1995). Today, federal district courts compare the financial stakes of the various plaintiffs and determine which has the most to gain from the lawsuit. Essentially, the test is a mechanical one based on which shareholder has the "largest financial interest" in the litigation, and therefore which one has the greatest relative incentive to pursue the litigation effectively on behalf of all shareholders. That plaintiff's law firm then represents the class.

Challenges of settlements. The settlement of lawsuits also presents policy challenges. Settlements occur more frequently in shareholder litigation than in other cases. Suits often are initiated by plaintiffs' attorneys who represent "figurehead" clients. Many plaintiffs' attorneys are committed to protecting the interests of the shareholders they represent, but almost all such attorneys work on a contingent fee basis. Thus, their personal financial interests lie in maximizing the fees they will earn for any given amount of work and minimizing the risk that they will receive no fee for their efforts. This produces a bias in favor of smaller, speedier settlements over trials that, if unsuccessful, will leave attorneys without compensation after years of work. In addition, plaintiffs' attorneys may find it financially attractive to initiate "strike suits" that have little prospect of success on the merits but that impose litigation costs on the defendant corporation and thus have nuisance, and therefore settlement, value.

Shareholders' financial interest, in contrast, lies in realizing the largest recovery, adjusted for litigation risk, that a suit has the potential to generate. At times, shareholders also may benefit from changes in the governance practices of the defendant corporation or from enhanced or corrective disclosure of material information.

Shareholders, however, realize no benefits from strike suits or from settlements that produce only symbolic governance changes or meaningless disclosures.

The key safeguard against opportunism in shareholder litigation is the requirement in F.R.C.P. 23 and 23.1, and the comparable requirement in most states' statutes or rules, that a court both approve any settlement, compromise, discontinuance, or dismissal of a derivative suit or shareholder class action and also determine what fee should be awarded to plaintiffs' attorneys.

It is up to the court to decide whether to approve a settlement that typically has been negotiated by plaintiffs' attorneys without input from many of the "clients" they represent. The courts attempt to ensure that settlements are fair to absent class members and other shareholders. The proponents of a settlement bear the burden of convincing the court that it is fair. In most cases, that determination will depend largely on the adequacy of the amount being recovered when compared to the potential recovery were plaintiff to succeed at trial. In making this evaluation, the court will discount the potential recovery at trial by the risk factors inherent in any litigation and the time value of money over the period during which recovery will be delayed.

> Important questions in evaluating settlements include the following:
>
> - How strong are the claims on the merits?
> - How much delay and expense would be involved in continued litigation?
> - Could any judgment actually be collected?
> - How much of a compromise is the settlement?
> - How do both parties view the settlement?

Evaluation of a settlement becomes more difficult when it involves non-pecuniary benefits to the corporation or the plaintiff class. For example, settlements of derivative suits may involve agreements to add outside directors to the board, to create more independent audit, compensation, or nominating committees, or to require managers to surrender stock options. Class action settlements may require additional disclosure before a planned transaction is consummated. Although settlements calling for improved governance mechanisms may reduce the prospect of future wrongdoing, they raise a separate problem (described by the ALI): "such therapeutic relief can sometimes represent a counterfeit currency by which the parties can increase the apparent value of the settlement and thereby justify higher attorney's fees for plaintiff's counsel, who is often the real party in interest." To deal with this problem, the ALI recommends that the court review the value of non-pecuniary relief both when evaluating the settlement and when computing plaintiff's counsel fees. ALI PRINCIPLES § 7.14, Comment c.

The integrity of the shareholder litigation process depends to a considerable degree on the rigor with which courts review proposed settlements and requests for attorneys' fees. However, a number of factors impair the effectiveness of courts' review. Perhaps the most important is that settlement hearings rarely are adversarial. As Judge Henry Friendly pointed out many years ago: "Once a settlement is agreed, the attorneys for the plaintiff stockholders link arms with their former adversaries to defend the joint handiwork." Absent a well prepared objector, courts thus must take the initiative in reviewing proposed settlements, yet courts often have an incentive to approve a proposed settlement, if for no other reason than to clear from their overcrowded dockets potentially complex cases that otherwise are likely to require a great deal of judicial attention.

Affected shareholders are made aware of proposed settlements through the notices required by F.R.C.P. 23 and 23.1 and comparable provisions of state law. Largely as a consequence of collective action problems, though, affected shareholders rarely object. They usually do not have detailed information about the merits of the action or the manner in which the settlement has been negotiated. To obtain this information, a shareholder has to challenge both the plaintiffs' attorneys, who nominally represent the shareholders' interests but who always have a strong interest in having the settlement approved, and the attorneys representing the defendants and the corporation. In addition, a shareholder often will have only a relatively brief period in which to object before the hearing on the settlement is scheduled to be held. Despite these problems, courts usually treat the absence of a large number of objections as a factor supporting approval of a proposed settlement. Even courts that are skeptical about the benefits of a proposed settlement often are reluctant to reject it.

Attorneys' fees. Under the "American" rule, which generally applies in litigation in the United States, the successful party is not entitled to recover attorneys' fees from the losing party. However, courts have created a partial exception to this rule for shareholder class and derivative litigation. If a defendant prevails, the American rule still applies. But if a plaintiff prevails on the merits or obtains a settlement, her attorneys can apply to the court for a fee award. In a class action, that fee will be payable out of whatever "common fund" the action creates. In a derivative suit, the corporation customarily is required to pay whatever fee is awarded on the grounds that it has derived a benefit, either monetary or non-monetary, from the successful prosecution or settlement of the suit.

Fees generally are calculated on either a "lodestar" or percentage of recovery basis. In 1985, a Third Circuit Task Force Report describes the "lodestar" method as follows:

> First, the court must determine the hours reasonably expended by coun-sel that created, protected, or preserved the fund. Second, the number of compensable hours is multiplied by a reasonable hourly rate for the attorney's services. Hourly rates may vary according to the status of the attorney who performed the work (that is, the attorney's experience, reputation, practice, qualifications, and similar factors) or the nature of the services provided. This multiplication of the number of compensable

hours by the reasonable hourly rate [constitutes] the "lodestar" of the court's fee determination.

The "lodestar" then could be increased or decreased based upon the contingent nature or risk in the particular case involved and the quality of the attorney's work. An increase or decrease of the lodestar amount is referred to as a "multiplier." In determining whether to increase the lodestar to reflect the contingent nature of the case, "the district court should consider any information that may help to establish the probability of success." However, "the court may find that the contingency was so slight or the amount found to constitute reasonable compensation for the hours worked was so large a proportion of the total recovery that an increased allowance for the contingent nature of the fee would be minimal." As to the quality multiplier, it was to be employed only for "an unusual degree of skill, superior or inferior, exhibited by counsel in the specific case before the court."

The percentage of recovery method, as its name implies, involves awarding a fee calculated as a percentage of the value of whatever the suit has produced. Fee awards generally range between 20–35% when the recovery is below $100 million and are lower percentages for higher amounts. Some retention agreements provide for a staggered schedule, so that the fee percentage declines as the settlement size increases.

Neither approach is entirely successful in resolving the structural conflicts inherent in shareholder litigation. If the lodestar formula is used, plaintiffs' attorneys have an interest in prolonging the litigation so as to maximize the amount of time for which they will be paid. Thus, counsel may reject an early settlement offer or engage in extended "confirmatory" discovery if a settlement has been negotiated. Defendants' counsel may tacitly acquiesce in such a scenario, as it also may benefit their interests. Such structural collusion may benefit all the attorneys involved, but it works against the plaintiff-shareholders and the corporation's interest in settling the case as favorably and quickly as possible. Moreover, because the fees to be awarded will not be directly linked to the amount of any settlement, counsel may be prepared to settle for less than the shareholders, if fully informed, would be prepared to accept.

The percentage of recovery method can be similarly problematic. Plaintiffs' attorneys may find it attractive to settle a case very early so as to avoid expending very much time. Their marginal return on their investment in a case generally will decline as the amount of time they invest in it increases. At some point, any increase in the amount recovered, even if it is attainable, will be unlikely to lead to any significant increase in their fee. Plaintiffs' attorneys also may be reluctant to include non-pecuniary terms in a settlement because no value may be attached to any benefits they provide when the attorneys' fees are calculated.

The percentage of recovery value method also tends to increase case splitting and fee splitting among different counsel. By diversifying the risks involved in any one case among a number of different lawyers, the lead counsel can reduce the effort put into the case and, hence, the costs that would be incurred if the case is not settled or litigated successfully. Such case splitting both decreases the incentive for plaintiff's counsel to settle early and reduces the effectiveness of counsel's work, thereby weakening the likelihood of a large recovery for the corporation.

———————————

CHAPTER 15

Voting

Voting is one of the central issues in corporate governance, and is the first of the shareholder rights that we mentioned early in the book: vote, sue, and sell. One of us refers to a shareholder rights poem of "vote, sue, sell, and yell," adding "yell," not only so the rights rhyme (and are easier to remember), but also because of the increasing importance of shareholder voice and shareholder activism, both of which are related to the policy questions posed in the previous chapter.

For some context, we will be discussing various shareholder rights throughout the next several chapters. After this chapter, we will cover shareholder litigation and the right to *sue*. At various points in the upcoming chapters, an important tactic for shareholders will be exiting their position, meaning the right to *sell* their shares (private corporations often restrict this right; exit is typically much easier in the public markets). We also will discuss shareholders proposing changes at companies: shareholders increasingly exercise their voice (i.e., *yell*), and make their concerns known publicly. But the most fundamental shareholder right, the one we cover now, is the right to *vote*.

In this chapter, we describe the basics of shareholder voting rights and how corporate law protects them. Shareholders are often called the "owners" of the corporation. But their governance role is limited by corporate law's tenet of centralized management. Remember that the board of directors, not the shareholders, has the authority to manage and direct the business and affairs of the corporation.

Shareholders exercise their limited corporate governance role mostly by voting. Shareholders annually elect the corporation's directors, and they can remove and replace directors in some circumstances. Shareholders frequently decide whether to approve certain *fundamental transactions*—such as mergers, sale of the corporation's significant business assets, and voluntary dissolution of the corporation. Shareholders also can make recommendations to the board concerning matters within the board's sphere of responsibility, and they have the power to amend the bylaws. Last but certainly not least, a shareholder vote is required to amend the articles of incorporation.

This chapter has four parts. First, we outline the basics of shareholder voting, including the annual election of directors to the board. Second, we consider the power of shareholders to initiate changes by making recommendations to the board, by altering the board's composition, and by amending the corporation's bylaws. Third, we consider how courts respond when the board seeks to interfere with shareholder initiatives. Finally, we address shareholder activism, one of the most important topics in business law, including shareholder proposals, which shareholders vote on annually at most public companies.

A. Basics of Shareholder Voting

1. Shareholder Meetings

Shareholders act at regularly scheduled annual meetings and at special meetings convened for particular purposes. At the annual meeting the only matter required of shareholders is to elect directors. Nonetheless, boards of directors often seek shareholder approval of other matters, such as the appointment of auditors, the adoption of management compensation plans, or the ratification of some decisions the board has made during the past year.

If an annual meeting has not been held in the previous 15 months (13 months under Delaware's statute), any holder of voting stock can require the corporation to convene an annual meeting, at which new directors can be elected. Special meetings may be called by the board or by a person authorized in the articles or bylaws, or under some statutes (but not in Delaware) by any 10% shareholder.

Shareholders can also act by means of written consent instead of a meeting. Some statutes require action by written consent to be unanimous, effectively limiting the procedure to closely held corporations. Under Delaware's statute, action by written consent can be taken by a majority of a corporation's voting shares. This gives shareholders of Delaware corporations the power—often useful in battles for corporate control—to act without waiting for a meeting and without having to provide advance notice to the company's management or to other shareholders. The consent procedure can be eliminated or restricted in the articles. The Delaware statute also contains a separate provision that requires unanimous written consent when shareholders elect directors by written consent in lieu of holding an annual meeting.

For many companies, the annual meeting is a mere formality, conducted electronically and quickly, or just on paper. But in other instances, the annual meeting can be great theatre, ranging from widely-attended celebrations in public venues to dramatic contests for corporate control featuring emotive speeches and close votes.

2. Shareholder Voting Procedures

Shareholders entitled to vote must receive written notice of the shareholder meeting. The notice, which typically must be sent at least 10 days, but no more than 60 days, before the meeting, describes the time and location of the meeting. The notice for special meetings must also describe the purpose of the meeting.

The shares entitled to be voted at the meeting are fixed on the "record date," a date set by the board before notice is sent to shareholders. Only those shareholders whose ownership is reflected on the corporation's books as of the record date are entitled to notice and to vote. In other words, shareholders who *sell* between the record date and the meeting date are entitled to vote, but shareholder who *buy* between the record date and the meeting date are not.

Most statutes require that shareholder meetings have a quorum equal to a majority of shares entitled to vote. The quorum may be increased or reduced in the articles or bylaws, though some statutes (including in Delaware) require a quorum of at least one-third. Quorum requirements protect against a minority faction calling a meeting and taking action without the presence of a majority.

Shareholders can vote in person at a meeting. Alternatively, unlike directors, shareholders can choose not to attend a meeting and instead vote by proxy. A proxy is simply the signed appointment in writing of an agent to appear and vote on behalf of the shareholder. The proxy may give the proxy holder discretion to vote as they please or it might direct a particular vote.

Large institutional shareholders of public companies typically direct how their shares are to be voted by submitting voting instructions for each of several thousand companies. These instructions are often based on advice from third-party proxy advisors. In contrast, individual shareholders more frequently delegate voting to their brokers, who submit proxies on their behalf.

Unless made irrevocable, the proxy can be revoked by the shareholder at any time by submitting a notice of revocation, signing a later-dated proxy, or appearing in person at the meeting. Many statutes limit proxies to 11 months, unless a longer term is specified.

> The two major "proxy advisory firms" are Glass Lewis and Institutional Shareholder Services, known as ISS. Proxy advisory firms provide recommendations on how to vote at shareholder meetings on a variety of topics. They became prominent in part because investment managers are expected to have policies and procedures for proxy voting, but it is expensive for each investment manager to produce recommendations for all of the companies whose shares they hold. The proxy advisory industry has been criticized for potential conflicts of interest and low competition given that two firms have captured more than 90% of the market.

Once proxy holders present their proxies and establish they are the agent for the shares represented, they cast their ballot. When questions arise about the validity of proxies, the board typically designates an election inspector—a professional hired to verify signatures, ensure proper voting by fiduciaries, confirm the dating of proxies, count ballots, and certify the result. Delaware's statute requires that public corporations appoint one or more inspectors in advance of any shareholder meeting.

3. Shareholder Voting Rights

The general corporate law rule is one-share/one-vote, unless the articles specify otherwise. Supermajority voting or voting caps on any shareholder who owns more than a specified percentage of shares are permissible, but mostly used in closely held corporations. Non-voting shares are also permissible, as are classes of shares that have greater or lesser votes. For example, many technology companies have Class A shares with one vote each, and Class B shares, controlled by the company's founders, which have, say, ten votes each. Other companies have issued public shares that have no vote at all. Obviously, shareholder voting rights are less important at companies that give shareholders less of a stake in voting.

As noted above, shareholders must approve certain fundamental transactions as specified in the relevant corporate statute. Some statutes specify a *simple majority* for shareholder approval of fundamental transactions: "the votes cast favoring the action exceed the votes cast opposing the action." Other statutes, including in Delaware, specify an *absolute majority*: "a majority of the outstanding stock of the corporation entitled to vote thereon." Shareholder voting on fundamental transactions is mandatory. Shareholder approval cannot be waived or be based on less than the specified majority.

Example

ABC Corporation has 100 shares outstanding, with 60 shares present or represented at a shareholders' meeting. If a simple majority is required for shareholder approval, the vote of 31 shares entitled to vote is sufficient. If an absolute majority is required, 51 of the 100 shares entitled to vote is required.

All directors are up for election at the annual meeting, unless the articles of incorporation provide for *staggered* terms, in which event shareholders elect directors for terms of two or three years. The power of shareholders to elect directors is exclusive, except when a board seat is vacant. In that case, the vacancy can be filled either by shareholders or by the remaining directors, unless the articles provide otherwise.

Directors can be elected either by *plurality voting*, which means that the top vote-getters for open directorships win those seats, or by *majority voting*, which means that each elected director must obtain a majority. Thus, under plurality voting, if a corporation has 9 open seats and the board nominates 9 directors and there are no other nominees, all of the board's nominees are elected so long as a quorum is present and each nominee receives at least one vote. In response to shareholder pressure, many public corporations—and most large public corporations—provide for majority voting in director elections. To be seated, each nominee must receive a majority of votes cast. Any nominee who does not receive a majority must resign (or act consistently with the majority voting bylaw provision). That seat is then filled by the board or left open until a future election.

Generally, the incumbent board uses corporate funds to call and conduct shareholder meetings. This includes soliciting proxies, the principal means by which shareholders in public corporations exercise their voting rights. Financial control by incumbent directors over the voting mechanism has substantial, long-standing support in the cases.

> Directors on a "staggered board" (sometimes called "classified board") are elected for multiple-year terms, typically three years. This means only part of the board (one-third) is up for election each year, making a takeover or voting insurgency more difficult.
>
> "Cumulative voting" allows shareholders to concentrate their votes for particular candidates, thus increasing the likelihood of minority representation on the board. Cumulative voting, once required in corporations, is now optional under most state corporate laws.

Incumbents thus have a tremendous advantage in voting contests. Insurgents seeking to displace the incumbent board must use their own funds to finance a proxy solicitation, and can recover their costs only if they prevail and receive shareholder ratification. We address the specifics of this allocation of power below, along with the question of whether such one-sided corporate is democratic.

Shareholders typically can remove directors with or without cause, unless the articles provide that directors can be removed only for cause. The power of shareholders to remove directors for cause is mandatory, and it cannot be restricted.

B. Shareholder Power to Initiate Action

Shareholder power to initiate action is limited. For example, shareholder rights to approve or veto fundamental transactions are passive. The board initiates the decision to merge or engage in a similar transaction. Shareholders react to that decision.

In this section, we consider three more "active" shareholder powers: to make recommendations, to remove and/or replace directors, and to amend bylaws. In this section, we consider how the shareholders (not the board) can initiate action. In the next section, we examine about the board can react to such initiatives.

Although corporate statutes give the board the power to "manage and direct" the business and affairs of the corporation, they do not specify when shareholders can direct or advise the board. Instead, the statutes leave open a broad continuum of possible roles for shareholders. At one extreme, shareholders might have the power to command the board to consider a specific decision. At the other extreme, shareholders might have no voice at all. Or shareholders might have some intermediate role: to suggest that the board take certain actions or report to them on particular matters, but not to require board action. Given the lack of specificity in corporate statutes, the challenge for judges over the years has been to determine where shareholder powers to initiate action should fall along this continuum.

Questions about what powers shareholders can initiate in a corporation resemble questions about what powers the electorate can initiate in a political democracy. Even in a representative government, voters can do more than vote: there are propositions, referenda, petitions, lobbying, and opinion polls. This section is about similar initiatives in the context of the corporation.

1. Shareholder Recommendations and Removal/Replacement of Directors

Shareholder recommendations are an important part of the shareholders' power to initiate action. For example, the SEC's shareholder proposal rule allows shareholders in public corporations to propose resolutions for the adoption by fellow shareholders through the corporate-financed proxy mechanism, provided the proposal is *proper under state law*. Accordingly, one important question is: what matters are proper?

The leading case establishing the ground rules for shareholder resolutions under state corporate law is *Auer v. Dressel*. The plaintiffs in that case owned a majority of the Class A stock of R. Hoe & Co., Inc. They brought an action for an order to compel the president of the corporation to call a special shareholders' meeting pursuant to a bylaw provision requiring such a meeting when requested by holders of a majority of the stock. The articles of incorporation provided for an eleven-member board, nine of whom were to be elected by the Class A stockholders and two of whom were to be elected by the Common stockholders.

The stated purposes of the special meeting were:

A. To vote on a resolution endorsing the administration of Joseph L. Auer, the former President and demanding his reinstatement;

B. To amend the articles of incorporation and bylaws to provide that vacancies on the board of directors arising from the removal of a director by the shareholders be filled only by the shareholders; and

C. To consider and vote on charges to remove four Class A directors for cause and to elect their successors.

The president refused to call the meeting on the grounds, among others, that the foregoing purposes were not proper subjects for a Class A shareholder meeting.

Auer v. Dressel

118 N.E.2d 590 (N.Y. 1954)

DESMOND, JUDGE.

The obvious purpose of the meeting here sought to be called (aside from the endorsement and reinstatement of former president Auer) is to hear charges against four of the class A directors, to remove them if the charges be proven, to amend the bylaws so that the successor directors be elected by the class A stockholders, and further to amend the bylaws so that an effective quorum of directors will be made up of no fewer than half of the directors in office and no fewer than one third of the whole authorized number of directors. No reason appears why the class A stockholders should not be allowed to vote on any or all of those proposals.

The stockholders, by expressing their approval of Mr. Auer's conduct as president and their demand that he be put back in that office [purpose (A)], will not be able, directly, to effect that change in officers, but there is nothing invalid in their so expressing themselves and thus putting on notice the directors who will stand for election at the annual meeting.

As to purpose (B), that is, amending the charter and bylaws to authorize the stockholders to fill vacancies as to class A directors who have been removed on charges or who have resigned, it seems to be settled law that the stockholders who are empowered to elect directors have the inherent power to remove them for cause [purpose (C)]. Of course, there must be the service of specific charges, adequate notice and full opportunity of meeting the accusations, but there is no present showing of any lack of any of those in this instance.

Since these particular stockholders have the right to elect nine directors and to remove them on proven charges, it is not inappropriate that they should use their further power to amend the bylaws to elect the successors of such directors as shall be removed after hearing, or who shall resign pending hearing. Such a change in the bylaws, dealing with the class A directors only, has no effect on the voting rights of the common stockholders, which rights have to do with the selection of the remaining two directors only. True, the certificate of incorporation authorizes the board of directors to remove any director on charges, but we do not consider that provision as an abdication by the stockholders of their own traditional, inherent power to remove their own directors. Rather, it provides an additional method. Were that not so, the stockholders might find themselves without effective remedy in a case where a majority of the directors were accused of wrongdoing and, obviously, would be unwilling to remove themselves from office.

We fail to see, in the proposal to allow class A stockholders to fill vacancies as to class A directors, any impairment or any violation of paragraph (h) of article

Third of the certificate of incorporation, which says that class A stock has exclusive voting rights with respect to all matters "other than the election of directors." That negative language should not be taken to mean that class A stockholders, who have an absolute right to elect nine of these eleven directors, cannot amend their bylaws to guarantee a similar right, in the class A stockholders and to the exclusion of common stockholders, to fill vacancies in the class A group of directors.

———

Points for Discussion

1. Court's holdings and dissent.

Judge Van Voorhis dissented in *Auer v. Dressel* on the ground that the cited purposes were not appropriate subjects for action by shareholders at the requested meeting. Proposal A, the endorsement of Auer's tenure as president, was only "an idle gesture." Proposal B was improper because the articles of incorporation authorized the directors to fill vacancies on the board, and the change sought would have denied the common stockholders their rights to a voice in the replacement of directors through their two representatives on the board. Proposal C, the removal of directors, was improper because a shareholders meeting was "altogether unsuited to the performance of duties which partake of the nature of the judicial function." Since most shareholders would vote by proxy, their decision would have to be made before the meeting at which the charges against the directors would be made and discussed.

Why should shareholders be allowed to state their non-binding preference and thus engage in "an idle gesture"? Why should shareholders be entitled to state their views on a matter entrusted to the board's discretion—namely, the selection of the corporate president? The shareholders cannot mandate whom the board selects as president.

2. Power over board composition.

The case also reflects a judicial attitude that voting by different shareholder classes should be separate and distinct. The Court upheld the power of Class A shareholders to remove and replace Class A directors, effectively sidestepping the directors elected by the common shareholders. Could the articles have specified that only the board could replace directors removed from office? Or is replacement of directors an inherent shareholder prerogative?

3. Power over articles and bylaws.

Notice that under Proposal B, the shareholders sought to amend the articles and the bylaws so that only shareholders would fill vacancies arising from the removal of directors. The court finessed the issue, by holding that shareholders could amend the bylaws, without mentioning whether they could also amend the articles in this regard. Why not? Remember that amendment of the articles, including in New York, must be initiated by the board and then approved by the shareholders.

The power of shareholders to elect directors would seem to imply a power to remove directors and to fill the resulting vacancies. But the power to remove and replace directors at any time could undermine board continuity and director independence, potentially leading to corporate instability.

Just as removing public officials in mid-term is generally more difficult than electing them, removal of corporate directors faces a number of obstacles under corporate law. A meeting must be called; notices must be sent; and proxies must be solicited. And, as the following case makes clear, when shareholders seek to remove a director *for cause*, sufficient charges must be proffered and a defense allowed.

The next case involved a battle for control of Loew's Inc. (a public corporation) by two factions, one headed by its President, Vogel, and the other by Tomlinson. At the February shareholders' meeting the two factions effected a compromise; each faction was to have six directors and a neutral director would complete the 13-member board. The peace was a short one. In July, two of the Vogel directors, one Tomlinson director and the neutral director resigned. On July 30, there was a board meeting attended only by the five Tomlinson directors, who attempted to fill two vacancies. The Delaware Chancery Court ruled the filling of the vacancies to be invalid for lack of a quorum. Meanwhile, on July 29, Vogel, as president, sent out a notice calling a special shareholders' meeting for September 12 for the following purposes:

1.   to fill director vacancies;

2.   to amend the bylaws to increase the number of board members from 13 to 19; to increase the quorum from 7 to 10; and to elect six additional directors;

3.   to remove Tomlinson and Stanley Meyer as directors and to fill the vacancies thus created.

The plaintiff sued to enjoin this special shareholder's meeting. The court first considered plaintiff's claim that Vogel, as president, lacked the power to call a stockholders' meeting to amend the bylaws and fill vacancies on the board. Relying on a bylaw explicitly granting the president power to call special meetings of stockholders "for any purpose," the court rejected this claim. Then the court considered the plaintiff's various arguments that the shareholders' powers to initiate action should be limited.

Campbell v. Loew's, Inc.

134 A.2d 852 (Del. Ch. 1957)

SEITZ, CHANCELLOR.

Plaintiff next argues that the stockholders have no power between annual meetings to elect directors to fill newly created directorships.

Plaintiff argues in effect that since the Loew's bylaws provide that the stockholders may fill "vacancies," and since our Courts have construed "vacancy" not to embrace "newly created directorships," the attempted call by the president for the purpose of filling newly created directorships was invalid.

Conceding that "vacancy" as used in the bylaws does not embrace "newly created directorships" does not resolve this problem. I say this because the stockholders have the inherent right between annual meetings to fill newly created directorships. The statute has since been amended to provide that not only vacancies but newly created directorships "may be filled by a majority of the directors then in office." 8 Del.C. § 223. Obviously, the amendment to include new directors is not worded so as to make the statute exclusive. It does not prevent the stockholders from filling the new directorships.

Plaintiff next argues that the shareholders of a Delaware corporation have no power to remove directors from office even for cause and thus the call for that purpose is invalid. The defendant naturally takes a contrary position.

While there are some cases suggesting the contrary, I believe that the stockholders have the power to remove a director for cause. This power must be implied when we consider that otherwise a director who is guilty of the worst sort of violation of his duty could nevertheless remain on the board. It is hardly to be believed that a director who is disclosing the corporation's trade secrets to a competitor would be immune from removal by the stockholders. Other examples, such as embezzlement of corporate funds, etc., come readily to mind.

But plaintiff correctly states that there is no provision in our statutory law providing for the removal of directors by stockholder action. In contrast he calls attention to § 142 of 8 Del.C., dealing with officers, which specifically refers to the possibility of a vacancy in an office by removal. He also notes that the Loew's bylaws provide for the removal of officers and employees but not directors. From these facts he argues that it was intended that directors not be removed even for cause. I believe the statute and bylaw are of course some evidence to support plaintiff's contention. But when we seek to exclude the existence of a power by implication, I think it is pertinent to consider whether the absence of the power can be said to subject the corporation to the possibility of real damage. I say this because we seek intention and such a factor would be relevant to that issue. Considering the damage a director might be able to inflict upon his corporation, I believe the doubt must be resolved by construing the statutes and bylaws as leaving untouched the question of director removal for cause. This being so, the Court is free to conclude on reason that the stockholders have such inherent power.

I therefore conclude that as a matter of Delaware corporation law the stockholders do have the power to remove directors for cause. I need not and do not decide whether the stockholders can by appropriate charter or bylaw provision deprive themselves of this right.

I turn next to plaintiff's charges relating to procedural defects and to irregularities in proxy solicitation by the Vogel group.

Plaintiff's first point is that the stockholders can vote to remove a director for cause only after such director has been given adequate notice of charges of grave impropriety and afforded an opportunity to be heard.

I am inclined to agree that if the proceedings preliminary to submitting the matter of removal for cause to the stockholders appear to be legal and if the charges are legally sufficient on their face, the Court should ordinarily not intervene. The sufficiency of the evidence would be a matter for evaluation in later proceedings. But where the procedure adopted to remove a director for cause is invalid on its face, a stockholder can attack such matters before the meeting. This conclusion is dictated both by the desirability of avoiding unnecessary and expensive action and by the importance of settling internal disputes, where reasonably possible, at the earliest moment. Otherwise a director could be removed and his successor could be appointed and participate in important board action before the illegality of the removal was judicially established. This seems undesirable where the illegality is clear on the face of the proceedings.

Turning now to plaintiff's contentions, it is certainly true that when the shareholders attempt to remove a director for cause," there must be the service of specific charges, adequate notice and full opportunity of meeting the accusation." *See Auer v. Dressel.* While it involved an invalid attempt by directors to remove a fellow director for cause, nevertheless, this same general standard was recognized in [an earlier decision by the Delaware Chancery Court]. The Chancellor said that the power of removal could not "be exercised in an arbitrary manner. The accused director would be entitled to be heard in his own defense."

Plaintiff asserts that no specific charges have been served upon the two directors sought to be ousted; that the notice of the special meeting fails to contain a specific statement of the charges; that the proxy statement which accompanied the notice also failed to notify the stockholders of the specific charges; and that it does not inform the stockholders that the accused must be afforded an opportunity to meet the accusations before a vote is taken.

Matters for stockholder consideration need not be conducted with the same formality as judicial proceedings. The proxy statement specifically recites that the two directors are sought to be removed for the reasons stated in the president's accompanying letter. Both directors involved received copies of the letter. Under the circumstances I think it must be said that the two directors involved were served with notice of the charges against them.

I next consider plaintiff's contention that the charges against the two directors do not constitute "cause" as a matter of law. It would take too much space to narrate in detail the contents of the president's letter. I must therefore give my summary of its charges. First of all, it charges that the two directors (Tomlinson and Meyer) failed to cooperate with Vogel in his announced program for rebuilding the company; that their purpose has been to put themselves in control; that they made baseless accusations against him and other management personnel and attempted to divert him from his normal duties as president by bombarding him with correspondence containing unfounded charges and other similar acts; that they moved into the company's building, accompanied by lawyers and accountants, and immediately proceeded upon a planned scheme of harassment. They called for many records, some going back twenty years, and were rude to the personnel. Tomlinson sent daily letters to the directors making serious charges directly and by means of innuendos and misinterpretations.

Are the foregoing charges, if proved, legally sufficient to justify the ouster of the two directors by the stockholders? I am satisfied that a charge that the directors desired to take over control of the corporation is not a reason for their ouster. Standing alone, it is a perfectly legitimate objective which is a part of the very fabric of corporate existence. Nor is a charge of lack of cooperation a legally sufficient basis for removal for cause.

The next charge is that these directors, in effect, engaged in a calculated plan of harassment to the detriment of the corporation. Certainly a director may examine books, ask questions, etc., in the discharge of his duty, but a point can be reached when his actions exceed the call of duty and become deliberately obstructive. In such a situation, if his actions constitute a real burden on the corporation then the stockholders are entitled to relief. The charges in this area made by the Vogel letter are legally sufficient to justify the stockholders in voting to remove such directors. In so concluding I of course express no opinion as to the truth of the charges.

I therefore conclude that the charge of "a planned scheme of harassment" as detailed in the letter constitutes a justifiable legal basis for removing a director.

I next consider whether the directors sought to be removed have been given a reasonable opportunity to be heard by the stockholders on the charges made.

There seems to be an absence of cases detailing the appropriate procedure for submitting a question of director removal for cause for stockholder consideration. I am satisfied, however, that to the extent the matter is to be voted upon by the use of proxies, such proxies may be solicited only after the accused directors are afforded an opportunity to present their case to the stockholders. This means, in my opinion, that an opportunity must be provided such directors to present their defense to the stockholders by a statement which must accompany or precede the initial solicitation of proxies seeking authority to vote for the removal of such director for cause. If not provided then such proxies may not be voted for removal. And the corporation has a duty to see that this opportunity is given the directors at its expense. Admittedly, no such opportunity was given the two directors involved.

I therefore conclude that the procedural sequence here adopted for soliciting proxies seeking authority to vote on the removal of the two directors is contrary to law. The result is that the proxy solicited by the Vogel group, which is based upon unilateral presentation of the facts by those in control of the corporate facilities, must be declared invalid insofar as they purport to give authority to vote for the removal of the directors for cause.

Points for Discussion

1. *What constitutes "cause"?*

The *Campbell v. Loew's* case arose before Delaware had enacted its statute (DGCL § 141(k) reproduced below) on director removal. The case's principal holding that shareholders have an inherent power to remove directors is now codified. In some instances, director removal requires "cause" and the case is useful in understanding how courts approach that issue. Notice that the court concludes that merely disagreeing with management or seeking to take control is not "cause" for removal, but "a planned scheme of harassment" is. When shareholders elect directors they face no constraints on whom they choose. Why should they be constrained when they seek to remove a director?

2. *Removal procedures.*

The case also lays out the procedures by which directors in a public corporation may be removed for cause. Given that shareholder voting in a public corporation happens through proxies, those seeking removal must proffer charges in a document, known as a proxy statement, distributed to all shareholders. The targeted director, according to the court, must be given a chance to respond to the charges. But notice how the court handles the question of timing. Rather than have the director respond to the charges *after* they have been distributed to the shareholders, the court requires that the director be permitted, at corporate expense, to respond *before* or *at the same time* as the charges are presented to the shareholders. Why is this? Remember that the rule in proxy voting is the proxy submitted "last in time" is the one that counts.

Couldn't shareholders who receive the proxy statement making charges against the director and send in a proxy voting to remove that director always revoke and change their proxy?

3. Removal as impeachment.

The rules on director removal seek to ensure continuity and independence for elected directors, while still providing some measure of protection against renegade directors. Why are fiduciary duties not enough? That is, why not require that shareholders bring a claim to enjoin a director's behavior that violates fiduciary duties and then elect a replacement at the next election of directors?

4. Delaware statute.

As noted above, Delaware's corporate statute now addresses the removal and replacement of directors.

DGCL § 141
Board of Directors; Removal

(k) Any director or the entire board of directors may be removed, with or without cause, by the holders of a majority of the shares then entitled to vote at an election of directors, except as follows:

  (1) Unless the certificate of incorporation otherwise provides, in the case of a corporation whose board is classified . . ., shareholders may effect such removal only for cause; or

  (2) In the case of a corporation having cumulative voting, if less than the entire board is to be removed, no director may be removed without cause if the votes cast against such director's removal would be sufficient to elect such director if then cumulatively voted at an election of the entire board of directors, or, if there be classes of directors, at an election of the class of directors of which such director is a part.

Does the language of Section 141(k) help describe the extent of shareholders' power to remove directors? What are the exceptions to the shareholders' power to remove directors without cause? Do they make sense?

Who has the power to fill vacancies on the board? What if the company has more than one class of shares? What if there are no directors left, or less than a majority of board seats are filled? DGCL Section 223 addresses some of the questions that can arise regarding vacancies and newly created directorships.

§ 223 Vacancies and Newly Created Directorships

(a) Unless otherwise provided in the certificate of incorporation or bylaws:

(1) Vacancies and newly created directorships . . . may be filled by a majority of the directors then in office, although less than a quorum, or by a sole remaining director;

(2) Whenever the holders of any class or classes of stock or series thereof are entitled to elect 1 or more directors by the certificate of incorporation, vacancies and newly created directorships of such class or classes or series may be filled by a majority of the directors elected by such class or classes or series thereof then in office, or by a sole remaining director so elected.

If at any time, by reason of death or resignation or other cause, a corporation should have no directors in office, then any officer or any stockholder . . . may call a special meeting of stockholders in accordance with the certificate of incorporation or the bylaws, or may apply to the Court of Chancery for a decree summarily ordering an election.

(c) If, at the time of filling any vacancy or any newly created directorship, the directors then in office shall constitute less than a majority of the whole board (as constituted immediately prior to any such increase), the Court of Chancery may, upon application of any stockholder or stockholders holding at least 10 percent of the voting stock at the time outstanding having the right to vote for such directors, summarily order an election to be held to fill any such vacancies or newly created directorships, or to replace the directors chosen by the directors then in office as aforesaid.

---

2. Bylaw Amendments

The power of shareholders to amend the bylaws has, in recent years, become a critical issue in corporate governance. A proper bylaw is binding on the board of directors, unlike most shareholder resolutions. For this reason, some activist shareholders have proposed bylaw amendments in public corporations, seeking to move the balance of power away from the board and toward shareholders. Some corporations have responded by trying to limit the ability of shareholders to amend the bylaws.

Bylaw amendments pose difficult questions, since in most corporations the power to amend the bylaws is *shared* by the board and the shareholders. Moreover, the authority over the corporation's business and affairs resides with the board, thus arguably limiting the extent to which shareholders can compel corporate action in the bylaws.

To illustrate some of the difficulties, consider a few passages of the Delaware General Corporation Law, which empowers the shareholders to adopt, amend, or repeal the corporation's bylaws and allows for the company's articles of incorporation to also give the board this power. However, there are tensions in various parts of the statute.

For example, Delaware's Section 109(a) provides:

> After a corporation has received any payment for any of its stock, the power to adopt, amend or repeal bylaws shall be in the stockholders entitled to vote; provided, however, any corporation may, in its certificate of incorporation, confer the power to adopt, amend or repeal bylaws upon the directors. The fact that such power has been so conferred upon the directors shall not divest the stockholders of the power, nor limit their power to adopt, amend or repeal bylaws.

The language "shall not divest" suggests that both the board and the shareholders can have the power with respect to the bylaws. This language suggests that only the Delaware legislature, not a company's board, can take away this shareholder power.

Then Section 109(b) provides:

> The bylaws may contain any provision, not inconsistent with law or with the certificate of incorporation, relating to the business of the corporation, the conduct of its affairs, and its rights or powers or the rights or powers of its stockholders, directors, officers or employees.

The language is broad: it suggests that the bylaws "may" contain "any" provision "relating to" shareholders' rights. Given that shareholders clearly have the right to vote, this language seems to suggest that the bylaws can include broad shareholder powers. But what if the board and shareholders disagree? Could the board amend the bylaws, and the shareholders change them, and so on? That back-and-forth obviously would be inefficient and indeterminate.

One might look to the articles of incorporation to address this puzzle. Section 102(b)(1) states that the articles "may" contain the following:

> Any provision for the management of the business and for the conduct of the affairs of the corporation, and any provision creating, defining, limiting and regulating the powers of the corporation, the directors and the stockholders, or any class of the stockholders; if such provisions are not contrary to the laws of this State. Any provision which is required or permitted by any section of this chapter to be stated in the bylaws may instead be stated in the certificate of incorporation.

This language suggests that articles may contain any provision limiting either the directors' or the shareholders' powers, and that the articles may contain anything that could be stated in the bylaws. Is that language helpful? Or does it simply permit the corporation to allocate power either in the articles (which require both shareholder and board approval) or the bylaws (which, once shareholders have delegated power, require only board approval)?

And then there is Delaware's Section 141(a):

> The business and affairs of every corporation organized under this chapter shall be managed by or under the direction of a board of directors, except as may be otherwise provided in this chapter or in its certificate of incorporation.

Delaware law explicitly states that the directors have the power to manage the business and affairs of the corporation. As we have seen, the shareholders lack such powers and instead play a more passive role, only voting on major questions such as the election of directors or fundamental corporate changes, when either the articles or the statute specifically authorizes a vote. Does this language give the directors the primary power to amend the bylaws as part of running the corporation, provided they do not violate their fiduciary duties in doing so? How much power can this language give the directors, without stripping away the express shareholder power to amend the bylaws in Section 109(a)?

The Delaware Supreme Court addressed this thorny question in *CA, Inc. v. AFSCME Employees Pension Plan*, 953 A.2d 227 (Del. 2008), a case involving a bylaw amendment proposed by shareholders that would require the board to reimburse shareholders' proxy expenses. The court analyzed the various statutory provisions above and concluded:

> It is at this juncture that the statutory language becomes only marginally helpful in determining what the Delaware legislature intended to be the lawful scope of the shareholders' power to adopt, amend and repeal bylaws. To resolve that issue, the Court must resort to different tools, namely, decisions of this Court and of the Court of Chancery that bear on this question.
>
> It is well-established Delaware law that a proper function of bylaws is not to mandate how the board should decide specific substantive business decisions, but rather, to define the process and procedures by which those decisions are made. As the Court of Chancery has noted: "Traditionally, the bylaws have been the corporate instrument used to set forth the rules by which the corporate board conducts its business. To this end, the DGCL is replete with specific provisions authorizing the bylaws to establish the procedures through which board and committee action is taken. There is a general consensus that bylaws that regulate the process by which the board acts are statutorily authorized."

The court cited several process-oriented bylaws that had been held appropriate, such as fixing number of directors on the board, some quorum and vote requirements, and even a few bylaws requiring unanimous board action. These were sufficiently procedural in nature that they did not improperly encroach upon the board's managerial authority under Section 141(a).

The court found that, in theory, a bylaw amendment requiring reimbursement of shareholder proxy expenses could be similarly process focused, and therefore would not violate any provision of Delaware law. However, the court also found that there was a risk that mandatory reimbursement could force the board to violate its fiduciary duties. What if the insurgent shareholder was a competitor? Or was motivated by "personal or petty concerns" or interests adverse to the corporations' interests? The court held that the particular bylaw at issue was problematic because it contained no language permitting the directors to deny reimbursement to shareholders when it would require the directors to breach their fiduciary duties.

Essentially, the court interpreted Section 109 as secondary to Section 141, which the court described as a "cardinal precept" of corporate law. Therefore, the power of shareholders to amend the bylaws must be consistent with the power of the board to manage the affairs and business of the corporation. Nonetheless, shareholders still have some room to operate. For example, the bylaws might provide for a "fiduciary out" so that the board could exercise discretionary power when fiduciary duties require that they do so? Could the bylaw be redrafted to satisfy the court's objections?

Another important type of bylaw is the "advance notice" bylaw, which requires that shareholders submit to the board in advance any proposals they want to bring up at a meeting. How far in advance? Often the requirement is months before the applicable meeting date, perhaps 90 or 120 days. One rationale for advance notice bylaws is that they help companies conduct more orderly meetings by ensuring that a shareholder will not suddenly raise a last-minute issue.

The Delaware courts have accepted this rationale and have permitted companies to implement such bylaws. However, the courts also have indicated that they will closely scrutinize advance notice bylaws if they intrude on shareholder rights. For example, if the bylaw mentions the nomination of directors but does not specifically cover shareholder proposals, then advance notice is not required for shareholder proposals. However, the line between which advance notice bylaw provisions are permissible, and which are not, remains unclear.

C. Board Responses to Shareholder Initiatives

What happens when the board interferes with the rights of shareholders to initiate action? The question is central to corporate law and we consider it in two contexts: board interference with shareholder voting, and board actions to preserve its future power.

1. Interference with Shareholder Voting

The following important case arose from a contest between a shareholder insurgent and an incumbent board about who would set the strategic direction of the corporation. To carry out its strategic plan, the insurgent proposed to obtain shareholder consents to increase the board size and pack the board with its nominees. But before the insurgent could solicit the consents, the board responded by engaging in its own board-packing—effectively undercutting the insurgent's plan. Both sides claimed they had a better vision for the corporation's future.

Below are the relevant provisions of the applicable Delaware statute:

DGCL § 228
Consent of Stockholders in Lieu of Meeting

(a) Unless otherwise provided in the certificate of incorporation, any action required by this chapter to be taken [or which may be taken] at any annual or special meeting of stockholders may be taken without a meeting, without prior notice and without a vote, if a consent or consents in writing, setting forth the action so taken, shall be signed by the holders of outstanding stock having not less than the minimum number of votes that would be necessary to authorize or take such action at a meeting at which all shares entitled to vote thereon were present and voted and shall be delivered to the corporation.

(c) Every written consent shall bear the date of signature of each stockholder, and no written consent shall be effective to take the corporate action referred to therein unless, within 60 days of the earliest dated consent delivered to the corporation, written consents signed by a sufficient number of holders or members to take action are delivered to the corporation.

The dispute occurred after Blasius Industries, Inc. began to accumulate shares of Atlas Corp. in July 1987. On October 29, Blasius disclosed that it owned 9.1% of Atlas' common stock and stated that it intended to encourage Atlas' management to consider a restructuring of the company. Blasius also disclosed that it was exploring the feasibility of obtaining control of Atlas.

Atlas' management did not welcome the prospect of Blasius' controlling shareholders involving themselves in Atlas' affairs. Atlas' new CEO, Weaver, had overseen a business restructuring of a sort and thought it should be given a chance to produce benefit before another restructuring was attempted.

Early in December, Blasius suggested that Atlas engage in a leveraged restructuring and distribute to its shareholders a one-time dividend of $35 million in cash and $125 million in subordinated debentures. Atlas' management responded coolly to this proposal. Mr. Weaver expressed surprise that Blasius would suggest using debt to accomplish a substantial liquidation of Atlas at a time when Atlas' future prospects were promising.

On December 30, Blasius delivered to Atlas a signed written consent (1) adopting a precatory resolution recommending that the board develop and implement a restructuring proposal, (2) amending the Atlas bylaws to, among other things, expand the size of the board from seven to fifteen members—the maximum number allowed by Atlas' articles of incorporation, and (3) electing eight named persons to fill the new directorships. Blasius also informed Atlas of its intent to solicit consents from other Atlas shareholders pursuant to DGCL § 228.

Mr. Weaver immediately conferred with Mr. Masinter, Atlas' outside counsel and a director, who viewed the consent as an attempt to take control of Atlas. They decided to call an emergency meeting of the board, even though a regularly scheduled meeting was to occur only one week hence, on January 6, 1988. In a telephone meeting held the next day, the board voted to amend Atlas' bylaws to increase the size of the board from seven to nine and then appointed John M. Devaney and Harry J. Winters, Jr. to fill the two newly created positions.

Blasius Industries, Inc. v. Atlas Corp.

564 A.2d 651 (Del. Ch. 1988)

ALLEN, CHANCELLOR.

Plaintiff attacks the December 31 board action as a selfishly motivated effort to protect the incumbent board from a perceived threat to its control of Atlas.

Defendants, of course, contest every aspect of plaintiffs' claims. They claim the formidable protections of the business judgment rule.

While I am satisfied that the evidence is powerful, indeed compelling, that the board was chiefly motivated on December 31 to forestall or preclude the possibility that a majority of shareholders might place on the Atlas board eight new members sympathetic to the Blasius proposal, it is less clear with respect to the more subtle motivational question: whether the existing members of the board did so because they held a good faith belief that such shareholder action would be self-injurious and shareholders needed to be protected from their own judgment.

On balance, I cannot conclude that the board was acting out of a self-interested motive in any important respect on December 31. I conclude rather that the board saw the "threat" of the Blasius recapitalization proposal as posing vital policy differences between itself and Blasius. It acted, I conclude, in a good faith effort to protect its incumbency, not selfishly, but in order to thwart implementation of the recapitalization that it feared, reasonably, would cause great injury to the Company.

The real question the case presents, to my mind, is whether, in these circumstances, the board, even if it *is* acting with subjective good faith, may validly act for the principal purpose of preventing the shareholders from electing a majority of new directors. The question thus posed is not one of intentional wrong (or even negligence), but one of authority *as between the fiduciary and the beneficiary.*

The shareholder franchise is the ideological underpinning upon which the legitimacy of directorial power rests. Generally, shareholders have only two protections against perceived inadequate business performance. They may sell their stock (which, if done in sufficient numbers, may so affect security prices as to create an incentive for altered managerial performance), or they may vote to replace incumbent board members.

It has, for a long time, been conventional to dismiss the stockholder vote as a vestige or ritual of little practical importance. It may be that we are now witnessing the emergence of new institutional voices and arrangements that will make the stockholder vote a less predictable affair than it has been. Be that as it may, however, whether the vote is seen functionally as an unimportant formalism, or as an important tool of discipline, it is clear that it is critical to the theory that legitimates the exercise of power by some (directors and officers) over vast aggregations of property that they do not own. Thus, when viewed from a broad, institutional perspective, it can be seen that matters involving the integrity of the shareholder voting process involve consideration not present in any other context in which directors exercise delegated power.

The distinctive nature of the shareholder franchise context also appears when the matter is viewed from a less generalized, doctrinal point of view. From this point of view, as well, it appears that the ordinary considerations to which the business judgment rule originally responded are simply not present in the shareholder voting context. That is, a decision by the board to act for the primary purpose of preventing the effectiveness of a shareholder vote inevitably involves the question who, as between the principal and the agent, has authority with respect to a matter of internal corporate governance. That, of course, is true in a very specific way in this case which deals with the question who should constitute the board of directors of the corporation, but it will be true in every instance in which an incumbent board seeks to thwart a shareholder majority. A board's decision to act to prevent the shareholders from creating a majority of new board positions and filling them does not involve the exercise of *the corporation's power* over its property, or with respect to *its* rights or obligations; rather, it involves allocation, between shareholders as a class and the board, of effective power with respect to governance of the corporation. Action designed principally to interfere with the effectiveness of a vote inevitably involves a conflict between the board and a shareholder majority. Judicial review of such action involves a determination of the legal and equitable obligations of an agent towards his principal. This is not, in my opinion, a question that a court may leave to the agent finally to decide so long as he does so honestly and competently; that is, it may not be left to the agent's business judgment.

Plaintiff argues for a rule of *per se* invalidity once a plaintiff has established that a board has acted for the primary purpose of thwarting the exercise of a shareholder vote.

A *per se* rule that would strike down, in equity, any board action taken for the primary purpose of interfering with the effectiveness of a corporate vote would have the advantage of relative clarity and predictability. It also has the advantage of most vigorously enforcing the concept of corporate democracy. The disadvantage it brings along is, of course, the disadvantage a *per se* rule always has: it may sweep too broadly.

In two recent cases dealing with shareholder votes, this court struck down board acts done for the primary purpose of impeding the exercise of stockholder voting power. In doing so, a *per se* rule was not applied. Rather, it was said that, in such a case, the board bears the heavy burden of demonstrating a compelling justification for such action.

In my view, our inability to foresee now all of the future settings in which a board might, in good faith, paternalistically seek to thwart a shareholder vote, counsels against the adoption of a *per se* rule invalidating, in equity, every board action taken for the sole or primary purpose of thwarting a shareholder vote, even though I recognize the transcending significance of the franchise to the claims to legitimacy of our scheme of corporate governance. It may be that some set of facts would justify such extreme action. This, however, is not such a case.

The board was not faced with a coercive action taken by a powerful shareholder against the interests of a distinct shareholder constituency (such as a public minority). It was presented with a consent solicitation by a 9% shareholder. Moreover, here it had time (and understood that it had time) to inform the shareholders of its views on the merits of the proposal subject to stockholder vote. The only justification that can, in such a situation, be offered for the action taken is that the board knows better than do the shareholders what is in the corporation's best interest. While that premise is no doubt true for any number of matters, it is irrelevant (except insofar as the shareholders wish to be guided by the board's recommendation) when the question is who should comprise the board of directors. The theory of our corporation law confers power upon directors as the agents of the shareholders; it does not create Platonic masters. It may be that the Blasius restructuring proposal was or is unrealistic and would lead to injury to the corporation and its shareholders if pursued. The board certainly viewed it that way, and that view, held in good faith, entitled the board to take certain steps to evade the risk it perceived. It could, for example, expend corporate funds to inform shareholders and seek to bring them to a similar point of view. But there is a vast difference between expending corporate funds to inform the electorate and exercising power for the primary purpose of foreclosing effective shareholder action. A majority of the shareholders, who were not dominated in any respect, could view the matter differently than did the board. If they do, or did, they are entitled to employ the mechanisms provided by the corporation law and the Atlas certificate of incorporation to advance that view. They are also entitled, in my opinion, to restrain their agents, the board, from acting for the principal purpose of thwarting that action.

I therefore conclude that, even finding the action taken was taken in good faith, it constituted an unintended violation of the duty of loyalty that the board owed to the shareholders. I note parenthetically that the concept of an unintended breach of the duty of loyalty is unusual but not novel. That action will, therefore, be set aside by order of this court.

Points for Discussion

1. *Platonic masters.*

Why aren't directors Platonic masters? Haven't shareholders deferred to their authority—as reflected in DGCL § 141—when they invested in the corporation?

2. *Power vs. duty.*

Blasius is a pillar of Delaware corporate law. It applies the principle announced in *Schnell v. Chris-Craft Indus., Inc.*, a case we saw early in our discussion of corporation basics, that involved an incumbent board's attempt to move forward the meeting date in a way that impeded an ongoing proxy contest. The Delaware Supreme Court said that "inequitable action does not become permissible simply because it is legally possible." Thus, even though there was no question that the Atlas board had the power to increase the board size and fill the resulting vacancies, the question was whether the power had been exercised consistently with the board's fiduciary duties. Why was it not enough that the board's motives were pure and the board was convinced in good faith that the recapitalization proposed by Blasius was a terrible idea?

3. *Compelling circumstances.*

Blasius rejects a *per se* rule of invalidity, contemplating the possibility of "compelling justifications" that would permit the board to interfere with shareholder voting in limited circumstances. When might interference be justified? Although the decision makes clear that the board's doubts about an insurgent's plans are not compelling, would it be justifiable for a board to impede a consent solicitation to replace the board on the eve of a shareholder vote to adopt a pending merger proposal?

2. Preserving the Power of the Board

There are two main ways for boards to preserve their power and defend against a hostile acquisition. A central idea behind both of these defenses is for boards to diminish the power of *subsequent* directors.

First, boards can implement a classified or staggered board, meaning that only a portion of the directors are up for reelection in a particular year. For example, if a board has three classes of directors, even shareholders who have enough votes to replace directors will have to wait through two annual election cycles to obtain control, because they will only to be able to elect one-third of the directors each year. The classified or staggered board is thus a way for boards to preserve their power, at least in the short term, by ensuring that any new directors will not constitute a majority of the board.

Second, since the 1980s, many public companies also have used "poison pills" to preserve the board's power, and specifically to deter hostile acquisitions. Poison pills make a hostile acquisition financially unattractive unless the target's board approves the deal. There are two keys to understanding poison pills: (1) the board can adopt a poison pill unilaterally, without shareholder approval, and (2) poison pills deter acquisitions because acquirers would lose a huge amount of money from the dilution in their share ownership if they were to move ahead with a takeover of the company. Subsequent directors are a central idea for poison pills, because they often seek to restrict the ability of future directors to redeem, or eliminate, them.

Many students find poison pills confusing, and they are. Keep in mind that poison pills are designed to deter potential acquirers by diluting their shareholdings. But poison pills are almost never actually triggered, and the threatened dilution almost never actually happens. That means the key to understanding poison pills is thinking about what *could* happen, not what actually does.

A poison pill is a "rights plan" that can be adopted by the board, typically without shareholder approval. The rights plan is a kind of placeholder: it gives every shareholder a placeholder right, with one important exception. Any shareholder who offers to buy or buys more than a stated percentage of the company's outstanding shares (such as 15%) will not receive the benefits of this placeholder right. Effectively, the rights plan divides the shareholders into two groups: the acquirer vs. the large group of shareholders not affiliated with the acquirer.

We call the right that attaches to each share a placeholder right, because initially it only gives each shareholder a right that is essentially worthless. This is a confusing part of the rights plan: each share has the right to buy new securities of the company, typically preferred stock, at an extremely high price. Why give each share such a strange, worthless right? One reason is that, because it involves preferred stock, the board can issue the right on its own, without shareholder approval. Another reason is that this right holds the place for a more important right, which can be triggered if the acquirer exceeds a specified ownership threshold.

The placeholder aspect of the rights becomes important if an acquirer buys more than the specified trigger amount of company's shares. This is the "first trigger," meaning that the rights attached to the shares are no longer merely placeholders. They instead are converted from a worthless right to acquire preferred shares into a very valuable right to acquire more common shares, at a significant discount. All of the shareholders get this right, except for the acquirer. For example, if a company had 100 shares, and the acquirer bought 20, the holders of 80 shares would have the right to buy more common shares at a discount, but the acquirer would not.

(The right to buy shareholders to buy more shares of their company, the target, is sometimes called a "flip-in" right. A poison pill can be designed so that if the target company is merged into the acquirer, the rights holders can "flip-over" their rights and buy shares of the acquiring company at half price, though these are more complex and are less frequently used.)

The holders of those 80 shares would only be able to execute this valuable right, and buy shares at a discount, if a "second trigger" occurs, meaning the takeover itself, typically through a merger. The acquirer's 20 shares would not have this valuable right. Again, the valuable right is to buy more shares at a significant discount.

Suppose the company is worth $1 million, so that the acquirer's 20% stake is worth $200,000. In other words, the other 80 shares could be converted into 160 shares, while the acquirer would still have just 20 shares. The total shares would be 180, meaning that the acquirer's stake would be diluted from 20% down to 11% (20 divided by 180).

The poison pill is an effective defense but an acquirer is not going to want to suffer losses from buying a 20% stake in a company and then immediately see that stake diluted to 11%. But remember that the key to understanding poison pills is thinking about what *could* happen, not what actually does. In this instance, the potential dilution deters the acquirer from making a hostile takeover and forces them to negotiate with the board, or seek to replace them.

The board holds the "antidote" to the "poison" in the poison pill, and can redeem the rights on terms based on their discretion. If the acquirer makes an offer that the board accepts, the board will redeem the rights and move forward with the deal. If the board rejects the acquirer, the acquirer can seek to replace the board with directors who will be willing to redeem the pill.

But what if the "poison pill" also restricts future directors? For example, the rights plan might provide that even, if the directors were replaced, any new directors would not be able to redeem the rights for a specified period of time. The Delaware courts have addressed this question in a line of cases.

In the case below, Mentor Graphics sought to acquire Quickturn Design Systems. Mentor was in the business of electronic design automation software and hardware, and Quickturn, a publicly traded Delaware corporation, was the market leader in emulation technology used to verify the design of silicon chips and electronics systems.

Although Quickturn had been a growth company with increasing earnings and revenues, its fortunes turned in the spring of 1998 when its growth and stock price declined because of the downturn in the semiconductor industry, especially in Asia. Smelling a bargain, Mentor began to explore the possibility of acquiring Quickturn. Mentor, which had been barred in patent litigation with Quickturn from competing in the U.S. emulation market, would realize a special benefit by acquiring Quickturn. If Mentor owned Quickturn, it could "unenforce" the Quickturn patents and enter the U.S. emulation market.

When Quickturn's stock price began to decline in May 1998, Mentor moved to acquire Quickturn for a cheap price. Mentor assembled financial and legal advisors, as well as proxy solicitors. And on August 12, Mentor made a cash tender offer for all outstanding common shares of Quickturn at $12.125 per share, representing a nearly 50% premium over Quickturn's pre-offer price, but a 20% discount from Quickturn's February 1998 stock price. Mentor announced that its tender offer, once consummated, would be followed by a second step merger in which Quickturn's nontendering stockholders would receive the same $12.125 per share.

Mentor also announced its intent to solicit proxies to replace the board at a special meeting. Using Quickturn's bylaw governing the call of special stockholders' meetings, Mentor began soliciting agent designations from Quickturn stockholders to satisfy the bylaw's stock ownership requirements to call such a meeting.

What is a hostile bid? It is a tender offer made to shareholders, without the approval or support of the target board. It is not "hostile" as to the shareholders, who may well be thrilled to be offered a premium for their shares over the current market price. Instead, it is "hostile" as to the board of directors (and often incumbent executives), who understand that if the bid succeeds they may lose their positions.

Under federal securities law, Quickturn was required to inform its shareholders of its response to Mentor's offer no later than ten business days after the offer was commenced. During that ten-day period, the Quickturn board met three times to consider Mentor's offer and ultimately to decide how to respond. Quickturn's board consisted of eight members, all but one of whom were outside, independent directors. All had distinguished careers and significant technological experience. Collectively, the board had more than 30 years of experience in the electronic design automation industry and held one million shares (about 5%) of Quickturn's common stock.

After hearing presentations from its financial advisers, the Quickturn board concluded that Mentor's offer was inadequate, and decided to recommend that Quickturn shareholders reject the offer. In addition, the Quickturn board adopted two defensive measures in response to Mentor's hostile takeover bid. First, the board amended Quickturn's bylaws, which permitted stockholders holding 10% or more of Quickturn's stock to call a special stockholders meeting. The amendment provided that if any special meeting is requested by shareholders, the board could determine the time and place of the meeting.

Second, the board amended Quickturn's shareholder Rights Plan or "poison pill" to add a Deferred Redemption Provision or DRP, under which no newly elected board could redeem the Rights Plan for six months after taking office, if the redemption would facilitate a transaction with an "Interested Person" (one who proposed, nominated or financially supported the election of the new directors to the board). Mentor would be an Interested Person.

The effect of the bylaw amendment would be to delay a shareholder-called special meeting for at least three months. The effect of the DRP would be to delay the ability of a newly-elected, Mentor-nominated board to redeem the Rights Plan for six months. Thus, their combined effect would be to delay any acquisition of Quickturn by Mentor for at least nine months.

Mentor challenged the legality of both defensive maneuvers in the Court of Chancery. After a trial on the merits, the Court of Chancery determined the bylaw amendment was valid, but the DRP was invalid on fiduciary grounds.

Quickturn appealed the DRP finding, but Mentor did not file a cross-appeal on the validity of the bylaw amendment. Consequently, the Delaware Supreme Court reviewed only the finding that Quickturn's directors breached their fiduciary duty by adopting the DRP.

Quickturn Design Systems, Inc. v. Shapiro

721 A.2d 1281 (Del. 1998)

HOLLAND, JUSTICE.

In this appeal, Mentor argues that the judgment of the Court of Chancery should be affirmed because the Delayed Redemption Provision (DRP) is invalid as a matter of Delaware law. According to Mentor, the DRP will impermissibly deprive any newly elected board of both its statutory authority to manage the corporation under 8 Del.C. § 141(a) and its concomitant fiduciary duty pursuant to that statutory mandate. We agree.

One of the most basic tenets of Delaware corporate law is that the board of directors has the ultimate responsibility for managing the business and affairs of a corporation. Section 141(a) requires that any limitation on the board's authority be set out in the certificate of incorporation. The Quickturn certificate of incorporation contains no provision purporting to limit the authority of the board in any way. The DRP, however, would prevent a newly elected board of directors from completely discharging its fundamental management duties to the corporation and its stockholders for six months. While the DRP limits the board of directors' authority in only one respect, the suspension of the Rights Plan, it nonetheless restricts the board's power in an area of fundamental importance to the shareholders—negotiating a possible sale of the corporation. Therefore, we hold that the DRP is invalid under Section 141(a), which confers upon any newly elected board of directors full power to manage and direct the business and affairs of a Delaware corporation.

In discharging the statutory mandate of Section 141(a), the directors have a fiduciary duty to the corporation and its shareholders. This unremitting obligation extends equally to board conduct in a contest for corporate control. The DRP prevents a newly elected board of directors from completely discharging its fiduciary duties to protect fully the interests of Quickturn and its stockholders.

This Court has recently observed that "although the fiduciary duty of a Delaware director is unremitting, the exact course of conduct that must be charted to properly discharge that responsibility will change in the specific context of the action the director is taking with regard to either the corporation or its shareholders." This Court has held "to the extent that a contract, or a provision thereof, purports to require a board to act or not act in such a fashion as to limit the exercise of fiduciary duties, it is invalid and unenforceable." The DRP "tends to limit in a substantial way the freedom of [newly elected] directors' decisions on matters of management policy." Therefore, "it violates the duty of each [newly elected] director to exercise his own best judgment on matters coming before the board."

In this case, the Quickturn board was confronted by a determined bidder that sought to acquire the company at a price the Quickturn board concluded was inadequate. Such situations are common in corporate takeover efforts. This Court has held that no defensive measure can be sustained when it represents a breach of the directors' fiduciary duty. *A fortiori*, no defensive measure can be sustained which would require a new board of directors to breach its fiduciary duty. In that regard, we note Mentor has properly acknowledged that in the event its slate of directors is elected, those newly elected directors will be required to discharge their unremitting fiduciary duty to manage the corporation for the benefit of Quickturn and its stockholders.

The DRP would prevent a new Quickturn board of directors from managing the corporation by redeeming the Rights Plan to facilitate a transaction that would serve the stockholders' best interests, even under circumstances where the board would be required to do so because of its fiduciary duty to the Quickturn stockholders. Because the DRP impermissibly circumscribes the board's statutory power under Section 141(a) and the directors' ability to fulfill their concomitant fiduciary duties, we hold that the DRP is invalid.

Points for Discussion

1. Beyond *Blasius?*

Notice that *Quickturn* does not say that the board violated its fiduciary duties by adopting a poison pill that tied the hands of future boards, but rather that limiting the board's future ability to exercise its fiduciary duties was beyond the board's power. In this sense, *Quickturn* goes beyond *Blasius* to declare some board actions as fundamentally inconsistent with shareholder voting rights—here the right to elect a fully-empowered board of directors. *Quickturn* does not mention a "compelling justifications" exception.

2. Dead hand pill.

Notice that to make the Rights Plan less susceptible to challenge, the Quickturn board eliminated a "dead hand" feature of the Rights Plan. This feature had provided that if an insurgent holding more than 15% of Quickturn's common stock successfully waged a proxy contest to replace a majority of the board, only "continuing directors" (those directors in office at the time the poison pill was adopted) could redeem the rights. In an earlier decision, not appealed to the Delaware Supreme Court, the Chancery Court had held that that such a "dead hand" poison pill was invalid both because it violated DGCL § 141 and because the directors had violated their fiduciary duties by adopting such a poison pill. *Carmody v. Toll Brothers, Inc.*, 723 A.2d 1180 (Del. Ch. 1998).

3. Consistency with CA, Inc. v. AFSCME?

The focus in *Quickturn* on the board's power in adopting the Rights Plan, rather than its fiduciary duties, suggests that any limits on the board's control of a poison pill must come (if at all) from the articles of incorporation. The decision suggests that a bylaw amendment initiated by shareholders to limit board prerogatives in creating or continuing a poison pill would face a statutory impediment. Some have read *Quickturn* merely to state that "the board's authority to manage the business and affairs of a corporation is inherently limited by the power of the stockholders to exercise decision-making authority for the voting and sale decisions assigned to them." Is this reading of *Quickturn* consistent with the more recent 2008 decision in *CA, Inc. v. AFSCME*, which holds that shareholders cannot impose procedures that limit the ability of directors to exercise their fiduciary duties?

4. *Shareholder duties in amending bylaws.*

The power of shareholders to amend the bylaws may also be constrained by fiduciary duties—that is, when a controlling shareholder seeks to amend the bylaws for its own selfish purposes. The Delaware courts have held that bylaw amendments initiated by a controlling shareholder are invalid if they have an inequitable purpose and effect. For example, bylaw amendments approved by a controlling shareholder to strip independent directors on the board of their power to consider a strategic direction that the controlling shareholder opposed have been held invalid. *Hollinger International, Inc. v. Black*, 844 A.2d 1022 (Del. Ch. 2004), *aff'd*, 872 A.2d 559 (Del. 2005).

D. Voting and Shareholder Activism

Shareholder activism is one of the most controversial topics in business and finance, for two reasons. First, from an economic perspective, there is a sharp divide between the directors and officers of companies and the shareholder activists who advocate new strategies or even replacing the board.

Many directors and officers view shareholder activists as short-term-oriented nuisances who impede their ability to manage corporations in the long-run economic interests of shareholders. Many shareholder activists view directors and officers as entrenched incompetents who line their pockets at the expense of shareholders.

There is overwhelming evidence that the announcement that an activist has a significant position in a target company's shares is on average associated with a significant increase in the value of those shares. But some commentators criticize this evidence as overly focused on the short-term, or say it reflects a transfer of value from stakeholders. Voting is important to this form of "economic" shareholder activism, especially when the activist seeks to replace either all or some of a company's directors in a proxy fight.

A second category of activism involves shareholders advocating changes related to the kinds of policy issues we discussed in the previous two chapters. For example, shareholder activists who focus on ESG issues typically take relatively small positions, and then request that the targeted company include a vote on a shareholder proposal as part of its annual meeting. There is less evidence that this category of activism impacts the value of shares, but it has been influential in pressing companies to confront a range of environmental, social, and governance issues.

Before we turn to some important legal issues related to activism, we briefly consider the ways in which the institutional nature of the holdings of shareholders impact activism of both categories.

---

1. Institutions as Shareholder Activists

As institutional ownership of shares has increased during the previous couple of decades, voting power in public corporations has become more concentrated. Today, large index funds families such as BlackRock, State Street, and Vanguard often control 15–20% of the outstanding shares of public companies. They are vocal proponents of corporate governance reforms and often push for boards to consider sustainability and other long-run objectives, as opposed to short-term shareholder gain.

In addition, large "hedge fund" activists control billions of dollars and frequently challenge boards to change their strategies, often with the support of the index funds. Collectively, shareholder activists have exercised a newfound voice and have pushed for a variety of governance reforms, such as new methods for electing directors, shareholder access to the nomination process, and greater say in corporate operations.

Shareholder activism is not a new phenomenon. Large block shareholders pressured the managers of corporations during late nineteenth and early twentieth centuries. During the 1980s, there was surge of takeover-driven shareholder activism, led by corporate "raiders" who bought large numbers of shares and then pushed for corporations to be sold or broken into pieces. Nevertheless, the recent increase in activism is noteworthy, if not unprecedented.

When we discuss shareholder activism, we often are talking about activism by institutions, not individuals, though a handful of individuals are very active in submitting shareholder proposals. In 1950, institutions held only 9% of U.S. stocks; in 1983 they crossed the 50% threshold; today, they hold the vast majority of shares. Equity ownership is also concentrated in the largest institutional shareholders. For most public companies, a majority of their shares are held by fewer than a hundred institutions; in many cases, the number of institutions is even smaller. If you invited one person from each of the top institutional shareholders of a typical company, you could fit representatives of a majority of the shares in a large law school classroom.

The shift from individuals to institutions promised improvements in corporate governance. Hopes ran high during the 1990s that institutional investors could overcome the rational apathy and collective action problems faced by individual investors. In theory, increasing institutionalization narrows the separation of ownership from control highlighted by Berle and Means. Voting apathy is less rational as shareholdings grow, and economies of scale make monitoring easier. An institution that votes on the same proposals at a number of companies reduces its per-company monitoring costs.

But institutional shareholders, themselves agents for their beneficiaries, face their own conflicting interests that discourage them from activism. That is, the institutional agents may not have incentives to act as principals. These conflicts are different for each institution:

- *Mutual funds.* Mutual funds (which obtain much of their business from employer-based savings plans, such as 401(k) plans) view portfolio companies as customers. Thus, fund managers face pressure, often subtle, from corporate management to vote according to management's interests or risk that management will withdraw its savings plan and move it elsewhere. This threat is even greater for mutual funds that are part of financial conglomerates, which also offer investment banking and corporate lending services.

- *Corporate pension plans.* Corporate pension plans (which invest corporate money to provide retirement benefits to employees) are managed by in-house plan administrators, usually corporate executives. These administrators face conflicts between managing the pension fund for the benefit of plan participants, as required by the Employee Retirement Income Security Act (ERISA), and managing it for the benefit of corporate management.

- *State pension plans.* State pension plans (which invest their assets for state employee retirement) face an entirely different set of pressures. Unlike their private counterparts, which worry about offending corporate management, public pension managers often have political aspirations and seek to be a thorn in the side of corporate management—to advance particular economic, social, or political causes that may be at odds with maximizing fund performance.

- *Insurance companies.* Insurance companies (which invest their assets to cover their insurance liabilities and also manage insurance-based retirement plans) face similar pressures as mutual funds. Activism risks antagonizing corporate clients and, even worse, creating a climate that invites scrutiny of corporate management across the board, including at insurance companies.

Besides these conflicts, institutional investors that index their investments (tracking the performance of a particular stock index, such as the S&P 500) have little incentive to undertake the expense of shareholder activism, even if it might improve portfolio performance. Since such institutions compete on cost, they have an incentive not to engage in corporate governance activities that would increase costs more than those of competitors. For many institutional investors, indexing is a significant part of their investment strategy.

Another explanation for institutional passivity is that institutions have a strong preference (sometimes mandated by law) for liquidity rather than control. Open-end mutual funds, for example, must stand ready to redeem their investors' shares. And many mutual funds and insurance companies see their business model as buying and selling stock in their portfolios, with annual turnover rates often exceeding 100%. They don't have time to treat portfolio companies as an owner. Only when an institution is constrained from selling the stock, because the size of its ownership will depress the market price, does an institution have the incentive to exercise voice in corporate affairs.

The institutional culture also is at odds with shareholder activism. Institutional managers often feel an "obedience to the mores of the financial community," which disdains shareholder activism. Institutional managers sometimes express their worry about developing a reputation as an activist, as though it were a communicable disease.

Marbled into these conflicts are various legal impediments to an institutional governance role—the result of a deep-seated American suspicion of concentrated financial power. As we will next see, the SEC proxy rules often discourage communications among shareholders seeking to make control changes. Federal law requires disgorgement of short-swing profits by 10% shareholders and federal securities disclosure rules applicable to 5% toehold positions impose additional costs on institutions seeking to take meaningful ownership positions. The possibility of disgorgement liability also discourages institutional investors from installing representatives on company boards. Regulation FD (the rule against selective corporate disclosures) raises questions about the legality of behind-the-scenes communications with corporate insiders on governance issues. And any legal liability that may arise from over-activism is borne by the institutional investor alone—another free-riding cost.

Despite these problems, there has been a steady increase over the past decade in institutional activism. Some institutions (primarily state pension plans and labor union pension funds) have become regular and effective users of the shareholder proposal rule. Their submissions on corporate governance reforms—such as majority voting in director elections, restrictions on poison pills, and redesigned executive compensation—have received regular majority support from fellow shareholders. And management implementation of some majority-supported proposals, particularly those dealing with majority voting for directors, has been widespread.

Other institutions, particularly the retirement fund for college professors (TIAA-CREF) and the largest state pension plan (CalPERS), have targeted under-performing companies and engaged in behind-the-scenes negotiations with corporate management to seek desired reforms. Studies indicate that some of these negotiations have produced positive effects on stock prices.

Institutional shareholders also have become subject to rules requiring that they vote the stock they hold. In carrying out these duties, institutional shareholders have often relied on the recommendations of proxy advisory firms, particularly the dominant Institutional Shareholder Services (ISS). Thus, for example, mutual funds often follow ISS recommendations on removing anti-takeover measures, even when opposed by management. By adhering to ISS recommendations, institutional investors assure themselves of being in the voting mainstream.

Over the past decade, shareholder proposals on topics of board structure and takeover defenses have regularly received majority support. This compares to the lukewarm reception that institutional shareholders have given proposals on social/political topics (such as child labor, global warming, political contributions, or environmental concerns).

Hedge funds are very different from the other types of institutional investors described above. Hedge funds are pooled, privately organized investment vehicles that are not widely available to the public and operate outside the securities regulation and registration requirements that apply to mutual funds and pension funds. Hedge funds are administered by professional investment managers with performance-based compensation and significant investments in the fund. Hedge funds typically charge their investors not only a fixed percentage fee based on the size of assets under management, but also a performance fee (often 20% of the profits). Thus, hedge fund managers typically have significantly greater financial incentives to achieve gains for shareholders than do the managers of other institutions.

The sharp financial incentives of hedge funds, and their size, have made them a more formidable threat to incumbent directors than other institutional investors. Recall that incumbent directors have significant advantages over insurgents in corporate elections: they control the distribution of proxy materials and can use corporate funds to pay for their reelection campaigns. It is difficult for shareholders to remove official director nominees.

Nevertheless, hedge fund activists have brought numerous campaigns against incumbent boards, and their proxy contests have succeeded more frequently than efforts by other institutions. The largest hedge funds, who have demonstrated the capacity to launch a proxy contest and oust one or more directors, have also been the most successful funds, and as a result are also among the largest.

Federal securities law provides that once a shareholder activist acquires 5% or more of the shares of a public corporation, it must disclose its ownership. The filing the shareholder must make is called a Schedule 13D: it must be filed with the Securities and Exchange Commission within 10 days by anyone who acquires beneficial ownership of a class of publicly traded securities of a public company. Studies of hedge fund activism consistently show that the announcement of activism, and the filing of a Schedule 13D, is associated with significant positive returns, in the range of 7% above other investments during the several days surrounding the announcement. There is a debate about whether those returns are sustained over the longer term, and whether the gains for shareholders come at the expense of other constituents.

Hedge fund activism has generated strong views and strident debate. Shareholder advocacy groups and institutional investors generally favor activism by hedge funds. Directors, officers, and lawyers who represent large public corporations frequently oppose it.

Points for Discussion

1. *Possible reforms.*

Given the emergence of institutional shareholders, can you think of any reforms to improve the mechanisms of "shareholder democracy"? For example, the Securities and Exchange Commission recently amended the federal proxy rules to require the use of "universal proxy cards," meaning that both management and shareholder candidates for election will be listed on the same universal proxy card. Shareholders presenting their own candidates must solicit holders of a minimum of 67 percent of the voting power of shareholders entitled to vote in the election. How might a shareholder activist solicit this many shareholders? How much do you think it would cost?

What do you think of a requirement that the board nominate at least two candidates for each open directorship, thus giving shareholders some choice? What if mutual funds and other institutional intermediaries solicited views from their investors, perhaps through scientific polling, on particular issues? Do you think a survey of shareholders might be useful in determining how they should vote on issues presented by activists?

2. *Re-theorizing the corporation.*

The theories of the corporation generally assume passive shareholders, who go along with management's slate of directors and their agenda. The "contract" theory assumes that markets (in which shareholders can sell their shares, and thus control, to an outside bidder) protect their interests. The "political product" theory assumes different institutions (such as securities markets and courts) serve this protective role. The "team production" theory assumes that mediator-directors balance the interests of shareholders with those of others. The "director primacy" theory assumes it is efficient for shareholders to have limited voting rights. Does the emergence of institutional investors affect the descriptive power of these theories?

2. State Law: Reimbursement Rules for Shareholder Activism

One barrier to shareholder activism is the law on shareholder voting. State law on the reimbursement of election-related expenses of shareholder insurgents chills activism. Generally, only the incumbent board can use corporate funds to solicit proxies. Insurgents must use their own funds to finance a proxy contest and can recover their election-related costs only if they win. But this edifice has been shifting.

The rule, described in the case below, essentially gives financial control over the voting mechanism to incumbent management. Is this good? On one hand, the rule limits wasteful spending by the corporation on shareholder initiatives supported by less than a shareholder majority. On the other hand, the rule discourages shareholder activism and helps entrench management.

Rosenfeld v. Fairchild Engine & Airplane Corp.

128 N.E.2d 291 (N.Y. 1955)

FROESSEL, JUDGE.

In a stockholder's derivative action brought by plaintiff, an attorney, who owns 25 out of the company's over 2,300,000 shares, he seeks to compel the return of $261,522, paid out of the corporate treasury to reimburse both sides in a proxy contest for their expenses. The Appellate Division has unanimously affirmed a judgment of an Official Referee dismissing plaintiff's complaint on the merits, and we agree.

Of the amount in controversy $106,000 were spent out of corporate funds by the old board of directors while still in office in defense of their position in said contest; $28,000 were paid to the old board by the new board after the change of management following the proxy contest, to compensate the former directors for such of the remaining expenses of their unsuccessful defense as the new board found was fair and reasonable; payment of $127,000, representing reimbursement of expenses to members of the prevailing group, was expressly ratified by a 16 to 1 majority vote of the stockholders.

The Appellate Division found that the difference between plaintiff's group and the old board 'went deep into the policies of the company,' and that among these [the former CEO's] contract was one of the 'main points of contention.'

Other jurisdictions and our own lower courts have held that management may look to the corporate treasury for the reasonable expenses of soliciting proxies to defend its position in a bona fide policy contest.

If directors of a corporation may not in good faith incur reasonable and proper expenses in soliciting proxies in these days of giant corporations with vast numbers of stockholders, the corporate business might be seriously interfered with because of stockholder indifference and the difficulty of procuring a quorum, where there is no contest. In the event of a proxy contest, if the directors may not freely answer the challenges of outside groups and in good faith defend their actions with respect to corporate policy for the information of the stockholders, they and the corporation may be at the mercy of persons seeking to wrest control for their own purposes, so long as such persons have ample funds to conduct a proxy contest. The test is clear. When the directors act in good faith in a contest over policy, they have the right to incur reasonable and proper expenses for solicitation of proxies and in defense of their corporate policies, and are not obliged to sit idly by.

It is also our view that the members of the so-called new group could be reimbursed by the corporation for their expenditures in this contest by affirmative vote of the stockholders. With regard to these ultimately successful contestants, as the Appellate Division below has noted, there was, of course, 'no duty of the corporation to pay for such expense'. However, where a majority of the stockholders chose in this case by a vote of 16 to 1 to reimburse the successful contestants for achieving the very end sought and voted for by them as owners of the corporation, we see no reason to deny the effect of their ratification nor to hold the corporate body powerless to determine how its own moneys shall be spent.

The rule then which we adopt is simply this: In a contest over policy, as compared to a purely personal power contest, corporate directors have the right to make reasonable and proper expenditures, subject to the scrutiny of the courts when duly challenged, from the corporate treasury for the purpose of persuading the stockholders of the correctness of their position and soliciting their support for policies which the directors believe, in all good faith, are in the best interests of the corporation. The stockholders, moreover, have the right to reimburse successful contestants for the reasonable and bona fide expenses incurred by them in any such policy contest, subject to like court scrutiny.

Points for Discussion

1. Actually, a close case.

At first glance, the *Rosenfeld* decision seems cut and dried. Incumbents (whether they win or lose) are paid their reasonable expenses in a proxy contest, so long as the contest is one of "policy." Insurgents can be reimbursed for their reasonable election expenses only if the shareholders vote for reimbursement—which as a practical matter means only when they win.

But three judges dissented, arguing that it should be illegal for incumbents (unless they receive the unanimous consent of shareholders) to use corporate funds in a proxy contest beyond that necessary to give notice of the meeting and the matters to be decided at the meeting. They argued against allowing corporate reimbursement of expenses incurred by incumbents on high-pressure election tactics (such as entertainment, limousines, public relations counsel, and proxy solicitors). In fact, prior cases had held that corporate payment of election expenses (to either side in a proxy contest) is *ultra vires*.

2. *Policy vs. personal.*

What are "policy" questions that warrant reimbursement, as opposed to "personal" questions that do not? For example, suppose that an insurgent thinks the corporation's CEO is "too high and mighty" and is paid more than he deserves. Is an election contest to remove the directors who hired the CEO a matter of policy or driven by personal motives?

3. *Compare to political voting.*

The government does not reimburse political candidates for their campaign expenditures, except for presidential candidates (whether or not incumbents) who qualify for matching funds. Although the government pays for the voting apparatus (polling places, voting machines, election officials), it leaves the candidates and their supporters to finance their own election campaigns. Why should the corporation be different? Why should corporate incumbents, but not insurgents, be allowed to use corporate funds as a matter of course to defray their election-related expenses?

4. *Consider the alternative.*

Consider the plight of insurgents in a corporate election contest. Their election-related expenses are reimbursable only if approved by shareholders. (Otherwise, reimbursement by the board would be self-dealing.) The practical effect is that insurgents are unlikely to seek to oust incumbents unless there is an excellent chance of winning. Thus, the reimbursement rule greatly reduces the chances that shareholders are offered an alternative slate of directors.

Would it be better if both sides were reimbursed their reasonable election expenses? Would that improve corporate governance? Or perhaps such an approach would be destabilizing. The reimbursement rule, which clearly favors incumbents, may simply reflect the assumption that shareholders are satisfied with current management. If not, they would not have elected them. There is no reason to promote dissension where none exists.

————————

3. Federal Regulation of Shareholder Communications

We discuss two aspects of federal law and voting: the federal regulation of shareholder communications and the federal regulation of shareholder proposals. First, the SEC proxy rules constitute the principal law of voting in public companies. The rules aim to ensure informed shareholder voting—whether proxies are solicited by incumbent management or outside insurgents. Although disclosure varies depending on who solicits proxies, the federal regime assumes that mandatory disclosure will best protect the shareholder franchise.

For shareholder voting in the public corporation, the basic disclosure document is the "proxy statement"—which must be filed with the SEC and disseminated to all shareholders whose votes are being solicited. Besides specifying its contents, SEC rules require that in voting contests the proxy statement be submitted to the SEC for pre-approval.

Any shareholder activity that qualifies as a "proxy solicitation" must comply with the filing and dissemination requirements of the SEC proxy rules. For example, sending a letter to fellow shareholders to organize a "shareholder revolt" or putting an ad in a newspaper to urge shareholders "to rise up" can violate the SEC rules—unless a proxy statement has been filed and disseminated to shareholders.

SEC Rule 14a–1
Securities Exchange Act of 1934

Proxy solicitation is defined:

(i) any request for a proxy whether or not accompanied by or included in a form of proxy;

(ii) any request to execute or not to execute, or to revoke, a proxy; or

(iii) the furnishing of a form of proxy or other communication to security holders under circumstances *reasonably calculated* to result in the procurement, withholding or revocation of a proxy.

Notice that "proxy solicitation" is defined to cover not only the usual requests for a proxy, but also communications reasonably calculated to result in requesting proxies. What does "reasonably calculated" mean? Most lower courts have held that there can be civil liability for misstatements in a proxy statement made negligently. Thus, a shareholder who sends a letter seeking shareholder support to inspect a shareholder list for the purpose of eventually asking shareholders to remove the incumbent board has been held to have engaged in a proxy solicitation. Before sending such a letter, the insurgent shareholders would have to file a proxy statement with the SEC and then disseminate it to all solicited shareholders. The theory has been that "one need only spread the misinformation adequately before beginning to solicit, and the Commission would be powerless to protect shareholders." In short, the SEC proxy rules assume shareholders in public corporations must be protected from ruthless, deceptive insurgents.

The rules governing "proxy solicitations" sometimes raise free speech implications. In one well-known case, *Long Island Lighting Co. v. Barbash*, 779 F.2d 793 (2d Cir. 1985), the court addressed whether a political advertisement accusing a utility of mismanagement was a "proxy solicitation." The ad claimed that managers were trying to have ratepayers pay needless costs relating to construction of a nuclear power plant, and urged that the utility be acquired by the public power authority. The managers complained that the ad was unlawful because no proxy statement had been filed and it was false and misleading.

Management sought to enjoin further ads by the group until their allegedly false statements were corrected and an appropriate SEC filing had been made. The district court declined to hold the ad constituted a "proxy solicitation" because it appeared in a general publication and could only indirectly affect the proxy contest at LILCO. The Second Circuit held that the ad was "reasonably calculated" to influence shareholder votes, even though it might not have been "targeted directly" at shareholders. Judge Ralph Winter dissented, arguing that when "advertisements are critical of corporate conduct but are facially directed solely to the public, in no way mention the exercise of proxies, and debate only matters of conceded public concern, I would construe federal proxy regulation as inapplicable, whatever the motive of those who purchase them."

In response to criticism that the proxy rules discouraged shareholder activism, the SEC responded with a set of "shareholder communications" rules to facilitate shareholder activism. But you'll notice it was a cautious reform. Here are the highlights:

- Solicitations by those who do not seek proxy authority and do not furnish shareholders with a form of proxy are exempted from the filing and dissemination requirements. Rule 14a–2.

- Shareholders generally can solicit other shareholders to vote in a particular way without filing notice with the SEC if the solicitation (1) is oral or (2) is by a shareholder who owns less than $5 million of the company's shares. But a shareholder who solicits in writing and owns more than $5 million in company shares must file a notice with the SEC within three days after sending the solicitation. The notice must state the solicitor's name and address, and attach the soliciting materials. The solicitation is subject only to the Rule 14a–9 prohibition against materially false and misleading statements in a proxy solicitation.

- Shareholders can announce how they intend to vote and explain their reasons. Such announcements can be published, broadcast, or disseminated to the media. And because they are not deemed a solicitation, the proxy rules do not apply.

4. Federal Law on Shareholder Proposals

Although shareholders can propose and adopt resolutions at shareholder meetings, shareholders of public corporations who do not have access to the proxy machinery, will find this approach difficult and expensive. Only in the most unusual circumstances would it be cost-justified to submit a proposal at the shareholder-proponent's expense.

The SEC shareholder proposal rule, adopted in 1942, attempted to solve the problem of shareholder access to the proxy machinery. Under Rule 14a–8, any shareholder who meets the ownership requirements of the rule and submits a proposal in a timely fashion and in proper form can have the proposal included in the company's proxy materials for a vote at the shareholders' annual meeting. That is, the rule compels the company to subsidize proper shareholder proposals.

Proposals have spanned the gamut. Some focus on governance issues (declassified boards, poison pills, shareholder ability to nominate directors); others deal with operational issues (pay for performance, shareholder approval of severance packages, longer vesting of stock options); and others present social/political issues (global warming, child labor, political contributions, equal employment, environment).

The mix of proposals has shifted over time, with more proposals recently dealing with governance issues. And the number of proposals that receive majority votes has increased steadily since the mid-1990s. (Before then, during the first 50 years of Rule 14a–8, only two shareholder proposals opposed by management received majority shareholder support.) In addition, many proposals are withdrawn or not even submitted after shareholder proponents enter into discussions with management and negotiate corporate changes that the proposal sought.

A growing number of precatory resolutions that receive majority support are soon implemented by management, despite initial objections. The broad adoption by companies of majority voting in director elections is an example. Although implementation rates were low at first, companies increased their adoption of majority voting. Today it is the prevalent method for electing directors in public corporations.

And even though social responsibility proposals rarely receive majority support, their proponents often find success by raising the issue with management. In fact, it is now common for proponents to withdraw their proposals after management agrees to undertake some or all of the proposed reforms. The company avoids annoying a vocal shareholder minority and gets a public relations victory.

a. Operation of Rule 14a–8

Rule 14a–8 uses a plain English "Q & A" format, sets forth procedural and substantive requirements that shareholder proponents must meet to have their proposals included in the company's proxy statement. The SEC has revised this rule frequently, so lawyers are well advised to check the most recent requirements when addressing any shareholder proposal.

Eligibility and procedural hoops. To be eligible, the proponent must have continuously held at least (1) $2,000 worth of the company voting shares for at least three years, (2) $15,000 worth of the company voting shares for at least two years, or (3) $25,000 worth of the company voting shares for at least one year. (Shareholders holding their shares in street name can establish beneficial ownership with a copy of their brokerage statement.) The proponent must then continue to hold the shares and present the proposal at the meeting.

A no-action letter by the SEC staff indicates that the staff will not recommend agency action should a company proceed as planned. A typical no-action letter involving a shareholder proposal reads: "There appears to be some basis for your view that the proposal may be excluded pursuant to Rule 14a–8." A refusal to state a no-action position reads: "The Division is unable to concur in your view that the proposal may be excluded."

A no-action letter is not binding on the SEC, but allows staff to communicate its legal views to interested parties. The no-action process is used in many areas of securities regulation.

A proponent may submit no more than one proposal per company for a particular shareholders' meeting. The proposal, including any accompanying supporting statement, may not exceed 500 words. The proposal must be received at the company's principal executive offices not less than 120 calendar days before the date of the company's last-year proxy statement.

If the company includes the proposal in its proxy materials, it typically will recommend that shareholders vote against the proposal and give reasons for its opposition. The proponent has no chance for rebuttal, but can contact the SEC staff if they believe the company's opposition contains materially false or misleading statements.

SEC no-action review. If the company omits the proposal from its proxy materials, it must notify the SEC by filing the proposal and the company's reasons for exclusion. The SEC staff (in the Division of Corporate Finance) then advises the company whether or not it will recommend that the Commission take any enforcement action if the company omits the proposal. If the answer is no, the staff response is known as a "no-action" letter.

The no-action process resembles a ritual dance. The shareholder first sends the proposal to the company, sometimes with a supporting legal opinion. The company then decides whether to include it in the proxy materials or exclude it. If included, the SEC is not involved. If excluded, the company must explain itself to the SEC, sometimes with an opinion of counsel that identifies the grounds for exclusion and analyzes past staff no-action letters—like a litigation brief. The proponent can submit a reply, sometimes with a contrary legal opinion.

Shareholders have an implied right of action to seek injunctive relief against the company's omission of a proposal. In addition, the SEC can seek an injunction to compel inclusion of a proper proposal. Rarely does either happen: shareholders rarely undertake the expense to sue and companies uniformly acquiesce in the SEC staff's views. Thus, the 14a–8 no-action process constitutes an alternative dispute mechanism in which the SEC staff decides the proper role of public shareholders in corporate governance. It is also worth noting that in some instances when a company receives a shareholder proposal, it negotiates behind the scenes with the shareholder to reach an agreed-upon solution, without involving the SEC in the process.

Are no-action letters binding law? The SEC has taken the position that no-action letters are not agency "rulings" or "decisions" on the merits. Courts have agreed and held that the no-action letters do not constitute a final order under the Administrative Procedure Act. Thus, a shareholder disappointed by an SEC no-action letter cannot sue the SEC.

> The SEC has authority under § 14(a) of the 1934 Act to ensure fair and full disclosure in proxy solicitations, but not to create new substantive rights. Rule 14a–8 can be seen as regulation of deception in the proxy solicitation process.
>
> Given that the company's proxy statement must reflect all the voting matters that management anticipates will come up at the shareholders meeting, it must disclose any *proper* shareholder proposals that will come up at the meeting. Failure to disclose (and describe) the proposal would be misleading.

b. Rule 14a-8 Exclusions

Rule 14a-8 includes <u>thirteen bases</u> for companies seeking to exclude a shareholder proposal. Some protect centralized corporate management, while others seek to prevent interference with management's solicitation of proxies or prevent misguided proposals that are illegal, deceptive, or abusive.

Three exclusions get the most use: (1) "improper under state law", (5) not "significantly related to business", and (7) "ordinary business operations." The precise language of these exclusions is set forth below:

(1) Improper under state law: If the proposal is not a proper subject for <u>action</u> by shareholders under the laws of the jurisdiction of the company's organization;

(5) Relevance: If the proposal relates to operations which account for less than 5 percent of the company's total assets at the end of its most recent fiscal year, and for less than 5 percent of its net earnings and gross sales for its most recent fiscal year, and is not otherwise significantly related to the company's business;

(7) Management functions: If the proposal deals with a matter relating to the company's ordinary business operations;

The "proper subject" exclusion is central, given that the shareholder proposal rule is essentially a federal mechanism to facilitate state-created shareholder voting rights. Recall from *Auer v. Dressel*, above, that the New York Court of Appeals decided that a shareholder proposal recommending the re-hiring of the company's president was proper under state law. In subsequent cases, courts found that a "proper subject" is one that a shareholder may properly bring to a vote under the law of the corporation's state of incorporation. For example, courts have found that proper proposals included proposals related to the election of auditors, reports of a company's financial condition, proposals to amend the bylaws, and proposals that the corporation send a report of the annual meeting to shareholders. Federal law now requires that companies disclose many of these subjects, and more.

In its note to the "proper purpose" exclusion (1), the SEC also states that resolutions *binding* the board (other than a bylaw amendment) are inconsistent with state law and thus not a "proper subject" for shareholder voting. In addition, the SEC deems resolutions dealing with "ordinary business" to be exclusively for the board. Thus, shareholders must fashion resolutions to be non-binding (precatory) and to address fundamental business strategies or matters of "public policy."

What about the "significantly related" exclusion (5)? Can a proposal be significant even though it fails to account for more than 5% of sales, assets, or earnings? The following case addresses the "otherwise significant" test.

Lovenheim v. Iroquois Brands, Ltd.

618 F. Supp. 554 (D.D.C. 1985)

GASCH, DISTRICT JUDGE.

Plaintiff Peter C. Lovenheim, owner of two hundred shares of common stock in Iroquois Brands, Ltd. (hereinafter "Iroquois/Delaware"), seeks to bar Iroquois/Delaware from excluding from the proxy materials being sent to all shareholders in preparation for an upcoming shareholder meeting information concerning a proposed resolution he intends to offer at the meeting. Mr. Lovenheim's proposed resolution relates to the procedure used to force-feed geese for production of paté de foie gras in France,[2] a type of paté imported by Iroquois/Delaware. Specifically, his resolution calls upon the Directors of Iroquois/Delaware to:

> form a committee to study the methods by which its French supplier produces paté de foie gras, and report to the shareholders its findings and opinions, based on expert consultation, on whether this production method causes undue distress, pain or suffering to the animals involved and, if so, whether further distribution of this product should be discontinued until a more humane production method is developed.

Iroquois/Delaware has refused to allow information concerning Mr. Lovenheim's proposal to be included in proxy materials being sent in connection with the next annual shareholders meeting. In doing so, Iroquois/Delaware relies on an exception to the general requirement of Rule 14a–8, Rule 14a–8(c)(5). [Before the 1998 amendments, the (i)(5) exclusion was numbered (c)(5).].

Iroquois/Delaware's reliance on the Rule 14a–8(c)(5) exception for proposals not "significantly related" to the company's business is based on the following information contained in the affidavit of its president: Iroquois/Delaware has annual revenues of $141 million with $6 million in annual profits and $78 million in assets. In contrast, its paté de foie gras sales were just $79,000 last year, representing a net loss on paté sales of $3,121. Iroquois/Delaware has only $34,000 in assets related to paté. Thus none of the company's net earnings and less than .05 percent of its assets are implicated by plaintiff's proposal. These levels are obviously far below the five percent threshold set forth in the first portion of the exception claimed by Iroquois/Delaware.

Plaintiff does not contest that his proposed resolution relates to a matter of little economic significance to Iroquois/Delaware. Nevertheless he contends that the Rule 14a–8(c)(5) exception is not applicable as it cannot be said that his proposal "is not otherwise significantly related to the issuer's business" as is required by the final portion of that exception. In other words, plaintiff's argument that Rule 14a–8 does not permit omission of his proposal rests on the assertion that the rule and statute on

---

[2] Paté de foie gras is made from the liver of geese. According to Mr. Lovenheim's affidavit, force-feeding is frequently used in order to expand the liver and thereby produce a larger quantity of paté. Mr. Lovenheim's affidavit also contains a description of the force-feeding process:

Force-feeding usually begins when the geese are four months old. On some farms where feeding is mechanized, the bird's body and wings are placed in a metal brace and its neck is stretched. Through a funnel inserted 10–12 inches down the throat of the goose, a machine pumps up to 400 grams of corn-based mash into its stomach. An elastic band around the goose's throat prevents regurgitation. When feeding is manual, a handler uses a funnel and stick to force the mash down.

Plaintiff contends that such force-feeding is a form of cruelty to animals. Plaintiff has offered no evidence that force-feeding is used by Iroquois/Delaware's supplier in producing the paté imported by Iroquois/Delaware. However his proposal calls upon the committee he seeks to create to investigate this question.

which it is based do not permit omission merely because a proposal is not economically significant where a proposal has "ethical or social significance."[8]

Iroquois/Delaware challenges plaintiff's view that ethical and social proposals cannot be excluded even if they do meet the economic or five percent test. Instead, Iroquois/Delaware views the exception solely in economic terms as permitting omission for any proposals relating to a de minimis share of assets and profits. Iroquois/ Delaware asserts that since corporations are economic entities, only an economic test is appropriate.

The Court would note that the applicability of the Rule 14a–8(c)(5) exception to Mr. Lovenheim's proposal represents a close question given the lack of clarity in the exception itself. In effect, plaintiff relies on the word "otherwise," suggesting that it indicates the drafters of the rule intended that other noneconomic tests of significance be used. Iroquois/Delaware relies on the fact that the rule examines other significance in relation to the issuer's business. Because of the apparent ambiguity of the rule, the Court considers the history of the shareholder proposal rule in determining the proper interpretation of the most recent version of that rule.

Prior to 1983, paragraph 14a–8(c)(5) excluded proposals "not significantly related to the issuer's business" but did not contain an objective economic significance test such as the five percent of sales, assets, and earnings specified in the first part of the current version. Although a series of SEC decisions through 1976 allowing issuers to exclude proposals challenging compliance with the Arab economic boycott of Israel allowed exclusion if the issuer did less than one percent of their business with Arab countries or Israel, the Commission stated later in 1976 that it did "not believe that subparagraph (c)(5) should be hinged solely on the economic relativity of a proposal." Thus the Commission required inclusion "in many situations in which the related business comprised less than one percent" of the company's revenues, profits or assets "where the proposal has raised *policy questions* important" enough to be considered " 'significantly related' to the issuer's business."

As indicated above, the 1983 revision adopted the five percent test of economic significance in an effort to create a more objective standard. Nevertheless, in adopting this standard, the Commission stated that proposals will be includible notwithstanding their "failure to reach the specified economic thresholds if a significant relationship

---

[8]   The assertion that the proposal is significant in an ethical and social sense relies on plaintiff's argument that "the very availability of a market for products that may be obtained through the inhumane force-feeding of geese cannot help but contribute to the continuation of such treatment." Plaintiff's brief characterizes the humane treatment of animals as among the foundations of western culture and cites in support of this view the Seven Laws of Noah, an animal protection statute enacted by the Massachusetts Bay Colony in 1641, numerous federal statutes enacted since 1877, and animal protection laws existing in all fifty states and the District of Columbia. An additional indication of the significance of plaintiff's proposal is the support of such leading organizations in the field of animal care as the American Society for the Prevention of Cruelty to Animals and The Humane Society of the United States for measures aimed at discontinuing use of force-feeding.

to the issuer's business is demonstrated on the face of the resolution or supporting statement." Thus it seems clear based on the history of the rule that "the meaning of" " 'significantly related' is not *limited* to economic significance."

The Court cannot ignore the history of the rule, which reveals no decision by the Commission to limit the determination to the economic criteria relied on by Iroquois/Delaware. The Court therefore holds that in light of the ethical and social significance of plaintiff's proposal and the fact that it implicates significant levels of sales, plaintiff has shown a likelihood of prevailing on the merits with regard to the issue of whether his proposal is "otherwise significantly related" to Iroquois/Delaware's business.

[The court then granted plaintiff's motion for a preliminary injunction.]

Points for Discussion

1. Amendments to Rule 14a–8.

The *Lovenheim* decision refers to a number of SEC amendments to Rule 14a–8. The SEC has actually amended the rule 17 times—apparently the record for any SEC rule. Why do you think the rule has been amended so often?

2. Ordinary business.

Could Mr. Lovenheim's proposal have been excluded as relating to "ordinary business decisions"—that is, the company's product line, its choice of suppliers, its public image? Doesn't the business judgment rule protect board decisions, and prevent shareholders from second-guessing the board's judgment, so long as there is a rational business purpose?

> Suppose that a national electronics retailer, such as Best Buy, receives a shareholder proposal from a religious group to keep minors from buying violent or sexually explicit video games. The group points out that some state legislatures are considering new laws that would fine store owners that sell such games to minors.
>
> Company management responds by agreeing to be more vigilant about preventing such sales. Is it because of corporate social responsibility or shareholder-value concerns?

3. Limits on shareholder access.

The 14a–8 exclusions represent the SEC's views on the proper role of public shareholders in corporate governance and shareholder voting. Notice that Rule 14a–8 does not allow shareholders to nominate their own board candidates [exclusion (8)], to oppose management proposals [exclusion (9)], or to question specific dividend payments [exclusion (13)]. Does state law prevent input by shareholders on these matters? Has the SEC defined the scope of shareholder rights under state law correctly?

When does corporate action go beyond "ordinary business" and become instead a matter of "public policy"? The boundary between these two concepts raises fundamental issues about corporate social responsibility. Both the courts and the SEC have long recognized this, as the following cases and line of SEC interpretations make clear.

The *Medical Committee (Napalm)* case. In 1970 during the height of the Vietnam War, a public interest group (Medical Committee for Human Rights) that opposed the War sought to end the manufacture of napalm for use in the War by Dow Chemical Company. (Napalm is an incendiary gel that was used by the U.S. military in the Vietnam War first to clear jungles, but later against people, producing terrible physical and psychological effects.) Although napalm constituted a small and not very profitable part of Dow's business, napalm was important to the government's war effort, and Dow management strongly defended its manufacture on patriotic grounds.

The Medical Committee submitted a shareholder proposal requesting that the Dow board amend Dow's certificate of incorporation to bar the sale of napalm unless the buyer gave assurances the napalm would not be used on human beings. Dow refused to include the proposal on the grounds that it promoted a political cause (which was then, but is no longer, a ground for exclusion under Rule 14a–8) and that it related to Dow's ordinary business.

The D.C. Circuit held that Dow could not omit the proposal. *Medical Committee for Human Rights v. SEC*, 432 F.2d 659 (D.C. Cir. 1970), *vacated as moot*, 404 U.S. 403 (1972). The "overriding purpose of Section 14(a) is to assure corporate shareholders the ability to exercise their right—some would say their duty—to control the important decisions which affect them as owners of the corporation." The court accepted that the shareholders could seek to have "their assets used in a manner which they believe to be more socially responsible but possibly less profitable than that which is dictated by present company policy." Moreover, since Dow management had proclaimed its support for making napalm "not *because* of business considerations, but *in spite of* them," management decisions involving "personal political or moral predilections" could not be insulated from shareholder oversight.

SEC interpretive release (1976). Does *Medical Committee* mean that any issue taken from the headlines (such as global warming, child labor, business outsourcing, and so on) becomes "significantly related" to a company's business and not "ordinary business"—thus a "proper subject" for shareholder consideration at company expense?

In 1976 the SEC attempted to draw the line in an interpretive release that continues to influence both the SEC and the courts.

The term "ordinary business operations" has been deemed on occasion to include certain matters which have significant policy, economic or other implications inherent in them. For instance, a proposal that a utility company not construct a proposed nuclear power plant has in the past been considered excludable. In retrospect, however, it seems apparent that the economic and safety considerations attendant to nuclear power plants are of such magnitude that a determination whether to construct one is not an "ordinary" business matter.

Where proposals involve business matters that are mundane in nature and do not involve any substantial policy or other considerations, the subparagraph may be relied upon to omit them.

The *Trinity Wall Street v. Wal-Mart* case. The issue of what constitutes an excludable ordinary business matter more recently arose in a shareholder proposal case concerning Wal-Mart's sale of high-capacity guns. The proposal was submitted by Trinity Church, an Episcopal parish in New York City with a long-held commitment to social justice. As a shareholder of Wal-Mart, it requested that the board develop and implement standards for management to use in deciding whether to sell a product that (1) "especially endangers public safety"; (2) "has the substantial potential to impair the reputation of Wal–Mart"; and/or (3) "would reasonably be considered by many offensive to the family and community values integral to the Company's promotion of its brand." *Trinity Wall Street v. Wal-Mart Stores, Inc.*, 792 F.3d 323, 327 (3d Cir. 2015). Wal-Mart sought to exclude the proposal from its proxy materials on the basis that it related to "ordinary business operations."

The district court ruled in favor of the church, viewing the proposal as one focused principally on board governance and raising a significant social policy issue—the sale of high-capacity guns by one of the world's largest retailers. The Third Circuit reversed, holding that the proposal was excludable: "Stripped to its essence, Trinity's proposal—although styled as promoting improved governance—goes to the heart of Wal–Mart's business: what it sells on its shelves." The court explained that when a proposal "targets day-to-day decision-making," the social policy issues do not "transcend a company's ordinary business" and the proposal is properly excluded.

The Third Circuit distinguished between "stop-selling" proposals aimed at "pure-play" manufacturers with a narrow product line, such as a tobacco or gun manufacturer, for which such proposals raise a transcendent issue that "relates to the seller's very existence," and retailers that sell thousands of products for which stop-selling proposals are enmeshed in management's daily business decisions. According to the court, Wal-Mart was in the latter category as a big-box retailer:

> Decisions relating to what products Wal–Mart sells in its rural locations versus its urban sites will vary considerably, and these are quintessentially calls made by management. Wal–Mart serves different Americas with

different values. Its customers in rural America want different products than its customers in cities, and that management decides how to deal with these differing desires is not an issue typical for its Board of Directors. And whether to put emphasis on brand integrity and brand protection, or none at all, is naturally a decision shareholders as well as directors entrust management to make in the exercise of their experience and business judgment.

In concluding, the court noted the difficulty of its job interpreting "hard-to-define exclusions," and suggested that the SEC "consider revising its regulation of proxy contests and issue fresh interpretive guidance."

Is discrimination in the workplace based on sexual orientation "ordinary business" or "public policy"? In 1992 the New York City Comptroller (manager of the city's employee retirement fund) submitted a proposal to Cracker Barrel Old Country Store to ends its practice of firing gay employees. The company excluded the proposal as an ordinary employment matter, and the SEC staff issued a "no-action" letter accepting the company's position. The full Commission later upheld the staff policy.

But the New York City Comptroller stuck with it, bringing an unsuccessful lawsuit and then urging the SEC to change its position. In 1998 the SEC changed its policy to allow proposals dealing with employment discrimination. Four annual meetings later, the Comptroller's proposal at Cracker Barrel received 58% shareholder support—the first ever CSR proposal to receive majority support. Soon after, the company's board announced it would accept the proposal as company policy.

Proxy access. Shareholders have tried various tactics to improve their access to the proxy machinery that is controlled by corporate directors and officers. Beginning in the early 2000s, some large institutions pressed for new rules that would permit shareholders who held a significant percentage of the companies' shares to nominate a few directors (though not a majority). Corporate managers opposed these rules. When the SEC proposed a new rule in 2003 that would give shareholders greater access to the director nomination process, management groups claimed the SEC was interfering with a matter of corporate governance beyond its authority and argued that shareholder-nominated board members would disrupt the collegial working relationships on corporate boards. At first the SEC dithered and then eventually decided not to pursue its rulemaking.

In response, several activist union and state pension funds began a company-by-company movement proposing amendments to company bylaws modeled on the abandoned SEC proxy access rule. The proponents sought to use the shareholder proposal rule to create a process for shareholders to nominate "short slates" to boards constituting fewer than a majority of directors. At first the SEC staff accepted such proposals as proper under the rule, but later reversed course and allowed their exclusion under the rule's then-existing exclusion (8): proposals that "relate to a nomination or an election for membership on the company's board of directors."

Disappointed by the SEC's flip-flop, one of the institutional proponents—the pension fund for the American Federation of State, County & Municipal Employees (AFSCME)—brought a lawsuit in federal district court against the American International Group to require that the Delaware-incorporated insurance company include a shareholder-submitted "proxy access" proposal in the company's proxy statement. The district court concluded that neither Rule 14a–8 nor state law required inclusion of the proposal, suggesting that the litigants (and the law professors who had filed an amicus brief in the case) look to the regulatory and legislative processes for their reform initiative.

> To give you a sense for the details of "proxy access," here is the proposal submitted by AFSCME in the AIG case:
>
> RESOLVED, pursuant to Section 6.9 of the By-laws (the "Bylaws") of American International Group Inc. ("AIG") and section 109(a) of the Delaware General Corporation Law, stockholders hereby amend the Bylaws to add section 6.10:
>
> "The Corporation shall include in its proxy materials for a meeting of stockholders the name, together with the Disclosure and Statement (both defined below), of any person nominated for election to the Board of Directors by a stockholder or group thereof that satisfies the requirements of this section 6.10 (the "Nominator"), and allow stockholders to vote with respect to such nominee on the Corporation's proxy card. Each Nominator may nominate one candidate for election at a meeting. To be eligible to make a nomination, a Nominator must:
>
> (a)   have beneficially owned 3 or more of the Corporation's outstanding common stock (the "Required Shares") for at least one year;
>
> (b)   provide written notice received by the Corporation's Secretary within the time period specified in section 1.11 of the Bylaws containing (i) with respect to the nominee, (A) the information required by Items 7(a), (b) and (c) of SEC Schedule 14A (such information is referred to herein as the "Disclosure") and (B) such nominee's consent to being named in the proxy statement and to serving as a director if elected; and (ii) with respect to the Nominator, proof of ownership of the Required Shares; and
>
> (c)   execute an undertaking that it agrees (i) to assume all liability of any violation of law or regulation arising out of the Nominator's communications with stockholders, including the Disclosure (ii) to the extent it uses soliciting material other than the Corporation's proxy materials, comply with all laws and regulations relating thereto.
>
> The Nominator shall have the option to furnish a statement, not to exceed 500 words, in support of the nominee's candidacy (the "Statement"), at the time the Disclosure is submitted to the Corporation's Secretary. The Board of Directors shall adopt a procedure for timely resolving disputes over whether notice of a nomination was timely given and whether the Disclosure and Statement comply with this section 6.10 and SEC Rules."

On appeal, the Second Circuit reversed and held that Rule 14a–8 (as then worded) permitted shareholders to propose bylaw amendments to create "proxy access." *See AFSCME v. AIG, Inc.*, 462 F.3d 121 (2d. Cir. 2006). The court concluded that such proposals "establish a procedure by which shareholder-nominated candidates may be included on the corporate ballot [and thus do] not relate to an election within the meaning of the Rule 14a–8." The case turned on the phrase "relates to an election," which the court interpreted (based on prior SEC interpretations) to mean that proposals were excludable when they related to a specific election for a particular director seat—but not to proposals creating general guidelines or procedures for director elections.

In response to the *AIG* decision, the SEC revised Rule 14a–8 to broaden the "election" exclusion to specifically cover proposals relating to procedures for nominating directors. The SEC said it saw the rule change as temporary while it sought a permanent resolution of the basic tension between board control of director nominations and shareholder voting rights.

In 2010 Congress put proxy access back on the corporate governance agenda in the Dodd-Frank Act, which specifically authorized the SEC to promulgate a proxy access rule. Within months of the law's enactment, the SEC accepted the Dodd-Frank invitation and repromulgated proxy access rules. The plot thickened when corporate managers, supported by the Business Roundtable and U.S. Chamber of Commerce, challenged the new rules, claiming the SEC failed to adequately consider the costs and benefits of the new governance rights. The D.C. Circuit agreed and held that the SEC had failed to consider the rule's effect on "efficiency, competition and capital formation." Even though Dodd-Frank seemed to have authorized the SEC to make this cost-benefit determination, the SEC decided not to appeal the decision to the Supreme Court and not to propose the rule again, apparently worried it could not meet the (unusually) high standard of review set by the D.C. Circuit.

In response, many shareholder activists adopted a company-by-company approach. The SEC has made it clear that shareholders can propose general procedures for nominating directors, and the Delaware legislature has provided that shareholders can amend company bylaws to provide for proxy access as well as mandatory reimbursement of proxy expenses incurred by shareholders in director elections. Under these revised corporate statutes, the bylaws can address such matters as ownership requirements for nominating shareholders, disclosure by the nominating shareholder, and caps on the number of shareholder-nominated directors. Hedge fund activists approach proxy access differently, by running either or "short slate" of directors to replace a portion of the board, or by mounting a proxy fight to replace the entire board. These activities are expensive, because the hedge fund does not have "proxy access," meaning it must pay for its own proxy materials and process. Proxy access remains a controversial issue.

————————

Points for Discussion

1. Company-by-company access vs. SEC rule.

Shareholders have the power to submit proxy access bylaw amendments for shareholder approval—with the question of whether this is "proper" largely resolved under state law. Thus, proxy access can vary from company to company. What are the pros and cons of shareholder access varying in this way, compared to a single uniform standard set by the SEC?

2. Just restrict shareholder proposals?

If the SEC shareholder proposal rule depends on state-created shareholder rights, can corporations prevent nettlesome shareholders from interfering with board-centric corporate governance? Could shareholders amend the articles or the bylaws to prohibit any company-financed shareholder proposals at all—or to fully permit such proposals, or to permit certain proposals, but not others? Is Rule 14a–8 mandatory? That is, could corporations opt out of the rule—by establishing either more or less shareholder democracy?

3. The power struggle over proxy access.

You might reflect on what is at stake in the debate about proxy access. Why would shareholder activists be so anxious to be able to put a minority of directors on the board? Can't these activists simply approach the board with their thoughts or plans? And why has corporate management fought this? Why would incumbent directors be so bothered about having co-directors on the board who were nominated by a sizeable group of shareholders and then elected by a majority of shareholders?

CHAPTER 16

Information

To exercise fully their right to vote, and especially their right to initiate corporate reforms, shareholders must often obtain information from the corporation. State and federal law create a mosaic of informational rights to support the shareholder franchise. State law allows shareholders to inspect corporate books and records if they have a "proper purpose." Federal law requires that shareholders in public corporations receive a formal disclosure document called a "proxy statement" when their vote is solicited. And federal law, as well as state fiduciary law, requires that any communication soliciting shareholder votes be honest and complete.

This chapter begins with a look at shareholder inspection rights, which have assumed increased importance as a pre-litigation tool for shareholders to obtain information from their corporations. Next, we summarize the *ex ante* rights of shareholders to information when they vote, both under state law and federal proxy rules. Finally, we consider the *ex post* rights of shareholders to complain about mis-information during the voting process, particularly in an implied private cause of action fashioned by federal courts.

A.   Shareholder Inspection Rights

Shareholders have long had equitable rights to inspect corporate books and records. State corporate statutes codify these rights, specifying when and how inspection can be had.

Here is an excerpt of the key provision in Delaware's statute:

DGCL § 220
Inspection of Books and Records

(b)   Any stockholder . . . shall, upon written demand under oath stating the
       purpose thereof, have the right during the usual hours for business to
       inspect for any proper purpose, and to make copies and extracts from:

---

(1) The corporation's stock ledger, a list of its stockholders, and its other books and records; and

(2) A subsidiary's books and records . . . [subject to certain conditions]. . .

A proper purpose shall mean a purpose reasonably related to such person's interest as a stockholder. . . The demand under oath shall be directed to the corporation at its registered office in this State or at its principal place of business. . .

(c) The Court of Chancery is . . . vested with exclusive jurisdiction to determine whether or not the person seeking inspection is entitled to the inspection sought. . . . Where a stockholder seeks to inspect the corporation's books and records, other than its stock ledger or list of stockholders, such stockholder shall first establish that:

(1) Such stockholder is a stockholder;

(2) Such stockholder has complied with this section respecting the form and manner of making demand for inspection of such documents; and

(3) The inspection such stockholder seeks is for a proper purpose.

Where the stockholder seeks to inspect the corporation's stock ledger or list of stockholders and establishes that such stockholder is a stockholder and has complied with this section respecting the form and manner of making demand for inspection of such documents, the burden of proof shall be upon the corporation to establish that the inspection such stockholder seeks is for an improper purpose. The Court may, in its discretion, prescribe any limitations or conditions with reference to the inspection, or award such other or further relief as the Court may deem just and proper. The Court may order books, documents and records, pertinent extracts therefrom, or duly authenticated copies thereof, to be brought within this State and kept in this State upon such terms and conditions as the order may prescribe.

Most statutes, including in Delaware and under the MBCA, permit inspection by both shareholders of record (whose names appears on the corporation's stock ledger) and beneficial shareholders (whose stock is held by another, such as a securities firm). Some states once limited inspection to shareholders owning a certain percentage of a corporation's shares or holding their shares for a minimum period. But over time the inspection right has been "democratized"—subject to the general requirement that the inspecting shareholder have a "proper purpose."

There is some variance in the statutes on what shareholders can inspect. As you can see, Delaware permits inspection of the stock ledger, the shareholder list, and other "books and records" upon the showing of a proper purpose. The burden for this showing depends on which item the shareholder seeks. The statute specifies that if the shareholder seeks books and records other than the stock ledger or list of shareholders, then such shareholder has the burden of showing a proper purpose as to each item sought. With regard to the stock ledger and list of shareholders, the burden is on the corporation to show that the shareholder seeks inspection for an improper purpose.

> Directors also have inspection rights. In Delaware, for example, under DGCL § 220(d), directors can seek inspection of "the corporation's stock ledger, a list of its stockholders and its other books and records for a purpose reasonably related to the director's position as a director." Whose inspection rights are broader—those of shareholders or those of directors?

Under the MBCA, ready inspection is available for the articles of incorporation, bylaws, minutes of shareholder meetings, the names of directors and officers, and like documents. But inspection of board minutes, accounting records, and shareholder lists requires that the shareholder make a demand in "good faith" and describe "with reasonable particularity" the records to be inspected and show that the records are "directly connected" with a "proper purpose." MBCA §§ 16.01–16.03.

The traditional remedy of a shareholder who is denied inspection is a judicial order compelling inspection. In fact, most statutes provide for a summary or expedited procedure. And to prevent obstruction of inspection rights, some statutes make the corporation pay the shareholder's costs, including reasonable attorneys' fees, unless the corporation can establish it acted reasonably in denying the shareholder's inspection request.

In recent years, shareholder inspection has become an important pre-filing tactic by plaintiffs bringing lawsuits to vindicate shareholder rights. Interestingly, Delaware courts have encouraged (even chastised) plaintiffs to seek inspection before bringing lawsuits. Inspection allows plaintiffs to obtain factual support for their allegations, thus avoiding dismissal of unsupported claims. (We look at the tough pleading standards for derivative suits, especially in Delaware, in Chapter 14, Litigation.) In addition, shareholders making claims of corporate fraud under the federal securities laws have increasingly relied on state inspection rights to obtain documents to plead securities fraud in federal court. (We look at these pleading standards in our chapter on class actions brought in federal court alleging fraud in securities markets. *See* Chapter 19, Securities Fraud.)

1. Proper Purpose and Inspection Requests

The key to inspection is showing a proper purpose. Statutes usually do not define the term or define it vaguely as "a purpose reasonably related to such person's interest as a stockholder."

The following three cases illustrate how shareholders have used inspection—and how courts view the role of shareholders in the corporation. The first case, *Pillsbury v. Honeywell*, is a well-known Minnesota case from the 1970s that takes a rather jaundiced view of shareholder activism, commenting that "the power to inspect may be the power to destroy." The case involved Charles A. Pillsbury, a scion of a prominent and wealthy Minneapolis family, who wanted to stop production by Honeywell, Inc. ("Honeywell") of anti-personnel fragmentation bombs used in Vietnam. He purchased 100 shares for the "sole purpose" of gaining a voice in Honeywell's affairs and then requested a shareholders' list to solicit proxies for the election of new directors. When Honeywell refused his request, he filed for a writ of mandamus. After discovery, the trial court denied him relief, holding that he had not stated a "proper purpose germane to his interest as a stockholder" under both Minnesota law and the law of Delaware, Honeywell's state of incorporation.

State ex rel. Pillsbury v. Honeywell, Inc.

191 N.W.2d 406 (Minn. 1971)

Kelly, Justice.

Petitioner contends that a stockholder who disagrees with management has an absolute right to inspect corporate records for purposes of soliciting proxies. He would have this court rule that such solicitation is per se a "proper purpose." Honeywell argues that a "proper purpose" contemplates concern with investment return. We agree with Honeywell.

This court has had several occasions to rule on the propriety of shareholders' demands for inspection of corporate books and records. Minn. St. 300.32, not applicable here, has been held to be declaratory of the common-law principle that a stockholder is entitled to inspection for a proper purpose germane to his business interests. While inspection will not be permitted for purposes of curiosity, speculation, or vexation, adverseness to management and a desire to gain control of the corporation for economic benefit does not indicate an improper purpose.

Several courts agree with petitioner's contention that a mere desire to communicate with other shareholders is, per se, a proper purpose. This would seem to confer an almost absolute right to inspection. We believe that a better rule would allow inspections only if the shareholder has a proper purpose for such communication.

The act of inspecting a corporation's shareholder ledger and business records must be viewed in its proper perspective. In terms of the corporate norm, inspection is merely the act of the concerned owner checking on what is in part his property. In the context of the large firm, inspection can be more akin to a weapon in corporate warfare. Because the power to inspect may be the power to destroy, it is important that only those with a bona fide interest in the corporation enjoy that power.

That one must have proper standing to demand inspection has been recognized by statutes in several jurisdictions. Courts have also balked at compelling inspection by a shareholder holding an insignificant amount of stock in the corporation.

Petitioner's standing as a shareholder is quite tenuous. He only owns one share in his own name, bought for the purposes of this suit. He had previously ordered his agent to buy 100 shares, but there is no showing of investment intent. While his agent had a cash balance in the $400,000 portfolio, petitioner made no attempt to determine whether Honeywell was a good investment or whether more profitable shares would have to be sold to finance the Honeywell purchase.

Petitioner had utterly no interest in the affairs of Honeywell before he learned of Honeywell's production of fragmentation bombs. Immediately after obtaining this knowledge, he purchased stock in Honeywell for the sole purpose of asserting ownership privileges in an effort to force Honeywell to cease such production. But for his opposition to Honeywell's policy, petitioner probably would not have bought Honeywell stock, would not be interested in Honeywell's profits and would not desire to communicate with Honeywell's shareholders. His avowed purpose in buying Honeywell stock was to place himself in a position to try to impress his opinions favoring a reordering of priorities upon Honeywell management and its other shareholders. Such a motivation can hardly be deemed a proper purpose germane to his economic interest as a shareholder.[5]

From the deposition, the trial court concluded that petitioner had already formed strong opinions on the immorality and the social and economic wastefulness of war long before he bought stock in Honeywell. His sole motivation was to change Honeywell's course of business because that course was incompatible with his political views. If unsuccessful, petitioner indicated that he would sell the Honeywell stock.

We do not mean to imply that a shareholder with a bona fide investment interest could not bring this suit if motivated by concern with the long- or short-term economic effects on Honeywell resulting from the production of war munitions. Similarly, this

---

[5]   We do not question petitioner's good faith incident to his political and social philosophy; nor did the trial court. In a well-prepared memorandum, the lower court stated: "This Court cannot but draw the conclusion that the Petitioner is sincere in his political and social philosophy, but this Court does not feel that this is a proper forum for the advancement of these political-social views by way of direct contact with the stockholders of Honeywell Company."

suit might be appropriate when a shareholder has a bona fide concern about the adverse effects of abstention from profitable war contracts on his investment in Honeywell.

In the instant case, however, the trial court, in effect, has found from all the facts that petitioner was not interested in even the long-term well-being of Honeywell or the enhancement of the value of his shares. His sole purpose was to persuade the company to adopt his social and political concerns, irrespective of any economic benefit to himself or Honeywell. This purpose on the part of one buying into the corporation does not entitle the petitioner to inspect Honeywell's books and records.

Petitioner argues that he wishes to inspect the stockholder ledger in order that he may correspond with other shareholders with the hope of electing to the board one or more directors who represent his particular viewpoint. While a plan to elect one or more directors is specific and the election of directors normally would be a proper purpose, here the purpose was not germane to petitioner's or Honeywell's economic interest. Instead, the plan was designed to further petitioner's political and social beliefs. Since the requisite propriety of purpose germane to his or Honeywell's economic interest is not present, the allegation that petitioner seeks to elect a new board of directors is insufficient to compel inspection.

The order of the trial court denying the writ of mandamus is affirmed.

Points for Discussion

1. *Shareholder wealth maximization.*

Would Pillsbury have been more successful if the request had been couched in terms of shareholder wealth maximization? For example, would the court have been more sympathetic if Pillsbury had sought to contact shareholders to urge them to demand that the company discontinue the production of anti-personnel fragmentation bombs on the grounds it could lead to legal liability, could result in consumer boycotts of the company's other products, or could damage the corporation's reputation? In short, was the problem one of poor lawyering?

2. *Purpose of the corporation.*

The case relates to a central question in corporate law and debate of the purpose of the corporation. Is the Minnesota Supreme Court correct in assuming that shareholders can only have an economic interest in the corporation and the corporation is only an economic institution? If corporations can have purposes other than shareholder wealth maximization, why shouldn't a shareholder be able to contact other shareholders to install a new board committed to corporate social responsibility?

3. *Multiple purposes?*

Shortly after *Pillsbury v. Honeywell*, the Supreme Court of Delaware gave shareholders breathing room, reiterating that under Section 220, "the desire to solicit proxies for a slate of directors in opposition to management is a purpose reasonably related to the stockholder's interest as a stockholder" and "any further or secondary purpose in seeking the list is irrelevant." *Credit Bureau Reports v. Credit Bureau of St. Paul*, 290 A.2d 689 (Del. Ch. 1972), *aff'd*, 290 A.2d 691 (Del. 1972). The Court affirmed an order that permitted a shareholder to inspect the shareholder list for the stated purpose of communicating with fellow shareholders as a prerequisite to a proxy contest. It was "irrelevant" that the shareholder hoped to "secondarily accomplish" changes in the company's managerial policy to deal more generously with its suppliers, of which the shareholder seeking inspection was one.

What is the optimal rule for calibrating a shareholder's access to corporate books and records? Should courts look only to confirm that a shareholder has stated a primary purpose that is proper?

Saito v. McKesson HBOC, Inc.

806 A.2d 113 (Del. 2002)

BERGER, JUSTICE.

In this appeal, we consider the limitations on a stockholder's statutory right to inspect corporate books and records. The statute, 8 Del. C. § 220, enables stockholders to investigate matters "reasonably related to [their] interest as [stockholders]" including, among other things, possible corporate wrongdoing. It does not open the door to the wide ranging discovery that would be available in support of litigation. For this statutory tool to be meaningful, however, it cannot be read narrowly to deprive a stockholder of necessary documents solely because the documents were prepared by third parties or because the documents predate the stockholder's first investment in the corporation. A stockholder who demands inspection for a proper purpose should be given access to all of the documents in the corporation's possession, custody or control, that are necessary to satisfy that proper purpose. Thus, where a § 220 claim is based on alleged corporate wrongdoing, and assuming the allegation is meritorious, the stockholder should be given enough information to effectively address the problem, either through derivative litigation or through direct contact with the corporation's directors and/or stockholders.

Factual and Procedural Background

On October 17, 1998, McKesson Corporation entered into a stock-for-stock merger agreement with HBO & Company ("HBOC"). On October 20, 1998, appellant, Noel Saito, purchased McKesson stock. The merger was consummated in January 1999 and the combined company was renamed McKesson HBOC, Incorporated. HBOC continued its separate corporate existence as a wholly-owned subsidiary of McKesson HBOC.

Starting in April and continuing through July 1999, McKesson HBOC announced a series of financial restatements triggered by its year-end audit process. During that four month period, McKesson HBOC reduced its revenues by $327.4 million for the three prior fiscal years. The restatements all were attributed to HBOC accounting irregularities. The first announcement precipitated several lawsuits, including a derivative action pending in the Court of Chancery, captioned Ash v. McCall, Civil Action No. 17132. Saito was one of four plaintiffs in the Ash complaint, which alleged that: (i) McKesson's directors breached their duty of care by failing to discover the HBOC accounting irregularities before the merger; (ii) McKesson's directors committed corporate waste by entering into the merger with HBOC; (iii) HBOC's directors breached their fiduciary duties by failing to monitor the company's compliance with financial reporting requirements prior to the merger; and (iv) McKesson HBOC's directors failed in the same respect during the three months following the merger. Although the Court of Chancery granted defendants' motion to dismiss the complaint, the dismissal was without prejudice as to the pre-merger and post-merger oversight claims.

In its decision on the motion to dismiss, the Court of Chancery specifically suggested that Saito and the other plaintiffs "use the 'tools at hand,' most prominently § 220 books and records actions, to obtain information necessary to sue derivatively." Saito was the only Ash plaintiff to follow that advice. The stated purpose of Saito's demand was:

> (1) to further investigate breaches of fiduciary duties by the boards of directors of HBO & Co., Inc., McKesson, Inc., and/or McKesson HBOC, Inc. related to their oversight of their respective company's accounting procedures and financial reporting; (2) to investigate potential claims against advisors engaged by McKesson, Inc. and HBO & Co., Inc. to the acquisition of HBO & Co., Inc. by McKesson, Inc.; and (3) to gather information relating to the above in order to supplement the complaint in Ash v. McCall, et al., in accordance with the September 15, 2000 Opinion of the Court of Chancery. Saito demanded access to eleven categories of documents, including those relating to Arthur Andersen's pre-merger review and verification of HBOC's financial condition; communications between or among HBOC, McKesson, and their investment bankers and accountants concerning HBOC's accounting practices; and discussions

among members of the Boards of Directors of HBOC, McKesson, and/ or McKesson HBOC concerning reports published in April 1997 and thereafter about HBOC's accounting practices or financial condition.

After trial, the Court of Chancery found that Saito stated a proper purpose for the inspection of books and records—to ferret out possible wrongdoing in connection with the merger of HBOC and McKesson. But the court held that Saito's proper purpose only extended to potential wrongdoing after the date on which Saito acquired his McKesson stock. The court also held that Saito did not have a proper purpose to inspect documents relating to potential claims against third party advisors who counseled the boards in connection with the merger. Finally, the court held that Saito was not entitled to HBOC documents because Saito was not a stockholder of pre-merger HBOC, and, with respect to post-merger HBOC, he did not establish a basis on which to disregard the separate existence of the wholly-owned subsidiary.

DISCUSSION

Stockholders of Delaware corporations enjoy a qualified common law and statutory right to inspect the corporation's books and records. Inspection rights were recognized at common law because, "as a matter of self-protection, the stockholder was entitled to know how his agents were conducting the affairs of the corporation of which he or she was a part owner." The common law right is codified in 8 Del. C. § 220, which provides in relevant part:

> (b) Any stockholder shall, upon written demand under oath stating the purpose thereof, have the right to inspect for any proper purpose the corporation's stock ledger, a list of its stockholders, and its other books and records, and to make copies or extracts therefrom. A proper purpose shall mean a purpose reasonably related to such person's interest as a stockholder.

Once a stockholder establishes a proper purpose under § 220, the right to relief will not be defeated by the fact that the stockholder may have secondary purposes that are improper. The scope of a stockholder's inspection, however, is limited to those books and records that are necessary and essential to accomplish the stated, proper purpose.

After trial, the Court of Chancery found "credible evidence of possible wrongdoing," which satisfied Saito's burden of establishing a proper purpose for the inspection of corporate books and records. But the Court of Chancery limited Saito's access to relevant documents in three respects. First, it held that, since Saito would not have standing to bring an action challenging actions that occurred before he purchased McKesson stock, Saito could not obtain documents created before October 20, 1998. Second, the court concluded that Saito was not entitled to documents relating to possible wrongdoing by the financial advisors to the merging companies. Third, the court denied Saito access to any HBOC documents, since Saito never was a stockholder of HBOC. We will consider each of these rulings in turn.

A. The Standing Limitation

By statute, stockholders who bring derivative suits must allege that they were stockholders of the corporation "at the time of the transaction of which such stockholder complains." 8 Del. C. § 327. The Court of Chancery decided that this limitation on Saito's ability to maintain a derivative suit controlled the scope of his inspection rights. As a result, the court held that Saito was "effectively limited to examining conduct of McKesson and McKesson HBOC's boards following the negotiation and public announcement of the merger agreement."

Although we recognize that there may be some interplay between the two statutes, we do not read § 327 as defining the temporal scope of a stockholder's inspection rights under § 220. The books and records statute requires that a stockholder's purpose be one that is "reasonably related" to his or her interest as a stockholder. The standing statute, § 327, bars a stockholder from bringing a derivative action unless the stockholder owned the corporation's stock at the time of the alleged wrong. If a stockholder wanted to investigate alleged wrongdoing that substantially predated his or her stock ownership, there could be a question as to whether the stockholder's purpose was reasonably related to his or her interest as a stockholder, especially if the stockholder's only purpose was to institute derivative litigation. But stockholders may use information about corporate mismanagement in other ways, as well. They may seek an audience with the board to discuss proposed reforms or, failing in that, they may prepare a stockholder resolution for the next annual meeting, or mount a proxy fight to elect new directors. None of those activities would be prohibited by § 327.

Even where a stockholder's only purpose is to gather information for a derivative suit, the date of his or her stock purchase should not be used as an automatic "cut-off" date in a § 220 action. First, the potential derivative claim may involve a continuing wrong that both predates and postdates the stockholder's purchase date. In such a case, books and records from the inception of the alleged wrongdoing could be necessary and essential to the stockholder's purpose. Second, the alleged post-purchase date wrongs may have their foundation in events that transpired earlier. In this case, for example, Saito wants to investigate how McKesson's merger was consummated. Due diligence documents generated before the merger agreement was signed may be essential to that investigation. In sum, the date on which a stockholder first acquired the corporation's stock does not control the scope of records available under § 220.

B. The Financial Advisors' Documents

The Court of Chancery denied Saito access to documents in McKesson HBOC's possession that the corporation obtained from financial and accounting advisors, on the ground that Saito could not use § 220 to develop potential claims against third parties. On appeal, Saito argues that he is seeking third party documents for the same reason he is seeking McKesson HBOC documents—to investigate possible wrongdoing by McKesson and McKesson HBOC. Since the trial court found that to be a proper purpose, Saito argues that he should not be precluded from seeing documents that are necessary to his purpose, and in McKesson HBOC's possession, simply because the documents were prepared by third party advisors.

We agree that, generally, the source of the documents in a corporation's possession should not control a stockholder's right to inspection under § 220. The issue is whether the documents are necessary and essential to satisfy the stockholder's proper purpose. In this case, Saito wants to investigate possible wrongdoing relating to McKesson and McKesson HBOC's failure to discover HBOC's accounting irregularities. Since McKesson and McKesson HBOC relied on financial and accounting advisors to evaluate HBOC's financial condition and reporting, those advisors' reports and correspondence would be critical to Saito's investigation.

C. HBOC Documents

Finally, the Court of Chancery held that Saito was not entitled to any HBOC documents because he was not a stockholder of HBOC before or after the merger. Although Saito is a stockholder of HBOC's parent, McKesson HBOC, stockholders of a parent corporation are not entitled to inspect a subsidiary's books and records, "absent a showing of a fraud or that a subsidiary is in fact the mere alter ego of the parent." The Court of Chancery found no basis to disregard HBOC's separate existence and, therefore, denied access to its records.

We reaffirm this settled principle, which applies to those HBOC books and records that were never provided to McKesson or McKesson HBOC. But it does not apply to relevant documents that HBOC gave to McKesson before the merger, or to McKesson HBOC after the merger. We assume that HBOC provided financial and accounting information to its proposed merger partner and, later, to its parent company. As with the third party advisors' documents, Saito would need access to relevant HBOC documents in order to understand what his company's directors knew and why they failed to recognize HBOC's accounting irregularities.

Points for Discussion

1. *"Proper purpose."*

The *Saito* decision identifies a number of proper purposes for shareholder inspection. Is there a unifying thread? For example, does the Delaware court address the question whether a shareholder could seek documents about the company's social or political activities?

By the way, who has the burden on the question of "proper purpose"? In Delaware, the statute splits the burden. With regard to the corporation's stock ledger or list of stockholders, the corporation must demonstrate the shareholder seeks inspection for an improper purpose. But the shareholder must establish a proper purpose for inspecting other books and records. *See* DGCL § 220(c). Does this make sense?

2. Nature of judicial review.

Notice that in *Saito* the Delaware Supreme Court, like the Court of Chancery, engages in a demand-by-demand review of the different categories of documents sought by the shareholder. Is this what the statute requires? Isn't this like judicial supervision of discovery during litigation? Why not simply make inspection a part of the litigation process, rather than its own separate procedure—and litigation? That is, wouldn't Delaware's stated purpose to provide a forum for corporate litigation be better served by not requiring (inspection) litigation prior to (derivative) litigation?

3. Fishing expeditions.

Like judges refereeing discovery disputes, Delaware judges in inspection cases frequently admonish shareholders that they will not permit "fishing expeditions." Why not? If, as the Delaware courts have required, shareholders seeking inspection must "present some credible basis from which the Court can infer that waste or mismanagement may have occurred," where does this pre-inspection information come from?

4. Inspection of subsidiary's documents.

Soon after the *Saito* decision, the Delaware legislature revised Section 220 to allow for inspection of the "books and records" of a Delaware corporation's subsidiaries, provided the corporation could obtain such documents through the exercise of control over the subsidiary. Under the provision, such inspection can be denied if it would violate an agreement between the corporation and the subsidiary or if the subsidiary has a legal right under applicable law (such as that of the jurisdiction of its incorporation) to deny inspection. Would you advise a corporation to enter into agreements with its subsidiaries that block inspection rights of the subsidiary's documents?

5. Confidentiality conditions.

Not only does DGCL Section 220 contemplate that the court may "prescribe conditions with reference to inspection," but Delaware courts have used "wide discretion" to decide the scope of inspection—including the execution of a confidentiality agreement as a condition for inspection. Is this like discovery? Should companies be able to impose confidentiality requirements on shareholders seeking inspection?

6. Publicly available information.

Should a shareholder be able to seek inspection of information or documents that are already publicly available? As we will see in the next section, the SEC requires the disclosure and filing of important documents in many transactions involving public corporations. The Delaware courts have carved out an exception to the statutory inspection rights when the "detailed information" available in SEC filings essentially discloses all facts material to the shareholder's purpose for inspection. Is this fair? For example, if SEC disclosures summarize opinion letters on company value in a going-private transaction (where the company buys its shares and as a result management acquires control), should shareholders seeking information about company value be denied inspection of the actual opinion letters and the documents on which they are based? Should the shareholder be forced to wait for discovery of this critical information in an appraisal lawsuit?

The next case involves a shareholder request to inspect books and records of AmerisourceBergen Corporation, one of the country's largest opioid distributors. In the wake of numerous government investigations and lawsuits concerning AmerisourceBergen's role in the national opioid crisis, two shareholders served the company with a Section 220 demand requesting to inspect various books and records regarding these issues, including board materials. The shareholders indicated several purposes for inspection, including to investigate possible breaches of fiduciary duty, mismanagement, and other violations of law, as well as to evaluate potential litigation. The company rejected the demand, and the stockholders filed an action in the Court of Chancery to compel production of the documents. The case went up to the Supreme Court of Delaware on interlocutory appeal.

AmerisourceBergen Corp. v. Lebanon County Employee's Retirement Fund

243 A.3d 417 (Del. 2020)

TRAYNOR, JUSTICE.

In this opinion, we hold that, when a Section 220 inspection demand states a proper investigatory purpose, it need not identify the particular course of action the stockholder will take if the books and records confirm the stockholder's suspicion of wrongdoing. We also hold that, although the actionability of wrongdoing can be a relevant factor for the Court of Chancery to consider when assessing the legitimacy of a stockholder's stated purpose, an investigating stockholder is not required in all cases to establish that the wrongdoing under investigation is actionable.

Factual Background & Procedural History

During the ongoing opioid epidemic, AmerisourceBergen, one of the country's largest opioid distributors, has been investigated by numerous law-enforcement and government agencies. AmerisourceBergen is also a defendant in multi-district litigation in the United States District Court (the "Multidistrict Litigation"), which "centralizes

1,548 different lawsuits." The plaintiffs in the Multidistrict Litigation, who also allege that AmerisourceBergen has failed to implement and maintain effective systems to flag suspicious orders, have successfully defended AmerisourceBergen's motion to dismiss and motion for summary judgment. In an effort to settle the ongoing Multidistrict Litigation, the Company and two other opioid distributors, offered to pay $10 billion. The regulators rejected the offer and demanded $45 billion. To date, AmerisourceBergen "has spent more than $1 billion in connection with opioid-related lawsuits and investigations." Analysts estimate that AmerisourceBergen could spend up to $100 billion to reach a global settlement.

In May 2019, amidst a "flood of government investigations and lawsuits relating to AmerisourceBergen's opioid practices," the Plaintiffs served a Section 220 demand on AmerisourceBergen, requesting inspection of thirteen categories of books and records. The Plaintiffs requested Board Materials from May 1, 2010 to date concerning certain settlements, acquisitions, investigations, and other events related to AmerisourceBergen's operations and its potential involvement in the opioid crisis.

The Demand listed four investigatory purposes:

(i) to investigate possible breaches of fiduciary duty, mismanagement, and other violations of law by members of the Company's Board of Directors and management . . . in connection with the Company's distribution of prescription opioid medications;

(ii) to consider any remedies to be sought in respect of the aforementioned conduct;

(iii) to evaluate the independence and disinterestedness of the members of the Board; and

(iv) to use information obtained through inspection of the Company's books and records to evaluate possible litigation or other corrective measures with respect to some or all of these matters.

AmerisourceBergen rejected the Demand in its entirety, claiming that the Demand did not state a proper purpose and that, even if the Plaintiffs' purpose were proper, the scope of the inspection was overbroad. In July 2019, the Plaintiffs filed this action in the Court of Chancery, seeking to compel production of the requested documents.

In its memorandum opinion following trial on a paper record, the Court of Chancery found that the Plaintiffs had demonstrated a proper purpose sufficient to warrant the inspection of Formal Board Materials. The Company moved for, and the Court of Chancery granted, certification of an interlocutory appeal.

DISCUSSION

A stockholder's right to inspect a corporation's books and records was "recognized at common law because '[a]s a matter of self-protection, the stockholder was entitled to know how his agents were conducting the affairs of the corporation of which he or she was a part owner.'" Section 220(c) provides that stockholders who seek to inspect a corporation's books and records must establish that "(1) such stockholder is a stockholder; (2) such stockholder has complied with § 220 respecting the form and manner of making demand for inspection of such documents; and (3) the inspection such stockholder seeks is for a proper purpose." A proper purpose is a "purpose reasonably related to such person's interest as a stockholder." Myriad proper purposes have been accepted under Delaware law including: "the determination of the value of one's equity holdings, evaluating an offer to purchase shares, inquiring into the independence of directors, investigation of a director's suitability for office, testing the propriety of the company's public disclosures, investigation of corporate waste, and investigation of possible mismanagement or self-dealing." Once a stockholder shows that its primary purpose is reasonably related to its interest as a stockholder, the fact that it may also have "a further or secondary purpose . . . is irrelevant. To avoid "indiscriminate fishing expeditions," a bare allegation of possible waste, mismanagement, or breach of fiduciary duty, without more, will not entitle a stockholder to a Section 220 inspection. Rather, a stockholder seeking to investigate wrongdoing must show, by a preponderance of the evidence, a credible basis from which the court can infer there is "possible mismanagement as would warrant further investigation." Although not an insubstantial threshold, the credible basis standard is the "lowest possible burden of proof." A stockholder need not show that corporate wrongdoing or mismanagement has occurred in fact, but rather the "threshold may be satisfied by a credible showing, through documents, logic, testimony or otherwise, that there are legitimate issues of wrongdoing." Once a stockholder has established a proper purpose, the stockholder will be entitled only to the "books and records that are necessary and essential to accomplish the stated, proper purpose."

A. The Plaintiffs' Proper Purpose

After a thoughtful analysis of Section 220's proper-purpose requirement, which included a review of a line of authority in the Court of Chancery requiring stockholders who want to investigate corporate wrongdoing "to state up-front what they plan to do with the fruits of the inspection," the court concluded that, although "the Demand did not recite ends to which the Plaintiffs might put the books and records, they were not required to do so. Instead the Plaintiffs reserved the ability to consider all possible courses of action that their investigation might warrant pursuing." We, too, reject AmerisourceBergen's characterization of the Plaintiffs' Demand as solely limited to pursuing derivative litigation. And we agree with the Court of Chancery's observation that a stockholder is not required to state the objectives of his investigation. AmerisourceBergen acknowledges that investigating corporate wrongdoing is a widely recognized proper purpose under Section 220. Yet it claims that "whether that purpose in a specific case is reasonably related to the stockholder's interest as a stockholder cannot be ascertained in a vacuum." According to AmerisourceBergen, "the objectives of the investigation will dictate whether the purpose is in fact a proper purpose." It concedes that this Court has not considered whether a stockholder must state in its demand the objectives of an investigation of corporate wrongdoing. Therefore, the Company relies heavily on a case involving a stockholder's request to inspect the company's list of stockholders. The majority in that case held that, in that context, a demand that contained "a mere statement" that the purpose of the inspection was "to communicate with other stockholders" was inadequate.

But a request to inspect a list of stockholders is fundamentally different than a request to inspect books and records in furtherance of an investigation of corporate wrongdoing. A corporation cannot discern whether the inspection of its list of stockholders for the purpose of communicating with other stockholders is related to the stockholder's interest as a stockholder without a disclosure of the substance of the intended communication. By contrast, corporate wrongdoing is, as the Court of Chancery noted, in and of itself "a legitimate matter of concern that is reasonably related to a stockholder's interest as a stockholder." We have recognized that, when a stockholder investigates meritorious allegations of possible mismanagement, waste, or wrongdoing, it serves the interests of all stockholders "and should increase stockholder return." It follows that, under such circumstances, the stockholder's purpose is proper. Of course, a mere statement of suspicion is inadequate. If the stockholder cannot present a credible basis from which the court can infer wrongdoing or mismanagement, it is likely that the stockholder's demand is an "indiscriminate fishing expedition." But where a stockholder meets this low burden of proof from which possible wrongdoing or mismanagement can be inferred, a stockholder's purpose will be deemed proper under Delaware law.

AmerisourceBergen contends that "this Court has expressly recognized that the objectives of an investigation are critical to a determination whether an investigative purpose is reasonably related to the stockholders' interests as a stockholder," citing *Saito v. McKesson HBOC, Inc.* AmerisourceBergen's reliance on *Saito* is misplaced. In that case, we addressed the interplay of the standing requirement in § 327 and books-and-records inspections under § 220. AmerisourceBergen omits, however, from the *Saito* quote the following qualification:

> But stockholders may use information about corporate mismanagement in other ways, as well. They may seek an audience with the board to discuss proposed reforms or, failing in that, they may prepare a stockholder resolution for the next annual meeting, or mount a proxy fight to elect new directors. None of those activities would be prohibited by § 327.

None of these post-inspection uses of the company's books and records were included in the purpose stated in Saito's demand, yet we recognized that they remained available to him. Thus, our reading of *Saito* undermines AmerisourceBergen's contention that a stockholder who seeks an inspection for the purpose of investigating mismanagement or wrongdoing must state in the demand all of the ways it might use the documents uncovered in the investigation. This is not to say that the stockholder's intended uses are irrelevant or that it is not advisable, in the interest of enhancing litigation efficiencies—to state the intended uses in the stockholder's demand. And we agree with the Court of Chancery that a corporation may challenge the bona fides of a stockholder's stated purpose and present evidence from which the court can infer that the stockholder's stated purpose is not its actual purpose. Or the court, when assessing the propriety of a stockholder's purpose, can imply . . . what the stockholders' intended use of the books and records will be. But when the purpose of an inspection of books and records under Section 220 is to investigate corporate wrongdoing, the stockholder seeking inspection is not required to specify the ends to which it might use the books and records.

B. Relevance of Actionability

The previous argument—that the Plaintiffs' sole purpose in seeking to inspect AmerisourceBergen's books and records is to pursue a *Caremark* claim and the court should not consider other potential uses of the documents—would not, standing alone, suffice to defeat the Plaintiffs' inspection rights. After all, AmerisourceBergen concedes that the evaluation of litigation options is an appropriate objective of an investigative Section 220 demand. As the Court of Chancery recognized, however, AmerisourceBergen's attempt to cabin the Plaintiffs' use of its books and records to their pursuit of a *Caremark* claim, merely set the stage for AmerisourceBergen's "launching [of] merits-based strikes on the lawsuit that AmerisourceBergen expects the Plaintiffs to file someday." Such strikes are justified, AmerisourceBergen contends, because the Plaintiffs must establish that the wrongdoing they seek to investigate is actionable wrongdoing. And, according to AmerisourceBergen, the Plaintiffs' claims are not actionable because they are legally barred by a Section 102(b)(7) exculpatory provision in its certificate of incorporation and by laches.

The Court of Chancery rejected AmerisourceBergen's argument on three grounds. First, the court found that the argument failed for the "threshold reason that the Plaintiffs are not seeking the books and records for the sole purpose of investigating a potential *Caremark* claim and thus can use the fruits of their investigation for other purposes." Second, the court held that "to obtain books and records, a stockholder does not have to introduce evidence from which a court could infer the existence of an actionable claim." Third, the court found that, in any event, AmerisourceBergen's Section 102(b)(7) and laches defenses were unavailing. As to the Section 102(b)(7) defense, the court found that "the issues that the Plaintiffs wish to investigate could well lead to non-exculpated claims." And as to the laches defense, it was not clear to the court that the Plaintiffs' potential derivative claims were time-barred, given the possibility that the doctrines of fraudulent concealment and equitable tolling could apply. Our agreement with the Court of Chancery on any one of these three grounds would be sufficient to lay AmerisourceBergen's argument to rest; we happen to agree on all three.

As mentioned, the *sine qua non* of AmerisourceBergen's contention that the Plaintiffs must establish a credible basis from which actionable wrongdoing can be inferred is that the Plaintiffs "are only seeking to investigate a *Caremark* claim." To support this claim, AmerisourceBergen contends that the Demand . . . is "littered with assertions" that the company's board of directors "ignored red flags"—language that suggests an investigation of a *Caremark* failed-oversight claim. AmerisourceBergen's assertions go too far.

A stockholder may state more than one purpose for inspection and use the information obtained for more than one purpose. As already mentioned, a stockholder may use the information supporting a claim of mismanagement obtained through an inspection for purposes other than bringing litigation. Although AmerisourceBergen correctly identifies several references to potential litigation in the Demand, the Demand also states that the information sought will be used "to evaluate other corrective measures with respect to all or some of these matters." The Demand also contemplates a "possible course of conduct to include making a demand on the Company's Board of Directors to take action." In our view, the Court of Chancery's determination that the Plaintiffs contemplated purposes other than litigation is supported by a fair reading of the Demand. We need go no further than that to dispose of AmerisourceBergen's "actionability" argument. We nevertheless take this opportunity to dispel the notion that a stockholder who demonstrates a credible basis from which the court can infer wrongdoing or mismanagement must demonstrate that the wrongdoing or mismanagement is actionable.

As noted above, under Section 220, a stockholder who wishes to investigate corporate wrongdoing must present a credible basis from which the court can infer that wrongdoing may have occurred. It bears repeating that this test "reflects judicial efforts to maintain a proper balance between the rights of shareholders to obtain information based upon credible allegations of corporation mismanagement and the rights of directors to manage the business of the corporation without undue interference from stockholders." Having struck that balance, this Court has not required stockholders to prove that the wrongdoing they seek to investigate is actionable. To the contrary, we have stated that a stockholder is not required to prove that wrongdoing occurred, only that there is "possible mismanagement that would warrant further investigation."

In the rare case in which the stockholder's sole reason for investigating mismanagement or wrongdoing is to pursue litigation and a purely procedural obstacle, such as standing or the statute of limitations, stands in the stockholder's way such that the court can determine, without adjudicating merits-based defenses, that the anticipated litigation will be dead on arrival, the court may be justified in denying inspection. But in all other cases, the court should—as the Court of Chancery did here—defer the consideration of defenses that do not directly bear on the stockholder's inspection rights, but only on the likelihood that the stockholder might prevail in another action.

———

Points for Discussion

1. *Investigating potential corporate wrongdoing.*

In *AmerisourceBergen,* the Court stated that "a stockholder is not required to state the objectives of his investigation" because "corporate wrongdoing is, as the Court of Chancery noted, in and of itself 'a legitimate matter of concern that is reasonably related to a stockholder's interest as a stockholder.'" Corporations may still "challenge the *bona fides* of a stockholder's stated purpose and present evidence from which the court can infer that the stockholder's stated purpose is not its actual purpose," but shareholders are nevertheless "not required to specify the ends to which they might use the books and records." How is investigating potential corporate wrongdoing related to a shareholder's interest as a shareholder? Why does a shareholder not have to present evidence that the wrongdoing be actionable in subsequent litigation?

2. *Scope of materials.*

After a data breach involving the unauthorized release of confidential user data to a data analytics firm, Facebook, Inc. (now known as Meta) faced investigation from the Federal Trade Commission ("FTC") regarding the potential violation of a consent decree the company had entered into in 2012 over previous data privacy breaches. The company settled with the FTC for $5 billion, and the settlement included a release for Facebook's CEO, Mark Zuckerberg. A shareholder subsequently served a demand to inspect Facebook's books and records to investigate whether the company had overpaid in the settlement to protect Zuckerberg from personal liability. Facebook produced thousands of pages, but some were heavily redacted, and it resisted the shareholder's request for board-level emails and text messages concerning the FTC settlement negotiations. The Court of Chancery rejected Facebook's arguments, explaining: "That a stockholder plaintiff believes it has a basis in facts already known to pursue claims of wrongdoing against company fiduciaries does not mean the stockholder should be denied use of the 'tools at hand' to develop those facts further so that it can well-plead its claims in a complaint, particularly a derivative complaint." The court commended the parties for focusing the trial on the scope of documents to be produced, rather than litigating the propriety of the shareholder's stated purpose at the outset. *See Employees' Retirement System of Rhode Island v. Facebook, Inc.,* 2021 WL 529439, at *6, n.11 (Del. Ch. Feb. 10, 2021); *see also In re Facebook, Inc. Section 220 Litig.,* 2019 WL 2320842 (Del. Ch. May 31, 2019).

Similarly, in *KT4 Partners LLC v. Palantir Technologies, Inc.* 203 A.3d 738 (Del. 2019), the Delaware Supreme Court validated a shareholder's request for e-mails related to amendments of an investors' rights agreement after the shareholder presented evidence that the company had acted through email in connection with the suspected wrongdoing. The Court explained: "Ultimately if a company observes traditional formalities, such as documenting its actions through board minutes, resolutions, and official letters, it will likely be able to satisfy a § 220 petitioner's needs solely by producing those books and records. But if a company instead decides to conduct formal corporate business largely through informal electronic communications, it cannot use its own choice of medium to keep shareholders in the dark about the substantive information to which § 220 entitles them."

As modern business correspondence shifts to e-mail and text messages, should these communications become "fair game" of Section 220 investigation by shareholders? How should the law balance the need for electronic communications with the burden of producing those communications?

————————

2.   "Stockholder List"

In the United States, unlike many other parts of the world, shares of stock are not issued in "bearer form" so that whoever holds the stock certificate (or its electronic equivalent) owns the stock. Instead, U.S. corporations are required to maintain records that list the names of *"stockholders of record"*—persons holding legal title to outstanding shares of stock.

> The "transfer agent," usually a bank or trust company, keeps the corporation's stock ledger. Among the services provided are issuing and canceling stock certificates to reflect changes in ownership, paying dividends or other distributions to shareholders, sending out proxy materials and other reports, exchanging a company's stock in a merger, or holding tendered shares in a tender offer.
>
> A "stock ledger" records all stock transactions in the corporation, such as initial issuance and any subsequent transfer. The stock ledger shows for each stock transaction the stock certificate number that is affected and the name of the shareholder who owns the certificate.
>
> The "list of stockholders" includes other lists of shareholders maintained by the corporation. For example, beneficial shareholders who agree (do not object) to having their names and addresses revealed to the company can be found on a Non-Objecting Beneficial Owner (NOBO) list.

Street name ownership. With the advent of electronic data storage and the disappearance of paper stock certificates, investors have changed how they own stock. Today, most investors in public corporations are not record holders, but instead hold their stock in nominee accounts in *"street name."* Even though corporations (or their transfer agents) often keep electronic records of current shareholders, these lists do not show who really (or beneficially) owns the stock. Thus, the requirement under the Delaware inspection statute that the corporation produce its "stock ledger" (a list of stockholders of record) is of little practical use. Such data lists mostly nominee holders and does not give information for contacting other shareholders.

Most stock brokerage firms and financial institutions—"first tier" nominees—are members of Depository Trust Company, which holds their customers' stock. Depository Trust registers all of its members' stock in one name, "CEDE & Co.," which allows it to simplify stock transfers among its members. As a result, most corporations' stockholder lists show only that CEDE & Co. owns a large portion of their stock—often more than 80%. The lists do not identify which brokerage firms and institutions hold their stock or who the beneficial owners are.

How can a corporation know who really owns its stock, for example to distribute disclosure documents? The corporation can ask Depository Trust to prepare a "CEDE breakdown"—a list of all brokerage firms and institutions holding stock in the name of CEDE & Co. Using this breakdown, the corporation then can contact the firms on the list to determine the number of beneficial owners each represents, to facilitate distribution of annual reports, notices of shareholder meetings, and other information. The brokerage firms and institutions generally will not volunteer the names of their customers since they consider that information confidential.

To get information on actual beneficial owners, corporations can ask brokerage firms for the names of those customers who do not object to having their identity revealed to the corporation. Brokerage firms are required by SEC rule to maintain a list of non-objecting beneficial owners ("NOBO list") and make it available to requesting corporations within seven days.

What can be inspected? Delaware courts have interpreted the "list of stockholders" mentioned in the Delaware inspection statute to include both CEDE breakdowns and NOBO lists within the corporation's possession. If the corporation does not already possess these lists, courts have required that the corporation request that the CEDE breakdown be produced, but have not required that the corporation request a NOBO list.

Information on the shareholders in public companies is available from other sources, as well. The federal securities laws require institutional shareholders (with more than $100 million in assets) to file reports of their securities holdings. In addition, shareholders that hold more than 10% of the outstanding shares of public companies must file reports on their holdings and any trading. In addition, public companies must list holdings by (certain) shareholders in their prospectuses and annual reports, as well as holdings of corporate directors and officers.

3. Shareholder Standing and "Encumbered Shares"

Which shareholders have inspection rights? Although most statutes permit both record and beneficial shareholders to seek inspection, the question is not as easy as it sounds. Given the proliferation of financial hedging techniques, shareholders frequently hold offsetting positions that reduce or eliminate the financial incentives associated with share ownership.

Suppose you buy a share for $100. If the share price goes up, you have made money; if it declines, you have lost. Now suppose that you also have "shorted" the same share. In a "short" transaction, you borrow a share from a broker and then sell the share. You get the money from the sale upfront, but you have the obligation to return the borrowed share to the broker. If the share price goes up, you lose money, because you have to buy a more expensive share to return to the broker. If the share price goes down, you make money, because you can buy a less expensive share to return. Financially, a "short" is like the mirror opposite of a share purchase.

In this example, if you both purchased a share ("long position") and shorted a share ("short position"), your net financial position would be zero. Upfront, the $100 you received from shorting would offset the $100 you paid for the share. And when you satisfied your obligation to return a share to the broker, you would simply give the broker the share you own. There would be no need to buy a share in the marketplace, so your fortunes would not depend at all on the share price. If the price went up to $110, you would make $10 on the share you bought, but lose $10 on your short. If the price dropped to $90, you would lose $10 on your share, but make $10 on your short.

Some investors only own shares long without short positions ("pure" shareholders). But some investors have both long and short positions. You can think of a short position as financially "encumbering" the long position, weighing down the shares owned by the investor with opposite positions that take away the upside when share prices rise (and reduce the downside when prices fall). In the extreme, an investor might have more shorts than longs, so that she would make money if the share price declined. Such an investor would not have the economic incentives of a shareholder—in fact, the opposite would be true. Should a shareholder with a net short position be entitled to the same rights as pure shareholders? Should courts or legislatures take into account short positions?

Delaware courts have sidestepped the issue. The Court of Chancery has held that an investor that held both long and short positions was entitled to exercise inspection rights based on its long positions—that is, beneficial ownership determines shareholder rights, not the investor's net financial position. *Deephaven Risk Arb Trading Ltd. v. UnitedGlobalCom, Inc.*, 2005 WL 1713067 (Del. Ch. 2005). In the case, an arb (an investment firm that places bets on corporate transactions, like mergers) was betting against a merger happening and had taken a net short position in the corporation that was planning the merger. When the corporation decided to curtail a planned rights offering, suggesting that the merger would go through, the arb sought inspection of documents concerning the rights offering.

The Vice Chancellor allowed inspection by the arb, even though it was net short—even though its shares were "encumbered" by short positions:

Practically, requiring an analysis of why and under what circumstances a § 220 plaintiff came to hold a company's shares could significantly complicate the nature of this summary and often expedited proceeding. [It] potentially would force courts to undertake a complex analysis to determine the plaintiff's financial position net of stock, options and other derivatives. One can imagine cases in which financial experts might be necessary to make such a determination. Moreover, the specter of being forced to disclose sophisticated and proprietary trading techniques could have a chilling effect on the use of § 220 by a substantial segment of stockholders. Finally, unlike in other situations such as voting, the § 220 analysis includes its own safeguard against plaintiffs with economic incentives that are not aligned with other stockholders: the proper purpose analysis.

The court then found a "credible basis" that the rights offering may have involved mismanagement and permitted the inspection.

Points for Discussion

1. Separation of ownership and control?

Does recognizing shareholder rights for investors who are betting against the corporation serve any corporate interest? Should short selling and use of other derivatives change the meaning of who is a "shareholder"?

2. Brave new world.

The *Deephaven* court understandably wanted to avoid the "complex analysis" of the true motivations of investors in the corporation. Can you suggest a way to deal with investors who hold "encumbered shares" and are "net short"—that is, investors who nominally own an interest in future corporate profitability, but whose true financial interests are aligned with corporate financial failure? Isn't this essentially the issue that the court faced in *Pillsbury v. Honeywell*?

B.   Information Required for Shareholder Voting

1.   State Law: Notice of Shareholder Meetings

As we saw when we looked at the basics of shareholder voting, state law requires only minimal information when shareholders vote. Shareholders receive notice of when and where the shareholder meeting will happen, but generally do not get information about the matters on which they will vote. Only if there is a special meeting (or a proposal to amend the articles) must shareholders be provided with notice of the matter to be voted on (or a copy or summary of the amendment).

2.   SEC Rules: Disclosure in Proxy Statements

Disclosure under federal law is a different story. Shareholders in public corporations receive extensive information on all matters (such as board elections, amendments of articles, approval of mergers) on which they are asked to vote. A comprehensive regulatory regime created by SEC rules requires that any solicitation, whether by management or by another shareholder, seeking shareholder proxies be accompanied by a disclosure document called a "proxy statement."

> Remember that state corporate statutes authorize shareholders to vote by proxy—that is, by giving an agent authority to vote in their place at a shareholder meeting. This is how most voting happens in public corporations—so it is no surprise that federal regulation of shareholder voting in public corporations is called "proxy regulation."

The extensive disclosure required under the SEC proxy regime stands in marked contrast to the bare-bones notice required by state corporate statutes. The federal rules cover companies whose shares are traded on public stock markets. They regulate all "proxy solicitations," a term defined broadly by SEC rules and court decisions. In most proxy solicitations, not only must shareholders receive a proxy statement, but the statement must be filed with (and sometimes reviewed by) the SEC. If shareholders are asked to vote, they must receive a "proxy card" with a specified format and voting options.

In short, the federal proxy regime creates a system of prior restraints and content regulation of corporate speech that relates to shareholder voting. Promulgated pursuant to § 14(a) of the Securities Exchange Act of 1934, the purpose is to ensure informed and fair suffrage in public corporations.

Public companies. What are public companies? The SEC proxy rules generally apply to every company that has a class of securities (equity or debt) listed on a stock exchange or has a class of equity securities owned by 2,000 or more holders of record and assets of at least $10,000,000. Securities Exchange Act § 12(b), (g).

There are approximately 4,000 U.S. publicly reporting companies. Besides having to provide information to shareholders when they vote, public companies must file informational reports annually (10-K), quarterly (10-Q), and when there are special events (8-K). Their insiders (directors, officers, and more than 10% shareholders) are required to disclose any trading in the company's equity shares.

One important note: you should be aware that foreign companies whose securities are traded on U.S. public markets are only subject to the periodic disclosure requirements, but not the requirements applicable to proxy voting or disclosure of insider trading.

Management proxy solicitations. Before soliciting shareholder proxies, management must prepare a proxy statement (a detailed disclosure document describing board candidates and the matters on which shareholders will vote) and a form of proxy (the instructions that specify how shareholders want their shares to be voted).

Schedule 14A is the SEC form (really a set of instructions) that specifies what must be disclosed in the management proxy statement. For a usual annual meeting, the bulk of the proxy statement includes information about director nominees and management's compensation arrangements.

If there are any proposals requiring a shareholder vote (such as an amendment of the corporate articles or approval of an executive compensation plan), the proxy statement must describe the proposal fully—including both its negative and positive aspects. Thus, for example, if management asks shareholders to approve a charter amendment that will create a staggered board, the proxy statement might read as follows:

Management must file preliminary copies of non-routine proxy statements and forms of proxy with the SEC at least 10 days before sending them to shareholders. The SEC staff endeavors to review and comment on preliminary proxy materials within this 10-day period. (The SEC permits limited confidential treatment for proxy filings related to business combinations or other extraordinary transactions.)

The SEC does not review routine proxy materials covering uncontested annual meetings (unopposed election of directors, ratification of company auditors, and voting on shareholder proposals). Instead, these materials are filed with the SEC when sent to shareholders.

Every "proxy solicitation" (basically, a request for the shareholder's proxy) by management must be accompanied or preceded by the *definitive* proxy statement, as filed with the SEC. In addition, if management is soliciting proxies for a meeting at which directors are to be elected, shareholders must also receive the company's annual report. Recent SEC rules permit these documents to be disseminated to shareholders, if they consent, by email or other electronic means.

Proxy card. The SEC proxy rules also regulate the "form of proxy"—that is, the voting ballot sent to shareholders. The proxy card must give shareholders an opportunity to vote either for or against each non-election matter. And if directors are to be elected, the proxy card must allow shareholders to withhold their votes on directors as a group or on individual candidates. (In companies that use "majority voting," shareholders must be able to vote for or against directors as a group or individually.)

The proxy holder (typically a member of the company's management) must vote according to the shareholder's instructions. A proxy may confer discretionary authority on matters where the shareholder does not specify a choice or if unforeseen matters come up at the meeting.

Example

Here is a typical proxy card, front and back:

The proxy card offers a treasure trove of insights into the proxy machinery. It is divided into two separate voting categories—those matters supported by management and those opposed by management. It does not allow shareholders to vote for write-in or alternative candidates. It requires that the proxy be signed and dated, since the last-dated proxy is the one that counts. It tells shareholders they can give their proxy online.

C. Proxy Fraud Litigation

Besides specifying the information that shareholders must receive in any proxy solicitation, the SEC rules under § 14(a) also require the information they receive to be full and complete. Under Rule 14a–9, false or misleading statements are prohibited:

SEC Rule 14a–9
Securities Exchange Act of 1934

(a) No solicitation subject to this regulation shall be made by means of any proxy statement . . . containing any statement which . . . is false or misleading with respect to any material fact, or which omits to state any material fact necessary in order to make the statements therein not false or misleading. . .

(b) The fact that a proxy statement has been filed with or examined by the Commission shall not be deemed a finding by the Commission that such material is accurate or complete or not false or misleading. . .

Notice that Rule 14a–9 prohibits misrepresentations in proxy statements, but does not specify a remedy. Although the 1934 Act authorizes the SEC to sue to enforce provisions of the statute and its rules, there is no explicit private enforcement mechanism for the rule. To fill this gap, federal courts fashioned an implied private action for misrepresentations that violate Rule 14a–9 on the theory that the SEC cannot review and ensure the accuracy of every proxy statement.

The private action tracks the elements of a typical fraud action. The plaintiff must show (1) a false or misleading statement (2) of material fact (3) upon which shareholder voters relied (4) causing them to suffer losses. Proxy fraud litigation has become more common in response to mergers, as it has become more difficult to challenge mergers in state court, particularly Delaware. The role of state law versus federal law in such litigation has shifted over time. When § 14(a) actions were common during the 1970s, state courts began to show an interest in ensuring honesty in communications to shareholders. In an important 1977 case, Delaware articulated a duty of "complete candor" that borrowed the framework, sometimes verbatim, of the federal proxy fraud action. *See Lynch v. Vickers Energy Corp.*, 383 A.2d 278 (Del. 1977). Stemming from the duties of care and loyalty, the duty of candor requires directors to disclose all material information, fully and fairly, to shareholders when seeking shareholder action.

Shareholders in Delaware corporations have used the duty of candor (which Delaware courts sometimes called the "duty of disclosure") to successfully challenge mergers, reorganizations, and charter amendments accomplished through false or misleading proxy statements. Over time, for many shareholders and their lawyers, Delaware has proved to be preferable to federal court. Under Delaware law, potential remedies for breach of the duty of candor include, depending on the context: rescissory damages, injunctive relief, compensatory damages, and disgorgement of fiduciary profit. In addition, Delaware allows attorneys' fees to be computed on the basis of class action results, not the less generous federal "lodestar" method.

———————

CHAPTER 17

Control

We have studied the fiduciary duties that *directors and officers* owe to the corporation and its shareholders. It might surprise you to learn that *shareholders* also can owe fiduciary duties. Specifically, controlling shareholders can owe fiduciary duties to minority shareholders.

Shareholder duties are the exception, not the rule, and they arise primarily when shareholders have control. In most other contexts, shareholders can act as they please. For example, they may vote their shares as they would like, without obligation to fellow shareholders. Compared to directors and officers, who voluntarily assume the role of fiduciary inherent in their corporate office, controlling shareholders never formally assent to fiduciary responsibilities. Yet courts impose special duties when shareholders have control—duties analogous to those of directors and officers, though as you will see they are different in subtle and important ways.

The fiduciary duties of controlling shareholders, and the standard of review, frequently are not as onerous as those of directors and officers. One reason for a lower standard is that controlling shareholders, unlike corporate managers, usually have paid for their control. Minority shareholders know this, or should, and courts recognize the prerogatives of the controlling shareholder. In other words, with power comes not only responsibility, but certain privileges as well.

We begin this chapter by introducing you to when a shareholder may be deemed to have control. Then, we examine the fiduciary duties of controlling shareholders in four settings, with four separate doctrines.

First, we consider intra-group transactions, such as parent-subsidiary dealings and dealings between a subsidiary and other corporations controlled by the parent, sometimes called affiliates.

Second, we discuss "cash-out" transactions, usually accomplished through a merger in which the controlling shareholder acquires the company and the minority shareholders receive cash for their shares. We also consider alternatives to cash-out mergers and examine how courts review these transactions. These topics—cash-out mergers and their alternatives—arise in an area of practice known as "M&A" that we examine in further detail in Chapter 18. Further, the case law involving controlling shareholder cash-out mergers has been evolving and is sometimes applied to other transactions in which a controlling shareholder has an interest or receives a non-ratable benefit that is not being shared proportionately with the minority shareholders.

Third, we examine issues of control in the closely held corporation. In this context, the focus is on the bargaining and contracting by which the parties structure their venture because there is not a public market in which shareholders can "exit" by selling their shares. Even with business planning, however, the relationships between shareholders in closely held corporations may sour or a shareholder or group of shareholders with control might act opportunistically to "oppress" a minority shareholder. Some jurisdictions have a special doctrine to deal with such circumstances, known as shareholder oppression, but we will see a variety of approaches.

Finally, we explore issues that can arise when a controlling shareholder sells their stock or transfers control. We consider the control premium and then look at the duties of shareholders who sell control to someone who loots the company and when selling control involves a corporate opportunity or puts others into board positions and whether this constitutes the illegal sale of a corporate office.

A.   What Constitutes Control?

When does a shareholder have "control" of a corporation and thus become subject to these various duties? Generally, control means the power to determine the policies of a corporation's business and affairs, and it can exist in several ways.

First, there can be *de jure* control. Absent special rules for board elections or shareholder voting, the owner of more than 50% of a corporation's voting power effectively controls that corporation because he can elect a majority of the board and decide any matters submitted to a shareholder vote.

Second, there can be *de facto* control. A shareholder owning less than 50% of the voting stock has de facto control (aka "effective control") if a majority of the board lacks independence from the shareholder (sometimes referred to as "ability to control" the corporation). The owner of a significant block of shares, less than 50%, can often mobilize sufficient votes to elect a board majority. For example, in a public corporation with dispersed shareholders, the SEC takes the position that holding more than 20% of the company's shares (without any other large block owners) generally constitutes effective control. The question is whether the block owner actually controls corporate conduct. The presumption is non-majority shareholders are not controlling, and the plaintiff bears the burden to prove control and they may plead either (or both) of the following: "(1) that the minority blockholder actually dominated and controlled the corporation, its board or the deciding committee with respect to the challenged transaction or (2) that the minority blockholder actually dominated and controlled the majority of the board generally." *In re Tesla Motors, Inc. S'holder Litig.*, 2018 WL 1560393 (Del. Ch. Mar. 28, 2018). To survive a motion to dismiss, the plaintiff must show control to a "reasonably conceivable" standard.

Sometimes a court will treat multiple shareholders as a collective "control group." Courts will do so where shareholders are "connected in some legally significant way" such as "by contract, common ownership, agreement, or other arrangement—to work together toward a shared goal." It is not sufficient, however, for there to be a "mere concurrence of self-interest" among certain shareholders.

Courts have a wide variety of factors in determining controlling shareholder status, including:

- The percentage of stock ownership and whether it is a large enough block to be a dominant force in a contest election

- The shareholder's relationship with directors, management, and advisors

- The shareholder's influence on or deference from directors

- The shareholder's influence within the company and whether they are important to business and operations

- Any contractual power of the shareholder including negative veto rights

As explained in *In re Tesla Motors, Inc. Stockholder Litigation*, 2020 WL 553902 (Del. Ch. Feb. 4, 2020):

> While every stockholder with majority voting control is a controller, not every controller is a majority stockholder. A minority blockholder can, as a matter of law, be a controlling stockholder through "a combination of potent voting power and management control such that the stockholder could be deemed to have effective control of the board without actually owning a majority of stock." "The requisite degree of control can be shown to exist generally or 'with regard to the particular transaction that is being challenged.' "

> While Musk's 22.1% voting share is well below the majority threshold, "there is no absolute percentage of voting power that is required in order for there to be a finding that a controlling stockholder exists ...." "[T]he focus of the [controller] inquiry [is] on the de facto power of a significant (but less than majority) shareholder, which, when coupled with other factors, gives that shareholder the ability to dominate the corporate decision-making process."

> This court has held that one of these "other factors" is "managerial supremacy." In *In re Cysive, Inc.*, when deciding post-trial that the plaintiffs had proven a minority blockholder was a controlling shareholder, the court gave great weight to the minority blockholder's role as a company's "hands-on" CEO and "inspirational force" who was "involved in all aspects of the company's business." Additional "other factors" might

include a company's public statements acknowledging that the minority blockholder "[is] able to exercise significant influence over our company" and that a loss of the blockholder "would have a material adverse effect on our business and operations."

The cases where this Court has found that a minority blockholder was, in fact, a controlling stockholder recognize that it is the controller's "ability to dominate the corporate decision-making process" that is important to the controlling stockholder analysis. The fact that the minority blockholder's "combination of stock voting power and managerial authority ... enables him to control the corporation, if he so wishes" is what makes him a controlling stockholder. In other words, the "ability" to control, rather than the actual exercise of control, is the determinative factor in our controlling stockholder jurisprudence.

In an earlier ruling in the case, excerpted below, the court had found that plaintiffs had adequately pleaded Elon Musk's controlling shareholder status, to a reasonably conceivable standard, in a dispute regarding Tesla's acquisition of SolarCity.

In re Tesla Motors, Inc. Stockholder Litigation

2018 WL 1560293 (Del. Ch. Mar. 28, 2018)

SLIGHTS, VICE CHANCELLOR.

The parties proffer several factors to inform the Court's determination of whether the Complaint adequately pleads Musk's controller status. They include: (1) Musk's ability to influence the stockholder vote to effect significant change at Tesla, including the removal of Board members; (2) Musk's influence over the Board as Tesla's visionary, CEO and Chairman of the Board; (3) Musk's strong connections with members of the Tesla Board and the fact that a majority of the Tesla Board was "interested," as that term is defined in our law, in the Acquisition; and (4) Tesla's and Musk's acknowledgement of Musk's control in its public filings. The parties' focus on these considerations is well-placed, as each is tied directly to our controlling stockholder jurisprudence.

1. Musk's Control of the Vote

Musk is a 22.1% stockholder. In the controlling stockholder context, this ownership stake is "relatively low" reflecting a "small block." Even so, "there is no absolute percentage of voting power that is required in order for there to be a finding that a controlling stockholder exists." Indeed, "[a]ctual control over business affairs may stem from sources extraneous to stock ownership." As illustrated in Crimson Exploration's thorough study of significant cases where the parties disputed whether a minority stockholder was a controlling stockholder, there is no "linear, sliding scale approach whereby a larger share percentage makes it substantially more likely that the court will find the stockholder was a controlling stockholder."

Before turning to the "other factors," it is appropriate to dilate for a moment on Defendants' position that Musk's relatively "small block" causes the controller analysis to break clearly in their favor. There is no question that the 28% delta between Musk's ownership stake and a voting majority is quite wide. Even so, it is perhaps conceivable that, of all people, Musk might be the minority blockholder who could rally other stockholders to bridge that gap, particularly if one accepts Plaintiffs' allegation that the public investments in Tesla actually reflect investments in Musk and his vision for Tesla's future. With that said, I agree with Defendants that this dynamic alone, even if true, would not be enough to carry Plaintiffs' controller argument across the "reasonably conceivable" threshold.

But there is more. Plaintiffs allege that Musk has demonstrated a willingness to facilitate the ouster of senior management when displeased, as evidenced by the fact that he "forced founder and then-CEO Eberhard out of the Company [and thereafter] appointed himself CEO." This history conceivably was not lost on members of the Tesla Board when they considered Musk's proposal that Tesla acquire SolarCity. Plaintiffs also point out that Tesla's bylaws contain several supermajority voting requirements. This supermajority standard allows Elon Musk significant control over corporate matters while only owning approximately 22% of Tesla's common stock.

2. Musk's Control Over Tesla's Board

That Musk is the "face of Tesla" cannot meaningfully be disputed. This fact alone, however, is not dispositive of the controller question.

According to the well-pled facts in the Complaint, there were practically no steps taken to separate Musk from the Board's consideration of the Acquisition. He brought the proposal to the Board not once, not twice, but three times. He then led the Board's discussions regarding the Acquisition throughout its laser focus on SolarCity and was responsible for engaging the Board's advisors. According to the Complaint, the Board never considered forming a committee of disinterested, independent directors to consider the bona fides of the Acquisition. It took that role upon itself, notwithstanding the obvious conflicts of its members. Under these circumstances, it is appropriate to consider whether Musk brought with him into the boardroom the kind of influence that would support a reasonable inference that he dominated the Board's decision-making with regard to the Acquisition.

When Musk rather insistently brought the proposed acquisition to the Board for consideration, the Board was well aware of Musk's singularly important role in sustaining Tesla in hard times and providing the vision for the Company's success. "As Tesla has acknowledged, '[i]n addition to serving as the CEO since October 2008, Mr. Musk has contributed significantly and actively to us since our earliest days in April 2004 by recruiting executives and engineers, contributing to the Tesla

Roadster's engineering and design, raising capital for us and bringing investors to us, and raising public awareness of the Company.' " When Tesla was on the ropes, Musk infused his own capital into the Company to keep it afloat. His "Master Plans," parts one and "deux," apparently the products of his mind alone, provide the architecture by which the Company has been and will be operated, right down to the acquisition of a solar energy company. Thus, setting aside Musk's and the Company's public acknowledgments of Musk's substantial influence (discussed below), and the obvious conflicts at the Board level (also discussed below), the pled facts reveal many of the markers that have been important to our courts when determining whether a minority blockholder is a controlling stockholder.

3. The Board Level Conflicts

The question of whether a board is comprised of independent or disinterested directors is relevant to the controlling stockholder inquiry because the answer, in turn, will inform the court's determination of whether the board was free of the controller's influence such that it could exercise independent judgment in its decision-making. Even an independent, disinterested director can be dominated in his decision-making by a controlling stockholder A director is even less likely to offer principled resistance when the matter under consideration will benefit him or a controller to whom he is beholden.

In this case, the Board did not form a special committee to consider the transaction, and it is reasonably conceivable that a majority of the five Board members who voted to approve the Offer and Acquisition (Musk and Gracias recused themselves) were interested in the Acquisition or not independent of Musk. Tesla's SEC filings concede Buss and Kimbal are not independent directors. Jurvetson has served on Tesla's Board for nearly a decade. The Complaint's well-pled facts allow a reasonable inference that he and Musk are acquainted beyond mere membership on the Board, as evidenced by Musk gifting to Jurvetson the first Tesla Model S and the second Tesla Model X ever made. DFJ, Jurvetson's venture capital firm, has invested in Tesla three times between 2006 and 2008, and held Tesla stock as recently as late 2014. DFJ also owned approximately 3.3% of SolarCity's outstanding common stock. And Jurvetson himself owned 417,450 shares of SolarCity common stock as of the Acquisition. Jurvetson also has substantial connections with the third entity in Musk's "pyramid," SpaceX. He serves as a member of the board of directors of SpaceX. And between 2009 and 2015, DFJ participated in four early venture funding rounds for SpaceX and remains a "significant stockholder." Musk, in turn, is a frequent investing partner with DFJ principals, including Jurvetson and DFJ co-founder, Tim Draper, and is invested in DFJ itself. "Although the actual extent of these relationships is not altogether clear at this point in the litigation, the existence of these interests and relationships is enough" to allow a reasonable inference that Jurvetson is beholden to Musk and may not have acted independently in voting to approve the Acquisition.

4. Musk and Tesla Acknowledge Musk's Influence

Plaintiffs argue that Tesla and Musk himself have made concessions of Musk's powerful influence over the Company and its Board. As for the Company, its public filings disclose:

- In addition to serving as the CEO since October 2008, Mr. Musk has contributed significantly and actively to us since our earliest days in April 2004 by recruiting executives and engineers, contributing to the Tesla Roadster's engineering and design, raising capital for us and bringing investors to us, and raising public awareness of the Company.

- [Tesla is] highly dependent on the services of Elon Musk, [who is] highly active in [the Company's] management, [and if Tesla were to lose his services, it could] disrupt our operations, delay the development and introduction of our vehicles and services, and negatively impact our business, prospects and operating results as well as cause our stock price to decline.

- The concentration of ownership among [Tesla's] existing executive officers, directors and their affiliates may prevent new investors from influencing significant corporate decisions, [such that] these stockholders will be able to exercise a significant level of control over all matters requiring stockholder approval, including the election of directors, amendment of our certificate of incorporation and approval of significant corporate transactions.

Musk himself has publically stated that: (1) Tesla, SolarCity and SpaceX form a "pyramid" on top of which he sits, and that it is "important that there not be some sort of house of cards that crumbles if one element of the pyramid ... falters"; and (2) Tesla is "his company."

Unlike *Zhongpin*, neither Tesla nor Musk have expressly conceded that Musk is a controlling stockholder. Indeed, if the public disclosures were all that Plaintiffs could point to as evidence of Musk's control, the pleading likely would come up short. The public acknowledgements of Musk's substantially outsized influence, however, do bear on the controlling stockholder inquiry when coupled with the other well-pled allegations of Musk's control over the Company and its Board.

* * * * * *

Whether Musk has regularly exercised control over Tesla's Board, or whether he did so only with respect to the Acquisition, is not entirely clear from the Complaint. For purposes of my decision on the motion, however, that distinction does not matter. At the very least, the Complaint pleads sufficient facts to support a reasonable inference that Musk exercised his influence as a controlling stockholder with respect to the Acquisition. Specifically, the combination of well-pled facts relating to Musk's voting influence, his domination of the Board during the process leading up to the Acquisition against the backdrop of his extraordinary influence within the Company generally, the Board level conflicts that diminished the Board's resistance to Musk's influence, and the Company's and Musk's own acknowledgements of his outsized influence, all told, satisfy Plaintiffs' burden to plead that Musk's status as a Tesla controlling stockholder is reasonably conceivable.

B.   Fiduciary Duties of Controlling Shareholders

As a general matter, shareholders have no obligations or duties to each other. Where a shareholder is elected to the board or hired as a corporate officer, the shareholder becomes a director or officer and in that role assumes fiduciary obligations towards the corporation and other shareholders. Between these two scenarios is the situation of a shareholder with control. Recognizing that a board in this context may not act independently of the controlling shareholder, courts began to extend aspects of the board's fiduciary duties to the controlling shareholder. As we noted at the outset, there is no singular rule or doctrine for controlling shareholders, and so we will study key areas in which issues arise involving controlling shareholders and their duties.

1. Transactions Within Corporate Groups

Controlling shareholders often use their control to engage in transactions with their controlled corporations—what else would you expect? Parent-subsidiary transactions occur regularly and rarely give rise to litigation. But fairness always is, or should be, on the mind of the parent. Corporate statutes generally do not address intra-group transactions. The following case, foundational in the U.S. law of corporate groups, illustrates the judicial approach to intra-group dealings, both between the parent and its partially-owned subsidiaries and between group affiliates.

Sinclair Oil Corp. v. Levien

280 A.2d 717 (Del. 1971)

WOLCOTT, CHIEF JUSTICE.

This is an appeal by the defendant, Sinclair Oil Corporation (hereafter Sinclair), from an order of the Court of Chancery, in a derivative action requiring Sinclair to account for damages sustained by its subsidiary, Sinclair Venezuelan Oil Company (hereafter Sinven), organized by Sinclair for the purpose of operating in Venezuela, as a result of dividends paid by Sinven, the denial to Sinven of industrial development, and a breach of contract between Sinclair's wholly-owned subsidiary, Sinclair International Oil Company, and Sinven.

Sinclair, operating primarily as a holding company, is in the business of exploring for oil and of producing and marketing crude oil and oil products. At all times relevant to this litigation, it owned about 97% of Sinven's stock. The plaintiff owns about 3000 of 120,000 publicly held shares of Sinven. Sinven, incorporated in 1922, has been engaged in petroleum operations primarily in Venezuela and since 1959 has operated exclusively in Venezuela.

> Sinclair Oil Corporation was founded by Harry Sinclair in 1916 and competed with Standard Oil, which had been founded by John D. Rockefeller. By the 1920s, Sinclair had expanded to Venezuela, where it acquired a majority interest in the company that would become Sinven. Sinclair established absolute control over Sinven by the late 1950s, with 97% of its stock and total domination of its board.

Sinclair nominates all members of Sinven's board of directors. The Chancellor found as a fact that the directors were not independent of Sinclair. Almost without exception, they were officers, directors, or employees of corporations in the Sinclair complex. By reason of Sinclair's domination, it is clear that Sinclair owed Sinven a fiduciary duty. Sinclair concedes this.

The Chancellor held that because of Sinclair's fiduciary duty and its control over Sinven, its relationship with Sinven must meet the test of intrinsic fairness. The standard of intrinsic fairness involves both a high degree of fairness and a shift in the burden of proof. Under this standard the burden is on Sinclair to prove, subject to careful judicial scrutiny, that its transactions with Sinven were objectively fair.

Sinclair argues that the transactions between it and Sinven should be tested, not by the test of intrinsic fairness with the accompanying shift of the burden of proof, but by the business judgment rule under which a court will not interfere with the judgment of a board of directors unless there is a showing of gross and palpable overreaching. A board of directors enjoys a presumption of sound business judgment, and its decisions will not be disturbed if they can be attributed to any rational business purpose. A court under such circumstances will not substitute its own notions of what is or is not sound business judgment.

We think, however, that Sinclair's argument in this respect is misconceived. When the situation involves a parent and a subsidiary, with the parent controlling the transaction and fixing the terms, the test of intrinsic fairness, with its resulting shifting of the burden of proof, is applied. The basic situation for the application of the rule is the one in which the parent has received a benefit to the exclusion and at the expense of the subsidiary.

A parent does indeed owe a fiduciary duty to its subsidiary when there are parent-subsidiary dealings. However, this alone will not evoke the intrinsic fairness standard. This standard will be applied only when the fiduciary duty is accompanied by self-dealing—the situation when a parent is on both sides of a transaction with its subsidiary. Self-dealing occurs when the parent, by virtue of its domination of the subsidiary, causes the subsidiary to act in such a way that the parent receives something from the subsidiary to the exclusion of, and detriment to, the minority stockholders of the subsidiary.

We turn now to the facts. The plaintiff argues that, from 1960 through 1966, Sinclair caused Sinven to pay out such excessive dividends that the industrial development of Sinven was effectively prevented, and it became in reality a corporation in dissolution.

From 1960 through 1966, Sinven paid out $108,000,000 in dividends ($38,000,000 in excess of Sinven's earnings during the same period). The Chancellor held that Sinclair caused these dividends to be paid during a period when it had a need for large amounts of cash. Although the dividends paid exceeded earnings, the plaintiff concedes that the payments were made in compliance with 8 Del.C. § 170, authorizing payment of dividends out of surplus or net profits. However, the plaintiff attacks these dividends on the ground that they resulted from an improper motive—Sinclair's need for cash. The Chancellor, applying the intrinsic fairness standard, held that Sinclair did not sustain its burden of proving that these dividends were intrinsically fair to the minority stockholders of Sinven.

Since it is admitted that the dividends were paid in strict compliance with 8 Del.C. § 170, the alleged excessiveness of the payments alone would not state a cause of action. Nevertheless, compliance with the applicable statute may not, under all circumstances, justify all dividend payments. If a plaintiff can meet his burden of proving that a dividend cannot be grounded on any reasonable business objective, then the courts can and will interfere with the board's decision to pay the dividend.

A dividend declaration by a dominated board will not inevitably demand the application of the intrinsic fairness standard. But if such a dividend is in essence self-dealing by the parent, then the intrinsic fairness standard is the proper standard. For example, suppose a parent dominates a subsidiary and its board of directors. The subsidiary has outstanding two classes of stock, X and Y. Class X is owned by the parent and Class Y is owned by minority stockholders of the subsidiary. If the subsidiary, at the direction of the parent, declares a dividend on its Class X stock only, this might well be self-dealing by the parent. It would be receiving something from the subsidiary to the exclusion of and detrimental to its minority stockholders. This self-dealing, coupled with the parent's fiduciary duty, would make intrinsic fairness the proper standard by which to evaluate the dividend payments.

Consequently it must be determined whether the dividend payments by Sinven were, in essence, self-dealing by Sinclair. The dividends resulted in great sums of money being transferred from Sinven to Sinclair. However, a proportionate share of this money was received by the minority shareholders of Sinven. Sinclair received nothing from Sinven to the exclusion of its minority stockholders. As such, these dividends were not self-dealing. We hold therefore that the Chancellor erred in applying the intrinsic fairness test as to these dividend payments. The business judgment standard should have been applied.

We conclude that the facts demonstrate that the dividend payments complied with the business judgment standard and with 8 Del.C. § 170. The motives for causing the declaration of dividends are immaterial unless the plaintiff can show that the dividend payments resulted from improper motives and amounted to waste. The plaintiff contends only that the dividend payments drained Sinven of cash to such an extent that it was prevented from expanding.

The plaintiff proved no business opportunities which came to Sinven independently and which Sinclair either took to itself or denied to Sinven. As a matter of fact, with two minor exceptions which resulted in losses, all of Sinven's operations have been conducted in Venezuela, and Sinclair had a policy of exploiting its oil properties located in different countries by subsidiaries located in the particular countries.

From 1960 to 1966 Sinclair purchased or developed oil fields in Alaska, Canada, Paraguay, and other places around the world. The plaintiff contends that these were all opportunities which could have been taken by Sinven. The Chancellor concluded that Sinclair had not proved that its denial of expansion opportunities to Sinven was intrinsically fair. He based this conclusion on the following findings of fact. Sinclair made no real effort to expand Sinven. The excessive dividends paid by Sinven resulted in so great a cash drain as to effectively deny to Sinven any ability to expand. During this same period Sinclair actively pursued a company-wide policy of developing through its subsidiaries new sources of revenue, but Sinven was not permitted to participate and was confined in its activities to Venezuela.

However, the plaintiff could point to no opportunities which came to Sinven. Therefore, Sinclair usurped no business opportunity belonging to Sinven. Since Sinclair received nothing from Sinven to the exclusion of and detriment to Sinven's minority stockholders, there was no self-dealing. Therefore, business judgment is the proper standard by which to evaluate Sinclair's expansion policies.

Since there is no proof of self-dealing on the part of Sinclair, it follows that the expansion policy of Sinclair and the methods used to achieve the desired result must, as far as Sinclair's treatment of Sinven is concerned, be tested by the standards of the business judgment rule. Accordingly, Sinclair's decision, absent fraud or gross overreaching, to achieve expansion through the medium of its subsidiaries, other than Sinven, must be upheld.

Even if Sinclair was wrong in developing these opportunities as it did, the question arises, with which subsidiaries should these opportunities have been shared? No evidence indicates a unique need or ability of Sinven to develop these opportunities. The decision of which subsidiaries would be used to implement Sinclair's expansion policy was one of business judgment with which a court will not interfere absent a showing of gross and palpable overreaching. No such showing has been made here.

Next, Sinclair argues that the Chancellor committed error when he held it liable to Sinven for breach of contract.

In 1961, Sinclair created Sinclair International Oil Company (hereafter International), a wholly owned subsidiary used for the purpose of coordinating all of Sinclair's foreign operations. All crude purchases by Sinclair were made thereafter through International.

On September 28, 1961, Sinclair caused Sinven to contract with International whereby Sinven agreed to sell all of its crude oil and refined products to International at specified prices. The contract provided for minimum and maximum quantities and prices. The plaintiff contends that Sinclair caused this contract to be breached in two respects. Although the contract called for payment on receipt, International's payments lagged as much as 30 days after receipt. Also, the contract required International to purchase at least a fixed minimum amount of crude and refined products from Sinven. International did not comply with this requirement.

Clearly, Sinclair's act of contracting with its dominated subsidiary was self-dealing. Under the contract Sinclair received the products produced by Sinven, and of course the minority shareholders of Sinven were not able to share in the receipt of these products. If the contract was breached, then Sinclair received these products to the detriment of Sinven's minority shareholders. We agree with the Chancellor's finding that the contract was breached by Sinclair, both as to the time of payments and the amounts purchased.

> Notice that intra-group dealings receive "intrinsic fairness" review. This means that the *substance* of the dealings are compared to the terms and price one would expect in an arm's-length, third-party transaction.
>
> Under the "entire fairness" test that Delaware courts use for "freeze-out mergers" (see below), judicial review encompasses both the *substance* of the transaction and the *process* by which the transaction was initiated, timed, negotiated, decided and disclosed. Thus, for business dealings between subsidiaries in a corporate group, it is worth noticing that the "intrinsic fairness" test does not mandate procedural hoops.

Although a parent need not bind itself by a contract with its dominated subsidiary, Sinclair chose to operate in this manner. As Sinclair has received the benefits of this contract, so must it comply with the contractual duties.

Under the intrinsic fairness standard, Sinclair must prove that its causing Sinven not to enforce the contract was intrinsically fair to the minority shareholders of Sinven. Sinclair has failed to meet this burden. Late payments were clearly breaches for which Sinven should have sought and received adequate damages. As to the quantities purchased, Sinclair argues that it purchased all the products produced by Sinven. This, however, does not satisfy the standard of intrinsic fairness. Sinclair has failed to prove that Sinven could not possibly have produced or someway have obtained the contract minimums. As such, Sinclair must account on this claim.

Finally, Sinclair argues that the Chancellor committed error in refusing to allow it a credit or setoff of all benefits provided by it to Sinven with respect to all the alleged damages. The Chancellor held that setoff should be allowed on specific transactions, e.g., benefits to Sinven under the contract with International, but denied an over all setoff against all damages claimed. We agree with the Chancellor, although the point may well be moot in view of our holding that Sinclair is not required to account for the alleged excessiveness of the dividend payments.

We will therefore reverse that part of the Chancellor's order that requires Sinclair to account to Sinven for damages sustained as a result of dividends paid between 1960 and 1966, and by reason of the denial to Sinven of expansion during that period. We will affirm the remaining portion of that order and remand the cause for further proceedings.

Points for Discussion

1. *Shareholder consent?*

Although not discussed in the opinion, Levien acquired his stock *after* Sinclair already owned 97% of Sinven. When he bought his stock, how did Levien expect Sinclair to conduct its business? Wasn't he on notice that Sinclair was likely to cause Sinven to pay large dividends at the end of each year? Should that affect the nature of the fiduciary duties that Sinclair owes to the minority shareholders of Sinven?

2. *Intra-group contracting.*

The *Sinclair Oil* court intervened with respect to the contract dealings between Sinven and other affiliates in the corporate group. What burdens does the court's holding place on such contract dealings? Is this burden greater or lesser than the burden a director faces in his dealing with the corporation?

Also, consider that Sinven won a judgment for $5.6 million on the contract claim, providing an (indirect) benefit for the public shareholders of approximately $168,000. Plaintiff's attorneys were awarded fees in excess of $1 million for recovering the $5.6 million.

3. *Cost-benefit analysis of intra-group dealings.*

Notice that the *Sinclair Oil* court, in reviewing intra-group costs, refused to offset the benefits of being in a group. For example, there may be advantages in being able to enter into intra-group transactions or to share group services, such as accounting, access to capital, personnel, and so on. Why should these benefits not be factored in? Will they be quantifiable—and by whom? Interestingly, some countries have laws that specifically permit controlling shareholders to claim offsetting benefits to group members. Would you feel comfortable investing in such corporate groups?

———————

2. "Cash-Out" Mergers and Other Controlling Shareholder Transactions

The next chapter covers an introduction to M&A in more detail, but we present here one issue that is unique to controlling shareholders in the M&A context. As the litigation in *Sinclair Oil* makes clear, parent corporations often have good reasons to eliminate minority shareholders, which is often referred to generally as a "freeze out." For example, a shareholder of a public corporation might want to "go private" by acquiring a controlling stake and then paying cash to the remaining shareholders. How can this be done? Normally, private parties cannot force others to sell to them—the power of eminent domain is generally reserved to the state.

But in a corporation, "majority rule" allows controlling shareholders to structure transactions that force minority shareholders to accept cash for their shares. This can be accomplished in different ways. Each of these involve a deal structure that would "cash out" or "freeze out" the minority shareholders such that they would no longer own stock in the subsidiary or the ownership structure of the subsidiary would change through a sale to an outside buyer. This discussion will introduce you to some new vocabulary relevant to M&A deals. Here are possible structures:

Cash-out merger. The parent corporation uses its control of the subsidiary's board and its voting majority to arrange a merger between the partially-owned subsidiary and a wholly-owned corporation of the parent (or the parent itself). In the process, the minority shareholders receive cash in the merger or, if they are dissatisfied with the merger terms, in a proceeding known as a judicial appraisal.

Tender offer followed by merger. A bidder corporation makes a tender offer conditioned on acquiring at least a specified percentage of a corporation's stock. (Historically, this specified percentage was 90%, though many modern statutes permit a merger once the bidder owns a majority of the target corporation's stock.) If successful, the bidder then merges with the corporation under a streamlined procedure that requires only approval of the parent corporation's board of directors.

Sale to outside buyer. The parent corporation, rather than acquiring 100% ownership of the subsidiary, arranges for the subsidiary to be merged with an outside buyer. In the merger, the parent corporation and minority shareholders receive consideration as specified in the merger plan.

What are the fiduciary duties of the parent corporation when it cashes out minority shareholders? The answer to that question has changed over time, in ways that are often confusing—and remain in flux. Our purpose here is not to cover all of the details of the jurisprudence of cash-out mergers and their alternatives, but instead to give you a sense of what the key issues have been, are, and are likely to be.

a. Cash-Out Mergers: Controlling Shareholders and the Entire Fairness Standard

Cash-out mergers are fraught with conflicts and the potential for coercion or retributive action by the controlling shareholder. If a controlling shareholder parent (P) owns a majority of subsidiary (S) stock, it can use its control of S's board and its ability to vote for approval of the merger to dictate the terms on which S's minority shareholders will be cashed out. Unless S's non-controlling shareholders can induce a court to intervene on equitable grounds, they are powerless to retain their equity interest in S or to alter the terms of the merger.

> Over the last two decades the cash-out merger has been widely used as the second step in corporate takeovers. When a corporate bidder acquires majority (but less than 100%) control of a target company, the cash-out merger provides the means to consolidate control.
>
> Once the target becomes a wholly-owned subsidiary, the parent is freed of nettlesome minority shareholders and thus any self-dealing duties to them. The parent can use the cash flow and assets of the target as it chooses, including to repay any debt it assumed in the acquisition.

Even if P has only de facto control of S and needs the support of other S shareholders to accomplish the cash-out, S's non-controlling shareholders may have trouble blocking an unfair cash-out merger. In a public corporation, the shareholders face collective action problems and lack a mechanism for bargaining with P. These problems are exacerbated by P's better understanding of S's business and assets—and therefore its value. P also will be in a position to time a cash-out merger so as to take advantage of shifts in interest rates, fluctuations in S's stock price, or drops in the value of S's assets (some of which P may have induced).

The availability of "appraisal rights," in which shareholders dissent from a merger and get a judicial valuation of their shares, only partially mitigates the potential for P's abuse. Dissenting shareholders (at least in Delaware) must bear the significant out-of-pocket costs of appraisal. Thus, even if they obtain an award higher than the merger price, the effort may not be economically worthwhile. And even if most of the non-controlling shareholders of S believe their stock is worth more than the merger price, collective action problems will impede them from coordinating their joint efforts to pursue appraisal. Recognizing this, P may try to set the merger price just high enough to make appraisal cost-ineffective.

Despite the potential for abuse, a cash-out merger is not inevitably exploitative. P may have bona fide reasons for the transaction. P may anticipate operating efficiencies by combining P and S. And P may wish to engage in concededly fair transactions with S without the threat of litigation. P may wish to eliminate the expense of having public shareholders, thus avoiding reporting requirements and regulatory burdens. Or if P has acquired a controlling interest in S through a cash tender offer, a subsequent cash-out merger will give P access to the cash flows and assets of S that can be used to repay the acquisition debt P incurred in the tender offer. Of course, whatever the business reasons for the cash-out, P may actually offer the minority shareholders a fair price for their stock.

A series of important cases have set out the standard of review that will apply if a minority shareholder brings fiduciary litigation against the controlling shareholder in connection with a cash-out merger. In ***Weinberger v. UOP***, 457 A.2d 701 (Del. 1983), the Delaware Supreme Court held in a "one-step" cash-out merger, where the board of a company with a controlling shareholder voted to approve a merger, the merger was subject to an "entire fairness" test.

The Court held that fairness has two basic aspects: fair dealing and fair price: "The former embraces questions of when the transaction was timed, how it was initiated, structured, negotiated, disclosed to the directors, and how the approvals of the directors and the stockholders were obtained. The latter aspect of fairness relates to the economic and financial considerations of the proposed merger, including all relevant factors: assets, market value, earnings, future prospects, and any other elements that affect the intrinsic or inherent value of a company's stock. However, the test for fairness is not a bifurcated one as between fair dealing and price. All aspects of the issue must be examined as a whole since the question is one of entire fairness. However, in a non-fraudulent transaction we recognize that price may be the preponderant consideration outweighing other features of the merger."

The Court criticized whether the vote by minority stockholders was fully informed. The court noted that the determination of fair value should include a variety of factors, including the factors relevant to a discount cash flow analysis (which we covered in Chapter 7). Accordingly, the Court found that basic aspects of both fair dealing and fair price were violated.

The Court noted in footnote 7 of the opinion that "the result here could have been entirely different if UOP had appointed an independent negotiating committee of its outside directors to deal with Signal at arm's length."

Accordingly, it became common after *Weinberger* for the boards of subsidiary corporations involved in cash-out mergers to create independent negotiating committees of outside directors to negotiate with the controlling shareholder and to condition such mergers on the approval of a majority of the minority shareholders. This led to a number of questions. For example, what is the standard of review if an independent committee negotiates on behalf of minority shareholders—entire fairness or BJR? And if the processes of the negotiating committee are inadequate, does the transaction automatically fail the "entire fairness" test?

Since *Weinberger*, the Delaware Supreme Court has attempted to answer the question posted in footnote 7, in various contexts. In ***Kahn v. Lynch Communication Sys., Inc.*** (*Lynch I*), 638 A.2d 1110 (Del. 1994), the Delaware Supreme Court refused to accept, as a general matter, that the outside directors on a special negotiating committee can ever be sufficiently "independent" to warrant BJR review. The court also made clear that the negotiating committee cannot be "forced" to accept the merger by threats of a lower-priced tender offer or other means.

The case was celebrated as a "high water" mark in the protection of minority shareholders.

On remand the Court of Chancery concluded that the controlling shareholder had borne its burden to show the cash-out merger satisfied the "entire fairness" test, despite the coercive pressure it had placed on the negotiating committee. Ultimately, the court accepted that the minority had done as well as they were going to do. The court found: (1) the cash-out was a viable financial alternative for the minority; (2) its initiation by the controlling shareholder did not financially disadvantage the minority; (3) any coercion was not "material" in the decision of the minority shareholders who approved the transaction; and (4) valuation reports and other information available to the negotiating committee indicated the price was fair.

The Delaware Supreme Court affirmed, pointing out that the *Weinberger* test "is not bifurcated or compartmentalized but one requiring an examination of all aspects of the transaction to gain a sense of whether the deal in its entirety is fair." *Kahn v. Lynch Communication Sys., Inc. (Lynch II)*, 669 A.2d 79 (Del. 1995). The Court had held that the effect of either approval by an independent special committee or a vote by a majority of the shareholders unaffiliated with the controlling shareholder (a "majority of the minority" vote) would shift the burden of proof under the entire fairness standard from the defendant to the plaintiff. It left open the question of what would be the combined effect if both procedural protections were used.

b. Evolving Standards in Controlling Shareholder Litigation

After *Weinberger* and *Lynch* controlling shareholders and their lawyers began to look for ways to avoid the demanding "entire fairness" review that the case lays out. There are other techniques, besides a negotiated cash-out merger, for a controlling shareholder to cash out minority shareholders: (1) under the expedited process for "short form" and "medium form" mergers permitted when the parent owns a specified percentage or more of the subsidiary's voting shares (DGCL §§ 253, 251(h)), and (2) by engaging first in a tender offer to reach a specified percentage threshold and then engaging in a short-form or medium-form merger. Under Delaware's doctrine of "independent legal significance," courts treat transactions differently by their structure. By structuring the deal other than as a *Weinberger*-style cash-out merger between the controlling shareholder and the company, planners avoid the heavy procedural requirements and judicial review that the "entire fairness" standard imposes, and will survive challenge so long as they disclosed material facts and did not coerce shareholders. *See Glassman v. Unocal Exploration*, 777A.2d 242 (Del. 2001); *In re Siliconix*, 2001 WL 716787 (Del. Ch. June 19, 2001); *In re Pure Resources*, 808 A.2d 421 (Del. Ch. 2002). Many legal observers criticized the disparity in treatment and argued that all controlling shareholder going-private transactions should be treated comparably.

And so, for years after *Kahn v. Lynch*, the question remained whether a *Weinberger*-style negotiated merger with a controlling shareholder could ever receive a standard of judicial scrutiny lighter than entire fairness. Finally, in 2014, **_Kahn v. M&F Worldwide Corp._**, 88 A.3d 635 (Del. 2014) ("*MFW*"), the Delaware Supreme Court addressed the effect of conditioning the deal from the outset on having dual shareholder protections:

> To summarize our holding, in controller buyouts, the business judgment standard of review will be applied *if and only if*: (i) the controller conditions the procession of the transaction on the approval of both a Special Committee and a majority of the minority stockholders; (ii) the Special Committee is independent; (iii) the Special Committee is empowered to freely select its own advisors and to say no definitively; (iv) the Special Committee meets its duty of care in negotiating a fair price; (v) the vote of the minority is informed; and (vi) there is no coercion of the minority.

The Court explained, per the lower court's opinion, that this conclusion "is consistent with the central tradition of Delaware law, which defers to the informed decisions of impartial directors, especially when those decisions have been approved by the disinterested stockholders on full information and without coercion." In its view, the rule will "be of benefit to minority stockholders because it will provide a strong incentive for controlling stockholders to accord minority investors the transactional structure that respected scholars believe will provide them the best protection, a structure where stockholders get the benefits of independent, empowered negotiating agents to bargain for the best price and say no if the agents believe the deal is not advisable for any proper reason, plus the critical ability to determine for themselves whether to accept any deal that their negotiating agents recommend to them." Further, "[t]he dual protection merger structure requires two price-related pretrial determinations: first, that a fair price was achieved by an empowered, independent committee that acted with care; and, second, that a fully-informed, uncoerced majority of the minority stockholders voted in favor of the price that was recommended by the independent committee."

After *MFW*, parties can structure a transaction that satisfies the listed conditions, and thereby hope to survive a challenge to the merger on a motion to dismiss. Of course, litigation remains possible as plaintiffs could attempt to challenge whether the independent special committee was truly independent and satisfied its duties, and whether the minority shareholder vote was informed and uncoerced, and so on. If the *MFW* conditions were not satisfied, the standard would remain entire fairness under *Weinberger*, with the burden depending on whether one procedural protection under *Kahn v. Lynch* was satisfied.

While *MFW* answered an important open question in the doctrine regarding controlling shareholder cash-out mergers, it opened up a new one as well: how far does *MFW* extend? Does it apply to any transaction in which a controlling shareholder has an interest or will receive a non-ratable benefit? Many of these questions are addressed in advanced courses in mergers and acquisitions.

3. Planning and Oppression in Closely Held Corporations

This section turns to the special problems related to control in closely held corporations. As we have seen, there is no generally agreed-upon definition of a "close" or "closely held" corporation. But there is a general sense in both case law and modern statutes that a closely held corporation is one with a relatively small number of shareholders and for whom there is no public market for the corporation's shares (aka "a private corporation").

Corporate statutes try to fit corporations closely held by a few shareholders into the same legal clothes worn by public corporations. But it's often a poor fit. The shareholders of a closely held corporation often find that the corporate rules of centralized management and majority control are at odds with their expectations and they want to customize the governance arrangements *ex ante*, or they may *ex post* end up in disputes and some minority shareholders might be "oppressed" by opportunistic conduct of majority shareholders. This section addresses both of these topics in turn.

a. Realignments of Shareholder Control

In the closely held corporation, the focus is on the bargaining and contracting by which the parties structure their own venture. The lawyer's job is to use the flexibility the law allows to anticipate potential problems and to create solutions from the outset, thus reducing the likelihood of problems or providing dispute resolution mechanisms should they arise.

Contracting to avoid disputes and specify rights has its limits. It can be expensive and time consuming. Even when shareholders are prepared to incur the expense, anticipating problems is difficult. For many years, planners of the closely held corporation also confronted judicial antagonism to special arrangements—whether

Many corporation statutes now permit flexibility in planning the closely held corporation. The most common statutory approach, which is the one taken by the MBCA, is to presume all corporations are alike but expressly to authorize close corporations to adopt governance structures that vary from the traditional model. A second approach is the "comprehensive" close corporation statute, which allows the corporation to elect treatment under a special statutory regime. DGCL §§ 341–356 provides a good example of such a statute. Only a corporation that meets certain tests and elects close corporation status can use the special provisions of the Delaware statute. A small percentage of eligible corporations have elected to use these statutory close corporation provisions.

embodied in the articles, bylaws, or a separate agreement—if they departed too far from the traditional statutory model. Two parallel developments, starting mostly in the 1960s, substantially loosened this judicial attitude. First, courts have become more realistic about the special demands of closely held corporations and became far more tolerant of departures from the norm. Second, legislatures recognized the unnecessary rigidity of the traditional structure and created special rules for the close corporation.

Closely held corporation participants can realign the traditional corporate structure either at the shareholder level (by creating special voting or liquidity rights) or at the management level (by prescribing special board prerogatives or manager duties). The most basic control devices are those designed to assure that all or certain shareholders are represented on the corporation's board. Three non-mutual choices are available: (1) arrangements that ensure board representation; (2) arrangements that give some or all shareholders the ability to veto board decisions with which they disagree; or (3) arrangements that provide for dispute resolution.

Cumulative Voting

There are two principal methods for conducting an election of directors. In straight voting (the default rule under most corporate statutes) each share is entitled to one vote for each open directorship, but a shareholder is limited in the number of votes she may cast for any given director to the number of shares she owns. Directors are elected by a plurality of the votes cast, so those who receive the most votes are elected, even if they receive less than a majority. This means that any shareholder or group of shareholders controlling 51% of the shares can elect all of the members of the board.

Cumulative voting, an alternative method, allows shareholder groups to elect directors in rough proportion to the shares held by each group and thus creates the possibility of minority representation on the board. Under cumulative voting, each share again by default carries one vote, but a shareholder may "cumulate" her votes across all of the directorships up for election and choose how to allocate her votes between them. Cumulating simply means multiplying the number of votes a shareholder is entitled to cast by the number of directors for whom she is entitled to vote. If there is cumulative voting, the shareholder may cast all her votes for one candidate or allocate them in any manner among a number of candidates.

The number of shares required to elect a given number of directors under a cumulative voting regime may be calculated by the following formula:

$$X = \frac{s \times d + 1}{D + 1}$$

Where
X = number of shares required to elect directors
s = number of shares represented at the meeting
d = number of directors it is desired to elect
D = total number of directors to be electeed

To understand this formula, let's work through a simple example. Suppose that four directors are to be elected at a meeting at which 1000 shares are represented and will vote. To elect one director, a minority group would have to control 201 shares. With that number, the minority would have 804 votes (201 × 4), which would all be cast for one candidate. The majority would have 3196 votes (799 × 4). Now if the majority distributed these equally among four candidates, each would receive 799 votes, and the one candidate receiving the minority's 804 votes would be guaranteed a seat. In other words, holding just over 20% of the shares guarantees the election of one of four directors.

Note that the reason for the "+ 1" at the end of the formula is to avoid the tie that would occur if, in this example, the minority controlled only 200 votes. Then it would be possible for five candidates each to receive 800 votes.

Under this formula, if only three directors were to be elected, the minority would need just over 25% to elect one director. What percentage is necessary to elect one member to a nine-member board? The answer: one vote more than 10%. The formula also can be used to calculate the number of votes needed to elect multiple directors to the board. Thus, to elect 5 members to the nine-member board would require one vote more than 50% (makes sense).

The availability of cumulative voting has varied significantly over time. During the early 20th century, many states made cumulative voting mandatory by statute or even state constitution. As corporate law became more permissive, many states came to treat cumulative voting as a matter of choice. In some states, cumulative voting arises unless the parties "opt out" in the articles of incorporation or sometimes the bylaws. Today, <u>in most states</u>, cumulative voting is available only if the parties "opt in" in the articles.

One question that might have occurred to you is the value of board representation to a minority shareholder, if the shareholder will remain in the minority on the board. If the factions are badly split, minority representation may exacerbate tensions and drive critical decision making by the controlling shareholders outside the boardroom. Critics of cumulative voting argue that injecting factionalism into the boardroom undermines the board's functioning as a team. On the other hand, cumulative voting gives larger minority shareholders a voice and promotes divergent points of view, which may result in better decision making. And minority representation may discourage self dealing and other improper conduct by the majority because of more information to the minority's board representative.

The majority may seek to undermine the effectiveness of cumulative voting. One method is to classify the board of directors and stagger the election of directors so each class will be elected in different years. By staggering the elections, there will be fewer vacancies to be filled each year, thereby making it more difficult for a minority group to place a representative on the board. With fewer directors to be elected each year, the majority has the advantage even under cumulative voting.

Another method to dilute the effect of cumulative voting is to decrease the board size. This increases the percentage of shares necessary for a minority shareholder to elect one director. The courts have generally upheld this technique, even though it undermines cumulative voting. A planner may guard against the implementation of these techniques by inserting anti-circumvention provisions in the articles, such as requiring a supermajority vote to stagger the board or reduce the number of directors.

Class Voting

A simple technique for ensuring shareholder representation on the board, which is somewhat more flexible than cumulative voting, is class voting for directors. Class voting is permitted by statute and entails dividing the voting stock into two or more classes, each of which is entitled to elect one or more directors.

In the simple case of a corporation with three shareholders, each wishing to elect one director, three classes of shares would be created (usually denominated, somewhat prosaically, classes "A," "B," and "C"). Each class would have the right to elect one director. Since it is not necessary to issue (or authorize) the same number of shares for each class, class voting can be used to guarantee board representation to a shareholder who owns too few shares to elect a director through cumulative voting or even to add a "tie breaker" to a board. For example, a corporation can issue to its attorney one share of stock without financial rights, but that entitles him to elect one of the corporation's five directors.

The rights of the different classes may be adjusted in other ways as well. For example, each class might be required to approve all or certain actions that require shareholder approval. In fact, the number and variety of changes that can be built on this basic device are limited only by the imagination of the drafter. Classes can be created with different numbers of shares, different rights in the event of liquidation, or different dividend or preemptive rights.

Class voting has its pitfalls. The principal problem is who fills the vacancy in a class when the director dies and is the sole holder of the stock. There are a number of possible answers to that question, but they all affect the future political balance within the company and introduce the possibility of an unwanted person being introduced into the corporate structure. The planner therefore must focus on the future implications of what appears to be a simple present solution.

Shareholder Voting Arrangements

Shareholders typically use one of three types of devices to limit or control the manner in which shares will be voted: (a) voting trusts, (b) irrevocable proxies, and (c) vote pooling agreements. Sometimes an arrangement may have attributes of each.

Voting trust. Shareholders create a *voting trust* by conveying legal title to their stock to a voting trustee or a group of trustees pursuant to the terms of a trust agreement. This transfer is normally registered on the corporation's stock transfer ledger,

Some companies have gone public with "dual-class" stock structures in which one share class is offered to the general public while the other is held by founders, executives, or a family. For example, when Google went public in 2004, the co-founders and CEO held Class B shares with ten times the voting power of the ordinary Class A shares that were sold to the public. In a letter to the public, one of the founders explained: "New investors will fully share in Google's long term economic future but will have little ability to influence its strategic decisions through their voting rights." Similarly, Facebook went public in 2012, offering Class A shares with a single vote per share, in contrast to Class B shares owned by corporate insiders that had ten votes per share. This structure allowed Facebook's founder-CEO, Mark Zuckerberg, to hold a majority of the voting power despite holding less than 10% of the economic value. When Lyft went public in 2019, the founders kept control because their Class B shares had twenty votes each, compared to one vote per share for Class A.

Multi-class stock structures can stir controversy. Supporters point out that they can allow visionary leaders to retain control and manage for the long-term interests of the corporation without having to bear excessive economic risk. Critics argue that these structures insulate corporate insiders from accountability and result in sub-optimal decision making. Some structures may even allow insiders to maintain control into perpetuity.

which shows the trustees as legal owners of the shares. The transferring shareholders—now beneficiaries of the trust—receive voting trust certificates in exchange for their shares; these evidence their equitable ownership of their stock. Voting trust certificates usually are transferable and entitle the owner to receive whatever dividends are paid on the underlying stock. They are, in effect, shares of stock shorn of their voting power. Most corporate statutes, however, permit holders of voting trust certificates to exercise non-voting shareholder rights, including the right to inspect corporate books and to institute a derivative suit on behalf of the corporation. Since the terms of the trust agreement are a matter of contract, the trustees may be given full discretion to vote the shares in the trust for the election of directors and for any other matter to come before the shareholders, or may be limited to voting on only certain matters.

Earlier courts tended to view voting trusts with suspicion, in many cases holding them void as against public policy because they separated shareholders' voting power and economic ownership. State legislatures responded by passing statutes permitting voting trusts but subjecting them to certain regulations, usually a <u>duration limit</u> (such as 10 years) and a requirement that their terms be made a matter of public record so that other shareholders would know, or could learn, that a voting trust exists. Today virtually all jurisdictions have legislation dealing with voting trusts.

Some of the judicial disdain for the voting trust has survived, however, in the doctrine that a shareholder arrangement that amounts to a voting trust in operation but does not comply with the terms of a voting trust statute is invalid. Although an interesting line of cases from the 1950s and 1960s in Delaware grappled with this issue, the Delaware courts ultimately concluded that the separation of voting power and economic ownership in a close corporation was <u>not against public policy</u> if the parties had agreed to the arrangement.

Irrevocable proxy. As we saw in the chapter on corporate voting, it is common for a shareholder to give a proxy to someone else to vote her shares, and even to give that person entire discretion in voting the shares. But the ordinary proxy, like any agency power, <u>may be revoked</u> at the will of the principal, and the proxy holder remains subject to the control of the principal.

Sometimes, however, the parties want to make the grant of the proxy *irrevocable*, perhaps subject to some contingency or for a specified time. Although earlier courts were reluctant to enforce irrevocable proxies, the modern trend in agency law and corporate law is to uphold irrevocable proxies that are "coupled with an interest." What sort of interest supports an irrevocable proxy? The more conservative view is that the interest must be in (or pertain to) the stock itself, such as when a shareholder pledges her stock and grants the pledgee an irrevocable proxy to vote the stock. Other courts, rejecting a formalistic application of agency principles, have recognized the value of close corporation arrangements. Irrevocable proxies have been upheld, for example, where proxies have been promised as an inducement to new investors in the corporation or even when two or more shareholders agree to grant each other irrevocable proxies, the consideration being merely the mutual promises of the parties. For example, the <u>MBCA</u> permits irrevocable proxies when given to (1) a pledgee; (2) a person who purchased or agreed to purchase the shares; (3) a creditor of the corporation who extended it credit under terms requiring the appointment; (4) an employee of the corporation whose employment contract requires the appointment; or (5) a party to a valid voting agreement.

Vote pooling agreements. A common close corporation control device is the *vote pooling agreement*. As with voting trusts and irrevocable proxies, its basic purpose is to bind some (or all) of the shareholders to vote together—either in a particular way or pursuant to some specified procedure—on designated questions or all questions that come before the shareholders.

Consistent with the general voting freedom of corporate shareholders, many corporate statutes recognize the validity of such agreements. Often the difficulty is enforcement. Famously, in an old Delaware case involving the Ringling Brothers circus company, the Delaware Supreme Court recognized the validity of a vote pooling agreement, but refused to infer any enforcement mechanism—thus rendering empty the parties' promises to pool their votes. The Official Comment to MBCA § 7.31 states:

> Section 7.31(a) explicitly recognizes agreements among two or more share-holders as to the voting of shares and makes clear that these agreements are not subject to the rules relating to a voting trust. The only formal requirements are that they be in writing and signed by all the participating shareholders. In other respects their validity is to be judged like any other contract. A voting agreement may provide its own enforcement mechanism, as by the appointment of a proxy to vote all shares subject to the agreement; the appointment may be made irrevocable under section 7.22. If no enforcement mechanism is provided, a court may order specific enforcement of the agreement and order the votes cast as the agreement contemplates. Section 7.31(b) recognizes that damages are not likely to be an appropriate remedy for breach of a voting agreement.

b.   Oppression in the Closely Held Corporation

Planning does not always avoid disputes. Dissension in the close corporation takes two recurring forms. First are cases in which the majority cuts off minority shareholders from any financial return, thus leaving them holding illiquid stock that generates no current income. Second are cases in which the majority exercises control to frustrate the preferences of the minority.

How courts respond to dissension in closely held corporations has turned on two factors. One is how the courts view closely held corporations. As we will see, courts in some states (such as Massachusetts) have analogized the relationship among closely held corporation participants to that of partners, holding shareholders to high standards of fairness. Courts in other states (particularly Delaware) have rejected the partnership analogy and held that when business participants adopt the corporate form, they also agree to the traditional norms of corporation law, including centralized management and majority rule.

The second factor is whether the state legislature has included in its corporate statute (as does the MBCA) provisions aimed at protecting shareholders in closely held corporations. Many state laws now authorize courts to order dissolution or to take other remedial actions to protect shareholders who show that the majority has oppressed the minority.

In the following case, the Massachusetts court wrestles with the appropriate standard for resolving a dispute in a close corporation, attempting to reconcile partnership-type rules of equal treatment and corporate rules of majority prerogative. How well does the court do?

Wilkes v. Springside Nursing Home, Inc.

353 N.E.2d 657 (Mass. 1976)

Hennessey, Chief Justice.

On August 5, 1971, the plaintiff (Wilkes) filed a bill in equity for declaratory judgment in the Probate Court for Berkshire County, naming as defendants T. Edward Quinn (Quinn), Leon L. Riche (Riche), the First Agricultural National Bank of Berkshire County and Frank Sutherland MacShane as executors under the will of Lawrence R. Connor (Connor), and the Springside Nursing Home, Inc. (Springside or the corporation). Wilkes alleged that he, Quinn, Riche and Dr. Hubert A. Pipkin (Pipkin) entered into a partnership agreement in 1951, prior to the incorporation of Springside, which agreement was breached in 1967 when Wilkes's salary was terminated and he was voted out as an officer and director of the corporation. Wilkes sought, among other forms of relief, damages in the amount of the salary he would have received had he continued as a director and officer of Springside subsequent to March, 1967.

A judgment was entered dismissing Wilkes's action on the merits. We granted direct appellate review. On appeal, Wilkes argued in the alternative that (1) he should recover damages for breach of the alleged partnership agreement; and (2) he should recover damages because the defendants, as majority stockholders in Springside, breached their fiduciary duty to him as a minority stockholder by their action in February and March, 1967.

We reverse so much of the judgment as dismisses Wilkes's complaint and order the entry of a judgment substantially granting the relief sought by Wilkes under the second alternative set forth above.

In 1951, Wilkes, Riche, Quinn, and Pipkin purchased a building to use as a nursing home. Ownership of the property was vested in Springside, a corporation organized under Massachusetts law.

Each of the four men invested $1,000 and subscribed to ten shares of $100 par value stock in Springside.[2] At the time of incorporation, it was understood by all of the parties that each would be a director of Springside and each would participate actively in the management and decision making involved in operating the corporation.[3] It was, further, the understanding and intention of all the parties that, corporate resources permitting, each would receive money from the corporation in equal amounts as long as each assumed an active and ongoing responsibility for carrying a portion of the burdens necessary to operate the business.

The work involved in establishing and operating a nursing home was roughly apportioned, and each of the four men undertook his respective tasks.

At some time in 1952, it became apparent that the operational income and cash flow from the business were sufficient to permit the four stockholders to draw money from the corporation on a regular basis. Each of the four original parties initially received $35 a week from the corporation. As time went on the weekly return to each was increased until, in 1955, it totalled $100.

In 1959, after a long illness, Pipkin sold his shares in the corporation to Connor, who was known to Wilkes, Riche and Quinn through past transactions with Springside in his capacity as president of the First Agricultural National Bank of Berkshire County. Connor received a weekly stipend from the corporation equal to that received by Wilkes, Riche and Quinn. He was elected a director of the corporation but never held any other office. He was assigned no specific area of responsibility in the operation of the nursing home but did participate in business discussions and decisions as a director and served additionally as financial adviser to the corporation.

In 1965 the stockholders decided to sell a portion of the corporate property to Quinn, who in addition to being a stockholder in Springside possessed an interest in another corporation that desired to operate a rest home on the property. Wilkes was successful in prevailing on the other stockholders of Springside to procure a higher sale price for the property than Quinn apparently wanted to pay. After the sale was consummated, the relationship between Quinn and Wilkes began to deteriorate.

The bad blood between Quinn and Wilkes affected the attitudes of both Riche and Connor. As a consequence of the strained relations among the parties, Wilkes, in January of 1967, gave notice of his intention to sell his shares for an amount based on an appraisal of their value. In February of 1967 a directors' meeting was held and

---

[2]   On May 2, 1955, and again on December 23, 1958, each of the four original investors paid for and was issued additional shares of $100 par value stock, eventually bringing the total number of shares owned by each to 115.

[3]   Wilkes testified before the master that, when the corporate officers were elected, all four men "were guaranteed directorships." Riche's understanding of the parties' intentions was that they all wanted to play a part in the management of the corporation and wanted to have some "say" in the risks involved; that, to this end, they all would be directors; and that "unless you [were] a director and officer you could not participate in the decisions of [the] enterprise."

the board exercised its right to establish the salaries of its officers and employees.[4] A schedule of payments was established whereby Quinn was to receive a substantial weekly increase and Riche and Connor were to continue receiving $100 a week. Wilkes, however, was left off the list of those to whom a salary was to be paid. The directors also set the annual meeting of the stockholders for March, 1967.

At the annual meeting in March, Wilkes was not reelected as a director, nor was he reelected as an officer of the corporation. He was further informed that neither his services nor his presence at the nursing home was wanted by his associates.

The meetings of the directors and stockholders in early 1967, the master found, were used as a vehicle to force Wilkes out of active participation in the management and operation of the corporation and to cut off all corporate payments to him. Though the board of directors had the power to dismiss any officers or employees for misconduct or neglect of duties, there was no indication in the minutes of the board of directors' meeting of February, 1967, that the failure to establish a salary for Wilkes was based on either ground. The severance of Wilkes from the payroll resulted not from misconduct or neglect of duties, but because of the personal desire of Quinn, Riche, and Connor to prevent him from continuing to receive money from the corporation. Despite a continuing deterioration in his personal relationship with his associates, Wilkes had consistently endeavored to carry on his responsibilities to the corporation in the same satisfactory manner and with the same degree of competence he had previously shown. Wilkes was at all times willing to carry on his responsibilities and participation if permitted so to do and provided that he receive his weekly stipend.

1. We turn to Wilkes's claim for damages based on a breach of the fiduciary duty owed to him by the other participants in this venture. In light of the theory underlying this claim, we do not consider it vital to our approach to this case whether the claim is governed by partnership law or the law applicable to business corporations. This is so because, as all the parties agree, Springside was at all times relevant to this action, a close corporation as we have recently defined such an entity in *Donahue v. Rodd Electrotype Co. of New England, Inc.*, 367 Mass. 578, 328 N.E.2d 505 (1975).

In *Donahue*, we held that "stockholders in the close corporation owe one another substantially the same fiduciary duty in the operation of the enterprise that partners owe to one another." As determined in previous decisions of this court, the standard of duty owed by partners to one another is one of "utmost good faith and loyalty." Thus, we concluded in *Donahue*, with regard to "their actions relative to the operations of the enterprise and the effects of that operation on the rights and invest-

---

[4] The bylaws of the corporation provided that the directors, subject to the approval of the stockholders, had the power to fix the salaries of all officers and employees. This power, however, up until February, 1967, had not been exercised formally; all payments made to the four participants in the venture had resulted from the informal but unanimous approval of all the parties concerned.

ments of other stockholders," "stockholders in close corporations must discharge their management and stockholder responsibilities in conformity with this strict good faith standard. They may not act out of avarice, expediency or self-interest in derogation of their duty of loyalty to the other stockholders and to the corporation."

In the *Donahue* case we recognized that one peculiar aspect of close corporations was the opportunity afforded to majority stockholders to oppress, disadvantage or "freeze out" minority stockholders. In *Donahue* itself, for example, the majority refused the minority an equal opportunity to sell a ratable number of shares to the corporation at the same price available to the majority. The net result of this refusal, we said, was that the minority could be forced to "sell out at less than fair value," since there is by definition no ready market for minority stock in a close corporation.

> The *Wilkes* court distances itself from *Donahue*, decided just a year earlier, which set out an equal opportunity rule that may have been overbroad and ill-conceived. In *Donahue*, a minority shareholder complained of unequal treatment when the corporation repurchased the majority shareholder's interest, without making the same offer to the minority shareholder. Arguably the majority shareholder was differently situated as he had been involved in management of the corporation and a business reason existed for the repurchase, but the court nevertheless concluded that the majority shareholder had breached a duty owed to the minority.

"Freeze outs," however, may be accomplished by the use of other devices. One such device which has proved to be particularly effective in accomplishing the purpose of the majority is to deprive minority stockholders of corporate offices and of employment with the corporation. F.H. O'Neal, "SQUEEZE-OUTS" OF MINORITY SHAREHOLDERS 59, 78–79 (1975). This "freeze-out" technique has been successful because courts fairly consistently have been disinclined to interfere in those facets of internal corporate operations, such as the selection and retention or dismissal of officers, directors and employees, which essentially involve management decisions subject to the principle of majority control. As one authoritative source has said, "Many courts apparently feel that there is a legitimate sphere in which the controlling directors or shareholders can act in their own interest even if the minority suffers." F.H. O'Neal, *supra* at 59 (footnote omitted).

The denial of employment to the minority at the hands of the majority is especially pernicious in some instances. A guaranty of employment with the corporation may have been one of the "basic reasons why a minority owner has invested capital in the firm." The minority stockholder typically depends on his salary as the principal return on his investment, since the "earnings of a close corporation are distributed in major part in salaries, bonuses and retirement benefits." 1 F.H. O'Neal, CLOSE CORPORATIONS § 1.07 (1971).[5] Other noneconomic interests of the minority

---

[5]   We note here that the master found that Springside never declared or paid a dividend to its stockholders.

stockholder are likewise injuriously affected by barring him from corporate office. Such action severely restricts his participation in the management of the enterprise, and he is relegated to enjoying those benefits incident to his status as a stockholder. In sum, by terminating a minority stockholder's employment or by severing him from a position as an officer or director, the majority effectively frustrate the minority stockholder's purposes in entering on the corporate venture and also deny him an equal return on his investment.

The distinction between the majority action in *Donahue* and the majority action in this case is more one of form than of substance. Nevertheless, we are concerned that untempered application of the strict good faith standard enunciated in *Donahue* to cases such as the one before us will result in the imposition of limitations on legitimate action by the controlling group in a close corporation which will unduly hamper its effectiveness in managing the corporation in the best interests of all concerned. The majority, concededly, have certain rights to what has been termed "selfish ownership" in the corporation which should be balanced against the concept of their fiduciary obligation to the minority.

Therefore, when minority stockholders in a close corporation bring suit against the majority alleging a breach of the strict good faith duty owed to them by the majority, we must carefully analyze the action taken by the controlling stockholders in the individual case. It must be asked whether the controlling group can demonstrate a legitimate business purpose for its action. In asking this question, we acknowledge the fact that the controlling group in a close corporation must have some room to maneuver in establishing the business policy of the corporation. It must have a large measure of discretion, for example, in declaring or withholding dividends, deciding whether to merge or consolidate, establishing the salaries of corporate officers, dismissing directors with or without cause, and hiring and firing corporate employees.

When an asserted business purpose for their action is advanced by the majority, however, we think it is open to minority stockholders to demonstrate that the same legitimate objective could have been achieved through an alternative course of action less harmful to the minority's interest. If called on to settle a dispute, our courts must weigh the legitimate business purpose, if any, against the practicability of a less harmful alternative.

Applying this approach to the instant case it is apparent that the majority stockholders in Springside have not shown a legitimate business purpose for severing Wilkes from the payroll of the corporation or for refusing to reelect him as a salaried officer and director. The master's subsidiary findings relating to the purpose of the meetings of the directors and stockholders in February and March, 1967, are supported by the evidence. There was no showing of misconduct on Wilkes's part as a director, officer or employee of the corporation which would lead us to approve the majority action as a legitimate response to the disruptive nature of an undesirable individual bent on injuring or destroying the corporation. On the contrary, it appears that Wilkes had always accomplished his assigned share of the duties competently, and that he had never indicated an unwillingness to continue to do so.

It is an inescapable conclusion from all the evidence that the action of the majority stockholders here was a designed "freeze out" for which no legitimate business purpose has been suggested. Furthermore, we may infer that a design to pressure Wilkes into selling his shares to the corporation at a price below their value well may have been at the heart of the majority's plan.[6]

> "Dissolution" is the formal extinguishment of the corporation's legal life. "Liquidation" is the process of reducing the corporation's assets to cash or liquid assets, after which the corporation becomes a liquid shell. "Winding up" is the process of liquidating the assets, paying off creditors, and distributing what remains to shareholders.

In the context of this case, several factors bear directly on the duty owed to Wilkes by his associates. At a minimum, the duty of utmost good faith and loyalty would demand that the majority consider that their action was in disregard of a long-standing policy of the stockholders that each would be a director of the corporation and that employment with the corporation would go hand in hand with stock ownership; that Wilkes was one of the four originators of the nursing home venture; and that Wilkes, like the others, had invested his capital and time for more than fifteen years with the expectation that he would continue to participate in corporate decisions. Most important is the plain fact that the cutting off of Wilkes's salary, together with the fact that the corporation never declared a dividend, assured that Wilkes would receive no return at all from the corporation.

2. The question of Wilkes's damages at the hands of the majority has not been thoroughly explored on the record before us. Wilkes, in his original complaint, sought damages in the amount of the $100 a week he believed he was entitled to from the time his salary was terminated up until the time this action was commenced. However, the record shows that, after Wilkes was severed from the corporate payroll, the schedule of salaries and payments made to the other stockholders varied from time to time. In addition, the duties assumed by the other stockholders after Wilkes was deprived of his share of the corporate earnings appear to have changed in significant respects. Any resolution of this question must take into account whether the corporation was dissolved during the pendency of this litigation.

Therefore our order is as follows: So much of the judgment as dismisses Wilkes's complaint and awards costs to the defendants is reversed.

---

6   This inference arises from the fact that Connor, acting on behalf of the three controlling stockholders, offered to purchase Wilkes's shares for a price Connor admittedly would not have accepted for his own shares.

Points for Discussion

1. Freeze-out tactics.

Notice the ways in which the majority owners sought to "freeze out" the minority owner Wilkes. After the majority removed Wilkes from his corporate position and discontinued his salary, they continued their long-standing policy of not paying dividends; they distributed to themselves corporate profits in the form of salaries and bonuses; and they offered to buy out Wilkes at a price they would not have accepted for their own shares. Does this seem fair? How might Wilkes have protected himself?

2. Compare to partnership.

If Wilkes had been a partner, partnership law would have allowed him to withdraw and demand payment in cash for the fair value of his ownership interest. Why did the court not treat this as a case governed by partnership law?

3. Equal treatment vs. balancing of interests.

The *Wilkes* court was not writing on a blank slate. The court's earlier decision in *Donahue* had set out a rule of "equal treatment" when majority shareholders preferentially redeemed the shares of one of their own, while excluding the minority shareholders. The *Wilkes* court decided not to extend the "equal treatment" rule to operational decisions—here the employment and compensation of a co-owner. Instead, the court articulated a balancing test. Does this approach overly involve the court, contrary to the wisdom of the business judgment rule, in inquiring into how majority owners run their business?

4. Non-contractual remedy.

In the end, the *Wilkes* court decided that the majority breached its fiduciary duties to the minority owner. The effect was to recognize rights for Wilkes that he had not obtained by contract. Does it make sense to assume that the co-owners would have negotiated for financial compensation if one of them were removed from the business without "legitimate business purposes" or without considering "less harmful alternatives"? That is, does the court leave enough room for legitimate freeze outs?

5. Valuation of minority interests.

Notice that the court does not resolve how Wilkes is to be compensated for the majority's breach of its fiduciary duties. Does it make sense that Wilkes would have continued to receive $100/month, even though he was no longer working in the business? Or should the court attempt to ascertain what portion of the $100/month was a return on investment and what was compensation for services? Can a court make those distinctions?

———————————

c. Prerogatives of Majority Control

Courts have shown varying degrees of sensitivity to claims of unequal treatment raised by minority shareholders. Most, like *Wilkes*, have rejected *Donahue*'s "utmost good faith and loyalty" test in favor of approaches that allow majority shareholders flexibility to manage the corporation's business as they see fit.

One recurring issue is whether a minority shareholder who is dismissed as an employee has a claim for a fiduciary breach. In many close corporations, shareholders view employment as an intrinsic aspect of their investment. And if the corporation is subject to double taxation on dividends, amounts paid as salary and bonuses often represent implicit dividends. Separating employment and corporate financial claims in the close corporation has proved difficult.

For example, in *Merola v. Exergen Corp.*, 668 N.E.2d 351 (Mass. 1996), a minority shareholder brought a fiduciary claim after being terminated from employment for commenting critically about an extra-marital relationship by the company's president and majority shareholder. The minority shareholder, Merola, claimed that he had joined the company on the understanding he would be able to invest in company shares and become a major shareholder. And after being hired, Merola had purchased a significant number of shares. The trial judge ruled that the majority shareholder, Pompei, had terminated Merola for no legitimate business purpose, thus breaching a fiduciary duty to honor the reasonable expectations that Merola had concerning his investment of time and money in the company.

On appeal, the Massachusetts Supreme Judicial Court rejected the linkage between Merola's shareholding and employment rights:

> Even in close corporations, the majority interest "must have a large measure of discretion, for example, in declaring or withholding dividends, deciding whether to merge or consolidate, establishing the salaries of corporate officers, dismissing directors with or without cause, and hiring and firing corporate employees." *Wilkes v. Springside Nursing Home, Inc.*, 370 Mass. 842, 851, 353 N.E.2d 657 (1976).

> Principles of employment law permit the termination of employees at will, with or without cause excepting situations within a narrow public policy exception.

> Here, although the plaintiff invested in the stock of Exergen with the reasonable expectation of continued employment, there was no general policy regarding stock ownership and employment, and there was no evidence that any other stockholders had expectations of continuing employment because they purchased stock. The investment in the stock was an investment in the equity of the corporation which was not tied to employment in any formal way.

Unlike the *Wilkes* case, there was no evidence that the corporation distributed all profits to shareholders in the form of salaries. On the contrary, the perceived value of the stock increased during the time that the plaintiff was employed. The plaintiff first purchased his stock at $2.25 per share and, one year later, he purchased more for $5 per share. This indicated that there was some increase in value to the investment independent of the employment expectation. Neither was the plaintiff a founder of the business, his stock purchases were made after the business was established, and there was no suggestion that he had to purchase stock to keep his job.

The plaintiff testified that, when he sold his stock back to the corporation four years after being terminated, he was paid $17 per share. This was a price that had been paid to other shareholders who sold their shares to the corporation at a previous date, and it is a price which, after consulting with his attorney, he concluded was a fair price. With this payment, the plaintiff realized a significant return on his capital investment independent of the salary he received as an employee.

We conclude that this is not a situation where the majority shareholder breached his fiduciary duty to a minority shareholder. Although there was no legitimate business purpose for the termination of the plaintiff, neither was the termination for the financial gain of Pompei or contrary to established public policy. Not every discharge of an at-will employee of a close corporation who happens to own stock in the corporation gives rise to a successful breach of fiduciary duty claim.

———

An "employee stock ownership plan" (or ESOP) is a retirement plan in which the company contributes its stock to the plan for the benefit of the company's employees. With an ESOP, the employee never buys or holds the stock directly.

An ESOP should not be confused with an employee stock option plan, which is not a retirement plan. Instead, employee stock option plans give employees the right (or option) to buy their company's stock at a set price within a certain period of time

The following case provides insight into Delaware's approach to close corporations. Specifically, the case addresses the question whether the board in a close corporation breached its fiduciary duties by failing to provide liquidity rights to non-employee minority shareholders, while providing such rights to employee-shareholders.

The plaintiffs were descendants of E.C. Barton, the founder of a successful closely-held lumber business incorporated in Delaware. As shareholders of non-voting Class B stock, they complained that the company's board had denied them liquidity rights that had been extended to themselves and other employees holding company shares. In particular, employees who owned Class B stock were allowed under the company's employee stock ownership plan (ESOP) to take cash for their shares when they left the company; this liquidity was not available to non-employee Class B shareholders.

Before his death, Mr. Barton had owned all the company's stock. Under his will, he directed that the company's Class A stock go to company employees, and that most of the Class B stock go to his family. Even though Class B stock represented 75% of the company's total equity, it did not have voting rights. In effect, the company became employee-operated, but primarily for the financial benefit of the founder's family.

Nixon v. Blackwell

626 A.2d 1366 (Del. 1993)

VEASEY, CHIEF JUSTICE.

V. Applicable Principles of Substantive Law

Defendants contend that the trial court erred in not applying the business judgment rule. Since the defendants benefited from the ESOP beyond that which benefited other stockholders generally, the defendants are on both sides of the transaction. For that reason, we agree with the trial court that the entire fairness test applies to this aspect of the case. Accordingly, defendants have the burden of showing the entire fairness of those transactions.

The trial court in this case, however, appears to have adopted the novel legal principle that Class B stockholders had a right to "liquidity" equal to that which the court found to be available to the defendants. It is well established in our jurisprudence that stockholders need not always be treated equally for all purposes. To hold that fairness necessarily requires precise equality is to beg the question:

> Many scholars, though few courts, conclude that one aspect of fiduciary duty is the equal treatment of investors. Their argument takes the following form: fiduciary principles require fair conduct; equal treatment is fair conduct; hence, fiduciary principles require equal treatment. The conclusion does not follow. The argument depends on an equivalence between *equal* and *fair* treatment. To say that fiduciary principles require equal treatment is to beg the question whether investors would contract for equal or even equivalent treatment.

Frank H. Easterbrook and Daniel R. Fischel, *The Economic Structure of Corporate Law* 110 (1991) (emphasis in original). This holding of the trial court overlooks the significant facts that the minority stockholders were not: (a) employees of the Corporation; (b) entitled to share in an ESOP; or (c) protected by specific provisions in the certificate of incorporation, bylaws, or a stockholders' agreement.

There is support in this record for the fact that the ESOP is a corporate benefit and was established, at least in part, to benefit the Corporation. Generally speaking, the creation of ESOPs is a normal corporate practice and is generally thought to benefit the corporation. If such corporate practices were necessarily to require equal treatment for non-employee stockholders, that would be a matter for legislative determination in Delaware. There is no such legislation to that effect. If we were to adopt such a rule, our decision would border on judicial legislation.

Accordingly, we hold that the Vice Chancellor erred as a matter of law in concluding that the liquidity afforded to the employee stockholders by the ESOP and the key man insurance required substantially equal treatment for the non-employee stockholders.

We hold on this record that defendants have met their burden of establishing the entire fairness of their dealings with the non-employee Class B stockholders, and are entitled to judgment. The record is sufficient to conclude that plaintiffs' claim that the defendant directors have maintained a discriminatory policy of favoring employee Class A stockholders over Class B non-employee stockholders is without merit.

The directors have followed a consistent policy originally established by Mr. Barton, the founder of the Corporation, whose intent from the formation of the Corporation was to use the Class A stock as the vehicle for the Corporation's continuity through employee management and ownership. The directors' actions following Mr. Barton's death are consistent with Mr. Barton's plan. An ESOP, for example, is normally established for employees. Accordingly, there is no inequity in limiting ESOP benefits to the employee stockholders. Indeed, it makes no sense to include non-employees in ESOP benefits. The fact that the Class B stock represented 75 percent of the Corporation's total equity is irrelevant to the issue of fair dealing. The Class B stock was given no voting rights because those stockholders were not intended to have a direct voice in the management and operation of the Corporation. They were simply passive investors—entitled to be treated fairly but not necessarily to be treated equally.

VI. No Special Rules for a "Closely-Held Corporation" Not Qualified as a "Close Corporation" Under DGCL Subchapter XIV

We wish to address one further matter which was raised at oral argument before this Court: Whether there should be any special, judicially-created rules to "protect" minority stockholders of closely-held Delaware corporations.

The case at bar points up the basic dilemma of minority stockholders in receiving fair value for their stock as to which there is no market and no market valuation. It is not difficult to be sympathetic, in the abstract, to a stockholder who finds himself or herself in that position. A stockholder who bargains for stock in a closely-held corporation and who pays for those shares can make a business judgment whether to buy into such a minority position, and if so on what terms. One could bargain for definitive provisions of self-ordering permitted to a Delaware corporation through the certificate of incorporation or bylaws by reason of the provisions in 8 Del.C. § 102, 109, and 141(a). Moreover, in addition to such mechanisms, a stockholder intending to buy into a minority position in a Delaware corporation may enter into definitive stockholder agreements, and such agreements may provide for elaborate earnings tests, buy-out provisions, voting trusts, or other voting agreements. *See, e.g.,* 8 Del. C. § 218.

The tools of good corporate practice are designed to give a purchasing minority stockholder the opportunity to bargain for protection before parting with consideration. It would do violence to normal corporate practice and our corporation law to fashion an ad hoc ruling which would result in a court-imposed stockholder buy-out for which the parties had not contracted.

In 1967, when the Delaware General Corporation Law was significantly revised, a new Subchapter XIV entitled "Close Corporations; Special Provisions," became a part of that law for the first time. Subchapter XIV is a narrowly constructed statute which applies only to a corporation which is designated as a "close corporation" in its certificate of incorporation, and which fulfills other requirements, including a limitation to 30 on the number of stockholders, that all classes of stock have to have at least one restriction on transfer, and that there be no "public offering." 8 Del. C. § 342. Accordingly, subchapter XIV applies only to "close corporations," as defined in section 342. "Unless a corporation elects to become a close corporation under this subchapter in the manner prescribed in this subchapter, it shall be subject in all respects to this chapter, except this subchapter." 8 Del. C. § 341. The corporation before the Court in this matter, is not a "close corporation." Therefore it is not governed by the provisions of Subchapter XIV.[7]

One cannot read into the situation presented in the case at bar any special relief for the minority stockholders in this closely-held, but not statutory "close corporation" because the provisions of Subchapter XIV relating to close corporations and other statutory schemes preempt the field in their respective areas. It would run counter to the spirit of the doctrine of independent legal significance, and would be inappropriate judicial legislation for this Court to fashion a special judicially-created rule for minority investors when the entity does not fall within those statutes, or when

---

[7]   We do not intend to imply that, if the Corporation had been a close corporation under Subchapter XIV, the result in this case would have been different. "Statutory close corporations have not found particular favor with practitioners. Practitioners have for the most part viewed the complex statutory provisions underlying the purportedly simplified operational procedures for close corporations as legal quicksand of uncertain depth and have adopted the view that the objectives sought by the subchapter are achievable for their clients with considerably less uncertainty by cloaking a conventionally created corporation with the panoply of charter provisions, transfer restrictions, bylaws, stockholders' agreements, buy-sell arrangements, irrevocable proxies, voting trusts or other contractual mechanisms which were and remain the traditional method for accomplishing the goals sought by the close corporation provisions." David A. Drexler, Lewis S. Black, Jr., and A. Gilchrist Sparks, III, Delaware Corporation Law and Practice § 43.01 (1993).

there are no negotiated special provisions in the certificate of incorporation, bylaws, or stockholder agreements.

——————

Points for Discussion

1. Discriminatory structure.

Notice that the Delaware approach places significant weight on the capital structure implemented by the corporate planner. In *Nixon v. Blackwell*, the corporation's founder chose to have his family provided for financially with non-voting Class B shares, for which no redemption rights were provided. The founder then assigned control of the corporation to voting Class A shares, the majority of which were held by employees through an ESOP under which redemption rights were provided in the event of the employee-shareholders' withdrawal or death. Is this differential treatment a violation of the majority's duty of "utmost good faith and loyalty" to minority shareholders?

2. Reconcile the approaches.

Can the Massachusetts "equal opportunity" and the Delaware "traditional" approach be reconciled? In theory, the Massachusetts approach requires that the minority receive the same shareholder-level rights as the majority, while the Delaware approach does not require equal treatment unless the parties have negotiated for it.

In the end, both approaches seek to enforce what the court assumes to be the parties' expectations. The real difference may lie in the willingness of the two courts to look beyond the formal corporate documents—and to forgive a failure in lawyering. In Massachusetts, the *Wilkes* court found no formal documents and created fiduciary duties to fill the perceived gaps. In Delaware, the *Nixon* court found a clear capital structure and refused to conclude that there were any gaps. While Wilkes got the benefit of the doubt in Massachusetts, would he (and his lawyer) have been treated the same way in Delaware? Or would they have been chastised for not obtaining contractual protections in the corporate documents? Why did the *Nixon* court apply the entire fairness standard?

3. Harsh rules and drafting incentives.

The "traditional" Delaware approach avoids the line-drawing required under the Massachusetts approach that seeks *ex post* to approximate the parties' expectations, whether under the "equal opportunity" test or the "legitimate business purposes" analysis. Such *ex post* judicial relief creates disincentives for the parties themselves to identify and negotiate their own relationship. Perhaps such judicial involvement makes sense when the parties, particularly in older corporations before formal contracting in close corporations became commonplace, failed formally to establish their rights.

Does it make sense in more recent corporations where special contracting is widely recognized and practiced?

4. Case-by-case duties?

If the role of courts in close corporation cases is to fill in the terms of the close corporation "contract," what aspects of the parties' relationship should the courts consider? For example, the *Wilkes* court looked at the long-standing informal practices and income expectations that the parties had developed; and the *Merola* court considered how the minority shareholder had actually acquired (and later sold) shares in the corporation. Should fiduciary duties vary according to the particular expectations and practices in the corporation?

5. Choosing a default rule.

On the assumption that the parties can negotiate for different levels of protection, what should be the default rule? Some commentators have argued for a default rule of strong fiduciary protections for minority shareholders, absent an agreement otherwise. How would such a rule affect investment in close corporations? Would strong fiduciary protections encourage or discourage investment? Arguably, if the rule overly favored minority investors, majority owners could negotiate (and pay) for limits on minority protections.

Another default rule might be to tailor fiduciary protections according to what the parties would likely have negotiated in their particular close corporation. To avoid the costs of *ex ante* bargaining, an *ex post* tailored default rule places the parties in the position they would have bargained for. Does such an approach give too much weight to the interests of minority shareholders, who are encouraged to obtain from a sympathetic judge what they could not get through negotiation with the majority? Or is this simply an efficient way to minimize bargaining costs?

----

d.   Statutory Remedies for Oppression

Over the last three decades, in relevant jurisdictions, courts have used involuntary dissolution statutes similar to MBCA § 14.30(2) to craft broad protections for minority shareholders who complain of "oppression" by majority shareholders. MBCA § 14.34 specifies a procedure for defendants to buyout plaintiffs when a claim of oppression is made. These statutes raise important interpretive questions. First, when is majority conduct "oppressive?" Second, when a court finds oppression, what remedy is appropriate—dissolution or buy-out? Third, where a corporation or shareholder elects to exercise buy-out rights under MBCA § 14.34, how is the "fair value" of the complaining shareholder's stock to be determined?

Corporate statutes usually provide that a corporation can be dissolved with the approval of the board of directors and the shareholders. *See* MBCA §§ 14.02–14.07. In the case of both voluntary and court-ordered dissolutions, corporate existence is terminated in an orderly fashion: the corporation sells off its assets, pays off its creditors, and distributes whatever remains to its shareholders. But a dissident shareholder who brings suit seeking dissolution often will be less interested in terminating the corporation's legal existence than in using the threat of dissolution as leverage to bargain for a better price for her stock.

Whether a threat of dissolution is effective may depend on the nature of the corporation's business. If a business derives its value almost entirely from the corporation's tangible assets, shareholders who wish to continue to operate the business probably will have to pay fair market value for those assets, since other prospective purchasers could use them to equally good effect. But if a business derives most of its value from its economic goodwill supplied by the presence of the majority owners, dissolution may disserve the minority's interests, because the majority may be able to purchase the corporation's tangible assets for its fair market value and to capture the associated goodwill at no additional cost. In such a situation, a mandatory buyout of her shares at their "fair market value" will better serve the minority's interests. That is so because, in valuing the minority's shares, most courts take account of the value of the corporation's economic goodwill.

At first glance, dissolution or a mandatory buyout may appear a sensible solution to oppression. But on closer examination, the problem is more complex. First, how might the forced sale of business assets affect the corporation's viability and thus other corporate constituents, such as employees or creditors? Second, will dissolution (or even a buyout) enable one shareholder group to acquire the business at a price unfair to others? Third, is the petitioning shareholder merely seeking to liquidate an investment or is there another, darker agenda?

What other relief is available in cases of oppression? Besides ordering dissolution or a buyout, courts have used their inherent equity authority to devise other remedies in deadlock or "freeze out" cases: (1) order dissolution at a specified future date, unless the shareholders resolve their differences; (2) appoint a receiver to operate the corporation, until the differences are resolved; (3) appoint a "special fiscal agent" to report to the court on ongoing business operations and treatment of the minority; (4) retain jurisdiction for the protection of the minority shareholders; (5) order an accounting by the majority for funds allegedly misappropriated; (6) enjoin continuing acts of "oppressive" conduct; (7) order the declaration of dividends; (8) award damages to minority shareholders for "oppressive" conduct by the majority.

See Baker v. Commercial Body Builders, Inc., 507 P.2d 387 (Or. 1973) (listing forms of relief).

Finally, a key issue in oppression cases is the valuation of the complaining shareholder's shares in a court-ordered buyout or when the corporation (or another shareholder) exercises buyout rights under MBCA § 14.34. The buyout statute, like the appraisal statutes that apply to valuing dissenters' shares in a merger or other fundamental corporate transactions, requires that the minority's shares be purchased at "fair value."

One important question is whether minority shares should be discounted to reflect their lack of control and non-marketability. A strict market-based approach (what a willing outside buyer would pay in a fully-disclosed arms-length transaction) would take account of the reality that minority shares are not proportionally as valuable as majority shares, since they lack meaningful control rights. Although minority shares have a right to the proportional payment of any dividends or other distributions, the discretion to make such payments lies with the majority. Moreover, minority shares in a close corporation, unlike minority shares in a publicly traded corporation or majority shares of a close corporation, lack a ready market—further diminishing their value.

Should a court's buyout order in an oppression case discount minority shares to reflect their lack of control and non-marketability? The question is significant since valuation experts often opine that the lack of control can diminish the value of minority shares by 30–40% compared to majority shares, and the lack of market-ability by another 30–40%. In all, minority shares may have a market value less than half of what a full-control, fully marketable ownership interest in the same business would command.

Most courts have concluded that it would be inequitable to apply a discount for lack of control or non-marketability in a close corporation valuation proceeding. Courts have explained that to allow the majority to buy out the minority at a discount would penalize the minority for exercising their statutory rights and tempt the majority to engage in activities creating dissension. That is, if the majority values the business at 100% of its earnings power or asset value, any discount applied to the minority's shares would reward the majority oppressor and penalize the minority. Thus, valuation of shares in a close corporation buyout is not just a matter of financial methodology but, rather, depends on what courts consider to be fair and equitable.

---

4. Sale of Control

The right of shareholders to sell their shares is part of the triumvirate of shareholder rights to vote, sue, and sell. As a general matter, shareholders are free to sell their shares, subject to securities law rules and any contractual transfer restrictions. One other proviso exists: there are limitations on controlling shareholders when they sell their shares. These limitations are somewhat narrow and we take a look at them here in concluding this chapter on controlling shareholders.

Sharing of control premium? Control shares command a premium. For example, if you own 60% of a corporation's shares and the other shares trade in a market at $20 per share, you should expect someone to pay more than that for your shares. In fact, studies show that control shares usually sell for 30–50% more than non-control shares. That is, your shares may well fetch $30 per share! That's because you get to elect the board and decide such matters as business strategy, executive pay, and dividend policy.

Should controlling shareholders be allowed to realize this "control premium"? One potential answer is that control sales are unfair to minority shareholders so that any control sale to an outsider should be made only as part of an offer to purchase shares on the same terms from all shareholders. After all, corporate law says all shares are by default equal.

But another potential answer is that such egalitarianism would discourage control transfers, potentially keeping corporate assets out of the hands of those who value them most and are best able to use them efficiently. On this theory, owners of control should be able to keep their control premiums, so long as other corporate constituents are no worse off as a result.

Corporate law sides with the second view: that it should be easy to transfer control. Accordingly, corporate law provides that control can be sold at a premium, subject to exceptions only in special circumstances.

> Recognizing that those who invest the capital necessary to acquire a dominant position in the ownership of a corporation have the right of controlling that corporation, it has long been settled law that, absent looting of corporate assets, conversion of a corporate opportunity, fraud or other acts of bad faith, a controlling stockholder is free to sell, and a purchaser is free to buy, that controlling interest at a premium price.

Zetlin v. Hanson Holdings, Inc., 48 N.Y.2d 684, 685 (1979).

Selling to a potential looter. Return to our example of the corporation whose shares are trading for $20. Suppose you own 60% of the corporation's shares and someone has offered to buy your entire stake for $30 per share. Does it matter what that person plans to do with the corporation after gaining control? Does it matter if you suspect the buyer will "loot" the corporation? Some courts have required a corporate seller to investigate the buyer if put on notice that the buyer is deceptive or not truthful. *See Harris v. Carter*, 582 A.2d 222 (Del. Ch. 1990).

Selling a corporate opportunity. Sometimes corporations have special business advantages—such as patents, market niches, customer relationships—that are particularly valuable to particular buyers. Should owners of control be able essentially to sell these business advantages without sharing the premium with other non-control shareholders? With limited exception, courts have generally accepted that a controlling shareholder can sell its controlling interest (even when the corporation has assets of particular value to the buyer) without sharing the control premium with noncontrolling shareholders or the corporation. *Cf. Perlman v. Feldmann*, 219 F.2d 173 (2d Cir. 1955).

Sale of office. Control of the corporation's business is vested in the board of directors. Just acquiring a majority of the corporation's shares does not give you immediate control of the business. Can corporate fiduciaries who are not selling a controlling block of stock accept payment for installing particular individuals into corporate positions? No, this would be considered a "sale of office" and per se illegal. However, it is generally legal for the seller of a control block to agree, as part of the sale of control, to insert the control buyer's nominees into corporate offices. The usual practice when a buyer acquires a control block is for the existing directors to resign (one by one) and to have the vacancies filled (one by one) by new directors chosen by the buyer. This latter practice is grounded on the premise that the buyer of the control block would eventually be able to vote her nominees into office at the next shareholders' meeting.

Test Your Knowledge

To assess your understanding of the Chapter 14, 15, 16, and 17 material in this module, click here to take a quiz.

MODULE VI – MARKETS

CHAPTER 18

M&A

"Mergers and acquisitions," or "M&A," is an advanced business law topic that typically is taught in a separate course. This chapter will give you a taste of some M&A basics in the context of an introductory course.

M&A involves the buying and selling of corporations, both public and private. Some see M&A as the most interesting topic of corporate law, filled with tales of high-powered takeover ploys and ingenious defensive gambits. Lurking behind every story are fundamental questions about the corporation in society and the role of corporate law: Who should share in the financial rewards of a M&A deal? Must corporate boards sell to the highest bidder? Are corporate takeovers good or bad? Are shareholders (and others) better served by activist boards or passive boards? What should be the attitude of corporate law toward takeovers?

This chapter is divided into three parts. First, we provide an overview of the basic structures of M&A deals, including shareholder voting and appraisal rights. Second, we describe the basic categories of anti-takeover devices boards use to discourage hostile takeovers, along with the deal protection devices they use to protect M&A deals. Third, we explore the fiduciary duties of directors in the M&A context, and the range of standards applied by the courts in different categories of scrutiny.

A. Basic M&A Deal Structures

In this section, we introduce you to four basic deal structures: (1) statutory merger, (2) triangular merger, (3) sale of assets, and (4) tender offer. We designate the principal corporation surviving the combination (the "parent" corporation) as P, any "subsidiary" of P as S, and the corporation to be acquired as T, the "target corporation." We also describe how shareholder voting and appraisal rights can vary depending on the deal structure.

Certain fundamental corporate changes, after being initiated by the board, must be approved by a shareholder majority. When is shareholder approval required? Although statutes vary, shareholders generally have the right to vote on amendments to the articles of incorporation, significant mergers, the sale of all or substantially all of a corporation's assets, and corporate dissolution—that is, transactions that change the corporation's form, scope, or continuity.

You can think of these shareholder voting rights as a veto power, since shareholders can block fundamental changes, but cannot initiate them. But shareholders do not have the power to veto every change. Many transactions that fundamentally change the corporation's business, such as the acquisition of a new division for cash or a major change in product focus, do not trigger shareholder voting rights, even though those changes are important.

Historically at common law, fundamental corporate changes required unanimous shareholder approval. Consequently, one shareholder could block any fundamental change, even a change as simple as extending the life of a corporation beyond its original term. The idea was that the charter was a contract, both among the corporation's shareholders and between the corporation and the state, and every shareholder had vested rights.

State legislatures began to recognize that the unanimity requirement created the potential for tyranny by the minority. Enterprising investors could purchase stock in a company in anticipation of a proposed fundamental change and threaten to veto the change, thus forcing the majority to repurchase their shares at a premium. Legislatures responded by amending corporate statutes to allow fundamental changes crafted by the board of directors and approved by a majority or super-majority of its shareholders.

Legislatures also granted dissenting shareholders a right to "opt out" of certain fundamental changes. Today shareholders can dissent from certain transactions and demand that the corporation pay them in cash the "fair value" of their shares as determined by a court in an appraisal proceeding, even though the requisite majority approves the transaction. Corporate statutes provide detailed procedural requirements that a shareholder must fulfill to perfect and exercise their right to appraisal. Requirements may include, for example, delivering to the corporation a written demand for appraisal and not voting in favor of the proposed merger. *See* DGCL § 262.

> What if a merging corporation has more than one class of shareholders? Some statutes require class voting—that is, the separate approval by each class of shares to be converted (or substantially changed) in the merger. Delaware does not require class voting, unless required in the plan of merger or in the certificate of incorporation.

Appraisal substitutes an exit right for the veto right. Appraisal also places a floor on the value of minority shares when the majority approves fundamental changes that affect the minority's interests. Whatever the rationale for appraisal statutes, three points are clear. First, every corporate statute authorizes shareholders to demand appraisal as to certain fundamental changes and to require the corporation to repurchase their stock in cash for its fair value. Second, corporation statutes vary from state to state on when shareholders have voting and appraisal rights.

Third, sometimes shareholders have voting rights in a transaction, but not appraisal rights.

1.   Statutory Merger

In a statutory merger, P and T begin as separate legal entities and end up as one entity. To do this, the boards of P and T must first adopt a *plan of merger* that—

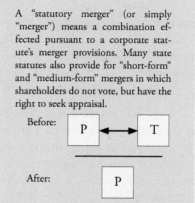

A "statutory merger" (or simply "merger") means a combination effected pursuant to a corporate statute's merger provisions. Many state statutes also provide for "short-form" and "medium-form" mergers in which shareholders do not vote, but have the right to seek appraisal.

- designates which corporation (here P) is to survive the merger

- describes the terms and conditions of the merger

- specifies how shares of T will be converted into shares of P (or other property, such as cash or bonds)

- sets forth any amendments to P's articles of incorporation necessary to effectuate the plan of merger.

The boards of each of the constituent corporations must approve the plan of merger. *See* DGCL § 251. The plan of merger then is submitted to the shareholders of T, as well as the shareholders of P if their approval is required. Once approved by shareholders, the plan of merger is filed with the secretary of state's office and the merger becomes effective.

What is the effect of a statutory merger? By operation of law, T immediately ceases to exist, the assets of T become the assets of P, and the liabilities of T become the liabilities of P. No formal conveyances or assignments need to be executed—it happens automatically. All shares of T are converted into shares of P, unless the plan of merger calls for consideration in the form of cash or other property. The shareholders of P retain their shares.

Voting rights. Voting rights vary from state to state. Many statutes, including in Delaware, require that statutory mergers be approved by an absolute majority of the shareholders of both P and T. But the vote of P shareholders is not required in a "whale-minnow merger" that does not increase by more than 20% the outstanding voting shares of P.

The MBCA requires that a statutory merger be approved only by a simple majority of the shareholders of T. The vote by P shareholders is required if the merger involves a *dilutive share issuance* where P is to issue new shares with voting power equal to at least 20% of the voting power that existed prior to the merger. In addition, the P shareholders must vote if the plan of merger would change the number of shares they hold after the merger or otherwise fundamentally affect their share rights.

Appraisal rights. Appraisal in a statutory merger also varies from state to state, with some statutes sometimes eliminating the appraisal remedy if shareholders have a market into which they can sell their shares. Other states, including Delaware, have restricted appraisal rights in some circumstances, including when sophisticated shareholders have waived their right to seek appraisal by agreement.

Some statutes (including those based on the pre-1999 MBCA) link appraisal rights to voting rights. Thus, T shareholders entitled to vote on the merger can dissent and seek an appraisal, and P shareholders have appraisal rights if the merger is significant enough to require their approval. The current MBCA generally makes appraisal rights available only to T shareholders entitled to vote on the merger and not subject to a "market out" exception (described below). P shareholders do not have appraisal rights, unless they are entitled to vote on the merger and their shares do not remain outstanding afterward. Delaware's statute also generally limits appraisal rights to T shareholders, whether or not they were entitled to vote on the merger, unless Delaware's "market out" exception applies (described next). P shareholders have appraisal rights if they were entitled to vote on the merger and the "market out" exception does not apply.

> The MBCA, as revised in 1999, asks whether a business combination, whatever its form, will dilute substantially the voting power of the acquiring corporation's shareholders. If the combination involves a "dilutive share issuance"—that is, the issuance of shares with voting power of more than 20% of the voting power that existed prior to the combination—the acquiring corporation's shareholders must vote to approve. MBCA § 6.21(f).
>
> The goal is substance over form. Voting rights in fundamental corporate changes are the same, regardless of how the transaction is structured. This approach follows a pattern adopted in some larger states, such as California and New Jersey. It also tracks rules of the New York Stock Exchange and NASDAQ, whose listing rules require a shareholder vote on any merger or other transaction that dilutes by more than 18.5% the voting power of existing shareholders (roughly the dilution when a corporation issues shares with voting power equal to more than 20% of existing voting power).

As noted, shareholders must follow the procedural requirements to perfect and exercise their right of appraisal. The use of appraisal rights in Delaware has become more common and controversial, as hedge funds have sought to profit by purchasing shares after a merger is announced. Note that the appraisal remedy is only valuable if a judge determines that the fair value of the shares is greater than the amount offered in the merger. If a judge says the merger price was fair, the appraisal remedy is zero.

> A "minority discount" reflects the lower price that minority shares command, compared to controlling shares. The discount arises both in public trading markets and in private transactions of closely held stock. *See* Chapter 17, Control.

The "market out" exception assumes shareholders dissatisfied with the terms of a merger do not need a judicial valuation remedy if there is a public market for their stock. The exception reflects the view that a stock's current market price is more likely to reflect accurately the stock's value than a later valuation by a judge or judicially appointed appraiser.

The MBCA "market out" exception prevents shareholders of T from seeking appraisal if their stock was publicly traded before the merger and they receive (or retain) cash or marketable stock in the merger. (Recall that P shareholders do not have appraisal rights if they retain their shares, whether publicly traded or not.) By contrast, Delaware's "market out" exception prevents shareholders of P or T from seeking appraisal if their stock was publicly traded before and will be publicly traded after the merger. Delaware law distinguishes between T shareholders who are "required" to take cash and T shareholders who have a choice among cash, shares, or other consideration. T shareholders who are "required" to take cash are entitled to appraisal rights, but T shareholders who have a choice of consideration are not. Thus, a stock-for-cash merger can trigger appraisal rights in Delaware, but not under the MBCA.

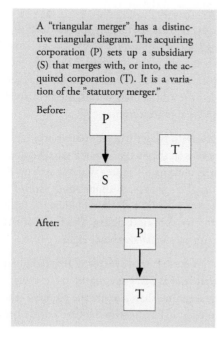

> A "triangular merger" has a distinctive triangular diagram. The acquiring corporation (P) sets up a subsidiary (S) that merges with, or into, the acquired corporation (T). It is a variation of the "statutory merger."
>
> Before:
>
> After:

Many have expressed misgivings about the "market out" exception, and the pre-1999 MBCA did not include it. Why not? Some questioned whether a stock's market value always equals its "true" value, and whether the market might be "demoralized" or be too thin to absorb a large sale of shares. Moreover a "market out" exception might not make sense if shareholders hold "restricted" stock that they could not sell publicly.

The current MBCA also reflects some concern that public markets might not adequately protect shareholders, particularly when a merger involves a conflict of interest. For example, the current MBCA "market out" exception does not apply to a squeeze-out merger that involves a 20% or more shareholder.

Nor does it apply to a management buyout, where an insider group has the power to elect one-fourth or more of the board.

2.   Triangular Merger

It is easy to transfer assets through a statutory merger. But a statutory merger can expose P to unknown or contingent liabilities associated with T's business. P can use a "triangular merger" to address such exposure.

> A *statutory share exchange* accomplishes the same result as a triangular merger. As with a statutory merger, the boards of P and T first must approve a plan of exchange that spells out the terms on which shares of T will be exchanged for P shares (or cash or other property). (Delaware law contains no provision for a statutory share exchange.) Under the MBCA, T shareholders then must approve the plan of exchange and may seek appraisal, subject to the market out exception. P shareholders have voting rights whenever the statutory share exchange involves a dilutive share issuance by P, but do not have appraisal rights, even if they are entitled to vote, since they retain their shares.

In a triangular merger, P creates a subsidiary corporation—we'll call it "S"—that merges with T. The merger between S and T can be done so that either is the surviving corporation. If S is the surviving corporation, we refer to the transaction as a "forward triangular merger." If T is the surviving corporation, it is a "reverse triangular merger." In either event, at the time of the merger, the consideration is transferred to the T shareholders and their T stock is cancelled. After the merger, P has a wholly-owned subsidiary that has the assets and liabilities of T.

Structuring the deal as a triangular merger can avoid exposing P to the liabilities associated with T's business, avoid disturbing the operations of T's business, and may be preferable from a tax perspective. For T's shareholders, it makes little difference whether the combination is structured as a statutory merger or a triangular merger. In either case, T's shareholders are entitled to vote on the merger and, if they dissent and do not have a market out, they can exercise appraisal rights.

Under many statutes, including Delaware's, structuring a combination as a triangular merger means only S shareholders vote on the merger—not P shareholders. Who are S's shareholders? Remember that P obtains S's shares when it sets up S. That means P's board can direct the voting of S's shares, without input from P's shareholders. Thus, a triangular merger effectively denies to P shareholders the right to vote on the business combination or exercise appraisal rights. The form of the combination determines the availability of substantive shareholder rights.

The current MBCA is very different. It favors substance over form. If a triangular merger involves a dilutive issuance by P—that is, if P will issue shares in the merger that will comprise more than 20% of P's outstanding shares *before* the merger—the approval of P shareholders is required. But even if P's shareholders are entitled to vote, they would not have appraisal rights, because they retain their shares in the transaction. This result is the same as in a statutory merger of T into P.

3. Sale of Assets

Alternatively, P can buy the assets of T, using as consideration some combination of its own stock, cash, or other securities. *See* DGCL § 271. Structuring an acquisition as a purchase of assets can have relatively high transaction costs, but can avoid liabilities of the target. The shareholders of T have the right to vote on the sale of assets. Under the MBCA, T shareholders also have appraisal rights, subject to the "market out" exception. But if T is a Delaware corporation, appraisal is not available in a sale of assets.

Under the current MBCA, which takes a unified approach to all dilutive share issuances, P shareholders have voting rights if P issues stock equal to more than 20% of its stock then outstanding as part of its purchase of T's assets. However, P shareholders do not have appraisal rights, because they retain their shares. Under most other statutes, including Delaware's, the issuance of stock to purchase assets (including all the assets of another corporation) is treated the same as any other transaction involving the issuance of previously authorized stock: it is a matter of board discretion. Thus, P shareholders have no voting or appraisal rights in an asset purchase.

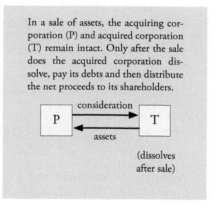

In a sale of assets, the acquiring corporation (P) and acquired corporation (T) remain intact. Only after the sale does the acquired corporation dissolve, pay its debts and then distribute the net proceeds to its shareholders.

Most notably, in a sale of assets transaction, P may, but need not, also assume some or all of T's liabilities. Structuring a deal as an asset sale may be attractive for this reason. For example, professional services firms often structure their business combinations as asset sales so that they acquire desired assets such as client lists, but leave behind liabilities such as those that arise from issuing opinions. Alternatively, T may retain sufficient liquid assets to pay off its liabilities.

In some circumstances, a purchaser may become responsible for liability associated with the assets. One such circumstance occurs when the asset purchase violates the Fraudulent Conveyances Act (discussed in Chapter 6, Limited Liability and Piercing the Corporate Veil). Also, in many states, statutory requirements or common law principles relating to "successor liability" may result in P being held responsible for certain of T's liabilities, even though they are not formally transferred in the deed or other sale documents. In response to this risk of successor liability, business lawyers sometimes use a separately incorporated subsidiary (the triangular form) for the asset purchase.

Example

Signal, a diversified conglomerate incorporated in Delaware, sells its wholly-owned subsidiary Oil & Gas to another oil company. Oil & Gas represents 26% of Signal's total assets, 41% of its net worth, and 15% of its revenues and earnings. Is approval of the sale by Signal's shareholders required? (DGCL § 271 requires shareholder approval for the sale of "all or substantially all" of the assets of a Delaware corporation.)

Shareholder approval is not required for every "major" corporate restructuring. Instead, the question is whether the "sale is in fact an unusual transaction that strikes at the heart of the corporate existence and purpose or one made in the regular course of business of the seller." The court further explained, "If the sale is of assets quantitatively vital to the operation of the corporation and is out of the ordinary and substantially affects the existence and purpose of the corporation," shareholder approval is required. Although Signal began as an oil and gas company, it expanded over time into other significant businesses, including snack foods, aircraft, aerospace, uranium enrichment, and truck manufacturing. Thus, the sale of Oil & Gas did not constitute a sale of "all or substantially all" of the conglomerate's assets.

See Gimbel v. Signal Cos., 316 A.2d 599 (Del. Ch. 1974), *aff'd per curium*, 316 A.2d 619 (Del. 1974); *see also Hollinger Inc. v. Hollinger, Intl., Inc.*, 858 A.2d 342 (Del. Ch. 2004) (applying the Gimbel test to a corporation's sale of a group of newspapers accounting for about 57% of the corporation's value and concluding that the sale did not constitute "substantially all" of the corporation's assets and no shareholder vote was required).

Now, for hypothetical purposes, assume instead that Signal is incorporated in an MBCA jurisdiction when it sells its Oil & Gas subsidiary. The MBCA jettisons the terms "all or substantially all" and instead requires shareholder approval "if the disposition would leave the corporation without a significant continuing business activity." MBCA § 12.02. Under a bright-line test, shareholder approval is not required if the selling corporation retains businesses that constitute at least 25% of its consolidated assets and 25% of either its consolidated revenues or pre-tax earnings from pre-transaction operations.

A stock-for-assets transaction can be functionally identical to a statutory merger if T is dissolved after the sale and P assumes T's liabilities. Then P will own all of T's assets and P will be owned by its shareholders and the former T shareholders.

Example

Loral buys for cash all of the assets of Arco, a Delaware corporation. Arco then dissolves and distributes its assets (the cash in the transaction) to its shareholders. The asset sale and dissolution are approved by a majority of Arco's shareholders, but some shareholders who voted against the transaction argue it's really a "de facto" merger—entitling them to appraisal rights. They assert that substance should trump form.

Delaware law does not provide for an appraisal in asset sales. Shareholders must abide by board decisions and majority rule. Any protection comes from the fiduciary duties of the directors who proposed the sale and the self-interest of fellow shareholders who approved it. *See Hariton v. Arco Electronics, Inc.*, 188 A.2d 123 (Del. 1963) (rejecting "de facto" merger doctrine in Delaware).

4. Tender Offers

P can also acquire control of T by offering to purchase T shares directly from T shareholders, either for P stock or for cash or other property. Through a *tender offer*, P can acquire control of T without the approval of T's board. Unlike the other combination techniques, T shareholders "approve" the transaction by individually accepting P's offer rather than through a formal vote. There are no appraisal rights. Instead, T shareholders who do not wish to accept P's offer can simply refuse to tender their shares.

> A "tender offer" is a contractual offer to buy shares from current shareholders, typically at a premium above prevailing market prices. The tender offer usually carries certain conditions, such as that shares be "tendered" (turned over to the offeror's agent) by a specified date and that a specified percentage of shares, such as 51%, be tendered.
>
> Shareholders can be offered cash or other consideration for their shares. If the offeror offers its own stock, it is known as an "exchange offer." Tender offers are the subject of federal securities regulation.

Once P purchases and can vote a majority of T shares, P can control T by electing its nominees to T's board. P shareholders have no right to approve the purchase, unless P offers its shares as consideration and either lacks sufficient authorized shares to effectuate the exchange or the issuance would constitute a dilutive share issuance. And P shareholders do not have appraisal rights in the tender offer, since their shares are not reduced in the transaction.

After acquiring a controlling interest, P may seek to acquire the remaining T shares in a "second-step" transaction, such as a statutory or short-form merger, so P can operate T free of minority T shareholders. Whether either corporation's shareholders have voting or appraisal rights in the second-step transactions will depend on the form of the transaction and the applicable corporate statutes.

Although "hostile" tender offers, undertaken without board approval, were common historically, the takeover defenses that companies began adopting during the 1980s takeover wave have effectively eliminated this use of tender offers. Instead, the more common use of tender offers today is as the mechanism for acquirers to obtain the target company's shares, after they have taken over control of the board or negotiated a friendly deal.

B. Anti-Takeover and Deal Protection

We next describe in greater detail the various anti-takeover measures that boards can use to deter hostile takeovers. We also describe the range of deal protection devices that boards use to protect deals.

There is some overlap between anti-takeover and deal protection concepts, but they are fundamentally different in practice. Anti-takeover devices are *ex ante* defensive tactics that are designed to minimize the chance of a hostile acquirer attempting to take over a company. Deal protection devices are *ex post* tactics that are designed to maximize the chance of an acquisition closing once a friendly acquirer already has appeared.

1. Anti-Takeover Devices

There are numerous ways for directors and officers to protect their corporations from unwanted suitors. Some are designed to prevent unsolicited acquisitions; others merely delay a takeover or make it more costly. Some require shareholder approval; others can be implemented by boards alone, sometimes even after a hostile bidder has emerged.

Takeover defenses are constantly in flux. Corporate lawyers adapt their takeover defense advice in response to new case law and changes in the markets. For now, the following basic list of anti-takeover devices will give you a good overview of the leading tools boards use as defenses.

Classified Boards

If shareholders have the right to elect every director annually, the corporation is subject to the risk that an insurgent could replace every director in a single election, and thereby take over the company. One way to prevent—or at least delay—a takeover is to "classify" or "stagger" the terms of directors, so that only a portion are elected each year. For example, if one-third of the directors are up for reelection each year, it will take a potential bidder two election cycles to obtain control of the board. Corporations frequently have boards that are classified or staggered into three groups.

Many states, including Delaware, permit corporations to create a classified board either in the articles of incorporation or the bylaws. DGCL § 141(d).

Poison Pills

Recall from our discussion of voting rights in Chapter 15 that "poison pills" are anti-takeover devices that dilute the stake of a potential acquirer. The term comes from the poisonous pills spies sometimes would carry to commit suicide before they were captured and interrogated by the enemy. In the corporate world, the term's meaning is less lethal. A corporate poison pill is intended to dilute the interests of an acquirer, to make a takeover less attractive by making the acquisition prohibitively expensive. It is the corporate version of a pill a spy might take to make it more difficult for the enemy to capture him or her.

Although "poison pill" is the commonly used term—many corporate lawyers simply just call it a "pill"—the actual anti-takeover device typically is labeled a "shareholder rights plan." In a shareholder rights plan, the corporation issues additional "rights" that attach to its outstanding shares. These new rights cannot be traded separately and initially have terms that make them have little value.

The rights plan specifies some "triggering" event, usually when a potential acquirer buys a specified percentage of the corporation's shares. For example, the trigger might occur when anyone purchases more than 15% of the outstanding shares.

Next, the rights plan provides that upon a triggering event, the holder has the option to buy additional shares at a low price. Importantly, the rights plan provides that the acquirer who triggered the change in the terms of the rights is not entitled to this benefit. In other words, after the triggering event, every shareholder *other than the potential acquirer* has the right to buy more shares of the corporation at a steep discount. When these shareholders exercise this option, the acquirer's position will be diluted.

Poison pills are almost never triggered. Nor do they prevent hostile takeovers entirely. Instead, they potentially strengthen a target board's powers in responding to a takeover attempt, and give it greater leverage in negotiations with a potential acquirer.

In practice, an acquirer typically will condition any deal on the redemption of the rights. Rights plans typically give the board the right to redeem the rights at a nominal price, such as $0.0001 per right, until a triggering event occurs. Rights holders do not have the rights of a shareholder, such as the right to vote or receive dividends, until the rights are exercised. The board retains the ability to amend the terms of the rights, other than the purchase price, as long as the rights are redeemable. After the rights are redeemed, the board may amend the rights as long as the amendments do not adversely affect the interests of the rights holders.

One key feature in a rights plan is that the board may unilaterally, without shareholder approval, authorize issuance of the rights, or redeem the rights without shareholder approval. If shareholders want to strip the board of such powers, they can do so by amending the articles of incorporation. Absent an amendment prohibiting a board from adopting a rights plan, the board has the power to adopt a plan, even after a potential acquirer has emerged. Thus, even corporations without a poison pill can be said to have a "shadow pill," a

Normally, poison pills are not triggered. But in late 2008, a poison pill with a low 5% threshold adopted by Selectica, Inc., a software company incorporated in Delaware, was actually triggered. This pill differed from traditional poison pills because of its low ownership trigger of just 5% (most poison pills have higher triggers, in the range of 15%). The rationale for the lower 5% trigger was to protect Selectica's "net operating losses," which could generate tax advantages for Selectica by offsetting future income (thereby reducing future taxes). Selectica claimed this tax benefit could be lost in a takeover. Meanwhile, Versata, Inc., a competitor with similar technologies and customers, had made several offers to acquire Selectica, but Selectica had rejected all of them. When Selectica adopted its 5% threshold pill, Versata intentionally triggered the pill and sued, claiming the pill was invalid. Versata was willing to incur the share dilution consequence of the pill as one cost in its overall strategy to take over Selectica. (Ultimately, the Delaware courts held that this pill was valid.)

takeover defense they can adopt if needed. Of course, courts might look skeptically on a board's decision to adopt a last-minute poison pill to thwart a takeover, but the board has that power nonetheless.

Moran v. Household International, Inc., 500 A.2d 1346 (Del. 1985), held that DGCL § 157 gives the board of a Delaware corporation authority to adopt a shareholder rights plan. Poison pills proliferated after *Moran*, and became many companies' first line of defense against hostile bids. Takeover cases decided after *Moran* focus on when a target's directors are obliged to redeem a poison pill and, in particular, whether and when a target's directors can rely on a pill to "just say no" to a bidder who offers to purchase all of a company's stock for a premium that most shareholders would find attractive.

Share Repurchases

Another way for the board to defend against a takeover is by purchasing the corporation's own shares. Directors can authorize the repurchase of shares, either by the corporation directly or through an employee stock ownership plan or pension plan. Share repurchases can signal support of shareholder interests, and their effect can be to increase the price of the corporation's shares. To the extent share repurchases increase the share price, they make a takeover more expensive and thereby deter potential acquirers.

> One key aspect of anti-takeover devices is who controls them. If shareholders can create or eliminate an anti-takeover device, the directors will not find it particularly useful in deterring acquirers. Thus, one key question to ask when analyzing a takeover defense is: who can create it and who can eliminate it? Classified boards are more effective defenses if they are in the articles, not merely in the bylaws. Conversely, poison pills are unlikely to be effective defenses if shareholders can remove them through changes in bylaws.

One form of share repurchase—known as "greenmail"—can be effective at deterring a particular unwanted acquirer. Greenmail is derived from the terms "blackmail" and "greenback," and involves the purchase of a potential acquirer's shares at a premium. Essentially, the acquirer agrees to give up a takeover in exchange for payment of a premium. The term "greenmail" has acquired a negative connotation, because some people see it as resembling a bribe to get the potential acquirer to go away. Like the adoption of a rights plan, the repurchase of shares is a decision the board can make unilaterally.

Lock-Ups

Boards can make the corporation a less attractive target by agreeing to transactions with third parties that "lock up" some or all of the value sought by a bidder. Lock ups are anti-takeover devices because they reduce or eliminate the financial incentives of a bidder to buy the corporation. If the bidder cannot "unlock" the value that has been transferred to a third party, it will have a reduced incentive to pursue a takeover.

For example, the board might agree to sell the corporation's "crown jewels," its most prized assets, to another corporation. Once those assets are off limits, the target corporation is no longer worth pursuing. Alternatively, the board might agree to give a third party an option to purchase unissued shares, thus diluting the bidder. These transactions also lock up value that a bidder might otherwise have obtained, and thus deter takeover attempts.

Anti-Takeover Statutes

Since the 1980s, many states have adopted anti-takeover statutes. The specific restrictions vary by statute. You might take a look at DGCL § 203 as an example.

The argument concerning the desirability of such statutes is a part of the larger debate over jurisdictional competition that we examined in Chapter 5, in which we saw that the basic argument in support of competition is that it promotes the development of more efficient corporation laws. In the setting of anti-takeover statutes, the argument appears to break down. Numerous econometric studies demonstrate that when a state adopts a strong anti-takeover law, the market value of corporations chartered in that state declines. Some see these studies as strong evidence that, at least in this respect, competition among the states reduces rather than maximizes shareholder wealth.

A further regulatory issue is the extent to which federal law should control tender offers. In *CTS Corp. v. Dynamics Corp. of America*, the Supreme Court suggested that states have considerable, but not unlimited, scope to regulate takeover bids. Of course, Congress has the constitutional power to preempt state law affecting tender offers and defenses against them. As a policy issue, it may not make sense to continue to allow state legislatures to make rules governing the affairs of national and multinational corporations. Because states' treatment of takeovers could be a "race for the bottom," some have argued that Congress should pass a federal law that lets the shareholders of every public corporation choose whether state or federal rules will govern managers' ability to resist hostile takeover bids.

---

2. Deal Protection Devices

Once the board has engaged with an acquirer, both the company and the acquirer have incentives to complete the deal with the terms they want. We next describe of the different tools corporations use to protect their deals. These devices can subsidize a deal with a wanted suitor, or they can impose costs on or obstacles to a deal with an unwanted suitor. These devices can be used on their own, or in tandem. Here are some key examples.

Termination Fees

Termination fees protect deals by requiring that the target corporation agree to pay a pre-agreed amount to the acquirer if the target terminates the deal. What triggers a termination fee can vary: examples include failing to close the deal by a specified date, failing to submit the deal to shareholders for approval, and doing a deal with another company. (This is why termination fees are sometimes called "break-up fees.") The size of termination fees also can vary: courts have approved termination fees ranging between 1–5% of the share price.

Deal protection devices that impose costs, such as termination fees, potentially deter deals, because they make it more expensive for another corporation to outbid the acquirer. For example, suppose you are considering challenging an acquirer that has agreed to pay $100 per share for the target in a deal with a $3 per share termination fee. You believe the acquirer is paying too little; you think the target really is worth $102 per share. But if you bid $102 per share, you will trigger the termination fee, which will make the target worth $3 per share less to you—or just $99 per share (even assuming your $102 estimate is correct). Because of the termination fee, you would only bid at most $99 per share, and therefore would not be a threat to the deal at $100 per share. Thus, the $3 per share termination fee would deter you from bidding.

Deal protection devices, such as termination fees, that impose costs on outside bidders also incentivize the acquirer and target to do a deal. They provide comfort to an acquirer worried about incurring the expense of negotiating with a target who might abandon the deal, by assuring that at minimum the acquirer will get the termination fee. And they provide an incentive for a target to complete a deal with the acquirer to avoid incurring the additional cost of the termination fee.

Lock-Ups

Just as lock-ups can be used to as an anti-takeover device to deter potential acquirers, they also can be used to favor an acquirer by giving them the right to buy certain assets of the target company for a bargain price. These assets are then "locked up"—no other potential acquirer can buy them for a comparable price. Like termination fees, lock-ups impose costs that make targets less attractive to competing acquirers. Indeed, termination fees and lock-ups have similar effects on the incentives of the various actors in a deal drama, even though they impose costs in different ways. Lock-ups frequently target the most valuable assets of a target (the "crown jewels").

In recent years, lawyers have invented and used increasingly complex lock-ups. For example, "matching rights" give bidders rights to match competing offers. "Information rights" can protect bidders by promising that they will receive all written and oral communications by others about competing offers.

No-Shops

No-shops prohibit the target from soliciting other acquirers. As with other deal protection devices, the specific terms can vary. For example, many no-shops permit targets to negotiate with a corporation that approaches the target and makes a sufficiently attractive unsolicited offer. Stronger provisions, known as "no-talks," prohibit companies from even speaking to third parties about a potential deal.

Like other devices, no-shops may include an exception for unsolicited offers that directors would be legally obligated to consider. Such limitations are a response to cases suggesting that target directors need to retain the ability to consider unsolicited offers in order to satisfy their fiduciary duties to shareholders. Such limitations are known as "fiduciary outs." Merger agreements can contain fiduciary outs that apply more generally to deal protection devices other than no-shops. Such fiduciary out clauses permit target directors to terminate a merger agreement if their fiduciary duties require them to do so.

A related deal protection device is a "go-shop" provision, which allows the target to seek other buyers for a specified period after an agreement with an acquirer is signed. As with a no-shop provision, the analysis of go-shops depends on specific terms, including the time period. Naturally, courts are more suspicious of go-shops that give a target only a few weeks than they are of go-shops that last for a few months.

Voting Agreements

Target directors can protect a deal by obtaining the agreement of shareholders to vote their shares to approve a merger. If enough shareholders agree to support a merger, the deal will be well protected; it would be a waste of time for another acquirer to approach a corporation whose shareholders already have agreed to a merger.

The protection of voting agreements can be made even stronger if the merger agreement also contains a provision *requiring* that the deal be submitted for shareholder approval. Such provisions are known as "Section 251(c) provisions," after DGCL Section 251(c), which permits target directors to submit a merger for shareholder approval even if they no longer recommend it. A Section 251(c) provision goes one step further than Delaware law, by making voluntary action mandatory. In other words, the parties agree upfront that the target directors will be required to submit their deal for shareholder approval. If the deal must be submitted for shareholder approval, and the shareholders already have agreed to approve it, it will be virtually impossible for another bidder to do a deal with the target, even if it offers a substantial premium.

Too Much Deal Protection: The Outlier Case of *Omnicare*

One of the most controversial cases in the area involving deal protections is *Omnicare, Inc. v. NCS Healthcare, Inc.*, 818 A.2d 914 (Del. 2003). The case does not represent the majority view, and it does not reflect the dominant practice with respect to deal protection devices but it does illustrate one of the two poles of the possible approaches to deal protection.

Here are the two poles.

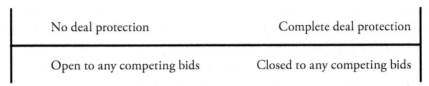

At one extreme, a target board might decide not to adopt any deal protection devices. It might instead elect to leave its deal open to any competing bids. Of course, an acquirer might never agree to such a deal, but it is at least a theoretical possibility: a deal with no protection at all.

At the other extreme, a target board might decide to adopt deal protection devices that are so restrictive as to make any competing bids impossible. Such a deal might be rare, but again it is possible: a deal with the ultimate protection.

Many of the deal protection devices you will encounter in the reported cases, and most of the devices you will see in practice, are somewhere in the middle of this spectrum. But *Omnicare* found that the protections at issue in that case were at the far right of the continuum above. Many commentators disagreed with this assessment, which is one reason the case is so controversial. Even so, *Omnicare* is at minimum a useful illustration of what can happen when deal protection is too strict, at least in the eyes of a few judges.

Omnicare involved a stock-for-stock merger agreement between NCS Health-care and Genesis Health Ventures. NCS was on the brink of bankruptcy and had thoroughly shopped the company in hopes of finding a buyer. Unable to find another bidder, the NCS board agreed that it was in the company's best interest to merge with Genesis. However, Genesis made it clear that it had no interest in being a "stalking horse" for NCS. To ensure that the merger went through, Genesis insisted on several aggressive deal-protection measures that would prevent NCS from accepting any competing proposals. First, Genesis obtained advance approval from two controlling NCS shareholders who agreed to vote all of their shares in favor of the merger. Second, the NCS board agreed to a "force the vote" provision that required the merger agreement to be submitted to a shareholder vote even if the NCS board later withdrew its recommendation for the merger. Finally, the NCS board agreed to omit any effective "fiduciary out" clause for these two provisions in the merger agreement.

When Omnicare subsequently launched a competing cash tender offer for all NCS stock, the defensive provisions in the merger agreement effectively prevented shareholders of NCS from accepting Omnicare's offer. Even though the NCS board recommended that its shareholders vote against the merger with Genesis, the deal protection measures operated to ensure that the NCS-Genesis merger would go through. Omnicare sued to enjoin the merger agreement between NCS and Genesis.

The Delaware Supreme Court, in a 3–2 decision, invalidated the combination of deal protection measures—the "force the vote" provision, the voting agreements, and the lack of a fiduciary out. The Supreme Court reasoned that Delaware law does not permit a target board to lock-up a transaction absolutely. Under these circumstances, the defensive measures "completely prevented the board from discharging its fiduciary responsibilities to the minority stockholders when Omnicare presented its superior transaction." As such, the majority held that this combination of deal protections was invalid and unenforceable under *Unocal*. The majority stated:

> Although the minority shareholders were not forced to vote for the Genesis merger, they were required to accept it because it was *a fait accompli*. The record reflects that the defensive devices employed by the NCS board were preclusive and coercive in the sense that they accomplished *a fait accompli*. In this case, despite the fact that the NCS board has withdrawn its recommendation for the Genesis transaction and recommended its rejection by the stockholders, the deal protection devices approved by the NCS board operated in concert to have a preclusive and coercive effect. Those tripartite defensive measures—the Section 251(c) provision, the voting agreements, and the absence of an effective fiduciary out clause— made it 'mathematically impossible' and 'realistically unattainable' for the Omnicare transaction or any other proposal to succeed, no matter how superior the proposal.

In a strongly worded dissent, Chief Justice Veasey argued that the majority failed to recognize the complex business reality in which the agreement was entered into. This was a situation where the NCS board and its controlling shareholders had "concluded a lengthy search and intense negotiation process in the context of insolvency and creditor pressure where no other viable bid had emerged." The Genesis deal was "the only game in town." In the dissent's view, the process by which the board agreed to the deal protection devices showed that the NCS board made an informed, good faith decision in a time of crisis. In these circumstances, the dissent argued, the NCS board had acted within the bounds of its fiduciary duties. The Court should not second guess the board's business judgment because in hindsight the Omnicare deal presented a superior offer for NCS's shareholders.

Omnicare was an unusual case in many ways, including the nature of the reported decision and dissent. Rarely are there dissenting opinions in Delaware Supreme Court decisions. More significantly, the sweeping language in the majority opinion seemed to change the rules surrounding the use of deal protection strategies in merger agreements. The decision was broadly worded and raised questions about the continued validity of deal protection devices that Delaware courts had previously upheld. Chief Justice Veasey expressed his hope that *Omnicare* would be interpreted narrowly.

Subsequent decisions by the Delaware courts suggest that deal protection provisions remain viable after *Omnicare*—just as they were before it—so long as they are used in the right combination and with the right limitations. The Delaware courts generally have limited *Omnicare* to its facts, and have considered carefully the risks and real-world factors that confront directors when they approve deal protection devices. Moreover, deal lawyers have been careful to include only devices that would be less onerous than those described in *Omnicare* (in other words, deal lawyers use only devices that would place their deal to the left of the devices used in *Omnicare* on the spectrum above). For example, some parties responded to *Omnicare* by structuring voting agreements so that the approval of a "majority of the minority" of public shareholders was required to complete the deal; that limitation meant there was no guarantee that a deal would be completed even though a majority of the other shareholders had agreed to vote in favor of the deal.

Nevertheless, you should keep *Omnicare* in mind, not only as an example of the kind deal protection devices a target board perhaps should not adopt, but also as a reminder that corporate lawyers and directors inevitably must adopt deal protection devices with a view to what a handful of judges ultimately might say. We now turn back to what judges actually have said in a few of the other leading deal protection cases. These cases continue to define the broad parameters governing the judicial assessment and corporate use of deal protection devices today.

C.   Fiduciary Duties and Standards of Review in M&A

What standard of review applies when a court is asked to review a claim that directors have breached their fiduciary duties in the M&A context? Anti-takeover tactics and deal protections can create a potential conflict between the interests of directors and shareholders. Did the directors act in their own interests to protect their own positions or to choose their favorite potential acquirer or fend off a disfavored bidder? Or were they instead acting in the best interests of the corporation and its shareholders in doing so? The courts have recognized the potential for conflict, but have struggled in deciding which standard of review to apply when evaluating a board's actions in the M&A context. Essentially, courts take one of three approaches depending on the circumstances.

First, courts can apply the business judgment rule. As we have discussed at several points in this book, a transaction approved by a majority of independent, disinterested directors receives the protection of the business judgment rule, a judicial presumption protecting the decision from review. The courts have made it clear that they often will apply the business judgment rule when an M&A transaction involves adequate process. For example, the business judgment rule standard applies when a transaction has been approved by a fully-informed, uncoerced majority of the disinterested shareholders. This doctrine has become known as the *Corwin* doctrine, based on *Corwin v. KKR Financial Holdings LLC*, 125 A.3d 304 (Del. 2015), which we will examine later in this chapter. Historically, courts applied the business judgment rule in other contexts as well, including selective repurchases of stock, as in the classic case of *Cheff v. Mathes*, 199 A.2d 548 (Del. Ch. 1964), which the Delaware courts continue to reference.

Second, courts can apply an intermediate level of scrutiny. As in the duty of loyalty context, courts recognize that when directors make decisions that might be motivated more by self-interest than the interests of shareholders, this conflict generates a need to examine the facts more closely. In these cases, board decisions are not protected by the business judgment rule. Instead, the courts inquire into the board's response to a perceived takeover threat and the question of whether the directors acted based on self-interest (to preserve their positions and those of the officers) or based on what the directors believed was in the best interests of the shareholders. *Unocal vs. Mesa Petroleum* is the leading case representing this intermediate standard.

Third, courts can apply a strict level of scrutiny. When it is apparent that a takeover attempt or attempts have proceeded so far that the corporation can be deemed "for sale," the role of the board shifts. Whereas the board typically is entitled to preserve the long-term interests of the corporation, even in the presence of a potential conflict of interest, once the company is for sale the board must act to maximize the value of the corporation in a sale for the benefit of the shareholders. Judges view anti-takeover measures with great skepticism once a company is for sale. *Revlon v. MacAndrews & Forbes Holdings* embodies this third, more rigorous approach. Companies that are for sale are often said to be in *"Revlon* mode."

Since the "classic" cases, the courts have filled in some of the gaps in the application of these tests. For example, one of the most significant cases during the 2010s involved the year-long battle for control of Airgas, Inc. The Airgas board defended against an offer by Air Products and Chemicals, Inc., rejecting the offer as "grossly inadequate," and refusing to redeem the company's poison pill, even when Air Products repeatedly raised its offer. Ultimately, the Delaware Chancery Court ruled in favor of Airgas, and Air Products withdrew its offer. *Air Prods. & Chem., Inc. v. Airgas, Inc.*, 16 A.3d 48, 128 (Del. Ch. 2011). Fortunately for the Airgas shareholders, the company eventually sold to another buyer for double the final bid that Air Products had offered. In contrast, the courts have been more likely to scrutinize directors' resistance to takeovers, including pressure from hedge fund activists, if the plaintiff shareholders allege that the directors faced a conflict of interest.

You will cover the details of these more recent cases in an M&A course. Our objective here is to familiarize you with the "classic" cases under each approach. Although they represent distinct standards of judicial review you might ask whether the lines between the different approaches are really as crisp as they might appear. When might a board facing a threat similar to the one in *Unocal* be deemed to be in *"Revlon* mode"? And what if the outside bid in *Revlon* had been an offer of stock and not cash? We begin with *Unocal*.

1. *Unocal* Proportionality Test: Intermediate Standard of Review

Most case law on corporation law issues develops at a snail's pace. Landmark decisions resolving major issues and changing the law's direction are sometimes separated by decades. However, beginning in 1985, the Delaware courts issued a series of decisions in rapid succession that almost completely reshaped the law governing corporate managers' responsibilities when they resist threats to control or agree to sell control. Many other jurisdictions have followed these cases.

Because these cases involved "real time" battles for corporate control, the Delaware courts faced serious logistical challenges, not only in keeping up with the cases at issue, but in anticipating the creativity of the lawyers and investment bankers who advised bidders and target companies. The Delaware judges knew these market actors would respond instantly to their decisions, so they wrote narrow opinions and avoided sweeping pronouncements. Many commentators have praised the flexibility of this approach, though others would have preferred greater certainty.

Unocal Corporation v. Mesa Petroleum Co. marks the beginning of Delaware's contemporary approach to regulating transactions involving a change of control. Mesa had made a hostile takeover bid for 51% of Unocal stock. Unocal believed this bid was both coercive and inadequate. In response, Unocal offered to repurchase its own securities from its shareholders but excluded Mesa from the offer. In determining the validity of excluding Mesa, the court declined to apply a business judgment rule standard of review. Instead, the court created an intermediate standard and applied a two-pronged "proportionality" test to determine (1) whether the board had reasonable grounds for believing a threat to the corporation existed and (2) whether the defensive measures taken were reasonable in relation to the perceived threat.

Unocal Corp. v. Mesa Petroleum Co.

493 A.2d 946 (Del. 1985)

MOORE, JUSTICE.

We confront an issue of first impression in Delaware—the validity of a corporation's self-tender for its own shares which excludes from participation a stockholder making a hostile tender offer for the company's stock.

The Court of Chancery granted a preliminary injunction to the plaintiffs, Mesa Petroleum Co., Mesa Asset Co., Mesa Partners II, and Mesa Eastern, Inc. (collectively "Mesa")[1] enjoining an exchange offer of the defendant, Unocal Corporation for its

---

[1] T. Boone Pickens, Jr., is President and Chairman of the Board of Mesa Petroleum and President of Mesa Asset and controls the related Mesa entities.

own stock. The trial court concluded that a selective exchange offer, excluding Mesa, was legally impermissible. We cannot agree with such a blanket rule. The factual findings of the Vice Chancellor, fully supported by the record, establish that Unocal's board, consisting of a majority of independent directors, acted in good faith, and after reasonable investigation found that Mesa's tender offer was both inadequate and coercive. Under the circumstances the board had both the power and duty to oppose a bid it perceived to be harmful to the corporate enterprise. On this record we are satisfied that the device Unocal adopted is reasonable in relation to the threat posed, and that the board acted in the proper exercise of sound business judgment. We will not substitute our views for those of the board if the latter's decision can be "attributed to any rational business purpose." Accordingly, we reverse the decision of the Court of Chancery and order the preliminary injunction vacated.

> T. Boone Pickens was one of the leading (and most colorful) takeover artists of the 1980s. He founded Mesa Petroleum in the 1950s, and by the 1980s it had become of the world's largest independent oil companies. Then, rather than drill for oil in the field, Mesa began to drill for oil on Wall Street by seeking to acquire other oil and gas companies. Some of the takeovers succeeded, but many failed—including bids for Unocal, Gulf Oil, and Philips Petroleum. In the 1990s, Pickens made acquisitions in other industries and later founded United Shareholders Association to influence corporate governance in large companies.

The factual background of this matter bears a significant relationship to its ultimate outcome.

On April 8, 1985, Mesa, the owner of approximately 13% of Unocal's stock, commenced a two-tier "front loaded" cash tender offer for 64 million shares, or approximately 37%, of Unocal's outstanding stock at a price of $54 per share. The "back-end" was designed to eliminate the remaining publicly held shares by an exchange of securities purportedly worth $54 per share. However, pursuant to an order entered by the United States District Court for the Central District of California on April 26, 1985, Mesa issued a supplemental proxy statement to Unocal's stockholders disclosing that the securities offered in the second-step merger would be highly subordinated, and that Unocal's capitalization would differ significantly from its present structure. Unocal has rather aptly termed such securities "junk bonds."

Unocal's board consists of eight independent, outside directors and six insiders. It met on April 13, 1985, to consider the Mesa tender offer. Thirteen directors were present, and the meeting lasted nine and one-half hours. The directors were given no agenda or written materials prior to the session. However, detailed presentations were made by legal counsel regarding the board's obligations under both Delaware corporate law and the federal securities laws. The board then received a presentation from Peter Sachs on behalf of Goldman Sachs & Co. and Dillon, Read & Co.

discussing the bases for their opinions that the Mesa proposal was wholly inadequate. Mr. Sachs opined that the minimum cash value that could be expected from a sale or orderly liquidation for 100% of Unocal's stock was in excess of $60 per share. In making his presentation, Mr. Sachs showed slides outlining the valuation techniques used by the financial advisors, and others, depicting recent business combinations in the oil and gas industry. The Court of Chancery found that the Sachs presentation was designed to apprise the directors of the scope of the analyses performed rather than the facts and numbers used in reaching the conclusion that Mesa's tender offer price was inadequate.

Mr. Sachs also presented various defensive strategies available to the board if it concluded that Mesa's two-step tender offer was inadequate and should be opposed. One of the devices outlined was a self-tender by Unocal for its own stock with a reasonable price range of $70 to $75 per share. The cost of such a proposal would cause the company to incur $6.1–6.5 billion of additional debt, and a presentation was made informing the board of Unocal's ability to handle it. The directors were told that the primary effect of this obligation would be to reduce exploratory drilling, but that the company would nonetheless remain a viable entity.

The eight outside directors, comprising a clear majority of the thirteen members present, then met separately with Unocal's financial advisors and attorneys. Thereafter, they unanimously agreed to advise the board that it should reject Mesa's tender offer as inadequate, and that Unocal should pursue a self-tender to provide the stockholders with a fairly priced alternative to the Mesa proposal. The board then reconvened and unanimously adopted a resolution rejecting as grossly inadequate Mesa's tender offer. Despite the nine and one-half hour length of the meeting, no formal decision was made on the proposed defensive self-tender.

On April 15, the board met again with one member still absent. This session lasted two hours. Unocal's Vice President of Finance and its Assistant General Counsel made a detailed presentation of the proposed terms of the exchange offer. A price range between $70 and $80 per share was considered, and ultimately the directors agreed upon $72. The board was also advised about the debt securities that would be issued, and the necessity of placing restrictive covenants upon certain corporate activities until the obligations were paid. The board's decisions were made in reliance on the advice of its investment bankers, including the terms and conditions upon which the securities were to be issued. Based upon this advice, and the board's own deliberations, the directors unanimously approved the exchange offer. Their resolution provided that if Mesa acquired 64 million shares of Unocal stock through its own offer (the Mesa Purchase Condition), Unocal would buy the remaining 49% outstanding for an exchange of debt securities having an aggregate par value of $72 per share. The board resolution also stated that the offer would be subject to other conditions that had been described to the board at the meeting, or which were deemed necessary by Unocal's officers, including the exclusion of Mesa from the proposal (the Mesa exclusion). Any such conditions were required to be in accordance with the "purport and intent" of the offer.

Unocal's exchange offer was commenced on April 17, 1985, and Mesa promptly challenged it by filing this suit in the Court of Chancery. On April 22, the Unocal board met again and was advised by Goldman Sachs and Dillon Read to waive the Mesa Purchase Condition as to 50 million shares. This recommendation was in response to a perceived concern of the shareholders that, if shares were tendered to Unocal, no shares would be purchased by either offeror. The directors were also advised that they should tender their own Unocal stock into the exchange offer as a mark of their confidence in it.

Another focus of the board was the Mesa exclusion. Legal counsel advised that under Delaware law Mesa could only be excluded for what the directors reasonably believed to be a valid corporate purpose. The directors' discussion centered on the objective of adequately compensating shareholders at the "back-end" of Mesa's proposal, which the latter would finance with "junk bonds." To include Mesa would defeat that goal, because under the proration aspect of the exchange offer (49%) every Mesa share accepted by Unocal would displace one held by another stockholder. Further, if Mesa were permitted to tender to Unocal, the latter would in effect be financing Mesa's own inadequate proposal.

On April 29, 1985, the Vice Chancellor temporarily restrained Unocal from proceeding with the exchange offer unless it included Mesa. The trial court recognized that directors could oppose, and attempt to defeat, a hostile takeover which they considered adverse to the best interests of the corporation. However, the Vice Chancellor decided that in a selective purchase of the company's stock, the corporation bears the burden of showing: (1) a valid corporate purpose, and (2) that the transaction was fair to all of the stockholders, including those excluded.

The issues we address involve these fundamental questions: Did the Unocal board have the power and duty to oppose a takeover threat it reasonably perceived to be harmful to the corporate enterprise, and if so, is its action here entitled to the protection of the business judgment rule?

Mesa contends that the discriminatory exchange offer violates the fiduciary duties Unocal owes it. Mesa argues that because of the Mesa exclusion the business judgment rule is inapplicable, because the directors by tendering their own shares will derive a financial benefit that is not available to all Unocal stockholders. Thus, it is Mesa's ultimate contention that Unocal cannot establish that the exchange offer is fair to all shareholders, and argues that the Court of Chancery was correct in concluding that Unocal was unable to meet this burden.

Unocal answers that it does not owe a duty of "fairness" to Mesa, given the facts here. Specifically, Unocal contends that its board of directors reasonably and in good faith concluded that Mesa's $54 two-tier tender offer was coercive and inadequate, and that Mesa sought selective treatment for itself. Furthermore, Unocal argues that the board's approval of the exchange offer was made in good faith, on an informed basis, and in the exercise of due care. Under these circumstances, Unocal contends that its directors properly employed this device to protect the company and its stockholders from Mesa's harmful tactics.

We begin with the basic issue of the power of a board of directors of a Delaware corporation to adopt a defensive measure of this type. Absent such authority, all other questions are moot. Neither issues of fairness nor business judgment are pertinent without the basic underpinning of a board's legal power to act.

The board has a large reservoir of authority upon which to draw. Its duties and responsibilities proceed from the inherent powers conferred by 8 Del. C. § 141(a), respecting management of the corporation's "business and affairs." Additionally, the powers here being exercised derive from 8 Del. C. § 160(a), conferring broad authority upon a corporation to deal in its own stock. From this it is now well established that in the acquisition of its shares a Delaware corporation may deal selectively with its stockholders, provided the directors have not acted out of a sole or primary purpose to entrench themselves in office.

Finally, the board's power to act derives from its fundamental duty and obligation to protect the corporate enterprise, which includes stockholders, from harm reasonably perceived, irrespective of its source. Thus, we are satisfied that in the broad context of corporate governance, including issues of fundamental corporate change, a board of directors is not a passive instrumentality.

Given the foregoing principles, we turn to the standards by which director action is to be measured. In *Pogostin v. Rice*, 480 A.2d 619 (Del. 1984), we held that the business judgment rule, including the standards by which director conduct is judged, is applicable in the context of a takeover.

When a board addresses a pending takeover bid it has an obligation to determine whether the offer is in the best interests of the corporation and its shareholders. In that respect a board's duty is no different from any other responsibility it shoulders, and its decisions should be no less entitled to the respect they otherwise would be accorded in the realm of business judgment. There are, however, certain caveats to a proper exercise of this function. Because of the omnipresent specter that a board may be acting primarily in its own interests, rather than those of the corporation and its shareholders, there is an enhanced duty which calls for judicial examination at the threshold before the protections of the business judgment rule may be conferred.

This Court has long recognized that:

We must bear in mind the inherent danger in the purchase of shares with corporate funds to remove a threat to corporate policy when a threat to control is involved. The directors are of necessity confronted with a conflict of interest, and an objective decision is difficult.

Bennett v. Propp, 187 A.2d 405, 409 (Del. 1962). In the face of this inherent conflict, directors must show that they had reasonable grounds for believing that a danger to corporate policy and effectiveness existed because of another person's stock ownership. *Cheff v. Mathes*, 199 A.2d at 554–55. However, they satisfy that burden "by showing good faith and reasonable investigation." Furthermore, such proof is materially enhanced, as here, by the approval of a board comprised of a majority of outside, independent directors who have acted in accordance with the foregoing standards.

In the board's exercise of corporate power to forestall a takeover bid, our analysis begins with the basic principle that corporate directors have a fiduciary duty to act in the best interests of the corporation's stockholders. As we have noted, their duty of care extends to protecting the corporation and its owners from perceived harm whether a threat originates from third parties or other shareholders. But such powers are not absolute. A corporation does not have unbridled discretion to defeat any perceived threat by any Draconian means available.

The restriction placed upon a selective stock repurchase is that the directors may not have acted solely or primarily out of a desire to perpetuate themselves in office. Of course, to this is added the further caveat that inequitable action may not be taken under the guise of law. The standard of proof established in *Cheff v. Mathes* is designed to ensure that a defensive measure to thwart or impede a takeover is indeed motivated by a good faith concern for the welfare of the corporation and its stockholders, which in all circumstances must be free of any fraud or other misconduct. However, this does not end the inquiry.

B.

A further aspect is the element of balance. If a defensive measure is to come within the ambit of the business judgment rule, it must be reasonable in relation to the threat posed. This entails an analysis by the directors of the nature of the takeover bid and its effect on the corporate enterprise. Examples of such concerns may include: inadequacy of the price offered, nature and timing of the offer, questions of illegality, the impact on "constituencies" other than shareholders (i.e., creditors, customers, employees, and perhaps even the community generally), the risk of non-consummation, and the quality of securities being offered in the exchange. While not a controlling factor, it also seems to us that a board may reasonably consider the basic stockholder interests at stake, including those of short-term speculators, whose actions may have fueled the coercive aspect of the offer at the expense of the long-term investor. Here, the threat posed was viewed by the Unocal board as a grossly inadequate two-tier coercive tender offer coupled with the threat of greenmail.

Specifically, the Unocal directors had concluded that the value of Unocal was substantially above the $54 per share offered in cash at the front end. Furthermore, they determined that the subordinated securities to be exchanged in Mesa's announced squeeze-out of the remaining shareholders in the "back-end" merger were "junk bonds" worth far less than $54. It is now well recognized that such offers are a classic coercive measure designed to stampede shareholders into tendering at the first tier, even if the price is inadequate, out of fear of what they will receive at the back end of the transaction. Wholly beyond the coercive aspect of an inadequate two-tier tender offer, the threat was posed by a corporate raider with a national reputation as a "greenmailer." [13]

In adopting the selective exchange offer, the board stated that its objective was either to defeat the inadequate Mesa offer or, should the offer still succeed, provide the 49% of its stockholders, who would otherwise be forced to accept "junk bonds," with $72 worth of senior debt. We find that both purposes are valid.

However, such efforts would have been thwarted by Mesa's participation in the exchange offer. First, if Mesa could tender its shares, Unocal would effectively be subsidizing Mesa's continuing effort to buy Unocal stock at $54 per share. Second, Mesa could not, by definition, fit within the class of shareholders being protected from its own coercive and inadequate tender offer.

Thus, we are satisfied that the selective exchange offer is reasonably related to the threats posed. The board's decision to offer what it determined to be the fair value of the corporation to the 49% of its shareholders, who would otherwise be forced to accept highly subordinated "junk bonds," is reasonable and consistent with the directors' duty to ensure that the minority stockholders receive equal value for their shares.

Mesa contends that it is unlawful, and the trial court agreed, for a corporation to discriminate in this fashion against one shareholder. It argues correctly that no case has ever sanctioned a device that precludes a raider from sharing in a benefit available to all other stockholders. However, as we have noted earlier, the principle of selective stock repurchases by a Delaware corporation is neither unknown nor unauthorized. The only difference is that heretofore the approved transaction was the payment of "greenmail" to a raider or dissident posing a threat to the corporate enterprise. All other stockholders were denied such favored treatment, and given Mesa's past history of greenmail, its claims here are rather ironic.

However, our corporate law is not static. It must grow and develop in response to, indeed in anticipation of, evolving concepts and needs. Merely because the General Corporation Law is silent as to a specific matter does not mean that it is prohibited. In the days when *Cheff, Bennett, Martin* and *Kors* were decided, the tender offer, while not an unknown device, was virtually unused, and little was known of such methods

---

[13] The Chancery Court noted that "Mesa has made tremendous profits from its takeover activities although in the past few years it has not been successful in acquiring any of the target companies on an unfriendly basis." Moreover, the trial court specifically found that the actions of the Unocal board were taken in good faith to eliminate both the inadequacies of the tender offer and to forestall the payment of "greenmail."

as two-tier "front-end" loaded offers with their coercive effects. Then, the favored attack of a raider was stock acquisition followed by a proxy contest. Various defensive tactics, which provided no benefit whatever to the raider, evolved. Thus, the use of corporate funds by management to counter a proxy battle was approved. Litigation, supported by corporate funds, aimed at the raider has long been a popular device.

More recently, as the sophistication of both raiders and targets has developed, a host of other defensive measures to counter such ever-mounting threats has evolved and received judicial sanction. These include defensive charter amendments and other devices bearing some rather exotic, but apt, names: Crown Jewel, White Knight, Pac Man, and Golden Parachute. Each has highly selective features, the object of which is to deter or defeat the raider.

Thus, while the exchange offer is a form of selective treatment, given the nature of the threat posed here the response is neither unlawful nor unreasonable. If the board of directors is disinterested, has acted in good faith and with due care, its decision in the absence of an abuse of discretion will be upheld as a proper exercise of business judgment.

To this Mesa responds that the board is not disinterested, because the directors are receiving a benefit from the tender of their own shares, which because of the Mesa exclusion, does not devolve upon all stockholders equally. However, Mesa concedes that if the exclusion is valid, then the directors and all other stockholders share the same benefit. The answer of course is that the exclusion is valid, and the directors' participation in the exchange offer does not rise to the level of a disqualifying interest.

Nor does this become an "interested-director transaction" merely because certain board members are large stockholders. As this Court has previously noted, that fact alone does not create a disqualifying "personal pecuniary interest" to defeat the operation of the business judgment rule.

Mesa also argues that the exclusion permits the directors to abdicate the fiduciary duties they owe it. However, that is not so. The board continues to owe Mesa the duties of due care and loyalty. But in the face of the destructive threat Mesa's tender offer was perceived to pose, the board had a supervening duty to protect the corporate enterprise, which includes the other shareholders, from threatened harm.

Mesa contends that the basis of this action is punitive, and solely in response to the exercise of its rights of corporate democracy. Nothing precludes Mesa, as a stockholder, from acting in its own self-interest. However, Mesa, while pursuing its own interests, has acted in a manner which a board consisting of a majority of independent directors has reasonably determined to be contrary to the best interests of Unocal and its other shareholders. In this situation, there is no support in Delaware law for the proposition that, when responding to a perceived harm, a corporation must guarantee a benefit to a stockholder who is deliberately provoking the danger being addressed. There is no obligation of self-sacrifice by a corporation and its shareholders in the face of such a challenge.

Here, the Court of Chancery specifically found that the "directors' decision [to oppose the Mesa tender offer] was made in the good faith belief that the Mesa tender offer is inadequate." Given our standard of review, we are satisfied that Unocal's board has met its burden of proof.

In conclusion, there was directorial power to oppose the Mesa tender offer, and to undertake a selective stock exchange made in good faith and upon a reasonable investigation pursuant to a clear duty to protect the corporate enterprise. Further, the selective stock repurchase plan chosen by Unocal is reasonable in relation to the threat that the board rationally and reasonably believed was posed by Mesa's inadequate and coercive two-tier tender offer. Under those circumstances the board's action is entitled to be measured by the standards of the business judgment rule. Thus, unless it is shown by a preponderance of the evidence that the directors' decisions were primarily based on perpetuating themselves in office, or some other breach of fiduciary duty such as fraud, overreaching, lack of good faith, or being uninformed, a Court will not substitute its judgment for that of the board.

In this case that protection is not lost merely because Unocal's directors have tendered their shares in the exchange offer. Given the validity of the Mesa exclusion, they are receiving a benefit shared generally by all other stockholders except Mesa. In this circumstance the test of *Aronson v. Lewis*, 473 A.2d at 812, is satisfied. If the stockholders are displeased with the action of their elected representatives, the powers of corporate democracy are at their disposal to turn the board out.

With the Court of Chancery's findings that the exchange offer was based on the board's good faith belief that the Mesa offer was inadequate, that the board's action was informed and taken with due care, that Mesa's prior activities justify a reasonable inference that its principle objective was greenmail, and implicitly, that the substance of the offer itself was reasonable and fair to the corporation and its stockholders if Mesa were included, we cannot say that the Unocal directors have acted in such a manner as to have passed an "unintelligent and unadvised judgment." The decision of the Court of Chancery is therefore REVERSED, and the preliminary injunction is VACATED.

Points for Discussion

1. *The rationale for excluding Mesa.*

What do the following two sentences from the opinion mean? "To include Mesa would defeat that goal, because under the proration aspect of the exchange offer (49%)

every Mesa share accepted by Unocal would displace one held by another stockholder. Further, if Mesa were permitted to tender to Unocal, the latter would in effect be financing Mesa's own inadequate proposal." Why was it necessary for Unocal to exclude Mesa from its exchange offer? (The Williams Act, a federal statute, regulates tenders offers and requires that if a tender offer is for less than all of the corporation's shares, the bidder must accept tendered shares on a pro-rata basis.) Why did Unocal waive the Mesa Purchase Condition?

2. *Other constituencies.*

The court says that in evaluating a threat, a target board may consider "the impact on 'constituencies' other than shareholders (i.e., creditors, customers, employees, and perhaps even the community generally)." Does this language dramatically expand the board's ability to resist an unwanted offer? If not, what limits are there on this concept?

3. *Effect on future cases.*

Unocal held that the "proportionality" requirement was satisfied because the Mesa exclusion, though discriminatory, was necessary to make Unocal's self-tender an effective response to Mesa's coercive and inadequate two-tier, front-end loaded takeover bid. Thus, the court effectively eliminated such bids. However, *Unocal* left unanswered several major questions. How would the court assess a similar response to a non-coercive bid? What defensive actions, if any, would the court consider proportionate if a bid threatened only the interests of non-shareholder constituencies?

4. **Unitrin.**

An important case involving application of the *Unocal* standard arose a decade later. In <u>*Unitrin, Inc. v. American General Corp.*</u>, 651 A.2d 1361 (Del. 1995), the target, Unitrin, rejected American General's bid and approved a stock repurchase plan that increased the board's stock ownership and thereby made a proxy contest more difficult. Did that tactic impermissibly impinge on the shareholder franchise? The Delaware Supreme Court said no. It reasoned that a target board's decision to fend off a hostile takeover bid—even an all-cash, all-shares bid at a substantial premium—should not be viewed as coercive so long as it does not preclude a successful proxy fight. However, *Unitrin* left open the possibility that the Delaware courts could invalidate a target board's response to an unsolicited offer that completely foreclosed a proxy contest or was unreasonably disproportionate to the threat. (Some commentators and courts group *Unocal* and *Unitrin* together as representing the intermediate approach to takeovers.)

5. *Remember* **Blasius.**

One challenge for courts assessing M&A disputes is determining whether they infringe upon the shareholder franchise. For example, does a defensive tactic or deal protection device at issue harm the shareholders' ability to exercise one of their fundamental rights, the right to vote? The courts have struggled with determining when a measure disenfranchises shareholders.

———————

Recall *Blasius Industries, Inc. v. Atlas Corp.*, the voting rights case holding that with respect to board elections, incumbent directors are not entitled to act as "Platonic masters" who "know better than do the shareholders what is in the corporation's best interest." *Blasius* requires that the board provide a "compelling justification" for any "acts done for the primary purpose of impeding the exercise of the stockholder voting power." Board actions that disenfranchise shareholders are subject to a kind of strict scrutiny.

The strict "compelling justification" standard of *Blasius* contrasts with the proportionality standard of *Unocal*, which allows a board considerable scope to decide whether a takeover bid is in the shareholders' best interests. Which standard should govern the target board's adoption of deal protection devices? Could *Blasius* be understood as a stricter application of the *Unocal* standard? How should judges, lawyers, and directors decide whether a particular device affects shareholder electoral rights? These are fundamental questions about how power is allocated between shareholders and directors, and they have puzzled the courts.

Ultimately, the question of which interest trumps—the protection of shareholder voting or the facilitating of deals—requires an analysis of some fundamental policy issues. Courts have varied in how they attempt to balance the importance of shareholder voting rights versus the realities of the marketplace for deals and devices to protect them.

2. *Revlon*: When the Corporation Is "For Sale"

As noted, the Delaware Supreme Court handed down a series of blockbuster cases in the 1980s amid a wave of M&A and hostile takeover activity. Corporate lawyers quickly adjusted how they counseled their clients in response to a series of major developments from the lightning strike of *Smith v. Van Gorkom*, which we saw in Chapter 9, Duty of Care , to the new standard set out in *Unocal* and the invention of the poison pill, which was validated in *Moran v. Household International, Inc.*

In the events leading up to the next big case, *Revlon, Inc. v. MacAndrews & Forbes Holdings, Inc.*, Ronald Perelman, a successful American businessman who was chairman of the board and CEO of Pantry Pride, met with Michel Bergerac, a Frenchman who was chairman of the board and CEO of Revlon, to discuss Pantry Pride's possible friendly acquisition of Revlon. The meeting, in August 1985, went badly, with Bergerac dismissing Perelman's offer of $40 to $50 a share as considerably below Revlon's intrinsic value. Perhaps in part because of Bergerac's strong personal antipathy for Perelman, Revlon rebuffed all of Pantry Pride's subsequent attempts to discuss a possible acquisition.

Perelman made another attempt. This time, Pantry Pride offered to acquire Revlon in a negotiated transaction at $42 to $43 per share or in a hostile tender offer at $45. Again, Bergerac rejected any possible Pantry Pride acquisition.

Faced with the possibility of a hostile takeover bid by Pantry Pride, Revlon's 14-member board took several defensive measures. (Six of the directors held senior management positions and two others owned significant blocks of Revlon stock. Four of the remaining six directors had been associated with entities that had business relationships with Revlon.) First, the Revlon board met with counsel and investment banker Lazard Freres to consider the impending hostile takeover bid. The board voted to repurchase up to 5 million shares of its common stock and to adopt a Note Purchase Rights plan. The plan permitted the rights holders to exchange their stock for a $65 one-year note unless someone acquired all the Revlon stock at $65 per share.

On August 23, Pantry Pride made an all-cash, all-shares tender offer at $47.50 per share, subject to obtaining financing and to the redemption of the rights. The Revlon board rejected the offer, then made its own offer to the Revlon shareholders to exchange notes for 10 million shares of common stock. The notes contained various covenants, the most important of which was a covenant against incurring future debt. Ultimately, Revlon accepted the full 10 million shares in the exchange offer.

On September 16, Pantry Pride announced a revised offer at $42 per share, conditioned on receiving 90% of the stock (or less, if Revlon removed the rights). Because of the exchange offer, the revised offer was the economic equivalent of Pantry Pride's earlier higher bid. Again the Revlon board rejected the offer. Pantry Pride increased its bid to $50 per share, then again to $53.

Meanwhile, the Revlon board agreed to a leveraged buyout in the form of a merger with Forstmann Little in which the Revlon shareholders would receive $56 per share, Forstmann would assume the debt incurred in the exchange offer, and Revlon would redeem the rights and waive the note covenants for Forstmann or any offer superior to Forstmann's. Immediately after the merger was announced, the market price of the notes fell substantially.

On October 7, Pantry Pride increased its bid to $56.25, subject to cancellation of the rights and the waiver of the note covenants. Two days later, it declared its intention to top any competing bid.

In response, Forstmann offered $57.25 per share and agreed to support the market price of the notes after the covenants were removed. The offer also required Revlon to grant Forstmann a lock-up option on two of its divisions at a price well below Lazard Freres' valuation if anyone else acquired 40% of the Revlon stock. Finally, Revlon was to pay a $25 million cancellation fee if the merger agreement was terminated or anyone else acquired more than 19.9% of Revlon's stock. The Revlon board accepted the offer because the price exceeded Pantry Pride's bid, the noteholders were protected against a decline in value of their notes, and Forstmann's financing was secure.

Pantry Pride promptly sued to invalidate the agreement and, on October 22, raised its bid to $58, conditioned upon the nullification of the rights, the waiver of the note covenants, and the granting of an injunction against the lock-up.

The *Revlon* court considered whether directors have unlimited powers to defend their corporation from threats to its policy and effectiveness or whether, at a certain point, their obligations to the corporation and shareholders change. As you read *Revlon*, consider at what point the board's duty changes from preserving the corporation to maximizing the corporation's value for the benefit of the shareholders and whether the board would have recognized that such a change had occurred.

Revlon, Inc. v. MacAndrews & Forbes Holdings, Inc.

506 A.2d 173 (Del. 1985)

Moore, Justice.

In this battle for corporate control of Revlon, Inc., the Court of Chancery enjoined certain transactions designed to thwart the efforts of Pantry Pride, Inc., to acquire Revlon.[1] The defendants are Revlon, its board of directors, and Forstmann Little & Co. and the latter's affiliated limited partnership (collectively, Forstmann). The injunction barred consummation of an option granted Forstmann to purchase certain Revlon assets (the lock-up option), a promise by Revlon to deal exclusively with Forstmann in the face of a takeover (the no-shop provision), and the payment of a $25 million cancellation fee to Forstmann if the transaction was aborted. The Court of Chancery found that the Revlon directors had breached their duty of care by entering into the foregoing transactions and effectively ending an active auction for the company. The trial court ruled that such arrangements are not illegal per se under Delaware law, but that their use under the circumstances here was impermissible. We agree. Thus, we granted this expedited interlocutory appeal to consider for the first time the validity of such defensive measures in the face of an active bidding contest for corporate control. Additionally, we address for the first time the extent to which a corporation may consider the impact of a takeover threat on constituencies other than shareholders. *See Unocal Corp. v. Mesa Petroleum Co.*, 493 A.2d 946, 955 (Del. 1985).

In our view, lock-ups and related agreements are permitted under Delaware law where their adoption is untainted by director interest or other breaches of fiduciary

---

[1]   The nominal plaintiff, MacAndrews & Forbes Holdings, Inc., is the controlling stockholder of Pantry Pride. For all practical purposes their interests in this litigation are virtually identical, and we hereafter will refer to Pantry Pride as the plaintiff.

duty. The actions taken by the Revlon directors, however, did not meet this standard. Moreover, while concern for various corporate constituencies is proper when addressing a takeover threat, that principle is limited by the requirement that there be some rationally related benefit accruing to the stockholders. We find no such benefit here.

Thus, under all the circumstances we must agree with the Court of Chancery that the enjoined Revlon defensive measures were inconsistent with the directors' duties to the stockholders. Accordingly, we affirm.

We turn first to Pantry Pride's probability of success on the merits. The ultimate responsibility for managing the business and affairs of a corporation falls on its board of directors. In discharging this function the directors owe fiduciary duties of care and loyalty to the corporation and its shareholders. These principles apply with equal force when a board approves a corporate merger; and of course they are the bedrock of our law regarding corporate takeover issues. While the business judgment rule may be applicable to the actions of corporate directors responding to takeover threats, the principles upon which it is founded—care, loyalty and independence must first be satisfied.

If the business judgment rule applies, there is a "presumption that in making a business decision the directors of a corporation acted on an informed basis, in good faith and in the honest belief that the action taken was in the best interests of the company." However, when a board implements anti-takeover measures there arises "the omnipresent specter that a board may be acting primarily in its own interests, rather than those of the corporation and its shareholders." This potential for conflict places upon the directors the burden of proving that they had reasonable grounds for believing there was a danger to corporate policy and effectiveness, a burden satisfied by a showing of good faith and reasonable investigation. In addition, the directors must analyze the nature of the takeover and its effect on the corporation in order to ensure balance—that the responsive action taken is reasonable in relation to the threat posed.

The first relevant defensive measure adopted by the Revlon board was the Rights Plan, which would be considered a "poison pill" in the current language of corporate takeovers—a plan by which shareholders receive the right to be bought out by the corporation at a substantial premium on the occurrence of a stated triggering event. By 8 *Del.C.* §§ 141 and 122(13), the board clearly had the power to adopt the measure. Thus, the focus becomes one of reasonableness and purpose.

The Revlon board approved the Rights Plan in the face of an impending hostile takeover bid by Pantry Pride at $45 per share, a price which Revlon reasonably concluded was grossly inadequate. Lazard Freres had so advised the directors, and had also informed them that Pantry Pride was a small, highly leveraged company bent on a "bust-up" takeover by using "junk bond" financing to buy Revlon cheaply, sell the acquired assets to pay the debts incurred, and retain the profit for itself.[1] In adopting the Plan, the board protected the shareholders from a hostile takeover at a price below the company's intrinsic value, while retaining sufficient flexibility to address any proposal deemed to be in the stockholders' best interests.

To that extent the board acted in good faith and upon reasonable investigation. Under the circumstances it cannot be said that the Rights Plan as employed was unreasonable, considering the threat posed. Indeed, the Plan was a factor in causing Pantry Pride to raise its bids from a low of $42 to an eventual high of $58. At the time of its adoption, the Rights Plan afforded a measure of protection consistent with the directors' fiduciary duty in facing a takeover threat perceived as detrimental to corporate interests. Far from being a "show-stopper," as the plaintiffs had contended in *Moran*, the measure spurred the bidding to new heights, a proper result of its implementation.

Although we consider adoption of the Plan to have been valid under the circumstances, its continued usefulness was rendered moot by the directors' actions on October 3 and October 12. At the October 3 meeting the board redeemed the Rights conditioned upon consummation of a merger with Forstmann, but further acknowledged that they would also be redeemed to facilitate any more favorable offer. On October 12, the board unanimously passed a resolution redeeming the Rights in connection with any cash proposal of $57.25 or more per share. Because all the pertinent offers eventually equaled or surpassed that amount, the Rights clearly were no longer any impediment in the contest for Revlon. This mooted any question of their propriety under *Moran* or *Unocal*.

The second defensive measure adopted by Revlon to thwart a Pantry Pride takeover was the company's own exchange offer for 10 million of its shares. The directors' general broad powers to manage the business and affairs of the corporation are augmented by the specific authority conferred under 8 *Del.C.* § 160(a), permitting the company to deal in its own stock. However, when exercising that power in an effort to forestall a hostile takeover, the board's actions are strictly held to the fiduciary standards outlined in *Unocal*. These standards require the directors to determine the best interests of the corporation and its stockholders, and impose an enhanced duty to abjure any action that is motivated by considerations other than a good faith concern for such interests.

The Revlon directors concluded that Pantry Pride's $47.50 offer was grossly inadequate. In that regard the board acted in good faith, and on an informed basis, with reasonable grounds to believe that there existed a harmful threat to the corporate enterprise. The adoption of a defensive measure, reasonable in relation to the threat

---

[1]   A "bust-up" takeover generally refers to a situation in which one seeks to finance an acquisition by selling off pieces of the acquired company, presumably at a substantial profit.

posed, was proper and fully accorded with the powers, duties, and responsibilities conferred upon directors under our law.

However, when Pantry Pride increased its offer to $50 per share, and then to $53, it became apparent to all that the break-up of the company was inevitable. The Revlon board's authorization permitting management to negotiate a merger or buyout with a third party was a recognition that the company was for sale. The duty of the board had thus changed from the preservation of Revlon as a corporate entity to the maximization of the company's value at a sale for the stockholders' benefit. This significantly altered the board's responsibilities under the *Unocal* standards. It no longer faced threats to corporate policy and effectiveness, or to the stockholders' interests, from a grossly inadequate bid. The whole question of defensive measures became moot. The directors' role changed from defenders of the corporate bastion to auctioneers charged with getting the best price for the stockholders at a sale of the company.

This brings us to the lock-up with Forstmann and its emphasis on shoring up the sagging market value of the Notes in the face of threatened litigation by their holders. Such a focus was inconsistent with the changed concept of the directors' responsibilities at this stage of the developments. The impending waiver of the Notes covenants had caused the value of the Notes to fall, and the board was aware of the noteholders' ire as well as their subsequent threats of suit. The directors thus made support of the Notes an integral part of the company's dealings with Forstmann, even though their primary responsibility at this stage was to the equity owners.

The original threat posed by Pantry Pride—the break-up of the company—had become a reality which even the directors embraced. Selective dealing to fend off a hostile-but-determined bidder was no longer a proper objective. Instead, obtaining the highest price for the benefit of the stockholders should have been the central theme guiding director action. Thus, the Revlon board could not make the requisite showing of good faith by preferring the noteholders and ignoring its duty of loyalty to the shareholders. The rights of the former already were fixed by contract. The noteholders required no further protection, and when the Revlon board entered into an auction-ending lock-up agreement with Forstmann on the basis of impermissible considerations at the expense of the shareholders, the directors breached their primary duty of loyalty.

The Revlon board argued that it acted in good faith in protecting the noteholders because Unocal permits consideration of other corporate constituencies. Although such considerations may be permissible, there are fundamental limitations upon that prerogative. A board may have regard for various constituencies in discharging its responsibilities, provided there are rationally related benefits accruing to the stockholders. However, such concern for non-stockholder interests is inappropriate when an auction among active bidders is in progress, and the object no longer is to protect or maintain the corporate enterprise but to sell it to the highest bidder.

Revlon also contended that it had contractual and good faith obligations to consider the noteholders. However, any such duties are limited to the principle that one may not interfere with contractual relationships by improper actions. Here, the rights of the noteholders were fixed by agreement, and there is nothing of substance to suggest that any of those terms were violated. The Notes covenants specifically contemplated a waiver to permit sale of the company at a fair price. The Notes were accepted by the holders on that basis, including the risk of an adverse market effect stemming from a waiver. Thus, nothing remained for Revlon to legitimately protect, and no rationally related benefit thereby accrued to the stockholders. Under such circumstances we must conclude that the merger agreement with Forstmann was unreasonable in relation to the threat posed.

A lock-up is not per se illegal under Delaware law. Its use has been approved in an earlier case. Such options can entice other bidders to enter a contest for control of the corporation, creating an auction for the company and maximizing shareholder profit. Current economic conditions in the takeover market are such that a "white knight" like Forstmann might only enter the bidding for the target company if it receives some form of compensation to cover the risks and costs involved. However, while those lock-ups which draw bidders into the battle benefit shareholders, similar measures which end an active auction and foreclose further bidding operate to the shareholders' detriment.

Recently, the United States Court of Appeals for the Second Circuit invalidated a lock-up on fiduciary duty grounds similar to those here. *Hanson Trust PLC v. ML SCM Acquisition Inc.*, 781 F.2d 264 (2d Cir. 1986).

The court stated:

In this regard, we are especially mindful that some lock-up options may be beneficial to the shareholders, such as those that induce a bidder to compete for control of a corporation, while others may be harmful, such as those that effectively preclude bidders from competing with the optionee bidder.

In *Hanson Trust*, the bidder, Hanson, sought control of SCM by a hostile cash tender offer. SCM management joined with Merrill Lynch to propose a leveraged buy-out of the company at a higher price, and Hanson in turn increased its offer. Then, despite very little improvement in its subsequent bid, the management group sought a lock-up option to purchase SCM's two main assets at a substantial discount. The SCM directors granted the lock-up without adequate information as to the size of the discount or the effect the transaction would have on the company. Their action effectively ended a competitive bidding situation. The *Hanson* court invalidated the lock-up because the directors failed to fully inform themselves about the value of a transaction in which management had a strong self-interest. "In short, the Board appears to have failed to ensure that negotiations for alternative bids were conducted by those whose only loyalty was to the shareholders."

The Forstmann option had a similar destructive effect on the auction process. Forstmann had already been drawn into the contest on a preferred basis, so the result of the lock-up was not to foster bidding, but to destroy it. The board's stated reasons for approving the transactions were: (1) better financing, (2) noteholder protection, and (3) higher price. As the Court of Chancery found, and we agree, any distinctions between the rival bidders' methods of financing the proposal were nominal at best, and such a consideration has little or no significance in a cash offer for any and all shares. The principal object, contrary to the board's duty of care, appears to have been protection of the noteholders over the shareholders' interests.

While Forstmann's $57.25 offer was objectively higher than Pantry Pride's $56.25 bid, the margin of superiority is less when the Forstmann price is adjusted for the time value of money. In reality, the Revlon board ended the auction in return for very little actual improvement in the final bid. The principal benefit went to the directors, who avoided personal liability to a class of creditors to whom the board owed no further duty under the circumstances. Thus, when a board ends an intense bidding contest on an insubstantial basis, and where a significant by-product of that action is to protect the directors against a perceived threat of personal liability for consequences stemming from the adoption of previous defensive measures, the action cannot withstand the enhanced scrutiny which *Unocal* requires of director conduct.

In addition to the lock-up option, the Court of Chancery enjoined the no-shop provision as part of the attempt to foreclose further bidding by Pantry Pride. The no-shop provision, like the lock-up option, while not per se illegal, is impermissible under the *Unocal* standards when a board's primary duty becomes that of an auctioneer responsible for selling the company to the highest bidder. The agreement to negotiate only with Forstmann ended rather than intensified the board's involvement in the bidding contest.

It is ironic that the parties even considered a no-shop agreement when Revlon had dealt preferentially, and almost exclusively, with Forstmann throughout the contest. After the directors authorized management to negotiate with other parties, Forstmann was given every negotiating advantage that Pantry Pride had been denied: cooperation from management, access to financial data, and the exclusive opportunity to present merger proposals directly to the board of directors. Favoritism for a white knight to the total exclusion of a hostile bidder might be justifiable when the latter's offer adversely affects shareholder interests, but when bidders make relatively similar offers, or dissolution of the company becomes inevitable, the directors cannot fulfill their enhanced Unocal duties by playing favorites with the contending factions. Market forces must be allowed to operate freely to bring the target's shareholders the best price available for their equity. Thus, as the trial court ruled, the shareholders' interests necessitated that the board remain free to negotiate in the fulfillment of that duty.

In conclusion, the Revlon board was confronted with a situation not uncommon in the current wave of corporate takeovers. A hostile and determined bidder sought the company at a price the board was convinced was inadequate. The initial defensive tactics worked to the benefit of the shareholders, and thus the board was able to sustain its *Unocal* burdens in justifying those measures. However, in granting an asset option lock-up to Forstmann, we must conclude that under all the circumstances the directors allowed considerations other than the maximization of shareholder profit to affect their judgment, and followed a course that ended the auction for Revlon, absent court intervention, to the ultimate detriment of its shareholders. No such defensive measure can be sustained when it represents a breach of the directors' fundamental duty of care. In that context the board's action is not entitled to the deference accorded it by the business judgment rule. The measures were properly enjoined. The decision of the Court of Chancery, therefore, is AFFIRMED.

Points for Discussion

1. Revlon *mode.*

What does it mean to say that a company is "for sale"? What factors would you point to in advising a target corporation's directors who have asked whether they are in "*Revlon* mode"? How would you decide when to advise a board that its duties are to conduct an auction to sell the company at the highest possible price?

2. *When is a sale inevitable?*

What is the basis for the court concluding that "when Pantry Pride increased its offer to $50 per share, and then to $53, it became apparent to all that the break-up of the company was inevitable"?

3. *Focus on the lock-up and no shop.*

What was the effect of the "lock-up option" and the "no shop provision" on Pantry Pride? Which "circumstances" made their use impermissible?

4. *Advising corporations in takeovers.*

What factors would you advise a board facing a takeover to focus on in determining both what their duties are and what they need to do to satisfy those duties? How should they determine what kind of scrutiny a court is likely to apply to their decisions?

---

3.   Developments Post-*Revlon*

Let's take a step back and remember that, in general, the board has the responsibility for managing the business and affairs of the corporation. The business judgment rule protects director decisions by presuming that the directors acted in the best interests of the corporation. Thus, one approach to assessing director decisions has been to apply the business judgment rule.

However, some courts have been concerned about applying the business judgment rule in assessing deal protection devices. Their concern is that, when control of the corporation is at stake, if target boards have too much freedom, then they will use these devices to further their own interests, not those of shareholders. A similar concern arose with takeover defenses and, as we have seen, the Delaware courts have established two other legal regimes—other than the business judgment rule—to govern disputes about sales of control and responses to threats to control.

In one approach, when a corporation is for sale, the strict standard of *Revlon* applies and the board must effectively conduct an auction to maximize shareholder value. Under *Revlon*, the board's duty shifts from preserving the corporate entity to getting the best price available for its stockholders. Long-term considerations disappear; the short-term selling price becomes supreme.

A second approach provides that, when a board takes defensive action in response to a hostile takeover bid, but does not seek to sell control, the intermediate standard of *Unocal* governs, and defensive actions can be permissible. The board can take into account long-term factors, and may consider corporate constituents other than shareholders. The important dividing line between *Revlon* and *Unocal* was—and is—whether a corporation is "for sale."

However, *Revlon* did not say when a corporation was "for sale." In *Revlon*, the court said the key moment arrived when "it became apparent to all that the break-up of the company was inevitable," and at that moment an auction was required. But that general statement didn't provide much guidance about the specific facts that would delineate when it was "apparent to all" that the break-up was "inevitable."

Nor did *Revlon* state precisely what a board was permitted to do when the corporation was "for sale." *Revlon* established that the board of a target company did not have unfettered discretion to counter a hostile bid. However, the court made it clear that, consistent with *Unocal*, a target company's board could use a poison pill and other takeover defenses to oppose a bid that it reasonably concluded was clearly inadequate. At the same time, the court said the board could not employ a takeover defense directed at protecting the interests of a non-shareholder constituency unless that defense also provided some significant financial benefit to the target company's shareholders.

a.   Clarification of *Revlon* Duties: *Paramount v. Time*

Paramount Communications, Inc. v. Time, Inc. attempted to clarify when the board's *Revlon* duties were triggered. The case stands, in contrast to *Revlon*, for the proposition that a corporation is not automatically "for sale" every time a board enters negotiations with a third party about a possible acquisition. Although the board has an obligation to secure the highest possible price for the corporation's shareholders, the board does not necessarily have to auction the corporation to the highest bidder. In other words, there are situations in which the board can "just say no."

The facts of the case are complicated, but are an interesting slice of entertainment industry history. Some members of the board of Time, Inc., a Delaware corporation, wanted to expand in the entertainment industry. Time's traditional business was book and magazine publishing, and it owned cable television franchises and provided pay television programming through its Home Box Office and Cinemax subsidiaries. However, several of Time's outside directors resisted the plan to expand. They viewed such a move as a threat to "Time Culture." They feared that a merger with an entertainment company would divert Time's focus from news journalism and threaten Time's editorial integrity.

In June 1988, management distributed a comprehensive long-range plan that examined strategies for the 1990s. Warner Communications was named as a potential acquisition candidate. Time's chairman and CEO J. Richard Munro and president and COO N.J. Nicholas then met with each outside director to discuss long-term strategies, specifically a combination with Warner, whose business they felt complemented Time better than other potential merger candidates. After these discussions, Time's board approved, in principle, a strategic plan for expansion and authorized continued merger discussions with Warner.

Talks between Time and Warner began in August 1988. Although Time had preferred an acquisition involving all cash or cash and securities, it agreed to a stock-for-stock exchange so that Warner's stockholders could retain an equity interest in the new corporation. Time also insisted on having control of the board in order to preserve "a management committed to Time's journalistic integrity." Negotiations failed when the parties could not agree on who would be the top executives of the new corporation. Time pursued other merger alternatives.

In January 1989, Time resumed talks with Warner. Time's board ultimately approved a stock-for-stock merger with Warner on March 3, 1989. The merger would give the Warner shareholders 62% of the combined company. The new company would have a 24-member board, with Time and Warner each initially represented by 12 directors. The board would have entertainment and editorial committees controlled respectively by Warner and Time directors. The rules of the New York Stock Exchange required Time's shareholders to approve the merger. However, because the transaction was cast as a triangular merger, Delaware law did not.

At the March 3 meeting, Time's board adopted several defensive tactics. It agreed to an automatic share exchange with Warner that gave Warner the right to receive 11.1% of Time's outstanding common stock. Time also sought and paid for "confidence letters" from its banks in which the banks agreed to not finance a hostile acquisition of Time. Time agreed to a no-shop clause preventing it from considering any other consolidation proposal regardless of the merits. After the announcement of the transaction, Time publicized the lack of debt in the transaction as being one of its chief benefits. Time scheduled the shareholder vote for June 23 and sent out its proxy materials for the merger on May 24.

On June 7, Paramount Communications announced a $175 per share, all-cash, all-shares "fully negotiable" offer for Time. Time's board found that Paramount's offer was subject to three conditions: (1) that Time terminate its merger agreement and share exchange agreement with Warner; (2) that Paramount obtain acceptable cable franchise transfers from Time; and (3) that DGCL § 203 (the anti-takeover statute) not apply to any subsequent Time-Paramount merger. Time believed that it would take at least several months to satisfy these conditions.

Although Time's financial advisers informed the board that Time's per share value was materially higher than Paramount's $175 offer, the board was concerned that shareholders would not appreciate the long-term benefits of the Warner merger if given the opportunity to accept the Paramount offer. Therefore, Time sought the NYSE's approval to complete the merger without stockholder approval. The NYSE refused.

A day after Paramount announced its offer, Time formally rejected it. Because it continued to believe that the offer presented a threat to Time's control of its own destiny and the "Time Culture," the board chose to recast the form of the Warner transaction. Under the new proposal, Time would make an immediate all-cash offer for 51% of Warner's outstanding stock at $70 per share. The remaining 49% would be purchased at some later date for a mixture of cash and securities worth $70 per share. Time would fund the acquisition of Warner by incurring $7 billion to $10 billion of debt, despite its original assertion that the debt-free nature of the combination was one of its principal benefits. Time also agreed to pay $9 billion to Warner for its goodwill. As a condition of accepting the revised transaction, Warner received a control premium and guarantee that the corporate governance provisions in the original merger agreement would remain. Time agreed not to employ its poison pill against Warner, and unless enjoined, to complete the transaction.

On June 23, 1989, Paramount raised its offer to $200 per share while continuing to maintain that all aspects of the offer were negotiable. On June 26, Time's board rejected the second offer on the grounds that it was still inadequate and that Time's acquisition of Warner "offered a greater long-term value for the stockholders and, unlike Paramount, was not a threat to Time's survival or 'culture.'"

Two groups of Time shareholders (collectively referred to as "Shareholder Plaintiffs") and Paramount sought to enjoin Time's tender offer. The Court of Chancery denied the plaintiffs' motions. The plaintiffs appealed.

Paramount Communications, Inc. v. Time, Inc.

571 A.2d 1140 (Del. 1989)

HORSEY, JUSTICE.

The Shareholder Plaintiffs first assert a *Revlon* claim. They contend that the March 4 Time-Warner agreement effectively put Time up for sale, triggering *Revlon* duties, requiring Time's board to enhance short-term shareholder value and to treat all other interested acquirers on an equal basis. The Shareholder Plaintiffs base this argument on two facts: (i) the ultimate Time-Warner exchange ratio of .465 favoring Warner, resulting in Warner shareholders' receipt of 62% of the combined company; and (ii) the subjective intent of Time's directors as evidenced in their statements that the market might perceive the Time-Warner merger as putting Time up "for sale" and their adoption of various defensive measures.

The Shareholder Plaintiffs further contend that Time's directors, in structuring the original merger transaction to be "takeover-proof," triggered *Revlon* duties by foreclosing their shareholders from any prospect of obtaining a control premium. In short, plaintiffs argue that Time's board's decision to merge with Warner imposed a fiduciary duty to maximize immediate share value and not erect unreasonable barriers to further bids. Therefore, they argue, the Chancellor erred in finding: that Paramount's bid for Time did not place Time "for sale;" that Time's transaction with Warner did not result in any transfer of control; and that the combined Time-Warner was not so large as to preclude the possibility of the stockholders of Time-Warner receiving a future control premium.

Paramount asserts only a *Unocal* claim in which the shareholder plaintiffs join. Paramount contends that the Chancellor, in applying the first part of the *Unocal* test, erred in finding that Time's board had reasonable grounds to believe that Paramount posed both a legally cognizable threat to Time shareholders and a danger to Time's corporate policy and effectiveness. Paramount also contests the court's finding that Time's board made a reasonable and objective investigation of Paramount's offer so as to be informed before rejecting it. Paramount further claims that the court erred in applying *Unocal*'s second part in finding Time's response to be "reasonable." Paramount points primarily to the preclusive effect of the revised agreement which denied Time shareholders the opportunity both to vote on the agreement and to respond to Paramount's tender offer. Paramount argues that the underlying motivation of Time's board in adopting these defensive measures was management's desire to perpetuate itself in office.

The Court of Chancery posed the pivotal question presented by this case to be: Under what circumstances must a board of directors abandon an in-place plan of corporate development in order to provide its shareholders with the option to elect and realize an immediate control premium? As applied to this case, the question becomes: Did Time's board, having developed a strategic plan of global expansion to be launched through a business combination with Warner, come under a fiduciary duty to jettison its plan and put the corporation's future in the hands of its shareholders?

While we affirm the result reached by the Chancellor, we think it unwise to place undue emphasis upon long-term versus short-term corporate strategy. Two key predicates underpin our analysis. First, Delaware law imposes on a board of directors the duty to manage the business and affairs of the corporation. This broad mandate includes a conferred authority to set a corporate course of action, including time frame, designed to enhance corporate profitability.[12] Thus, the question of "long-term" versus "short-term" values is largely irrelevant because directors, generally, are obliged to chart a course for a corporation which is in its best interests without regard to a fixed investment horizon. Second, absent a limited set of circumstances as defined under *Revlon*, a board of directors, while always required to act in an informed manner, is not under any *per se* duty to maximize shareholder value in the short term, even in the context of a takeover. In our view, the pivotal question presented by this case is: "Did Time, by entering into the proposed merger with Warner, put itself up for sale?" A resolution of that issue through application of *Revlon* has a significant bearing upon the resolution of the derivative *Unocal* issue.

We first take up plaintiffs' principal *Revlon* argument, summarized above. In rejecting this argument, the Chancellor found the original Time-Warner merger agreement not to constitute a "change of control" and concluded that the transaction did not trigger *Revlon* duties. The Chancellor's conclusion is premised on a finding that "before the merger agreement was signed, control of the corporation existed in a fluid aggregation of unaffiliated shareholders representing a voting majority—in other words, in the market." The Chancellor's findings of fact are supported by the record and his conclusion is correct as a matter of law. However, we premise our rejection of plaintiffs' *Revlon* claim on different grounds, namely, the absence of any substantial evidence to conclude that Time's board, in negotiating with Warner, made the dissolution or break-up of the corporate entity inevitable, as was the case in *Revlon*.

Under Delaware law there are, generally speaking and without excluding other possibilities, two circumstances which may implicate *Revlon* duties. The first, and clearer one, is when a corporation initiates an active bidding process seeking to sell

---

12   In endorsing this finding, we tacitly accept the Chancellor's conclusion that it is not a breach of faith for directors to determine that the present stock market price of shares is not representative of true value or that there may indeed be several market values for any corporation's stock. We have so held in another context.

itself or to effect a business reorganization involving a clear break-up of the company. However, Revlon duties may also be triggered where, in response to a bidder's offer, a target abandons its long-term strategy and seeks an alternative transaction involving the breakup of the company. Thus, in *Revlon,* when the board responded to Pantry Pride's offer by contemplating a "bust-up" sale of assets in a leveraged acquisition, we imposed upon the board a duty to maximize immediate shareholder value and an obligation to auction the company fairly. If, however, the board's reaction to a hostile tender offer is found to constitute only a defensive response and not an abandonment of the corporation's continued existence, *Revlon* duties are not triggered, though *Unocal* duties attach.[14]

The plaintiffs insist that even though the original Time-Warner agreement may not have worked "an objective change of control," the transaction made a "sale" of Time inevitable. Plaintiffs rely on the subjective intent of Time's board of directors and principally upon certain board members' expressions of concern that the Warner transaction *might* be viewed as effectively putting Time up for sale. Plaintiffs argue that the use of a lock-up agreement, a no-shop clause, and so-called "dry-up" agreements prevented shareholders from obtaining a control premium in the immediate future and thus violated *Revlon.*

We agree with the Chancellor that such evidence is entirely insufficient to invoke *Revlon* duties; and we decline to extend *Revlon*'s application to corporate transactions simply because they might be construed as putting a corporation either "in play" or "up for sale." The adoption of structural safety devices alone does not trigger *Revlon.* Rather, as the Chancellor stated, such devices are properly subject to a *Unocal* analysis.

Finally, we do not find in Time's recasting of its merger agreement with Warner from a share exchange to a share purchase a basis to conclude that Time had either abandoned its strategic plan or made a sale of Time inevitable. The Chancellor found that although the merged Time-Warner company would be large (with a value approaching approximately $30 billion), recent takeover cases have proven that acquisition of the combined company might nonetheless be possible. The legal consequence is that *Unocal* alone applies to determine whether the business judgment rule attaches to the revised agreement.

We turn now to plaintiffs' *Unocal* claim. We begin by noting, as did the Chancellor, that our decision does not require us to pass on the wisdom of the board's decision to enter into the original Time-Warner agreement. That is not a court's task. Our task is simply to review the record to determine whether there is sufficient evi-

---

14   Within the auction process, any action taken by the board must be reasonably related to the threat posed or reasonable in relation to the advantage sought. Thus, a Unocal analysis may be appropriate when a corporation is in a *Revlon* situation and *Revlon* duties may be triggered by a defensive action taken in response to a hostile offer. Since *Revlon,* we have stated that differing treatment of various bidders is not actionable when such action reasonably relates to achieving the best price available for the stockholders.

dence to support the Chancellor's conclusion that the initial Time-Warner agreement was the product of a proper exercise of business judgment.

There is detailed the evidence of the Time board's deliberative approach to expand, beginning in 1983. Time's decision to combine with Warner was made only after what could be fairly characterized as an exhaustive appraisal of Time's future as a corporation. After concluding that the corporation must expand to survive, and beyond journalism into entertainment, the board combed the field of available entertainment companies. By 1987, Time had focused upon Warner; by late July 1988 Time's board was convinced that Warner would provide the best "fit" for Time to achieve its strategic objectives. The record attests to the zealousness of Time's executives, fully supported by their directors, in seeing to the preservation of Time's "culture," i.e., its perceived editorial integrity in journalism. We find ample evidence in the record to support the Chancellor's conclusion that the Time board's decision to expand the business of the company through its March 3 merger with Warner was entitled to the protection of the business judgment rule.

The Chancellor reached a different conclusion in addressing the Time-Warner transaction as revised three months later. He found that the revised agreement was defense-motivated and designed to avoid the potentially disruptive effect that Paramount's offer would have had on consummation of the proposed merger were it put to a shareholder vote. Thus, the court declined to apply the traditional business judgment rule to the revised transaction and instead analyzed the Time board's June 16 decision under *Unocal*. The court ruled that *Unocal* applied to all director actions taken, following receipt of Paramount's hostile tender offer, that were reasonably determined to be defensive. Clearly that was a correct ruling and no party disputes that ruling.

Unocal involved a two-tier, highly coercive tender offer. In such a case, the threat is obvious: shareholders may be compelled to tender to avoid being treated adversely in the second stage of the transaction. In subsequent cases, the Court of Chancery has suggested that an all-cash, all-shares offer, falling within a range of values that a shareholder might reasonably prefer, cannot constitute a legally recognized "threat" to shareholder interests sufficient to withstand a *Unocal* analysis. *AC Acquisitions Corp. v. Anderson, Clayton & Co.*, 519 A.2d 103 (Del. Ch. 1986); *Grand Metropolitan, PLC v. Pillsbury Co.*, 558 A.2d 1049 (Del. Ch. 1988); *City Capital Associates v. Interco, Inc.*, 551 A.2d 787 (Del. Ch. 1988). In those cases, the Court of Chancery determined that whatever threat existed related only to the shareholders and only to price and not to the corporation.

From those decisions, Paramount and the individual plaintiffs extrapolate a rule of law that an all-cash, all-shares offer with values reasonably in the range of acceptable price cannot pose any objective threat to a corporation or its shareholders. Thus, Paramount would have us hold that only if the value of Paramount's offer were determined to be clearly inferior to the value created by management's plan to merge with Warner could the offer be viewed—objectively—as a threat.

Implicit in the plaintiffs' argument is the view that a hostile tender offer can pose only two types of threats: the threat of coercion that results from a two-tier offer promising unequal treatment for non-tendering shareholders; and the threat of inadequate value from an all-shares, all-cash offer at a price below what a target board in good faith deems to be the present value of its shares. Since Paramount's offer was all-cash, the only conceivable "threat," plaintiffs argue, was inadequate value. We disapprove of such a narrow and rigid construction of *Unocal*, for the reasons which follow.

Plaintiffs' position represents a fundamental misconception of our standard of review under *Unocal* principally because it would involve the court in substituting its judgment as to what is a "better" deal for that of a corporation's board of directors. To the extent that the Court of Chancery has recently done so in certain of its opinions, we hereby reject such approach as not in keeping with a proper *Unocal* analysis.

The usefulness of *Unocal* as an analytical tool is precisely its flexibility in the face of a variety of fact scenarios. *Unocal* is not intended as an abstract standard; neither is it a structured and mechanistic procedure of appraisal. Thus, we have said that directors may consider, when evaluating the threat posed by a takeover bid, the "inadequacy of the price offered, nature and timing of the offer, questions of illegality, the impact on 'constituencies' other than shareholders, the risk of nonconsummation, and the quality of securities being offered in the exchange." The open-ended analysis mandated by *Unocal* is not intended to lead to a simple mathematical exercise: that is, of comparing the discounted value of Time-Warner's expected trading price at some future date with Paramount's offer and determining which is the higher. Indeed, in our view, precepts underlying the business judgment rule militate against a court's engaging in the process of attempting to appraise and evaluate the relative merits of a long-term versus a short-term investment goal for shareholders. To engage in such an exercise is a distortion of the *Unocal* process and, in particular, the application of the second part of *Unocal*'s test, discussed below.

In this case, the Time board reasonably determined that inadequate value was not the only legally cognizable threat that Paramount's all-cash, all-shares offer could present. Time's board concluded that Paramount's eleventh-hour offer posed other threats. One concern was that Time shareholders might elect to tender into Paramount's cash offer in ignorance or a mistaken belief of the strategic benefit which a business combination with Warner might produce. Moreover, Time viewed the conditions attached to Paramount's offer as introducing a degree of uncertainty that skewed a comparative analysis. Further, the timing of Paramount's offer to follow issuance of Time's proxy notice was viewed as arguably designed to upset, if not confuse, the Time stockholders' vote. Given this record evidence, we cannot conclude that the Time board's decision of June 6 that Paramount's offer posed a threat to corporate policy and effectiveness was lacking in good faith or dominated by motives of either entrenchment or self-interest.

Paramount also contends that the Time board had not duly investigated Paramount's offer. Therefore, Paramount argues, Time was unable to make an informed decision that the offer posed a threat to Time's corporate policy. Although the Chancellor did not address this issue directly, his findings of fact do detail Time's exploration of the available entertainment companies, including Paramount, before determining that Warner provided the best strategic "fit." In addition, the court found that Time's board rejected Paramount's offer because Paramount did not serve Time's objectives or meet Time's needs. Thus, the record does, in our judgment, demonstrate that Time's board was adequately informed of the potential benefits of a transaction with Paramount. We agree with the Chancellor that the Time board's lengthy pre-June investigation of potential merger candidates, including Paramount, mooted any obligation on Time's part to halt its merger process with Warner to reconsider Paramount. Time's board was under no obligation to negotiate with Paramount. Time's failure to negotiate cannot be fairly found to have been uninformed. The evidence supporting this finding is materially enhanced by the fact that twelve of Time's sixteen board members were outside, independent directors.

We turn to the second part of the *Unocal* analysis. The obvious requisite to determining the reasonableness of a defensive action is a clear identification of the nature of the threat. As the Chancellor correctly noted, this "requires an evaluation of the importance of the corporate objective threatened; alternative methods of protecting that objective; impacts of the 'defensive' action, and other relevant factors." It is not until both parts of the *Unocal* inquiry have been satisfied that the business judgment rule attaches to defensive actions of a board of directors. As applied to the facts of this case, the question is whether the record evidence supports the Court of Chancery's conclusion that the restructuring of the Time-Warner transaction, including the adoption of several preclusive defensive measures, was a *reasonable response* in relation to a perceived threat.

Paramount argues that, assuming its tender offer posed a threat, Time's response was unreasonable in precluding Time's shareholders from accepting the tender offer or receiving a control premium in the immediately foreseeable future. Once again, the contention stems, we believe, from a fundamental misunderstanding of where the power of corporate governance lies. Delaware law confers the management of the corporate enterprise to the stockholders' duly elected board representatives. The fiduciary duty to manage a corporate enterprise includes the selection of a time frame for achievement of corporate goals. That duty may not be delegated to the stockholders. Directors are not obliged to abandon a deliberately conceived corporate plan for a short-term shareholder profit unless there is clearly no basis to sustain the corporate strategy.

Although the Chancellor blurred somewhat the discrete analyses required under *Unocal*, he did conclude that Time's board reasonably perceived Paramount's offer to be a significant threat to the planned Time-Warner merger and that Time's response was not "overly broad." We have found that even in light of a valid threat, management actions that are coercive in nature or force upon shareholders a management-sponsored alternative to a hostile offer may be struck down as unreasonable and non-proportionate responses.

Here, on the record facts, the Chancellor found that Time's responsive action to Paramount's tender offer was not aimed at "cramming down" on its shareholders a management-sponsored alternative, but rather had as its goal the carrying forward of a pre-existing transaction in an altered form. Thus, the response was reasonably related to the threat. The Chancellor noted that the revised agreement and its accompanying safety devices did not preclude Paramount from making an offer for the combined Time-Warner company or from changing the conditions of its offer so as not to make the offer dependent upon the nullification of the Time-Warner agreement. Thus, the response was proportionate. We affirm the Chancellor's rulings as clearly supported by the record. Finally, we note that although Time was required, as a result of Paramount's hostile offer, to incur a heavy debt to finance its acquisition of Warner, that fact alone does not render the board's decision unreasonable so long as the directors could reasonably perceive the debt load not to be so injurious to the corporation as to jeopardize its well being.

Applying the test for grant or denial of preliminary injunctive relief, we find plaintiffs failed to establish a reasonable likelihood of ultimate success on the merits. Therefore, we affirm.

---

b. Aftermath of *Paramount* and Importance of "Change of Control"

After the court sustained the strategic Time-Warner merger in *Paramount v. Time*, it appeared that *Revlon* duties might apply only when the company put itself up for sale or took steps as to make the break-up of the company inevitable. Paramount read that analysis as providing some hope, and perhaps a road map. Paramount's board was committed to acquiring or merging with other companies in the entertainment, media, or communications industry. The unsuccessful bid for Time had been part of Paramount's goal of strategic expansion. It decided to try again, this time with a different target.

In 1990, Paramount first considered a possible combination with Viacom, which had a range of entertainment operations. Viacom was controlled by its Chairman and CEO Sumner M. Redstone, who indirectly owned approximately 85.2% of Viacom's voting Class A stock and approximately 69.2% of Viacom's nonvoting Class B stock through National Amusements, Inc., an entity 91.7% owned by Redstone.

In September 1993, after a few months of negotiations between the companies, the Paramount board unanimously approved an agreement to merge Paramount into Viacom. Under that agreement, the Paramount board agreed to amend its poison pill plan to exempt the proposed merger with Viacom. In addition, the agreement had several defensive provisions designed to make competing bids more difficult, including a no-shop provision, a termination fee, and a stock option agreement.

Under the no-shop provision, Paramount agreed not to solicit, encourage, discuss, negotiate, or endorse any competing transaction unless: (a) a third party made an unsolicited proposal not subject to any material financing contingencies and (b) the Paramount board determined that it must negotiate with the third party to comply with its fiduciary duties.

The termination fee provision provided that Viacom would receive $100 million if: (a) Paramount terminated the merger agreement because of a competing transaction; (b) Paramount's stockholders did not approve the merger; or (c) the Paramount Board recommended a competing transaction.

The most significant defensive measure, the stock option agreement, gave Viacom an option to purchase approximately 19.9% of Paramount's outstanding common stock at $69.14 per share if the termination fee was triggered. The agreement also had two unusual provisions that were highly beneficial to Viacom: (a) Viacom was to pay for the shares with a senior subordinated note of questionable marketability rather than cash, avoiding the need to raise the $1.6 billion purchase price; and (b) Viacom could require Paramount to pay a cash sum equal to the difference between the purchase price and the market price of Paramount's stock. The stock option agreement had no limit to its maximum dollar value.

Paramount and Viacom publicly announced their proposed merger and indicated that it was a virtual certainty. Redstone described it as a "marriage" that would "never be torn asunder" and stated that only a "nuclear attack" could break the deal. Further, aware that QVC was also interested in acquiring Paramount, Redstone called QVC Chairman and CEO Barry Diller to discourage him from making a competing bid.

QVC was not discouraged. Instead, it proposed a merger with Paramount in which QVC would acquire Paramount for approximately $80 per share (0.893 shares of QVC common stock and $30 in cash) and indicated its willingness to negotiate further with Paramount. The Paramount board ignored this proposal without investigating its value. Thereafter, QVC moved to enjoin the Paramount-Viacom merger and announced an $80 tender offer for 51% of Paramount's outstanding shares (the remaining shares to be converted into QVC common stock in a second-step merger). This bid was $10 more per share than the consideration the Paramount shareholders would receive in the proposed Viacom merger. Viacom realized that it needed to revise the terms of the merger agreement and thus, as the Delaware Supreme Court stated, "in effect, the opportunity for a 'new deal' with Viacom was at hand for the Paramount Board. With the QVC hostile bid offering greater value to the Paramount stockholders, the Paramount Board had considerable leverage with Viacom."

The amended merger agreement did not substantially change the terms of the transaction other than offering the Paramount shareholders more consideration and providing the Paramount board slightly more flexibility. The defensive measures were not removed. Paramount did not use its leverage to eliminate the no-shop provision, the termination fee or the stock option agreement.

A bidding war between Viacom and QVC ensued. Viacom's highest tender offer price was $85 a share. QVC's was $90. The Paramount board continued to reject QVC's bid, despite its higher price, because the board determined that QVC's offer was not in the best interests of the shareholders. Several directors believed the Viacom merger would be more advantageous to Paramount's future business prospects than a QVC merger would be.

The Court of Chancery preliminarily enjoined Paramount's defensive measures designed to facilitate the strategic alliance with Viacom and thwart QVC's unsolicited, more valuable tender offer. The Delaware Supreme Court affirmed, holding that Paramount's merger agreement with Viacom constituted a sale of control, triggering the board's *Revlon* duties to auction the corporation to the highest bidder. *Paramount Communications v. QVC Network*, 637 A.2d 34 (Del. 1994). The court determined that the board violated its fiduciary duties in favoring the less-valuable Viacom merger over the QVC offer without adequately informing itself as to the terms of the QVC offer.

First, the Delaware Supreme Court explained in the *QVC* case, public shareholders owned a majority of Paramount's voting stock, so control of the corporation was maintained in "the fluid aggregation of unaffiliated shareholders" and not by a single entity. In the Paramount-Viacom transaction, the Paramount shareholders would receive a minority voting position in the new company. The new controlling shareholder would have the voting power to effect various corporate changes, including materially altering the nature of the corporation. Even though the Paramount board intended the merger with Viacom to further Paramount's long-term strategy, upon sale of control, the new controlling stockholder would have the power to alter that vision. Further, after the sale of the control, the former Paramount shareholders would no longer have leverage to demand a control premium for their shares. "As a result, the Paramount stockholders are entitled to receive, and should receive, a control premium and/or protective devices of significant value. There being no such protective provisions in the Viacom-Paramount transaction, the Paramount directors had an obligation to take the maximum advantage of the current opportunity to realize for the stockholders the best value reasonably available."

The court then held that when *Revlon* applies, the target board has a primary obligation to act reasonably to realize the best value available for the shareholders. This obligation requires the board to be particularly diligent and adequately informed in its negotiations, including a consideration of the cash value, non-cash value, and future value of a strategic alliance in the context of the entire situation and the likelihood of each alternative.

Most important, the court rejected Paramount's argument that the proposed merger did not trigger *Revlon* duties because the transaction did not contemplate a break-up or dissolution of the corporation as *Paramount* had suggested. Rather, returning to Chancellor Allen's decision in *Time-Warner*, the court noted that there had been "no change of control in the original stock-for-stock merger between Time and Warner because Time would be owned by a fluid aggregation of stockholders both before and after the merger." By contrast, if the Paramount-Viacom merger took effect, because CEO Redstone had 89% voting control of Viacom, control of the surviving corporation would no longer exist in a fluid market and the minority shareholders (the former Paramount shareholders) could no longer demand a control premium for their stock.

The court emphasized that in *Paramount v. Time*, it had stated that there were "generally speaking and *without excluding other possibilities*, two circumstances which may implicate *Revlon* duties." Here, the Paramount board did in fact contemplate a change in control because it unintentionally initiated a bidding war by agreeing to sell control of the corporation to Viacom when there was another potential acquirer, QVC, equally interested in bidding on the corporation. Thus the court held that:

> When a corporation undertakes a transaction which will cause: (a) a change in corporate control; or (b) a break-up of the corporate entity, the directors' obligation is to seek the best value reasonably available to the stockholders. This obligation arises because the effect of the Viacom-Paramount transaction, if consummated, is to shift control of Paramount from the public stockholders to a controlling stockholder, Viacom. Neither *Paramount v. Time* nor any other decision of this Court holds that a "break-up" of the company is essential to give rise to this obligation where there is a sale of control.

The court held that the Paramount board had breached its fiduciary obligations by: (1) ignoring QVC's offer, failing to examine critically the competing transactions; (2) failing to obtain and act with due care on reasonably available information that was necessary to compare the two offers to determine which transaction, or an alternative course of action, would provide the best value reasonably available to the shareholders; and (3) by failing to negotiate with both Viacom and QVC to achieve that value.

Even though provisions in the Paramount-Viacom merger agreement precluded the board from negotiating with QVC, the court held that the board's fiduciary duties overrode the terms of the contract. The court noted that the QVC offer gave Paramount an opportunity to renegotiate its contract with Viacom and modify the favorable defensive measures, which impeded the board's ability to realize the best value available for the Paramount shareholders, and was harshly critical of Paramount's failure to make any such effort in an attempt to "cling to its vision of a strategic alliance with Viacom." While Paramount was not obligated to sell the corporation to QVC, it was obligated to carefully evaluate QVC's bid. Indeed, as the court found, at one point, QVC's offer exceeded Viacom's by $1 billion, yet the Paramount board never considered it.

After *Revlon* and *QVC*, Chancellor Allen described the duties of a target board in a sale of control as follows:

> Existing uncertainty respecting the meaning of "*Revlon* duties" was substantially dissipated by the Delaware Supreme Court's opinion in *QVC*. The case teaches a great deal, but it may be said to support these generalizations at least: (1) where a transaction constituted a "change in corporate control", such that the shareholders would thereafter lose a further opportunity to participate in a change of control premium, (2) the board's duty of loyalty requires it to try in good faith to get the best price reasonably available (which specifically means that the board must at least discuss an interest expressed by any financially capable buyer), and (3) in such context courts will employ an (objective) "reasonableness" standard of review (both to the process and the result!) to evaluate whether the directors have complied with their fundamental duties of care and good faith (loyalty). Thus, QVC in effect mediates between the "normalizing" tendency of some prior cases and the more highly regulatory approach of others. It adopts an intermediate level of judicial review which recognizes the broad power of the board to make decisions in the process of negotiating and recommending a "sale of control" transaction, so long as the board is informed, motivated by good faith desire to achieve the best available transaction, and proceeds "reasonably."
>
> With respect to the important question of when these duties are enhanced—specifically, the duty to try in good faith to maximize current share value and the duty to reasonably explore all options (i.e., to talk with all financially responsible parties)—the court's teaching ironically narrowed the range of corporate transactions to which the principle of *Revlon* applies. That is, it explicitly recognized that where a stock for stock merger is involved, the business judgment of the board, concerning the quality and prospects of the stock the shareholders would receive in the merger, would be reviewed deferentially, as in other settings. The holding of *QVC*, however, was that where the stock to be received in the merger was the stock of a corporation under the control of a single individual or a control group, then the transaction should be treated for "*Revlon*

duty" purposes as a cash merger would be treated. How this "change in control" trigger works in instances of mixed cash and stock or other paper awaits future cases.

Equity-Linked Investors, L.P. v. Adams, 705 A.2d 1040 (Del. Ch. 1997).

Points for Discussion

1. Substance vs. process.

Should courts apply different substantive standards to the different kinds of deal protection devices, based on the facts of each case? For example, should courts assess termination fees based on estimates of the acquirer's bidding costs and the chances that a competing bid will emerge? Should courts look specifically at the effect of voting agreements on shareholders, or the effect of no-shops on bidders? Or should courts look more to the process of adopting deal protection devices, which would not necessarily vary by type of device? How important should substance vs. process be in the judicial assessment of deal protection devices?

2. Short-term value vs. long-term value.

In deal protection cases, the courts often assess how the board compared its own assessment of the value of the corporation's shares with the value of an acquirer's offer. What is the rationale for a board's assessment that the current share price does not reflect the long-run value of the corporation? For example, could the board implement deal protection devices, and effectively "just say no," to an offer of double the current price of the corporation's shares? What could support a board's conclusion that the current price accurately reflected the value of the corporation?

3. The spectrum.

Is it possible to assess whether particular deal protection devices will pass judicial muster based on the degree of protection they offer? Put another way, is the key to assessing deal protection devices how much less attractive they make the target to other bidders? If so, why don't the courts explicitly frame their analysis in terms of weighing the costs of making a target less attractive vs. the benefits of ensuring that a deal is completed? Can you describe where the deal protection devices in the cases in this chapter would fit on the spectrum of deal protection, from none to absolute?

4. Shareholder Ratification and the Business Judgment Rule

Finally, we consider the effects of shareholder ratification on judicial review of an M&A deal. One of the most important developments in Delaware law is known as the *Corwin* doctrine. We conclude with some key language from that case.

Corwin v. KKR Financial Holdings LLC

125 A.3d 304 (Del. 2015)

STRINE, CHIEF JUSTICE.

In a well-reasoned opinion, the Court of Chancery held that the business judgment rule is invoked as the appropriate standard of review for a post-closing damages action when a merger that is not subject to the entire fairness standard of review has been approved by a fully informed, uncoerced majority of the disinterested stockholders. For that and other reasons, the Court of Chancery dismissed the plaintiffs' complaint. In this decision, we find that the Chancellor was correct in finding that the voluntary judgment of the disinterested stockholders to approve the merger invoked the business judgment rule standard of review and that the plaintiffs' complaint should be dismissed. For sound policy reasons, Delaware corporate law has long been reluctant to second-guess the judgment of a disinterested stockholder majority that determines that a transaction with a party other than a controlling stockholder is in their best interests.

I. The Court Of Chancery Properly Held That The Complaint Did Not Plead Facts Supporting An Inference That KKR Was A Controlling Stockholder of Financial Holdings

The plaintiffs filed a challenge in the Court of Chancery to a stock-for-stock merger between KKR & Co. L.P. ("KKR") and KKR Financial Holdings LLC ("Financial Holdings") in which KKR acquired each share of Financial Holdings's stock for 0.51 of a share of KKR stock, a 35% premium to the unaffected market price. Below, the plaintiffs' primary argument was that the transaction was presumptively subject to the entire fairness standard of review because Financial Holdings's primary business was financing KKR's leveraged buyout activities, and instead of having employees manage the company's day-to-day operations, Financial Holdings was managed by KKR Financial Advisors, an affiliate of KKR, under a contractual management agreement that could only be terminated by Financial Holdings if it paid a termination fee. As a result, the plaintiffs alleged that KKR was a controlling stockholder of Financial Holdings, which was an LLC, not a corporation.

After carefully analyzing the pled facts and the relevant precedent, the Chancellor held:

[T]here are no well-pled facts from which it is reasonable to infer that KKR could prevent the [Financial Holdings] board from freely exercising its independent judgment in considering the proposed merger or, put differently, that KKR had the power to exact retribution by removing the [Financial Holdings] directors from their offices if they did not bend to KKR's will in their consideration of the proposed merger.

Although the plaintiffs reiterate their position on appeal, the Chancellor correctly applied the law and we see no reason to repeat his lucid analysis of this question.

II. The Court of Chancery Correctly Held That The Fully Informed, Uncoerced Vote Of The Disinterested Stockholders Invoked The Business Judgment Rule Standard Of Review

On appeal, the plaintiffs further contend that, even if the Chancellor was correct in determining that KKR was not a controlling stockholder, he was wrong to dismiss the complaint because they contend that if the entire fairness standard did not apply, *Revlon* did, and the plaintiffs argue that they pled a *Revlon* claim against the defendant directors. But, as the defendants point out, the plaintiffs did not fairly argue below that *Revlon* applied and even if they did, they ignore the reality that Financial Holdings had in place an exculpatory charter provision, and that the transaction was approved by an independent board majority and by a fully informed, uncoerced stockholder vote. Therefore, the defendants argue, the plaintiffs failed to state a non-exculpated claim for breach of fiduciary duty.

But we need not delve into whether the Court of Chancery's determination that *Revlon* did not apply to the merger is correct for a single reason: it does not matter. Because the Chancellor was correct in determining that the entire fairness standard did not apply to the merger, the Chancellor's analysis of the effect of the uncoerced, informed stockholder vote is outcome-determinative, even if *Revlon* applied to the merger.

As to this point, the Court of Chancery noted, and the defendants point out on appeal, that the plaintiffs did not contest the defendants' argument below that if the merger was not subject to the entire fairness standard, the business judgment standard of review was invoked because the merger was approved by a disinterested stockholder majority. The Chancellor agreed with that argument below, and adhered to precedent supporting the proposition that when a transaction not subject to the entire fairness standard is approved by a fully informed, uncoerced vote of the disinterested stockholders, the business judgment rule applies.

Furthermore, although the plaintiffs argue that adhering to the proposition that a fully informed, uncoerced stockholder vote invokes the business judgment rule would impair the operation of *Unocal* and *Revlon*, or expose stockholders to unfair action by directors without protection, the plaintiffs ignore several factors. First, *Unocal* and *Revlon* are primarily designed to give stockholders and the Court of Chancery the tool of injunctive relief to address important M & A decisions in real time, before closing. They were not tools designed with post-closing money damages claims in mind, the standards they articulate do not match the gross negligence standard for director due care liability under *Van Gorkom*, and with the prevalence of exculpatory charter provisions, due care liability is rarely even available.

Second and most important, the doctrine applies only to fully informed, uncoerced stockholder votes, and if troubling facts regarding director behavior were not disclosed that would have been material to a voting stockholder, then the business judgment rule is not invoked. Here, however, all of the objective facts regarding the board's interests, KKR's interests, and the negotiation process, were fully disclosed.

Finally, when a transaction is not subject to the entire fairness standard, the long-standing policy of our law has been to avoid the uncertainties and costs of judicial second-guessing when the disinterested stockholders have had the free and informed chance to decide on the economic merits of a transaction for themselves. There are sound reasons for this policy. When the real parties in interest—the disinterested equity owners—can easily protect themselves at the ballot box by simply voting no, the utility of a litigation-intrusive standard of review promises more costs to stockholders in the form of litigation rents and inhibitions on risk-taking than it promises in terms of benefits to them. The reason for that is tied to the core rationale of the business judgment rule, which is that judges are poorly positioned to evaluate the wisdom of business decisions and there is little utility to having them second-guess the determination of impartial decision-makers with more information (in the case of directors) or an actual economic stake in the outcome (in the case of informed, disinterested stockholders). In circumstances, therefore, where the stockholders have had the voluntary choice to accept or reject a transaction, the business judgment rule standard of review is the presumptively correct one and best facilitates wealth creation through the corporate form.

For these reasons, therefore, we affirm the Court of Chancery's judgment on the basis of its well-reasoned decision.

———

Points for Discussion

1. *What is left of* Revlon?

After *Corwin*, in a post-closing suit for damages, what avenues are available for challenging directors for breach of fiduciary duty? When does *Revlon* still apply? What effect do you think *Corwin* has had on shareholder litigation? Why were the plaintiffs in *Corwin* attempting to cast KKR as a controlling shareholder?

2. How can the board obtain BJR?

One challenging question for management is what they should do to ensure that a transaction is reviewed under the business judgment rule. In an advanced M&A course, you will study numerous issues that matter in this context, including factors set forth by the Delaware Supreme Court in *Kahn v. M&F Worldwide Corp.*, 88 A.3d 635 (2014). Among the conditions that this case, known as *MFW*, considered important were (1) approval by an independent special committee, and (2) approval by an informed and uncoerced "majority of the minority" of shareholders. Courts closely examine whether a special committee truly is independent and empowered to negotiate and make decisions about the deal, and whether the minority shareholders truly are informed and not coerced.

How might a board ensure that the transaction is reviewed under the BJR? What if the approval vote is "bundled" with a shareholder vote on another topic? What if the deal has a very high termination fee, which might "coerce" shareholders into voting yes? One important factor is when the "economic" negotiations begin, meaning a substantive discussion of deal terms. But when does that occur? After the first meeting with the other side's bankers and lawyers? Before that meeting? What if the deal is mentioned by one CEO to the other at their country club? These are difficult fact-based questions, but they can be determinative in litigation over the standard that applies to a deal.

3. When does entire fairness apply?

Corwin refers to its posture as a "post-closing damages action when a merger that is not subject to the entire fairness standard of review has been approved by a fully informed, uncoerced majority of the disinterested stockholders." This raises the question, by distinction, of when does the entire fairness standard apply to a merger?

We have already seen several examples of when this heightened standard applies. Recall the discussion of *Weinberger* and controller cash-out mergers in Chapter 17. Further, recall *Smith v. Van Gorkom* in Chapter 9, when the board breaches its duty of care and the directors are not exculpated from liability under DGCL §102(b)(7). We also saw in Chapter 10 that entire fairness can apply in interested director transactions, such as when a majority of the board has an interest in the transaction or lacks independence from or is dominated by an interested party. For example, in *In re Trados Inc. Shareholder Litigation*, 73 A.3d 17 (Del. Ch. 2013), involving a venture-backed startup, the court applied the entire fairness standard to a board's decision to approve a merger that provided consideration to the preferred shareholders and management, where a majority of the directors were affiliated with either the preferred shareholders or management.

4. *Legal challenges to M&A?*

Shareholders, and their lawyers, often challenge M&A deals, for various reasons. However, consistent with *Corwin*, the Delaware courts have tightened the standards for such challenges, and they have become much less common. One of the key cases in this area, *In re Trulia, Inc. Stockholder Litigation*, 129 A.3d 884 (Del. Ch. 2016), was especially influential, because it rejected settlements of lawsuits challenging M&A deals if the plaintiffs only obtained improvements in disclosures related to the deal. Courts have subsequently rejected settlements of cases unless they obtained "plainly material" disclosures.

Other jurisdictions have followed Delaware in restricting M&A litigation. But that, and many other issues, are for an advanced M&A course!

CHAPTER 19

Securities Fraud and Markets

This chapter covers securities fraud and markets, topics that have been featured in popular films and are a constant source of gossip and news chatter. These topics will be relevant to you even if you are planning a career that has nothing to do with business law. No one wants to be defrauded, and most people would like to understand at least a little bit about stock markets.

On average, a few hundred public companies are sued in securities class actions every year. Recall that *sue* is one of the shareholder rights in our poem of vote, sue, sell, and yell. The securities fraud class action is an important shareholder right, and it is the key private enforcement mechanism for investors. A federal securities lawsuit is direct, not derivative; it thus contrasts with the state law derivative suits for breaches of fiduciary duty that we have encountered in earlier chapters. Securities fraud litigation is controversial, and complicated. Many lawyers spend their entire careers on securities class actions, some of which can last for a decade or longer.

Unlike derivative suits, securities fraud class actions do not require that demand be made on directors. They do not have the same state law procedural requirements as derivative suits. Instead, securities fraud class actions have elements specified under federal law that purchasers and sellers of securities must plead and prove in order to recover. When a large corporate disaster or fraud is announced, shareholders often will file both forms of litigation—derivative suits and securities class actions—and these two separate lawsuits will move forward in parallel.

We begin this chapter with an overview of securities markets, including a discussion of the theory of market efficiency and some historical background and context. An understanding of the securities markets is important in part because investors who have traded on the basis of company misinformation are essentially alleging that they traded at an unfair price and that they should be able to recover their trading losses from the company and insiders (or others) responsible for the deception.

We then turn to the statute that governs most securities class actions: Section 10(b) of the Securities Exchange Act of 1934. Rule 10b–5 promulgated under Section 10(b) compels honest and full disclosure in all securities-related communications. It creates an important shareholder protection against management deception to securities markets. The possibility of liability for making false or misleading statements of material fact disciplines corporate management perhaps as much as state-based fiduciary duties. In fact, many corporate executives say they worry more about being sued for securities fraud under federal law than for breach of fiduciary duties under state law.

Rule 10b–5 has created a sprawling area of law, and there are whole law courses devoted to the topic of securities litigation. We will focus here on how the Supreme Court, and to some extent Congress, have shaped the contours of the law, and how their changes have become part of the regulatory infrastructure of U.S. stock markets, guiding management of public companies in their public communications and dealings with shareholders.

Finally, we examine three important elements of a securities class action: the *materiality* of alleged misrepresentations, the *scienter* (or state of mind) of any defendants, and the *reliance* of shareholders in public markets on the misrepresentations. In particular, you will notice how the Supreme Court has created a separate, non-overlapping body of disclosure law that regulates corporate governance as a co-equal with state fiduciary law.

"Going public" refers to a private corporation's decision to issue securities to the public and thereby be subject to the system of federal regulation of securities markets. In contrast, "going private" refers to the mirror opposite: the decision by a public corporation to go back to being a private corporation. Most of the world's largest corporations are public (their shares are publicly traded on stock exchanges), but there are some prominent examples of large private corporations. For example, Koch Industries, Cargill, and IKEA are privately owned and a number of startups have grown to significant size before being acquired by other companies or going public. Startups that have done private rounds of financing with valuations of $1 billion or more are sometimes called "unicorns."

We will only scratch the surface of these issues. Securities regulation courses cover more details about these topics, in greater depth. That said, we offer this background about the securities markets and their regulation in the hope you will better understand the ways corporations are regulated and to put into context the chapter that follows on insider trading.

The central message of this chapter is that securities markets are governed primarily by federal law and involve primarily public corporations. Private corporations, sometimes referred to as close or closely held, issue securities, but those securities do not trade in public securities markets. The distinction between public and private corporations already has been important in this course, but now it comes to occupy center stage. Indeed, a private corporation's decision about whether to "go public" or a public corporation's decision about whether to "go private" is among the most important in the corporation's life. The decision is driven by the benefits and costs of accessing the public securities markets and operating as a public company, including the possibility of becoming a defendant in a federal securities class action.

A.   Overview of Securities Markets

We begin by discussing two important background issues: market efficiency and the historical background of the securities markets. Market efficiency relates to how the securities markets generate prices. Understanding some history and context of securities markets also should help you understand some of the issues that follow in this module.

1.   Market Efficiency

One important idea that permeates legal issues related to securities fraud and markets is the notion of "market efficiency." The idea is that information known to some participants in a market is impounded into the market price so it's as though all participants are aware of the information at the same time. Participants in securities markets absorb information from news sources, government reports, company disclosures, and stock trading patterns. They use this data to estimate future cash flows and the risk that such cash flows may not materialize and thus to establish the current price at which they are willing to buy or sell the stock. That is, they engage in a constant ongoing process of valuing corporate securities using the techniques we described in our chapter on accounting and valuation. When they decide a stock is undervalued, their demand to buy the stock leads to an increase in price (in general, greater demand in a market results in higher prices). Conversely, when participants sell stock that they believe is overvalued, their selling depresses the price. Thus, the information that market participants absorb from various sources is impounded into the price of the company's stock.

Of all the existing information about a company, how much actually is impounded into stock prices? If the stock market is completely "informationally efficient"—that is, it reflects *all* information, *both publicly available and privately held*, about risks and cash flows, we would expect that trading by insiders would not be profitable because whatever information an insider possessed would already be reflected in the stock price. We would also predict that dissemination of false or misleading information about a public company would cause no harm because the market price would reflect that the misinformation was false or misleading.

Although there is substantial evidence that stock markets in the United States respond to new information almost instantaneously (for example, company earnings announcements are sometimes read by computers and trading happens in less than a second) and with relative efficiency (new prices remain stable until new information changes them), they are not perfectly informationally efficient. Corporate insiders, who have access to information about anticipated changes in their companies' businesses, can earn abnormal returns (that is returns in excess of market averages, adjusted for risk) when they trade their companies' stock. Nevertheless, because of the relatively high degree of informational efficiency, non-insiders generally cannot expect to earn abnormal returns by trading on the basis of publicly available information. This is an important point: it means (and many studies confirm) that even sophisticated investors, such as mutual fund managers, generally cannot and do not outperform the market after expenses—except through luck. As a result, many pension plans and even individual investors have abandoned the hope of beating the market and have turned to low-cost index funds, which simply hold the stocks in a market segment, such as the S&P 500, at the lowest possible cost. In fact, the largest institutional investors today are Blackrock and Vanguard, both offering mostly low-cost index funds.

There is a good deal of evidence that U.S. public stock markets are relatively efficient at impounding publicly available information. The securities laws are built on this assumption, requiring that companies disclose relevant information when they sell securities to investors and when their securities are traded in public stock markets. In this way, market intermediaries have enough company-specific information to ensure that market prices reflect relevant information—and thus that investors are trading at that price. Likewise, the securities antifraud rules assume that if investors buy or sell when the market price is skewed by materially false or misleading information, the investors will suffer losses because, when the truth is revealed, the market can be expected to re-price the security to reflect the true information.

How informationally efficient are U.S. securities markets? Opinions vary, although the global financial crisis of 2007–08 and the "meme stock" frenzy of early 2021 created some challenges for the proponents of market efficiency. Why didn't bank stocks reflect the risk of insolvency much earlier in the crisis, when many people thought they were essentially insolvent? How much of the fluctuation in bank stock prices was due to changing expectations about a government rescue? And what about GameStop Corp., which was trading below $5 per share in late 2020, but skyrocketed to more than $80 per share on January 25, 2021? What stories might support such wild fluctuations in stock prices?

These questions matter to securities class actions, because the courts are trying to determine whether purchases and sellers of securities were harmed by misrepresentations and omissions by the company and its officers. It can be very challenging to parse how much of a stock's decline (or rise) is due to fraud, as opposed to other factors.

2.   Securities Markets Background

Depending on how you define a security, there have been securities markets for hundreds, or perhaps thousands, of years. In Europe, merchants traded financial interests in a range of business ventures. Over time, this trading became centrally located. For example, in the seventeenth century the Dutch traded shares of companies at the Amsterdam Stock Exchange.

In the United States, securities trading began in New York in 1792, when two dozen stock traders signed the "Buttonwood Agreement" (under a buttonwood tree on Wall Street). During the following century, some trading moved indoors, where a few brokers had rented space; other brokers continued to trade outdoors, on the curb of Wall Street. One of the indoor groups established the organization now known as the New York Stock Exchange, or the NYSE, and it became the premier location for trading securities of U.S. corporations.

After the stock market crash of 1929, investment in all kinds of securities plummeted. During the following three years, reports emerged about many massive corporate frauds. Congress convened a set of hearings on "Stock Exchange Practices" to investigate some of the most wide-ranging scandals, particularly the fraudulent sale of shares by corporations founded by Samuel Insull and Ivar Kreuger, two of the most notorious financiers of the era. By 1933, the American public was outraged about these frauds and was losing faith in securities markets.

> How can so many smart people, with so many tools and so much information, be so fundamentally mistaken? One answer is that investors are simply trying to anticipate what other investors believe particular securities are worth. Fundamental analysis of risk and return has become a game of out-guessing the crowd. As John Maynard Keynes observed after the stock market crash of 1929:
>
> > Professional investment may be likened to those newspaper competitions in which the competitors have to pick the six prettiest faces from a hundred photographs, the prize being awarded to the competitor whose choice most nearly corresponds to the average preference of the competitors as a whole; so that each competitor has to pick, not those faces which he himself finds prettiest, but those which he thinks likeliest to catch the fancy of the other competitors, all of whom are looking at the problem from the same point of view.
>
> John Maynard Keynes, THE GENERAL THEORY OF EMPLOYMENT, INTEREST AND MONEY 156 (1936).

Federal securities laws. In response, Congress enacted the Securities Act of 1933, a federal securities law aimed at restoring public confidence in corporate securities and the stock markets in general. To reassure investors of the soundness of corporate securities, Congress created a kind of "truth in securities" system for the issuance of securities to the public. Like today's requirement that food producers attach a label describing their product's ingredients, calorie count, and fat content, the Securities Act of 1933 requires issuers of securities to "register" their stock issuance and provide investors with detailed information about the company, its management, its plans and finances, and the securities being offered. The theme of the 1933 Securities Act is disclosure, built on a philosophy that information will help protect investors and promote confidence in the integrity of the markets.

In 1934, Congress adopted a companion statute, the Securities Exchange Act of 1934, which created the Securities and Exchange Commission (SEC) to administer the 1933 Securities Act. The 1934 Act also creates periodic disclosure obligations, and regulates the buying and selling of securities by investors in securities trading markets. It contains the prohibitions against fraud that form the basis for securities fraud class actions and insider trading cases.

These federal laws began a dramatic shift away from state regulation of securities markets. Originally, § 18 of the 1933 Securities Act expressly preserved state securities laws, better known as "blue sky" laws after (some say) an early judicial opinion condemning "speculative schemes which have no more basis than so many feet of blue sky." Blue sky laws generally prohibited fraudulent statements in connection with the sales of securities and also required the registration of securities with a state regulator before they could be sold or traded. Because of the overlapping federal and state requirements, when large public offerings were sold in many states, someone (usually counsel for the underwriters) had to "blue sky" the issue to be sure it complied with the laws of every state in which securities were to be offered.

Today, trading of stocks in the United States is highly fractured, and securities are frequently traded "off-exchange." Still, the two major stock exchanges where public companies list their securities for trading remain important: the New York Stock Exchange (NYSE) and NASDAQ (the National Association of Securities Dealers Automated Quotations). The primary difference between the NYSE and NASDAQ is the method of trading. On the NYSE, orders are routed centrally, mostly through "Designated Market Makers," formerly known as "specialists," who act as intermediaries for buyers and sellers. On the NASDAQ, shares are traded in an "over the counter" system, where dealer members post online the prices at which they will buy and sell securities, and other dealers then transact online at those prices. Older, more established firms tend to list their shares on the NYSE, while newer technology firms tend to prefer the NASDAQ.

In 1996, Congress responded to claims that state "blue sky" laws imposed significant costs on U.S. capital formation with few benefits and amended § 18 of the 1933 Securities Act to preempt state regulation for many securities offerings. Specifically, § 18 now precludes state registration requirements for many offerings of securities, including securities that will be listed on the NYSE or NASDAQ and securities that will be exempt from registration under SEC rules as "private placements."

However, some powers are still available to the states. Section 18 still allows states to bring antifraud proceedings, and many state attorneys general do. States also may require that issuers of securities not listed on an exchange pay fees and file documents "substantially similar" to those filed with the SEC. In addition, states may require registration of offerings subject to the intrastate exemption and small-offering exemptions. These issues are covered in courses on securities regulation.

Broker agreements. In addition to federal and state law, securities trading also is governed by contract. Most of you will buy and sell securities at some point, and your likely entry point will be through a broker (whether at an office or online). When you open an account to trade securities, the broker will require that you sign an agreement. Few people read these agreements carefully, just as few people read the financial statements and filings of the companies whose shares they buy. The agreements are mostly boilerplate, but they include some important "private law" provisions that govern much securities trading. For example, brokerage agreements typically provide that disputes will be subject to arbitration, not litigation.

Another important, but often overlooked, provision in many brokerage agreements relates to the voting of corporate shares. In simple terms, private contracts in securities markets frequently remove the ability of shareholders to vote the shares they hold. This disenfranchisement would be a surprise to many shareholders, if they were aware of it.

Here's how it happens. When you open a brokerage account, you have several alternatives, some of which include a provision permitting brokers to lend out your shares. As a result, and often without your knowledge, your broker will take the shares in your account and lend them to someone else.

As long as your shares are loaned out, you technically do not hold the rights, including the voting rights, associated with those shares. In order to vote those shares, you would have to ask your broker to recall the loaned out shares and put them back in your account. Most people are not aware when their shares are loaned-out and do not understand the consequences. The shares that have been loaned out can be sold to another buyer, and that buyer—not the original holder of the shares—will hold the rights associated with those shares. Large institutional investors demand that brokers pay them for the right to lend out their shares, but individual investors frequently permit brokers to lend their shares for free. Individuals often do not read their brokerage agreements, which give this permission, or realize that their brokers can make significant profits by lending out their customer's shares.

This chapter, however, is not meant to be a deep dive into the complex, ever-changing securities markets. Many of the key issues in securities law are covered in advanced securities regulation courses, such as the requirement that offerings of securities must be registered by filing a registration statement with the Securities and Exchange Commission. This "registration requirement" marks a key distinction between public and private corporations. We mention it here to emphasize the limited role played by the SEC. According to the SEC, the purpose of registration is to require enough disclosure to enable investors and their intermediaries to make informed judgments about whether to buy a corporation's securities. The SEC reviews registration statements in an effort to ensure that corporations issuing securities *ex ante* disclose required information. However, the SEC does not guarantee the accuracy of the information contained in a registration statement or a prospectus. Instead, the securities laws, particularly the system of securities litigation, give investors the right to recovery if a corporation made incomplete or inaccurate disclosures. This is why securities litigation *ex post* is such an important part of securities markets. We turn to this category of litigation next.

B. Overview of Private Securities Fraud Actions Under Rule 10b–5

Section 10(b) of the Securities Exchange Act of 1934, and Rule 10b–5 promulgated under this section, do not provide much guidance about what constitutes a violation of the statute and rule. Instead, the federal courts, with the Supreme Court showing the way, have used Rule 10b–5 to create an impressive judge-made regime.

Before we describe an overview of the judge-made elements of securities class actions, and then some statutory provisions added by Congress, take a look at how little Section 10(b) actually says:

Securities Exchange Act of 1934
§ 10—Manipulative and Deceptive Devices

It shall be unlawful for any person . . .

(b) to use or employ, in connection with the purchase or sale of any security, any manipulative or deceptive device or contrivance in contravention of such rules and regulations as the Commission may prescribe.

You might imagine, that with so little guidance from Congress, the Securities and Exchange Commission would set forth a more detailed rule to guide potential litigants, and judges. But here is Rule 10b–5, in its entirety:

---

§ 10b–5 Employment of Manipulative and Deceptive Devices.

It shall be unlawful for any person, directly or indirectly, by the use of any means or instrumentality of interstate commerce, or of the mails or of any facility of any national securities exchange,

(a) To employ any device, scheme, or artifice to defraud,

(b) To make any untrue statement of a material fact or to omit to state a material fact necessary in order to make the statements made, in the light of the circumstances under which they were made, not misleading, or

(c) To engage in any act, practice, or course of business which operates or would operate as a fraud or deceit upon any person,

in connection with the purchase or sale of any security.

Reading the statute and the rule is a useful exercise, if only to show that these words leave a lot of room for judicial interpretation!

1. Judge-Made Elements

Over time, federal courts have articulated the elements of a private cause of action under Rule 10b–5. Basically, any purchaser or seller of a security can sue any person (including a corporation) that (1) makes materially false or misleading statements (2) with an intent to deceive (3) upon which the plaintiff relies (4) causing losses to the plaintiff. The action can be brought as a class action, thus consolidating many smaller claims into one large lawsuit. The action must be brought in federal court, subject to a statute of limitations that runs for 5 years after the fraud (though within two years after the plaintiff has notice of the fraud).

These elements might sound straightforward, but there are numerous subtleties and complexities. We'll just mention a few of them. First, who are the parties to a 10b–5 action? The plaintiffs must have been actual purchasers and sellers. Someone who was fraudulently induced not to trade does not have standing. Defendants include only persons were "primary violators," meaning that their statements induced investors to trade; aiding and abetting does not create private liability. In addition, defendants are liable under 10b–5 only if they had "ultimate control" over false statements. There are many other limitations on as well.

What constitutes a false or deceptive statement? Rule 10b–5 only covers deception, not unfair corporate transactions or breaches of fiduciary duties. That means, for example, that claims of an unfair merger price are not actionable. There are difficult questions about what degree of falsity or deception is required, and when an omission can be misleading.

There also are difficult questions about causation and damages. Plaintiffs typically must establish causation by showing that there was a relationship between one or more "corrective disclosures" (meaning disclosures that revealed the truth about a false or deceptive statement) and a decline in the price of the stock. In practice, expert witnesses testify about the dates on which stock price declines were statistically significant, and whether there were "corrective disclosures" associated with those stock price declines. Experts also testify about the "inflation ribbon" during the class period, the amount by which a stock's price was artificially inflated by the false or misleading statement, and damages are based on the difference between the price a purchaser of the stock actually paid and the lower price they would have paid if the defendants had been truthful.

In the next section, we address specific issues related to three elements of the securities fraud action: materiality, scienter, and reliance. We summarize these three issues briefly here. Information is *material* if there is a substantial likelihood that a reasonable investor would consider it important in deciding whether to buy or sell securities. Courts determine whether information about future events is material by balancing the probability the event will occur and the anticipated magnitude of the event to the affected company.

Scienter is a challenging concept, even in its pronunciation ("sahy-ent-er" is preferred, but many people say "see-ent-er"). Scienter is a mental state that is more than mere negligence, but not necessarily complete knowledge of every aspect of the fraud. Scienter requires some degree of deceptive, manipulative, or fraudulent intent.

Individualized so-called "eyeball" reliance is often not required in securities class actions, meaning that plaintiffs do not need to prove they actually read and relied on the allegedly false or deceptive statements. Instead, reliance by investors in developed securities markets is presumed when publicly available information is reflected in market prices. Expert testimony addresses this concept as well. When plaintiffs seek to certify their class based on allegedly false statements in the public stock market, defendants may attempt to defeat the presumption of reliance by submitting evidence that alleged misrepresentation did not actually affect market price of stock.

> Rule 10b–5 requires that the fraud be "in connection with" the purchase or sale of securities. What does "in connection with" mean? Courts have interpreted the term broadly. For one, there is no requirement of privity. Thus, public statements by a corporation are actionable even if the corporation does not engage in any securities trading itself.
>
> In addition, there is no requirement that the fraud be related to the price of the securities that are traded. Thus, the Supreme Court has held that a stockbroker who falsely assures a customer that his securities account will be safe and then sells securities from the account and pockets the proceeds has committed a fraud "in connection with" securities trading.

There are numerous cases on each of the above points, and the law is constantly developing. One of the key questions in this area, including in Supreme Court cases, is balancing concerns about securities fraud actions being used as "vexatious litigation" brought merely for their settlement value against the recognition that securities litigation likely would not occur without certain presumptions in favor of plaintiffs.

2.   Statutory Requirements

Although the elements of a Rule 10b–5 action are judge-made, Congress has added a number of legislative glosses. The most important come from the Private Securities Litigation Reform Act of 1995 (PLSRA), which sought to tighten some of the procedures and pleading standards in securities fraud litigation. The PSLRA, aimed mostly at abusive class actions alleging securities fraud, affects several 10b–5 elements.

For example, Section 21D(a)(3) of the PSLRA provides that the plaintiff leading a securities class action must be the "most adequate plaintiff," meaning the purchaser or seller with the largest financial stake in the litigation. There are often battles between potential lead plaintiffs to determine who will play that role, and defendants simply wait on the sidelines where plaintiffs exchange their trading records and argue about who suffered greater damages during the class period.

As to materiality, Section 21E(c)(1)(A)(i) provides that statements a company identifies as "forward-looking statements" are not actionable if they are accompanied by "meaningful cautionary statements." As a result, companies often will seek to identify many statements as "forward looking" and provide additional disclosure meant to be cautionary. As to scienter, Section 21D(b)(2) provides that plaintiffs must, for every false or misleading statement, "state with particularity facts giving rise to a strong inference that the defendant acted with the required state of mind." In addition, Section 21D(e) caps damages at the difference between trading price and the average daily price during the 90-day period after corrective disclosure.

Points for Discussion

1. Ebb and flow.

In the 1970s the Supreme Court pared back the reach of the private 10b–5 cause of action. The Court reversed lower court decisions that 10b–5 private liability could be based on negligent misstatements, could arise when an investor was induced not to trade, and could extend to unfair transactions argued to be tantamount to fraud. The Court was adamant that Rule 10b–5 referred to fraud, given the "manipulative or deceptive device or contrivance" language of § 10(b).

In the 1980s and 1990s, the Court clarified what constitutes material information in public stock markets and opened the federal courthouse doors to securities fraud class actions, though carefully limiting who could be sued as defendants. In the 2000s, post-PSLRA, the Court adjusted how open the door is for private securities fraud litigation. It tightened even further who could be defendants, made it more difficult to prove losses arising from securities fraud, and limited the ability of plaintiffs to circumvent the federal procedural restrictions by going to state court. But the Court also clarified how plaintiffs could get past the pleading phase with well-pled inferences of intentional wrongdoing.

More recently, the Court has reaffirmed the "fraud on the market" theory on which securities fraud class actions are based, while providing defendants additional tools to seek early dismissal of cases when the alleged misstatements had not affected market prices and the entity sued did not have ultimate control over the alleged misstatements.

Overall, Congress seems conflicted about securities fraud litigation. Some of the PSLRA provisions add requirements or constraints on private enforcement. Yet

Congress also has breathed life into securities fraud actions, by leaving intact the judicial presumption of reliance in public markets and, in the Sarbanes-Oxley Act, lengthening the statute of limitations to its period of five years or two years from the time a fraud is discovered. Why the ebb and flow?

2. Corporate federalism.

One of the most important decisions in the Supreme Court's extensive 10b–5 jurisprudence came in *Santa Fe Industries v. Green*, 430 U.S. 462 (1977). The case squarely presented the issue whether *unfair corporate practices* could be tantamount to fraud. The stakes were high. If Rule 10b–5 covered unfair practices, corporate governance disputes could easily migrate from state courts enforcing fiduciary duties to federal courts enforcing broad securities fraud standards.

The case arose from a squeeze-out merger at an allegedly unfair price, the corporate defendant had disclosed all of the relevant facts in the merger, including that the minority shareholders were to be paid $150 per share, even though the company's net assets had a value of $640 per share. The Court stated:

> The "fundamental purpose" of the Act is to implement a "philosophy of full disclosure"; once full and fair disclosure has occurred, the fairness of the terms of the transaction is at most a tangential concern of the statute.

> There was no "omission" or "misstatement" in the information statement accompanying the notice of merger. On the basis of the information provided, minority shareholders could either accept the price offered or reject it and seek an appraisal in the Delaware Court of Chancery. Their choice was fairly presented, and they were furnished with all relevant information on which to base their decision.

> The reasoning behind a holding that the complaint in this case alleged fraud under Rule 10b–5 could not be easily contained. The result would be to bring within the Rule a wide variety of corporate conduct traditionally left to state regulation. This extension of the federal securities laws would overlap and quite possibly interfere with state corporate law.

In short, claims of *unfair* treatment of shareholders are a matter for state corporate law—in particular, state court claims for breaches of fiduciary duty and state procedures for appraisal of fair value.

C. Selected Elements of a Securities Fraud Class Action

Recall that in a private securities fraud action the plaintiff must prove the defendant (1) made materially false or misleading statements (2) with an intent to deceive (3) upon which the plaintiff relied (4) causing losses to the plaintiff. The following cases explore the materiality, scienter, and reliance elements. We have broken the first case, *Basic Inc. v. Levinson*, into two parts—the first dealing with standards of materiality in public stock markets and the second dealing with whether investor reliance should be presumed in public markets. The second case, *Tellabs v. Makor Issues & Rights*, deals with the demanding "scienter" pleading standards of the PSLRA.

The excerpts that follow are meant to give you a sense of the arguments surrounding the critical issues of materiality, scienter, and reliance. As you read these cases, notice the importance that the Court (and the parties) attach to resolving these issues at the pleading stage. Because securities fraud class actions rarely go to trial, the effect of a case surviving a motion to dismiss is that it will almost always then be settled.

1. Materiality

Basic Inc. v. Levinson

485 U.S. 224 (1988)

JUSTICE BLACKMUN delivered the opinion of the Court.

This case requires us to apply the materiality requirement of § 10(b) of the Securities Exchange Act of 1934, and the Securities and Exchange Commission's Rule 10b–5, in the context of preliminary corporate merger discussions.

I

Prior to December 20, 1978, Basic Incorporated was a publicly traded company primarily engaged in the business of manufacturing chemical refractories for the steel industry. As early as 1965 or 1966, Combustion Engineering, Inc., a company producing mostly alumina-based refractories, expressed some interest in acquiring Basic, but was deterred from pursuing this inclination seriously because of antitrust concerns it then entertained. In 1976, however, regulatory action opened the way to a renewal of Combustion's interest.

Beginning in September 1976, Combustion representatives had meetings and telephone conversations with Basic officers and directors, including petitioners here, concerning the possibility of a merger. During 1977 and 1978, Basic made three public statements denying that it was engaged in merger negotiations.[4] On December 18,

---

[4]   On October 21, 1977, after heavy trading and a new high in Basic stock, the following news item appeared in the Cleveland Plain Dealer:

> "Basic President Max Muller said the company knew no reason for the stock's activity and that no negotiations were under way with any company for a merger. He said Flintkote recently denied Wall Street rumors that it would make a tender offer of $25 a share for control of the Cleveland- based maker of refractories for the steel industry."

1978, Basic asked the New York Stock Exchange to suspend trading in its shares and issued a release stating that it had been "approached" by another company concerning a merger. On December 19, Basic's board endorsed Combustion's offer of $46 per share for its common stock, and on the following day publicly announced its approval of Combustion's tender offer for all outstanding shares.

Respondents are former Basic shareholders who sold their stock after Basic's first public statement of October 21, 1977, and before the suspension of trading in December 1978. Respondents brought a class action against Basic and its directors, asserting that the defendants issued three false or misleading public statements and thereby were in violation of § 10(b) of the 1934 Act and of Rule 10b–5. Respondents alleged that they were injured by selling Basic shares at artificially depressed prices in a market affected by petitioners' misleading statements and in reliance thereon.

The District Court held that, as a matter of law, any misstatements were immaterial: there were no negotiations ongoing at the time of the first statement, and although negotiations were taking place when the second and third statements were issued, those negotiations were not "destined, with reasonable certainty, to become a merger agreement in principle."

The United States Court of Appeals for the Sixth Circuit reversed the District Court's summary judgment, and remanded the case.

We granted certiorari to resolve the split among the Courts of Appeals as to the standard of materiality applicable to preliminary merger discussions.

II

The 1934 Act was designed to protect investors against manipulation of stock prices. Underlying the adoption of extensive disclosure requirements was a legislative philosophy: "There cannot be honest markets without honest publicity. Manipulation and dishonest practices of the market place thrive upon mystery and secrecy."

The Court previously has addressed various positive and common-law requirements for a violation of § 10(b) or of Rule 10b–5. The Court also explicitly has defined a standard of materiality under the securities laws, *see TSC Industries, Inc. v. Northway, Inc.,* 426 U.S. 438 (1976), concluding in the proxy-solicitation context

---

On September 25, 1978, in reply to an inquiry from the New York Stock Exchange, Basic issued a release concerning increased activity in its stock and stated that

> "management is unaware of any present or pending company development that would result in the abnormally heavy trading activity and price fluctuation in company shares that have been experienced in the past few days."

On November 6, 1978, Basic issued to its shareholders a "Nine Months Report 1978." This Report stated:

> "With regard to the stock market activity in the Company's shares we remain unaware of any present or pending developments which would account for the high volume of trading and price fluctuations in recent months."

that "an omitted fact is material if there is a substantial likelihood that a reasonable shareholder would consider it important in deciding how to vote." It further explained that to fulfill the materiality requirement "there must be a substantial likelihood that the disclosure of the omitted fact would have been viewed by the reasonable investor as having significantly altered the 'total mix' of information made available." We now expressly adopt the *TSC Industries* standard of materiality for the § 10(b) and Rule 10b–5 context.

III

The application of this materiality standard to preliminary merger discussions is not self-evident. Where the impact of the corporate development on the target's fortune is certain and clear, the *TSC Industries* materiality definition admits straight-forward application. Where, on the other hand, the event is contingent or speculative in nature, it is difficult to ascertain whether the "reasonable investor" would have considered the omitted information significant at the time. Merger negotiations, because of the ever-present possibility that the contemplated transaction will not be effectuated, fall into the latter category.

A

Petitioners urge upon us a Third Circuit test for resolving this difficulty. Under this approach, preliminary merger discussions do not become material until "agreement-in-principle" as to the price and structure of the transaction has been reached between the would-be merger partners. By definition, then, information concerning any negotiations not yet at the agreement-in-principle stage could be withheld or even misrepresented without a violation of Rule 10b–5.

Three rationales have been offered in support of the "agreement-in-principle" test. The first derives from the concern that an investor not be overwhelmed by excessively detailed and trivial information, and focuses on the substantial risk that preliminary merger discussions may collapse: because such discussions are inherently tentative, disclosure of their existence itself could mislead investors and foster false optimism. The other two justifications for the agreement-in-principle standard are based on management concerns: because the requirement of "agreement-in-principle" limits the scope of disclosure obligations, it helps preserve the confidentiality of merger discussions where earlier disclosure might prejudice the negotiations; and the test also provides a usable, bright-line rule for determining when disclosure must be made.

The first rationale "assumes that investors are nitwits, unable to appreciate—even when told—that mergers are risky propositions up until the closing." Disclosure, and not paternalistic withholding of accurate information, is the policy chosen and expressed by Congress. We have recognized time and again, a "fundamental purpose" of the various Securities Acts, "was to substitute a philosophy of full disclosure for the philosophy of caveat emptor and thus to achieve a high standard of business ethics in the securities industry."

The second rationale, the importance of secrecy during the early stages of merger discussions, also seems irrelevant to an assessment whether their existence is significant to the trading decision of a reasonable investor. We need not ascertain whether secrecy necessarily maximizes shareholder wealth for this case does not concern the timing of a disclosure; it concerns only its accuracy and completeness. We face here the narrow question whether information concerning the existence and status of preliminary merger discussions is significant to the reasonable investor's trading decision. The "secrecy" rationale is simply inapposite to the definition of materiality.

The final justification offered in support of the agreement-in-principle test seems to be directed solely at the comfort of corporate managers. A bright-line rule indeed is easier to follow than a standard that requires the exercise of judgment in the light of all the circumstances. But ease of application alone is not an excuse for ignoring the purposes of the Securities Acts and Congress' policy decisions.

We therefore find no valid justification for artificially excluding from the definition of materiality information concerning merger discussions, which would otherwise be considered significant to the trading decision of a reasonable investor, merely because agreement-in-principle as to price and structure has not yet been reached by the parties or their representatives.

C

Even before this Court's decision in *TSC Industries*, the Second Circuit had explained the role of the materiality requirement of Rule 10b–5, with respect to contingent or speculative information or events. Under such circumstances, materiality "will depend at any given time upon a balancing of both the indicated probability that the event will occur and the anticipated magnitude of the event in light of the totality of the company activity."

In a subsequent decision, the late Judge Friendly, writing for a Second Circuit panel, applied the *Texas Gulf Sulphur* probability/magnitude approach in the specific context of preliminary merger negotiations. After acknowledging that materiality is something to be determined on the basis of the particular facts of each case, he stated:

> "Since a merger in which it is bought out is the most important event that can occur in a small corporation's life, to wit, its death, we think that inside information, as regards a merger of this sort, can become material at an earlier stage than would be the case as regards lesser transactions—and this even though the mortality rate of mergers in such formative stages is doubtless high."

We agree with that analysis.

Whether merger discussions in any particular case are material therefore depends on the facts. Generally, in order to assess the probability that the event will occur, a factfinder will need to look to indicia of interest in the transaction at the highest corporate levels. Without attempting to catalog all such possible factors, we note by way of example that board resolutions, instructions to investment bankers, and actual negotiations between principals or their intermediaries may serve as indicia of interest. To assess the magnitude of the transaction to the issuer of the securities allegedly manipulated, a factfinder will need to consider such facts as the size of the two corporate entities and of the potential premiums over market value. No particular event or factor short of closing the transaction need be either necessary or sufficient by itself to render merger discussions material.[17]

As we clarify today, materiality depends on the significance the reasonable investor would place on the withheld or misrepresented information. Because the standard of materiality we have adopted differs from that used by both courts below, we remand the case for reconsideration of the question whether a grant of summary judgment is appropriate on this record.

Points for Discussion

1. *Securities fraud class action.*

The case shows you the structure of a securities fraud class action. Shareholders claimed they sold their shares because of false and misleading statements by the corporation, which corporate officials knew were false, and then sought damages from the corporation equal to the difference between the price at which they sold and the eventual merger price that they lost out on. The claims were brought as a class action in which one representative (Levinson) and class counsel (a specialized part of the corporate bar) sought to vindicate the principle of full and honest disclosure in securities markets.

---

[17]   To be actionable, of course, a statement must also be misleading. Silence, absent a duty to disclose, is not misleading under Rule 10b–5. "No comment" statements are generally the functional equivalent of silence. *See* New York Stock Exchange Listed Company Manual § 202.01 (premature public announcement may properly be delayed for valid business purpose and where adequate security can be maintained).

It has been suggested that given current market practices, a "no comment" statement is tantamount to an admission that merger discussions are underway. That may well hold true to the extent that issuers adopt a policy of truthfully denying merger rumors when no discussions are underway, and of issuing "no comment" statements when they are in the midst of negotiations. There are, of course, other statement policies firms could adopt; we need not now advise issuers as to what kind of practice to follow, within the range permitted by law. Perhaps more importantly, we think that creating an exception to a regulatory scheme founded on a prodisclosure legislative philosophy, because complying with the regulation might be "bad for business," is a role for Congress, not this Court.

2. *Reasonable investor in public markets.*

The *TSC Industries* materiality standard refers to what a "reasonable investor" would consider important in a securities transaction. Who is this investor? The Supreme Court's probability plus magnitude test in *Basic* essentially frames the question as one of expected value: what does particular information tell you about the likelihood of a corporate event taking place (like a merger or payment of dividends) and the financial significance of that event? This is precisely the calculation that stock analysts perform in evaluating information and its relevance to prices in public stock markets.

> Normally, silence is not actionable under Rule 10b–5. But as we will see when we study insider trading, there is a duty to speak when defendants have a relationship of trust and confidence with the plaintiff. *See Chiarella v. United States*, 445 U.S. 222 (1980). A duty to speak also arises when majority owners deal with minority shareholder-employees in a close corporation. *See Jordan v. Duff & Phelps, Inc.*, 815 F.2d 429 (7th Cir. 1987) (holding securities firm liable for remaining silent when the firm repurchased the shares of an employee who resigned on the eve of a lucrative merger offer).

3. *Duty to disclose?*

What if the corporate officials in *Basic* had simply stayed quiet and said nothing about the merger negotiations? Is failure to disclose *material* information a violation of Rule 10b–5? The Supreme Court distinguishes a "duty to disclose" and the question of whether particular statements are material. Unless there is a duty to disclose in an SEC filing or to update or correct statements that are "still alive," a company need not disclose material information—no matter how important investors might find it. That is, there is no duty of continuous disclosure under the U.S. securities laws.

4. *Meaning of "no comment."*

Often when we hear politicians say "no comment," we can infer they have something to hide. What about corporate "no comment" statements? The Supreme Court addressed this in *Basic v. Levison* in its important footnote 17. Is that clarification convincing?

> The SEC has issued guidance permitting public companies to *not* disclose pending merger negotiations in their disclosure filings, in recognition of the value of confidential negotiations.
>
> How would you advise the corporate executives in *Basic* to have responded to press inquiries about rumors that the company was engaged in merger negotiations?

---

2.   Scienter

As we have seen, the Supreme Court has required plaintiffs in 10b–5 actions to prove the defendant's scienter, a "mental state embracing intent to deceive, manipulate, or defraud." Generally, this means plaintiffs must show that the defendant was aware of the truth and appreciated the propensity of his statement to mislead.

In addition, Congress has sought to make it hard for shareholders who claim they were misled in their stock trading by creating a heightened pleading standard in 10b–5 actions. Under the PSLRA a complaint alleging securities fraud must "state with particularity facts giving rise to a strong inference that the defendant acted with the required state of mind." Exchange Act § 21D(b)(2). Failure to adequately plead scienter is a frequent basis for dismissal. What "facts" must be pled? What constitutes a "strong inference"? Those were the questions before the Supreme Court in the next case.

Tellabs, Inc. v. Makor Issues & Rights, Ltd.

551 U.S. 308 (2007)

Justice Ginsburg delivered the opinion of the Court.

Exacting pleading requirements are among the control measures Congress included in the PSLRA. The PSLRA requires plaintiffs to state with particularity both the facts constituting the alleged violation, and the facts evidencing scienter, i.e., the defendant's intention "to deceive, manipulate, or defraud." *Ernst & Ernst v. Hochfelder*, 425 U.S. 185, 194, & n. 12 (1976); *see* 15 U.S.C. § 78u–4(b)(1), (2). This case concerns the latter requirement. As set out in § 21D(b)(2) of the PSLRA, plaintiffs must "state with particularity facts giving rise to a strong inference that the defendant acted with the required state of mind." 15 U.S.C. § 78u–4(b)(2).

I

Petitioner Tellabs, Inc., manufactures specialized equipment used in fiber optic networks. During the time period relevant to this case, petitioner Richard Notebaert was Tellabs' chief executive officer and president. Respondents (Shareholders) are persons who purchased Tellabs stock between December 11, 2000, and June 19, 2001. They accuse Tellabs and Notebaert (as well as several other Tellabs executives) of engaging in a scheme to deceive the investing public about the true value of Tellabs' stock.

Beginning on December 11, 2000, the Shareholders allege, Notebaert (and by imputation Tellabs) "falsely reassured public investors, in a series of statements that Tellabs was continuing to enjoy strong demand for its products and earning record revenues," when, in fact, Notebaert knew the opposite was true. From December 2000 until the spring of 2001, the Shareholders claim, Notebaert knowingly misled the public in four ways. First, he made statements indicating that demand for Tellabs' flagship networking device, the TITAN 5500, was continuing to grow, when in fact demand for that product was waning. Second, Notebaert made statements indicating that the TITAN 6500, Tellabs' next-generation networking device, was available for delivery, and that demand for that product was strong and growing, when in truth the product was not ready for delivery and demand was weak. Third, he falsely represented Tellabs' financial results for the fourth quarter of 2000 (and, in connection with those results, condoned the practice of "channel stuffing," under which Tellabs flooded its customers with unwanted products). Fourth, Notebaert made a series of overstated revenue projections, when demand for the TITAN 5500 was drying up and production of the TITAN 6500 was behind schedule. Based on Notebaert's sunny assessments, the Shareholders contend, market analysts recommended that investors buy Tellabs' stock.

The first public glimmer that business was not so healthy came in March 2001 when Tellabs modestly reduced its first quarter sales projections. In the next months, Tellabs made progressively more cautious statements about its projected sales. On June 19, 2001, the last day of the class period, Tellabs disclosed that demand for the TITAN 5500 had significantly dropped. Simultaneously, the company substantially lowered its revenue projections for the second quarter of 2001. The next day, the price of Tellabs stock, which had reached a high of $67 during the period, plunged to a low of $15.87.

On December 3, 2002, the Shareholders filed a class action in the District Court for the Northern District of Illinois. After the first complaint was dismissed for failing to plead their case with the particularity the PSLRA requires, the Shareholders amended their complaint, adding references to 27 confidential sources and making further, more specific, allegations concerning Notebaert's mental state. The District Court again dismissed, this time with prejudice, determining they had insufficiently alleged that he acted with scienter.

The Court of Appeals for the Seventh Circuit reversed in relevant part. It concluded that the Shareholders had sufficiently alleged that Notebaert acted with the requisite state of mind.

We granted certiorari to resolve disagreement among the Circuits on whether, and to what extent, a court must consider competing inferences in determining whether a securities fraud complaint gives rise to a "strong inference" of scienter.

II

In an ordinary civil action, the Federal Rules of Civil Procedure require only "a short and plain statement of the claim showing that the pleader is entitled to relief." Fed. Rule Civ. Proc. 8(a)(2). Prior to the enactment of the PSLRA, the sufficiency of a complaint for securities fraud was governed not by Rule 8, but by the heightened pleading standard set forth in Rule 9(b). Rule 9(b) applies to "all averments of fraud or mistake"; it requires that "the circumstances constituting fraud . . . be stated with particularity" but provides that "malice, intent, knowledge, and other condition of mind of a person may be averred generally."

Setting a uniform pleading standard for § 10(b) actions was among Congress' objectives when it enacted the PSLRA. Designed to curb perceived abuses of the § 10(b) private action—"nuisance filings, targeting of deep-pocket defendants, vexatious discovery requests and manipulation by class action lawyers," the PSLRA installed both substantive and procedural controls. Notably, Congress prescribed new procedures for the appointment of lead plaintiffs and lead counsel. Congress also "limited recoverable damages and attorney's fees, provided a 'safe harbor' for forward-looking statements, . . . mandated imposition of sanctions for frivolous litigation, and authorized a stay of discovery pending resolution of any motion to dismiss." And in § 21D(b) of the PSLRA, Congress "imposed heightened pleading requirements in actions brought pursuant to § 10(b) and Rule 10b–5."

Under the PSLRA's heightened pleading instructions, any private securities complaint alleging that the defendant made a false or misleading statement must: "state with particularity facts giving rise to a strong inference that the defendant acted with the required state of mind." In the instant case the District Court and the Seventh Circuit disagreed on whether the Shareholders "stated with particularity facts giving rise to a strong inference that Notebaert acted with scienter."

> As you read the rest of the material on Rule 10b–5, think about why the Court refers to these suits as "lawyer-driven litigation." Who benefits the most from Rule 10b–5 actions?

With no clear guide from Congress other than its "intention to strengthen existing pleading requirements," Courts of Appeals have diverged in construing the term "strong inference." Among the uncertainties, should courts consider competing inferences in determining whether an inference of scienter is "strong"? Our task is to prescribe a workable construction of the "strong inference" standard, a reading geared to the PSLRA's twin goals: to curb frivolous, lawyer-driven litigation, while preserving investors' ability to recover on meritorious claims.

III

A

We establish the following prescriptions: *First*, faced with a Rule 12(b)(6) motion to dismiss a § 10(b) action, courts must, as with any motion to dismiss for failure to plead a claim on which relief can be granted, accept all factual allegations in the complaint as true.

Second, courts must consider the complaint in its entirety, as well as other sources courts ordinarily examine when ruling on Rule 12(b)(6) motions to dismiss, in particular, documents incorporated into the complaint by reference, and matters of which a court may take judicial notice. The inquiry is whether *all* of the facts alleged, taken collectively, give rise to a strong inference of scienter, not whether any individual allegation, scrutinized in isolation, meets that standard.

Third, in determining whether the pleaded facts give rise to a "strong" inference of scienter, the court must take into account plausible opposing inferences. The Seventh Circuit expressly declined to engage in such a comparative inquiry. A complaint could survive, that court said, as long as it "alleges facts from which, if true, a reasonable person could infer that the defendant acted with the required intent." But in § 21D(b)(2), Congress did not merely require plaintiffs to "provide a factual basis for their scienter allegations," *i.e.*, to allege facts from which an inference of scienter rationally *could* be drawn. Instead, Congress required plaintiffs to plead with particularity facts that give rise to a "strong"—*i.e.*, a powerful or cogent—inference.

The strength of an inference cannot be decided in a vacuum. The inquiry is inherently comparative: How likely is it that one conclusion, as compared to others, follows from the underlying facts? To determine whether the plaintiff has alleged facts that give rise to the requisite "strong inference" of scienter, a court must consider plausible, nonculpable explanations for the defendant's conduct, as well as inferences favoring the plaintiff. Yet the inference of scienter must be more than merely "reasonable" or "permissible"—it must be cogent and compelling, thus strong in light of other explanations. A complaint will survive, we hold, only if a reasonable person would deem the inference of scienter cogent and at least as compelling as any opposing inference one could draw from the facts alleged.[5]

Tellabs contends that when competing inferences are considered, Notebaert's evident lack of pecuniary motive will be dispositive. The Shareholders, Tellabs stresses, did not allege that Notebaert sold any shares during the class period. While it is true that motive can be a relevant consideration, and personal financial gain may weigh heavily in favor of a scienter inference, we agree with the Seventh Circuit that the absence of a motive allegation is not fatal.

Tellabs also maintains that several of the Shareholders' allegations are too vague or ambiguous to contribute to a strong inference of scienter. For example, the Shareholders alleged that Tellabs flooded its customers with unwanted products, a practice known as "channel stuffing." But they failed, Tellabs argues, to specify whether the channel stuffing allegedly known to Notebaert was the illegitimate kind (*e.g.*, writing orders for products customers had not requested) or the legitimate kind (*e.g.*, offering customers discounts as an incentive to buy). We agree that omissions and ambiguities

---

5   Justice Scalia objects to this standard on the ground that "if a jade falcon were stolen from a room to which only A and B had access," it could not "possibly be said there was a 'strong inference' that B was the thief." We suspect, however, that law enforcement officials as well as the owner of the precious falcon would find the inference of guilt as to B quite strong—certainly strong enough to warrant further investigation.

count against inferring scienter. We reiterate, however, that the court's job is not to scrutinize each allegation in isolation but to assess all the allegations holistically. In sum, the reviewing court must ask: When the allegations are accepted as true and taken collectively, would a reasonable person deem the inference of scienter at least as strong as any opposing inference?

IV

We emphasize that under our construction of the "strong inference" standard, a plaintiff is not forced to plead more than she would be required to prove at trial. A plaintiff alleging fraud in a § 10(b) action, we hold today, must plead facts rendering an inference of scienter *at least as likely as* any plausible opposing inference. At trial, she must then prove her case by a "preponderance of the evidence." Stated otherwise, she must demonstrate that it is *more likely* than not that the defendant acted with scienter.

Neither the District Court nor the Court of Appeals had the opportunity to consider the matter in light of the prescriptions we announce today. We therefore vacate the Seventh Circuit's judgment and remand the case so it may be reexamined in accord with our construction of § 21D(b)(2).

JUSTICE SCALIA, concurring in the judgment.

I fail to see how an inference that is merely "at least as compelling as any opposing inference," can conceivably be called what the statute here at issue requires: a "strong inference." If a jade falcon were stolen from a room to which only A and B had access, could it *possibly* be said there was a "strong inference" that B was the thief? I think not, and I therefore think that the Court's test must fail. In my view, the test should be whether the inference of scienter (if any) is *more plausible* than the inference of innocence.

Points for Discussion

1. *True to the spirit of PLSRA?*

Based on your understanding of the PSLRA, in which Congress sought to discourage frivolous 10b–5 lawsuits, whose position seems more consistent with the statute's purpose? Shouldn't allegations by shareholders (and their counsel) of intentional deceit be subjected to a higher threshold of proof? Or did *Tellabs* seek to encourage 10b–5 lawsuits when they seem meritorious?

2. *What's the big deal?*

Why does it matter whether the tie goes to the plaintiff? Isn't this a theoretical exercise? Won't a judge, looking at the allegations in a complaint, be able to determine which inferences (intent to mislead or innocent mistake) are more "cogent and compelling"?

3. Guidance from the Court?

Does *Tellabs* provide useful guidance to lower courts that must decide whether or not to allow securities fraud actions to proceed? For example, the Court says the inferences pointing to scienter must be "cogent and compelling," not simply "reasonable and permissible." What does this mean? The Court also says that for there to be scienter the corporate insider need not be motivated by personal gain, but would evidence that the insider had sold his stock after making a false statement provide a "cogent and compelling" inference of scienter?

Think about the allegations in the case. Given that the CEO Notebaert was aware of internal reports that the company's flagship product was experiencing difficulties, would it be reasonable to infer that he knew his optimistic statements were false? Why did the Supreme Court remand the case?

---

3.   Reliance in Public Markets (and Shareholder Losses)

The SEC has the authority to bring enforcement actions under Rule 10b–5, seeking injunctive relief or civil penalties. The SEC need not prove reliance or causation, but simply that there were materially false or misleading statements made with scienter.

Reliance and causation, elements of traditional common-law deceit, are also elements of a private 10b–5 action. The reliance requirement tests whether the plaintiff's trading was linked to the alleged misrepresentations—it weeds out claims where the misrepresentation had little or no impact on the plaintiff's investment decision. The causation requirement, like proximate cause in tort law, tests the link between the misrepresentation and the plaintiff's loss—it weeds out claims where the securities fraud was not "responsible" for the investor's loss.

Basic Inc. v. Levinson

485 U.S. 224 (1988)

[The part of the opinion laying out the facts and addressing materiality appear earlier in this chapter.]

We must also determine whether a person who traded a corporation's shares on a securities exchange after the issuance of a materially misleading statement by the corporation may invoke a rebuttable presumption that, in trading, he relied on the integrity of the price set by the market.

IV

A

We turn to the question of reliance and the fraud-on-the-market theory. Succinctly put:

> The fraud on the market theory is based on the hypothesis that, in an open and developed securities market, the price of a company's stock is determined by the available material information regarding the company and its business. . . . Misleading statements will therefore defraud purchasers of stock even if the purchasers do not directly rely on the misstatements. . . . The causal connection between the defendants' fraud and the plaintiffs' purchase of stock in such a case is no less significant than in a case of direct reliance on misrepresentations." *Peil v. Speiser*, 806 F. 2d 1154, 1160–1161 (3d Cir. 1986).

Our task, of course, is not to assess the general validity of the theory, but to consider whether it was proper for the courts below to apply a rebuttable presumption of reliance, supported in part by the fraud-on-the-market theory.

In their amended complaint, the named plaintiffs alleged that in reliance on Basic's statements they sold their shares of Basic stock in the depressed market created by petitioners. Requiring proof of individualized reliance from each member of the proposed plaintiff class effectively would have prevented respondents from proceeding with a class action, since individual issues then would have overwhelmed the common ones. The District Court found that the presumption of reliance created by the fraud-on-the-market theory provided "a practical resolution to the problem of balancing the substantive requirement of proof of reliance in securities cases against the procedural requisites of Fed. Rule Civ. Proc. 23." The District Court thus concluded that with reference to each public statement and its impact upon the open market for Basic shares, common questions predominated over individual questions, as required by Fed. Rule Civ. Proc. 23(a)(2) and (b)(3).

Petitioners and their amici complain that the fraud-on-the-market theory effectively eliminates the requirement that a plaintiff asserting a claim under Rule 10b–5 prove reliance. They note that reliance is and long has been an element of common-law fraud, and argue that because the analogous express right of action includes a reliance requirement, so too must an action implied under § 10(b).

We agree that reliance is an element of a Rule 10b–5 cause of action. Reliance provides the requisite causal connection between a defendant's misrepresentation and a plaintiff's injury. There is, however, more than one way to demonstrate the causal connection. Indeed, we previously have dispensed with a requirement of positive proof of reliance, where a duty to disclose material information had been breached, concluding that the necessary nexus between the plaintiffs' injury and the defendant's wrongful conduct had been established. *See Affiliated Ute Citizens v. United States*, 406 U.S. at 153–154.

The modern securities markets, literally involving millions of shares changing hands daily, differ from the face-to-face transactions contemplated by early fraud cases, and our understanding of Rule 10b–5's reliance requirement must encompass these differences.

> The importance of the fraud-on-the market theory was recognized when the case went to the Supreme Court. Amicus briefs urging the Court not to create a presumption of reliance were filed for the American Corporate Counsel Association, various accounting firms, including Arthur Andersen & Co., and the American Institute of Certified Public Accountants. The United States Department of Justice, with the support of the SEC, filed an amicus brief favoring a presumption of reliance.

"In face-to-face transactions, the inquiry into an investor's reliance upon information is into the subjective pricing of that information by that investor. With the presence of a market, the market is interposed between seller and buyer and, ideally, transmits information to the investor in the processed form of a market price. Thus the market is performing a substantial part of the valuation process performed by the investor in a face-to-face transaction. The market is acting as the unpaid agent of the investor, informing him that given all the information available to it, the value of the stock is worth the market price." *In re LTV Securities Litigation*, 88 F. R. D. 134, 143 (N.D. Tex. 1980).

B

Presumptions typically serve to assist courts in managing circumstances in which direct proof, for one reason or another, is rendered difficult. Requiring a plaintiff to show a speculative state of facts, i.e., how he would have acted if omitted material information had been disclosed, or if the misrepresentation had not been made, would place an unnecessarily unrealistic evidentiary burden on the Rule 10b–5 plaintiff who has traded on an impersonal market.

Arising out of considerations of fairness, public policy, and probability, as well as judicial economy, presumptions are also useful devices for allocating the burdens of proof between parties. The presumption of reliance employed in this case is consistent with, and, by facilitating Rule 10b–5 litigation, supports, the congressional policy embodied in the 1934 Act.

The presumption is also supported by common sense and probability. Recent empirical studies have tended to confirm Congress' premise that the market price of shares traded on well-developed markets reflects all publicly available information, and, hence, any material misrepresentations. It has been noted that "it is hard to imagine that there ever is a buyer or seller who does not rely on market integrity. Who would knowingly roll the dice in a crooked crap game?" An investor who buys or sells stock at the price set by the market does so in reliance on the integrity of that price. Because most publicly available information is reflected in market price, an investor's reliance on any public material misrepresentations, therefore, may be presumed for purposes of a Rule 10b–5 action.

C

The Court of Appeals found that petitioners "made public material misrepresentations and plaintiffs sold Basic stock in an impersonal, efficient market. Thus the class, as defined by the district court, has established the threshold facts for proving their loss." The court acknowledged that petitioners may rebut proof of the elements giving rise to the presumption, or show that the misrepresentation in fact did not lead to a distortion of price or that an individual plaintiff traded or would have traded despite his knowing the statement was false.

Any showing that severs the link between the alleged misrepresentation and either the price received (or paid) by the plaintiff, or his decision to trade at a fair market price, will be sufficient to rebut the presumption of reliance. For example, if petitioners could show that the "market makers" were privy to the truth about the merger discussions here with Combustion, and thus that the market price would not have been affected by their misrepresentations, the causal connection could be broken. Similarly, if, despite petitioners' allegedly fraudulent attempt to manipulate market price, news of the merger discussions credibly entered the market and dissipated the effects of the misstatements, those who traded Basic shares after the corrective statements would have no direct or indirect connection with the fraud. Petitioners also could rebut the presumption of reliance as to plaintiffs who would have divested themselves of their Basic shares without relying on the integrity of the market.

JUSTICE WHITE, with whom JUSTICE O'CONNOR joins, concurring in part and dissenting in part.

I

A

At the outset, I note that there are portions of the Court's fraud-on-the-market holding with which I am in agreement. Most importantly, I agree the fraud-on-the-market presumption must be capable of being rebutted by a showing that a plaintiff did not "rely" on the market price. For example, a plaintiff who decides, months in advance of an alleged misrepresentation, to purchase a stock; one who buys or sells a stock for reasons unrelated to its price; one who actually sells a stock "short" days before the misrepresentation is made—surely none of these people can state a valid claim under Rule 10b–5.

B

For while the economists' theories which underpin the fraud-on-the-market presumption may have the appeal of mathematical exactitude and scientific certainty, they are—in the end—nothing more than theories which may or may not prove accurate upon further consideration. Thus, while the majority states that, for purposes of reaching its result it need only make modest assumptions about the way in which "market professionals generally" do their jobs, and how the conduct of market professionals affects stock prices, I doubt that we are in much of a position to assess which theories aptly describe the functioning of the securities industry.

> Do you agree with Justice White—should the Court rely on economic theories to prove legal concepts, or adhere to historical precedents, such as requiring a specific showing of reliance?

Consequently, I cannot join the Court in its effort to reconfigure the securities laws, based on recent economic theories, to better fit what it perceives to be the new realities of financial markets. I would leave this task to others more equipped for the job than we.

C

At the bottom of the Court's conclusion that the fraud-on-the-market theory sustains a presumption of reliance is the assumption that individuals rely "on the integrity of the market price" when buying or selling stock in "impersonal, well-developed markets for securities." It is this aspect of the fraud-on-the-market hypothesis which most mystifies me.

The meaning of this phrase "integrity of the market price" eludes me, for it implicitly suggests that stocks have some "true value" that is measurable by a standard other than their market price. While the scholastics of medieval times professed a means to make such a valuation of a commodity's "worth," I doubt that the federal courts of our day are similarly equipped.

Even if securities had some "value"—knowable and distinct from the market price of a stock—investors do not always share the Court's presumption that a stock's price is a "reflection of [this] value." Indeed, "many investors purchase or sell stock because they believe the price *inaccurately* reflects the corporation's worth." If investors really believed that stock prices reflected a stock's "value," many sellers would never sell, and many buyers never buy.

I do not propose that the law retreat from the many protections that § 10(b) and Rule 10b–5, as interpreted in our prior cases, provide to investors. But any extension of these laws, to approach something closer to an investor insurance scheme, should come from Congress, and not from the courts.

Points for Discussion

1. *Effect of presumption.*

According to the Court, what must a plaintiff show to avoid having to prove that each class member relied on the alleged misrepresentations? What is the effect of the Court's presumption of reliance in "well-developed stock markets"? What must the plaintiffs show to get the presumption? What must the defendant show to overcome the presumption? How likely is it that a defendant would be able to overcome the presumption?

Notice, as did the Court, that without a presumption of reliance private securities fraud class actions often would not be possible. Why does the Court seem to believe that private enforcement is necessary to combat securities fraud in stock markets? Wouldn't it be better if the SEC, using its public enforcement powers, were the one to decide what deceptions harmed investors and which ones undermined the integrity of the stock markets? Or, perhaps, the stock markets themselves (especially the NYSE and NASDAQ) should do the policing, given their strong interest in market integrity.

2. *Should reliance be presumed?*

In his dissent Justice White asserted that the courts are not institutionally well-suited to decide whether one economic theory is better than another one. Does the majority base its presumption of reliance on an economic theory? Or was the majority just making law?

Justice White also points out (in a part of the opinion we did not include) that nearly all of the plaintiffs made money from their sale of Basic stock, which during the class period rose from $20 to $30. Does it make sense to protect these shareholders, who sold in a rising market? Did they believe in the integrity of the market price?

In short, there is reason to question the presumption of reliance. Perhaps the Supreme Court was making law—though maybe for a good cause. For many years after *Basic*, corporate reformers urged that the case be overruled. In 2014, the Supreme Court had its chance—and seriously considered overruling or modifying *Basic*'s presumption of reliance—but ended up declining to do so. *Halliburton Co. v. Erica P. John Fund, Inc.*, 573 U.S. 258 (2014) (*Halliburton II*). The Court seemed to accept that too much water had already passed under the bridge. Congress, which over the years had tinkered with many of the elements of a 10b–5 action, seemed to agree with the Court's conclusion in *Basic* that a presumption of reliance in developed stock markets is good law.

3. *Circularity of recovery from corporation.*

On average, a few hundred securities fraud class actions are filed annually in the United States, most of them "classic" cases of corporate misrepresentations that, when disclosed, usually result in dramatic price drops. Eventually, many of these cases are settled, with class members recovering (some) of their trading losses.

Who pays when a corporation defrauds the market? In the typical case, when the corporation issues fraudulently optimistic news, those investors who bought at artificially-inflated prices recover from the corporation (and sometimes from D&O insurance maintained by the corporation). Payment by the corporation, assuming it is solvent, is thus ultimately borne by the shareholders, including the luckless shareholders who held during the period of false optimism. (The lucky shareholders who sold to the plaintiffs keep their windfall gains.) In short, 10b–5 recovery against the corporation essentially results in one shareholder group (the unlucky holders) subsidizing another shareholder group (the buying victims).

Given that most shareholders (particularly institutional shareholders) are diversified, corporate recovery essentially involves the flow of money from one pocket to another. The only "dead weight" losses come from the costs of litigation—especially the fees paid to lawyers for the plaintiffs and to lawyers for the defendants. Is there any way to justify such a circular system?

For some, the answer is deterrence. To the extent that corporate managers (specifically and generally) respond to litigation by improving disclosure and corporate governance might the system be seen as cost-effective. Although studies indicate that companies that settle securities fraud class actions subsequently undertake corporate governance reforms and then financially out-perform their peers, many continue to question whether the benefits of litigation are worth their costs.

4. *State liability for securities fraud?*

So an obvious question is how state law, particularly in Delaware, handles fraudulent corporate statements in public markets. The simple answer: incompletely. Although Delaware courts recognize that corporate officials have a "duty of disclosure" that permits shareholders to sue for materially false or misleading statements, there is no state-law presumption of reliance for "fraud on the market." The result is that except in corporate acquisitions where shareholders must decide whether to sell their shares or seek appraisal, state disclosure law is mostly dead letter.

The leading Delaware case on the "duty of disclosure" that arises when directors make false statements in public markets offers a curious lesson in double-speak. *Malone v. Brincat*, 722 A.2d 5 (Del.1998). In the following excerpt, notice how the Delaware court speaks in grandiloquent terms about the duties of corporate directors to be completely honest in their communications to shareholders, but then backs away (without much explanation) from creating an effective remedy:

Whenever directors communicate publicly or directly with shareholders about the corporation's affairs, with or without a request for shareholder action, directors have a fiduciary duty to shareholders to exercise due care, good faith and loyalty. It follows *a fortiori* that when directors communicate publicly or directly with shareholders about corporate matters the *sine qua non* of directors' fiduciary duty to shareholders is honesty.

Shareholders are entitled to rely upon the truthfulness of all information disseminated to them by the directors: public statements made to the market, including shareholders; statements informing shareholders about the affairs of the corporation without a request for shareholder action; and, statements to shareholders in conjunction with a request for shareholder action.

When corporate directors impart information they must comport with the obligations imposed by both the Delaware law and the federal statutes and regulations of the United States Securities and Exchange Commission. In deference to the panoply of federal protections that are available to investors in connection with the purchase or sale of securities of Delaware corporations, this Court has decided not to recognize a state common law cause of action against the directors of Delaware corporations for "fraud on the market."

As we have seen, the Delaware courts require disclosure by directors and controlling shareholders when shareholders are asked to sell their shares or seek appraisal—whether in a traditional merger, a tender offer by a controlling shareholder, or a tender offer by the corporation for its own shares (a self-tender). The duty has also been applied in the context of mergers, including short-form mergers, even though no shareholder vote is required and appraisal rights are available.

When the directors are not seeking shareholder action, but are deliberately misinforming shareholders about the business of the corporation, either directly or by a public statement, there is a violation of fiduciary duty. That violation may result in a derivative claim on behalf of the corporation or a cause of action for damages.

Here the complaint alleges (if true) an egregious violation of fiduciary duty by the directors in knowingly disseminating materially false information. Then it alleges that the corporation lost about $2 billion in value as a result. Then it merely claims that the action is brought on behalf of the named plaintiffs and the putative class. It is a *non sequitur* rather than a syllogism.

The plaintiffs never expressly assert a derivative claim on behalf of the corporation or allege compliance with Court of Chancery Rule 23.1, which requires pre-suit demand or cognizable and particularized allegations that demand is excused. If the plaintiffs intend to assert a derivative claim, they should be permitted to replead to assert such a claim and any damage or equitable remedy sought on behalf of the corporation. Likewise, the plaintiffs should have the opportunity to replead to assert any individual cause of action and articulate a remedy that is appropriate on behalf of the named plaintiffs individually, or a properly recognizable class consistent with Court of Chancery Rule 23, and our decision in *Gaffin*.[47]

In the case, the plaintiffs had claimed that the directors had systematically and intentionally overstated corporate earnings over the course of four years. When the company finally corrected its financials, the stock price plummeted. While troubled by the fraud, the Court made clear that the only shareholder remedies would be in a derivative suit showing that the fraud affected *company value* or by individual shareholders showing they had individually relied to their detriment on the false financials.

Does this explain why shareholders (and plaintiffs' counsel) rarely bring "duty of disclosure" cases in Delaware?

————————

[47] Gaffin v. Teledyne, Inc., 611 A.2d at 474 ("A class action may not be maintained in a purely common law or equitable fraud case since individual questions of law or fact, particularly as to the element of justifiable reliance, will inevitably predominate over common questions of law or fact.").

CHAPTER 20

Insider Trading

Suppose you have inside information about a company that, when revealed to the public, is sure to cause the price of the company's stock to skyrocket. Perhaps you have advance notice about a new blockbuster product. Or maybe you learned the company is about to disclose record earnings. When are you prohibited from using this information to buy securities? That, in a nutshell, is the question we address in this chapter.

Insider trading is the subject of considerable regulatory focus and enforcement. The SEC and Department of Justice can be aggressive in targeting illegal insider trading, in the belief that it is crucial to deter such trading to maintain confidence in our financial markets. They bring dozens of high-profile cases every year.

Like the other securities markets issues addressed in this casebook, the law of insider trading today is defined primarily by federal law. Yet its history is rooted in state law and the basic fiduciary duties that we addressed in earlier chapters. Accordingly, we begin this chapter with a discussion of state law. We then describe the three main Supreme Court insider trading cases, which set forth the current law on insider trading. But before we discuss the law of insider trading, we first address the reasons for prohibiting insider trading and ask the most basic question: what is wrong with trading while in possession of inside information?

A. Insider Trading Policy

Imagine two possible approaches to insider trading in financial markets. In the first, which we might label the "Wild West," anyone would be permitted to trade based on any information advantage. Even CEOs could buy and sell shares of their companies before they or the company disclosed important details to the public. In the second, which we might label the "level playing field," no one would be permitted to trade based on any information advantage. Even investors who had scrutinized a company's financial statements and determined that its shares were undervalued would be prohibited from buying shares unless they first disclosed their analysis to the market.

There are downsides to each of these polar approaches. In the "Wild West," insiders could take unfair advantage of other stock traders and cause investors to lose confidence in stock investing. In the "level playing field," those with an information advantage (even if fairly obtained) would not be able to profit from their insights and investors would have little incentive to participate in the stock markets. But what, precisely, would be the harm of a "Wild West"? And what exactly are the costs of a "level playing field"? To address these questions, we consider arguments for and against insider trading.

1. Arguments for Insider Trading

Some have made the provocative (and controversial) argument that insider trading is good and should not be prohibited. That is, investors and stock markets would be better off in the "Wild West."

Recall our earlier discussion about the "informational efficiency" of stock markets. As information about a company enters the market—whether good news or bad news—the forces of supply and demand cause the market price to adjust. Buying on favorable inside information will put upward pressure on the price of the stock; and selling on unfavorable inside information will put downward pressure on the stock price. As the stock price moves, it will more accurately reflect the value of the stock. One view of insider trading is that it will help to direct capital to its highest-valued use.

Insider trading signals information to stock markets. Those who *argue* for insider trading point out that such trading transmits critical and difficult-to-communicate information to the stock markets, permitting smoother price movements before inside information is ultimately disclosed. Insiders who buy on undisclosed good news drive up the price, and insiders who sell on undisclosed bad news drive it down. Moreover, competitively-sensitive information can be transmitted to stock markets, without disclosing its specific contents.

But the argument raises questions. Wouldn't stock markets and investors prefer full disclosure, as opposed to smoother prices? And isn't actual disclosure of good or bad news clearer and more effective than signaling through insider trading? And if widespread insider trading did signal information the company might not want to disclose, such as a top-secret new product or a disastrous earnings report, wouldn't the corporate preference for nondisclosure be compromised?

Moreover, even when markets know that insiders are trading (as required by federal reporting requirements), price responses are skewed. Studies show that markets react quickly when insiders buy (presumably on the basis of good news), but only slightly when insiders sell (perhaps uncertain why the insider is selling).

Insider trading compensates management. Those who argue for insider trading point out that it can be seen as a form of executive compensation that creates incentives for managers to take risks that benefit investors. Because managers are inherently risk-averse, the possibility of profitable insider trading encourages managers to make business decisions with net positive value, even if the decisions are highly risky. If the risks pay off, everyone—insiders and outsiders—shares in a larger pie.

But again, there are questions. If managers can profit by selling company stock or stock options before bad news is disclosed, doesn't this create an incentive to produce bad results? And if insider trading on bad news is a reward for taking risks that sometimes don't pan out, why wouldn't managers simply aim for failure?

Perhaps insider trading could be limited to trading on good news. But this form of executive compensation raises additional questions. How can insider trading accurately measure the insider's contribution, if any, to particular good news in the firm? And, if all the insiders are given carte blanche to trade on good news, who will mind the store? Won't insiders become focused on maximizing their individual stock trading positions, instead of advancing the company's best interests?

2. Arguments Against Insider Trading

The arguments against insider trading and for its prohibition are varied—and suggest different legal approaches based on concerns ranging from fairness to economics.

Insider trading is unfair. The most fundamental argument against insider trading is that insiders should not be allowed to benefit from information generated for a corporate purpose. Accordingly, insiders who trade on inside information unfairly exploit shareholders in the company (or investors about to become shareholders) who trusted the insiders to be working for the company's best interest, not their own.

But is this intuitive argument valid? Trading in the securities of publicly held companies occurs primarily on anonymous stock markets in which buyers and sellers are randomly matched with each other. It has been argued that insider trading does not harm investors who trade with insiders, but rather harms those whose trades are affected by the insider's trades. Under this analysis, if the insider's buying causes the price to rise, those investors induced to sell are harmed when they fail to profit from the subsequent good news. Similarly, if an insider's selling causes the price to fall, those investors induced to buy suffer a price decrease when bad news is ultimately disclosed.

But remember that it is unclear whether trading volume actually affects trading patterns and the stock price. In informationally efficient markets, additional buying or selling may not constitute "new information" that changes stock valuations. Therefore, concerns about the unfairness of insider trading could perhaps be better expressed in terms of a harm to perceptions of the integrity and fairness of the market more generally rather than specific harm to individuals trading with insiders.

Insider trading distorts company disclosures. Another argument is that insider trading, if permitted, would interfere with informational efficiency in stock markets. Insiders would be encouraged to manipulate corporate disclosures or time truthful

The concern that insider trading would induce insiders to manipulate corporate disclosures may have been at the heart of the regulation of short-swing trading by designated insiders. As we will see at the end of this chapter, § 16 of the Securities Exchange Act of 1934 calls for the disgorgement of any insider-trading profits based on trades during a six-month window, thus reducing the incentives of corporate insiders to manipulate stock prices for their own trading benefit.

disclosure to the markets so they could exploit their informational advantage. At the extreme, investors might regard markets as so distorted that they would be unwilling to trade.

According to this argument, informational flows in and out of the company would be distorted if insider trading were permitted. Disclosure delays would be predictable as information flowed up the corporate ladder and insiders at each rung took advantage of it before passing it along. Further, once particular insiders had traded, they would seek to release the information expeditiously to assure their trading profits—even when disclosure might be contrary to the company's best interests.

But, as some have asserted, why would insiders want to manipulate the content or timing of disclosures if doing so would undermine the credibility of the firm in its communications to investors? This rejoinder may be wishful thinking. It assumes that the incentives for insiders to bolster corporate credibility outweigh their personal incentives to trade profitably in their company's stock. As we have seen, many securities fraud class actions involve the release by corporate executives of false or misleading information aimed at making more profitable their personal trading in the company's stock.

Insider trading is theft of company information. Others argue that insider trading is essentially the use of private information owned by the company. As such, prohibitions against insider trading can be seen as protection of intellectual property.

Just as trade secrets, patents, and other informational property are protected to encourage the production of socially valuable information, inside information is protected to encourage companies to create it. For example, a mining company that strikes a rich ore deposit will want to use this information to obtain mining rights from adjacent property owners, without running the risk that insider trading will reveal the strike.

Insider trading prohibitions simply recognize that as between the company and the insider, valuable company information belongs to the company, not the insider. The prohibition against insider trading is a way of protecting company information. Not only does treating inside information as company property encourage its production (good news), but protecting adverse information from insider exploitation (bad news) also reduces the company's cost of capital and increases its reputation for integrity.

But if insider trading exploits company property, why don't we see private enforcement of insider trading rules? Certainly, companies enforce their rights in patents, trademarks, and other valuable proprietary information; but the norm in insider trading cases is *public enforcement* (often prosecutions of insiders). Perhaps lack of private enforcement reflects doubts about whether insider trading actually causes harm to the corporation. For example, it is unclear whether insider trading causes companies to lose opportunities, such as the acquisition of mineral rights, or injures the corporate reputation.

Nonetheless, viewing insider trading as theft of proprietary information—where detection is costly and difficult, and valuing the loss may be impossible—explains why public enforcement may be necessary. Since detection of insider trading requires systems of securities surveillance, private civil enforcement may be inadequate to create sufficient disincentives. Only through public systems of surveillance, such as stock markets and government regulators, and through public enforcement, including criminal sanctions, is inside information adequately protected from insider exploitation.

> Countries without insider trading regulation or enforcement often experience wide spreads in bid-ask prices. What does this mean? Normally, the difference between the broker's buying price (bid) and selling price (ask) reflects the "commission" the broker charges for acting as intermediary between sellers and buyers. Thus, if the bid price is $19.90 and the ask price is $20.10, the broker is effectively charging $0.20 for buying stock from one investor and selling it to another investor. But if there is a risk of stock traders using undisclosed inside information, the broker will protect herself by charging a bigger spread—let's say, bid $19.50 and ask $20.50. In this way, if a trader with inside information knows more than the broker, the spread protects the broker. But the effect is a less liquid market. Who wants to pay a one dollar spread, buying stock for $20.50 and knowing that you could resell it for only $19.50?

Insider trading increases firms' cost of capital. Many argue that insider trading undermines investor confidence in stock markets. According to this argument, if insider trading were permitted, investors would take precautions and discount the company's stock price, thereby raising the company's cost of capital (the price at which the company can borrow money or sell securities). When investors in a stock market can't figure out whether insiders are trading on material, nonpublic information, they will assume the worst. They will either not invest in the market or discount the stock of all companies by the risk of insider trading. In jurisdictions without insider trading regulation and enforcement, studies show that this investor self-insurance increases firms' cost of capital.

Why don't firms proactively respond to this possible problem by incurring bonding and monitoring costs to signal to investors their lower likelihood of insider trading? The answer is that many do. For example, most U.S. public companies now limit when insiders can trade in their company's stock. Using "blackouts" and "trading windows," many companies permit insiders to trade only for a specified period (typically 7–30 days) after earnings announcements and other important corporate information is released. One study found that this self-regulation both suppresses trading by insiders and narrows the bid-ask spread for the company's stock. Not only do company-imposed policies affect insider trading but market intermediaries such as brokers price securities to reflect the reduced risk of insider trading once companies adopt such policies.

B.   State Law on Insider Trading

We've observed that contemporary insider trading law and enforcement is primarily focused at the federal level and has developed under § 10(b) of the 1934 Act and Rule 10b–5. Why is this? The following case, *Goodwin v. Agassiz*, offers a window into understanding the limitations of state law on insider trading.

Historically, state courts developed different common law rules regulating insider trading. The "majority rule" rejected imposing an affirmative duty on corporate directors and officers to disclose information that they acquired through their corporate responsibilities. Under this approach, state law on insider trading had limited reach and applicability. In some instances, the plaintiff or prosecutor could complain only of a director or officer's silence, not an actual misrepresentation or misleading disclosure in a purchase or sale of stock. Furthermore, even where there was actionable conduct, the common law tort requirement of privity was often lacking because the stock transaction took place over a stock exchange with an unknown person instead of in a face-to-face dealing.

A few courts, by contrast, adopted a "minority rule," which created a duty to disclose material information acquired by the corporate director or officer to shareholders before trading with them. *See Hotchkiss v. Fischer*, 16 P.2d 531 (Kan. 1932). The "minority rule" (sometimes known as the "Kansas rule") was still limited in certain regards, however. It generally did not apply to impersonal stock markets. In addition, some interpreted it to apply only to transactions between insiders and existing shareholders; selling to a new investor would not be covered.

With that background, let's turn now to our illustrative state law case, *Goodwin v. Agassiz*. The case arose when a stockholder of the Cliff Mining Company, whose stock was listed on the Boston Stock Exchange, sought relief for losses suffered when he sold on the exchange 700 shares of the company's stock to the defendants, who were officers and directors of the corporation. The court accepted the trial judge's findings that the company had started exploration for copper on its land in 1925, acting on certain geological surveys. However, the exploration was not successful, and the company removed its equipment in May 1926.

Meanwhile, in March 1926, an experienced geologist wrote a report theorizing about the existence of copper deposits in the region of the company's holdings. The defendants, believing there was merit to the theory, secured options to land adjacent to the copper belt. Also, anticipating an increase in the value of the stock if the theory proved correct, the defendants purchased shares of the company's stock through an agent.

When the plaintiff learned of the termination of the original exploratory operations from a newspaper article—for which defendants were in no way responsible—he immediately sold his stock. The plaintiff did not know that the purchasers of his stock were officers and directors of the corporation, nor was there any communication between them.

Goodwin v. Agassiz

186 N.E. 659 (Mass. 1933)

RUGG, CHIEF JUSTICE.

The contention of the plaintiff is that the purchase of his stock in the company by the defendants without disclosing to him as a stockholder their knowledge of the geologist's theory, their belief that the theory was true, the keeping secret the existence of the theory, discontinuance by the defendants of exploratory operations begun in 1925 on property of the Cliff Mining Company and their plan ultimately to test the value of the theory, constitute actionable wrong for which he as stockholder can recover.

The trial judge ruled that based on all the circumstances developed by the trial there was no fiduciary relation requiring such disclosure by the defendants to the plaintiff before buying his stock in the manner in which they did.

The directors of a commercial corporation stand in a relation of trust to the corporation and are bound to exercise the strictest good faith in respect to its property and business. The contention that directors also occupy the position of trustee toward individual stockholders in the corporation is plainly contrary to repeated decisions of this court and cannot be supported. In *Smith v. Hurd*, 12 Metc. (Mass.) 371 (1847), it was said by Chief Justice Shaw: "There is no legal privity, relation, or immediate connection, between the holders of shares in a bank, in their individual capacity, on the one side, and the directors of the bank on the other."

The principle thus established is supported by an imposing weight of authority in other jurisdictions.

While the general principle is as stated, circumstances may exist requiring that transactions between a director and a stockholder as to stock in the corporation be set aside. The knowledge naturally in the possession of a director as to the condition of a corporation places upon him a peculiar obligation to observe every requirement of fair dealing when directly buying or selling its stock. Mere silence does not usually amount to a breach of duty, but parties may stand in such relation to each other that an equitable responsibility arises to communicate facts. Purchases and sales of stock dealt in on the stock exchange are commonly impersonal affairs. An honest director would be in a difficult situation if he could neither buy nor sell on the stock exchange shares of stock in his corporation without first seeking out the other actual ultimate party to the transaction and disclosing to him everything which a court or jury might later find that he then knew affecting the real or speculative value of such shares. Business of that nature is a matter to be governed by practical rules. Fiduciary obligations of directors ought not to be made so onerous that men of experience and ability will be deterred from accepting such office. Law in its sanctions is not coextensive with morality. It cannot undertake to put all parties to every contract on an equality as to knowledge, experience, skill and shrewdness. It cannot undertake to relieve against hard bargains made between competent parties without fraud.

On the other hand, directors cannot rightly be allowed to indulge with impunity in practices which do violence to prevailing standards of upright businessmen. Therefore, where a director personally seeks a stockholder for the purpose of buying his shares without making disclosure of material facts within his peculiar knowledge and not within reach of the stockholder, the transaction will be closely scrutinized and relief may be granted in appropriate instances. *Strong v. Repide*, 213 U.S. 419 (1909).

The precise question to be decided in the case at bar is whether on the facts found the defendants as directors had a right to buy stock of the plaintiff, a stockholder. Every element of actual fraud or misdoing by the defendants is negatived by the findings. Fraud cannot be presumed; it must be proved. The facts found afford no ground for inferring fraud or conspiracy. The only knowledge possessed by the defendants not open to the plaintiff was the existence of a theory formulated in a thesis by a geologist as to the possible existence of copper deposits where certain geological conditions existed common to the property of the Cliff Mining Company and that of other mining companies in its neighborhood. This thesis did not express an opinion that copper deposits would be found at any particular spot or on property of any specified owner. Whether that theory was sound or fallacious, no one knew, and so far as appears has never been demonstrated. The defendants made no representations to anybody about the theory. No facts found placed upon them any obligation to disclose the theory. A few days after the thesis expounding the theory was brought to the attention of the defendants, the annual report by the directors of the Cliff Mining Company for the calendar year 1925, signed by Agassiz for the directors, was issued. It did not cover the time when the theory was formulated. The report described the status of the operations under the exploration which had been begun in 1925. At the annual meeting of the stockholders of the company held early in April, 1926, no reference was made to the theory. It was then at most a hope, possibly an expectation. It had not passed the nebulous stage. No disclosure was made of it. The Cliff Mining Company was not harmed by the nondisclosure. There would have been no advantage to it, so far as appears, from a disclosure. The disclosure would have been detrimental to the interests of another mining corporation in which the defendants were directors. In the circumstances there was no duty on the part of the defendants to set forth to the stockholders at the annual meeting their faith, aspirations and plans for the future.

The stock of the Cliff Mining Company was bought and sold on the stock exchange. The identity of buyers and sellers of the stock in question in fact was not known to the parties and perhaps could not readily have been ascertained. The plaintiff was no novice. He was a member of the Boston Stock Exchange and had kept a record of sales of Cliff Mining Company stock. He acted upon his own judgment in selling his stock. He made no inquiries of the defendants or of other officers of the company. The result is that the plaintiff cannot prevail.

Decree dismissing bill affirmed with costs.

Points for Discussion

1. *Majority rule and candor.*

As noted, *Goodwin* reflects the so-called "majority rule" that, absent fraud or application of the "special facts" doctrine, directors and officers have no state-based fiduciary duty to disclose material nonpublic information when trading company securities in an impersonal market. Is this consistent with other doctrines that we have studied in corporate law such as the "duty of candor" that corporate fiduciaries have to be honest in their communications with shareholders?

2. *Materiality.*

Perhaps *Goodwin* did not actually involve insider trading because the information available to the insiders (the geologist's theory) was not material—that is, it was not information that reasonable investors would have considered important in valuing Cliff Mining's stock. Is that why the court rejected the plaintiff's claim? Would the outcome have been different if the insiders had traded after learning of a major mineral strike on the company's land?

3. *Special facts.*

Goodwin recognized that a different rule or "exception" to the "majority rule" exists—the "special facts doctrine" enunciated in *Strong v. Repide*, 213 U.S. 419 (1909). Under this doctrine, although an insider normally owes no fiduciary duty to individual shareholders, a plaintiff may have a remedy "where, by reason of the special facts, such duty exists." In *Strong v. Repide*, the defendant was a director, majority shareholder, and general manager of the corporation. He was in negotiations to sell otherwise worthless property owned by the corporation to the U.S. government at a substantial price. To hide his identity from the selling shareholder, he used an undisclosed agent to purchase the plaintiff's shares at a price that did not reflect the pending (and very lucrative) deal with the government.

What counts as "special facts"? Courts have not provided a bright-line rule or definition, but have usually applied the doctrine in instances in which the director or officer had knowledge of the likelihood or certainty of a significant event such as a forthcoming merger or takeover bid, a sale of assets, or a liquidation (as in *Strong v. Repide*).

It is also worth noting that, ironically, the "majority rule" may be inaptly labeled. In *Bailey v. Vaughn*, 359 S.E. 2d 599, 603–04 (W. Va. 1987), the Supreme Court of West Virginia surveyed a number of "majority rule" cases and observed that when they are closely analyzed, it is "difficult to conclude that the court intends to create a per se rule of no liability as there is often some limiting language." It found that "there is presently no majority rule that enables a director to utilize insider information which points to substantial undervaluation of the corporate shares and then to purchase shares from an uninformed shareholder without any liability." Furthermore, it noted that the distinction between the so-called "minority rule" and "special facts doctrine" is "shadowy at best" and reflect significant overlap in logic.

4. Fraud.

Goodwin left open the possibility that shareholders may have recourse against insiders who commit fraud when they trade in their company's securities. The common law tort of deceit, which varies somewhat from state to state, basically requires the plaintiff to prove five elements: (1) The defendant misrepresented a material fact (2) with knowledge of its falsity or with reckless disregard for the truth and (3) with the intention that the plaintiff rely, and (4) the plaintiff justifiably relied on defendant's misrepresentation (5) to her detriment.

Traditional fraud law suffers from several serious drawbacks from a plaintiff's perspective. In a typical case of insider trading the defendant makes no statements, material or otherwise, when trading in company stock. Even if silence could be actionable—because of a special relationship between the parties—the plaintiff must prove her reliance on the silence, which may be nearly impossible.

5. Corporate recovery.

Isn't the corporation, given its interest in the faithfulness of its fiduciaries and the integrity of trading in its stock, harmed by insider trading? Shouldn't the corporation be able to recover the ill-gotten gains of corporate fiduciaries who misused inside information?

Before the development of federal insider trading law, which began in earnest in the 1980s, some state courts held that the corporation could recover trading profits realized by insiders, even though it had suffered no loss. In 1949, the Delaware

Chancery Court said that a corporation engaged in an undisclosed stock repurchase program could recover from insiders who knew about the program and had competed against the corporation by purchasing stock for themselves. *Brophy v. Cities Service Co.,* 70 A.2d 5 (Del. Ch. 1949). According to the court, corporate recovery was possible even if the corporation did not suffer any actual financial loss. In 1969, the New York Court of Appeals came to a similar conclusion, holding that a corporation could recover against insiders who traded on nonpublic corporate information, even though the corporation suffered no loss. *Diamond v. Oreamuno,* 248 N.E.2d 910 (N.Y. 1969).

These state law fiduciary duty cases for harm to the corporation by insider trading are still on the books and widely cited, but the cause of action has not been frequently asserted. In subsequent years, a large body of federal law addressing insider trading developed and has been the focus of greater enforcement activity.

C. Federal Law on Insider Trading

Despite these forays of state law into insider trading, most regulation in this area is federal. Congress's earliest attempt to rein in insider trading was through the enactment of § 16 of the Securities Exchange Act of 1934. But § 16—which we describe more fully in the final section of this chapter—only applies to purchases and sales by specified insiders of their own company's stock within a six-month period. It creates a remedy that forces the insider to disgorge their trading profits, but has proved to be ineffective against the most common forms of insider trading. For example, it does not apply to trading by insiders who have held their stock more than six months; nor does it apply to trading by outsiders on the basis of material nonpublic information.

Instead, the SEC and the courts have relied primarily on the SEC's Rule 10b–5 to regulate the intentional misuse of inside information. Rule 10b–5—which was the subject of the previous chapter on securities fraud—frequently has been described as a "judicial oak" that grew from little more than a "legislative acorn." Authority for the rule—the legislative acorn—comes from § 10(b) of the Securities Exchange Act of 1934, which authorizes the SEC to promulgate rules forbidding the use of "any manipulative or deceptive device or contrivance" in connection with the purchase or sale of any security. Borrowing language from § 17(a) of the Securities Act of 1933, which applies to deception in the sale of securities, the SEC drafted Rule 10b–5 to cover deception "in connection with the *purchase* or *sale* of securities."

When it adopted Rule 10b–5, the SEC had little idea that courts would seize on the rule to make it the mainstay of U.S. securities fraud regulation. Significantly, the rule itself contains no express language prohibiting insider trading. The SEC did not use the rule to pursue insider trading activity until several decades after its adoption.

An early SEC enforcement action, *In the Matter of Cady, Roberts & Co.*, 40 S.E.C. 907 (1961), provided the theoretical basis for early federal judicial cases on insider trading.

In that action, Curtiss-Wright Corporation, a major aircraft manufacturer, had announced that it was developing a new internal combustion engine. As you might guess, the company's stock price rose dramatically. A few weeks later, the company's board of directors met and decided, surprisingly, to cut the company's dividend rate by 40%. One of the directors, a member of a securities firm, left the board meeting during a recess and called from a payphone to tell his office about the dividend cut. On hearing this, a sales rep at the firm sold Curtiss-Wright stock held in various customer accounts. Later that day when news of the dividend cut was released to various financial wire services, the stock price fell 15%.

In a disciplinary case against the firm and the sales rep, the SEC began by intoning that Rule 10b–5 was meant to protect investors and had created "managerial duties and liabilities unknown to the common law." Then, citing the "special facts" cases from state law, the SEC said that when corporate insiders have material nonpublic information they are under a duty to disclose the information before trading or to "forego the transaction." The SEC explained this disclose-or-abstain duty "rests on two principal elements; first, the existence of a relationship giving access to information intended to be available only for a corporate purpose and not for the personal benefit of anyone, and second, the inherent unfairness involved where a party takes advantage of such information knowing it is unavailable to those with whom he is dealing." The SEC acknowledged that it might have been a different case if the securities firm had surmised there would be a dividend cut based on "perceptive analysis of generally known facts." In the end, the SEC suspended the sales rep for 20 days—and the interpretation of Rule 10b–5 as an insider-trading prohibition had arrived.

Following *Cady, Roberts & Co.*, the first major federal court case was *Securities and Exchange Commission v. Texas Gulf Sulphur Co.*, 401 F.2d 833 (2d Cir. 1968). This case presents a classic fact pattern involving insider trading. Texas Gulf Sulphur Co. (TGS) was drilling on a site in Canada and found highly valuable mineral content. As a result, TGS wanted to purchase the site of the minerals, but did not want to attract any competitors. Thus, TGS concealed the mineral content from the public. In the meantime, some officers of TGS were aware of the mineral content and began to buy and sell stock based on this information and pass along the "tip" to outside individuals. When reports that minerals were found in the area began to surface, TGS released a statement that stated that reports of mineral content were "inconclusive." Four days later, TGS officially announced the presence of a major copper-ore strike. In the time between the two statements, a TGS secretary and a TGS engineer bought TGS stock. Also, a TGS director bought TGS stock immediately after the announcement of the mineral content, and his son-in-law, a broker, bought shares for himself and his customers. The Second Circuit held that people with knowledge of material non-public information must either disclose it to the public or refrain from trading in the securities that are affected by the inside information while it is undisclosed. The TGS secretary, officers, and engineer were not permitted to buy TGS stock (or cause others to buy stock) until there was public disclosure of the material information about the minerals at the drilling site. They violated Section 10(b) and Rule 10b–5 of the Securities Exchange Act of 1934 because they traded based on material inside information. In addition, the TGS director was also in violation of Rule 10b–5 because he purchased the stock before the information was fully disseminated and before the market could reflect the information. Note that while this case provides a useful starting point through which to understand insider trading, this case is no longer good law, as some of the holdings have not been adopted by the Supreme Court.

Nevertheless, over the years the SEC and the Supreme Court have inventively interpreted Rule 10b–5 to prohibit insider trading through different theories of liability, which can be applied in open-market transactions as well as in face-to-face dealings. Specifically, the Court has built a federal common law regime built on the notion that it is "deceptive" when a person trades in securities in breach of fiduciary duties or a relationship of trust and confidence.

We turn next to the triumvirate of landmark Supreme Court insider trading cases—the classical theory (*Chiarella*), the tipper-tippee theory (*Dirks*), and the misappropriation theory (*O'Hagan*)—each an important branch of the 10b–5 "judicial oak."

- *Chiarella* establishes the "classical theory" of insider trading—a Rule 10b–5 violation can occur when there is a duty to disclose arising from a relationship of trust and confidence (fiduciary duty) between the parties to the transaction, such as the relationship that the Court said corporate insiders have to the corporation and its shareholders.

- *Dirks* extends the classical theory to "tippers" and "tippees." Tipping by an insider can be a breach of fiduciary duty if "the insider will benefit, directly or indirectly, from his disclosure" and a "tippee" violates Rule 10b–5 if she "knows or should know that there has been a breach." In its famous footnote 14, *Dirks* also indicates that an outsider (such as an underwriter, accountant, attorney, or consultant who receives nonpublic corporate information with the expectation that it will be kept confidential) is considered a "temporary" or "constructive" insider for insider trading law purposes.

O'Hagan establishes the "misappropriation theory" of insider trading—trading on the basis of material nonpublic information in breach of a duty owed to the source of the information. This conduct violates Rule 10b–5, even though the misappropriator owes no duty to the person with whom she trades.

Note that all three cases, and subsequent district and appellate court cases, focus on fiduciary duty. As you read the cases, ask whether this focus on fiduciary duty is consistent with our earlier policy discussion of the pros and cons of insider trading.

1. *Chiarella* and the "Classical" Theory

Chiarella sets out the theory for regulating "classical" insider trading—that is, insider trading by company insiders in their own company's stock. The theory proceeds from the notion that insiders have a duty of "trust and confidence" to the company and its shareholders. But, as we have seen, state law imposes such a duty only in limited circumstances. As you read this case and those that follow, some important questions arise. Where does the duty not to trade on inside information come from? Where does the Supreme Court get the authority to define the contours of that duty? And what does any of this have to do with the reasons to prohibit insider trading?

Chiarella v. United States

445 U.S. 222 (1980)

JUSTICE POWELL delivered the opinion of the Court.

The question in this case is whether a person who learns from the confidential documents of one corporation that it is planning an attempt to secure control of a second corporation violates § 10(b) of the Securities Exchange Act of 1934 if he fails to disclose the impending takeover before trading in the target company's securities.

Petitioner is a printer by trade. In 1975 and 1976, he worked as a "markup man" in the New York composing room of Pandick Press, a financial printer. Among documents that petitioner handled were five announcements of corporate takeover bids. When these documents were delivered to the printer, the identities of the acquiring and target corporations were concealed by blank spaces or false names. The true names were sent to the printer on the night of the final printing.

The petitioner, however, was able to deduce the names of the target companies before the final printing from other information contained in the documents. Without disclosing his knowledge, petitioner purchased stock in the target companies and sold the shares immediately after the takeover attempts were made public. By this method, petitioner realized a gain of slightly more than $30,000 in the course of 14 months. Subsequently, the SEC began an investigation of his trading activities. In May 1977, petitioner entered into a consent decree with the SEC in which he agreed to return his profits to the sellers of the shares. On the same day, he was discharged by Pandick Press.

In January 1978, petitioner was indicted on 17 counts of violating § 10(b) of the Securities Exchange Act of 1934 and SEC Rule 10b–5. After petitioner unsuccessfully moved to dismiss the indictment, he was brought to trial and convicted on all counts.

The Court of Appeals for the Second Circuit affirmed petitioner's conviction. We granted certiorari, and we now reverse.

This case concerns the legal effect of the petitioner's silence. The District Court's charge permitted the jury to convict the petitioner if it found that he willfully failed to inform sellers of target company securities that he knew of a forthcoming takeover bid that would make their shares more valuable. In order to decide whether silence in such circumstances violates § 10(b), it is necessary to review the language and legislative history of that statute as well as its interpretation by the Commission and the federal courts.

Although the starting point of our inquiry is the language of the statute, § 10(b) does not state whether silence may constitute a manipulative or deceptive device. Section 10(b) was designed as a catchall clause to prevent fraudulent practices. But neither the legislative history nor the statute itself affords specific guidance for the resolution of this case. When Rule 10b–5 was promulgated in 1942, the SEC did not discuss the possibility that failure to provide information might run afoul of § 10(b).

The SEC took an important step in the development of § 10(b) when it held that a broker-dealer and his firm violated that section by selling securities on the basis of undisclosed information obtained from a director of the issuer corporation who was also a registered representative of the brokerage firm. In *Cady, Roberts & Co.*, the Commission decided that a corporate insider must abstain from trading in the shares of his corporation unless he has first disclosed all material inside information known to him. The obligation to disclose or abstain derives from

> an affirmative duty to disclose material information which has been traditionally imposed on corporate "insiders," particular officers, directors, or controlling stockholders. We, and the courts have consistently held that insiders must disclose material facts which are known to them by virtue of their position but which are not known to persons with whom they deal and which, if known, would affect their investment judgment.

The Commission emphasized that the duty arose from (i) the existence of a relationship affording access to inside information intended to be available only for a corporate purpose, and (ii) the unfairness of allowing a corporate insider to take advantage of that information by trading without disclosure.

That the relationship between a corporate insider and the stockholders of his corporation gives rise to a disclosure obligation is not a novel twist of the law. At common law, misrepresentation made for the purpose of inducing reliance upon the false statement is fraudulent. But one who fails to disclose material information prior to the consummation of a transaction commits fraud only when he is under a duty to do so. And the duty to disclose arises when one party has information "that the other party is entitled to know because of a fiduciary or similar relation of trust and confidence between them." In its *Cady, Roberts* decision, the Commission recognized a relationship of trust and confidence between the shareholders of a corporation and those insiders who have obtained confidential information by reason of their position with that corporation. This relationship gives rise to a duty to disclose because of the "necessity of preventing a corporate insider from taking unfair advantage of the uninformed minority stockholders."

Thus, silence in connection with the purchase or sale of securities may operate as a fraud actionable under § 10(b) despite the absence of statutory language or legislative history specifically addressing the legality of nondisclosure. But such liability is premised upon a duty to disclose arising from a relationship of trust and confidence between parties to a transaction. Application of a duty to disclose prior to trading guarantees that corporate insiders, who have an obligation to place the shareholder's welfare before their own, will not benefit personally through fraudulent use of material nonpublic information.

The petitioner was convicted of violating § 10(b) although he was not a corporate insider and he received no confidential information from the target company. Moreover, the "market information" upon which he relied did not concern the earning power or operations of the target company, but only the plans of the acquiring company. Petitioner's use of that information was not a fraud under § 10(b) unless he was subject to an affirmative duty to disclose it before trading. In this case, the jury instructions failed to specify any such duty. In effect, the trial court instructed the jury that petitioner owed a duty to everyone; to all sellers, indeed, to the market as a whole. The jury simply was told to decide whether petitioner used material, nonpublic information at a time when "he knew other people trading in the securities market did not have access to the same information."

The Court of Appeals affirmed the conviction by holding that "*anyone*—corporate insider or not—who regularly receives material nonpublic information may not use that information to trade in securities without incurring an affirmative duty to disclose." Although the court said that its test would include only persons who regularly receive material nonpublic information, its rationale for that limitation is unrelated to the existence of a duty to disclose. The Court of Appeals, like the trial court, failed to identify a relationship between petitioner and the sellers that could give rise to a duty. Its decision thus rested solely upon its belief that the federal securities laws have "created a system providing equal access to information necessary for reasoned and intelligent investment decisions."

The use by anyone of material information not generally available is fraudulent, this theory suggests, because such information gives certain buyers or sellers an unfair advantage over less informed buyers and sellers.

This reasoning suffers from two defects. First not every instance of financial unfairness constitutes fraudulent activity under § 10(b). Second, the element required to make silence fraudulent—a duty to disclose— is absent in this case. No duty could arise from petitioner's relationship with the sellers of the target company's securities, for petitioner had no prior dealings with them. He was not their agent, he was not a fiduciary, he was not a person in whom the sellers had placed their trust and confidence. He was, in fact, a complete stranger who dealt with the sellers only through impersonal market transactions.

We cannot affirm petitioner's conviction without recognizing a general duty between all participants in market transactions to forgo actions based on material, nonpublic information. Formulation of such a broad duty, which departs radically from the established doctrine that duty arises from a specific relationship between two parties, should not be undertaken absent some explicit evidence of congressional intent.

As we have seen, no such evidence emerges from the language or legislative history of § 10(b). Moreover, neither the Congress nor the Commission ever has adopted a parity-of-information rule. Instead the problems caused by misuse of market information have been addressed by detailed and sophisticated regulation that recognizes when use of market information may not harm operation of the securities markets. For example, the Williams Act limits but does not completely prohibit a tender offeror's purchases of target corporation stock before public announcement of the offer. Congress' careful action in this and other areas contrasts, and is in some tension, with the broad rule of liability we are asked to adopt in this case.

We see no basis for applying such a new and different theory of liability in this case. As we have emphasized before, the 1934 Act cannot be read "more broadly than its language and the statutory scheme reasonably permit." Section 10(b) is aptly described as a catch-all provision, but what it catches must be fraud. When an allegation of fraud is based upon nondisclosure, there can be no fraud absent a duty to speak. We hold that a duty to disclose under § 10(b) does not arise from the mere possession of nonpublic market information. The contrary result is without support in the legislative history of § 10(b) and would be inconsistent with the careful plan that Congress has enacted for regulation of the securities markets.

In its brief to this Court, the United States offers an alternative theory to support petitioner's conviction. It argues that petitioner breached a duty to the acquiring corporation when he acted upon information that he obtained by virtue of his position as an employee of a printer employed by the corporation. The breach of this duty is said to support a conviction under § 10(b) for fraud perpetrated upon both the acquiring corporation and the sellers.

We need not decide whether this theory has merit for it was not submitted to the jury.

The jury instructions demonstrate that petitioner was convicted merely because of his failure to disclose material, nonpublic information to sellers from whom he bought the stock of target corporations. The jury was not instructed on the nature or elements of a duty owed by petitioner to anyone other than the sellers. Because we cannot affirm a criminal conviction on the basis of a theory not presented to the jury, we will not speculate upon whether such a duty exists, whether it has been breached, or whether such a breach constitutes a violation of § 10(b).

The judgment of the Court of Appeals is reversed.

CHIEF JUSTICE BURGER, dissenting.

I believe that the jury instructions in this case properly charged a violation of § 10(b) and Rule 10b–5, and I would affirm the conviction.

As a general rule, neither party to an arm's-length business transaction has an obligation to disclose information to the other unless the parties stand in some confidential or fiduciary relation. This rule permits a businessman to capitalize on his experience and skill in securing and evaluating relevant information; it provides incentive for hard work, careful analysis, and astute forecasting. But the policies that underlie the rule also should limit its scope. In particular, the rule should give way when an informational advantage is obtained, not by superior experience, foresight, or industry, but by some unlawful means. I would read § 10(b) and Rule 10b–5 to encompass and build on this principle: to mean that a person who has misappropriated nonpublic information has an absolute duty to disclose that information or to refrain from trading.

The Court's opinion, as I read it, leaves open the question whether § 10(b) and Rule 10b–5 prohibit trading on misappropriated nonpublic information. Instead, the Court apparently concludes that this theory of the case was not submitted to the jury. In the Court's view, the instructions given the jury were premised on the erroneous notion that the mere failure to disclose nonpublic information, however acquired, is a deceptive practice. And because of this premise, the jury was not instructed that the means by which Chiarella acquired his informational advantage—by violating a duty owed to the acquiring companies—was an element of the offense.

The evidence shows beyond all doubt that Chiarella, working literally in the shadows of the warning signs in the printshop, misappropriated—stole to put it bluntly—valuable nonpublic information entrusted to him in the utmost confidence.

He then exploited his ill-gotten informational advantage by purchasing securities in the market. In my view, such conduct plainly violates § 10(b) and Rule 10b–5. Accordingly, I would affirm the judgment of the Court of Appeals.

Points for Discussion

1. *Type of trading.*

What type of insider trading—"classical" or "misappropriation"—did Chiarella engage in? Who was hurt by his trading?

2. *Nature of duty.*

The Court decides that § 10(b) and Rule 10b–5 regulate trading on material nonpublic information when there is a relation of "trust and confidence" between the trading parties. Under state law, do corporate fiduciaries have such a duty to shareholders—or to investors who are buying company stock from them? Where does the duty inferred by the Supreme Court come from?

3. *Chiarella's conviction.*

Note that *Chiarella* frames the prohibition against insider trading as arising from an insider's duty to "disclose or abstain." Does this mean that if an insider discloses material nonpublic information and then trades on the basis of that information, there's no 10b–5 violation? Technically, the answer would seem to be yes—provided that the disclosure sufficiently alerts shareholders (or the market) of the material nonpublic information and gives the market time to absorb the information. Of course, once this happens and the trading price reflects the information, there is no incentive for the insider to trade on it. And it is possible that the disclosure would violate some other duty under the law.

But the question remains. When is disclosure of material nonpublic information sufficient so an insider has satisfied his "disclose or abstain" duty—and need no longer abstain? For example, would posting the inside information on a social media site, such as Facebook, be enough to then trade on that information? Or what about a "tweet" by a CEO who had millions of followers on Twitter? Or is the answer that only disclosure that effectively eliminates any informational advantage will do? That is, the "disclose or abstain" duty is really a duty to abstain.

Chiarella's criminal conviction was overturned. Why? If the jury had been instructed to find a violation of § 10(b) if Chiarella had used information that he was obligated to keep confidential, would this conviction have stood?

---

2. *Dirks* and the Tipper-Tippee Liability

Chiarella clarified that § 10(b) and Rule 10b–5 make it unlawful for a corporate insider to use material nonpublic information to trade in that corporation's stock. Does the same prohibition apply to a noninsider who has obtained material nonpublic information from an insider? In other words, how do the insider trading prohibitions apply to tippers and tippees?

First, some vocabulary. A *tipper* is a person who discloses material nonpublic information. A *tippee* is a person who receives material nonpublic information from a tipper. If the tippee then discloses the information, he becomes a tipper, and the person to whom he discloses becomes a *subtippee*.

Note that the tipper can hold different positions. The tipper might be an insider, such as a director, officer or employee of the corporation. Or the tipper might be a constructive insider, such as a corporate lawyer or accountant, who has a confidential relationship with the corporation. (We will later see that the tipper could alternatively be a misappropriator.)

Likewise, a tippee might hold a range of positions. The tippee's relationship with the tipper can vary, from spouses to more distant family members to friends to a range of professional and nonprofessional relationships (doctor-patient, priest-penitent, softball team captain-first base-person, and so on).

Finally, who actually trades on the information can vary. Both the tipper and the tippee might trade. Or just the tippee. Or only a subtippee (or remote sub-subtippees). All of these permutations affect the analysis, and the facts in tipper-tippee case can be quite complex. But we start with the basic tipper-tippee case, so you have a sense of the key factors courts look to in assessing tipper-tippee liability.

As you read the following case, keep in mind that the market's ability to accurately price securities depends on market participants having access to new information on a timely basis. What happens if there are unfair disparities in the information available to market participants? Does the Court's approach to tipper-tippee liability account for these policy questions?

Dirks v. Securities and Exchange Commission

463 U.S. 646 (1983)

JUSTICE POWELL delivered the opinion of the Court.

Petitioner Raymond Dirks received material nonpublic information from "insiders" of a corporation with which he had no connection. He disclosed this information to investors who relied on it in trading in the shares of the corporation. The question is whether Dirks violated the antifraud provisions of the federal securities laws by this disclosure.

In 1973, Dirks was an officer of a New York broker-dealer firm who specialized in providing investment analysis of insurance company securities to institutional investors. On March 6, Dirks received information from Ronald Secrist, a former officer of Equity Funding of America. Secrist alleged that the assets of Equity Funding, a diversified corporation primarily engaged in selling life insurance and mutual funds, were vastly overstated as the result of fraudulent corporate practices. Secrist also stated that various regulatory agencies had failed to act on similar charges made by Equity Funding employees. He urged Dirks to verify the fraud and disclose it publicly.

Dirks decided to investigate the allegations. He visited Equity Funding's headquarters in Los Angeles and interviewed several officers and employees of the corporation. The senior management denied any wrongdoing, but certain corporation employees corroborated the charges of fraud. Neither Dirks nor his firm owned or traded any Equity Funding stock, but throughout his investigation he openly discussed the information he had obtained with a number of clients and investors. Some of these persons sold their holdings of Equity Funding securities, including five investment advisers who liquidated holdings of more than $16 million.[2]

While Dirks was in Los Angeles, he was in touch regularly with William Blundell, the *Wall Street Journal*'s Los Angeles bureau chief. Dirks urged Blundell to write a story on the fraud allegations. Blundell did not believe, however, that such a massive fraud could go undetected and declined to write the story. He feared that publishing such damaging hearsay might be libelous.

During the two-week period in which Dirks pursued his investigation and spread word of Secrist's charges, the price of Equity Funding stock fell from $26 per share to less than $15 per share. This led the New York Stock Exchange to halt trading on March 27. Shortly thereafter California insurance authorities impounded Equity Funding's records and uncovered evidence of the fraud. Only then did the SEC file a complaint against Equity Funding[3] and only then, on April 2, did the *Wall Street Journal* publish a front-page story based largely on information assembled by Dirks. Equity Funding immediately went into receivership.

The SEC began an investigation into Dirks' role in the exposure of the fraud. After a hearing by an administrative law judge, the SEC found that Dirks had aided and abetted violations of § 17(a) of the Securities Act of 1933, § 10(b) of the Securities Exchange Act of 1934, and SEC Rule 10b–5, by repeating the allegations of fraud to members of the investment community who later sold their Equity Funding stock. The SEC concluded: "Where 'tippees'—regardless of their motivation or occupation—come into possession of material 'information that they know is confidential and know or should know came from a corporate insider,' they must either publicly disclose that information or refrain from trading." Recognizing, however, that Dirks

---

[2]   Dirks received from his firm a salary plus a commission for securities transactions above a certain amount that his clients directed through his firm. But "it is not clear how many of those with whom Dirks spoke promised to direct some brokerage business through Dirks' firm to compensate Dirks, or how many actually did so."

[3]   On March 9, 1973, an official of the California Insurance Department informed the SEC's regional office in Los Angeles of Secrist's charges of fraud. Dirks himself voluntarily presented his information at the SEC's regional office beginning on March 27.

"played an important role in bringing Equity Funding's massive fraud to light," the SEC only censured him.

Dirks sought review in the Court of Appeals for the District of Columbia Circuit. The court entered judgment against Dirks "for the reasons stated by the Commission in its opinion." Judge Wright, a member of the panel, issued an opinion stating that "the obligations of corporate fiduciaries pass to all those to whom they disclose their information before it has been disseminated to the public at large."

In view of the importance to the SEC and to the securities industry of the question presented by this case, we granted a writ of certiorari. We now reverse.

We were explicit in *Chiarella* in saying that there can be no duty to disclose where the person who has traded on inside information "was not the corporation's agent, was not a fiduciary, or was not a person in whom the sellers of the securities had placed their trust and confidence." Not to require such a fiduciary relationship, we recognized, would "depart radically from the established doctrine that duty arises from a specific relationship between two parties" and would amount to "recognizing a general duty between all participants in market transactions to forego actions based on material, nonpublic information." This requirement of a specific relationship between the shareholders and the individual trading on inside information has created analytical difficulties for the SEC and courts in policing tippees who trade on inside information. Unlike insiders who have independent fiduciary duties to both the corporation and its shareholders, the typical tippee has no such relationships.[14] In view of this absence, it has been unclear how a tippee acquires the *Cady, Roberts* duty to refrain from trading on inside information.

The SEC's position in this case is that a tippee "inherits" the *Cady, Roberts* obligation to shareholders whenever he receives inside information from an insider. This view differs little from the view that we rejected as inconsistent with congressional intent in *Chiarella*. In that case, the Court of Appeals agreed with the SEC and affirmed Chiarella's conviction, holding that "*anyone*—corporate insider or not—who regularly receives material nonpublic information may not use that information to trade in securities without incurring an affirmative duty to disclose." Here, the SEC maintains that anyone who knowingly receives nonpublic material information from an insider has a fiduciary duty to disclose before trading.

---

[14]　Under certain circumstances, such as where corporate information is revealed legitimately to an underwriter, accountant, lawyer, or consultant working for the corporation, these outsiders may become fiduciaries of the shareholders. The basis for recognizing this fiduciary duty is not simply that such persons acquired nonpublic corporate information, but rather that they have entered into a special confidential relationship in the conduct of the business of the enterprise and are given access to information solely for corporate purposes. When such a person breaches his fiduciary relationship, he may be treated more properly as a tipper than a tippee. For such a duty to be imposed, however, the corporation must expect the outsider to keep the disclosed nonpublic information confidential, and the relationship at least must imply such a duty.

In effect, the SEC's theory of tippee liability appears rooted in the idea that the antifraud provisions require equal information among all traders. This conflicts with the principle set forth in *Chiarella* that only some persons, under some circumstances, will be barred from trading while in possession of material nonpublic information. We reaffirm today that "a duty to disclose arises from the relationship between parties and not merely from one's ability to acquire information because of his position in the market." Imposing a duty to disclose or abstain solely because a person knowingly receives material nonpublic information from an insider and trades on it could have an inhibiting influence on the role of market analysts, which the SEC itself recognizes is necessary to the preservation of a healthy market. It is commonplace for analysts to "ferret out and analyze information," and this often is done by meeting with and questioning corporate officers and others who are insiders. And information that the analysts obtain normally may be the basis for judgments as to the market worth of a corporation's securities. The analyst's judgment in this respect is made available in market letters or otherwise to clients of the firm. It is the nature of this type of information, and indeed of the markets themselves, that such information cannot be made simultaneously available to all of the corporation's stockholders or the public generally.

The conclusion that recipients of inside information do not invariably acquire a duty to disclose or abstain does not mean that such tippees always are free to trade on the information. The need for a ban on some tippee trading is clear. Not only are insiders forbidden by their fiduciary relationship from personally using undisclosed corporate information to their advantage, but they may not give such information to an outsider for the same improper purpose of exploiting the information for their personal gain. Similarly, the transactions of those who knowingly participate with the fiduciary in such a breach are "as forbidden" as transactions "on behalf of the trustee himself." Thus, the tippee's duty to disclose or abstain is derivative from that of the insider's duty.

Thus, some tippees must assume an insider's duty to the shareholders not because they receive inside information, but rather because it has been made available to them *improperly*. Thus, a tippee assumes a fiduciary duty to the shareholders of a corporation not to trade on material nonpublic information only when the insider has breached his fiduciary duty to the shareholders by disclosing the information to the tippee and the tippee knows or should know that there has been a breach.

In determining whether a tippee is under an obligation to disclose or abstain, it thus is necessary to determine whether the insider's "tip" constituted a breach of the insider's fiduciary duty. All disclosures of confidential corporate information are not inconsistent with the duty insiders owe to shareholders. In contrast to the extraordinary facts of this case, the more typical situation in which there will be a question whether disclosure violates the insider's *Cady, Roberts* duty is when insiders disclose information to analysts. Whether disclosure is a breach of duty depends in large part on the purpose of the disclosure. This standard was identified by the SEC itself in *Cady, Roberts*: a purpose of the securities laws was to eliminate "use of inside information for personal advantage." Thus, the test is whether the insider personally will benefit, directly or indirectly, from his disclosure. Absent some personal gain, there has been no breach of duty to stockholders. And absent a breach by the insider, there is no derivative breach.

To determine whether the disclosure itself "deceives, manipulates, or defrauds" shareholders, the initial inquiry is whether there has been a breach of duty by the insider. This requires courts to focus on objective criteria, i.e., whether the insider receives a direct or indirect personal benefit from the disclosure, such as a pecuniary gain or a reputational benefit that will translate into future earnings. There are objective facts and circumstances that often justify such an inference. For example, there may be a relationship between the insider and the recipient that suggests a *quid pro quo* from the latter, or an intention to benefit the particular recipient. The elements of fiduciary duty and exploitation of nonpublic information also exist when an insider makes a gift of confidential information to a trading relative or friend. The tip and trade resemble trading by the insider himself followed by a gift of the profits to the recipient.

Determining whether an insider personally benefits from a particular disclosure, a question of fact, will not always be easy for courts. But it is essential, we think, to have a guiding principle for those whose daily activities must be limited and instructed by the SEC's inside-trading rules, and we believe that there must be a breach of the insider's fiduciary duty before the tippee inherits the duty to disclose or abstain. In contrast, the rule adopted by the SEC in this case would have no limiting principle.

Under the inside-trading and tipping rules set forth above, we find that there was no actionable violation by Dirks. It is undisputed that Dirks himself was a stranger to Equity Funding, with no pre-existing fiduciary duty to its shareholders. He took no action, directly or indirectly, that induced the shareholders or officers of Equity Funding to repose trust or confidence in him. There was no expectation by Dirks' sources that he would keep their information in confidence. Nor did Dirks misappropriate or illegally obtain the information about Equity Funding. Unless the insiders breached their *Cady, Roberts* duty to shareholders in disclosing the nonpublic information to Dirks, he breached no duty when he passed it on to investors as well as to the *Wall Street Journal*.

It is clear that neither Secrist nor the other Equity Funding employees violated their *Cady, Roberts* duty to the corporation's shareholders by providing information to Dirks. The tippers received no monetary or personal benefit for revealing Equity Funding's secrets, nor was their purpose to make a gift of valuable information to Dirks. As the facts of this case clearly indicate, the tippers were motivated by a desire to expose the fraud. In the absence of a breach of duty to shareholders by the insiders, there was no derivative breach by Dirks.

Points for Discussion

1. Basis for tipping liability.

Does the Court explain how § 10(b) and Rule 10b–5 extend beyond those who have a relation of "trust and confidence" to encompass those who obtain information from such a person?

2. Stock analysts.

What attitude does the majority opinion take toward stock analysts, whose job is to ascertain price-sensitive information and share it with clients?

3. Benefit to tipper.

After *Dirks*, lower courts wrestled with what constitutes a "personal benefit" sufficient to create tipping liability—coming to conflicting conclusions. Some courts narrowly interpreted *Dirks* and held that the personal benefit received by the tipper had to be tangible, a sort of kickback for passing confidential information, or otherwise part of a meaningfully close relationship. Other courts interpreted *Dirks* to cover situations in which the tipper was in a friend or family relationship with the tippee and had a personal reason for tipping inside information. The question thus came down to whether the tipper had to receive a "tangible" benefit or whether receiving a "psychic" benefit was enough and if so how close of a relationship would suffice.

Here's a colorful case applying the "personal benefit" test of *Dirks*. In *SEC v. Switzer*, 590 F. Supp. 756 (W.D. Okla. 1984), Switzer, then the football coach of the University of Oklahoma, was sitting in the bleachers at a track meet. He overheard Platt, the CEO of Phoenix Resources Company, tell his wife that he might be out of town the following week because there was a chance that Phoenix would be liquidated. Platt's purpose in telling his wife about the trip, according to the court, was so she could make child care arrangements. The Platts did not know that Switzer was on a bench behind them during this conversation. Switzer, who knew of Platt's position with Phoenix, along with several of Switzer's friends, bought Phoenix stock in the expectation that its liquidation would lead to a price spike. The SEC argued that Switzer and his friends were liable under Rule 10b–5 as tippees. The court held, however, that Platt did not breach a fiduciary duty to Phoenix's shareholders by disclosing the information because he did not personally benefit, directly or indirectly, from the disclosure. Accordingly, under *Dirks*, Switzer and his friends were not liable as tippees.

Suppose the CEO had turned to Switzer, "Hey, coach, I know you like to play the stock market. You might be interested to know that my company might be liquidated." Would the result be different?

In 2016, the Supreme Court resolved this circuit split. *United States v. Salman*, 137 S. Ct. 420 (2016). The Court reaffirmed the original language of *Dirks* and held that a family member is personally benefitted (and thus breaches a duty) by giving confidential information to a relative who trades on the tip. The Court viewed *Dirks* as "easily" resolving the question and concluded that "giving a gift of trading information [to a trading relative] is the same thing as trading by the tipper followed by a gift of the proceeds." In the case, which involved the trading by a sub-tippee, a Citigroup insider had given his brother confidential information about M&A clients of the bank with the expectation that his brother would trade on it. The Court held the insider's tip to his brother was a breach of his duty of trust and confidence to Citigroup and its clients. Then when his brother passed this information to their brother-in-law Salman, this duty was acquired and breached by Salman when he traded on the information with full knowledge that it had been improperly tipped originally. The Court made clear that the lower court's view that the tipper must receive something of a "pecuniary or similarly valuable nature" was "inconsistent" with *Dirks.*

4. *Remote tippees.*

Tipper/tippee liability can become more complicated when the information gets passed along a chain to "remote tippees." A number of questions can arise when determining remote tippee liability. Must the recipient know the identity of the original tipper for liability to attach to a remote tippee? Must they know that the tipper disclosed the material nonpublic information for a personal benefit or is it enough that the recipient know that the information came to them improperly? What happens if the information has been so distorted through the chain of people that it no longer resembles the original material nonpublic information (similar to the children's game of "telephone")? A recipient may claim that the tip was just a generalized recommendation. Should remote tippees have a duty to inquire about the source of the securities information and whether the information was received through a breach of duty?

---

3.   *O'Hagan* and the "Misappropriation" Theory

Chiarella and *Dirks* resolved three major issues. First, they confirmed that § 10(b) and Rule 10b–5 made it unlawful for an insider or temporary insider of a corporation to trade that corporation's stock on the basis of material nonpublic information. Second, they confirmed that it was unlawful for an insider or temporary insider, acting in breach of a fiduciary duty owed to the corporation, to disclose to another (to "tip") material nonpublic information about that corporation for personal benefit. Third, they rejected the "level playing field" principle—in other words, they held that § 10(b) and Rule 10b–5 did not bar outsiders and nontippees from trading simply because they possessed material nonpublic information not available to other traders.

However, *Chiarella* and *Dirks* left an important question open. What about traders who were neither insiders nor tippees? What about *outsiders* who obtained material nonpublic information and traded on the basis of that information? When did such outsiders violate § 10(b) and Rule 10b–5? After *Chiarella* and *Dirks*, the circuit courts were split on the question of whether such outsider trading was unlawful and the theory on which such liability might be based.

In their attempts to go after outsiders, prosecutors had developed the "misappropriation" theory, referenced in *Chiarella* but not ruled upon in that case. According to the theory, it was unlawful even for a person who had no connection to a corporation to trade in the corporation's securities on the basis of material nonpublic information if the person had misappropriated the information from some third party.

The misappropriation theory faced several potential challenges. Most prominently, the Supreme Court had made clear that § 10(b) addressed only deception, not trading that was financially unfair. Misappropriating inside information might be unfair, but how was it "deceptive"? Wasn't there something different about deceiving the source of information and deceiving a participant in the marketplace? And wasn't "theft" different from "deception"?

For example, if I broke into a corporation's headquarters, stole some valuable information and then sold that information to one of the corporation's competitors, I would be guilty of theft. But had I violated § 10(b)? That would seem a stretch; after all, such a theft did not even involve the trading of securities. Would it matter if I used the proceeds from the theft to buy the corporation's securities? Again, that seemed too attenuated; the securities purchase was only incidental to the theft of information.

However, what if the valuable information I stole was inside information that I could profit from *only* by trading the corporation's securities? Or if the *ordinary* way to profit from such information was by trading? Was there a way to distinguish the theft of material nonpublic information that typically was valuable in the securities markets (such as early information on a merger, an earnings release, or a new product launch)? Could § 10(b) be stretched to cover the theft of information and subsequent securities trading, even by an outsider?

In applying the "classical" theory, the courts had interpreted the "deception" component of § 10(b) as requiring a breach of fiduciary duty. But was a breach of duty to the source of the information (the "misappropriation" theory) deceptive in the same way as a breach of duty to the corporation and shareholders (the "classical" theory)? The nature of the relationship between the person trading and the source of the information, and whether there was disclosure to the source of the plan to trade on the basis of the material nonpublic information, was crucial to the analysis of whether the misappropriation theory prohibited trading under § 10(b). Did it make sense for liability to depend on these factors?

Moreover, why should liability depend on whether there was a breach of fiduciary duty? If § 10(b) was directed at ensuring the integrity of securities markets, why did it matter whether the "misappropriation" from the source of the information was wrongful? For example, what if the source of the information told the outsider it was permissible to trade on the information? In that case, the outsider would not breach a fiduciary duty because there would be no "deception" of the source. But does that conclusion make sense? Why should § 10(b) liability depend on whether the source of the information gave the outsider permission to use it to his or her advantage?

Finally, Rule 10b–5 required that the deception be "in connection with" the trading of securities. Did the misappropriation theory satisfy this "in connection with" requirement? What if the source of the information, presumably injured by the misappropriator's breach of fiduciary duty, was not a participant in any relevant securities transaction? Was there a way to connect (1) the misappropriator's breach of a fiduciary duty owed to the source of the information with (2) the misappropriator's trading in securities?

> In 1980, after *Chiarella*, and relying on its rulemaking authority under § 14(e) of the Exchange Act, the SEC adopted Rule 14e–3(a) which specifically prohibits trading on the basis of material, nonpublic information about tender offers.
>
> The rule applies once "a substantial step or steps to commence" a tender offer has occurred. It prohibits any person who knows or has reason to know material nonpublic information about a pending tender offer, originating from a bidder or target company, from trading on the basis of this information. For the full text, see Rule 14e–3(a).
>
> In *O'Hagan*, the Supreme Court validated the SEC's authority to promulgate Rule 14e–3. In addition, the case raised the bigger question of the viability of the misappropriation theory of insider trading liability under Rule 10b–5, which is not limited to the tender offer context.

These questions were thorny, but without the misappropriation theory, the government would be unable to prosecute many instances of unfair trading that prosecutors believed to be wrongful. Interestingly, the trading by James O'Hagan in the case that you are about to read was *not* an example of wrongful trading that would have fallen through the cracks without the misappropriation theory. The government could, and did, prosecute and convict O'Hagan for other violations of law such as Rule 14e–3 concerning trading in connection with a tender offer. Nevertheless, *O'Hagan* became the vehicle for the Supreme Court to answer these fundamental questions and to set forth a roadmap for future cases.

United States v. O'Hagan

<u>521 U.S. 642 (1997)</u>

JUSTICE GINSBURG delivered the opinion of the Court.

Respondent James Herman O'Hagan was a partner in the law firm of Dorsey & Whitney in Minneapolis, Minnesota. In July 1988, Grand Metropolitan PLC (Grand Met), a company based in London, England, retained Dorsey & Whitney as local counsel to represent Grand Met regarding a potential tender offer for the common stock of the Pillsbury Company, headquartered in Minneapolis. Both Grand Met and Dorsey & Whitney took precautions to protect the confidentiality of Grand Met's tender offer plans. O'Hagan did no work on the Grand Met representation. Dorsey & Whitney withdrew from representing Grand Met on September 9, 1988. Less than a month later, on October 4, 1988, Grand Met publicly announced its tender offer for Pillsbury stock.

On August 18, 1988, while Dorsey & Whitney was still representing Grand Met, O'Hagan began purchasing call options for Pillsbury stock. Each option gave him the right to purchase 100 shares of Pillsbury stock. By the end of September, he owned 2,500 unexpired Pillsbury options, apparently more than any other individual investor. O'Hagan also purchased, in September 1988, some 5,000 shares of Pillsbury common stock, at a price just under $39 per share. When Grand Met announced its tender offer in October, the price of Pillsbury stock rose to nearly $60 per share. O'Hagan then sold his Pillsbury call options and common stock, making a profit of more than $4.3 million.

The Securities and Exchange Commission initiated an investigation into O'Hagan's transactions, culminating in a 57-count indictment. The indictment alleged that O'Hagan defrauded his law firm and its client, Grand Met, by using for his own trading purposes material, nonpublic information regarding Grand Met's planned tender offer. According to the indictment, O'Hagan used the profits he gained through this trading to conceal his previous embezzlement and conversion of unrelated client trust funds. A jury convicted O'Hagan on all counts, and he was sentenced to a 41-month term of imprisonment.

A divided panel of the Court of Appeals for the Eighth Circuit reversed all of O'Hagan's convictions. Liability under § 10(b) and Rule 10b–5, the Eighth Circuit held, may not be grounded on the "misappropriation theory" of securities fraud on which the prosecution relied.

Decisions of the Courts of Appeals are in conflict on the propriety of the misappropriation theory under § 10(b) and Rule 10(b)–5. We granted certiorari and now reverse the Eighth Circuit's judgment.

We address first the Court of Appeals' reversal of O'Hagan's convictions under § 10(b) and Rule 10b–5. Following the Fourth Circuit's lead, the Eighth Circuit rejected the misappropriation theory as a basis for § 10(b) liability. We hold, in accord with several other Courts of Appeals that criminal liability under § 10(b) may be predicated on the misappropriation theory.

Section 10(b) proscribes (1) using any deceptive device (2) in connection with the purchase or sale of securities, in contravention of rules prescribed by the Commission. The provision, as written, does not confine its coverage to deception of a purchaser or seller of securities; rather, the statute reaches any deceptive device used "in connection with the purchase or sale of any security."

Under the "traditional" or "classical theory" of insider trading liability, § 10(b) and Rule 10b–5 are violated when a corporate insider trades in the securities of his corporation on the basis of material, nonpublic information. Trading on such information qualifies as a "deceptive device" under § 10(b), we have affirmed, because "a relationship of trust and confidence exists between the shareholders of a corporation and those insiders who have obtained confidential information by reason of their position with that corporation." That relationship, we recognized, "gives rise to a duty to disclose or to abstain from trading because of the 'necessity of preventing a corporate insider from taking unfair advantage of uninformed stockholders.' " The classical theory applies not only to officers, directors, and other permanent insiders of a corporation, but also to attorneys, accountants, consultants, and others who temporarily become fiduciaries of a corporation.

The "misappropriation theory" holds that a person commits fraud "in connection with" a securities transaction, and thereby violates § 10(b) and Rule 10b–5, when he misappropriates confidential information for securities trading purposes, in breach of a duty owed to the source of the information. Under this theory, a fiduciary's undisclosed, self-serving use of a principal's information to purchase or sell securities, in breach of a duty of loyalty and confidentiality, defrauds the principal of the exclusive use of that information. In lieu of premising liability on a fiduciary relationship between company insider and purchaser or seller of the company's stock, the misappropriation theory premises liability on a fiduciary-turned-trader's deception of those who entrusted him with access to confidential information.

The two theories are complementary, each addressing efforts to capitalize on nonpublic information through the purchase or sale of securities. The classical theory targets a corporate insider's breach of duty to shareholders with whom the insider transacts; the misappropriation theory outlaws trading on the basis of nonpublic information by a corporate "outsider" in breach of a duty owed not to a trading party, but to the source of the information. The misappropriation theory is thus designed to "protect the integrity of the securities markets against abuses by 'outsiders' to a corporation who have access to confidential information that will affect the corporation's security price when revealed, but who owe no fiduciary or other duty to that corporation's shareholders."

In this case, the indictment alleged that O'Hagan, in breach of a duty of trust and confidence he owed to his law firm, Dorsey & Whitney, and to its client, Grand Met, traded on the basis of nonpublic information regarding Grand Met's planned tender offer for Pillsbury common stock. This conduct, the Government charged, constituted a fraudulent device in connection with the purchase and sale of securities.[5]

—————————

5   The Government could not have prosecuted O'Hagan under the classical theory, for O'Hagan

We agree with the Government that misappropriation, as just defined, satisfies § 10(b)'s requirement that chargeable conduct involve a "deceptive device or contrivance" used "in connection with" the purchase or sale of securities. We observe, first, that misappropriators, as the Government describes them, deal in deception. A fiduciary who "pretends loyalty to the principal while secretly converting the principal's information for personal gain," "dupes" or defrauds the principal.

Deception through nondisclosure is central to the theory of liability for which the Government seeks recognition. As counsel for the Government stated in explanation of the theory at oral argument: "To satisfy the common law rule that a trustee may not use the property that has been entrusted to him, there would have to be consent. To satisfy the requirement of the Securities Act that there be no deception, there would only have to be disclosure." [6]

The misappropriation theory advanced by the Government trains on conduct involving manipulation or deception. Because the deception essential to the misappropriation theory involves feigning fidelity to the source of information, if the fiduciary discloses to the source that he plans to trade on the nonpublic information, there is no "deceptive device" and thus no § 10(b) violation—although the fiduciary-turned-trader may remain liable under state law for breach of a duty of loyalty.[7]

We turn next to the § 10(b) requirement that the misappropriator's deceptive use of information be "in connection with the purchase or sale of a security." This element is satisfied because the fiduciary's fraud is consummated, not when the fiduciary gains the confidential information, but when, without disclosure to his principal, he uses the information to purchase or sell securities. The securities transaction and the breach of duty thus coincide. This is so even though the person or entity defrauded is not the other party to the trade, but is, instead, the source of the nonpublic information. A misappropriator who trades on the basis of material, nonpublic information, in short,

---

was not an "insider" of Pillsbury, the corporation in whose stock he traded. Although an "outsider" with respect to Pillsbury, O'Hagan had an intimate association with, and was found to have traded on confidential information from, Dorsey & Whitney, counsel to tender offeror Grand Met. Under the misappropriation theory, O'Hagan's securities trading does not escape Exchange Act sanction, as it would under the dissent's reasoning, simply because he was associated with, and gained nonpublic information from, the bidder, rather than the target.

[6]   Under the misappropriation theory urged in this case, the disclosure obligation runs to the source of the information, here, Dorsey & Whitney and Grand Met. Chief Justice Burger, dissenting in *Chiarella*, advanced a broader reading of § 10(b) and Rule 10b–5; the disclosure obligation, as he envisioned it, ran to those with whom the misappropriator trades. 445 U.S. at 240 ("a person who has misappropriated nonpublic information has an absolute duty to disclose that information or to refrain from trading"). The Government does not propose that we adopt a misappropriation theory of that breadth.

[7]   Where, however, a person trading on the basis of material, nonpublic information owes a duty of loyalty and confidentiality to two entities or persons—for example, a law firm and its client—but makes disclosure to only one, the trader may still be liable under the misappropriation theory.

gains his advantageous market position through deception; he deceives the source of the information and simultaneously harms members of the investing public.

The misappropriation theory targets information of a sort that misappropriators ordinarily capitalize upon to gain no-risk profits through the purchase or sale of securities. Should a misappropriator put such information to other use, the statute's prohibition would not be implicated. The theory does not catch all conceivable forms of fraud involving confidential information; rather, it catches fraudulent means of capitalizing on such information through securities transactions.

The Government notes another limitation on the forms of fraud § 10(b) reaches: "The misappropriation theory would not apply to a case in which a person defrauded a bank into giving him a loan or embezzled cash from another, and then used the proceeds of the misdeed to purchase securities." In such a case, the Government states, "the proceeds would have value to the malefactor apart from their use in a securities transaction, and the fraud would be complete as soon as the money was obtained." In other words, money can buy, if not anything, then at least many things; its misappropriation may thus be viewed as sufficiently detached from a subsequent securities transaction that § 10(b)'s "in connection with" requirement would not be met.

The misappropriation theory comports with § 10(b)'s language, which requires deception "in connection with the purchase or sale of any security," not deception of an identifiable purchaser or seller. The theory is also well-tuned to an animating purpose of the Exchange Act: to insure honest securities markets and thereby promote investor confidence. Although informational disparity is inevitable in the securities markets, investors likely would hesitate to venture their capital in a market where trading based on misappropriated nonpublic information is unchecked by law. An investor's informational disadvantage vis-a-vis a misappropriator with material, nonpublic information stems from contrivance, not luck; it is a disadvantage that cannot be overcome with research or skill.

In sum, the misappropriation theory, as we have examined and explained it in this opinion, is both consistent with the statute and with our precedent. Vital to our decision that criminal liability may be sustained under the misappropriation theory, we emphasize, are two sturdy safeguards Congress has provided regarding scienter. To establish a criminal violation of Rule 10b–5, the Government must prove that a person "willfully" violated the provision. *See* 15 U.S.C. § 78ff(a). Furthermore, a defendant may not be imprisoned for violating Rule 10b–5 if he proves that he had no knowledge of the rule. O'Hagan's charge that the misappropriation theory is too indefinite to permit the imposition of criminal liability, thus fails not only because the theory is limited to those who breach a recognized duty. In addition, the statute's "requirement of the presence of culpable intent as a necessary element of the offense does much to destroy any force in the argument that application of the statute" in circumstances such as O'Hagan's is unjust.

The Eighth Circuit erred in holding that the misappropriation theory is inconsistent with § 10(b).

JUSTICE THOMAS, with whom THE CHIEF JUSTICE joins, concurring in the judgment in part and dissenting in part.

Central to the majority's holding is the need to interpret § 10(b)'s requirement that a deceptive device be "use[d] or employ[ed], in connection with the purchase or sale of any security." Because the Commission's misappropriation theory fails to provide a coherent and consistent interpretation of this essential requirement for liability under § 10(b), I dissent.

I cannot accept the Commission's interpretation of when a deceptive device is "use[d] . . . in connection with" a securities transaction. Although the Commission and the majority at points seem to suggest that any relation to a securities transaction satisfies the "in connection with" requirement of § 10(b), both ultimately reject such an overly expansive construction and require a more integral connection between the fraud and the securities transaction. The majority states, for example, that the misappropriation theory applies to undisclosed misappropriation of confidential information "for securities trading purposes," thus seeming to require a particular intent by the misappropriator in order to satisfy the "in connection with" language.

The Commission's construction of the relevant language in § 10(b), and the incoherence of that construction, become evident as the majority attempts to describe why the fraudulent theft of information falls under the Commission's misappropriation theory, but the fraudulent theft of money does not. The majority correctly notes that confidential information "qualifies as property to which the company has a right of exclusive use." It then observes that the "undisclosed misappropriation of such information, in violation of a fiduciary duty, . . . constitutes fraud akin to embezzlement—the fraudulent appropriation to one's own use of the money or goods entrusted to one's care by another." What the embezzlement analogy does not do, however, is explain how the relevant fraud is "use[d] or employ[ed], in connection with" a securities transaction." Neither the Commission nor the majority has a coherent theory regarding § 10(b)'s "in connection with" requirement.

Accepting the Government's description of the scope of its own theory, it becomes plain that the majority's explanation of how the misappropriation theory supposedly satisfies the "in connection with" requirement is incomplete. The touchstone required for an embezzlement to be "use[d] or employ[ed], in connection with" a securities transaction is not merely that it "coincide" with, or be consummated by, the transaction, but that it is necessarily and only consummated by the transaction. Where the property being embezzled has value "apart from [its] use in a securities transaction"—even though it is in fact being used in a securities transaction—the Government contends that there is no violation under the misappropriation theory.

The relevant distinction is not that the misappropriated information was used for a securities transaction . . . but rather that it could only be used for such a transaction.

Once the Government's construction of the misappropriation theory is accurately described and accepted–along with its implied construction of § 10(b)'s "in connection with" language–that theory should no longer cover cases, such as this one, involving fraud on the source of information where the source has no connection with the other participant in a securities transaction. It seems obvious that the undisclosed misappropriation of confidential information is not necessarily consummated by a securities transaction. In this case, for example, upon learning of Grand Met's confidential takeover plans, O'Hagan could have done any number of things with the information: He could have sold it to a newspaper for publication; he could have given or sold the information to Pillsbury itself . . .

Under any theory of liability, however, these activities would not violate § 10(b). That O'Hagan actually did use the information to purchase securities is thus no more significant here than it is in the case of embezzling money used to purchase securities. If the relevant test under the "in connection with" language is whether the fraudulent act is necessarily tied to a securities transaction, then the misappropriation of confidential information used to trade no more violates § 10(b) than does the misappropriation of funds used to trade.

Moreover, as we have repeatedly held, use of nonpublic information to trade is not itself a violation of § 10(b). Rather, it is the use of fraud "in connection with" a securities transaction that is forbidden. Where the relevant element of fraud has no impact on the integrity of the subsequent transactions as distinct from the nonfraudulent element of using nonpublic information, one can reasonably question whether the fraud was used in connection with a securities transaction.

The absence of a coherent and consistent misappropriation theory . . . is particularly problematic in the context of this case . . . . [I]n this case we do not even have a formal regulation embodying the agency's misappropriation theory. Certainly Rule 10b–5 cannot be said to embody the theory although it deviates from the statutory language by the addition of the words "any person," it merely repeats, unchanged, § 10(b)'s "in connection with" language. Given that the validity of the misappropriation theory turns on the construction of that language in § 10(b), the regulatory language is singularly uninformative.

I find wholly unpersuasive a litigating position by the Commission that, at best, embodies an inconsistent and incoherent interpretation of the relevant statutory language and that does not provide any predictable guidance as to what behavior contravenes the statute. That position is no better than an ad hoc interpretation of statutory language and in my view can provide no basis for liability.

JUSTICE SCALIA, concurring in part and dissenting in part.

I do not entirely agree with Justice Thomas's analysis . . . principally because it seems to me irrelevant whether the Government's theory of why respondent's acts were covered is "coherent and consistent." In point of fact, respondent's actions either violated § 10(b) and Rule 10b–5, or they did not–regardless of the reasons the Government gave. And it is for us to decide.

While the Court's explanation of the scope of § 10(b) and Rule 10b–5 would be entirely reasonable in some other context, it does not seem to accord with the principle of lenity we apply to criminal statutes. In light of that principle, it seems to me that the unelaborated statutory language: "[t]o use or employ, in connection with the purchase or sale of any security . . . any manipulative or deceptive device or contrivance," § 10(b), must be construed to require the manipulation or deception of a party to a securities transaction.

Points for Discussion

1. *Outsider trading.*

Would Justice Powell, who wrote the opinions in *Chiarella* and *Dirks*, have decided *O'Hagan* the same way that Justice Ginsburg did? Notice that in *Chiarella* Justice Powell explained that liability under the antifraud provisions of § 10(b) and Rule 10b–5 arose because of a relationship of "trust and confidence *between the parties.*" Was there such a relationship in *O'Hagan*? How is the misappropriation theory of insider trading liability broader than the classical theory?

2. *Evaluating the misappropriation theory.*

Do you agree with Justice Thomas that the majority's explanation of the misappropriation theory is confusing, incomplete, and hard to apply? What do you think of Justice Scalia's contention that applying the misappropriation theory of liability to O'Hagan was inconsistent with the principle of lenity and that it should only apply when there is "manipulation or deception of a party to a securities transaction"? When do you think the misappropriation theory of liability should apply?

3. *We are family.*

The misappropriation theory hinges on a breach of duty to the source of the information. But does the theory apply only to established business relationships, such as lawyer-client or employer-employee? Or does it apply to more informal nonbusiness relationships, such as in a family? In one well-known case, *United States v. Chestman,* 947 F.2d 551 (2d Cir. 1991) *(en banc), cert. denied* 503 U.S. 1004 (1992), the court held that a son-in-law who learned of plans to sell a family-controlled corporation did not owe a duty to the family, despite being asked to keep the plans confidential, because "kinship alone does not create the necessary relationship." Other cases, however, held family members to a duty of trust and confidence.

In Rule 10b5–2, the SEC responded to ambiguities about when a person owes a duty to the source of information for purposes of misappropriation theory. The SEC's view was insider trading by family members harms the market just as much as other forms of insider trading. Moreover, the SEC wanted to establish a bright-line rule to avoid intrusive inquiries into family relationships. Subpart (b) of the rule enumerated three non-exclusive circumstances in which "duties of trust and confidence" would exist under the misappropriation theory. Existence of such a duty, in turn, would support a finding of liability under Rule 10b–5. Here are the key provisions of the SEC rule. Does this clear things up?

Rule 10b5–2
Securities and Exchange Act of 1934

(b)   *Enumerated "duties of trust or confidence."* For purposes of [the "misappropriation" theory of insider trading under Section 10(b) of the Act and Rule 10b–5], a "duty of trust or confidence" exists in the following circumstances, among others:

1.   Whenever a person agrees to maintain information in confidence;

2.   Whenever the person communicating the material nonpublic information and the person to whom it is communicated have a history, pattern, or practice of sharing confidences, such that the recipient of the information knows or reasonably should know that the person communicating the material nonpublic information expects that the recipient will maintain its confidentiality; or

3.   Whenever a person receives or obtains material nonpublic information from his or her spouse, parent, child, or sibling; provided, however, that the person receiving or obtaining the information may demonstrate that no duty of trust or confidence existed with respect to the information, by establishing that he or she neither knew nor reasonably should have known that the person who was the source of the information expected that the person would keep the information confidential, because of the parties' history, pattern, or practice of sharing and maintaining confidences, and because there was no agreement or understanding to maintain the confidentiality of the information.

4. *State of mind.*

What state of mind triggers liability in a case of insider trading? In *O'Hagan*, the Supreme Court said only that the trading must be "on the basis" of material nonpublic information. Lower courts have split on whether insider trading liability requires a showing that the trader was in "knowing possession" of inside information or a heightened requirement that the trader "used" the information in trading. The Second Circuit accepted the "knowing possession" standard when a young attorney tipped inside information about transactions involving clients of his law firm. The court justified the lower "knowledge" standard as simpler to apply and consistent with the expansive nature of Rule 10b–5 and its focus on the duty to disclose or abstain from insider trading. Other courts, however, have insisted on a showing the trader "used" the information, particularly when a defendant's state of mind is at issue in criminal cases.

In 2000, the SEC adopted Rule 10b5–1 to clarify this aspect of insider trading liability. Rule 10b5–1(b) provides that, for purposes of insider trading, a person trades "on the basis" of material nonpublic information if the trader is "aware" of the material nonpublic information when making the purchase or sale. In its release accompanying the rule, the SEC explained that "aware" is a commonly used English word, implying "conscious knowledge," with clearer meaning than "knowing possession." What level of knowledge or intent should be required before a trader (or tipper) will be liable for insider trading? And who has the authority to determine what state of mind is necessary, the SEC or the courts?

5. *Tipping in misappropriation cases.*

Courts have applied the same "benefit to tipper" analysis in cases involving misappropriated information as is used when insiders disclose company secrets. Does this make sense? In *United States v. Libera*, 989 F.2d 596 (2d Cir. 1993), employees of a publishing company with access to advance copies of *Business Week* magazine sent the copies to tippees. The publishing company had a policy prohibiting its employees from disclosing the magazine's contents before publication. The Second Circuit concluded that, as a matter of law, the employer-employee relationship was sufficient to establish a duty not to disclose, a duty the printer's employees breached by providing advance copies of the magazine to others. The court also held that a tipper could be liable even if the tipper did not know that the tippee would trade on the basis of the information. The tipper's knowledge she is breaching a duty to the owner of the information "suffices to establish the tipper's expectation that the breach will lead to some kind of misuse." The court reasoned, "This is so because it may be presumed that the tippee's interest in the information is, in contemporary jargon, not for nothing. To allow a tippee to escape liability because the government cannot prove to a jury's satisfaction that the tipper knew exactly what misuse would result from the tipper's wrongdoing would not fulfill the purpose of the misappropriation theory, which is to protect property rights in information."

Misappropriator-Tippers

Consider the facts of *SEC v. Yun*, 327 F.3d 1263 (11th Cir. 2003). David Yun, the president of Scholastic Book Fairs, explained to his wife Donna that his Scholastic stock options had become less valuable because he believed the company's stock price would drop after an upcoming earnings announcement. David told Donna not to disclose this information to anyone, and Donna agreed to keep the information secret. The next evening, Donna attended an awards banquet and apparently talked to some of her co-workers about the pending Scholastic earnings announcement. One of her co-workers, Jerry Burch, called his broker the next day and, based on information he said he obtained at a cocktail party, purchased put options. When Scholastic announced its unexpectedly weak earnings and its share price dropped 40%, Burch realized a profit of $269,000.

Did Donna have a fiduciary duty to David (or Scholastic) that prevented her from tipping Burch? The Eleventh Circuit concluded that "a spouse who trades in breach of a reasonable and legitimate expectation of confidentiality held by the other spouse sufficiently subjects the former to insider trading liability." Based on evidence that David had granted Donna access to confidential information "in reasonable reliance on a promise that she would safeguard the information" and that "Donna had agreed in this instance to keep the information confidential," the court concluded a jury could find that a duty of confidentiality existed between them.

Must Donna have intended to gain a personal benefit when she tipped Burch? The Eleventh Circuit reasoned that the "personal benefit" requirement is the same whether the tip is from an insider (classical theory) or from an outsider (misappropriation theory). Thus, the court concluded "an outsider who tips (rather than trades) is liable if he intends to benefit from the disclosure." As *Dirks* held, a benefit can include a gift to a trading relative or friend. In the case, the court concluded there was enough evidence that Donna had expected to benefit from her tip to Burch by maintaining a good relationship between a friend and a frequent partner in real estate deals.

6. 10b5–1 plans.

SEC Rule 10b5–1 clarifies when trading is "on the basis" of inside information and sets forth affirmative defenses designed to allow corporate insiders and others to structure securities trading plans when they are not aware of inside information and cannot influence these trading plans even if they later become aware of inside information. Courts have recognized that individual trading plans executed in good faith pursuant to Rule 10b5–1 may provide a defense against insider trading charges.

10b5–1 plans have been controversial. Because these plans allow insiders to trade in their company's stock, it is not surprising that they are subject to detailed rules. For example, after adopting a 10b5–1 plan, an individual must wait for a mandatory "cooling off period" to expire before engaging in any trades in accordance with the plan. There have been concerns that insiders might strategically use these plans to appear to be engaging only in pre-planned purchases and sales of stock, when in fact they are taking advantage of inside information.

To illustrate this idea, imagine a client is a director or officer of a company and wanted to set up fifty-two 10b5–1 plans, one for each week in the upcoming year. One concern is that they might sell stock pursuant to a plan during a week when inside information suggests the stock price is high, but cancel the plan for a different week when inside information suggests the stock price is low. SEC amendments to Rule 10b5–1, effective in 2023, addressed some of these concerns by restricting overlapping plans and imposing a "good faith" requirement.

7. *Trading by members of Congress.*

So what happens when the source of material nonpublic information is Congress? Do members of Congress and congressional staffers have duties not to trade on information they learn in their official roles, where that information could affect stock prices of particular companies or industries? In the Stop Trading on Congressional Knowledge (STOCK) Act of 2012, Congress specified that congressional persons owe duties to the United States, as well as to Congress and the U.S. citizens, with respect to material nonpublic information derived from their position or gained from performing their official responsibilities. Thus, members of Congress and their aides—as well as any recipients who trade on congressionally sourced information—can be liable for insider trading under a misappropriation theory.

In addition, just as corporate insiders must report their trading in their corporation's stock, members of Congress and their aides must report their stock trades above $1,000 within 30 to 45 days of the trade. Not only does such reporting allow the public (and the press) to compare congressional stock trading with congressional activities, it also can serve as the basis for public and private insider-trading actions.

The STOCK Act has raised many questions. Evidentiary barriers created by the Constitution's "Speech or Debate" clause immunize lawmakers for their official legislative activities. Moreover, many members of Congress have failed to report their trades accurately, or in a timely manner. Likewise, numerous legislators have traded in shares of companies that are impacted by their legislative work, including investigations. As a result of such criticism, some have argued that lawmakers should be banned entirely from trading individual stocks.

4.   Remedies for Insider Trading

As we have seen, insider trading can be punished as a crime with the possibility of prison time and fines. But what about civil remedies? Section 20A of the Exchange Act creates a private right of action on behalf of contemporaneous traders against insiders, constructive insiders, tippers, and tippees (as well as their controlling persons) who trade while in possession of material, nonpublic information. Liability in such cases is limited to the actual profits realized or losses avoided reduced by the amount of any disgorgement obtained by the SEC under its broad authority to seek injunctive relief.

Pursuant to § 21A of the Exchange Act, which has been used significantly more than § 20A, the SEC is authorized to seek judicially imposed civil penalties against insiders, constructive insiders, tippers, and tippees of up to three times the profits gained or the losses avoided in unlawful insider trading. These civil penalties are *in addition* to other remedies. Thus, an insider, tipper, or tippee may be required to disgorge her profits, whether in an SEC or private action, and pay a treble damage penalty. The civil penalty can be imposed only at the insistence of the SEC.

Section 21A also permits the imposition of civil penalties on controlling persons, such as employers, of up to $1 million or three times the insider's profits (whichever is greater) if the controlling person knowingly or recklessly disregards the insider trading by persons under its control. It also encourages private watchdogs by providing for the payment of bounties to people who provide information concerning insider trading.

In other areas of corporate law that we have covered in this casebook, plaintiffs' securities lawyers have played a prominent role in enforcing violations of law. Should this approach also be followed for insider trading violations? Or should the SEC be the primary enforcer? More generally, should insider trading civil remedies be expanded to match those in other areas of corporate and securities law, or should the remedies in those other areas be restricted to match those of insider trading?

5.   Regulatory Reform

Some advocates believe that insider trading legislation and common law are vague and produce inconsistent findings of insider trading liability. One attempt at regulatory reform is the Insider Trading Prohibition Act ("ITPA") (draft legislation that was passed by the House of Representatives in 2021; as you read this, you can go online to check the current status). Subsection (a) would make it illegal to trade when one is "aware of material, nonpublic information relating to such security or any nonpublic information, from whatever source, that has, or would reasonably be expected to have, a material effect on the market price of any such security. . . if such person knows, or recklessly disregards, that such information has been obtained wrongfully, or that such purchase or sale would constitute a wrongful use of such information."

Subsection (b) defines tipper liability, which includes that a tipper can be liable if the tipper wrongfully communicates material, nonpublic information relating to a security to a tippee if it is "reasonably foreseeable" that the tippee will purchase or sell the security after learning of the information or communicate the information to another tippee. However, the ITPA does not completely eliminate the personal benefit requirement. Subsection (c)(2) adds that the tipper is only liable if the tipper received a direct or indirect personal benefit, described in subsection (c)(1)(D) as "including pecuniary gain, reputational benefit, or a gift of confidential information to a trading relative or friend."

Subsection (c)(1) clarifies that "wrongful use" or "wrongful communication," involves when information has been obtained or is used through improper means such as theft, bribery, violation of Federal law protecting computer data, misappropriation, breach of fiduciary duty, breach of a relationship of trust and confidence for direct or indirect personal benefit, and others.

Representative Himes, the Act's chief sponsor, explained that the Act is meant to clarify the existing insider trading law and would not expand liability. Some scholars, like Stephen Bainbridge, disagree. Bainbridge expressed that the Act, contrary to Himes's articulation, expands the risk of insider trading liability because of the many actions that could fall under the new, broad "wrongful use" definition. New questions could also arise such as what it means to be "aware of" information and what constitutes an "indirect personal benefit." Further, Bainbridge has argued that the Act's expansion of liability could stifle market analysts' and investment professionals' research into public companies, which is essential for market efficiency. Which view do you find more convincing? Do you think regulatory reform is needed?

D. Section 16: Disgorgement of Short-Swing Trading Profits

Insider trading was one of the problems Congress attempted to address in the Securities Exchange Act of 1934. Responding to a public outcry against reports of insider trading and the perceived inadequacy of state common law, Congress created a novel regulatory scheme. Rather than prohibit trading on the basis of material nonpublic information, Congress attacked one narrow type of stock trading often associated with the misuse of inside information, namely "short-swing" trading—the purchase and resale by insiders of public company stock within a relatively short period of time.

Since the capital gains period of the tax laws at the time was six months, there was good reason to suspect that in most cases someone with access to inside information who bought and sold within six months (and therefore forewent the favorable tax treatment available for profits made on trades separated by a longer period) was doing so to take advantage of some special knowledge. It was only a step from this perception to the simple and readily enforceable, if crude, principle of § 16(b) of the 1934 Act, which provides:

"For the purpose of preventing the unfair use of information which may have been obtained by such beneficial owner, director, or officer by reason of his relationship to the issuer, any profit realized by him from any purchase and sale, or any sale and purchase, of any equity security of such issuer . . . within any period of less than six months . . . shall inure to and be recoverable by the issuer, irrespective of any intention on the part of such beneficial owner, director or officer in entering into such transaction . . ."

Although the section explicitly states that its purpose is "preventing the unfair use of information," there is no need to show any such "unfair use." It is a rule of strict liability and all that needs to be shown are offsetting trades within six months by someone with the necessary relationship to the corporation.

Section 16 applies to the directors and officers, as well as any person who is the "beneficial owner" of more than 10% of a class of equity securities, of any public corporation (one registered under § 12 of the 1934 Act). For purposes of § 16, an "officer" includes executive officers, chief financial or accounting officers, as well as any person, regardless of title, who performs significant "policy-making functions" in the corporation. Further, courts have concluded that a corporation or partnership may be considered to be a "director" under § 16 if a member or officer of the entity is "deputized" to represent the partnership or corporation as a director of the corporation in whose shares it trades. Section 16(b) applies to officers and directors trading in their corporation's securities while they are in office and extends to purchases or sales they make after they leave office, so long as still within six months.

For purposes of determining a person's status as a more than 10% shareholder of any class of stock, it is necessary to count the beneficial ownership of all "equity securities," including those securities that could be acquired through the exercise of conversion rights, and to consider classes of stock separately. Unlike officers and directors, a beneficial owner may be liable under § 16(b) only if he owned more than 10% of the stock at the time of *both* purchase and sale. Officers and directors are treated differently from beneficial owners because the former are deemed to have more ready access to confidential business information. The following case establishes this interpretation of the beneficial ownership requirement for purposes of § 16(b).

Foremost-McKesson, Inc. v. Provident Securities Co.

423 U.S. 232 (1976)

JUSTICE POWELL delivered the opinion of the Court.

This case presents an unresolved issue under § 16(b) of the Securities Exchange Act of 1934. That section of the Act was designed to prevent a corporate director or officer or "the beneficial owner of more than 10 per centum" of a corporation from profiteering through short-swing securities transactions on the basis of inside information. It provides that a corporation may capture for itself the profits realized on a purchase and sale, or sale and purchase, of its securities within six months by a director, officer, or beneficial owner. Section 16(b)'s last sentence, however, provides that it "shall not be construed to cover any transaction where such beneficial owner was not such both at the time of the purchase and sale, or the sale and purchase, of the security involved   ." The question presented here is whether a person purchasing securities that put his holdings above the 10% level is a beneficial owner "at the time of the purchase" so that he must account for profits realized on a sale of those securities within six months. The United States Court of Appeals for the Ninth Circuit answered this question in the negative. We affirm.

Respondent, Provident Securities Co., was a personal holding company. In 1968 Provident decided tentatively to liquidate and dissolve, and it engaged an agent to find a purchaser for its assets. Petitioner, Foremost-McKesson, Inc., emerged as a potential purchaser, but extensive negotiations were required to resolve a disagreement over the nature of the consideration Foremost would pay. Provident wanted cash in order to facilitate its dissolution, while Foremost wanted to pay with its own securities.

Eventually a compromise was reached, and Provident and Foremost executed a purchase agreement embodying their deal on September 25, 1969. The agreement provided that Foremost would buy two-thirds of Provident's assets for $4.25 million in cash and $49.75 million in Foremost convertible subordinated debentures. The agreement further provided that Foremost would register under the Securities Act of 1933 $25 million in principal amount of the debentures and would participate in an underwriting agreement by which those debentures would be sold to the public. At the closing on October 15, 1969, Foremost delivered to Provident the cash and a $40 million debenture which was subsequently exchanged for two debentures in the principal amounts of $25 million and $15 million. Foremost also delivered a $2.5 million debenture to an escrow agent on the closing date. On October 20 Foremost delivered to Provident a $7.25 million debenture representing the balance of the purchase price. These debentures were immediately convertible into more than 10% of Foremost's outstanding common stock.

On October 21 Provident, Foremost, and a group of underwriters executed an underwriting agreement to be closed on October 28. The agreement provided for sale to the underwriters of the $25 million debenture. On October 24 Provident distributed the $15 million and $7.25 million debentures to its stockholders, reducing the amount of Foremost common into which the company's holdings were convertible to less than 10%. On October 28 the closing under the underwriting agreement was accomplished. Provident thereafter distributed the cash proceeds of the debenture sale to its stockholders and dissolved.

Provident's holdings in Foremost debentures as of October 20 were large enough to make it a beneficial owner of Foremost within the meaning of § 16. Having acquired and disposed of these securities within six months, Provident faced the prospect of a suit by Foremost to recover any profits realized on the sale of the debenture to the underwriters. Provident therefore sued for a declaration that it was not liable to Foremost under § 16(b). The District Court granted summary judgment for Provident, and the Court of Appeals affirmed.

The meaning of the exemptive provision has been disputed since § 16(b) was first enacted. The discussion has focused on the application of the provision to a purchase-sale sequence, the principal disagreement being whether "at the time of the purchase" means "before the purchase" or "immediately after the purchase." The difference in construction is determinative of a beneficial owner's liability in cases such as Provident's where such owner sells within six months of purchase the securities the acquisition of which made him a beneficial owner. The commentators divided immediately over which construction Congress intended, and they remain divided. The Courts of Appeals also are in disagreement over the issue.

The general purpose of Congress in enacting § 16(b) is well known. Congress recognized that insiders may have access to information about their corporations not available to the rest of the investing public. By trading on this information, these persons could reap profits at the expense of less well informed investors. In § 16(b) Congress sought to "curb the evils of insider trading (by) . . . taking the profits out of a class of transactions in which the possibility of abuse was believed to be intolerably great." *Reliance Elec. Co. v. Emerson Elec. Co.*, 404 U.S. 418, 422 (1972). It accomplished this by defining directors, officers, and beneficial owners as those presumed to have access to inside information and enacting a flat rule that a corporation could recover the profits these insiders made on a pair of security transactions within six months.

The exemptive provision, which applies only to beneficial owners and not to other statutory insiders, must have been included in § 16(b) for a purpose. Although the extensive legislative history of the Act is bereft of any explicit explanation of Congress' intent, the evolution of § 16(b) from its initial proposal through passage does shed significant light on the purpose of the exemptive provision.

The legislative record reveals that the drafters focused directly on the fact that S. 2693 covered a short-term purchase-sale sequence by a beneficial owner only if his status existed before the purchase, and no concern was expressed about the wisdom of this requirement. But the explicit requirement was omitted from the operative language of the section when it was restructured to cover sale-repurchase sequences. In the same draft, however, the exemptive provision was added to the section. On this record we are persuaded that the exemptive provision was intended to preserve the requirement of beneficial ownership before the purchase. We hold that, in a purchase-sale sequence, a beneficial owner must account for profits only if he was a beneficial owner "before the purchase."

Our construction of § 16(b) also is supported by the distinction Congress recognized between short-term trading by mere stockholders and such trading by directors and officers. The legislative discourse revealed that Congress thought that all short-swing trading by directors and officers was vulnerable to abuse because of their intimate involvement in corporate affairs. But trading by mere stockholders was viewed as being subject to abuse only when the size of their holdings afforded the potential for access to corporate information. These different perceptions simply reflect the realities of corporate life.

It would not be consistent with this perceived distinction to impose liability on the basis of a purchase made when the percentage of stock ownership requisite to insider status had not been acquired. To be sure, the possibility does exist that one who becomes a beneficial owner by a purchase will sell on the basis of information attained by virtue of his newly acquired holdings. But the purchase itself was not one posing dangers that Congress considered intolerable, since it was made when the purchaser owned no shares or less than the percentage deemed necessary to make one an insider.

Points for Discussion

1. Bright-line rule.

How might § 16(b) be both over- and under-inclusive if the goal of the prohibition was to target corporate insiders trading on the basis of information they had access to that was not available to the rest of the investing public?

Now that you have studied insider trading law under § 10(b) and Rule 10b–5 as well as the short-swing trading rule of § 16(b), how might you assess the pros and cons of the bright-line nature of the latter?

2. Reporting obligations.

To ensure that potential plaintiffs can learn about short-swing trading, § 16(a) requires those covered by the statute to file reports with the SEC disclosing the ownership of their equity securities, as well as any changes in that ownership. Initial reports must be filed electronically 10 days after a person becomes an insider, and updated reports must be filed electronically 2 days after any changes in the insider's holdings.

3. Maximum recovery.

The remedy for short-swing trading is a self-contained, hybrid derivative suit set forth in § 16(b). A security holder, who need not be a contemporaneous owner, must first make a demand on the directors unless demand would be futile. Thereafter, the corporation has 60 days to decide whether to institute suit. If it does not, the action may be maintained by the holder, who must hold shares at suit and through trial. Any "profit" that is recovered, which courts compute by matching purchases and sales by the insider within any six-month period, goes to the corporation. Courts interpret the statute to allow for matching a purchase and sale in any order (e.g., sale followed by purchase) that would theoretically give rise to profits within six months and will calculate § 16(b) liability so as to maximize the amount recovered by the company.

In *Gratz v. Claughton*, 187 F.2d 46 (2d Cir.), cert. denied, 341 U.S. 920 (1951), the defendant had suffered a net loss of $400,000 on his trading in the company's stock, yet he was charged with liability for a $300,000 "profit" given the theoretical possibility of matching transactions in such a way under § 16(b). The court explained: "[T]he statute makes all such dealings unlawful, and makes the fiduciary accountable to the corporation. Although it is impossible in the case at bar to compute the defendant's profits, except that they must fall between two limits—the minimum and the maximum-the cause of this uncertainty is the number of transactions within six months: that is, the number of defendant's derelictions." It continued that "since the days of the 'Chimney Sweeper's Jewel Case,' . . . when damages are at some unascertainable amount below an upper limit and when the uncertainty arises from the defendant's wrong, the upper limit will be taken as the proper amount."

Would you compute damages so as to maximize recovery to the corporation even if a defendant had suffered trading losses in actuality? Why or why not?

4. *Fees, of course.*

Why would a security holder bring a § 16(b) action if any recovery goes to the corporation, producing only the remotest benefit to him? As with conventional derivative suits, attorneys' fees are available for a successful § 16(b) plaintiff. The plaintiff's counsel thus becomes the moving force in § 16(b) litigation. Indeed, courts have held that it is no defense to a § 16(b) action that the suit was motivated primarily by the desire to obtain such fees.

———————

Test Your Knowledge

To assess your understanding of the Chapter 18, 19, and 20 material in this module, click here to take a quiz.